www.wadsworth.com

www.wadsworth.com is the World Wide Web site for Thomson Wadsworth and is your direct source to dozens of online resources.

At *www.wadsworth.com* you can find out about supplements, demonstration software, and student resources. You can also send email to many of our authors and preview new publications and exciting new technologies.

www.wadsworth.com
Changing the way the world learns®

Criminal Procedure

Sixth Edition

JOEL SAMAHA
University of Minnesota

THOMSON

WADSWORTH

Australia • Canada • Mexico • Singapore • Spain • United Kingdom • United States

THOMSON
WADSWORTH

Senior Executive Editor, Criminal Justice: Sabra Horne
Development Editor: Julie Sakaue
Assistant Editor: Jana Davis
Editorial Assistant: Elise Smith
Technology Project Manager: Susan DeVanna
Marketing Manager: Terra Schultz
Marketing Assistant: Annabelle Yang
Advertising Project Manager: Stacey Purviance
Project Manager, Editorial Production: Jennie Redwitz
Art Director: Vernon Boes/Carolyn Deacy
Print/Media Buyer: Becky Cross

Permissions Editor: Sommy Ko
Production Service: Ruth Cottrell Books
Text Designer: Adriane Bosworth
Copy Editor: Lura Harrison
Illustrator: Judith Ogus, Random Arts
Cover Designer: Bill Stanton
Cover Images: U.S. Seal: Bettman/Corbis; Constitution Hall: © Catherine Karnow/Corbis
Compositor: R&S Book Composition
Printer: RR Donnelley

For more information about our products,
contact us at:
Thomson Learning Academic Resource Center
1-800-423-0563
For permission to use material from this text or
product, submit a request online at
http://www.thomsonrights.com.
Any additional questions about permissions can be
submitted by email to
thomsonrights@thomson.com.

Library of Congress Control Number: 2004104327

Student Edition: ISBN 0-534-62928-8

Instructor's Edition: ISBN 0-534-62929-6

Image credits: p. 37: photo, *The Crisis,* April 1935 #3. p. 51; p. 105: illustration, A. Balz; p. 287: two photos, Arizona State Library, Archives Division; p. 356: illustration, A. Balz/photo, Courtesy of Capt. Carl Delau, C.P.D.; p. 444: illustration, A. Balz

Thomson Wadsworth
10 Davis Drive
Belmont, CA 94002-3098
USA

Thomson Learning
5 Shenton Way #01-01
UIC Building
Singapore 068808

Australia/New Zealand
Thomson Learning
102 Dodds Street
Southbank, Victoria 3006
Australia

Canada
Nelson
1120 Birchmount Road
Toronto, Ontario M1K 5G4
Canada

Europe/Middle East/Africa
Thomson Learning
High Holborn House
50/51 Bedford Row
London WC1R 4LR
United Kingdom

Latin America
Thomson Learning
Seneca, 53
Colonia Polanco
11560 Mexico D.F.
Mexico

Spain/Portugal
Paraninfo
Calle Magallanes, 25
28015 Madrid, Spain

For Steve, Doug, and my students

About the Author

Professor Joel Samaha teaches Criminal Law, Criminal Procedure, Introduction to Criminal Justice, and The Supreme Court and the Bill of Rights at the University of Minnesota. He is both a lawyer and an historian whose primary research interest is constitutional and legal history. He received his B.A., J.D., and Ph.D. from Northwestern University. Professor Samaha also studied under the late Sir Geoffrey Elton at Cambridge University, England.

Professor Samaha was admitted to the Illinois Bar in 1962 and practiced law briefly in Chicago. He taught at UCLA before going to the University of Minnesota in 1971. At the University of Minnesota, he served as Chair of the Department of Criminal Justice Studies from 1974 to 1978. He now teaches and writes full time. He has taught both television and radio courses in criminal justice and has co-taught a National Endowment for the Humanities seminar in legal and constitutional history. He was named Distinguished Teacher at the University of Minnesota in 1974.

In addition to *Law and Order in Historical Perspective* (1974), an analysis of law enforcement in pre-industrial English society, Professor Samaha has transcribed and written a scholarly introduction to a set of criminal justice records in the reign of Elizabeth I. He has also written several articles on the history of criminal justice, published in *Historical Journal, The American Journal of Legal History, Minnesota Law Review, William Mitchell Law Review,* and *Journal of Social History.* In addition to *Criminal Procedure,* he has written two other textbooks, *Criminal Law,* now in its eighth edition, and *Criminal Justice,* now in its sixth edition.

Brief Contents

Contents

4 Stop and Frisk   94

5 Seizures of Persons: Arrest   157

6 Searches for Evidence   193

Preface

Balancing the power of government to enforce the criminal law against the rights of individuals to come and go as they please without government interference is the central problem in the law of criminal procedure in a constitutional democracy. It's also the heart of *Criminal Procedure* 6. It's a problem that always fascinates my students, stimulates them to think, and provokes them to discuss it not only in class but also with their friends and family outside class. (Of course it's also a topic that's of special concern since September 11, 2001.) I'm not surprised. The balance between government power and individual rights has fascinated me since 1958 when I was lucky enough to study criminal procedure at Northwestern University Law School under the sparkling Claude R. Sowle and the legendary Fred E. Inbau. Professor Sowle, a brilliant advocate and a distinguished teacher, emphasized the philosophical underpinnings of the law of criminal procedure. Professor Inbau, a famous interrogator and a highly respected student of the law of interrogation, spoke from the 1930s right up to his death in the late 1990s with the authority of one who has actually applied abstract principles to everyday police practices.

In 1968, I began work on what would eventually become my *Law and Order in Historical Perspective*, a reconstruction of the criminal process in sixteenth-century England. In 1971, I taught criminal procedure for the first time. I've done so ever since—during the regular terms, during the summers, and in the evenings. My students have included undergraduates, graduate students, and law students. That many of these students are now police officers, corrections officers, prison wardens, criminal defense attorneys, prosecutors, and judges testifies to their enduring interest in the law of criminal procedure and to their commitment to the application of formal law to informal real-life decision making.

Criminal Procedure 6, like its predecessors, reflects my conviction that the best way to learn the law of criminal procedure is to understand **general principles** and critically examine the application of these principles to real problems. By "critically" I don't mean "negatively"; *Criminal Procedure* isn't aimed at "bashing the system." Rather, it examines and weighs the principles that govern the balance between government power and individual life, liberty, privacy, and property. It tests the weight of strong, honest feelings about this balance in the bright light of reason, logic, and facts. *Criminal Procedure* proceeds on the assumptions that the general principles governing the balance between government and individuals have real meaning only in the context of a specific reality, and that reality makes sense only when seen in the light of general principles applied to facts.

BALANCING CONFLICTING INTERESTS

Criminal Procedure is organized according to the central theme of **balancing conflicting interests.** First, the law of criminal procedure balances the interest in obtaining the **correct result in particular cases** against the interest in upholding a **fair process in all cases.** This balancing of result and process is an example of the timeless puzzle of whether the ends justify the means. In criminal procedure, the ends are the correct result in the case at hand; the means is the process by which the result is obtained. The law of criminal procedure recognizes the importance of obtaining the correct result—namely, the ends of both freeing the innocent and convicting the guilty. But the law of criminal procedure also promotes the value of enforcing the law according to fair procedures. In other words, in the law of criminal procedure the ends don't justify the means. In fact, when forced to choose, the framers of our constitutional system decided that the means of fair procedures have to trump the ends of correct results. Or, to put it another way, ensuring fair proceedings for all people is more important than convicting even one guilty person by unfair means.

Facts, Not Hunches

Hunches or whims aren't enough to back up government invasions of liberty, privacy, and property. The U.S. Constitution and the constitutions of the states demand that the government back up all invasions of liberty, privacy, and property with facts. No police officer can justify detaining a person by claiming that she had a "hunch" that something was wrong. The greater the invasion, the more facts government officers have to produce to back up their invasions. So, to detain a person briefly on the street, police officers need only a few facts that create a "reasonable suspicion" that a crime may be afoot. But to convict defendants and send them to prison, the government has to prove they are guilty "beyond a reasonable doubt." This reliance on facts **(objective basis)** to back up government action lies at the heart of our constitutional democracy.

Hearing Before Condemnation

"A law that hears before it condemns" is the foundation of our constitutional system, said the great nineteenth-century lawyer Daniel Webster. A law that "hears before it condemns" is a law that deprives persons of life, liberty, privacy, and property only according to fair procedures. In the case of invasions before conviction, courts review street stops and frisks, arrests, searches, interrogations, and the conduct of identification procedures. In the case of conviction, courts are required to "hear" cases, either by trials or by approving guilty pleas, before defendants are "condemned." This review by courts, known as *judicial review,* is an essential element of our legal system.

TEXT AND CASES

Criminal Procedure is and has always been a **text-case book,** meaning that it contains both text and excerpts of actual court opinions that apply the general principles discussed in the text to concrete cases. The text and case excerpts complement each other. The text enriches the understanding of the cases, while the cases enhance the understanding of the text. The cases aren't just examples, illustrations, or attention grabbers (although surely they're all of these); the cases explain, clarify, elaborate, and, most of all, apply the general principles and constitutional provisions to real-life situations. Moreover, the cases are excellent tools for developing the critical thinking skills of students of all levels.

The cases and the text are independent enough of each other that they can stand alone. They are set off clearly from each other in design (the text appears in a one-column format; edited cases appear in two columns). This separation of text from cases allows instructors who favor the case analysis approach to emphasize cases over text, leaving the text for students to read if they need to in order to understand the cases. Instructors who favor the text approach can focus on the text, allowing students to read the cases as enrichment or as examples of the principles, constitutional provisions, and rules discussed in the text.

The case excerpts (edited carefully for nonlawyers) present students with a full statement of the facts of the case; the court's application of the law to the facts of the case; key portions of the reasoning of the court; and its decision. Excerpts also contain portions of the dissenting opinions and, when appropriate, parts of the concurring opinions.

A case question at the beginning of the case focuses on the main point in the edited case. The case history gives a brief procedural history of the case. And the questions at the end of the case excerpts test whether students know the facts of the case, whether they understand the law of the case, and whether they comprehend the application of the law to the facts of the case. The questions also provide the basis for developing critical thinking skills, not to mention provoking exciting class discussions on the legal, ethical, and policy issues raised by the edited case.

NEW AND ENHANCED FEATURES IN *CRIMINAL PROCEDURE* 6

New Cases. A number of new cases and many re-edited existing cases appear in *Criminal Procedure* 6. I added, replaced, and re-edited cases for three reasons. First, I wanted to reflect new developments in the law since the last edition. Second, I included new cases I've found since the last edition that explain the law better and apply the law to the facts in clearer and more interesting ways for students. Third, experiences through actual use in the classroom made it necessary to re-edit some cases.

Chapter Streamlining. Chapter 1 is the result of combining and streamlining Chapters 1 and 2 of *Criminal Procedure* 5. Chapters 12 through 14 are streamlined to include only what students really need to know and understand about the highly complicated, technical, difficult, and rare procedures that take place after cases enter the court system.

New Chapter 15, "Criminal Procedure in Crisis Times." This chapter reflects the impact of the September 11, 2001, terrorist attacks on the law of criminal procedure.

The coverage of the procedural changes enacted in the **USA Patriot Act,** and the cases applying the law, build on the broad and enduring theme of criminal procedure stressed in previous chapters—the problem of balancing the power of government and the rights of individuals in a constitutional democracy. The chapter stresses the need for recalibration of the balance during emergencies and then applies this general recalibration to the specific readjustments made (and still being made) since September 11, 2001, to provide for national security.

More Emphasis on State Constitutional Law. One of the most overlooked aspects of the law of criminal procedure is that states have the power to interpret their own constitutions differently from parallel provisions in the U.S. Constitution. States can't lower a federal constitutional right, but they can raise the federal minimum constitutional standard. I've continued my search for state cases that raise constitutional minimums under their own constitutions. Several of the new cases reflect this emphasis.

Exploring Further Feature. This feature enhances the Decision Points feature in previous editions. It provides examples of how the interpretation and application of the principle of the main case excerpt can vary depending on the facts of each case and the interpretation by courts. By exploring such variations, this feature reinforces and deepens students' understanding of the law of criminal procedure while also prompting them to think critically about the practical appliction of these procedures to real life.

Chapter Summaries in Detailed Outline Form. Reviewers and students have always praised the summary outline I provided in the chapter on criminal homicide in my *Criminal Law* text-case book. In *Criminal Procedure 6*, I expanded this concept so that every chapter now contains a summary outline. I have also included the outlines in electronic format on the enclosed CD-ROM. The electronic versions are formatted so that students can expand the outline by adding their own notes from class, their reading assignments, and so on. Students are thus encouraged to build their own outline, which they can then use to study and review.

A New, More Accessible Design. The design for *Criminal Procedure 6* was created with greater accessibility in mind. Thus, it has more visible Web site and CD-ROM references throughout the text to guide students to the relevant sections of these helpful resources. These and other design enhancements were made to help focus and guide students through the chapter content more effectively.

Interactive Criminal Procedure 6 CD-ROM

The interactive CD-ROM made its debut in *Criminal Procedure 5*. Based on my own use, comments from students at the University of Minnesota, and from adopters of *Criminal Procedure 5*, the CD-ROM now contains the following components for each chapter.

- **Interactive Summary Outlines.** The CD-ROM contains an interactive copy of each chapter's Summary Outline, which students can annotate with their lecture notes, notes from reading, and recommendations from their instructors.

- **Assignments.** There are a variety of assignments that instructors may use either as required work or for extra credit enrichment. The assignments allow for more in-depth learning and critical thinking about balances in the law of criminal procedure as it operates in a constitutional democracy. Each assignment asks specific questions about the statutes, cases, and other sources and includes specific instructions on how to find the materials included in the assignments.

  Many students and adopters complained that *Criminal Procedure* 5 had too many assignments requiring connection to the Internet—I heard you. Many assignments in the *Criminal Procedure* 6 CD-ROM don't require connecting to the Internet. The instructions make it clear which assignments don't require such a connection.

- **Link to "Exploring Further" cases.** Full case reports of all case excerpts in the "Exploring Further" features are included.

- **Link to Review Questions.** All end-of-chapter Review Questions are included on the CD-ROM.

- **The U.S. Constitution.** A complete version of the U.S. Constitution is now provided on the CD-ROM, and complete versions of the Fourth, Fifth, Sixth, Eighth, and Fourteenth Amendments are included in the appendix of the text for easy access.

- **Links to many of the features on the Book Companion Web Site.**

ORGANIZATION AND CHAPTER-BY-CHAPTER REVISIONS

Criminal Procedure 6, like its predecessors, is based on the assumption that thinking critically about criminal procedure requires an understanding of the structure and process of the law and practice of criminal procedure in a constitutional democracy. **Chapter 1** is an overview of that structure and process. In that respect, it combines and streamlines the content of Chapters 1 and 2 in *Criminal Procedure* 5. A new section, "The Big Picture," provides a road map for students' journeys through the criminal process in our U.S. version of constitutional democracy. Chapter 1 also contains a revised special section from Chapter 2 in *Criminal Procedure* 5, "The Text-Case Method." It describes and explains the significance of the book's text/case method, then goes on to provide detailed instructions and examples of how to "brief" cases (summarize the facts, issue, decision, and reasoning of the case excerpts).

Chapter 2 covers the basic constitutional principles that govern the whole of the criminal process (mainly due process and equal protection of the law). An understanding of these principles is a necessary prerequisite to understanding (and thinking critically about) the content in the rest of the book.

Chapters 3 through 9 arrange the specific constitutional provisions of criminal procedure chronologically as they occur in real life. The chronology begins with the encounters between law enforcement officers and individuals on the street and other public places, followed by those at the police station. Chapters 3 through 7 describe and critically examine searches and seizures. Why so many chapters on the subject of searches and seizures? Because government searches and seizures affect far more people than any other criminal procedure. Probably as a result of both this disproportionate effect and the complicated business of applying it in real life, there are more search and seizure cases than on any other subject in the law of criminal procedure.

Chapter 3 describes and analyzes the search and seizure clause of the Fourth Amendment. It requires students not only to understand but also to think critically about the answers to two questions: When is a government action a search? When is a government action a seizure? In discussing when a government action is a search, I've added the U.S. Supreme Court's latest word on thermal imaging (*Kyllo v. U.S.*) to show students how this complex issue arises relative to technological advances.

Chapter 4 describes and critically examines the myriad brief encounters between police and individuals that take place on the street. It requires students to think critically about when brief detentions and pat downs on the street are "reasonable searches and seizures." Chapter 4 includes new cases on race as a factor in reasonable suspicion (*U.S. v. Weaver*); the reasonable length of Fourth Amendment stops (*U.S. v. Sharpe*); the reasonableness of taking a suspect to the station as part of a stop (*People v. Courtney*); and the reasonableness of an "apartment checkpoint" for trespassers (*Wilson v. Commonwealth of Virginia*).

Chapter 5 focuses on arrest, the Fourth Amendment seizure that consists of taking suspects into custody, usually by taking them to the police station. It requires students to think critically about three questions: When is a detention an arrest? What amounts to probable cause? What is the proper manner of arrest? To help students address these questions, I've added new tables, one on the characteristics of arrest and a second on what information is acceptable in probable cause determination. Chapter 5 also includes new cases on the reasonableness of entering a home without a warrant to make a DWI arrest (*Welsh v. Wisconsin*) and of making a full custodial arrest for violation of a fine-only violation of a seat-belt law (*Atwater v. City of Lago Vista*).

Chapter 6 examines searches for evidence, both with and without warrants. It requires students to think critically about when warrants are required, the exceptions to the warrant requirement, and the manner in which searches are conducted. I've added a new case on the reasonableness of using a battering ram to enter a home after officers announced their presence with the intent to execute a search warrant (*State v. Ross*), as well as a state constitutional law case (*Commonwealth v. Gelineau and Theobald*) that raises the standard for searches of vehicles incident to arrest announced by the U.S. Supreme Court in *New York v. Belton*.

Chapter 7 describes and critically examines special-needs searches, in which the purpose isn't to obtain evidence. These searches go beyond ordinary law enforcement inventory searches that take place after arrest. Chapter 7 also addresses school searches, employee drug testing, and searches of prison visitors. It requires students to think critically about the application of the Fourth Amendment to subjects not directly related to criminal law enforcement. The principles and concepts examined in this chapter are brought to life in such new cases as *Cochrane v. Quattrochi*, which addresses the reasonableness of strip-searching a prison visitor, and *Commonwealth v. Neilson*, which addresses the reasonableness of searching college students' dorm rooms.

Chapters 8 and 9 describe two highly publicized and widely known procedures: police interrogation and confessions and police identification procedures, including lineups, "mug shots," and DNA testing. These chapters require students to think critically about the right to remain silent and the use of physical evidence to convict criminal defendants. Students must also consider the need for, the fairness of, and the reliability of interrogation and identification procedures in obtaining the truth. Chapter 8 has new cases on the meaning of "custody" in relation to the requirement of giving the *Miranda* warnings (*Berkemer v. McCarty*); the public safety exception to *Miranda* (*U.S. v. Reyes*); and the valid waiver of the right to remain silent (*North Carolina v. Butler*). There are also two new tables, one on circumstances relevant to showing a valid waiver of the right to remain silent and the other on cases where courts found there was a valid waiver. Chapter 9 has two new cases on the reliability of lineups (*McFadden v. Cabana* and *State v. Smith*), as well as a new table on the five reliability factors of identification procedures.

Chapters 10 and 11 critically examine the remedies against the government when officials violate the constitutional rights discussed in Chapters 3 through 9. Chapter 10 focuses on what we call *process remedies*, taking a look at the main process remedy, the exclusionary rule, as well as entrapment, expungement, and others. In Chapter 10, I strengthened the section on the scope of the exclusionary rule by adding a new section on the major exceptions to the rule (collateral use, cross-examination, attenuation, independent source, and inevitable discovery). I also added a new section, "Illegally Seized (Arrested) Persons," which examines whether charges against illegally arrested persons are "fruit of a poisonous tree" and therefore have to be dismissed. A new case (*Matta-Ballesteros v. Henman*) elaborates on the jurisdiction of courts over illegally arrested persons. Chapter 11 concentrates on the right to sue the government for the injuries that result from constitutional violations and other illegal official actions. Both chapters invite students to think critically about the nature, value, and purposes of the various remedies against mistakes and misconduct by government officials in the enforcement, prosecution, and disposition of criminal laws.

Chapter 12 covers court proceedings before trial (the decision to charge, bail, and the right to counsel). **Chapter 13** describes and assesses the determination of guilt, both by formal trial and by guilty pleas. **Chapter 14** describes and evaluates proceedings following conviction (sentencing, appeal, and habeas corpus). I streamlined these chapters to weed out the highly technical and difficult-to-follow procedures that are rarely used in practice and that non-law students don't need to know. The result is a cleaner, leaner, more accessible and useful treatment of these complicated procedures.

A completely new **Chapter 15,** "Criminal Procedure in Crisis Times," examines the effects of 9/11 on criminal procedure.

PEDAGOGICAL AIDS

However it's organized and presented, the law of criminal procedure is a complicated subject that embraces a lot of technical concepts. I've tried to help students work through these complexities, primarily by writing clear, direct prose. But there are special features as well. Each chapter contains a **Chapter Outline** and a list of the **Chapter Main Points.** I've also boldfaced key terms in the text, which appear in a list of **Key Terms** at the end of each chapter as well as in the **Glossary** at the end of the book. **Review Questions** at the end of each chapter provide a good test of whether students have identified and understood the main points in the chapter. Students frequently comment that the combination of the Chapter Outline and Chapter Main Points at the beginning of the chapter tell them what they should look for as they read and that the Key Terms and Review Questions at the end of each chapter tell them whether they have found and understood what they looked for.

"Putting the people back in 'We the People'"—this is how Professor Michael Dorf introduces *Constitutional Law Stories* (2004). The Rest of the Story feature I introduced in *Criminal Procedure* 5 is my effort to put the people back into a few of the leading criminal procedure cases. The feature demonstrates that the cases involve real people; they don't just decide an impersonal legal principle. Students frequently want to get beyond the confines of the case excerpt; they wonder what happened to criminals and their victims before, during, and after the crime, and they even want to know what they looked like. It's impossible to present this information in most cases; but, I've been able to do it for five case excerpts: the historic forced confession case of *Brown v. Mississippi* (Chapter 2); the landmark U.S. Supreme Court stop-and-frisk case *Terry v. Ohio* (Chapter 4); the famous *Miranda v. Arizona* (Chapter 8); the landmark case of *Mapp v. Ohio* on the exclusionary rule (Chapter 10); and another landmark case, *Gideon v. Wainwright* (Chapter 12).

In addition to these pedagogical aids, I've also included a few others that I described in detail in the section "New and Enhanced Features in *Criminal Procedure* 6" earlier in this Preface. Based on positive feedback from reviewers and classroom testing, I've modified such pedagogical features as the State Constitutional Law boxes, the Decision Points feature (now called the Exploring Further feature), and the Chapter Summaries to strengthen the characteristics of each feature that reviewers found successful and to introduce a few new characteristics to keep the features fresh and effective.

MEETING THE NEEDS OF A VARIETY OF CLASS DESIGNS

Some criminal procedure courses and many criminal procedure texts (particularly those designed for undergraduates) cover only the law of arrest, search and seizure, interrogation, and identification procedures. In other words, these courses and texts focus on police practices (the contacts between individuals and the police on the street and at the police station). They usually cover the constitutional framework of criminal procedure, and they sometimes include discussions of the exclusionary rule. *Criminal Procedure* 6 lends itself to this type of course because instructors can use Chapters 3 through 9, which can stand alone, without covering either Chapters 1 and 2 on the general principles and constitutional provisions or Chapters 10 and 11 on remedies for illegal official conduct. Instructors who want to teach the exclusionary rule and the constitutional provisions can add Chapter 2 on criminal procedure and the Constitution and Chapter 10, which covers the exclusionary rule.

Criminal Procedure 6 is also suitable for courses that cover the entire criminal process, from the early encounters between individuals and the police on the street to procedures following conviction. And, for students in courses covering only police practices, Chapters 1, 2, and 10 through 15 should fill the gap if they want to read about the other subjects covered in the study of the law of criminal procedure.

ANCILLARIES

A number of ancillaries to accompany *Criminal Procedure* 6 are available to qualified adopters. Please consult your local sales representative for details.

For the Instructor

Instructor's Manual. This Instructor's Manual includes Learning Objectives, Chapter Outlines, Key Terms and Concepts, Chapter Summaries, Discussion Topics, Student Activities, and Recommended Readings. Also included is a test bank that contains multiple-choice, true/false, fill-in-the-blank, and essay questions, with answer keys and rejoinders.

ExamView® Computerized Testing. Instructors can create, deliver, and customize tests and study guides (both print and online) in minutes with this easy-to-use assessment and tutorial system. ExamView offers both a Quick Test Wizard and an Online Test Wizard that guide instructors step by step through the process of creating tests, while the unique WYSIWYG capability allows instructors to see the tests they are creating on the screen exactly as they'll print or display online. Instructors can build tests of up to 250 questions using up to twelve question types. With ExamView, instructors can also enter an unlimited number of new questions or edit existing questions.

WebTutor™ ToolBox for Blackboard and WebCT. NEW to *Criminal Procedure* 6, this great supplement comes preloaded with content and is available for free via pin code when packaged with this text. WebTutor Toolbox pairs all the content of this text's rich Book Companion Web site with all the sophisticated course management functionality of a WebCT or BlackBoard product. Instructors can assign materials (including online quizzes) and have the results flow automatically to their gradebooks. ToolBox is ready to use at log on, or instructors can customize its preloaded content by uploading images and other resources, adding Web links or creating their own practice materials. Students only have access to student resources on the Web site; instructors can enter a pin code for access to password-protected instructor resources.

Criminal Procedure: A Microsoft® PowerPoint® Tool. FREE to adopters of this text, this dual platform CD-ROM is designed to work with PowerPoint® presentation software and includes detailed outlines that will help you develop your criminal procedure lecture presentations.

Wadsworth Criminal Justice Video Library. Choose from hundreds of videos featuring topics covered in criminal justice courses, from such respected sources as

CNN, Court TV, Films for the Humanities and Sciences, and the American Society of Criminology's Oral History Project. For a complete listing, please contact your local Thomson Wadsworth representative.

For the Student

Samaha's Companion Website for *Criminal Procedure* 6.
http://cj.wadsworth.com/samaha/crim_pro6e

This student-friendly companion Web site includes chapter summary outlines, flashcards and a glossary of key terms, crossword puzzles, tutorial quizzing, Internet activities, InfoTrac® College Edition exercises, Web links, an exciting interactive simulation "Where's Melanie?" and much more!

Key Cases, Comments, and Questions on Substantive Criminal Law. Written by Henry F. Fradella (The College of New Jersey), this book examines cases with comments, analyses, and discussion questions to help students grasp challenging material and test their knowledge. For more information, contact your Thomson Wadsworth representative.

Careers in Criminal Justice Interactive CD-ROM, Version 3.0. This CD provides students with extensive career profiling information and self-assessment testing and is designed to help them investigate and focus on the criminal justice career choices that are right for them. With links and tools to assist students in finding a professional position, this new version includes ten new "Career Profiles" and two new "Video Interviews," bringing the total number of careers covered to fifty-eight.

Guide to Criminal Procedure for California; Guide to Criminal Procedure for Florida; Guide to Criminal Procedure for Illinois; Guide to Criminal Procedure for New York; Guide to Criminal Procedure for Texas. These brief guides explore state-specific procedures and cases and include chapter introductions, overviews of codes and implications, and exercises about state-specific penal codes.

InfoTrac College Edition Student Guide for Criminal Justice. This twenty-four-page booklet provides detailed user guides illustrating how to use the InfoTrac College Edition database. Special features include log-in help, a complete search tips cheat sheet, and a topic list of suggested keyword search terms for criminal justice.

ACKNOWLEDGMENTS

Writing a book always accumulates a lot of debts. Acknowledging these debts hardly repays them, but the past (and hopefully the future) success of *Criminal Procedure* requires that I acknowledge some of the people I'm indebted to for its success, even if I can't repay them.

The thousands of University of Minnesota students (including police officers, corrections officers, probation and parole officers, prison wardens, prosecutors, defense attorneys, and judges) who've taken my courses in the last thirty-three years contributed more than they can ever know or than I can ever put into words. They asked stimulating questions, participated in lively discussions, and told me bluntly (sometimes even irreverently) what they *really* thought about *Criminal Procedure*. The book is a lot better because of their blunt honesty.

I'm also grateful for the guidance of the following pre-revision reviewers, whose excellent suggestions are reflected in this edition of *Criminal Procedure:*

Michael Benza, Case Western Reserve University

Craig Hemmens, Boise State University

Gene Straughan, Lewis-Clark State College

Beth Webber, Indiana University–Purdue University at Fort Wayne

I'd also like to thank the many survey respondents who provided me with valuable feedback that helped me to shape parts of the Sixth Edition:

Charles Adams, Savannah State University

Dana Cook Baer, Waynesburg College

Shelley Bannister, Northeastern Illinois University

Ken Barnes, Arizona Western College

Edward Bohlander, Western Kentucky University

Michael W. Buckley, Texas A&M University

Frank Butler, Temple University

Jack E. Call, Radford University

Rick Castberg, University of Hawaii at Hilo

Nigel Cohen, University of Texas–Pan American

Chris De Lay, University of Louisiana at Lafayette

Charles Dolan, Western New England College

Ken Egbo, Iowa Wesleyan College

Marie Henry, Sullivan County Community College

G. G. Hunt, Wharton County Junior College

Robert Hunt, Delta State University

Jennifer Lanterman, Rutgers University

Collin Lau, Chaminade University of Honolulu

Robert Lockwood, Portland State University

Edward Mott, Bellevue Community College

John C. Mott, Mansfield University of Pennsylvania

Lee G. Nollau, Pennsylvania State University

William R. Parks, II, University of South Carolina, Spartanburg

Martin S. Redmann, Madison Area Technical College

Sheri Short, Navarro College

John W. Steinberg, St. Philips College

Jeff Stockner, Tiffin University

Martha J. Sullivan, Stephen F. Austin State University

Bradford Timbers, Elizabethtown Community & Technical College

Paul Weizer, Fitchburg State College

Past teachers, without even knowing it, have also influenced *Criminal Procedure*. Professors Claude Sowle and Fred Inbau, who taught me the law of criminal procedure at Northwestern University Law School, sparked an interest that became a lifelong fascination with the subject. My dear friend and mentor, the late Sir Geoffrey Elton, Clare College, Cambridge, guided and stimulated my curiosity about the history of criminal procedure and taught me how to conduct disciplined research in the primary sources of sixteenth-century criminal justice administration. Finally, Professor Lacey Baldwin Smith, Northwestern University, the best teacher I've ever had (and I've had lots!), provided me with an outstanding example of how to transfer my own excitement about a subject I love to my students. He also taught me how to transform my convoluted English into readable prose.

Ruth Cottrell, the best production editor ever, as always made the production of the book seem easy when I know better. The application of Lura Harrison's careful editing saved the book from a lot of errors and made it clearer. The people at Wadsworth deserve special mention. Sabra Horne encouraged me throughout the revision of *Criminal Procedure* 6. Julie Sakaue and Jennie Redwitz kept me on track with deadlines and details that I'm not good at keeping or even noticing. Susan DeVanna helped me with the CD-ROM, and Jana Davis worked to provide the other wonderful supplements that are offered with this text.

What would I do without Doug and Steve? Doug takes me here and gets me there and everywhere, day in and day out, days that now have stretched into years. And my old and dear friend Steve, who from the days when he watched over my kids to now decades later—he takes care of (and loves) the Irish Wolfhounds and the Siamese cat all the time and the Standard Poodle when I'm not here. And both Doug and Steve do all this while putting up with what Sir Geoffrey called "Joel's mercurial temperament." Only those who really know me can understand how I can try the patience of Job!

I'm happy to give credit to my students, my teachers, my editors, and others at Wadsworth, and Steve and Doug for making *Criminal Procedure* 6 a better book. Of course, I take the blame for all its shortcomings.

Joel Samaha
Minneapolis

Criminal Procedure: The Big Picture

1

Chapter Main Points

- *Criminal Procedure* 6 is a road map and a guidebook to help you find your way and keep you from getting lost in your journey through the United States law of criminal procedure.
- Your journey will take you through these stages:
  - *On the street.* Brief encounters between law enforcement officers and individuals on the street
  - *At the police station.* More-intensive contacts between officers and suspects at the police station
  - *In court.* Contacts between lawyers and criminal defendants before conviction and between lawyers and offenders after conviction
- Chapter 1 describes and explains the elements of this big picture of your journey, so that you can stay on the road and understand everything you see along the way.
- The big picture in U.S. criminal procedure consists of balancing our two most priceless values: safety and the freedom that lets us come and go as we please.
- Most criminal procedure cases are in court because defendants want the court to throw out "good" evidence obtained by "bad" methods.
- The history of criminal procedure is a pendulum swing between the *ends* of crime control and the *means* of fair procedures.
- At the end of the day, our history and our criminal procedure show that we don't believe in crime control at any price. The means of fair procedure always trump the ends of crime control.
- Decision making in criminal procedure is both formal (according to written rules) and informal (based on unwritten discretionary judgments).
- Hunches aren't good enough to back up official decisions. Officials have to back up with facts every restraint on individuals' freedom to come and go as they please.
- *Criminal Procedure* 6 is a text-case book. The text element defines, describes, and explains what you'll see on your journey; the cases apply and make you think about what you see.

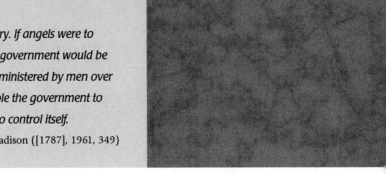

If men were angels, no government would be necessary. If angels were to govern men, neither external nor internal controls on government would be necessary. In framing a government which is to be administered by men over men, the great difficulty lies in this: You must first enable the government to control the governed; and in the next place, oblige it to control itself.

James Madison ([1787], 1961, 349)

THE CRIMINAL PROCEDURE ROADMAP

Criminal Procedure 6 takes you on a journey through three stages in crime control in the United States (Figure 1.1).

1. *On the street.* Encounters between law enforcement officers and persons suspected of committing crimes

2. *At the police station.* Encounters between law enforcement officers and persons arrested for committing crimes

3. *In court.* Encounters between defendants and their lawyers, prosecutors, judges, juries, and appeals courts

In this journey, our focus will be on describing, explaining, and critically examining the power and the limits of the government's power to control crime. (Right from the start, here's a warning: Don't misunderstand what I mean by "critically examining." I don't mean "dissing" ("trashing" or "putting down"); I mean forming and basing your opinions about crime control procedures on what you *know,* not on how you *feel.* This will be tough because most people have strong feelings about controlling crime.)

But before we begin the journey from the first contact between people and law enforcement officers on the streets to the last review of offenders' convictions in the U.S. Supreme Court, let's look at some preliminary concepts, definitions, and other tools to help you get and keep a grip on all you're going to learn.

THE "BIG PICTURE" IS BALANCE

If we lived in a police state, officials could break into our houses in the dead of night and shoot us in our beds based on nothing more than the whim of the current dictator. If we lived in a *pure* democracy, the majority who won the last election could pass and enforce a law to lock up everyone who protests the war on terror. But, we live in a **constitutional democracy,** where neither a single dictator nor an overwhelming majority of the people has total power over us as individuals. We focus on two balances

A GENERAL VIEW OF THE CRIMINAL JUSTICE SYSTEM

This chart seeks to present a simple yet comprehensive view of the movement of cases through the criminal justice system. Procedures in individual jurisdictions may vary from the pattern shown here. The differing weights of the line indicate the relative volumes of cases disposed of at various points in the system, but this is only suggestive since no nationwide data of this sort exists.

Police

Crimes Observed by the Police — Investigation 1 — Unsolved or Not Arrested — Released Without Prosecution — Arrest — Released Without Prosecution

Undetected Crimes

Crime

Crimes Reported to the Police

Unreported Crimes

Prosecution

Booking 2 — Initial Appearance 3 — Charges Dropped or Dismissed

Courts

Preliminary Hearing 4 — Charges Dropped or Dismissed

Felonies

Information 5 — Grand Jury 6 — Refusal to Indict — Arraignment — Charges Dismissed — Trial 7 — Acquitted — Guilty Pleas — Reduction of Charges 8 — Sentencing

Misdemeanors

Information — Arraignment — Charges Dismissed — Trial — Acquitted — Guilty Pleas — Sentencing

Petty Offenses

Released — Released — Intake Hearing 11 — Adjudicatory Hearing — Nonadjudicatory Disposition 12

Police Juvenile Unit 10 — Release or Station Adjustment

Juvenile Offenses

Non-Police Referrals

Corrections

Probation — Revocation — Penitentiary — Parole — Parole — Revocation — Habeas Corpus 9 — **Out of System**

Appeal

Probation — Fine — Nonpayment — Jail — Revocation — **Out of System**

Probation — Revocation — Juvenile Institution — Parole — Revocation — **Out of System**

1 May continue until trial.

2 Administrative record of arrest. First step at which temporary release on bail may be available.

3 Before magistrate, commissioner, or justice of peace. Formal notice of charge, advice of rights. Bail set. Summary trials for petty offenses usually conducted here without further processing.

4 Preliminary testing of evidence against defendant. Charge may be reduced. No separate preliminary hearing for misdemeanors in some systems.

5 Charge filed by prosecutor on basis of information submitted by police or citizens. Alternative to grand jury indictment; often used in felonies, almost always in misdemeanors.

6 Reviews whether Government evidence sufficient to justify trial. Some States have no grand jury system; others seldom use it.

7 Appearance for plea; defendant elects trial by judge or jury (if available); counsel for indigent usually appointed here in felonies. Often not at all in other cases.

8 Charge may be reduced at any time prior to trial in return for plea of guilty or for other reasons.

9 Challenge on constitutional grounds to legality of detention. May be sought at any point in process.

10 Police often hold informal hearings, dismiss or adjust many cases without further processing.

11 Probation officer decides desirability of further court action.

12 Welfare agency, social services, counseling, medical care, etc., for cases where adjudicatory handling not needed.

FIGURE 1.1 A General View of the Criminal Justice System

in criminal procedure: between community security and individual autonomy and between ends and means.

Safety and Autonomy

The heart of our *constitutional* democracy is balance between two values that make life in a free society worth living. The first is **community security,** where *we* as a *community* are safe: our lives are safe from murder; our bodies are safe from rape and other assaults; our homes are safe from burglars, arsonists, and trespassers; and our "stuff" is safe from thieves and vandals. The second is **individual autonomy,** where *I* alone control *my* life: I can come and go as I please; develop my body and my mind as I wish to do; believe whatever or whomever I want; worship any god I like; "hang" with anybody I pick to hang with; have consensual sex in the privacy of my own home; and do pretty much anything else I want to do (assuming, of course, I'm a competent adult and what I want doesn't include committing crimes that violate the community's safety or other persons against their will). In other words, I can't tip the balance between community safety and individual autonomy in my favor whenever and however I want.

Weighed on one side of the balance is the amount of government power needed to control crime for everybody's safety and security. Weighed on the other side of the balance is the amount of control individuals have over their own lives. James Madison (see the passage quoted on p. 2) and others who wrote and adopted the U.S. Constitution in the 1700s were realists; they accepted human nature for what it is: Humans aren't angels. Left to do as they please, ordinary people will break the law. And, because they're people, too, government officials left to do as *they* please will abuse *their* power. So, the Founders expected excesses from both ordinary people and government officials who live in a *real* world inhabited by *imperfect* people. Let me be clear right at the beginning of our journey through the criminal process: I subscribe to Madison's view of human nature and the world.

A few words of caution: Since both security and autonomy are equally important, striking the balance between them is difficult, and where it's struck never satisfies anyone completely. U.S. Supreme Court Chief Justice William Rehnquist (1974) expressed the challenge this way:

> Throughout the long history of political theory and the development of constitutional law in our country, the most difficult cases to decide have been those in which two competing values, each able to marshal respectable claims on its behalf, meet in a contest in which one must prevail over the other. (1)

Another important point: The balance between crime control and individual rights is flexible. Where the balance is exactly struck shifts, depending on the circumstances. Put another way, the right balance falls within a zone; it's not a point on the spectrum between total control and total freedom. The most extreme examples are emergencies, especially in wartime. As one lawyer prosecuting suspected disloyalists during the Civil War put it [I'm paraphrasing here], "During wartime the Bill of Rights is put to sleep. We'll wake it up when the emergency passes" (Gayarré 1903, 601). But, it's not just during emergencies like wars that we'll see the balance struck in various places in the zone. We'll see many examples where courts move around in the zone between order and liberty.

Ends and Means

Crime control in a constitutional democracy depends on a second balance—between ends and means. (To be more precise, I'll call it the **balance between result and process.**) In criminal procedure, the "ends" side of the balance consists of the search for the truth to obtain the correct result in individual cases. The correct result has two dimensions: (1) catching, convicting, and punishing *guilty* people and (2) freeing as soon as possible *innocent* people caught up in government efforts to control crime. Keep in mind these words of the late Professor Jerome Hall (1942) as we make our journey through the law of criminal procedure:

> [Criminal law's] ultimate ends are dual and conflicting. It must be designed from inception to end to acquit the innocent as readily as to convict the guilty. This presents the inescapable dilemma of criminal procedure... that the easier it is made to prove guilt, the more difficult it becomes to establish innocence. (728)

At the "means" end of the **end–means balance** is the commitment to fairness in dealing with suspects, defendants, and offenders. In our constitutional democracy, we don't believe in catching, convicting, and punishing criminals at any price. The U.S. Constitution and provisions in every state constitution limit public officials' power to control crime in two ways (Chapter 2). The body of the Constitution defines the structure of criminal procedure as federal and state governments with separation of powers into branches that make (legislatures), interpret (courts), and carry out (executive) laws. **Bills of rights** guarantee individuals' rights against government power, like the prohibition against self-incrimination (Chapter 9); unreasonable searches and seizures (Chapters 3–7); and others we'll discuss throughout the rest of the book.

Balancing ends and means creates an uncomfortable tension. The rules that protect everybody against government abuses of power also can get in the way of the search for truth in individual cases. This interference can and probably does reduce the security of all people. Some guilty individual will go free in one case today to make sure the government will play by the rules in all cases tomorrow!

It might help you to understand and accept this balance between ends and means if you frequently remind yourself that the principles and rules we make to control crime apply to *all* government officials and *all* suspects, defendants, and offenders. In other words, the rules don't apply just to *good* cops catching and prosecutors convicting *bad* (guilty) people. They also apply to *bad* cops and prosecutors apprehending and prosecuting *innocent* people.

The balance between result and process never rests easily at a point that satisfies everyone. Throughout our history, it has caused great frustration, even anger. Those who fear criminals more than they fear government abuses of power stress the importance of correct result in particular cases. They complain of rules or "technicalities" that "handcuff the police" and allow criminals to go free. Those who fear government abuses of power more than they fear criminals complain that we haven't obligated the government to "control itself," as Madison warned us to do.

The great U.S. Court of Appeals Judge Learned Hand clearly took the side of government power in this debate. According to Judge Hand (1922):

> Under our criminal procedure the accused has every advantage. While the prosecution is held rigidly to the charge, he need not disclose the barest outline of his defense. He is immune from question or comment on his silence; he cannot be convicted when there is the

least fair doubt in the minds of any one of the twelve. . . . Our dangers do not lie in too little tenderness to the accused. Our procedure has been always haunted by the ghost of the innocent man convicted. It is an unreal dream. What we need to fear is the archaic formalism and the watery sentiment that obstructs, delays, and defeats the prosecution of crime. (659)

Professor Joseph Goldstein (1960), weighing in on the side of controlling government, strongly disagrees with Judge Hand's position. Goldstein believes the process favors the government, not criminal suspects and defendants:

The fact is that . . . [Judge Hand's] view does not accurately represent the process. . . . Criminal procedure . . . does not give the accused "every advantage" but, instead, gives overwhelming advantage to the prosecution. The real effect of the "modern" approach has been to aggravate this condition by loosening standards of . . . proof without introducing compensatory safeguards earlier in the process. Underlying this development has been a . . . rejection of the presumption of innocence in favor of a presumption of guilt. (1152)

At the end of the day, though, in our constitutional democracy the trump card is the means of fair procedures, not the end of crime control, *except in extreme emergencies.*

"Good" Evidence and "Bad" Methods

Most criminal procedure cases are in court because defendants want to take advantage of the trump card of fair procedures—the **exclusionary rule** (Chapter 10). This rule forces courts to throw out **"good" evidence** (evidence that proves defendants are guilty) if the government got it by **"bad" methods** (methods that violate the U.S. or state Constitutions). Referring to the exclusionary rule, the great judge Benjamin Cardozo once asked, "Should the culprit go free because the constable blundered?" The answer by supporters of the rule, "Well, if the culprit goes free, it's the *Constitution* that set him free." The exclusionary rule is an excellent, and maybe the most controversial, rule in criminal procedure; it is used only in the United States. Its application triggered many of the cases you're going to read about in this book. Because it will be very important to your understanding of the ends–means feature that is at the heart of criminal procedure in our constitutional democracy, we'll discuss it more fully later in Chapter 10.

A CAPSULE HISTORY OF BALANCE IN CRIMINAL PROCEDURE

The tensions between, and the attempt to balance, the conflicting interests of society and the individual and result and process—captured in James Madison's famous passage from *The Federalist* (quoted in the chapter opening) and in the disagreement between Judge Hand and Professor Goldstein—is as old as Western law. The early twentieth-century legal scholar Roscoe Pound (1921) wrote that the history of criminal procedure is a pendulum swing between the two extremes of these tensions. According to Pound, no system has perfectly balanced the power of the government to enforce the social interest in crime control and the rights of individuals in procedures to control crime. Throughout Western history, societies have swung back and forth between putting crime control first and then, in reaction, putting individuals first (1– 16). Let's take a brief journey through the many centuries of history that lie behind what you're going to study this term. We'll begin with a look at conflicts between crime control and procedures to protect individuals, beginning with the Roman republic and moving forward to modern-day debates.

The Roman Republic and Empire

The early Roman republic established strong safeguards for individuals against government power in its law of criminal procedure. As a result, according to Professor James Leigh Strachan-Davidson (1912), the Romans created a criminal law "that in spite of abundant threats of capital punishment became in practice the mildest ever known in the history of mankind." In reaction to this mildness and its commitment to process, the government of the Roman Empire went to the other extreme. In Imperial Rome, provincial governors acted as both prosecutors and judges. The emperor Hadrian noted that full-fledged trials weren't necessary; the governors' mere act of sending accused criminals to trial was unchallengeable proof of their guilt (114, 168).

England

Several centuries later, in thirteenth-century England, the same conflict between crime control and procedures to protect individuals arose. In the Magna Carta, King John's barons successfully placed a number of checks on royal power. These checks emphasized process at the expense of result. During the sixteenth and seventeenth centuries, as in Imperial Rome, this excess of process led to power grabbing by the English monarchs. By the reign of King Charles I in the early 1600s, the royal court of the Star Chamber had abandoned the common-law procedural safeguards for the accused in favor of royal power to convict the guilty. This expansion of royal power didn't stop with creating new royal courts; it extended to the kings' political domination of the common-law judges. Through intimidation, favor, and other influence, the seventeenth-century English kings brought about decisions favorable to their own and the aristocracy's interests.

Although interference in the business of the courts was by no means new, a growing middle class, hungry for political influence to match their growing economic worth, regarded royal interference in judicial proceedings as intolerable. The English revolution—and the founding of the American colonies—was, at least in part, a reaction by the middle classes to this expansion of royal power and its capacity to use that power to trump process with result.

United States, 1776–1899

The Articles of Confederation, reacting to what Americans saw as British tyranny, went to the other extreme, creating a government too weak to govern. The U.S. Constitution is one of the most famous efforts in history to write into constitutional law a permanent balance between government power—particularly, national government power— and individual liberty. According to Alexander Hamilton:

In the commencement of a revolution which received its birth from the usurpations of tyranny, nothing was more natural than that the public mind should be influenced by an extreme spirit of jealousy. To resist these encroachments, and to nourish this spirit, was the great object of all our public and private institutions. The zeal for liberty became predominant and excessive. In forming our Confederation, this passion alone seemed to actuate us, and we appear to have had no other view than to secure ourselves from despotism. The object certainly was a valuable one, and deserves our utmost attention; but, sir, there is another object, equally important, and which our enthusiasm rendered us little capable of regarding: I mean a principle of strength and stability in the organization of our government, and vigor in its operations.

Storing 1981, 71

Even this balance didn't satisfy Anti-Federalists. They feared government power too much to rely on such a general protection. The Bill of Rights, added as amendments to the Constitution, reflects the deep suspicion, even hostility, to government power among some of the middle classes who'd experienced firsthand both a royal executive and an appointed judiciary eager to use their power to trump individual rights. The Bill of Rights shows the determination of the Anti-Federalists to protect individual rights against government intrusions and deprivations (McDonald 1985; Rutland 1955).

United States, 1900–1959

By the early 1900s, the United States was increasingly urban, industrial, and densely populated with immigrants whose values conflicted with the dominant Anglo-Saxon Protestant culture. These changes produced a perception of uncertainty and disorder. That perception led to calls for more government power to control a rapidly growing list of crimes. These calls took place during a "crime wave" the public believed was of epidemic proportions.

Complaints spread that "technicalities" set criminals free and that constitutional safeguards made it difficult to convict known criminals. The newspapers, the new middle-class magazines, national conventions of criminal justice officials, professors, and lawyers loudly complained about how the criminal justice system favored criminals over innocent citizens. Put in terms of this brief history, there was a widespread belief (at least among those whose voices were left behind for us to hear) that the pendulum had swung too far from crime control toward individual rights.

These complaints provoked open demands to amend the Constitution, sometimes drastically. At the 1910 annual meeting of the American Academy of Political and Social Science, a prestigious New York criminal lawyer, Samuel Untermeyer, told the conference that the Fourth Amendment protection against unreasonable searches and seizures and the Fifth Amendment protection against self-incrimination gave too much protection to criminals, especially corporate criminals. He recommended a "shocking" solution: abolish the Fourth and Fifth Amendments to the U.S. Constitution (American Academy of Political and Social Science 1910). Other reformers demanded similar treatment for the jury trial. Critics argued that this "palladium of liberty" and democracy ought to be abolished because sentimental jurors set criminals free to prey on innocent people. The complaints of the early 1900s created a tough law-and-order atmosphere and nourished a growing police power that continued from the 1920s through the 1950s (Walker 1980).

United States, 1960–2004

During the 1960s, this enhanced police power spawned a reaction we call the **due process revolution.** Led by the U.S. Supreme Court (called the Warren Court after its chief justice, Earl Warren), this revolution tilted the balance of power toward process and individual rights. According to its critics, it tilted the balance too far—so far that it created a criminal procedure soft on criminals and hard on victims (Cronin and others 1981).

Since 1971, there's been a definite pendulum swing from process back to result. In 1968, presidential candidate Richard Nixon promised to appoint "law and order" judges. And President Nixon did what Candidate Nixon promised. He started in 1969 by nominating a "tough on crime" U.S. Court of Appeals judge, Warren Burger, to succeed the retiring Earl Warren as chief justice of the U.S. Supreme Court. Presidents Nixon, Reagan, and George H. W. Bush were able to appoint the majority of the federal bench with like-minded judges. President George W. Bush promised to do the same. As I write this chapter, President G. W. Bush is trying to keep Candidate Bush's promise; not surprisingly, the process critics are fighting his efforts.

Let's be clear about something: There's nothing wrong with or unusual about presidents nominating judges who share their beliefs. Whatever the blather to the contrary by politicians, this is the way it's always been done, by every president, beginning with George Washington.

But there's a more important point to make here than that judicial appointments are political. It's not fair to explain the judicial participation in the crime control swing as simply the result of judges' personal belief in being tough on crime. The participation is also due to their commitment to a firm and old principle—**judicial restraint.** Judges are bound to defer to the will of the people expressed through their elected representatives—namely, presidents, governors, and federal and state legislatures. Led by the U.S. Supreme Court under Chief Justices Warren Burger (1971–1986) and William Rehnquist (1986–present), judges have increasingly followed the principle of judicial restraint by deferring to the judgments of the elected branches of government—the executive branch, which controls law enforcement, and the legislative branch, which defines crimes.

Despite the emphasis on the protection of society over the rights of criminal defendants, balancing the interests of "process," which protects individuals, and result, which protects the interests of society, remains at the heart of the law of criminal procedure (Packer 1968). Why? Because individual freedom is worthless without safety and security from criminal attacks. In the words of Chief Justice Rehnquist (1974), "Unregulated freedom is anarchy, and absolute order is despotism" (2). So, society has an interest in protecting people both from attacks by criminals who prey upon law-abiding individuals and from government excesses that threaten the autonomy associated with life in a free society.

Nothing in recent history has tested the balances between society and the individual and between ends and means more than two "wars": first the war on drugs (Chapters 3–6) and now the war on terror. (These two wars might be candidates, like the Civil War and World War II, for a **wartime emergency exception to the Bill of Rights** [Chapter 16].) Putting aside ordinary rules during extraordinary emergencies is a fact of life in every society under every form of government (Rossiter 1948).

Even during ordinary times, individuals demand extraordinary measures when they're victims or feel like victims. I remember back in the 1970s a woman came into the Minneapolis Police Department precinct office and demanded the officer in charge go into her neighbor's house and get a television set she was sure the neighbor had taken. "We can't just go in there because you tell us to," said the officer. "Why not?" the woman asked. "Because you need a warrant," the officer explained. "And you can't get a warrant without probable cause, and you don't have probable cause. That's the law." Without pausing for a second the woman asked, "How do we get this rule changed?"

LAW AND DISCRETION IN CRIMINAL PROCEDURE

Another way to view the swings in the pendulum from result to process is to contrast them with the swings in the balance between formal and informal criminal procedure. (You can't really understand what's happening in your journey through the law of criminal procedure without understanding this balance.) **Formal criminal procedure** focuses on decision making according to rules spelled out in the Constitution, laws, judicial opinions, and other written sources (Chapter 2). **Discretionary decision making**—informal decision making, or judgments by professionals based on unwritten rules, their training, and their experience—is how the process works on a day-to-day basis.

Think of each step in the criminal process as a decision point. Each step presents a criminal justice professional with the opportunity to decide whether or not to start, continue, or end the criminal process. The police can investigate suspects, or not, and arrest them, or not—initiating the formal criminal process, or stopping it. Prosecutors can charge suspects and continue the criminal process, divert suspects to some social service agency, or take no further action—effectively terminating the criminal process. Defendants can plead guilty (usually on their lawyers' advice) and avoid trial. Judges can suspend sentences or sentence convicted offenders to the maximum allowable penalty—hence, either minimizing or maximizing the punishment the criminal law prescribes.

Justice, fairness, and predictability all require the certainty and the protection against abuses provided by written rules. These same goals also require discretion to soften the rigidity of written rules. The tension between formal law and informal discretion—a recurring theme in criminal procedure—is as old as law; arguments raged over it in Western civilization as early as the Middle Ages.

One example of the need for discretionary decision making comes up when laws are applied to behavior that "technically" violates a criminal statute but was never intended by the legislature to be criminalized. This happens because it's impossible for legislators to predict all the ramifications of the statutes they enact. For example, it's a misdemeanor to drink in public parks in many cities, including Minneapolis. Yet, when a gourmet group had a brunch in a city park, because they thought the park had just the right ambience in which to enjoy their salmon mousse and imported French white wine, not only did the police not arrest the group for drinking in the park, but the city's leading newspaper wrote it up as a perfectly respectable social event. However, a young public defender wasn't pleased with the nonarrest. He pointed out that the police had arrested, and the prosecutor was at that moment prepared to prosecute, a Native American caught washing down a tuna fish sandwich with cheap red wine in another Minneapolis park. The public defender—a bit of a wag—noted that both the gourmet club and the Native American were consuming items from the same food groups. These incidents display both the strengths and weaknesses of discretion. The legislature obviously didn't intend the statute to cover drinking of the type the gourmet club engaged in; arresting them would have been foolish. On the other hand, arresting and prosecuting the Native American might well have been discriminatory, a wholly unintended and unacceptable result of law enforcement that is discretionary and selective.

In the end, the criminal process in practice is a blend of the formal law of criminal procedure and informal influences that enter the process by way of discretion. Discretion and law complement each other in promoting and balancing the interests in criminal procedure.

HUNCHES AREN'T ENOUGH

However much play in the joints discretion creates in the formal rules of law, one thing is certain: The agents of crime control aren't free to do whatever they please. That's because of another principle of criminal procedure you need to carry with you in your journey through the law of criminal procedure, the **objective basis requirement.** According to this principle, the government has to back up with *facts* every officially triggered restraint on the rights of individuals to come and go as they please and be let alone by the government. Hunches or whims are *never* enough. There's also a related principle (there's no official name for it; we'll call it the **graduated objective basis requirement**) that goes like this: The greater the limit, the more facts required to back it up. So, to arrest a person, police have to have enough facts to add up to probable cause (Chapter 5), but to convict a defendant, the government has to marshal enough evidence to prove guilt beyond a reasonable doubt (Chapter 14).

DUE PROCESS: HEARING BEFORE CONDEMNATION

One last principle is **hearing before condemnation.** "A law that hears before it condemns" is the foundation of our constitutional system, said the great nineteenth-century lawyer Daniel Webster (*Powell v. Alabama* 1932, 68). A law that "hears before it condemns" is a law that deprives persons of life, liberty, privacy, and property only according to fair procedures. In the case of invasions before conviction, courts review street stops and frisks, arrest, searches, interrogation, and the conduct of identification procedures. In the case of conviction, courts are required to "hear" cases, either by trials or by approving guilty pleas, before defendants are "condemned" by conviction. This review by courts, known as **judicial review** (deciding whether the actions of other branches of the government square with the Constitution), is an essential element of our legal system.

THE TEXT-CASE METHOD

Criminal Procedure 6 is what I call a text-case book; it's part text and part excerpts from real-life criminal procedure cases, edited for nonlawyers. The text part of the book explains the general principles and practices of the law of criminal procedure. The case excerpts provide you with real-life encounters between criminal suspects, defendants, and offenders and law enforcement officers, prosecutors, defense lawyers, and judges. The case excerpts let you see the general information in the text applied to the specifics of real-life situations, allowing you to think critically about the principles and their application. I believe the best way to test whether you understand a general concept is to apply it to concrete situations. So, although you can learn a lot from the text alone, you won't get the full benefit of what you've learned without applying and thinking about it by reading the case excerpts.

Throughout this book, you're going to read excerpts of cases from four levels of courts: the U.S. Supreme Court, the U.S. Courts of Appeals, state supreme courts, and state intermediate appeals courts (Figure 1.2). Most of the excerpted cases are U.S.

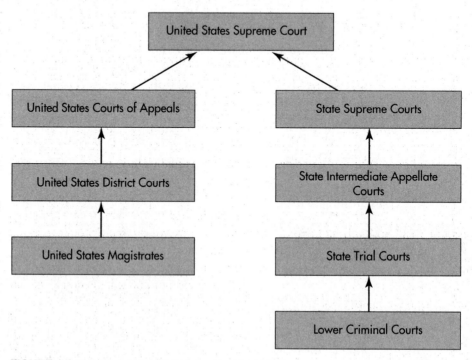

FIGURE 1.2 Court Structure in Our Federal and State System

Supreme Court cases. Why? Because the U.S. Supreme Court has the final word in interpreting the U.S. Constitution, and the Constitution is the source of authority for all the balances we've discussed in this chapter and will discuss throughout the rest of the book. The Constitution defines all of these balances only generally, and that's the way it's supposed to be. Constitutions aren't instruction manuals; they're a set of general principles.

Legislatures, courts, prosecutors and defense attorneys, and police departments write the instruction manuals. They have lots of leeway to write the instructions; the only limit is they can't write an instruction that violates the general principles set out in the Constitution. They also have lots of leeway in carrying out the instructions they've written; again, the only limit is they can't violate the Constitution's general principles.

Some of the constitutional provisions establishing the general principles don't need much clarification (separation of powers and federalism). Others need a lot. In fact, the two provisions we'll deal with most in the book are also the ones that need the most interpretation because they're so general and vague. These provisions are the right to "due process of law" and the right against "unreasonable searches and seizures." (I don't know if it's coincidental or not, but the provisions needing the most interpretation are also the ones dealing with the balances we discussed earlier.) Unfortunately, the Constitution doesn't come with a glossary.

What does all this business about general principles, instruction manuals, actions to carry out instructions, and glossaries have to do with the U.S. Supreme Court? The Court gets the last word (it writes the glossary) on what the principles mean, and it decides whether the instruction manuals and the actions carrying out the instructions comply with the constitutional principles it has defined.

The U.S. Supreme Court has the last word but not the only word. In fact, most cases on these weighty matters never get to the U.S. Supreme Court. The great bulk of judicial review never gets to the U.S. Supreme Court. So, occasionally, you'll read excerpts from **U.S. Courts of Appeals** cases (Figure 1.3). These intermediate federal appeals courts are distributed geographically throughout the country. U.S. Courts of Appeals usually review **U.S. District Court** (federal trial court) decisions. Sometimes, U.S. Courts of Appeals cases deal with issues not yet decided by the U.S. Supreme Court; at other times, they apply rules already established by the Supreme Court.

Occasionally, you'll read cases from state courts, too (see Figure 1.2). State cases are important for at least two reasons. First, every state has a bill of rights that contains provisions similar or identical to those in the U.S. Bill of Rights. State courts decide for themselves how to interpret and apply their own state constitutional provisions. Second, most criminal procedure cases never get into the federal courts. So, state courts are the first, and most of the time the only, courts that apply the U.S. Constitution to criminal procedure cases. The bottom line: The Supreme Court reviews only a few of the tens of thousands of decisions made by police officers, prosecutors, trial judges, and state appellate courts.

Before we begin examining excerpts from some of the decisions from these courts throughout the book, let's take a closer look at what you'll be reading. We'll begin with a look at the parts of case excerpts, the importance of precedent and stare decisis, appellate cases, and, finally, an approach to briefing the cases.

District of Columbia Circuit
District of Columbia
First Circuit
Maine, Massachusetts, New Hampshire, Puerto Rico, Rhode Island
Second Circuit
Connecticut, Eastern District New York, Southern District New York, Western District New York, Vermont
Third Circuit
Delaware, New Jersey, Eastern District Pennsylvania, Middle District Pennsylvania, Western District Pennsylvania, Virgin Islands
Fourth Circuit
Maryland, Eastern District North Carolina, Middle District North Carolina, Western District North Carolina, South Carolina, Eastern District Virginia, Western District Virginia, Southern District West Virginia
Fifth Circuit
Eastern District Louisiana, Middle District Louisiana, Western District Louisiana, Northern District Mississippi, Southern District Mississippi, Eastern District Texas, Northern District Texas, Southern District Texas, Western District Texas
Sixth Circuit
Eastern District Kentucky, Western District Kentucky, Eastern District Michigan, Western District Michigan, Northern District Ohio, Southern District Ohio, Eastern District Tennessee, Middle District Tennessee, Western District Tennessee
Seventh Circuit
Central District Illinois, Northern District Illinois, Southern District Illinois, Northern District Indiana, Southern District Indiana, Eastern District Wisconsin, Western District Wisconsin
Eighth Circuit
Eastern District Arkansas, Western District Arkansas, Northern District Iowa, Southern District Iowa, Minnesota, Eastern District Missouri, Western District Missouri, Nebraska, North Dakota, South Dakota
Ninth Circuit
Alaska, Arizona, Central District California, Eastern District California, Northern District California, Southern District California, Guam, Hawaii, Idaho, Montana, Nevada, Oregon, Eastern District Washington, Western District Washington
Tenth Circuit
Colorado, Kansas, Eastern District Oklahoma, Western District Oklahoma, Utah, Wyoming
Eleventh Circuit
Middle District Alabama, Northern District Alabama, Southern District Alabama, Middle District Florida, Northern District Florida, Southern District Florida, Middle District Georgia, Northern District Georgia, Southern District Georgia
Federal Circuit
Washington, D.C.

FIGURE 1.3 Federal Circuit and District Courts

Parts of Case Excerpts

Don't worry if reading cases intimidates you at first. Like so many students before you, you'll get the hang of it before long. To help you get the most out of the case excerpts, in this section I've included a set of detailed instructions for reading and analyzing the excerpts. (Since they're excerpts, I've also included instructions for finding cases. That way you can read the whole case to find out what I've left out.) The notes or annotations I've included will help you understand the cases; the annotations appear as footnotes. Next, I've outlined the main parts of each case, the (1) title, (2) citation, (3) procedural history, (4) judge, (5) facts, (6) decision, and (7) opinion. Learn them right at the beginning, and I'm sure you'll catch on to how to read cases sooner.

1. *Title.* The title in criminal cases consists of two names, one on either side of *"v."* (standing for "versus" or "against"). The name to the left of *"v."* is the party that brought the case to the court that's deciding the case. The name to the right of *"v."* is the party that lost the case in the lower court. The government (U.S. or Minnesota) is always the first party in the trial court because the government starts all criminal cases in the United States. The name on the right in the trial court that decided the case is the defendant. There are no trial court cases in this book because, unfortunately, trial records aren't published. We enter the case after the trial court has decided an issue in the case, a higher court has reviewed the trial court's decision, and it has decided to publish its opinion. (Reviewing courts don't have to publish their opinions; the decision to publish is discretionary.)

   Let's suppose the title of our first case is *Bostick v. State.* Why is this the title? Because Bostick was convicted in the trial court. The name of the party who's appealing her loss in the trial court appears first (**first party** or **appellant**); the party who won at the trial (**second party** or **appellee**) appears second. So, the title tells us Bostick is the defendant (appellant) who lost in the trial court; Florida is the government (appellee) that won. It's important to keep in mind that the government can't appeal a verdict of "not guilty." Why? Because the double jeopardy clause of the U.S. Constitution forbids it (Chapter 13). The government can appeal some trial court decisions (which we'll encounter) but *never* an acquittal.

2. *Citation.* After the title of the case, you'll see a string of letters and numbers. These are called the case **citation.** The case citation, like a footnote, endnote, or other reference in articles and books, tells you the source of the material quoted or relied upon. So, the citation tells you where you can find the published report of the case. The information in the citation tells you:
   a. The court that's reporting the case
   b. The date the court decided the case
   c. The book, volume, and page where the case is reported

   In *Bostick v. State,* the citation reads 554 So.2d 1153 (Fla. 1989). This means the Florida Supreme Court decided this case in 1989, and you can find the case printed in Volume 554 of the *Southern Reporter,* second series, on page 1153. Let me explain how I already (and you soon *will*) know this. The "(Fla. 1989)" tells us the name of the court and the year it was decided. How do I know it was the Florida Supreme Court and not the Florida intermediate court of appeals? If it were the intermediate court, it would've read "(Fla.App. 1989)." Now let's look at the 554 So.2d 1153. The state case excerpts in this book are published in several sets of books called regional reporters. The So.2d is an abbreviation for the *Southern Reporter,* second series. The 554 refers to the volume and the 1153 to the page in the volume where *Bostick v. State* is printed. So, the first number is the volume number, the abbreviation is the reporter name, the second number is the page in the volume, and the abbreviation and year in parentheses is the state court that decided the case and the year the court decided it.

   The U.S. courts follow the same scheme of citation. The U.S. Supreme Court cases appear in three major publications: the official reports published by the U.S. government, called the *United States Reports,* abbreviated U.S.; the *Supreme Court Reporter,* abbreviated S.Ct.; and the *Lawyer's Edition,* abbreviated L.Ed. The U.S. Court of Appeals are reported by *The Federal Reporter,* abbreviated F., F.2d. (second series), and F.3d. (third series).

3. *Procedural history.* The case history is a brief description of the procedural steps and judgments (decisions) made by each court that has heard the case.

4. *Judge.* This is the name of the judge who wrote the opinion and issued the court's judgment in the case.

5. *Facts.* The facts of the case are the critical starting point in reading and analyzing cases. If you don't know the facts, you can't understand the principle the case is teaching. One of my favorite law professors used to tell us again and again: "Remember cases are stories with a point. You can't get the point if you don't know the story." He also told us something else I think will help you: "Forget you're lawyers. Tell me the story as if you were telling it to your grandmother who doesn't know anything about the law." Take Professor Hill's advice. I do, because it's still good advice.

6. *Judgment (decision).* The court's judgment (sometimes called the court's decision) is how the court disposes of the case. In the trial court, the judgments are almost always guilty or not guilty. In appeals courts, the judgments are affirmed, reversed, or reversed and remanded. This is the most important legal action of the court, because it's what decides what happens to the defendant and the government.

7. *Opinion.* **Court opinions** explain why courts decided and entered the judgment in the case. The opinion contains two essential ingredients:
   a. The court's holding—the legal rule the court has decided to apply to the facts of the cases
   b. The court's reasoning—the reasons the court gives to support its holding
   Most of the cases, particularly those of the U.S. Supreme Court, consist of two types of opinions: majority and dissent. Four types of opinions can be offered by the court:
   - *Majority opinion.* The U.S. Supreme Court consists of nine justices, each of whom has a vote and the right to submit an opinion. The **majority opinion** (one that five justices agree to) is the law.
   - *Concurring opinions.* Sometimes, justices agree with the decision reached in another opinion but write separate opinions giving their own reasons for reaching the decision. Opinions that agree with the result of another opinion whether majority or dissent are called **concurring opinions.**
   - *Plurality opinions.* If a majority of the justices agree with the result in a case but they can't agree on the reasons for the result, the opinion with the reasoning agreed to by the largest number of justices is called a **plurality opinion.** For example, suppose that seven justices agree with the result and four give one set of reasons, three give another set of reasons, and two dissent. The opinion to which the four subscribe is the plurality opinion. A plurality opinion is *not* the law.
   - *Dissenting opinions.* If justices don't agree with the court's decision and/or its reasoning, they can write their own **dissenting opinions** explaining why they don't agree with either the reasoning, the result, or both. Often, the dissenting opinions point to the future; many majority opinions of today are based on dissents from the past. The late chief justice Charles Evans Hughes once said a dissent should be "an appeal to the brooding spirit of the law, to the intelligence of a future day" (Lewis 1994, A13).

The conflicting arguments and reasoning in the majority, plurality, concurring, and dissenting opinions challenge you to think about the issues in the cases because, most of the time, all of the justices convincingly argue their views of the case. First, the majority opinion, then the concurring opinion(s), and finally the dissenting opinion(s) present convincing arguments that will cause you to sway one way and then another. This is good. It teaches you that there is more than one reasonable position on all the important issues in the law of criminal procedure. Yes, reasonable people do disagree!

Precedent and Stare Decisis

You'll notice that court opinions refer to past cases to back up their reasons and their decision in the present case. These prior decisions are called **precedent.** The ancient and firmly entrenched doctrine called **stare decisis** binds judges to follow precedent. But, stare decisis only binds judges to the prior decisions of either their own court or of courts superior to them in their own *jurisdiction*. **Jurisdiction** means the power to hear and decide cases in a specific geographical area (like a county, a state, or a federal district) or the subject matter (like criminal appeals) the court controls.

Supreme Court Justice and respected judicial philosopher Benjamin Cardozo (1921) once said this about precedent and the doctrine of stare decisis:

> It is easier to follow the beaten track than it is to clear another. In doing this, I shall be treading in the footsteps of my predecessors, and illustrating the process that I am seeking to describe, since the power of precedent, when analyzed, is the power of the beaten path. (62)

The idea of precedent isn't special to the law of criminal procedure, nor is it the basis only of legal reasoning (Schauer 1987, 571). We're accustomed to the basic notion of precedent in ordinary life. We like to do things the way we've done them in the past. For example, if a professor asks multiple-choice questions covering only material in the text on three exams, you expect multiple-choice questions on the fourth exam. If you get an essay exam instead, you won't like it. Not only won't you like it; you'll probably think it's "unfair." Why? Precedent—the way we've done things before—makes life stable and predictable. Knowing what to expect, and counting on it, guides our actions in the future so we can plan for and meet challenges and solve problems. Changing this without warning is unfair. In ordinary life, then, as in criminal procedure, following past practice gives stability, predictability, and a sense of fairness and justice to decisions.

Of course, doing things the way we've always done them isn't always right or good. When we need to, we change (usually reluctantly) and do things differently. These changes themselves become guides to future action—so, too, with legal precedent. Courts change precedent, but they do it reluctantly. Courts, like individuals in ordinary life, don't like to change, particularly when they have to admit they were wrong. That's why, as you read the case excerpts, you'll rarely find one that comes right out and says, "We overrule our prior decision." Instead, when courts decide to get off the beaten path they do it by distinguishing cases. This means that a court decides that a prior decision doesn't apply to the current case because the facts are different. For example, the rule that controls the right to a lawyer in death penalty cases doesn't have to apply to a case punishable by a fine. As the Court has noted, "Death is different" (Schauer 1987, 571).

Appellate Cases

Most of the cases in this textbook are appellate court cases. This means that a lower court has already taken some action in the case and that one of the parties has asked a higher court to review the lower court's action. Parties seek appellate review of what they claim were errors by the trial court or unlawful actions by police, judges, prosecutors, or defense lawyers. Sometimes, a convicted defendant appeals. Only defendants can appeal convictions; the government can never appeal acquittals. However, many appellate reviews arise out of proceedings before trial and convictions. Both the government and the defendant can appeal pretrial proceedings.

Most appellate cases in this book arise out of defendants' motions to throw out evidence obtained by law enforcement officers during searches and seizures, interrogation, and identification procedures, such as lineups. These motions are heard in a proceeding called a **suppression hearing.**

Courts call parties in appellate courts by different names. The most common parties in the appellate courts are the appellant (the party appealing) and appellee (the party appealed against). Both of these terms originate from the word appeal. In the excerpts of older cases, you'll find other names for the parties. The older cases refer to the "plaintiff in error," the party that claims the lower courts erred in their rulings, and to the "defendant in error," the party who won in the lower court. These names stem from an old and no longer used writ called the writ of error.

A **petitioner** is a defendant who asks the higher court to review a decision made either by a lower court or some other official. The two main petitions are *habeas corpus,* Latin for "you have the body," and *certiorari,* Latin for "to be certified":

- *Habeas corpus.* Called a collateral attack because it's a separate proceeding from the criminal case, habeas corpus is a *civil action* (a noncriminal proceeding) that reviews the constitutionality of the petitioner's detention or imprisonment. Let's say a prisoner sues his jailers, prison administrators, and other officials who are holding him in custody. The suit petitions the court to order the official to prove that he is locked up legally. You can recognize these proceedings by their title. Instead of the name of a state or the United States, you'll see two individuals' names, such as in *Adams v. Williams.* Here, Adams is the warden of the prison that is holding Williams prisoner.

- *Certiorari.* Most appeals to the U.S. Supreme Court are based on writs of certiorari. **Certiorari** is a proceeding used only in the U.S. Supreme Court to review decisions of lower courts. These proceedings begin when petitioners ask for reviews of court decisions. It's important to understand right away that the Court doesn't grant certiorari to prevent the punishment of innocent defendants. Petitioners would get nowhere if their petitions said, "I'm innocent; they convicted the wrong person." As a legal matter, the Court isn't interested in whether individual defendants are innocent or guilty; that's the job of the lower courts. The Supreme Court grants certiorari because a case raises an important constitutional issue that affects large numbers of individuals; in a sense the defendant in the case reviewed represents these other individuals.

Granting certiorari is wholly discretionary, and the Court grants it—that is, it issues a writ of certiorari (an order to the court that decided the case to send up the record of its proceedings to the U.S. Supreme Court for review)—in only a tiny percentage of petitions. Four of the nine Supreme Court justices have to vote to review a case—a requirement known as the **rule of four**—before the Court will hear an appeal on certiorari.

Briefing the Cases

To guide your reading and to help you get the most out of the case excerpts, you should summarize the main parts of the case. Law students call this "briefing" a case. Whether you call it a brief, a summary, or a study guide, you should sort out the parts of the opinion and write out short summaries of each part. I recommend using a separate card or piece of paper for each case. At the top of each card or sheet, put the name and the citation of the case. Then, summarize briefly and accurately the (1) history, (2) facts, (3) issue, (4) decision, (5) opinions, and (6) disposition of the case.

1. *History.* The history of the case refers to the formal procedural steps the case has taken and the decisions at each of these steps, beginning usually with the indictment and moving through the trial court and appellate courts to the court whose excerpt you're briefing. This part of your brief puts the excerpt in its correct place so that you'll know where the case has been, what decisions were made before it got to the appellate court, and the decision of the appellate court in the case whose excerpted facts and opinion you're about to read.

2. *Facts.* You can't understand the principles and policies of a case unless you know the facts of the case. All the cases apply principles to facts; principles alone have no meaning without applying them to the facts of the case. There are two types of **relevant facts** in criminal procedure cases: acts by government officials and the objective basis for the actions.
   a. *Acts by government officials.* List the specific acts by government officials that the defendant claims violated the Constitution or other law. List each act by the government accurately and in chronological order. Also, include circumstances surrounding the acts. I recommend that you put each act and circumstance on a separate line of your brief. Think of these facts as notes for a story you're going to tell someone who isn't familiar at all with what government officials did and the circumstances surrounding the acts.
   b. *Objective basis (quantum of proof).* Objective basis (also called the **quantum of proof**) means the facts and circumstances that back up the act by government officials. As you'll learn over and over in your study of criminal procedure, government officials can't restrict your freedom of movement or your privacy on a whim; they have to justify their actions by facts and circumstances that lead them to reasonably suspect or believe that you've committed a crime. For example, an officer can't back up patting you down by claiming she had a "hunch" you were carrying a gun. But she can back it up by saying there was a bulge at your waist inside your shirt.

3. *Constitutional (legal) question.* Think of criminal procedure cases as stories with a point. The facts tell the story. The point is that the story raises a question(s) (the lawyers call it an *issue* in the case) about the U.S. Constitution, state constitutions,

or prior cases involving those constitutions. Specifically, the **issue in criminal procedure cases** (also called the **legal question in the case**) is whether acts by law enforcement officers, prosecutors, defense counsel, or judges violated a specific constitutional provision, statute, or rule. In this part of your brief, make sure you identify:

    a. The specific type of government official (law enforcement officer, etc.)
    b. The specific actions taken by the official (ordered the suspect to halt, chased her, and tackled her)
    c. The specific provision or part of a provision that is in question (unreasonable seizure clause of the Fourth Amendment of the U.S. Constitution)

      So, in our pat-down example, the question might ask: Is a police officer pat-down, backed up by seeing a bulge at the suspect's waist, a reasonable Fourth Amendment search?

4. *Decision or holding.* The **decision of the court** part of your brief should state the court's answer to the question—for example, a law enforcement officer feeling the suspect's outer clothing backed up by seeing a bulge at the suspect's waist was a reasonable Fourth Amendment search.

5. *Opinions.* State in simple English the arguments and reasons that the majority, plurality, concurring, and dissenting present.

6. *Judgment (disposition).* Courts don't have to write opinions. Many times (and in trial courts in almost every case) they don't, which as students is our loss (or maybe to you it's a blessing). The **judgment of the case** is the only binding action of the court. It states what's going to happen to the judgment of the court below and, ultimately, to the defendant or convicted offender. Common judgments in criminal cases include affirmed, reversed and remanded, or remanded.

    a. *Affirmed.* **Affirmed** means the appellate court upheld a lower court's decision.
    b. *Reversed and/or remanded.* **Reversed** means the appellate court set aside, or nullified, the lower court's judgment. **Remanded** means that the appellate court sent the case back to the court from which it came for further action. Notice that neither reversed nor remanded means that the defendant automatically goes free. Fewer than half the defendants who win Supreme Court cases ultimately triumph when their cases are reversed and/or remanded to lower courts, particularly to state courts. For example, in the famous *Miranda v. Arizona*, the prison gates didn't open for Ernesto Miranda. He was detained in jail while he was retried without the confession he made, promptly convicted, and sent from jail to prison (Chapter 8).

SUMMARY

    I. The criminal procedure road map
      A. Follows three stages:
        1. On the street—brief encounters between law enforcement officers and individuals

2. At the police station—more extensive contacts between law enforcement officers and suspects
3. In court proceedings—contacts before trial between prosecutors, judges, and defense lawyers with defendants and after trial with offenders
B. The focus will be on examining power and the limits on power to control crime

II. The "big picture": balance
A. We live in a constitutional democracy, where neither government nor the majority has all the power
B. Balancing community safety and individual freedom is the heart of criminal procedure in a constitutional democracy; it has three objectives:
1. Ensuring we feel safe and secure as a community from crimes against our bodies, our homes, and our property
2. Maximizing the individual autonomy to come and go as we please and be free of government invasion of our lives
3. Giving government enough power to control the people *and* guarantee government will control itself
C. Balance between ends and means
1. Is a balance between result and process
2. "Ends" consists of the search for the truth to obtain the correct result in individual cases
a. Catching, convicting, and punishing *guilty* people
b. Freeing as soon as possible *innocent* people caught up in government efforts to control crime
3. "Means" is the commitment to fairness in dealing with suspects, defendants, and offenders
D. The trump card is the means of fair procedure, not the ends of crime control, *except in dire emergencies*
E. The exclusionary rule is the most frequent way to play the trump card of fair procedures

III. A capsule history of balance in criminal procedure
A. The history is a pendulum swing between result (crime control) and process (fair procedures)
B. Roman republic focused on the process; the Roman Empire on the result
C. English monarchs shifted to royal power and control of governed; restive aristocrats, then middle classes, and American colonies focused on process and individual rights
D. From independence to 1900, the Bill of Rights and other measures emphasized individual rights and the process
E. 1900–1960 saw a swing to crime control
F. 1960–2004 saw a swing first to process and individual rights in the 1960s "due process revolution" and then back to community safety and government power ("law and order," war on drugs, and war on terror) since the 1970s

IV. Law and discretion in criminal procedure
A. Formal and informal decision making co-exist in U.S. criminal procedure
B. Formal decision making is according to formal rules to guarantee uniformity, certainty, and predictability

C. Informal discretionary decision making is to insure flexibility, fairness, and individualized responses

D. Formal and informal decision making complement each other to promote the values of crime control in a constitutional democracy

V: Hunches aren't enough

A. Government restrictions on individual liberty and privacy require an objective basis

B. Facts, not hunches, have to back up government restrictions

C. The greater the restriction, the higher the objective basis (the more facts needed to back it up)

VI. Due process: hearing before condemnation

A. Hallmark of a constitutional democracy

B. Every government action restricting individual rights is subject to review in court

 Go to the Criminal Procedure 6e CD to download this summary outline. The outline has been formatted so that you can add notes to it during class lectures, or later create a customized chapter outline to use while reviewing. Either way, the summary outline will help you understand the "big picture" and fill in the details as you study.

REVIEW QUESTIONS

1. Identify and describe the three stages in U.S. crime control.

2. Explain the difference between "dissing" and critically examining a criminal procedure.

3. Explain the difference between crime control in a dictatorship, a pure democracy, and a constitutional democracy.

4. Identify and describe the balance of values at the heart of our constitutional democracy.

5. Explain what James Madison meant in the quotation, "If men were angels…" that's reprinted in the chapter opening.

6. Explain how and why the balances you identified in (4) are flexible.

7. Describe how our system tries to strike a balance between ends and means. Describe the controversy this creates.

8. What's the significance of the exclusionary rule in the ends–means balance?

9. Describe the history of criminal procedure, and explain why it's described as a pendulum swing.

10. Describe the difference between formal and informal criminal procedure, and explain why both are essential to crime control in our constitutional democracy.

11. Explain why "hunches aren't enough" in criminal procedure.

12. What does "hearing before condemnation" mean in the law of criminal procedure, and what's the significance of the idea?

KEY TERMS

constitutional democracy p. 2
community security p. 4
individual autonomy p. 4
balance between result and
    process p. 5
ends–means balance p. 5
bills of rights p. 5
exclusionary rule p. 6
"good" evidence p. 6
"bad methods" p. 6
due process revolution p. 9
judicial restraint p. 9
wartime emergency exception to
    the Bill of Rights p. 9
formal criminal procedure p. 10
discretionary decision making
    p. 10
objective basis requirement p. 11

graduated objective basis
    requirement p. 11
hearing before condemnation
    p. 11
judicial review p. 12
U.S. Courts of Appeals p. 13
U.S. District Court p. 13
first party p. 15
appellant p. 15
second party p. 15
appellee p. 15
citation p. 15
court opinions p. 16
majority opinion p. 16
concurring opinion p. 16
plurality opinion p. 16
dissenting opinion p. 16
precedent p. 17

stare decisis p. 17
jurisdiction p. 17
suppression hearing p. 18
petitioner p. 18
habeas corpus p. 18
certiorari p. 18
rule of four p. 19
relevant facts p. 19
quantum of proof p. 19
issue in criminal procedure cases
    p. 20
legal question in the case p. 20
decision of the court p. 20
judgment of the case p. 20
affirmed p. 20
reversed p. 20
remanded p. 20

THE COMPANION WEB SITE
FOR *CRIMINAL PROCEDURE,* SIXTH EDITION

http://cj.wadsworth.com/samaha/crim_pro6e

Supplement your review of this chapter by going to the companion Web site to take one of the Tutorial Quizzes, use the flash cards to test yourself on the key terms from each chapter, and check out the many other study aids you'll find there. You'll find valuable data and resources at your fingertips to help you study for that big exam or write that important paper.

2 The Constitution and Criminal Procedure

Chapter Outline

Constitutionalism

The Sources of Criminal Procedure
The U.S. Constitution and
    Federal Courts
State Constitutions and Courts
Federal and State Statutes
    and Rules
Model Codes and Rules

Due Process of Law
The Fundamental Fairness
    Doctrine
The Incorporation Doctrine

**Equal Protection
of the Law**

Chapter Main Points

- Laws passed by legislatures are constantly changing, detailed rules; constitutions adopted by the whole people are permanent (or at least very hard to change), general principles.
- Criminal procedure is the method government has to follow in controlling crime.
- The sources of criminal procedure consist of U.S. and state constitutions, statutes, court opinions, and administrative rules.
- The U.S. Constitution is the supreme law of the land.
- The Constitution doesn't come with an instruction manual to interpret its meaning.
- The U.S. Supreme Court is the final interpreter of the meaning of the U.S. Constitution.
- The U.S. Constitution is a set of minimum standards that states are bound to follow.
- States can raise the minimum standards in the U.S. Constitution, but they can't lower them.
- State courts have the final word in interpreting their own state constitutions.
- Most day-to-day criminal procedure takes place at the local and state level.
- Until the Civil War amendments to the U.S. Constitution, the Bill of Rights applied only to federal criminal procedures.
- During the 1960s, the U.S. Supreme Court declared that the Fourteenth Amendment turned the Bill of Rights into national rights that are binding on all state and local criminal procedures.
- The U.S. Supreme Court also declared that the equal protection clause of the Fourteenth Amendment to the U.S. Constitution created a national guarantee that is binding on all state and local criminal procedures.
- Equal protection doesn't require officials to treat everyone exactly alike; it means they can't classify people according to unacceptable group characteristics, especially race or ethnicity.
- The burden of proving claims of official discrimination that violate the guarantee of equal protection is very high; the burden is on those who claim discrimination, and, in practice, the burden is hardly ever met.

Cliff Dial, a deputy sheriff, accompanied by others, came to the home of Ellington, one of the defendants, and requested him to accompany them to the house of the deceased, and there a number of white men were gathered, who began to accuse the defendant of the crime. Upon his denial they seized him, and with the participation of the deputy they hanged him by a rope to the limb of a tree, and, having let him down, they hung him again, and when he was let down the second time, and he still protested his innocence, he was tied to a tree and whipped, and, still declining to accede to the demands that he confess, he was finally released, and he returned with some difficulty to his home, suffering intense pain and agony. The record of the testimony shows that the signs of the rope on his neck were plainly visible during the so-called trial. A day or two thereafter the deputy returned to the home of the defendant and arrested him, and departed with the prisoner towards the jail and while on the way, the deputy stopped and again severely whipped the defendant, declaring that he would continue the whipping until he confessed, and the defendant then agreed to confess to such a statement as the deputy would dictate, and he did so, after which he was delivered to jail.

Brown v. Mississippi (1936), U.S. Supreme Court

No State ... shall deny any person of life, liberty, or property without due process of law; nor deny to any person within its jurisdiction equal protection of the law.

U.S. Constitution, Amendment XIV

CONSTITUTIONALISM

"We must never forget that it is a *constitution* we are expounding," Chief Justice John Marshall wrote in the great case *McCulloch v. Maryland* (1819). The chief justice was referring to a deeply embedded idea in our constitutional democracy—the idea of **constitutionalism.** The core of the idea is that constitutions adopted by the whole people are a higher form of law than ordinary laws passed by legislatures. As such, constitutions are forever; other laws are for now. **Laws** are detailed, constantly changing rules passed by legislatures; **constitutions** are a set of permanent (or at least very hard to change), general principles. We can boil down the difference between laws and constitutions into six contrasting characteristics (Gardner 1991, 814):

1. Constitutions are a higher form of law that speak with a political authority that no ordinary law or other government action can ever match.

2. Constitutions express the will of the whole people.

3. Constitutions always bind the government.

4. Constitutions can't be changed by the government.

5. Only the direct action of the whole people themselves can change constitutions.

6. Constitutions embody the fundamental values of the people.

THE SOURCES OF CRIMINAL PROCEDURE

Criminal procedures are the rules government has to follow to detect and investigate crimes, apprehend suspects, prosecute and convict defendants, and punish criminals. We find these rules and the principles governing them in four federal and state sources (Table 2.1):

1. Constitutions

2. Court decisions

3. Statutes

4. Administrative rules

TABLE 2.1
Sources of Criminal Procedure Law

1. *United States Constitution.* The supreme law of the land, the ultimate source of authority in criminal procedure.

2. *State constitutions.* Instruments with provisions that are parallel to those of the United States Constitution.

3. *United States Supreme Court decisions.* Decisions that interpret, amplify, and apply federal constitutional standards to specific cases. These decisions are the law of the land.

4. *United States Court of Appeals and District Court opinions.* Decisions that are the law only in the territory covered by their jurisdiction. If the United States Supreme Court rules on the question, its decision takes precedence. Although not law beyond their own jurisdiction, these decisions address important issues and suggest results that other jurisdictions may follow.

5. *State court opinions.* Decisions that are the law only within a state. States can raise standards under provisions in state constitutions that are parallel to provisions in the federal Constitution, but they cannot reduce those standards below the minimum set by the United States Constitution as interpreted by the United States Supreme Court.

6. Federal Rules of Criminal Procedure. The rules established by the United States Supreme Court that govern practices in all federal courts, from the filing of a criminal complaint to appeals from (and other challenges to) convictions in federal courts. Most states have adopted rules similar to the *Federal Rules of Criminal Procedure.*

7. *State rules of criminal procedure.* Rules similar to the *Federal Rules* that govern procedure in state courts.

8. Model Code of Pre-arraignment Procedure. The American Law Institute's *Model Code* to govern practice in police-citizen encounters on the street not covered by the *Federal Rules* but sometimes found in state "stop-and-frisk" statutes. The code and commentary embody the arguments and recommendations of distinguished professionals and scholars of criminal justice. The code is not law, but courts often cite both its model provisions and the authoritative commentary accompanying the provisions.

TABLE 2.2

Criminal Procedure Protections in the Bill of Rights

FOURTH AMENDMENT
Guarantee against

1. unreasonable searches and seizures. The right of the people to be secure in their persons, houses, papers, and effects, against unreasonable searches and seizures, shall not be violated, and no warrants shall issue, but upon probable cause, supported by oath or affirmation, and particularly describing the place to be searched, and the persons or things to be seized.

FIFTH AMENDMENT
Guarantees of

2. grand jury indictment

3. no double jeopardy

4. due process

5. protection against self-incrimination. No person shall be held to answer for a capital, or otherwise infamous crime, unless on a presentment or indictment of a Grand Jury, except in cases arising in the land or naval forces, or in the militia, when in actual service in time of war or public danger; nor shall any person be subject for the same offence to be twice put in jeopardy of life or limb; nor shall be compelled in any criminal case to be a witness against himself, nor be deprived of life, liberty, or property, without due process of law....

SIXTH AMENDMENT
Rights to

6. public and speedy trial

7. impartial jury

8. notice of the nature and cause of the accusation

9. confrontation with opposing witnesses

10. compulsory process

11. assistance of counsel. In all criminal prosecutions, the accused shall enjoy the right to a speedy and public trial, by an impartial jury of the State and district wherein the crime shall have been committed, which districts shall have been previously ascertained by law, and to be informed of the nature and cause of the accusation; to be confronted with the witnesses against him; to have compulsory process for obtaining witnesses in his favor; and to have the assistance of counsel for his defense.

EIGHTH AMENDMENT
Prohibitions against

12. excessive bail

13. excessive fines

14. cruel and unusual punishment. Excessive bail shall not be required, nor excessive fines imposed, nor cruel and unusual punishments inflicted.

The U.S. Constitution is the highest authority in criminal procedure; it trumps all other sources. There are two criminal procedure provisions in the body of the Constitution: Article I, § 9, recognizes **habeas corpus** (the right of individuals to challenge any government detention) (Chapter 14), and Article III, § 2, guarantees trial by jury in the community where the crimes were committed.

Most criminal provisions are in the amendments to the Constitution, the part known as the Bill of Rights (12 out of the 28 provisions are guarantees made to persons suspected of, charged with, or convicted of crimes) (Table 2.2). Originally, the guarantees listed in Table 2.2 applied only to the *federal* government, but since the 1960s, they've applied to state and local governments, too.

The U.S. Constitution and Federal Courts

According to the U.S. Constitution, Article VI (the **supremacy clause**):

> This constitution, and the laws of the United States which shall be made in pursuance thereof...shall be the supreme law of the land; and the judges in every state shall be bound thereby, anything in the constitution or laws of any state to the contrary notwithstanding.

In other words, the U.S. Constitution is the final authority in criminal procedure. True as this may be, the Constitution doesn't come with an instruction manual. It requires—and gets—a lot of interpretation. Who tells officials (and us, too, of course) what the Constitution means? Chief Justice John Marshall answered the question in the great case of *Marbury v. Madison* (1803). Writing for the Court, Marshall established what later courts would call the principle of **judicial review.** According to that principle, courts, and ultimately the U.S. Supreme Court, not the Congress and not the president, have the final word in saying what the Constitution means.

Alexander Hamilton defended this startlingly vast power of judicial review in the *Federalist Papers* ([1788]; 1961):

> The interpretation of the laws is the proper and peculiar province of the courts. A constitution is, in fact, and must be regarded by the judges as, a fundamental law. It therefore belongs to them to ascertain its meaning, as well as the meaning of any particular act proceeding from the legislative body. If there should happen to be an irreconcilable variance between the two, that which has the superior obligation and validity ought, of course, to be preferred; or, in other words, the Constitution ought to be preferred to the statute, the intention of the people to the intention of their agents. (485–486)

So, the supremacy clause and judicial review together establish that criminal procedure has to answer to the U.S. Constitution, and *courts* determine which procedures are in line with the Constitution. All courts can interpret the Constitution, but the U.S. Supreme Court has the last word; its decisions bind all other courts, legislatures, executives, and criminal justice officials. But it's important for you to keep in mind two important limits on this enormous power: First, the U.S. Constitution and Supreme Court are at the top of a pyramid with a very wide state and local base of criminal justice administration. So, the Supreme Court has to depend on local courts and police to apply its decisions to day-to-day operations. Second, and just as important, U.S. Courts of Appeals, U.S. District Courts, and state courts answer constitutional questions the Supreme Court hasn't answered yet—and maybe never will (Amsterdam 1970, 785).

One final point: The U.S. Supreme Court has more power over criminal procedure in lower federal courts than it does over state courts. Why? Because of what's called its **supervisory power**—the power to make rules to manage how lower federal courts conduct their business. The Court can only control criminal procedures in state courts if the states' rules violate the U.S. Constitution. Many procedures (some of them very important for defendants and the state) don't violate the Constitution, like the rule banning the use of illegally obtained evidence (Chapter 10).

State Constitutions and Courts

Every state constitution guarantees its citizens **parallel rights**—rights similar to those in the U.S. Constitution and Bill of Rights. For example, every state constitution guarantees rights against self-incrimination and unreasonable searches and seizures as well as the right to counsel and to jury trial. Also, some state constitutions provide rights not specifically mentioned in the U.S. Constitution, like the right to privacy.

State courts are a source of criminal procedure law in two types of cases: (1) those involving the U.S. Constitution and (2) those involving their own state constitutions. In cases involving the U.S. Constitution, state court decisions aren't final. They can always be appealed to federal courts. Many cases excerpted in this book started in state courts and ended in the U.S. Supreme Court. But, in practice, most criminal cases never get past state courts.

State courts are the final authority in cases based on state constitutions and statutes. The federal courts—even the U.S. Supreme Court—can't interpret state constitutions and statutes if the state provisions and state courts interpreting them meet the standards set by the U.S. Constitution. The U.S. Constitution sets *minimum* standards. In referring to this federal rights floor, a Supreme Court justice once said, "It doesn't pay a law much of a compliment to declare it constitutional." States are free to raise the minimum, and sometimes they do. The special feature "State Constitutional Law" you'll see in most chapters includes cases where states have raised the U.S. constitutional minimum rights floor.

Federal and State Statutes and Rules

As you now know, constitutions aren't detailed codes of criminal procedure (see "Constitutionalism"). Details are the business of federal and state legislatures, courts, and criminal justice agencies. The federal government and most states have adopted some rules of criminal procedure. Most of these rules apply to proceedings in court and are written by judges and approved by legislatures. Most police departments and prosecutors' offices also have rules of procedure.

One set of these rules, the *Federal Rules of Criminal Procedure,* grew out of a deep dissatisfaction with the administration of justice during the early decades of the twentieth century. In 1940, Congress authorized the Supreme Court to adopt rules of criminal procedure for the federal courts. Pursuant to this authorization, the Court appointed "a group of eminent practitioners and scholars" to research and draft rules that would effectively put the ideals of the Constitution into daily practice. According to criminal law scholar Professor Gerhard O. Mueller (1966), "In three and one half years of hard labor the group produced the *Federal Rules of Criminal Procedure.* For the first time in history the premises of procedure had been assembled in a body, neatly organized, expressed tersely and concisely" (xiv).

Model Codes and Rules

The *Federal Rules of Criminal Procedure*—and the state rules fashioned after them—don't address the period *before* arrest, specifically encounters between individuals and police officers on the street (Chapters 3–4). The **American Law Institute** (1975), a group of distinguished judges, lawyers, criminal justice professionals, law enforcement professionals, and scholars, filled this gap in its *Model Code of Pre-Arraignment Procedure.* Although it's not law, courts sometimes cite both the code and the authoritative commentary that accompanies it in their decisions.

DUE PROCESS OF LAW

One of the major results of the 1960s "due process revolution" (Chapter 1) was the expansion of individual rights. How was this expansion accomplished? First, more classes of people (the vulnerable as well as the powerful, including criminal suspects, defendants, and offenders) were included within the scope of constitutional protection, and, second, states as well as the federal government were compelled to guarantee those rights to these vulnerable classes. The bases for this two-pronged expansion are two guarantees states have to provide according to the Fourteenth Amendment: due process and equal protection of the law. The Fourteenth Amendment commands that

> No state shall . . . deprive any citizen of life, liberty, or property without due process of law; nor deny to any person within its jurisdiction the equal protection of the laws.

From colonial times until the Civil War, criminal justice was a local affair. In view of this history, it's not surprising that the Bill of Rights wasn't applied to the states. As early as 1833, Chief Justice John Marshall noted that the question of whether the Bill of Rights extended to the states was "of great importance, but not of much difficulty." If the Congress that created the Bill of Rights had meant to take the highly unusual step of applying them to the states, it would have said so, "in plain and intelligible language" (*Barron v. Baltimore* 1833, 250).

The Fourteenth Amendment, adopted in the aftermath of the Civil War, changed all that (Nelson 1988, Chapter 2). A main goal of the Civil War (vindicated in the crushing defeat of the Confederacy) was to establish federal supremacy over states' rights. A second principle, that everyone was entitled to equal rights, triumphed at least on paper in the abolition of slavery. The drafters of the amendment purposely left the definitions of due process and equal protection general (and not by accident, vague). You should already know one reason why: They were constitutional provisions, not ordinary laws. The other reason is rooted in the history of the time: States' rights and equality were enormously controversial issues. No matter how decisive in strictly military terms the victory of the Union and the crushing defeat of the secessionists were, the outcome couldn't guarantee the triumph of the great principles that millions had fought and died for. Don't forget this history. It'll help you to understand the struggle to define the (purposely) vague due process and equal protection guarantees.

How do the courts, particularly the U.S. Supreme Court, define **due process,** this broad and vague idea that lends itself to many interpretations? Some emphasize the "process" part, contending that due process guarantees fair procedures for deciding cases. (A piece of advice: Whenever you see "due process" think "fair process.") We call this definition **procedural due process.** (This is the meaning we'll discuss in this book. We leave aside **substantive due process,** the other meaning of due process, which is a topic for a course in constitutional law, not criminal procedure.) But what fair procedures are guaranteed by due process? The Bill of Rights lists several. Are these the ones due process guarantees? Yes, say some experts. The framers of the Bill of

Rights were codifying a specific list of hard-fought and proudly won procedures to protect private persons against government excesses.

No, say others. If due process is just shorthand for the Bill of Rights, then the Fourteenth Amendment due process clause is wasted language, because the Fifth Amendment already includes a due process clause, "No person shall be denied life, liberty, or property without due process of law" (*Adamson v. California* 1947). Besides, they say, the framers wouldn't have frozen criminal procedure at a particular eighteenth-century moment. The authors of the Constitution looked forward; they hoped the meaning of due process would evolve and expand to meet the needs and wants of an ever-advancing society.

Until the 1930s, the U.S. Supreme Court time and again—sometimes exasperated that lawyers didn't get the message—stubbornly refused to apply the Fourteenth Amendment due process clause to state criminal proceedings. *Hurtado v. California* (1884), decided in 1884, began a line of cases that rejected the idea that due process was shorthand for the application of the specific provisions in the Bill of Rights to state criminal proceedings. The case involved Joseph Hurtado and José Estuardo, who'd been close friends for several years. Then Hurtado discovered Estuardo was having an affair with his wife. When confronted, Estuardo admitted it and said, "I'm the meat and you're the knife; kill me if you like." Instead, Hurtado demanded that Estuardo leave Sacramento. Estuardo promised to leave but then reneged and renewed his pursuit of Hurtado's wife. The case began with a brawl in a Sacramento tavern. Hurtado assaulted Estuardo. A few days later, Hurtado shot Estuardo in the chest. Estuardo turned to flee; Hurtado shot him in the back. Estuardo fell to the ground; Hurtado shot him again, then bludgeoned him with the pistol (Cortner 1981, 18–19).

In the federal courts, and in most state courts of the time, a grand jury would've decided whether to indict Hurtado. But California didn't follow the practice of indictment by grand jury review. California was one of a number of states that during the 1800s replaced the grand jury with a procedure known as **charging by information.** In proceeding by information, prosecutors charged criminal defendants directly; they didn't have to rely on grand juries. But, there was a problem: the Fifth Amendment requires grand jury indictment in capital or otherwise "infamous" crimes. Following Hurtado's conviction, the judge sentenced him to "be hung by the neck until he is dead." After losing an appeal based on trial errors, Hurtado appealed to the U.S. Supreme Court. The basis of his appeal was that failure to indict him by grand jury review violated his Fifth Amendment right to grand jury indictment in a capital case. Hurtado's lawyer made the novel argument that *Fourteenth Amendment due process* commanded *states* to provide *Fifth Amendment grand jury indictment* in capital cases.

Hurtado's lawyer relied on an earlier U.S. Supreme Court case that decided due process required "a fair trial in a court of justice, according to the modes of proceeding applicable to such case." Hurtado's lawyer argued that due process meant more than that; namely, it included all the ancient common-law rights inherited from England and recognized as fundamental to free people. Grand jury indictment, he maintained, was one of these fundamental rights. The Court rejected this argument, affirming Hurtado's conviction. According to Justice Stanley Matthews, including only procedures adopted in the past would be to deny every quality of the law but its age, and to render it incapable of progress or improvement. It would be to stamp on our jurisprudence the unchangeableness attributed to the laws of the Medes and Persians. [The Constitution and due process were made] for an undefined and expanding future, and for a people gathered from many nations and of many tongues.... [Because the common law drew] its inspiration from every fountain of justice, we are not to assume that the sources of its supply have been exhausted. On the contrary, we should expect that the new and various experiences of our own situation and system will mold and shape it into new and not less useful forms. (530)

Justice John Marshall Harlan, the lone dissenter, argued that the Fourteenth Amendment due process clause "imposed upon the states the same restrictions, in respect of proceedings involving life, liberty, and property, which had been imposed upon the general government." Lawyers tried more than once to get the Court to see things the way Justice Harlan did. (In the 1960s, the Court would adopt Justice Harlan's position when it subscribed to the *incorporation doctrine*, discussed later.) But for the time being, the Court stuck steadfastly to its position that state criminal procedure was a local matter and none of the federal government's business.

Then came the German war machine of the First World War and the rise of fascism and other totalitarian governments of the 1920s and 1930s. These developments revived old American suspicions of arbitrary government. It was probably no coincidence that the U.S. Supreme Court first applied the Fourteenth Amendment due process clause to state criminal procedures in a case the Court decided just when Hitler was rising to power in Nazi Germany (Allen 1978, 157–158).

That first case began in northern Alabama one morning in March 1931, when seven scruffy white boys came into a railway station in northern Alabama and told the stationmaster that a "bunch of Negroes" had picked a fight with them and thrown them off a freight train. The stationmaster phoned ahead to Scottsboro, where a deputy sheriff deputized every man who owned a gun. When the train got to Scottsboro, the posse rounded up nine black boys and two white girls. The girls were dressed in men's caps and overalls. Five of the boys were from Georgia and four from Tennessee. They ranged in age from 12 to 20. One was blind in one eye and had only 10 percent vision in the other; one walked with a cane; all were poor and illiterate. After the deputy sheriff had tied the boys together and was loading them into his truck, Ruby Bates told the sheriff that the boys had raped her and her friend, Victoria Price. By nightfall a mob of several hundred people surrounded the little Scottsboro jail, vowing to avenge the rape by lynching the boys.

When the trial began on Monday morning April 6, 1931, 102 National Guardsmen struggled to keep several thousand people at least 100 feet away from the courthouse. Inside the courtroom, Judge Alfred E. Hawkins offered the job of defense attorney to anyone who would take it. Only Chattanooga lawyer Stephen Roddy—an alcoholic already drunk at 9:00 A.M.—who admitted he didn't know anything about Alabama law, accepted. Judge Hawkins then appointed "all members" of the local bar present in the courtroom as counsel. By Thursday, eight of the boys were tried, convicted, and sentenced to death. Only 12-year-old Roy Wright remained because the jury hung, with seven demanding death and five holding out for life imprisonment. Judge Hawkins declared a mistrial in Roy Wright's trial and sentenced the others to death by electrocution.

Liberals, radicals, and Communists around the country rallied to the defense of the "Scottsboro boys," as the defendants were popularly known. In March 1932, the Alabama Supreme Court upheld all of the convictions except for Eugene Williams, who was granted a new trial as a juvenile. In November, the U.S. Supreme Court ruled in *Powell v. Alabama* (1932) that Alabama had denied the boys due process of law. According to Justice Sutherland:

> Notwithstanding the sweeping character of the language in the *Hurtado* Case [that the criminal procedure amendments in the Bill of Rights do not apply to the states], the rule laid down is not without exceptions. The rule . . . in some instances may be conclusive; but it must yield to more compelling considerations whenever such considerations exist. The fact that the right involved is of such a character that it cannot be denied without violating those "fundamental principles of liberty and justice which lie at the base of all our civil and political institutions" is obviously one of those compelling considerations which must prevail in determining whether it is embraced within the due process clause of the Fourteenth Amendment, although it be specifically dealt with in another part of the Federal Constitution. . . . If this is so, it is not because those rights are enumerated in the first eight Amendments, but because they are of such a nature that they are included in the conception of due process of law. While the question has never been categorically determined by this court, a consideration of the nature of the right and a review of the expressions of this and other courts makes it clear that the right to the aid of counsel is of this fundamental character. . . .
>
> In the light of the facts . . . the ignorance and illiteracy of the defendants, their youth, the circumstances of public hostility, the imprisonment and the close surveillance of the defendants by the military forces, the fact that their friends and families were all in other states and communication with them necessarily difficult, and above all that they stood in deadly peril of their lives—we think the failure of the trial court to give them reasonable time and opportunity to secure counsel was a clear denial of due process. But passing that, and assuming their inability, even if opportunity had been given, to employ counsel, as the trial court evidently did assume, we are of opinion that, under the circumstances just stated, the necessity of counsel was so vital and imperative that the failure of the trial court to make an effective appointment of counsel was likewise a denial of due process within the meaning of the Fourteenth Amendment. . . .

Two members of the Court dissented because they objected to imposing the Bill of Rights on state criminal justice. Writing for himself and Justice McReynolds, Justice Pierce Butler wrote:

> The Court . . . declares that "the failure of the trial court to make an effective appointment of counsel was . . . a denial of due process within the meaning of the Fourteenth Amendment." This is an extension of federal authority into a field hitherto occupied exclusively by the several States. . . . The record wholly fails to reveal that petitioners have been deprived of any right guaranteed by the Federal Constitution, and I am of opinion that the judgment should be affirmed.

With monsters like Hitler, Stalin, Mussolini, and Franco in the background providing hideous examples of what governments can do to individuals not protected by rights, the Court soon revisited state criminal justice. In 1936, the Court inched ahead the process of applying the due process clause to state criminal proceedings in *Brown v. Mississippi*. Since this is the first case excerpt, before you read it, you should review the "The Text-Case Method" section in Chapter 1 (pp. 12–20).

Brown et al. v. Mississippi
297 U.S. 278 (1936)

Ed Brown, Henry Shields, and Yank Ellington were convicted of murder. The Supreme Court of the State of Mississippi affirmed their convictions. The defendants petitioned the U.S. Supreme Court for a writ of certiorari. The Court granted the petition and reversed the judgment of the Mississippi Supreme Court.

HUGHES, C.J.

FACTS*

The crime with which these defendants, all ignorant negroes, are charged, was discovered about 1 o'clock P.M. on Friday, March 30, 1934. On that night one Dial, a deputy sheriff, accompanied by others, came to the home of Ellington, one of the defendants, and requested him to accompany them to the house of the deceased, and there a number of white men were gathered, who began to accuse the defendant of the crime. Upon his denial they seized him, and with the participation of the deputy they hanged him by a rope to the limb of a tree, and, having let him down, they hung him again, and when he was let down the second time, and he still protested his innocence, he was tied to a tree and whipped, and, still declining to accede to the demands that he confess, he was finally released, and he returned with some difficulty to his home, suffering intense pain and agony. The record of the testimony shows that the signs of the rope on his neck were plainly visible during the so-called trial. A day or two thereafter the said deputy, accompanied by another, returned to the home of the said defendant and arrested him, and departed with the prisoner towards the jail in an adjoining county, but went by a route which led into the state of Alabama; and while on the way, in that state, the deputy stopped and again severely whipped the defendant, declaring that he would continue the whipping until he confessed, and the defendant then agreed to confess to such a statement as the deputy would dictate, and he did so, after which he was delivered to jail.

The other two defendants, Ed Brown and Henry Shields, were also arrested and taken to the same jail. On Sunday night, April 1, 1934, the same deputy, accompanied by a number of white men, one of whom was also an officer, and by the jailer, came to the jail, and the two last named defendants were made to strip and they were laid over chairs and their backs were cut to pieces with a leather strap with buckles on it, and they were likewise made by the said deputy definitely to understand that the whipping would be continued unless and until they confessed, and not only confessed, but confessed in every matter of detail as demanded by those present; and in this manner the defendants confessed the crime, and, as the whippings progressed and were repeated, they changed or adjusted their confession in all particulars of detail so as to conform to the demands of their torturers. When the confessions had been obtained in the exact form and contents as desired by the mob, they left with the parting admonition and warning that, if the defendants changed their story at any time in any respect from that last stated, the perpetrators of the outrage would administer the same or equally effective treatment.

Further details of the brutal treatment to which these helpless prisoners were subjected need not be pursued. It is sufficient to say that in pertinent respects the transcript reads more like pages torn from some medieval account than a record made within the confines of a modern civilization which aspires to an enlightened constitutional government.

All this having been accomplished, on the next day, that is, on Monday, April 2, when the defendants had been given time to recuperate somewhat from the tortures to which they had been subjected, the two sheriffs, one of the county where the crime was committed, and the other of the county of the jail in which the prisoners were confined, came to the jail, accompanied by eight other persons, some of them deputies, there to hear the free and voluntary confession of these miserable and abject defendants. The sheriff of the county of the crime admitted that he had heard of the whipping, but averred that he had no personal knowledge of it. He admitted that one of the defendants, when brought before him to confess, was limping and did not sit down, and that this particular defendant then and there stated that he had been strapped so severely that he could not sit down, and, as already stated, the signs of the rope on the neck of another of the defendants were plainly visible to all. Nevertheless the solemn farce of hearing the free and voluntary confessions was gone through with, and these two sheriffs and one other person then present were the three witnesses used in court to establish the so-called confessions, which were received by the court and admitted in evidence over the objections of the defen-

---

*The statement of facts is taken from Mississippi Supreme Court Justice Griffith's dissenting opinion in *State v. Brown*.

dants duly entered of record as each of the said three witnesses delivered their alleged testimony. There was thus enough before the court when these confessions were first offered to make known to the court that they were not, beyond all reasonable doubt, free and voluntary; and the failure of the court then to exclude the confessions is sufficient to reverse the judgment, under every rule of procedure that has heretofore been prescribed, and hence it was not necessary subsequently to renew the objections by motion or otherwise.

The spurious confessions having been obtained—and the farce last mentioned having been gone through with on Monday, April 2d—the court, then in session, on the following day, Tuesday, April 3, 1934, ordered the grand jury to reassemble on the succeeding day, April 4, 1934, at 9 o'clock, and on the morning of the day last mentioned the grand jury returned an indictment against the defendants for murder. Late that afternoon the defendants were brought from the jail in the adjoining county and arraigned, when one or more of them offered to plead guilty, which the court declined to accept, and, upon inquiry whether they had or desired counsel, they stated that they had none, and did not suppose that counsel could be of any assistance to them. The court thereupon appointed counsel, and set the case for trial for the following morning at 9 o'clock, and the defendants were returned to the jail in the adjoining county about thirty miles away.

The defendants were brought to the courthouse of the county on the following morning, April 5th, and the so-called trial was opened, and was concluded on the next day, April 6, 1934, and resulted in a pretended conviction with death sentences. The evidence upon which the conviction was obtained was the so-called confessions. Without this evidence, a peremptory instruction to find for the defendants would have been inescapable. The defendants were put on the stand, and by their testimony the facts and the details thereof as to the manner by which the confessions were extorted from them were fully developed, and it is further disclosed by the record that the same deputy, Dial, under whose guiding hand and active participation the tortures to coerce the confessions were administered, was actively in the performance of the supposed duties of a court deputy in the courthouse and in the presence of the prisoners during what is denominated, in complimentary terms, the trial of these defendants. This deputy was put on the stand by the state in rebuttal, and admitted the whippings. It is interesting to note that in his testimony with reference to the whipping of the defendant Ellington, and in response to the inquiry as to how severely he was whipped, the deputy stated, "Not too much for a negro; not as much as I would have done if it were left to me." Two others who had participated in these whippings were

introduced and admitted it—not a single witness was introduced who denied it. The facts are not only undisputed, they are admitted, and admitted to have been done by officers of the state, in conjunction with other participants, and all this was definitely well known to everybody connected with the trial, and during the trial, including the state's prosecuting attorney and the trial judge presiding.*

Petitioners were indicted for the murder of one Raymond Stewart, whose death occurred on March 30, 1934. They were indicted on April 4, 1934, and were then arraigned and pleaded not guilty. Counsel were appointed by the court to defend them. Trial was begun the next morning and was concluded on the following day, when they were found guilty and sentenced to death.

Aside from the confessions, there was no evidence sufficient to warrant the submission of the case to the jury. After a preliminary inquiry, testimony as to the confessions was received over the objection of defendants' counsel. Defendants then testified that the confessions were false and had been procured by physical torture. The case went to the jury with instructions, upon the request of defendants' counsel, that if the jury had reasonable doubt as to the confessions having resulted from coercion, that they were not to be considered as evidence. On their appeal to the Supreme Court of the State, defendants assigned as error the inadmissibility of the confessions. The judgment was affirmed.

Defendants then moved in the Supreme Court of the State to arrest the judgment and for a new trial on the ground that all the evidence against them was obtained by coercion and brutality known to the court and to the district attorney, and that defendants had been denied the benefit of counsel or opportunity to confer with counsel in a reasonable manner. The motion was supported by affidavits. At about the same time, defendants filed in the Supreme Court a "suggestion of error" explicitly challenging the proceedings of the trial, in the use of the confessions and with respect to the alleged denial of representation by counsel, as violating the due process clause of the Fourteenth Amendment of the Constitution of the United States. The state court entertained the suggestion of error, considered the federal question, and decided it against defendants' contentions. Two judges dissented. We granted a writ of certiorari.

OPINION

The state is free to regulate the procedure of its courts in accordance with its own conceptions of policy, unless in so

_____

*The remainder of this excerpt is taken from Chief Justice Hughes's opinion in the U.S. Supreme Court.

doing it "offends some principle of justice so rooted in the traditions and conscience of our people as to be ranked as fundamental." The state may abolish trial by jury. It may dispense with indictment by a grand jury and substitute complaint or information. But the freedom of the state in establishing its policy is the freedom of constitutional government and is limited by the requirement of due process of law.

Because a state may dispense with a jury trial, it does not follow that it may substitute trial by ordeal. The rack and torture chamber may not be substituted for the witness stand. The state may not permit an accused to be hurried to conviction under mob domination—where the whole proceeding is but a mask—without supplying corrective process. The state may not deny to the accused the aid of counsel. Nor may a state, through the action of its officers, contrive a conviction through the pretense of a trial which in truth is "but used as a means of depriving a defendant of liberty through a deliberate deception of court and jury by the presentation of testimony known to be perjured."

And the trial equally is a mere pretense where the state authorities have contrived a conviction resting solely upon confessions obtained by violence. The due process clause requires "that state action, whether through one agency or another, shall be consistent with the fundamental principles of liberty and justice which lie at the base of all our civil and political institutions." It would be difficult to conceive of methods more revolting to the sense of justice than those taken to procure the confessions of these petitioners, and the use of the confessions thus obtained as the basis for conviction and sentence was a clear denial of due process.

It is in this view that the further contention of the State must be considered. That contention rests upon the failure of counsel for the accused, who had objected to the admissibility of the confessions, to move for their exclusion after they had been introduced and the fact of coercion had been proved. It is a contention which proceeds upon a misconception of the nature of petitioners' complaint. That complaint is not of the commission of mere error, but of a wrong so fundamental that it made the whole proceeding a mere pretense of a trial and rendered the conviction and sentence wholly void.

We are not concerned with a mere question of state practice, or whether counsel assigned to petitioners were competent or mistakenly assumed that their first objections were sufficient. In an earlier case the Supreme Court of the State had recognized the duty of the court to supply corrective process where due process of law had been denied. In *Fisher v. State*, 110 So. 361, 365, the court said:

Coercing the supposed state's criminals into confessions and using such confessions so coerced from them against them in trials has been the curse of all countries. It was the chief iniquity, the crowning infamy of the Star Chamber, and the Inquisition, and other similar institutions. The Constitution recognized the evils that lay behind these practices and prohibited them in this country. The duty of maintaining constitutional rights of a person on trial for his life rises above mere rules of procedure, and wherever the court is clearly satisfied that such violations exist, it will refuse to sanction such violations and will apply the corrective.

In the instant case, the trial court was fully advised by the undisputed evidence of the way in which the confessions had been procured. The trial court knew that there was no other evidence upon which conviction and sentence could be based. Yet it proceeded to permit conviction and to pronounce sentence. The conviction and sentence were void for want of the essential elements of due process, and the proceeding thus vitiated could be challenged in any appropriate manner. *Mooney v. Holohan*, supra. It was challenged before the Supreme Court of the State by the express invocation of the Fourteenth Amendment. That court entertained the challenge, considered the federal question thus presented, but declined to enforce petitioners' constitutional right. The court thus denied a federal right fully established and specially set up and claimed, and the judgment must be reversed.

Questions

1. What does the Court mean when it says that this case is not about the Fifth Amendment right against self-incrimination? How can that be?

2. How can the torture of these defendants not be a violation of the Fifth Amendment words "no person shall be compelled in any criminal case to be a witness against himself"?

3. State the fundamental fairness doctrine as the Court understands it in this case.

4. How did the Court apply the doctrine to the facts of this case?

5. If defendants don't meet deadlines for making objections to errors in the proceedings, should they be barred from making them? Make an argument in favor of "timely" objections, even if you don't agree with the argument.

 Go to Exercise 2-1 on the Criminal Procedure 6e CD to learn more about the trial record of *Brown v. Mississippi* and Exercise 2-2 to learn more about due process and state criminal justice.

Brown v. Mississippi

February 5, 1935

In the Supreme Court of the State of Mississippi
Affidavit of John A. Clark—Filed Feb. 5, 1935

Personally appeared before me, the undersigned authority authorized to administer oaths under the laws of the state of Mississippi, John A. Clark, of DeKalb, Mississippi, who says upon oath that on or about the 29th of March, 1934, Mr. Stewart was found in a dying condition at his home, and shortly thereafter, during the 29th day of March, 1934, died; and that the next week, or to be exact, on the 4th day of April, which was on a Wednesday of the week, a grand jury was called together, returned a bill of indictment against the three defendants Ed Brown, Henry Shields and Yank Ellington, and the Negroes were confined in jail at the time in Meridian, Mississippi, which is in Lauderdale county, some thirty miles from DeKalb, the county seat of Kemper county. That each of the three parties charged in the indictment of murder for the killing of Mr. Stewart were ignorant, pauper Negroes. That they were brought over from Meridian on the 4th day of April, in the afternoon, and brought into the court house, and they were arraigned on the bill of indictment, and one of them, speaking for the trio, said, "We just as well plead guilty." There was present standing near the defendants Mr. Cliff Dial, a deputy sheriff. The court then told the defendants that they were to be tried, and asked them if they wanted a lawyer, and they said they didn't suppose it would be any use to have one. Thereupon the court said, "I will appoint Mr. Spinks and Mr. Clark to defend you," and said the case would be called for trial tomorrow morning. Thereupon the three defendants were taken immediately from the court room and into an adjoining room for about a thirty or forty minute conference with said attys and then carried back to Meridian, Mississippi.

The next morning about nine or ten o'clock the defendants were brought into the court room again by the officers of the law, and the two parties ap- pointed to defend them requested a conference with the defendants, and they were sent into a room in the court house for this conference along with the deputy sheriffs guarding them, and Mr. Cliff Dial started to come into the room where they were un- dertaking to confer with their counsel, and there- upon objection was made to him coming into the room because of certain matters, which will hereafter be referred to. That within a short while, not exceed- ing thirty or forty minutes, a messenger was sent into the room by the court with the statement made to us that the court does not want to unduly hurry you gentlemen in your conference with the defendants, but to get through as quickly as you can, as the court desires to proceed with the trial, and in the course of an hour or two spent in the conference the court sent two or three times with this message to the de- fendants' counsel in order to hurry them up with the conference.

When Mr. Cliff Dial, a Special deputy sheriff, was excluded from the room, he stood just outside of the door where he could be observed by the defendants and their counsel, and he would hold his ear down near the keyhole in the door, as if he were trying to hear what was said by the defendants to their coun- sel, and he repeated this effort to the knowledge of the defendants and the affiant, as they could see him through the glass in the door, and the defendants ex- pressed themselves secretly to the affiant that they were afraid to talk about the case. On two or three occasions while the conference was going on, Mr. Cliff Dial opened the door a little ajar and poked his head in the door and stated that he wanted to deliver a message to the sheriff who was in the room, and after this conference had been hurried two or three different times by the courier announcing that the court did not want to unduly hurry the conference but wanted them to hurry up and come on and begin the trial, the defendants and their counsel came out and had had no time to confer with their witnesses and no opportunity to learn anything about the case except a smattered effort at whispered conversations in the room in this way to their counsel.

The case was then called against all three of the said defendants; they were not advised that they were entitled to a severance or that they were entitled to a special venire from which to draw a jury, but the court announced that he had appointed two other counsel to assist in the defense, Mr. Daws and Mr. Davis, and they came out and took seats at the bar in the case, but affiant states that neither of the three men assigned with him in the trial of said cause were at all in sympathy with the defendants, but all prejudiced the case, and thought they should be convicted. That affiant himself had heard from the officers that they had voluntarily confessed to the murder and he himself at that time had no doubt about their guilt and was simply going through the form of a trial in this way. Twelve men then were called into the box by the court and they began taking evidence, the court having had pleas of Not Guilty entered for them. The trial continued until late in the afternoon, and it had developed that the Negroes had been terrifically whipped and abused and clearly the confessions extorted from them. All of the defendants were very much excited and bewildered from the time they were brought in court until the court took a recess late in the afternoon, this being the 5th day of April, and ordered the prisoners taken back to Meridian. They were immediately hustled into the conveyances and left for Meridian without any opportunity to confer with their counsel or witnesses or any one else.

The next morning, being the 6th day of April, 1934, the defendants were brought into court and immediately the trial began and continued through the day, and during the day it developed that Mr. Cliff Dial, who made the arrest of each of them, did so terrorize them by the most cruel and brutal whippings and beatings and by hanging one of them by the neck until his neck was all scarred up with a ring around it that could be observed clear across the court room, and this had been brought out in evidence and admitted by Mr. Cliff Dial and others, and we could then see why the ignorant Negroes were in such desperate fear of Mr. Dial, and that they had upon their bodies tremendous sores and stripes placed there by the whippings and this was brought to the attention of the court and the district attorney [John C. Stennis] and the jury and in open court, and that then the evidence rested in the case; the jury went out after hearing a feeble argument, and re-

turned in open court a verdict of guilty of murder against each of the defendants, and as soon as the court could look at a calendar and arrange the date for the execution, upon the motion of the district attorney, they were called to the bar of the court and sentenced to be hanged, and the date set for their execution, and as soon as this was done, the prisoners were immediately hand-cuffed, taken out of the court room, and driven away for Meridian, the county seat of another county thirty miles away with no opportunity to make a motion for a new trial; it being after dark on the night of the 6th, no money in the hands of anybody to pay for going down there to visit them or have any talk with them, and without their having been brought back or given any opportunity to make a motion for a new trial or confer with counsel making one.

The court next morning signed the minutes and adjourned the court for the term, and affiant states upon oath that such was the manner and haste in which the trial was conducted, and that just before the date of the execution, he went at his own expense down to Meridian, and had a conference with each of the defendants and so impressed was he with their innocence that he prepared and executed a papers' oath and petition for appeal, two of the other attorneys declining to have anything to do with any effort at appeal in said cause, and the 3rd only permitted his name to be used, but took no part (Davis) and procured the stenographer to transcribe the notes of the evidence, and had the record certified to the supreme court.

(Signed) *John A. Clark*
Sworn to and subscribed before me
this 5th day of February, 1935.

(Signed) *Mae Nunn, Notary Public (Seal)*

December 12, 1935

MRS. JOHN A. CLARK
Democratic National Committee Woman
De Kalb, Mississippi

December 12, 1935
Hon. Arthur Garfield Hays, New York, N.Y.

Dear Mr. Hays:

Your letter with check, coming just as Mr. Clark is recovering from a long and critical illness, is deeply appreciated.

Our physicians tell us that Mr. Clark's illness was caused to a great extent by the work and worry of the fight for the lives of the three negroes. He was a sick man when the Judge appointed him to defend the negroes, and for that reason asked to be excused from the case. The Judge insisted on his defending the clients, and when Mr. Clark entered the case he put his whole heart and ability in his defense.

He has been very unjustly criticized and has worried quite a bit because of the lack of help he has had in the hard fight he has waged. He has "fought a good fight and kept the faith." I have encouraged him and helped in every way possible.

We are now hoping that Mr. Clark will be able to take up the defense anew, if the United States Supreme Court grants a new trial. DeKalb is a rural village, the county site of Kemper county and there are only three lawyers here—if Mr. Clark should not be able to carry on the case, if we have a new trial, it simply means that the trial will be a farce and a Roman holiday for the citizenry of the County and State. Racial prejudice runs high here, and the gallows erected for the hanging, scheduled last year, is a Mecca for people from all over the State...of course, the justice loving, law abiding people here are in sympathy with Mr. Clark's efforts but many of them dare not express their opinions because of inflamed public sentiment.

I am sure that your letter is going to do lots toward helping to brighten my husband's convalescing days.

I would appreciate you having other friends write Mr. Clark; the letters will strengthen his determination to get well and renew the fight with courage and the consciousness that he is upholding the high standard of the legal profession.

Thanking you again for your letter, I am

Very cordially yours,
/s/ MRS. JOHN A. CLARK

January 21, 1936

DeKalb, Mississippi
January 21, 1936
Hon. Arthur Garfield Hays, New York, N.Y.

Dear Mr. Hays:

I wish I could adequately express how deeply Mr. Clark and I appreciate your interest in "the negro case," which has caused us so much worry and unhappiness.

Since the article appeared in the "Nation" we have received many letters and a few telegrams from readers who wanted to express their commendation for the fight Mr. Clark has made.

A majority of the letters, tho,' were written by friends you had contacted and whose interest you have enlisted. Some of the writers have sent checks to the total of $176.00. This money, which is indeed a God

send, I am placing in a separate account to be used solely for the defense of the negroes. I feel sure that if I can have sufficient money I can guarantee that they get a fair trial and splendid defense.

Mr. Clark continues to improve, and is now sitting up a few hours each day—the many letters and lovely magazine articles have done much to help him gain his strength and *fighting spirits.*

When Mr. Clark filed his suggestion of error with the Mississippi Supreme Court, I realized that he had reached the breaking point, physically and nervously.

I went to one of my closest friends, Ex-Governor Earl Brewer, who seems almost like a father to me, and begged him to help Mr. Clark in the fight he was making for a humane cause. I told him all the horrible details of the case and he was very indignant and consented to help us solely because of his personal love for Mr. Clark and for the purpose of helping to right a grievous wrong. I told Governor Brewer that he could not count upon a fee, as the negroes were the poorest and most illiterate type of share croppers. Their families could not raise five dollars if all of their lives depended upon their so doing.

So intense is public sentiment against the negroes that our Circuit Judge told Mr. Clark that he would not allow the $25.00 per client that our law says must be allowed the attorney who is appointed by the Court to defend a prisoner unable to employ counsel.

I quietly contacted some of the negro preachers in the State and enlisted their help in securing sufficient money to pay Governor Brewer's expenses to Washington, where he argued the case before the United States Supreme Court, January 9th (inst). I am certainly proud of his work in the Court, and feel sure that we will secure a new hearing. I am sending you some press clippings which will show you why I am so optimistic about the future developments in the case.

You will note that when the Mississippi Supreme Court affirmed the death sentence a year ago, Judge Anderson rendered a dissenting opinion almost as caustic as that of Judge Griffith's later on.

When Mr. Clark filed his suggestion of error with the Mississippi Supreme Court we were sure of Judge Anderson's position, and were very happy to have Judge Griffith join him in dissent, when the suggestion of error was over-ruled by a two to four decision.

Judge Marion W. Reily, of Meridian, Mississippi, is considered the State's leading criminal lawyer. He is one of our closest personal and political friends. He and Mr. Clark are frequently associated in the defense of mutual clients. Judge Reily has been wonderfully kind since Mr. Clark's illness. He has taken over all of his cases to be tried in our March term of Circuit Court, and will give his time and service to Mr. Clark's clients because of his friendship for Mr. Clark. He has strongly disapproved of Mr. Clark "wasting his time and strength for a losing cause." He told me that my husband was too valuable and greatly needed in Mississippi public affairs to be permitted to sacrifice his life for the three negroes.

At last I have won Judge Reily over to our view point, but I can not afford to ask him to come into the case without the assurance of some kind of fee. So you can understand why I am so happy to know that you are not only giving us your moral support but are helping us to raise the money to make a strong fight when the case is remanded back for trial.

One of the Supreme Court Judges is a brother-in-law of mine, and my brother, O. G. Tann, is Supt. of the Mississippi State Penitentiary. I am telling you this so that you may know some thing of my affiliations in the State.

I have always been active in any civic or political movement, in the States which tended to promote the welfare and happiness of others.

I have reached the conclusion that all of my public welfare and political activities are to be the means for giving me prestige and contacts I shall need for what I have decided to do in the future. I shall from now on be active in helping the poor unfortunate negroes in their vain efforts to secure justice in Courts.

This case has brought to me the realization that we are our brother's keeper and I feel that it is my duty to help the unfortunate victims of race hatred and prejudice.

I do not recall whether or not I told you that Mr. Clark was defeated for re-election to the State Senate this summer in the Democratic primaries, after having served this District faithfully and efficiently for eight years. The only issue in the campaign was his defense of the negroes.

We have paid a great price for being true to our conception of duty, and I know that the future will bring more disappointments and unhappiness because of our stand in face of so much local prejudice and intolerance, but you can be assured that we will always be fighting for the cause in which you have manifested a friendly interest.

I am inclosing you a picture of Mr. Clark and myself so that you may visualize your Southern friends as we stand on the firing line.

Mr. Clark, just fifty-two years old, has a brilliant record as Senate floor leader for the out going Governor's administration. This picture shows him at his desk in the State Senate.

I am expecting to be called to Washington during the month of February for some Party conferences. If I am financially able, I hope to visit in New York before coming back home. In the event I make the trip to New York I will certainly avail myself of the pleasure of seeing you while there.

Thanking you for the great encouragement and renewing of our determination to go on with our fight, I am

Cordially yours,
(signed) Mrs. John A. Clark

February 17, 1936

Chief Justice Charles Evans Hughes, writing for the U.S. Supreme Court:

The trial court was fully advised by the undisputed evidence of the way in which the confessions had been procured. The trial court knew that there was no other evidence upon which conviction and sentence could be based. Yet it proceeded to permit conviction and to pronounce sentence. The conviction and sentence were void for want of the essential elements of due process, and the proceeding thus vitiated could be challenged in any appropriate manner. It was challenged before the Supreme Court of the State by the express invocation of the Fourteenth Amendment. That court entertained the challenge, considered the federal question thus presented, but declined to enforce petitioners' constitutional right. The court thus denied a federal right fully established and specially set up and claimed, and the judgment must be reversed. It is so ordered.

February 18, 1936

Earl Brewer, the lawyer who won the reversal of the convictions and death sentences in the U.S. Supreme Court visited Ed Brown, Henry Shields, and Yank Ellington in jail where they had been locked up since March 31, 1934, to tell them that "freedom is in sight."

"God bless you guvner!" shouted all three. They spent the rest of the day singing black spirituals and praising God for the Supreme Court.

Brewer told the press that "it seems certain that no further prosecution of the cases is to be expected."

February 22, 1936

The African American newspaper *The Chicago Defender* warned that the U.S. Supreme Court's decision "in no way guarantees the freedom of the oppressed defendants as the case must be returned to Mississippi courts where feeling against the men is high for retrial."

February 24, 1936

District Attorney John Stennis, the prosecutor at the trial, announced that he would seek a new trial of the defendants.

April 12, 1936

The Mississippi Supreme Court reversed the convictions. "In obedience to the mandate" of the U.S. Supreme Court, "the judgment of the court below will be reversed and the case remanded for further proceedings...."

September 5, 1936

Earl Brewer, attorney for Brown, Shields, and Ellington filed a petition for a writ of habeas corpus in a county court in Jackson, Mississippi, seeking the immediate release of his clients on the ground that the only evidence against them was their confessions obtained by torture.

Chancellor V.J. Stricker issued the writ and ordered a hearing to be held on September 10, 1936.

September 19, 1936

The hearing on the writ of habeas corpus was held. Judge Andrew Longino ordered Brown, Shields, and Ellington released from jail.

District Attorney Stennis appealed Judge Longino's order to Chief Justice Sydney Smith of the Mississippi Supreme Court. Chief Justice Smith reversed the order to release the three defendants. The chief justice ruled that although the U.S. Supreme Court had reversed the convictions it had not invalidated the indictment. Therefore, the three were still under indictment for capital murder. He ordered the men to remain in jail until their case was decided.

October 25, 1936

The trial was set for November 30, 1936.

November 28, 1936

Ed Brown, Henry Shields, and Yank Ellington accepted a plea bargain. They pleaded nolo contendere (no contest) to manslaughter. Brown was sentenced to 10 years in prison, Shields to 5, and Ellington to 3. They were convinced that a Mississippi jury would convict them, and the judge would sentence them to death.

December 1, 1936

Editorial, Jackson, Mississippi, *Daily Clarion-Legend:*

> The bargain may seem illogical to many citizens who are not lawyers. The three negroes were either guilty of a murder deserving the death sentence, or they were innocent of all crime. In the former case, these sentences are ridiculous. In the latter case, the sentences are unjust. Many plain citizens will think it would be better for the state's repute either to have forced the three to trial again on the murder indictments, or to have released them.

July 2, 2000

A now elderly nephew of Yank Ellington related that after his uncle was released from jail he told him that he didn't kill Stewart, but that Cliff Dial "beat me until the blood was running into my boots" (Remme 2000).

The Fundamental Fairness Doctrine

The two great cases *Powell v. Alabama* and *Brown v. Mississippi* established what came to be called the fundamental fairness doctrine of due process. According to the **fundamental fairness doctrine,** due process is a command to the states to provide the basics of a fair trial. What are the basics?

1. Give defendants notice of the charges against them.

2. Assure a full hearing of the facts before convicting and punishing defendants.

The specifics of notice and hearing facts are left to the individual states and to developing notions of natural law.

During the 1930s through the 1950s, except for cases of extreme physical brutality like *Brown*—and *Powell,* where Alabama provided no real hearing at all—a majority of the Court continued to reject the claim that the Bill of Rights applied to state criminal justice. In *Palko v. Connecticut* (1937), "one of the most influential [opinions] in the history of the court," Justice Cardozo conceded that some rights are "implicit in the concept of ordered liberty and thus, through the Fourteenth Amendment, became valid as against the states." But, the Fourteenth Amendment imposes on the states only the rights that are "of the very essence of a scheme of ordered liberty." The Bill of Rights *might* include some of these fundamental rights. In *Palko,* the question was whether double jeopardy was one of these rights. Justice Cardozo put it this way: Did exposing Frank Palko to double jeopardy subject him to

> a hardship so shocking that our polity will not endure it? Does it violate those "fundamental principles of liberty and justice which lie at the base of all our civil and political institutions? [No.] . . . The edifice of justice stands, in its symmetry, to many, greater than before. (328)

Justice Felix Frankfurter, the greatest defender of fundamental fairness, tried to capture its essence in two phrases: "procedures that offend the community's sense of fair play and decency" and "conduct that shocks the conscience." Writing for the Court, Justice Frankfurter applied the fundamental fairness doctrine in *Rochin v. California* (1952).

C A S E | *Did the Police Actions "Shock the Conscience"?*

Rochin v. California
342 U.S. 165 (1952)

Antonio Rochin was convicted of the illegal possession of two capsules of morphine. He challenged the use of the two capsules as evidence against him. The trial court admitted the morphine capsules. Rochin appealed. The California District Court of Appeal affirmed the conviction. The California Supreme Court denied Rochin's petition to rehear the case without writing an opinion. The U.S. Supreme Court reversed.

FRANKFURTER, J.

FACTS

Having "some information that Rochin was selling narcotics," three deputy sheriffs of the County of Los Angeles, on the morning of July 1, 1949, made for the two-story dwelling house in which Rochin lived with his mother, common-law wife, brothers and sisters. Finding the outside door open, they entered and then forced open the door to Rochin's room on the second floor. Inside they found petitioner sitting partly dressed on the side of his bed, upon which his wife was lying. On a "night stand" beside the bed the deputies spied two capsules. When asked, "Whose stuff is this?" Rochin seized the capsules and put them in his mouth. A struggle ensued, in the course of which the three officers "jumped upon him" and attempted to extract the capsules. The force they applied proved unavailing against Rochin's resistance.

He was handcuffed and taken to a hospital. At the direction of one of the officers a doctor forced an emetic solution through a tube into Rochin's stomach against his will. This "stomach pumping" produced vomiting. In the vomited matter were found two capsules which proved to contain morphine.

Rochin was brought to trial before a California Superior Court, sitting without a jury, on the charge of possessing "a preparation of morphine" in violation of the California Health and Safety Code 1947, § 11500. Rochin was convicted and sentenced to sixty days' imprisonment. The chief evidence against him was the two capsules. They were admitted over petitioner's objection, although the means of obtaining them was frankly set forth in the testimony by one of the deputies, substantially as here narrated.

On appeal, the District Court of Appeal affirmed the conviction, despite the finding that the officers "were guilty of unlawfully breaking into and entering defendant's room and were guilty of unlawfully assaulting and battering defendant while in the room," and "were guilty of unlawfully assaulting, battering, torturing and falsely imprisoning the defendant at the alleged hospital." One of the three judges, while finding that "the record in this case reveals a shocking series of violations of constitutional rights," concurred only because he felt bound by decisions of his Supreme Court. These, he asserted, "have been looked upon by law enforcement officers as an encouragement, if not an invitation, to the commission of such lawless acts." The Supreme Court of California denied without opinion Rochin's petition for a hearing. Two justices dissented from this denial, and in doing so expressed themselves thus:

> A conviction which rests upon evidence of incriminating objects obtained from the body of the accused by physical abuse is as invalid as a conviction which rests

upon a verbal confession extracted from him by such abuse.... Had the evidence forced from defendant's lips consisted of an oral confession that he illegally possessed a drug...he would have the protection of the rule of law which excludes coerced confessions from evidence. But because the evidence forced from his lips consisted of real objects the People of this state are permitted to base a conviction upon it. (We) find no valid ground of distinction between a verbal confession extracted by physical abuse and a confession wrested from defendant's body by physical abuse.

This Court granted certiorari, because a serious question is raised as to the limitations which the Due Process Clause of the Fourteenth Amendment imposes on the conduct of criminal proceedings by the States.

OPINION

In our federal system the administration of criminal justice is predominantly committed to the care of the States.... Broadly speaking, crimes in the United States are what the laws of the individual States make them.... Accordingly, in reviewing a State criminal conviction under a claim of right guaranteed by the Due Process Clause of the Fourteenth Amendment...we must be deeply mindful of the responsibilities of the States for the enforcement of criminal laws, and exercise with due humility our merely negative function in subjecting convictions from state courts to the very narrow scrutiny which the Due Process Clause of the Fourteenth Amendment authorizes. Due process of law, itself a historical product, is not to be turned into a destructive dogma against the States in the administration of their systems of criminal justice.

However, this Court too has its responsibility. Regard for the requirements of the Due Process Clause inescapably imposes upon this court an exercise of judgment upon the whole course of the proceedings...in order to ascertain whether they offend those canons of decency and fairness which express the notions of justice of English-speaking peoples even toward those charged with the most heinous offenses. These standards of justice are not authoritatively formulated anywhere as though they were specifics. Due process of law is a summarized constitutional guarantee of respect for those personal immunities which, as Mr. Justice Cardozo twice wrote for the Court, are "so rooted in the traditions and conscience of our people as to be ranked as fundamental," or are "implicit in the concept of ordered liberty."

The Court's function in the observance of this settled conception of the Due Process Clause does not leave us without adequate guides in subjecting State criminal procedures to constitutional judgment. In dealing not with the machinery of government but with human rights, the absence of formal exactitude, or want of fixity of meaning, is not an unusual or even regrettable attribute of constitutional provisions. Words being symbols do not speak without a gloss explanation....

When the gloss...is a function of the process of judgment, the judgment is bound to fall differently at different times and differently at the same time through different judges. Even more specific provisions, such as the guaranty of freedom of speech and the detailed protection against unreasonable searches and seizures, have inevitably evoked as sharp divisions in this Court as the least specific and most comprehensive protection of liberties, the Due Process Clause.

The vague contours of the Due Process Clause do not leave judges at large. We may not draw on our merely personal and private notions and disregard the limits that bind judges in their judicial function. Even though the concept of due process of law is not final and fixed, these limits are derived from considerations that are fused in the whole nature of our judicial process. These are considerations deeply rooted in reason and in the compelling traditions of the legal profession. The Due Process Clause places upon this Court the duty of exercising a judgment...upon interests of society pushing in opposite directions.... In each case "due process of law" requires an evaluation based on a...detached consideration of conflicting claims, on a judgment...duly mindful of reconciling the needs both of continuity and of change in a progressive society.

Applying these general considerations to the circumstances of the present case, we are compelled to conclude that the proceedings by which this conviction was obtained do more than offend some fastidious squeamishness or private sentimentalism about combating crime too energetically. This is conduct that shocks the conscience. Illegally breaking into the privacy of Rochin, the struggle to open his mouth and remove what was there, the forcible extraction of his stomach's contents—this course of proceeding by agents of government to obtain evidence is bound to offend even hardened sensibilities. They are methods too close to the rack and the screw to permit of constitutional differentiation....

On the facts of this case the conviction of Rochin has been obtained by methods that offend the Due Process Clause. The judgment below must be reversed.

CONCURRING OPINION

BLACK, J.

...I believe that faithful adherence to the specific guarantees in the Bill of Rights insures a more permanent protection of individual liberty than that which can be afforded by the nebulous standards stated by the majority. What the majority hold is that the Due Process Clause empowers this Court to nullify any state law if its application "shocks the conscience," offends "a sense of justice" or runs counter to the "decencies of civilized conduct." The majority emphasize that these statements do not refer to their own consciences or to their senses of justice and decency. For we are told that "we may not draw on our merely personal and private notions"; our judgment must be grounded on "considerations deeply rooted in reason and in the compelling traditions of the legal profession." We are further admonished to measure the validity of state practices, not by our reason, or by the traditions of the legal profession, but by "the community's sense of fair play and decency"; by the "traditions and conscience of our people"; or by "those canons of decency and fairness which express the notions of justice of English-speaking peoples." These canons are made necessary, it is said, because of "interests of society pushing in opposite directions."

If the Due Process Clause does vest this Court with such unlimited power to invalidate laws, I am still in doubt as to why we should consider only the notions of English-speaking peoples to determine what are immutable and fundamental principles of justice. Moreover, one may well ask what avenues of investigation are open to discover "canons" of conduct so universally favored that this Court should write them into the Constitution? All we are told is that the discovery must be made by an "evaluation based on a disinterested inquiry pursued in the spirit of science, on a balanced order of facts.". . .

Of even graver concern, however, is the use of philosophy to nullify the Bill of Rights. I long ago concluded that the accordion-like qualities of this philosophy must inevitably imperil all the individual liberty safeguards specifically enumerated in the Bill of Rights. . . .

Questions

1. Why did the police actions violate Rochin's due process?

2. Does the police conduct in this case "shock your conscience"? Why or why not?

3. Are "shocks the conscience," offending the "community's sense of fair play and decency," "traditions and conscience of our people," and "those canons of decency and fairness which express the notions of justice of English-speaking peoples" purely a matter of personal opinion, or are they objective tests? Explain.

4. Summarize how Justice Frankfurter defines and defends the fundamental fairness doctrine.

5. Summarize how Justice Black defines and defends the incorporation doctrine.

6. In your opinion, which doctrine is better? Back up your answer with the facts of the case and the arguments of the majority and concurring opinions.

7. After you've read the next section on incorporation, decide if you've changed your mind about your answer to (6). Explain why or why not.

The Incorporation Doctrine

During the 1940s and 1950s, all the justices came to accept the idea that the Bill of Rights *does* impose limits on state criminal procedure. But, they disagreed hotly over exactly why and what those limits are. The fundamental fairness doctrine, or the idea that some higher law than the Bill of Rights defined due process, fueled a great debate on and off the Court. A growing minority on the Court rejected the fundamental fairness doctrine. In its place, they accepted the **incorporation doctrine,** which defined Fourteenth Amendment due process as applying the specific provisions of the Bill of Rights to state criminal procedure. By the 1960s, incorporation claimed a majority of the Court as advocates. Part of the explanation for this were changes in the Court's membership. The leader of fundamental fairness, Justice Felix Frankfurter, suffered a stroke in 1962 and retired. Justice Charles Whittaker, an ally of Justice Frankfurter, retired the same year. President John F. Kennedy replaced them with two incorporationists, Justices Byron R. White and Arthur J. Goldberg. They were helped by the leadership of the staunch incorporationist Chief Justice Warren.

The fundamental fairness doctrine and the incorporation doctrine differed significantly. First, the fundamental fairness doctrine focused on general fairness and the incorporation doctrine on specific procedures. According to Professor Jerold Israel (1982):

> The concept of due process dated back to the Magna Carta, and English and American commentators had discussed it at length. The proponents of fundamental fairness viewed those authorities as having established a flexible standard of justice that focused on the essence of fairness rather than the familiarity of form. Due process, under this view, was "a concept less rigid and more fluid than those envisaged in other specific and particular provisions of the Bill of Rights." Indeed, Justice Frankfurter described it as "perhaps, the least frozen concept of our law—the least confined to history and the most absorptive of powerful social standards of a progressive society." Its basic objective was to provide "respect enforced by law" for that feeling of just treatment which has evolved through centuries of Anglo American constitutional history and civilization. Thus, it had a "natural law" background, which extended beyond procedural fairness and imposed limits as well on the substance of state regulation.

So, according to proponents of the fundamental fairness doctrine, due process might include some of the specific procedural rights in the Bill of Rights, but, if it does, it's purely by chance.

On the other hand, the incorporation doctrine says that due process is shorthand for the specific procedural guarantees in the Bill of Rights. Justice Hugo L. Black, the incorporation doctrine's strongest advocate, maintained that due process grants only a "right to be tried by an independent and unprejudiced court using established procedures and applying valid preexisting laws." According to Justice Black (*Duncan v. Louisiana* 1968, 169), due process absorbs every specific right listed in the Bill of Rights.

Second, fundamental fairness and incorporation differ over the degree of uniformity of procedures required in state and local systems of criminal justice. According to the fundamental fairness doctrine, states could define most of their own criminal procedure law. The incorporation doctrine says that the states have to apply the procedures outlined in the Bill of Rights.

When the Court finally adopted the incorporation doctrine, justices continued to disagree strongly over which provisions the Fourteenth Amendment incorporated. A few justices, like Justice Black called for **total incorporation,** meaning that all the provisions were incorporated under the due process clause. Most supported the more moderate **selective incorporation,** meaning that some rights were incorporated and others were not (Table 2.3).

During the 1960s, the majority of the Supreme Court opted for the selective incorporation doctrine. According to Justice William Brennan, by 1970 the incorporation doctrine had changed the "face of the law." The decisions of that decade incorporated

---

TABLE 2.3

Comparison of Fundamental Fairness and Total and Selective Incorporation

Fundamental Fairness	Total Incorporation	Selective Incorporation
General fairness	All provisions in Bill of Rights incorporated	Some provisions in Bill of Rights incorporated
States can define their own procedures	States have to follow procedures as they're practiced in federal courts	States have to follow procedures as they're practiced in federal courts

TABLE 2.4
Bill of Rights Provisions Incorporated as of 2004

Unreasonable searches and seizures	*Wolf v. Colorado* (1949)
Exclusionary rule applied to state searches and seizures	*Mapp v. Ohio* (1961)
Self-incrimination	*Malloy v. Hogan* (1964)
Assistance of counsel	*Gideon v. Wainwright* (1963)
Confrontation of witnesses against the accused	*Pointer v. Texas* (1965)
Compulsory process to obtain witnesses	*Washington v. Texas* (1967)
Speedy trial	*Klopfer v. North Carolina* (1967)
Cruel and unusual punishment	*Robinson v. California* (1962)

all but four of the Bill of Rights guarantees relating to criminal justice: public trial, notice of charges, prohibition of excessive bail, and prosecution by indictment (Table 2.4). In cases decided since the 1960s, the Court has suggested that the Fourteenth Amendment due process absorbs all but indictment by grand jury.

Incorporated rights apply to the states exactly as in federal proceedings, according to the Supreme Court—"jot-for-jot and case for case," as one of the doctrine's severest critics, Justice John Harlan, put it. Justice Brennan defended the **"jot for jot" approach** this way: "Only impermissible subjective judgments can explain stopping short of the incorporation of the full sweep of the specific being absorbed (Friendly 1965, 936).

The Court didn't just shift its reason for intervening in state criminal procedure, it did something far more consequential and controversial for day-to-day criminal procedure. As we'll see in other chapters, it also expanded its intervention from the courtroom to the police station (interrogation and right to counsel [Chapter 8]; search and seizure [Chapters 3–7]; identification procedures [Chapter 9]; and even onto the street and other public places (stop and frisk [Chapter 4]). The labels used to describe this enormous expansion of federal intervention in local law enforcement ("handcuffing the police," "constitutionalizing criminal procedure," "policing the police," "judicial lawmaking") only hint at the firestorm of controversy set off by the highest court in the land (and the least democratic branch of the government) when the U.S. Supreme Court got involved in reviewing the day-to-day activities of police officers in every city, town, and village in the country (Graham 1970).

The critics of incorporation—it had and still has many—charged that incorporation destroys federalism, interferes with local criminal justice, and eviscerates the need for both local variety and experiments with different solutions to problems in criminal justice administration. They maintain that the great differences among the states and among federal, state, and local systems of criminal justice demand local control and variation.

Critics rightly observe that federal criminal justice consists mainly of cases involving fraud, tax evasion, and other complex crimes. Investigation takes place largely in offices, not in the field. Local law enforcement deals mainly with the hurly-burly street crimes that bring local police into contact with violent individuals and strangers who are difficult to identify, apprehend, and bring to trial. As a result, the critics say, the Bill of Rights works well for federal but not state and local criminal justice. Furthermore, most local police aren't highly trained college graduates, as are the federal police, particularly FBI agents. So, according to the critics, the incorporation doctrine works effectively for the 0.6 percent of federal criminal cases but not for the remaining 99.4 percent of state cases (Graham 1970).

The criticisms target all criminal justice agencies, but perhaps nothing generates more controversy than whether or not uniform standards ought to apply to local police departments. Cries that the U.S. Supreme Court was "running local police departments" from Washington and "handcuffing" local police by doing so were common during the late 1960s, following the decision in the famous *Miranda* case (Chapter 8). So damaging to the Court's prestige was *Miranda v. Arizona* (1966) that the decision was labeled one of three times in its history that the Court was the object of a "self-inflicted wound" (Graham 1970).

The Court may have wounded itself, but, by most accounts, contrary to its opponents' fears, the incorporation doctrine hasn't wounded criminal justice. The Supreme Court's flexible interpretations of the constitutional protections permit plenty of local diversity and experimentation. The Court paid deference to local variation and experiment in *Chandler v. Florida* (1981). Noel Chandler argued that Florida's practice of televising trials violated his right to a fair trial. The Court rejected Chandler's claim. Chief Justice Warren Burger, personally no fan of television in the courts, supported the right of local jurisdictions to follow their own practices:

> Dangers lurk in this, as in most experiments, but unless we were to conclude that television coverage under all conditions is prohibited by the Constitution, the state must be free to experiment. We are not empowered by the Constitution to oversee or harness state procedural experimentation; only when the state action infringes fundamental guarantees are we authorized to intervene. We must assume state courts will be alert to any factors that impair the fundamental rights of the accused. Absent a showing of prejudice of constitutional dimensions to these defendants, there is no reason for this Court either to endorse or to invalidate Florida's experiment. (582)

EQUAL PROTECTION OF THE LAW

Constitutional democracy couldn't survive without protecting our right to fair procedures as guaranteed by due process of law. But neither could it survive without the equal protection of those procedures for everybody. Equality is deeply embedded in the concept of U.S. constitutionalism. In the years just prior to the Revolution, one commentator wrote the following: "The least considerable man among us has an interest equal to the proudest nobleman, in the laws and constitution of his country" (Inbau and others 1980, 209). In the 1960s, we used to state this value on equality in blunter terms: "If the rich can beat the rap, then everyone should get to beat the rap."

Equality before the law is more than a slogan in criminal justice; since 1868, it has been a constitutional command. According to the Fourteenth Amendment to the U.S. Constitution,

> No state shall . . . deny to any person within its jurisdiction the equal protection of the laws.

Equal protection of the law doesn't mean state officials have to treat everybody exactly alike. It means they can't investigate, apprehend, convict, and punish people for unacceptable reasons. So, courts look suspiciously at certain classifications, particularly those based on race or ethnicity. In practice, it's very difficult to prove claims that officials denied equal protection. Claimants have to prove two difficult facts: First, the official action had a discriminatory effect. Specifically, this means proving race or some other illegal group characteristic (not some legitimate criterion like seriousness of the offense or criminal record) accounts for the official decision. Second, and much more difficult, claimants have to prove specific officials intended to discriminate against the specific claimant because of race or other illegal criteria. For example, proving an official said (and meant) "I hate Hispanics" isn't good enough to win an equal protection case. The claimant has to prove that the prosecutor decided to charge him because of his Hispanic ethnicity. So, proving the prosecutor said (and meant), "I charged him because he was Hispanic would be good enough." Of course, in this day and age of political correctness, it's unlikely any prosecutor would say that, and if so, it's not likely the claimant could prove it.

In addition to the difficulty of proving discriminatory effect and discriminatory purpose, there's another hurdle: the **presumption of regularity.** The presumption is that government actions are lawful in the absence of "clear evidence to the contrary." The claimant has to disprove the presumption. In *United States v. Armstrong* (1996), the U.S. Supreme Court applied the presumption of regularity to a claim by two African-American men that race was behind a U.S. attorney's decision to prosecute them for drug and firearm offenses.

| CASE | *Is Selective Enforcement of the Drug Laws Provable?* |

U.S. v. Armstrong
517 U.S. 456 (1996)

The respondents in this case (Christopher Lee Armstrong, Aaron Hampton, Freddie Mack, Shelton Martin, and Robert Rozelle) were indicted for selling crack and using firearms in connection with drug trafficking. They moved for discovery on a claim of selective prosecution. [*Discovery* is a legal action asking for a court order to compel one side—the U.S. Attorney's office in this case—to turn over information that may help the other side—in this case, the respondents.] The U.S. District Court for the Central District of California granted the motion. The Government appealed. A three-judge panel of the 9th Circuit Court of Appeals reversed. Rehearing en banc [by the all the judges on the Court] was granted. The full Court of Appeals affirmed the District Court. The U.S. Supreme Court granted certiorari and reversed and remanded the case.

REHNQUIST, C.J., joined by O'CONNOR, SCALIA, KENNEDY, SOUTER, THOMAS, and GINSBURG, JJ.

FACTS

In this case, we consider the showing necessary for a defendant to be entitled to discovery on a claim that the prosecuting attorney singled him out for prosecution on the basis of his race. We conclude that respondents failed to satisfy the threshold showing: They failed to show that the Government declined to prosecute similarly situated suspects of other races.

In April 1992, respondents were indicted in the U.S. District Court for the Central District of California on charges of conspiring to possess with intent to distribute more than 50 grams of cocaine base (crack) and conspiring to distribute the same, in violation of 21 U.S.C. §§ 841 and 846 (1988 ed. and Supp. IV), and federal firearms offenses.

For three months prior to the indictment, agents of the Federal Bureau of Alcohol, Tobacco, and Firearms and the Narcotics Division of the Inglewood, California, Police Department had infiltrated a suspected crack distribution ring by using three confidential informants. On seven separate occasions during this period, the informants had bought a total of 124.3 grams of crack from respondents and witnessed respondents carrying firearms during the sales. The agents searched the hotel room in which the sales were transacted, arrested respondents Armstrong and Hampton in the room, and found more crack and a loaded gun. The agents later arrested the other respondents as part of the ring.

In response to the indictment, respondents filed a motion for discovery or for dismissal of the indictment, alleging they were selected for federal prosecution because they are black. In support of their motion, they offered only an affidavit by a "Paralegal Specialist," employed by the Office of the Federal Public Defender representing one of the respondents. The only allegation in the affidavit was that, in every one of the 24 § 841 or § 846 cases closed by the office during 1991, the defendant was black. Accompanying the affidavit was a "study" listing the 24 defendants, their race, whether they were prosecuted for dealing cocaine as well as crack, and the status of each case.*

The Government opposed the discovery motion, arguing... that there was no evidence or allegation "that the Government has acted unfairly or has prosecuted nonblack defendants or failed to prosecute them." The District Court granted the motion. It ordered the Government

(1) to provide a list of all cases from the last three years in which the Government charged both cocaine and firearms offenses,

(2) to identify the race of the defendants in those cases,

(3) to identify what levels of law enforcement were involved in the investigations of those cases, and

(4) to explain its criteria for deciding to prosecute those defendants for federal cocaine offenses.

The Government moved for reconsideration of the District Court's discovery order. With this motion it submitted affidavits and other evidence to explain why it had chosen to prosecute respondents and why respondents' study did not support the inference that the Government was singling out blacks for cocaine prosecution. The federal and local agents participating in the case alleged in affidavits that race played no role in their investigation. An Assistant

United States Attorney explained in an affidavit that the decision to prosecute met the general criteria for prosecution, because

> there was over 100 grams of cocaine base involved, over twice the threshold necessary for a ten year mandatory minimum sentence; there were multiple sales involving multiple defendants, thereby indicating a fairly substantial crack cocaine ring; ... there were multiple federal firearms violations intertwined with the narcotics trafficking; the overall evidence in the case was extremely strong, including audio and videotapes of defendants; ... and several of the defendants had criminal histories including narcotics and firearms violations.

The Government also submitted sections of a published 1989 Drug Enforcement Administration report which concluded that "large-scale, interstate trafficking networks controlled by Jamaicans, Haitians and Black street gangs dominate the manufacture and distribution of crack." J. Featherly & E. Hill, Crack Cocaine Overview 1989.

In response, one of respondents' attorneys submitted an affidavit alleging that an intake coordinator at a drug treatment center had told her that there are "an equal number of Caucasian users and dealers to minority users and dealers." Respondents also submitted an affidavit from a criminal defense attorney alleging that in his experience many non blacks are prosecuted in state court for crack offenses, and a newspaper article reporting that federal "crack criminals ... are being punished far more severely than if they had been caught with powder cocaine, and almost every single one of them is black." The District Court denied the motion for reconsideration. When the Government indicated it would not comply with the court's discovery order, the court dismissed the case. ...

A divided three-judge panel of the Court of Appeals for the Ninth Circuit reversed, holding that, because of the proof requirements for a selective-prosecution claim, defendants must "provide a colorable basis for believing that 'others similarly situated have not been prosecuted'" to obtain discovery. The Court of Appeals voted to rehear the case en banc, and the en banc panel affirmed the District Court's order of dismissal, holding that "a defendant is not required to demonstrate that the government has failed to prosecute others who are similarly situated." We granted certiorari to determine the appropriate standard for discovery for a selective-prosecution claim.

OPINION

A selective-prosecution claim is ... [based] an assertion that the prosecutor has brought the charge for reasons

---

*Other defendants had introduced this study in support of similar discovery motions in at least two other Central District cocaine prosecutions. Both motions were denied. One District Judge explained from the bench that the 23-person sample before him was "statistically insignificant," and that the evidence did not indicate "whether there is a bias in the distribution of crime that says black people use crack cocaine, hispanic people use powdered cocaine, caucasian people use whatever it is they use."

forbidden by the Constitution. Our cases delineating the necessary elements to prove a claim of selective prosecution have taken great pains to explain that the standard is a demanding one. These cases afford a "background presumption" that the showing necessary to obtain discovery should itself be a significant barrier to the litigation of insubstantial claims.

A selective-prosecution claim asks a court to exercise judicial power over a "special province" of the Executive. The Attorney General and United States Attorneys retain "'broad discretion'" to enforce the Nation's criminal laws. They have this latitude because they are designated by statute as the President's delegates to help him discharge his constitutional responsibility to "take Care that the Laws be faithfully executed." U.S. Const., Art. II, § 3. As a result, "the presumption of regularity [government actions are presumed to be lawful] supports" their prosecutorial decisions and, "in the absence of clear evidence to the contrary, courts presume that they have properly discharged their official duties." In the ordinary case, "so long as the prosecutor has probable cause to believe that the accused committed an offense defined by statute, the decision whether or not to prosecute, and what charge to file or bring before a grand jury, generally rests entirely in his discretion."

Of course, a prosecutor's discretion is "subject to constitutional constraints." One of these constraints, imposed by the equal protection clause . . . is that the decision whether to prosecute may not be based on "an unjustifiable standard such as race, religion, or other arbitrary classification." A defendant may demonstrate that the administration of a criminal law is "directed so exclusively against a particular class of persons . . . with a mind so unequal and oppressive" that the system of prosecution amounts to "a practical denial" of equal protection of the law.

In order to dispel the presumption that a prosecutor has not violated equal protection, a criminal defendant must present "clear evidence to the contrary." We explained in *Wayte* why courts are "properly hesitant to examine the decision whether to prosecute." Judicial deference to the decisions of these executive officers rests in part on an assessment of the relative competence of prosecutors and courts. "Such factors as the strength of the case, the prosecution's general deterrence value, the Government's enforcement priorities, and the case's relationship to the Government's overall enforcement plan are not readily susceptible to the kind of analysis the courts are competent to undertake." It also stems from a concern not to unnecessarily impair the performance of a core executive constitutional function. "Examining the basis of a prosecution delays the criminal proceeding, threatens to chill law enforcement by subjecting the prosecutor's motives and decision making to outside inquiry, and may undermine prosecutorial effectiveness by revealing the Government's enforcement policy."

The requirements for a selective-prosecution claim draw on "ordinary equal protection standards." The claimant must demonstrate that the federal prosecutorial policy "had a discriminatory effect and that it was motivated by a discriminatory purpose." To establish a discriminatory effect in a race case, the claimant must show that similarly situated individuals of a different race were not prosecuted. . . .

The similarly situated requirement does not make a selective-prosecution claim impossible to prove. . . . In *Yick Wo v. Hopkins* (1886), we invalidated an ordinance . . . that prohibited the operation of laundries in wooden buildings. Yick Wo successfully demonstrated that the ordinance was applied against Chinese nationals but not against other laundry-shop operators. The authorities had denied the applications of 200 Chinese subjects for permits to operate shops in wooden buildings, but granted the applications of 80 individuals who were not Chinese subjects to operate laundries in wooden buildings "under similar conditions." . . .

Having reviewed the requirements to prove a selective-prosecution claim [itself], we turn to the showing necessary to obtain discovery in support of such a claim. If discovery is ordered, the Government must assemble from its own files documents which might corroborate or refute the defendant's claim. Discovery thus imposes many of the costs present when the Government must respond to a prima facie case of selective prosecution. It will divert prosecutors' resources and may disclose the Government's prosecutorial strategy. The justifications for a rigorous standard for the elements of a selective-prosecution claim thus require a correspondingly rigorous standard for discovery in aid of such a claim. . . .

In this case we consider what evidence constitutes "some evidence tending to show the existence" of the discriminatory effect element. The Court of Appeals held that a defendant may establish a colorable basis for discriminatory effect without evidence that the Government has failed to prosecute others who are similarly situated to the defendant. We think it was mistaken in this view. . . .

The Court of Appeals reached its decision in part because it started "with the presumption that people of all races commit all types of crimes—not with the premise that any type of crime is the exclusive province of any particular racial or ethnic group." It cited no authority for this proposition, which seems contradicted by the most recent statistics of the United States Sentencing Commission. Those statistics show: More than 90% of the persons sentenced in 1994 for crack cocaine trafficking were black; 93.4% of convicted LSD dealers were white; and 91% of those convicted for pornography or prostitution were white. Presumptions at war with presumably reliable statistics have no proper place in the analysis of this issue.

The Court of Appeals also expressed concern about the "evidentiary obstacles defendants face." But all of its sister Circuits that have confronted the issue have required that defendants produce some evidence of differential treatment of similarly situated members of other races or protected classes. In the present case, if the claim of selective prosecution were well founded, it should not have been an insuperable task to prove that persons of other races were being treated differently than respondents. For instance, respondents could have investigated whether similarly situated persons of other races were prosecuted by the State of California and were known to federal law enforcement officers, but were not prosecuted in federal court. We think the required threshold—a credible showing of different treatment of similarly situated persons—adequately balances the Government's interest in vigorous prosecution and the defendant's interest in avoiding selective prosecution.

In the case before us, respondents' "study" did not constitute "some evidence tending to show the existence of the essential elements of" a selective-prosecution claim. The study failed to identify individuals who were not black and could have been prosecuted for the offenses for which respondents were charged, but were not so prosecuted. This omission was not remedied by respondents' evidence in opposition to the Government's motion for reconsideration. The newspaper article, which discussed the discriminatory effect of federal drug sentencing laws, was not relevant to an allegation of discrimination in decisions to prosecute. Respondents' affidavits, which recounted one attorney's conversation with a drug treatment center employee and the experience of another attorney defending drug prosecutions in state court, recounted hearsay and reported personal conclusions based on anecdotal evidence. The judgment of the Court of Appeals is therefore reversed, and the case is remanded for proceedings consistent with this opinion.

DISSENT

STEVENS, J.

Federal prosecutors are respected members of a respected profession. Despite an occasional misstep, the excellence of their work abundantly justifies the presumption that "they have properly discharged their official duties." Nevertheless, the possibility that political or racial animosity may infect a decision to institute criminal proceedings cannot be ignored. For that reason, it has long been settled that the prosecutor's broad discretion to determine when criminal charges should be filed is not completely unbri-

dled. As the Court notes, however, the scope of judicial review of particular exercises of that discretion is not fully defined.

The United States Attorney for the Central District of California is a member and an officer of the bar of that District Court. As such, she has a duty to the judges of that Court to maintain the standards of the profession in the performance of her official functions. If a District Judge has reason to suspect that she, or a member of her staff, has singled out particular defendants for prosecution on the basis of their race, it is surely appropriate for the judge to determine whether there is a factual basis for such a concern. . . .

The Court correctly concludes that in this case the facts presented to the District Court in support of respondents' claim that they had been singled out for prosecution because of their race were not sufficient to prove that defense. Moreover, I agree with the Court that their showing was not strong enough to give them a right to discovery. . . . Like Chief Judge Wallace of the Court of Appeals, however, I am persuaded that the District Judge did not abuse her discretion when she concluded that the factual showing was sufficiently disturbing to require some response from the United States Attorney's Office. Perhaps the discovery order was broader than necessary, but I cannot agree with the Court's apparent conclusion that no inquiry was permissible.

The District Judge's order should be evaluated in light of three circumstances that underscore the need for judicial vigilance over certain types of drug prosecutions. First, the Anti-Drug Abuse Act of 1986 and subsequent legislation established a regime of extremely high penalties for the possession and distribution of so-called "crack" cocaine. Those provisions treat one gram of crack as the equivalent of 100 grams of powder cocaine. The distribution of 50 grams of crack is thus punishable by the same mandatory minimum sentence of 10 years in prison that applies to the distribution of 5,000 grams of powder cocaine. The Sentencing Guidelines extend this ratio to penalty levels above the mandatory minimums: For any given quantity of crack, the guideline range is the same as if the offense had involved 100 times that amount in powder cocaine.*

Second, the disparity between the treatment of crack cocaine and powder cocaine is matched by the disparity between the severity of the punishment imposed by federal law and that imposed by state law for the same conduct. For a variety of reasons, often including the absence of mandatory minimums, the existence of parole, and lower

---

*These penalties result in sentences for crack offenders that average three to eight times longer than sentences for comparable powder offenders.

baseline penalties, terms of imprisonment for drug offenses tend to be substantially lower in state systems than in the federal system. The difference is especially marked in the case of crack offenses. The majority of States draw no distinction between types of cocaine in their penalty schemes; of those that do, none has established as stark a differential as the Federal Government. For example, if respondent Hampton is found guilty, his federal sentence might be as long as a mandatory life term. Had he been tried in state court, his sentence could have been as short as 12 years, less worktime credits of half that amount.

Under California law at the time of the offenses, possession for sale of cocaine base involving 50 grams carried a penalty of imprisonment for either three, four, or five years. If the defendant had no prior convictions, he could be granted probation. § 11370. For each prior felony drug conviction, the defendant received an additional 3-year sentence. § 11370.2. Thus, with three priors and the possibility of work time reductions, Hampton could have served as little as six years under California law. Since the time of the offenses, California has raised several of these penalties, but the new punishments could not be applied to respondents.

Finally, it is undisputed that the brunt of the elevated federal penalties falls heavily on blacks. While 65% of the persons who have used crack are white, in 1993 they represented only 4% of the federal offenders convicted of trafficking in crack. Eighty-eight percent of such defendants were black. During the first 18 months of full guideline implementation, the sentencing disparity between black and white defendants grew from preguideline levels: Blacks on average received sentences over 40% longer than whites. See Bureau of Justice Statistics, Sentencing in the Federal Courts: Does Race Matter? 6–7 (Dec. 1993). Those figures represent a major threat to the integrity of federal sentencing reform, whose main purpose was the elimination of disparity (especially racial) in sentencing. . . .

The extraordinary severity of the imposed penalties and the troubling racial patterns of enforcement give rise to a special concern about the fairness of charging practices for crack offenses. Evidence tending to prove that black defendants charged with distribution of crack in the Central District of California are prosecuted in federal court, whereas members of other races charged with similar offenses are prosecuted in state court, warrants close scrutiny by the federal judges in that district. In my view, the District Judge, who has sat on both the federal and the state benches in Los Angeles, acted well within her discretion to call for the development of facts that would demonstrate what standards, if any, governed the choice of forum where similarly situated offenders are prosecuted.

Respondents submitted a study showing that of all cases involving crack offenses that were closed by the Fed-

eral Public Defender's Office in 1991, 24 out of 24 involved black defendants. To supplement this evidence, they submitted affidavits from two of the attorneys in the defense team. The first reported a statement from an intake coordinator at a local drug treatment center that, in his experience, an equal number of crack users and dealers were Caucasian as belonged to minorities. The second was from David R. Reed, counsel for respondent Armstrong. Reed was both an active court-appointed attorney in the Central District of California and one of the directors of the leading association of criminal defense lawyers who practice before the Los Angeles County courts. Reed stated that he did not recall "ever handling a [crack] cocaine case involving non-black defendants" in federal court, nor had he even heard of one. He further stated that "there are many crack cocaine sales cases prosecuted in state court that do involve racial groups other than blacks."

The majority discounts the probative value of the affidavits, claiming they recounted "hearsay" and reported "personal conclusions based on anecdotal evidence." But the Reed affidavit plainly contained more than mere hearsay; Reed offered information based on his own extensive experience in both federal and state courts. Given the breadth of his background, he was well qualified to compare the practices of federal and state prosecutors. In any event, the Government never objected to the admission of either affidavit on hearsay or any other grounds. It was certainly within the District Court's discretion to credit the affidavits of two members of the bar of that Court, at least one of whom had presumably acquired a reputation by his frequent appearances there, and both of whose statements were made on pains of perjury.

The criticism that the affidavits were based on "anecdotal evidence" is also unpersuasive. I thought it was agreed that defendants do not need to prepare sophisticated statistical studies in order to receive mere discovery in cases like this one. Certainly evidence based on a drug counselor's personal observations or on an attorney's practice in two sets of courts, state and federal, can "'tend to show the existence'" of a selective prosecution.

Even if respondents failed to carry their burden of showing that there were individuals who were not black but who could have been prosecuted in federal court for the same offenses, it does not follow that the District Court abused its discretion in ordering discovery. There can be no doubt that such individuals exist, and indeed the Government has never denied the same. In those circumstances, I fail to see why the District Court was unable to take judicial notice of this obvious fact and demand information from the Government's files to support or refute respondents' evidence. The presumption that some whites are prosecuted in state court is not "contradicted" by the statistics the majority cites, which show only that high percentages of blacks are convicted of certain federal crimes, while high percentages of whites are convicted of other federal crimes. Those figures are entirely consistent with the allegation of selective prosecution. The relevant comparison, rather, would be with the percentages of blacks and whites who commit those crimes. But, as discussed above, in the case of crack far greater numbers of whites are believed guilty of using the substance. The District Court, therefore, was entitled to find the evidence before it significant and to require some explanation from the Government.*

In sum, I agree with the Sentencing Commission that "while the exercise of discretion by prosecutors and investigators has an impact on sentences in almost all cases to some extent, because of the 100-to-1 quantity ratio and federal mandatory minimum penalties, discretionary decisions in cocaine cases often have dramatic effects." The severity of the penalty heightens both the danger of arbitrary enforcement and the need for careful scrutiny of any colorable claim of discriminatory enforcement. In this case, the evidence was sufficiently disturbing to persuade the District Judge to order discovery that might help explain the conspicuous racial pattern of cases before her court. I cannot accept the majority's conclusion that the District Judge either exceeded her power or abused her discretion when she did so. I therefore respectfully dissent.

---

*Also telling was the Government's response to respondents' evidentiary showing. It submitted a list of more than 3,500 defendants who had been charged with federal narcotics violations over the previous three years. It also offered the names of 11 nonblack defendants whom it had prosecuted for crack offenses. All 11, however, were members of other racial or ethnic minorities. See 48 F.3d 1508, 1511 (CA9 1995). The District Court was authorized to draw adverse inferences from the Government's inability to produce a single example of a white defendant, especially when the very purpose of its exercise was to allay the court's concerns about the evidence of racially selective prosecutions. As another court has said: "Statistics are not, of course, the whole answer, but nothing is as emphatic as zero...."

Questions

1. Summarize the facts presented by the defendants in favor of the discovery of information to support a claim of selective enforcement of the drug laws.

2. Summarize the facts presented by the government against the discovery of information to support a claim of selective enforcement of the drug laws.

3. Assume that you're the defendants' lawyer. Argue the case in favor of discovery.

4. Assume that you're the prosecutor. Argue the case against discovery.

5. Now, assume that you're the judge. Rule on the motion to discover. State your reasons for your ruling on the motion.

SUMMARY

 I. Constitutionalism
   A. Is deeply embedded in our philosophy of government
   B. Constitutions are forever; laws are for now
   C. Six characteristics of constitutions
       1. Are a higher form of law
       2. Express the will of the whole people
       3. Always bind the government
       4. Can't be changed by government
       5. Can only be changed through direct action by the whole people
       6. Embody the fundamental values of the people

 II. The sources of criminal procedure
   A. Criminal procedure—the method government has to follow to detect and investigate crime; apprehend, prosecute, and convict defendants; and punish criminals

B. Sources of criminal procedure are
   1. U.S. and state constitutions
   2. Court decisions
   3. Statutes
   4. Administrative rules
C. The U.S. Constitution and federal courts
   1. The U.S. Constitution trumps all other sources (supremacy clause)
   2. Courts interpret the Constitution's general principles
   3. All criminal procedure has to answer to the Constitution and the courts' interpretation of it (judicial review)
   4. The U.S. Supreme Court has more power over lower federal courts than over state courts
   5. The U.S. Constitution sets minimum standards for criminal procedure
D. State constitutions and courts
   1. Most day-to-day operations of criminal procedure take place in state and local courts and law enforcement agencies
   2. State constitutions guarantee criminal procedure rights parallel to the U.S. Bill of Rights
   3. State constitutions can raise but not lower the minimum standards set by the U.S. Constitution
E. Federal and state statutes and rules
   1. Statutes and administrative rules fill in the details of criminal procedure
   2. Some rules of procedure are found in statutes
   3. Courts formulate rules for proceeding in court
   4. Law enforcement agencies and prosecutors' offices also adopt rules for their agencies
F. Model codes and rules
   1. Most rules don't address the period before arrest
   2. Most street encounters between police and individuals take place before arrest
   3. The American Law Institute adopted a model set of rules to fill the gap

III. Due process of law
   A. Constitutional democracy couldn't survive without the due process guarantee of fair procedures (when you see "due process," think "fair process")
   B. Until the Civil War, due process was a guarantee directed only at the national government, not the states
   C. The Civil War created on paper a national right to due process, but, in practice, criminal procedure was left entirely to the states
   D. The fundamental fairness doctrine
      1. Debated from 1900 to 1960
      2. Fundamental fairness—due process is not frozen in the Bill of Rights; it's forward looking and responds to evolving standards of fairness
      3. Contains two basics:
         a. Give defendants notice of charges against them
         b. Ensure a fair hearing of the facts
      4. Fundamental fairness was the rule until fears of totalitarian police states abroad and racist criminal justice at home stirred fears of arbitrary government

5. Incorporation—due process is shorthand for Bill of Rights criminal procedure guarantees
   E. The incorporation doctrine
      1. During the 1960s due process revolution, the U.S. Supreme Court ruled that due process required states to guarantee the criminal procedure rights in the Bill of Rights to state criminal justice
      2. Two parts of the expansion:
         a. Apply national standards to state court proceedings
         b. Extend judicial supervision beyond the courtroom to police encounters with individuals in police stations and on the street and other public places
      3. National supervision of state court proceedings was reluctantly accepted, but extending federal court supervision to police stations and the street set off a firestorm of controversy

IV. Equal protection of the law
   A. Constitutional democracy couldn't survive without a guarantee of equality before the law
   B. Equality before the law is more than a slogan; it's a constitutional command
   C. Since the Civil War, it's a command to federal, state, and local governments
   D. Equal protection doesn't mean state officials have to treat everybody exactly alike; they can't use unacceptable classifications by group characteristics, especially race or ethnicity
   E. Proving government discrimination requires a very high burden of proof; claimants have to carry the burden, and, in practice, rarely succeed

 Go to the Criminal Procedure 6e CD to download this summary outline. The outline has been formatted so that you can add notes to it during class lectures, or later create a customized chapter outline to use while reviewing. Either way, the summary outline will help you understand the "big picture" and fill in the details as you study.

REVIEW QUESTIONS

1. What's the meaning and significance of Chief Justice Marshall's remark, "We must never forget that it is a *constitution* we are expounding"?

2. List six characteristics of constitutionalism.

3. Identify the four sources of the rules of criminal procedure.

4. Why do we say, "The Constitution doesn't come with an instruction manual"?

5. Who has the final word in telling us what the Constitution means?

6. Explain why the U.S. Supreme Court has more power over lower federal courts than it does over state courts.

7. Identify two types of cases where state courts are a source of criminal procedure law.

8. Explain the meaning and significance of the phrase, "It doesn't pay a law much of a compliment to declare it constitutional."

9. What's the importance of the *Model Code of Pre-Arraignment Procedure*?

10. Identify the major results of the 1960s "due process revolution."

11. Briefly trace the history of due process from the adoption of the U.S. Constitution to the present.

12. Describe and explain the significance of *Hurtado v. California*.

13. Identify domestic and foreign events that may have influenced the U.S. Supreme Court to begin to supervise state criminal procedures.

14. Describe, state the holding of the Court, and explain the significance of *Powell v. Alabama*.

15. Identify the characteristics of cases the U.S. Supreme Court accepted for due process review from 1930 to 1960.

16. Summarize the differences among the fundamental fairness, total incorporation, and selective incorporation doctrines as they affect state criminal procedures.

17. Summarize the controversy generated by the U.S. Supreme Court's 1960s incorporation decisions.

18. Explain the significance of the term "self-inflicted wound" as it applies to the U.S. Supreme Court's 1960s criminal justice decisions.

19. Identify the two facts individuals have to prove to succeed in their claims the government denied them equal protection of the laws.

20. Explain why it's difficult to win claims that the government denied a person equal protection of the law.

KEY TERMS

constitutionalism p. 25
laws p. 25
constitutions p. 25
criminal procedures p. 26
habeas corpus p. 27
supremacy clause p. 28
judicial review p. 28

supervisory power p. 28
parallel rights p. 28
American Law Institute p. 29
due process p. 30
procedural due process p. 30
substantive due process p. 30
charging by information p. 31

fundamental fairness doctrine p. 41
incorporation doctrine p. 44
total incorporation p. 45
selective incorporation p. 45
"jot for jot" approach p. 46
equal protection of the law p. 47
presumption of regularity p. 48

THE COMPANION WEB SITE
FOR *CRIMINAL PROCEDURE,* SIXTH EDITION

http://cj.wadsworth.com/samaha/crim_pro6e

Supplement your review of this chapter by going to the companion Web site to take one of the Tutorial Quizzes, use the flash cards to test yourself on the key terms from each chapter, and check out the many other study aids you'll find there. You'll find valuable data and resources at your fingertips to help you study for that big exam or write that important paper.

Searches and Seizures

3

Chapter Main Points

- Crime control depends on information, but that information usually comes from reluctant sources.
- The Fourth Amendment was originally created to make sure the government didn't use illegal methods to get evidence in sedition and customs cases.
- The Fourth Amendment balances government power to control crime and the right of people to be let alone by the government; so, it doesn't ban *all* searches and seizures, only "unreasonable" ones.
- Government actions aren't searches unless they invade a person's reasonable expectation of privacy.
- Discoveries of evidence in plain view, in public places, in open fields, or on abandoned property aren't searches, and so the Fourth Amendment doesn't apply to them.
- Searches aren't unreasonable if they're backed up by an objective basis (facts); the more invasive the search, the greater the objective basis required.
- People aren't "seized" *whenever* officers approach them and ask questions; they're seized only when they're either physically detained or submit to an officer's display of authority.

The right of the people to be secure in their persons, houses, papers, and effects, against unreasonable searches and seizures, shall not be violated, and no warrants shall issue but upon probable cause, supported by Oath or affirmation, and particularly describing the place to be searched, and the persons or things to be seized.

Amendment IV, U.S. Constitution

Individuals may feel a moral obligation or psychological pressure to cooperate with police officers who approach them and question them, but they aren't required to do so unless they are "seized."

Florida v. Royer (1983), U.S. Supreme Court Justice Byron White

Every week for two months, and at least once more a month later, the Laguna Beach police clawed through the trash that Greenwood left in opaque, sealed bags on the curb outside his home. Complete strangers minutely scrutinized their bounty, undoubtedly dredging up intimate details of Greenwood's private life and habits. The intrusions proceeded without a warrant, and no court before or since has concluded that the police acted on probable cause to believe Greenwood was engaged in any criminal activity.

California v. Greenwood (1988), Dissent, U.S. Supreme Court

SEARCHES AND SEIZURES

Crime control in a constitutional democracy depends on information, but the information usually comes from reluctant (sometimes stubborn, fearful, and even hostile) sources—criminals, suspects, victims, and witnesses. Criminals don't want to incriminate themselves. Potential criminals don't want to give away their criminal schemes. Victims and other witnesses often are afraid to talk, or they don't want to give up their friends and family. So, law enforcement officers have to rely on four involuntary methods to get information—searches and seizures (Chapters 3–7), interrogation (Chapter 8), and identification procedures (Chapter 9).

Although getting information to control crime is the *main* purpose of searches and seizures, there are also some special needs for searches and seizures that go beyond law enforcement purposes. These **special-needs searches** include searches and seizures to

1. Protect officers from armed suspects (Chapters 4, 6)
2. Protect the property of detained suspects from loss or damage (Chapter 7)
3. Protect officials from lawsuits (Chapter 7)

4. Detect drug use among students and public employees (Chapter 7)

5. Prevent drunk driving (Chapter 7)

In this section, we'll look at the purpose of the Fourth Amendment (quoted on p. 58); the three-step criteria for determining whether law enforcement has complied with the Fourth Amendment; and the objective basis required by the law to back up a lawful search.

Purpose of the Fourth Amendment

The Fourth Amendment was created to make sure the government doesn't use illegal methods to get evidence. To understand why, let's look at a little history. Search and seizure law began a long time ago with the invention of the printing press and didn't have anything to do with the kinds of crimes we're familiar with today. To protect English monarchs from their critics, royal agents were sent out to conduct search and destroy missions against **seditious libels** (printed criticism of the government). The low respect the English had for their imported German kings in the eighteenth century (the four Georges of the House of Hanover) raised the number of seditious libels to epidemic proportions. To fight this epidemic the Crown relied on the **general warrant** (officially called a **writ of assistance**), a document in two parts. The first part gave royal agents the power to search anyone, anywhere, anytime. The second part (for which it's named) gave the agents the power to order anyone who happened to be nearby to help execute the warrant.

Writs of assistance were issued at the beginning of a new monarch's reign and were good for the life of the monarch. Like the holder of a blank check who can fill in the amount, the writ permitted the officer to fill in names of persons, homes, shops, offices, private papers, and other items the officer wanted to search. So, for the life of the monarch, officers of the Crown had total discretion as to whom, where, and what to search and seize. In the case of George III, that meant the authority was good from 1760 to 1820!

Writs of assistance weren't just used to search for and destroy seditious libels. They were used to collect taxes on a long list of items used by everybody, like cider, beer, and paper. The British hated paying these taxes, and the American colonists hated paying customs duties on the same stuff; both were notorious for not paying any of them. Smuggling into and out of the American colonies was rampant. The writs of assistance became a weapon used to collect the hated customs in the American colonies. Notice what these original searches and seizures were *not* directed at: looking for and taking evidence of common felonies against individuals and their property, drug crimes—and now terrorism—and arresting suspects involved in these activities. So, their purposes were very different from what they're used for today (Taylor 1969, Part I).

It was the use of the hated writs of assistance in these tax and political cases that prompted William Pitt in the House of Commons to speak the most famous words ever uttered against the power of government to search:

> The poorest man may in his cottage bid defiance to all the forces of the Crown. It may be frail—its roof may shake—the wind may blow through it—the storm may enter—but the King of England cannot enter—all his force dares not cross the threshold of the ruined tenement.
>
> Hall 1993, 2:4

And, in America, it was in a customs case that the young lawyer and future president John Adams watched the great colonial trial lawyer James Otis attack the writs of assistance in a Boston courtroom. Otis argued that writs of assistance were illegal. Only searches with specific dates, naming the places or persons to be searched and seized, and based on probable cause, were lawful where free people lived. Otis's argument moved John Adams to write years later: "There was the Child Independence born" (Smith 1962, 56). But, the powerful oratory hurled against the writs of assistance didn't stop either the English Crown or American governors from using them. The authors of the Bill of Rights didn't forget their hatred for the general warrant, and they wrote their opposition to it into the Fourth Amendment to the U.S. Constitution (see p. 58).

The Fourth Amendment isn't directed solely against government power. It balances two basic interests: government power and individual rights. So, it's supposed to make sure the government has enough power to look for and get the evidence it needs to control crime, protect officers, seize suspects, and meet special needs beyond criminal law enforcement. But, the government can't do any of these by means of "unreasonable searches and seizures." The *reasonableness* limit is to protect the deepest values in a free society: (1) **liberty**, the right to come and go as we please, sometimes called the **right of locomotion**, and (2) **privacy**, the right to be let alone by the government. Keep in mind that the Fourth Amendment protects us from invasions by *government officials*; it doesn't protect us from invasions by *private persons*.

Three-Step Fourth Amendment Analysis

Determining whether the government has complied with the Fourth Amendment is a three-step process intended to answer the questions:

1. Was the government action a search or a seizure? (this chapter)

2. If the government action was a search or a seizure, was it an *unreasonable* search or seizure? (Chapters 4–7)

3. If the government search or seizure was unreasonable, should evidence obtained during the search be excluded? (Chapter 10)

The first question focuses on a broad range of encounters between individuals and law enforcement officers. These encounters include everything from trivial to severe and from consensual to forced invasions of liberty and privacy. Only some of these encounters are Fourth Amendment searches or seizures.

Degrees of Objective Basis Required

Government actions that *might* be Fourth Amendment searches and/or seizures take place in three stages:

1. Initial encounters between individuals and police officers on the street and in other public places (Chapters 3–6)

2. Encounters between individuals and officers after they've been taken to the police station (Chapter 6)

3. Encounters after conviction between prisoners and officers in jails and prisons (and in special-needs searches, between school officials and students in schools and colleges and employers and employees in public agencies) (Chapter 7)

When encounters between individuals and the government move from the street to the police station and then to jails and prisons, they don't just change locations, they invade more deeply privacy and liberty. As the degree of invasion increases, so does the **objective basis** (facts and circumstances) required to back it up. Officers don't need any objective basis to justify voluntary encounters because they're neither Fourth Amendment searches nor seizures. Officers need only a few facts and circumstances—**reasonable suspicion** (Chapter 4)—to justify stops and frisks (analyzed in Chapter 4). However, it takes more facts—**probable cause**—to back up full-blown arrests (Chapter 5) and searches (Chapter 6). It takes varying degrees of objective bases to support the invasions for special-needs searches (Chapter 7).

SEARCHES

Until 1967, the U.S. Supreme Court defined searches according to what was called the **trespass doctrine.** According to the doctrine, to amount to a "search," officers had to invade physically a "constitutionally protected area." Constitutionally protected areas were the places named in the Fourth Amendment—persons, houses, papers, and effects (personal stuff). According to the Supreme Court, searching persons includes touching their bodies, rummaging through their pockets, taking blood tests, and performing surgery to remove bullets. On the other hand, the Court ruled that ordering suspects to give handwriting samples, voice samples, or hair specimens aren't searches of their person because they're less invasive. Houses include apartments, hotel rooms, garages, business offices, stores, and even warehouses. Papers include a broad range of personal writings, including diaries and letters. Effects include many items of personal property: cars, purses, briefcases, and packages (*Silverman v. U.S.* 1961).

The privacy doctrine began with a famous dissent in a Prohibition Era case, *Olmstead v. United States* (1928). In *Olmstead*, the defendants' telephones were tapped without a warrant to find evidence of violations of alcohol laws. The government collected more than 775 pages of notes from the wiretaps and, based on this information, indicted more than seventy people. The Supreme Court applied the trespass doctrine to the case, holding that the government wiretaps were not Fourth Amendment searches of the defendants' houses, papers, or effects because no officers physically entered the defendants' buildings. Justice Louis Brandeis wrote one of the most famous dissents in the history of the Court. He conceded that wiretaps were not physical trespasses; nevertheless:

> The makers of the Constitution . . . recognized the significance of man's spiritual nature, of his feelings and of his intellect. They knew that only a part of the pain, pleasure and satisfactions of life are to be found in material things. They sought to protect Americans in their beliefs, their thoughts, their emotions and their sensations. They conferred, as against the Government, the right to be let alone—the most comprehensive of rights and the right most valued by civilized men. (478)

The late senator and constitutional scholar Sam Ervin (1983) reaffirmed the Brandeis notion of the right to privacy in 1983:

> The oldest and deepest hunger in the human heart is for a place where one may dwell in peace and security and keep inviolate from public scrutiny one's innermost aspirations and thoughts, one's most intimate associations and communications, and one's most private activities. This truth was documented by Micah, the prophet, 2,700 years ago when he described the Mountain of the Lord as a place where "they shall sit every man under his own vine and fig tree and none shall make them afraid." (283)

In 1967, Justice Brandeis's dissent became the law of the land when, in the landmark case *Katz v. United States*, the Supreme Court replaced the trespass doctrine with the **privacy doctrine**. According to the privacy doctrine, the Fourth Amendment protects persons, not places, whenever they have an expectation of privacy that society is prepared to recognize.

In theory, the privacy doctrine is a fine example of balancing the government's power to control crime and the individual's right to be let alone. In practice, as you'll soon find out, courts nearly always weigh the balance in favor of the government. As a result, courts give a lot of leeway to the police in their encounters with private individuals on the street and in other public places. According to former prosecutor and Fourth Amendment specialist John Wesley Hall, Jr. (1993):

> When [society's need for security and the individual's need for privacy] are balanced, the former usually weighs heavily.... While this is perhaps a valid purpose in the administration of criminal justice, we must not lose sight of the fundamental precepts of the Fourth Amendment that the individual is to be free from arbitrary and oppressive governmental intrusions. (6)

In this section, we'll see how the right to privacy translates in practice by looking at what amounts to a reasonable "expectation of privacy," what is and what isn't a "plain-view search," and what places aren't protected by the Fourth Amendment, including open fields, public places, and abandoned property.

The "Expectation of Privacy"

Justice John Marshall Harlan's concurring opinion in *Katz v. United States* (1967) established a two-pronged privacy test to determine whether a government action is a search:

1. *Subjective privacy prong.* Whether the "person exhibited an actual [personal] expectation of privacy"

2. *Objective privacy prong.* Whether the subjective expectation of privacy is reasonable—that is, an expectation "that society is prepared to recognize as 'reasonable'"

Almost every case since *Katz* has phrased the privacy test as Justice Harlan stated it. In *Katz*, the Supreme Court not only adopted and applied the privacy doctrine but defined the "expectation of privacy."

Katz v. United States
389 U.S. 347, 88 S.Ct. 507, 19 L.Ed.2d 576 (1967)

Charles Katz was convicted under a federal statute of transmitting wagering information by telephone across state lines. The court of appeals affirmed the conviction. The Supreme Court granted certiorari and reversed.

STEWART, J.

FACTS

[The facts are taken from *Katz v. U.S.*, 369 F.2d 130 [9th Cir. 1966].] In February of 1965 Charles Katz was seen placing calls from a bank of three public telephone booths during certain hours and on an almost daily basis. He was never observed in any other telephone booth. In the period of February 19 to February 25, 1965, at set hours, Special Agents of the Federal Bureau of Investigation placed microphones on the tops of two of the public telephone booths normally used by Katz. The other phone was placed out of order by the telephone company. The microphones were attached to the outside of the telephone booths with tape. There was no physical penetration inside of the booths. The microphones were activated only while Katz was approaching and actually in the booth. Wires led from microphones to a wire recorder on top of one of the booths. Thus the F.B.I. obtained a record of Katz's end of a series of telephone calls. A study of the transcripts of the recordings made of Katz's end of the conversations revealed that the conversations had to do with the placing of bets and the obtaining of gambling information by Katz.

On February 23, 1965, F.B.I. Agent Allen Frei rented a room next to Katz's apartment residence. He listened to conversations through the common wall without the aid of any electronic device. He overheard Katz's end of a series of telephone conversations and took notes on them. These notes and the tapes made from the telephone booth recordings were the basis of a search warrant, which was obtained to search Katz's apartment. The search warrant called for "bookmaking records, wagering paraphernalia, including, but not limited to, bet slips, betting markers, run-down sheets, schedule sheets indicating the lines, adding machines, money, telephones, telephone address listings." The articles seized are described in the return. They are all related to the categories described in the warrant.

During the conversations overheard by Agent Frei, Katz made numerous comments to the effect that "I have

Northwestern minus 7," and "Oregon plus 3." Also, there was a statement by Katz such as, "Don't worry about the line. I have phoned Boston three times about it today."

At the trial evidence was introduced to show that from February 19 to February 25, 1965, inclusive, the appellant placed calls from two telephone booths located in the 8200 block of Sunset Boulevard in Los Angeles. The conversations were overheard and recorded every day except February 22. The transcripts of the recordings and the normal business records of the telephone company were used to determine that the calls went to Boston, Massachusetts, and Miami, Florida.

The testimony of Joseph Gunn of the Administrative Vice Division of the Los Angeles Police Department, who was the expert called by the government in the area of bookmaking, was that the transcripts of the conversations showed that bets were made and information assisting in the placing of bets was transmitted on the dates and at the times alleged in the indictment. Bets were recorded like "Give me Duquesne minus 7 for a nickel." Information relating to the line and the acquiring of credit was also transmitted. In correlating the transcript of the telephone conversations and line sheets and markers found in appellant's residence during the search pursuant to the warrant, Officer Gunn concluded that Katz was placing wagers with a bookmaker for another person for a consideration.

On February 25, 1965, Katz was advised by a Special Agent of the F.B.I., Emmett Doherty, that he had a right to remain silent, he had a right to consult counsel, and that any statements he made could be used against him in a court of law. Katz was arrested on the street. He was later present in his apartment where another agent of the F.B.I. was involved in the search authorized by the search warrant. Katz asked when he could have his records back. He stated that without them he was out of business and that he knew no other trade. During this exchange, in response to a question about interstate betting, Katz said that he could not bet locally because the bookmakers would not pay off.

The next day, which was February 26, 1965, Agent Donovan of the F.B.I. met Katz in the lobby of his apartment building to return two personal items, which had been taken at the time of the search. Donovan had been with Agent Doherty the day before when Doherty advised Katz of his rights with respect to statements made to the Federal Agents. Katz again asked why he could not have his records back. He stated without them he was out of business and that he had been a handicapper and a bettor most of his life. He suggested that if he got his records back he would continue to bet.

From all of the evidence in the case the court found the volume of business being done by Katz indicated that it was not a casual incidental occupation of Katz. The court found that he was engaged in the business of betting or wagering at the time of the telephone conversations, which were transmitted and recorded.

... Katz was convicted of transmitting wagering information by telephone from Los Angeles to Miami and Boston, in violation of a federal statute. We granted certiorari to consider the constitutional questions thus presented.

OPINION

Katz has phrased those questions as follows:

A. Whether a public telephone booth is a constitutionally protected area so that evidence obtained by attaching an electronic listening recording device to the top of such a booth is obtained in violation of the right to privacy of the user of the booth.

B. Whether physical penetration of a constitutionally protected area is necessary before a search and seizure can be said to be violative of the Fourth Amendment to the United States Constitution.

We decline to adopt this formulation of the issues. In the first place, the correct solution of Fourth Amendment problems is not necessarily promoted by incantation of the phrase "constitutionally protected area." Secondly, the Fourth Amendment cannot be translated into a general constitutional "right to privacy." That Amendment protects individual privacy against certain kinds of governmental intrusion, but its protections go further, and often have nothing to do with privacy at all. Other provisions of the Constitution protect personal privacy from other forms of governmental invasion. But the protection of a person's general right to privacy—his right to be let alone by other people—is, like the protection of his property and of his very life, left largely to the law of the individual states.

Because of the misleading way the issues have been formulated, the parties have attached great significance to the characterization of the telephone booth from which the petitioner placed his calls. Katz has strenuously argued that the booth was a "constitutionally protected area." The Government has maintained with equal vigor that it was not. But this effort to decide whether or not a given "area" is "constitutionally protected" deflects attention from the problem presented by this case. For the Fourth Amendment protects people, not places. What a person knowingly exposes to the public, even in his own home or office, is not a subject of Fourth Amendment protection. But what he seeks to preserve as private, even in an area accessible to the public, may be constitutionally protected.

The Government stresses that the telephone booth from which the petitioner made his calls was constructed partly of glass, so that he was visible after he entered it as he would have been if he had remained outside. But what he sought to exclude when he entered the booth was not the intruding eye—it was the uninvited ear. He did not shed his right to do so simply because he made calls from a place where he might be seen. No less than an individual in a business office, in a friend's apartment, or in a taxicab, a person in a telephone booth may rely upon the protection of the Fourth Amendment. One who occupies it, shuts the door behind him, and pays the toll that permits him to place a call is surely entitled to assume that the words he utters into the mouthpiece will not be broadcast to the world. To read the Constitution more narrowly is to ignore the vital role that the public telephone booth has come to play in private conversation.

The Government contends, however, that the activities of its agents in this case should not be tested by the Fourth Amendment requirements, for the surveillance technique they employed involved no physical penetration of the telephone booth from which Katz placed his calls. It is true that the absence of such penetration was at one time thought to foreclose further Fourth Amendment inquiry, for that Amendment was thought to limit only searches and seizures of tangible property.... Although a closely divided Court supposed in *Olmstead* that surveillance without any trespass and without the seizure of any material object fell outside the ambit of the Constitution, we have since departed from the narrow view on which that decision rested.... Once this much is acknowledged, and once it is recognized that the Fourth Amendment protects people—and not simply "areas"—against unreasonable searches and seizures it becomes clear that the reach of that Amendment cannot turn upon the physical presence or absence of a physical intrusion into any given enclosure.

We conclude ... the "trespass" doctrine ... can no longer be regarded as controlling. The Government's activities in electronically listening to and recording Katz's words violated the privacy upon which he justifiably relied while using the telephone booth and thus constituted a "search and seizure" within the meaning of the Fourth Amendment. The fact that the electronic device employed to achieve that end did not happen to penetrate the wall of the booth can have no constitutional significance.*

_____

*The Court reversed the conviction because the FBI agents did not get a search warrant, which they could easily have gotten (Chapter 6).

CONCURRING OPINION

HARLAN, J.

...As the Court's opinion states, "the Fourth Amendment protects people, not places." The question, however, is what protection it affords to those people. Generally, as here, the answer to that question requires reference to a "place." My understanding...is there is a twofold requirement, first a person exhibited an actual (subjective) expectation of privacy and, second, the expectation be one that society is prepared to recognize as "reasonable." Thus a man's home is, for most purposes, a place where he expects privacy, but objects, activities, or statements that he exposes to "plain view" of outsiders are not "protected" because no intention to keep them to himself has been exhibited. On the other hand, conversations in the open would not be protected against being overhead, for the expectation of privacy under the circumstances would be unreasonable.

DISSENT

BLACK, J.

If I could agree with the Court that eavesdropping carried on by electronic means (equivalent to wiretapping) constitutes a "search" or "seizure," I would be happy to join the Court's opinion.... My basic objection is twofold: (1) I do not believe that the words of the Amendment will bear the meaning given them by today's decision, and (2) I do not believe that it is the proper role of this Court to rewrite the Amendment in order "to bring it into harmony with the times" and thus reach a result that many people believe to be desirable....

Tapping telephone wires, of course, was an unknown possibility at the time the Fourth Amendment was adopted. But eavesdropping (and wiretapping is nothing more than eavesdropping by telephone) was..."an ancient practice which at common law was condemned as a nuisance. In those days the eavesdropper listened by naked ear under the eaves of houses or their windows, or beyond their walls seeking out private discourse." There can be no doubt that the Framers were aware of this practice, and if they had desired to outlaw or restrict the use of evidence obtained by eavesdropping, I believe that they would have used the appropriate language to do so in the Fourth Amendment. They certainly would not have left such a task to the ingenuity of language-stretching judges.

No one, it seems to me, can read the debates on the Bill of Rights without reaching the conclusion that its Framers and critics well knew the meaning of the words they used, what they would be understood to mean by others, their scope and their limitations. Under these circumstances it strikes me as a charge against their scholarship, their common sense and their candor to give to the Fourth Amendment's language the eavesdropping meaning the Court imputes to it today.... The Fourth Amendment was aimed directly at the abhorred practice of breaking in, ransacking and searching homes and other buildings and seizing people's personal belongings without warrants issued by magistrates....

In interpreting the Bill of Rights, I willingly go as far as a liberal construction of the language takes me, but I simply cannot in good conscience give a meaning to words which they have never before been thought to have and which they certainly do not have in common ordinary usage. I will not distort the words of the Amendment in order to "keep the Constitution up to date" or "bring it into harmony with the times." It was never meant that this Court have such power, which in effect would make us a continuously functioning constitutional convention.

With this decision the Court has completed, I hope, its rewriting of the Fourth Amendment, which started only recently when the Court began referring incessantly to the Fourth Amendment not so much as a law against unreasonable searches and seizures as one to protect an individual's privacy. By clever word juggling the Court finds it plausible to argue that language aimed specifically at searches and seizures of things that can be searched and seized may, to protect privacy, be applied to eavesdropped evidence of conversations that can neither be searched nor seized. Few things happen to an individual that do not affect his privacy in one way or another. Thus, by arbitrarily substituting the Court's language, designed to protect privacy, for the Constitution's language, designed to protect against unreasonable searches and seizures, the Court has made the Fourth Amendment its vehicle for holding all laws violative of the Constitution which offend the Court's broadest concept of privacy.

As I said in *Griswold v. Connecticut* (1965), "The Court talks about a constitutional 'right of privacy' as though there is some constitutional provision or provisions forbidding any law ever to be passed which might abridge the 'privacy' of individuals. But there is not." I made clear in that dissent my fear of the dangers involved when this Court uses the "broad, abstract and ambiguous concept" of "privacy" as a "comprehensive substitute" for the Fourth Amendment's guarantee against "unreasonable searches and seizures."

The Fourth Amendment protects privacy only to the extent that it prohibits unreasonable searches and seizures of "persons, houses, papers, and effects." No general right is created by the Amendment so as to give this Court the unlimited power to hold unconstitutional everything which affects privacy. Certainly the Framers, well acquainted as they were with the excesses of governmental power, did not intend to grant this Court such omnipotent lawmaking authority as that. The history of governments proves that it is dangerous to freedom to repose such powers in courts.

For these reasons I respectfully DISSENT.

Questions

1. List the specific government invasions in the case.

2. State the privacy and trespass doctrines.

3. Why did the Court reject the trespass doctrine?

4. What values does the privacy doctrine promote? How do the two doctrines differ in the values they protect?

5. Which test would you adopt? Defend your answer.

6. Is Justice Black right in his dissent that there is no right to privacy in the Fourth Amendment? Explain your answer.

7. What if it's true that the framers of the Fourth Amendment didn't intend to protect us from government eavesdropping? Should something written over two hundred years ago bind the Court (and us) today? Explain your answer.

8. Do you agree that the Supreme Court doesn't have the authority to keep the Constitution "up to date"? Explain your answer.

EXPLORING THE EXPECTATION OF PRIVACY FURTHER

 Go to the Criminal Procedure 6e CD to read the full text versions of the cases featured here.

1. *Was There a Reasonable Expectation of Privacy in His Bank Records?*

FACTS

In response to an informant's tip, a deputy sheriff from Houston County, Georgia, stopped a van-type truck occupied by two of Mitch Miller's alleged co-conspirators. The truck contained distillery apparatus and raw material. A few weeks later, a fire broke out in a Kathleen, Georgia, warehouse rented to Miller. During the blaze firefighters and sheriff's department officials discovered a 7500-gallon-capacity distillery, 175 gallons of nontax-paid whiskey, and related paraphernalia.

Two weeks later agents from the Treasury Department's Alcohol, Tobacco, and Firearms Bureau presented grand jury subpoenas to the presidents of the Citizens & Southern National Bank of Warner Robins and the Bank of Byron, where Miller maintained accounts. The subpoenas required the two presidents to appear in court and to produce all records of accounts—savings, checking, loan or otherwise, in the name of Mr. Mitch Miller.

The banks didn't tell Miller about the subpoenas but ordered their employees to make the records available and to provide copies of any documents the agents desired. At the Bank of Byron, an agent was shown microfilm records of the relevant account and provided with copies of one deposit slip and one or two checks. At the Citizens & Southern National Bank microfilm records also were shown to the agent, and he was given copies of the records of the respondent's account during the applicable period. These included all checks, deposit slips, two financial statements, and three monthly statements. The bank presidents were then told that it wouldn't be necessary to appear in person before the grand jury.

In a motion to suppress the bank records, Miller contended that the bank records were illegally seized. Did Miller have a reasonable expectation of privacy in his bank records?

DECISION AND REASONS

The trial court overruled the motion, and the U.S. Supreme Court agreed. According to the Court:

> Miller urges that he has a Fourth Amendment interest in the records kept by the banks because . . . he has a reasonable expectation of privacy [in the records]. He relies on this Court's statement in *Katz v. United States* that "we have . . . departed from the narrow view" that " 'property interests control the right of the Government to search and seize,' " and that a "search and seizure" become unreasonable when the Government's activities violate "the privacy upon which a person justifiably relies." But in *Katz* the Court also stressed that "what a person knowingly exposes to the public . . . is not a subject of Fourth Amendment protection." We . . . perceive no legitimate "expectation of privacy" in their contents. The checks are not confidential communications but negotiable instruments to be used in commercial transactions. All of the documents obtained, including financial statements and deposit slips, contain only information voluntarily conveyed to the banks and exposed to their employees in the ordinary course of business. . . .
>
> The depositor takes the risk, in revealing his affairs to another, that the information will be conveyed by that person to the Government. This Court has held repeatedly that the Fourth Amendment does not prohibit the obtaining of information revealed to a third party and conveyed by him to Government authorities, even if the information is revealed on the assumption that it will be used only for a limited purpose and the confidence placed in the third party will not be betrayed.
>
> BRENNAN, J., dissenting.
>
> The customer of a bank expects that the documents, such as checks, which he transmits to the bank in the course of his business operations, will remain private, and that such an expectation is reasonable. The prosecution concedes as much, although it asserts that this expectation is not constitutionally cognizable. Representatives of several banks testified at the suppression hearing that information in their possession regarding a customer's account is deemed by them to be confidential.
>
> *United States v. Miller*, 425 U.S. 435 1976

2. Was There a Reasonable Expectation of Privacy in the Numbers He Dialed from His Home Telephone?

FACTS

In Baltimore, Maryland, Patricia McDonough was robbed. She gave the police a description of the robber and of a 1975 Monte Carlo automobile she had observed near the scene of the crime. After the robbery, McDonough began receiving threatening and obscene phone calls from a man identifying himself as the robber. On one occasion, the caller asked that she step out on her front porch; she did so, and saw the 1975 Monte Carlo she had earlier described to police moving slowly past her home. On March 16, police spotted a man who met McDonough's description driving a 1975

Monte Carlo in her neighborhood. By tracing the license plate number, police learned that the car was registered in the name of Michael Lee Smith.

The next day, the telephone company, at police request, installed a pen register at its central offices to record the numbers dialed from the telephone at Smith's home. The police didn't get a warrant or court order before having the pen register installed. The register revealed that on March 17 a call was placed from Smith's [the defendant's] home to McDonough's phone. On the basis of this and other evidence, the police obtained a warrant to search the petitioner's residence. The search revealed that a page in Smith's phone book was turned down to the name and number of Patricia McDonough; the phone book was seized. Smith was arrested, and a six-man lineup was held on March 19. McDonough identified the petitioner as the man who had robbed her.

Smith was indicted in the Criminal Court of Baltimore for robbery. He moved to suppress "all fruits derived from the pen register" on the ground that the police had failed to secure a warrant prior to its installation. Did he have a reasonable expectation of privacy in the numbers he dialed from his home telephone?

DECISION AND REASONS

The trial court denied the motion. The U.S. Supreme Court agreed. According to the majority:

> ...We doubt that people in general entertain any actual expectation of privacy in the numbers they dial....Petitioner can claim no legitimate expectation of privacy here. When he used his phone, petitioner voluntarily conveyed numerical information to the telephone company and "exposed" that information to its equipment in the ordinary course of business. In so doing, petitioner assumed the risk that the company would reveal to police the numbers he dialed. The switching equipment that processed those numbers is merely the modern counterpart of the operator who, in an earlier day, personally completed calls for the subscriber....

STEWART, J., dissenting:

I think that the numbers dialed from a private telephone—like the conversations that occur during a call—are within the constitutional protection recognized in *Katz*. It seems clear to me that information obtained by pen register surveillance of a private telephone is information in which the telephone subscriber has a legitimate expectation of privacy. The information captured by such surveillance emanates from private conduct within a person's home or office—locations that without question are entitled to Fourth and Fourteenth Amendment protection....

The numbers dialed from a private telephone—although certainly more prosaic than the conversation itself—are not without "content." Most private telephone subscribers may have their own numbers listed in a publicly distributed directory, but I doubt there are any who would be happy to have broadcast to the world a list of the local or long distance numbers they have called. This is not because such a list might in some sense be incriminating, but because it easily could reveal the identities of the persons and the places called, and thus reveal the most intimate details of a person's life.

MARSHALL, J., dissenting:

Since I remain convinced that constitutional protections are not abrogated whenever a person apprises another of facts valuable in criminal investigations, I respectfully dissent....Just as one who enters a public telephone booth is "entitled to assume that the words he utters into the mouthpiece will not be broadcast to the world," so too, he should be entitled to assume that the numbers he dials in the privacy of his home will be recorded, if at all, solely for the phone company's business purposes. Accordingly, I would require law enforcement officials to obtain a warrant before they enlist telephone companies to secure information otherwise beyond the government's reach.

Smith v. Maryland, 442 U.S. 745 (1979)

Plain View, Hearing, Smell, and Touch

What officers discover by the ordinary senses of seeing, touching, smelling, and hearing are called **plain-view searches**. We really should call them *non*searches, because what officers discover by means of their senses are *not* Fourth Amendment searches (and *non*seizures, because what they seize as a result of the discovery aren't "seizures").

The **plain-view doctrine** of nonsearch applies only if three conditions are met at the time of the discovery:

1. Officers are where they have a legal right to be.

2. Officers don't beef up their ordinary senses with advanced technology.

3. The officers' discovery is by chance.

A variety of situations can satisfy the three conditions. While conducting a search with a warrant for specific items related to one crime, officers may see evidence of another crime. Or they may be conducting a lawful search without a warrant and see contraband in plain view. The conditions are also satisfied when officers are conducting noncriminal business and accidentally discover incriminating evidence. For example, suppose police officers approach a car to check its registration. While talking to the driver, the officers happen to see marijuana lying on the passenger seat. It's not a search to see it, and it's not a seizure to take it. Why? Because the officers have a lawful right to approach drivers. They're where they have a legal right to be, and they happen to see the marijuana without the aid of some hi-tech sense enhancer. But, if the marijuana was under some newspapers, and the officers reached inside the car and moved the papers, then they *would* be searching because they had to take some further action to discover the marijuana. In other words, they didn't discover it by sight alone.

High-Tech Enhancements of Ordinary Senses

The plain-view doctrine only applies to detection by the ordinary senses, not to discovery enhanced by technology. But, there's a difference between technological enhancements that many people use and anyone can get easily—flashlights, bifocals, and magnifying glasses—and high-powered devices that only a few people have or can get easily. So, eyesight enhanced by a flashlight is treated like ordinary eyesight; eyesight enhanced by X ray isn't. In *U.S. v. Kim* (1976), for example, FBI agents used an 800-millimeter telescope with a 60-millimeter opening to observe activities in Earl "The Old Man" Kim's apartment. The surveillance took place nearly a quarter mile from the apartment. The telescope was so powerful the agents could even see what Kim was reading. According to the court, "It is inconceivable that the government can intrude so far into an individual's home that it can detect the material he is reading and still not be considered to have engaged in a search...."

But the U.S. Supreme Court came to a different result when it applied the plain-view doctrine in *California v. Ciraolo* (1986). The police saw marijuana growing in Dante Ciraolo's yard from a plane 1000 feet in the air. The police had hired the plane because two privacy fences blocked their view from the ground. According to the Court, the use of the plane didn't enhance the officers' naked eye such that it turned the observation into a Fourth Amendment search.

In a similar case, *Dow Chemical Corporation v. U.S.* (1986), Dow maintained elaborate security around a 2000-acre chemical plant that bars ground-level observation. When Dow refused the Environmental Protection Agency's (EPA's) request for an on-site inspection, the EPA employed a commercial air photographer to fly over the plant and take photographs to determine whether Dow was complying with EPA standards. The U.S. Supreme Court ruled that such aerial observation and photography weren't Fourth Amendment searches.

In *United States v. White* (1971), the U.S. Supreme Court dealt with the application of the Fourth Amendment to electronic eavesdropping.

CASE	*Is Electronic Eavesdropping a "Search"?*

United States v. White
401 U.S. 745 (1971)

James A. White was tried and convicted, fined and sentenced to 25 years in prison for drug law violations. The conviction was based on evidence overheard by means of radio transmissions from an informant wired for sound. The U.S. Court of Appeals reversed the conviction. The U.S. Supreme Court granted certiorari and reversed the Court of Appeals.

WHITE, J., joined by BURGER, CJ., and STEWART and BLACKMUN, JJ.

FACTS

... James A. White was tried and convicted for dealing in illegal drugs. He was fined and sentenced as a second offender to 25-year concurrent sentences. The issue before us is whether the Fourth Amendment bars from evidence the testimony of government agents who related certain conversations between White and a government informant, Harvey Jackson, and which the agents overheard by monitoring the frequency of a radio transmitter carried by Jackson and concealed on his person. On four occasions the conversations took place in Jackson's home; each of these conversations was overheard by an agent concealed in a kitchen closet with Jackson's consent and by a second agent outside the house using a radio receiver. Four other conversations—one in respondent's home, one in a restau-

rant, and two in Jackson's car—were overheard by the use of radio equipment. The prosecution was unable to locate and produce Jackson at the trial and the trial court overruled objections to the testimony of the agents who conducted the electronic surveillance. The jury returned a guilty verdict and defendant appealed.

The Court of Appeals ... interpreted the Fourth Amendment to forbid the introduction of the agents' testimony in the circumstances of this case. Accordingly, the court reversed. ... In our view, the Court of Appeals misinterpreted ... the Fourth Amendment. ...

OPINION

... The Court of Appeals understood *Katz v. United States* [see p. 63] to render inadmissible against White the agents' testimony concerning conversations that Jackson broadcast to them. We cannot agree. *Katz* involved no revelation to the Government by a party to conversations with the defendant nor did the Court indicate in any way that a defendant has a justifiable and constitutionally protected expectation that a person with whom he is conversing will not then or later reveal the conversation to the police. ...

Our problem is not what the privacy expectations of particular defendants in particular situations may be or the extent to which they may in fact have relied on the discretion of their companions. Very probably, individual defendants neither know nor suspect that their colleagues have gone or will go to the police or are carrying recorders or transmitters. Otherwise, conversation would cease.... Our problem, in terms of the principles announced in *Katz*, is what expectations of privacy are constitutionally "justifiable"—what expectations the Fourth Amendment will protect in the absence of a warrant. So far, the law permits the frustration of actual expectations of privacy by permitting authorities to use the testimony of those associates who for one reason or another have determined to turn to the police, as well as by authorizing the use of informants. If the law gives no protection to the wrongdoer whose trusted accomplice is or becomes a police agent, neither should it protect him when that same agent has recorded or transmitted the conversations which are later offered in evidence to prove the State's case.

Inescapably, one contemplating illegal activities must realize and risk that his companions may be reporting to the police. If he sufficiently doubts their trustworthiness, the association will very probably end or never materialize. But if he has no doubts, or allays them, or risks what doubt he has, the risk is his. In terms of what his course will be, what he will or will not do or say, we are unpersuaded that he would distinguish between probable informers with transmitters [and] the other. Given the possibility or probability that one of his colleagues is cooperating with the police, it is only speculation to assert that the defendant's utterances would be substantially different or his sense of security any less if he also thought it possible that the suspected colleague is wired for sound....

Nor should we be too ready to erect constitutional barriers to relevant and probative evidence which is also accurate and reliable. An electronic recording will many times produce a more reliable rendition of what a defendant has said than will the unaided memory of a police agent....

DISSENT

DOUGLAS, J.

...What the ancients knew as "eavesdropping," we now call "electronic surveillance"; but to equate the two is to treat man's first gunpowder on the same level as the nuclear bomb. Electronic surveillance is the.greatest leveler of human privacy ever known. How most forms of it can be held "reasonable" within the meaning of the Fourth Amendment is a mystery. To be sure, the Constitution and Bill of Rights are not to be read as covering only the technology known in the 18th century. Otherwise its concept of "commerce" would be hopeless when it comes to the management of modern affairs. At the same time, the concepts of privacy which the Founders enshrined in the Fourth Amendment vanish completely when we slavishly allow an all-powerful government, proclaiming law and order, efficiency, and other benign purposes, to penetrate all the walls and doors which men need to shield them from the pressures of a turbulent life around them and give them the health and strength to carry on....

[According to the Court's decision] must everyone live in fear that every word he speaks may be transmitted or recorded and later repeated to the entire world? I can imagine nothing that has a more chilling effect on people speaking their minds and expressing their views on important matters. The advocates of the regime should spend some time in totalitarian countries and learn first-hand the kind of regime they are creating here.

HARLAN, J.

...The critical question...is whether under our system of government...we should impose on our citizens the risks of the electronic listener or observer without at least the protection of a warrant requirement. This question must, in my view, be answered by assessing the nature of a particular practice and the likely extent of its impact on the individual's sense of security balanced against the utility of the conduct as a technique of law enforcement. For those more extensive intrusions that significantly jeopardize the sense of security which is the paramount concern of Fourth Amendment liberties, I am of the view that more than self-restraint by law enforcement officials is required and at the least warrants should be necessary.

The impact of the practice of third-party bugging must, I think, be considered such as to undermine that confidence and sense of security in dealing with one another that is characteristic of individual relationships between citizens in a free society. It goes beyond the impact on privacy occasioned by the ordinary type of "informer" investigation....The argument of the plurality opinion, to the effect that it is irrelevant whether secrets are revealed by the mere tattletale or the transistor, ignores the differences occasioned by third-party monitoring and recording which insures full and accurate disclosure of all that is said, free of the possibility of error and oversight that inheres in human reporting.

Authority is hardly required to support the proposition that words would be measured a good deal more carefully and communication inhibited if one suspected his conversations were being transmitted and transcribed. Were third-party bugging a prevalent practice, it might well smother that spontaneity—reflected in frivolous, impetuous, sacrilegious, and defiant discourse—that liberates daily life. Much offhand exchange is easily forgotten and one may count on the obscurity of his remarks, protected by the very fact of a limited audience, and the likelihood that the listener will either overlook or forget what is said, as well as the listener's inability to reformulate a conversation without having to contend with a documented record.

All these values are sacrificed by a rule of law that permits official monitoring of private discourse limited only by the need to locate a willing assistant.

Questions

1. Is the court saying it's reasonable to expect people we confide in may be wired for sound to the police? Do you expect this?

2. What values is the Court balancing in this case?

3. Which is most intrusive: listening to James White in his home, in Harvey Jackson's home, in a restaurant, on the street, or in a car? Or are they all about the same? Why? Why not?

4. Does the dissent have a point that everyone will live in fear that what she or he says will be reported, or transmitted by radio, to the police?

5. Should the police have been required to get a warrant here? Explain your answer.

 Go to Exercise 3-1 on the Criminal Procedure 6e CD to learn more about *U.S. v. White.*

Technology that allows officers to get information about possible suspects has advanced significantly since 1971 when the Court decided *U.S. v. White.* One of those advances is **thermal imagers**, devices that detect, measure, and record infrared radiation not visible to the naked eye. The imagers convert radiation into images based on the amount of heat (black is cool, white is hot, shades of gray are in between). What if unbeknown to you, police officers parked on the street outside your house, aimed a thermal imager at your house, and measured and recorded the amount of heat coming out of various parts of your house? Do you have an expectation of privacy in these heat waves? If you do, is it an expectation society is prepared to recognize? The U.S. Supreme Court answered the question of whether discovery and measurement of heat—something invisible to the naked eye—escaping from your home is a Fourth Amendment search in *Kyllo v. U.S.* (2001).

| CASE | *Was the Thermal Imaging of a Private Home a Search?* |

Kyllo v. U.S.
533 U.S. 27 (2001)

After unsuccessfully moving to suppress evidence, Danny Kyllo entered a conditional guilty plea to manufacturing marijuana and appealed. Following remand, the U.S. District Court for the District of Oregon again denied Kyllos's suppression motion, and Kyllo appealed. The Ninth Circuit Court of Appeals affirmed. Certiorari was granted. The U.S. Supreme Court reversed and remanded.

SCALIA, J., joined by SOUTER, THOMAS, GINSBURG, and BREYER, JJ.

FACTS

In 1991 Agent William Elliott of the United States Department of the Interior came to suspect that marijuana was being grown in the home belonging to petitioner Danny Kyllo, part of a triplex on Rhododendron Drive in Florence, Oregon. Indoor marijuana growth typically requires high-intensity lamps. In order to determine whether an amount of heat was emanating from petitioner's home consistent with the use of such lamps, at 3:20 A.M. on January 16, 1992, Agent Elliott and Dan Haas used an Agema Thermovision 210 thermal imager to scan the triplex. Thermal imagers detect infrared radiation, which virtually all objects emit but which is not visible to the naked eye. The imager converts radiation into images based on relative warmth—black is cool, white is hot, shades of gray connote relative differences; in that respect, it operates somewhat like a video camera showing heat images.

The scan of Kyllo's home took only a few minutes and was performed from the passenger seat of Agent Elliott's vehicle across the street from the front of the house and also from the street in back of the house. The scan showed that the roof over the garage and a side wall of Kyllo's home were relatively hot compared to the rest of the home and substantially warmer than neighboring homes in the triplex. Agent Elliott concluded that Kyllo was using halide lights to grow marijuana in his house, which indeed he was.

Based on tips from informants, utility bills, and the thermal imaging, a Federal Magistrate Judge issued a warrant authorizing a search of Kyllo's home, and the agents found an indoor growing operation involving more than 100 plants.

Kyllo was indicted on one count of manufacturing marijuana, in violation of 21 U.S.C. § 841(a)(1). He unsuccessfully moved to suppress the evidence seized from his home and then entered a conditional guilty plea. The Court of Appeals for the Ninth Circuit remanded the case for an evidentiary hearing regarding the intrusiveness of thermal imaging. On remand the District Court found that the Agema 210 "is a non-intrusive device which emits no rays or beams and shows a crude visual image of the heat being radiated from the outside of the house"; it "did not show any people or activity within the walls of the structure"; "the device used cannot penetrate walls or windows to reveal conversations or human activities"; and "no intimate details of the home were observed." Based on these findings, the District Court upheld the validity of the warrant that relied in part upon the thermal imaging, and reaffirmed its denial of the motion to suppress. A divided Court of Appeals initially reversed, but that opinion was withdrawn and the panel (after a change in composition) affirmed, with Judge Noonan dissenting. The court held that Kyllo had shown no subjective expectation of privacy because he had made no attempt to conceal the heat escaping from his home, and even if he had, there was no objectively reasonable expectation of privacy because the imager "did not expose any intimate details of Kyllo's life," only "amorphous 'hot spots' on the roof and exterior wall." We granted certiorari.

OPINION

... "At the very core" of the Fourth Amendment "stands the right of a man to retreat into his own home and there be free from unreasonable governmental intrusion." With few exceptions, the question whether a warrantless search of a home is reasonable and hence constitutional must be answered no.

On the other hand, the antecedent question whether or not a Fourth Amendment "search" has occurred is not so simple.... As Justice Harlan's oft-quoted concurrence described it, a Fourth Amendment search occurs when the government violates a subjective expectation of privacy that society recognizes as reasonable....

The present case involves officers on a public street engaged in more than naked-eye surveillance of a home. We have previously reserved judgment as to how much technological enhancement of ordinary perception from such a vantage point, if any, is too much....

It would be foolish to contend that the degree of privacy secured to citizens by the Fourth Amendment has been entirely unaffected by the advance of technology. For example, as the cases discussed above make clear, the technology enabling human flight has exposed to public view (and hence, we have said, to official observation) uncovered portions of the house and its curtilage [area immediately surrounding a home] that once were private. The question we confront today is what limits there are upon this power of technology to shrink the realm of guaranteed privacy.

The *Katz* test—whether the individual has an expectation of privacy that society is prepared to recognize as reasonable—has often been criticized as circular, and hence subjective and unpredictable. While it may be difficult to refine *Katz* when the search of areas such as telephone booths, automobiles, or even the curtilage and uncovered portions of residences is at issue, in the case of the search of the interior of homes ... there is a ready criterion, with roots deep in the common law, of the minimal expectation of privacy that *exists*, and that is acknowledged to be *reasonable*. To withdraw protection of this minimum expectation would be to permit police technology to erode the privacy guaranteed by the Fourth Amendment. We think that obtaining by sense-enhancing technology any information regarding the interior of the home that could not otherwise have been obtained without physical "intrusion into a constitutionally protected area," constitutes a search—at least where (as here) the technology in question is not in general public use. This assures preservation of that degree of privacy against government that existed when the Fourth Amendment was adopted. On the basis of this criterion, the information obtained by the thermal imager in this case was the product of a search.

The Government maintains, however, that the thermal imaging must be upheld because it detected "only heat radiating from the external surface of the house."... We rejected such a mechanical interpretation of the Fourth Amendment in *Katz*, where the eavesdropping device picked up only sound waves that reached the exterior of the phone booth. Reversing that approach would leave the homeowner at the mercy of advancing technology—including imaging technology that could discern all human activity in the home. While the technology used in the present case was relatively crude, the rule we adopt must take account of more sophisticated systems that are already in use or in development....

The Government also contends that the thermal imaging was constitutional because it did not "detect private activities occurring in private areas."...The Fourth Amendment's protection of the home has never been tied to measurement of the quality or quantity of information obtained. In *Silverman*, for example, we made clear that any physical invasion of the structure of the home, "by even a fraction of an inch," was too much, and there is certainly no exception to the warrant requirement for the officer who barely cracks open the front door and sees nothing but the nonintimate rug on the vestibule floor. In the home, our cases show, *all* details are intimate details, because the entire area is held safe from prying government eyes. Thus, in *Karo*, the only thing detected was a can of ether in the home; and in *Arizona v. Hicks*, the only thing detected by a physical search that went beyond what officers lawfully present could observe in "plain view" was the registration number of a phonograph turntable. These were intimate details because they were details of the home, just as was the detail of how warm—or even how relatively warm—Kyllo was heating his residence....

We have said that the Fourth Amendment draws "a firm line at the entrance to the house." That line, we think, must be not only firm but also bright—which requires clear specification of those methods of surveillance that require a warrant. While it is certainly possible to conclude from the videotape of the thermal imaging that occurred in this case that no "significant" compromise of the homeowner's privacy has occurred, we must take the long view, from the original meaning of the Fourth Amendment forward....

Where, as here, the Government uses a device that is not in general public use, to explore details of the home that would previously have been unknowable without physical intrusion, the surveillance is a "search" and is presumptively unreasonable without a warrant. Since we hold the Thermovision imaging to have been an unlawful search, it will remain for the District Court to determine whether, without the evidence it provided, the search warrant issued in this case was supported by probable cause—and if not, whether there is any other basis for supporting admission of the evidence that the search pursuant to the warrant produced.

The judgment of the Court of Appeals is reversed; the case is remanded for further proceedings consistent with this opinion.

DISSENT

STEVENS, J., joined by REHNQUIST, CJ.,
and O'CONNOR and KENNEDY, JJ.

There is, in my judgment, a distinction of constitutional magnitude between "through-the-wall surveillance" that gives the observer or listener direct access to information in a private area, on the one hand, and the thought processes used to draw inferences from information in the public domain, on the other hand. The Court has crafted a rule that purports to deal with direct observations of the inside of the home, but the case before us merely involves indirect deductions from "off-the-wall" surveillance, that is, observations of the exterior of the home. Those observations were made with a fairly primitive thermal imager that gathered data exposed on the outside of petitioner's home but did not invade any constitutionally protected interest in privacy....

...This case...is controlled by established principles from our Fourth Amendment jurisprudence. One of those core principles, of course, is that "searches and seizures *inside a home* without a warrant are presumptively unreasonable." [Emphasis added.] But it is equally well settled that searches and seizures of property in plain view are presumptively reasonable. Whether that property is residential or commercial, the basic principle is the same: What a person knowingly exposes to the public, even in his own home or office, is not a subject of Fourth Amendment protection. That is the principle implicated here....

The notion that heat emissions from the outside of a dwelling are a private matter implicating the protections of the Fourth Amendment (the text of which guarantees the right of people "to be secure *in* their...houses" against unreasonable searches and seizures is...quite difficult to take seriously. Heat waves, like aromas that are generated in a kitchen, or in a laboratory or opium den, enter the public domain if and when they leave a building. A subjective expectation that they would remain private is not only implausible but also surely not "one that society is prepared to recognize as 'reasonable.'"...

There is a strong public interest in avoiding constitutional litigation over the monitoring of emissions from homes, and over the inferences drawn from such monitoring. Just as "the police cannot reasonably be expected to avert their eyes from evidence of criminal activity that could have been observed by any member of the public," so too public officials should not have to avert their senses or their equipment from detecting emissions in the public domain such as excessive heat, traces of smoke, suspicious odors, odorless gases, airborne particulates, or radioactive emissions, any of which could identify hazards to the community. In my judgment, monitoring such emissions with "sense-enhancing technology," and drawing useful conclusions from such monitoring, is an entirely reasonable public service.

On the other hand, the countervailing privacy interest is at best trivial. After all, homes generally are insulated to keep heat in, rather than to prevent the detection of heat going out, and it does not seem to me that society will suffer from a rule requiring the rare homeowner who both intends to engage in uncommon activities that produce extraordinary amounts of heat, and wishes to conceal that production from outsiders, to make sure that the surrounding area is well insulated. The interest in concealing the heat escaping from one's house pales in significance to "the chief evil against which the wording of the Fourth Amendment is directed," the "physical entry of the home," and it is hard to believe that it is an interest the Framers sought to protect in our Constitution.

Since what was involved in this case was nothing more than drawing inferences from off-the-wall surveillance, rather than any "through-the-wall" surveillance, the officers' conduct did not amount to a search and was perfectly reasonable....

I respectfully DISSENT.

Questions

1. Describe specifically the information officers Elliott and Haas got from Kyllo's house.

2. Describe exactly how the officers got the information.

3. Summarize the arguments the majority makes to support its conclusion that getting and recording thermal images are searches and seizures.

4. Summarize the arguments the dissent makes to support its conclusions they aren't searches.

Unprotected Places

The Fourth Amendment protects our right to be secure in our persons, houses, papers, and effects, but through its decisions, the Supreme Court has made it clear that this protection does not extend everywhere. Unprotected places include open fields, public places, and abandoned property.

Open Fields

Open fields are any privately owned land not included within the area immediately surrounding a house (Lafave and Israel 1987, 1:425). According to the **open fields doctrine**, "the special protection accorded by the Fourth Amendment to the people in their 'persons, houses, papers, and effects' is not extended to the open fields." In *Oliver v. U.S.* (1984), the U.S. Supreme Court concluded that society isn't prepared to recognize any reasonable expectation of privacy in open fields:

> Open fields do not provide the setting for those intimate activities that the Amendment is intended to shelter from government interference or surveillance. There is no societal interest in protecting the privacy of those activities, such as the cultivation of crops, that occur in open fields. (178)

What if owners give notice they expect privacy—like building fences or putting up "No Trespassing" signs? Does the doctrine still apply? Yes, says the Supreme Court. Why? Because of the practical difficulties officers would face in administering it:

> Police officers would have to guess before every search whether landowners had erected fences sufficiently high, posted a sufficient number of warning signs, or located contraband in an area sufficiently secluded to establish a right of privacy. (181)

On the other hand, the ground and buildings immediately surrounding a home (the **curtilage**), like garages, patios, and pools, *aren't* open fields. Why? Because this is where family and other private activities take place. The Supreme Court has identified the following criteria to determine whether an area falls within the curtilage:

- Distance from the house
- Presence or absence of a fence around the area
- Use or purpose of the area
- Measures taken to prevent public view

In applying these criteria in *U.S. v. Dunn* (1987), the Court concluded that Ronald Dunn's barn wasn't part of the curtilage because it was 60 yards from the house; it was 50 yards beyond a fence surrounding the house; it wasn't used for family purposes; and Dunn took no measures to hide it from public view. So, the crystal meth lab the officers discovered by shining a flashlight through a window in the barn wasn't a search.

Public Places

The Fourth Amendment doesn't protect what officers can discover through their ordinary senses in **public places**, including streets, parks, and other publicly owned areas. Public places also include privately owned businesses that are open to the public. But "employees only" areas, like offices, restrooms, basements, and other places not open to the public aren't public places. Public restrooms are public places, too, even enclosed stalls—at least as much as officers can see over and under partitions or through cracks or other gaps in partitions (Hall 1993, 543–548).

Abandoned Property

According to the U.S. Supreme Court, there's no "reasonable expectation of privacy" in **abandoned property**. But what does *abandoned* mean? There's a physical *and* a mental element to abandonment:

- Physically giving up possession of something
- Intending to give up the expectation of privacy

So, I legally abandon an apple core when I throw it away after I've eaten what I want of the apple. But, I don't abandon my car when I park it in the University of Minnesota parking ramp while I teach my "Criminal Law in U.S. Society" class. I've given it up only for the purpose of safekeeping until I'm ready to go home. How does this relate to the law of searches? An officer's actions don't amount to a search if there's proof that the person gave up physical possession of something *and* that person also intended to give up a reasonable expectation of privacy in that something.

The U.S. Supreme Court has adopted a **totality-of-circumstances test** (a test you'll encounter frequently in the text and case excerpts) to determine whether throwing away property proves the intent to give up the reasonable expectation of privacy protected by the Fourth Amendment. The Court looks at all the facts in each case to determine the intent to abandon, the actions indicating abandonment, and therefore the termination of a reasonable expectation of privacy in the items seized by the government. In the leading abandonment case decided during the Prohibition era, *Hester v. United States* (1924), revenue agents chased Hester through open fields. When the agents fired a shot, Hester dropped the illegal liquor he was carrying. The Supreme Court held that the facts indicated that Hester intended to abandon the alcohol. Later, in a famous Cold War case, immigration officials arrested suspected Communist spy Rudolf Abel. After Abel checked out of the hotel where FBI agents had arrested him, the agents searched his hotel room. They seized several items Abel had left behind in a wastepaper basket. The U.S. Supreme Court held that Abel had abandoned the room and, therefore, intended to give up his reasonable expectation of privacy in what he left behind in the wastepaper basket (*Abel v. U.S.* 1960).

In *California v. Greenwood* (1988), the U.S. Supreme Court applied the totality-of-circumstances test to determine whether Billy Greenwood had abandoned trash he left at the curbside for collection.

CASE	*Was the Trash "Abandoned"?*

California v. Greenwood
486 U.S. 35, 108 S.Ct. 1625, 100 L.Ed.2d 30 (1988)

Billy Greenwood and Dyanne Van Houten (respondents) were arrested and charged with felony possession of cocaine and hashish seized under two search warrants. Greenwood moved to set aside the warrants on the ground they violated the Fourth Amendment. A California superior court granted the motion, and a California intermediate appellate court affirmed. The California Supreme Court denied the state's petition for review. The U.S. Supreme Court granted certiorari and reversed the judgment of the California Court of Appeals.

WHITE J., joined by REHNQUIST, CJ., and BLACKMUN, STEVENS, O'CONNOR, and SCALIA, JJ.

FACTS

In early 1984, Investigator Jenny Stracner of the Laguna Beach Police Department received information indicating that respondent Greenwood might be engaged in narcotics trafficking. Stracner learned that a criminal suspect had informed a federal drug-enforcement agent in February 1984 that a truck filled with illegal drugs was en route to the Laguna Beach address at which Greenwood resided. In addition, a neighbor complained of heavy vehicular traffic late at night in front of Greenwood's single-family home. The neighbor reported that the vehicles remained at Greenwood's house for only a few minutes.

Stracner sought to investigate this information by conducting a surveillance of Greenwood's home. She observed several vehicles make brief stops at the house during the late-night and early-morning hours, and she followed a truck from the house to a residence that had previously been under investigation as a narcotics trafficking location.

On April 6, 1984, Stracner asked the neighborhood's regular trash collector to pick up the plastic garbage bags that Greenwood had left on the curb in front of his house and to turn the bags over to her without mixing their contents with garbage from other houses. The trash collector cleaned his truck bin of other refuse, collected the garbage bags from the street in front of Greenwood's house, and turned the bags over to Stracner. The officer searched through the rubbish and found items indicative of narcotics use. She recited the information that she had gleaned from the trash search in an affidavit in support of a warrant to search Greenwood's home.

Police officers encountered both Greenwwod and Van Houten at the house later that day when they arrived to execute the warrant. The police discovered quantities of cocaine and hashish during their search of the house. Greenwood and Van Houten were arrested on felony narcotics charges. They subsequently posted bail. The police continued to receive reports of many late-night visitors to the Greenwood house. On May 4, Investigator Robert Rahaeuser obtained Greenwood's garbage from the regular trash collector in the same manner as had Stracner. The garbage again contained evidence of narcotics use. Rahaeuser secured another search warrant for Greenwood's home based on the information from the second trash search. The police found more narcotics and evidence of narcotic trafficking when they executed the warrant. Greenwood was again arrested.

The Superior Court dismissed the charges against respondents. The Court of Appeal affirmed. The California Supreme Court denied the State's petition for review of the Court of Appeal's decision. We granted certiorari, and now reverse.

OPINION

The warrantless search and seizure of the garbage bags left at the curb outside the Greenwood house would violate the Fourth Amendment only if Greenwood and Van

Houten (respondents) manifested a subjective expectation of privacy in their garbage that society accepts as objectively reasonable. Respondents do not disagree with this standard. They assert, however, that they had, and exhibited, an expectation of privacy with respect to the trash that was searched by the police: The trash, which was placed on the street for collection at a fixed time, was contained in opaque plastic bags, which the garbage collector was expected to pick up, mingle with the trash of others, and deposit at the garbage dump. The trash was only temporarily on the street, and there was little likelihood that it would be inspected by anyone.

It may well be that respondents did not expect that the contents of their garbage bags would become known to the police or other members of the public. An expectation of privacy does not give rise to Fourth Amendment protection, however, unless society is prepared to accept that expectation as objectively reasonable. Here, we conclude that respondents exposed their garbage to the public sufficiently to defeat their claim to Fourth Amendment protection. It is common knowledge that plastic garbage bags left on or at the side of a public street are readily accessible to animals, children, scavengers, snoops, and other members of the public. Moreover, respondents placed their refuse at the curb for the express purpose of conveying it to a third party, the trash collector, who might himself have sorted through respondents' trash or permitted others, such as the police, to do so. Accordingly, having deposited their garbage "in an area particularly suited for public inspection and, in a manner of speaking, public consumption, for the express purpose of having strangers take it," respondents could have had no reasonable expectation of privacy in the inculpatory items that they discarded.

Furthermore, as we have held, the police cannot reasonably be expected to avert their eyes from evidence of criminal activity that could have been observed by any member of the public. Hence, "what a person knowingly exposes to the public, even in his own home or office, is not a subject of Fourth Amendment protection."...

Our conclusion that society would not accept as reasonable respondents' claim to an expectation of privacy in trash left for collection in an area accessible to the public is reinforced by the unanimous rejection of similar claims by the Federal Courts of Appeals. In *United States v. Thornton* (1984), the court observed that "the overwhelming weight of authority rejects the proposition that a reasonable expectation of privacy exists with respect to trash discarded outside the home and the curtilage thereof." In addition, of those state appellate courts that have considered the issue, the vast majority have held that the police may con-

duct warrantless searches and seizures of garbage discarded in public areas.*

...The judgment of the California Court of Appeal is therefore reversed, and this case is remanded for further proceedings not inconsistent with this opinion. It is so ordered.

DISSENT

BRENNAN, J., joined by MARSHALL, J.
Every week for two months, and at least once more a month later, the Laguna Beach police clawed through the trash that Greenwood left in opaque, sealed bags on the curb outside his home. Complete strangers minutely scrutinized their bounty, undoubtedly dredging up intimate details of Greenwood's private life and habits. The intrusions proceeded without a warrant, and no court before or since has concluded that the police acted on probable cause to believe Greenwood was engaged in any criminal activity....

The Framers of the Fourth Amendment understood that "unreasonable searches" of "papers and effects"—no less than "unreasonable searches" of "persons and houses"—infringe privacy.... So long as a package is "closed against inspection," the Fourth Amendment protects its contents, "wherever they may be," and the police must obtain a warrant to search it just "as is required when papers are subjected to search in one's own household."... In *Robbins v. California* [1981], for example, Justice Stewart, writing for a plurality of four, pronounced that "unless the container is such that its contents may be said to be in plain view, those contents are fully protected by the Fourth Amendment," and soundly rejected any distinction for Fourth Amendment purposes among various opaque, sealed containers....

More recently, in *United States v. Ross* (1982), the Court, relying on the "virtually unanimous" agreement in *Robbins*...that a constitutional distinction between "worthy" and "unworthy" containers would be improper, held that a distinction among "paper bags, locked trunks, lunch buckets, and orange crates" would be inconsistent with "the central purpose of the Fourth Amendment....A traveler who carries a toothbrush and a few articles of clothing in a paper bag or knotted scarf may claim an equal right to conceal his possessions from official inspection as the sophisticated executive with the locked attaché case."...

---

*Given that the dissenters are among the tiny minority of judges whose views are contrary to ours, we are distinctly unimpressed with the dissent's prediction that "society will be shocked" to learn of today's decision.

A trash bag, like any of the above-mentioned containers, "is a common repository for one's personal effects" and, even more than many of them, is "therefore...inevitably associated with the expectation of privacy. Almost every human activity ultimately manifests itself in waste products....". ..."If you want to know what is really going on in a community, look at its garbage." A single bag of trash testifies eloquently to the eating, reading, and recreational habits of the person who produced it. A search of trash, like a search of the bedroom, can relate intimate details about sexual practices, health, and personal hygiene. Like rifling through desk drawers or intercepting phone calls, rummaging through trash can divulge the target's financial and professional status, political affiliations and inclinations, private thoughts, personal relationships, and romantic interests. It cannot be doubted that a sealed trash bag harbors telling evidence of the "intimate activity associated with the 'sanctity of a man's home and the privacies of life,'" which the Fourth Amendment is designed to protect....

Beyond a generalized expectation of privacy, many municipalities, whether for reasons of privacy, sanitation, or both, reinforce confidence in the integrity of sealed trash containers by "prohibiting anyone, except authorized employees of the Town...to rummage into, pick up, collect, move or otherwise interfere with articles or materials placed on...any public street for collection.". ..

That is not to deny that isolated intrusions into opaque, sealed trash containers occur. When, acting on their own, "animals, children, scavengers, snoops, [or] other members of the general public," actually rummage through a bag of trash and expose its contents to plain view, "police cannot reasonably be expected to avert their eyes from evidence of criminal activity that could have been observed by any member of the public.". ..

Had Greenwood flaunted his intimate activity by strewing his trash all over the curb for all to see, or had some nongovernmental intruder invaded his privacy and done the same, I could accept the Court's conclusion that an expectation of privacy would have been unreasonable. Similarly, had police searching the city dump run across incriminating evidence that, despite commingling with the trash of others, still retained its identity as Greenwood's, we would have a different case. But all that Greenwood "exposed...to the public" were the exteriors of several opaque, sealed containers. Until the bags were opened by police, they hid their contents from the public's view.... Faithful application of the warrant requirement does not require police to "avert their eyes from evidence of criminal activity that could have been observed by any member of the public." Rather, it only requires them to adhere to

norms of privacy that members of the public plainly acknowledge.

The mere possibility that unwelcome meddlers might open and rummage through the containers does not negate the expectation of privacy in its contents any more than the possibility of a burglary negates an expectation of privacy in the home; or the possibility of a private intrusion negates an expectation of privacy in an unopened package; or the possibility that an operator will listen in on a telephone conversation negates an expectation of privacy in the words spoken on the telephone. "What a person... seeks to preserve as private, even in an area accessible to the public, may be constitutionally protected."

Nor is it dispositive that "respondents placed their refuse at the curb for the express purpose of conveying it to a third party...who might himself have sorted through respondents' trash or permitted others, such as police, to do so." In the first place, Greenwood can hardly be faulted for leaving trash on his curb when a county ordinance commanded him to do so, and prohibited him from disposing of it in any other way. Unlike in other circumstances where privacy is compromised, Greenwood could not "avoid exposing personal belongings...by simply leaving them at home."

More importantly, even the voluntary relinquishment of possession or control over an effect does not necessarily amount to a relinquishment of a privacy expectation in it. Were it otherwise, a letter or package would lose all Fourth Amendment protection when placed in a mail box or other depository with the "express purpose" of entrusting it to the postal officer or a private carrier; those bailees are just as likely as trash collectors (and certainly have greater incentive) to "sort through" the personal effects entrusted to them, "or permit others, such as police to do so." Yet, it has been clear for at least 110 years that the possibility of such an intrusion does not justify a warrantless search by police in the first instance.

In holding that the warrantless search of Greenwood's trash was consistent with the Fourth Amendment, the Court paints a grim picture of our society. It depicts a society in which local authorities may command their citizens to dispose of their personal effects in the manner least protective of the "sanctity of [the] home and the privacies of life," and then monitor them arbitrarily and without judicial oversight—a society that is not prepared to recognize as reasonable an individual's expectation of privacy in the most private of personal effects sealed in an opaque container and disposed of in a manner designed to commingle it imminently and inextricably with the trash of others. The American society with which I am familiar "chooses to dwell in reasonable security and freedom from surveillance," and is more dedicated to individuals' liberty and more sensitive to intrusions on the sanctity of the home than the Court is willing to acknowledge.

I DISSENT.

Questions

1. List all the facts relevant to determining whether Billy Greenwood and Dyanne Van Houten intended to give up their reasonable expectation of privacy in their trash.

2. What values did the Court balance in this case? In your opinion, did the Court balance them appropriately? Explain your answer.

3. When you throw your own trash away, do you abandon it totally or only for the purpose of having it destroyed?

4. What does the dissent mean when it says that the Court "paints a grim picture of our society"? Do you agree? Explain your answer.

5. Do you think that this case is important enough to get to the Supreme Court? Explain your answer?

 Go to Exercise 3-2 on the Criminal Procedure 6e CD to learn more about this *California v. Greenwood*.

◆ STATE CONSTITUTIONAL LAW ◆

State v. Morris
165 Vt. 111, 680 A.2d 90 (1996)

Did They "Search" His Trash?

Richard Morris, the defendant, entered a conditional plea of no contest to possession of marijuana in the District Court, Unit No. 1, Windham Circuit, and he appealed. The Vermont Supreme Court reversed and remanded.

JOHNSON, J.

FACTS

Sometime before March 1993, a confidential informant told an officer of the Brattleboro Police Department that defendant was selling marijuana from his apartment and from the parking lot of a certain grocery store. On March 1, 1993, a regularly scheduled trash collection day, two police officers went to the apartment building where defendant resided and seized the five or six opaque trash bags that had been set out for collection near the curb about five or six feet from the building. From the exterior of the bags, there was no way to identify which tenant had deposited which bags. All of the bags were transported to the police station and searched without a warrant. Inside defendant's bags, which were identified through discarded pieces of mail, the police found marijuana seeds and stems and baggies containing flakes of marijuana.

Based on the items found in the trash, the information supplied by the confidential informant, and an unidentified neighbor's report that defendant had received many different visitors during the past month, the police sought and obtained a warrant to search defendant's residence. Approximately four ounces of marijuana were found, and defendant was charged with possession of marijuana. Defendant moved to suppress all evidence seized from his apartment on the ground that the search warrant was defective because it was based primarily on evidence discovered during an illegal warrantless search of his garbage. The district court denied defendant's motion to suppress, ruling that defendant had no expectation of privacy in his discarded garbage.

OPINION

Our task is to discover and protect the core value of privacy embraced by Chapter I, Article 11 of the Vermont Constitution. Chapter I, Article 11 of the Vermont Constitution provides:

> That the people have a right to hold themselves, their houses, papers, and possessions, free from search or seizure; and therefore warrants, without oath or affirmation first made, affording sufficient foundation for them, and whereby by any officer or messenger may be commanded or required to search suspected places, or to seize any person or persons, his, her or their property, not particularly described, are contrary to that right, and ought not to be granted.

The first and foremost line of protection is the warrant requirement. Requiring advance judicial approval before subjecting persons to police searches represents a balance in which an individual's privacy interest outweighs the burdens on law enforcement in obtaining a warrant. Thus, absent exceptional circumstances, the government's decision to invade a person's privacy must be made by a neutral judicial officer rather than the police.

Of course, Article 11 does not "protect areas or activities that have been willingly exposed to the public." In determining whether persons have a privacy interest in any given area or activity, we examine both private subjective expectations and general social norms. The manifested privacy interest must be a reasonable one, but as we have cautioned before, constitutional rights are not limited by waning expectations of privacy resulting from increased governmental intrusion into people's lives. Ultimately, the question is "'whether, if the particular form of surveillance practiced by the police is permitted to go unregulated by constitutional constraints, the amount of privacy and freedom remaining to citizens would be diminished to a compass inconsistent with the aims of a free and open society.'"

Given the facts of this case, we believe that defendant manifested a privacy interest recognized by society, and we conclude that unconstrained government inspection of people's trash is not consistent with a free and open society. As Justice Brennan stated in his dissent in *California v. Greenwood*, "Scrutiny of another's trash is contrary to commonly accepted notions of civilized behavior."... See *State v. Hempele*, 576 A.2d 793, 803 (1990) (undoubtedly, most people would be upset to see another person sifting through their garbage, perusing their discarded mail, reading their bank statements, looking at their empty pharmaceutical bottles, and checking receipts to see what videotapes they rent).

Further, that privacy interest is not lost merely because people follow the customary practice of depositing their garbage in closed containers at curbside for collection and disposal.... Most people today have little choice but to place their garbage at curbside for collection by public or private trash haulers. It is often unreasonably burdensome or unlawful to privately burn or bury unwanted refuse; thus, people must necessarily rely upon governmental or commercial trash collection systems to achieve anonymous disposal of garbage....

Notwithstanding the possibility that their garbage will be tampered with by scavengers or snoops, people reasonably expect that, once their refuse is placed on the curb in the customary and accepted manner, it will be collected, taken to the landfill, and commingled with other garbage without being intercepted and examined by the police. The Vermont Constitution does not require the residents of this state to employ extraor-

dinary or unlawful means to keep government authorities from examining discarded private effects.

Persons should not be denied protection from unregulated police intrusion into their affairs merely because they are discarding rather than transporting their private effects. Although a person placing trash at curbside for collection and disposal undoubtedly relinquishes a proprietary interest in the trash, it does not necessarily follow that the person intends to renounce a privacy interest in it.... Thus, the question is not whether the person abandoned the garbage itself but rather whether the person relinquished an expectation of privacy in the garbage.

Our focus must be on the objective reasonableness of one's privacy interest, not one's proprietary interest, in curbside garbage. This focus is consistent with our prior case law on Article 11, in which we have emphasized that the core value of privacy is the quintessence of Article 11, and that we must determine in such cases whether those persons searched have a reasonable expectation of privacy in the affairs or possessions intruded upon....

In addition to the abandonment theory, the State relies principally on the...rationale espoused by the *Greenwood* majority in holding that the Fourth Amendment does not constrain police from warrantless searches of curbside garbage....We decline, as have the California, Hawaii, New Jersey, and Washington state supreme courts, to follow this...analysis. Broken down into its component parts, the *Greenwood* analysis states that there is no objectively reasonable expectation of privacy in the contents of opaque garbage bags placed at curbside for collection because (1) animals, scavengers and snoops might get at them; (2) the bags are relinquished to third parties who may do as they please with them; and (3) police cannot be expected to ignore that which is exposed to the public....

We acknowledge that today's decision limits, to some extent, tactics that police may use in investigating reports of criminal activity. But improving the efficiency of law enforcement cannot come at the expense of the protection provided by Article 11 against unconstrained governmental intrusion into our private lives. We will not countenance under Article 11 a society in which authorities require citizens to dispose of their personal effects in a manner that is then deemed unworthy of protection from arbitrary governmental monitoring without judicial oversight.

In this case, defendant exposed to public view only the exterior of opaque trash bags, and in doing so, he sought to dispose of his personal possessions in the accepted manner that normally would result in commingling them inextricably with the trash of others. Nevertheless, without probable cause or judicial oversight, police searched through defendant's trash, as well as the trash of other apartment dwellers who had the misfortune of placing their garbage bags alongside those of someone suspected of having committed a crime. Such unconstrained governmental intrusion into people's private lives is inconsistent with Article 11 and a free and open society. Because the warrantless search of defendant's trash violated Article 11, the evidence obtained from that search, which was used to obtain a warrant to search defendant's home, must be suppressed and expunged from the affidavit supporting the search warrant....

REVERSED and REMANDED.

DISSENT

DOOLEY, J.

...I have no doubt that examining people's waste has been an investigative tool of law enforcement throughout recorded history....Defendant lived in an apartment building. He and the other tenants in the building put out their trash in plastic bags at curbside for Monday pick-up. Five or six bags were placed outside a fence which was located six feet from the apartment building. I think it is clear from our precedents that Article 11 does not extend to the trash bags put out on the curb by defendant and other tenants. By putting them in a public place, defendant no longer had a possessory interest in the trash and had no protected interest in the area from which it was taken. The trash fell outside the protection of Article 11....The trash bags were subject to the hands and eyes of any member of the public who, without legal restriction, opened them or took them.

[The majority relies] on a law review article for the proposition that "most people today have little choice but to place their garbage at curbside for collection by public or private trash haulers," the majority asserts that citizens cannot avoid subjecting their trash to police scrutiny unless Article 11 restricts that scrutiny. I am not surprised that the proposition comes from an article published in New York, one of the most population-dense of American states, but find it incredible that the majority would apply it to Vermont, the most rural of states, where most residences do not have curbs at all. Although modern solid waste management may have taken some of the cultural charm out of the weekly trip to the "dump" in favor of large regional landfills and transfer stations, defendant can still exercise the time-honored tradition of self-disposal, ensuring his garbage is mixed in anonymously with that of many of his fellow citizens. Moreover, he could have chosen a living arrangement, whether single-family or an apartment, that did not leave his garbage outside the curtilage waiting for pick-up....

I DISSENT. I am authorized to state that the Chief Justice joins in this dissent.

Questions

1. Compare and contrast the reasoning of the Vermont Supreme Court with that of the majority and dissenting opinions in *California v. Greenwood*.

2. Do you think the Vermont court did the right thing in defining the police actions as searches of Morris's trash? Defend your answer.

3. Can you formulate a general rule for when and how state courts should raise the constitutional rights of its own citizens above that of the minimum required by the U.S. Constitution? State what that rule would be.

SEIZURES

Seizure (as far as the Fourth Amendment is concerned) takes place when an officer takes away your right to leave or stay in a place you want to be. According to the U.S. Supreme Court, there are two kinds of Fourth Amendment seizures known as "stops" (Table 3.1):

1. *Actual-seizure stops*. Officers physically grab suspects with the intent to keep them from leaving.

TABLE 3.1	
Two Kinds of Fourth Amendment Stops	
Actual-Seizure Stops	**Show-of-Authority Stops**
1. Suspect is grabbed and held by officer	1. Officer displays authority by order, display of weapon, etc.
2. Officer intends to keep suspect from leaving	2. Suspect submits to authority
	3. No physical restraint

2. *Show-of-authority stops.*
   a. Officers display their authority by ordering suspects to stop, drawing their weapons, or otherwise acting such that a reasonable person would not feel free to leave or "otherwise terminate the encounter, *and*
   b. Suspects submit to the show of authority.

So, according to the U.S. Supreme Court,

> Law enforcement officers do not violate the Fourth Amendment by merely approaching an individual on the street or in another public place, by asking him if he is willing to answer some questions, [or] by putting questions to him if the person is willing to listen. . . . Nor would the fact that the officer identifies himself as a police officer without more, convert the encounter into a seizure.

> *Florida v. Royer* 1983, 497

Because they're not "seized," individuals can walk away and ignore the officer's request. And, walking away doesn't by itself provide the objective basis required to "seize" persons. Again in Justice White's words:

> The person approached, however, need not answer any question put to him; indeed, he may decline to listen to the questions at all and may go on his way. He may not be detained, even momentarily without reasonable, objective grounds for doing so; and his refusal to listen or answer does not, without more, furnish such grounds. (497–498)

Adding intimidation or coercion to questioning will convert a voluntary encounter into a seizure. See Table 3.2 for other examples of what the Supreme Court has ruled are show-of-force stops.

Notice two kinds of restraints on your freedom of movement have no Fourth Amendment significance: psychological pressure and a sense of moral duty. You may

TABLE 3.2	
Show-of-Force Stops	
Show of Force	**Not a Show of Force**
Setting up a roadblock	Approaching a citizen in public
Flashing an emergency light	Identifying oneself as a police officer
Ordering a person to leave a car	Merely asking questions
Surrounding a car	Requesting to search
Drawing a weapon	Following a pedestrian in a police car
Being in the presence of several officers	
Using a commanding tone of voice	

feel a psychological pressure—and, as responsible members of your community you should also feel a moral duty—to cooperate with police officers. But, neither psychological pressure nor your sense of moral duty can turn a police encounter into a Fourth Amendment seizure (*INS v. Delgado* 1984 [Chapter 5]). Why? Because these are self-imposed restraints; law enforcement officers didn't impose them on you.

The American Law Institute (1975) also takes the position that simple questioning by law enforcement officers is not a seizure. Its respected *Model Code of Pre-Arraignment Procedure* provides:

> §110.1 Requests for Cooperation by Law Enforcement Officers (1) Authority to Request Cooperation. A law enforcement officer may...request any person to furnish information or otherwise cooperate in the investigation or prevention of crime. The officer may request the person to respond to questions, to appear at a police station, or to comply with any other reasonable request. In making requests...no officer shall indicate that a person is legally obliged to furnish information or otherwise to cooperate if no such legal obligation exists. Compliance with a request for information or other cooperation...shall not be regarded as involuntary or coerced solely on the ground that such request was made by one known to be a law enforcement officer. (3)

The U.S. Supreme Court addressed the distinction between actual-seizure and show-of-authority stops and applied it in *California v. Hodari D.* (1991).

| CASE | *When Did the Police "Seize" Him?* |

California v. Hodari D.
499 U.S. 621, 111 S.Ct. 1547, 113 L.Ed.2d 690 (1991)

Hodari D., a juvenile, appealed from an order of the Superior Court, Alameda County, denying his motion to suppress and finding that he was in possession of cocaine. The California Court of Appeal reversed. The California Supreme Court denied the state's application for review. Certiorari was granted. The Supreme Court reversed and remanded.

SCALIA, J., joined by REHNQUIST, CJ., and BLACKMUN, O'CONNOR, KENNEDY, and SOUTER, JJ.

FACTS

Late one evening in April 1988, Officers Brian McColgin and Jerry Pertoso were on patrol in a high-crime area of Oakland, California. They were dressed in street clothes but wearing jackets with "Police" embossed on both front and back. Their unmarked car proceeded west on Foothill Boulevard, and turned south onto 63rd Avenue. As they rounded the corner, they saw four or five youths huddled around a small red car parked at the curb. When the youths saw the officers' car approaching they apparently panicked, and took flight. The respondent here, Hodari D., and one companion ran west through an alley; the others fled south. The red car also headed south, at a high rate of speed. The officers were suspicious and gave chase. McColgin remained in the car and continued south on 63rd Avenue.

Pertoso left the car, ran back north along 63rd, then west on Foothill Boulevard, and turned south on 62nd Avenue. Hodari, meanwhile, emerged from the alley onto 62nd and ran north. Looking behind as he ran, he did not turn and see Pertoso until the officer was almost upon him, whereupon he tossed away what appeared to be a small rock. A moment later, Pertoso tackled Hodari, handcuffed him, and radioed for assistance. Hodari was found to be carrying $130 in cash and a pager; and the rock he had discarded was found to be crack cocaine.

In the juvenile proceeding brought against him, Hodari moved to suppress the evidence relating to the cocaine. The court denied the motion without opinion. The California Court of Appeal reversed, holding that Hodari had been "seized" when he saw Officer Pertoso running toward him, that this seizure was unreasonable under the Fourth

Amendment, and that the evidence of cocaine had to be suppressed as the fruit of that illegal seizure. The California Supreme Court denied the state's application for review. We granted certiorari.

OPINION

[The only question the Court decided was] "whether, at the time he dropped the drugs, Hodari had been seized within the meaning of the Fourth Amendment." [The reason this was the only question is because] California conceded below that Officer Pertoso did not have the 'reasonable suspicion' required to justify stopping Hodari. That it would be unreasonable to stop, for brief inquiry, young men who scatter in panic upon the mere sighting of the police is not self-evident, and arguably contradicts proverbial common sense. See Proverbs 28:1 ("The wicked flee when no man pursueth"). We do not decide that point here, but rely entirely upon the state's concession.

[If Pertoso had seized him at the time he dropped the drugs], Hodari argues, the drugs were the fruit of that seizure and the evidence concerning them was properly excluded. If not, the drugs were abandoned by Hodari and lawfully recovered by the police, and the evidence should have been admitted. (In addition, of course, Pertoso's seeing the rock of cocaine, at least if he recognized it as such, would provide reasonable suspicion for the unquestioned seizure that occurred when he tackled Hodari.)

We have long understood that the Fourth Amendment's protection against "unreasonable . . . seizures" includes seizure of the person. From the time of the founding to the present, the word "seizure" has meant a "taking possession.". . . Hodari contends (and we accept as true for purposes of this decision) that Pertoso's pursuit qualified as a "show of authority" calling upon Hodari to halt. The narrow question before us is whether, with respect to a show of authority as with respect to application of physical force, a seizure occurs even though the subject does not yield. We hold that it does not. . . .

Respondent contends that his position is sustained by the so-called **Mendenhall test**, formulated by Justice Stewart's opinion in *United States v. Mendenhall* (1980):

> A person has been "seized" within the meaning of the Fourth Amendment only if, in view of all the circumstances surrounding the incident, a reasonable person would have believed that he was not free to leave.

In seeking to rely upon that test here, Hodari fails to read it carefully. It says that a person has been seized "only if," not that he has been seized "whenever"; it states a necessary, but not a sufficient, condition for seizure—or, more precisely, for seizure effected through a "show of authority." *Mendenhall* establishes that the test for existence of a "show of authority" is an objective one: not whether the citizen perceived that he was being ordered to restrict his movement, but whether the officer's words and actions would have conveyed that to a reasonable person. Application of this objective test was the basis for our decision in the other case principally relied upon by respondent, where we concluded that the police cruiser's slow following of the defendant did not convey the message that he was not free to disregard the police and go about his business. We did not address in *Michigan v. Chesternut*, however, the question whether, if the *Mendenhall* test was met—if the message that the defendant was not free to leave had been conveyed—a Fourth Amendment seizure would have occurred.

Quite relevant to the present case, however, was our decision in *Brower v. Inyo County* (1989). In that case, police cars with flashing lights had chased the decedent for 20 miles—surely an adequate "show of authority"—but he did not stop until his fatal crash into a police-erected blockade. The issue was whether his death could be held to be the consequence of an unreasonable seizure in violation of the Fourth Amendment. We did not even consider the possibility that a seizure could have occurred during the course of the chase because, as we explained, that "show of authority" did not produce his stop. . . .

In sum, assuming that Pertoso's pursuit in the present case constituted a "show of authority" enjoining Hodari to halt, since Hodari did not comply with that injunction he was not seized until he was tackled. The cocaine abandoned while he was running was in this case not the fruit of a seizure, and his motion to exclude evidence of it was properly denied. We reverse the decision of the California Court of Appeal, and remand for further proceedings not inconsistent with his opinion.

It is so ordered.

DISSENT

STEVENS, J., joined by MARSHALL, J.

The court's narrow construction of the word "seizure" represents a significant, and in my view, unfortunate, departure from prior case law construing the Fourth Amendment. Almost a quarter of a century ago, in two landmark cases—one broadening the protection of individual privacy [*Katz v. United States*] and the other broadening the powers of law enforcement officers [*Terry v. Ohio*]—we rejected the method of Fourth Amendment analysis that today's majority endorses. In particular, the Court now adopts a definition of "seizure" that is unfaithful to a long line of Fourth Amendment cases. Even if the Court were defining seizure for the first time, which it is not, the definition that it chooses today is profoundly unwise. In its decision, the Court assumes, without acknowledging, that a police officer may now fire his weapon at an innocent citizen and not implicate the Fourth Amendment—as long as he misses his target. . . .

The Court's gratuitous quotation from Proverbs 28:1, mistakenly assumes that innocent residents have no reason to fear the sudden approach of strangers. We have previously considered, and rejected, this ivory-towered analysis of the real world for it fails to describe the experience of many residents, particularly if they are members of a minority. It has long been "a matter of common knowledge" that men who are entirely innocent do sometimes fly from the scene of a crime through fear of being apprehended as the guilty parties, or from an unwillingness to appear as witnesses. Nor is it true as an accepted axiom of criminal law that "the wicked flee when no man pursueth, but the righteous are as bold as a lion.". . .

Whatever else one may think of today's decision, it unquestionably represents a departure from earlier Fourth Amendment case law. The notion that our prior cases contemplated a distinction between seizures effected by a touching on the one hand, and those effected by a show of force on the other hand, and that all of our repeated descriptions of the *Mendenhall* test stated only a necessary, but not a sufficient, condition for finding seizures in the latter category, is nothing if not creative lawmaking. Moreover, by narrowing the definition of the term seizure, instead of enlarging the scope of reasonable justifications for seizures, the Court has significantly limited the protection provided to the ordinary citizen by the Fourth Amendment. . . .

In this case the officer's show of force—taking the form of a head-on chase—adequately conveyed the message that respondent was not free to leave. . . . There was an interval of time between the moment that respondent saw the officer fast approaching and the moment when he was tackled, and thus brought under the control of the officer. The question is whether the Fourth Amendment was implicated at the earlier or the later moment.

Because the facts of this case are somewhat unusual, it is appropriate to note that the same issue would arise if the show of force took the form of a command to "freeze," a warning shot, or the sound of sirens accompanied by a patrol car's flashing lights. In any of these situations, there may be a significant time interval between the initiation of the officer's show of force and the complete submission by the citizen. At least on the facts of this case, the Court concludes that the timing of the seizure is governed by the citizen's reaction, rather than by the officer's conduct. One consequence of this conclusion is that the point at which the interaction between citizen and police officer becomes a seizure occurs, not when a reasonable citizen believes he

or she is no longer free to go, but rather, only after the officer exercises control over the citizen. . . .

It is too early to know the consequences of the Court's holding. If carried to its logical conclusion, it will encourage unlawful displays of force that will frighten countless innocent citizens into surrendering whatever privacy rights they may still have. . . . The Court today defines a seizure as commencing, not with egregious police conduct, but rather, with submission by the citizen. Thus, it both delays the point at which "the Fourth Amendment becomes relevant" to an encounter and limits the range of encounters that will come under the heading of "seizure." Today's qualification of the Fourth Amendment means that innocent citizens may remain "secure in their persons . . . against unreasonable searches and seizures" only at the discretion of the police.

Some sacrifice of freedom always accompanies an expansion in the executive's unreviewable law enforcement powers. A court more sensitive to the purposes of the Fourth Amendment would insist on greater rewards to society before decreeing the sacrifice it makes today. Alexander Bickel presciently wrote that "many actions of government have two aspects: their immediate, necessarily intended, practical effects, and their perhaps unintended or unappreciated bearing on values we hold to have more general and permanent interest." The Court's immediate concern with containing criminal activity poses a substantial, though unintended, threat to values that are fundamental and enduring.

I respectfully DISSENT.

Questions

1. What are the relevant facts in determining when the officer seized Hodari D.?

2. What criteria does the Court use in determining when seizures occur?

3. Why does the dissent see a danger in distinguishing between show-of-force stops and actual-seizure stops? Do you agree that this poses a danger?

4. When do you think the officer stopped Hodari? Why is it important in this case?

5. Why is it important generally?

6. Consider the following remarks of Professor Richard Uviller, who observed the police in New York City for a period of a year:

[T]he manifest confidence [exuded by the police] begets submission. And the cops learn the firm tone and hand that informs even the normally aggressive customer of the futility of resistance. It's effective. In virtually every encounter I have witnessed, the response of the person approached was docile, compliant, and respectful.

Do you think Professor Uviller's observations support the argument that no reasonable person feels free to leave the presence of a police officer? Do you believe that it supports the argument that a request by a police officer is really a command that citizens are not free to deny? Defend your answer.

 Go to Exercise 3-3 on the Criminal Procedure 6e CD to learn more about *California v. Hodari D.*

◆ STATE CONSTITUTIONAL LAW ◆

In the Matter of the WELFARE of E.D.J.
502 N.W.2d 779 (MN 1993)

Was He "Seized"?

After determining that a juvenile, E.D.J., abandoned drugs before he was seized, the District Court entered a judgment finding that E.D.J. had committed a delinquent act, and E.D.J. appealed. The Court of Appeals affirmed, and further review was sought. The Supreme Court reversed, and the adjudication of delinquency was vacated.

KEITH, CJ.

FACTS

At 6:45 P.M. on February 22, 1992, two Minneapolis police officers on routine patrol saw three men—two were adults, one was a juvenile—standing on the southeast corner of 38th Street and Fourth Avenue South. The officers knew this corner to be an area of heavy trafficking in crack cocaine. When the three men saw the police car approaching from the west, they turned and began walking in an easterly direction on 38th, looking back again as they did so. The officers pulled up behind the men and ordered them to stop. The two older men stopped instantly. However, E.D.J., the juvenile, continued walking for approximately five steps, dropped something, took two more steps, then stopped and turned around.

E.D.J. was arrested and subsequently charged in juvenile court with having committed a delinquent act, specifically, fifth-degree possession of a controlled substance, namely crack cocaine. Minn.Stat. §152.025, subd. 2(1) (1992). The trial court denied E.D.J.'s motion to suppress. Relying on *California v. Hodari D.*, it reasoned that E.D.J. abandoned the cocaine before he was seized and that therefore the abandonment was not the suppressible fruit of any illegal conduct. At the trial on the merits, the trial court found that E.D.J. had committed a delinquent act. The trial court then placed E.D.J. on probation and ordered him to perform 40 hours of community service. The court of appeals, also relying on *Hodari*, affirmed. We granted E.D.J.'s petition for review.

OPINION

In a series of decisions, we have articulated and reiterated the standard to be used by a trial court in determining at a suppression hearing in a criminal case whether an investigatory "seizure" of the person of the defendant by the police occurred. We have made it clear that the trial court should determine objectively, on the basis of the totality of the circumstances, whether a reasonable person in the defendant's shoes would have concluded that he or she was not free to leave. Recently, the United States Supreme Court, in a sharp departure from this approach, concluded that, under the Fourth Amendment, a "seizure" of the person occurs only when police use physical force to restrain a person or, absent that, when a person physically submits to a show of authority by the police.

Exercising our independent authority to interpret our own state constitution, we have concluded that trial courts in Minnesota, in determining whether a "seizure" of the person of the defendant by police occurred, should not follow the recently adopted *Hodari* approach but should continue to apply the familiar approach we have previously articulated and reiterated. Following this familiar approach, we conclude that an unlawful "seizure" of the person occurred in this case and that the trial court erred in denying the motion to suppress evidence abandoned by appellant in response to the unlawful conduct of the police. Accordingly, we reverse the decision of the court of appeals and vacate the district court's determination that appellant, a juvenile, committed a delinquent act.

In *State v. Fuller*, 374 N.W.2d 722 (Minn. 1985), in an opinion by Justice Peterson, we said:

It is axiomatic that a state supreme court may interpret its own state constitution to offer greater protection of individual rights than does the federal constitution. Indeed, as the highest court of this state, we are "'independently responsible for safeguarding the rights of [our] citizens.'" State courts are, and should be, the first line of defense for individual liberties within the federalist system. This, of course, does not mean that we will or should cavalierly construe our constitution more expansively than the United States Supreme Court has construed the federal constitution. Indeed, a decision of the United States Supreme Court interpreting a comparable provision of the federal constitution that, as here, is textually identical to a provision of our constitution, is of inherently persuasive, although not necessarily compelling, force.

The language of Minn. Const. art. I, §10, is identical to that of the Fourth Amendment of the United States Constitution. The decisions of the United States Supreme Court interpreting and applying the Fourth Amendment are therefore decisions to which we invariably turn in the first instance whenever we are asked in a criminal case whether the police conduct constitutes an unreasonable search and seizure.

In this case the issue is whether a "seizure" occurred when the police pulled up and ordered E.D.J. to stop or whether it occurred moments later when he actually submitted to the order. The answer to the question given by the United States Supreme Court in its recent decision in *Hodari* is that the "seizure" did not occur until E.D.J. actually submitted to the authority of the police by stopping.

We do not "cavalierly" reject the *Hodari* approach. Rather, we reject it because (a) we have had considerable experience in applying the standard which the Court in *Hodari* rejected, (b) we are not persuaded by the arguments favoring the *Hodari* approach, and (c) we are persuaded that there is no need to depart from the pre-*Hodari* approach.

In *Terry v. Ohio*, 392 U.S. 1, 19 n. 16, 88 S.Ct. 1868, 1879 n. 16, 20 L.Ed.2d 889 (1968), Chief Justice Warren, speaking for the United States Supreme Court, stated that "not all personal intercourse between policemen and citizens involves 'seizures' of persons" and that a "seizure" occurs only "when the officer, by means of physical force or show of authority, has in some way restrained the liberty of a citizen."

In *United States v. Mendenhall*, 446 U.S. 544, 100 S.Ct. 1870, 64 L.Ed.2d 497 (1980), the Court elaborated on this. Justice Stewart, announcing the judgment of the Court in an opinion joined by one other justice, said:

We conclude that a person has been "seized" within the meaning of the Fourth Amendment only if, in view of all of the circumstances surrounding the incident, a reasonable person would have believed that he was not free to leave. Examples of circumstances that might indicate a seizure, even where the person did not attempt to leave, would be the threatening presence of several officers, the display of a weapon by an officer, some physical touching of the person of the citizen, or the use of language or tone of voice indicating that compliance with the officer's request might be compelled. In the absence of some such evidence, otherwise inoffensive contact between a member of the public and the police cannot, as a matter of law, amount to a seizure of that person.

On the facts of this case, no "seizure" of the respondent occurred. The events took place in the public concourse. The agents wore no uniforms and displayed no weapons. They did not summon the respondent to their presence, but instead approached her and identified themselves as federal agents. They requested, but did not demand, to see the respondent's identification and ticket. Such conduct, without more, did not amount to an intrusion upon any constitutionally protected interest. The respondent was not seized simply by reason of the fact that the agents approached her, asked if she would show them her ticket and identification, and posed to her a few questions. Nor was it enough to establish a seizure that the person asking the question was a law enforcement official.

Three concurring justices did not comment on the Stewart standard; four dissenters did not question the standard used by Stewart but said he had overlooked certain facts that would support a determination that a "seizure" occurred. The standard articulated by Justice Stewart in *Mendenhall* was fully accepted by a majority of the Court in *Florida v. Royer*, 460 U.S. 491 (1984). Specifically, a majority of the Court agreed that it was not a "seizure" for the police to merely approach the defendant in the airport and ask to see his ticket and his driver's license. In *Royer* the "line was crossed" only when the police went beyond this and identified themselves as narcotics officers, told Royer that he was suspected of transporting narcotics, and asked him to accompany them to a police room without telling him that he was free to leave....

We have been applying the *Mendenhall/Royer* standard ever since it was first articulated by Justice Stewart....We believe that the *Hodari* decision represents a departure from the *Mendenhall/Royer* approach. This is a belief shared by some of the leading commentators on the law of search and seizure. In our view, *Hodari* adds another level of analysis, allowing a trial court to conclude that a seizure occurs only if (a) the *Mendenhall/Royer* test is satisfied and (b) the police either used physical force or the defendant submitted to the assertion of authority....Accordingly, exercising our independent authority to interpret our own state constitution, we have decided to continue to adhere to the pre-*Hodari* approach of determining, objectively and on the basis of the totality of the circumstances, whether a reasonable person in the defendant's shoes would have concluded that he or she was not free to leave.

We emphasize that following this approach does not mean that police necessarily must possess articulable suspicion before they follow a person in public or before they approach a person in public. What it does mean is that if a trial court later determines that, under all the circumstances, a reasonable person would have believed that because of the conduct of the police he was not free to leave, then there was a "seizure," and the police must be able to articulate reasonable suspicion justifying the seizure, else any evidence that is the fruit of the seizure is suppressible. Here, as we have said,

there clearly was a "seizure" once the police directed E.D.J. to stop, and the question becomes whether the police articulated a sufficient basis for the stop. We conclude that they did not.

Since there was a "seizure" of the person of E.D.J., and since the police did not articulate a sufficient basis for the "seizure," the cocaine should have been suppressed if it was a fruit of the illegality. Since E.D.J. abandoned the cocaine after he was unlawfully directed to stop, the abandonment was the suppressible fruit of the illegality. Without the evidence seized there was an insufficient basis for the delinquency adjudication. We therefore reverse the court of appeals and vacate the trial court's determination that E.D.J. committed a delinquent act.

REVERSED and adjudication of delinquency [decision that E.D.J. was a juvenile delinquent] vacated.

Questions

1. What exactly were the reasons why the Minnesota Supreme Court decided not to follow *Hodari*?

2. What is the definition of seizure adopted by the Minnesota Supreme Court?

3. Which definition, in your opinion, is better? Defend your answer.

4. Which definition sets the proper balance between "controlling the governed" and "controlling the government"? Explain your answer.

SUMMARY

   I.   Searches and seizures
       A. Crime control in a constitutional democracy depends on information
       B. Most information comes from reluctant sources
           1. Criminals
           2. Suspects
           3. Victims
           4. Witnesses
       C. Special-needs searches go beyond searches for evidence of crime; they
           1. Protect officers
           2. Protect property of detained suspects
           3. Protect officers from lawsuits

        4. Detect drug use among students and employees

        5. Prevent drunk driving

   D. Purpose of the Fourth Amendment

        1. Searches and seizures were aimed originally at sedition (criticism of English monarchs) and tax evasions, not crimes against persons (like murder) and their property (theft)

        2. Balance government power and individual rights

           a. Give government enough power to control crimes

           b. Protect individuals' right to be let alone by the government (not by private individuals)

        3. Ensure only "reasonable" searches and seizures take place

        4. "Reasonable" limit meant to protect individuals' rights to

           a. Locomotion—come and go as they please

           b. Privacy

   E. Three-step Fourth Amendment analysis

        1. Was government action a search or a seizure?

        2. If it was, was it reasonable?

        3. If it was unreasonable, should evidence be excluded?

   F. Degrees of objective basis required

        1. All searches and seizures require an objective basis (facts to back them up)

        2. Three stages of Fourth Amendment–based encounters between police and private individuals

           a. On the street and other public places

           b. At the police station

           c. In jails before and in prisons after conviction

        3. Each creates progressively deeper invasions of liberty and privacy

        4. The greater the government invasion, the greater the objective basis needed to back it up

II. Searches

   A. Definition—government actions that invade a person's expectation of privacy

   B. Becomes a search when it invades a reasonable expectation of privacy (when society is prepared to recognize the expectation as reasonable)

   C. Theory and practice

        1. Theory—balance the power of government to control crime against individuals' right to be let alone by government

        2. Practice—balance is weighted in favor of government power

   D. Plain-view discoveries aren't searches

        1. Plain-view searches (nonsearches), discovery of evidence by ordinary senses (sight, touch, smell, and hearing), aren't searches

        2. Three conditions to meet plain-view doctrine requirements

           a. Officers are lawfully present at the scene

           b. Officers don't enhance their ordinary senses by hi-tech devices

           c. Discovery is inadvertent (by chance)

   E. High-tech enhancements don't meet the plain-view standard

        1. Technology in wide use and easily obtained (flashlights and glasses) isn't high-tech

        2. Technology rarely used and not easily obtained (X ray and thermal imaging) is high-tech

F. Unprotected places
  1. Open fields discoveries aren't searches
    a. No reasonable expectation of privacy in open fields
    b. Open fields don't include curtilage (area immediately surrounding house) judged by
      (1) Distance from house
      (2) Fences
      (3) Use or purpose of area
      (4) Measures taken to prevent public view
  2. Public-place discoveries aren't searches if they're in
    a. Publicly owned (sidewalks, parks, stadiums) areas
    b. Businesses open to the public (restaurants and stores)
    c. Parts of business not open to the public
G. Abandoned property not protected by Fourth Amendment
  1. Abandonment includes two elements
    a. Physical—giving up physical possession
    b. Mental—intention to give up expectation of privacy
  2. Test of abandonment
    a. Burden on government to prove
    b. Totality of circumstances judged on a case-by-case basis

III. Seizures
  A. Officers don't subject individuals to Fourth Amendment seizures when they approach and question them
  B. Individuals don't have to stop or talk to officers who approach them, unless officers "seize" them
  C. Stopping because of psychological pressure or a sense of public duty doesn't qualify as a Fourth Amendment seizure
  D. Two types of seizure
    1. Physical detention (grabbing)
    2. Submission to official show of authority

 Go to the Criminal Procedure 6e CD to download this summary outline. The outline has been formatted so that you can add notes to it during class lectures, or later create a customized chapter outline to use while reviewing. Either way, the summary outline will help you understand the "big picture" and fill in the details as you study.

REVIEW QUESTIONS

1. What's the importance of information in a constitutional democracy?

2. Identify the four types of sources of information in crime control, and explain why we call these sources reluctant.

3. Describe the origins and original purposes of searches and seizures.

4. Identify and describe the balance of interests the Fourth Amendment is supposed to protect.

5. Identify two values the "reasonableness" limit is supposed to protect.

6. Identify the three steps in determining whether the government has complied with the Fourth Amendment.

7. Identify three stages of citizen-police encounters in which government actions might be searches and seizures.

8. Explain how the degree of objective basis required changes based on the stages you identified in (7).

9. Compare the trespass doctrine with the privacy doctrine in defining Fourth Amendment searches.

10. Compare the privacy doctrine in theory and practice.

11. State the privacy test of whether a government action is a search as Justice Harlan formulated it.

12. Why can plain-view searches be called *non*searches?

13. Identify and describe the situations when the three conditions of the plain-view doctrine apply.

14. Define two kinds of "high tech" enhancement to ordinary senses, give examples of each, and state the effect of each on the plain-view doctrine.

15. Why is there no reasonable expectation of privacy in open fields?

16. Why does the open fields doctrine apply even when owners post a "No Trespassing" sign?

17. Why is the curtilage excepted from the open fields doctrine?

18. Identify four criteria used to determine whether an area is within the curtilage.

19. Identify and give examples of "public places" that aren't subject to Fourth Amendment protection.

20. Identify and give an example of each of the two elements that determines whether property is abandoned for Fourth Amendment purposes.

21. Identify the two conditions that each turns an encounter with the police into a Fourth Amendment seizure.

22. What can a citizen do when an officer without enough objective basis approaches and asks him questions?

23. What's the effect of walking away from an officer on the objective basis required for a seizure?

24. Identify two kinds of restraint on your freedom of movement that have no Fourth Amendment significance.

KEY TERMS

special-needs searches p. 58
seditious libels p. 59
general warrant p. 59
writs of assistance p. 59

liberty p. 60
right of locomotion p. 60
privacy p. 60
objective basis p. 61

reasonable suspicion p. 61
probable cause p. 61
trespass doctrine p. 61
privacy doctrine p. 62

THE COMPANION WEB SITE
FOR *CRIMINAL PROCEDURE,* SIXTH EDITION

http://cj.wadsworth.com/samaha/crim_pro6e

 Supplement your review of this chapter by going to the companion Web site to take one of the Tutorial Quizzes, use the flash cards to test yourself on the key terms from each chapter, and check out the many other study aids you'll find there. You'll find valuable data and resources at your fingertips to help you study for that big exam or write that important paper.

4 Stop and Frisk

Chapter Main Points

- Stops are Fourth Amendment "seizures" that allow officers to briefly "freeze" suspicious people on the street to check out whether "crime may be afoot."

- Frisks are Fourth Amendment "searches" that allow officers to protect themselves during stops by patting-down the outer clothing of people they stop.

- The reasonableness of stops depends on whether there's reasonable suspicion to back them up and whether they're brief and close to the scene of suspicious activity.

- Anonymous tips corroborated with other evidence can amount to reasonable suspicion.

- Race and ethnicity *by themselves* don't amount to reasonable suspicion, but they can be *part* of the totality of circumstances that make up reasonable suspicion.

- It's reasonable for officers to remove passengers from vehicles stopped because of the driver's suspicious activity.

- Controlling who and what enters and leaves the country justifies substantial reductions of liberty and privacy at international borders.

- Frisks for the protection of officers are reasonable, if officers have already lawfully stopped a suspect and they reasonably suspect that person is armed.

- Frisks are reasonable only if officers use a once-over-lightly pat-down of outer clothing to detect weapons.

A customs inspector told Elvira Montoya de Hernandez, a passenger arriving at Los Angeles International Airport on a flight from Bogotá, Colombia, that he suspected she was smuggling drugs in her alimentary canal. The officer placed her in a customs office under observation and told her that if she went to the toilet she would have to use a wastebasket in the women's restroom so that female inspectors could inspect her stool for balloons or capsules carrying narcotics. The inspector refused Montoya de Hernandez's request to call her husband in Colombia. Montoya de Hernandez remained detained under watch in the customs office, for most of the time curled up in a chair leaning to one side. She refused all offers of food and drink, and refused to use the toilet facilities. She exhibited symptoms of discomfort with "heroic efforts to resist the usual calls of nature." At the shift change at 4:00 P.M. the next afternoon, almost 16 hours after her flight had landed, Montoya de Hernandez still had not defecated or urinated or partaken of food or drink.

U.S. v. Montoya de Hernandez (1985), U.S. Supreme Court

STOPS, FRISKS, AND THE FOURTH AMENDMENT

The power to stop and question suspicious persons is ancient. From at least the Middle Ages, English constables could—and were bound by their office to—detain suspicious people, especially the dreaded "nightwalkers." (Anyone walking around between dusk and dawn was automatically suspected of being up to no good [Stern 1967, 532].) The English brought "stop and frisk" to their American colonies, and nobody challenged it until the 1960s.

During the due process revolution of that decade (Chapter 2), civil libertarians did challenge the power of police to detain suspicious people on a hunch. On what basis? Private individuals, they argued, especially "outsiders," need the courts to protect their rights whenever they're out on the streets and other public places. Not surprisingly, law enforcement officers didn't see it that way. They argued that until they made an *arrest* (Chapter 5)—took suspects to the police station and kept them there against their will—their good judgment, based on their professional expertise gained from training and experience, was enough. Formal rules written by judges who had no knowledge and experience of the "street" and "street people" would only interfere with crime control (Remington 1960, 390).

Fourth Amendment stops are brief detentions that allow law enforcement officers to freeze suspicious situations briefly so they can investigate them. Fourth Amendment *seizures* of persons include everything from these brief street stops to lengthy jail detentions (Figure 4.1). **Fourth Amendment frisks** are once-over-lightly pat-downs of outer clothing to protect officers by taking away suspects' weapons. (We don't expect officers to risk their lives when they approach a person to check out possible danger.) Fourth Amendment *searches* of persons include everything from these protective pat-downs for weapons to strip and body-cavity searches. Chapters 5 and 6 analyze the greater invasions of arrests and full-blown searches in the unfamiliar and isolated surroundings of police stations and jails. This chapter examines stops and frisks, the least-invasive seizures and searches of persons in familiar and more comfortable public places like streets, parks, and malls.

We've already touched on how the U.S. Constitution requires government officers to have an **objective basis** (suspicious facts and circumstances), not just hunches, to back up official unwanted interferences with individuals' rights (Chapters 2–3). We further noted that the greater the invasion, the greater the objective basis required by the Constitution to back it up. With specific reference to Fourth Amendment searches and seizures, this means officers need to prove fewer suspicious facts and circumstances to back up stops and frisks than they do for arrests (Chapter 5) and full-blown searches (Chapter 6). Stops and frisks represent the beginning of a chronological path through the criminal process from more frequent and more visible (but less-intrusive) searches and seizures in public to more-intrusive (but less-visible) searches and seizures out of sight in police stations.

Stops and frisks aren't just fine points for constitutional lawyers and courts to debate. They also reflect broad public policies aimed at balancing the values of crime control and individual liberty and privacy. As we've just seen, although they may take place in the less-intimidating atmosphere of public places, and invade liberty and privacy less than arrests and searches, stops and frisks affect a lot more people. The ratio of stops to arrests is about one arrest out of every nine stops (Spitzer 1999, Table I.B.1). In fact, for most people stops and frisks are the only uninvited (and unwanted) contact with the police they'll ever have. Just as important, because stops and frisks take place in public, the display of police power is there for everybody to see. Because of this visibility (*transparency,* we call it today), stops and frisks probably shape public opinion of police power more than the greater invasions of arrest and searches that we never see. Deciding which is more important in a constitutional democracy—crime control by means of less-intrusive public stops and frisks affecting more people or often invisible arrests and searches affecting fewer people—is both a constitutional and public policy question.

As we examine the realities of stop and frisk, keep in mind these very important facts:

- Officers are going to stop many people who haven't done anything wrong; and they'll frisk lots of people who aren't armed.

- Most of these same people *want* police protection and (at least in high-crime neighborhoods) *need* it more than people who live in safe neighborhoods.

- Both lawbreakers *and* law-abiders in high-street-crime neighborhoods form lasting opinions about the police from street encounters they've either watched or experienced.

In this section, we'll look at stop-and-frisk law; the two clauses of the Fourth Amendment and how evolving interpretations of them by the Supreme Court have led to a reasonableness test for searches and seizures; and the historic case of *Terry v. Ohio,* in which the test was first explained and applied.

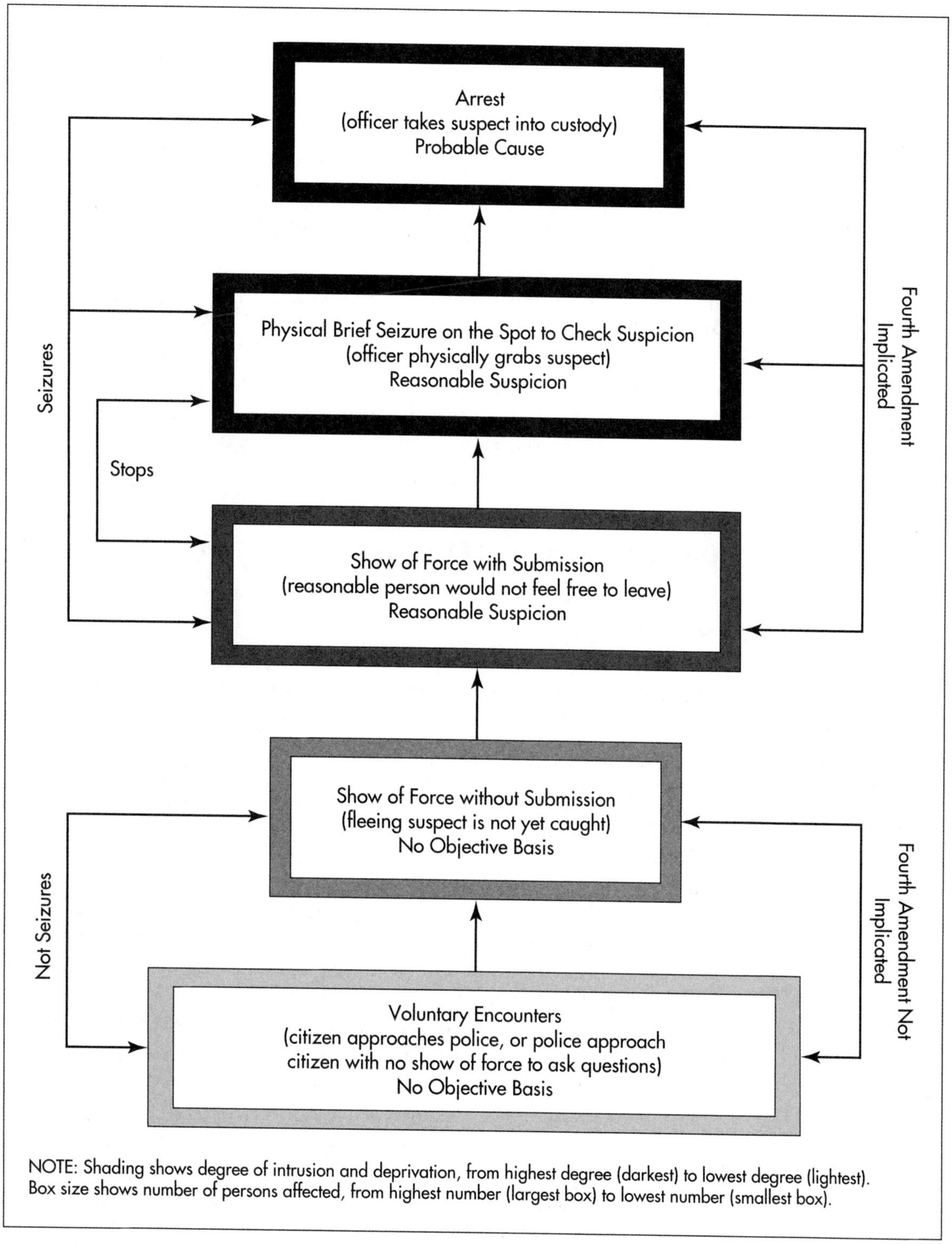
Arrest
(officer takes suspect into custody)
Probable Cause
Physical Brief Seizure on the Spot to Check Suspicion
(officer physically grabs suspect)
Reasonable Suspicion
Show of Force with Submission
(reasonable person would not feel free to leave)
Reasonable Suspicion
Show of Force without Submission
(fleeing suspect is not yet caught)
No Objective Basis
Voluntary Encounters
(citizen approaches police, or police approach citizen with no show of force to ask questions)
No Objective Basis
Seizures
Stops
Not Seizures
Fourth Amendment Implicated
Fourth Amendment Not Implicated
NOTE: Shading shows degree of intrusion and deprivation, from highest degree (darkest) to lowest degree (lightest).
Box size shows number of persons affected, from highest number (largest box) to lowest number (smallest box).

FIGURE 4.1 Seizures

Stop-and-Frisk Law

Stop-and-frisk law follows a slight alteration of the three-step analysis used to decide whether an officer's action was a search or seizure at all (Chapter 3):

1. Was the officer's action a stop or a frisk?

2. If the government action was a stop and/or a frisk, was it "unreasonable"?

3. If the stop or frisk was "unreasonable," should evidence obtained during the stop and/or frisk be excluded from legal proceedings against the defendants (Chapter 10)?

If the action wasn't a stop or a frisk (step 1, Chapter 3), then the Fourth Amendment doesn't apply at all. Practically speaking, this means the courts don't have authority to review what officers do in such situations; it's left to officers' discretion. If the action *was* a stop or a frisk, then the analysis proceeds to decide whether it was reasonable (step 2, this chapter). If it was reasonable, the analysis is over. If it was *unreasonable*, the analysis proceeds to decide whether the evidence has to be excluded (step 3, (Chapter 10).

Two Approaches to Fourth Amendment Analysis

Before we analyze stops and frisks, you need to understand the two parts of the Fourth Amendment:

1. *The reasonableness clause.* "The right of the people to be secure in their persons, houses, papers, and effects against unreasonable searches and seizures shall not be violated."

2. *The warrant clause.* "... and no warrants shall issue but upon probable cause, supported by oath or affirmation, and particularly describing the place to be searched, and the persons or things to be seized."

Until the 1960s, the U.S. Supreme Court adopted what we call the **conventional Fourth Amendment approach,** which says the warrant and reasonableness clauses are firmly connected. Specifically, the reasonableness clause is just a stirring introduction to the heart of the people's right against unreasonable searches and seizures—the warrant clause. The warrant clause guarantees that only searches and seizures based on warrants and probable cause are reasonable. In the 1960s, the Supreme Court shifted from this conventional approach to the **reasonableness Fourth Amendment approach.** It says the two clauses are separate, and they address separate problems. The warrant clause tells us what the Fourth Amendment requires only when law enforcement officers want to obtain warrants. Because only a tiny fraction of searches and seizures are made with warrants, and many searches and seizures don't require probable cause either, the warrant clause then isn't very important. So, according to the Court, we can't read the Fourth Amendment to mean searches and seizures without warrants and probable cause are *always* "unreasonable."

Since the 1960s, the Court has spent a lot of its time reviewing, case by case, the circumstances that make a search or seizure unreasonable. By now it should be clear to *you* that the Court's decisions *aren't* always clear. But don't blame the Court; after all, "unreasonable" is probably the vaguest and so also one of the toughest to define words in the Constitution. The Fourth Amendment has generated more cases, and takes up more pages in criminal procedure books including this one, than any other subject in the law of criminal procedure. Why? All lower courts have to follow these decisions. State legislatures also consult them when they write criminal procedure rules. And, most important, local police departments and police officers know their stop-and-frisk rules and actions *might* be reviewed by at least *some* court and *could* go all the way to the Supreme Court.

Reasonableness is a broad—and some say too subjective—standard. According to Professor John M. Copacino (1994), in balancing the interest of the government in crime control and special needs against the invasions of individual liberty and privacy:

> [T]he Supreme Court has been satisfied by broad characterization of the government's interest, usually unaccompanied by any hard evidence. Similarly, in assessing the harm caused to the individual by the intrusion, the Court does not cite any empirical evidence, expert testimony, or individual testimony from those who have been affected by the search or seizure. It simply proclaims its subjective judgment of the citizen's likely reactions. (236)

Now, let's make a stab at explaining what Fourth Amendment reasonableness means.

When the U.S. Supreme Court decided there were more reasonable searches and seizures without than with warrants, it created two major challenges: (1) when does the Fourth Amendment require warrants, and (2) what does "unreasonable" mean? The Court has formulated a method for meeting these challenges. One type of reasonable search and seizure is based on warrants and probable cause. The other type—which in practice includes the vast majority of searches and seizures—has to pass the **reasonableness test.**

The reasonableness test consists of two elements the government has to prove:

1. *Balancing element.* The need to search and/or seize outweighs the invasion of liberty and privacy rights of the individuals.

2. *Objective basis.* There are enough facts to back up the search and/or seizure.

Still, there's no **"bright line" (clear) rule** to tell officers, courts, or us what's reasonable. According to the U.S. Supreme Court, courts have to decide whether searches and seizures are reasonable on a **case-by-case basis.** How do they do it? They look at the **totality of circumstances** surrounding the specific searches and seizures in individual cases. Officers make a *preliminary* (usually on the spur-of-the-moment under pressure) reasonableness decision on the street and in police stations. In making their decision, officers are allowed to view the totality of circumstances through the lens of their professional training and experience. But officers' decisions aren't final. That's left to judges. They review the totality of the circumstances the officers acted on and decide whether they meet the constitutional standard of reasonableness.

The test of reasonableness also requires a case-by-case evaluation of whether there was enough objective basis to back up the searches and seizures. The objective basis ranges from probable cause required to back up full-blown searches (Chapter 6) and seizures (arrests, Chapter 5) to reasonable suspicion required to back up stops and frisks. Both probable cause (always) and reasonable suspicion (usually) require **individualized suspicion,** meaning suspicion that points to specific individuals. However, DWI roadblocks (discussed later in this chapter) and some noncriminal law enforcement searches (Chapter 7) don't require individualized suspicion. In these cases, the objective basis consists of such things as random stops.

Terry v. Ohio and Stop and Frisk

Today's stop-and-frisk law grew out of the practical problems police officers face in preventing and investigating crime on the streets and other public places in our largest cities. In these investigations, officers are usually dealing with people they don't know and probably won't ever see again. Usually, these strangers' suspicious behavior doesn't add up to the probable cause needed to arrest them (Chapter 5). For example, officers don't have enough facts and circumstances viewed through the lens of their professional experience and training to arrest two men who peer into a store window, look around as if to see if anyone's watching them, and pace up and down repeating this pattern for 10 minutes. What should the officers do? Nothing? Keep watching them? Briefly detain them and pat them down for weapons? Take them to the police station? These were the issues raised in the famous *Terry v. Ohio* case.

The answer depends on three possible interpretations of the Fourth Amendment (Dix 1985, 853–855):

1. The Fourth Amendment applies only to full searches and arrests, so what officers do is left to their discretion.

2. Even brief street detentions are arrests, and pat-downs are searches; so the police can't do anything unless they've got probable cause.

3. Stops and frisks are searches and seizures, but they're "minor" ones; so officers have to back them up with facts, but they need fewer facts than they'd need to arrest and search.

If officers can't take any action until they've got probable cause (alternative 2), crime control suffers because they'll probably never see the suspects again. But, if the Constitution doesn't apply at all to these street encounters (alternative 1), then people on the street are subject to the whims of every officer. So, both alternatives 1 and 2 are unacceptable; the U.S. Supreme Court chose alternative 3.

According to the Court, the Fourth Amendment gives the police enough power to "freeze" suspicious events and people briefly to find out if criminal activity "may be afoot." The Fourth Amendment also gives officers the power to protect themselves by frisking the people they stop. But officers can't freeze all the events and lay hands on all the people they've got a hunch may be up to no good; their stops and frisks have to be "reasonable." Courts can later review their stops and frisks to make sure they were reasonable.

What's reasonable? First, in the balance between crime control and individual freedom and privacy, in each case, the need to control crime has to outweigh the invasions against the individuals' rights. Second, officers can't stop and frisk people on a hunch, whim, or "mere suspicion." They need facts—not as many as would add up to probable cause (Chapters 5–6), but enough so later a neutral judge can decide if there was enough objective basis to back up both the stop and the frisk.

The U.S. Supreme Court explained and applied the reasonableness test to stops and frisks in the case of *Terry v. Ohio* (1968).

Terry v. Ohio
392 U.S. 1 (1968)

John Terry and Richard Chilton were prosecuted for carrying a concealed weapon. An Ohio trial court overruled a pretrial motion to suppress as evidence a gun seized during a stop and frisk on a Cleveland street. Terry and Chilton were convicted. Terry appealed. An intermediate Ohio appeals court affirmed the conviction. The Ohio Supreme Court dismissed Terry's appeal. The U.S. Supreme Court granted certiorari and affirmed.

WARREN, CJ.

FACTS

. . . Officer McFadden testified that while he was patrolling in plain clothes in downtown Cleveland at approximately 2:30 in the afternoon of October 31, 1963, his attention was attracted by two men, Chilton and Terry, standing on the corner of Huron Road and Euclid Avenue. He had never seen the two men before, and he was unable to say precisely what first drew his eye to them. However, he testified that he had been a policeman for 39 years and a detective for 35 and that he had been assigned to patrol this vicinity of downtown Cleveland for shoplifters and pickpockets for 30 years. He explained that he had developed routine habits of observation over the years and that he would "stand and watch people or walk and watch people at many intervals of the day." He added: "Now, in this case when I looked over they didn't look right to me at the time."

His interest aroused, Officer McFadden took up a post of observation in the entrance to a store 300 to 400 feet away from the two men. "I get more purpose to watch them when I seen their movements," he testified. He saw one of the men leave the other one and walk southwest on Huron Road, past some stores. The man paused for a moment and looked in a store window, then walked on a short distance, turned around and walked back toward the corner, pausing once again to look in the same store window. He rejoined his companion at the corner, and the two conferred briefly. Then the second man went through the same series of motions, strolling down Huron Road, looking in the same window, walking on a short distance, turning back, peering in the store window again, and returning to confer with the first man at the corner.

The two men repeated this ritual alternately between five and six times apiece—in all, roughly a dozen trips. At one point, while the two were standing together on the corner, a third man approached them and engaged them briefly in conversation. This man then left the two others and walked west on Euclid Avenue. Chilton and Terry resumed their measured pacing, peering and conferring. After this had gone on for 10 to 12 minutes, the two men walked off together, heading west on Euclid Avenue, following the path taken earlier by the third man.

By this time Officer McFadden had become thoroughly suspicious. He testified that after observing their elaborately casual and oft-repeated reconnaissance of the store window on Huron Road, he suspected the two men of "casing a job, a stick-up," and that he considered it his duty as a police officer to investigate further. He added that he feared "they may have a gun." Thus, Officer McFadden followed Chilton and Terry and saw them stop in front of Zucker's store to talk to the same man who had conferred with them earlier on the street corner.

Deciding that the situation was ripe for direct action, Officer McFadden approached the three men, identified himself as a police officer and asked for their names. At this point his knowledge was confined to what he had observed. He was not acquainted with any of the three men by name or by sight, and he had received no information concerning them from any other source.

When the men "mumbled something" in response to his inquiries, Officer McFadden grabbed petitioner Terry, spun him around so that they were facing the other two, with Terry between McFadden and the others, and patted down the outside of his clothing. In the left breast pocket of Terry's overcoat Officer McFadden felt a pistol. He reached inside the overcoat pocket, but was unable to remove the gun.

At this point, keeping Terry between himself and the others, the officer ordered all three men to enter Zucker's store. As they went in, he removed Terry's overcoat completely, removed a .38-caliber revolver from the pocket and ordered all three men to face the wall with their hands raised. Officer McFadden proceeded to pat down the outer clothing of Chilton and the third man, Katz. He discovered another revolver in the outer pocket of Chilton's overcoat, but no weapons were found on Katz. The officer testified that he only patted the men down to see whether they had weapons, and that he did not put his hands beneath the outer garments of either Terry or Chilton until he felt their guns. So far as appears from the record, he never placed his hands beneath Katz' outer garments.

Officer McFadden seized Chilton's gun, asked the proprietor of the store to call a police wagon, and took all three men to the station, where Chilton and Terry were formally charged with carrying concealed weapons.

[The trial court denied Terry's motion to suppress the gun as evidence] . . . on the ground that Officer McFadden, on the basis of his experience, "had reasonable cause to believe . . . that the defendants were conducting themselves suspiciously, and some interrogation should be made of their action." Purely for his own protection, the court held, the officer had the right to pat down the outer clothing of these men, who he had reasonable cause to believe might be armed. . . .

After the court denied their motion to suppress, Chilton and Terry waived jury trial and pleaded not guilty. The court adjudged them guilty, and the Court of Appeals for the Eighth Judicial District, Cuyahoga County, affirmed. The Supreme Court of Ohio dismissed their appeal. . . . We granted certiorari, to determine whether the admission of the revolvers in evidence violated petitioner's rights under the Fourth Amendment, made applicable to the States by the Fourteenth. We affirm the conviction.

OPINION

The Fourth Amendment . . . right . . . against unreasonable searches and seizures . . . belongs as much to the citizen on the streets of our cities as to the homeowner closeted in his study to dispose of his secret affairs. . . . Unquestionably Terry was entitled to the protection of the Fourth Amendment as he walked down the street in Cleveland. The question is whether in all the circumstances of this on-the-street encounter, his right to personal security was violated by an unreasonable search and seizure. . . .

Our first task is to establish at what point in this encounter . . . Officer McFadden "seized" Terry and whether and when he conducted a "search." There is some suggestion in the use of such terms as "stop" and "frisk" that such police conduct is outside the purview of the Fourth Amendment because neither action rises to the level of a "search" or "seizure" within the meaning of the Constitution. We emphatically reject this notion.

It is quite plain that the Fourth Amendment governs "seizures" of the person which do not eventuate in a trip to the station house and prosecution for crime—"arrests" in traditional terminology. It must be recognized that whenever a police officer accosts an individual and restrains his freedom to walk away, he has "seized" that person. And it is nothing less than sheer torture of the English language to suggest that a careful exploration of the outer surfaces of a person's clothing all over his or her body in an attempt to find weapons is not a "search." Moreover, it is simply fantastic to urge that such a procedure performed in public by a policeman while the citizen stands helpless, perhaps facing a wall with his hands raised, is a "petty indignity." It is a serious intrusion upon the sanctity of the person, which may inflict great indignity and arouse strong resentment, and it is not to be undertaken lightly. . . .

The . . . central inquiry under the Fourth Amendment [is]—the reasonableness in all the circumstances of the particular governmental invasion of a citizen's personal security. . . . In this case there can be no question that Officer McFadden "seized" petitioner and subjected him to a "search" when he took hold of him and patted down the outer surfaces of his clothing. We must decide whether at that point it was reasonable for Officer McFadden to have interfered with petitioner's personal security as he did.

. . . [I]n determining whether the seizure and search were "unreasonable" our inquiry is a dual one—whether the officer's action was justified at its inception, and whether it was reasonably related in scope to the circumstances which justified the interference in the first place. . . .

. . . [I]n justifying the particular intrusion the police officer must be able to point to specific and articulable facts which, taken together with rational inferences from those facts, reasonably warrant that intrusion. . . . [T]he Fourth Amendment is meaningful only if at some point the conduct of those charged with enforcing the laws can be subjected to the more detached, neutral scrutiny of a judge who must evaluate the reasonableness of a particular search or seizure. . . . [I]n making that assessment it is imperative that the facts be judged against an objective standard: would the facts available to the officer at the moment of the seizure or the search "warrant a man of reasonable caution in the belief" that the action taken was appropriate? Anything less would invite intrusions upon constitutionally guaranteed rights based on nothing more substantial than inarticulate hunches. . . . And simple "good faith on the part of the arresting officer is not enough." . . . If subjective good faith alone were the test, the protections of the Fourth Amendment would evaporate, and the people would be "secure in their persons, houses, papers, and effects" only in the discretion of the police.

Applying these principles to this case, we consider first the nature and extent of the government interests involved. One general interest is of course that of effective crime prevention and detection; it is this interest which underlies the recognition that a police officer may in appropriate circumstances and in an appropriate manner approach a person for purposes of investigating possibly criminal behavior even though there is no probable cause to make an arrest. It was this legitimate investigative function Officer McFadden was discharging when he decided to approach Terry and his companions. He had observed Terry, Chilton, and Katz go through a series of acts, each of them perhaps innocent in itself, but which taken together warranted further investigation.

There is nothing unusual in two men standing together on a street corner, perhaps waiting for someone. Nor is there anything suspicious about people in such circumstances strolling up and down the street, singly or in pairs. Store windows, moreover, are made to be looked in. But the story is quite different where, as here, two men hover about a street corner for an extended period of time, at the end of which it becomes apparent that they are not waiting for anyone or anything; where these men pace alternately along an identical route, pausing to stare in the same store window roughly 24 times; where each completion of this route is followed immediately by a conference between the two men on the corner; where they are joined in one of these conferences by a third man who leaves swiftly; and where the two men finally follow the third and rejoin him a couple of blocks away. It would have been poor police work indeed for an officer of 30 years' experience in the detection of thievery from stores in this same neighborhood to have failed to investigate this behavior further.

The crux of this case, however, is not the propriety of Officer McFadden's taking steps to investigate Terry's suspicious behavior, but rather, whether there was justification for McFadden's invasion of Terry's personal security by searching him for weapons in the course of that investigation. We are now concerned with more than the governmental interest in investigating crime; in addition, there is the more immediate interest of the police officer in taking steps to assure himself that the person with whom he is dealing is not armed with a weapon that could unexpectedly and fatally be used against him. Certainly it would be unreasonable to require that police officers take unnecessary risks in the performance of their duties....

We must still consider, however, the nature and quality of the intrusion on individual rights which must be accepted if police officers are to be conceded the right to search for weapons in situations where probable cause to arrest for crime is lacking. Even a limited search of the outer clothing for weapons constitutes a severe, though brief, intrusion upon cherished personal security, and it must surely be an annoying, frightening, and perhaps humiliating experience....

Our evaluation of the proper balance that has to be struck in this type of case leads us to conclude that there must be a narrowly drawn authority to permit a reasonable search for weapons for the protection of the police officer, where he has reason to believe that he is dealing with an armed and dangerous individual.... [I]n determining whether the officer acted reasonably in such circumstances, due weight must be given, not to his inchoate and unparticularized suspicion or "hunch," but to the specific reasonable inferences which he is entitled to draw from the facts in light of his experience.

We must now examine the conduct of Officer McFadden in this case to determine whether his search and seizure of petitioner were reasonable, both at their inception and as conducted. He had observed Terry, together with Chilton and another man, acting in a manner he took to be preface to a "stick-up." We think on the facts and circumstances Officer McFadden detailed before the trial judge a reasonably prudent man would have been warranted in believing petitioner was armed and thus presented a threat to the officer's safety while he was investigating his suspicious behavior.

The actions of Terry and Chilton were consistent with McFadden's hypothesis that these men were contemplating a daylight robbery—which, it is reasonable to assume, would be likely to involve the use of weapons—and nothing in their conduct from the time he first noticed them until the time he confronted them and identified himself as a police officer gave him sufficient reason to negate that hypothesis. Although the trio had departed the original scene, there was nothing to indicate abandonment of an intent to commit a robbery at some point.

The manner in which the seizure and search were conducted is, of course, as vital a part of the inquiry as whether they were warranted at all. The Fourth Amendment proceeds as much by limitations upon the scope of governmental action as by imposing preconditions upon its initiation.

... [S]uch a search ... is not justified by any need to prevent the disappearance or destruction of evidence of crime. The sole justification of the search in the present situation is the protection of the police officer and others nearby, and it must therefore be confined in scope to an intrusion reasonably designed to discover guns, knives, clubs, or other hidden instruments for the assault of the police officer.

The scope of the search in this case presents no serious problem in light of these standards. Officer McFadden patted down the outer clothing of petitioner and his two companions. He did not place his hands in their pockets or under the outer surface of their garments until he had felt weapons, and then he merely reached for and removed the guns.... Officer McFadden confined his search strictly to what was minimally necessary to learn whether the men were armed and to disarm them once he discovered the weapons. He did not conduct a general exploratory search for whatever evidence of criminal activity he might find.

We conclude that the revolver seized from Terry was properly admitted in evidence against him....

Each case of this sort will, of course, have to be decided on its own facts. We merely hold today that where a police officer observes unusual conduct which leads him reasonably to conclude in light of his experience that criminal activity may be afoot and that the persons with whom he is dealing may be armed and presently dangerous, where in the course of investigating this behavior he identifies himself as a policeman and makes reasonable inquiries, and where nothing in the initial stages of the encounter serves to dispel his reasonable fear for his own or others' safety, he is entitled for the protection of himself and others in the area to conduct a carefully limited search of the outer clothing of such persons in an attempt to discover weapons which might be used to assault him. Such a search is a reasonable search under the Fourth Amendment, and any weapons seized may properly be introduced in evidence against the person from whom they were taken.

AFFIRMED.

CONCURRING OPINION

HARLAN, J.

...Where...a stop is reasonable...the right to frisk must be immediate and automatic if the reason for the stop is, as here, an articulable suspicion of a crime of violence.... There is no reason why an officer, rightfully but forcibly confronting a person suspected of a serious crime, should have to ask one question and take the risk that the answer might be a bullet....

DISSENT

DOUGLAS, J.

...The infringement on personal liberty of any "seizure" of a person can only be "reasonable" under the Fourth Amendment if we require the police to possess "probable cause" before they seize him. Only that line draws a meaningful distinction between an officer's mere inkling and the presence of facts within the officer's personal knowledge which would convince a reasonable man that the person seized has committed, is committing, or is about to commit a particular crime....

To give the police greater power than a magistrate is to take a long step down the totalitarian path. Perhaps such a step is desirable to cope with modern forms of lawlessness. But if it is taken, it should be the deliberate choice of the people through a constitutional amendment. Until the Fourth Amendment, ... is rewritten, the person and the effects of the individual are beyond the reach of all government agencies until there are reasonable grounds to believe (probable cause) that a criminal venture has been launched or is about to be launched.

There have been powerful hydraulic pressures throughout our history that bear heavily on the Court to water down constitutional guarantees and give the police the upper hand. That hydraulic pressure has probably never been greater than it is today. Yet if the individual is no longer to be sovereign, if the police can pick him up whenever they do not like the cut of his jib, if they can "seize" and "search" him in their discretion, we enter a new regime. The decision to enter it should be made only after a full debate by the people of this country.

Questions

1. List in chronological order all of McFadden's specific actions from the time he started watching Terry until he arrested him.

2. For each of McFadden's actions, state the objective basis, if any.

3. According to the Court, at what point did McFadden *seize* Terry? Summarize the Court's reasons for picking that point.

4. According to the Court, at what point did McFadden *search* Terry? Summarize the Court's reasons for picking that point.

5. What was the objective basis (facts and circumstances) for McFadden's "stop" of Terry?

6. What was the objective basis (facts and circumstances) for McFadden's "frisk" of Terry?

7. During the oral argument before the Supreme Court, it came out that in all of Officer McFadden's experience, he'd never investigated a robbery; his experience was limited to shoplifting and pick-pocketing. Does this matter? Explain your answer.

8. It was also learned during oral argument that Terry, Chilton, and Katz were a lot bigger than Officer McFadden. Does it matter? Why?

9. Consider the following excerpt from the amicus curiae brief filed in *Terry v. Ohio*:

> In the litigation now before the Court—as is usual in cases where police practices are challenged—two parties essentially are represented. Law enforcement officers, legal representatives of their respective States, ask the Court to broaden police powers, and thereby to sustain what has proved to be a "good pinch." Criminal defendants caught with the goods through what in retrospect appears to be at least shrewd and successful (albeit constitutionally questionable) police work ask the Court to declare that work illegal and to reverse their convictions. Other parties intimately affected by the issues before the Court are not represented. The many thousands of our citizens who have been or may

be stopped and frisked yearly, only to be released when the police find them innocent of any crime, are not represented. The records of their cases are not before the Court and cannot be brought here. Yet it is they, far more than those charged with crime, who will bear the consequences of the rules of constitutional law which this Court establishes. The determination of the quantum of "belief" or "suspicion" required to justify the exercise of intrusive police authority is precisely the determination of how far afield from instances of obvious guilt the authority stretches. To lower that quantum is to broaden the police net and, concomitantly, to increase the number (and probably the proportion) of innocent people caught up in it. The innocent are those this Court will never see. (Kurland and Casper 1975)

10. What's the point the brief makes? What's the importance of the point?

11. During oral arguments of the case before the Supreme Court, Louis Stokes, Terry's lawyer, revealed some of what happened at the suppression hearing. Stokes said, among other things, that Officer McFadden testified that he did not know the men, that they walked normally, that they were standing in front of a store talking normally, and that they were facing away from the store windows. When asked why he approached Terry, Chilton, and Katz, Officer McFadden replied, "Because... I didn't like them." Is this testimony important? Also, McFadden was white and Terry and Chilton were black. Is this important?

THE REST OF THE STORY

Terry v. Ohio

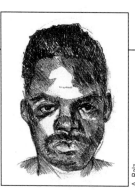

A. Balz

HONORABLE MICHAEL R. JUVILER

After the Terry opinions were filed, we felt perhaps like the makers of the hydrogen bomb. What had we created? What had we contributed to? Would this lead to further racial divisions, police abuse, police "testilying [police perjury]"? (*St. Johns Law Review* 1998, 741)

Judge Juviler was a prosecutor in 1968. He argued in favor of the power to stop and frisk in a New York case argued before the U.S. Supreme Court at the same time that *Terry v. Ohio* was heard.

RICHARD D. CHILTON, DEFENDANT

Richard Chilton, a black male, was 26 years old when his case went to trial in 1964. According to his own testimony, he had some prior work experience as a printer and had moved from Chicago to Cleveland in 1962. Chilton had no criminal record until he was arrested by Detective McFadden on October 31, 1963. He was convicted of carrying a concealed weapon in the 1964 bench trial that is transcribed here. He served a 13-month sentence in the Ohio State Reformatory for this conviction. The U.S. Supreme Court granted Chilton and Terry's petition for a writ of certiorari on May 29, 1967. A few weeks later, Chilton was killed during a shootout that erupted as he and three other armed men attempted to rob a drugstore in Columbus, Ohio.

JOHN W. TERRY, DEFENDANT

John Terry, a black male, was a heroin addict with a criminal record. Following his conviction in 1964 for carrying a concealed weapon in this case, Terry was sentenced to prison, served his time, and then was paroled. In August 1966, Terry was arrested again, this time for possession of heroin. While his gun case was pending in the U.S. Supreme Court, and while he faced return to the state penitentiary for violating his parole, Terry was confined in State Hospital for the criminally insane at Lima, Ohio, because he was a heroin addict. The last we know of John Terry is that on May 7, 1990, he was arrested for breaking into a pharmacy in West Virginia. His attorney, Louis Stokes, said this of him:

> I knew Terry from his hanging around with another person whom I represented, a fellow by the name of Billy Cox. Billy Cox was a rather notorious individual around

Cleveland. I represented Billy Cox in a couple of murder cases and knew Terry from his hanging around Billy Cox, because Terry liked to be around the more notorious type of individuals in the community. After his arrest, Terry called me. I went down to see him, and he asked me if I would represent both him and Chilton. Both of them were able at that time to retain me. Later on, it was determined they were both really indigent. Not only could they not afford me, they could not afford to take this case up to the United States Supreme Court. (*St. Johns Law Review* 1998, 727)

DETECTIVE MARTIN J. MCFADDEN, CLEVELAND POLICE DEPARTMENT

Martin McFadden, a white male, was born in Cleveland. After attending high school and working as a Cleveland Railway Company timekeeper, he joined the Cleveland Police Department in 1925. In 1930, McFadden was promoted to the detective bureau. He joined its fraud unit in 1934, where he specialized in detecting pickpockets and other perpetrators of frauds against Cleveland's downtown department stores. As a tribute to his years of service, he was selected to be Cleveland's representative to the security force at the inaugurations of Presidents Eisenhower (in 1957), Kennedy, Johnson, and Nixon (in 1969). Detective McFadden retired, after forty-six years on the job, in 1970.

Although McFadden's arrests of Terry and Chilton on Halloween 1963 produced the most notable court decision of the detective's career, he was more famous in Cleveland during his lifetime for his frequent arrests of Louis "Louie the Dip" Finkelstein, one of the city's most notorious pickpockets. "I remember four straight years I arrested Louie at the Ice Capades," recalls Marty. "In those days all we had to do was see Louis in a crowd and we arrested him." Finkelstein called McFadden "the persecutor."

Detective McFadden was happy with the decision in *Terry v. Ohio*. "I knew I was right, and I was, because the U.S. Supreme Court in Washington said I was." Martin McFadden died of cancer in 1981.

Thirty years after *Terry v. Ohio*, Louis Stokes, Terry and Chilton's lawyer, reminisced about McFadden:

I think I need to take a couple of minutes to talk about Detective McFadden. He was a real character—a tall, stately guy, and basically a good policeman. "Mac," as we called him, was really a guy that we really liked. He was straight. One thing about him—as a police officer, he came straight down the line. You did not have to worry about him misrepresenting what the facts were. He would come straight down the line, and as a defense lawyer I could appreciate that.

When I put him on as my witness on the motion to suppress, I, of course, did not know what he would say. All I could rely upon was what my clients had told me. I could not believe his testimony as it came out of his mouth on the stand. He said to us that he had seen these two fellows standing across the street from him, and he described them as being two Negroes, and then he talked of the white fellow who came up to them and talked with them. Then he went on down the street. Mac then admitted to us they weren't doing anything, except one of the black fellows would leave the other one, walk down the street a little bit, turn around, peer into the window at either the United Airlines or the jewelry store window, then walk back up to where the other fellow was. Then the other fellow would take a walk in a similar manner.

He was asked specifically what attracted him to them. On one occasion he said, "Well, to tell the truth, I just didn't like 'em." He was asked how long he'd been a police officer. "39 years." How long had he been a detective? "35 years." What did he think they were doing? "Well," he said, "I suspected that they were casing a joint for the purpose of robbing it." "Well," he was asked, "have you ever in your 39 years as a police officer, 35 as a detective, had the opportunity to observe anybody casing a place for a stickup?" He said, "No, I haven't." "Have you ever arrested anybody for that purpose?" "No, I haven't." "Then what attracted you to them?" He indicated he just didn't like them. He suspected they might be up to a stickup. That also is the reason why he thought they might have guns. (*St. Johns Law Review* 1998, 741)

Reuben Payne, who prosecuted Terry, remembered McFadden differently:

Detective McFadden…was an exceptional police officer. He had been on the force for thirty-nine years at the time of the Terry incident. I do not recall a case that McFadden brought to the court wherein the matter was thrown out or the defendant acquitted. There were many arrests and convictions in the performance of his job. He had an ability to enunciate the facts, describe clearly what took place, and was renowned for the number of arrests and convictions made in the performance of his duty. He had a keen sense of intuition…McFadden was an exceptional, outstanding police officer.

McFadden had been on the force thirty-nine years. He was on duty when he observed two men on Euclid Avenue. The streets were crowded and McFadden, true enough, testified, "I didn't like them." Knowing McFadden, that statement had not one single thing to do with their race. It had to do with his previous observations studying people in general, as well as people who commit crimes and people who are involved in criminal activity. His statement referred to the classification of people which his duty called for him to be on the look-out for when he said he didn't like them. (*St. Johns Law Review* 1998, 733)

REUBEN M. PAYNE, ASSISTANT COUNTY PROSECUTOR

Reuben Payne, a black male, was born in Scio, Ohio, in 1922. A World War II veteran, he served in the U.S. Army in North Africa, Sicily, and Italy. Payne worked his way through Western Reserve University at the Cleveland Transit System, and in 1953, graduated with honors from Cleveland-Marshall College of Law. He then worked as a state parole officer, at the U.S. General Accounting Office, as assistant law librarian at Cleveland-Marshall, and in private legal practice. He was also an active member of the NAACP.

After running unsuccessfully to become an Ohio state senator and later for state representative, Payne became an assistant county prosecutor in Cuyahoga County, Ohio, in 1957. In 1962, Ohio Governor Michael DiSalle appointed Payne to serve on the State Personnel Board of Review, where he was one of three board members who heard appeals by civil service employees and reviewed civil service job reclassification requests.

By early 1964, Payne had returned to the Cuyahoga County Prosecutor's Office. By chance, he was assigned to prosecute Terry and Chilton. Payne successfully opposed their pretrial motions to suppress the gun (Terry and Chilton argued that McFadden's stop and frisk violated the Fourth Amendment and that *Mapp v. Ohio* [excerpted in Chapter 10] required the court to throw out the gun as evidence). Payne then obtained convictions and prison sentences for Chilton and Terry at their trial without a jury before Judge Bernard Friedman. Later, he successfully defended Chilton's and Terry's convictions and sentences in the Ohio Court of Appeals, in the Ohio Supreme Court, and after Chilton's death, Terry's conviction and sentence in the U.S. Supreme Court.

In early 1968, after fourteen years in public service, during which he was active in Democratic Party politics and ran for election to Cleveland's city council and to the trial court bench in Cuyahoga County, Payne left government and became one of Cleveland's leading criminal defense attorneys. He relocated to Arizona in 1975 and now is retired.

LOUIS STOKES, DEFENSE ATTORNEY

Louis Stokes, a black male, who was born in 1925, attended Western Reserve University and received his law degree from the Cleveland-Marshall College of Law in 1953. He became a member of Stokes,

Stokes, Character, & Terry law firm and was one of Cleveland's leading criminal defense lawyers. In late 1963, he agreed to defend Richard Chilton and John Terry against charges that they had been carrying concealed weapons illegally when they were stopped and frisked by Detective McFadden. Stokes represented them at trial and on appeal, including in the U.S. Supreme Court.

In 1967, Stokes helped his younger brother Carl B. Stokes win election as mayor of Cleveland. The next year, within months of the Supreme Court's *Terry* decision, Louis Stokes was elected to represent Ohio's 21st Congressional District in the U.S. House of Representatives. He was reelected to Congress fourteen times. Representative Stokes decided not to seek reelection in 1998.

JUDGE BERNARD FRIEDMAN, TRIAL JUDGE

Bernard Friedman, a white male, was born in Poland in 1909. He immigrated with his family to the United States as a child. He graduated from a Cleveland high school and, in 1931, from Ohio State University. After obtaining his law degree from Western Reserve School of Law in 1934, Friedman served in a variety of public positions. In 1936, he was special counsel to the attorney general of the state of Ohio. From 1937 to 1938, he was a Public Works Administration attorney in Chicago and Columbus. He served from 1950 to 1960, on a part-time basis, as city appraiser in Cleveland's law department. His private law practice focused on labor negotiations, including many years representing the Cleveland transit employees' union. From 1959 to 1963, he was Cuyahoga County's deputy registrar of motor vehicles. He was appointed to the Cuyahoga County, Court of Common Pleas in 1963 and was assigned to try the Chilton and Terry cases the following year.

In 1968, Judge Friedman said that he was "very pleased" by the Supreme Court's *Terry* decision, which affirmed his denial of the motions to suppress the gun as evidence in the original trial. But Judge Friedman stressed that he did not approve of unlimited power to stop and frisk:

> The court's decision gives police a vehicle through which to properly stop and search a suspicious person. In the [Chilton and Terry] trial, I limited this right to stopping and searching for weapons. This is necessary for the protection of the officer when he is acting on the basis of his experience and there is strong suspicion of wrongdoing. I don't believe there should be indiscriminate frisking for other contraband and I so indicated in this case. (*St. Johns Law Review* 1998, 727)

Judge Friedman was elected to a six-year term in 1964 and reelected in 1970 and 1976. He also was appointed by Ohio's governor in 1971 to chair a citizens' task force that investigated conditions in Ohio's seven adult prisons. Judge Friedman, who served on Cuyahoga County's trial court bench until 1983, died in 1987. Terry's defense attorney, Louis Stokes, remembered the following about him:

Judge Friedman was very liberal, a civil libertarian type of judge. He also was a very courageous type of judge.

If he agreed with you that the law was on your side, whether you were against the police or anyone else, he would have the guts to throw that case out and do whatever was right by your client. So I didn't hesitate to try a case before Judge Bernie Friedman. He was a well-respected, highly regarded judge. I tried several other matters before him where I had these types of facts, and he had always come right down the line. So I knew that if I had any chance at all, my best chance was with Judge Bernie Friedman.

St. Johns Law Review 1998, 727

STOPS AND THE FOURTH AMENDMENT

Beginning with *Terry v. Ohio*, the framework for analyzing police encounters with individuals can be divided into three categories (Table 4.1):

1. *Voluntary encounters.* Fall outside the Fourth Amendment—that is, "communication between police and individuals involving no coercion or detection"
2. *Stops.* Brief "seizures" that require reasonable suspicion to back them up
3. *Arrests.* Longer detentions in police stations that require probable cause to justify them (see earlier Figure 4.1) (Chapter 5)

We've already examined the difference between voluntary encounters with the police (which are left to police discretion) and the two kinds of stops to investigate suspicious persons and circumstances that qualify as Fourth Amendment seizures (see Chapter 3, actual-seizure and show-of-authority stops). Remember, the first question in the three-step analysis of Fourth Amendment seizures is, "Was the police action a stop?" If it wasn't, then the Fourth Amendment doesn't apply at all, and the analysis stops. But, if the action was a stop, then the analysis proceeds to answering the question in step 2, "Was the stop *reasonable*?" What's a reasonable stop? It depends on two elements:

1. Does the objective basis for the stop add up to reasonable suspicion?
2. Are the requirements of the "scope of the stop" met?
   a. Duration is short
   b. Location of investigation is at the scene of the stop

According to *Terry*, as long as officers have nameable facts amounting to reasonable suspicion, officers can "freeze" suspicious people and situations in time and space. But, the freeze can last only long enough (duration) either to get enough information to arrest suspects or to let them go. And, it has to take place (location) on the spot or very near the place where the stop took place. How many facts are enough to add up to reasonable suspicion? How long is "only long enough"; or, in Fourth Amendment terms, how long is reasonable? And, exactly what is "on the spot"? Or, how far, if any distance at all, is it reasonable for officers to move suspects from the spot? Let's try to answer these questions by looking at the objective basis for reasonable suspicion and the scope of the **reasonableness test of Fourth Amendment stops.**

TABLE 4.1		
Three Kinds of Encounters Between Officers and Individuals		
Voluntary Encounters	**Stops**	**Arrests**
Encounters without force or coercion	Brief (usually measured in minutes) involuntary seizures in public places	Longer (usually measured in hours) involuntary detentions (usually in police stations)
Fourth Amendment doesn't apply	Fourth Amendment requires reasonable suspicion	Fourth Amendment requires probable cause

Reasonable Suspicion

The U.S. Supreme Court in *Terry v. Ohio* called the objective basis for a stop "articulable facts" that showed "criminal activity may be afoot." Simply put, **articulable facts** are facts we can name. In *Terry*, the nameable facts included Officer McFadden's direct observation of Terry and Chilton pacing up and down and peering into a store window in downtown Cleveland. Seeing this aroused his suspicion that the three men were "casing" the store and were about to rob it. The *Terry* Court never used the words **reasonable suspicion**, but that's the name the Court now gives to the articulable facts required to back up Fourth Amendment stops.

Reasonable suspicion refers to the totality of articulable facts and circumstances that would lead an officer to *suspect* that crime *may* be afoot. (Notice the emphasis on "suspect" and "may" in contrast to the definition of *arrest*, which requires officers to *believe* that crime *is* afoot [Chapter 5]). The totality-of-facts-and-circumstances test—usually called just the **totality-of-circumstances test**—is a favorite standard the Court applies to decide whether official actions are constitutional. (You'll notice this as we work our way through the rest of the book.) It might help you to call the test the **whole picture test,** an idea of Chief Justice Warren Burger's, who wrote that the "essence" of reasonable suspicion is "that the totality of circumstances—the whole picture—must be taken into account. Based upon that whole picture, the detaining officers must have a particularized and objective basis for suspecting the particular person stopped of criminal activity." What appears innocent to the untrained and inexperienced person may well look suspicious to trained officers with practical experience. Officers are entitled to view the whole picture (the totality of facts and circumstances) in the light of their experience and training, and courts have to take their trained and experienced view into account when they decide whether officers' suspicions were reasonable. In this section, we'll look more closely at the two main types of information officers can rely on to build reasonable suspicion: direct and hearsay information. We'll also look at two other, more controversial, factors the courts say can be considered in meeting the totality-of-circumstances test: race and profiles.

Direct Information

There are two kinds of facts officers can rely on to build reasonable suspicion:

1. *Direct information*. Facts officers learn firsthand from what they themselves see, hear, smell, and touch

2. *Hearsay information*. Facts officers learn secondhand from what victims, witnesses, other police officers, and anonymous, professional, or paid informants tell them they've seen, heard, smelled, and felt

TABLE 4.2

Direct and Hearsay Bases for Reasonable Suspicion

Direct Information	Hearsay
Flight	Victim statement
Furtive movement	Eyewitness statement
Hiding	Fellow officer statement
Resisting an officer	Informant statement
Attempting to destroy evidence	Anonymous tip
Evasive answers	
Contradictory answers	
Weapons or contraband in plain view	

TABLE 4.3

Reasons Insufficient by Themselves to Amount to Reasonable Suspicion

1. General suspicion that drug dealing went on in a tavern. *Ybarra v. Illinois*, 444 U.S. 85 (1979)
2. Driver double-parked within 10 feet of a pedestrian in a drug-trafficking location. *Rivera v. Murphy*, 979 F.2d 259 (1st Cir. 1992)
3. Other bar patrons, not the one detained, possessed weapons and contraband. *U.S. v. Jaramillo*, 25 F.3d 1146 (2d Cir. 1994)
4. Passenger leaving airplane appeared nervous in the presence of officers. *U.S. v. Caicedo*, 85 F.3d 1184 (6th Cir. 1996)
5. Driver of a car with out-of-state license plates and no noticeable luggage avoided eye contact with a police car. *U.S. v. Halls*, 40 F.3d 275 (8th Cir. 1995)
6. "Hispanic-looking" males in a heavy truck near the border looked nervous, did not acknowledge police presence, and drove faster than the flow of traffic. *U.S. v. Garcia-Camacho*, 53 F.3d 244 (9th Cir. 1995)
7. Generalized suspicion of criminal activity in a high-crime neighborhood. *Brown v. Texas*, 443 U.S. 47 (1979)
8. Nervous man traveling alone who left an airline terminal quickly after picking up one suitcase and had a one-way ticket that he had bought with cash from a drug-source city. *U.S. v. Lambert*, 46 F.3d 1064 (10th Cir. 1995)
9. Driver failed to look at patrol car late at night. *U.S. v. Smith*. 799 F.2d 704 (11th Cir. 1986)
10. "Mexican-appearing" person, driving a car with out-of-state license plates and no suitcases, appeared nervous in talking with officers during discussion of a speeding ticket. *U.S. v. Tapia*, 912 F.2d 1367 (11th Cir. 1990)

Direct information consists of facts and circumstances that the officer knows firsthand. These facts and circumstances include flight, furtive movements, hiding, attempts to destroy evidence, resisting officers, evasive answers, contradictory explanations, fingerprints, hair samples, blood samples, and DNA information. Table 4.2 elaborates on direct and hearsay bases for reasonable suspicion; Table 4.3 lists factors the courts have ruled insufficient by themselves to demonstrate reasonable suspicion.

In *Illinois v. Wardlow* (2000), the U.S. Supreme Court decided whether police officers' firsthand observation of a suspect running away from them in a high-crime neighborhood amounted to reasonable suspicion to stop him.

Illinois v. Wardlow
528 U.S. 119 (2000)

William "Sam" Wardlow (respondent) was arrested and charged with unlawful use of a weapon by a felon. The Illinois trial court denied his motion to suppress. Wardlow was convicted. The Illinois Appellate Court reversed. The Illinois Supreme Court affirmed. The U.S. Supreme Court granted certiorari and reversed.

REHNQUIST, CJ., joined by O'CONNOR, SCALIA, KENNEDY, and THOMAS, JJ.

FACTS

On September 9, 1995, Officers Nolan and Harvey were working as uniformed officers in the special operations section of the Chicago Police Department. The officers were driving the last car of a four-car caravan converging on an area known for heavy narcotics trafficking in order to investigate drug transactions. The officers were traveling together because they expected to find a crowd of people in the area, including lookouts and customers.

As the caravan passed 4035 West Van Buren, Officer Nolan observed respondent Wardlow standing next to the building holding an opaque bag. Wardlow looked in the direction of the officers and fled. Nolan and Harvey turned their car southbound, watched him as he ran through the gangway and an alley, and eventually cornered him on the street. Nolan then exited his car and stopped Wardlow. He immediately conducted a protective pat-down search for weapons because in his experience it was common for there to be weapons in the near vicinity of narcotics transactions. During the frisk, Officer Nolan squeezed the bag Wardlow was carrying and felt a heavy, hard object similar to the shape of a gun. The officer then opened the bag and discovered a .38-caliber handgun with five live rounds of ammunition. The officers arrested Wardlow.

The Illinois trial court denied Wardlow's motion to suppress, finding the gun was recovered during a lawful stop and frisk. Following a stipulated bench trial, Wardlow was convicted of unlawful use of a weapon by a felon. The Illinois Appellate Court reversed Wardlow's conviction, concluding that the gun should have been suppressed because Officer Nolan did not have reasonable suspicion sufficient to justify an investigative stop pursuant to *Terry v. Ohio*.

The Illinois Supreme Court agreed. While rejecting the Appellate Court's conclusion that Wardlow was not in a high crime area, the Illinois Supreme Court determined that sudden flight in such an area does not create a reasonable suspicion justifying a *Terry* stop.... The court explained that although police have the right to approach individuals and ask questions, the individual has no obligation to respond. The person may decline to answer and simply go on his or her way, and the refusal to respond, alone, does not provide a legitimate basis for an investigative stop. The court then determined that flight may simply be an exercise of this right to "go on one's way," and, thus, could not constitute reasonable suspicion justifying a *Terry* stop.

The Illinois Supreme Court also rejected the argument that flight combined with the fact that it occurred in a high crime area supported a finding of reasonable suspicion because the "high crime area" factor was not sufficient standing alone to justify a *Terry* stop. Finding no independently suspicious circumstances to support an investigatory detention, the court held that the stop and subsequent arrest violated the Fourth Amendment. We granted certiorari, and now reverse.

OPINION

In *Terry v. Ohio*, we held that an officer may... conduct a brief, investigatory stop when the officer has a reasonable, articulable suspicion that criminal activity is afoot. While "reasonable suspicion" is a less demanding standard than probable cause and requires a showing considerably less than preponderance of the evidence, the Fourth Amendment requires at least a minimal level of objective justification for making the stop. The officer must be able to articulate more than an "inchoate and unparticularized suspicion or hunch" of criminal activity.

Nolan and Harvey were among eight officers in a four-car caravan that was converging on an area known for heavy narcotics trafficking, and the officers anticipated encountering a large number of people in the area, including drug customers and individuals serving as lookouts. It was in this context that Officer Nolan decided to investigate Wardlow after observing him flee. An individual's presence in an area of expected criminal activity, standing alone, is not enough to support a reasonable, particularized suspicion that the person is committing a crime. But officers are not required to ignore the relevant characteristics of a location in determining whether the circumstances are sufficiently suspicious to warrant further investigation. Accordingly, we have previously noted the stop occurred in a "high crime area" among the relevant contextual considerations in a *Terry* analysis. *Adams v. Williams* (1972).

In this case, moreover, it was not merely Wardlow's presence in an area of heavy narcotics trafficking that aroused the officers' suspicion but his unprovoked flight upon noticing the police. Our cases have also recognized that nervous, evasive behavior is a pertinent factor in determining reasonable suspicion. Headlong flight—wherever it occurs—is the consummate act of evasion: it is not necessarily indicative of wrongdoing, but it is certainly suggestive of such. In reviewing the propriety of an officer's conduct, courts do not have available empirical studies dealing with inferences drawn from suspicious behavior, and we cannot reasonably demand scientific certainty from judges or law enforcement officers where none exists. Thus, the determination of reasonable suspicion must be based on commonsense judgments and inferences about human behavior. We conclude Officer Nolan was justified in suspecting that Wardlow was involved in criminal activity, and, therefore, in investigating further.

Such a holding is entirely consistent with our decision in *Florida v. Royer* (1983), where we held that when an officer, without reasonable suspicion or probable cause, approaches an individual, the individual has a right to ignore the police and go about his business. And any "refusal to cooperate, without more, does not furnish the minimal level of objective justification needed for a detention or seizure." But unprovoked flight is simply not a mere refusal to cooperate. Flight, by its very nature, is not "going about one's business"; in fact, it is just the opposite. Allowing officers confronted with such flight to stop the fugitive and investigate further is quite consistent with the individual's right to go about his business or to stay put and remain silent in the face of police questioning.

Wardlow and amici* also argue that there are innocent reasons for flight from police and that, therefore, flight is not necessarily indicative of ongoing criminal activity. This fact is undoubtedly true, but does not establish a violation of the Fourth Amendment. Even in *Terry*, the conduct justifying the stop was ambiguous and susceptible of an innocent explanation. The officer observed two individuals pacing back and forth in front of a store, peering into the window and periodically conferring. All of this conduct was by itself lawful, but it also suggested that the individuals were casing the store for a planned robbery. *Terry* recognized that the officers could detain the individuals to resolve the ambiguity.

In allowing such detentions, *Terry* accepts the risk that officers may stop innocent people. Indeed, the Fourth Amendment accepts that risk in connection with more drastic police action; persons arrested and detained on probable cause to believe they have committed a crime may turn out to be innocent. The *Terry* stop is a far more minimal intrusion, simply allowing the officer to briefly investigate further. If the officer does not learn facts rising to the level of probable cause, the individual must be allowed to go on his way. But in this case the officers found Wardlow in possession of a handgun, and arrested him for violation of an Illinois firearms statute. . . .

The judgment of the Supreme Court of Illinois is reversed, and the cause is remanded for further proceedings not inconsistent with this opinion. It is so ordered.

CONCURRING AND DISSENTING OPINIONS

STEVENS, J., joined by SOUTER, GINSBURG, and BREYER, JJ., concurring in part and dissenting in part. The State of Illinois asks this Court to announce a "bright-line rule" authorizing the temporary detention of anyone who flees at the mere sight of a police officer. Wardlow counters by asking us to adopt the opposite per se rule—that the fact that a person flees upon seeing the police can never, by itself, be sufficient to justify a temporary investigative stop of the kind authorized by *Terry v. Ohio*. The Court today wisely endorses neither per se rule. Instead, it rejects the proposition that "flight is . . . necessarily indicative of ongoing criminal activity," adhering to the view that "the concept of reasonable suspicion . . . is not readily, or even usefully, reduced to a neat set of legal rules," but must be determined by looking to "the totality of the circumstances—the whole picture." Abiding by this framework, the Court concludes that "Officer Nolan was justified in suspecting that Wardlow was involved in criminal activity."

Although I agree with the Court's rejection of the per se rules proffered by the parties, unlike the Court, I am persuaded that in this case the brief testimony of the officer who seized Wardlow does not justify the conclusion that he had reasonable suspicion to make the stop. . . .

The question in this case concerns "the degree of suspicion that attaches to" a person's flight—or, more precisely, what "commonsense conclusions" can be drawn respecting the motives behind that flight. . . .**

---

*These are briefs filed with the permission of the Court by those who are interested in the case but not parties to it.

**Compare, e.g., Proverbs 28:1 ("The wicked flee when no man pursueth: but the righteous are as bold as a lion") with Proverbs 22:3 ("A shrewd man sees trouble coming and lies low; the simple walk into it and pay the penalty"). I have rejected reliance on the former proverb in the past, because its "ivory-towered analysis of the real world" fails to account for the experiences of many citizens of this country, particularly those who are minorities. That this pithy expression fails to capture the total reality of our world, however, does not mean it is inaccurate in all instances.

Given the diversity and frequency of possible motivations for flight, it would be profoundly unwise to endorse either per se rule. The inference we can reasonably draw about the motivation for a person's flight, rather, will depend on a number of different circumstances. Factors such as the time of day, the number of people in the area, the character of the neighborhood, whether the officer was in uniform, the way the runner was dressed, the direction and speed of the flight, and whether the person's behavior was otherwise unusual might be relevant in specific cases. This number of variables is surely sufficient to preclude either a bright-line rule that always justifies, or that never justifies, an investigative stop based on the sole fact that flight began after a police officer appeared nearby.

Still, Illinois presses for a per se rule regarding "unprovoked flight upon seeing a clearly identifiable police officer." The phrase "upon seeing," as used by Illinois, apparently assumes that the flight is motivated by the presence of the police officer.*

Even assuming we know that a person runs because he sees the police, the inference to be drawn may still vary from case to case. Flight to escape police detection ... may have an entirely innocent motivation:

It is a matter of common knowledge that men who are entirely innocent do sometimes fly from the scene of a crime through fear of being apprehended as the guilty parties, or from an unwillingness to appear as witnesses. Nor is it true as an accepted axiom of criminal law that "the wicked flee when no man pursueth, but the righteous are as bold as a lion." Innocent men sometimes hesitate to confront a jury—not necessarily because they fear that the jury will not protect them, but because they do not wish their names to appear in connection with criminal acts, are humiliated at being

obliged to incur the popular odium of an arrest and trial, or because they do not wish to be put to the annoyance or expense of defending themselves. *Alberty v. United States,* 162 U. S. 499, 511 (1896).

In addition to these concerns, a reasonable person may conclude that an officer's sudden appearance indicates nearby criminal activity. And where there is criminal activity there is also a substantial element of danger—either from the criminal or from a confrontation between the criminal and the police. These considerations can lead to an innocent and understandable desire to quit the vicinity with all speed.

Among some citizens, particularly minorities and those residing in high crime areas, there is also the possibility that the fleeing person is entirely innocent, but, with or without justification, believes that contact with the police can itself be dangerous, apart from any criminal activity associated with the officer's sudden presence....**

For such a person, unprovoked flight is neither "aberrant" nor "abnormal."...†

Many stops never lead to an arrest, which further exacerbates the perceptions of discrimination felt by racial minorities and people living in high crime areas....‡

Even if these data were race neutral, they would still indicate that society as a whole is paying a significant cost in infringement on liberty by these virtually random stops.

Moreover, these concerns and fears are known to the police officers themselves, and are validated by law enforcement investigations into their own practices....

---

*I have rejected reliance on the former proverb in the past, because its "ivory-towered analysis of the real world" fails to account for the experiences of many citizens of this country, particularly those who are minorities....

[Note: Nowhere in Illinois' briefs does it specify what it means by "unprovoked." At oral argument, Illinois explained that if officers precipitate a flight by threats of violence, that flight is "provoked." But if police officers in a patrol car—with lights flashing and siren sounding—descend upon an individual for the sole purpose of seeing if he or she will run, the ensuing flight is "unprovoked."] Illinois contends that unprovoked flight is "an extreme reaction," because innocent people simply do not "flee at the mere sight of the police." To be sure, Illinois concedes, an innocent person—even one distrustful of the police—might "avoid eye contact or even sneer at the sight of an officer," and that would not justify a *Terry* stop or any sort of per se inference. But, Illinois insists, unprovoked flight is altogether different. Such behavior is so "aberrant" and "abnormal" that a per se inference is justified.

**See Casimir, Minority Men: We Are Frisk Targets, *N.Y. Daily News,* Mar. 26, 1999, p. 34 (informal survey of 100 young black and Hispanic men living in New York City; 81 reported having been stopped and frisked by police at least once; none of the 81 stops resulted in arrests); Brief for NAACP Legal Defense & Educational Fund as Amicus Curiae 17–19 (reporting figures on disproportionate street stops of minority residents in Pittsburgh and Philadelphia, Pennsylvania, and St. Petersburg, Florida); U.S. Dept. of Justice, Bureau of Justice Statistics, S. Smith, Criminal Victimization and Perceptions of Community Safety in 12 Cities 25 (June 1998) (African-American residents in 12 cities are more than twice as likely to be dissatisfied with police practices than white residents in same community).

†See, e.g., Kotlowitz, Hidden Casualties: Drug War's Emphasis on Law Enforcement Takes a Toll on Police, *Wall Street Journal,* Jan. 11, 1991 ("Black leaders complained that innocent people were picked up in the drug sweeps.... Some teen-agers were so scared of the task force they ran even if they weren't selling drugs.").

‡See Goldberg, "The Color of Suspicion," *N.Y. Times Magazine,* June 20, 1999, (reporting that in a 2-year period, New York City Police Department Street Crimes Unit made 45,000 stops, only 9,500, or 20%, of which resulted in arrest); Casimir (reporting that in 1997, New York City's Street Crimes Unit conducted 27,061 stop-and-frisks, only 4,647 of which, 17%, resulted in arrest).

...The Massachusetts Attorney General investigated... allegations of egregious police conduct toward minorities. The report stated:

> Perhaps the most disturbing evidence was that the scope of a number of *Terry* searches went far beyond anything authorized by that case and indeed, beyond anything that we believe would be acceptable under the federal and state constitutions even where probable cause existed to conduct a full search incident to an arrest. Forcing young men to lower their trousers, or otherwise searching inside their underwear, on public streets or in public hallways, is so demeaning and invasive of fundamental precepts of privacy that it can only be condemned in the strongest terms. The fact that not only the young men themselves, but independent witnesses complained of strip searches, should be deeply alarming to all members of this community.

Accordingly, the evidence supporting the reasonableness of these beliefs is too pervasive to be dismissed as random or rare, and too persuasive to be disparaged as inconclusive or insufficient. In any event, just as we do not require "scientific certainty" for our commonsense conclusion that unprovoked flight can sometimes indicate suspicious motives, neither do we require scientific certainty to conclude that unprovoked flight can occur for other, innocent reasons....

"Unprovoked flight," in short, describes a category of activity too broad and varied to permit a per se reasonable inference regarding the motivation for the activity. While the innocent explanations surely do not establish that the Fourth Amendment is always violated whenever someone is stopped solely on the basis of an unprovoked flight, neither do the suspicious motivations establish that the Fourth Amendment is never violated when a *Terry* stop is predicated on that fact alone....

Guided by that totality-of-the-circumstances test, the Court concludes that Officer Nolan had reasonable suspicion to stop respondent. In this respect, my view differs from the Court's. The entire justification for the stop is articulated in the brief testimony of Officer Nolan. Some facts are perfectly clear; others are not. This factual insufficiency leads me to conclude that the Court's judgment is mistaken.

Wardlow was arrested a few minutes after noon on September 9, 1995. Nolan was part of an eight-officer, four-car caravan patrol team. The officers were headed for "one of the areas in the 11th District [of Chicago] that's high [in] narcotics traffic." The reason why four cars were in the caravan was that "normally in these different areas there's an enormous amount of people, sometimes lookouts, customers." Officer Nolan testified that he was in uniform on

that day, but he did not recall whether he was driving a marked or an unmarked car.

Officer Nolan and his partner were in the last of the four patrol cars that "were all caravaning eastbound down Van Buren." Nolan first observed respondent "in front of 4035 West Van Buren." Wardlow "looked in our direction and began fleeing." Nolan then "began driving southbound down the street observing [respondent] running through the gangway and the alley southbound," and observed that Wardlow was carrying a white, opaque bag under his arm. After the car turned south and intercepted respondent as he "ran right towards us," Officer Nolan stopped him and conducted a "protective search," which revealed that the bag under respondent's arm contained a loaded handgun.

This terse testimony is most noticeable for what it fails to reveal. Though asked whether he was in a marked or unmarked car, Officer Nolan could not recall the answer. He was not asked whether any of the other three cars in the caravan were marked, or whether any of the other seven officers were in uniform. Though he explained that the size of the caravan was because "normally in these different areas there's an enormous amount of people, sometimes lookouts, customers," Officer Nolan did not testify as to whether anyone besides Wardlow was nearby 4035 West Van Buren. Nor is it clear that that address was the intended destination of the caravan. As the Appellate Court of Illinois interpreted the record, "it appears that the officers were simply driving by, on their way to some unidentified location, when they noticed defendant standing at 4035 West Van Buren." Officer Nolan's testimony also does not reveal how fast the officers were driving. It does not indicate whether he saw respondent notice the other patrol cars. And it does not say whether the caravan, or any part of it, had already passed Wardlow by before he began to run.

Indeed, the Appellate Court thought the record was even "too vague to support the inference that...defendant's flight was related to his expectation of police focus on him." Presumably, respondent did not react to the first three cars, and we cannot even be sure that he recognized the occupants of the fourth as police officers. The adverse inference is based entirely on the officer's statement: "He looked in our direction and began fleeing."

No other factors sufficiently support a finding of reasonable suspicion. Though respondent was carrying a white, opaque bag under his arm, there is nothing at all suspicious about that. Certainly the time of day—shortly after noon—does not support Illinois' argument. Nor were the officers "responding to any call or report of suspicious activity in the area." Officer Nolan did testify that he expected to find "an enormous amount of people," including drug customers or lookouts, and the Court points out that "[i]t was in this context that Officer Nolan decided to investigate Wardlow after observing him flee." This observation, in my view, lends insufficient weight to the reasonable suspicion analysis; indeed, in light of the absence of testimony that anyone else was nearby when respondent began to run, this observation points in the opposite direction.

The State, along with the majority of the Court, relies as well on the assumption that this flight occurred in a high crime area. Even if that assumption is accurate, it is insufficient because even in a high crime neighborhood unprovoked flight does not invariably lead to reasonable suspicion. On the contrary, because many factors providing innocent motivations for unprovoked flight are concentrated in high crime areas, the character of the neighborhood arguably makes an inference of guilt less appropriate, rather than more so. Like unprovoked flight itself, presence in a high crime neighborhood is a fact too generic and susceptible to innocent explanation to satisfy the reasonable suspicion inquiry.

It is the State's burden to articulate facts sufficient to support reasonable suspicion. In my judgment, Illinois has failed to discharge that burden. I am not persuaded that the mere fact that someone standing on a sidewalk looked in the direction of a passing car before starting to run is sufficient to justify a forcible stop and frisk.

I therefore respectfully DISSENT from the Court's judgment to reverse the court below.

◆ ◆ ◆

Questions

1. Identify the "articulable" facts Officer Nolan relied on to stop Wardlow.

2. List the Court's reasons for concluding these facts added up to reasonable suspicion.

3. Compare the facts Nolan possessed with those possessed by Officer McFadden in *Terry v. Ohio*. In your opinion, which officer had more articulable facts?

4. Even if one had more than the other, did they both have reasonable suspicion? Defend your answer.

5. Is reasonable suspicion enough of a safeguard to the right of all people, innocent and guilty, to come and go as they please? Defend your answer.

6. List and summarize the empirical evidence Justice Stevens includes in his dissenting opinion. Is the evidence reliable? Assuming the evidence is reliable, does it have anything to do with whether Nolan's stop and frisk of Wardlow was reasonable? Defend your answer.

Go to Exercise 4-1 on the Criminal Procedure 6e CD to learn more about reasonable suspicion.

Hearsay and Anonymous Tips

Remember, in *Terry v. Ohio* reasonable suspicion was based on Officer McFadden's firsthand observations. In 1968, when *Terry* was decided, those of us old enough to remember believed (wrongly) that reasonable suspicion *had* to be based on firsthand observations like McFadden's; hearsay information of informants wasn't good enough. Four years later, in an appeal in a habeas corpus action (see Chapters 1 and 14 on habeas corpus) *Adams, Warden, Connecticut State Prison v. Williams* (1972), the Court was faced with an officer who relied on an informant's hearsay to build reasonable suspicion. In that case, an informant walked up to Sergeant John Connelly and told him Robert Williams was sitting in a car nearby with heroin in his pocket and a gun at his waist. Officer Connelly knew the informant because he'd previously told him about criminal activity in the local railway station. The Court allowed the use of the hearsay and decided the informant's tip plus the time (2:00 A.M.) and the location (a high-crime neighborhood) added up to reasonable suspicion to stop Williams. So, officers can rely on secondhand information, or hearsay, either partly or completely. Officers usually get information secondhand through victims, witnesses, other police officers, and professional informants.

In *Williams,* Officer Connelly *knew* the informant (even though he never named him). But what about *anonymous* tips? Are they enough to add up to reasonable suspicion? In 2000, the Court answered this question in *Florida v. J.L.,* an illegal weapons possession case involving a juvenile.

| CASE | *Did the Anonymous Tip Add Up to Reasonable Suspicion?* |

Florida v. J.L.
529 U.S. 266 (2000)

J.L., Juvenile, being tried on weapons charge moved to suppress evidence. The Circuit Court of Dade County granted the motion, and the state appealed. The District Court of Appeal reversed. The Juvenile petitioned for review, and the Florida Supreme Court reversed the Court of Appeal. After granting the state's petition for certiorari, the Supreme Court affirmed the Florida Supreme Court.

GINSBURG, J., delivered the opinion for
a unanimous Court.

FACTS

On October 13, 1995, an anonymous caller reported to the Miami-Dade Police that a young black male standing at a particular bus stop and wearing a plaid shirt was carrying a gun. So far as the record reveals, there is no audio recording of the tip, and nothing is known about the informant. Sometime after the police received the tip—the record does not say how long—two officers were instructed to respond. They arrived at the bus stop about six minutes later and saw three black males "just hanging out [there]." One of the three, respondent J.L., was wearing a plaid shirt. Apart from the tip, the officers had no reason to suspect any of the three of illegal conduct. The officers did not see a firearm, and J.L. made no threatening or otherwise unusual movements. One of the officers approached J.L., told him to put his hands up on the bus stop, frisked him, and seized a gun from J.L.'s pocket. The second officer frisked the other two individuals, against whom no allegations had been made, and found nothing.

J.L., who was at the time of the frisk "10 days shy of his 16th birthday," was charged under state law with carrying a concealed firearm without a license and possessing a firearm while under the age of 18. He moved to suppress the gun as the fruit of an unlawful search, and the trial court granted his motion. The intermediate appellate court reversed, but the Supreme Court of Florida quashed that

decision and held the search invalid under the Fourth Amendment.

Anonymous tips, the Florida Supreme Court stated, are generally less reliable than tips from known informants and can form the basis for reasonable suspicion only if accompanied by specific indicia of reliability, for example, the correct forecast of a subject's "not easily predicted" movements. The tip leading to the frisk of J.L., the court observed, provided no such predictions, nor did it contain any other qualifying indicia of reliability. Two justices dissented. The safety of the police and the public, they maintained, justifies a "firearm exception" to the general rule barring investigatory stops and frisks on the basis of bare-boned anonymous tips.

Seeking review in this Court, the State of Florida noted that the decision of the State's Supreme Court conflicts with decisions of other courts declaring similar searches compatible with the Fourth Amendment. We granted certiorari, and now affirm the judgment of the Florida Supreme Court.

OPINION

. . . Officers' suspicion that J.L. was carrying a weapon arose not from any observations of their own but solely from a call made from an unknown location by an unknown caller. Unlike a tip from a known informant whose reputation can be assessed and who can be held responsible if her allegations turn out to be fabricated, an anonymous tip alone seldom demonstrates the informant's basis of knowledge or veracity. As we have recognized, however, there are situations in which an anonymous tip, suitably corroborated, exhibits "sufficient indicia of reliability to provide reasonable suspicion to make the investigatory stop." The question we here confront is whether the tip pointing to J.L. had those indicia of reliability.

In *Alabama v. White* (1990), the police received an anonymous tip asserting that a woman was carrying cocaine and predicting that she would leave an apartment building at a specified time, get into a car matching a particular description, and drive to a named motel. Standing alone, the tip would not have justified a *Terry* stop. Only after police observation showed that the informant had accurately predicted the woman's movements, we explained, did it become reasonable to think the tipster had inside knowledge about the suspect and therefore to credit his assertion about the cocaine. Although the Court held that the suspicion in *White* became reasonable after police surveillance, we regarded the case as borderline. Knowledge about a person's future movements indicates some familiarity with that person's affairs, but having such knowledge does not necessarily imply that the informant knows, in particular, whether that person is carrying hidden contraband. We accordingly classified *White* as a "close case."

The tip in the instant case lacked the moderate indicia of reliability present in *White* and essential to the Court's decision in that case. The anonymous call concerning J.L. provided no predictive information and therefore left the police without means to test the informant's knowledge or credibility. That the allegation about the gun turned out to be correct does not suggest that the officers, prior to the frisks, had a reasonable basis for suspecting J.L. of engaging in unlawful conduct: The reasonableness of official suspicion must be measured by what the officers knew before they conducted their search. All the police had to go on in this case was the bare report of an unknown, unaccountable informant who neither explained how he knew about the gun nor supplied any basis for believing he had inside information about J.L. If *White* was a close case on the reliability of anonymous tips, this one surely falls on the other side of the line.

Florida contends that the tip was reliable because its description of the suspect's visible attributes proved accurate: There really was a young black male wearing a plaid shirt at the bus stop. The United States as *amicus curiae* makes a similar argument, proposing that a stop and frisk should be permitted "when (1) an anonymous tip provides a description of a particular person at a particular location illegally carrying a concealed firearm, (2) police promptly verify the pertinent details of the tip except the existence of the firearm, and (3) there are no factors that cast doubt on the reliability of the tip...." These contentions misapprehend the reliability needed for a tip to justify a *Terry* stop.

An accurate description of a subject's readily observable location and appearance is of course reliable in this limited sense: It will help the police correctly identify the person whom the tipster means to accuse. Such a tip, however, does not show that the tipster has knowledge of concealed criminal activity. The reasonable suspicion here at issue requires that a tip be reliable in its assertion of illegality, not just in its tendency to identify a determinate person.

A second major argument advanced by Florida . . . is, in essence, that the standard *Terry* analysis should be modi-

fied to license a "firearm exception." Under such an exception, a tip alleging an illegal gun would justify a stop and frisk even if the accusation would fail standard pre-search reliability testing. We decline to adopt this position.

Firearms are dangerous, and extraordinary dangers sometimes justify unusual precautions. Our decisions recognize the serious threat that armed criminals pose to public safety; *Terry's* rule, which permits protective police searches on the basis of reasonable suspicion rather than demanding that officers meet the higher standard of probable cause, responds to this very concern. But an automatic firearm exception to our established reliability analysis would rove too far. Such an exception would enable any person seeking to harass another to set in motion an intrusive, embarrassing police search of the targeted person simply by placing an anonymous call falsely reporting the target's unlawful carriage of a gun. Nor could one securely confine such an exception to allegations involving firearms. Several Courts of Appeals have held it *per se* foreseeable for people carrying significant amounts of illegal drugs to be carrying guns as well. If police officers may properly conduct *Terry* frisks on the basis of bare-boned tips about guns, it would be reasonable to maintain under the above-cited decisions that the police should similarly have discretion to frisk based on bare-boned tips about narcotics. As we clarified when we made indicia of reliability critical in *Adams* and *White,* the Fourth Amendment is not so easily satisfied.*

The facts of this case do not require us to speculate about the circumstances under which the danger alleged in an anonymous tip might be so great as to justify a search even without a showing of reliability. We do not say, for example, that a report of a person carrying a bomb need bear the indicia of reliability we demand for a report of a person carrying a firearm before the police can constitutionally conduct a frisk. Nor do we hold that public safety officials in quarters where the reasonable expectation of Fourth

---

*At oral argument, petitioner also advanced the position that J.L.'s youth made the stop and frisk valid, because it is a crime in Florida for persons under the age of 21 to carry concealed firearms. See Fla. Stat. § 790.01 (1997) (carrying a concealed weapon without a license is a misdemeanor), § 790.06(2)(b) (only persons aged 21 or older may be licensed to carry concealed weapons). This contention misses the mark. Even assuming that the arresting officers could be sure that J.L. was under 21, they would have had reasonable suspicion that J.L. was engaged in criminal activity only if they could be confident that he was carrying a gun in the first place. The mere fact that a tip, if true, would describe illegal activity does not mean that the police may make a *Terry* stop without meeting the reliability requirement, and the fact that J.L. was under 21 in no way made the gun tip more reliable than if he had been an adult.

Amendment privacy is diminished, such as airports, and schools, cannot conduct protective searches on the basis of information insufficient to justify searches elsewhere.

Finally, the requirement that an anonymous tip bear standard indicia of reliability in order to justify a stop in no way diminishes a police officer's prerogative, in accord with *Terry*, to conduct a protective search of a person who has already been legitimately stopped. We speak in today's decision only of cases in which the officer's authority to make the initial stop is at issue. In that context, we hold that an anonymous tip lacking indicia of reliability of the kind contemplated in *Adams* and *White* does not justify a stop and frisk whenever and however it alleges the illegal possession of a firearm.

The judgment of the Florida Supreme Court is affirmed.

Questions

1. Describe the details of the tip that led the officers to stop J.L.

2. Summarize the reasons the Court rejected the tip that led to the stop of J.L.

3. Under what circumstances might an anonymous tip amount to reasonable suspicion?

4. Why did the Court reject the argument that anonymous tips about weapons should be enough to add up to reasonable suspicion? Do you agree? Defend your answer.

5. In an article criticizing the use of anonymous tips, Professor David S. Rudstein wrote the following:

> Any person with a bit of knowledge of another individual can make that individual the target of a prank, or if he harbors a grudge against the individual, can maliciously attempt to inconvenience and embarrass him, by formulating a tip about the individual similar to the one in *White* and then anonymously passing it on to the police. (679)

Do you agree? Explain your answer.

Race

Should officers be allowed to view race through the lens of their training and experience as part of the totality of circumstances adding up to reasonable suspicion? Even asking this question generates explosive controversy (Kennedy 1997, Chapter 4). The courts have made it clear that race by itself can never amount to reasonable suspicion. But, courts have made it just as clear that reasonable suspicion doesn't have to be color-blind. In fact, say the courts, when it comes to reasonable suspicion, color is part of reality, however uncomfortable that reality may be. So, say the courts, officers can use race as part of the totality of circumstances that add up to reasonable suspicion. In *U.S. v. Weaver* (1992), the Eighth Circuit U.S. Court of Appeals addressed the issue of race and reasonable suspicion.

| CASE | *Was Race Alone the Basis of Reasonable Suspicion?* |

U.S. v. Weaver
966 F.2d 391 (8th Cir. 1992)

Arthur Weaver, (defendant) conditionally pled guilty in the U.S. District Court for the Western District of Missouri, to possession of cocaine with intent to distribute and was convicted and sentenced to 151 months' imprisonment, supervised release of five years, a fine of ten thousand dollars, and a special assessment. Weaver appealed the denial of his motion to suppress all physical evidence obtained from his person and baggage. The Court of Appeals affirmed.

WOLLMAN, J.

FACTS

In the early morning hours of March 8, 1989, Drug Enforcement Administration (DEA) agent Carl Hicks and Platte County Detectives Paul Carrill and Tully Kessler were at the Kansas City International Airport awaiting the arrival of Braniff Flight 650, a direct flight to Kansas City from Los Angeles due in at 6:45 A.M. As Weaver disembarked from Flight 650 he caught Officer Hick's attention because he was a "roughly dressed" young black male who was carrying two bags and walking rapidly, almost running, down the concourse toward a door leading to a taxi stand. Because Hicks was aware that a number of young roughly dressed black males from street gangs in Los Angeles frequently brought cocaine into the Kansas City area and that walking quickly towards a taxicab was a common characteristic of narcotics couriers at the airport, he became suspicious that Weaver was a drug trafficker.

Hicks and his fellow officers began running down the concourse after Weaver. Weaver stopped, turned around, saw the three men approaching him, and hesitated. Hicks displayed his badge and asked Weaver if he would answer some questions. In response to Hicks' question, Weaver said that he had been in Los Angeles trying to find his sister who had been missing for several years. Hicks requested to see Weaver's airline ticket, but after searching his pockets Weaver said that he must have left it on the plane. When Hicks asked Weaver if he had any identification, Weaver replied that he did not, but gave Hicks his name and Kansas City address. Hicks testified that while it is extremely uncommon for adults not to have identification, it is common for persons carrying narcotics not to have any. Hicks also testified that Weaver appeared to be very nervous: his voice was unsteady, his speech was rapid, his hands shook, and his body swayed. Officer Carrill testified that although people often become nervous when approached by a police officer, Weaver exhibited more nervousness than innocent people usually do.

Hicks again displayed his badge, identified himself as a DEA agent looking for drugs, and asked to search Weaver's bags. After telling Hicks that he did not have any drugs, Weaver initially assented to Hicks' searching his bags, but then changed his mind and told Hicks that he could not search the bags without a warrant. Weaver then said that he needed to catch a taxi to see his mother in the hospital, picked up his bags, and walked out of the terminal towards a taxicab.

Hicks decided at this point to detain Weaver's bags and apply for a search warrant. He and the other officers followed Weaver to the sidewalk outside the terminal, where Hicks told Weaver that he was going to detain his bags and attempt to get a search warrant. Weaver stopped, set down the bags, opened one of them and removed a sweater, saying, "[L]ook, there's no drugs in my bag," but would not let Hicks look in the bag. Weaver again picked up the bags and walked toward a taxi.

Hicks followed Weaver and again told him that he was going to seize his bags and attempt to get a search warrant. Hicks told Weaver that he was free to remove anything he needed in order to continue his trip. Weaver said he needed a coat out of the bag. Hicks told him that that was fine and that he would give Weaver a receipt for the bag. Nevertheless, Weaver got into the back seat of a taxi with both bags. Hicks grabbed one of the bags and tried to take it out of the taxi. When Weaver began hitting Hicks' hand in an attempt to pry it off his bag, Hicks placed him under arrest.

The officers then conducted a pat down search on Weaver. They found a plastic bag filled with crack cocaine and a smoking pipe, along with $2,532 in currency. Hicks obtained a warrant and searched both of Weaver's bags. One of the bags contained more than six pounds of crack cocaine.

Weaver moved to suppress all physical evidence obtained from his person and baggage. Following a hearing, the district court denied the motion. Weaver entered a conditional guilty plea, reserving the right to appeal the denial of the suppression motion. The district court sentenced Weaver to 151 months' imprisonment, supervised release of five years, a fine of ten thousand dollars, and a special assessment. This appeal followed.

OPINION

Weaver contends that the law enforcement officers did not have a reasonable, articulable suspicion of criminal activity and thus violated his Fourth Amendment right to be free from unreasonable searches and seizures.

Police may, without a warrant, briefly stop and ask questions of a person whom they reasonably suspect of criminal activity.... Reasonable suspicion must derive from more than an "inchoate and unparticularized suspicion or 'hunch.'" For a stop to be valid, the police must point to particular facts and inferences rationally drawn from those facts that, when viewed under the totality of the circumstances and in light of the officer's experience, create a reasonable suspicion of criminal activity. "The relevant inquiry is not whether particular conduct is 'innocent' or 'guilty,' but the degree of suspicion that attaches to particular types of non-criminal acts." Thus, a series of acts that appear innocent, when viewed separately, may warrant further investigation when viewed together. "Conduct typical of a broad category of innocent people provides a weak basis for suspicion."

Because Weaver felt free to leave when the officers first questioned him, that encounter was consensual and did not constitute a seizure. It was only when Hicks told

Weaver that he intended to seize Weaver's bags that a seizure for Fourth Amendment purposes occurred. Our decision therefore turns on whether the officers had a reasonable, articulable suspicion that Weaver was engaged in criminal activity when they pursued him to detain his baggage after he attempted to leave.

Hicks testified that he took the following factors into consideration when he decided to detain Weaver's bags:

(1) that Weaver got off a direct flight from Los Angeles, a source city for drugs;

(2) that he was a roughly dressed young black male who might be a member of a Los Angeles street gang that had been bringing narcotics into the Kansas City area;

(3) that he moved rapidly from the airplane toward a taxicab;

(4) that he had two carry-on bags and no checked luggage;

(5) that he had no identification on his person;

(6) that he did not have a copy of his ticket;

(7) that he appeared very nervous when he talked to Hicks;

(8) and that he made no mention of visiting his mother until the last second before he tried to leave the consensual interview.

Regarding the matter of race, Hicks testified that several different factors caused him to suspect that Weaver might be carrying drugs: "Number one, we have intelligence information and also past arrest history on two black—all black street gangs from Los Angeles called the Crips and the Bloods. They are notorious for transporting cocaine into the Kansas City area from Los Angeles for sale. Most of them are young, roughly dressed male blacks."

We agree with the dissent that large groups of our citizens should not be regarded by law enforcement officers as presumptively criminal based upon their race. We would not hesitate to hold that a solely race-based suspicion of drug courier status would not pass constitutional muster. Accordingly, had Hicks relied solely upon the fact of Weaver's race as a basis for his suspicions, we would have a different case before us. As it is, however, facts are not to be ignored simply because they may be unpleasant—and the unpleasant fact in this case is that Hicks had knowledge, based upon his own experience and upon the intelligence reports he had received from the Los Angeles authorities, that young male members of black Los Angeles gangs were flooding the Kansas City area with cocaine. To that extent, then, race, when coupled with the other factors Hicks relied upon, was a factor in the decision to approach and ul-

timately detain Weaver. We wish it were otherwise, but we take the facts as they are presented to us, not as we would like them to be. . . .

It is true that some or all of the facts relied upon by Agent Hicks could, and might when viewed by those having no experience in surveilling and apprehending drug couriers, be viewed as innocent, nonsuspicion-raising details. Indeed, when juxtaposed against each other, the facts in similar cases can be made to appear wildly inconsistent and contradictory. Nevertheless, we must review these cases one at a time and on their particular facts. Having done so here, we conclude that Agent Hicks possessed a reasonable, articulable suspicion that Weaver was carrying drugs, and we therefore affirm the order denying the motion to suppress.

The judgment of conviction is AFFIRMED.

DISSENT

ARNOLD, CJ.

One of the most disturbing aspects of this case is the agents' reference to Weaver as "a roughly dressed young black male." Most young people on airplanes are roughly dressed, or at least they look that way to one of my age and stage. (This could be said of older people, too, I suspect.) And large numbers of travelers carry two or even three bags on planes with them, apparently mistrusting the airlines' baggage service. . . .

Finally, a word about the reliance placed on Weaver's race. This factor is repeated several times in the Court's opinion. I am not prepared to say that it could never be relevant. If, for example, we had evidence that young blacks in Los Angeles were more prone to drug offenses than young whites, the fact that a young person is black might be of some significance, though even then it would be dangerous to give it much weight. I do not know of any such evidence. Use of race as a factor simply reinforces the kind of stereotyping that lies behind drug-courier profiles. When public officials begin to regard large groups of citizens as presumptively criminal, this country is in a perilous situation indeed.

Airports are on the verge of becoming war zones, where anyone is liable to be stopped, questioned, and even searched merely on the basis of the on-the-spot exercise of discretion by police officers. The liberty of the citizen, in my view, is seriously threatened by this practice. The sanctity of private property, a precious human right, is endangered. It's hard to work up much sympathy for Weaver. He's getting what he deserves, in a sense. What is missing here, though, is an awareness that law enforcement is a broad concept. It includes enforcement of the Bill of

Rights, as well as enforcement of criminal statutes. Cases in which innocent travelers are stopped and impeded in their lawful activities don't come to court. They go on their way, too busy to bring a lawsuit against the officious agents who have detained them. If the Fourth Amendment is to be enforced, therefore, it must be by way of motions to suppress in cases like this.

Questions

1. List the facts on which Officer Hicks and his fellow officers based their stop of Weaver.

2. How important do you think Weaver's race was in the decision to stop him?

3. When, if ever, can race (or any "group" characteristic) be taken into account when officers stop individuals?

Profiles

In addition to direct observation and hearsay, government agents also rely on profiles to alert them to possible criminal activity. Profiles have been popular since the 1970s when the government introduced an airline hijacker profile. Drug Enforcement Agent Paul Markonni developed the **drug courier profile** in 1974 while he was assigned to the Detroit DEA office and trained other agents in its use. Since then, it has become a "nationwide law enforcement tool." Officers stationed at airports observe travelers, looking for seven primary and four secondary characteristics (Table 4.4, *U.S. v. Elmore* 1979, 1039, n. 3).

If their suspicions are aroused, agents approach travelers, identify themselves, seek their consent to be questioned, and ask to see their identification and ticket. If this doesn't put to rest their suspicion, the agents continue the questioning, asking travelers to come with them to another location, usually a room used by law enforcement officers. Once inside the room, agents ask travelers to consent to searches of their persons and luggage. If travelers refuse, agents have to either let them go or "seize" them (Cloud 1985, 848–849).

Since the introduction of the airport drug courier profile, law enforcement has introduced a number of other profiles, including for those entering illegally into the United States; international drug smugglers; customers of suspected domestic drug dealers; and highway drug couriers.

Notice that profiles are neither direct observation nor hearsay. Direct observation and hearsay are based on individualized suspicion—that is, facts pointing to particular suspects. The drug courier profile, on the other hand, is derived from suspicion based on statistical data that put individuals into a suspect category. The U.S. Supreme

TABLE 4.4	
Primary and Secondary Characteristics of Drug Couriers	
Primary Characteristics	**Secondary Characteristics**
Arriving or departing from "source" cities	Using public transportation when leaving airports
Carrying little or no luggage, or empty suitcases	
Traveling by an unusual itinerary	Making telephone calls immediately after getting off the plane
Using an alias	Leaving false or fictitious callback numbers when leaving the plane
Carrying unusually large amounts of cash	
Purchasing tickets with large numbers of small bills	Making excessively frequent trips to source or distribution cities
Appearing unusually nervous	

Court has never ruled that a drug courier profile *by itself* amounts to reasonable suspicion, but in *United States v. Sokolow* (1989), it did answer the question of whether a drug courier profile could be *part* of reasonable suspicion.

CASE	*Is a "Profile" Reasonable Suspicion?*

United States v. Sokolow
490 U.S. 1 (1989)

Andrew Sokolow (respondent) was convicted in the U.S. District Court for the District of Hawaii of possessing cocaine with intent to distribute. He appealed. The Court of Appeals reversed and remanded. Certiorari was granted. The U.S. Supreme Court reversed.

REHNQUIST, J., joined by WHITE, BLACKMUN, STEVENS, O'CONNOR, SCALIA, and KENNEDY, JJ.

FACTS

This case involves a typical attempt to smuggle drugs through one of the nation's airports. On a Sunday in July 1984, Andrew Sokolow went to the United Airlines ticket counter at Honolulu Airport, where he purchased two round-trip tickets for a flight to Miami leaving later that day. The tickets were purchased in the names of "Andrew Kray" and "Janet Norian," and had open return dates. Sokolow paid $2,100 for the tickets from a large roll of $20 bills, which appeared to contain a total of $4,000. He also gave the ticket agent his home telephone number. The ticket agent noticed that Sokolow seemed nervous; he was about 25 years old; he was dressed in a black jumpsuit and wore gold jewelry; and he was accompanied by a woman, who turned out to be Janet Norian. Neither Sokolow nor his companion checked any of their four pieces of luggage.

After the couple left for their flight, the ticket agent informed Officer John McCarthy of the Honolulu Police Department of Sokolow's cash purchase of tickets to Miami. Officer McCarthy determined that the telephone number Sokolow gave to the ticket agent was subscribed to a "Karl Herman," who resided at 348-A Royal Hawaiian Avenue in Honolulu. Unbeknownst to McCarthy (and later to the DEA agents), Sokolow was Herman's roommate. The ticket agent identified Sokolow's voice on the answering machine at Herman's number. Officer McCarthy was unable to find any listing under the name "Andrew Kray" in Hawaii. McCarthy subsequently learned that return reservations from Miami to Honolulu had been made in the names of Kray and Norian, with their arrival scheduled for

July 25, three days after respondent and his companion had left. He also learned that Kray and Norian were scheduled to make stopovers in Denver and Los Angeles.

On July 25, during the stopover in Los Angeles, DEA agents identified Sokolow. He "appeared to be very nervous and was looking all around the waiting area." Later that day, at 6:30 P.M., Sokolow and Norian arrived at Honolulu. As before, they had not checked their luggage. Sokolow was still wearing a black jumpsuit and gold jewelry. The couple proceeded directly to the street and tried to hail a cab, where Agent Richard Kempshall and three other DEA agents approached them. Kempshall displayed his credentials, grabbed respondent by the arm and moved him back onto the sidewalk. Kempshall asked respondent for his airline ticket and identification; respondent said that he had neither. He told the agents that his name was "Sokolow," but that he was traveling under his mother's maiden name, "Kray."

Sokolow and Norian were escorted to the DEA office at the airport. There, the couple's luggage was examined by "Donker," a narcotics detector dog, which alerted to Sokolow's brown shoulder bag. The agents arrested Sokolow. He was advised of his constitutional rights and declined to make any statements. The agents obtained a warrant to search the shoulder bag. They found no illicit drugs, but the bag did contain several suspicious documents indicating Sokolow's involvement in drug trafficking. The agents had Donker reexamine the remaining luggage, and this time the dog alerted to a medium sized Louis Vuitton bag. By now, it was 9:30 P.M., too late for the agents to obtain a second warrant. They allowed Sokolow to leave for the night, but kept his luggage. The next morning, after a second dog confirmed Donker's alert, the agents obtained a warrant and found 1,063 grams of cocaine inside the bag.

Sokolow was indicted for possession with the intent to distribute cocaine in violation of 21 U.S.C. §841(a)(1). The U.S. District Court for Hawaii denied his motion to suppress the cocaine and other evidence seized from his luggage, finding that the DEA agents had a reasonable suspicion that he was involved in drug trafficking when they stopped him at the airport. Sokolow then entered a conditional plea of guilty to the offense charged. The U.S. Court of Appeals for the Ninth Circuit reversed Sokolow's conviction by a divided vote, holding that the DEA agents did not have a reasonable suspicion to justify the stop.... We granted certiorari to review the decision of the Court of Appeals because of its serious implications for the enforcement of the federal narcotics laws. We now reverse.

OPINION

The Fourth Amendment requires "some minimal level of objective justification" for making the stop. That level of suspicion is considerably less than proof of wrongdoing by a preponderance of the evidence.... The concept of reasonable suspicion, like probable cause, is not "readily, or even usefully, reduced to a neat set of legal rules.". . .

Paying $2,100 in cash for two airplane tickets is out of the ordinary, and it is even more out of the ordinary to pay that sum from a roll of $20 bills containing nearly twice that amount of cash. Most business travelers, we feel confident, purchase airline tickets by credit card or check so as to have a record for tax or business purposes, and few vacationers carry with them thousands of dollars in $20 bills. We also think the agents had a reasonable ground to believe that Sokolow was traveling under an alias; the evidence was by no means conclusive, but it was sufficient to warrant consideration. While a trip from Honolulu to Miami, standing alone, is not a cause for any sort of suspicion, here there was more: surely, few residents of Honolulu travel from that city for 20 hours to spend 48 hours in Miami during the month of July.

Any one of these factors is not by itself proof of any illegal conduct and is quite consistent with innocent travel. But we think taken together they amount to reasonable suspicion....

We do not agree with respondent that our analysis is somehow changed by the agents' belief that his behavior was consistent with one of the DEA's "drug courier profiles.". . . .*

A court sitting to determine the existence of reasonable suspicion must require the agent to articulate the factors leading to that conclusion, but the fact that these factors may be set forth in a "profile" does not somehow detract from their evidentiary significance as seen by a trained agent.

REVERSED AND REMANDED. . . .

---

*Court Note: Agent Kempshall testified that Sokolow's behavior "had all the classic aspects of a drug courier." Since 1974, the DEA has trained narcotics officers to identify drug smugglers on the basis of the sort of circumstantial evidence at issue here.

DISSENT

MARSHALL, J., joined by BRENNAN, J.

Because the strongest advocates of Fourth Amendment rights are frequently criminals, it is easy to forget that our interpretations of such rights apply to the innocent and the guilty alike. In the present case, the chain of events set in motion when respondent Andrew Sokolow was stopped by Drug Enforcement Administration (DEA) agents at Honolulu International Airport led to the discovery of cocaine, and, ultimately, to Sokolow's conviction for drug trafficking. But in sustaining this conviction on the ground that the agents reasonably suspected Sokolow of ongoing criminal activity, the Court diminishes the rights of all citizens. . . "to be secure in their persons," as they traverse the nation's airports. Finding this result constitutionally impermissible, I dissent. . . .

. . . [T]he facts about Andrew Sokolow known to the DEA agents at the time they stopped him fall short of reasonably indicating that he was engaged at the time in criminal activity. It is highly significant that the DEA agents stopped Sokolow because he matched one of the DEA's "profiles" of a paradigmatic drug courier.

In my view, a law enforcement officer's mechanistic application of a formula of personal and behavioral traits in deciding who to detain can only dull the officer's ability and determination to make sensitive and fact-specific inferences "in light of his experience," particularly in ambiguous or borderline cases. Reflexive reliance on a profile of drug courier characteristics runs a far greater risk than does ordinary, case-by-case police work, of subjecting innocent individuals to unwarranted police harassment and detention. This risk is enhanced by the profile's "chameleon-like way of adapting to any particular set of observations."

Questions

1. What were the facts upon which DEA agents based the "stop"?

2. Which of the facts point to Sokolow specifically, and which are facts that make him fit the drug courier profile?

3. If you don't count the profile facts, was there reasonable suspicion to suspect Sokolow possessed cocaine with the intent to distribute it? Defend your answer.

4. Under what conditions, if any, should "circumstantial" evidence like the drug courier profile provide the basis for stops?

The Scope of Reasonable Stops

A brief freeze in time and space. That's what the "scope of a reasonable stop" refers to. So, there are two elements to the scope of a reasonable stop: short duration and on-the-spot location of the investigation. Let's look at each.

Short Duration

According to the American Law Institute's (a group of distinguished prosecutors, defense lawyers, law enforcement officers, and academics) *Model Code of Pre-Arraignment Procedure* (1975), there ought to be a bright-line rule controlling the length of stops. Here's the model duration rule:

> SECTION 110.2. STOPPING OF PERSONS
>
> A law enforcement officer, lawfully present in any place, may...order a person to remain in the officer's presence...for such period as is reasonably necessary...but in no case for more than twenty minutes...if such action is reasonably necessary to obtain or verify the identification of such person, to obtain or verify an account of such person's presence or conduct, or to determine whether to arrest such person.

The U.S. Supreme Court has so far declined to adopt this rule. Why? Because the Court prefers to keep its options open and to give officers plenty of room for discretionary decision making. That way neither the Court nor officers are nailed down to a bright-line rule that may hamper crime control. You can see the Court's hesitation to limit reasonable duration to an exact number of minutes in *U.S. v. Sharpe and Savage* (1985), the leading case dealing with duration of stops.

CASE | *Was the Duration "Brief"?*

U.S. v. Sharpe and Savage
470 U.S. 675 (1985)

William Sharpe and Donald Savage were convicted in the United States District Court for the District of South Carolina of possession of a controlled substance with intent to distribute, and they appealed. The Court of Appeals for the Fourth Circuit reversed the convictions, and the Government petitioned for certiorari. The Supreme Court vacated and remanded for further consideration. On remand, the Court of Appeals again reversed the convictions, and the Government petitioned for certiorari. The Supreme reversed and remanded.

BURGER, CJ.

FACTS

On the morning of June 9, 1978, Agent Cooke of the Drug Enforcement Administration (DEA) was on patrol in an unmarked vehicle on a coastal road near Sunset Beach, North Carolina, an area under surveillance for suspected drug trafficking. At approximately 6:30 A.M., Cooke noticed a blue pickup truck with an attached camper shell traveling on the highway in tandem with a blue Pontiac Bonneville. Donald Savage was driving the pickup, and William Sharpe was driving the Pontiac. The Pontiac also carried a passenger, Davis, the charges against whom were later dropped. Observing that the truck was riding low in the rear and that the camper did not bounce or sway appreciably when the truck drove over bumps or around curves, Agent Cooke concluded that it was heavily loaded. A quilted material covered the rear and side windows of the camper.

Cooke's suspicions were sufficiently aroused to follow the two vehicles for approximately 20 miles as they proceeded south into South Carolina. He then decided to make an "investigative stop" and radioed the State Highway Patrol for assistance. Officer Thrasher, driving a marked patrol car, responded to the call. Almost immediately after

Thrasher caught up with the procession, the Pontiac and the pickup turned off the highway and onto a campground road. Cooke and Thrasher followed the two vehicles as the latter drove along the road at 55 to 60 miles an hour, exceeding the speed limit of 35 miles an hour. The road eventually looped back to the highway, onto which Savage and Sharpe turned and continued to drive south.

At this point, all four vehicles were in the middle lane of the three right-hand lanes of the highway. Agent Cooke asked Officer Thrasher to signal both vehicles to stop. Thrasher pulled alongside the Pontiac, which was in the lead, turned on his flashing light, and motioned for the driver of the Pontiac to stop. As Sharpe moved the Pontiac into the right lane, the pickup truck cut between the Pontiac and Thrasher's patrol car, nearly hitting the patrol car, and continued down the highway. Thrasher pursued the truck while Cooke pulled up behind the Pontiac.

Cooke approached the Pontiac and identified himself. He requested identification, and Sharpe produced a Georgia driver's license bearing the name of Raymond J. Pavlovich. Cooke then attempted to radio Thrasher to determine whether he had been successful in stopping the pickup truck, but he was unable to make contact for several minutes, apparently because Thrasher was not in his patrol car. Cooke radioed the local police for assistance, and two officers from the Myrtle Beach Police Department arrived about 10 minutes later. Asking the two officers to "maintain the situation," Cooke left to join Thrasher.

In the meantime, Thrasher had stopped the pickup truck about one-half mile down the road. After stopping the truck, Thrasher had approached it with his revolver drawn, ordered the driver, Savage, to get out and assume a "spread eagled" position against the side of the truck, and patted him down. Thrasher then holstered his gun and asked Savage for his driver's license and the truck's vehicle registration. Savage produced his own Florida driver's license and a bill of sale for the truck bearing the name of Pavlovich. In response to questions from Thrasher concerning the ownership of the truck, Savage said that the truck belonged to a friend and that he was taking it to have its shock absorbers repaired. When Thrasher told Savage that he would be held until the arrival of Cooke, whom Thrasher identified as a DEA agent, Savage became nervous, said that he wanted to leave, and requested the return of his driver's license. Thrasher replied that Savage was not free to leave at that time.

Agent Cooke arrived at the scene approximately 15 minutes after the truck had been stopped. Thrasher handed Cooke Savage's license and the bill of sale for the truck; Cooke noted that the bill of sale bore the same name as Sharpe's license. Cooke identified himself to Savage as a DEA agent and said that he thought the truck was loaded with marihuana. Cooke twice sought permission to search the camper, but Savage declined to give it, explaining that he was not the owner of the truck. Cooke then stepped on the rear of the truck and, observing that it did not sink any lower, confirmed his suspicion that it was probably overloaded. He put his nose against the rear window, which was covered from the inside, and reported that he could smell marihuana. Without seeking Savage's permission, Cooke removed the keys from the ignition, opened the rear of the camper, and observed a large number of burlap-wrapped bales resembling bales of marihuana that Cooke had seen in previous investigations. Agent Cooke then placed Savage under arrest and left him with Thrasher.

Cooke returned to the Pontiac and arrested Sharpe and Davis. Approximately 30 to 40 minutes had elapsed between the time Cooke stopped the Pontiac and the time he returned to arrest Sharpe and Davis. Cooke assembled the various parties and vehicles and led them to the Myrtle Beach police station. That evening, DEA agents took the truck to the Federal Building in Charleston, South Carolina. Several days later, Cooke supervised the unloading of the truck, which contained 43 bales weighing a total of 2,629 pounds. Acting without a search warrant, Cooke had eight randomly selected bales opened and sampled. Chemical tests showed that the samples were marihuana.

Sharpe and Savage were charged with possession of a controlled substance with intent to distribute it in violation of 21 U.S.C. § 841(a)(1) and 18 U.S.C. § 2. The U.S. District Court for the District of South Carolina denied (Sharpe's and Savage's motion to suppress the contraband), and they were convicted.

OPINION

The Fourth Amendment is not a guarantee against *all* searches and seizures, but only against *unreasonable* searches and seizures.... The Court of Appeals...concluded that the 30- to 40-minute detention of Sharpe and the 20-minute detention of Savage "failed to meet the [Fourth Amendment's] requirement of brevity."...

The Court of Appeals' decision would effectively establish a *per se* rule that a 20-minute detention is too long to be justified under the *Terry* doctrine [excerpted earlier in this chapter]. Such a result is clearly and fundamentally at odds with our approach in this area.

In assessing whether a detention is too long in duration to be justified as an investigative stop, we consider it appropriate to examine whether the police diligently pursued a means of investigation that was likely to confirm or dispel their suspicions quickly, during which time it was necessary to detain the defendant. A court making this assessment should take care to consider whether the police are acting in a swiftly developing situation, and in such cases the court should not indulge in unrealistic second-guessing. A creative judge engaged in [after the fact] evaluation of police conduct can almost always imagine some alternative means by which the objectives of the police might have been accomplished. But "the fact that the protection of the public might, in the abstract, have been accomplished by 'less intrusive' means does not, itself, render the search unreasonable." The question is not simply whether some other alternative was available, but whether the police acted unreasonably in failing to recognize or to pursue it.

We readily conclude that, given the circumstances facing him, Agent Cooke pursued his investigation in a diligent and reasonable manner. During most of Savage's 20-minute detention, Cooke was attempting to contact Thrasher and enlisting the help of the local police who remained with Sharpe while Cooke left to pursue Officer Thrasher and the pickup. Once Cooke reached Officer Thrasher and Savage, he proceeded expeditiously: within the space of a few minutes, he examined Savage's driver's license and the truck's bill of sale, requested (and was denied) permission to search the truck, stepped on the rear bumper and noted that the truck did not move, confirming his suspicion that it was probably overloaded. He then detected the odor of marihuana. . . .

We reject the contention that a 20-minute stop is unreasonable when the police have acted diligently and a suspect's actions contribute to the added delay about which he complains. The judgment of the Court of Appeals is reversed, and the case is remanded for further proceedings consistent with this opinion.

DISSENT

BRENNAN, J.

. . . The Framers did not enact the Fourth Amendment to further the investigative powers of the authorities, however, but to curtail them: *Terry's* exception to the probable-cause safeguard must not be expanded to the point where the constitutionality of a citizen's detention turns only on whether the individual officers were coping as best they could given inadequate training, marginal resources, negli-

gent supervision, or botched communications. Our precedents require more—the demonstration by the Government that it was infeasible to conduct the training, ensure the smooth communications, and commit the sort of resources that would have minimized the intrusions.

The Court today has evaded these requirements, failed even to acknowledge the evidence of bungling, miscommunication, and reasonable investigative alternatives, and pronounced simply that the individual officers "acted diligently." Thus the Court has moved a step or two further in what appears to be "an emerging tendency on the part of the Court to convert the *Terry* decision into a general statement that the Fourth Amendment requires only that any seizure be reasonable," a balancing process in which the judicial thumb apparently will be planted firmly on the law enforcement side of the scales.

Justice Douglas, the lone dissenter in *Terry,* warned that "there have been powerful hydraulic pressures throughout our history that bear heavily on the Court to water down constitutional guarantees and give the police the upper hand." Those hydraulic pressures are readily apparent in the outcome of this case. The Court's . . . breed of decision making breaches faith with our high constitutional duty "to prevent wholesale intrusions upon the personal security of our citizenry." . . .

Questions

1. Describe what happened during the 30 to 40 minutes the officers detained Sharpe.

2. Explain the court's reasons for concluding the detention satisfied the "brevity" requirement of reasonable stops.

3. According to the dissent, why did the 30- to 40-minute detention not satisfy the brevity requirement?

4. Compare the length of the detention in this case with that of Officer McFadden's detention of Terry in *Terry v. Ohio* (excerpted earlier). In your opinion, was the 30- to 40-minute detention reasonable based on *Terry?* Back up your answer with facts and arguments from the opinions in *Terry* and in this case.

5. Should there be a bright-line 20-minute duration rule? Defend your answer.

"On the Spot" Investigation Requirement

According to the **"on the spot" requirement,** the brief freeze of a stop has to take place where the officers stop the suspect. But officers have some leeway; "some movement in the general vicinity of the stop is permissible" (LaFave and Israel 1987, 3:393). Remember that Officer McFadden moved Terry, Chilton, and Katz into the nearest store, and the Court didn't question this move. According to the court in *People v. Courtney* (1970):

> No exact formula exists for determining reasonableness; each case must be decided on the facts and circumstances presented to the officers at the time they were required to act. We note that an otherwise permissible detention of a person for investigation is clearly not restricted to the precise point of accostation. It is proper in such a case for the police to require one to step out of an automobile, or to "step back to the police vehicle." It is common and, so far as we know, accepted practice to continue questioning of a suspect in a nearby police car. And it has been held not per se unreasonable to take a person under investigation "to the police station ... for further investigation."

But, it's not reasonable to take someone down to the station (*Hayes v. Florida* 1985) for further investigation, unless there's an emergency, as the California Court of Appeals concluded there was in *People v. Courtney* (1970).

| CASE | *Would Taking Him to the Station Be Reasonable?* |

People v. Courtney
90 Cal.Rptr. 370 (Cal. App.3d 1970)

Jack Courtney, Defendant, was convicted in the Superior Court, Santa Clara County, John S. McInerny, J., of possession of marijuana, and he appealed from an order placing him on probation. The Court of Appeal affirmed.

ELKINGTON, J.

FACTS

George Bruschi was employed as a police officer by Stanford University, a private educational institution. During midafternoon of December 1, 1968, he was on mobile patrol in a residential area which was the private property of the university. There had been an alarming number of crimes in the area. The officer had had an "extreme" amount of trouble there, including burglaries and indecent exposures. The home of the university's president was nearby and he had personally been threatened. His office had been fire bombed and gasoline had been found in his garage. There had been other threats of bombings and actual bombings on the university grounds. Another problem was "a run of people stealing women's underclothing" from clotheslines. The university's police were advised to "be cautious."

Officer Bruschi observed defendant Jack Courtney walking through the area. He was dressed in unusual garb and when he saw the uniformed officer he turned his head away "kind of like to avoid me." Courtney appeared to be a stranger to the neighborhood so the officer pulled up to "ascertain if he had business" and identification. Courtney showed a draft card in his name and said he was going to a certain residence. The occupant of the residence to which he said he was going was known by the officer to have a police record.

The officer "felt it was necessary" to investigate further so he told Courtney "that I was going to run a check through police radio to further his identification." The officer testified, "And at that time before I even had a chance—I just had my hand on the receiver of the police radio—he stated he had no driver's license because it was revoked for hit and run; (that he had been) busted for dope, whatever that meant and also carrying a concealed .38 weapon on his person." At that point the officer observed an unusual "bulge" under Courtney's jacket, and felt concern for his safety. He called for assistance over the police radio. Asked what the bulge was, Courtney replied that it was none of the officer's business because he was not under arrest. Officer Bruschi then reached out toward the bulge "to possibly identify by the feel if it could be a weapon." But Courtney pulled back; the officer couldn't "get a good enough feel of the thing" except that it felt firm—"rather hard." At one time Courtney pulled out the object briefly and said, "Here it is" and quickly replaced it in his pocket. The object was a bag but its contents could not be seen.

In the meantime another officer arrived and a crowd of 18 to 20 people had gathered. Further inquiry as to the nature of the bulge was futile, Courtney insisting, "he was not under arrest, and he did not have to reveal what was in his pocket." Since other officers had had trouble with crowds while making "investigations on the campus," Officer Bruschi told Courtney he "was going to hold him for further investigation because there was a crowd gathering on the corner. For both our welfare—"; he felt "it was common sense to get us both off the street." He further testified: "I told him that I would have to transport him to the Stanford Police Station for further interrogation because there was a crowd gathering, and I felt it wasn't common sense to stay out there at that intersection any longer than we had already been."

Officer Sanguinetti who had responded to the radio call testified: "I arrived there, and I got out of my vehicle, and Officer Bruschi came to me and said, 'I have a problem here that I'd like you to stand by with for a few minutes.'" I said, "All right." I said, "What seems to be the trouble?" He said, "Well, this fellow has got something concealed under his coat." I stated, "Did you ask him what it was?" And he said, "Yes, but he won't tell me." And I said—well, I believe I addressed the defendant then—I said, "Son, what do you have under your coat?" And he said, "You will have to arrest me before I show you. . . ." I was standing behind the defendant off to the side where I could watch him because we thought he had a dangerous weapon or something on him, which Officer Bruschi said that he told him that he had been in trouble before. And also hit run with something to do with narcotics. And so with this bulge under this pea coat, we presumed it could be possibly a dangerous weapon. . . . We had to keep watching him, make sure he wasn't going to produce a weapon. . . . (W)e finally decided we weren't getting anywhere with the young fellow; so Officer Bruschi said, "We are going to have to take you to the Stanford Police Department and continue this," because there was a crowd of people gathering, and on Stanford a crowd of people can sometimes be hostile to police; let's face it. . . .

Both officers testified that Courtney was not under arrest at this point.

OPINION

It is now established law "that circumstances short of probable cause to make an arrest may still justify an officer's stopping pedestrians or motorists on the streets for questioning. . . ." Because of the stranger's paucity of identification and his statement that he was headed for the home of one known to have a police record, the officer's decision to detain him while he ran a radio check was proper. . . . In the meantime a large and apparently hostile crowd had gathered.

The issue seems to narrow to whether an adjournment of the investigation and weapon search to the university police station would have been unreasonable and therefore violative of Fourth Amendment standards. If so, then any evidence resulting from a threat to do so would be constitutionally inadmissible.

No exact formula exists for determining reasonableness; each case must be decided on the facts and circumstances presented to the officers at the time they were required to act. We note that an otherwise permissible detention of a person for investigation is clearly not restricted to the precise point of accostation. It is proper in such a case for the police to require one to step out of an automobile, or to "step back to the police vehicle." It is common and, so far as we know, accepted practice to continue questioning of a suspect in a nearby police car. And it has been held not per se unreasonable to take a person under investigation "to the police station . . . for further investigation.

A recapitulation of the totality of "facts and circumstances" here presented to the officers is helpful. They observed a person in a private (university) community who apparently had no business there. The area had been the scene of much crime and violence including bombing and threats of bombing. Without constitutional infringement they learned that the person had a police record for "hit and run" driving, narcotics violation, and carrying a concealed .38 caliber weapon. They were refused an opportunity to determine the contents of a bag which caused a bulge in the suspect's clothing. Under the circumstances the police could reasonably suspect that it contained a weapon, or even explosives which today may take a wide variety of shapes and consistencies. Further investigation would obviously require some force which if used on the street would probably antagonize a growing and apparently hostile crowd of bystanders.

Certainly there was no Fourth Amendment compulsion on the police to choose between an on-the-spot continuation of their investigation at the probable cost of their own safety, or abandoning the investigation, thus allowing the suspect to continue his mission, whatever it might be, without further inquiry. We recognize that it is only in a rare case where, absent probable cause for arrest, the removal of a suspect to a police station for further investigation is constitutionally permissible. Nevertheless we are constrained to hold, and we do hold, that under the totality of facts and circumstances here known to the police, it was reasonable for them to remove Courtney to the university policy station for that purpose. The Fourth Amendment test of reasonableness has been met. . . .

AFFIRMED.

Questions

1. State the facts and circumstances that backed up Officers Sanguinetti and Bruschi's decision to take Jack Courtney to the station for further investigation.

2. State the court's test for deciding whether or not the officers' decision was consistent with the on-the-spot rule.

3. Summarize the court's reasons for ruling the decision didn't violate the Fourth Amendment.

4. Do you agree with the court's decision? Defend your answer.

SPECIAL SITUATION STOPS

Not all reasonable seizures without probable cause fit neatly into the picture of brief, on-the-spot "freezes" based on reasonable suspicion. Under some special situations it's reasonable to move suspects based on no articulable facts (passengers in stopped vehicles); to detain suspects for a whole day on reasonable suspicion (individuals entering the country); and to detain all persons in a particular place with no individualized suspicion (DWI roadblocks). Let's look at why these three special situation stops are reasonable seizures.

Removing Passengers from Stopped Vehicles

In *Pennsylvania v. Mimms* (1977), the U.S. Supreme Court ruled that officers can order *drivers* out of cars they lawfully stop. Why? For the safety of the officers. According to the Court, talking to a driver while an officer is exposed to traffic puts the officer in danger. Removing the driver from the car is a "trivial invasion" because the driver's already stopped. Balancing the possible danger to the officer clearly outweighs the trivial invasion of removing the driver from the car. But, is it a trivial invasion to order *passengers* (who officers don't suspect of any wrongdoing) out of the car while officers sort out their suspicions of the driver? The Supreme Court answered the question in *Maryland v. Wilson* (1997).

CASE	*Was the Order to Get Out of the Car Reasonable?*

Maryland v. Wilson
519 U.S. 408 (1997)

Jerry Lee Wilson (respondent) moved to suppress crack cocaine seized by a police officer during a traffic stop. The trial court granted the motion. The State appealed. The Maryland Court of Special Appeals affirmed. The Maryland Court of Appeals denied certiorari. The U.S. Supreme Court granted certiorari and reversed and remanded the case.

REHNQUIST, CJ., joined by O'CONNOR, SCALIA, SOUTER, THOMAS, GINSBURG, and BREYER, JJ.

FACTS

At about 7:30 P.M. on a June evening, Maryland state trooper David Hughes observed a passenger car driving southbound on I-95 in Baltimore County at a speed of 64 miles per hour. The posted speed limit was 55 miles per hour, and the car had no regular license tag; there was a torn piece of paper reading "Enterprise Rent-A-Car" dangling from its rear. Hughes activated his lights and sirens, signaling the car to pull over, but it continued driving for another mile and a half until it finally did so.

During the pursuit, Hughes noticed there were three occupants in the car and that the two passengers turned to look at him several times, repeatedly ducking below sight level and then reappearing. As Hughes approached the car on foot, the driver alighted and met him halfway. The driver was trembling and appeared extremely nervous, but nonetheless produced a valid Connecticut driver's license. Hughes instructed him to return to the car and retrieve the rental documents, and he complied. During this encounter, Hughes noticed that the front-seat passenger, Jerry Lee Wilson (the respondent), was sweating and also appeared extremely nervous. While the driver was sitting in the driver's seat looking for the rental papers, Hughes ordered Wilson out of the car.

When Wilson exited the car, a quantity of crack cocaine fell to the ground. Wilson was then arrested and charged with possession of cocaine with intent to distribute. Before trial, Wilson moved to suppress the evidence, arguing that Hughes' ordering him out of the car constituted an unreasonable seizure under the Fourth Amendment. The Circuit Court for Baltimore County agreed, and granted respondent's motion to suppress. On appeal, the Court of Special Appeals of Maryland affirmed, ruling that *Pennsylvania v. Mimms* does not apply to passengers. The Court of Appeals of Maryland denied certiorari. We granted certiorari, and now reverse.

OPINION

In *Mimms*, we considered a traffic stop much like the one before us today. There, Mimms had been stopped for driving with an expired license plate, and the officer asked him to step out of his car. When Mimms did so, the officer noticed a bulge in his jacket that proved to be a .38-caliber revolver, whereupon Mimms was arrested for carrying a concealed deadly weapon. Mimms, like Wilson, urged the suppression of the evidence on the ground that the officer's ordering him out of the car was an unreasonable seizure, and the Pennsylvania Supreme Court, like the Court of Special Appeals of Maryland, agreed.

We reversed, explaining that "the touchstone of our analysis under the Fourth Amendment is always 'the reasonableness in all the circumstances of the particular governmental invasion of a citizen's personal security,'" and that reasonableness "depends 'on a balance between the public interest and the individual's right to personal security free from arbitrary interference by law officers.'" On the public interest side of the balance, we noted that the State "freely conceded" that there had been nothing unusual or suspicious to justify ordering Mimms out of the car, but that it was the officer's "practice to order all drivers [stopped in traffic stops] out of their vehicles as a matter of course" as a "precautionary measure" to protect the officer's safety. We thought it "too plain for argument" that this justification—officer safety—was "both legitimate and weighty." In addition, we observed that the danger to the officer of standing by the driver's door and in the path of oncoming traffic might also be "appreciable."

On the other side of the balance, we considered the intrusion into the driver's liberty occasioned by the officer's ordering him out of the car. Noting that the driver's car was already validly stopped for a traffic infraction, we deemed the additional intrusion of asking him to step outside his car "de minimis" [trivial]. Accordingly, we concluded that "once a motor vehicle has been lawfully detained for a traffic violation, the police officers may order the driver to get out of the vehicle without violating the Fourth Amendment's proscription of unreasonable seizures."

Wilson urges, and the lower courts agreed, that this per se rule does not apply to Wilson because he was a passenger, not the driver....We must therefore now decide whether the rule of *Mimms* applies to passengers as well as to drivers. On the public interest side of the balance, the same weighty interest in officer safety is present regardless of whether the occupant of the stopped car is a driver or passenger. Regrettably, traffic stops may be dangerous encounters. In 1994 alone, there were 5,762 officer assaults and 11 officers killed during traffic pursuits and stops. Federal Bureau of Investigation, Uniform Crime Reports: Law Enforcement Officers Killed and Assaulted 71, 33 (1994). In the case of passengers, the danger of the officer's standing in the path of oncoming traffic would not be present except in the case of a passenger in the left rear seat, but the fact that there is more than one occupant of the vehicle increases the possible sources of harm to the officer.

On the personal liberty side of the balance, the case for the passengers is in one sense stronger than that for the driver. There is probable cause to believe that the driver has committed a minor vehicular offense, but there is no such reason to stop or detain the passengers. But as a practical matter, the passengers are already stopped by virtue of the stop of the vehicle. The only change in their circumstances which will result from ordering them out of the car is that they will be outside of, rather than inside of, the stopped car. Outside the car, the passengers will be denied access to any possible weapon that might be concealed in the interior of the passenger compartment. It would seem that the possibility of a violent encounter stems not from the ordinary reaction of a motorist stopped for a speeding violation, but from the fact that evidence of a more serious crime might be uncovered during the stop. And the motivation of a passenger to employ violence to prevent apprehension of such a crime is every bit as great as that of the driver. . . .

In summary, danger to an officer from a traffic stop is likely to be greater when there are passengers in addition to the driver in the stopped car. While there is not the same basis for ordering the passengers out of the car as there is for ordering the driver out, the additional intrusion on the passenger is minimal. We therefore hold that an officer making a traffic stop may order passengers to get out of the car pending completion of the stop.

The judgment of the Court of Special Appeals of Maryland is reversed, and the case is remanded for proceedings not inconsistent with this opinion. It is so ordered.

DISSENT

STEVENS, J., joined by KENNEDY, J.
. . . My concern is not with the ultimate disposition of this particular case, but rather with the literally millions of other cases that will be affected by the rule the Court announces. Though the question is not before us, I am satisfied that—under the rationale of *Terry v. Ohio*—if a police officer conducting a traffic stop has an articulable suspicion of possible danger, the officer may order passengers to exit the vehicle as a defensive tactic without running afoul of the Fourth Amendment. Accordingly, I assume that the facts recited in the majority's opinion provided a valid justification for this officer's order commanding the passengers to get out of this vehicle. But the Court's ruling goes much farther. It applies equally to traffic stops in which there is not even a scintilla of evidence of any potential risk to the police officer. In those cases, I firmly believe that the Fourth Amendment prohibits routine and arbitrary seizures of obviously innocent citizens.

The majority suggests that the personal liberty interest at stake here . . . is outweighed by the need to ensure officer safety. The Court correctly observes that "traffic stops may be dangerous encounters." The magnitude of the danger to police officers is reflected in the statistic that, in 1994 alone, "there were 5,762 officer assaults and 11 officers killed during traffic pursuits and stops." There is, unquestionably, a strong public interest in minimizing the number of such assaults and fatalities. The Court's statistics, however, provide no support for the conclusion that its ruling will have any such effect.

Those statistics do not tell us how many of the incidents involved passengers. Assuming that many of the assaults were committed by passengers, we do not know how many occurred after the passenger got out of the vehicle, how many took place while the passenger remained in the vehicle, or indeed, whether any of them could have been prevented by an order commanding the passengers to exit. There is no indication that the number of assaults was smaller in jurisdictions where officers may order passengers to exit the vehicle without any suspicion than in jurisdictions where they were then prohibited from doing so. Indeed, there is no indication that any of the assaults occurred when there was a complete absence of any articulable basis for concern about the officer's safety—the only condition under which I would hold that the Fourth Amendment prohibits an order commanding passengers to exit a vehicle. In short, the statistics are as consistent with the hypothesis that ordering passengers to get out of a vehicle increases the danger of assault as with the hypothesis that it reduces that risk.

Furthermore, any limited additional risk to police officers must be weighed against the unnecessary invasion that will be imposed on innocent citizens under the majority's rule in the tremendous number of routine stops that occur each day. We have long recognized that "because of the extensive regulation of motor vehicles and traffic . . . the extent of police–citizen contact involving automobiles will be substantially greater than police–citizen contact in a home or office." Most traffic stops involve otherwise law-abiding citizens who have committed minor traffic offenses. A strong interest in arriving at a destination—to deliver a patient to a hospital, to witness a kick-off, or to get to work on time—will often explain a traffic violation without justifying it. In the aggregate, these stops amount to significant law enforcement activity.

Indeed, the number of stops in which an officer is actually at risk is dwarfed by the far greater number of routine stops. If Maryland's share of the national total is about average, the State probably experiences about 100 officer assaults each year during traffic stops and pursuits. Making the unlikely assumption that passengers are responsible for one-fourth of the total assaults, it appears that the Court's new rule would provide a potential benefit to Maryland officers in only roughly 25 stops a year. These stops represent a minuscule portion of the total. In Maryland alone, there are something on the order of one million traffic stops each year. Assuming that there are passengers in about half of the cars stopped, the majority's rule is of some possible advantage to police in only about one out of every twenty thousand traffic stops in which there is a passenger in the car. And, any benefit is extremely marginal. In the overwhelming majority of cases posing a real threat, the officer would almost certainly have some ground to suspect danger that would justify ordering passengers out of the car.

In contrast, the potential daily burden on thousands of innocent citizens is obvious. That burden may well be "minimal" in individual cases. But countless citizens who cherish individual liberty and are offended, embarrassed, and sometimes provoked by arbitrary official commands may well consider the burden to be significant. In all events, the aggregation of thousands upon thousands of petty indignities has an impact on freedom that I would characterize as substantial, and which in my view clearly outweighs the evanescent safety concerns pressed by the majority....

To order passengers about during the course of a traffic stop, insisting that they exit and remain outside the car, can hardly be classified as a *de minimis* intrusion. The traffic violation sufficiently justifies subjecting the driver to detention and some police control for the time necessary to conclude the business of the stop. The restraint on the liberty of blameless passengers that the majority permits is, in contrast, entirely arbitrary.

In my view, wholly innocent passengers in a taxi, bus, or private car have a constitutionally protected right to decide whether to remain comfortably seated within the vehicle rather than exposing themselves to the elements and the observation of curious bystanders. The Constitution should not be read to permit law enforcement officers to order innocent passengers about simply because they have the misfortune to be seated in a car whose driver has committed a minor traffic offense.

Unfortunately, the effect of the Court's new rule on the law may turn out to be far more significant than its immediate impact on individual liberty. Throughout most of our history the Fourth Amendment embodied a general rule requiring that official searches and seizures be authorized by a warrant, issued "upon probable cause, supported by Oath or affirmation, and particularly describing the place to be searched, and the persons or things to be seized." During the prohibition era, the exceptions for warrantless searches supported by probable cause started to replace the general rule. In 1968, in the landmark "stop and frisk" case *Terry v. Ohio*, the Court placed its stamp of approval on seizures supported by specific and articulable facts that did not establish probable cause. The Court crafted *Terry* as a narrow exception to the general rule that "the police must, whenever practicable, obtain advance judicial approval of searches and seizures through the warrant procedure." The intended scope of the Court's major departure from prior practice was reflected in its statement that the "demand for specificity in the information upon which police action is predicated is the central teaching of this Court's Fourth

Amendment jurisprudence." In the 1970s, the Court twice rejected attempts to justify suspicionless seizures that caused only "modest" intrusions on the liberty of passengers in automobiles. Today, however, the Court takes the unprecedented step of authorizing seizures that are unsupported by any individualized suspicion whatsoever.

The Court's conclusion seems to rest on the assumption that the constitutional protection against "unreasonable" seizures requires nothing more than a hypothetically rational basis for intrusions on individual liberty. How far this ground-breaking decision will take us, I do not venture to predict. I fear, however, that it may pose a more serious threat to individual liberty than the Court realizes.

I respectfully DISSENT.

KENNEDY, J.

Traffic stops, even for minor violations, can take upwards of 30 minutes. When an officer commands passengers innocent of any violation to leave the vehicle and stand by the side of the road in full view of the public, the seizure is serious, not trivial. As Justice Stevens concludes, the command to exit ought not to be given unless there are objective circumstances making it reasonable for the officer to issue the order. (We do not have before us the separate question whether passengers, who, after all are in the car by choice, can be ordered to remain there for a reasonable time while the police conduct their business.)...

Coupled with *Whren v. U.S.* [excerpted in Chapter 7] the Court puts tens of millions of passengers at risk of arbitrary control by the police. If the command to exit were to become commonplace, the Constitution would be diminished in a most public way. As the standards suggested in dissent are adequate to protect the safety of the police, we ought not to suffer so great a loss....

Most officers, it might be said, will exercise their new power with discretion and restraint; and no doubt this often will be the case. It might also be said that if some jurisdictions use today's ruling to require passengers to exit as a matter of routine in every stop, citizen complaints and political intervention will call for an end to the practice. These arguments, however, would miss the point. Liberty comes not from officials by grace but from the Constitution by right.

For these reasons, and with all respect for the opinion of the Court, I dissent.

Questions

1. List the specific invasions Jerry Lee Wilson experienced *after* the vehicle he was a passenger in was stopped.

2. Identify the government interest that was furthered by ordering Wilson out of the car.

3. In your opinion, did the government interest outweigh the degree of invasion against Wilson? In your answer, consider both the majority and dissenting opinions.

4. State specifically the objective basis for ordering Wilson out of the car.

5. State the Court's "bright line rule" governing officers' power to order passengers out of cars they've stopped.

6. Summarize the arguments the majority gave to back up its bright-line rule.

7. Describe the empirical evidence the majority's opinion was based on. In view of the dissenting justices' criticism of the statistics, how much weight do they carry in your opinion?

8. How do the dissenting justices answer the majority's arguments in (7)? Which side has the better arguments? Defend your answer.

 Go to Exercise 4-2 on the Criminal Procedure 6e CD to learn more about *Maryland v. Wilson.*

◆ STATE CONSTITUTIONAL LAW ◆

Commonwealth v. Gonsalves
429 Mass. 658, 711 N.E.2d 108 (1999)

When Is It Reasonable for Officers to Order Passenger to Get Out of a Stopped Car?

GREANEY, J.

FACTS

John Gonsalves was charged with trafficking in cocaine in violation of G.L. c. 94C, § 32E (b). The cocaine was seized by a State trooper...while on routine traffic patrol about 9 P.M. on March 5, 1997. When the State trooper observed the taxi traveling partly in the breakdown lane of the highway which he was patrolling, he became concerned that the driver might be under the influence of an intoxicant, and signaled for the driver to stop. The trooper approached the stopped taxi, spoke to the driver, and noted that there were also two passengers in the car, including Gonsalves, who was the sole occupant of the back seat. The trooper took the taxi driver's license and registration. He questioned the driver about his driving over the marked lane, and the driver told the trooper that he had trouble with his night vision.

In the course of questioning the driver, the trooper trained his flashlight on the occupants of the car, something which he routinely did on such stops for his personal safety. The trooper thought Gonsalves was extremely nervous. His hands were trembling and moving from his lap to the seat and back to his lap again, and he appeared to be breathing heavily. Because Gonsalves appeared nervous, the trooper ordered him to step out of the taxi. Gonsalves complied, and the trooper conducted a pat frisk, which revealed nothing. He asked Gonsalves why he was nervous, and Gonsalves replied that there were warrants outstanding against him for driving without a license. At that point, the trooper "secured" Gonsalves in the rear seat of the police cruiser. He obtained permission from the driver of the taxi to search the vehicle's back seat, where the trooper saw a portion of a plastic bag protruding from between the seat cushion and the seat back. The plastic bag contained white powder which the trooper suspected was cocaine.

OPINION

To determine whether an exit order was justified, we ask "whether a reasonably prudent man in the policeman's position would be warranted in the belief that the safety of the police or that of other persons was in danger. The rule that a police officer must, at least, have a reasonable suspicion of danger before compelling a driver to leave his motor vehicle has been affirmed by this court well after the United States Supreme Court abandoned that requirement in *Mimms.* Because we have departed from the Federal view of a citizen's Fourth Amendment rights in the area, our long-standing rule expresses a principle of State constitutional law under art. 14. [Article 14 reads in part that "Every subject has a right to be secure from all unreasonable searches, and seizures, of his person, his houses, his papers, and all his possessions."]

We have expressly granted other protections to drivers and occupants of motor vehicles under art. 14 in a variety of areas, and we have done so to guarantee protections that, in some cases, may not be recognized under the Fourth Amendment. In view of these protections we conclude that art. 14 requires that a police officer, in a routine traffic stop, must have a reasonable belief that the officer's safety, or the safety of others, is in danger before ordering a driver out of a motor vehicle. The fact that we do not follow *Mimms* in this type of case necessarily leads to the conclusion that we shall not follow *Wilson* either, because *Wilson* extends *Mimms* in a manner incompatible with the rights guaranteed Massachusetts citizens under art. 14....

Such an intrusion into a driver or a passenger's privacy is not minimal. As was expressed by a dissent in *Mimms*, "a woman stopped at night may fear for her own safety; a person in poor health may object to standing in the cold or rain; another who left home in haste to drive children or spouse to school or to the train may not be fully dressed; an elderly driver who presents no possible threat of violence may regard the police command as nothing more than an arrogant and unnecessary display of authority." Routine traffic stops may also pose unique hardships on minorities who, it has been argued, are often the subject of stops on pretext. The rules in *Mimms* and *Wilson*, which permit automobile exit orders during any traffic stop, but which do not require that such orders be given, are a clear invitation to discriminatory enforcement of the rule.

The Declaration of Rights was adopted in 1780, as part of the Massachusetts Constitution, some seven years before the United States Constitution was approved. The Declaration of Rights was written in the historical context of the abuses of governmental power inflicted on the colonists by British officials, and art. 14 was directed at the unlawful invasion of privacy rights by those officials. That the drafters of the Fourth Amendment subsequently chose to replicate the words used in art. 14 cannot support a conclusion that we are compelled to act in lockstep with the United States Supreme Court when it interprets that amendment. Such a conclusion posits a serious misunderstanding of the authority of this court to interpret and enforce the various provisions of the Massachusetts Constitution, particularly those in the area of civil liberties.

Chief Justice Wilkins has stated that, "the United States Supreme Court... describes a common base from which we can go up," but the Justices of this court "are, however, entitled to their own views, indeed constitutionally required to have them." The nature of federalism requires that State Supreme Courts and State Constitutions be strong and independent repositories of authority in order to protect the rights of their citizens.

The foregoing discussion explains the foundation of our rule that, once a stopped driver has produced the necessary papers and they are found to be in order, he and his passengers are to be promptly released, and why we choose not to follow *Mimms–Wilson*. We, of course, respect the United States Supreme Court's judgment in the matter under the Fourth Amendment. That judgment was reached after balancing the interests of the police against the liberty interests of citizens, with the Court's concluding that the former should prevail over the latter. For the reasons stated, we conclude that, under art. 14, the balancing of interests requires that Massachusetts citizens should not be subjected to unjustified exit orders during routine traffic stops.

Order allowing motion to suppress AFFIRMED.

Stops at International Borders

Ever since colonial times, U.S. Customs officers have had the power to detain without probable cause travelers who cross our borders. According to the U.S. Supreme Court, the high government need to control what and who comes into the country greatly reduces the liberty and privacy interests of international travelers and also the objective basis officials need to back up searches and seizures of anyone who crosses the borders into the United States. Most invasions, like opening suitcases for a brief peek with few—or even no—facts to back them up hardly cause notice, let alone comment. But long, incommunicado detentions accompanied by intense interrogation and strip and body-cavity searches are another story. They've set off major controversies over the balance of power between government power and individual liberty and privacy.

Border stops, and the controversy surrounding them, took on an air of urgency during the 1980s war on drugs when border control became a major tactic in the war on drugs. Although we don't have much information yet, border seizures and searches probably also are going to be a major tactic in preventing future terrorist attacks and apprehending terrorist suspects (Chapter 15). We'll limit our discussion to illegal drug control, particularly the difficulty for law enforcement created by **balloon swallowers.** These are smugglers who bring illegal drugs into the country in their alimentary canal. Couriers and/or users who hide illegal drugs in their rectums or vaginas present another problem.

The U.S. Supreme Court addressed the application of the Fourth Amendment to detentions at international borders for purposes of investigating "balloon swallowers" in *United States v. Montoya de Hernandez* (1985).

CASE | *Was the Detention Reasonable?*

United States v. Montoya de Hernandez
473 U.S. 531 381 (1985)

Rosa Elvira Montoya de Hernandez was charged with narcotics violations. She moved to suppress the narcotics; the district court denied the motion and admitted the cocaine in evidence. Montoya de Hernandez was convicted of possessing cocaine with intent to distribute and unlawful importation of cocaine. A divided U.S. Court of Appeals for the 9th Circuit reversed the conviction. The government appealed to the U.S. Supreme Court. The Supreme Court reversed.

REHNQUIST, J., joined by BURGER, CJ., and WHITE, BLACKMUN, POWELL, and O'CONNOR, JJ.

FACTS

Montoya de Hernandez arrived at Los Angeles International Airport shortly after midnight, March 5, 1983, on Avianca Flight 080, a direct 10-hour flight from Bogotá, Colombia. Her visa was in order so she was passed through Immigration and proceeded to the customs desk. At the customs desk she encountered Customs Inspector Talamantes, who reviewed her documents and noticed from her passport that she had made at least eight recent trips to either Miami or Los Angeles. Talamantes referred respondent to a secondary customs desk for further questioning. At this desk Talamantes and another inspector asked Montoya de Hernandez general questions concerning herself and the purpose of her trip. Montoya de Hernandez revealed that she spoke no English and had no family or friends in the United States. She explained in Spanish that she had come to the United States to purchase goods for her husband's store in Bogotá. The customs inspectors recognized Bogotá as a "source city" for narcotics. Montoya de

Hernandez possessed $5,000 in cash, mostly $50 bills, but had no billfold. She indicated to the inspectors that she had no appointments with merchandise vendors, but planned to ride around Los Angeles in taxicabs visiting retail stores such as J.C. Penney and K-Mart in order to buy goods for her husband's store with the $5,000.

Montoya de Hernandez admitted she had no hotel reservations, but said she planned to stay at a Holiday Inn. Montoya de Hernandez could not recall how her airline ticket was purchased. When the inspectors opened Montoya de Hernandez's one small valise they found about four changes of "cold weather" clothing. Montoya de Hernandez had no shoes other than the high-heeled pair she was wearing. Although Montoya de Hernandez possessed no checks, waybills, credit cards, or letters of credit, she did produce a Colombian business card and a number of old receipts, waybills, and fabric swatches displayed in a photo album.

At this point Talamantes and the other inspector suspected that Montoya de Hernandez was a "balloon swallower," one who attempts to smuggle narcotics into this country hidden in her alimentary canal. Over the years Inspector Talamantes had apprehended dozens of alimentary canal smugglers arriving on Avianca Flight 080....

The inspectors requested a female customs inspector to take Montoya de Hernandez to a private area and conduct a pat down and strip search. During the search the female inspector felt Montoya de Hernandez's abdomen area and noticed a firm fullness, as if Montoya de Hernandez were wearing a girdle. The search revealed no contraband, but the inspector noticed that Montoya de Hernandez was wearing two pairs of elastic underpants with a paper towel lining the crotch area.

When Montoya de Hernandez returned to the customs area and the female inspector reported her discoveries, the inspector in charge told Montoya de Hernandez that he suspected she was smuggling drugs in her alimentary canal.... The inspector then gave Montoya de Hernandez the option of returning to Colombia on the next available flight, agreeing to an x-ray, or remaining in detention until she produced a monitored bowel movement that would confirm or rebut the inspectors' suspicions. Montoya de Hernandez chose the first option and was placed in a customs office under observation. She was told that if she went to the toilet she would have to use a wastebasket in the women's restroom, in order that female inspectors could inspect her stool for balloons or capsules carrying narcotics. The inspectors refused Montoya de Hernandez's request to place a telephone call....

Montoya de Hernandez sat in the customs office, under observation, for the remainder of the night.... She remained detained in the customs office under observation, for most of the time curled up in a chair leaning to one side. She refused all offers of food and drink, and refused to use the toilet facilities. The Court of Appeals noted that she exhibited symptoms of discomfort with "heroic efforts to resist the usual calls of nature."...

At the shift change at 4:00... the next afternoon, almost 16 hours after her flight had landed, Montoya de Hernandez still had not defecated or urinated or partaken of food or drink. At that time customs officials sought a court order authorizing... an x-ray, and a rectal examination. The Federal Magistrate issued an order just before midnight that evening, which authorized a rectal examination and involuntary x-ray.... A physician conducted a rectal examination and removed from Montoya de Hernandez's rectum a balloon containing a foreign substance. Montoya de Hernandez was then placed formally under arrest. By 4:10 A.M. Montoya de Hernandez had passed 6 similar balloons; over the next four days she passed 88 balloons containing a total of 528 grams of 80% pure cocaine hydrochloride.

After a suppression hearing the District Court admitted the cocaine in evidence against Montoya de Hernandez. She was convicted of possession of cocaine with intent to distribute...[a]nd unlawful importation of cocaine.... A divided panel of the United States Court of Appeals for the Ninth Circuit reversed Montoya de Hernandez's convictions....

OPINION

The Fourth Amendment commands that searches and seizures be reasonable. What is reasonable depends upon all of the circumstances surrounding the search or seizure itself.... The permissibility of a particular law enforcement practice is judged by "balancing its intrusion on the individual's Fourth Amendment interest against its promotion of legitimate governmental interests."...

Here the seizure of Montoya de Hernandez took place at the international border. Since the founding of our Republic, Congress has granted the Executive plenary authority to conduct routine searches and seizures at the border, without probable cause or a warrant, in order to regulate the collection of duties and to prevent the introduction of contraband into this country.... The Fourth Amendment's balance of reasonableness is qualitatively different at the international border than in the interior. Routine searches of the persons and effects of entrants are not subject to any requirement of reasonable suspicion, probable cause, or warrant, and first-class mail may be opened without a warrant on less than probable cause....

These cases reflect long-standing concern for the protection of the integrity of the border. This concern is, if anything, heightened by the veritable national crisis in law enforcement caused by smuggling of illicit narcotics... and in particular by the increasing utilization of alimentary canal smuggling. This desperate practice appears to be a relatively recent addition to the smugglers' repertoire of deceptive practices, and it also appears to be exceedingly difficult to detect....

Balanced against the sovereign's interests at the border are the Fourth Amendment rights of Montoya de Hernandez. Having presented herself at the border for admission, and having subjected herself to the criminal enforcement powers of the Federal Government... she was entitled to be free from unreasonable search and seizure. But not only is this expectation of privacy less at the border than in the interior... the Fourth Amendment balance between the interests of the Government and the privacy right of the individual is also struck much more favorably to the Government at the border....

We have not previously decided what level of suspicion would justify a seizure of an incoming traveler for purposes other than a routine border search.... The Court of Appeals viewed "clear indication" as an intermediate standard between "reasonable suspicion" and "probable cause."...No other court, including this one, has ever adopted..."clear indication" language as a Fourth Amendment standard.... We do not think that the Fourth Amendment's emphasis upon reasonableness is consistent with the creation of a third verbal standard in addition to "reasonable suspicion" and "probable cause."...

We hold that detention of a traveler at the border, beyond the scope of a routine customs search and inspection, is justified at its inception if customs agents, considering all the facts surrounding the traveler and her trip, reasonably suspect that the traveler is smuggling contraband in her alimentary canal.... The facts, and their rational inferences, known to customs inspectors in this case clearly supported a reasonable suspicion that Montoya de Hernandez was an alimentary canal smuggler. . . . The trained customs inspectors had encountered many alimentary canal smugglers and certainly had more than an "inchoate and unparticularized suspicion or 'hunch,'" . . . that Montoya de Hernandez was smuggling narcotics in her alimentary canal. The inspectors' suspicion was a "'common-sense conclusion about human behavior' upon which 'practical people,' . . . including government officials, are entitled to rely." . . .

The final issue in this case is whether the detention of Montoya de Hernandez was reasonably related in scope to the circumstances which justified it initially. In this regard we have cautioned that courts should not indulge in "unrealistic second-guessing," . . . and we have noted that "creative judges, engaged in [after the fact] evaluations of police conduct can almost always imagine some alternative means by which the objectives of the police might have been accomplished." . . . The rudimentary knowledge of the human body which judges possess in common with the rest of humankind tells us that alimentary canal smuggling cannot be detected in the amount of time in which other illegal activity may be investigated through brief *Terry*-type stops. It presents few, if any external signs; a quick frisk will not do, nor will even a strip search.

In the case of Montoya de Hernandez the inspectors had available, as an alternative to simply awaiting her bowel movement, an x-ray. They offered her the alternative of submitting herself to that procedure. But when she refused that alternative, the customs inspectors were left with only two practical alternatives: detain her for such a time as necessary to confirm their suspicions, a detention which would last much longer than the typical *Terry* stop, or turn her loose into the interior carrying the reasonably suspected contraband drugs. . . . The inspectors in this case followed this former procedure. They no doubt expected that Montoya de Hernandez, having recently disembarked from a 10-hour direct flight with a full and stiff abdomen, would produce a bowel movement without extended delay. But her visible efforts to resist the call of nature, which the court below labeled "heroic," disappointed this expectation and in turn caused her humiliation and discomfort.

Our prior cases have refused to charge police with delays in investigatory detention attributable to the suspect's evasive actions. . . . Montoya de Hernandez alone was responsible for much of the duration and discomfort of the seizure. Under these circumstances, we conclude that the detention was not unreasonably long. It occurred at the international border, where the Fourth Amendment balance of interests leans heavily to the Government. . . . Montoya de Hernandez's detention was long, uncomfortable indeed, humiliating; but both its length and its discomfort resulted solely from the method by which she chose to smuggle illicit drugs into this country. . . .

CONCURRING OPINION

STEVENS, J.

If a seizure and search of the person of the kind disclosed by this record may be made on the basis of reasonable suspicion, we must assume that a significant number of innocent persons will be required to undergo similar procedures. The rule announced in this case cannot, therefore, be supported on the ground that Montoya de Hernandez's prolonged and humiliating detention "resulted solely from the method by which she chose to smuggle illicit drugs into this country." . . . The prolonged detention of Montoya de Hernandez was, however, justified by a different choice that Montoya de Hernandez made; she withdrew her consent to an x-ray examination that would have easily determined whether the reasonable suspicion that she was concealing contraband was justified. . . .

DISSENT

BRENNAN, J., joined by MARSHALL, J.

We confront a "disgusting and saddening episode" at our Nation's border. . . . "That Montoya de Hernandez so degraded herself as to offend the sensibilities of any decent citizen is not questioned." That is not what we face. For "it is a fair summary of history to say that the safeguards of liberty have frequently been forged in controversies involving not very nice people." . . . The standards we fashion to govern the ferreting out of the guilty apply equally to the detention of the innocent, and "may be exercised by the most unfit and ruthless officers as well as by the fit and reasonable." . . . Nor is the issue whether there is a "veritable national crisis in law enforcement caused by smuggling illicit narcotics." . . . "In our democracy such enforcement presupposes a moral atmosphere and a reliance upon intelligence whereby the effective administration of justice can be achieved with due regard for those civilized standards in the use of the criminal law which are formulated in our Bill of Rights."

The issue, instead, is simply this: Does the Fourth Amendment permit an international traveler, citizen or alien, to be subjected to the sort of treatment that occurred in this case without the sanction of a judicial officer and based on nothing more than the "reasonable suspicion" of low ranking investigative officers that something might be amiss? The Court today concludes that the Fourth Amendment grants such sweeping and unmonitored authority to customs officials. . . . I dissent.

Indefinite involuntary incommunicado detentions "for investigation" are the hallmark of a police state, not a free society. . . . In my opinion, Government officials may no more confine a person at the border under such circumstances for purposes of criminal investigation than they may within the interior of the country. The nature and duration of the detention here may well have been tolerable for spoiled meat or diseased animals, but not for human beings held on simple suspicion of criminal activity.... Finally, I believe that the warrant and probable cause safeguards equally govern Justice STEVENS' proffered alternative of exposure to x-irradiation for criminal investigative purposes....

...The available evidence suggests that the number of highly intrusive border searches of suspicious-looking but ultimately innocent travelers may be very high. One physician who at the request of customs officials conducted many "internal searches"—rectal and vaginal examinations and stomach pumping—estimated that he had found contraband in 15 to 20 percent of the persons he had examined. It has similarly been estimated that only 16 percent of women subjected to body cavity searches at the border were in fact found to be carrying contraband. It is precisely to minimize the risk of harassing so many innocent people that the Fourth Amendment requires the intervention of a judicial officer....

The Court argues, however, that the length and "discomfort" of de Hernandez' detention "resulted solely from the method by which she chose to smuggle illicit drugs into this country," and it speculates that only her "heroic" efforts prevented the detention from being brief and to the point.... Although we now know that de Hernandez was indeed guilty of smuggling drugs internally, such *post hoc* rationalizations have no place in our Fourth Amendment jurisprudence, which demands that we "prevent hindsight from coloring the evaluation of the reasonableness of a search or seizure."...At the time the authorities simply had, at most, a reasonable suspicion that de Hernandez might be engaged in such smuggling.

Neither the law of the land nor the law of nature supports the notion that petty government officials can require people to excrete on command; indeed, the Court relies elsewhere on "the rudimentary knowledge of the human body" in sanctioning the "much longer than... typical" duration of detentions such as this. And, with all respect to the Court, it is not "unreasonable second-guessing," to predict that an innocent traveler, locked away in incommunicado detention in unfamiliar surroundings in a foreign land, might well be frightened and exhausted as to be unable so to "cooperate" with the authorities....

It is tempting, of course, to look the other way in a case that so graphically illustrates the "veritable national crisis" caused by narcotics trafficking. But if there is one enduring lesson to be learned in the long struggle to balance individual rights against society's need to defend itself against lawlessness, it is that

> it is easy to make light of insistence on scrupulous regard for the safeguards of civil liberties when invoked on behalf of the unworthy. It is too easy. History bears testimony that by such disregard are the rights of liberty extinguished, heedlessly at first, then stealthily, and brazenly in the end.

Questions

1. Identify the government interests the invasions of Montoya de Hernandez's liberty and privacy were intended to protect.

2. Compare the duration, location, and subjective invasiveness of Montoya de Hernandez's detention with that of John Terry in *Terry v. Ohio*.

3. Assume first you're a prosecutor and then a defense lawyer. Relying on the facts and opinion in *Terry v. Ohio*, argue, first, that the detention and searches of Montoya de Hernandez pass the reasonableness test and, then, that they fail the reasonableness test. Make sure you include all of the elements of reasonableness we've discussed in this chapter.

4. Now, assume you're a judge. Based on your view of the law, write an opinion supporting your decision whether the government actions in this case were reasonable under the Fourth Amendment.

 Go to Exercise 4-3 on the Criminal Procedure 6e CD to learn more about *U.S. v. Montoya de Hernandez*.

◆ ◆ ◆

Roadblocks

The government sets up **roadblocks**—barricades for stopping vehicles and questioning their occupants—that invade drivers' and passengers' liberty and privacy to protect a number of legitimate public interests. So, we see roadblocks for checking vehicles and their occupants, including:

- Driver's license and vehicle safety checks
- Weigh stations for trucks

- Game warden road checks

- Agricultural inspection stops

- Criminal investigation stops (to solve a specific crime)

- Border stops (to check for smuggled goods, contraband, and/or illegal aliens)

- Sobriety checkpoints

- Drug stops (to check for the possession and transport of illegal drugs)

Roadblocks to apprehend fleeing felons, to check vehicle safety requirements, and to prevent illegal aliens from entering the country are all legal. Amid a lot of controversy, a number of states have created roadblocks to prevent drunk driving and apprehend and prosecute drunk drivers (Hickey and Axline 1992; Weiner and Royster 1991). Are DWI roadblocks unreasonable stops? As you might expect by this point in reading the book, the U.S. Supreme Court answered, "It all depends...," in *Michigan v. Sitz* (1990).

| CASE | *Was the DWI Roadblock an Unreasonable Seizure?* |

Michigan v. Sitz
496 U.S. 444 (1990)

Rick Sitz and other drivers (respondents) brought an action to challenge the constitutionality of a highway sobriety checkpoint program. The Circuit Court of Wayne County, Michigan, invalidated the program, and the Michigan Department of State Police (petitioners) appealed. The Court of Appeals of Michigan affirmed. The U.S. Supreme Court granted certiorari. The Supreme Court reversed and remanded the case.

REHNQUIST, CJ., joined by WHITE, O'CONNOR, SCALIA, and KENNEDY, JJ.

FACTS

The Michigan Department of State Police and its Director (petitioners), established a sobriety checkpoint pilot program in early 1986....[Under the plan] checkpoints would be set up at selected sites along state roads. All vehicles passing through a checkpoint would be stopped and their drivers briefly examined for signs of intoxication. In cases where a checkpoint officer detected signs of intoxication, the motorist would be directed to a location out of the traffic flow where an officer would check the motorist's driver's license and car registration and, if warranted, conduct further sobriety tests. Should the field tests and the officer's observations suggest that the driver was intoxicated, an arrest would be made. All other drivers would be permitted to resume their journey immediately.

The first—and to date the only—sobriety checkpoint operated under the program was conducted in Saginaw County with the assistance of the Saginaw County Sheriff's Department. During the hour-and-fifteen-minute duration of the checkpoint's operation, 126 vehicles passed through the checkpoint. The average delay for each vehicle was approximately 25 seconds. Two drivers were detained for field sobriety testing, and one of the two was arrested for driving under the influence of alcohol. A third driver who drove through without stopping was pulled over by an officer in an observation vehicle and arrested for driving under the influence.

On the day before the operation of the Saginaw County checkpoint, Sitz and the other drivers (respondents) filed a complaint in the Circuit Court of Wayne County seeking declaratory and injunctive relief from potential subjection to the checkpoints. Sitz and each of the other drivers "is a licensed driver in the State of Michigan...who regularly travels throughout the State in his automobile." During pretrial proceedings, the Michigan Department of State Police (petitioners) agreed to delay further implementation of the checkpoint program pending the outcome of this litigation.

After the trial, at which the court heard extensive testimony concerning...the "effectiveness" of highway sobriety checkpoint programs, the court ruled that the Michigan program violated the Fourth Amendment and Art. 1, §11, of the Michigan Constitution. On appeal, the Michigan Court of Appeals affirmed the holding that the program violated the Fourth Amendment and, for that reason, did not consider whether the program violated the Michigan Constitution. After the Michigan Supreme Court denied Department of State Police's application for leave to appeal, we granted certiorari.

To decide this case the trial court performed a balancing test derived from our opinion in *Brown v. Texas* (1979). As described by the Court of Appeals, the test involved

1. "balancing the state's interest in preventing accidents caused by drunk drivers,

2. the effectiveness of sobriety checkpoints in achieving that goal, and

3. the level of intrusion on an individual's privacy caused by the checkpoints."

The Court of Appeals agreed that "the *Brown* three-prong balancing test was the correct test to be used to determine the constitutionality of the sobriety checkpoint plan." As characterized by the Court of Appeals, the trial court's findings with respect to the balancing factors were that the State has "a grave and legitimate" interest in curbing drunken driving; that sobriety checkpoint programs are generally "ineffective" and, therefore, do not significantly further that interest; and that the checkpoints' "subjective intrusion" on individual liberties is substantial. According to the court, the record disclosed no basis for disturbing the trial court's findings, which were made within the context of an analytical framework prescribed by this Court for determining the constitutionality of seizures less intrusive than traditional arrests.

OPINION

The Department of State police (petitioners) concede, correctly in our view, that a Fourth Amendment "seizure" occurs when a vehicle is stopped at a checkpoint.... The question thus becomes whether such seizures are "reasonable" under the Fourth Amendment.

...We address only the initial stop of each motorist passing through a checkpoint and the associated preliminary questioning and observation by checkpoint officers. Detention of particular motorists for more extensive field sobriety testing may require satisfaction of an individualized suspicion standard. No one can seriously dispute the magnitude of the drunken driving problem or the States' interest in eradicating it.... "Drunk drivers cause an annual death toll of over 25,000 and in the same time span cause nearly one million personal injuries and more than five billion dollars in property damage." For decades, this Court has "repeatedly lamented the tragedy."

Conversely, the weight bearing on the other scale—the measure of the intrusion on motorists stopped briefly at sobriety checkpoints—is slight.... The trial court and the

Court of Appeals, thus, accurately gauged the "objective" intrusion, measured by the duration of the seizure and the intensity of the investigation, as minimal.

With respect to what it perceived to be the "subjective" intrusion on motorists, however, the Court of Appeals found such intrusion substantial. The court first affirmed the trial court's finding that the guidelines governing checkpoint operation minimize the discretion of the officers on the scene. But the court also agreed with the trial court's conclusion that the checkpoints have the potential to generate fear and surprise in motorists. This was so because the record failed to demonstrate that approaching motorists would be aware of their option to make U-turns or turnoffs to avoid the checkpoints. On that basis, the court deemed the subjective intrusion from the checkpoints unreasonable.

We believe the Michigan courts misread our cases concerning the degree of "subjective intrusion" and the potential for generating fear and surprise. The "fear and surprise" to be considered are not the natural fear of one who has been drinking over the prospect of being stopped at a sobriety checkpoint but, rather, the fear and surprise engendered in law-abiding motorists by the nature of the stop....

The Court of Appeals went on to consider as part of the balancing analysis the "effectiveness" of the proposed checkpoint program. Based on extensive testimony in the trial record, the court concluded that the checkpoint program failed the "effectiveness" part of the test, and that this failure materially discounted petitioners' strong interest in implementing the program. We think the Court of Appeals was wrong on this point as well.... Experts in police science might disagree over which of several methods of apprehending drunken drivers is preferable as an ideal. But for purposes of Fourth Amendment analysis, the choice among such reasonable alternatives remains with the governmental officials who have a unique understanding of, and a responsibility for, limited public resources, including a finite number of police officers.

...This case involves neither a complete absence of empirical data nor a challenge of random highway stops. During the operation of the Saginaw County checkpoint, the detention of each of the 126 vehicles that entered the checkpoint resulted in the arrest of two drunken drivers. Stated as a percentage, approximately 1.5 percent of the drivers passing through the checkpoint were arrested for alcohol impairment. In addition, an expert witness testified at the trial that experience in other states demonstrated that, on the whole, sobriety checkpoints resulted in drunken driving arrests of around 1 percent of all motorists stopped....

In sum, the balance of the state's interest in preventing drunken driving, the extent to which this system can reasonably be said to advance that interest, and the degree of intrusion upon individual motorists who are briefly stopped, weighs in favor of the state program. We therefore hold that it is consistent with the Fourth Amendment. The judgment of the Michigan Court of Appeals is accordingly reversed, and the case is remanded for further proceedings not inconsistent with this opinion.

REVERSED.

DISSENT

BRENNAN, J., joined by MARSHALL, J.

... Some level of individualized suspicion is a core component of the protection the Fourth Amendment provides against arbitrary government action. By holding that no level of suspicion is necessary before the police may stop a car for the purpose of preventing drunken driving, the Court potentially subjects the general public to arbitrary or harassing conduct by the police....

I do not dispute the immense social cost caused by drunken drivers, nor do I slight the government's efforts to prevent such tragic losses. Indeed, I would hazard a guess that today's opinion will be received favorably by a majority of our society, who would willingly suffer the minimal intrusion of a sobriety checkpoint stop in order to prevent drunken driving. But consensus that a particular law enforcement technique serves a laudable purpose has never been the touchstone of constitutional analysis.

The Fourth Amendment was designed not merely to protect against official intrusions whose social utility was less as measured by some "balancing test" than its intrusion on individual privacy; it was designed in addition to grant the individual a zone of privacy whose protections could be breached only where the "reasonable" requirements of the probable cause standard were met. Moved by whatever momentary evil has aroused their fears, officials—perhaps even supported by a majority of citizens—may be tempted to conduct searches that sacrifice the liberty of each citizen to assuage the perceived evil. But the Fourth Amendment rests on the principle that a true balance between the individual and society depends on the recognition of "the right to be let alone—the most comprehensive of rights and the right most valued by civilized men." *Olmstead v. United States* (1928) (Brandeis, J., dissenting).

In the face of the "momentary evil" of drunken driving, the Court today abdicates its role as the protector of that fundamental right. I respectfully dissent.

STEVENS, J., joined by BRENNAN and MARSHALL, JJ.

... The record in this case makes clear that a decision holding these suspicionless seizures unconstitutional would not impede the law enforcement community's remarkable progress in reducing the death toll on our highways. Be-

cause the Michigan program was patterned after an older program in Maryland, the trial judge gave special attention to that state's experience. Over a period of several years, Maryland operated 125 checkpoints; of the 41,000 motorists passing through those checkpoints, only 143 persons (0.3%) were arrested. The number of man-hours devoted to these operations is not in the record, but it seems inconceivable that a higher arrest rate could not have been achieved by more conventional means.

... Any relationship between sobriety checkpoints and an actual reduction in highway fatalities is even less substantial than the minimal impact on arrest rates. As the Michigan Court of Appeals pointed out,

> Maryland had conducted a study comparing traffic statistics between a county using checkpoints and a control county. The results of the study showed that alcohol-related accidents in the checkpoint county decreased by ten percent, whereas the control county saw an eleven percent decrease; and while fatal accidents in the control county fell from sixteen to three, fatal accidents in the checkpoint county actually doubled from the prior year.

In light of these considerations, it seems evident that the Court today... overvalues the law enforcement interest in using sobriety checkpoints [and] undervalues the citizen's interest in freedom from random, unannounced investigatory seizures....

... A Michigan officer who questions a motorist at a sobriety checkpoint has virtually unlimited discretion to detain the driver on the basis of the slightest suspicion. A ruddy complexion, an unbuttoned shirt, bloodshot eyes or a speech impediment may suffice to prolong the detention. Any driver who had just consumed a glass of beer, or even a sip of wine, would almost certainly have the burden of demonstrating to the officer that her driving ability was not impaired.

... These fears are not, as the Court would have it, solely the lot of the guilty. To be law abiding is not necessarily to be spotless, and even the most virtuous can be unlucky. Unwanted attention from the local police need not be less discomforting simply because one's secrets are not the stuff of criminal prosecutions. Moreover, those who have found—by reason of prejudice or misfortune—that encounters with the police may become adversarial or unpleasant without good cause will have grounds for worrying at any stop designed to elicit signs of suspicious behavior. Being stopped by the police is distressing even when it should not be terrifying, and what begins mildly may by happenstance turn severe....

... In my opinion, unannounced investigatory seizures are, particularly when they take place at night, the hallmark of regimes far different from ours; the surprise intrusion upon individual liberty is not minimal. On that issue, my difference with the Court may amount to nothing less than a difference in our respective evaluations of the importance of individual liberty, a serious albeit inevitable source of constitutional disagreement. On the degree to which the sobriety checkpoint seizures advance the public interest, however, the Court's position is wholly indefensible. . . .

. . . The evidence in this case indicates that sobriety checkpoints result in the arrest of a fraction of one percent of the drivers who are stopped, but there is absolutely no evidence that this figure represents an increase over the number of arrests that would have been made by using the same law enforcement resources in conventional patrols. Thus, although the gross number of arrests is more than zero, there is a complete failure of proof on the question whether the wholesale seizures have produced any net advance in the public interest in arresting intoxicated drivers. . . .

The most disturbing aspect of the Court's decision today is that it appears to give no weight to the citizen's interest in freedom from suspicionless unannounced investigatory seizures. . . . On the other hand, the Court places a heavy thumb on the law enforcement. . . . Perhaps this tampering with the scales of justice can be explained by the Court's obvious concern about the slaughter on our highways, and a resultant tolerance for policies designed to alleviate the problem by "setting an example" of a few motorists. . . .

This is a case that is driven by nothing more than symbolic state action—an insufficient justification for an otherwise unreasonable program of random seizures. Unfor-

tunately, the Court is transfixed by the wrong symbol—the illusory prospect of punishing countless intoxicated motorists—when it should keep its eyes on the road plainly marked by the Constitution.

I respectfully DISSENT.

Questions

1. According to the Court, why are DWI checkpoints Fourth Amendment seizures?

2. Why, according to the Court, are they reasonable seizures?

3. What interests does the Court balance in reaching its result?

4. What does Justice Stevens mean when he says that he and the majority disagree over the meaning of freedom? What does he have to say about the need and effectiveness of DWI checkpoints?

5. What does Justice Brennan mean when he says that the degree of the intrusion begins, not ends, the inquiry about whether DWI checkpoints are reasonable seizures?

6. How would you identify and balance the interests at stake in the DWI checkpoints? Are the checkpoints effective? Explain.

7. According to the American Civil Liberties Union (ACLU), "highly publicized local law enforcement efforts such as random roadblocks" are "Orwellian intrusions into individual privacy." What does the ACLU mean? Do you agree? Explain.

After the U.S. Supreme Court decision, the *Sitz* case went back to Michigan, where the Michigan Supreme Court ruled that suspicionless stops are unreasonable seizures.

◆ STATE CONSTITUTIONAL LAW ◆

Sitz v. Michigan Department of State Police
506 N.W.2d 209 (Mich. 1993)

Does the Michigan Constitution Require "Individualized" Suspicion?

FACTS

[The Facts of this case appear in the case excerpt *Michigan v. Sitz* (1990).]

OPINION

. . . [O]ur jurisprudence conclusively demonstrates that, in the context of automobile seizures, we have extended more expansive protection to our citizens than that extended in *Sitz*. This Court has never recognized the right of the state, without any level of suspicion whatsoever, to detain members of the population at large for criminal investigatory purposes. Nor has Michigan completely acquiesced to the judgment of "politically accountable officials" when determining reasonableness in such a context. In these circumstances, the Michigan Constitution offers more protection than the United States Supreme Court's interpretation of the Fourth Amendment....

The Michigan Constitution has historically treated searches and seizures for criminal investigatory purposes differently than those for regulatory or administrative purposes. These administrative or regulatory searches and seizures have traditionally been regarded as "reasonable" in a constitutional sense. However, seizures with the primary goal of enforcing the criminal law have generally required some level of suspicion, even if that level has fluctuated over the years.

As long ago as 1889, the justices of this Court stated:

> Personal liberty, which is guaranteed to every citizen under our Constitution and laws, consists of the right of locomotion—to go where one pleases, and when, and to do that which may lead to one's business or pleasure, only so far restrained as the rights of others may make it necessary for the welfare of all other citizens. One may travel along the public highways or in public places; and while conducting themselves in a decent and orderly manner, disturbing no other, and interfering with the rights of no other citizens, there, they will be protected under the law, not only in their persons, but in their safe conduct. The Constitution and the laws are framed for the public good, and the protection of all citizens, from the highest to the lowest; and no one may be restrained of his liberty, unless he has transgressed some law. [*Pinkerton v. Verberg*, 78 Mich. 573, 584, 44 N.W. 579 (1889).]

We do not suggest that in a different context we might not reach a similar result under the balancing test of reasonableness employed in *Sitz*. Indeed, our precedent regarding automobiles implicitly incorporates a balancing test that is inherent in assessing the reasonableness of warrantless searches and seizures. We

hold only that the protection afforded to the seizures of vehicles for criminal investigatory purposes has both an historical foundation and a contemporary justification that is not outweighed by the necessity advanced. Suspicionless criminal investigatory seizures, and extreme deference to the judgments of politically accountable officials is, in this context, contrary to Michigan constitutional precedent....

DISSENT

BRICKLEY, J.

...There are distinct advantages to uniformity in the interpretation of search and seizure constitutional provisions. The interstate flow of traffic on our intrastate and interstate highway system argues for uniformity in highway safety enforcement.... Technological advances in miniaturization and the concomitant development of easily concealed destructive devices (not to mention the lethal force of an automobile driven by an intoxicated person), coupled with increasing levels of violence and the threat of international terrorism, are going to continue to prompt the need for and the public acceptance of surveillance–inspection techniques that involve minimum inconveniences and intrusions as a necessary trade-off for the personal safety and security of the population at large. Such systematic and evenly enforced measures need not erode the traditional and accepted standards of probable cause and articulable suspicion when employed in the customary criminal investigation context....

Accordingly, this is not, in my view, the time, nor does this case present the circumstances, to have the Michigan Constitution digress from the evolving Fourth Amendment standards as interpreted by the United States Supreme Court.

EXPLORING ROADBLOCKS FURTHER

 Go to the Criminal Procedure 6e CD to read the full text versions of the cases featured here.

1. *Is a "Pretext" Roadblock a Reasonable Stop?*

FACTS

During the summer of 1989, Larry Buck, a detective with the Stark County Sheriff's Office, Sgt. Don Glarum of the State Highway Patrol, and Stark County Deputy Sheriff

Mike Adolph were assigned by their supervisors to establish a highway checkpoint in Stark County to coincide with the upcoming annual motorcycle rally in Sturgis, South Dakota. On June 26, 1989, District Eight Highway Patrol Captain David Messer issued Operation Order 2–89, which stated in part:.

> Due to the rally in Sturgis, South Dakota, and the large volume of drugs on our highways, the North Dakota Highway Patrol along with the Stark County Sheriff's Office and other agencies will conduct a driver's license and registration check. If probable cause presents its self [sic], for drugs and other contraband, a search will be conducted. The check will be conducted on Highway 85 on 5–6 and 13–14 August, 1989. It will be the mission of the North Dakota Highway Patrol to attempt to alleviate the problem of drugs being transported by vehicle, on state highway's [sic] in North Dakota.

On July 17, 1989, Stark County Sheriff James Rice issued a memorandum in preparation for the operation that stated the following:

Checkpoints will be set up and operated as listed below:

1. All vehicles heading in an assigned direction will be stopped.

2. Vehicle registration will be checked for current status.

3. Driver of vehicle will be checked for current operator's driver's license.

4. A vehicle inspection will be conducted. Checkpoints will be located on #85, #22, #8 and #10 during assigned times.

On August 5–6 and 13–14, 1989, law enforcement officers conducted a checkpoint 12 miles south of Belfield on U.S. Highway 85. Personnel from the Stark, Billings, and Slope County Sheriff's Offices; the State Highway Patrol; the State Drug Enforcement Unit; the U.S. Border Patrol; and the Minot Police Department participated in the operation. On August 5 and 6, which coincided with the beginning of the motorcycle rally, all southbound traffic was stopped. On August 13 and 14, which coincided with the conclusion of the rally, all northbound traffic was stopped. The checkpoint was located in a small valley so that oncoming traffic could not see it from a long distance. A driver would first see a large sign that said, "Please stop." The actual checkpoint was located approximately two-tenths of one mile from the sign. The checkpoint was conducted only during daylight hours.

Every vehicle was stopped at the checkpoint. The driver would first encounter three fluorescent orange traffic cones and an officer referred to as the "point man," who was located at an intersection of the highway and a gravel road. Parked on the gravel road on the driver's right were sheriffs' cars, a camper used as a command post, and Drug Enforcement Unit vehicles. Drug Enforcement Unit officers and sheriffs' deputies conducted searches of vehicles referred to this area if the driver consented to a search. Two Highway Patrol officers were stationed farther down the highway to conduct vehicle-safety inspections.

Keith Everson, one of the motorcyclists who was stopped and who had amphetamines and marijuana in his possession, argued that the search and seizure violated the Fourth Amendment. Was the checkpoint legal?

DECISION AND REASONS

The trial court ruled the roadblock was "pretextual." According to the court:

> Although the State characterizes this roadblock as multi-purpose, the main purpose was to search for controlled substances. This is reflected by the lead person being a criminal

investigator not a traffic officer, by the operation order for the Highway Patrol stating that the purpose was "to alleviate the problem of drugs being transported by the [sic] vehicle," by the point man having unconstrained discretion to send vehicles to the search area or the inspection area, and by the first and main area at the roadblock being the search area.

The North Dakota Supreme Court disagreed with the trial court:

> In analyzing the constitutionality of the checkpoint in this case, we begin by noting the trial court's apparent determination that the checkpoint was unconstitutional because it was conducted as a pretext or subterfuge to check for the presence of controlled substances. The State does not challenge the trial court's finding that the primary purpose of the checkpoint was to look for controlled substances, but asserts that this fact should not in itself invalidate the checkpoint. We agree.

Applying the reasoning and the holding of *Michigan v. Sitz* to the North Dakota roadblock, the court wrote the following:

> If a state may validly conduct a checkpoint for the purpose of apprehending drunk drivers, we think the state may validly conduct a checkpoint for the purpose of apprehending drug traffickers, a societal harm at least equal in magnitude to drunk driving....

In a strong dissent, the dissenting judge wrote:

> If we are to extend *Sitz* to condone a nonrandom roadblock whose purpose is to look for illegal drugs, then any nonrandom roadblock whose purpose is to look for evidence of any criminal conduct is permissible under the Fourth Amendment. But the war on drugs cannot suspend constitutional guarantees.... I assume, until the United States Supreme Court tells me otherwise, that the Fourth Amendment still has some application to vehicles. Drivers' expectations of privacy in those vehicles, so long as those drivers are obeying traffic laws, are not in the vicinity of or crossing a border, and are not drinking or otherwise using illegal substances, still find some protection under the Fourth Amendment and its requirement of reasonable suspicion in order to make a seizure reasonable. At least, I hope so.

State v. Everson, 474 N.W.2d 695 (N.D. 1991)

2. Is An Apartment "Checkpoint" for Trespassers a Reasonable Stop?

FACTS

On December 8, 1996, Officer Sayas was instructed by his lieutenant to establish a "security" checkpoint at the Hoffler Apartment Complex (Hoffler), which was owned by the Suffolk Public Housing Authority (the Authority). The Authority requested police assistance in response to resident complaints about trespassers and drug dealers on the premises. Sayas testified that he had patrolled Hoffler previously, but that this was the first time he had conducted a checkpoint there.

Sayas and another officer established the checkpoint just inside the entrance to Hoffler. They were told to stop all persons, whether traveling in a vehicle or on foot, entering the complex between midnight and 2:00 A.M. The officers were to ascertain the identity of each person entering the complex and that person's purpose for being there. Andra Wilson was stopped as he approached the checkpoint at approximately 1:35 A.M. Sayas arrested Wilson after determining that he was intoxicated. Did the officers at the checkpoint seize Andra Wilson unreasonably?

DECISION AND REASONS

Yes, according to the Court of Appeals of Virginia:

Stopping a motor vehicle and detaining its operator at a roadblock [checkpoint] constitutes a "seizure" within the meaning of the Fourth Amendment. If the stop is made without probable cause or reasonable suspicion of criminal activity, then the seizure must be carried out pursuant to a plan embodying explicit, neutral limitations on the conduct of individual officers. (*Brown v. Texas*, 443 U.S. 47, 51 [1979])

To determine whether a checkpoint stop is constitutionally valid, we apply the balancing test established in *Brown*. The *Brown* test involves a weighing of three criteria: "(1) the gravity of the public concerns served by the seizure, (2) the degree to which the seizure advances the public interest, and (3) the severity of the interference with individual liberty...." A "central concern" in balancing the foregoing competing considerations has been to make certain that "an individual's reasonable expectation of privacy is not subject to arbitrary invasions solely at the unfettered discretion of officers in the field."

The United States Supreme Court has stated that the second prong of the *Brown* test was not meant to transfer from politically accountable officials to the courts the decision as to which among reasonable alternative law enforcement techniques should be employed to deal with a serious public danger.... For purposes of Fourth Amendment analysis, the choice among such reasonable alternatives remains with the governmental officials who have a unique understanding of, and responsibility for, limited public resources, including a finite number of police officers. *Michigan Dept. of State Police v. Sitz*, 496 U.S. 444, 453–54 (1990).

Nevertheless, the Commonwealth must present some evidence establishing that the method employed will be an effective tool for addressing the public concern involved.

Assuming that combating drug dealing satisfies the "gravity of the public concerns served" prong of the *Brown* balancing test, the Commonwealth presented insufficient evidence proving that the security checkpoint at Hoffler effectively addressed this concern. The only evidence presented regarding the circumstances leading to the checkpoint's establishment was that Hoffler residents had complained to the Authority about trespassers and drug dealers on the property. The Commonwealth, however, presented no empirical evidence that there was a problem with drug dealers at Hoffler. There was no evidence that any drug-related arrests were made as a result of the checkpoint that night. Cf. *Sitz*, 496 U.S. at 454–55, 110 S.Ct. 2481 (noting the number of drunk drivers arrested as a result of the challenged roadblock). Although Sayas testified that he had previously patrolled at Hoffler, there was no evidence that he had ever made any arrests there for drug dealing. There was also no evidence that security checkpoints like this one are an effective tool in combating drug dealing.

In the absence of sufficient evidence to satisfy the second prong of the *Brown* test, we hold that the interference with individual liberty inherent in this checkpoint outweighed the public interest in establishing it. Because appellant's detention at the checkpoint was unlawful, the trial court should have suppressed all evidence seized as a result of the stop. Accordingly, the judgment of the trial court is reversed and the case is remanded for retrial, if the Commonwealth be so advised.

REVERSED AND REMANDED.

Wilson v. Commonwealth of Virginia, 509 S.E.2d 540 (1999)

FRISKS AND THE FOURTH AMENDMENT

Frisks and stops are closely linked, but they're not the same: Stops are seizures; **frisks** are searches. According to the court in a leading stop-and-frisk case from New York, *People v. Rivera* (1964), a frisk is a

> contact or patting of the outer clothing of a person to detect by the sense of touch, if a concealed weapon is being carried. . . . The sense of exterior touch here involved is not very far different from the sense of sight or hearing upon which police customarily act. . . . [It is] a minor inconvenience and petty indignity. (35)

The justification for stops is criminal law enforcement; for frisks, it's to protect officers during stops. A lawful stop has to come *before* a frisk. It works like this. First, officers have to reasonably suspect crime is afoot; then they have to stop a suspect; then (and *only*) if they reasonably suspect the person they stopped may be armed, they can frisk (once-over-lightly pat-down) the suspect (Table 4.5). Understand that the facts that back up a stop don't automatically back up a frisk. The facts have to point to a suspicion the suspects may be armed.

Frisks are the least-invasive searches; body-cavity searches stand at the other extreme. However, to say that frisks are the least-invasive doesn't mean they're not invasions of privacy. After all, even a slight touch, when it's not wanted, can be highly offensive. So, it's not surprising that the U.S. Supreme Court has never wavered from calling frisks Fourth Amendment searches. The reasonableness of frisks depends on balancing the government interest in criminal law enforcement against the individual privacy right not to be touched by an officer. The basic idea is that we shouldn't expect police officers to risk their lives unnecessarily to investigate suspicious persons and circumstances. At the same time, we have to obey the Fourth Amendment command to keep people "secure in their persons" against unreasonable searches.

So what does constitute reasonable suspicion to frisk? And, what is the scope of lawful frisks? Let's look at both of these issues.

Reasonable Suspicion to Back Up Frisks

There's no magic formula to tell us the number and quality of facts that add up to reasonable suspicion a suspect is armed. But, some examples suggest the kind of objective basis that justifies particular frisks. In *Terry v. Ohio*, it was the nature of the crime. Officer McFadden reasonably suspected that Terry and his companions were about to commit armed robbery. If it was reasonable to suspect that they were going to commit armed robbery, it was, of course, also reasonable to suspect they would use weapons

TABLE 4.5
Elements of a Lawful Frisk

A stop is backed up by a reasonable suspicion a crime may be afoot.

Officers must have reasonable suspicion the suspect may be armed.

Officers may do a once-over-lightly pat-down to detect weapons (*not* contraband or evidence).

TABLE 4.6

Examples of Scope of Frisk That Justify More Than Outer-Clothing Pat-Down

Feeling a hard object inside a coat pocket that could be a weapon authorizes reaching inside the coat.

Encountering unusually bulky winter clothing may require feeling underneath the outer clothing.

Suspecting the contents of a closed handbag may be illegal can justify opening the handbag.

to do so. So, it was reasonable to frisk Terry and his companions for guns. Other examples of what courts have accepted include bulges in clothing, sudden movement toward a pocket or other place that might contain a weapon, and knowledge that the suspect had been armed on a previous occasion.

Reasonable suspicion to frisk requires only that officers reasonably *suspect* the person stopped *may* be armed. Officers are allowed to rely on their training and experience in forming suspicion. So, officers can read more into facts than the rest of us. For example, the average person knows nothing about a drug operation, but experienced narcotics officers quickly grasp them. As in most Fourth Amendment situations, reasonable suspicion to frisk allows officers a lot of discretion to protect themselves.

The Scope of Lawful Frisks

On the same day the U.S. Supreme Court decided *Terry v. Ohio*, it decided another case, rejecting emphatically the government's argument that after a lawful stop an automatic frisk for evidence and contraband was lawful. In *Sibron v. New York* (1968), the Court held that frisks are so intrusive that only saving officers from wounding and death justifies the invasion of a frisk during the brief "freeze" of a stop to investigate suspicious people and circumstances. In other words, there are two elements in a lawful frisk: (1) First, there has to be a lawful stop. (2) Second, there has to be reasonable suspicion the persons stopped are armed.

This doesn't mean that it's always unreasonable to seize evidence and contraband during a frisk. Suppose an officer is patting down a suspect who was lawfully stopped and is reasonably suspected of being armed. She pats down the suspect and comes upon marijuana. Can she seize it? Yes, as long as the frisk for weapons isn't a pretext for looking for marijuana. However, critics fear that allowing such seizures will lead to abuse of the power to frisk. To avoid abuse, they recommend that stops be allowable only when there's the suspicion that the person has committed violent crimes. Referring to the power to seize contraband found during frisks, the reporters for the American Law Institute's *Model Code of Pre-Arraignment Procedure* (1975) wrote:

> It is hard to ignore the fact that . . . any power will be abused. The courts have made it quite clear that in the name of police safety, they will always allow a frisk of extensive proportions, and it is difficult to see how this can be avoided. A corollary hard reality is that police will use this power not really to protect themselves but to seize and confiscate weapons and other contraband.

Once officers reasonably suspect suspects might be armed, they're allowed to use only the amount of bodily contact necessary to detect weapons. In most cases, this means officers may lightly touch suspects' outer clothing to locate and seize concealed weapons. Courts are vague about how much further police officers may lawfully go (Table 4.6).

The Pennsylvania Superior Court examined how far officers can go in frisking suspects in *Commonwealth v. Guillespie.*

Commonwealth v. Guillespie
745 A.2d 654 (PA Sup. Ct. 2000)

Derrick Guillespie, defendant, was convicted in the Court of Common Pleas, Dauphin County, Criminal Division, of possession with intent to deliver, possession of drug paraphernalia, and possession of marijuana and sentenced to 3 to 6 years in prison. He appealed. The Pennsylvania Superior Court reversed and remanded.

CIRILLO, J.

FACTS

On November 8, 1997 at approximately 8:15 P.M., the Harrisburg Police Bureau received a report that a robbery had just occurred at 13th and Chestnut Streets. A police officer patrolling the vicinity spotted two men, the Appellant and his co-defendant, who fit the general description of the alleged robbers. Officers then attempted to stop the individuals. When the police moved in to effectuate the investigatory stop, the officers observed appellant's co-defendant discard something. Officer Luis Rodriguez then frisked appellant and felt from the outside of his pockets what appeared to be two pill bottles. When appellant was asked what was in his pockets, he stated that it was candy.

The facts that follow the preceding events are critical to our decision today. The testimony reveals that Officer Rodriguez did not immediately search Guillespie further once he initially felt the pill bottles. Rather, the officer's testimony is sketchy on the events that followed. From the record, we glean that at some point, either before or after his initial pat-down, Officer Rodriguez handcuffed Guillespie. At this time he did not have any concerns that Guillespie had a weapon on his person.

Subsequent to this initial pat-down, the robbery victim arrived at the scene where the police had detained Guillespie and his co-defendant; he indicated that neither of them were the perpetrators of the robbery. Another officer then checked for any outstanding arrest warrants on Guillespie's co-defendant. Thereafter, the police revealed that the items initially discarded by Guillespie's co-defendant were drugs. It was at this time that Officer Rodriguez conducted a second pat-down of Guillespie and removed the items from his pockets. At some point thereafter, officers determined that there were outstanding arrest warrants for Guillespie. He was then taken to the police station where the substances inside the pill bottles were inventoried, among other personal items on his person.

Prior to trial, Guillespie filed a motion to suppress the evidence found on his person during Officer Rodriguez' pat-down. The trial court denied this request and ultimately found him guilty and sentenced him to three to six years' incarceration.

OPINION

Guillespie sets forth the following claim for our review: Whether the search of Appellant beyond a pat-down for weapons was illegal.

…Under Pennsylvania case law, a police officer may conduct "a limited search of an individual's outer clothing in an attempt to discover the presence of weapons which may be used to endanger the safety of police or others." Such procedure is known as a *Terry* stop and frisk or pat-down.

…Since the sole justification for a *Terry* search is the protection of the police and others nearby, such a protective search must be strictly "limited to that which is necessary for the discovery of weapons which might be used to harm the officer or others nearby." Thus, the purpose of this limited search is not to discover evidence, but to allow the officer to pursue his investigation without fear of violence. If the protective search goes beyond what is necessary to determine if the suspect is armed, it is no longer valid under *Terry* and its fruits will be suppressed.

In *Commonwealth v. Graham,* the Pennsylvania Supreme Court was careful to note that this exception to the warrant requirement should be construed in an extremely narrow fashion, finding that even a "squeeze" of the defendant's pocket went beyond the scope of the search authorized by *Terry.* The court also articulated that Pennsylvania jurisprudence follows the principle that a *Terry* frisk must relate, in nature and scope, to the sole justification for the search: a pat-down for weapons to ensure the safety of the police and those nearby.

The *Graham* court stated that "therefore, a *Terry* frisk will only support the seizure of contraband discovered via the officer's plain feel [Chapter 3] when the incriminating nature of that contraband is immediately apparent to the officer, based solely on the officer's initial pat-down of the suspect's outer garments. Once the initial pat-down dispels the officer's suspicion that the suspect is armed, any further poking, prodding, squeezing, or other manipulation of any objects discovered during that pat-down is outside the scope of the search authorized under as noted in Graham…that the plain feel doctrine is only applicable if the incriminating nature of the contraband is immediately apparent.

In the present case, the facts reveal that Officer Rodriguez felt, during his pat-down of Guillespie, what appeared to be pill bottles in his pockets. When questioned as to what was actually in his pockets, Guillespie stated that it was candy. Rodriguez, however, did not immediately search Guillespie's pockets to remove the bottles. Rather, he waited until another officer arrested Guillespie's co-defendant, before he emptied Guillespie's pockets and uncovered uncontrolled substances and drug paraphernalia. Subsequently, the officers also discovered that there were outstanding warrants for Guillespie's arrest; the officers then charged and arrested Guillespie.

...At the time Officer Rodriguez conducted the "pat-down" of Guillespie, it was not immediately apparent that the objects in Guillespie's pockets were incriminatingly indicative of the presence of contraband. First, any innocuous small objects could have been contained within the pill bottles. Second, if the officer had thought that the objects in the pockets were "immediately apparent" as contraband, he should not have stopped his search and later decided to resume a more detailed search of Guillespie's pockets once he received evidence of drugs having been discarded by his co-defendant. Under such circumstances, the second search clearly went beyond that justified for a *Terry* stop—the search was no longer needed to protect Officer Rodriguez from a suspiciously armed suspect....

We must keep in mind that an "investigative detention" or *Terry* stop must be supported by reasonable suspicion; it subjects the suspect to a stop and a period of detention, but does not involve such coercive conditions as to constitute the functional equivalent of arrest. Between the time when Officer Rodriguez searched Guillespie a second time and when the other officers actually found out that there were outstanding arrest warrants for Guillespie, Officer Rodriguez no longer had reasonable suspicion to detain him....

Instantly, because Officer Rodriguez no longer had reasonable suspicion at the point that the robbery victim came to the scene and eliminated Guillespie as a robbery suspect, any further detention of him was improper....He was free to leave at this point and the officer's handcuffing and subsequent (second) pat-down and seizure of the pill bottles was illegal. Accordingly, we reverse Guillespie's judgment of sentence.

Judgment of sentence reversed. Case remanded for a new trial. Jurisdiction relinquished.

Questions

1. List all of the facts relevant to deciding whether the officers had reasonable suspicion to frisk Guillespie. Be sure to separate the facts to support Guillespie's stop and frisk from those supporting the stop and frisk of his co-defendant.

2. Summarize the court's argument in favor of suppressing the evidence.

3. Should the officers have been allowed to frisk Guillespie for drugs as long as they had reasonable suspicion to stop him? To stop and frisk his co-defendant? Defend your answer.

EXPLORING REASONABLE SUSPICION FOR FRISKS FURTHER

 Go to the Criminal Procedure 6e CD to read the full text versions of these cases.

1. Was the Roadside Frisk Reasonable?

FACTS

Two deputies saw a car swerve into a ditch and stopped to investigate. David Long, the only occupant, met the deputies at the rear of the car and showed them his driver's license. He had started back toward the open door of the car when the deputies asked him for the car registration. The officers saw a large hunting knife on the floorboard, so one of the deputies frisked Long. The other then entered the vehicle and found an open pouch of marijuana under an armrest. Was the frisk lawful?

DECISION AND REASONS

Yes, according to the U.S. Supreme Court, because

> roadside encounters between police and suspects are especially hazardous, and ... danger may arise from the possible presence of weapons in the area surrounding a suspect, [the] search of the passenger compartment of an automobile, limited to those areas in which a weapon may be placed or hidden, is permissible if the police officer possesses a reasonable belief based on "specific and articulable facts which, taken together with the rational inferences from those facts, reasonably warrant" the officer in believing that the suspect is dangerous and may gain immediate control of weapons.

> *Michigan v. Long,* 463 U.S. 1032 (1983)

2. Was the Frisk of the "Bikers" Reasonable?

FACTS

Patrick Robinson (Defendant) and his companion, Mark Guardado, both of whom were wearing Hell's Angels jackets and insignia, were traveling by motorcycle through Brecksville, Ohio, on the morning of June 13, 1996. At approximately 7:00 A.M., Defendant's motorcycle began to sputter, and both men pulled their bikes over to the side of the road. Two police officers who had observed the sputtering pulled up beside Robinson and Guardado and were quickly joined by a third officer. Upon the request of the officers, both men produced valid out-of-state licenses and registrations, and no outstanding warrants were discovered. Defendant was asked where he and Guardado were heading, and he said they were on their way from Chicago, Illinois, to Rochester, New York.

During the encounter, Officer Craig Mares spotted part of a knife sheath protruding from under Guardado's jacket. Mares asked Guardado to lift up his jacket and then asked him to put the knife, which had a 5-inch blade, on the ground. Guardado complied and was informed by Officer Mares that he would be patted down. Before beginning the pat-down, Mares asked Guardado if he had any additional weapons, and when Guardado indicated that he had a gun, he was handcuffed and searched. A loaded 9-millimeter pistol was recovered.

Officer Mares called out to Officer William Reppa, who was standing next to Defendant Robinson, and told Reppa that he had found a pistol on Guardado and that Reppa should pat down Defendant. Reppa told Defendant to put his hands behind his back and asked him if he had any weapons. Defendant indicated that he did and ultimately produced two folding knives with 5-inch blades. Reppa then patted Defendant down, with Officer Mares assisting. During the patdown, Officer Reppa felt a plastic bag in Defendant's pocket, reached in, and discovered that the bag contained three marijuana cigarettes and a small amount of white powder that turned out to be methamphetamine. Defendant was handcuffed and advised that he was under arrest. Officers Mares and Reppa then resumed their search of Defendant and found a .38 caliber revolver and ammunition in a fanny pack inside Defendant's pants.

Did the officers have the automatic power to frisk Robinson because he was Guardado's companion?

DECISION AND REASONS

No, according to the U.S. Sixth Circuit Court of Appeals:

> We turn ... to the central issue in this case, which is whether the officers, when they decided to pat down Defendant, had reasonable suspicion based on specific and articulable facts that Defendant was armed and dangerous or was engaging in criminal activity. If the officers had reasonable suspicion, the revolver and ammunition were lawfully recovered from Defendant and can be used at trial. Otherwise, the evidence must be suppressed.
>
> In arguing that the officers had the requisite reasonable suspicion to justify the patdown of Defendant, the Government relies heavily on the fact that Guardado was found to be carrying a loaded and concealed pistol, as well as a knife. ... This court has rejected a rule under which "companions of the arrestee within the immediate vicinity [can be] constitutionally subjected to the cursory pat-down reasonably necessary to give assurance that they are unarmed." We stated that "the *Terry* requirement of reasonable suspicion under the circumstances has [not] been eroded to the point that an individual may be frisked based upon nothing more than an unfortunate choice of associates." While Defendant's proximity to Guardado can "be considered as a factor in determining the legitimacy of a frisk ... proximity cannot be the sole legitimizing factor." Thus, the Government must point to additional specific and articulable facts if it is to establish that reasonable suspicion existed for the patdown of Defendant. It is here that the Government's case falls short. ...
>
> In sum, if the officers based their patdown of Defendant on objectively reasonable suspicion, rather than, say, prejudice towards motorcycle riders, members of the Hell's Angels, or people from out-of-state, they must have been relying almost entirely on the fact that a pistol and knife were recovered from Guardado. Such reliance comes so close to making Defendant's companion the sole justification for the search of Defendant, that it is at odds with the spirit, if not the letter, of the ... prohibition against basing a *Terry* frisk on "nothing more than an unfortunate choice of associates." While additional factors were involved, it is difficult to imagine a case where police officers could not point to something to provide slight additional justification for a frisk, as they did here. In the instant case, the additional factors gave the officers nothing more than "a mere inchoate and unparticularized suspicion or hunch [that they were] dealing with an armed and dangerous individual." That is not enough. Therefore ... we AFFIRM the district court's decision to grant the suppression motion.
>
> *U.S. v. Robinson,* 149 F.3d 1185 (6th Cir. 1998)

SUMMARY

    I. Stops, frisks, and the Fourth Amendment
      A. The discretionary power to stop and question suspicious persons is ancient
      B. First challenged during the 1960s due process revolution
      C. Stops and frisks
        1. Fourth Amendment stops are brief detentions, allowing officers to briefly freeze situations to investigate them
        2. Fourth Amendment frisks are once-over-lightly pat-downs of outer clothing to protect officers from concealed weapons

3. Stops and frisks most often take place on the street and other public places
4. Stops and frisks are the least-invasive invasions of liberty and privacy but they affect a lot more people

D. Fourth Amendment seizures include everything from brief stops on the street to long detentions in jail

E. Fourth Amendment searches include everything from outer-clothing pat-downs to body-cavity searches

F. Stop-and-frisk law
1. Three-step analysis
   a. Was the action a stop or frisk?
   b. If it was a stop or frisk, was it reasonable?
   c. It was reasonable, should evidence be excluded?
2. Consequences:
   a. If action wasn't a stop or frisk, the Fourth Amendment doesn't apply; no further court analysis, action left to officer discretion
   b. If action was a stop or frisk, then proceed to decide if either was reasonable
   c. If the stop or frisk was unreasonable, then proceed to decide if evidence has to be excluded

G. Two approaches to Fourth Amendment analysis
1. Two parts to the amendment
   a. Reasonableness clause
   b. Warrant clause
2. Conventional and reasonableness approaches by the Court
   a. Conventional approach, reasonableness depends on two elements
      (1) Warrant
      (2) Probable cause
   b. Reasonableness approach
      (1) Reasonableness depends on two elements
         (a) Balancing—the need to search outweighs the invasion of individual liberty and privacy
         (b) Objective basis—level depends on the kind of seizure or search
            i. Reasonable suspicion required for stops and frisks
            ii. Probable cause required for arrests and full-blown searches
            iii. Both require individualized suspicion—suspicion that points to specific individuals
      (2) Case-by-case totality-of-circumstances test (not "bright line") used to determine both elements

H. *Terry v. Ohio* and Stop and Frisk
1. Stop-and-frisk law responded to practical problems of checking out suspicious strangers on the streets of big cities
2. Conflict—officers don't have probable cause to arrest but they can't just let them go, and yet to stop and frisk them is a serious invasion of their personal liberty and privacy
3. Three possible interpretations of the Fourth Amendment
   a. Leave response to officer discretion because stops aren't seizures and frisks aren't searches, so the amendment doesn't apply
   b. Ban officer response unless there's probable cause to arrest or search

      c. Even though stops are less-invasive than arrests, and frisks are less-invasive than full-blown searches, officers must back them up with facts

    4. Court created a middle ground between banning the police from doing anything and leaving what they do entirely to police discretion

      a. Officers can "freeze" the situation to conduct a brief on-the-spot investigation if they reasonably suspect that criminal activity may be afoot

      b. Officers can conduct a superficial search for weapons to protect themselves, if they reasonably suspect the persons stopped may be armed

II. Stops and the Fourth Amendment

  A. Fall somewhere between voluntary encounters and full-blown arrests

  B. Two elements of reasonable stops

    1. Objective basis of reasonable suspicion

    2. Scope of stop

      a. Short duration

      b. Location of the investigation is near the scene of the stop

  C. Reasonable suspicion

    1. Definition—the totality (whole picture) of articulable facts (nameable) leads officer to *suspect* a crime *may* be afoot

    2. Types of articulable facts

      a. Direct information

      b. Hearsay, including anonymous tips plus corroboration

      c. Race plus other articulable facts and circumstances

      b. Profiles plus other articulable facts and circumstances of individualized suspicion

  D. The scope of reasonable stops

    1. Two elements

      a. Duration has to be brief

        (1) No specific time limit

        (2) Reasonableness depends on the totality of circumstances

      b. Location of the investigation has to be near the scene of the stop

        (1) Not limited to exact spot

        (2) General vicinity included

        (3) Removing suspect from general vicinity can be reasonable in "extraordinary" circumstances

III. Special situation stops

  A. Removing passengers from stopped vehicles

    1. No reasonable suspicion needed

    2. Officer safety outweighs trivial invasion of passenger rights

  B. Stops at international borders

    1. Objective—balance

      a. Government interest in border control

      b. Rights of persons entering country

    2. Interest in controlling borders justifies substantial reduction in individual rights of freedom of movement and privacy

    3. Can detain suspects for longer period based on reasonable suspicion

  C. Roadblocks

    1. Strong interest in preventing crime and apprehending criminals

2. No individualized suspicion required
3. Random stops satisfy the objective basis requirement
IV. Frisks and the Fourth Amendment
   A. Frisk is a pat-down of outer-clothing to detect a concealed weapon after a Fourth Amendment stop
   B. Differences between stops and frisks
      1. Frisks are searches; stops are seizures
      2. Purpose of stop to investigate crime; purpose of frisk to protect officers
   C. Elements of reasonable frisk
      1. Reasonable stop before the frisk
      2. Reasonable *suspicion* (not belief) the person stopped *may* be (not is) armed
      3. Scope of frisk consists of an outer-clothing pat-down to discover and seize weapons (not contraband or evidence)

 Go to the Criminal Procedure 6e CD to download this summary outline. The outline has been formatted so that you can add notes to it during class lectures, or later create a customized chapter outline to use while reviewing. Either way, the summary outline will help you understand the "big picture" and fill in the details as you study.

REVIEW QUESTIONS

1. Identify the three steps in the analysis used to decide whether stops and frisks are reasonable Fourth Amendment seizures and searches.

2. Identify the two parts of the Fourth Amendment and the role they play in the conventional and reasonableness approach to the Fourth Amendment.

3. Identify and describe the two elements of the reasonableness test to the Fourth Amendment.

4. Describe the role of officers and judges in deciding the reasonableness of searches and seizures.

5. Explain how the "totality of circumstances" test works in practice.

6. Describe the background and summarize the significance of *Terry v. Ohio*.

7. Identify the three possible alternatives for applying the Fourth Amendment to stops and frisks, and explain why the U.S. Supreme Court adopted alternative 3.

8. Identify and describe three stages of police encounters with individuals.

9. Identify and describe the two elements of a reasonable stop.

10. Identify and define two types of facts officers can rely on in building reasonable suspicion.

11. Why are officers entitled to interpret facts differently from the rest of us?

12. Does unprovoked flight + high-crime area = reasonable suspicion? Explain.

13. Does an anonymous tip amount to reasonable suspicion? Explain.

14. When can race be used in building reasonable suspicion?

15. When can profiles be used in building reasonable suspicion?

16. What's the difference between individualized suspicion and a profile?

17. Why is it reasonable to remove a passenger from a stopped vehicle when there's no suspicion the passenger may be involved in crime?

18. Why are the rights to free movement and personal privacy substantially reduced at international borders?

19. Identify the legitimate purposes for roadblocks, and explain the objective basis that makes roadblocks reasonable Fourth Amendment seizures.

20. State the reasonable suspicion that justifies a frisk, and describe the scope of a reasonable frisk.

KEY TERMS

Fourth Amendment stops p. 95
Fourth Amendment frisks p. 95
objective basis p. 96
reasonableness clause p. 98
warrant clause p. 98
conventional Fourth Amendment approach p. 98
reasonableness Fourth Amendment approach p. 98
reasonableness test (Fourth Amendment) p. 99

balancing element (of reasonableness test) p. 99
"bright line" (clear) rule p. 99
case-by-case basis p. 99
totality of circumstances p. 99
individualized suspicion p. 99
voluntary encounters p. 108
stops p. 108
arrests p. 108
reasonableness test of Fourth Amendment stops p. 108

articulable facts p. 109
reasonable suspicion p. 109
totality-of-circumstances test p. 109
whole picture test p. 109
direct information p. 109
hearsay information p. 109
drug courier profile p. 121
"on the spot" requirement p. 126
balloon swallowers p. 135
roadblocks p. 138
frisks p. 147

THE COMPANION WEB SITE FOR *CRIMINAL PROCEDURE,* SIXTH EDITION

http://cj.wadsworth.com/samaha/crim_pro6e

 Supplement your review of this chapter by going to the companion Web site to take one of the Tutorial Quizzes, use the flash cards to test yourself on the key terms from each chapter, and check out the many other study aids you'll find there. You'll find valuable data and resources at your fingertips to help you study for that big exam or write that important paper.

Seizures of Persons: Arrest

5

Chapter Main Points

- Arrests are more invasive than stops, but the line between them is hard to draw.
- The power to arrest is vital to crime control, but officers can't violate the Fourth Amendment to control crime.
- The reasonableness of arrests depends on the objective basis to back them up and the manner of the arrest.
- Arrests require probable cause to back them.
- Arrests with warrants require affidavits supporting probable cause and identification of the person to be arrested.
- Arrests in homes require arrest warrants, except in emergencies.
- Officers can only use reasonable force to arrest and bring suspects under control.
- Officers can only use *deadly* force when it's necessary to apprehend dangerous felons and doesn't endanger innocent people.
- After being arrested, most (not all) misdemeanor suspects are released; felony suspects are subjected to some or all of the actions of full custodial arrests.

At about 10:45 P.M. Memphis Police Officers Elton Hymon and Leslie Wright were dispatched to answer a "prowler inside call." Upon arriving at the scene they saw a woman standing on her porch gesturing toward the adjacent house. She told them she had heard glass breaking and that "they" or "someone" was breaking in next door. While Wright radioed the dispatcher to say that they were on the scene, Hymon went behind the house. He heard a door slam and saw someone run across the backyard. The fleeing suspect, 15-year-old Edward Garner, stopped at a 6-feet-high chain link fence at the edge of the yard. With the aid of a flashlight, Hymon was able to see Garner's face and hands. He saw no sign of a weapon, and though not certain, was "reasonably sure" and "figured" that Garner was unarmed. He thought Garner was 17 or 18 years old and about 5'5" or 5'7" tall. While Garner was crouched at the base of the fence, Hymon called out "police, halt" and took a few steps toward him. Garner began to climb over the fence. Convinced that if Garner made it over the fence he would elude capture, Hymon shot him. The bullet hit Garner in the back of the head. Garner was taken by ambulance to a hospital, where he died on the operating table. Ten dollars and a purse taken from the house were found on his body.

Tennessee v. Garner (1985), U.S. Supreme Court

THE ISSUES OF ARRESTS

Arrests are a vital tool that can help law enforcement catch the guilty and free the innocent. But, the *way* officers arrest people has to square with the requirements of the U.S. Constitution. Remember, the noble end of crime control doesn't justify unreasonable arrests to attain that end.

So, just what is an *arrest*? And, what makes an arrest reasonable? What happens to suspects after they're arrested? These are the issues we'll tackle in this chapter.

THE DEFINITION OF *ARREST*

Arrests, in which suspects are seized and detained for a period, are more invasive seizures than stops (Chapter 4). Stops are measured in minutes; arrests (what we call **full custodial arrests**) can last hours, sometimes even days. So, the duration of the seizure is one difference. Stops begin and end on streets and in other public places with other people around; arrested people are taken to the isolated and intimidating surroundings of the local police department and jail where they're held against their will for hours, sometimes even days. So, a change in location is a second distinction.

TABLE 5.1		
Characteristics of a Full Custodial Arrest		

The police officer says to the suspect, "You're under arrest."

The suspect is put into a squad car.

The suspect is taken to the police station.

The suspect is photographed, booked, and fingerprinted.

The suspect is searched.

The suspect is locked up either at the police station or in a jail cell.

The suspect is interrogated.

The suspect may be put into a lineup.

And, whereas most stops don't get "written up," arrests produce written documents that become part of a person's record, or "rap sheet." Stops (unless accompanied by frisks) don't involve body searches. Full-body searches (usually) and strip and body-cavity searches (sometimes) accompany arrests (Chapter 6). Interrogations (Chapter 8) and lineups (Chapter 9) can also accompany arrests (Table 5.1). Arrests can produce fear, anxiety, and loss of liberty; further, they can cause temporary loss of income and even the permanent loss of a job. More, these losses don't just affect the suspects; they also embarrass and cause economic hardship to their families. These embarrassments and hardships rarely accompany a Fourth Amendment stop.

Full custodial arrests are the most invasive of all arrests, but considerably less invasive seizures are also arrests. Think of arrest as a zone, not as a point on a spectrum of invasions between investigatory stops at one end and imprisonment at the other end (see Table 5.2). That zone begins when stops end and continues through full custodial arrests (detention) that involve all the invasions listed in Table 5.1. Within that zone,

TABLE 5.2				
Deprivations of Liberty				
Deprivation	**Objective Basis**	**Duration**	**Location**	**Degree of Invasion**
Voluntary contact	None	Brief	On the spot	Moral and psychological pressure
Stop	Reasonable suspicion	Minutes	At or near the stop, on the street, or in another public place	Reveal identification and explain whereabouts
Arrest	Probable cause	Hours to a few days	Usually removal to a police station	Fingerprints, booking, photograph, interrogation, identification procedures
Detention	Probable cause promptly verified by magistrate	Days to months	Jail	Inventory, full-body, strip, and body-cavity searches; restricted contact with outside
Imprisonment	Proof beyond a reasonable doubt	Years to life	Prison	Same as detention, with heightened invasions of privacy, liberty, and property

arrests may contain only some of the characteristics in the table. The duration and location also may vary significantly from the full custodial arrest depicted in the table.

How long does a seizure have to last to turn a stop into an arrest? How far do officers have to move an individual to turn a stop into an arrest? No "bright line" separates stops from arrests. Why does it matter where we draw the line? Because of one element common to all arrests in the zone: The Fourth Amendment requires probable cause to make them reasonable.

REASONABLE ARREST

What makes an arrest reasonable? An arrest is an "unreasonable seizure" unless the government can prove two elements:

1. *Objective basis.* The arrest was backed up by probable cause.

2. *Manner of arrest.* The way the arrest was made was reasonable.

Let's look at each of these elements.

Probable Cause

Probable cause to arrest means that there are enough facts and circumstances to lead police officers, in the light of their experience, to the reasonable belief that the person arrested has committed, is committing, or is about to commit a crime. (Contrast this definition with the reasonable-grounds-to-suspect standard for stops discussed in Chapter 4.) It lies on a continuum between reasonable suspicion on one end and proof beyond a reasonable doubt on the other. Table 5.2 shows the increasing objective basis requirements as the level of invasiveness increases in criminal procedure.

The probable cause requirement balances the societal interest in crime control and the individual right of *locomotion*—the freedom to come and go as we please. According to the classic probable cause case *Brinegar v. U.S.* (1949):

> These long prevailing standards [of probable cause] seek to safeguard citizens from rash and unreasonable interferences with privacy and from unfounded charges of crime. They also seek to give fair leeway for enforcing the law in the community's protection. Because many situations which confront officers in the course of executing their duties are more or less ambiguous, room must be allowed for some mistakes on their part. But the mistakes must be those of reasonable men, acting on facts leading sensibly to their conclusions of probability. The rule of probable cause is a practical, nontechnical conception affording the best compromise that has been found for accommodating these often opposing interests. Requiring more would unduly hamper law enforcement. To allow less would be to leave law-abiding citizens at the mercy of the officers' whim or caprice. (176)

Probable cause is a commonsense rule; that is, its day-to-day application rests mainly with officers on the street who have to make quick decisions. They don't have the luxury that professors in their studies and judges in their chambers have to think deeply about technical matters. According to the Court in *Brinegar* (1949), "In dealing with probable cause...as the very name implies, we deal with probabilities. These are not technical; they are the factual and practical considerations of everyday life on which reasonable and prudent men, not legal technicians, act."

So, although officers can't arrest on hunch, whim, or mere suspicion, and although judges have the final say on whether the officers had probable cause, courts tend to accept the facts as police see them. According to one judge:

> Police officers patrolling the streets do not prearrange the setting within which they operate. They do not schedule their steps in the calm reflective atmosphere of some remote law library. Events occur without warning and policemen are required as a matter of duty to act as a reasonably prudent policeman would under the circumstances as those circumstances unfold before him.
>
> *People v. Brown* 1969, 869

Notice that probable cause is an *objective* standard. The belief has to be reasonable—nameable facts have to back it up. An officer's personal, even if totally honest, belief isn't good enough. The basis for reasonable belief can be based either **direct information** (information known personally to officers) or **hearsay** (information officers received from someone else). Let's look at these two kinds of information; in many cases, officers have some direct and some hearsay. Let's look at direct information and hearsay.

Direct Information

Direct information is firsthand information known to arresting officers by what they see, hear, feel, taste, and smell. Direct information doesn't automatically make the case for probable cause. The courts look for patterns, or a totality of circumstances, that build the case for probable cause.

Table 5.3 lists some of the facts and circumstances officers usually acquire firsthand, and which either alone or in combination a judge may rule amounts to probable cause.

Hearsay

To make their case for probable cause officers don't have to rely on direct information. They can (and often do) rely on hearsay. Officers get information secondhand from victims, witnesses, other police officers, and professional informants.

According to the **hearsay rule,** courts won't admit secondhand evidence to prove guilt, but, if it's reliable and truthful, they'll accept it to show probable cause to arrest. Why? Because arrests aren't trials. (Of course, they can still cost suspects their liberty—

TABLE 5.3
Probable Cause Information Officers Know Firsthand

Fleeing ("flight")	Giving contradictory explanations
Making furtive movements	Fingerprints
Hiding	Hair samples
Attempting to destroy evidence	Blood samples
Resisting officers	DNA information
Giving evasive answers	

but only long enough to decide whether there's enough evidence to charge them with a crime [Chapter 11] and put them on trial [Chapter 12].) At trial, there are legal experts in the courtroom to testify and plenty of time to weigh the evidence. However, police officers on the street—and at the precinct station—aren't lawyers, and they aren't supposed to be. They don't have the leisure to sort out the evidence they've acquired. They have to either act immediately or forever lose their chance to arrest suspects. So, allowing hearsay to show probable cause reflects the deference that courts concede to the realities of police work.

Not all hearsay carries equal weight; some informants are more trustworthy than others. In determining probable cause, magistrates weigh both the trustworthiness and the source of the information. So, according to the court in *Allison v. State* (1974), "If the citizen or victim informant is an eyewitness this will be enough to support probable cause even without specific corroboration of reliability." But, this isn't true if victims or witnesses refuse to identify themselves. So, anonymous tips standing alone are never enough to establish probable cause to arrest (see *Draper v. U.S.*, p. 163).

There's another problem. Bystander eyewitnesses aren't the source of most hearsay information; professional informants (almost always) are. And, snitches create greater problems with credibility than victims and nonprofessional eyewitnesses. In *Jones v. United States* (1959), the U.S. Court of Appeals for the District of Columbia wrote the following:

> It is notorious that the narcotics informer is often himself involved in the narcotics traffic and is often paid for his information in cash, narcotics, immunity from prosecution, or lenient punishment.... The reliability of such persons is obviously suspect.... [T]he present informer practice amounts to condoning felonies on condition that the confessed or suspected felon brings about the conviction of others. Under such stimulation it is to be expected that the informer will not infrequently reach for shadowy leads, or even seek to incriminate the innocent. The practice of paying fees to the informer for the cases he makes may also be expected from time to time, to induce him to lure no-users into the drug habit and then entrap them into law violations. (928)

Until 1983, courts tested the worth of informants' information according to a **two-pronged test of reliability,** also called the *Spinelli–Aguilar* test after the two cases that established the test. The first prong, called the **veracity prong,** asks whether informants are basically honest people. One way to prove the veracity prong is to show that the informant has a "good track record." For example, an affidavit stating the informant has given the police truthful information in the past demonstrates the informant's veracity (*McCray v. Illinois* 1967). In *Draper v. U.S.* (1959; see the next case), the informant, Hereford's, record of being right every time for six months surely impressed the Court to accept his truthfulness. An informant's giving information that goes against his or her own interest can also satisfy the veracity prong (*U.S. v. Harris* 1971). For example, if an informant tells the police that she has bought "crystal meth" from the suspect for two years, this satisfies the veracity test because "people do not lightly admit a crime and place critical evidence in the hands of the police in the form of their own admission."

Still, just because the informant is honest doesn't guarantee the accuracy of the information. The second prong, or the **basis-of-knowledge prong,** focuses on the information itself. This prong asks questions like: How do informants know what they know? In a suspected drug arrest, for example, do they know Michelle has marijuana in her pocket because Nathan saw her put it there? Or did Nathan believe that the "grass" was in Michelle's pocket because she kept checking her pocket while she looked around "furtively"? Or did Doug tell Nathan (hearsay on hearsay) that Michelle had marijuana in her pocket?

If the officer doesn't know or tell how the informant knows what she knows, the amount of detail provided by the informant might satisfy the basis-of-knowledge prong. In *Draper v. U.S.*, Hereford's impressive detailed knowledge of Draper's physical appearance, his clothing, his mannerisms, and what he was carrying is a powerful example of how detail, if necessary, might have made up for a lack of knowledge about how the officer, Marsh, knew what he knew. This amount of detail led the Court to conclude that Hereford gave so many details that the officers could "reasonably infer that the informant had gained his information in a reliable way."

What if informants don't prove either the veracity or the basis-of-knowledge prong? Under the two-pronged *Spinelli–Aguilar* test, there's no probable cause, the arrest is illegal, the evidence seized during the arrest is illegally obtained, and the evidence is excluded. The two-pronged test is another one of these bright-line rules, which prescribe specific behavior. These rules are supposed to send clear directions to law enforcement officers about what they can and can't do. They reduce discretion and uncertainty but also enforce rigidity.

To make it easier to establish probable cause, the Supreme Court created another one of its favorite totality-of-circumstances tests—this one called the **totality of circumstances of informant reliability test.** In evaluating informants' information, this test takes veracity and basis of knowledge into account as two of many pieces of information that might add up to probable cause.

One of the best discussions of probable cause, and one of the clearest explanations of its application to the facts of an arrest based on a combination of direct and hearsay information (hearsay corroborated by an officer's direct observations), appears in *Draper v. U.S.* (1959).

| CASE | *Was There Probable Cause to Arrest?* |

Draper v. United States
358 U.S. 307 (1959)

James Alonzo Draper was prosecuted for knowingly concealing and transporting heroin in violation of federal narcotics laws. The U.S. District Court for the District of Colorado denied Draper's motion to suppress the heroin, and Draper was convicted. Draper appealed. The U.S. Court of Appeals affirmed the conviction. The U.S. Supreme Court granted certiorari and affirmed.

WHITTAKER, J.

FACTS

The evidence offered at the hearing on the motion to suppress . . . established that . . . Marsh, a federal narcotic agent with 29 years' experience, was stationed at Denver; that . . . Hereford had been engaged as a "special employee" of the Bureau of Narcotics at Denver for about six months, and from time to time gave information to Marsh regarding violations of the narcotics laws, for which Hereford was paid small sums of money, and that Marsh had always found the information given by Hereford to be accurate and reliable. On September 3, 1956, Hereford told Marsh that

James Draper (petitioner) recently had taken up abode at a stated address in Denver and "was peddling narcotics to several addicts" in that city. Four days later, on September 7, Hereford told Marsh "that Draper had gone to Chicago the day before (September 6) by train and that he was going to bring back three ounces of heroin and that he would return to Denver either on the morning of the 8th of September or the morning of the 9th of September also by train." Hereford also gave Marsh a detailed physical description of Draper and of the clothing he was wearing, and said that he would be carrying "a tan zipper bag," and that he habitually "walked real fast."*

On the morning of September 8, Marsh and a Denver police officer went to the Denver Union Station and kept watch over all incoming trains from Chicago, but they did not see anyone fitting the description that Hereford had given. Repeating the process on the morning of September 9, they saw a person, having the exact physical attributes and wearing the precise clothing described by Hereford, alight from an incoming Chicago train and start walking "fast" toward the exit. He was carrying a tan zipper bag in his right hand and the left was thrust in his raincoat pocket. Marsh, accompanied by the police officer, overtook, stopped and arrested him. They then searched him and found the two "envelopes containing heroin" clutched in his left hand in his raincoat pocket, and found the syringe in the tan zipper bag. Marsh then took him (petitioner) into custody. Hereford died four days after the arrest and therefore did not testify at the hearing on the motion.

OPINION

The Narcotic Control Act of 1956, provides, in pertinent part:

> The Commissioner . . . and agents, of the Bureau of Narcotics . . . may—(2) make arrests without warrant for violations of any law of the United States relating to narcotic drugs . . . where the violation is committed in the presence of the person making the arrest or where such person has reasonable grounds to believe that the person to be arrested has committed or is committing such violation.

The crucial question for us then is whether knowledge of the related facts and circumstances gave Marsh "probable cause" within the meaning of the Fourth Amendment, and "reasonable grounds" within the meaning of § 104(a)

to believe that petitioner had committed or was committing a violation of the narcotics laws.**

If it did, the arrest, though without a warrant, was lawful and the subsequent search of petitioner's person and the seizure of the found heroin were validly made incident to a lawful arrest, and therefore the motion to suppress was properly overruled and the heroin was competently received in evidence at the trial.

Petitioner contends (1) that the information given by Hereford to Marsh was "hearsay" and, because hearsay is not legally competent evidence in a criminal trial, could not legally have been considered, but should have been put out of mind, by Marsh in assessing whether he had "probable cause" and "reasonable grounds" to arrest petitioner without a warrant, and (2) that, even if hearsay could lawfully have been considered, Marsh's information should be held insufficient to show "probable cause" and "reasonable grounds" to believe that petitioner had violated or was violating the narcotic laws and to justify his arrest without a warrant.

Considering the first contention, we find petitioner entirely in error. The criterion of admissibility in evidence, to prove the accused's guilt, of the facts relied upon to show probable cause goes much too far in confusing and disregarding the difference between what is required to prove guilt in a criminal case and what is required to show probable cause for arrest or search. It approaches requiring (if it does not in practical effect require) proof sufficient to establish guilt in order to substantiate the existence of probable cause. There is a large difference between the two things to be proved (guilt and probable cause), as well as between the tribunals which determine them, and therefore a like difference in the quanta and modes of proof required to establish them. . . .

Nor can we agree with petitioner's second contention that Marsh's information was insufficient to show probable cause and reasonable grounds to believe that petitioner had violated or was violating the narcotic laws and to justify his arrest without a warrant. The information given to narcotic agent Marsh by "special employee" Hereford may have been hearsay to Marsh, but coming from one employed for that purpose and whose information had always been found accurate and reliable, it is clear that Marsh would have been derelict in his duties had he not pursued it. And when, in pursuing that information, he saw a man, having the exact physical attributes and wearing the precise clothing and carrying the tan zipper bag that Hereford had described, alight

---

*Note: Hereford told Marsh that Draper was a Negro of light brown complexion, 27 years of age, 5 feet 8 inches tall, weighed about 160 pounds, and that he was wearing a light colored raincoat, brown slacks, and black shoes.

**Note: The terms *probable cause* as used in the Fourth Amendment and *reasonable grounds* as used in § 104 (a) of the Narcotic Control Act, 70 Stat. 570, are substantial equivalents of the same meaning.

from one of the very trains from the very place stated by Hereford and start to walk at a "fast" pace toward the station exit, Marsh had personally verified every facet of the information given him by Hereford except whether petitioner had accomplished his mission and had the three ounces of heroin on his person or in his bag. And surely, with every other bit of Hereford's information being thus personally verified, Marsh had "reasonable grounds" to believe that the remaining unverified bit of Hereford's information—that Draper would have the heroin with him—was likewise true.

"In dealing with probable cause . . . as the very name implies, we deal with probabilities. These are not technical; they are the factual and practical considerations of everyday life on which reasonable and prudent men, not legal technicians, act." Probable cause exists where "the facts and circumstances within their (the arresting officers') knowledge and of which they had reasonably trustworthy information are sufficient in themselves to warrant a man of reasonable caution in the belief that" an offense has been or is being committed.

We believe that, under the facts and circumstances here, Marsh had probable cause and reasonable grounds to believe that petitioner was committing a violation of the laws of the United States relating to narcotic drugs at the time he arrested him. The arrest was therefore lawful, and the subsequent search and seizure, having been made incident to that lawful arrest, were likewise valid. It follows that petitioner's motion to suppress was properly denied and that the seized heroin was competent evidence lawfully received at the trial.

AFFIRMED.

DISSENT

DOUGLAS, J.

Decisions under the Fourth Amendment, taken in the long view, have not given the protection to the citizen which the letter and spirit of the Amendment would seem to require. One reason, I think, is that wherever a culprit is caught red-handed, as in leading Fourth Amendment cases, it is difficult to adopt and enforce a rule that would turn him loose. A rule protective of law-abiding citizens is not apt to flourish where its advocates are usually criminals. Yet the rule we fashion is for the innocent and guilty alike. If the word of the informer on which the present arrest was made is sufficient to make the arrest legal, his word would also protect the police who, acting on it, hauled the innocent citizen off to jail.

Of course, the education we receive from mystery stories and television shows teaches that what happened in this case is efficient police work. The police are tipped off that a man carrying narcotics will step off the morning train. A man meeting the precise description does alight from the train. No warrant for his arrest has been—or, as I see it,

could then be—obtained. Yet he is arrested; and narcotics are found in his pocket and a syringe in the bag he carried. This is the familiar pattern of crime detection which has been dinned into public consciousness as the correct and efficient one. It is, however, a distorted reflection of the constitutional system under which we are supposed to live. . . .

The Court is quite correct in saying that proof of "reasonable grounds" for believing a crime was being committed need not be proof admissible at the trial. It could be inferences from suspicious acts, e.g., consort with known peddlers, the surreptitious passing of a package, an intercepted message suggesting criminal activities, or any number of such events coming to the knowledge of the officer. But, if he takes the law into his own hands and does not seek the protection of a warrant, he must act on some evidence known to him. The law goes far to protect the citizen. Even suspicious acts observed by the officers may be as consistent with innocence as with guilt. That is not enough, for even the guilty may not be implicated on suspicion alone. The reason is, as I have said, that the standard set by the Constitution and by the statute is one that will protect both the officer and the citizen. For if the officer acts with "probable cause" or on "reasonable grounds," he is protected even though the citizen is innocent. This important requirement should be strictly enforced, lest the whole process of arrest revert once more to whispered accusations by people. When we lower the guards as we do today, we risk making the role of the informer—odious in our history—once more supreme. I think the correct rule was stated in *Poldo v. United States*. "Mere suspicion is not enough; there must be circumstances represented to the officers through the testimony of their senses sufficient to justify them in a good-faith belief that the defendant had violated the law."

Here the officers had no evidence—apart from the mere word of an informer—that petitioner was committing a crime. The fact that petitioner walked fast and carried a tan zipper bag was not evidence of any crime. The officers knew nothing except what they had been told by the informer. If they went to a magistrate to get a warrant of arrest and relied solely on the report of the informer, it is not conceivable to me that one would be granted. For they could not present to the magistrate any of the facts which the informer may have had. They could swear only to the fact that the informer had made the accusation. They could swear to no evidence that lay in their own knowledge. They could present, on information and belief, no facts which the informer disclosed. No magistrate could issue a warrant on the mere word of an officer, without more. We are not justified in lowering the standard when an arrest is made without a warrant and allowing the officers more leeway than we grant the magistrate.

With all deference I think we break with tradition when we sustain this arrest. We said in *United States v. Di Re*, "A search is not to be made legal by what it turns up. In law it is good or bad when it starts and does not change character from its success." In this case it was only after the arrest and search were made that there was a shred of evidence known to the officers that a crime was in the process of being committed.

Questions

1. List all the facts and circumstances supporting the conclusion there was probable cause to arrest Draper.

2. Identify which were firsthand, hearsay, or a combination of the two.

3. Do you think Justice Douglas is overreacting to the decision in this case? Or does he have a point that the hearsay provided by the informant amounts to nothing of substance that would lead a reasonable person to conclude that a crime was committed or in progress and that James Draper committed it?

4. Does the majority ruling favor crime control at the expense of procedural regularity and controlling government?

5. Does the Court give clear guidelines in regard to what constitutes probable cause to arrest? Explain.

 Go to Exercise 5-1 on the Criminal Procedure 6e CD to learn more about probable cause.

EXPLORING PROBABLE CAUSE FURTHER

 Go to the Criminal Procedure 6e CD to read the full text versions of the cases featured here.

1. *Did Their Observations and Other Knowledge Amount to Probable Cause?*

FACTS

Des Moines police officers Gary Bryan and Michael Stueckrath were patrolling the vicinity of the Another World Lounge at about 11:00 P.M. They noticed Claude Bumpus, Marvin Taylor, and another man they didn't recognize in the parking lot of the lounge crouching behind a car. The officers observed that the men were exchanging something, but they couldn't see what it was. The Another World Lounge was a notorious site for drug transactions. Based on their past experience with the location, the nature and furtiveness of the three men's actions, the notoriety of the location, and the lateness of the hour, the officers pulled their patrol car into the parking lot. Bumpus ran away from them into the bar. Once inside, Bumpus tried to conceal a black pouch from the officer who pursued him. Officer Bryan grabbed Bumpus's arm and asked him to step outside. Once outside, Bumpus threw the pouch over a fence and tried to flee. After a brief struggle, Bryan seized and arrested Bumpus. The trial court decided that Officer Bryan arrested Bumpus not when he said, "You're under arrest," but when he grabbed his arm inside the bar and escorted him outside. Did Bryan have probable cause at the moment of the arrest?

DECISION AND REASONS

The Iowa Supreme Court said yes: "While flight alone does not give rise to probable cause . . . in this case not only did Bumpus flee from officers but he also attempted to conceal the pouch." Therefore, when he grabbed Bumpus's arm, Officer Bryan had probable cause to arrest him.

State v. Bumpus, 459 N.W.2d 619 (Iowa 1990)

2. Was There Probable Cause to Believe a Drug Deal Had Taken Place?

FACTS

Detective Odesto, the arresting officer, testified at a suppression hearing that at 11:45 P.M., in a high-crime area in Manhattan, he observed Nathaniel Brown, in the "company of someone he suspected of being a narcotics addict." The suspected addict walked away from Brown and entered a building, returning shortly to Brown. The two came "close together," Detective Odesto said, adding: "I observed what appeared to be a movement of hand. At that time I started to go across the street and intercepted the two persons when Mr. Brown walked in my direction with 'a fast shuffling gait' and the other person walked in the opposite direction." Detective Odesto arrested Brown for possession of a narcotic drug. At the suppression hearing, Detective Odesto explained that this was typical behavior for drug transactions in that neighborhood:

> Most of its persons engaged in the selling of narcotics do not carry narcotics on them. They usually have a place where it is stored in or carried by someone else.... [U]sually the person would have a conversation with the potential seller, give him his money... and then... the potential seller will go to his place where he stores the narcotics and bring it back, give it to that person, and they'll go in opposite directions.

Did Detective Odesto have probable cause to arrest Brown?

DECISION AND REASONS

The trial judge said yes; the appellate court reversed:

> Although the observed acts of the defendant and the suspected narcotic addict were not inconsistent with a culpable narcotics transaction, they were also susceptible of many innocent interpretations, even between persons with a narcotics background. The behavior, at most "equivocal and suspicious," was not supplemented by any additional behavior raising "the level of inference from suspicion to probable cause." Thus, for example only, there was no recurring pattern of conduct sufficient to negate inferences of innocent activity, no overheard conversation between the suspects that might clarify the acts observed, no flight at the approach of the officer, and no misstatements when questioned about observed activity.

> The logical and practical problem is that even accepting ungrudgingly, as one should, the police officer's expertness in detecting a pattern of conduct characteristic of a particular criminal activity, the detected pattern, being only the superficial part of a sequence, does not provide probable cause for arrest if some sketchy pattern occurs just as frequently or even more frequently in innocent transactions. The point is that the pattern is equivocal and is neither uniquely nor generally associated with criminal conduct, and unless it is there is no probable cause. Thus, for example, the observation of a known or obvious prostitute talking to a man she meets (or accosts) on the street does not establish probable cause. More of a pattern must be shown, either by proof of the conversation or ensuing culpable conduct.

People v. Brown, 248 N.E.2d 867 (N.Y. 1969)

3. Was "Flight" Enough to Amount to Probable Cause?

FACTS

Officers Lewis and Griffin were in the vicinity of 1232 Buchanan Street. They observed Michael Washington, the defendant, along with four other individuals in a courtyard area between 1133 Laguna and 1232 Buchanan. Washington and the others were observed talking in a "huddle" formation with "a lot of hand movement" inside the huddle, but the officers could not see what was in the hands of any member of the group. The officers then walked toward the group, at which point everyone looked in the officers' direction, whispered, and quickly dispersed. When Washington saw the officers, he immediately turned around and started walking at a fast pace through the lobby of 1232 Buchanan. The officers followed him for a quarter of a block when Officer Griffin called out to Washington. He replied, "Who, me?" Officer Griffin answered, "Yes," and Washington immediately ran away. The officers chased him. Two minutes later, while still chasing Washington, Officer Lewis saw him discard a plastic bag containing five white bundles. Officer Lewis scooped up the bag as he continued to give chase. Shortly thereafter, the officers apprehended Washington.

Officer Lewis testified that during the four years he had been a patrolman he had made at least one hundred arrests concerning cocaine in the area frequented by the defendant that night. On cross-examination, Officer Lewis answered yes when asked if most of the black men he saw in the area usually had something to hide if they ran from police. The officer stated that prior to the chase he saw no contraband, nor was anything about the group's dispersal significant. Nor did the officer explain why they singled out the defendant to follow. The trial court denied the defendant's motion to suppress. Did Officers Lewis and Griffin have probable cause to arrest Washington?

DECISION AND REASONS

The court said no:

> Prior to defendant's abandonment of the cocaine, the police lacked the "articulable suspicion that a person has committed or is about to commit a crime." The officers spotted the group of men in an open courtyard at 6:15 P.M.; the men made no attempt to conceal themselves and did not exhibit any furtive behavior. The hand gestures were, on the police officer's own testimony, inconclusive and unrevealing. Furthermore, the time at which the detention occurred is not the "late or unusual hour . . . from which any inference of criminality may be drawn." The fact that defendant was seen in what was a high crime area also does not elevate the facts into a reasonable suspicion of criminality. Courts have been "reluctant to conclude that a location's crime rate transforms otherwise innocent-appearing circumstances into circumstances justifying the seizure of an individual."

> Once the officers made their approach visible, they gave no justification for their decision to follow defendant apart from the others in the group. Neither officer knew defendant or knew of defendant's past criminal record, nor did Officer Lewis testify that defendant appeared to be a principal or a leader in the group. Further, the defendant had the right to walk away from the officers. He had no legal duty to submit to the attention of the officers; he had the freedom to "go on his way," free of stopping even momentarily for the officers. By walking at a brisk rate away from the officers, defendant could have been exercising his right to avoid the officers or avoid any other person, or could have simply walked rapidly through sheer nervousness at the sight of a police officer.

We see no change in the analysis when defendant decided to run from the officers. Flight alone does not trigger an investigative detention; rather, it must be combined with other objective factors that give rise to an articulable suspicion of criminal activity. No such factors existed, nor does Officer Lewis's assertion that the "black men [they] see in the project usually have something to hide when they run" justify a detention. "[M]ere subjective speculation as to the [person's] purported motives...carries no weight." Thus, prior to defendant's abandonment of the contraband, the circumstances of defendant's actions were not reasonably consistent with criminal activity.

Here, the officers conceded they had no objective factors upon which to base any suspicions that the group was involved in illegal activity, and the officers offered no explanation why they singled out defendant to follow. Indeed, the only justification for engaging in pursuit was that defendant was a Black male, and that it was the officer's subjective belief that Black men run from police when they have something to hide. Thus, a single factor—the defendant's race—triggered the detention....

People v. Washington, 236 Cal.Rptr. 840 (Cal.App. 1987)

The Manner of Arrest

Probable cause by itself isn't enough to make an arrest a reasonable Fourth Amendment seizure; there's also a **reasonable manner of arrest requirement.** This means the *way* officers conduct the arrest also has to be reasonable. What's a reasonable manner? Two points are clear from the cases: First, officers have to get warrants, based on the totality of the circumstances, before they enter homes to arrest suspects. Second, officers can't use excessive force to arrest suspects, wherever they're arrested.

The Warrant Requirement

Constitutionally speaking, warrants aren't required to make arrests reasonable except when officers want to arrest someone in a home. Practically, that makes arrest warrants extremely rare. Still, warrants are very useful because they mean judges make the probable cause decision *before* arrests, so officers don't have to guess whether they've got the arrest backed up. To meet the requirements of the Fourth Amendment warrant clause, arrest warrants have to include three elements:

1. *A neutral magistrate.* A judge decides whether there is probable cause before officers arrest suspects.

2. *An **affidavit*** (sworn statement). This is made by someone (nearly always a law enforcement officer) who swears under oath to the facts and circumstances amounting to probable cause.

3. *The name of the person to be arrested.* The warrant has to identify specifically the person(s) the officers are going to arrest.

Let's look more closely at each of these requirements.

- *A neutral magistrate.* The requirement that officers get approval from a neutral magistrate (one who will fairly and adequately review the warrant) before they arrest assumes that magistrates carefully review the information that law enforcement officers supply them. However, both the outcomes of cases and social science research suggest otherwise:

There is little reason to be reassured by what we know about magistrates in operation. The magistrate can know there are factual issues to be explored only if he looks behind the particulars presented. Yet it is rare for such initiatives to be taken. Most magistrates devote very little time to appraising the affidavit's sufficiency. They assume that the affiant is being honest.... They tend to ask no questions and to issue warrants in routine fashion. Over the years the police have adapted their practice not only to the law's requirements but also to the opportunities presented by the manner in which the law is administered. They have often relied on the magistrate's passivity to insulate from review affidavits that are only apparently sufficient—sometimes purposely presenting them through officers who are "ignorant of the circumstances" and, therefore, less likely to provide awkward details in the unlikely event that questions are asked....

Goldstein 1987, 1182

Summarizing the results of a study of probable cause determination, Professor Abraham S. Goldstein (1987) found:

Proceedings before magistrates generally lasted only two to three minutes and the magistrate rarely asked any questions to penetrate the boilerplate language or the hearsay in the warrant. Witnesses other than the police applicant were never called. And the police often engaged in "magistrate shopping" for judges who would give only minimal scrutiny to the application. (1183)

Whether a judge is, in fact, neutral can become an issue, when the validity of a warrant is challenged because it is charged that the magistrate failed to properly determine whether the requirements for showing probable cause had been met before issuing the warrant. This happened in *Barnes v. State* (1975):

At the hearing held by the trial court (challenging the issuance of a warrant) in the absence of the jury, Justice of the Peace Matthews testified that, although he did not read all of the three-page, single-spaced affidavit presented him by Officers Blaisdale and Bridges, but only "touched the high parts," he did question the officers in detail about its contents and about the necessity of issuing the warrant. Further, he was acquainted with the requirements for showing probable cause, and it was only after satisfying himself that probable cause existed for the search of the premises described that he issued the warrant. According to the court, the charge that J. P. Matthews wasn't a "neutral and detached magistrate" had no merit. (401)

- *An affidavit.* The Fourth Amendment requires that magistrates base their probable cause determination on information sworn to under oath. The pain of **perjury** (the crime of lying under oath) encourages truthfulness. If the affidavit establishes probable cause, the magistrate issues the warrant.

  The written statement isn't always enough to establish probable cause; sometimes it's purposely vague. For example, police officers who want to preserve the anonymity of undercover agents make only vague references to the circumstances surrounding the information (*Fraizer v. Roberts* 1971). In these cases, supplemental oral information can satisfy the requirement in some jurisdictions. However, other courts require that all information be in writing (*Orr v. State* 1980).

  Officers usually appear before magistrates with the written affidavit, but not all jurisdictions require officers to appear in person. For example, the *Federal Rules of Criminal Procedure* 2002, 41(d)(3), authorize officers to phone or radio their information to a federal magistrate. The magistrate records the information verbatim. If the information satisfies the probable cause requirement, the magistrate authorizes the officer to sign the magistrate's name to a warrant.

Some argue that modern electronic advances should eliminate the need for most warrantless arrests. According to this argument, officers always can obtain advance judicial approval for arrests, except in emergencies, without hindering effective law enforcement. According to Professor Craig Bradley (1985), a former clerk to Chief Justice Rehnquist, if courts adopted this practice:

> The Supreme Court could actually enforce the warrant doctrine to which it has paid lip service for so many years. That is, a warrant is always required for every search and seizure when it is practicable to obtain one. However, in order that this requirement be workable and not be swallowed by its exception, the warrant need not be in writing but rather may be phoned or radioed into a magistrate (where it will be tape recorded and the recording preserved) who will authorize or forbid the search orally. By making the procedure for obtaining a warrant less difficult (while only marginally reducing the safeguards it provides), the number of cases where "emergencies" justify an exception to the warrant requirement should be very small. (1471)

- *The name of the person to be arrested.* The Fourth Amendment requires specific identification of the person to be arrested. To satisfy this particularity requirement, the *Federal Rules of Criminal Procedure* provide that an arrest warrant "shall contain the name of the defendant or, if his name is unknown, any name or description by which he can be identified with reasonable certainty."

According to the U.S. Supreme Court in *Welsh v. Wisconsin* (1984), the "physical entry of the home is the chief evil against which the wording of the Fourth Amendment is directed." This is especially true of entries into suspects' homes to arrest them. The Court regards warrants as the chief protection against "unnecessary intrusions into private dwellings." The Court applied its **no arrests in homes without a warrant rule** in *Payton v. New York* (1980).

| CASE | *Did They Need a Warrant to Enter the Homes?* |

Payton v. New York
445 U.S. 573 (1980)

Theodore Payton was convicted of murder, and Obie Riddick was convicted of armed robbery. The New York trial court judge denied their motions to suppress evidence seized during a search of their houses without warrants. The New York Court of Appeals affirmed. The U.S. Supreme Court reversed.

STEVENS, J., joined by BRENNAN, STEWART, MARSHALL, BLACKMUN, and POWELL, JJ.

FACTS

... On January 14, 1970, after two days of intensive investigation, New York detectives had assembled evidence sufficient to establish probable cause to believe that Theodore Payton had murdered the manager of a gas station two days earlier. At about 7:30 A.M. on January 15, six officers went to Payton's apartment in the Bronx, intending to arrest him. They had not obtained a warrant. Although light and music emanated from the apartment, there was no response to their knock on the metal door. They summoned emergency assistance and, about 30 minutes later, used crowbars to break open the door and enter the apartment. No one was there. In plain view, however, was a .30-caliber shell casing that was seized and later admitted into evidence at Payton's murder trial.

In due course Payton surrendered to the police, was indicted for murder, and moved to suppress the evidence taken from his apartment. The trial judge held that the warrantless and forcible entry was authorized by the New York Code of Criminal Procedure, and that the evidence in plain view was properly seized. He found that exigent circumstances justified the officers' failure to announce their purpose before entering the apartment as required by the statute. He had no occasion, however, to decide whether those circumstances also would have justified the failure to obtain a warrant, because he concluded that the warrantless entry was adequately supported by the statute without regard to the circumstances. The Appellate Division, First Department, summarily affirmed.

On March 14, 1974, Obie Riddick was arrested for the commission of two armed robberies that had occurred in 1971. He had been identified by the victims in June 1973, and in January 1974 the police had learned his address. They did not obtain a warrant for his arrest. At about noon on March 14, a detective, accompanied by three other officers, knocked on the door of the Queens house where Riddick was living. When his young son opened the door, they could see Riddick sitting in bed covered by a sheet. They entered the house and placed him under arrest. Before permitting him to dress, they opened a chest of drawers two feet from the bed in search of weapons and found narcotics and related paraphernalia. Riddick was subsequently indicted on narcotics charges. At a suppression hearing, the judge held that the warrantless entry into his home was authorized by the revised New York Statute....

The New York Court of [A]ppeals affirmed the convictions.

OPINION

...The Fourth Amendment protects the individual's privacy in a variety of settings. In none is the zone of privacy more clearly defined than when bounded by the unambiguous physical dimensions of an individual's home—a zone that finds its roots in clear and specific constitutional terms: "The right of the people to be secure in their... houses...shall not be violated." That language unequivocally establishes the proposition that "at the very core of the Fourth Amendment stands the right of a man to retreat into his own home and there be free from unreasonable governmental intrusion." In terms that apply equally to seizures of property and to seizures of persons, the Fourth Amendment has drawn a firm line at the entrance to the house. Absent exigent circumstances, that threshold may not reasonably be crossed without a warrant....

A majority of the States that have taken a position on the question permit warrantless entry into the home to arrest even in the absence of exigent circumstances....But these current figures reflect a significant decline during the last decade in the number of States permitting warrantless entries for arrest....A long-standing, widespread practice is not immune from constitutional scrutiny. But neither is it to be lightly brushed aside....Seven state courts have re-

cently held that warrantless home arrests violate their respective State constitutions....That is significant because by invoking a state constitutional provision, a state court immunizes its decision from review by this Court....

The parties have argued at some length about the practical consequences of a warrant requirement as a precondition to a felony arrest in the home. In the absence of any evidence that effective law enforcement has suffered in those States that already have such a requirement...we are inclined to view such argument with skepticism. More fundamentally, however, such arguments of policy must give way to a constitutional command that we consider to be unequivocal....

Thus, for Fourth Amendment purposes, an arrest warrant founded on probable cause implicitly carries with it the limited authority to enter a dwelling in which the suspect lives when there is reason to believe the suspect is within.

Because no arrest warrant was obtained in either of these cases, the judgments must be REVERSED and the cases REMANDED to the New York Court of Appeals for further proceedings not inconsistent with this opinion.

DISSENT

WHITE, J., joined by BURGER, CJ., and REHNQUIST, J. These four restrictions on home arrests—felony, knock and announce, daytime, and stringent probable cause—constitute powerful and complementary protections for the privacy of interests associated with the home. The felony requirement guards against abusive or arbitrary enforcement and ensures that invasions of the home occur only in case of the most serious crimes. The knock-and-announce and daytime requirements protect individuals against fear, humiliation, and embarrassment of being roused from their beds in states of partial or complete undress. And these requirements allow the arrestee to surrender at his front door, thereby maintaining his dignity and preventing the officers from entering other rooms of the dwelling. The stringent probable-cause requirement would help ensure against the possibility that the police would enter when the suspect was not home, and, in searching for him, frighten members of the family or ransack parts of the house, seizing items in plain view. In short, these requirements, taken together, permit an individual suspected of a serious crime to surrender at the front door of his dwelling and thereby avoid most of the humiliation and indignity that the Court seems to believe necessarily accompany a house entry....

All of these limitations on warrantless arrest entries are satisfied on the facts of the present cases. The arrests here were for serious felonies—murder and armed robbery—and both occurred during daylight hours. The authorizing statutes required that the police announce their business and demand entry; neither Payton nor Riddick makes any contention that these statutory requirements were not fulfilled. And it is not argued that the police had no probable cause to believe that both Payton and Riddick were in their dwellings at the time of the entries....

While exaggerating the invasion of personal privacy involved in home arrests, the Court fails to account for the danger that its rule will "severely hamper effective law enforcement."...The policeman on his beat must now make subtle discriminations that perplex even judges in their chambers.

...Police will sometimes delay making an arrest, even after probable cause is established, in order to be sure that they have enough evidence to convict. Then, if they suddenly have to arrest, they run the risk that the subsequent exigency will not excuse their prior failure to obtain a warrant. This problem cannot effectively be cured by obtaining a warrant as soon as probable cause is established because of the chance that the warrant will go stale before the arrest is made.

Further, police officers will often face the difficult task of deciding whether the circumstances are sufficiently exigent to justify their entry to arrest without a warrant. This is a decision that must be made quickly in the most trying of circumstances. If the officers mistakenly decide that the exigent circumstances are lacking, they may refrain from making the arrest, thus creating the possibility that a dangerous criminal will escape into the community. The police could reduce the likelihood of escape by staking out all possible exits until the circumstances become clearly exigent or a warrant is obtained. But the costs of such a stakeout seem excessive in an era of risking crime and scarce police resources.

Questions

1. Should there be a bright-line rule that officers may never enter a home to arrest without a warrant?

2. What exigent circumstances (emergencies) justify relaxing the warrant requirement, in your opinion?

3. Is the dissent right that the four restrictions already imposed on warrantless arrests in homes satisfy the Fourth Amendment reasonableness standard? Defend your answer.

There's one exception to the rule of no arrests in homes without a warrant—emergencies. What qualifies as an emergency? So far, the Supreme Court has recognized only the **hot pursuit** of fleeing felons as an emergency. Why? Because it would be outrageous and dangerous to compel officers to stop chasing a mugger they saw roll a victim while they go get a warrant. But, would it also be outrageous and dangerous to compel officers to get a warrant before they enter the home of a drunk driver when doing so would allow his blood alcohol to go down? The Court answered the question in *Welsh v. Wisconsin* (1984).

| CASE | *Was It Unreasonable to Enter the House of a Drunk Driver Without a Warrant?* |

Welsh v. Wisconsin
466 U.S. 470 (1984)

The Circuit Court of Dane County, Wisconsin revoked Edward Welsh's motor vehicle operator's license for 60 days for unreasonable refusal to submit to a breathalyzer test, and he appealed. The Court of Appeals reversed, and the State sought review. The Wisconsin Supreme Court reversed. The U.S. Supreme Court granted certiorari and vacated and remanded the case.

BRENNAN, J.

FACTS

Shortly before 9 o'clock on the rainy night of April 24, 1978, a lone witness, Randy Jablonic, observed a car being driven erratically. After changing speeds and veering from side to side, the car eventually swerved off the road and came to a stop in an open field. No damage to any person or property occurred. Concerned about the driver and fearing that the car would get back on the highway, Jablonic drove his truck up behind the car so as to block it from returning to the road. Another passerby also stopped at the scene, and Jablonic asked her to call the police. Before the police arrived, however, the driver of the car emerged from his vehicle, approached Jablonic's truck, and asked Jablonic for a ride home. Jablonic instead suggested that they wait for assistance in removing or repairing the car. Ignoring Jablonic's suggestion, the driver walked away from the scene.

A few minutes later, the police arrived and questioned Jablonic. He told one officer what he had seen, specifically noting that the driver was either very inebriated or very sick. The officer checked the motor vehicle registration of the abandoned car and learned that it was registered to Welsh, Edward G. Welsh. In addition, the officer noted that Welsh's residence was a short distance from the scene, and therefore easily within walking distance.

Without securing any type of warrant, the police proceeded to Welsh's, arriving about 9 P.M. When Welsh's stepdaughter answered the door, the police gained entry into the house. Proceeding upstairs to Welsh's bedroom, they found him lying naked in bed. At this point, Welsh was placed under arrest for driving or operating a motor vehicle while under the influence of an intoxicant, in violation of Wis.Stat. § 346.63(1) (1977). Welsh was taken to the police station, where he refused to submit to a breath-analysis test. . . .

The State filed a criminal complaint against Welsh for driving while intoxicated. Welsh was charged with a criminal misdemeanor because this was his second such citation in the previous five years. Although Welsh was subject to a criminal charge, the police conducting the warrantless entry of his home did not know that Welsh had ever been charged with, or much less convicted of, a prior violation for driving while intoxicated. It must be assumed, therefore, that at the time of the arrest the police were acting as if they were investigating and eventually arresting for a nonjailable traffic offense that constituted only a civil violation under the applicable state law. Welsh responded by filing a motion to dismiss the complaint, relying on his contention that the underlying arrest was invalid. After receiving evidence at a hearing on this motion in July 1980, the trial court concluded that the criminal complaint would not be dismissed because the existence of both probable cause and exigent circumstances justified the warrantless arrest. . . .

Contrary to the trial court, the appellate court concluded that the warrantless arrest of Welsh in his home violated the Fourth Amendment because the State, although demonstrating probable cause to arrest, had not established the existence of exigent circumstances. Welsh's refusal to submit to a breath test was therefore reasonable. The Supreme Court of Wisconsin in turn reversed the Court of Appeals, relying on the existence of three factors that it believed constituted exigent circumstances: the need for "hot pursuit" of a suspect, the need to prevent physical harm to the offender and the public, and the need to prevent destruction of evidence. Because of the important Fourth Amendment implications of the decision below, we granted certiorari. . . .

OPINION

It is axiomatic that the "physical entry of the home is the chief evil against which the wording of the Fourth Amendment is directed." And a principal protection against unnecessary intrusions into private dwellings is the warrant requirement imposed by the Fourth Amendment on agents of the government who seek to enter the home for purposes of search or arrest. It is not surprising, therefore, that the Court has recognized, as "a 'basic principle of Fourth Amendment law,' that searches and seizures inside a home without a warrant are presumptively unreasonable." In *Johnson v. U.S.*, Justice Jackson eloquently explained the warrant requirement in the context of a home search:

> The point of the Fourth Amendment, which often is not grasped by zealous officers, is not that it denies law enforcement the support of the usual inferences which reasonable men draw from evidence. Its protection consists in requiring that those inferences be drawn by a neutral and detached magistrate instead of being judged by the officer engaged in the often competitive enterprise of ferreting out crime. . . . The right of officers to thrust themselves into a home is . . . a grave concern, not only to the individual but to a society which chooses to dwell in reasonable security and freedom from surveillance. When the right of privacy must reasonably yield to the right of search is, as a rule, to be decided by a judicial officer, not by a policeman or government enforcement agent.

Consistently with these long-recognized principles, the Court decided in *Payton v. New York*, that warrantless felony arrests in the home are prohibited by the Fourth Amendment, absent probable cause and exigent circumstances. At the same time, the Court declined to consider the scope of any exception for exigent circumstances that might justify warrantless home arrests, thereby leaving to the lower courts the initial application of the exigent-circumstances exception. Prior decisions of this Court, however, have emphasized that exceptions to the warrant requirement are "few in number and carefully delineated," and that the police bear a heavy burden when attempting to demonstrate an urgent need that might justify warrantless searches or arrests. Indeed, the Court has recognized only a few such emergency conditions, see, e.g., *United States v. Santana*, 427 U.S. 38, 42–43, 96 S.Ct. 2406, 2409–2410, 49 L.Ed.2d 300 (1976) (hot pursuit of a fleeing felon); *Schmerber v. California*, 384 U.S. 757, 770–771, 86 S.Ct. 1826, 1835–1836, 16L.Ed.2d 908 (1966) (destruction of evidence); *Michigan v. Tyler*, 436 U.S. 499, 509, 98 S.Ct. 1942, 1949, 56 L.Ed.2d 486 (1978) (ongoing fire), and has actually applied only the "hot pursuit" doctrine to arrests in the home.

Our hesitation in finding exigent circumstances, especially when warrantless arrests in the home are at issue, is particularly appropriate when the underlying offense for which there is probable cause to arrest is relatively minor. Before agents of the government may invade the sanctity of the home, the burden is on the government to demonstrate exigent circumstances that overcome the presumption of unreasonableness that attaches to all warrantless home entries. When the government's interest is only to arrest for a minor offense, that presumption of unreasonableness is difficult to rebut, and the government usually should be allowed to make such arrests only with a warrant issued upon probable cause by a neutral and detached magistrate.

Consistently with this approach, the lower courts have looked to the nature of the underlying offense as an important factor to be considered in the exigent circumstances calculus. In a leading federal case defining exigent circumstances, for example, the en banc United States Court of Appeals for the District of Columbia Circuit recognized that the gravity of the underlying offense was a principal factor to be weighed. . . . Many other lower courts have also considered the gravity of the offense an important part of their constitutional analysis. . . .

We therefore conclude that the common-sense approach utilized by most lower courts is required by the Fourth Amendment prohibition on "unreasonable searches and seizures," and hold that an important factor to be considered when determining whether any exigency exists is the gravity of the underlying offense for which the arrest is being made. Moreover, although no exigency is created simply because there is probable cause to believe that a serious crime has been committed, application of the exigent- circumstances exception in the context of a home entry should rarely be sanctioned when there is probable cause to believe that only a minor offense, such as the kind at issue in this case, has been committed.

Application of this principle to the facts of the present case is relatively straightforward. Welsh was arrested in the privacy of his own bedroom for a non criminal, traffic offense. The State attempts to justify the arrest by relying on the hot-pursuit doctrine, on the threat to public safety, and on the need to preserve evidence of Welsh's blood-alcohol level. On the facts of this case, however, the claim of hot pursuit is unconvincing because there was no immediate or continuous pursuit of Welsh from the scene of a crime. Moreover, because Welsh had already arrived home, and had abandoned his car at the scene of the accident, there was little remaining threat to the public safety. Hence, the only potential emergency claimed by the State was the need to ascertain Welsh's blood-alcohol level.

Even assuming, however, that the underlying facts would support a finding of this exigent circumstance, mere similarity to other cases involving the imminent destruction of evidence is not sufficient. The State of Wisconsin has chosen to classify the first offense for driving while intoxicated as a noncriminal, civil forfeiture offense for which no imprisonment is possible. This is the best indication of the State's interest in precipitating an arrest, and is one that can be easily identified both by the courts and by officers faced with a decision to arrest. Given this expression of the State's interest, a warrantless home arrest cannot be upheld simply because evidence of Welsh's blood-alcohol level might have dissipated while the police obtained a warrant. To allow a warrantless home entry on these facts would be to approve unreasonable police behavior that the principles of the Fourth Amendment will not sanction.

The Supreme Court of Wisconsin let stand a warrantless, nighttime entry into Welsh's home to arrest him for a civil traffic offense. Such an arrest, however, is clearly prohibited by the special protection afforded the individual in his home by the Fourth Amendment. Welsh's arrest was therefore invalid, the judgment of the Supreme Court of Wisconsin is vacated, and the case is REMANDED for further proceedings not inconsistent with this opinion. On remand, the state courts may consider whether Welsh's arrest was justified because the police had validly obtained consent to enter his home.

It is so ordered.

CONCURRING OPINION

BLACKMUN, J.

I join the Court's opinion but add a personal observation. I yield to no one in my profound personal concern about the unwillingness of our national consciousness to face up to—and to do something about—the continuing slaughter upon our Nation's highways, a good percentage of which is due to drivers who are drunk or semi-incapacitated because of alcohol or drug ingestion. I have spoken in these Reports to this point before.

And it is amazing to me that one of our great States—one which, by its highway signs, proclaims to be diligent and emphatic in its prosecution of the drunken driver—still classifies driving while intoxicated as a civil violation that allows only a money forfeiture of not more than $300 so long as it is a first offense. The State, like the indulgent parent, hesitates to discipline the spoiled child very much, even though the child is engaging in an act that is dangerous to others who are law abiding and helpless in the face of the child's act. Our personal convenience still weighs heavily in the balance, and the highway deaths and injuries continue. But if Wisconsin and other States choose by legislation thus to regulate their penalty structure, there is, unfortunately, nothing in the United States Constitution that says they may not do so.

DISSENT

WHITE, J. joined by REHNQUIST, J.
. . . Warrantless nonfelony arrests in the home are prohibited by the Fourth Amendment absent probable cause and exigent circumstances. Although I continue to believe that the Court erred in *Payton v. New York* in requiring exigent circumstances to justify warrantless in-home felony arrests, I do not reject the obvious logical implication of the Court's decision. But I see little to commend an approach that looks to "the nature of the underlying offense as an important factor to be considered in the exigent-circumstances calculus."

The gravity of the underlying offense is, I concede, a factor to be considered in determining whether the delay that attends the warrant-issuance process will endanger officers or other persons. The seriousness of the offense with which a suspect may be charged also bears on the likelihood that he will flee and escape apprehension if not arrested immediately. But if, under all the circumstances of a particular case, an officer has probable cause to believe that the delay involved in procuring an arrest warrant will gravely endanger the officer or other persons or will result in the suspect's escape, I perceive no reason to disregard those exigencies on the ground that the offense for which the suspect is sought is a "minor" one. . . .

A warrantless home entry to arrest is no more intrusive when the crime is "minor" than when the suspect is sought in connection with a serious felony. The variable factor, if there is one, is the governmental interest that will be served by the warrantless entry. Wisconsin's Legislature and its Supreme Court have both concluded that warrantless in-home arrests under circumstances like those present here promote valid and substantial state interests. In determining whether the challenged governmental conduct was

reasonable, we are not bound by these determinations. But nothing in our previous decisions suggests that the fact that a State has defined an offense as a misdemeanor for a variety of social, cultural, and political reasons necessarily requires the conclusion that warrantless in-home arrests designed to prevent the imminent destruction or removal of evidence of that offense are always impermissible. If anything, the Court's prior decisions support the opposite conclusion.

A test under which the existence of exigent circumstances turns on the perceived gravity of the crime would significantly hamper law enforcement and burden courts with pointless litigation concerning the nature and gradation of various crimes. . . . The decision to arrest without a warrant typically is made in the field under less-than-optimal circumstances; officers have neither the time nor the competence to determine whether a particular offense for which warrantless arrests have been authorized by statute is serious enough to justify a warrantless home entry to prevent the imminent destruction or removal of evidence.

Even if the Court were correct in concluding that the gravity of the offense is an important factor to consider in determining whether a warrantless in-home arrest is justified by exigent circumstances, it has erred in assessing the seriousness of the civil-forfeiture offense for which the officers thought they were arresting Welsh. As the Court observes, the statutory scheme in force at the time of Welsh's arrest provided that the first offense for driving under the influence of alcohol involved no potential incarceration. Nevertheless, this Court has long recognized the compelling state interest in highway safety, the Supreme Court of Wisconsin identified a number of factors suggesting a substantial and growing governmental interest in apprehending and convicting intoxicated drivers and in deterring alcohol-related offenses, and recent actions of the Wisconsin Legislature evince its "belief that significant benefits, in the reduction of the costs attributable to drunk driving, may be achieved by the increased apprehension and conviction of even first time . . . offenders."

The Court ignores these factors and looks solely to the penalties imposed on first offenders in determining whether the State's interest is sufficient to justify warrantless in-home arrests under exigent circumstances. Although the seriousness of the prescribed sanctions is a valuable objective indication of the general normative judgment of the seriousness of the offense, other evidence is available and should not be ignored. Although first offenders are subjected only to civil forfeiture under the Wisconsin statute, the seriousness with which the State regards the crime for which Welsh was arrested is evinced by (1) the fact that defendants charged with driving under the influence are guaranteed the right to a jury trial; (2) the legislative authorization of warrantless arrests for traffic offenses occurring outside the officer's presence; and (3) the collateral consequence of mandatory license revocation that attaches to all convictions for driving under the influence. It is possible, moreover, that the legislature consciously chose to limit the penalties imposed on first offenders in order to increase the ease of conviction and the overall deterrent effect of the enforcement effort.

In short, the fact that Wisconsin has chosen to punish the first offense for driving under the influence with a fine rather than a prison term does not demand the conclusion that the State's interest in punishing first offenders is insufficiently substantial to justify warrantless in-home arrests under exigent circumstances. As the Supreme Court of Wisconsin observed, "this is a model case demonstrating the urgency involved in arresting the suspect in order to preserve evidence of the statutory violation." We have previously recognized that "the percentage of alcohol in the blood begins to diminish shortly after drinking stops, as the body functions to eliminate it from the system." Moreover, a suspect could cast substantial doubt on the validity of a blood or breath test by consuming additional alcohol upon arriving at his home. In light of the promptness with which the officers reached Welsh's house, therefore, I would hold that the need to prevent the imminent and ongoing destruction of evidence of a serious violation of Wisconsin's traffic laws provided an exigent circumstance justifying the warrantless in-home arrest.

I respectfully dissent.

Questions

1. List all the evidence for and against the argument that entering Welsh's house was an emergency.

2. Identify the values the Court balanced in applying the no-arrest-in-homes-without-warrants rule.

3. Summarize the majority opinion's reasons for deciding the case didn't qualify as an emergency.

4. Summarize the dissent's arguments that entering Welsh's home was an emergency.

5. Should it matter whether Wisconsin considers drunk driving a minor offense? Defend your answer.

EXPLORING WARRANTLESS ARRESTS FURTHER

 Go to the Criminal Procedure 6e CD to read the full text version of the case featured here.

Was the Arrest Unreasonable Because the Officer Had Time to Get a Warrant and Didn't?

FACTS

On August 17, an informant of proven reliability delivered a stolen credit card to a federal postal inspector. The informant alleged that he had received the card from Henry Watson, who had instructed him to purchase airline tickets with it. Although authorities had probable cause to arrest Watson, they neither arrested him immediately nor applied for an arrest warrant. Instead, they arranged for a meeting between the informant and Watson on August 22. The meeting was postponed until August 23, at which time the informant signaled to postal inspectors that Watson had indicated that he presently had additional stolen credit cards in his possession. The inspectors entered the restaurant where the meeting had taken place, arrested Watson without a warrant, and searched his person, finding nothing. Watson, however, consented to a search of his nearby car; that search yielded the stolen credit cards. Was the arrest illegal because the officers had time to get a warrant but did not do so?

DECISION AND REASONS

The Court of Appeals for the Ninth Circuit ruled that when they have time, police have to get a warrant to arrest someone, even in a public place. Not so, said the U.S. Supreme Court:

> Law enforcement officers may find it wise to seek arrest warrant[s] where practicable to do so, and their judgments about probable cause may be more readily accepted where backed by a warrant issued by a magistrate. But we decline to transform this judicial preference into a constitutional rule when the judgment of the Nation . . . has for so long been to authorize warrantless public arrests on probable cause rather than to encumber criminal prosecutions with endless litigation with respect to the existence of exigent circumstances, whether it was practicable to get a warrant, whether the suspect was about to flee, and the like.

In a dissenting opinion, Marshall, J., observed:

> The Government's assertion that a warrant requirement would impose an intolerable burden stems, in large part, from the specious supposition that procurement of an arrest warrant would be necessary as soon as probable cause ripens. There is no requirement that a search warrant be obtained the moment police have probable cause to search. The same rule should obtain for arrest warrants, where it may even make more sense. . . .

> This approach obviates most of the difficulties that have been suggested with an arrest warrant rule. Police would not have to cut their investigation short the moment they obtain probable cause to arrest, nor would undercover agents be forced suddenly to terminate their work and forfeit their covers. Moreover, if in the course of continued police investigation exigent circumstances develop that demand an immediate arrest, the arrest may be made without fear of unconstitutionality, so long as the exigency was unanticipated and not used to avoid the arrest warrant requirement. . . . [T]he requirement that officers about to arrest a suspect ordinarily obtain a warrant before they do so does not seem unduly burdensome. . . .

U.S. v. Watson, 423 U.S. 411 (1976)

Arrest by Force

Whether the manner of an arrest was reasonable is also affected by whether the level of force applied (if any) was reasonable. Usually, when we hear about the use of force to make an arrest, it is when the officers have shot and killed a suspect. This tends to distort the public's view of the frequency of the use of **deadly force**—that is, restraint capable of producing death. In reality, there are far more forcible arrests using nondeadly force than deadly force. And, of course the vast majority of all arrests are made without the use of any force at all. Keeping these facts in mind, let's look at the use of deadly and nondeadly force to arrest suspects.

- *Deadly force.* Throughout most of our history, states have followed the ancient common-law rule that allowed officers to use deadly force when it was necessary to apprehend fleeing felons. By the 1960s, many police departments had adopted rules that restricted this common-law rule. The gist of these rules is that officers can use deadly force only when (1) it's necessary to apprehend "dangerous" suspects, and (2) it doesn't put innocent people in danger. In *Tennessee v. Garner* (1985), the U.S. Supreme adopted these two rules as Fourth Amendment requirements in using deadly force to make arrests. Here's how it applied the rules to the facts of the case.

Tennessee v. Garner
471 U.S. 1 (1985)

Fifteen-year-old Edward Garner was killed by the Memphis Police Department when he fled the scene of a suspected burglary. His father, Cleamtree Garner, sued the Department under U.S.C.A. § 1983* for violating his son's Fourth Amendment right against unreasonable seizures. The U.S. District Court ruled that the shooting was not an unreasonable seizure. The U.S. Court of Appeals reversed. The U.S. Supreme Court affirmed.

WHITE, J., joined by BRENNAN, MARSHALL, BLACKMUN, POWELL, and STEVENS, JJ.

FACTS

At about 10:45 P.M. on October 3, 1974, Memphis Police Officers Elton Hymon and Leslie Wright were dispatched to answer a "prowler inside call." Upon arriving at the scene they saw a woman standing on her porch gesturing toward the adjacent house. She told them she had heard glass breaking and that "they" or "someone" was breaking in next door. While Wright radioed the dispatcher to say that they were on the scene, Hymon went behind the house. He heard a door slam and saw someone run across the backyard. The fleeing suspect, who was appellee–respondent's descendent, Edward Garner, stopped at a 6-feet-high chain link fence at the edge of the yard. With the aid of a flashlight, Hymon was able to see Garner's face and hands. He saw no sign of a weapon, and though not certain, was "reasonably sure" and "figured" that Garner was unarmed. He thought Garner was 17 or 18 years old and about 5'5" or 5'7" tall. While Garner was crouched at the base of the fence, Hymon called out "police, halt" and took a few steps toward him. Garner began to climb over the fence. Convinced that if Garner made it over the fence he would elude capture, Hymon shot him. The bullet hit Garner in the back of the head. Garner was taken by ambulance to a hospital, where he died on the operating table. Ten dollars and a purse taken from the house were found on his body.

In using deadly force to prevent escape, Hymon was acting under the authority of a Tennessee statute and pursuant to Police Department policy. The statute provides that "if, after notice of the intention to arrest the defen-

dant, he either flee or forcibly resist, the officer may use all the necessary means to effect the arrest." Tenn. Code Ann. § 40-7-108 (1982). The Department policy was slightly more restrictive than the statute, but still allowed the use of deadly force in cases of burglary. The incident was reviewed by the Memphis Police Firearm's Review Board and presented to a grand jury. Neither took any action.

Garner's father then brought this action in the Federal District Court for the Western District of Tennessee, seeking damages under 42 U.S.C. § 1983 for asserted violations of Garner's constitutional rights. The complaint alleged that the shooting violated the Fourth, Fifth, Sixth, Eighth, and Fourteenth Amendments of the United States Constitution. It named as defendants Officer Hymon, the Police Department, its Director, and the Mayor and City of Memphis. After a 3-day bench trial, the District Court entered judgment for all defendants. It dismissed the claims against the Mayor and the Director for lack of evidence. It then concluded that Hymon's actions were authorized by the Tennessee statute, which in turn was constitutional. Hymon had employed the only reasonable and practicable means of preventing Garner's escape. Garner had "recklessly and heedlessly attempted to vault over the fence to escape, thereby assuming the risk of being fired upon."

The District Court . . . found that the statute, and Hymon's actions, were constitutional. The Court of Appeals reversed and remanded. . . .

OPINION

. . . Whenever an officer restrains the freedom of a person to walk away, he has seized that person. . . . There can be no question that apprehension by the use of deadly force is a seizure subject to the reasonableness requirement of the Fourth Amendment.

A police officer may arrest a person if he has probable cause to believe that person committed a crime. Petitioners and appellant argue that if this requirement is satisfied the Fourth Amendment has nothing to say about how that seizure is made. The submission ignores the many cases in which this Court, by balancing the extent of the intrusion against the need for it, has examined the reasonableness of the manner in which a search or seizure is conducted. . . .

The use of deadly force to prevent the escape of all felony suspects, whatever the circumstances, is constitutionally

---

*See Chapter 11.

unreasonable. It is not better that all felony suspects die than that they escape. Where the suspect poses no immediate threat to the officer and no threat to others, the harm resulting from failing to apprehend him does not justify the use of deadly force to do so. It is no doubt unfortunate when a suspect who is in sight escapes, but the fact the police arrive a little late or are a little slower afoot does not always justify killing the suspect. A police officer may not seize an unarmed, nondangerous suspect by shooting him dead. The Tennessee statute is unconstitutional insofar as it authorizes the use of deadly force against such fleeing suspects. . . .

Officer Hymon could not reasonably have believed that Garner—young, slight, and unarmed—posed any threat. Indeed, Hymon never attempted to justify his actions on any basis other than the need to prevent escape. . . . The fact that Garner was a suspected burglar could not, without regard to the other circumstances, automatically justify the use of deadly force. Hymon did not have probable cause to believe that Garner, whom he correctly believed to be unarmed, posed any physical danger to himself or to others.

DISSENT

O'CONNOR, J., joined by BURGER, CJ.,
and REHNQUIST, J.

For purposes of Fourth Amendment analysis, I agree with the Court that Officer Hymon "seized" Garner by shooting him. Whether that seizure was reasonable and therefore permitted by the Fourth Amendment requires a careful balancing of the important public interest in crime prevention and detection and the nature and quality of the intrusion upon legitimate interests of the individual. In striking this balance here, it is crucial to acknowledge that police use of deadly force to apprehend a fleeing criminal suspect falls within the "rubric of police conduct . . . necessarily [invoking] swift action predicated upon the on-the-spot observations of the officer on the beat.". . .

The public interest involved in the use of deadly force as a last resort to apprehend a fleeing burglary suspect relates primarily to the serious nature of the crime. Household burglaries represent not only the illegal entry into a person's home, but also "pose a real risk of serious harm to others." According to recent Department of Justice statistics, "Three-fifths of all rapes in the home, three-fifths of all home robberies, and about a third of home aggravated and simple assaults are committed by burglars.". . .

Against the strong public interests justifying the conduct at issue here must be weighed the individual interests implicated in the use of deadly force by police officers. The majority declares that "the suspect's fundamental interest in his own life need not be elaborated upon." This blithe assertion hardly provides an adequate substitute for the majority's failure to acknowledge the distinctive manner in which the suspect's interest in his life is even exposed to risk. For purposes of this case, we must recall that the police officer, in the course of . . . investigating a nighttime burglary, had reasonable cause to arrest the suspect and ordered him to halt. The officer's use of force resulted because the suspected burglar refused to heed this command and the officer reasonably believed that there was no means short of firing his weapon to apprehend the suspect. . . ." The policeman's hands should not be tied merely because of the possibility that the suspect will fail to cooperate with legitimate actions by law enforcement personnel.". . .

Questions

1. Should the Fourth Amendment apply to the manner of arrest? Defend your answer.

2. Professor H. Richard Uviller (1986), a longtime student of police power and the Constitution, commented on the decision in *Tennessee v. Garner:*

> It is embarrassing for a law professor to be blindsided in his own territory. But the truth is, I didn't see it coming. It had never occurred to me that a police officer shooting to kill a fleeing felon might be engaging in an unconstitutional search and seizure. Of course, I can see the connection now that it has been explained to me, but I did not spontaneously equate a deadly shot with an arrest. And I have had some prior acquaintance not only with the fourth amendment, but specifically with the issue of the bullet aimed at the back of a retreating felon. (706)

Is shooting a suspect a "seizure"?

3. Professor Uviller asks the following questions: Would the rule in this case permit an officer to shoot a drunk driver swerving erratically down the road headed toward a town? A person wanted for a series of violent crimes but not presently armed who flees from the police? How would you answer Professor Uviller's questions? Defend your answers.

4. Will this rule embolden criminals? Did the Court tilt the balance too far toward process and societal interests and too far away from the interest in results? Defend your answer.

◆   ◆   ◆

- *Nondeadly force.* Shooting is the most dramatic and publicized use of force to arrest suspects, but, in practice, officers are far more likely to use nondeadly force. In one case, the U.S. Supreme Court decided that the use of chokeholds can be reasonable seizures. In *Graham v. Connor* (1989), the Court adopted an **objective standard of reasonable force.** According to the standard, the Fourth Amendment permits officers to use the amount of force necessary to apprehend and bring suspects under control. The standard is objective because it doesn't depend on the officer's intent or motives. So, as long as an officer uses a reasonable amount of force, it doesn't matter that he might have used it out of malice or prejudice; it doesn't make the manner of arrest or use of force unreasonable. By the same token, no amount of good intentions and noble motive will make the use of excessive force reasonable.

CASE	*Did the Officers Use Excessive Force?*

Graham v. Connor
490 U.S. 386 (1989)

Dethorne Graham, a diabetic, brought a § 1983 action to recover damages for injuries sustained when law enforcement officers used physical force against him during an investigatory stop. The U.S. District Court directed a verdict for the defendant police officers. The court of appeals affirmed. The U.S. Supreme Court granted certiorari and reversed.

REHNQUIST, J., joined by WHITE, STEVENS, O'CONNOR, SCALIA, and KENNEDY, JJ.

FACTS

On November 12, 1984, Dethorne Graham, a diabetic, felt the onset of an insulin reaction. He asked a friend, William Berry, to drive him to a nearby convenience store so he could purchase some orange juice to counteract the reaction. Berry agreed, but when Graham entered the store, he saw a number of people ahead of him in the checkout line. Concerned about the delay, he hurried out of the store and asked Berry to drive him to a friend's house instead. Respondent Connor, an officer of the Charlotte, North Carolina, Police Department, saw Graham hastily enter and leave the store. The officer became suspicious that something was amiss and followed Berry's car. About one-half mile from the store, he made an investigative stop. Although Berry told Connor that Graham was simply suffering from a "sugar reaction," the officer ordered Berry and Graham to wait while he found out what, if anything, had happened at the convenience store. When Officer Connor returned to his patrol car to call for backup assistance, Graham got out of the car, ran around it twice, and finally sat down on the curb, where he passed out briefly.

In the ensuing confusion, a number of other Charlotte police officers arrived on the scene in response to Officer Connor's request for backup. One of the officers rolled Graham over on the sidewalk and cuffed his hands tightly behind his back, ignoring Berry's pleas to get him some sugar. Another officer said: "I've seen a lot of people with sugar diabetes that never acted like this. Ain't nothing wrong with the M. F. but drunk. Lock the S. B. up." Several officers then lifted Graham up from behind, carried him over to Berry's car, and placed him face down on its hood. Regaining consciousness, Graham asked the officers to check in his wallet for a diabetic decal that he carried. In response, one of the officers told him to "shut up" and shoved his face down against the hood of the car. Four officers grabbed Graham and threw him headfirst into the police car. A friend of Graham's brought some orange juice to the car, but the officers refused to let him have it. Finally, Officer Connor received a report that Graham had done nothing wrong at the convenience store, and the officers drove him home and released him.

At some point during his encounter with the police, Graham sustained a broken foot, cuts on his wrists, a bruised forehead, and an injured shoulder; he also claims to have developed a loud ringing in his right ear that continues to this day. He commenced this action under 42 U.S.C. § 1983 against the individual officers involved in the incident, all of whom are respondents here, alleging that they had used excessive force in making the investigatory stop, in violation of "rights secured to him under the

Fourteenth Amendment to the United States Constitution and 42 U.S.C. § 1983." The case was tried before a jury. At the close of petitioner's evidence, respondents moved for a directed verdict. In ruling on that motion, the District Court considered the following four factors, which it identified as "[t]he factors to be considered in determining when the excessive use of force gives rise to a cause of action under § 1983":

1. the need for the application of force;

2. the relationship between that need and the amount of force that was used;

3. the extent of the injury inflicted; and

4. whether the force was applied in a good faith effort to maintain and restore discipline or maliciously and sadistically for the very purpose of causing harm.

Finding that the amount of force used by the officers was "appropriate under the circumstances," that "there was no discernable injury inflicted," and that the force used "was not applied maliciously or sadistically for the very purpose of causing harm," but in "a good faith effort to maintain or restore order in the face of a potentially explosive situation," the District Court granted respondents' motion for a directed verdict.

A divided panel of the Court of Appeals for the Fourth Circuit affirmed.... We granted certiorari, and now reverse.

OPINION

Fifteen years ago, in *Johnson v. Glick* [1974], the Court of Appeals for the Second Circuit addressed a § 1983 damages claim filed by a pretrial detainee who claimed that a guard had assaulted him without justification. In evaluating the detainee's claim, Judge Friendly applied neither the Fourth Amendment nor the Eighth, the two most textually obvious sources of constitutional protection against physically abusive governmental conduct. Instead, he looked to "substantive due process," holding that "quite apart from any 'specific' of the Bill of Rights, application of undue force by law enforcement officers deprives a suspect of liberty without due process of law." As support for this proposition, he relied upon our decision in *Rochin v. California* (1952),* which used the Due Process Clause to void a state criminal conviction based on evidence obtained by pumping the defendant's stomach. If a police officer's use of force which "shocks the conscience" could justify setting aside a criminal conviction, Judge Friendly reasoned, a correctional officer's use of similarly excessive force must give

rise to a due process violation actionable under § 1983. Judge Friendly went on to set forth four factors to guide courts in determining "whether the constitutional line has been crossed" by a particular use of force—the same four factors relied upon by the courts below in this case.

In the years following *Johnson v. Glick*, the vast majority of lower federal courts have applied its four-part "substantive due process" test indiscriminately to all excessive force claims lodged against law enforcement and prison officials under § 1983, without considering whether the particular application of force might implicate a more specific constitutional right governed by a different standard. Indeed, many courts have seemed to assume, as did the courts... in this case, that there is a generic "right" to be free from excessive force, grounded not in any particular constitutional provision but rather in "basic principles of § 1983 jurisprudence."

We reject this notion that all excessive force claims brought under § 1983 are governed by a single generic standard. As we have said many times, § 1983 "is not itself a source of substantive rights," but merely provides "a method for vindicating federal rights elsewhere conferred." In addressing an excessive force claim brought under §1983, analysis begins by identifying the specific constitutional right allegedly infringed by the challenged application of force.... In most instances, that will be either the Fourth Amendment's prohibition against unreasonable seizures of the person, or the Eighth Amendment's ban on cruel and unusual punishments, which are the two primary sources of constitutional protection against physically abusive governmental conduct. The validity of the claim must then be judged by reference to the specific constitutional standard which governs that right, rather than to some generalized "excessive force" standard. See *Tennessee v. Garner* (claim of excessive force to effect arrest analyzed under a Fourth Amendment standard); *Whitley v. Albers* (1986) (claim of excessive force to subdue convicted prisoner analyzed under an Eighth Amendment standard).

Where, as here, the excessive force claim arises in the context of an arrest or investigatory stop of a free citizen, it is most properly characterized as one invoking the protections of the Fourth Amendment, which guarantees citizens the right "to be secure in their persons... against unreasonable... seizures" of the person.... Today we... hold that all claims that law enforcement officers have used excessive force—deadly or not—in the course of an arrest, investigatory stop, or other "seizure" of a free citizen should be analyzed under the Fourth Amendment and its "reasonableness" standard, rather than under a "substantive due process" approach. Because the Fourth Amendment provides an explicit textual source of constitutional

---

*See Chapter 2.

protection against this sort of physically intrusive governmental conduct, that Amendment, not the more generalized notion of "substantive due process," must be the guide for analyzing these claims....

Determining whether the force used to effect a particular seizure is "reasonable" under the Fourth Amendment requires a careful balancing of "the nature and quality of the intrusion on the individual's Fourth Amendment interests" against the countervailing governmental interests at stake. Our Fourth Amendment jurisprudence has long recognized that the right to make an arrest or investigatory stop necessarily carries with it the right to use some degree of physical coercion or threat thereof to effect it.... With respect to a claim of excessive force, the ... standard of reasonableness at the moment applies: "Not every push or shove, even if it may later seem unnecessary in the peace of a judge's chambers," *Johnson v. Glick*, violates the Fourth Amendment. The calculus of reasonableness must embody allowance for the fact that police officers are often forced to make split-second judgments—in circumstances that are tense, uncertain, and rapidly evolving—about the amount of force that is necessary in a particular situation.

As in other Fourth Amendment contexts, however, the "reasonableness" inquiry in an excessive force case is an objective one: the question is whether the officers' actions are "objectively reasonable" in light of the facts and circumstances confronting them, without regard to their underlying intent or motivation. An officer's evil intentions will not make a Fourth Amendment violation out of an objectively reasonable use of force; nor will an officer's good intentions make an objectively unreasonable use of force constitutional.

Because petitioner's excessive force claim is one arising under the Fourth Amendment, the Court of Appeals erred in analyzing it under the four-part *Johnson v. Glick* test. That test, which requires consideration of whether the individual officers acted in "good faith" or "maliciously and sadistically for the very purpose of causing harm," is incompatible with a proper Fourth Amendment analysis. We do not agree with the Court of Appeals' suggestion, that the "malicious and sadistic" inquiry is merely another way of describing conduct that is objectively unreasonable under the circumstances. Whatever the empirical correlations between "malicious and sadistic" behavior and objective unreasonableness may be, the fact remains that the "malicious and sadistic" factor puts in issue the subjective motivations of the individual officers, which our prior cases make clear has no bearing on whether a particular seizure is "unreasonable" under the Fourth Amendment.

Nor do we agree with the Court of Appeals' conclusion, that because the subjective motivations of the individual officers are of central importance in deciding whether force used against a convicted prisoner violates the Eighth Amendment, it cannot be reversible error to inquire into them in deciding whether force used against a suspect or arrestee violates the Fourth Amendment. Differing standards under the Fourth and Eighth Amendments are hardly surprising: the terms "cruel" and "punishment" clearly suggest some inquiry into subjective state of mind, whereas the term "unreasonable" does not. Moreover, the less protective Eighth Amendment standard applies "only after the State has complied with the constitutional guarantees traditionally associated with criminal prosecutions." *Ingraham v. Wright* (1977). The Fourth Amendment inquiry is one of "objective reasonableness" under the circumstances, and subjective concepts like "malice" and "sadism" have no proper place in that inquiry.

Because the Court of Appeals reviewed the District Court's ruling on the motion for directed verdict under an erroneous view of the governing substantive law, its judgment must be vacated and the case REMANDED to that court for reconsideration of that issue under the proper Fourth Amendment standard.

CONCURRING OPINION

BLACKMUN, J., joined by BRENNAN and MARSHALL, JJ. I join the Court's opinion insofar as it rules that the Fourth Amendment is the primary tool for analyzing claims of excessive force in the prearrest context, and I concur in the judgment remanding the case to the Court of Appeals for reconsideration of the evidence under a reasonableness standard. In light of respondents' concession, however, that the pleadings in this case properly may be construed as raising a Fourth Amendment claim, I see no reason for the Court to find it necessary further to reach out to decide that prearrest excessive force claims are to be analyzed under the Fourth Amendment rather than under a substantive due process standard. I also see no basis for the Court's suggestion, that our decision in *Tennessee v. Garner* implicitly so held. Nowhere in *Garner* is a substantive due process standard for evaluating the use of excessive force in a particular case discussed; there is no suggestion that such a standard was offered as an alternative and rejected....

Questions

1. List all the specific uses of force by the officers.

2. State the standard that the Court adopted for determining whether the use of force violated the Fourth Amendment.

3. How does the Court's standard differ from the test that the Court of Appeals applied in the case?

4. Why did the Court change the standard? Which test do you favor? Explain your answer.

5. What is the main point of Justice Blackmun's concurring opinion? Do you agree with it? Explain.

6. If you were applying the tests to the facts of this case, what decision would you reach? Defend your answer.

 Go to Exercise 5-2 on the Criminal Procedure 6e CD to learn more about the manner of arrest.

AFTER THE ARREST

Immediately after an arrest, as we've just seen, police officers may use force to subdue unruly suspects; to prevent escape; and to protect suspects, officers, other people, or property. When they arrest suspects for felonies, officers almost always take the following actions:

1. Search suspects (see Chapter 6)

2. Take suspects to the police station, and then "book" them by putting their name and address, the time the crime was committed, and other information into the police blotter

3. Photograph and fingerprint them

4. Interrogate them (Chapter 8)

5. Put them into lineups (Chapter 9)

6. Turn the results of the initial investigations over to prosecutors (Chapter 12)

7. Present prisoners to a magistrate (Chapter 12)

Misdemeanor suspects are not usually arrested; they're usually issued a citation. But not always. Sometimes, officers make a custodial arrest and take some or all of the seven actions in the list above. Are these full custodial arrests reasonable Fourth Amendment seizures? A sharply divided U.S. Supreme Court answered the question in *Atwater v. City of Lago Vista.*

CASE | ***Was the Custodial Arrest for Violating the Fine-Only Seat Belt Law Reasonable?***

Atwater v. City of Lago Vista
532 U.S. 318 (2001)

Gail Atwater was charged with driving without her seatbelt fastened, failing to secure her children in seatbelts, driving without a license, and failing to provide proof of insurance. She pleaded no contest to the misdemeanor seatbelt offenses and paid a $50 fine; the other charges were dismissed. Atwater and her husband, Michael Haas, sued Officer Bart Turek, the City of Lago Vista, and the Lago Vista Chief of Police Frank Miller. The City removed the suit to the U.S. District Court for the Western District of Texas. The District Court granted the City's summary judgment motion. A panel of the U.S. Court of Appeals for the Fifth

Circuit reversed. Sitting en banc, the Court of Appeals vacated the panel's decision and affirmed the District Court's summary judgment for the City. The U.S. Supreme Court affirmed.

SOUTER, J., joined by REHNQUIST, CJ.,
and SCALIA, KENNEDY, THOMAS, JJ.

FACTS

In Texas, if a car is equipped with safety belts, a front-seat passenger must wear one, Tex. Tran. Code Ann. §545.413(a) (1999), and the driver must secure any small child riding in front, §545.413(b). Violation of either provision is "a misdemeanor punishable by a fine not less than $25 or more than $50." §545.413(d). Texas law expressly authorizes "[a]ny peace officer [to] arrest without warrant a person found committing a violation" of these seatbelt laws, §543.001, although it permits police to issue citations in lieu of arrest, §§543.003–543.005.

In March 1997, Gail Atwater was driving her pickup truck in Lago Vista, Texas, with her 3-year-old son and 5-year-old daughter in the front seat. None of them was wearing a seatbelt. Bart Turek, a Lago Vista police officer at the time, observed the seatbelt violations and pulled Atwater over. According to Atwater's complaint (the allegations of which we assume to be true for present purposes), Turek approached the truck and "yelled" something to the effect of "we've met before" and "you're going to jail."* He then called for backup and asked to see Atwater's driver's license and insurance documentation, which state law required her to carry. Tex. Tran. Code Ann. §§521.025, 601.053 (1999). When Atwater told Turek that she did not have the papers because her purse had been stolen the day before, Turek said that he had "heard that story two-hundred times."

Atwater asked to take her "frightened, upset, and crying" children to a friend's house nearby, but Turek told her, "you're not going anywhere." As it turned out, Atwater's friend learned what was going on and soon arrived to take charge of the children. Turek then handcuffed Atwater, placed her in his squad car, and drove her to the local police station, where booking officers had her remove her shoes, jewelry, and eyeglasses, and empty her pockets. Officers took Atwater's "mug shot" and placed her, alone, in a jail cell for about one hour, after which she was taken before a magistrate and released on $310 bond.

---

*Turek had previously stopped Atwater for what he had thought was a seatbelt violation, but had realized that Atwater's son, although seated on the vehicle's armrest, was in fact belted in. Atwater acknowledged that her son's seating position was unsafe, and Turek issued a verbal warning.

OPINION

The question is whether the Fourth Amendment forbids a warrantless arrest for a minor criminal offense, such as a misdemeanor seatbelt violation punishable only by a fine. We hold that it does not.

The Fourth Amendment safeguards "the right of the people to be secure in their persons, houses, papers, and effects, against unreasonable searches and seizures.". . . If we were to derive a rule exclusively to address the uncontested facts of this case, Atwater might well prevail. She was a known and established resident of Lago Vista with no place to hide and no incentive to flee, and common sense says she would almost certainly have buckled up as a condition of driving off with a citation. In her case, the physical incidents of arrest were merely gratuitous humiliations imposed by a police officer who was (at best) exercising extremely poor judgment. Atwater's claim to live free of pointless indignity and confinement clearly outweighs anything the City can raise against it specific to her case. [Atwater argues for a new]. . . arrest rule . . . forbidding custodial arrest, even upon probable cause, when conviction could not ultimately carry any jail time and when the government shows no compelling need for immediate detention.

But we have traditionally recognized that a responsible Fourth Amendment balance is not well served by standards requiring sensitive, case-by-case determinations of government need, lest every discretionary judgment in the field be converted into an occasion for constitutional review. Often enough, the Fourth Amendment has to be applied on the spur (and in the heat) of the moment, and the object in implementing its command of reasonableness is to draw standards sufficiently clear and simple to be applied with a fair prospect of surviving judicial second-guessing months and years after an arrest or search is made. Courts attempting to strike a reasonable Fourth Amendment balance thus credit the government's side with an essential interest in readily administrable rules.** (Fourth Amendment rules "ought to be expressed in terms that are readily applicable by the police in the context of the law enforcement activities in which they are necessarily engaged" and not "qualified by all sorts of ifs, ands, and buts"). . . .

. . . Atwater's . . . rule . . . promises very little in the way of administrability. It is no answer that the police routinely make judgments on grounds like risk of immediate repetition; they surely do and should. But there is a world of difference between making that judgment in choosing between the discretionary leniency of a summons in place of a clearly lawful arrest, and making the same judgment when the question is the lawfulness of the warrantless

---

**See *New York v. Belton*, excerpted in Chapter 6.

arrest itself. It is the difference between no basis for legal action challenging the discretionary judgment, on the one hand, and the prospect of evidentiary exclusion or (as here) personal §1983 liability for the misapplication of a constitutional standard, on the other. Atwater's rule therefore would not only place police in an almost impossible spot but would guarantee increased litigation over many of the arrests that would occur. For all these reasons, Atwater's various distinctions between permissible and impermissible arrests for minor crimes strike us as "very unsatisfactory lines" to require police officers to draw on a moment's notice.

One may ask, of course, why these difficulties may not be answered by a simple tie breaker for the police to follow in the field: if in doubt, do not arrest. . . . Whatever help the tie breaker might give would come at the price of a systematic disincentive to arrest in situations where . . . arresting would serve an important societal interest. [For example,] an officer not quite sure that drugs weighed enough to warrant jail time or not quite certain about a suspect's risk of flight would not arrest, even though it could perfectly well turn out that, in fact, the offense called for incarceration and the defendant was long gone on the day of trial. Multiplied many times over, the costs to society of such under enforcement could easily outweigh the costs to defendants of being needlessly arrested and booked, as Atwater herself acknowledges.

Just how easily the costs could outweigh the benefits may be shown by asking, as one Member of this Court did at oral argument, "how bad the problem is out there." The very fact that the law has never jelled the way Atwater would have it leads one to wonder whether warrantless misdemeanor arrests need constitutional attention, and there is cause to think the answer is no. So far as such arrests might be thought to pose a threat to the probable-cause requirement, anyone arrested for a crime without formal process, whether for felony or misdemeanor, is entitled to a magistrate's review of probable cause within 48 hours, and there is no reason to think the procedure in this case atypical in giving the suspect a prompt opportunity to request release, see Tex. Tran. Code Ann. §543.002 (1999) (persons arrested for traffic offenses to be taken "immediately" before a magistrate).

Many jurisdictions, moreover, have chosen to impose more restrictive safeguards through statutes limiting warrantless arrests for minor offenses. . . . It is, in fact, only natural that States should resort to this sort of legislative regulation, for . . . it is in the interest of the police to limit petty-offense arrests, which carry costs that are simply too great to incur without good reason. Finally, . . . the preference for categorical treatment of Fourth Amendment claims gives way to individualized review when a defendant makes a colorable argument that an arrest, with or without a warrant, was "conducted in an extraordinary manner, unusually harmful to [his] privacy or even physical interests."

The upshot of all these influences, combined with the good sense (and, failing that, the political accountability) of most local lawmakers and law-enforcement officials, is a dearth of horribles demanding redress. Indeed, when Atwater's counsel was asked at oral argument for any indications of comparably foolish, warrantless misdemeanor arrests, he could offer only one. We are sure that there are others, but just as surely the country is not confronting anything like an epidemic of unnecessary minor-offense arrests. That fact caps the reasons for rejecting Atwater's request for the development of a new and distinct body of constitutional law.

Accordingly, we confirm today what our prior cases have intimated: the standard of probable cause "applies to all arrests, without the need to 'balance' the interests and circumstances involved in particular situations." If an officer has probable cause to believe that an individual has committed even a very minor criminal offense in his presence, he may, without violating the Fourth Amendment, arrest the offender.

Atwater's arrest satisfied constitutional requirements. There is no dispute that Officer Turek had probable cause to believe that Atwater had committed a crime in his presence. She admits that neither she nor her children were wearing seat belts, as required by Tex. Tran. Code Ann. §545.413 (1999). Turek was accordingly authorized (not required, but authorized) to make a *custodial* [italics added] arrest without balancing costs and benefits or determining whether or not Atwater's arrest was in some sense necessary.

Nor was the arrest made in an "extraordinary manner, unusually harmful to her privacy or . . . physical interests." . . . The question whether a search or seizure is "extraordinary" turns, above all else, on the manner in which the search or seizure is executed. *Tennessee v. Garner* (1985) ("seizure by means of deadly force"),* *Wilson v. Arkansas,* (1995) ("unannounced entry into a home"),** *Welsh v. Wisconsin,* (1984) ("entry into a home without a warrant"),† and *Winston v. Lee* (1985) ("physical penetration of the body").

Atwater's arrest was surely "humiliating," as she says in her brief, but it was no more "harmful to . . . privacy or . . . physical interests" than the normal custodial arrest. She was handcuffed, placed in a squad car, and taken to the

---

*Excerpted earlier in this chapter, on p. 179.

**Excerpted in Chapter 6.

†Excerpted earlier in this chapter, on p. 173.

local police station, where officers asked her to remove her shoes, jewelry, and glasses, and to empty her pockets. They then took her photograph and placed her in a cell, alone, for about an hour, after which she was taken before a magistrate, and released on $310 bond. The arrest and booking were inconvenient and embarrassing to Atwater, but not so extraordinary as to violate the Fourth Amendment.

The Court of Appeals' en banc judgment is AFFIRMED ...

DISSENT

O'CONNOR, J., joined by STEVENS, GINSBURG, and BREYER, JJ.

... The Court recognizes that the arrest of Gail Atwater was a "pointless indignity" that served no discernible state interest, and yet holds that her arrest was constitutionally permissible. Because the Court's position is inconsistent with the explicit guarantee of the Fourth Amendment, I dissent. A full custodial arrest, such as the one to which Ms. Atwater was subjected, is the quintessential seizure. When a full custodial arrest is effected without a warrant, the plain language of the Fourth Amendment requires that the arrest be reasonable. ...

The touchstone of our analysis under the Fourth Amendment is always the reasonableness in all the circumstances of the particular governmental invasion of a citizen's personal security." ... [We] evaluate the search or seizure under traditional standards of reasonableness by assessing, on the one hand, the degree to which it intrudes upon an individual's privacy and, on the other, the degree to which it is needed for the promotion of legitimate governmental interests." In other words, in determining reasonableness, "each case is to be decided on its own facts and circumstances." ...

A custodial arrest exacts an obvious toll on an individual's liberty and privacy, even when the period of custody is relatively brief. The arrestee is subject to a full search of her person and confiscation of her possessions. If the arrestee is the occupant of a car, the entire passenger compartment of the car, including packages therein, is subject to search as well. The arrestee may be detained for up to 48 hours without having a magistrate determine whether there in fact was probable cause for the arrest. Because people arrested for all types of violent and nonviolent offenses may be housed together awaiting such review, this detention period is potentially dangerous. And once the period of custody is over, the fact of the arrest is a permanent part of the public record.

... If the State has decided that a fine, and not imprisonment, is the appropriate punishment for an offense, the State's interest in taking a person suspected of committing that offense into custody is surely limited, at best. This is not to say that the State will never have such an interest. A full custodial arrest may on occasion vindicate legitimate state interests, even if the crime is punishable only by fine. Arrest is the surest way to abate criminal conduct. It may also allow the police to verify the offender's identity and, if the offender poses a flight risk, to ensure her appearance at trial. But when such considerations are not present, a citation or summons may serve the State's remaining law enforcement interests every bit as effectively as an arrest. ...

Because a full custodial arrest is such a severe intrusion on an individual's liberty, its reasonableness hinges on "the degree to which it is needed for the promotion of legitimate governmental interests." In light of the availability of citations to promote a State's interests when a fine-only offense has been committed, I cannot concur in a rule which deems a full custodial arrest to be reasonable in every circumstance. Giving police officers constitutional carte blanche to effect an arrest whenever there is probable cause to believe a fine-only misdemeanor has been committed is irreconcilable with the Fourth Amendment's command that seizures be reasonable.

Instead, I would require that when there is probable cause to believe that a fine-only offense has been committed, the police officer should issue a citation unless the officer is "able to point to specific and articulable facts which, taken together with rational inferences from those facts, reasonably warrant [the additional] intrusion" of a full custodial arrest. ...

The majority insists that a bright-line rule focused on probable cause is necessary to vindicate the State's interest in easily administrable law enforcement rules. ... While clarity is certainly a value worthy of consideration in our Fourth Amendment jurisprudence, it by no means trumps the values of liberty and privacy at the heart of the Amendment's protections. ...

The record in this case makes it abundantly clear that Ms. Atwater's arrest was constitutionally unreasonable. Atwater readily admits—as she did when Officer Turek pulled her over—that she violated Texas' seatbelt law. While Turek was justified in stopping Atwater, neither law nor reason supports his decision to arrest her instead of simply giving her a citation. The officer's actions cannot sensibly be viewed as a permissible means of balancing Atwater's Fourth Amendment interests with the State's own legitimate interests.

There is no question that Officer Turek's actions severely infringed Atwater's liberty and privacy. Turek was loud and accusatory from the moment he approached Atwater's car. Atwater's young children were terrified and hysterical. Yet when Atwater asked Turek to lower his voice because he was scaring the children, he responded by jabbing his finger in Atwater's face and saying, "You're going to jail." Having made the decision to arrest, Turek did not inform Atwater of her right to remain silent. He instead asked for her license and insurance information.

Atwater asked if she could at least take her children to a friend's house down the street before going to the police station. But Turek—who had just castigated Atwater for not caring for her children—refused and said he would take the children into custody as well. Only the intervention of neighborhood children who had witnessed the scene and summoned one of Atwater's friends saved the children from being hauled to jail with their mother.

With the children gone, Officer Turek handcuffed Ms. Atwater with her hands behind her back, placed her in the police car, and drove her to the police station. Ironically, Turek did not secure Atwater in a seat belt for the drive. At the station, Atwater was forced to remove her shoes, relinquish her possessions, and wait in a holding cell for about an hour. A judge finally informed Atwater of her rights and the charges against her, and released her when she posted bond. Atwater returned to the scene of the arrest, only to find that her car had been towed.

Ms. Atwater ultimately pleaded no contest to violating the seatbelt law and was fined $50. Even though that fine was the maximum penalty for her crime, and even though Officer Turek has never articulated any justification for his actions, the city contends that arresting Atwater was constitutionally reasonable because it advanced two legitimate interests: "the enforcement of child safety laws and encouraging [Atwater] to appear for trial."

It is difficult to see how arresting Atwater served either of these goals any more effectively than the issuance of a citation. With respect to the goal of law enforcement generally, Atwater did not pose a great danger to the community. She had been driving very slowly—approximately 15 miles per hour—in broad daylight on a residential street that had no other traffic. Nor was she a repeat offender; until that day, she had received one traffic citation in her life—a ticket, more than 10 years earlier, for failure to signal a lane change. Although Officer Turek had stopped Atwater approximately three months earlier because he thought that Atwater's son was not wearing a seatbelt, Turek had been mistaken, Moreover, Atwater immediately accepted responsibility and apologized for her conduct. Thus, there was every indication that Atwater would have buckled herself and her children in had she been cited and allowed to leave.

With respect to the related goal of child welfare, the decision to arrest Atwater was nothing short of counterproductive. Atwater's children witnessed Officer Turek yell at their mother and threaten to take them all into custody.

Ultimately, they were forced to leave her behind with Turek, knowing that she was being taken to jail. Understandably, the 3-year-old boy was "very, very, very traumatized." After the incident, he had to see a child psychologist regularly, who reported that the boy "felt very guilty that he couldn't stop this horrible thing…he was powerless to help his mother or sister." Both of Atwater's children are now terrified at the sight of any police car. According to Atwater, the arrest "just never leaves us. It's a conversation we have every other day, once a week, and it's—it raises its head constantly in our lives."

Citing Atwater surely would have served the children's interests well. It would have taught Atwater to ensure that her children were buckled up in the future. It also would have taught the children an important lesson in accepting responsibility and obeying the law. Arresting Atwater, though, taught the children an entirely different lesson: that "the bad person could just as easily be the policeman as it could be the most horrible person they could imagine."

The City also contends that the arrest was necessary to ensure Atwater's appearance in court. Atwater, however, was far from a flight risk. A 16-year resident of Lago Vista, population 2,486, Atwater was not likely to abscond. Although she was unable to produce her driver's license because it had been stolen, she gave Officer Turek her license number and address. In addition, Officer Turek knew from their previous encounter that Atwater was a local resident.

The city's justifications fall far short of rationalizing the extraordinary intrusion on Gail Atwater and her children. Measuring "the degree to which [Atwater's custodial arrest was] needed for the promotion of legitimate governmental interests," against "the degree to which it intruded upon her privacy," it can hardly be doubted that Turek's actions were disproportionate to Atwater's crime. The majority's assessment that "Atwater's claim to live free of pointless indignity and confinement clearly outweighs anything the City can raise against it specific to her case," is quite correct. In my view, the Fourth Amendment inquiry ends there.

The Court's error, however, does not merely affect the disposition of this case. The per se rule that the Court creates has potentially serious consequences for the everyday lives of Americans. A broad range of conduct falls into the category of fine-only misdemeanors. In Texas alone, for example, disobeying any sort of traffic warning sign is a misdemeanor punishable only by fine, as is failing to pay a highway toll, and driving with expired license plates. Nor are fine-only crimes limited to the traffic context. In several States, for example, littering is a criminal offense punishable only by fine.

To be sure, such laws are valid and wise exercises of the States' power to protect the public health and welfare. My concern lies not with the decision to enact or enforce these laws, but rather with the manner in which they may be enforced. Under today's holding, when a police officer has probable cause to believe that a fine-only misdemeanor offense has occurred, that officer may stop the suspect, issue a citation, and let the person continue on her way. Or, if a traffic violation, the officer may stop the car, arrest the driver, search the driver, search the entire passenger compartment of the car including any purse or package inside, and impound the car and inventory all of its contents. Although the Fourth Amendment expressly requires that the latter course be a reasonable and proportional response to the circumstances of the offense, the majority gives officers unfettered discretion to choose that course without articulating a single reason why such action is appropriate.

Such unbounded discretion carries with it grave potential for abuse. The majority takes comfort in the lack of evidence of "an epidemic of unnecessary minor-offense arrests." But the relatively small number of published cases dealing with such arrests proves little and should provide little solace. Indeed, as the recent debate over racial profiling demonstrates all too clearly, a relatively minor traffic infraction may often serve as an excuse for stopping and harassing an individual. After today, the arsenal available to any officer extends to a full arrest and the searches permissible concomitant to that arrest. An officer's subjective motivations for making a traffic stop are not relevant considerations in determining the reasonableness of the stop. But it is precisely because these motivations are beyond our purview that we must vigilantly ensure that officers' post stop actions—which are properly within our reach—comport with the Fourth Amendment's guarantee of reasonableness.

The Court neglects the Fourth Amendment's express command in the name of administrative ease. In so doing, it cloaks the pointless indignity that Gail Atwater suffered with the mantle of reasonableness. I respectfully dissent.

Questions

1. List all of Officer Turek's actions leading up to, during, and following Gail Atwater's arrest.

2. List all the actions taken by booking officers after Officer Turek turned her over to them.

3. According to the majority opinion, what is the bright-line rule regarding arrests for fine-only offenses?

4. Summarize the majority's arguments supporting the bright-line rule.

5. According to the majority, what are the exceptions to the bright-line rule?

6. Summarize the dissent's arguments against the bright-line rule.

7. State the rule the dissent recommends for fine-only offenses.

8. Summarize the dissent's arguments in favor of the rule it recommends.

9. List the exceptions the dissent recommends should apply to its rule.

Go to Exercise 5-3 on the Criminal Procedure 6e CD to learn more about *Atwater v. Lago Vista*.

◆ ◆ ◆

SUMMARY

  I. The issues of arrest
    A. Definition
    B. Reasonableness
    C. Post-arrest actions
 II. The definition of arrest
    A. More invasive than stops
       1. Duration—lasts longer than stops
       2. Location—suspects are moved from the place of the stop
    B. Arrest is a zone, not a point on a spectrum of invasions

  1. From seizures lasting slightly longer, where suspects are moved beyond the immediate vicinity (but not taken to the station) when there's no emergency

  2. To full custodial arrest lasting days in confinement accompanied by booking, mug shots, searches, interrogation, and lineups

III. Reasonable arrest

 A. Two elements

  1. Objective basis, in which the arrest is backed up by probable cause

  2. The manner of arrest was reasonable

 B. Probable cause

  1. Purpose—balance social interest in crime control and individual right of locomotion

  2. Decision making

   a. Police officers make a *preliminary* decision about probable cause

   b. Judges review and make the final decision later

    (1) Decision is based on day-to-day reality of police officers who have to make quick decisions on the street

    (2) Decision is not based on what judges would decide in the leisurely atmosphere of their chambers

  3. Can include hearsay and direct information

  4. The totality of circumstances determines whether the objective basis adds up to probable cause

 C. The manner of arrest

  1. The totality of circumstances determines the reasonableness of the manner of arrest (the way the suspect was arrested)

  2. Arrests with warrants

   a. Most arrests don't require warrants to make them reasonable

   b. Elements of lawful warrants

    (1) Neutral magistrate decides probable cause *before* officers arrest

    (2) Officer swears to the truth of facts supporting probable cause in an affidavit

    (3) Person to be arrested is named in the warrant

   c. Warrants are required to enter homes to arrest suspects, except in emergencies ("hot pursuit")

  3. Arrests by force

   a. Deadly force arrests are the most talked about; nondeadly force arrests are the most common

   b. Deadly force

    (1) Common-law rule—use of deadly force is justified when it's necessary to apprehend a fleeing felon

    (2) *Tennessee v. Garner*—the reasonable manner requirement is satisfied if

     (a) Deadly force is necessary to apprehend "dangerous" suspects

     (b) Use of deadly force doesn't put innocent people in danger

   c. Nondeadly force

    (1) The amount of force was reasonable if it was necessary either to apprehend a suspect or get control of a suspect already apprehended

    (2) The reasonableness of force is judged by the totality of circumstances

    (3) The motive of the officer isn't relevant

IV. After the arrest
    A. Felony arrests—suspects are taken to a police station for further processing
    B. Misdemeanor arrests—suspects usually are released

 Go to the Criminal Procedure 6e CD to download this summary outline. The outline has been formatted so that you can add notes to it during class lectures, or later create a customized chapter outline to use while reviewing. Either way, the summary outline will help you understand the "big picture" and fill in the details as you study.

REVIEW QUESTIONS

1. Contrast a full custodial arrest with a stop.
2. Identify the characteristics of a full custodial arrest.
3. Why do we call arrests a zone and not a point?
4. Identify the common element in all arrests within the zone.
5. Identify the two elements of a reasonable arrest.
6. Compare the definition of reasonable suspicion with probable cause.
7. What two interests does probable cause balance?
8. Why is probable cause called a "common sense" rule?
9. Make a list of facts officers can take into account in building probable cause.
10. What, if any, use can officers make of hearsay in building probable cause?
11. Identify the sources of hearsay information in building probable cause.
12. Identify and provide details about the three elements of arrest warrants that satisfy the requirements of the Fourth Amendment warrant clause.
13. Identify the one situation where arrest warrants are required by the Fourth Amendment, and state one exception to the requirement.
14. What's the most common kind of force used in making arrests?
15. State the common-law rule regarding the use of deadly force to arrest.
16. According to *Tennessee v. Garner,* when is the use of deadly force reasonable?
17. What's the importance of officer intent and motive in the "objective standard of reasonable force"?
18. Describe the period after arrest for persons arrested for misdemeanors and those arrested for felonies.

KEY TERMS

arrest p. 158
full custodial arrest p. 158
probable cause p. 160

direct information p. 161
hearsay p. 161
hearsay rule p. 161

two-pronged test of reliability
  p. 162
Spinelli–Aguilar test p. 162

THE COMPANION WEB SITE
FOR *CRIMINAL PROCEDURE,* SIXTH EDITION

http://cj.wadsworth.com/samaha/crim_pro6e

Supplement your review of this chapter by going to the companion Web site to take one of the Tutorial Quizzes, use the flash cards to test yourself on the key terms from each chapter, and check out the many other study aids you'll find there. You'll find valuable data and resources at your fingertips to help you study for that big exam or write that important paper.

Searches for Evidence

6

Chapter Main Points

- Crime control couldn't survive without searches, but, like all good things, the power to search comes at a price—individual privacy.
- The Fourth Amendment requires officers to "knock and announce" their presence before entering places they search, but when necessary "no knock" entries are legal.
- Most searches fall within exceptions to the warrant requirement for two reasons: necessity and practicality.
- Officers can search individuals they arrest without warrants because of the need to protect themselves, preserve evidence, and prevent escape.
- Searches for drugs incident to pretext arrests for minor offenses are reasonable if the arrests are based on probable cause.
- Consent searches without probable cause or warrants aren't unreasonable searches as long as they're voluntary.
- Searches based on one person consenting for someone else are reasonable as long as officers reasonably believe the person consenting had the authority.
- Vehicle searches without warrants that are based on probable cause are reasonable because of the mobility and reduced expectation of privacy in vehicles.
- To be reasonable, container (purses, briefcases, luggage) searches usually require warrants unless the containers are in vehicles.
- Emergency searches without warrants are reasonable when it's dangerous and impractical to require officers to get warrants.

Robert D. Robinette was clocked at 69 miles per hour as he drove his car along a stretch of Interstate 70 north of Dayton, Ohio, where the posted speed limit was 45 miles per hour because of construction. He was stopped by Deputy Roger Newsome of the Montgomery County Sheriff's office. Newsome asked for and Robinette gave him his driver's license. Newsome ran a computer check that didn't turn up any previous violations. Then Newsome asked Robinette to step out of his car, turned on his mounted video camera, gave a verbal warning to Robinette, and gave his license back. At this point, Newsome asked, "One question before you get gone: Are you carrying any illegal contraband in your car? Any weapons of any kind, drugs, anything like that?" Robinette said "no," to these questions, after which Deputy Newsome asked if he could search the car. Robinette consented. In the car, Deputy Newsome discovered a small amount of marijuana and, in a film container, a pill that was later determined to be methamphetamine.

Ohio v. Robinette (1996), U.S. Supreme Court

THE POWER TO SEARCH

Crime control couldn't survive without searches, but, like all good things, the power to search comes at a price. Searches invade the privacy of individuals, their homes, and their "stuff." And, the power to search, like all power, tempts those who hold it to abuse it. No one appreciated the price and the temptation to abuse the power to search more than U.S. Supreme Court Justice Robert H. Jackson. At the end of World War II, President Truman appointed Justice Jackson chief prosecutor at the Nazi war crimes trials in Nuremberg, Germany. There, Justice Jackson learned details of the Nazis' atrocities against the German people's "persons, houses, papers and effects" (Hockett 1991, 257–299).

These discoveries were a defining moment for Justice Jackson, and when he returned to the Supreme Court, he spoke eloquently of the right against unreasonable searches and seizures. Worried that Americans didn't fully appreciate the importance of the Fourth Amendment, Justice Jackson disapproved what he believed was the Supreme Court's tendency to treat the rights against unreasonable searches and seizures as "second-class rights":

> I protest, [the rights against unreasonable searches and seizures] are not mere second-class rights but belong in the catalog of indispensable freedoms. Among deprivations of rights, none is so effective in cowing a population, crushing the spirit of the individual and putting terror in every heart. Uncontrolled search and seizure is one of the first and most effective weapons in the arsenal of every arbitrary government. And one need only briefly to

have dwelt and worked among a people possessed of many admirable qualities but deprived of these rights to know that the human personality deteriorates and dignity and self-reliance disappear where homes, persons and possessions are subject at any hour to unheralded search and seizure by the police. But the right against searches and seizures is one of the most difficult to protect. Since the officers are themselves the chief invaders, there is no enforcement outside of court.

Brinegar v. U.S. 1949, 180–181

Notice that Justice Jackson didn't condemn *all* searches, only "uncontrolled" searches." He knew very well how important searches are in controlling crime. (Jackson was an aggressive prosecutor at one point in his life.) But, he also knew the Fourth Amendment doesn't just confer the power on good officers searching bad people, their homes, and stuff; it bestows the same power on bad officers searching good people. So, Jackson urged, courts had to balance the need for searches against the privacies they invade.

The three-step analysis we used to examine the government actions in Chapter 3, the stops and frisks in Chapter 4, and the arrests in Chapter 5 also applies to the searches we'll examine in this chapter:

1. Was the government action a search? (Chapter 3)

2. If it was a search, was it reasonable?

3. If it was unreasonable, then should the evidence be excluded? (Chapter 10)

But, we won't repeat the first step in the analysis (the definition of search) because we already examined it in Chapter 3. To consider the issues affecting the reasonableness of searches, we'll divide our discussion into searches for evidence of crime (this chapter) and special-needs searches that go beyond crime control (Chapter 7).

Let's look first at searches with warrants and then searches without warrant.

SEARCHES WITH WARRANTS

The Fourth Amendment commands that "no warrants shall issue, but upon probable cause, supported by oath or affirmation, and particularly describing the place to be searched, and the persons or things to be seized." (See the discussion on neutral magistrates in the Probable Cause section of Chapter 5.) According to the distinguished U.S. Supreme Court Justice Felix Frankfurter, "[W]ith minor and severely confined exceptions . . . every search . . . is unreasonable when made without a magistrate's authority expressed through a validly issued warrant" (*Harris v. U.S.* 1947, 162). That may be true, but there are a lot of exceptions to the warrant requirement (up to thirty, depending on how you count them).

Three elements are required to meet the Fourth Amendment's warrant requirement:

1. Particularity

2. Affidavit supporting probable cause

3. "Knock and announce" rule

The Particularity Requirement

To comply with the Fourth Amendment, search warrants have to "particularly describe the place to be searched"; this is known as the **particularity requirement.** The address of a single-dwelling house, "404 Blake Road," particularly describes the place to be searched; a warrant to search "1135 Stone Street," a sixteen-floor apartment complex doesn't. Warrants also have to "particularly describe the things to be seized." A warrant to search for and seize "one book entitled *Criminal Procedure*, 6th edition, by Joel Samaha" is good enough. So are warrants naming whole classes of items, like, "address books, diaries, business records, documents, receipts, warranty books, guns, stereo equipment, and a color television" in a list of stolen property. Catchall categories might also meet the requirement. For example, a search warrant that named "records, notes, and documents indicating involvement in and control of prostitution activity" was particular enough in one case because the officers were directed to seize only items related to prostitution.

The Probable Cause Affidavit

This is the same as the requirement for arrest warrants (Chapter 5), so we won't repeat the details here, except to point out that the probable cause in search warrant affidavits is evidence to support the claim that the items or classes of items named in the warrant will be found in the place to be searched.

The "Knock-and-Announce" Rule

Most states and the U.S. government have many specific requirements for how search warrants are supposed to be executed. One of these rules, the **knock-and-announce rule,** has 700 years of English and U.S. history behind it—and centuries of controversy surrounding it. According to the rule, officers have to knock and announce they're officers with a search warrant before they enter the places they're about to search. But, does the Fourth Amendment require this knock-and-announce rule or is a **no-knock entry** reasonable, too? Oddly enough, for all the history behind the rule, and the controversy surrounding it, the U.S. Supreme Court didn't answer this important question until 1995, when it decided *Wilson v. Arkansas.*

CASE | *Was the "No-Knock" Entry an Unreasonable Search?*

Wilson v. Arkansas
514 U.S. 927, 115 S.Ct. 1914 (1995)

Sharlene Wilson was charged with illegal possession of marijuana and methamphetamine. The Circuit Court, Hot Springs County, Arkansas, denied Wilson's motion to suppress marijuana, amphetamines, and other evidence seized during a "no knock" search of her house. She was convicted and sentenced to 32 years in prison. She appealed and the Arkansas Supreme Court affirmed. The U.S. Supreme Court granted certiorari and reversed and remanded.

THOMAS, J. for a unanimous court.

FACTS

During November and December 1992, Sharlene Wilson made a series of narcotics sales to a Joann Potts, an informant acting at the direction of the Arkansas State Police. In late November, Potts purchased marijuana and methamphetamine at the home that Wilson shared with Bryson Jacobs. On December 30, Potts telephoned Wilson at her home and arranged to meet her at a local store to buy some marijuana. According to testimony presented below, Wilson produced a semiautomatic pistol at this meeting and waved it in Potts's face, threatening to kill her if she turned out to be working for the police. Wilson then sold Potts a bag of marijuana.

The next day, police officers applied for and obtained warrants to search Wilson's home and to arrest both Wilson and Jacobs. Affidavits filed in support of the warrants set forth the details of the narcotics transactions and stated that Jacobs had previously been convicted of arson and firebombing. The search was conducted later that afternoon. Police officers found the main door to Wilson's home open. While opening an unlocked screen door and entering the residence, they identified themselves as police officers and stated that they had a warrant. Once inside the home, the officers seized marijuana, methamphetamine, valium, narcotics paraphernalia, a gun, and ammunition. They also found Wilson in the bathroom, flushing marijuana down the toilet. Wilson and Jacobs were arrested and charged with delivery of marijuana, delivery of methamphetamine, possession of drug paraphernalia, and possession of marijuana.

Before trial, Wilson filed a motion to suppress the evidence seized during the search. Wilson asserted that the search was invalid on various grounds, including that the officers had failed to "knock and announce" before entering her home. The trial court summarily denied the suppression motion. After a jury trial, Wilson was convicted of all charges and sentenced to 32 years in prison.

The Arkansas Supreme Court affirmed Wilson's conviction on appeal. The court noted that "the officers entered the home while they were identifying themselves," but it rejected Wilson's argument that "the Fourth Amendment requires officers to knock and announce prior to entering the residence." Finding "no authority for [Wilson's] theory that the knock and announce principle is required by the Fourth Amendment," the court concluded that neither Arkansas law nor the Fourth Amendment required suppression of the evidence.

We granted certiorari to resolve the conflict among the lower courts as to whether the common-law knock-and-announce principle forms a part of the Fourth Amendment reasonableness inquiry. We hold that it does, and accordingly reverse and remand.

OPINION

Although the common law generally protected a man's house as "his castle of defense and asylum," common-law courts long have held that "when the King is party, the sheriff (if the doors be not open) may break the party's house, either to arrest him, or to do other execution of the King's process, if otherwise he cannot enter." Semayne's Case, 5 Co. Rep. 91a, 91b, 77 Eng.Rep. 194, 195 (K.B.1603). To this rule, however, common-law courts appended an important qualification:

> But before he breaks it, he ought to signify the cause of his coming, and to make request to open doors . . . , for the law without a default in the owner abhors the destruction or breaking of any house (which is for the habitation and safety of man) by which great damage and inconvenience might ensue to the party, when no default is in him; for perhaps he did not know of the process, of which, if he had notice, it is to be presumed that he would obey it. . . .

Several prominent founding-era commentators agreed on this basic principle. According to Sir Matthew Hale, the "constant practice" at common law was that "the officer may break open the door, if he be sure the offender is there, if after acquainting them of the business, and demanding the prisoner, he refuses to open the door." William Hawkins propounded a similar principle: "the law doth never allow" an officer to break open the door of a dwelling "but in cases of necessity," that is, unless he "first signify to those in the house the cause of his coming, and request them to give him admittance." Sir William Blackstone stated simply that the sheriff may "justify breaking open doors, if the possession be not quietly delivered."

The common-law knock-and-announce principle was woven quickly into the fabric of early American law. Most of the States that ratified the Fourth Amendment had enacted constitutional provisions or statutes generally incorporating English common law. . . . Our own cases have acknowledged that the common law principle of announcement is "embedded in Anglo-American law," but we have never squarely held that this principle is an element of the reasonableness inquiry under the Fourth Amendment. We now so hold. Given the long-standing common-law endorsement of the practice of announcement, we have little doubt that the Framers of the Fourth

Amendment thought that the method of an officer's entry into a dwelling was among the factors to be considered in assessing the reasonableness of a search or seizure. Contrary to the decision below, we hold that in some circumstances an officer's unannounced entry into a home might be unreasonable under the Fourth Amendment.

This is not to say, of course, that every entry must be preceded by an announcement. The Fourth Amendment's flexible requirement of reasonableness should not be read to mandate a rigid rule of announcement that ignores countervailing law enforcement interests. As even Wilson concedes, the common-law principle of announcement was never stated as an inflexible rule requiring announcement under all circumstances....

Thus, because the common-law rule was justified in part by the belief that announcement generally would avoid "the destruction or breaking of any house...by which great damage and inconvenience might ensue," courts acknowledged that the presumption in favor of announcement would yield under circumstances presenting a threat of physical violence. See for example, *Mahomed v. The Queen* 13 Eng.Rep. 293, 296 (P.C.1843) ("While he was firing pistols at them, were they to knock at the door, and to ask him to be pleased to open it for them? The law in its wisdom only requires this ceremony to be observed when it possibly may be attended with some advantage, and may render the breaking open of the outer door unnecessary").

Similarly, courts held that an officer may dispense with announcement in cases where a prisoner escapes from him and retreats to his dwelling. Proof of "demand and refusal" was deemed unnecessary in such cases because it would be a "senseless ceremony" to require an officer in pursuit of a recently escaped arrestee to make an announcement prior to breaking the door to retake him.

Finally, courts have indicated that unannounced entry may be justified where police officers have reason to believe that evidence would likely be destroyed if advance notice were given.

We need not attempt a comprehensive catalog of the relevant countervailing factors here. For now, we leave to the lower courts the task of determining the circumstances under which an unannounced entry is reasonable under the Fourth Amendment. We simply hold that although a search or seizure of a dwelling might be constitutionally defective if police officers enter without prior announcement, law enforcement interests may also establish the reasonableness of an unannounced entry.

Arkansas contends that the judgment below should be affirmed because the unannounced entry in this case was justified for two reasons. First, Arkansas argues that police officers reasonably believed that a prior announcement would have placed them in peril, given their knowledge that Wilson had threatened a government informant with a semiautomatic weapon and that Mr. Jacobs had previously been convicted of arson and firebombing. Second, Arkansas suggests that prior announcement would have produced an unreasonable risk that Wilson would destroy easily disposable narcotics evidence.

These considerations may well provide the necessary justification for the unannounced entry in this case. Because the Arkansas Supreme Court did not address their sufficiency, however, we remand to allow the state courts to make any necessary findings of fact and to make the determination of reasonableness in the first instance. The judgment of the Arkansas Supreme Court is REVERSED, and the case is REMANDED for further proceedings not inconsistent with this opinion.

It is so ordered.

Questions

1. What does the history Justice Thomas relates have to do with whether the Fourth Amendment requires officers to "knock and announce"?

2. Did the officers satisfy the knock-and-announce rule? List the facts that might indicate that the officers satisfied the requirement.

3. Identify the three exceptions to the knock-and-announce rule Justice Thomas referred to in the excerpt from the Court's opinion. What do they all have in common? Do you agree that they should be exceptions? Explain.

4. Assume you're the prosecutor when the case is remanded. Argue that the facts of the case fit into one or more of the exceptions.

5. Assume you're the judge on remand. Decide the case and give your reasons.

◆   ◆   ◆

EXPLORING THE KNOCK-AND-ANNOUNCE RULE FURTHER

 Go to the Criminal Procedure 6e CD to read the full text version of the case featured here.

Were the Officers' Actions After an Announced Entry Reasonable?

FACTS

At approximately 6:15 P.M. on June 27, 2000, West Allis, Wisconsin, police officers executed a search warrant for Ryan Ross's house. Detective Jeffrey Nohelty testified that on arrival at Ross's residence, police officers got out of their vehicles with guns drawn and ordered Ross, who was outside mowing his lawn, to the ground. Police then knocked on his front door, identified themselves, and announced that they had a search warrant. No one responded, but the officers heard dogs barking inside the house. They knocked and announced their presence a second time and then tried the door but found it locked. Detective Nohelty asked Ross if anyone was inside, and Ross answered no. The officers then used a battering ram to open the door. Inside, the officers found four or five pit bulls and approximately 25 grams of marijuana. Following his arrest, Ross moved to suppress the evidence recovered in the search of his home. He argued that *Wilson v. Arkansas* (1995) and *Richards v. Wisconsin* (1997) support his claim that the officers' actions were unreasonable. The State contended that *Wilson* and *Richards* didn't apply to this case, because they involved unannounced entries and Ross's case involved an announced entry. Who was right, the state or Ross?

DECISION AND REASONS

The state, according to the Wisconsin Court of Appeals:

> This court concludes that, clearly, under the circumstances presented to the officers at the time they executed the warrant, their entry was reasonable.

> Detective Nohelty testified that the officers knocked and announced their presence two times before trying to enter the residence, thereby putting any occupant on notice of their presence and intent. By knocking and announcing twice and waiting a reasonable time before entering, police gave any occupants the opportunity to open the door. At the time of entry, police only had Ross's word that the house was unoccupied. The dogs were barking, thus making it difficult to discern whether anyone was in the house or to determine what the police might face on entry.

> Ross contends that the police officers should have asked for his keys rather than entering by force. He fails, however, to present any legal authority to support his contention. Moreover, as the State notes, "There is no indication in the record that [Ross] had been removed from the immediate vicinity nor is there any indication that Ross made any attempt to assist the police by indicating he had the keys to open the door. . . ." Further, Detective Nohelty clarified that asking Ross for his keys would have delayed the entry, thus increasing the potential for destruction of evidence. And finally, Detective Nohelty added, forcibly entering the residence, while leaving Ross on the ground outside, prevented Ross from commanding the dogs to attack.

> *State v. Ross*, 639 N.W.2d 225 (Wisc.App. 2001)

After *Wilson v. Arkansas,* we know the "knock and announce rule" is part of the Fourth Amendment. We also know there are three major exceptions to the rule: to prevent violence, the destruction of evidence, and the escape of suspects. And there may be more to come. In the following excerpt from *Wilson v. Arkansas,* Justice Thomas sent a not-too-subtle invitation to lower courts to come up with more exceptions to the knock-and-announce rule:

> We need not attempt a comprehensive catalog of the relevant countervailing factors here. For now, we leave to the lower courts the task of determining the circumstances under which an unannounced entry is reasonable under the Fourth Amendment. We simply hold that although a search or seizure of a dwelling might be constitutionally defective if police officers enter without prior announcement, law enforcement interests may also establish the reasonableness of an unannounced entry. (936)

The state of Wisconsin Supreme Court accepted Justice Thomas's invitation in *State v. Richards* (1996) when it created a blanket exception to the knock-and-announce rule. Because of the seriousness of the drug problem, the court ruled that "the police are never required to adhere to the rule of announcement when executing a search warrant involving felonious drug delivery."

Wisconsin's acceptance of Justice Thomas's invitation raises an extremely important question: Should the definition of reasonable search depend on the times we live in? That's a question that's always aroused controversy but one that gets especially hot during wartime.

 Go to Exercise 6-1 on the Criminal Procedure 6e CD to learn more about the knock-and-announce rule.

SEARCHES WITHOUT WARRANTS

The U.S. Supreme Court has repeatedly said the Fourth Amendment expresses a strong preference for search warrants with only a few well-defined exceptions. That's the *law,* but what's the *practice*? The vast number of searches are made without warrants, because the exceptions are interpreted broadly to satisfy the strong preference of law enforcement officers and the clear practical need for searches without warrants (Haddad 1977, 198–225; Sutton 1986, 411).

One former Washington, D.C., assistant U.S. attorney said of this practical element in searches without warrants: "As anyone who has worked in the criminal justice system knows, searches conducted pursuant to these exceptions, particularly searches incident to arrest, automobile and 'stop and frisk' searches, far exceed searches performed pursuant to warrants." According to this attorney, the reason "is simple: the clear rule that warrants are required is unworkable and to enforce it would lead to exclusion of evidence in many cases where the police activity was essentially reasonable" (Bradley 1985, 1475).

Law enforcement officers frequently express frustration with the delay in getting search warrants. One police officer said it takes four hours from the time he decides he wants a warrant until the time he has one in his hand:

And that's if everything goes right. You find people and . . . get 'em typed and you can find the judges when they are sitting at the bench—because a lot of judges won't see people in their offices. [If you miss them there,] they leave and go to lunch and you have to wait until they come back for the afternoon dockets, and if they are already into the afternoon dockets, they are not going to interrupt the procedures [for a warrant]. So you sit and wait through three or four docket sessions. . . . It can take all day.

Sutton 1986, 411

Frustration tempts officers to "get around" the Fourth Amendment. One detective explained how he gets around the warrant requirement by "shamming" consent:

You tell the guy, "Let me come in and take a look at your house." And he says, "No, I don't want to." And then you tell him, "Then I'm going to leave Sam here, and he's going to live with you until we come back. Now we can do it either way." And very rarely do the people say, "Go get your search warrant, then."

Sutton 1986, 415

Let's look at the five major exceptions to the warrant requirement approved by the U.S. Supreme Court:

1. Searches incident to arrest
2. Consent searches
3. Vehicle searches
4. Container searches
5. Emergency searches (also called exigent circumstances searches)

Searches Incident to (at the time of) Arrest

The brilliant constitutional lawyer and historian Telford Taylor's research revealed that searches of people at the time of their arrest without either warrants or probable cause "is as old as arrest itself." **Searches incident to arrest** are old, but are they reasonable Fourth Amendment searches? Yes, says the U.S. Supreme Court. Why? Three reasons:

- They protect officers suspects might injure or kill.
- They prevent arrested suspects from escaping.
- They preserve evidence suspects might destroy or damage.

Forty years ago, Associate Justice Hugo Black put the case for the reasonableness of searches incident to arrest this way:

One thing is clear. . . . Search of an arrested man and of the items within his immediate reach must in almost every case be reasonable. There is always a danger that the suspect will try to escape, seizing concealed weapons with which to overpower and injure the arresting officers, and there is a danger that he may destroy evidence vital to the prosecution. Circumstances in which these justifications would not apply are sufficiently rare that inquiry is not made into searches of this scope, which have been considered reasonable throughout.

Chimel v. California 1969, 773

The Supreme Court discussed both the purposes and the scope of this ancient and most common of all searches in *Chimel v. California* (1969).

Chimel v. California
395 U.S. 752 (1969)

Ted Chimel was prosecuted for the burglary of a coin shop. He was convicted in the Superior Court, Orange County, California, and appealed. The California Supreme Court affirmed, and Chimel petitioned the U.S. Supreme Court for a writ of certiorari. The Supreme Court granted the writ and reversed.

STEWART, J.

FACTS

...Late in the afternoon of September 13, 1965, three police officers arrived at the Santa Ana, California, home of Ted Chimel with a warrant authorizing his arrest for the burglary of a coin shop. The officers knocked on the door, identified themselves to Chimel's wife, and asked if they might come inside. She ushered them into the house, where they waited 10 or 15 minutes until Chimel returned home from work. When Chimel entered the house, one of the officers handed him the arrest warrant and asked for permission to "look around." Chimel objected, but was advised that "on the basis of the lawful arrest," the officers would nonetheless conduct a search. No search warrant had been issued.

Accompanied by Chimel's wife, the officers then looked through the entire three-bedroom house, including the attic, the garage, and a small workshop. In some rooms the search was relatively cursory. In the master bedroom and sewing room, however, the officers directed Mrs. Chimel to open drawers and "to physically move contents of the drawers from side to side so that (they) might view any items that would have come from (the) burglary." After completing the search, they seized numerous items—primarily coins, but also several medals, tokens, and a few other objects. The entire search took between 45 minutes and an hour.

At Chimel's subsequent state trial on two charges of burglary, the items taken from his house were admitted into evidence against him, over his objection that they had been unconstitutionally seized. He was convicted, and the judgments of conviction were affirmed by both the California Court of Appeal, and the California Supreme Court....We granted certiorari in order to consider Chimel's substantial constitutional claims.

OPINION

Without deciding the question, we proceed on the hypothesis that the California courts were correct in holding that Chimel's arrest was valid under the Constitution. This brings us directly to the question whether the warrantless search of Chimel's entire house can be constitutionally justified as incident to that arrest....

When an arrest is made, it is reasonable for the arresting officer to search the person arrested in order to remove any weapons that the latter might seek to use in order to resist arrest or effect his escape. Otherwise, the officer's safety might well be endangered, and the arrest itself frustrated. In addition, it is entirely reasonable for the arresting officer to search for and seize any evidence on the arrestee's person in order to prevent its concealment or destruction. And the area into which an arrestee might reach in order to grab a weapon or evidentiary items must, of course, be governed by a like rule. A gun on a table or in a drawer in front of one who is arrested can be as dangerous to the arresting officer as one concealed in the clothing of the person arrested.

There is ample justification, therefore, for a search of the arrestee's person and the area "within his immediate control"—construing that phrase to mean the area from within which he might gain possession of a weapon or destructible evidence. There is no comparable justification, however, for routinely searching any room other than that in which an arrest occurs—or, for that matter, for searching through all the desk drawers or other closed or concealed areas in that room itself. Such searches, in the absence of well-recognized exceptions, may be made only under the authority of a search warrant. The "adherence to judicial processes" mandated by the Fourth Amendment requires no less....

It is argued in the present case that it is "reasonable" to search a man's house when he is arrested in it. But that argument is founded on little more than a subjective view regarding the acceptability of certain sorts of police conduct, and not on consideration relevant to Fourth Amendment interests. Under such an unconfined analysis, Fourth Amendment protection in this area would approach the evaporation point....

After arresting a man in his house, to rummage at will among his papers in search of whatever will convict him, appears to us to be indistinguishable from what might be done under a general warrant; indeed, the warrant would give more protection, for presumably it must be issued by a magistrate....Application of sound Fourth Amendment principles to the facts of this case produces a clear result. The search here went far beyond the petitioner's person and the area from within which he might have obtained either a weapon or something that could have been used as evidence against him. There was no constitutional justification, in the absence of a search warrant, for extending the search beyond that area. The scope of the search was, therefore, "unreasonable" under the Fourth and Fourteenth Amendments and the petitioner's conviction cannot stand. . . .

REVERSED. . . .

DISSENT

WHITE, J., joined by BLACK, J.

. . . The Fourth Amendment does not proscribe "warrantless searches" but instead it proscribes "unreasonable searches" and this Court has never held nor does the majority today assert that warrantless searches are necessarily unreasonable. . . . This case provides a good illustration . . . that it is unreasonable to require police to leave the scene of an arrest in order to obtain a search warrant when they already have probable cause to search and there is a clear danger that the items for which they may reasonably search will be removed before they return with a warrant.

Chimel was arrested in his home. . . . There was doubtless probable cause not only to arrest Chimel, but also to search his house. He had obliquely admitted, both to a neighbor and to the owner of the burglarized store, that he

had committed the burglary. In light of this, and the fact that the neighbor had seen other admittedly stolen property in petitioner's house, there was surely probable cause on which a warrant could have issued to search the house for the stolen coins.

Moreover, had the police simply arrested Chimel, taken him off to the station house, and later returned with a warrant, it seems very likely that Chimel's wife, who in view of Chimel's generally garrulous nature must have known of the burglary, would have removed the coins. For the police to search the house while the evidence they had probable cause to search out and seize was still there cannot be considered unreasonable.

Questions

1. Describe the search that followed Chimel's arrest.

2. How does the Court define the area "within [a suspect's] immediate control"?

3. If you were defining the phrase, would you have included the whole house within the scope of the rule? Explain your answer, including what interests you consider paramount in formulating your definition.

4. Does Justice White, in his dissent, have the better argument in the case? Summarize his argument and then evaluate it.

Now, let's look at other issues raised by searches incident to arrests, including how the courts define the "grabbable"—or searchable—area and whether it extends to vehicles; the time frame officers have to conduct a search before it is no longer considered incident to the arrest; and searches incident to misdemeanors and pretext arrests.

The Grabbable Area

According to *Chimel v. California*, law enforcement officers can only search the "**grabbable area**—namely, the arrested person and the area under her or his immediate physical control." The rule seems clear enough, but confusion arose when police were faced with applying the rule to arrests of suspects in vehicles. The courts were divided over whether the grabbable area rule even applied to searches of vehicles. Some courts quickly said it did; others were reluctant.

New York is a good example of the division. A trial court said the "grabbable area" rule applied even when the arrested person was outside the car and under the control of the police, and so highly unlikely to escape, grab a weapon, or destroy evidence inside the vehicle. The intermediate appeals court agreed, but a divided Court of Appeals, New York's highest court, said the rule didn't include a search of the car when the arrested suspects were outside the car. The U.S. Supreme Court resolved the problem, not only for New York but for the country, in *New York v. Belton* (1981).

New York v. Belton
453 U.S. 454 (1981)

Roger Belton was convicted in the Ontario County Court, of attempted criminal possession of a small amount of cocaine, and he appealed. The Supreme Court, Appellate Division, affirmed. The Court of Appeals reversed. The U.S. Supreme Court granted certiorari and reversed.

STEWART, J.

FACTS

On April 9, 1978, Trooper Douglas Nicot, a New York State policeman driving an unmarked car on the New York Thruway, was passed by another automobile traveling at an excessive rate of speed. Nicot gave chase, overtook the speeding vehicle, and ordered its driver to pull it over to the side of the road and stop. There were four men in the car, one of whom was Roger Belton. The policeman asked to see the driver's license and automobile registration, and discovered that none of the men owned the vehicle or were related to its owner.

Meanwhile, the policeman had smelled burnt marijuana and had seen on the floor of the car an envelope marked "Supergold" that he associated with marijuana. He therefore directed the men to get out the car, and placed them under arrest for the unlawful possession of marijuana. He patted down each of the men and "split them up into four separate areas of the Thruway at this time so they would not be in physical touching area of each other." He then picked up the envelope marked "Supergold" and found that it contained marijuana.

After giving the arrestees the warnings required by *Miranda v. Arizona*, the state policeman searched each one of them. He then searched the passenger compartment of the car. On the back seat he found a black leather jacket belonging to Belton. He unzipped one of the pockets of the jacket and discovered cocaine. Placing the jacket in his automobile, he drove the four arrestees to a nearby police station.

Belton was subsequently indicted for criminal possession of a controlled substance. In the trial court he moved that the cocaine the trooper had seized from the jacket pocket be suppressed. The court denied the motion. Belton then pleaded guilty to a lesser included offense, but preserved his claim that the cocaine had been seized in violation of the Fourth and Fourteenth Amendments. The Appellant Division of the New York Supreme Court upheld the constitutionality of the search and seizure, reasoning that "once defendant was validly arrested for possession of marijuana, the officer was justified in searching the immediate area for other contraband."

The New York Court of Appeals reversed, holding that "a warrantless search of the zippered pockets of an unaccessible jacket may not be upheld as a search incident to a lawful arrest where there is no longer any danger that the arrestee or a confederate might gain access to the article." Two judges dissented. They pointed out that the "search was conducted by a lone peace officer who was in the process of arresting four unknown individuals whom he had stopped in a speeding car owned by none of them and apparently containing an uncertain quantity of a controlled substance. The suspects were standing by the side of the car as the officer gave it a quick check to confirm his suspicions before attempting to transport them to police headquarters...." We granted certiorari to consider the constitutionally permissible scope of a search in circumstances such as these.

OPINION

It is a first principle of Fourth Amendment jurisprudence that the police may not conduct a search unless they first convince a neutral magistrate that there is probable cause to do so. This Court has recognized, however, that "the exigencies of the situation" may sometimes make exemption from the warrant requirement "imperative." Specifically, the Court held in *Chimel v. California*,* that a lawful custodial arrest creates a situation which justifies the contemporaneous search without a warrant of the person arrested and of the immediately surrounding area. Such searches have long been considered valid because of the need "to remove any weapons that [the arrestee] might seek to use in order to resist arrest or effect his escape" and the need to prevent the concealment or destruction of evidence.

The Court's opinion in *Chimel* emphasized the principle that, as the Court had said in *Terry v. Ohio*,** "the scope of a search must be 'strictly tied to and justified by' the circumstances which rendered its initiation permissible." Thus while the Court in *Chimel* found "ample justifi-

---

*See the case excerpt, on p. 202.

**Excerpted in Chapter 4.

cation" for a search of "the area from within which [an arrestee] might gain possession of a weapon or destructible evidence," the Court found "no comparable justification... for routinely searching any room other than that in which an arrest occurs—or, for that matter, for searching through all the desk drawers or other closed or concealed areas in that room itself."

Although the principle that limits a search incident to a lawful custodial arrest may be stated clearly enough, courts have discovered the principle difficult to apply in specific cases. Yet, as one commentator has pointed out, the protection of the Fourth and Fourteenth Amendments "can only be realized if the police are acting under a set of rules which, in most instances, makes it possible to reach a correct determination beforehand as to whether an invasion of privacy is justified in the interest of law enforcement." In short, "a single, familiar standard is essential to guide police officers, who have only limited time and expertise to reflect on and balance the social and individual interests involved in the specific circumstances they confront.". . .

But no straightforward rule has emerged... respecting the question involved here—the question of the proper scope of a search of the interior of an automobile incident to a lawful custodial arrest of its occupants. . . . When a person cannot know how a court will apply a settled principle to a recurring factual situation, that person cannot know the scope of his constitutional protection, nor can a policeman know the scope of his authority. While the *Chimel* case established that a search incident to an arrest may not stray beyond the area within the immediate control of the arrestee, courts have found no workable definition of "the area within the immediate control of the arrestee" when that area arguably includes the interior of an automobile and the arrestee is its recent occupant.

Our reading of the cases suggests the generalization that articles inside the relatively narrow compass of the passenger compartment of an automobile are in fact generally, even if not inevitably, within "the area into which an arrestee might reach in order to grab a weapon or evidentiary item." In order to establish the workable rule this category of cases requires, we read *Chimel*'s definition of the limits of the area that may be searched in light of that generalization.

Accordingly, we hold that when a policeman has made a lawful custodial arrest of the occupant of an automobile, he may, as a contemporaneous incident of that arrest, search the passenger compartment of that automobile. It follows from this conclusion that the police may also examine the contents of any containers found within the passenger compartment, for if the passenger compartment

is within reach of the arrestee, so also will containers in it be within his reach.*

Such a container may... be searched whether it is open or closed, since the justification for the search is not that the arrestee has no privacy interest in the container, but that the lawful custodial arrest justifies the infringement of any privacy interest the arrestee may have. Thus, while the Court in *Chimel* held that the police could not search all the drawers in an arrestee's house simply because the police had arrested him at home, the Court noted that drawers within an arrestee's reach could be searched because of the danger their contents might pose to the police.

It is true... that these containers will sometimes be such that they could hold neither a weapon nor evidence of the criminal conduct for which the suspect was arrested. However, in *United States v. Robinson*, the Court rejected the argument that such a container—there a "crumpled up cigarette package"—located during a search of Robinson incident to his arrest could not be searched: "The authority to search the person incident to a lawful custodial arrest, while based upon the need to disarm and to discover evidence, does not depend on what a court may later decide was the probability in a particular arrest situation that weapons or evidence would in fact be found upon the person of the suspect. A custodial arrest of a suspect based on probable cause is a reasonable intrusion under the Fourth Amendment; that intrusion being lawful, a search incident to the arrest requires no additional justification.". . .

It is not questioned that Belton was the subject of a lawful custodial arrest on a charge of possessing marijuana. The search of Belton's jacket followed immediately upon that arrest. The jacket was located inside the passenger compartment of the car in which Belton had been a passenger just before he was arrested. The jacket was thus within the area which we have concluded was "within the arrestee's immediate control" within the meaning of the *Chimel* case. The search of the jacket, therefore, was a search incident to a lawful custodial arrest, and it did not violate the Fourth and Fourteenth Amendments.

Accordingly, the judgment is REVERSED.

---

*"Container" here denotes any object capable of holding another object. It thus includes closed or open glove compartments, consoles, or other receptacles located anywhere within the passenger compartment, as well as luggage, boxes, bags, clothing, and the like. Our holding encompasses only the interior of the passenger compartment of an automobile and does not encompass the trunk.

DISSENT

BRENNAN, J., joined by MARSHALL, J.

...As the facts of this case make clear, the Court today substantially expands the permissible scope of searches incident to arrest by permitting police officers to search areas and containers the arrestee could not possibly reach at the time of arrest. These facts demonstrate that at the time Belton and his three companions were placed under custodial arrest—which was after they had been removed from the car, patted down, and separated—none of them could have reached the jackets that had been left on the back seat of the car....

By approving the constitutionality of the warrantless search in this case, the Court carves out a dangerous precedent that is not justified by the concerns underlying *Chimel*.... The Court for the first time grants police officers authority to conduct a warrantless "area" search under circumstances where there is no chance that the arrestee "might gain possession of a weapon or destructible evidence." Under the approach taken today, the result would presumably be the same even if Officer Nicot had handcuffed Belton and his companions in the patrol car before placing them under arrest, and even if his search had extended to locked luggage or other inaccessible containers located in the back seat of the car....

The Court seeks to justify its departure from the principles underlying *Chimel* by proclaiming the need for a new "bright-line" rule to guide the officer in the field.... However, "the mere fact that law enforcement may be made more efficient can never by itself justify disregard of the Fourth Amendment.".... Because the Court's new rule abandons the justifications underlying *Chimel*, it offers no guidance to the police officer seeking to work out these answers for himself. As we warned in *Chimel*: "No consideration relevant to the Fourth Amendment suggests any point of rational limitation, once the search is allowed to go beyond the area from which the person arrested might obtain weapons or evidentiary items." By failing to heed this warning, the Court has undermined rather than furthered the goal of consistent law enforcement: it has failed to offer any principles to guide the police and the courts in their application of the new rule to nonroutine situations.

The standard announced in *Chimel* is not nearly as difficult to apply as the Court suggests. To the contrary, I continue to believe that *Chimel* provides a sound, workable rule for determining the constitutionality of a warrantless search incident to arrest. Under *Chimel*, searches incident to arrest may be conducted without a warrant only if limited to the person of the arrestee, or to the area within the arrestee's "immediate control." While it may be difficult in some cases to measure the exact scope of the arrestee's immediate control, relevant factors would surely include the relative number of police officers and arrestees, the manner of restraint placed on the arrestee, and the ability of the arrestee to gain access to a particular area or container. Certainly there will be some close cases, but when in doubt the police can always turn to the rationale underlying *Chimel*—the need to prevent the arrestee from reaching weapons or contraband—before exercising their judgment. A rule based on that rationale should provide more guidance than the rule announced by the Court today. Moreover, unlike the Court's rule, it would be faithful to the Fourth Amendment.

Questions

1. Describe the details of the searches Officer Nicot conducted following his arrests of Belton and the other occupants in the car.

2. State the Court's definition of "grabbable area" in this case, and compare it with the definition in *Chimel v. California* (p. 202). Are the definitions consistent? Explain.

3. In your opinion, which definition best balances the government's interest in controlling illegal drugs and Belton's right against unreasonable seizure? Defend your answer.

4. Do you prefer the bright-line rule that the Court adopted or the case-by-case approach that the dissent favors? Why?

5. Should the officer be permitted to search not only the interior of the car but also the trunk? under the hood? a locked glove compartment?

6. Should the officer be restricted to patting down the outer part of Belton's jacket? Is the Court's expansion of the grabbable area applicable only to vehicle cases, or should it apply to houses, too?

7. After the case was decided one commentator (Hancock 1982) noted:

> Ten years ago most state court judges might have welcomed the Supreme Court's...decision. The new automobile search rule for arrested motorists [that deems the interior of an automobile always to be within the "grabbing area"]...certainly makes it easier for courts to apply the law of searches incident to arrest in such cases....This new rule not only allows police to be more certain about the precise scope of their search powers, it also frees lower courts from the burden of case-by-case adjudication of the frequently disputed factual issue of actual grabbing area. (1085)

Do you agree? Do you favor the rule per se for that reason? Why or why not?

8. Consider the concerns expressed by Professor Wayne LaFave (1993), an expert on the law of search and seizure:

> There is good reason to be...concerned with the Court's...holding in *New York v. Belton* that in every instance in which "a policeman has made a lawful custodial arrest of the occupant of an automobile, he may, as a contemporaneous incident of that arrest, search the passenger compartment of that automobile." In all such instances..."there is always the possibility that a police officer, lacking probable cause to obtain a search warrant, will use a traffic arrest as a pretext to conduct a search." Given that very few drivers can traverse any appreciable distance without vio-

lating some traffic regulation, this is indeed a frightening possibility. It is apparent that virtually anyone who ventures out onto the public streets and highways may then, with little effort by the police, be placed in a position where his or her person and vehicle are subject to search. (243)

Do you agree with Professor LaFave's contention that the ruling in *New York v. Belton* has created a "frightening possibility"?

 Go to Exercise 6-2 on the Criminal Procedure 6e CD to learn more about *New York v. Belton*.

STATE CONSTITUTIONAL LAW

Search Incident to Arrest

Commonwealth v. Gelineau and Theobald
696 A.2d 188 (Pa.Sup.Ct. 1997)

Richard Gelineau and James Theobald were charged with unlawful possession with intent to deliver a controlled substance, criminal conspiracy to commit possession of a controlled substance, unlawful possession of a controlled substance, and possession of drug paraphernalia. The Court of Common Pleas, Lackawanna County granted the defendants' motion to suppress evidence. Commonwealth appealed. The Superior Court, Philadelphia affirmed.

CAVANAUGH, J.

FACTS

On March 31, 1995, Richard L. Gelineau and James Theobald were traveling on Interstate 81 in Lackawanna County when they were stopped by Trooper Scott R. Walck for failing to use a turn signal when changing lanes of traffic. Theobald exited the vehicle he was driving and walked toward the police car but was ordered back into the car by Trooper Walck. Subsequently, Trooper Walck approached the stopped vehicle and asked Theobald for his driver's license, registration and proof of insurance. The passenger, Gelineau, stated that the vehicle belonged to his father.

While standing by the driver side door, Trooper Walck detected a strong odor of burnt marijuana emanating from the interior of the car. He immediately called for back-up, whereupon Trooper James Seamon and

Trooper Richard Seaberg arrived on the scene. The officers conducted a pat-down search of the two men and discovered marijuana residue and seeds in Gelineau's shirt pocket. At this time, Gelineau was handcuffed and placed in the back seat of a police vehicle and Theobald was handcuffed and placed on the side of the highway. The officers told appellees (Theobald and Gelineau) that they were going to search the vehicle; if they did not find anything, the men would be free to go. However, while searching the engine compartment of the vehicle, the officers found 78 one-gram baggies of a substance which, after a field test, tested positive for marijuana.

After being advised of his *Miranda* rights, Gelineau stated that the marijuana was his and that Theobald had nothing to do with it. Both men were then arrested on charges of Unlawful Possession With the Intent to Deliver a Controlled Substance, Criminal Conspiracy to Commit Possession of a Controlled Substance, Unlawful Possession of a Controlled Substance and Possession of Drug Paraphernalia.... After a suppression hearing...the trial court held that the warrantless search of the Gelineau vehicle constituted an illegal search incident to arrest....

OPINION

A well-recognized exception to the warrant requirement is where the search is conducted incident to arrest. It is the precise scope of the search that has been the subject of much debate. The Supreme Court of our Commonwealth has consistently given greater deference to an individual's privacy than has the United States Supreme Court. For example, in *Commonwealth v. Timko* (1980), our Supreme Court limited the warrantless search of an automobile incident to an arrest to areas and clothing immediately accessible to the person arrested. The purpose of this search is to prevent the arrestee from securing a weapon or destroying evidence of criminal activity. Once the danger is removed, a search of any property not immediately associated with the person of the arrestee to their exclusive control is no longer a search incident to the arrest.

To the contrary, the United States Supreme Court held, one year later, in *New York v. Belton*, 453 U.S. 454 (1981), that "when a policeman has made a lawful custodial arrest of the occupant of an automobile, he may, as a contemporaneous incident of that arrest, search the passenger compartment of that automobile." Despite the holding in *Belton*, our Supreme Court stated . . . that *Timko* is still the law of this Commonwealth regarding the scope of a search incident to arrest:

It is axiomatic that the Supreme Court of Pennsylvania may provide more protection for the citizens of Pennsylvania under the Pennsylvania Constitution than the federal courts provide under the United States Constitution, and it is our view that the rule of *Timko* is as valid today as it was fifteen years ago when *Timko* was decided. In fact, the thrust of *Timko* is even more compelling today than it was in 1980 because this court has increasingly emphasized the privacy interests inherent in Article I, Section 8 of the Pennsylvania Constitution. By contrast, the United States Supreme Court has deemphasized the privacy interests inherent in the Fourth Amendment.

[Our cases] . . . require us to uphold the trial court's finding that this was an illegal search incident to arrest. Searching under the hood of this car was well beyond the area and clothing immediately accessible to appellees. The danger of either appellee securing a weapon or destroying the contraband was removed the moment they were handcuffed and placed at a distance from the subject vehicle. As our Supreme Court has announced a very clear and precise rule, we are required to follow that rule.

. . . AFFIRMED.

EXPLORING SEARCH INCIDENT TO ARREST FURTHER

 Go to the Criminal Procedure 6e CD to read the full text versions of the cases featured here.

1. *Was the Search of the Suitcase on the Road Next to the Suspect Reasonable?*

FACTS

A California police officer discovered a pistol and drugs on a hitchhiker during a lawful pat-down, arrested and handcuffed him, and put him in a police vehicle. Only then did a second officer open an unlocked suitcase that had been sitting on the road next to the suspect at the time of the arrest; inside the suitcase were more drugs. Was the search of the suitcase incident to the arrest?

DECISION AND REASONS

The California Court of Appeals said it was, holding that if a container is close enough that the arrested suspect could have reached it at the moment of arrest:

[A] search does not become unlawful because the police first separate the arrestee from the reach of the article, or handcuff or otherwise restrain the arrestee, so long as the search is made immediately thereafter, while the arrestee is still nearby at the scene of the arrest and before the arresting officers have turned their attention to tasks unrelated to securing the safety of persons and property involved in the arrest.

People v. Brooks (Cal.App. 1989)

2. Was the Search of the Suspect's Jacket While He Was Held at the Other End of the Room Reasonable?

FACTS

Alaska police officers entered a tavern and arrested the bartender for selling drugs moments earlier to an informer. Fifteen minutes later, while the suspect was being held at the other end of the room, an officer searched the jacket from which the suspect had gotten the drugs, which had been hanging all along on a coatrack some 10 to 15 feet from the bar. Was the search of the jacket incident to the arrest?

DECISION AND REASONS

The Alaska Supreme Court ruled that it was not because the jacket was not accessible to the suspect at the moment of the arrest: "Physical proximity at the time of the arrest—with the consequent threat to safety and risk of destruction—is the basic requirement upon which the search incident to arrest exception is predicated." The majority held that the exigencies of the situation at the point of the suspect's arrest did not call for a search of the jacket.

State v. Ricks (Alaska.App. 1989)

The Time Frame of "Incident to Arrest"

What's the time frame of "at the time of arrest," or as the courts call it "incident to arrest"? According to the U.S. Supreme Court, "incident to" includes the time before, during, and after arrest. For example, in *Cupp v. Murphy* (1973), right before Portland, Oregon, police officers arrested Daniel Murphy, they scraped his fingernails for blood residue to see if it was his strangled wife's. The U.S. Supreme Court held that because the officers *could've* arrested Murphy before they searched him (they had probable cause), the search was incident to the arrest.

In *U.S. v. Edwards* (1974), Eugene Edwards was arrested shortly after 11:00 P.M. and put in jail. The next morning, officers took his clothing and searched it for paint chips that would link Edwards to a burglary. Despite the 10-hour gap between the arrest and the search, and over a strong dissent arguing the officers had plenty of time to present their evidence to a neutral magistrate to get a search warrant, the Supreme Court ruled that the search was incident to the arrest.

Searches Incident to Arrests for Misdemeanors

Until now, we've looked at the reasonableness of searches incident to *felony* arrests, but what about the reasonableness of searches incident to arrests for misdemeanors? The U.S. Supreme Court answered the question in *U.S. v. Robinson* (1973). Officer Richard Jenks, a 15-year veteran of the Washington, D.C., Police Department, arrested Willie Robinson for driving without a license (a misdemeanor). Jenks then searched Robinson. During the search, Jenks felt a lump in Robinson's coat pocket. Reaching inside, he found a crumpled-up cigarette package. Jenks took the package out of Robinson's pocket, opened it, and found heroin inside.

Robinson was charged with illegally possessing narcotics. He moved to suppress the evidence, but the court denied his motion and admitted the heroin. The heroin was the main evidence that convicted Robinson. The Supreme Court upheld the conviction and formulated a "bright line" *Robinson* **rule**: Officers *can* always search anyone they're authorized to take into custody. (Be clear that officers don't *have* to search; many times they won't, but whether they do is a matter of individual officer discretion.) According to Justice Rehnquist, writing for the majority:

> A police officer's determination as to how and where to search the person of a suspect whom he has arrested is necessarily a quick ad hoc judgment which the Fourth Amendment does not require to be broken down in each instance into an analysis of each step in the search. The authority to search the person incident to a lawful custodial arrest, while based upon the need to disarm and to discover evidence, does not depend upon what a court may later decide was the probability in a particular arrest situation that weapons or evidence would in fact be found upon the person of the suspect. A custodial arrest of a suspect based on probable cause is a reasonable intrusion under the Fourth Amendment; that intrusion being lawful, a search incident to the arrest requires no additional justification. It is the fact of the lawful arrest which establishes the authority to search, and we hold that in the case of a lawful custodial arrest a full search of the person is not only an exception to the warrant requirement of the Fourth Amendment, but is also a "reasonable" search under that Amendment. (234–235)

What's the justification for the "bright line" *Robinson* rule? Two reasons, according to the Court:

1. The possible danger to police officers taking suspects into custody
2. The logical impossibility of the Court's reviewing every police decision

The *Robinson* bright-line rule shows the Court's reluctance to second-guess law enforcement decisions. However, six state courts—Alaska, California, Hawaii, New York, Oregon, and West Virginia—haven't been so reluctant; they rejected the bright-line *Robinson* rule. (Five—Illinois, Michigan, Montana, New Hampshire, and Texas—have adopted it [Latzer 1991, 64].)

Are searches incident to traffic **citations** reasonable under the *Robinson* rule? (As most of you probably know, citations are substitutes for arrests.) A unanimous U.S. Supreme Court answered the question in *Knowles v. Iowa* (1998), a case challenging an Iowa statute that created a search-incident-to-citation exception to the warrant requirement.

CASE | *Was the Search Incident to Citation Reasonable?*

Knowles v. Iowa
525 U.S. 113 (1998)

Patrick Knowles was charged with possession of marijuana and keeping marijuana in a car. After the court denied his motion to suppress the marijuana as evidence, he was convicted of both offenses. The Iowa Supreme Court affirmed. The U.S. Supreme Court granted certiorari and reversed and remanded the case.

REHNQUIST, C.J.

An Iowa police officer stopped Knowles for speeding, but issued him a citation rather than arresting him. The question presented is whether such a procedure authorizes the officer, consistently with the Fourth Amendment, to conduct a full search of the car. We answer this question "no."

FACTS

Patrick Knowles was stopped in Newton, Iowa, after having been clocked driving 43 miles per hour on a road where the speed limit was 25 miles per hour. The police officer issued a citation to Knowles, although under Iowa law he might have arrested him. The officer then conducted a full search of the car, and under the driver's seat he found a bag of marijuana and a "pot pipe." Knowles was then arrested and charged with violation of state laws dealing with controlled substances.

Before trial, Knowles moved to suppress the evidence so obtained. He argued that the search could not be sustained under the "search incident to arrest" exception recognized in *United States v. Robinson* (1973), because he had not been placed under arrest. At the hearing on the motion to suppress, the police officer conceded that he had neither Knowles' consent nor probable cause to conduct the search. He relied on Iowa law dealing with such searches.

Iowa Code Ann. § 321.485(1)(a) (West 1997) provides that Iowa peace officers having cause to believe that a person has violated any traffic or motor vehicle equipment law may arrest the person and immediately take the person before a magistrate. Iowa law also authorizes the far more usual practice of issuing a citation in lieu of arrest or in lieu of continued custody after an initial arrest. Section 805.1(4) provides that the issuance of a citation in lieu of an arrest "does not affect the officer's authority to conduct an otherwise lawful search." The Iowa Supreme Court has interpreted this provision as providing authority to officers to conduct a full-blown search of an automobile and driver in those cases where police elect not to make a custodial arrest and instead issue a citation—that is, a search incident to citation.

Based on this authority, the trial court denied the motion to suppress and found Knowles guilty. The Supreme Court of Iowa, sitting en banc, affirmed by a divided vote. Relying on its earlier opinion in *State v. Doran* (Iowa 1997), the Iowa Supreme Court upheld the constitutionality of the search under a bright-line "search incident to citation" exception to the Fourth Amendment's warrant requirement, reasoning that so long as the arresting officer had probable cause to make a custodial arrest, there need not in fact have been a custodial arrest. We granted certiorari, and we now reverse.

OPINION

In *United States v. Robinson*, we noted the two historical rationales for the "search incident to arrest" exception: (1) the need to disarm the suspect in order to take him into custody, and (2) the need to preserve evidence for later use at trial. But neither of these underlying rationales for the search incident to arrest exception is sufficient to justify the search in the present case.

We have recognized that the first rationale—officer safety—is "both legitimate and weighty," *Maryland v. Wil-*

son.* The threat to officer safety from issuing a traffic citation, however, is a good deal less than in the case of a custodial arrest. In *Robinson*, we stated that a custodial arrest involves "danger to an officer" because of "the extended exposure which follows the taking of a suspect into custody and transporting him to the police station." We recognized that "the danger to the police officer flows from the fact of the arrest, and its attendant proximity, stress, and uncertainty, and not from the grounds for arrest." A routine traffic stop, on the other hand, is a relatively brief encounter and "is more analogous to a so-called 'Terry stop'... than to a formal arrest." See *Cupp v. Murphy*, 412 U.S. 291, 296 (1973) ("Where there is no formal arrest... a person might well be less hostile to the police and less likely to take conspicuous, immediate steps to destroy incriminating evidence").

This is not to say that the concern for officer safety is absent in the case of a routine traffic stop. It plainly is not. But while the concern for officer safety in this context may justify the "minimal" additional intrusion of ordering a driver and passengers out of the car, it does not by itself justify the often considerably greater intrusion attending a full field-type search. Even without the search authority Iowa urges, officers have other, independent bases to search for weapons and protect themselves from danger. For example, they may order out of a vehicle both the driver; perform a "patdown" of a driver and any passengers upon reasonable suspicion that they may be armed and dangerous *Terry v. Ohio* (1968);** conduct a "Terry patdown" of the passenger compartment of a vehicle upon reasonable suspicion that an occupant is dangerous and may gain immediate control of a weapon; and even conduct a full search of the passenger compartment, including any containers therein, pursuant to a custodial arrest, *New York v. Belton* (1981).†

Nor has Iowa shown the second justification for the authority to search incident to arrest—the need to discover and preserve evidence. Once Knowles was stopped for speeding and issued a citation, all the evidence necessary to prosecute that offense had been obtained. No further evidence of excessive speed was going to be found either on the person of the offender or in the passenger compartment of the car.

Iowa nevertheless argues that a "search incident to citation" is justified because a suspect who is subject to a routine traffic stop may attempt to hide or destroy evidence related to his identity (e.g., a driver's license or vehicle

---

*Excerpted in Chapter 4.

**Excerpted in Chapter 4.

†See earlier in this chapter, p. 204.

registration), or destroy evidence of another, as yet undetected crime. As for the destruction of evidence relating to identity, if a police officer is not satisfied with the identification furnished by the driver, this may be a basis for arresting him rather than merely issuing a citation. As for destroying evidence of other crimes, the possibility that an officer would stumble onto evidence wholly unrelated to the speeding offense seems remote.

In *Robinson*, we held that the authority to conduct a full field search as incident to an arrest was a "bright-line rule," which was based on the concern for officer safety and destruction or loss of evidence, but which did not depend in every case upon the existence of either concern. Here we are asked to extend that "bright-line rule" to a situation where the concern for officer safety is not present to the same extent and the concern for destruction or loss of evidence is not present at all. We decline to do so. The judgment of the Supreme Court of Iowa is REVERSED, and the cause REMANDED for further proceedings not inconsistent with this opinion.

It is so ordered.

Questions

1. Summarize the reasons for Iowa's claim that the search incident to a citation is reasonable. Do you agree? Explain.

2. Summarize the reasons why the U.S. Supreme Court decided that the Iowa statute was unconstitutional. Do you agree? Explain.

3. Do you think the Supreme Court retreated from its sweeping decision in *U.S. v. Robinson*? If so, do you think it's a good idea that it did? Defend your answer.

Searches Incident to Pretext Arrests

Suppose an officer has only a hunch that a college student has marijuana in her car. The officer sees her make a left turn without signaling. What luck, he thinks, now I've got my chance. He stops her for turning without signaling so that he can search the car for marijuana—the arrest is simply a pretext for the search. **Pretext arrests** are powerful investigative tools in the "drug war." Most people commit traffic offenses, so officers can use this fact of life to act on their hunches that drivers are committing drug crimes. Critics argue that pretext traffic arrest searches put a heavy thumb on the government side of the balance between government and individuals. According to Professor Daniel S. Jonas (1989):

> The conflict between liberty and law enforcement is particularly sharp in the area of pretextual police conduct. Police would have a powerful investigative tool if it were constitutional, for example, to arrest a felony suspect on the basis of a parking ticket that had not been paid, when the facts relating to the felony did not provide probable cause. Precisely because its investigative potential is so great, pretextual police conduct poses an alarming threat to individual freedom from government intrusion. (1792)

A unanimous U.S. Supreme Court decided whether a search for drugs incident to a pretext traffic violation arrest was reasonable in *Whren v. U.S.* (1996).

CASE	*Was the Search Incident to a Pretext Search Reasonable?*

Whren v. U.S.
517 U.S 806 (1996)

Michael A. Whren and James L. Brown were convicted in the U.S. District Court for the District of Columbia of drug offenses, and they appealed. The Court of Appeals affirmed. The U.S. Supreme Court granted certiorari. The U.S. Supreme Court affirmed.

SCALIA, J.

FACTS

On the evening of June 10, 1993, plainclothes vice-squad officers of the District of Columbia Metropolitan Police Department were patrolling a "high drug area" of the city in an unmarked car. Their suspicions were aroused when they passed a dark Nissan Pathfinder with temporary license plates and youthful occupants waiting at a stop sign, the driver looking down into the lap of the passenger at his right. The Pathfinder remained stopped at the intersection for what seemed an unusually long time—more than 20 seconds. When the police car executed a U-turn in order to head back toward the truck, the Pathfinder turned suddenly to its right, without signaling, and sped off at an "unreasonable" speed. The policemen followed, and in a short while overtook the Pathfinder when it stopped behind other traffic at a red light. They pulled up alongside, and Officer Ephraim Soto stepped out and approached the driver's door, identifying himself as a police officer and directing the driver, James Brown, to put the vehicle in park. When Soto drew up to the driver's window, he immediately observed two large plastic bags of what appeared to be crack cocaine in James Whren's hands. Brown and Whren were arrested, and quantities of several types of illegal drugs were retrieved from the vehicle.

Brown and Whren were charged in a four-count indictment with violating various federal drug laws, including 21 U.S.C. §§ 844(a) and 860(a). At a pretrial suppression hearing, they challenged the legality of the stop and the resulting seizure of the drugs. They argued that the stop had not been justified by probable cause to believe, or even reasonable suspicion, that they were engaged in illegal drug-dealing activity; and that Officer Soto's asserted ground for approaching the vehicle—to give the driver a warning concerning traffic violations—was pretextual. The District Court denied the suppression motion, concluding that "the facts of the stop were not controverted," and "there was nothing to really demonstrate that the actions of the officers were contrary to a normal traffic stop."

Whren and Brown were convicted.... The Court of Appeals affirmed the convictions, holding with respect to the suppression issue that, "regardless of whether a police officer subjectively believes that the occupants of an automobile may be engaging in some other illegal behavior, a traffic stop is permissible as long as a reasonable officer in the same circumstances *could* [emphasis added] have stopped the car for the suspected traffic violation." We granted certiorari.

OPINION

...As a general matter, the decision to stop an automobile is reasonable where the police have probable cause to believe that a traffic violation has occurred. Brown and Whren accept that Officer Soto had probable cause to believe that various provisions of the District of Columbia traffic code had been violated:

1. 18 D.C. Mun. Regs. §§ 2213.4 (1995) ("An operator shall...give full time and attention to the operation of the vehicle");

2. 2204.3 ("No person shall turn any vehicle...without giving an appropriate signal");

3. 2200.3 ("No person shall drive a vehicle...at a speed greater than is reasonable and prudent under the conditions").

They argue, however, that "in the unique context of civil traffic regulations" probable cause is not enough. Since, they contend, the use of automobiles is so heavily and minutely regulated that total compliance with traffic and safety rules is nearly impossible, a police officer will almost invariably be able to catch any given motorist in a technical violation. This creates the temptation to use traffic stops as a means of investigating other law violations, as to which no probable cause or even articulable suspicion exists. Whren and Brown, who are both black, further contend that police officers might decide which motorists to stop based on decidedly impermissible factors, such as the race of the car's occupants. To avoid this danger, they say, the Fourth Amendment test for traffic stops should be, not the normal one (applied by the Court of Appeals) of whether probable cause existed to justify the stop; but rather, whether a police officer, acting reasonably, *would* [emphasis added] have made the stop for the reason given.

Whren and Brown contend that the standard they propose is consistent with our past cases' disapproval of police attempts to use valid bases of action against citizens as pretexts for pursuing other investigatory agendas. We are reminded that in *Florida v. Wells*, 495 (1990), we stated that "an inventory search must not be used as a ruse for a general rummaging in order to discover incriminating evidence"; that in *Colorado v. Bertine*, 479 U.S. 367, 372 (1987), in approving an inventory search, we apparently thought it significant that there had been "no showing that the police, who were following standard procedures, acted in bad faith or for the sole purpose of investigation"; and that in *New York v. Burger*, 482 U.S. 691 (1987), we observed, in upholding the constitutionality of a warrantless administrative inspection, that the search did not appear to be a pretext for obtaining evidence of...violation of... penal laws.

...Not only have we never held, outside the context of inventory search or administrative inspection (discussed above), that an officer's motive invalidates objectively justifiable behavior under the Fourth Amendment; but we have repeatedly held and asserted the contrary. . . . In *United States v. Robinson*, 414 U.S. 218 (1973), we held that a traffic-violation arrest (of the sort here) would not be rendered invalid by the fact that it was "a mere pretext for a narcotics search," and that a lawful post arrest search of the person would not be rendered invalid by the fact that it was not motivated by the officer-safety concern that justifies such searches. . . . *Robinson* . . . established that "the fact that the officer does not have the state of mind which is hypothecated by the reasons which provide the legal justification for the officer's action does not invalidate the action taken as long as the circumstances, viewed objectively, justify that action."

We think these cases foreclose any argument that the constitutional reasonableness of traffic stops depends on the actual motivations of the individual officers involved. We of course agree with Whren and Brown that the Constitution prohibits selective enforcement of the law based on considerations such as race. But the constitutional basis for objecting to intentionally discriminatory application of laws is the Equal Protection Clause, not the Fourth Amendment. Subjective intentions play no role in ordinary, probable-cause Fourth Amendment analysis. . . .

Whren and Brown's claim that a reasonable officer *would* [emphasis added] not have made this stop is based largely on District of Columbia police regulations which permit plainclothes officers in unmarked vehicles to enforce traffic laws "only in the case of a violation that is so grave as to pose an immediate threat to the safety of others." . . . This basis of invalidation would not apply in jurisdictions that had a different practice. And it would not have applied even in the District of Columbia, if Officer Soto had been wearing a uniform or patrolling in a marked police cruiser.

. . . Whren and Brown argue that the balancing inherent in any Fourth Amendment inquiry requires us to weigh the governmental and individual interests implicated in a traffic stop such as we have here. That balancing, they claim, does not support investigation of minor traffic infractions by plainclothes police in unmarked vehicles; such investigation only minimally advances the government's interest in traffic safety, and may indeed retard it by producing motorist confusion and alarm—a view said to be supported by the Metropolitan Police Department's own regulations generally prohibiting this practice. . . .

It is of course true that in principle every Fourth Amendment case, since it turns upon a "reasonableness" determination, involves a balancing of all relevant factors. With rare exceptions not applicable here, however, the result of that balancing is not in doubt where the search or seizure is based upon probable cause. . . .

Where probable cause has existed, the only cases in which we have found it necessary actually to perform the "balancing" analysis involved searches or seizures conducted in an extraordinary manner, unusually harmful to an individual's privacy or even physical interests—such as, for example, seizure by means of deadly force, see *Tennessee v. Garner*, 471 U.S. 1 (1985),* unannounced entry into a home, see *Wilson v. Arkansas,* 514 U.S.—(1995),** entry into a home without a warrant, see *Welsh v. Wisconsin,* 466 U.S. 740 (1984),† or physical penetration of the body, see *Winston v. Lee,* 470 U.S. 753 (1985). The making of a traffic stop out-of-uniform does not remotely qualify as such an extreme practice, and so is governed by the usual rule that probable cause to believe the law has been broken "outbalances" private interest in avoiding police contact.

Whren and Brown urge as an extraordinary factor in this case that the "multitude of applicable traffic and equipment regulations" is so large and so difficult to obey perfectly that virtually everyone is guilty of violation, permitting the police to single out almost whomever they wish for a stop. But we are aware of no principle that would allow us to decide at what point a code of law becomes so expansive and so commonly violated that infraction itself can no longer be the ordinary measure of the lawfulness of enforcement. And even if we could identify such exorbitant codes, we do not know by what standard (or what right) we would decide, as Whren and Brown would have us do, which particular provisions are sufficiently important to merit enforcement.

For the run-of-the-mine case, which this surely is, we think there is no realistic alternative to the traditional common-law rule that probable cause justifies a search and seizure. Here the District Court found that the officers had probable cause to believe that petitioners had violated the traffic code. That rendered the stop reasonable under the Fourth Amendment, the evidence thereby discovered admissible, and the upholding of the convictions by the Court of Appeals for the District of Columbia Circuit correct.

Judgment AFFIRMED.

Questions

1. List all the actions Officer Soto and his partner took that affected Whren and Brown's liberty and privacy.

2. What's the evidence that Officer Soto and his partner conducted a pretext search?

---

*See Chapter 5.

**See the excerpt in this chapter, on p. 196.

†See Chapter 5.

3. For what "crimes" did the officers have probable cause to arrest Brown and Whren?

4. Did Officer Soto and his partner have probable cause to arrest Whren and Brown? List the relevant facts and circumstances relevant to deciding whether they had probable cause.

5. Explain the "*could* have" and "*would* have" tests to determine the reasonableness of the pretext search. What test did the Court adopt? Why?

6. Do you agree with Professor Jonas in the quotation at the opening of this section that pretext searches threaten individual rights too much? That they give the government too much power? Or do you believe that the government needs this power to fight the "war on drugs"?

7. Consider the following excerpt from the Petitioner's Brief (1996) in *Whren v. U.S.*:

> Justice Jackson's observation nearly a half-century ago is no less true today: "I am convinced that there are . . . many unlawful searches of homes and automobiles of innocent people which turn up nothing incriminating, in which no arrest is made, about which courts do nothing, and about which we never hear." *Brinegar v. United States,* 338 U.S. 160 (1949) (JACKSON, J., dissenting).
>
> Because police do not generally keep records of traffic stops that turn up nothing and in which no one is ticketed, it is no simple matter to substantiate Justice Jackson's suspicions. However, reporters from the *Orlando Sentinel* had the unique opportunity to document this phenomenon when they obtained 148 hours of videotaped "traffic" stops of 1,084 motorists along Interstate 95 in Florida (Brazil and Berry, "Color of Driver is Key to Stops in I-95 Videos," *Orlando Sentinel,* Aug. 23, 1992). Although all of the stops were purportedly based on traffic violations, only nine drivers (less than one percent) were issued citations. Searches were made in almost half the stops, but only 5 percent of all stops resulted in an arrest. Most shocking is how racially disproportionate the stops were. Although blacks and Hispanics made up only 5 percent of the drivers on that stretch of I-95 and only 15 percent of traffic convictions statewide, approximately 70 percent of those stopped were black or Hispanic. On average, stops of minority drivers lasted more than twice as long as stops of white drivers. For some, the tapes showed it was not the first time they had been singled out: "There is the bewildered black man who stands on the roadside trying to explain to the deputies that it is the seventh time he has been stopped. And the black man who shakes his head in frustration as his car is searched; it is the

second time in minutes he has been stopped." This kind of baseless "checking out" of racial minorities generally gets public attention only when someone well-known speaks out.

Materials in a class action involving pretextual traffic stops along Interstate 95 near Philadelphia show a similar pattern. The class representatives alleged that, while returning from a church celebration in 1991, they were stopped and subjected to a sniff by a police dog before being told, "in order to make this a legitimate stop, I'm going to give you a warning for obstruction of your car's rear-view mirror." The only object hanging from the mirror was a thin piece of string on which an air freshener had once been attached. When the driver pointed out that the officer could not have seen the string, the officer stated that they were stopped "because you are young, black and in a high drug-trafficking area, driving a nice car." Materials and follow-up interviews in the Tinicum Township case showed:

> First, the interdiction program is based on the power to make a pretextual traffic stop. Numerous vehicles have been stopped, for example, for having small items tied to their rearview mirrors, for outdated inspection stickers, or for other minor violations, all supposedly observed as the car passed the police at sixty miles per hour. Second, the stops are racially disproportionate. Third, claims of consent are rebutted by numerous innocent individuals who give consistent accounts of being told that they would have to wait for a police dog, have their car towed, or suffer other types of roadside detention unless they consented to a search. (24–27)

How does this passage affect your opinion of the reasonableness of pretext searches? Is it more relevant to claims under the equal protection than the due process clause? (Refer to Chapter 2 on due process and equal protection.)

8. Consider the following remarks made by a police officer to researchers Lawrence Tiffany and his colleagues (1967):

> You can always get a guy legitimately on a traffic violation if you tail him for a while, and then a search can be made. You don't have to follow a driver very long before he will move to the other side of the yellow line and then you can arrest and search him for driving on the wrong side of the highway. In the event that we see a suspicious automobile or occupant and wish to search the person or the car, or both, we will usually follow the vehicle until the driver makes a technical

violation of a traffic law. Then we have a means of making a legitimate search. (131)

9. Present arguments that both defense lawyers and prosecutors might make to support the reasonableness and the unreasonableness of searches incident to pretext traffic arrests. Then assume the role of judge, and decide the reasonableness of pretext traffic arrest searches in light of Fourth Amendment reasonableness.

 Go to Exercise 6-3 on the Criminal Procedure 6e CD to learn more about *Whren v. U.S.*

◆ STATE CONSTITUTIONAL LAW ◆

Was the Seizure of a Gun During a Pretext Stop Reasonable?

State v. Ladson
979 P.2d 833 (1999)

Thomas Ladson was prosecuted for possession of a stolen firearm and possession of marijuana with intent to deliver while armed with a deadly weapon. The Superior Court, Thurston County, Washington, suppressed the gun and marijuana as evidence because they were seized during a pretext stop. The state appealed, and the Washington Court of Appeals reversed. A petition for review was granted by the Washington Supreme Court, and the Supreme Court reversed.

SANDERS, J.

FACTS

On October 5, 1995 City of Lacey police officer Jim Mack and Thurston County sheriff's detective Cliff Ziesmer were on proactive gang patrol. The officers explained they do not make routine traffic stops while on proactive gang patrol although they use traffic infractions as a means to pull over people in order to initiate contact and questioning. The trial court factually found that "While on gang patrol, officer Mack selectively enforces traffic violations depending on whether he believes there is the potential for intelligence gathering in such stops."

On the day in question Richard Fogle attracted the attention of officers Mack and Ziesmer as he drove by. Fogle and his passenger Thomas Ladson are both African-American. Although the officers had never seen Ladson before, they recognized Fogle from an unsubstantiated street rumor that Fogle was involved with drugs. The trial court found that "Officer Mack's suspicions about Fogle's reputed drug dealing was his motivation in finding a legal reason to initiate the stop of Fogle's vehicle."

The officers tailed the Fogle vehicle looking for a legal justification to stop the car. They shadowed the vehicle while it refueled at a local filling station and then finally pulled Fogle over several blocks later on the grounds that Fogle's license plate tabs had expired five days earlier. The officers do not deny the stop was pretextual.

The police then discovered Fogle's driver's license was suspended and arrested him on the spot. After securing Fogle in handcuffs in the squad car, the police conducted a full search of the car "incident to Fogle's arrest." Then they turned their attention to the passenger, Thomas Ladson. They ordered Ladson to exit the vehicle, patted him down, and required him to stand against the car while they searched its interior. The police searched Ladson's jacket which was in the passenger's seat and found a small handgun. Ladson was placed under arrest and searched. On Ladson's person and in his jacket the police found several baggies of marijuana and some $600 in cash.

Ladson was charged with unlawful possession of a controlled substance with intent to deliver while armed with a deadly weapon, and possession of a stolen firearm. Ladson filed a pretrial motion to suppress the evidence on the grounds it was obtained during an unconstitutional pretextual traffic stop. The trial court agreed and granted the motion ruling, "Pretextual stops by law enforcement officers are violative of the Constitution." The State appealed and shortly thereafter the United States Supreme Court decided *Whren v. United States*, holding pretextual traffic stops do not violate the Fourth Amendment to the United States Constitution. Accordingly the Court of Appeals, relying on Whren, reversed the suppression order. However, the Court of Appeals refused to address the state constitutional claim, stating Ladson inadequately briefed the issue. Ladson then sought review by this court. His petition for review, which thoroughly addressed the state law issue, argued article I, section 7, of the state constitution provides broader protection than does the Fourth Amendment in the area of pretextual traffic stops and contended article I, section 7, renders pretextual traffic stops unconstitutional. We granted review of that discrete issue.

OPINION

...It is already well established that article I, section 7, of the state constitution has broader application than does the Fourth Amendment of the United States Constitution. Washington Constitution article I, section 7, provides: "No person shall be disturbed in his private affairs, or his home invaded, without authority of law." Article I, section 7, is explicitly broader than that of the Fourth Amendment as it clearly recognizes an individual's right to privacy with no express limitations and places greater emphasis on privacy. Further, while the Fourth Amendment operates on a downward ratcheting mechanism of diminishing expectations of privacy, article I, section 7, holds the line by pegging the constitutional standard to those privacy interests which citizens of this state have held, and should be entitled to hold, safe from governmental trespass absent a warrant.

We begin our analysis by acknowledging the essence of this, and every, pretextual traffic stop is that the police are pulling over a citizen, not to enforce the traffic code, but to conduct a criminal investigation unrelated to the driving. Therefore the reasonable articulable suspicion that a traffic infraction has occurred which justifies an exception to the warrant requirement for an ordinary traffic stop does not justify a stop for criminal investigation....

We conclude the citizens of Washington have held, and are entitled to hold, a constitutionally protected interest against warrantless traffic stops or seizures on a mere pretext to dispense with the warrant when the true reason for the seizure is not exempt from the warrant requirement. We therefore hold pretextual traffic stops violate article I, section 7, because they are seizures absent the "authority of law" which a warrant would bring. Const. art. I, § 7.

When determining whether a given stop is pretextual, the court should consider the totality of the circumstances, including both the subjective intent of the officer as well as the objective reasonableness of the officer's behavior....An objective test may not fully answer the critical inquiry: Was the officer conducting a pretextual traffic stop or not?

...Here, the initial stop, which is a seizure for constitutional purposes, was without authority of law because the reason for the stop (investigation) was not exempt from the warrant requirement. It is elementary that if the initial stop was unlawful, the subsequent search and fruits of that search are inadmissible.... Suppression is required.

REVERSED.

Consent Searches

Consent searches, in which individuals give officers permission to look through their belongings or conduct a pat-down, make law enforcement officers' job easier because they don't have to go through the hassle of either getting warrants before they search or proving probable cause to a judge later. Lawrence P. Tiffany, Donald M. McIntyre, Jr., and Daniel L. Rotenberg, in their classic *The Detection of Crime* (1967), studied consent searches as part of the distinguished American Bar Foundation's massive research into the day-to-day operations of criminal justice in America. They found that officers prefer to search by consent even when they have probable cause to obtain warrants because consent searches are convenient. "Search warrant procedure is overly technical and time-consuming, and...has no corresponding advantages for them or meaningful protections for the individual" (157–161).

But, convenience isn't the only reason for consent searches. Necessity also drives police officers to ask individuals to consent to searches. Officers need consent when they don't have probable cause to search. For example, it's well known that drug dealers travel by bus or plane, but officers don't have probable cause to search most passengers. So, they approach travelers, ask if they can talk to them, explain the seriousness of the drug problem, and ask them if they mind having officers search them and their belongings. According to the anecdotal evidence supplied by officers, most travelers give their consent, especially when officers are polite and respectful.

In *U.S. v. Blake* (1988), Detective Perry Kendrick, who worked the Fort Lauderdale Airport, testified that people willingly consent even to searches of their crotches in the public part of airports. According to Kendrick, on just one day, he

> talked with 16 to 20 people and most consented, but one or two did not. He testified further that initially some complain after the search, but that after the deputies explain their mission in interdicting narcotics moving from airport to airport within the United States, that the persons understand and many "thank us for the job we're doing." (927)

Many legal issues surround consent, including the test of whether consent was given; how much can be searched, or the scope of consent; whether consent can be withdrawn once given; and when searches based on consent by a third party are valid. We'll look at each.

The Test of Consent

When police officers ask for consent to search, they're *really* asking individuals to give up their rights against unreasonable searches and seizures. Because it's a serious matter to give up one of the fundamental rights our ancestors fought the Revolutionary War to protect, the U.S. Supreme Court demands that as a minimum requirement, the government has to prove the consent was voluntary. The **voluntariness test of consent searches** looks at the totality of circumstances in each case to determine if the suspect consented voluntarily. These circumstances can include all of the following:

- Knowledge of constitutional rights in general
- Knowledge of the right to refuse consent
- Sufficient age and maturity to make an independent decision
- Intelligence to understand significance of consent
- Education of or experience with the workings of the criminal justice system
- Cooperation with officers, such as saying, "Sure, go ahead and search"
- Attitude toward the likelihood that officers will discover contraband
- Length of detention and nature of questioning regarding consent
- Coercive police behavior surrounding the consent

A signed consent form (like the type in Figure 6.1) is another example of how officers can demonstrate consent to search was given voluntarily by a suspect.

The U.S. Supreme Court created the totality-of-circumstances test of voluntariness and applied it to the facts of the leading consent search case, *Schneckloth v. Bustamonte* (1973).

WAIVER AND CONSENT TO SEARCH

The undersigned _____

residing at _____

_____ hereby authorizes

the following named St. Paul Police Officers _____

to search the _____

_____

(insert description of place or auto, lic. number, etc.)

owned by/or in possession of the undersigned.
I do hereby waive any and all objections that may be made by me to said search and declare that this waiver and consent is freely and voluntarily given of my own free will and accord.

Signed _____ day of _____ 19___ at _____ PM   AM

Signed _____

Witnessed _____

FIGURE 6.1 St. Paul, MN, Consent Search Form

CASE | *Did Bustamonte Voluntarily Consent?*

Schneckloth v. Bustamonte
412 U.S. 218 (1973)

Clyde Bustamonte was brought to trial in a California court upon a charge of possessing a check with intent to defraud. The trial judge denied his motion to suppress and Bustamonte was convicted. The California Court of Appeals affirmed. The California Supreme Court denied review. Bustamonte brought a petition for habeas corpus in the U.S. District Court for the Northern District of California. The District Court denied the petition. The U.S. Court of Appeals for the Ninth Circuit vacated the District Court's order, and remanded. The U.S. Supreme Court reversed.

STEWART, J.

FACTS

While on routine patrol in Sunnyvale, California, at approximately 2:40 in the morning, Police Officer James Rand stopped an automobile when he observed that one headlight and its license plate light were burned out. Six men were in the vehicle. Joe Alcala and Robert Clyde Bustamonte were in the front seat with Joe Gonzales, the driver. Three older men were seated in the rear. When, in response to the policeman's question, Gonzales could not produce a driver's license, Officer Rand asked if any of the other five had any evidence of identification. Only Alcala produced a license, and he explained that the car was his brother's.

After the six occupants had stepped out of the car at the officer's request and after two additional policemen had arrived, Officer Rand asked Alcala if he could search the car. Alcala replied, "Sure, go ahead." Prior to the search no one was threatened with arrest and, according to Officer Rand's uncontradicted testimony, it "was all very congenial at this time." Gonzales testified that Alcala actually helped in the search of the car, by opening the trunk and glove compartment. In Gonzales' words: The police officer asked Joe (Alcala), he goes, "Does the trunk open?" And Joe said,

"Yes." He went to the car and got the keys and opened up the trunk.

Wadded up under the left rear seat, the police officers found three checks that had previously been stolen from a car wash.

OPINION

It is well settled under the Fourth Amendment... that one of the specifically established exceptions to the requirements of both a warrant and probable cause is a search that is conducted pursuant to consent.... The precise question in this case... is what must the prosecution prove to demonstrate that a consent was "voluntarily" given. And upon that question there is a square conflict of views between the state and federal courts that have reviewed the search involved in the case before us. The Court of Appeals for the Ninth Circuit concluded that it is an essential part of the State's initial burden to prove that a person knows he has a right to refuse consent. The California courts have followed the rule that voluntariness is a question of fact to be determined from the totality of all the circumstances, and that the state of a defendant's knowledge is only one factor to be taken into account in assessing the voluntariness of a consent.

The most extensive judicial exposition of the meaning of "voluntariness" has been developed in those cases in which the Court has had to determine the "voluntariness" of a defendant's confession... This Court's [confession] decisions reflect a frank recognition that the Constitution requires the sacrifice of neither security nor liberty. The Due Process Clause does not mandate that the police forgo all questioning, or that they be given carte blanche to extract what they can from a suspect. The ultimate test remains... [the same] test in Anglo-American courts for two hundred years: the test of voluntariness. Is the confession the product of an essentially free and unconstrained choice by its maker? If it is, if he has willed to confess, it may be used against him. If it is not, if his will has been overborne and his capacity for self-determination critically impaired, the use of his confession offends due process.

In determining whether a defendant's will was overborne in a particular case, the Court has assessed the totality of all the surrounding circumstances—both the characteristics of the accused and the details of the interrogation. Some of the factors taken into account have included the youth of the accused, his lack of education, or his low intelligence, the lack of any advice to the accused of his constitutional rights, the length of detention, the repeated and prolonged nature of the questioning, and the use of physical punishment such as the deprivation of food or sleep, In all of these cases, the Court determined the factual circumstances surrounding the confession, assessed the psychological impact on the accused, and evaluated the legal significance of how the accused reacted.

The significant fact about all of these decisions is that none of them turned on the presence or absence of a single controlling criterion; each reflected a careful scrutiny of all the surrounding circumstances. In none of them did the Court rule that the Due Process Clause required the prosecution to prove as part of its initial burden that the defendant knew he had a right to refuse to answer the questions that were put. While the state of the accused's mind, and the failure of the police to advise the accused of his rights, were certainly factors to be evaluated in assessing the "voluntariness" of an accused's responses, they were not in and of themselves determinative.

Similar considerations lead us to agree with the courts of California that the question whether a consent to a search was in fact "voluntary" or was the product of duress or coercion... is a question of fact to be determined from the totality of all the circumstances. While knowledge of the right to refuse consent is one factor to be taken into account, the government need not establish such knowledge as [indispensable to] an effective consent. As with police questioning, two competing concerns must be accommodated in determining the meaning of a voluntary consent—the legitimate need for such searches and the equally important requirement of assuring the absence of coercion.

In situations where the police have some evidence of illicit activity, but lack probable cause to arrest or search, a search authorized by a valid consent may be the only means of obtaining important and reliable evidence. In the present case for example, while the police had reason to stop the car for traffic violations, the State does not contend that there was probable cause to search the vehicle or that the search was incident to a valid arrest of any of the occupants. Yet, the search yielded tangible evidence that served as a basis for a prosecution, and provided some assurance that others, wholly innocent of the crime, were not mistakenly brought to trial.... In short, a search pursuant to consent may result in considerably less inconvenience for the subject of the search, and, properly conducted, is a constitutionally permissible and wholly legitimate aspect of effective police activity.

But the Fourth Amendment requires that a consent not be coerced.... In examining all the surrounding circumstances to determine if in fact the consent to search was coerced, account must be taken of subtly coercive police questions, as well as the possibly vulnerable subjective state of the person who consents. Those searches that are the product of police coercion can thus be filtered out without undermining the continuing validity of consent searches....

The approach of the Court of Appeals for the Ninth Circuit...that the State must affirmatively prove that the subject of the search knew that he had a right to refuse consent, would, in practice, create serious doubt whether consent searches could continue to be conducted. There might be rare cases where it could be proved from the record that a person in fact affirmatively knew of his right to refuse—such as a case where he announced to the police that if he didn't sign the consent form, "you (police) are going to get a search warrant."... But more commonly where there was no evidence of any coercion...the prosecution would nevertheless be unable to demonstrate that the subject of the search in fact had known of his right to refuse consent....

[Bustamonte also argues] that the Court's decision in the *Miranda* case requires the conclusion that knowledge of a right to refuse is an indispensable element of a valid consent....In *Miranda* the Court found that the techniques of police questioning and the nature of custodial surroundings produce an inherently coercive situation.... The Court noted that "without proper safeguards the process of in-custody interrogation of persons suspected or accused of crime contains inherently compelling pressures which work to undermine the individual's will to resist and to compel him to speak where he would not otherwise do so freely."

In this case, there is no evidence of any inherently coercive tactics—either from the nature of the police questioning or the environment in which it took place. Indeed, since consent searches will normally occur on a person's own familiar territory, the specter of incommunicado police interrogation in some remote station house is simply inapposite. There is no reason to believe, under circumstances such as are present here, that the response to a policeman's question is presumptively coerced; and there is, therefore, no reason to reject the traditional test for determining the voluntariness of a person's response....

It is also argued that the failure to require the Government to establish knowledge as a prerequisite to a valid consent, will relegate the Fourth Amendment to the special province of "the sophisticated, the knowledgeable and the privileged." We cannot agree. The traditional definition of voluntariness we accept today has always taken into account evidence of minimal schooling, low intelligence, and the lack of any effective warnings to a person of his rights; and the voluntariness of any statement taken

under those conditions has been carefully scrutinized to determine whether it was in fact voluntarily given....

Our decision today is a narrow one. We hold only that when the subject of a search is not in custody and the State attempts to justify a search on the basis of his consent, the Fourth Amendment requires that it demonstrate that the consent was in fact voluntarily given, and not the result of...coercion....Voluntariness is a question of fact to be determined from all the circumstances, and while the subject's knowledge of a right to refuse is a factor to be taken into account, the prosecution is not required to demonstrate such knowledge as a prerequisite to establishing a voluntary consent.

Judgment of Court of Appeals REVERSED.

DISSENT

MARSHALL, J.

Several years ago, Mr. Justice Stewart reminded us that "the Constitution guarantees...a society of free choice. Such a society presupposes the capacity of its members to choose." I would have thought that the capacity to choose necessarily depends upon knowledge that there is a choice to be made. But today the Court reaches the curious result that one can choose to relinquish a constitutional right— the right to be free of unreasonable searches—without knowing that he has the alternative of refusing to accede to a police request to search....

Consent...is a mechanism by which substantive requirements...are avoided. In the context of the Fourth Amendment, the relevant substantive requirements are that searches be conducted only after evidence justifying them has been submitted to an impartial magistrate for a determination of probable cause....

...Consent searches are permitted, not because [of]... an exception to the requirements of probable cause and warrant is essential to proper law enforcement, but because we permit our citizens to choose whether or not they wish to exercise their constitutional rights. Our prior decisions do not support the view that a meaningful choice has been made solely because no coercion was brought to bear on the subject....

I am at a loss to understand why consent cannot be taken literally to mean a "knowing choice." In fact, I have difficulty in comprehending how a decision made without knowledge of available alternatives can be treated as a choice at all....I can think of no other situation in which we would say that a person agreed to some course of action if he convinced us that he did not know that there was some other course he might have pursued....

The Court contends that if an officer paused to inform the subject of his rights, the informality of the exchange would be destroyed. I doubt that a simple statement by an officer of an individual's right to refuse consent would do much to alter the informality of the exchange, except to alert the subject to a fact that he surely is entitled to know. It is not without significance that for many years the agents of the Federal Bureau of Investigation have routinely informed subjects of their right to refuse consent, when they request consent to search. The reported cases in which the police have informed subjects of their right to refuse consent show, also, that the information can be given without disrupting the casual flow of events. What evidence there is, then, rather strongly suggests that nothing disastrous would happen if the police, before requesting consent, informed the subject that he had a right to refuse consent and that his refusal would be respected.

I must conclude with some reluctance that when the Court speaks of practicality, what it really is talking of is the continued ability of the police to capitalize on the ignorance of citizens so as to accomplish by subterfuge what they could not achieve by relying only on the knowing relinquishment of constitutional rights. Of course it would be "practical" for the police to ignore the commands of the Fourth Amendment, if by practicality we mean that more criminals will be apprehended, even though the constitutional rights of innocent people also go by the board. But such a practical advantage is achieved only at the cost of permitting the police to disregard the limitations that the Constitution places on their behavior, a cost that a constitutional democracy cannot long absorb.

I find nothing in the opinion of the Court to dispel my belief that . . . under many circumstances a reasonable person might read an officer's "May I" as the courteous expression of a demand backed by force of law. [In] most cases, in my view . . . consent is ordinarily given as acquiescence in an implicit claim of authority to search. Permitting searches in such circumstances, without any assurance at all that the subject of the search knew that, by his consent, he was relinquishing his constitutional rights, is something that I cannot believe is sanctioned by the Constitution.

The proper resolution of this case turns, I believe, on a realistic assessment of the nature of the interchange between citizens and the police. . . . Although the Court's says it "cannot agree," the holding today confines the protection of the Fourth Amendment against searches con-

ducted without probable cause to the sophisticated, the knowledgeable, and, I might add, the few. The Court's half-hearted defense, that lack of knowledge is to be "taken into account," rings rather hollow, in light of the apparent import of the opinion that even a subject who proves his lack of knowledge may nonetheless have consented "voluntarily," under the Court's peculiar definition of voluntariness. In the final analysis, the Court now sanctions a game of blindman's buff, in which the police always have the upper hand, for the sake of nothing more than the convenience of the police. But the guarantees of the Fourth Amendment were never intended to shrink before such an ephemeral and changeable interest. The Framers of the Fourth Amendment struck the balance against this sort of convenience and in favor of certain basic civil rights. It is not for this Court to restrike that balance because of its own views of the needs of law enforcement officers. I fear that that is the effect of the Court's decision today. . . .

Questions

1. State the elements of the voluntariness test created by the U.S. Supreme Court.

2. List all the facts and circumstances relevant to deciding whether Clyde Bustamonte consented to the search of the car.

3. Describe the Court's application of the voluntariness test to consent in the case.

4. Explain why the Court says there's a fundamental difference between rights guaranteeing a fair trial and the rights against searches and seizures.

5. According to Justice Marshall, do individuals ever voluntarily consent to police requests, or are all police requests polite orders? Do you agree with Justice Marshall? Defend your answer.

6. State the elements of the waiver test favored by Justice Marshall.

7. Apply the majority voluntariness and the dissent's waiver test to the facts of the consent in the case.

8. Consider the consent form used by the St. Paul, Minnesota, Police Department in Figure 6.1. If Bustamonte had signed this form, would his consent have been voluntary? Why or why not? Would it matter if the officer just handed the form to him without explaining its importance? Explain your answer.

◆   ◆   ◆

EXPLORING CONSENT SEARCHES FURTHER

 Go to the Criminal Procedure 6e CD to read the full text versions of the cases featured here.

1. Was Consent Voluntary When Given While in Handcuffs and After Promises and Threats?

FACTS

Secret Service agents had information that Abraham Ceballos and Efrian Adames were counterfeiting U.S. currency. After a number of agents entered the P & J Printing Company where Ceballos worked, they handcuffed and escorted him out. Later, they advised him of his right to remain silent. Ceballos was taken to the field office and questioned. The agents warned him of the seriousness of a counterfeiting offense and threatened to get a search warrant unless he consented to a search of his apartment. They offered to help Ceballos obtain low bail and retain his job if he cooperated. After a couple of hours, Ceballos consented to a search of his apartment. At the apartment, Ceballos located counterfeit plates and surrendered them to the agents. He was taken back to the field office, whereupon he and Adames were indicted on counterfeiting and conspiracy charges.

Did Ceballos voluntarily consent to the search of his apartment?

DECISION AND REASONS

Yes, according to the U.S. Second Circuit of Appeals:

> [T]he agents forcibly removed Ceballos from his place of work in handcuffs. There is also no question that the agents sought to persuade Ceballos to consent to a search and to confess. They warned him of the disruption to his household of execution of a court-ordered search warrant. They promised him aid in obtaining low bail and retaining his job if he cooperated.

> Nonetheless, the totality of the circumstances suggest that Ceballos' consent to search...was voluntarily given. The record indicates that the only use of force was in connection with the arrest. Thereafter the agents gave Ceballos a *Miranda* warning. They questioned him at their field office for a couple of hours before he consented to the search....We find that the warnings made and promises offered by the agents did not overbear Ceballos' free will.

U.S. v. Ceballos, 812 F.2d 42 (2d Cir. 1987)

2. Was Consent Voluntary When Given After the Trooper Asked to Search the Stopped Car?

FACTS

This case arose on a stretch of Interstate 70 north of Dayton, Ohio, where the posted speed limit was 45 miles per hour because of construction. Robert D. Robinette was clocked at 69 miles per hour as he drove his car along this stretch of road, and he was stopped by Deputy Roger Newsome of the Montgomery County Sheriff's office. Newsome asked for and was handed Robinette's driver's license, and he ran a computer check, which indicated that Robinette had no previous violations. Newsome then asked Robinette to step out of his car, turned on his mounted video camera, issued a verbal warning to Robinette, and returned his license.

At this point, Newsome asked, "One question before you get gone: Are you carrying any illegal contraband in your car? Any weapons of any kind, drugs, anything like that?" Robinette answered "no" to these questions, after which Deputy Newsome asked if he could search the car. Robinette consented. In the car, Deputy Newsome discovered a small amount of marijuana and, in a film container, a pill that was later determined to be methylenedioxymethamphetamine (MDMA). Robinette was then arrested and charged with knowing possession of a controlled substance, MDMA, in violation of Ohio Rev.Code Ann. § 2925.11(A) (1993). Did Robinette voluntarily consent to the search?

DECISION AND REASONS

Yes, said the U.S. Supreme Court:

> We have long held that the "touchstone of the Fourth Amendment is reasonableness." Reasonableness, in turn, is measured in objective terms by examining the totality of the circumstances. In applying this test we have consistently eschewed bright-line rules, instead emphasizing the fact-specific nature of the reasonableness inquiry.... In *Schneckloth v. Bustamonte*, 412 U.S. 218 (1973), it was argued that such a consent could not be valid unless the defendant knew that he had a right to refuse the request. We rejected this argument: "While knowledge of the right to refuse consent is one factor to be taken into account, the government need not establish such knowledge as the sine qua non of an effective consent." And just as it "would be thoroughly impractical to impose on the normal consent search the detailed requirements of an effective warning," so too would it be unrealistic to require police officers to always inform detainees that they are free to go before a consent to search may be deemed voluntary.
>
> *Ohio v. Robinette*, 117 S.Ct. 417 (1996)

The Scope of Consent

How far can officers go in searching after they get permission to search? Only as far as the person who gave it consented to. But, how far is that? As far as the person who gave it intended the search to be, or as far as the officer believes the consent goes? According to the U.S. Supreme Court, the consent is as broad as the officers reasonably believe it to be. In *Florida v. Jimeno* (1991), officers asked for permission to search Jimeno's "car." He agreed. The police searched not only the car itself but also a brown paper bag found in the trunk of the car. (The officer found drugs in the paper bag.) The U.S. Supreme Court upheld the reasonableness of the search. According to the Court, "The Fourth Amendment is satisfied when, under the circumstances, it is objectively reasonable for the officer to believe that the scope of the suspect's consent permitted him to open a particular container within the automobile" (248–249).

The scope of consent searches is a major issue in so-called crotch searches, a tactic used in drug law enforcement. Specially trained officers who patrol bus stations, airports, and railway stations approach people with no reasonable suspicion. They get into some light conversation and then ask, "Do you mind if I search you?" If the people agree, the officers immediately pat down their crotch area. The U.S. Supreme

Court hasn't decided whether consent to search "you" includes searching the genital area, especially if the search occurs in the public areas of busy airports, bus stations, and railway stations. The U.S. Circuit Courts are divided. Some say consent to search "you" includes the groin area. Others say officers have to ask specifically, "Can I search your genital area?" The District of Columbia Circuit Court analyzed the reasonableness of consent crotch searches in *U.S. v. Rodney* (1992).

CASE	*Did He Consent to a Search of His Crotch?*

United States v. Rodney
956 F.2d 295 (C.A.D.C. 1992)

Dylan Rodney pleaded guilty to possession with intent to distribute crack cocaine. After the court denied his motion to suppress, Rodney appealed. The court of appeals affirmed before WALD, BADER-GINSBERG, and THOMAS, JJ.

THOMAS, J.

FACTS

...On February 17, 1990, Dylan Rodney stepped off a bus that had arrived in Washington, D.C., from New York City. As Rodney left the bus station, Detective Vance Beard, dressed in plainclothes and carrying a concealed weapon, approached him from behind. A second officer waited nearby. Beard displayed identification and asked if Rodney would talk to him. Rodney agreed. Beard asked Rodney whether he lived in either Washington or New York. Rodney replied that he lived in Florida, but had come to Washington to try to find his wife. She lived on Georgia Avenue, Rodney said, although he was unable to identify any more precise location. Beard asked Rodney whether he was carrying drugs in his travel bag. After Rodney said no, Beard obtained permission to search the bag. As he did so, the other officer advanced to within about five feet of Rodney. The search failed to turn up any contraband.

Beard then asked Rodney whether he was carrying drugs on his person. After Rodney again said no, Beard requested permission to conduct a body search. Rodney said "Sure" and raised his arms above his head. Beard placed his hands on Rodney's ankles and, in one sweeping motion, ran them up the inside of Rodney's legs. As he passed over the crotch area, Beard felt small, rock-like objects. Rodney exclaimed: "That's me!" Detecting otherwise, Beard placed Rodney under arrest. At the police station, Beard unzipped Rodney's pants and retrieved a

plastic bag containing a rock-like substance that was identified as cocaine base. Rodney was charged with possession and intent to distribute.

Rodney moved to suppress the crack. Rodney argued... that...the consent did not include a search of his crotch area....The DC District Court...denied the motion, finding that Rodney had "given his consent voluntarily to the search of his person and belongings." Rodney entered a conditional guilty plea, reserving the right to withdraw it if this court [DC Circuit] reversed the denial of his suppression motion.

OPINION

Rodney first contends that the District Court erred in finding that his consent to the body search was voluntary, and therefore not prohibited by the Fourth Amendment. In determining the voluntariness of a consent, a district court must examine "the totality of all the surrounding circumstances—both the characteristics of the accused and the details of the interrogation." *Schneckloth v. Bustamonte*, 412 U.S. 218 (1973). Relevant factors include: the youth of the accused; his lack of education; or his low intelligence; the lack of any advice to the accused of his constitutional rights; the length of detention; the repeated and prolonged nature of the questioning; and the use of physical punishment such as the deprivation of food or sleep. We review only for clear error....

Rodney...argues that...he did not consent to the search of his crotch area. A consensual search cannot exceed the scope of the consent. The scope of the consent is measured by a test of "'objective' reasonableness": it depends on how broadly a reasonable observer would have interpreted the consent under the circumstances. *Florida v. Jimeno*, 500 U.S. 248 (1991). Here, Rodney clearly consented to a search of his body for drugs. We conclude that a reasonable person would have understood that consent to encompass the search undertaken here.

Under *Jimeno*, "the scope of a search is generally defined by its expressed object." In this case, Rodney authorized a search for drugs. Dealers frequently hide drugs near their genitals. Indeed, Beard testified that his colleagues make up to 75 percent of their drug recoveries from around the crotch area. For these reasons, we conclude that a request to conduct a body search for drugs reasonably includes a request to conduct some search of that area.

Although *Jimeno* states the test "generally" used to determine the scope of a consent to search, we doubt that the Supreme Court would have us apply that test unflinchingly in the context of body searches. At some point, we suspect, a body search would become so intrusive that we would not infer consent to it from a generalized consent, regardless of the stated object of the search. For example, although drugs can be hidden virtually anywhere on or in one's person, a generalized consent to a body search for drugs surely does not validate everything up to and including a search of body cavities.

The search undertaken here, however, was not unusually intrusive, at least relative to body searches generally. It involved a continuous sweeping motion over Rodney's outer garments, including the trousers covering the crotch area. In this respect, the search was no more invasive than the typical pat-down frisk for weapons described by the Supreme Court over two decades ago:

> The officer must feel with sensitive fingers every portion of the [defendant's] body. A thorough search must be made of the defendant's arms and armpits, waistline and back, the groin and area about the testicles, and entire surface of the legs down to the feet. *Terry v. Ohio*, 392 U.S. 1 (1968)

We conclude that the frisk of Rodney's fully clothed body involved nothing so intrusive, relative to body searches generally, as to require a separate consent above and beyond the consent to a body search that Rodney had given voluntarily.... We hold only that Rodney's generalized consent authorized the kind of "traditional frisk search" undertaken here, and we express no view on questions involving...consensual searches of a more intrusive nature.... We conclude that Rodney voluntarily consented to a search of his body for drugs, which encompassed the frisk undertaken here....

Accordingly, the judgment of conviction is AFFIRMED.

DISSENT

WALD, J.

I disagree with the panel ruling that a citizen's consent to a search of his "person" on a public thoroughfare, given in response to a police request made in the absence of probable cause or even "reasonable suspicion" to believe that he has committed a crime, encompasses authority to conduct a palpation of the person's genital area in an effort to detect drugs. Because I believe that in this case such an intimate and intrusive search exceeded the scope of any general permission to search granted, I would find the search nonconsensual and the drugs seized inadmissible....

...The issue before us is whether a person against whom there is no articulable suspicion of wrongdoing who is asked to submit to a body search on a public street expects that search to include manual touching of the genital area. I do not believe any such expectation exists at the time a cooperative citizen consents to an on-the-street search. Rather, that citizen anticipates only those kinds of searches that unfortunately have become a part of our urban living, searches ranging from airport security personnel passing a hand-held magnometer over a person's body, to having a person empty his pockets, and subject himself to a patting-down of sides, shoulders, and back. Any search that includes touching genital areas or breasts would not normally be expected to occur in public.

In all aspects of our society, different parts of the body are subject to very different levels of privacy and expectations about intrusions. We readily bare our heads, arms, legs, backs, even midriffs, in public, but, except in the most unusual circumstances, certainly not our breasts or genitals. On the streets, in elevators, and on public transportation, we often touch, inadvertently or even casually, each others' hands, arms, shoulders, and backs, but it is a serious affront, and sometimes even a crime, to intentionally touch another's intimate body parts without explicit permission; and while we feel free to discuss other people's hair, facial features, weight, height, noses or ears, similar discussions about genitals or breasts are not acceptable. Thus in any consensual encounter, it is not "objectively reasonable" for a citizen desiring to cooperate with the police in a public place to expect that permission to search her body includes feeling, even "fully clothed," the most private areas of her body. Under our social norms that requires "special permission," given with notice of the areas to be searched....

The mere fact that drug couriers often hide their stash in the crotch area [can't] justify the search of such area without some elementary form of notice to the citizen that such an offensive procedure is about to take place. The ordinary citizen's expectation of privacy in intimate parts of her body is certainly well enough established to merit a particularized request for consent to such an intimate search in public....

A general consent to a search of a citizen's "person" in a public place does not include consent to touch the genital or breast areas. The majority today upholds a practice that allows police under the rubric of a general consent to conduct intimate body searches, and in so doing defeats the legitimate expectations of privacy that ordinary citizens should retain during cooperative exchanges with the police on the street. I believe the search was impermissible.

Questions

1. State the specific rule the majority adopted to cover the scope of consent searches of a person.

2. State exactly what the officers asked Rodney to consent to.

3. Assume you're Rodney's lawyer. Relying on the facts as they're outlined in the case, argue that Rodney didn't consent to a search of his crotch.

4. Now assume you're the prosecutor, and argue that Rodney voluntarily consented to the search of his crotch.

5. Now assume you are the judge. Rule on the consent and its scope.

Withdrawing Consent

A police officer saw Frank Martinez sitting in his car at 2:00 A.M. in a neighborhood where frequent narcotics arrests were made. The officer came up to the car and asked Martinez for identification. Martinez showed the officer identification. When the officer asked him if he could "look around inside the car," Martinez agreed. The officer searched the inside of the car, including the glove compartment. Then, he asked if he could "look in the trunk." Martinez opened the trunk, and the officer started to go through the trunk. Up to this point, the search had taken about 15 minutes, and Martinez had been cooperative. But, now he told the officer to stop the search. The officer continued the search anyway even though he testified, "I didn't know what I was looking for." He eventually found methamphetamine.

Did Martinez's withdrawal of consent invalidate the search and seizure of the drugs? The answer's far from clear. Conventional wisdom among police officers argues against taking back consent. The wisdom's based on the assumption that guilty people will consent just to throw officers off the track. Then, if their ploy starts to fail because the officers are about to uncover incriminating evidence, contraband, or weapons, guilty people will withdraw their consent. Despite this argument, the *Model Code of Pre-Arraignment Procedure* (American Law Institute 1975) includes a withdrawal provision:

> Section 24.3(3) Withdrawal or Limitation of Consent. A consent . . . may be withdrawn or limited at any time prior to the completion of the search, and if so withdrawn or limited, the search . . . shall cease, or be restricted to the new limits, as the case may be. Things discovered and subject to seizure prior to such withdrawal or limitation of consent shall remain subject to seizure despite such change or termination of the consent. (151)

Case authority on this point is limited and divided, but, in *People v. Martinez* (1968), the court said:

> The serious question presented in the case . . . is whether a voluntary consent to a search . . . may be withdrawn before the search is completed. Our answer . . . is . . . yes. We find [no] reason to hold that a consent, once given, may not be withdrawn. It is true that the contrary view has been expressed. We do not believe that this is the present law, particularly in

TABLE 6.1
Examples of Valid Third-Party Consent Searches

One lover consents to a search of the room shared with the other lover.

One roommate consents to a search of an entire apartment, including the other roommate's separate bedroom.

A homeowner consents to a search of the room that a houseguest occupies.

One joint user of a duffel bag consents to a search of the shared duffel bag.

A high-school principal consents to a search of high-school students' lockers.

A college dean permits a search of students' rooms for marijuana.

---

view of the explicit statement in the *Miranda* case [Chapter 8] that a defendant consenting to answer police questioning without a lawyer may withdraw such waiver at any time. We see no reason, in this respect, to distinguish between withdrawal of waiver of legal representation during investigation and withdrawal of consent to search once given. We, therefore, reverse the judgment.

Third-Party Consent Searches

Can you consent to a search of your roommate's bedroom? It depends. Sometimes, one person can consent to a search for another person; this is called a **third-party consent search.** Authority to search for others usually comes up in common relationships: spouse–spouse, parent–child, roommate–roommate, employer–employee, landlord–tenant, and school administrator–student. But, these relationships don't *automatically* give one person the authority to consent for the other person. For example, consent to search given out of spite can invalidate the consent. Also, employers can't consent to searches of their employees' desks where employees have a reasonable expectation of privacy. So, a principal couldn't consent to searching a guidance counselor's desk that was locked; was located in the counselor's office; and contained psychological profiles and other confidential student records. On the other hand, a factory manager can consent to searching items on top of an employee's workbench. Janitors, clerks, and drivers can't consent to searches of their employers' premises, but managers can. (Table 6.1 lists examples of valid third-party consent searches.)

There is both an objective and a subjective rule to decide whether one person can consent to a search for someone else.

1. *Actual authority (objective) third-party consent.* Only someone who *in fact* has the *legal* authority to consent for someone else can give law enforcement officers permission to search that other person's house or stuff.

2. *Apparent authority (subjective) third-party consent.* Consent given by someone who law enforcement officers *reasonably believe* (but who in fact *doesn't*) have the authority to consent for another makes the search reasonable.

Federal and state courts used to be split over which of these two tests to adopt. The U.S. Supreme settled the question of what the minimum standard required by the Fourth Amendment is in *Illinois v. Rodriguez* (1990).

Illinois v. Rodriguez
497 U.S. 177 (1990)

Edward Rodriguez who was charged with possession of a controlled substance with intent to deliver moved to suppress seized evidence. The Circuit Court, Cook County, Illinois, granted the motion, and the People appealed. The Appellate Court affirmed. The People petitioned for leave to appeal. The Supreme Court denied the petition without published opinion. The People petitioned for a writ of certiorari. The Supreme Court granted the writ and reversed and remanded.

SCALIA, J., joined by REHNQUIST, C.J., and WHITE, BLACKMUN, O'CONNOR, and KENNEDY, JJ.

FACTS

On July 26, 1985, police were summoned to the residence of Dorothy Jackson on South Wolcott in Chicago. They were met by Ms. Jackson's daughter, Gail Fischer, who showed signs of a severe beating. She told the officers that she had been assaulted by Edward Rodriguez earlier that day in an apartment on South California. Fischer stated that Rodriguez was then asleep in the apartment, and she consented to travel there with the police in order to unlock the door with her key so that the officers could enter and arrest him. During this conversation, Fischer several times referred to the apartment on South California as "our" apartment, and said that she had clothes and furniture there. It is unclear whether she indicated that she currently lived at the apartment, or only that she used to live there.

The police officers drove to the apartment on South California, accompanied by Fischer. They did not obtain an arrest warrant for Rodriguez, nor did they seek a search warrant for the apartment. At the apartment, Fischer unlocked the door with her key and gave the officers permission to enter. They moved through the door into the living room, where they observed in plain view drug paraphernalia and containers filled with white powder that they believed (correctly, as later analysis showed) to be cocaine. They proceeded to the bedroom, where they found Rodriguez asleep and discovered additional containers of white powder in two open attaché cases. The officers arrested Rodriguez and seized the drugs and related paraphernalia.

Rodriguez was charged with possession of a controlled substance with intent to deliver. He moved to suppress all evidence seized at the time of his arrest, claiming that Fischer had vacated the apartment several weeks earlier and had no authority to consent to the entry. The Cook County Circuit Court granted the motion, holding that at the time she consented to the entry Fischer did not have common authority over the apartment. The Court concluded that Fischer was not a "usual resident" but rather an "infrequent visitor" at the apartment on South California, based upon its findings that Fischer's name was not on the lease, that she did not contribute to the rent, that she was not allowed to invite others to the apartment on her own, that she did not have access to the apartment when Rodriguez was away, and that she had moved some of her possessions from the apartment. The Circuit Court also rejected the State's contention that, even if Fischer did not possess common authority over the premises, there was no Fourth Amendment violation if the police reasonably believed at the time of their entry that Fischer possessed the authority to consent. The Appellate Court of Illinois affirmed the Circuit Court in all respects. The Illinois Supreme Court denied the State's petition for leave to appeal, and we granted certiorari.

OPINION

The Fourth Amendment prohibits the warrantless entry of a person's home, whether to make an arrest or to search for specific objects. The prohibition does not apply, however, to situations in which voluntary consent has been obtained, either from the individual whose property is searched (*Schneckloth v. Bustamonte*, 412 U.S. 218 (1973), or from a third party who possesses common authority over the premises (*United States v. Matlock*, 415 U.S., at 171). The State of Illinois contends that that exception applies in the present case.

As we stated in *Matlock, supra,* "common authority" rests "on mutual use of the property by persons having joint access or control...." The burden of establishing that common authority rests upon the State. On the basis of this record, it is clear that burden was not sustained. The evidence showed that although Fischer, with her two small children, had lived with Rodriguez beginning in December 1984, she had moved out on July 1, 1985, almost a month before the search at issue here, and had gone to live with her mother. She took her and her children's clothing with her, though leaving behind some furniture and household effects. During the period after July 1 she sometimes spent the night at Rodriguez's apartment, but never invited her friends there, and never went there herself when he was not home. Her name was not on the lease nor did she contribute to the rent. She had a key to the apartment, which she said at trial she had taken without Rodriguez's knowledge (though she testified at the preliminary hearing that Rodriguez had given her the key). On these facts the State has not established that, with respect to the South California apartment, Fischer had "joint access or control for most purposes." To the contrary, the Appellate Court's determination of no common authority over the apartment was obviously correct.

The State contends that, even if Fischer did not in fact have authority to give consent, it suffices to validate the entry that the law enforcement officers reasonably believed she did. . . . Rodriguez asserts that permitting a reasonable belief of common authority to validate an entry would cause a defendant's Fourth Amendment rights to be "vicariously waived." We disagree.

We have been unyielding in our insistence that a defendant's waiver of his trial rights cannot be given effect unless it is "knowing" and "intelligent." We would assuredly not permit, therefore, evidence seized in violation of the Fourth Amendment to be introduced [at trial] on the basis of a trial court's mere "reasonable belief"—derived from statements by unauthorized persons—that the defendant has waived his objection. But one must make a distinction between, on the one hand, trial rights that derive from the violation of constitutional guarantees and, on the other hand, the nature of those constitutional guarantees themselves.

What Rodriguez is assured by the trial right of the exclusionary rule . . . is that no evidence seized in violation of the Fourth Amendment will be introduced at his trial unless he consents. What he is assured by the Fourth Amendment itself, however, is not that no government search of his house will occur unless he consents; but that no such search will occur that is "unreasonable." There are various elements that can make a search of a person's house "reasonable"—one of which is the consent of the person or his cotenant. The essence of Rodriguez's argument is that we should impose upon this element a requirement that we have not imposed upon other elements that regularly compel government officers to exercise judgment regarding the facts: namely, the requirement that their judgment be not only responsible but correct.

The fundamental objective that alone validates all unconsented government searches is the seizure of persons who have committed or are about to commit crimes, or of evidence related to crimes. But "reasonableness," with respect to this necessary element, does not demand that the

government be factually correct in its assessment that that is what a search will produce. . . . What is demanded . . . is not that [officers] always be correct, but that they always be reasonable. As we put it in *Brinegar v. United States*, 338 U.S. 160 (1949):

> Because many situations which confront officers in the course of executing their duties are more or less ambiguous, room must be allowed for some mistakes on their part. But the mistakes must be those of reasonable men, acting on facts leading sensibly to their conclusions of probability.

We see no reason to depart from this general rule with respect to facts bearing upon the authority to consent to a search. Whether the basis for such authority exists is the sort of recurring factual question to which law enforcement officials must be expected to apply their judgment; and all the Fourth Amendment requires is that they answer it reasonably. The Constitution is no more violated when officers enter without a warrant because they reasonably (though erroneously) believe that the person who has consented to their entry is a resident of the premises, than it is violated when they enter without a warrant because they reasonably (though erroneously) believe they are in pursuit of a violent felon who is about to escape. . . .

What we hold today does not suggest that law enforcement officers may always accept a person's invitation to enter premises. Even when the invitation is accompanied by an explicit assertion that the person lives there, the surrounding circumstances could conceivably be such that a reasonable person would doubt its truth and not act upon it without further inquiry. As with other factual determinations bearing upon search and seizure, determination of consent to enter must "be judged against an objective standard: would the facts available to the officer at the moment . . . 'warrant a man of reasonable caution in the belief'" that the consenting party had authority over the premises? *Terry v. Ohio*, 392 U.S. 1, 21–22, 88 S.Ct. 1868, 1880, 20 L.Ed.2d 889 (1968). If not, then warrantless entry without further inquiry is unlawful unless authority actually exists. But if so, the search is valid.

In the present case, the Appellate Court found it unnecessary to determine whether the officers reasonably believed that Fischer had the authority to consent, because it ruled as a matter of law that a reasonable belief could not validate the entry. Since we find that ruling to be in error, we remand for consideration of that question. The judgment of the Illinois Appellate Court is REVERSED, and the case is REMANDED for further proceedings not inconsistent with this opinion.

DISSENT

MARSHALL, J., joined by BRENNAN and STEVENS, JJ. Dorothy Jackson summoned police officers to her house to report that her daughter Gail Fischer had been beaten. Fischer told police that Ed Rodriguez, her boyfriend, was her assaulter. During an interview with Fischer, one of the officers asked if Rodriguez dealt in narcotics. Fischer did not respond. Fischer did agree, however, to the officers' request to let them into Rodriguez's apartment so that they could arrest him for battery. The police, without a warrant and despite the absence of an exigency, entered Rodriguez's home to arrest him. As a result of their entry, the police discovered narcotics that the State subsequently sought to introduce in a drug prosecution against Rodriguez.

The Court holds that the warrantless entry into Rodriguez's home was nonetheless valid if the officers reasonably believed that Fischer had authority to consent. The majority's defense of this position rests on a misconception of the basis for third-party consent searches. That such searches do not give rise to claims of constitutional violations rests not on the premise that they are "reasonable" under the Fourth Amendment, but on the premise that a person may voluntarily limit his expectation of privacy by allowing others to exercise authority over his possessions. Thus, an individual's decision to permit another "joint access [to] or control [over the property] for most purposes," *United States v. Matlock*, 415 U.S. 164, 171, n. 7, 94 S.Ct. 988, 993, n. 7, 39 L.Ed.2d 242 (1974), limits that individual's reasonable expectation of privacy and to that extent limits his Fourth Amendment protections. If an individual has not so limited his expectation of privacy, the police may not dispense with the safeguards established by the Fourth Amendment.

...We have recognized that the "physical entry of the home is the chief evil against which the wording of the Fourth Amendment is directed." We have further held that "a search or seizure carried out on a suspect's premises without a warrant is per se unreasonable, unless the police can show that it falls within one of a carefully defined set of exceptions."...The Court has often heard, and steadfastly rejected, the invitation to carve out further exceptions to the warrant requirement for searches of the home because of the burdens on police investigation and prosecution of crime. Our rejection of such claims is not due to a lack of appreciation of the difficulty and importance of effective law enforcement, but rather to our firm commitment to "the view of those who wrote the Bill of Rights that the privacy of a person's home and property may not be totally sacrificed in the name of maximum simplicity in enforcement of the criminal law."

The weighty constitutional interest in preventing unauthorized intrusions into the home overrides any law enforcement interest in relying on the reasonable but potentially mistaken belief that a third party has authority to consent to such a search or seizure.... Against this law enforcement interest in expediting arrests is "the right of a man to retreat into his own home and there be free from unreasonable governmental intrusion."

To be sure, in some cases in which police officers reasonably rely on a third party's consent, the consent will prove valid, no intrusion will result, and the police will have been spared the inconvenience of securing a warrant. But in other cases, such as this one, the authority claimed by the third party will be false.... The concerns of expediting police work and avoiding paperwork are never very convincing reasons and, in these circumstances, certainly are not enough to by-pass the constitutional requirement. In this case, no suspect was fleeing or likely to take flight. The search was of permanent premises, not of a movable vehicle. No evidence or contraband was threatened with removal or destruction.... If the officers in this case were excused from the constitutional duty of presenting their evidence to a magistrate, it is difficult to think of a case in which it should be required.

Unlike searches conducted pursuant to the recognized exceptions to the warrant requirement, see supra, at 2802–2803, third-party consent searches are not based on an exigency and therefore serve no compelling social goal. Police officers, when faced with the choice of relying on consent by a third party or securing a warrant, should secure a warrant and must therefore accept the risk of error should they instead choose to rely on consent.

...A search conducted pursuant to an officer's reasonable but mistaken belief that a third party had authority to consent is thus on an entirely different constitutional footing from one based on the consent of a third party who in fact has such authority. Even if the officers reasonably believed that Fischer had authority to consent, she did not, and Rodriguez's expectation of privacy was therefore undiminished. Rodriguez accordingly can challenge the warrantless intrusion into his home as a violation of the Fourth Amendment. This conclusion flows directly from *Stoner v. California*, 376 U.S. 483 (1964). There, the Court required the suppression of evidence seized in reliance on a hotel clerk's consent to a warrantless search of a guest's room. The Court reasoned that the guest's right to be free of unwarranted intrusion "was a right...which only [he] could waive by word or deed, either directly or through an agent." Accordingly, the Court rejected resort to "unrealistic doctrines of 'apparent authority'" as a means of upholding the search to which the guest had not consented....

Our cases demonstrate that third-party consent searches are free from constitutional challenge only to the extent that they rest on consent by a party empowered to do so. The majority's conclusion to the contrary ignores the legitimate expectations of privacy on which individuals are entitled to rely. That a person who allows another joint access to his property thereby limits his expectation of privacy does not justify trampling the rights of a person who has not similarly relinquished any of his privacy expectation.

Questions

1. List all the facts relevant to determining whether the search in this case was a lawful search.

2. How does the majority define third-party consent? How does the dissent define it?

3. Why did the Supreme Court hold that Fischer's consent made the search of Rodriguez's apartment a lawful search?

4. Do you agree that someone can consent for another even when the person giving consent doesn't have the authority to do so?

5. Do you agree that if you share your property with someone else you "assume the risk" that the other person may give the police permission to search the property?

6. What arguments does the dissent make to reject the validity of Fischer's consent to search Rodriguez's apartment?

7. How do the majority and dissent balance differently Rodriguez's rights and law enforcement's needs for consent searches? How would you balance the interests in the case?

 Go to Exercise 6-4 on the Criminal Procedure 6e CD to learn more about *Illinois v. Rodriguez.*

◆ STATE CONSTITUTIONAL LAW ◆

Did the Grandfather Have Authority to Consent to the Search of His Grandson's Apartment?

State v. McLees
994 P.2d 683 (Mont. 2000)

Travis McLees was convicted in the District Court, Madison County, on his plea of guilty to two counts of burglary, two counts of theft, and one count of criminal mischief, and he appealed. The Supreme Court reversed and remanded.

HUNT, J.

FACTS

On November 25, 1995, the Madison County Sheriff's Department received reports of two burglaries and thefts. Chief Deputy Sheriff, Merlin Ehlers (Deputy Ehlers) investigated the break-ins, one at the Harrison school, the other at the studio of Michelle Walker in Harrison, Montana. With some reason to suspect Travis McLees, Ehlers went to Travis's grandfather Earl McLees (Earl) who Travis was living with. Earl told Deputy Ehlers that Travis was living in the apartment which Earl owned next door. Earl told Deputy Ehlers that

Travis had slept in the apartment the night before but had left that morning. Deputy Ehlers didn't have a search warrant but asked Earl if he could look in the apartment for possible evidence of one of the burglaries. Earl and Deputy Ehlers went to the front door of the apartment, but found it locked. Because Earl didn't have a key to the front door, he and Deputy Ehlers went around to the shop which adjoined the apartment from the rear; both entered the apartment through an unlocked door leading from the shop to the apartment.

Upon entering the apartment, Deputy Ehlers noticed some drug paraphernalia and what he believed to be items taken from the Harrison school. Ehlers then telephoned the Gallatin County Sheriff's Office to have them send out an officer from that jurisdiction. Three Forks Marshall Keith King (Officer King) responded to the scene and entered the apartment. At that time, Officer King and Deputy Ehlers discussed whether they should have a search warrant. Officer King returned to his office in Three Forks where he called the Gallatin County Attorney's office and received the opinion that based on Officer King's description of the situation, a consent search would be sufficient. During Officer King's absence, Deputy Ehlers stayed at the apartment to secure the site.

Officer King returned to the apartment with a consent-to-search form, which Earl signed. Deputy

Ehlers and Officer King then searched and photographed the apartment and seized several items of evidence. A few days later, Deputy Ehlers returned without a warrant, and Earl again allowed him to enter the apartment. A warrant for Travis's arrest was issued on November 30, 1995, and Travis was arrested several months later. Reserving the right to appeal the denial of his motion to suppress, Travis pleaded guilty to two counts of burglary, two counts of theft, and one count of criminal mischief.

OPINION

[The court found Earl didn't have actual authority to consent for Travis.] The State contends that even if Earl did not have authority to give consent, representations made by Earl to the officers at the time of the search support a finding that the officers believed Earl had authority to consent, even if he did not. They maintain that under the doctrine of "apparent authority," a search is valid if consent is given by a person who police reasonably, but mistakenly, believe has joint authority over the premises. This issue was first addressed by the United States Supreme Court in *Illinois v. Rodriguez* (1990), 497 U.S. 177. [The U.S. Supreme Court ruled that apparent authority was enough to satisfy the Fourth Amendment reasonableness requirement.]...

In Montana, however, we analyze such a situation in light of our citizens' enhanced right to privacy. "Except in certain carefully defined classes of cases, a search of property without proper consent is 'unreasonable' unless it has been authorized by a valid search warrant."... Allowing warrantless searches of an individual's home without the consent of someone authorized to give it... [except in emergencies] would fly in the face of this protection. Indeed, an invasion of privacy is no less of an "invasion" if the governmental officials are "reasonable" in their mistaken belief that the third party possesses the authority to consent. This is because, regardless of whether the police acted in good faith, the individual's "privacy" is still invaded when the police search his or her personal belongings without permission.

REVERSED and REMANDED.

Vehicle Searches

The vehicle exception to the warrant requirement began with a 1789 act of Congress. This was the same Congress that had adopted the Fourth Amendment, so the hated British general warrants were fresh in their minds. Despite these bitter memories, the 1789 statute authorized law enforcement officers without a warrant "to enter any ship or vessel, in which they shall have reason to suspect any goods, wares or merchandise subject to duty shall be concealed; and therein to search for, seize, and secure any such goods, wares or merchandise."

Ships were one thing; homes were quite another. Officers who suspected people were hiding taxable stuff in their houses had to get a warrant based on probable cause before they searched. Why the difference between boats and houses? Necessity: "Goods in course of transportation and concealed in a movable vessel...readily could be put out of reach of a search warrant." Later, the U.S. Supreme Court added another reason for the vehicle exception: the reduced expectation of privacy in vehicles.

Throughout the nineteenth and twentieth centuries, Congress continued to enact search and seizure statutes with a vehicle exception. In 1815, Congress authorized officers "not only to board and search vessels within their own and adjoining districts, but also to stop, search, and examine any vehicle, beast, or person on which or whom they should suspect there was merchandise which was subject to duty." In 1917, Congress authorized officers in the Indian country

having reason to suspect or being informed that any white person or Indian is about to introduce, or has introduced, any spirituous liquor or wine into the Indian country, in violation of law, may cause the boats, stores, packages, wagons, sleds and places of deposit of such person to be searched and if any liquor is found therein, then it, together with the vehicles, shall be seized and . . . forfeited.

And, by the Indian Appropriation Act of 1917, officers without warrants could seize and forfeit "automobiles used in introducing or attempting to introduce intoxicants into the Indian territory."

Not a single U.S. Supreme Court case ever challenged this exception until 1925 during Prohibition, when the modern history of the vehicle exception began. The landmark case *Carroll v. U.S.* (1925) reflected a fear of alcohol-related crimes during the 1920s. The fear of illegal drugs still drives the interpretation of the Fourth Amendment (as so many cases in Chapters 3 through 6 clearly demonstrate).

| CASE | *Was the Search of the Car for Liquor Reasonable?* |

Carroll v. United States
267 U.S. 132 (1925)

George Carroll and John Kiro were indicted and convicted in the U.S. District Court, Michigan Western Division, of transporting 68 quarts of whisky, gin whisky, and gin in an automobile in violation of the National Prohibition Act. Defendants moved to get their liquor back. The District Court denied the motion. The U.S. Supreme Court affirmed.

TAFT, CJ.

FACTS

The search and seizure were made by Cronenwett, Scully, and Thayer, federal prohibition agents, and one Peterson, a state officer, in December, 1921, as the car was going westward on the highway between Detroit and Grand Rapids at a point 16 miles outside of Grand Rapids. The facts leading to the search and seizure were as follows: On September 29th, Cronenwett and Scully were in an apartment in Grand Rapids. Three men came to that apartment, a man named Kurska, and the two defendants, Carroll and Kiro. Cronenwett was introduced to them as one Stafford working in the Michigan Chair Company in Grand Rapids, who wished to buy three cases of whisky. The price was fixed at $130 a case. The three men said they had to go to the east end of Grand Rapids to get the liquor and that they would be back in half or three-quarters of an hour.

They went away, and in a short time Kruska came back and said they could not get it that night, that the man who had it was not in, but that they would deliver it the next day. They had come to the apartment in an automobile known as an Oldsmobile roadster, the number of which Cronenwett then identified, as did Scully. The proposed vendors did not return the next day, and the evidence disclosed no explanation of their failure to do so. One may surmise that it was suspicion of the real character of the proposed purchaser, whom Carroll subsequently called by his first name when arrested in December following.

Cronenwett and his subordinates were engaged in patrolling the road leading from Detroit to Grand Rapids, looking for violations of the Prohibition Act. This seems to have been their regular tour of duty. On the 6th of October, Carroll and Kiro going eastward from Grand Rapids in the same Oldsmobile roadster, passed Cronenwett and Scully some distance out from Grand Rapids. Cronenwett called to Scully, who was taking lunch, that the Carroll boys had passed them going toward Detroit, and sought with Scully to catch up with them to see where they were going. The officers followed as far as East Lansing, half way to Detroit, but there lost trace of them.

On the 15th of December, some two months later, Scully and Cronenwett, on their regular tour of duty with Peterson, the state officer, were going from Grand Rapids to Ionia, on the road to Detroit, when Kiro and Carroll met and passed them in the same automobile, coming from the direction of Detroit to Grand Rapids. The government agents turned their car and followed the defendants to a point some 16 miles east of Grand Rapids, where they stopped them and searched the car. They found behind the upholstering of the seats, the filling of which had been removed, 68 bottles. These had labels on them, part purporting to be certificates of English chemists that the contents were blended Scotch whiskies, and the rest that the contents were Gordon gin made in London. When an expert witness was called to prove the contents, defendants admitted the nature of them to be whisky and gin.

When the defendants were arrested, Carroll said to Cronenwett, "Take the liquor and give us one more chance, and I will make it right with you," and he pulled out a roll of bills, of which one was for $10. Peterson and another took the two defendants and the liquor and the car to Grand Rapids, while Cronenwett, Thayer, and Scully remained on the road looking for other cars, of whose coming they had information. The officers were not anticipating that the defendants would be coming through on the highway at that particular time, but when they met them there they believed they were carrying liquor, and hence the search, seizure, and arrest.

OPINION

The constitutional and statutory provisions involved in this case include the Fourth Amendment and...the National Prohibition Act, passed to enforce the Eighteenth Amendment, which makes it unlawful to have or possess any liquor intended for use in violating the act, or which has been so used, and provides that no property rights shall exist in such liquor. A search warrant may issue and such liquor, with the containers thereof, may be seized under the warrant and be ultimately destroyed....

Section 26, title 2, under which the seizure herein was made, provides in part as follows:

When the commissioner, his assistants, inspectors, or any officer of the law shall discover any person in the act of transporting in violation of the law, intoxicating liquors in any wagon, buggy, automobile, water or air craft, or other vehicle, it shall be his duty to seize any and all intoxicating liquors found therein being transported contrary to law. Whenever intoxicating liquors transported or possessed illegally shall be seized by an officer he shall take possession of the vehicle and team or automobile, boat, air or water craft, or any other conveyance, and shall arrest any person in charge thereof.

The section then provides that the court upon conviction of the person so arrested shall order the liquor destroyed, and except for good cause shown shall order a sale by public auction of the other property seized, and that the proceeds shall be paid into the Treasury of the United States....

The guaranty of freedom from unreasonable searches and seizures by the Fourth Amendment has been construed, practically since the beginning of the government, as recognizing a necessary difference between a search of a store, dwelling house, or other structure in respect of which a proper official warrant readily may be obtained and a search of a ship, motor boat, wagon, or automobile for contraband goods, where it is not practicable to secure a warrant, because the vehicle can be quickly moved out of the locality or jurisdiction in which the warrant must be sought.

Having thus established that contraband goods concealed and illegally transported in an automobile or other vehicle may be searched for without a warrant, we come now to consider under what circumstances such search may be made. It would be intolerable and unreasonable if a prohibition agent were authorized to stop every automobile on the chance of finding liquor, and thus subject all persons lawfully using the highways to the inconvenience and indignity of such a search. Travelers may be so stopped in crossing an international boundary because of national self-protection reasonably requiring one entering the country to identify himself as entitled to come in, and his belongings as effects which may be lawfully brought in. But those lawfully within the country, entitled to use the public highways, have a right to free passage without interruption or search unless there is known to a competent official, authorized to search, probable cause for believing that their vehicles are carrying contraband or illegal merchandise.

Section 26, title 2, of the National Prohibition Act [Volstead Act]...was enacted primarily to accomplish the seizure and destruction of contraband goods; secondly, the automobile was to be forfeited; and, thirdly, the driver was to be arrested. Under section 29, title 2, of the act the latter might be punished by not more than $500 fine for the first offense, not more than $1,000 fine and 90 days' imprisonment for the second offense, and by a fine of $500 or more and by not more than 2 years' imprisonment for the third offense. Thus he is to be arrested for a misdemeanor for his first and second offenses, and for a felony if he offends the third time.

The main purpose of the act obviously was to deal with the liquor and its transportation, and to destroy it. The mere manufacture of liquor can do little to defeat the policy of the Eighteenth Amendment and the Prohibition Act, unless the forbidden product can be distributed for illegal sale and use. Section 26 was intended to reach and destroy the forbidden liquor in transportation and the provisions for forfeiture of the vehicle and the arrest of the transporter were incidental....Under section 28, title 2, of the Prohibition Act, the Commissioner of Internal Revenue, his assistants, agents and inspectors are to have the power and protection in the enforcement of the act conferred by the existing laws relating to the manufacture or sale of intoxicating liquors....

[The existing laws provide that] if an officer seizes an automobile or the liquor in it without a warrant, and the facts as subsequently developed do not justify a judgment of condemnation and forfeiture, the officer may escape costs or a suit for damages by a showing that he had reasonable or probable cause for the seizure. The measure of legality of such a seizure is therefore, that the seizing officer shall have reasonable or probable cause for believing that the automobile which he stops and seizes has contraband liquor therein which is being illegally transported....

Such a rule fulfills the guaranty of the Fourth Amendment. In cases where the securing of a warrant is reasonably practicable, it must be used and when properly supported by affidavit and issued after judicial approval protects the seizing officer against a suit for damages. In cases where seizure is impossible except without warrant, the seizing officer acts unlawfully and at his peril unless he can show the court probable cause....

The judgment is AFFIRMED.

DISSENT

MCREYNOLDS, J.

The damnable character of the "bootlegger's" business should not close our eyes to the mischief which will surely follow any attempt to destroy it by unwarranted methods. "To press forward to a great principle by breaking through every other great principle that stands in the way of its establishment; in short, to procure an eminent good by means that are unlawful, is as little consonant to private morality as to public justice." Sir William Scott, The Le Louis, 2 Dodson, 210, 257.

While quietly driving an ordinary automobile along a much frequented public road, Carroll and Kiro were arrested by federal officers without a warrant and upon mere suspicion—ill-founded, as I think. The officers then searched the machine and discovered carefully secreted whisky, which was seized and thereafter used as evidence against plaintiffs in error when on trial for transporting intoxicating liquor contrary to the Volstead Act [National Prohibition Act]. 41 Stat. 305, c. 85. They maintain that both arrest and seizure were unlawful and that use of the liquor as evidence violated their constitutional rights....

The arrest of the defendants was unauthorized, illegal, and violated the guaranty of due process given by the Fifth Amendment. The liquor offered in evidence was obtained by the search which followed this arrest and was therefore obtained in violation of their constitutional rights. Articles found upon or in the control of one lawfully arrested may be used as evidence for certain purposes, but not at all when secured by the unlawful action of a federal officer....

The facts known by the officers who arrested plaintiffs in error were wholly insufficient to create a reasonable belief that they were transporting liquor contrary to law....

The negotiation concerning three cases of whisky on September 29th was the only circumstance which could have subjected the defendants to any reasonable suspicion. No whisky was delivered, and it is not certain that they ever intended to deliver any. The arrest came 2½ months after the negotiation. Every act in the meantime is consistent with complete innocence. Has it come about that merely because a man once agreed to deliver whisky, but did not, he may be arrested whenever thereafter he ventures to drive an automobile on the road to Detroit!

...To me it seems clear enough that the judgment should be reversed.

Questions

1. State the vehicle exception to the Fourth Amendment warrant requirement as outlined by the majority opinion.

2. Summarize the majority opinion's arguments for the vehicle exception.

3. State the facts of the case as elaborated by the dissent.

4. In your opinion, was the search reasonable? Back up your answer with the facts of the case and the arguments of the majority and/or dissenting opinions.

Searches of Vehicle Passengers

Recall that one of the reasons for the vehicle exception to the warrant requirement is a reduced expectation of privacy in vehicles. Do passengers as well as drivers have a reduced expectation of privacy? And, if they do, can officers search a woman passenger's purse when they have no probable cause to suspect her of the crime they arrested the driver for? The U.S. Supreme Court answered these questions in *Wyoming v. Houghton* (1999).

Wyoming v. Houghton
526 U.S. 295 (1999)

Sandra Houghton was convicted in the District Court, Natrona County, Wyoming, of felony possession of methamphetamine, and she appealed. The Wyoming Supreme Court reversed and remanded. The U.S. Supreme Court granted certiorari and reversed.

SCALIA, J., joined by REHNQUIST, CJ., and O'CONNOR, KENNEDY, THOMAS, and BREYER, JJ.

FACTS

In the early morning hours of July 23, 1995, a Wyoming Highway Patrol officer (Officer Baldwin) stopped an automobile for speeding and driving with a faulty brake light. There were three passengers in the front seat of the car: David Young (the driver), his girlfriend, and Houghton. While questioning Young, the officer noticed a hypodermic syringe in Young's shirt pocket. He left the occupants under the supervision of two backup officers as he went to get gloves from his patrol car. Upon his return, he instructed Young to step out of the car and place the syringe on the hood. The officer then asked Young why he had a syringe; with refreshing candor, Young replied that he used it to take drugs.

At this point, the backup officers ordered the two female passengers out of the car and asked them for identification. Houghton falsely identified herself as "Sandra James" and stated that she did not have any identification. Meanwhile, in light of Young's admission, the officer searched the passenger compartment of the car for contraband. On the back seat, he found a purse, which Houghton claimed as hers. He removed from the purse a wallet containing Houghton's driver's license, identifying her properly as Sandra K. Houghton. When the officer asked her why she had lied about her name, she replied: "In case things went bad."

Continuing his search of the purse, the officer found a brown pouch and a black wallet-type container. Houghton denied that the former was hers, and claimed ignorance of how it came to be there; it was found to contain drug paraphernalia and a syringe with 60 cc's of methamphetamine. Houghton admitted ownership of the black container, which was also found to contain drug paraphernalia, and a syringe (which Houghton acknowledged was hers) with 10 cc's of methamphetamine—an amount insufficient to support the felony conviction at issue in this case. The officer also found fresh needle-track marks on Houghton's arms. He placed her under arrest.

The State of Wyoming charged Houghton with felony possession of methamphetamine in a liquid amount greater than three-tenths of a gram. After a hearing, the trial court denied her motion to suppress all evidence obtained from the purse as the fruit of a violation of the Fourth and Fourteenth Amendments. The court held that the officer had probable cause to search the car for contraband, and, by extension, any containers therein that could hold such contraband. A jury convicted Houghton as charged.

The Wyoming Supreme Court, by divided vote, reversed the conviction and announced the following rule:

> Generally, once probable cause is established to search a vehicle, an officer is entitled to search all containers therein which may contain the object of the search. However, if the officer knows or should know that a container is the personal effect of a passenger who is not suspected of criminal activity, then the container is outside the scope of the search unless someone had the opportunity to conceal the contraband within the personal effect to avoid detection.

The court held that the search of Houghton's purse violated the Fourth and Fourteenth Amendments because the officer "knew or should have known that the purse did not belong to the driver, but to one of the passengers," and because "there was no probable cause to search the passengers' personal effects and no reason to believe that contraband had been placed within the purse."

OPINION

. . . It is uncontested in the present case that the police officers had probable cause to believe there were illegal drugs in the car. *Carroll v. United States,* 267 U.S. 132 (1925),* similarly involved the warrantless search of a car that law enforcement officials had probable cause to believe contained contraband—in that case, bootleg liquor. The Court concluded that the Framers would have regarded such a search as reasonable in light of legislation enacted by Congress from 1789 through 1799—as well as subsequent

---

*See the case excerpt, on p. 234.

legislation from the Founding era and beyond—that empowered customs officials to search any ship or vessel without a warrant if they had probable cause to believe that it contained goods subject to a duty. Thus, the Court held that "contraband goods concealed and illegally transported in an automobile or other vehicle may be searched for without a warrant" where probable cause exists.

We have furthermore read the historical evidence to show that the Framers would have regarded as reasonable (if there was probable cause) the warrantless search of containers within an automobile. In *United States v. Ross*, 456 U.S. 798 (1982), we upheld as reasonable the warrantless search of a paper bag and leather pouch found in the trunk of Ross's car by officers who had probable cause to believe that the trunk contained drugs. . . .

Ross summarized its holding as follows: "If probable cause justifies the search of a lawfully stopped vehicle, it justifies the search of every part of the vehicle and its contents that may conceal the object of the search." And our later cases describing *Ross* have characterized it as applying broadly to all containers within a car, without qualification as to ownership.

To be sure, there was no passenger in *Ross*, and it was not claimed that the package in the trunk belonged to anyone other than the driver. Even so . . . , neither *Ross* itself nor the historical evidence it relied upon admits of a distinction among packages or containers based on ownership. When there is probable cause to search for contraband in a car, it is reasonable for police officers—like customs officials in the Founding era—to examine packages and containers without a showing of individualized probable cause for each one. A passenger's personal belongings, just like the driver's belongings or containers attached to the car like a glove compartment, are "in" the car, and the officer has probable cause to search for contraband in the car.

Even if the historical evidence . . . were thought to be equivocal, we would find that the balancing of the relative interests weighs decidedly in favor of allowing searches of a passenger's belongings. Passengers, no less than drivers, possess a reduced expectation of privacy with regard to the property that they transport in cars. . . .

Whereas the passenger's privacy expectations are . . . considerably diminished, the governmental interests at stake are substantial. Effective law enforcement would be appreciably impaired without the ability to search a passenger's personal belongings when there is reason to believe contraband or evidence of criminal wrongdoing is hidden in the car. As in all car-search cases, the "ready mobility" of an automobile creates a risk that the evidence or contraband will be permanently lost while a warrant is obtained. In addition, a car passenger . . . will often be engaged in a common enterprise with the driver, and have the same interest in concealing the fruits or the evidence of their wrongdoing. . . .

To be sure, these factors favoring a search will not always be present, but the balancing of interests must be conducted with an eye to the generality of cases. To require that the investigating officer have positive reason to believe that the passenger and driver were engaged in a common enterprise, or positive reason to believe that the driver had time and occasion to conceal the item in the passenger's belongings, surreptitiously or with friendly permission, is to impose requirements so seldom met that a "passenger's property" rule would dramatically reduce the ability to find and seize contraband and evidence of crime.

Of course these requirements would not attach (under the Wyoming Supreme Court's rule) until the police officer knows or has reason to know that the container belongs to a passenger. But once a "passenger's property" exception to car searches became widely known, one would expect passenger-confederates to claim everything as their own. And one would anticipate a bog of litigation—in the form of both civil lawsuits and motions to suppress in criminal trials—involving such questions as whether the officer should have believed a passenger's claim of ownership, whether he should have inferred ownership from various objective factors, whether he had probable cause to believe that the passenger was a confederate, or to believe that the driver might have introduced the contraband into the package with or without the passenger's knowledge. When balancing the competing interests, our determinations of "reasonableness" under the Fourth Amendment must take account of these practical realities. We think they militate in favor of the needs of law enforcement, and against a personal-privacy interest that is ordinarily weak. . . .

We hold that police officers with probable cause to search a car may inspect passengers' belongings found in the car that are capable of concealing the object of the search.

The judgment of the Wyoming Supreme Court
is REVERSED.

CONCURRING OPINION

BREYER, J.

. . . I . . . point out certain limitations upon the scope of the bright-line rule that the Court describes. Obviously, the rule applies only to automobile searches. Equally obviously, the rule applies only to containers found within automobiles. And it does not extend to the search of a person found in that automobile. As the Court notes, and as *United States v. Di Re*, relied on heavily by Justice STEVENS' dissent, makes clear, the search of a person, including even "a limited search of the outer clothing," is a very different matter in respect to which the law provides "significantly heightened protection."

Less obviously, but in my view also important, is the fact that the container here at issue, a woman's purse, was found at a considerable distance from its owner, who did not claim ownership until the officer discovered her identification while looking through it. Purses are special containers. They are repositories of especially personal items that people generally like to keep with them at all times. So I am tempted to say that a search of a purse involves an intrusion so similar to a search of one's person that the same rule should govern both. However, given this Court's prior cases, I cannot argue that the fact that the container was a purse automatically makes a legal difference, for the Court has warned against trying to make that kind of distinction. But I can say that it would matter if a woman's purse, like a man's billfold, were attached to her person. It might then amount to a kind of "outer clothing." In this case, the purse was separate from the person, and no one has claimed that, under those circumstances, the type of container makes a difference. For that reason, I join the Court's opinion.

DISSENT

STEVENS, J., joined by SOUTER and GINSBURG, JJ.
...In all of our prior cases applying the automobile exception to the Fourth Amendment's warrant requirement, either the defendant was the operator of the vehicle and in custody of the object of the search, or no question was raised as to the defendant's ownership or custody. In the only automobile case confronting the search of a passenger defendant—*United States v. Di Re* (addressing searches of the passenger's pockets and the space between his shirt and underwear, both of which uncovered counterfeit fuel rations)—the Court held that the exception to the warrant requirement did not apply.

In *Di Re*, as here, the information prompting the search directly implicated the driver, not the passenger. Today, instead of adhering to the settled distinction between drivers and passengers, the Court fashions a new rule that is based on a distinction between property contained in clothing worn by a passenger and property contained in a passenger's briefcase or purse. In cases on both sides of the Court's newly minted test, the property is in a "container"

(whether a pocket or a pouch) located in the vehicle. Moreover, unlike the Court, I think it quite plain that the search of a passenger's purse or briefcase involves an intrusion on privacy that may be just as serious as was the intrusion in *Di Re*.

...I [am not] persuaded that the mere spatial association between a passenger and a driver provides an acceptable basis for presuming that they are partners in crime or for ignoring privacy interests in a purse. Whether or not the Fourth Amendment required a warrant to search Houghton's purse, at the very least the trooper in this case had to have probable cause to believe that her purse contained contraband. The Wyoming Supreme Court concluded that he did not.

Finally, in my view, the State's legitimate interest in effective law enforcement does not outweigh the privacy concerns at issue. I am as confident in a police officer's ability to apply a rule requiring a warrant or individualized probable cause to search belongings that are—as in this case—obviously owned by and in the custody of a passenger as is the Court in a "passenger-confederate's" ability to circumvent the rule. Certainly the ostensible clarity of the Court's rule is attractive. But that virtue is insufficient justification for its adoption. Moreover, a rule requiring a warrant or individualized probable cause to search passenger belongings is every bit as simple as the Court's rule; it simply protects more privacy....

Instead of applying ordinary Fourth Amendment principles to this case, the majority extends the automobile warrant exception to allow searches of passenger belongings based on the driver's misconduct. Thankfully, the Court's automobile-centered analysis limits the scope of its holding. But it does not justify the outcome in this case.

I respectfully dissent.

Questions

1. State the rule for searching passengers' "containers" adopted by the majority of the Court.

2. Explain how the majority applied the rule to the search of Sandra Houghton's purse.

3. Summarize the dissent's arguments for concluding the purse search was unreasonable.

4. Summarize Justice Breyer's hesitation about supporting the majority decision.

5. Consider your summaries. Which opinion do you think is the most convincing? Defend your answer.

◆   ◆   ◆

Container Searches

The U.S. Supreme Court has decided that people have a reasonable expectation of privacy in their briefcases, purses, luggage, and other **containers** where they keep their stuff. The expectation of privacy in containers is less than it is in homes but more than it is in vehicles. So, under ordinary circumstances law enforcement officers need both a warrant and probable cause to search containers. But, under special circumstances, officers can seize and search containers without warrants. For example, when officers reasonably suspect there's evidence of crime in containers, they can briefly seize the containers, but they can't search them until they get a warrant backed up by probable cause (*U.S. v. Teslim* 1989).

Officers can also search containers without warrants in vehicles if they have probable cause to believe there's evidence of crime inside. Until 1990, officers could only search containers in vehicles if they had separate probable cause to search both the vehicle and the container. If they had probable cause to search the container but not the vehicle, they had to get a warrant. The Court cleared up this silly glitch in *California v. Acevedo* (1991). Police officers observed Charles Acevedo leave an apartment where officers knew there was marijuana. Acevedo was carrying a brown paper bag the size of marijuana packages they'd seen earlier. Acevedo put the bag into the trunk of his car. As he drove away, the police stopped his car, opened the trunk, opened the bag, and found marijuana in it. The Court held it was reasonable to search the container without a warrant because they had probable cause to believe the bag contained marijuana. The Court recognized Acevedo's expectation of privacy in the brown bag but concluded the risk the car might drive off and the marijuana disappear trumped Acevedo's expectation of privacy.

Emergency Searches

Emergency searches (also called **exigent circumstance searches**) are based on the idea that it's sometimes impractical (even dangerous) to require officers to obtain warrants before they search. The danger might be to officers' safety, justifying frisks, or pat-downs for weapons (Chapter 4); that suspects or others might destroy evidence during the time it takes to get a search warrant; that fleeing felons might escape while officers are trying to obtain search warrants, or that individuals in the community are in immediate danger. Since we've already examined frisks, in which officers' reasonable suspicion that a lawfully stopped suspect is armed justifies a pat-down for weapons (Chapter 4), we won't repeat that discussion here. Let's look at the other three types of emergencies.

Destruction of Evidence

If police officers have probable cause to search, and they reasonably believe evidence is about to be destroyed now, they can search without a warrant. For example, in *Cupp v. Murphy* (1973), the U.S. Supreme Court held that police officers who had probable cause to believe Daniel Murphy had strangled his wife didn't need a warrant to take scrapings of what looked like blood under his fingernails. Why? Because Murphy knew the officers suspected he was the strangler, so he had a motive to destroy the short-lived bloodstain evidence. In *Schmerber v. California* (1966, Chapter 8), the

Supreme Court held that rapidly declining blood alcohol levels justified giving a blood alcohol test to Schmerber without a warrant. And in *Ker v. California* (1963), the Court held that a warrantless entry into a home was justified by the reasonable fear that Ker was about to destroy or hide marijuana.

Hot Pursuit

Hot pursuit is another emergency created by the need to apprehend a fleeing suspect. If officers are chasing a suspect whom they have probable cause to arrest, they can follow the suspect into a house without getting a warrant (*U.S. v. Santana* 1976). So, officers wouldn't need a warrant to enter a home to search for a fleeing armed robbery suspect and weapons. But, how extensive can the search be? Only as extensive as is necessary to prevent the suspect from escaping or resisting. So, officers can't search every nook and cranny of a house just because they got in lawfully during a hot pursuit (*Warden v. Hayden* 1967). For example, they can't search dresser drawers for contraband. Nor can they search every room of a hotel because a robber entered the hotel (*U.S. v. Winsor* 1988).

Danger to the Community

Police officers can sidestep the warrant requirement if they have probable cause to believe either that a suspect has committed a violent crime or that they or others in the community are in immediate danger. So, officers could enter and search a house in a residential area because they reasonably believed guns and bombs were in the house (*U.S. v. Lindsey* 1989). It was also reasonable to enter a house without a warrant to search for a weapon when police found a dead body on the front porch (*U.S. v. Doe* 1985).

Other dangers to the public include fires and explosions. Police officers at the scene of a fire don't need a warrant to stay inside a burned building long enough to look for possible injured victims and to investigate the cause of the fire or explosion. But, once they determine the cause of the fire, officers have to get a warrant if they want to search for evidence of a crime (*Michigan v. Clifford* 1984). Furthermore, they can't enter just because a fire or explosion might be in the offing. For example, a court ruled that it wasn't reasonable for officers to enter a house where they knew a man had kept dangerous chemicals in his house for two weeks and wasn't at home (*U.S. v. Warner* 1988).

SUMMARY

I. The power to search
   A. Crime control depends on searches
   B. The Fourth Amendment balances the need for searches and the invasion of individuals' privacy resulting from searches
   C. Two types of searches
      1. With warrants
      2. Without warrants

II. Searches with warrants
   A. The Fourth Amendment requires officers to get search warrants but exceptions to the warrant requirement result in far more searches without than with warrants
   B. Warrant requirements
      1. Particularity
         a. Describe the place to be searched
         b. Describe the things to be seized
      2. Probable cause affidavit containing facts supporting the claim that the evidence listed in the warrant will be found in the place to be searched
      3. "Knock and announce"
         a. Officers have to knock, identify themselves as officers, and pause briefly before entering places to be searched
         b. Exceptions
            (1) Prevent violence
            (2) Prevent destruction of evidence
            (3) Prevent escape

III. Searches without warrants
   A. Most searches fall under exceptions to warrant requirements because of the needs and preference of law enforcement
   B. Five major exceptions to warrant requirements
      1. Searches incident to arrest
      2. Consent searches
      3. Vehicle searches
      4. Container searches
      5. Emergency searches
   C. Searches incident to arrest
      1. Don't require warrants *or* probable cause
      2. Requirements
         a. Lawful arrest
         b. Limited to person arrested and "grabbable area"—area under immediate control of arrested person
         c. Vehicles included in "grabbable area" (*New York v. Belton*)
         d. Time frame—before, during, and after arrest as long as there's probable cause to arrest
      3. Searches incident to misdemeanors
         a. Misdemeanors have to qualify for custodial arrest—for example, moving traffic violations
         b. Search doesn't apply to citations
      4. Searches incident to pretext arrests
         a. Powerful investigative tool in drug law enforcement
         b. Scenario
            (1) Officer has a hunch but no objective basis that suspect is carrying contraband (almost always drugs)
            (2) Officer has probable cause to believe suspect has committed a crime unrelated to drugs (typically a traffic violation)
            (3) Officer uses the pretext of a traffic arrest to search for drugs

      c. U.S. Supreme Court in *Whren v. U.S.*—as long as officers have probable cause to arrest, the motive for the search incident to it is irrelevant

D. Consent searches
1. Significance—consent searches involve waiving the constitutional right against unreasonable searches
2. The test of consent
    a. Whether a suspect voluntarily consented is measured by the totality of circumstances
    b. Knowledge and waiver of right to refuse consent is one circumstance but not required
    c. Burden to prove voluntary consent is on the government
3. The scope of consent
    a. Depends on how broad officers believe the consent to be
    b. Does not depend on what the consenting person intended the scope of the search to be
4. Withdrawing consent
    a. Not clear whether consent once given can be withdrawn during a search
    b. *Model Code of Pre-Arraignment* procedure adopted the rule that a search has to stop immediately if the person withdraws consent
5. Third-party consent searches
    a. One person can give up another person's right against unreasonable searches if the person has the authority to consent for the other person—for example, a parent consents for a minor child
    b. Test of authority to consent for another
       (1) Test isn't actual authority of person to consent for another
       (2) Test is apparent authority—namely, officers' reasonable belief the third person had authority to consent

E. Vehicle searches
1. Searches of vehicles based on probable cause don't require warrants
2. Two reasons
    a. Mobility of vehicles
    b. Reduced expectation of privacy
3. Personal containers belonging to passengers found in the car can be searched

F. Container searches
1. Require probable cause to believe there's evidence of crime inside the containers
2. Reasonable expectation of privacy in containers is greater than in cars but less than in homes

G. Emergency searches
1. Rationale for no warrant and sometimes no probable cause—impractical and even dangerous to get a warrant or require probable cause
2. Frisks to protect officers based on reasonable suspicion
3. The need to prevent the destruction of evidence justifies an exception to the warrant requirement if officers have probable cause to believe evidence is about to be destroyed

4. The need to apprehend a fleeing felon entering a house removes the need to get a warrant
5. Officers can sidestep the warrant requirement if they have probable cause to believe a suspect has created an immediate danger to the community or committed a violent crime

 Go to the Criminal Procedure 6e CD to download this summary outline. The outline has been formatted so that you can add notes to it during class lectures, or later create a customized chapter outline to use while reviewing. Either way, the summary outline will help you understand the "big picture" and fill in the details as you study.

REVIEW QUESTIONS

1. Identify the three steps in the analysis of whether government actions are searches.
2. Identify three elements required in a search warrant that meets Fourth Amendment requirements.
3. Identify three exceptions to the "knock and announce" rule.
4. What's the U.S. Supreme Court's preference when it comes to searches with or without warrants?
5. Identify three reasons why searches incident to arrest are reasonable.
6. Describe the division of opinion over including passenger compartments of vehicles within the "grabbable" area. How did the U.S. Supreme Court resolve the division in *N.Y. v. Belton*?
7. Describe the "time frame" of searches incident to arrest, and explain how it was applied in *U.S. v. Edwards*.
8. What's the rule regarding searches incident to arrests for minor offenses? Describe how and why the U.S. Supreme Court created and applied the rule in *U.S. v. Robinson*.
9. Describe a search incident to a pretext arrest, and explain its significance.
10. When police officers ask for consent to search, what are they *really* asking?
11. State the voluntariness test of consent.
12. List nine circumstances that qualify as part of the "totality of circumstances" relevant to voluntary consent.
13. According to the U.S. Supreme Court, what's the test of the scope of consent? Explain how the Court applied the test in *Florida v. Jimeno*.
14. When and how can a person who consents to a search withdraw consent and stop the search according to the *Model Code of Pre-Arraignment Procedure*?
15. Give examples of who can consent to a search for someone else.
16. Explain the difference between actual and apparent authority to consent for another person.

17. Identify the two reasons why vehicle searches are reasonable without warrants.

18. What's the rule regarding searches of containers of passengers in vehicles (*Wyoming v. Houghton*)?

19. What's the rule regarding the container exception to the warrant requirement?

20. Identify four emergency searches, and describe why each falls under the exception to the warrant requirement.

KEY TERMS

particularity requirement p. 196
knock-and-announce rule p. 196
no-knock entry p. 196
searches incident to arrest p. 201
grabbable area p. 203
Robinson rule p. 210
citations p. 210
pretext arrests p. 212

consent search p. 217
voluntariness test of consent
    searches p. 218
third-party consent searches p. 228
actual authority (objective)
    third-party consent p. 228
apparent authority (subjective)
    third-party consent p. 228

containers p. 240
emergency searches p. 240
exigent circumstance searches
    p. 240
hot pursuit p. 241

THE COMPANION WEB SITE
FOR *CRIMINAL PROCEDURE,* SIXTH EDITION

http://cj.wadsworth.com/samaha/crim_pro6e

Supplement your review of this chapter by going to the companion Web site to take one of the Tutorial Quizzes, use the flash cards to test yourself on the key terms from each chapter, and check out the many other study aids you'll find there. You'll find valuable data and resources at your fingertips to help you study for that big exam or write that important paper.

7

Special-Needs Searches

Chapter Main Points

- Searches for criminal evidence aren't the only kind of Fourth Amendment searches; there are also searches based on special needs beyond law enforcement.

- The reasonableness of special-needs searches depends on balancing the special needs against the invasiveness of the search.

- The objective basis for special-needs searches isn't limited to individualized suspicion but can extend to profiles, routine procedures, and random selection.

- The reasonableness of inventory searches depends on balancing individuals' privacy against the special needs to protect individuals' property; government's liability for that property; and jails' security against dangerous contraband.

- Searches at international borders balance the privacy of individuals against the special need to protect international borders.

- Airport searches don't require warrants or probable cause.

- Prisoners, probationers, and parolees have no reasonable expectation they won't be searched (except for strip and body-cavity searches).

- The reasonableness of prison visitor and employee searches depends on balancing the need to prevent smuggling of contraband against the invasion of visitors' and employees' privacy.

- Searches of high-school students balance the need to maintain a learning environment against students' reasonable expectation of privacy.

- College students have a reasonable expectation of privacy against searches of their dormitory rooms.

Mary Beth G. and Sharon N. were stopped for traffic violations; they were arrested and taken to detention centers because there were outstanding parking tickets against their cars. They were subjected to the strip search policy of the city of Chicago. That policy, as described by the city, required each woman placed in detention facilities of the Chicago Police Department to be searched by female personnel to:

1. *lift her blouse or sweater and unhook and lift her brassiere to allow a visual inspection of the breast area, to replace these articles of clothing and then*

2. *pull up her skirt or dress or lower her pants and pull down any undergarments, to squat two or three times facing the detention aide, and to bend over at the waist to permit visual inspection of the vaginal and anal area.*

The city claimed that all searches were conducted in a closed room away from the view of all persons except the person conducting the search. The strip search policy was not applied to males. Men were searched thoroughly by hand. The male detainee would place his hands against the wall and stand normally while the searching officer, with his fingers, would go through the hair, into the ears, down the back, under the armpits, down both arms, down the legs, into the groin area, and up the front. The officer would also search the waistband and require the detainee to remove his shoes and sometimes his socks.

Mary Beth G. v. City of Chicago (1983), U.S. Court of Appeals (7th Cir.)

SPECIAL NEEDS VS. THE EXPECTATION OF PRIVACY

Until now, we've discussed searches and seizures conducted for the purpose of gathering evidence of crime, but crime control isn't the only legitimate purpose for searches. The U.S. Supreme Court has applied the Fourth Amendment to a wide range of searches to meet "special needs" that go beyond criminal law enforcement. **Special-needs searches** include:

1. *Inventory searches.* Documenting inventory searches of persons and containers in government custody to protect the owners from theft and damage, government agencies from lawsuits, and jails from danger

2. *International border searches.* Conducting international border checks to control who and what comes into and goes out of the country

3. *Airport searches.* Examining airport passengers and their baggage to protect the safety of travelers

4. *Custody-related searches.* Searching prisoners, probationers and parolees, and visitors and employees of prisons and jails to control contraband

5. *Student searches.* Searching students to maintain a thriving learning environment

6. *Employee drug testing.* Testing employees for drug use to increase workplace safety

Other special-needs searches include "inspecting" businesses like restaurants and bars to make sure they're complying with health and safety codes and conducting vehicle safety checks to make the roads safer.

The variety of special-needs searches shouldn't hide four characteristics they have in common:

1. They're directed at people generally, not criminal suspects and defendants specifically.

2. They can result in criminal prosecution and conviction.

3. They don't require warrants or probable cause.

4. Their reasonableness depends on balancing the special government needs against invasions of individual privacy.

We'll look at several of these special-needs searches to gain a greater understanding of how they serve the aims of protecting the public.

INVENTORY SEARCHES

Inventory searches consist of making a list of people's personal property and *containers* held in government custody. **Containers** include vehicles, purses, clothing, or anything else where people in custody might put their "stuff." After looking through ("searching") the containers, officials make a list of the items and put them away ("seize") for safekeeping. According to the U.S. Supreme Court, in *Colorado v. Bertine* 1987, inventory searches are Fourth Amendment searches, but they're reasonable without either probable cause or warrants. Why? Because they're not searches for the purpose of gathering evidence to prosecute crime. Inventory searches satisfy three special needs not related to searching for evidence of a crime:

1. To protect owners' stuff while it's in police custody

2. To protect law enforcement agencies against lawsuits for the loss, destruction, or theft of owners' stuff

3. To protect law enforcement officers, detained suspects, and offenders from the danger of bombs, weapons, and illegal drugs that might be hidden in owners' "stuff"

The reasonableness of an inventory search depends on balancing the government's special need to inspect against the invasion of individuals' privacy caused by the search. If the government special need outweighs (it almost always does) the individual right to privacy, the search is reasonable.

Second, reasonableness depends on the objective basis—which in inventory searches isn't probable cause; it's not even reasonable suspicion. According to the U.S. Supreme Court, "The standard of probable cause is peculiarly related to criminal investigations, not routine, noncriminal proceedings." This doesn't mean special-needs searches are left entirely to officer discretion. Following routine, department-approved, written procedures take the place of probable cause and reasonable suspicion in inventory searches. Why? First, because following routine procedures is objective because the procedures apply to all searches. Second, they keep law enforcement officers from searching on a ruse and roaming too far and deep in making the inventory. In the words of the U.S. Supreme Court, inventory searches

> must not be a ruse for a general rummaging in order to discover incriminating evidence. The policy or practice governing inventory searches should be designed to produce an inventory. The individual police officer must not be allowed so much latitude that inventory searches are turned into "a purposeful and general means of discovering evidence of crime."
>
> *Whren v. U.S.* 1996

Despite this **routine written procedure requirement,** law enforcement officers have plenty of elbow room when they conduct inventory searches (*Colorado v. Bertine* 1987). The U.S. Supreme Court discussed how much room for discretion officers have in an inventory search of a college student's impounded car in *South Dakota v. Opperman* (1976).

| ## *Was the Marijuana Found During a Reasonable Search?*

South Dakota v. Opperman
428 U.S. 364 (1976)

Donald Opperman was convicted in a South Dakota court of possession of less than one ounce of marijuana, fined $100, and sentenced to 14 days in jail. He appealed. The South Dakota Supreme Court reversed. The U.S. Supreme Court granted certiorari, reversed the South Dakota Supreme Court, and remanded the case.

BURGER, CJ.

FACTS

Local ordinances prohibit parking in certain areas of downtown Vermillion, S.D., between the hours of 2 A.M. and 6 A.M. During the early morning hours of December 10, 1973, a Vermillion police officer observed Opperman's unoccupied car illegally parked in the restricted zone. At approximately 3 A.M., the officer issued an overtime parking ticket and placed it on the car's windshield. The citation warned: "Vehicles in violation of any parking ordinance may be towed from the area." At approximately 10 o'clock on the same morning, another officer issued a second ticket for an overtime parking violation. These circumstances were routinely reported to police headquar-

ters, and after the vehicle was inspected, the car was towed to the city impound lot.

From outside the car at the impound lot, a police officer observed a watch on the dashboard and other items of personal property located on the back seat and floor. At the officer's direction, the car door was then unlocked and, using a standard inventory form pursuant to standard police procedures, the officer inventoried the contents of the car, including the contents of the glove compartment which was unlocked. There he found marihuana contained in a plastic bag. All items, including the contraband, were removed to the police department for safekeeping.*

---

*At Opperman's trial, the officer who conducted the inventory testified as follows:

Q. "And why did you inventory this car?"
A. "Mainly for safekeeping, because we have had a lot of trouble in the past of people getting into the impound lot and breaking into cars and stealing stuff out of them."
Q. "Do you know whether the vehicles that were broken into . . . were locked or unlocked?"
A. "Both of them were locked, they would be locked."

In describing the impound lot, the officer stated:

A. "It's the old county highway yard. It has a wooden fence partially around part of it, and kind of a dilapidated wire fence, a makeshift fence."

During the late afternoon of December 10, Opperman appeared at the police department to claim his property. The marihuana was retained by police. Opperman was subsequently arrested on charges of possession of marihuana. His motion to suppress the marijuana was denied; he was convicted after a jury trial and sentenced to a fine of $100 and 14 days incarceration in the county jail. On appeal, the Supreme Court of South Dakota reversed the conviction. The court concluded that the evidence had been obtained in violation of the Fourth Amendment prohibition against unreasonable searches and seizures. We granted certiorari, and we reverse.

OPINION

In discharging their varied responsibilities for ensuring the public safety, law enforcement officials are necessarily brought into frequent contact with automobiles. Most of this contact is distinctly noncriminal in nature. In the interests of public safety and as part of what the Court has called "community caretaking functions," automobiles are frequently taken into police custody.... To permit the uninterrupted flow of traffic and in some circumstances to preserve evidence, disabled or damaged vehicles will often be removed from the highways or streets at the behest of police engaged solely in caretaking and traffic-control activities. Police will also frequently remove and impound automobiles which violate parking ordinances and which thereby jeopardize both the public safety and the efficient movement of vehicular traffic. The authority of police to seize and remove from the streets vehicles impeding traffic or threatening public safety and convenience is beyond challenge.

When vehicles are impounded, local police departments generally follow a routine practice of securing and inventorying the automobiles' contents. These procedures developed in response to three distinct needs: the protection of the owner's property while it remains in police custody, the protection of the police against claims or disputes over lost or stolen property, and the protection of the police from potential danger. The practice has been viewed as essential to respond to incidents of theft or vandalism.... In applying the reasonableness standard adopted by the Framers, this Court has consistently sustained police intrusions into automobiles impounded or otherwise in lawful police custody where the process is aimed at securing or protecting the car and its contents.... It would be unreasonable to hold that the police, having to retain the car in their custody for such a length of time, had no right, even for their own protection, to search it ...

The Vermillion police were indisputably engaged in a caretaking search of a lawfully impounded automobile.

The inventory was conducted only after the car had been impounded for multiple parking violations. The owner, having left his car illegally parked for an extended period, and thus subject to impoundment, was not present to make other arrangements for the safekeeping of his belongings. The inventory itself was prompted by the presence in plain view of a number of valuables inside the car. As in Cady, there is no suggestion whatever that this standard procedure, essentially like that followed throughout the country, was a pretext concealing an investigatory police motive.

On this record we conclude that in following standard police procedures, prevailing throughout the country and approved by the overwhelming majority of courts, the conduct of the police was not "unreasonable" under the Fourth Amendment. The judgment of the South Dakota Supreme Court is therefore REVERSED, and the case is REMANDED for further proceedings not inconsistent with this opinion.

DISSENT

MARSHALL, J., joined by BRENNAN and STEWART, JJ. The Court's opinion appears to suggest that its result may ... be justified because the inventory search procedure is a "reasonable" response to "three distinct needs: the protection of the owner's property while it remains in police custody ...; the protection of the police against claims or disputes over lost or stolen property ...; and the protection of the police from potential danger." This suggestion is flagrantly misleading ... because the record of this case explicitly belies any relevance of the last two concerns. In any event it is my view that none of these "needs," separately or together, can suffice to justify the inventory search procedure approved by the Court.

First, this search cannot be justified ... as a safety measure, for though the Court ignores it, the sole purpose given by the State for the Vermillion police's inventory procedure was to secure valuables.... Even aside from the actual basis for the police practice in this case, however, I do not believe that any blanket safety argument could justify a program of routine searches of the scope permitted here....

Second, the Court suggests that the search for valuables in the closed glove compartment might be justified as a measure to protect the police against lost property claims. Again, this suggestion is belied by the record, since although the Court declines to discuss it the South Dakota Supreme Court's interpretation of state law explicitly absolves the police, as "gratuitous depositors," from any obligation beyond inventorying objects in plain view and locking the car....

Finally, the Court suggests that the public interest in protecting valuables that may be found inside a closed compartment of an impounded car may justify the inventory procedure. I recognize the genuineness of this governmental interest in protecting property from pilferage. But even if I assume that the posting of a guard would be fiscally impossible as an alternative means to the same protective end, I cannot agree with the Court's conclusion. The Court's result authorizes, indeed it appears to require, the routine search of nearly every car impounded. In my view, the Constitution does not permit such searches as a matter of routine; absent specific consent, such a search is permissible only in exceptional circumstances of particular necessity. . . .

Because the record in this case shows that the procedures followed by the Vermillion police in searching Opperman's car fall far short of these standards, in my view the search was impermissible and its fruits must be suppressed. First, so far as the record shows, the police in this case had no reason to believe the glove compartment of the impounded car contained particular property of any substantial value. Moreover, the owner had apparently thought it adequate to protect whatever he left in the car overnight on the street in a business area simply to lock the car, and there is nothing in the record to show that the impoundment lot would prove a less secure location against pilferage, particularly when it would seem likely that the owner would claim his car and its contents promptly, at least if it contained valuables worth protecting.

Even if the police had cause to believe that the impounded car's glove compartment contained particular valuables, however, they made no effort to secure the owner's consent to the search. Although the Court relies, as

it must, upon the fact that Opperman was not present to make other arrangements for the care of his belongings, in my view that is not the end of the inquiry. Here the police readily ascertained the ownership of the vehicle, yet they searched it immediately without taking any steps to locate respondent and procure his consent to the inventory or advise him to make alternative arrangements to safeguard his property. Such a failure is inconsistent with the rationale that the inventory procedure is carried out for the benefit of the owner.

The Court's result in this case elevates the conservation of property interests indeed mere possibilities of property interests above the privacy and security interests protected by the Fourth Amendment. For this reason I dissent. On the remand it should be clear in any event that this Court's holding does not preclude a contrary resolution of this case or others involving the same issues under any applicable state law.

Questions

1. What are the justifications for allowing inventory searches without either warrants or probable cause?

2. Why should the evidence of a crime obtained in an inventory search be admitted to convict a person when the purpose of the search was for noncriminal law enforcement purposes?

3. Assume you're the lawyer for the government in this case. Answer the dissent's arguments that the inventory search of Donald Opperman's car didn't serve any of the purposes for inventory searches the Court says justifies setting aside the warrant and probable cause requirements.

STATE CONSTITUTIONAL LAW

State v. Opperman
247 N.W.2d 673 (S.D. 1976)

Was the Inventory Search Reasonable?

WINANS, J.

FACTS

On April 15, 1975, this court reversed a judgment against Donald Opperman because we found that the contraband used to convict petitioner had been seized pursuant to an inventory search which was unreasonable under the Fourth Amendment to the United States Constitution. On November 3, 1975, the U.S. Supreme Court granted certiorari; in a 5–4 decision it reversed the judgment of this court and remanded for further proceedings not inconsistent with its opinion. On August 26, 1976, this court granted a rehearing to ascertain whether the inventory search of petitioner's automobile was in violation of his rights under Article VI, § 11 of the South Dakota Constitution. We find that the inventory procedure followed in this instance constitutes an unreasonable search under our state constitution; accordingly we reverse the decision of the trial court.

OPINION

We are mindful that the United States Supreme Court found that the inventory procedure followed in this case did not amount to an unreasonable search in violation of the Fourth Amendment. That decision is binding on this court as a matter of federal constitutional law. However, manifestly the question remains for us to decide whether it offends any of the provisions of our own constitution and we are under no compulsion to follow the United States Supreme Court in that regard.

There can be no doubt that this court has the power to provide an individual with greater protection under the state constitution than does the United States Supreme Court under the federal constitution. This court is the final authority on interpretation and enforcement of the South Dakota Constitution. We have always assumed the independent nature of our state constitution regardless of any similarity between the language of that document and the federal constitution. Admittedly the language of Article VI, § 11 is almost identical to that found in the Fourth Amendment;

however, we have the right to construe our state constitutional provision in accordance with what we conceive to be its plain meaning. We find that logic and a sound regard for the purposes of the protection afforded by S.D.Const., Art. VI, § 11 warrant a higher standard of protection for the individual in this instance than the United States Supreme Court found necessary under the Fourth Amendment.

Article VI, § 11 of our state constitution guarantees our citizens the right to be free from "unreasonable searches and seizures." We have held that a determination of reasonableness requires a balancing of the need for a search in a particular case against the scope of the particular intrusion. . . . We now conclude that as a matter of protection under S.D.Const., Art. VI, § 11, "minimal interference" with a citizen's constitutional rights means that noninvestigative police inventory searches of automobile without a warrant must be restricted to safeguarding those articles which are within plain view of the officer's vision. We therefore AFFIRM . . . our original decision as a matter of state constitutional law.

INTERNATIONAL BORDER SEARCHES

According to the U.S. Supreme Court in *U.S. v. Ramsey* (1977), searches at international borders are reasonable even without warrants or probable cause. This is known as the **border search exception.** The special need of border searches is the right to control who and what comes into and goes out of the country. In *Ramsey,* a batch of incoming, letter-sized airmail envelopes from Thailand (a known source of narcotics) was bulky and much heavier than normal airmail letters. So, a customs inspector opened the envelopes for inspection at the General Post Office in New York City (considered a "border") and found heroin in them. The inspector seized the heroin and used it to convict the recipient. The customs inspector didn't obtain a warrant to search the envelopes, even though he had time to get one.

Still, according to the U.S. Supreme Court, it wasn't an illegal search and seizure:

> That searches made at the border, pursuant to the long-standing right of the sovereign to protect itself by stopping and examining persons and property crossing into this country, are reasonable simply by virtue of the fact that they occur at the border, should, by now, require no extended demonstration. The Congress which proposed the Bill of Rights, including the Fourth Amendment, to the state legislatures on September 25, 1789, had, some two months prior to that proposal, enacted the first customs statute. . . . This statute granted customs officials "full power and authority" to enter and search "any ship or vessel, in which they shall have reason to suspect any goods, wares or merchandise subject to duty shall be

concealed. . . ." The historical importance of the enactment of this customs statute by the same Congress which proposed the Fourth Amendment is, we think, manifest. (606)

Applying the balancing test to border searches, the U.S. Supreme Court found that the national interest in controlling our international borders outweighs the invasions of individual privacy caused by border searches. So, border checks require neither warrants nor individualized suspicion. However, reasonable suspicion is required to back up strip searches for contraband and weapons because people coming into the country are "forced to disrobe to a state which would be offensive to the average person." Body-cavity searches at the border are reasonable only if they're backed up by probable cause (LaFave and Israel 1984, 1:327–328).

AIRPORT SEARCHES

Since a series of airline hijackings and terrorist bombings in the 1970s, travelers have had to pass through detectors before they can board airplanes. Passengers also must pass their luggage through X-ray machines for examination. Additionally, sometimes inspectors open and look through baggage. If they discover suspicious items, they investigate further. Applying the balancing test of Fourth Amendment reasonableness, the U.S. Supreme Court has held that airport searches are reasonable even without warrants or probable cause. According to the Court, airport searches serve extremely important special needs—the security and the safety of air travelers. These special needs clearly outweigh the minimal invasion of privacy caused by having passengers pass through metal detectors and allow their luggage to be observed by X ray. Further, these invasions apply equally to all passengers, who are notified in advance that they're subject to them. So, passengers are free not to board the airplane if they don't want to subject their person and luggage to these intrusions (LaFave and Israel 1984, 1:332–333).

Since September 11, 2001, the searches have become more frequent and more intrusive, but so has the sense of urgency about security. No court challenge to these security changes that I'm aware of has arisen. But should a court challenge arise, it's not likely the balance will be struck against the current practice. Of course, if passengers are singled out for more-frequent and more-invasive measures because of their Middle Eastern background and/or their Muslim religion, that's a different matter.

CUSTODY-RELATED SEARCHES

Prisoners and their cells; prison visitors and employees; prisoners released on parole; probationers who could be but aren't locked up, and even defendants detained before they're convicted—all can be searched without warrants or probable cause, and sometimes without any individualized suspicion at all. Why? Because the balance between the special need to maintain safety, security, and discipline over people locked up in jails and prisons (and over people in custody but in the community) outweighs the significantly reduced expectation of privacy society grants to people in the custody of the criminal justice system. Let's examine this balance as it applies to prisoners, probationers and parolees, and prison visitors and employees.

Prisoners

Historically, prisoners had no Fourth Amendment rights; the Constitution stopped at the prison gate. Referring to convicted prisoners, the Virginia court in *Ruffin v. Commonwealth* (1871) said, "[T]he bill of rights is a declaration of general principles to govern a society of freemen." Prisoners "are the slaves of the State" (1025). As for people detained in jails before they're convicted, in *Lanza v. New York* (1962), the U.S. Supreme Court ruled that "a jail shares none of the attributes of privacy of a home, automobile, an office or hotel room, . . . and official surveillance has traditionally been the order of the day in prisons" (139). In the 1980s, the Court conceded that prisoners have an expectation of privacy that society recognizes. According to the Court, in *Hudson v. Palmer* (1984), "We have repeatedly held that prisons are not beyond the reach of the Constitution. No 'iron curtain' separates one from the other" [but] "imprisonment carries with it the circumscription or loss of many significant rights" (523).

To address searches of prisoners, the Court adopted a balancing approach borrowed from stop-and-frisk law (Chapter 4). The reasonableness of prisoner searches depends on balancing the need to maintain prison and jail security, safety, and discipline against the invasion of prisoners' substantially reduced reasonable expectation of privacy. The Court applied the balancing approach in *Hudson v. Palmer* (1984)— and it accepted the prisoner's, Russell Thomas Palmer's, version of the facts:

> On 9-16-81 around 5:50 P.M., officer Hudson shook down my locker and destroyed a lot of my property, i.e.: legal materials, letters, and other personal property only as a means of harassment. Officer Hudson has violated my Constitutional rights. The shakedown was no routine shakedown. It was planned and carried out only as harassment. Hudson stated the next time he would really mess my stuff up. I have plenty of witnesses to these facts. (541)

Then Chief Justice Burger, writing for the majority, held that the **shakedown** routine— unannounced searches of prisoners and their cells for weapons and contraband—was not a search at all:

> Notwithstanding our caution in approaching claims that the Fourth Amendment is inapplicable in a given context, we hold that society is not prepared to recognize as legitimate any . . . expectation of privacy that a prisoner might have in his prison cell and that, accordingly, the Fourth Amendment proscription against unreasonable searches does not apply within the confines of the prison cell. The recognition of privacy rights for prisoners in their individual cells simply cannot be reconciled with the concept of incarceration and the needs and objectives of penal institutions. (525–526)

The Court ruled the Fourth Amendment doesn't apply even if the motive behind the shakedown was harassment, as Palmer claimed it was. Four justices disagreed. According to Justice Stevens, writing for the dissenters:

> Measured by the conditions that prevail in a free society, neither the possessions nor the slight residuum of privacy that a prison inmate can retain in his cell, can have more than the most minimal value. From the standpoint of the prisoner, however, that trivial residuum may mark the difference between slavery and humanity (542). . . .

Personal letters, snapshots of family members, a souvenir, a deck of cards, a hobby kit, perhaps a diary or a training manual for an apprentice in a new trade, or even a Bible—a variety of inexpensive items may enable a prisoner to maintain contact with some part of his past and an eye to the possibility of a better future. Are all of these items subject to un-restrained perusal, confiscation, or mutilation at the hands of a possibly hostile guard? Is the Court correct in its perception that "society" is not prepared to recognize any privacy or possessory interest of the prison inmate—no matter how remote the threat to prison security may be (542–543)?

...The view once held that an inmate is a mere slave is now totally rejected. The re-straints and the punishment which a criminal conviction entails do not place the citizen beyond the ethical tradition that accords respect to the dignity and intrinsic worth of every individual "Liberty" and "custody" are not mutually exclusive concepts.".... By telling pris-oners that no aspect of their individuality, from a photo of a child to a letter from a wife, is entitled to constitutional protection, the Court breaks with the ethical tradition that I had thought was enshrined forever in our jurisprudence. (557–558)

The Court accepts that full-body, strip, and body-cavity searches are Fourth Amendment searches, but they're reasonable without either warrants or probable cause if in the particular situation, the need for security, safety, or discipline out-weighs prisoners' reasonable expectation of privacy in the particular circumstances of the case. For example, in *Bell v. Wolfish* (1979; Chapter 12), the U.S. Supreme Court said it was reasonable to require jail inmates awaiting trial to expose their body cavi-ties for visual inspection after every visit with a person from outside the jail. The Court said these body-cavity searches were reasonable to maintain safety and order in the jail. Broad as this power is, the Fourth Amendment doesn't leave prisoners completely at the discretion of government officials. Sometimes, the balance between the special need and individual privacy weighs in favor of prisoners. Highly intrusive custodial searches when security, safety, and discipline don't require them can violate the rights of prisoners. Also, they require an objective basis of reasonable suspicion to back them up. The Seventh Circuit Court of Appeals addressed the question of strip-searching all women confined in the Cook County Jail in *Mary Beth G. v. City of Chicago* (1983).

| CASE | *Was the Strip Search Reasonable?* |

Mary Beth G. v. City of Chicago
723 F.2d 1263 (7th Cir. 1983)

Mary B. G., Sharon N., Mary Ann Tikalsky, and Hinda Hoffman were arrested for misdemeanor traffic violations. While they were awaiting bail in lockups, jail matrons strip-searched them. The four women challenged the con-stitutionality of Chicago's strip search policy. The U.S. Dis-trict Court entered judgment in favor of the women. The U.S. Seventh Circuit Court of Appeals held that the strip search policy violated the Fourth Amendment, that the

jury awards were not excessive, and that plaintiffs were en-titled to attorney's fees.

WOOD, J.

FACTS

Mary Beth G. and Sharon N. were stopped for traffic viola-tions, arrested, and taken to detention centers because there were outstanding parking tickets on their cars. Hinda Hoffman was stopped for making an improper left turn, arrested, and taken to the police station when she failed to produce her driver's license. All four women were subjected to the strip search policy of the City of Chicago. That policy, as described by the City, required each woman placed in detention facilities of the Chicago Police Department and searched by female personnel to:

1. lift her blouse or sweater and unhook and lift her brassiere to allow a visual inspection of the breast area, to replace these articles of clothing and then

2. pull up her skirt or dress or to lower her pants and pull down any undergarments, to squat two or three times facing the detention aide and to bend over at the waist to permit visual inspection of the vaginal and anal area....

The strip search policy wasn't applied to males. Male detainees were subject to a strip search only if the arresting officers or detention aides had reason to believe the detainee was concealing weapons or contraband. Otherwise, men were searched thoroughly by hand. The male detainee would place his hands against the wall and stand normally while the searching officer, with his fingers, would go through the hair, into the ears, down the back, under the armpits, down both arms, down the legs, into the groin area, and up the front. The officer would also search the waistband and require the detainee to remove his shoes and sometimes his socks.

Originally, women detainees were also searched in this manner, but in 1952 the City changed its policy and began conducting the strip searches.

OPINION

...The City argues that its strip search policy is valid under two recognized exceptions to the warrant requirement. One exception allows warrantless searches [because the Fourth Amendment]...permits warrantless searches incident to the detention of persons lawfully arrested....

Our starting point is the balancing test announced in *Bell v. Wolfish* (1979), beginning with the magnitude of the invasion of personal rights. Strip searches involving the visual inspection of the anal and genital areas are "demeaning, dehumanizing, undignified, humiliating, terrifying, unpleasant, embarrassing, and repulsive, signifying degradation and submission...." Balanced against this invasion of personal privacy is the governmental interest in conducting the particular searches in question. In these cases, the governmental interest alleged by the City to justify these particular strip searches was the need to maintain the security of the City lockups by preventing misdemeanor offenders from bringing in weapons or contraband; the need was apparently felt to be so great that women misde-

meanants were strip searched even when there was no reason to believe they were hiding weapons or contraband on their persons.

The evidence the City offered to demonstrate the need for requiring strip searches of women minor offenders to maintain jail security, however, belies its purported concerns. The affidavits of the lockup personnel, which lack specificity, suggests that only a few items have been recovered from the body cavities of women arrested on minor charges over the years. In the only analytical survey submitted by the City, conducted over a thirty-five day period in June and July of 1965, all of the items found in the body orifices of the 1,800 women searched during that period were taken from women charged with either prostitution (7 items), assault (1 item), or a narcotics violation (1 item).

These are the kinds of crimes, unlike traffic or other offenses, that might give rise to a reasonable belief that the woman arrestee was concealing an item in a body cavity. Although a detention center may be a place "fraught with serious security dangers," the evidence does not support the view that those dangers are created by women minor offenders entering the lockups for short periods while awaiting bail. Here, the "need for the particular search," a strip search, is hardly substantial enough, in light of the evidence regarding the incidence of weapons and contraband found in the body cavities of women minor offenders, to justify the severity of the governmental intrusion.

Balancing the citizen's right to be free from substantial government intrusions against the mission of law enforcement personnel to ensure a safer society is often a difficult task. While the need to assure jail security is a legitimate and substantial concern, we believe that, on the facts here, the strip searches bore an insubstantial relationship to security needs so that, when balanced against plaintiffs–appellees' privacy interests, the searches cannot be considered "reasonable." The reasonableness standard usually requires, "at a minimum, that the facts upon which an intrusion is based be capable of measurement against 'an objective standard,' whether this be probable cause or a less stringent test." The more intrusive the search, the closer governmental authorities must come to demonstrating probable cause for believing that the search will uncover the objects for which the search is being conducted. Based on these principles, we agree with the District Court that insuring the security needs of the City by strip searching plaintiffs–appellees was unreasonable without a reasonable suspicion by the authorities that either of the twin dangers of concealing weapons or contraband existed....

Accordingly, because the court and jury...could reasonably conclude that the strip search policy of the City as applied in these cases was unreasonable under the fourth amendment, we uphold their determinations on this issue.

AFFIRMED.

Questions

1. Identify the special government need and the searches used to meet the need.

2. How did the court balance the need to maintain jails and the privacy rights of Mary Beth G. and the other women who sued the city? How would you balance these interests?

3. Identify the objective basis the court decided was necessary to back up the searches, and explain why the court decided on this level of objective basis.

4. Is labeling someone a "prisoner" ever enough to justify the kind of searches used in this case? Or should this kind of search always require individualized suspicion?

5. Would you go further and say that these searches should require probable cause to believe the person searched is concealing weapons or contraband? Why or why not?

6. The jury awarded the plaintiffs $25,000 each, except for Hinda Hoffman, who received $60,000 because male officers had watched and uttered rude remarks during her search. The city of Chicago claimed the awards were excessive. Do you agree? How do you assess how much money these intrusions are worth? Why do you suppose the Chicago policy remained unchallenged for so many years?

Probationers and Parolees

Probationers and parolees have diminished Fourth Amendment rights, even though they're not locked up (LaFave and Israel 1984, 1:336–338). Their reduced expectation of privacy subjects probationers and parolees to arrest and searches of their persons, their vehicles, and their houses without warrants or probable cause. Why? Some courts say it's because they're still in state custody and conditional release is a *privilege,* not a *right.* After all, they could still be locked up; it's only by the grace of the state they're conditionally released, and one of the conditions is to be searched at the discretion of the state. Other courts say they're consent searches and seizures—signed and agreed to in their "contract" of release. Still other courts adopt a balancing approach to the searches of probationers and parolees. Probation and parole are risks taken to help rehabilitate convicted offenders, and, therefore, to protect society from further crimes, reduced Fourth Amendment protections for probationers and parolees are reasonable.

Visitors and Employees

The special need for prison and jail safety, security, and order extends to searches without warrants or probable cause of prison visitors and employees. What are the searches looking for? Smuggled contraband like drugs, weapons, and money. The court in *State v. Putt* (1997) had this to say about smuggling in one Tennessee prison:

> Turney Center is plagued, as many correctional facilities are, with serious problems as a result of drugs being smuggled into the facility by prison visitors. The warden at the time of the defendant's arrest testified that drug smuggling had led to stabbings among the inmates as well as other general outbursts of violence. As one court has noted, "it is vital that contraband articles be kept out of a prison. This is necessary for the protection of the inmates, employees of the institution and law enforcement officials assigned to that institution." The United States Supreme Court has stated, "a detention facility is a unique place fraught with serious security dangers. Smuggling of money, drugs, weapons, and other contraband

is all too common an occurrence." Thus, we have no trouble concluding that the first element [balancing need for search against invasion of visitor's privacy] of the reasonableness test weighs heavily in the state's favor. (644)

How invasive can these searches be? It depends on the need for the search, the invasiveness of the search, and the objective basis for it. All the following invasions of prison visitors' and employees' privacy are reasonable without any facts pointing to their smuggling contraband into the prison or jail:

- A pat-down search

- Removal of outer clothing

- Emptying of pockets

- Screening by a metal detection device or other device that doesn't require disrobing

- Inspection of papers, bags, books, or other items carried into the facility (*Black v. Amico* 1974, 92)

Whoever does the search has to conduct it "in a manner least likely to embarrass or delay the passage" into the facility (*Black v. Amico* 1974, 92).

What about strip searches? They're a different story. Courts are tougher in applying the balancing test to strip searches, particularly when it comes to the objective basis for them. Almost all courts that have decided strip-search cases say jail and prison officials must have at least reasonable suspicion that the visitor or employee is smuggling contraband into the facility. The U.S. First Circuit Court of Appeals applied the balancing test in *Cochrane v. Quattrocchi* (1991), a prison visitor case.

| C A S E | *Was the Strip Search Reasonable?* |

Cochrane v. Quattrocchi
949 F.2d 11 (1st Cir. 1991)

Dawn Cochrane, a prison visitor, who was required to submit to a strip search before she would be permitted to visit her inmate father, brought action for damages asserting civil rights violations under 42 U.S.C. § 1983* and state law claims for battery, intentional infliction of emotional distress, false imprisonment, and assault. The U.S. District Court for the District of Rhode Island directed verdicts against Cochrane at the conclusion of her case in chief,** and she appealed. The Court of Appeals vacated and remanded for new trial.

CYR, J.

---

*See Chapter 11.

**Presenting the government's case as opposed to cross-examining defense witnesses and otherwise challenging the defense case (Chapter 13).

FACTS

Appellant [Dawn Cochrane], the teenage daughter of ACI inmate Rickie A. Cochrane ("Cochrane"), has been a regular visitor at ACI since she was very young. She has never violated a prison visitation rule or presented any threat to institutional security. Cochrane, on the other hand, has spent most of his adult life in prison and admits to having used contraband drugs on ten to twenty occasions while incarcerated.

On arrival at ACI on June 10, 1989, appellant was informed that she would not be allowed to visit her father that day, or ever again, until she submitted to a strip search. Appellant was presented with a form containing a consent to search, which she signed. Two female correctional officers then led her into a bathroom, where she was told to remove her clothing. A correctional officer checked her hair and her ears. Appellant was instructed to squat, hold her head to her chest and cough, while two female correction officers stood behind her. No contraband was discovered and appellant was permitted to visit her father. Appellant was emotionally shaken by the experience.

During October 1988, inmate Cochrane had been found unconscious in his cell following an overdose of cocaine, which Cochrane told a police officer was supplied by appellee Deputy Quattrocchi or his son, a correctional officer at ACI. Upon learning that Cochrane had mentioned him and his son, appellee Quattrocchi became angry and warned Cochrane, "I'm going to get you for that."

The district court first ruled that appellant had no constitutional right to visit her father in prison. The court then concluded that there could be no fourth amendment violation, since appellant had consented to the strip search and the search was reasonable in scope. The court directed the challenged verdicts before the defendants presented their case.

OPINION

Like every other circuit that has considered the question, we have held that a prison visitor retains a fourth amendment right to be free from unreasonable searches and seizures. Reasonableness, of course, depends on the context within which a search takes place. In deciding to what standard of reasonableness prison officials strip searching visitors should be held, we must balance the official interest in maintaining security against the intrusion entailed by a strip search, bearing in mind both that the preservation of internal security is central to all other corrections goals, and that prison visitors possess a diminished expectation of privacy. Those visiting a prison cannot credibly claim to carry with them the full panoply of rights they normally enjoy.

On the other hand, we recognize that a strip search, by its very nature, constitutes an extreme intrusion upon personal privacy, as well as an offense to the dignity of the individual. *Arruda v. Fair*, 710 F.2d 886, 887 (1st Cir.1983) (recognizing the "severe if not gross interference with a person's privacy that occurs when guards conduct a visual inspection of body cavities"); *Hunter v. Auger*, 672 F.2d 668, 674 (8th Cir.1982) ("a strip search, regardless how professionally and courteously conducted, is an embarrassing and humiliating experience"). These latter considerations have prompted us to hold that some as-yet undefined "level of *individualized* suspicion" is necessary before a strip search of a prison visitor can be reconciled with the requirements of the fourth amendment.

Appellees contend that the strip search was reasonable, as it was based both on information from a reliable informant and on the uncontroverted evidence of Cochrane's repeated drug use while incarcerated....

Appellant argues that two factors undermine the validity of the strip search: (1) it was done in retaliation for Cochrane's allegations against appellee Quattrocchi (2) there were insufficient indicia of reliability surrounding the evidence that appellant had, in the past, brought drugs into the correctional facility. On this record we conclude that a reasonable person, crediting Cochrane's testimony, as we are presently required to do, could have found that the strip search was conducted in retaliation for Cochrane's allegations—whether made seriously or sardonically—that Quattrocchi or his son supplied the cocaine used by Cochrane in October, 1988. Moreover, absent any evidence that appellant ever violated a prison visitation rule, or ever supplied Cochrane with drugs, a reasonable juror could have concluded that Cochrane's contraband drugs were supplied by prison officials or other inmates. Thus, the jury could have found that the strip search of appellant was unreasonable because it was based on *no* "individualized suspicion."

Our conclusion finds further support in Quattrocchi's testimony as to the reliability of his confidential informant. On direct examination, Quattrocchi admitted that until the morning of the trial, he had been unable to remember the name of the informant who told him that Dawn Cochrane had been carrying drugs to her father. Thereafter, he vouched for the reliability of the informant in only the most general terms, stating in formulaic fashion that the inmate was "a reliable informant, who had proved reliable in the past."

Only much later, ironically on cross-examination by appellant's lawyer, was there any approach to specificity. Even then, the indicia of reliability were meager. Quattrocchi was unable to recall the date when he began to use the informant, and was unwilling to specify the time period during which the information was supplied, or to describe the information received in any detail, stating only that "whenever [the informant] did give me information, it was reliable." With considerable prodding by appellant's counsel, Quattrocchi eventually testified that the informant had, over roughly a six month period, provided reliable information regarding the introduction of narcotics and weapons into the correctional facility.

While this evidence, standing alone, might be viewed as sufficient to justify the strip search of appellant, it is fragile enough to be overcome by a finding that a retaliatory motive, rather than "individualized suspicion," was the real basis for the search.

Since it is the province of the jury to judge witness credibility, and it is for the jury to determine the reasonableness of a search in a section 1983 action, the motion for directed verdict submitted at the conclusion of appellant's case in chief should have been denied.

The district court ruling that appellant's execution of the consent form mooted any question as to whether there was a reasonable basis for the strip search runs counter to our decision in *Blackburn, supra*. There we considered whether a prison visitor who had provided written consents to successive strip searches had waived any fourth amendment claim. The *Blackburn* panel decided . . . that a prison visitor confronted with the choice between submitting to a strip search or foregoing a visit cannot provide a "legally cognizable consent," [Without considering] . . . the question whether a visitor possessed a constitutional right, or merely a privilege, to visit the prison, *Blackburn* concluded that conditioning "access to the Jail upon sacrifice of [the visitor's] right to be free of an otherwise unreasonable strip search" was "dispositive of the consent issue." rejected the argument that the visitor's right to leave rather than submit to search, or to decline to return after the first strip search, in any way affected the issue; "for it is the *very choice to which she was put* that is constitutionally intolerable. . . ." (emphasis in original); *see also Thorne*, 765 F.2d at 1276 (consent does not render a groundless strip search reasonable).

Given that appellant in the instant case was confronted with a similar, and no less "constitutionally intolerable,"

choice between being denied prison visitation access indefinitely or waiving her constitutional right to be free from unreasonable search, *Blackburn* requires the conclusion that appellant gave no "legally cognizable consent." The directed verdicts must be vacated.

The district court judgment is vacated and the case is REMANDED for a new trial. Costs are awarded to appellant.

Questions

1. Identify the interests the court balanced in the case.

2. According to the court, are prison visitors protected by the Fourth Amendment? If so, why?

3. According to the court, why didn't Dawn Cochrane waive her Fourth Amendment right, assuming she had one?

4. List the relevant facts necessary to decide whether there was reasonable suspicion to strip-search Dawn Cochrane. Summarize the court's reasons for ruling the facts didn't add up to reasonable suspicion.

5. Assume you're the prison's lawyer, and argue that the strip search was reasonable. Back up your answer with facts from the case.

EXPLORING CUSTODY-RELATED SEARCHES FURTHER

 Go to the Criminal Procedure 6e CD to read the full text version of this case.

Was the Strip Search of the Corrections Officer Reasonable?

FACTS

Some time before noon, Cook County Corrections investigator Leison Linzy received a phone call from a man identifying himself as Agent Gary Miller of the Federal Bureau of Investigation. Agent Miller told Linzy that an Officer Kennedy would be transporting heroin into Division 5 later that day. He didn't know the officer's first name, nor did he indicate the source of his information. Linzy then called the FBI and confirmed that they employed a man by the name of Gary Miller. Linzy also checked the personnel roster and confirmed that an Officer Kennedy—Alphonso Kennedy—was assigned to work the late shift at Division 5. At this point, Linzy decided he would search Kennedy later that day, and informed Investigators Alfred Brown and Leonard Peterson they'd have to work a little overtime that evening.

As Cook County Corrections Officer Alphonso Kennedy was about to begin his 4:00 P.M.-to-midnight shift, Director of Cook County Department of Corrections Roy Patrick approached Kennedy while he was standing at roll call and ordered him into the nearby men's locker room. Patrick also contacted Linzy, Peterson, and Brown and told them to come to the locker room. Once there, they surrounded Kennedy and searched him, his briefcase, and his locker, forcing him to remove all of his clothes. Then, in plain view of other officers, they examined his body cavities. They found nothing. Was the strip search reasonable?

DECISION AND REASONS

No, according to the District Court:

> In this case, a reasonable jury could certainly conclude that the extensive search of plaintiff was unreasonable. The search was initiated by Patrick who knew, at most, that an FBI agent had informed Linzy that an Officer Kennedy would be bringing drugs into the prison. He did not know the source of the agent's information, the first name of the accused officer, or the intended recipient of the drugs. Nor does it appear that he, or any of the investigators, had any information regarding the quantity of drugs that the officer would be bringing into the prison.

> Nevertheless, he authorized an extensive strip/body cavity search of an officer in a place where the officer's friends and colleagues would be almost certain to witness it. Under these circumstances, this court cannot say that the search was reasonable as a matter of law.... A bare anonymous tip does not provide the requisite "reasonable suspicion" for an extensive strip/body cavity search such as the one involved here. The only "corroboration" Patrick had of the anonymous tip was that an Officer Kennedy did indeed work in Division 5, a fact no more indicative that he sold drugs than that he had an inmate who did not like him.

> Further, there is no evidence in the record that the officer or officers who conducted the body cavity search had any more information than did Patrick regarding the identity or the reliability of the informant. Thus, this court cannot say as a matter of law that the search was reasonable under clearly established legal principles.

> *Kennedy v. Hardiman*, 684 F.Supp. 540
> (U.S. District Court, N.D. Illinois, Eastern Division 1988)

STUDENT SEARCHES

For centuries, minors have lacked some fundamental rights enjoyed by adults, including the right to be let alone by the government. This is especially true while they're in school. According to the legal doctrine *in loco parentis,* school administrators are substitute parents while students are in school. Inspections of students and their stuff during school hours and activities are searches. To determine whether they're *reasonable* searches, courts weigh the special need for schools to maintain an environment where learning can thrive against students' privacy.

The U.S. Supreme Court had to balance the special need of high schools and high-school students' privacy in *New Jersey v. T.L.O* (1985). A teacher at a New Jersey high school caught T.L.O., a 14-year-old freshman, and a friend smoking cigarettes in the girls' bathroom. The teacher took them to the principal's office. T.L.O. denied she was smoking; in fact, she denied she smoked at all. The assistant vice-principal demanded to see her purse, opened it, and found a pack of cigarettes and also noticed a package of cigarette rolling papers commonly used in smoking marijuana. So, he searched the purse more thoroughly and found marijuana, a pipe, plastic bags, a fairly substantial amount of money, and two letters that implicated T.L.O. in marijuana dealing. The state brought delinquency charges, and the case eventually reached the U.S. Supreme Court where the Court had to decide whether the Fourth Amendment applied to searches by school officials.

Two questions confronted the Court: Does the Fourth Amendment apply to school searches? And, was this search reasonable? According to the U.S. Supreme Court, the answer to both questions is yes. The Court held that the Fourth Amendment's ban on unreasonable searches and seizures applies to searches conducted by public school officials. Furthermore, school officials can't escape the commands of the Fourth Amendment because of their authority over schoolchildren. When they search students, they aren't *in loco parentis* (acting as parents); so, students have a reasonable expectation of privacy. But that expectation is limited. Striking a balance between students' reasonable expectations of privacy and the school's legitimate need to maintain a healthy learning environment calls for easing the restrictions on searches of students. So, school officials don't have to get warrants, and they don't need probable cause before they search students. Reasonable suspicion is enough.

But, what about searches of college students? The rules are somewhat different because the setting is different. Most searches are of dormitory rooms, and more often than not law enforcement officers (municipal or college police) participate in the searches. Also, college students are older and are entitled to a greater expectation of privacy. Do these differences matter to the Fourth Amendment? The Supreme Court hasn't answered the question of how much protection the Fourth Amendment guarantees to college students in their dormitory rooms, but federal and state courts have. One such decision was in the Massachusetts case *Commonwealth v. Neilson* (1996).

| CASE | *Was the Search of the Dormitory Room Reasonable?* |

Commonwealth v. Neilson
666 N.E.2d 984 (Mass. 1996)

The defendant, Eric W. Neilson, is charged with illegal possession of marihuana and cultivating and distributing marihuana, in violation of G.L. c. 94C, § § 32C, 34 (1994 ed.). A District Court judge allowed the defendant's motion to suppress evidence and contraband obtained in a search of his dormitory room at Fitchburg State College. A single justice of this court granted the Commonwealth's application for an interlocutory appeal from the allowance of the defendant's motion and transmitted the case to the Appeals Court. We transferred the case here on our own initiative and now affirm the decision of the District Court.

LYNCH, J.

FACTS

At the time of his arrest, Eric Neilson (defendant) was a twenty-three-year-old student living in a dormitory at Fitchburg State College, a public institution. Before moving into the dormitory, the defendant signed a residence hall contract, which stated, in relevant part, that "residence life staff members will enter student rooms to inspect for hazards to health or personal safety."

On the morning of April 30, 1993, a maintenance worker heard a cat inside a dormitory suite containing four bedrooms, including the defendant's. He reported the information to college officials, who visited the suite and informed one of the residents (not the defendant) that any cat must be removed pursuant to the college's health and safety regulations. That afternoon, a college official posted notices on all four bedroom doors of the suite, informing the students of the possible violation of college policy and alerting them that a "door to door check" would be conducted by 10 P.M. that night to ensure that the cat had been removed.

That night, the officials returned; the defendant was not present. While searching the defendant's bedroom, the officials noticed a light emanating from the closet. The officials, fearing a fire hazard, opened the closet door. There, they discovered two four-foot tall marihuana plants, along with lights, fertilizer, and numerous other materials for marihuana cultivation and use.

The officials stopped their investigation at that point, and requested the assistance of the Fitchburg State College campus police, who have powers of arrest. The police arrived at the suite, entered the bedroom, and observed the marihuana plants and other apparatus. They took photographs of the evidence and then, with the help of the college officials, removed it from the room. At no time did the police seek, obtain, or possess a warrant for the search.

OPINION

...The right to be free from unreasonable searches and seizures as guaranteed by the Fourth Amendment to the United States Constitution applies when the police search a dormitory room in a public college. *Morale v. Grigel,* 422 F.Supp. 988, 997 (D.N.H.1976) ("dormitory room is a student's home away from home"); *Commonwealth v. Mc-Closkey,* 217 Pa.Super. 432, 435, 272 A.2d 271 (1970) ("dormitory room is analogous to an apartment or a hotel room"). See also *Tinker v. Des Moines Indep. Community Sch. Dist.,* 393 U.S. 503, 506, 89 S.Ct. 733, 736, 21 L.Ed.2d 731 (1969) (students do not "shed their constitutional rights ... at the schoolhouse gate"). To be reasonable in the constitutional sense, a search usually must be supported by probable cause and be accompanied by a search warrant, unless there are circumstances excusing the use of a warrant.

The probable cause and warrant requirements are relaxed, however, in the case of searches that occur in elementary and secondary public schools. There is no constitutional violation when a high school official conducts a warrantless search that is "reasonable in all the circumstances." This reduced standard was prompted by "concerns about school officials' vital responsibility to preserve a proper educational environment" and "the special need for an immediate response to behavior that threatens either the safety of schoolchildren and teachers or the educational process itself...."

The Commonwealth urges us to extend the lesser protections afforded to high school students into the collegiate arena. Although the courts that have examined the issue are split on whether the Fourth Amendment requires probable cause and a warrant in college searches, when police are involved and the evidence obtained is to be used in a criminal proceeding, courts generally require probable cause and a warrant, absent express consent or exigent circumstances. *People v. Haskins,* 48 A.D.2d 480, 484, 369 N.Y.S.2d 869 (N.Y.1975) ("A more strict standard would certainly apply if the search had been instigated by law enforcement officials or if law enforcement personnel had participated in the search to any significant degree, thereby directly tainting the search by the school official with State action"); *State v. Hunter,* 831 P.2d 1033, 1037 (Utah Ct.App.1992) ("Nor did university officials attempt to delegate their right to inspect rooms to the police, which would result in the circumvention of traditional restrictions on police activity"). See also *New Jersey v. T.L.O., supra* at 341 n. 7, 105 S.Ct. at 743 n. 7 (not deciding whether probable cause and a warrant might be required when police are involved in a high school search); *Picha v. Wielgos,* 410 F.Supp. 1214, 1219–1221 (N.D.Ill.1976) (junior high school search by police required probable cause).

The defendant does not contend (and the District Court judge did not find) that the initial search of the dormitory room by college officials was improper. The defendant consented to reasonable searches to enforce the college's health and safety regulations when he signed the residence contract. The hunt for the elusive feline fit within the scope of that consent. Similarly, when the college officials opened the closet door they were reasonably concerned about health and safety. Thus, the initial search was reasonable because it was intended to enforce a legitimate health and safety rule that related to the college's function as an educational institution. See *Piazzola v. Watkins, supra* at 289 (search must further legitimate educational function).

Instead, the crux of the defendant's argument is that constitutional violation occurred when the campus police searched the room and seized evidence. We agree. The police entered the room without a warrant, consent, or exigent circumstances. This search was unreasonable and violated the defendant's Fourth Amendment rights. The Commonwealth contends that, since the college officials were in the room by consent, and observed the drugs in plain view while pursuing legitimate objectives, the police officers' warrantless entry was proper. Furthermore, the Commonwealth argues, the police action was lawful because it did not exceed the scope of the prior search and seizure by college officials. We disagree.

First, there was no consent to the police entry and search of the room. "The [defendant's] consent [was] given, not to police officials, but to the University and the latter cannot fragmentize, share or delegate it." While the college officials were entitled to conduct a health and safety inspection, they "clearly . . . had no authority to consent to or join in a police search for evidence of crime." *Piazzola v. Watkins, supra* at 290.

Second, the plain view doctrine does not apply to the police seizure, where the officers were not lawfully present in the dormitory room when they made their plain view observations. While the college officials were legitimately present in the room to enforce a reasonable health and safety regulation, the sole purpose of the warrantless police entry into the dormitory room was to confiscate contraband for purposes of a criminal proceeding. An entry for such a purpose required a warrant where, as here, there was no showing of express consent or exigent circumstances.

We conclude that, when the campus police entered the defendant's dormitory room without a warrant, they violated the defendant's Fourth Amendment rights. All evidence obtained as a result of that illegal search was properly suppressed by the judge below.

Judgment AFFIRMED.

Questions

1. Explain why the court concluded Neilson gave consent to the officials but not to the campus police to enter and search his room. Do you agree? Defend your answer.

2. List the specific invasions on Neilson's privacy.

3. Summarize the reasons why the court decided the search by college officials was reasonable and the search by campus police was unreasonable.

4. Assume you're Neilson's lawyer, and argue that the search by college officials was unreasonable. Back up your answer with facts and arguments made by the state in the case.

5. Do you think Neilson's privacy outweighs the college's special needs? Back up your answer.

6. Does it matter whether the officials or campus police or city police conduct the search? Defend your answer.

◆　　◆　　◆

EMPLOYEE DRUG SEARCHES

Searches for employee drug use through drug testing are directed at the special need to reduce the danger to public safety caused by pilots, bus drivers, railway engineers, and others who work while they're under the influence of alcohol and other drugs. But, meeting that need obviously conflicts with the privacy of the employees. According to Associate U.S. Supreme Court Justice Sandra Day O'Connor, dissenting in *Vernonia School District v. Acton* (1995, 672): "State-compelled, state-monitored collecting of urine, while perhaps not the most intrusive of searches (visual body cavity searches) is still particularly destructive of privacy and offensive to personal dignity." The Supreme Court dealt with the problem of balancing the government's need and employees' privacy in *National Treasury Employees Union v. Von Raab* (1989).

| CASE | *Was the Urine Test a Reasonable Search?* |

National Treasury Employees Union v. Von Raab
489 U.S. 656, 109 S.Ct. 1384, 103 L.Ed.2d 685 (1989)

The National Treasury Employees Union and its president brought an action against the U.S. Customs Service to get an injunction (court order) and to challenge the constitu-

tionality of a drug-testing program that analyzed urine specimens of employees who applied for promotion to positions connected to the interdiction of illegal drugs, the required carrying of firearms, or the handling of classified materials. The Customs Service moved to dismiss. The U.S. District Court denied a motion to dismiss and granted the injunction. The Customs Service appealed. The Court of Appeals for the Fifth Circuit vacated the injunction. The U.S. Supreme Court granted certiorari. The U.S. Supreme Court reversed.

KENNEDY, J., joined by REHNQUIST, CJ., and WHITE, BLACKMUN, and O'CONNOR, JJ.

FACTS

The United States Customs Service, a bureau of the Department of the Treasury, is the federal agency responsible for processing persons, carriers, cargo, and mail into the United States, collecting revenue from imports, and enforcing customs and related laws. An important responsibility of the Service is the interdiction and seizure of contraband, including illegal drugs. In 1987 alone, Customs agents seized drugs with a retail value of nearly 9 billion dollars.

In the routine discharge of their duties, many Customs employees have direct contact with those who traffic in drugs for profit. Drug import operations, often directed by sophisticated criminal syndicates, may be effected by violence or its threat. As a necessary response, many Customs operatives carry and use firearms in connection with their official duties. In December 1985, respondent, the Commissioner of Customs, established a Drug Screening Task Force to explore the possibility of implementing a drug screening program within the Service.

After extensive research and consultation with experts in the field, the Task Force concluded "that drug screening through urinalysis is technologically reliable, valid and accurate." Citing this conclusion, the Commissioner announced his intention to require drug tests of employees who applied for, or occupied, certain positions within the Service. The Commissioner stated his belief that "Customs is largely drug-free," but noted also that "unfortunately no segment of society is immune from the threat of illegal drug use." Interdiction has become the agency's primary enforcement mission, and the Commissioner stressed that "there is no room in the Customs Service for those who break the laws prohibiting the possession and use of illegal drugs."

In May 1986, the Commissioner announced implementation of the drug-testing program. Drug tests were made a condition of placement or employment for positions that meet one or more of three criteria. The first is direct involvement in drug interdiction or enforcement of related laws, an activity the Commissioner deemed fraught with obvious dangers to the mission of the agency and the lives of customs agents. The second criterion is a requirement that the incumbent carry firearms, as the Commissioner concluded that "public safety demands that em-

ployees who carry deadly arms and are prepared to make instant life or death decisions be drug free." The third criterion is a requirement for the incumbent to handle "classified" material, which the Commissioner determined might fall into the hands of smugglers if accessible to employees who, by reason of their own illegal drug use, are susceptible to bribery or blackmail.

After an employee qualifies for a position covered by the Customs testing program, the Service advises him by letter that his final selection is contingent upon successful completion of drug screening. An independent contractor contacts the employee to fix the time and place for collecting the sample. On reporting for the test, the employee must produce photographic identification and remove any outer garments, such as a coat or a jacket, and personal belongings. The employee may produce the sample behind a partition, or in the privacy of a bathroom stall if he so chooses. To ensure against adulteration of the specimen, or substitution of a sample from another person, a monitor of the same sex as the employee remains close at hand to listen for the normal sounds of urination. Dye is added to the toilet water to prevent the employee from using the water to adulterate the sample.

Upon receiving the specimen, the monitor inspects it to ensure its proper temperature and color, places a tamper-proof custody seal over the container, and affixes an identification label indicating the date and the individual's specimen number. The employee signs a chain-of-custody form, which is initialed by the monitor, and the urine sample is placed in a plastic bag, sealed, and submitted to a laboratory. . . . The laboratory tests the sample for the presence of marijuana, cocaine, opiates, amphetamines, and phencyclidine. . . .

Petitioners, a union of federal employees and a union official, commenced this suit in the United States District Court for the Eastern District of Louisiana on behalf of current Customs Service employees who seek covered positions. Petitioners alleged that the Custom Service drug-testing program violated the Fourth Amendment. The District Court agreed. The court acknowledged "the legitimate governmental interest in a drug-free work place and work force," but concluded that "the drug testing plan constitutes an overly intrusive policy of searches and seizures without probable cause or reasonable suspicion, in violation of legitimate expectations of privacy." The court enjoined the drug testing program, and ordered the Customs Service not to require drug tests of any applicants for covered positions.

A divided panel of the United States Court of Appeals for the Fifth Circuit vacated the injunction. . . . We granted certiorari. We now affirm so much of the judgment of the court of appeals as upheld the testing of employees directly involved in drug interdiction or required to carry firearms. We vacate the judgment to the extent it upheld the testing of applicants for positions requiring the incumbent to handle classified materials, and remand for further proceedings.

OPINION

...While we have often emphasized, and reiterate today, that a search must be supported, as a general matter, by a warrant issued upon probable cause,...neither a warrant nor probable cause, nor, indeed, any measure of individualized suspicion, is an indispensable component of reasonableness in every circumstance....Our cases establish that where a Fourth Amendment intrusion serves special governmental needs, beyond the normal need for law enforcement, it is necessary to balance the individual's privacy expectations against the Government's interests to determine whether it is impractical to require a warrant or some level of individualized suspicion in the particular context.

It is clear that the Customs Service's drug testing program is not designed to serve the ordinary needs of law enforcement. Test results may not be used in a criminal prosecution of the employee without the employee's consent. The purposes of the program are to deter drug use among those eligible for promotion to sensitive positions within the Service and to prevent the promotion of drug users to those positions. These substantial interests...present a special need that may justify departure from the ordinary warrant and probable cause requirements....

The Customs Service is our Nation's first line of defense against one of the greatest problems affecting the health and welfare of our population. We have adverted before to "the veritable national crisis in law enforcement caused by smuggling of illicit narcotics." Our cases also reflect the traffickers' seemingly inexhaustible repertoire of deceptive practices and elaborate schemes for importing narcotics, e.g., *United States v. Montoya de Hernandez.**...The record in this case confirms that, through the adroit selection of source locations, smuggling routes, and increasingly elaborate methods of concealment, drug traffickers have managed to bring into this country increasingly large quantities of illegal drugs. The record also indicates, and it is well known, that drug smugglers do not hesitate to use violence to protect their lucrative trade and avoid apprehension. Many of the Service's employees are often exposed to this criminal element and to the controlled substances they seek to smuggle into the country....

Where the Government requires its employees to produce urine samples to be analyzed for evidence of illegal

drug use, the collection and subsequent chemical analysis of such samples are searches that must meet the reasonableness requirement of the Fourth Amendment. Because the testing program adopted by the Customs Service is not designed to serve the ordinary needs of law enforcement, we have balanced the public interest in the Service's testing program against the privacy concerns implicated by the tests, without reference to our usual presumption in favor of the procedures specified in the Warrant Clause, to assess whether the tests required by Customs are reasonable.

We hold that the suspicionless testing of employees who apply for promotion to positions directly involving the interdiction of illegal drugs, or to positions which require the incumbent to carry a firearm, is reasonable. The Government's compelling interests in preventing the promotion of drug users to positions where they might endanger the integrity of our Nation's borders or the life of the citizenry outweigh the privacy interests of those who seek promotion to these positions, who enjoy a diminished expectation of privacy by virtue of the special, and obvious, physical and ethical demands of those positions.

DISSENT

SCALIA, J., joined by STEVENS, J.
...The issue here is what steps can constitutionally be taken to detect drug use. The Government asserts it can demand that employees perform "an excretory function traditionally shielded by great privacy," while "a monitor of the same sex...remains close at hand to listen for the normal sounds," and that the excretion thus produced be turned over to the Government for chemical analysis. The Court agrees that this constitutes a search for purposes of the Fourth Amendment—and I think it obvious that it is a type of search particularly destructive of privacy and offensive to personal dignity.

Until today this court had upheld a bodily search separate from arrest and without individualized suspicion of wrongdoing only with respect to prison inmates, relying upon the uniquely dangerous nature of that environment. Today, [in a companion case upholding urine tests of railway workers] we allow a less intrusive bodily search of railroad employees involved in train accidents. I joined the Court's opinion there because the demonstrated frequency of drug and alcohol use by the targeted class of employees, and the demonstrated connection between such use and grave harm, rendered the search a reasonable means of protecting society. I decline to join the Court's opinion in the present case because neither frequency of use nor connection to harm is demonstrated or even likely. In my view the Customs Service rules are a kind of immolation of privacy and human dignity in symbolic opposition to drug use....

---

*See Chapter 4.

The Court's opinion in the present case will be searched in vain for real evidence of a real problem that will be solved by urine testing of Customs Service employees.... The only pertinent points, it seems to me, are supported by nothing but speculation, and not very plausible speculation at that.... What is absent in the Government's justifications—notably absent, revealingly absent, and as far as I am concerned dispositively absent—is the recitation of even a single instance in which any of the speculated horribles actually occurred: an instance, that is, in which the cause of bribe-taking, or of poor aim, or of unsympathetic law enforcement, or of compromise of classified information, was drug use....

The Court's response to this lack of evidence is that "there is little reason to believe that American workplaces are immune from the pervasive social problem" of drug abuse. Perhaps such a generalization would suffice if the workplace at issue could produce such catastrophic social harm that no risk whatever is tolerable—the secured areas of a nuclear power plant. But if such a generalization suffices to justify demeaning bodily searches, without particularized suspicion, to guard against the bribing or blackmailing of a law enforcement agent, or the careless use of a firearm, then the Fourth Amendment has become frail protection indeed.

...I do not believe for a minute that the driving force behind these drug-testing rules was any of the feeble justifications put forward by counsel here and accepted by the Court. The only plausible explanation, in my view, is what the Commissioner himself offered in the concluding sentence of his memorandum to Customs Service employees announcing the program: "Implementation of the drug screening program would set an important example in our country's struggle with this most serious threat to our national health and security." Or as respondent's brief to this Court asserted: "if a law enforcement agency and its employees do not take the law seriously, neither will the public on which the agency's effectiveness depends."

What better way to show that the Government is serious about its "war on drugs" than to subject its employees on the front line of that war to this invasion of their privacy and affront to their dignity? To be sure, there is only a slight chance that it will prevent some serious public harm resulting from Service employee drug use, but it will show to the world that the Service is "clean," and—most important of all—will demonstrate the determination of the Government to eliminate this scourge of our society!

I think it obvious that this justification is unacceptable; that the impairment of individual liberties cannot be the means of making a point; that symbolism, even symbolism for so worthy a cause as the abolition of unlawful drugs, cannot validate an otherwise unreasonable search. There is irony in the Government's citation, in support of its position, of Justice BRANDEIS's statement in *Olmstead v. United States* (1928) that "for good or for ill, (our Government) teaches the whole people by its example." BRANDEIS was there dissenting from the Court's admission of evidence obtained through an unlawful Government wiretap. He was not praising the Government's example of vigor and enthusiasm in combating crime, but condemning its example that "the end justifies the means." An even more apt quotation from that famous BRANDEIS dissent would have been the following:

It is...immaterial that the intrusion was in aid of law enforcement. Experience should teach us to be most on our guard to protect liberty when the Government's purposes are beneficent. Men born to freedom are naturally alert to repel invasion of their liberty by evil-minded rulers. The greatest dangers to liberty lurk in insidious encroachment by men of zeal, well-meaning but without understanding.

Those who lose because of the lack of understanding that begot the present exercise in symbolism are not just the Custom Service employees, whose dignity is thus offended, but all of us—who suffer a coarsening of our national manners that ultimately give the Fourth Amendment its content, and who become subject to the administration of federal officials whose respect for our privacy can hardly be greater than the small respect they have been taught to have for their own.

Questions

1. What compelling government interest and what privacy interests did the Court balance in reaching its result in this case?

2. What precise intrusions and deprivations do employees suffer in the Customs Service's drug-testing program?

3. Does Justice Scalia have a point that no evidence established a link between the interest the government seeks to protect in the drug testing and the method used to protect the interest?

4. Should the Court require empirical proof before it accepts plans to further governmental interests?

5. Does the Court promote the interests of drug control at too high a cost to individual privacy? Or does it balance them properly? Explain your answer.

Go to Exercise 7-1 on the Criminal Procedure 6e CD to learn more about drug testing.

◆   ◆   ◆

SUMMARY

I. Special needs vs. the expectation of privacy
   A. The Fourth Amendment applies to special-needs searches beyond searches for evidence of a crime
   B. Common characteristics of special-needs searches
      1. Directed at everybody, not just criminal suspects
      2. Can result in criminal prosecution and conviction
      3. Don't require warrants or probable cause
      4. Balancing test of Fourth Amendment reasonableness
         a. Special need
         b. Individual privacy

II. Inventory searches
   A. Definition—making a list of people's personal property and containers held in government custody
   B. No need for warrant or probable cause
   C. Balancing test of reasonableness
      1. Protection of three special needs
         a. People's personal "stuff" and their containers
         b. Law enforcement agencies from lawsuits
         c. Officers, suspects, and defendants from the dangers posed by smuggled-in bombs, weapons, and drugs
      2. Invasion of individual privacy
   D. Objective basis
      1. Routine written procedures substitute for individualized suspicion
      2. Routine written procedures guarantee against using inventory as a pretext for searches for evidence of a crime

III. International border searches
   A. Reasonable even without warrants or probable cause
   B. Special government need to control what enters and leaves the country outweighs the invasions of individual privacy
   C. Objective basis
      1. Routine searches—none
      2. Strip—reasonable suspicion
      3. Body cavity—probable cause

IV. Airport searches
   A. Reasonable even without warrants or individualized suspicion
   B. Balance
      1. Special needs of passenger security and safety
      2. Minimal invasion of passengers privacy with advance notice they'll have to go through metal detectors and pass baggage through X-ray machines
   C. Objective basis
      1. No individualized suspicion required
      2. All passengers affected by the same routine procedure of metal detectors and X-ray machines

V. Custody-related searches
   A. Applies to
      1. Prisoners (in jails before conviction and in jails and prisons after conviction)
      2. Probationers and parolees
      3. Visitors and employees
   B. Reasonable even without warrants or probable cause
   C. Balances
      1. Safety, security, and discipline in prisons
      2. Significantly reduced expectation of privacy of individuals
   D. Prisoners
      1. General
         a. Greatly reduced expectation of privacy society is prepared to recognize
         b. Surveillance the order of the day in prisons
         c. No "iron curtain" between prison and constitution
      2. Balance need for security, safety, and discipline against prisoners' reduced right against unreasonable searches and seizures
      3. No objective basis required for shakedowns because they're not Fourth Amendment searches
      4. Strip and body-cavity searches are protected by the Fourth Amendment but only to the extent they require reasonable suspicion (not probable cause) to back them up
   E. Probationers and parolees
      1. Searches of probationers and parolees don't require warrants or probable cause to be reasonable (probation and parole are *privileges,* not *rights,* so probationers' and parolees' rights are substantially reduced)
      2. Balancing approach—special need to protect community from convicted criminals free in the community outweighs probationers' and parolees' Fourth Amendment rights (probationers and parolees are still in custody even though they're released into the community)
   F. Visitors and employees
      1. Searches are reasonable even without warrants or probable cause
      2. Balancing test of reasonableness
         a. Special need to prevent smuggled drugs, weapons, and money from entering prisons
         b. Substantially reduced expectation of privacy for prison employees and visitors
      3. Objective basis
         a. No individualized suspicion needed for
            (1) Pat-downs
            (2) Removal of outer clothing
            (3) Emptying pockets
            (4) Screening by metal detectors
            (5) Inspection of papers, books, and containers
         b. Substitute for individualized suspicion—carried out in a "manner least likely to embarrass or delay the passage" (*Black v. Amico*)
      4. Strip searches are different—individualized reasonable suspicion required

VI. Student searches
   A. High school
      1. Reduced expectation of privacy in school
      2. Searches reasonable even without warrants or probable cause
      3. Balancing test
         a. Special need to preserve safe learning environment
         b. Reduced expectation of privacy for high-school students
      4. Objective basis—individualized reasonable suspicion required to search students and their lockers
   B. College
      1. Circumstances different from high school
         a. Searches are usually of dorm rooms ("home away from home")
         b. Law enforcement usually participates (municipal or campus)
         c. College students are entitled to a greater expectation of privacy
      2. No warrants or probable cause required for college officials to conduct safety and health inspections that aren't intended to gather evidence of crime
      3. Warrants based on probable cause are required for municipal or campus police to search dorm rooms

VII. Employee drug searches
   A. Reasonable without warrants or individualized suspicion
   B. Balancing test
      1. Special need to protect public safety of travelers
      2. Minimal invasion (urine sample) of employees' privacy
   C. Objective basis—random testing

 Go to the Criminal Procedure 6e CD to download this summary outline. The outline has been formatted so that you can add notes to it during class lectures, or later create a customized chapter outline to use while reviewing. Either way, the summary outline will help you understand the "big picture" and fill in the details as you study.

REVIEW QUESTIONS

1. Identify four characteristics all special-needs searches have in common.

2. Why are inventory searches reasonable even without warrants or probable cause?

3. Identify three special needs satisfied by inventory searches.

4. Describe the balancing test of reasonableness as it applies to inventory searches.

5. What substitutes for probable cause as the objective basis for inventory searches?

6. Why are searches at international borders reasonable without warrants or probable cause?

7. Describe the special need, the degree of invasion, and the objective basis in airport searches.

8. Identify and describe the special need and the expectation of privacy in custody-related searches.

9. Identify the special need for searches of prisoners and prisoners' expectation of privacy.

10. What effect does searching for the purpose of harassing prisoners have on the reasonableness of prison shakedowns?

11. When are strip and body-cavity searches of prisoners "reasonable"? Explain.

12. What's the objective basis required to back up strip searches?

13. Give two explanations for why searches of probationers and parolees don't require warrants or probable cause to be reasonable.

14. List five invasions of prison employees' and visitors' privacy that are reasonable even without any facts backing them up.

15. Describe the manner in which searches of prison visitors and employees have to be conducted.

16. Identify the special need and the expectation of privacy balanced in searches of high-school students as outlined by the U.S. Supreme Court in *T.L.O. v. New Jersey.*

17. Why are searches of high-school students reasonable without warrants or probable cause?

18. How does the setting of searches of college students differ from the setting of searches of high-school students?

19. According to *Commonwealth v. Nielson,* why are searches of college students' dorm rooms reasonable only if backed up by warrants and probable cause?

20. Why are employee drug tests reasonable without warrants or probable cause?

KEY TERMS

special-needs searches p. 247
inventory searches p. 247
international border searches
   p. 247
airport searches p. 247
custody-related searches p. 248

student searches p. 248
employee drug testing p. 248
containers p. 248
routine written procedure
   requirement p. 249
border search exception p. 252

shakedown p. 254
in loco parentis p. 261

THE COMPANION WEB SITE
FOR *CRIMINAL PROCEDURE,* SIXTH EDITION

http://cj.wadsworth.com/samaha/crim_pro6e

Supplement your review of this chapter by going to the companion Web site to take one of the Tutorial Quizzes, use the flash cards to test yourself on the key terms from each chapter, and check out the many other study aids you'll find there. You'll find valuable data and resources at your fingertips to help you study for that big exam or write that important paper.

8 Police Interrogation and Confessions

Chapter Main Points

- *Miranda v. Arizona* is part of our culture and of our "culture wars."
- Interrogation of suspects isn't pleasant—and it's not supposed to be.
- Interrogation may be unpleasant, but it helps convict guilty people *and* free innocent people.
- Interrogators rarely coerce suspects to confess, and most interrogations are short.
- Voluntariness, fairness, and truth are the rationales for the right against self-incrimination.
- The right to remain silent applies only to *testimony,* not to physical evidence.
- *Pressure* during interrogation is constitutional; *coercion* isn't.
- Custodial interrogation is *inherently* coercive without the *Miranda* warnings.
- The *Miranda* warnings are only required if suspects are in custody and are being interrogated.
- The *Miranda* warnings aren't required if giving them would endanger an officer or someone nearby.
- Most suspects give up (waive) their constitutional rights to remain silent and to counsel.
- Due process requires that all confessions have to be voluntary.
- Confessions are involuntary only if officers engaged in coercive conduct during the interrogation *and* the coercion *caused* the suspect to confess.

No person shall be compelled in any criminal case to be a witness against himself.

U.S. Constitution, Fifth Amendment

Miranda has become embedded in routine police practice to the point where the warnings have become part of our national culture.

Chief Justice William Rehnquist (June 26, 2000)

THE INTERROGATION AND CONFESSION SETTING

What was the occasion for Chief Justice Rehnquist's comment? He was reading the U.S. Supreme Court's decision in *Dickerson v. U.S* (2000). In that case, the Court ruled that Congress doesn't have the power to overrule *Miranda v. Arizona* (1966), something it had tried to do in 1968. In that year, in a burst of "get tough on criminals" legislation, Congress passed a law saying officers don't have to warn suspects of their rights to a lawyer and against self-incrimination before they interrogate them. The law was ignored by federal and state officials until 1997 when a Virginia federal court relied on the 1968 statute to admit Charles Dickerson's confession obtained after FBI agents gave him defective *Miranda* warnings. The 1968 law, the 1997 case relying on it, and the Supreme Court's decision declaring the law unconstitutional reflect a long and emotional debate over the right against self-incrimination.

The Chief Justice was right: *Miranda* is part of our culture, but what he left out is it's also part of our culture wars. Perhaps no procedure has generated more hostility between social conservatives and social liberals. On the popular TV cop show *NYPD Blue*, the "good cops" Andy Sipowitz and whoever his current partner is (it's getting to be a long list) wage a "war on *Miranda*." In almost every episode, a "scumbag" murderer—or his lawyer—makes a "mockery of the system" by taunting the cops with his "rights." Then, Sipowitz and his partner threaten, shove, and usually wind up beating a confession out of the "worthless animal" called a suspect. We all know he's guilty (it's always a man by the way), and we're invited to hate not only the murderer but also the system that provides such scumbags with rights.

But, this popular portrayal of saintly cops and satanic criminals hides the complexity of real police interrogation and confessions. The atmosphere in police stations is (and it's supposed to be) strange, intimidating, and hostile to criminal suspects. It's not like being stopped, asked a few questions, and frisked in the familiar surroundings of public places (Chapter 4). In police stations, suspects are thoroughly searched—sometimes strip-searched and, occasionally, subjected to body-cavity searches (Chapter 6); they have to stand in lineups (Chapter 9); and, they're interrogated incommunicado. (Let's be clear, this isn't a criticism; it's a description.) Being taken to police stations isn't supposed to be pleasant for suspects. The atmosphere and the actions are supposed to flush out the truth about suspects' possible criminal behavior or what they know about someone else's criminal behavior.

By the time officers bring arrested suspects to police stations, their investigation has focused on those particular suspects. This period when the police have shifted their attention from a general investigation of a crime to building a case against a named individual is called the **accusatory stage** of the criminal process. During this stage, balancing the needs of law enforcement against the interests of individual privacy and liberty carries higher stakes for both suspects and law enforcement. Defining the proper balance between these competing social interests during the period when the police hold suspects in custody but before prosecutors have charged them with crimes has always generated controversy over how much the U.S. Constitution protects criminal suspects in police custody.

These aren't black-and-white issues. Consider the following hypothetical situations. In which cases can the persons "be compelled to be witnesses" against themselves?

1. A police officer asks a man he has stopped on the street, "What are you doing out at 1:30 A.M.?" The man replies, "I'm trying to buy some crystal meth, as if it's any of your business."

2. An officer hears screams coming from an apartment. He enters without knocking and asks, "What's going on here?" A woman answers, "I just beat up my baby."

3. An elderly woman is beaten when she won't give her purse to three muggers. She is left on the street and dies of exposure. Officers in relays question an 18-year-old suspect for six hours without a break. Some officers get tough, bullying the youth and telling him he's in "big trouble" if he doesn't talk. But, they never touch him. One officer befriends him, telling him the officer knows whoever took the purse didn't mean to kill the woman and that, anyway, it was really her fault for resisting. The young man finally weakens and confesses.

4. A police officer, while interrogating a suspect in the police station, promises, "If you'll just tell me the truth about raping the college student, I'll see to it that the prosecutor only charges you with misdemeanor assault." The suspect asks, "You can do that?" The officer replies, "Sure, I wouldn't tell you something I couldn't do." The suspect says, "O.K., I did it." He later puts the confession in writing.

5. An officer tells a suspect brought to the police station for questioning, "You might as well admit you killed your husband, because your neighbor already told us he saw the whole thing." The officer is lying. The suspect replies, "My God, I knew I should've pulled the shades; that nosy bastard's always spying on me."

Reconsider your answers after you've read the rest of the chapter. In the meantime, to better understand interrogation and confessions, we'll examine their importance and look at the potential for the abuse of interrogation.

The Importance of Interrogation and Confessions

Almost a half century ago, in *Culombe v. Connecticut* (1961), U.S. Supreme Court Justice Felix Frankfurter explained why he believed police interrogation and confessions were important:

Despite modern advances in the technology of crime detection, offenses frequently occur about which things cannot be made to speak. And where there cannot be found innocent human witnesses to such offenses, nothing remains—if police investigation is not to be balked before it has fairly begun—but to seek out possible guilty witnesses and ask them questions, witnesses, that is, who are suspected of knowing something about the offense precisely because they are suspected of implication in it. (571)

Fred Inbau—for sixty years a professor of law, author of the leading manual on police interrogation, and one of the best interrogators of his time—gave three reasons why he supported Justice Frankfurter's position (Kamisar 1977):

1. Police can't solve many crimes unless guilty people confess or suspects give police information that can convict someone else who's guilty.

2. Criminals don't confess unless the police either catch them in the act or interrogate them in private.

3. Police have to use "less refined methods" when they interrogate suspects than are "appropriate for the transaction of ordinary, every-day affairs by and between law-abiding citizens" (Inbau 1961).

We'll probably never know empirically how close to the truth Justice Frankfurter and Professor Inbau were about the importance of interrogations and confessions. U.S. Supreme Court Chief Justice Earl Warren—himself an experienced and effective former prosecutor—explained why: "Interrogation still takes place in privacy. Privacy results in secrecy and this in turn results in a gap in our knowledge as to what in fact goes on in the interrogation room" (*Miranda v. Arizona,* 1966). But some recent empirical research is closing this gap. Sociologist Richard Leo (1998, 65–74) spent more than five hundred hours inside the interrogation rooms of a major urban police department and also viewed videotaped **custodial interrogations** (police questioning suspects while holding them against their will, usually in a police station but sometimes in other places) from two other departments. His observations produced important findings, including:

1. Interrogators rarely coerce suspects to confess.

2. Almost all interrogations last less than an hour.

3. One in four suspects invokes his *Miranda* rights.

4. Interrogators make up evidence and use "good guy–bad guy" routines to undermine the confidence of suspects and overcome their rational decision making.

The Abuse of Interrogation

What amounts to abuse of police power to interrogate suspects? Answers vary radically. At one extreme are those who maintain that *all* incommunicado interrogation is an abuse of police power. At the other extreme are those who contend that only beating, whipping, or threats of violence are out of line. In the middle are those who say *pressure* is okay; *coercion* isn't. But, what's the difference between pressure and coercion? Coercion obviously includes using force or threatening to use force. It can also include tricks, lies, or false promises that "overbear the will" of the suspect (Kamisar 1977; Caplan 1985; Schulhofer 1981, 1987; White 1986).

Those who say all incommunicado interrogation is coercive take this extreme position because they're worried about three possibilities:

1. Innocent people might be convicted.

2. The government might not bear its burden of carrying the whole load of proving suspects are guilty.

3. The police might abuse their power.

Those who favor broad police interrogation power stress three needs:

1. Get the facts.

2. Convict the guilty.

3. Convict the guilty quickly, so offenders can be punished and get on with the business of redemption.

Those who say "pressure yes; coercion no" adopt to some degree the reasons given by both extremes. At the end of the day, disagreement over defining the abuse of interrogation boils down to balancing the interest in obtaining the correct result in individual cases against guaranteeing fairness in all cases.

THE CONSTITUTION AND SELF-INCRIMINATION

The right to remain silent in the face of an accusation has ancient religious *and* legal origins. The ancient Talmudic law, which put the teachings of Moses into writing, contained an absolute prohibition against self-incrimination. There was no way you could waive your right against self-incrimination because it violated the right of survival. Jesus was probably exercising this right when he stood before the Roman governor Pontius Pilate, who demanded to know if Jesus was guilty of treason. When Pilate asked, "Art thou King of the Jews?"

> Jesus artfully replied, "Thou sayest." Then the chief priests and elders accused Jesus of many crimes. Jesus stood and "answered them nothing." Surprised at Jesus' obstinacy, Pilate demanded, "Hearest thou not how many things they witness against thee?" And still Jesus answered him to never a word, insomuch that the governor marveled greatly.
>
> Matthew 27: 11-14

The origin of the right to remain silent is also tied to another ancient rule, the common-law rule that confessions had to be voluntary.

By the time the right to remain silent appeared in the Fifth Amendment to the U.S. Constitution, it had followed a controversial and complicated history (Levy 1968). We'll learn more about this Fifth Amendment right as we look at three constitutional approaches to controlling interrogation and confessions. Each is based on interpretations of constitutional clauses, including those that guarantee individual rights to due process, the "right to counsel," and not being compelled to be witnesses against ourselves.

Three Constitutional Approaches

The U.S. Supreme Court has relied on three provisions in the U.S. Constitution to develop rules to control police interrogation and confessions (Table 8.1):

TABLE 8.1

The U.S. Constitution and Self-Incrimination

Amendment	Stage of Criminal Process
Fifth and Fourteenth Amendment due process clauses	All stages
Sixth Amendment right-to-counsel clause	All stages after formal proceedings begin
Fifth Amendment self-incrimination clause	Custodial interrogation and all stages following

1. *Fourteenth Amendment* **due process clause.** "No state shall... deprive any person of life, liberty, or property without due process of law."

2. *Sixth Amendment* **right-to-counsel clause.** "In all criminal prosecutions, the accused shall... have the assistance of counsel for his defense."

3. *Fifth Amendment* **self-incrimination clause.** "No person... shall be compelled in any criminal case to be a witness against himself."

Each of these constitutional provisions has led to a different approach to police interrogation and suspects' confessions. Let's look at these three approaches.

Due Process

The due process, right-to-counsel, and self-incrimination approaches overlap, but they follow a roughly chronological line. In 1936, in *Brown v. Mississippi,* the U.S. Supreme Court applied the Fourteenth Amendment due process clause to the confessions extracted by torture in that tragic case (Chapter 2). The basic idea behind the **due process approach** to confessions is voluntariness. Involuntary confessions violate due process, not because they're "compelled," but because they're not reliable (meaning they may be false). The **reliability rationale** for due process is that admitting unreliable evidence to prove guilt denies defendants the right to their lives (Brown, Stewart, and Ellington were sentenced to death) without due process of law. In *Brown,* the confessions were the only evidence against the defendants. Here's what Chief Justice Hughes wrote for the Court:

> The state is free to regulate the procedure of its courts in accordance with its own conceptions of policy.... But the freedom of the state in establishing its policy... is limited by the requirement of due process of law.... The rack and torture chamber may not be substituted for the witness stand.... And the trial... is a mere pretense where the state authorities have contrived a conviction resting solely on the confessions obtained by violence. The due process clause requires that "state action... shall be consistent with the fundamental principles of liberty and justice which lie at the base of all our civil and political institutions." It would be difficult to conceive of methods more revolting to the sense of justice than those taken to procure the confessions of these petitioners, and the use of the confessions thus obtained as the basis for conviction and sentence was a clear denial of due process. (286)

The unreliability of coerced confessions provided the rationale for the reviews of most of the early state confessions cases decided by the U.S. Supreme Court after *Brown v. Mississippi.* In 1944 in *Ashcraft v. Tennessee,* the Court added a second rationale, the **accusatory system rationale.** According to the accusatory system rationale, forced confessions violate due process even if they're true, because under our system the government alone has the burden of proving guilt beyond a reasonable doubt. In applying the accusatory system rationale in *Rogers v. Richmond* (1961), the Court threw out a confession that the police got after they threatened to bring Rogers's arthritic wife in for questioning. According to Justice Felix Frankfurter:

> Our decisions under [the Fourteenth Amendment] have made clear that convictions following the admission...of confessions which are involuntary, i.e., the product of coercion, either physical or psychological, cannot stand. This is so not because such confessions are unlikely to be true but because the methods used to extract them offend an underlying principle in the enforcement of our criminal law: that ours is an accusatorial and not an inquisitorial system—a system in which the State must establish guilt by evidence independently and freely secured and may not by coercion prove its charge against an accused out of his own mouth. To be sure, confessions cruelly extorted may be and have been...found to be untrustworthy. But the constitutional principle of excluding confessions that are involuntary does not rest on this consideration. Indeed, in many of the cases in which the command of the Due Process clause has compelled us to reverse...convictions involving the use of confessions obtained by impermissible methods, independent corroborating evidence left little doubt of the truth of what the defendant had confessed. (540)

The Court relied on a third rationale for reviewing state confessions in *Spano v. New York* (1959). According to what came to be called the **fundamental fairness rationale**, coerced confessions aren't just unreliable and contrary to the accusatory system of justice; they offend the fundamental fairness required by the due process clause. According to Chief Justice Warren, writing for a unanimous Court in *Spano v. New York*:

> The abhorrence of society to the use of involuntary confessions does not turn alone on their inherent untrustworthiness. It also turns on the deep-rooted feeling that the police must obey the law while enforcing the law; that in the end life and liberty can be as much endangered from illegal methods used to convict those thought to be criminals as from the actual criminals themselves. Accordingly, the actions of police in obtaining confessions have come under scrutiny in a long series of cases. (319)

During the thirty years from *Brown v. Mississippi* in 1936 to *Miranda v. Arizona* in 1966, the Supreme Court threw out forty state confessions because they violated due process. Most of the early cases involved southern white mobs who had rounded up poor, illiterate blacks and tortured them until they confessed. The Court was much more reluctant to overturn the convictions of less "sympathetic criminals" from other parts of the country. In *Lisenba v. California* (1941), for example, Ray Lisenba (an educated white business executive from California) confessed he'd "tied his wife to a chair, subjected her to rattlesnake bites, and then drowned her in a pond." The police grilled Lisenba in several all-night sessions for two weeks, refusing to grant his repeated demands to see a lawyer and to remain silent until he did. But even in the face of these tactics, the Court refused to overturn Lisenba's conviction by throwing out his confession. According to the Court, his incriminating statements, looked at in the light of his intelligence and business experience, were not caused by police "overbearing his will" but instead were "a calculated attempt to minimize his culpability after carefully considering statements by the accomplice."

In *Stein v. New York* (1953), another case of "unsympathetic criminals," this time involving clever, experienced white robbers in rural New York State, Justice Jackson impatiently referred to the defendants as criminals who were "convinced their dance was over and the time had come to pay the fiddler." According to Justice Jackson:

> The limits in any case depend upon a weighing of the circumstances of pressure against the power of resistance of the person confessing. What would be overpowering to the weak of will or mind might be utterly ineffective against an experienced criminal. (184)

The Right to Counsel

At the same time the U.S. Supreme Court was developing the due process approach to the review of state confessions cases, a growing minority of the Court was looking for tougher measures to control police interrogation. They found one of these tougher measures in the Sixth Amendment, which reads: "In all criminal prosecutions, the accused shall . . . have the assistance of counsel for his defense." The problem is the phrase "all criminal prosecutions"; it suggests proceedings in *court* not in police stations. But by 1958, four of nine justices, including Chief Justice Warren and Associate Justices Black, Douglas, and Brennan, were calling custodial interrogation a **critical stage in criminal prosecutions** (the point when suspects' right to a lawyer kicked in).

In *Crooker v. California* (1958), John Russell Crooker, Jr., was a former law student working as a houseboy for a woman he was having an affair with. She broke off the affair when she found another boyfriend. After 14 hours in police custody, Crooker confessed to stabbing and strangling her. Although the police wouldn't let Crooker call his lawyer, there was no evidence officers had forced him to confess. He was allowed to eat, drink, and smoke, and interrogation sessions lasted only about an hour at a time. The U.S. Supreme Court affirmed Crooker's conviction, but Chief Justice Warren and Justices Black, Douglas, and Brennan dissented. Justice Douglas explained:

> The mischief and abuse of the third degree will continue as long as an accused can be denied the right to counsel at the most critical period of his ordeal. For what takes place in the secret confines of the police station may be more critical than what takes place at trial. (444–445)

A change in Court membership brought to a slim majority of 5–4 the number of justices who favored the right-to-counsel approach to police interrogation. In 1964, in *Escobedo v. Illinois* (1964), the Supreme Court by a 5–4 vote turned to the Sixth Amendment right-to-counsel clause as the basis for reviewing state confessions cases. Danny Escobedo asked his Chicago police interrogators to let him see his lawyer. They refused. His lawyer came to the station at Escobedo's mother's request, but the officers repeatedly refused his requests to see Danny. Finally, Escobedo confessed. The Supreme Court threw out the confession because Escobedo had given it without the advice of his lawyer. According to the Court, as soon as a police investigation focuses on a particular suspect (the accusatory stage), criminal prosecution begins and the right to counsel attaches. If defendants don't have a right to a lawyer until they go to trial and they confess before trial without a lawyer, then the trial is "no more than an appeal from the interrogation."

Four dissenting justices argued that allowing lawyers in interrogation rooms would kill the use of confessions. Why? Because—"Any lawyer worth his salt will tell the suspect in no uncertain terms to make no statement to the police under any circumstances" (*Watts v. Indiana* 1949, 59). According to Justice White, dissenting in *Escobedo:*

I do not suggest for a moment that law enforcement will be destroyed by the rule announced today. The need for peace and order is too insistent for that. But it will be crippled and its task made a great deal more difficult.... (499)

Self-Incrimination

In 1966, just two years after adopting the right-to-counsel approach to custodial interrogations, the Court abruptly dropped it. In a 5–4 decision in the landmark *Miranda v. Arizona* (1966) case, the Court majority relied on the Fifth Amendment self-incrimination clause to decide the constitutionality of custodial interrogation.

The due process, right-to-counsel, and self-incrimination doctrines are all still applied in combination to decide cases. To decide whether police custodial interrogation was inherently coercive *before* formal charges, the Court relies on the Fifth Amendment self-incrimination clause. To decide whether coercion was used *after* formal charges, the Court relies on the Sixth Amendment right to counsel. To review whether suspects and defendants have knowingly and voluntarily made incriminating statements *whenever* they take place, the Court relies on the Fourteenth Amendment due process clause.

The Meaning of *Witness Against Himself*

The Fifth Amendment says you can't be compelled to be a "witness" against yourself, but what does this mean? According to the U.S. Supreme Court, it means the government can't force you to give **testimony** (the *content* of what you say and write) against yourself. But, content doesn't include the *voice* that spoke the words. So, the government can compel you to speak particular words that might help a witness identify your voice. Also, drivers involved in accidents don't incriminate themselves when they have to give their names and addresses to the police. And, if some law says you have to turn over information in your personal books, papers, bank accounts, and other records, you aren't being compelled to incriminate yourself. (See Table 8.2 for more examples.)

Finally, the government can take other kinds of incriminating evidence against your will, like physical evidence "seized" during reasonable searches and seizures (Chapters 5–7) and evidence gotten from identification procedures (Chapter 9). In *Schmerber v. California* (1966), the Supreme Court decided whether taking blood alcohol samples against Armando Schmerber's will compelled him to be a witness against himself.

TABLE 8.2	
Incriminating Evidence Not Protected by the Fifth Amendment	
Weapons	Photographs
Contraband	Appearance in lineup
Stolen property	Bullets removed from the body
Handwriting samples	Products of consent searches
Hair samples	Books, papers, documents
Voice samples	Records required by law to be kept
Fingerprints	

Can Blood "Talk"?

Schmerber v. California
384 U.S. 757, 86 S.Ct. 1826 (1966)

Armando Schmerber was convicted in the Los Angeles Municipal Court of driving an automobile while under the influence of intoxicating liquor, and he appealed. The Appellate Department of the California Superior Court affirmed. The U.S. Supreme Court granted certiorari and affirmed.

BRENNAN, J.

FACTS

Armando Schmerber was convicted in Los Angeles Municipal Court of the criminal offense of driving an automobile while under the influence of intoxicating liquor. He had been arrested at a hospital while receiving treatment for injuries suffered in an accident involving the automobile that he had apparently been driving. Schmerber and a companion had been drinking at a tavern and bowling alley. There was evidence showing that Schmerber was driving from the bowling alley about midnight November 12, 1964, when the car skidded, crossed the road and struck a tree. Both Schmerber and his companion were injured and taken to a hospital for treatment. At the direction of a police officer, a blood sample was then withdrawn from Schmerber's body by a physician at the hospital.

The chemical analysis of this sample revealed a percent by weight of alcohol in his blood at the time of the offense which indicated intoxication, and the report of this analysis was admitted in evidence at the trial. Schmerber objected to receipt of this evidence of the analysis on the ground that the blood had been withdrawn despite his refusal, on the advice of his counsel, to consent to the test. He contended that in that circumstance the withdrawal of the blood and the admission of the analysis in evidence denied him due process of law under the Fourteenth Amendment, as well as specific guarantees of the Bill of Rights secured against the States by that Amendment: his privilege against self-incrimination under the Fifth Amendment; his right to counsel under the Sixth Amendment; and his right not to be subjected to unreasonable searches and seizures in violation of the Fourth Amendment. The Appellate Department of the California Superior Court rejected these contentions and affirmed the conviction.... We granted certiorari. We AFFIRM.

OPINION

...In *Malloy v. Hogan,* we held that the

> Fourteenth Amendment secures against state invasion the same privilege that the Fifth Amendment guarantees against federal infringement—the right of a person to remain silent unless he chooses to speak in the unfettered exercise of his own will, and to suffer no penalty for such silence.

We therefore must now decide whether the withdrawal of the blood and admission in evidence of the analysis involved in this case violated petitioner's privilege. We hold that the privilege protects an accused only from being compelled to testify against himself, or otherwise provide the State with evidence of a testimonial or communicative nature, and that the withdrawal of blood and use of the analysis in question in this case did not involve compulsion to these ends.

It could not be denied that in requiring Schmerber to submit to the withdrawal and chemical analysis of his blood the State compelled him to submit to an attempt to discover evidence that might be used to prosecute him for a criminal offence. He submitted only after the police officer rejected his objection and directed the physician to proceed. The officer's direction to the physician to administer the test over Schmerber's objection constituted compulsion for the purposes of the privilege. The critical question, then, is whether petitioner was thus compelled "to be a witness against himself.".....

The withdrawal of blood necessarily involves puncturing the skin for extraction, and the percent by weight of alcohol in that blood, as established by chemical analysis, is evidence of criminal guilt. Compelled submission fails on one view to respect the "inviolability of the human personality." Moreover, since it enables the State to rely on evidence forced from the accused, the compulsion violates at least one meaning of the requirement that the State procure the evidence against an accused "by its own independent labors."

...However,...history and a long line of authorities in lower courts have consistently limited [the self-incrimination] protection to situations in which the State seeks to...obtain evidence against an accused through "the cruel, simple expedient of compelling it from his own mouth. In sum, the privilege is fulfilled only when the person is guaranteed the right to remain silent unless he chooses to speak in the unfettered exercise of his own will." The leading case in this Court is *Holt v. United States*. There the question was whether evidence was admissible that the accused, prior to trial and over his protest, put on a blouse that fitted him. It was contended that compelling the accused to submit to the demand that he model the blouse violated the privilege. Mr. Justice Holmes, speaking for the Court, rejected the argument as "based upon an extravagant extension of the 5th Amendment," and went on to say:

> The prohibition of compelling a man in a criminal court to be witness against himself is a prohibition of the use of physical or moral compulsion to extort communications from him, not an exclusion of his body as evidence when it may be material. The objection in principle would forbid a jury to look at a prisoner and compare his features with a photograph in proof.

> ... Both federal and state courts have usually held that [the privilege against self-incrimination] offers no protection against compulsion to submit to fingerprinting, photographing, or measurements, to write or speak for identification, to appear in court, to stand, to assume a stance, to walk, or to make a particular gesture. The distinction which has emerged, often expressed in different ways, is that the privilege is a bar against compelling "communications" or "testimony," but that compulsion which makes a suspect or accused the source of "real or physical evidence" does not violate it.... Not even a shadow of testimonial compulsion upon or enforced communication by the accused was involved either in the extraction or in the chemical analysis. Schmerber's testimonial capacities were in no way implicated; indeed, his participation, except as a donor, was irrelevant to the results of the test, which depend on chemical analysis and on that alone.

Since the blood test evidence, although an incriminating product of compulsion, was neither Schmerber's testimony nor evidence relating to some communicative act or writing by Schmerber, it was admissible....

AFFIRMED.

DISSENT

BLACK, J., joined by DOUGLAS, J.

The Court admits that "the State compelled Schmerber to submit to an attempt to discover evidence (in his blood) that might be (and was) used to prosecute him for a criminal offense." To reach the conclusion that compelling a person to give his blood to help the State convict him is not equivalent to compelling him to be a witness against himself strikes me as quite an extraordinary feat....

It seems to me that the compulsory extraction of petitioner's blood for analysis so that the person who analyzed it could give evidence to convict him had both a "testimonial" and a "communicative nature." The sole purpose of this project which proved to be successful was to obtain "testimony" from some person to prove that Schmerber had alcohol in his blood at the time he was arrested. And the purpose of the project was certainly "communicative" in that the analysis of the blood was to supply information to enable a witness to communicate to the court and jury that petitioner was more or less drunk....

How can it reasonably be doubted that the blood test evidence was not in all respects the actual equivalent of "testimony" taken from Schmerber when the result of the test was offered as testimony, was considered by the jury as testimony, and the jury's verdict of guilt rests in part on that testimony?... Believing with the Framers that constitutional safeguards broadly construed by independent tribunals of justice provide our best hope for keeping our people free from governmental oppression, I deeply regret the Court's holding....

Questions

1. Describe the details of the blood test performed on Schmerber.

2. According to the Court, why doesn't the self-incrimination clause apply to the blood test?

3. Summarize the dissent's arguments presented by Justices Black and Douglas in favor of applying the self-incrimination clause to the blood test. Is the dissent more persuasive than the majority? Why?

The Meaning of *Compelled*

The due process approach to self-incrimination relied on the voluntariness test to decide whether suspects were "compelled" to be witnesses against themselves. According to the **voluntariness test of self-incrimination,** confessions and other incriminating statements violate due process if the totality of circumstances surrounding the statements shows that suspects didn't confess voluntarily. In 1966, a combination of three factors produced one of the most famous (and most controversial and hated, too) decisions in U.S. constitutional history—*Miranda v. Arizona*:

1. Uneasiness about tactics used against suspects in the intimidating atmosphere of police stations

2. Dissatisfaction with the vagueness of the totality-of-circumstances approach

3. Impatience with the case-by-case approach to deciding whether confessions were voluntarily given and gotten

MIRANDA V. ARIZONA

In *Miranda v. Arizona* (1966), a bare 5–4 majority of the U.S. Supreme Court established a "bright line" rule to govern custodial interrogation. According to the Court majority, custodial interrogation is "inherently coercive." Why? First, because suspects are held in strange surroundings where they're not free to leave or even to call for emotional support from relatives and friends. Second, skilled police officers use tricks, lies, and psychological pressure to "crack" the will of suspects. These circumstances, according to the Court, require strong measures to prevent involuntary confessions. Those measures (what we all know as the *Miranda* warnings) and the reasons for them were hotly debated and decided in *Miranda v. Arizona*.

CASE | *Does the Fifth Amendment Apply to Custodial Interrogation?*

Miranda v. Arizona
384 U.S. 436 (1966)

Ernesto Miranda was convicted of rape and robbery in the Superior Court, Maricopa County, Arizona, and sentenced to twenty to thirty years in prison for each crime. He appealed. The Arizona Supreme Court affirmed. The U.S. Supreme Court granted certiorari and reversed.

WARREN, CJ.

FACTS

On March 13, 1963, petitioner, Ernesto Miranda, was arrested at his home and taken into custody to a Phoenix police station. He was there identified by the complaining witness. The police then took him to "Interrogation Room No. 2" of the detective bureau, where two police officers questioned him. The officers admitted at trial Miranda was

not advised he had a right to have an attorney present.... Two hours later, the officers emerged from the interrogation room with a written confession signed by Miranda. At the top of the statement was a typed paragraph stating the confession was made voluntarily, without threats or promises of immunity and "with full knowledge of my legal rights, understanding any statement I make may be used against me." One of the officers testified he read this paragraph to Miranda. Apparently, however, he did not do so until after Miranda had confessed orally.

At his trial before a jury, the written confession was admitted into evidence over the objection of defense counsel, and the officers testified to the prior oral confession made by Miranda during the interrogation. Miranda was found guilty of kidnapping and rape. He was sentenced to 20 to 30 years' imprisonment on each count, the sentences to run concurrently. On appeal, the Supreme Court of Arizona held that Miranda's constitutional rights were not violated in obtaining the confession and affirmed the conviction. In reaching its decision, the court emphasized heavily the fact that Miranda did not specifically request counsel.

OPINION

The constitutional issue we decide . . . is the admissibility of statements obtained from a defendant questioned while in custody or otherwise deprived of his freedom of action in any significant way. . . .

The modern practice of in-custody interrogation is psychologically rather than physically oriented. . . . Interrogation takes place in privacy [and] privacy results in secrecy. [But] from . . . representative samples of interrogation techniques,* the setting . . . becomes clear: To be alone with the subject is essential to prevent distraction and to deprive him of any outside support. The aura of confidence in his guilt undermines his will to resist. He merely confirms the preconceived story the police seek to have him describe. Patience and persistence, at times relentless questioning, are employed. . . . When normal procedures fail to produce the needed result, the police may resort to deceptive stratagems such as giving false legal advice. It is important to keep the subject off balance, for example, by trading on his insecurity about himself or his surroundings. The police then persuade, trick, or cajole him out of exercising his constitutional rights.

In *Miranda*, we concern ourselves primarily with this interrogation atmosphere and the evils it can bring. The police arrested Miranda and took him to a special interrogation room where they secured a confession. . . . Miranda was thrust into an unfamiliar atmosphere and run through menacing police interrogation procedures. The potentiality for compulsion is forcefully apparent, for example, where the indigent Mexican defendant was a seriously disturbed individual with pronounced sexual fantasies. To be sure, the records do not evince overt physical coercion or patent psychological ploys. . . .

We have concluded that without proper safeguards the process of in-custody interrogation . . . contains inherently compelling pressures which work to undermine the individual's will to resist and to compel him to speak where he would not otherwise do so freely. In order to combat these pressures and to permit a full opportunity to exercise the privilege against self-incrimination, the accused must be adequately and effectively apprised of his rights and the exercise of those rights must be fully honored. . . .

If a person in custody is to be subjected to interrogation, he must first be informed in clear and unequivocal terms that he has the right to remain silent. . . . Such a warning is an absolute prerequisite in overcoming the inherent pressures of the interrogation atmosphere. . . . The Fifth Amendment privilege is so fundamental to our system of constitutional rule and the expedient of giving an adequate warning as to the availability of the privilege so simple, we will not pause to inquire in individual cases whether the defendant was aware of his rights without a warning being given. . . .

The warning of the right to remain silent must be accompanied by the explanation that anything said can and will be used against the individual in court. This warning is needed in order to make him aware not only of the privilege, but also of the consequences of forgoing it . . . This warning may serve to make the individual more acutely aware that he is faced with a phase of the adversary system—that he is not in the presence of persons acting solely in his interest.

. . . We hold that an individual held for interrogation must be clearly informed that he has the right to consult with a lawyer and to have the lawyer with him during interrogation under the system for protecting the privilege we delineate today. As with the warnings of the right to remain silent and that anything stated can be used in evidence against him, this warning is an absolute prerequisite to interrogation. No amount of circumstantial evidence that the person may have been aware of this right will suffice to stand in its stead. . . .

. . . In order fully to apprise a person interrogated of the extent of his rights under this system, it is necessary to warn him not only that he has the right to consult with an attorney, but also that if he is indigent [poor] a lawyer will be appointed to represent him. Without this additional warning, the admonition of the right to consult with counsel would often be understood as meaning only that he can consult with a lawyer if he has one or has the funds to obtain one. The warning of a right to counsel would be hollow if not couched in terms that would convey to the indigent . . . that he too has a right to have counsel present. . . .

Once warnings have been given, the subsequent procedure is clear. If the individual indicates in any manner, at any time prior to or during questioning, that he wishes to remain silent, the interrogation must cease. . . . If the individual states that he wants an attorney, the interrogation must cease until an attorney is present. . . . If the individual cannot obtain an attorney and he indicates that he wants one before speaking to police, they must respect his decision to remain silent. . . .

If the interrogation continues without the presence of an attorney and a statement is taken, a heavy burden rests on the government to demonstrate that the defendant knowingly and intelligently waived his privilege against self-incrimination and his right to retained or appointed coun-

---

*Found in police manuals and texts on interrogation.

sel.... Since the State is responsible for establishing the isolated circumstances under which the interrogation takes place and has the only means of making available corroborated evidence of warnings given during incommunicado interrogation, the burden is rightly on its shoulders....

In dealing with statements obtained through interrogation, we do not purport to find all confessions inadmissible. Confessions remain a proper element in law enforcement. Any statement given freely and voluntarily without any compelling influences is, of course, admissible in evidence....

A recurrent argument made in these cases is that society's need for interrogation outweighs the privilege.... [But] if the individual desires to exercise his privilege, he has the right to do so. This is not for the authorities to decide. An attorney may advise his client not to talk to police until he has had an opportunity to investigate the case, or he may wish to be present with his client during any police questioning.... This is not cause for considering the attorney a menace to law enforcement. He is merely carrying out what he is sworn to do under his oath—to protect to the extent of his ability the rights of his client. In fulfilling this responsibility the attorney plays a vital role in the administration of criminal justice under our Constitution....

Over the years the Federal Bureau of Investigation has compiled an exemplary record of effective law enforcement while advising any suspect or arrested person, at the outset of an interview, that he is not required to make a statement, that any statement may be used against him in court, that the individual may obtain the services of an attorney of his own choice and, more recently, that he has a right to free counsel if he is unable to pay. A letter received from the Solicitor General in response to a question from the Bench makes it clear that the present pattern of warnings and respect for the rights of the individual followed as a practice by the FBI is consistent with the procedure which we delineate today.... The practice of the FBI can readily be emulated by state and local enforcement agencies. The argument that the FBI deals with different crimes than are dealt with by state authorities does not mitigate the significance of the FBI experience.

It is also urged upon us that we withhold decision on this issue until state legislative bodies and advisory groups have had an opportunity to deal with these problems by rule making.... The Constitution does not require any specific code of procedures for protecting the privilege against self-incrimination during custodial interrogation. Congress and the States are free to develop their own safeguards for the privilege, so long as they are fully as effective as those described above in informing accused persons of their right of silence and in affording a continuous opportunity to exercise it. [But] the issues presented are of constitutional dimensions and must be determined by the courts. The admissibility of a statement in the face of a claim that it was obtained in violation of the defendant's constitutional rights is an issue the resolution of which has long since been undertaken by this Court. Judicial solutions to problems of constitutional dimension have evolved decade by decade. As courts have been presented with the need to enforce constitutional rights, they have found means of doing so.... Where rights secured by the Constitution are involved, there can be no rule making or legislation which would abrogate them....

From the testimony of the officers and by the admission of Arizona, it is clear that Miranda was not in any way apprised of his right to consult with an attorney and to have one present during the interrogation, nor was his right not to be compelled to incriminate himself effectively protected in any other manner. Without these warnings the statements were inadmissible. The mere fact that he signed a statement which contained a typed-in clause stating that he had "full knowledge" of his "legal rights" does not approach the knowing and intelligent waiver required to relinquish constitutional rights.

Judgment of the Supreme Court of Arizona REVERSED.

DISSENT

CLARK, J.

It is with regret that I find it necessary to write in this case. However, I am unable to join... in the Court's criticism of the present practices of police and investigatory agencies as to custodial interrogation. The materials it refers to as "police manuals" are, as I read them, merely writings in this filed by professors and some police officers. Not one is shown by the record here to be the official manual of any police department, much less in universal use in crime detection. Moreover the examples of police brutality mentioned by the Court are rare exceptions to the thousands of cases that appear every year in the law reports. The police agencies—all the way from municipal and state forces to the federal bureaus—are responsible for law enforcement and public safety in this country. I am proud of their efforts, which in my view are not fairly characterized by the Court's opinion.

HARLAN, J., joined by STEWART and WHITE, JJ.

... The new rules are not designed to guard against police brutality or other unmistakably banned forms of coercion.... Rather, the thrust of the new rules is to negate all pressures, to reinforce the nervous or ignorant suspect, and ultimately to discourage any confession at all. The aim in short is toward "voluntariness" in a utopian sense, or to view it from a different angle, voluntariness with a vengeance....

Without at all subscribing to the generally black picture of police conduct painted by the Court, I think it must be frankly recognized at the outset that police questioning... may inherently entail some pressure on the suspect and may seek advantage in his ignorance or weaknesses. The atmosphere and questioning techniques, proper and fair though they be, can in themselves exert a tug on the suspect to confess.... Until today, the role of the Constitution has been only to sift out undue pressure, not to assure spontaneous confessions....

The Court largely ignores that its rules impair, if they will not eventually serve wholly to frustrate, an instrument of law enforcement that has long and quite reasonably been thought worth the price paid for it. There can be little doubt that the Court's new code would markedly decrease the number of confessions. To warn the suspect that he may remain silent and remind him that his confession may be used in court are minor obstructions. To require also an express waiver by the suspect and an end to questioning whenever he demurs must heavily handicap questioning. And to suggest or provide counsel for the suspect simply invites the end of the interrogation.

How much harm this decision will inflict on law enforcement cannot fairly be predicted with accuracy. Evidence on the role of confessions is notoriously incomplete...[But] we do know that some crimes cannot be solved without confessions, that ample expert testimony attests to their importance in crime control, and that the Court is taking a real risk with society's welfare in imposing its new regime on the country. The social costs of crime are too great to call the new rules anything but a hazardous experimentation....

WHITE, J., joined by HARLAN and STEWART, JJ.
Only a tiny minority of our judges who have dealt with the question, including today's majority, have considered in custody interrogation...to be a violation of the Fifth Amendment. And this Court, as every member knows, has left standing literally thousands of criminal convictions that rested at least in part on confessions taken in the course of interrogation by the police after arrest.

...More than the human dignity of the accused is involved; the human personality of others in the society must also be preserved. Thus the values reflected by the privilege are not the sole desideratum; society's interest in the general security is of equal weight.

The obvious underpinning of the Court's decision is a deep-seated distrust of all confessions.... This is the not so subtle overtone of the opinion—that it is inherently wrong for the police to gather evidence from the accused himself. And this is precisely the nub of this dissent. I see nothing wrong or immoral, and certainly nothing unconstitutional, in the police's asking a suspect whom they have reasonable cause to arrest whether or not he killed his wife or in confronting him with the evidence on which the arrest was based, at least where he has been plainly advised that he may remain completely silent....Moreover, it is by no means certain that the process of confessing is injurious to the accused. To the contrary it may provide psychological relief and enhance the prospects for rehabilitation.

...There is, in my view, every reason to believe that a good many criminal defendants who otherwise would have been convicted on what this Court has previously thought to be the most satisfactory kind of evidence will now under this new version of the Fifth Amendment, either not be tried at all or will be acquitted if the State's evidence, minus the confession, is put to the test of litigation. I have no desire whatsoever to share the responsibility for any such impact on the present criminal process. In some unknown number of cases the Court's rule will return a killer, a rapist or other criminal to the streets and to the environment which produced him, to repeat his crime whenever it pleases him. As a consequence, there will not be a gain, but a loss, in human dignity. The real concern is not the unfortunate consequences of this new decision on the criminal law as an abstract, disembodied series of authoritative proscriptions, but the impact on those who rely on the public authority for protection and who without it can only engage in violent self-help with guns, knives and the help of their neighbors similarly inclined....

Questions

1. According to the Supreme Court, what do the words *custody* and *interrogation* mean?

2. Why is custodial interrogation "inherently coercive," according to the majority?

3. Identify and explain the criteria for waiving the right against self-incrimination in custodial interrogation.

4. On what grounds do the dissents disagree with the majority's decision? What interests are in conflict, according to the Court?

5. How do the majority and the dissent explain the balance of interests established by the Constitution?

6. Which makes more sense regarding the law of police interrogation, the majority's bright-line rule requiring warnings or the dissent's due process test weighing the totality of circumstances on a case-by-case basis? Defend your answer.

 Go to Exercise 8-1 on the Criminal Procedure 6e CD to learn more about *Miranda v. Arizona.*

Miranda v. Arizona

(Baker 1985)

Born in Mesa, Arizona, in 1940, Ernesto Arturo Miranda was the fifth son of Manuel Miranda, a house painter and a Mexican immigrant. When Ernesto was 6, his mother died. The next year, his father remarried, but Ernesto didn't get along with his stepmother. He drifted apart from his father and wasn't close with his older brothers.

According to the priests and nuns at Queen of Peace Elementary School in Mesa, Arizona, Ernesto wasn't an ideal student. Frequently truant, when he was in school he was in trouble. He completed the eighth grade in 1954; that's when his troubles began:

1954: He committed his first felony, car theft, and was put on probation.

1955: He was arrested for burglary in May, sent to Arizona Industrial School for Boys, and released in December.

1956: In January, he was arrested for attempted rape and assault. According to Ernesto, he was walking past a house where he saw a naked woman lying on a bed. He walked through the unlocked front door, slid into bed with the woman, and stayed there until her husband came home and called the police. Ernesto was sent back to the School for Boys for one year.

1957: Released from the School for Boys in January, he moved to Los Angeles. In May, Los Angeles police picked him up for curfew violations and Peeping Tom activities. He spent three days in the Los Angeles County Detention Home. When he was released, he got a job as a supermarket carryout. In September, he was arrested for, but not convicted of, armed robbery. Shortly after, he was arrested again for "suspicion of" armed robbery. This time he was put in the custody of the California Youth Authority for forty-five days and then deported back to Arizona.

1958: Ernesto joined the U.S. Army. Six of his fifteen months in the army he spent at hard labor in the stockade for going AWOL and getting caught in a Peeping Tom act.

1959: Ernesto received an "undesirable discharge" from the U.S. Army. He traveled around and wound up spending two weeks in the county jail in Peco, Texas, for vagrancy. On December 6, a deputy sheriff in Nashville caught him driving a car that had been reported missing. According to Ernesto, he was supporting himself by selling stolen cars. He pleaded guilty and was sentenced to one year and one day in prison.

1961: On January 4, 1961, he was released from prison. The day before his release, Ernesto lost a finger when the electric prison gate slammed shut on it while he was waving good-bye to visitors. Shortly after he got out of prison, 21-year-old Ernesto met 29-year-old Twila Hoffman. They fell in love, and he moved in with her, her 11-year-old son, and her 10-year-old daughter. In 1962, they had a daughter of their own. Twila found a job in a nursery school in Mesa, and Ernesto went to work for United Produce in Phoenix. His employer liked him, "He was one of the best workers I've ever had. I wish I had a hundred more like him."

FROM THE RAPE TO THE FIRST TRIAL

1963 (March 2): Ernesto kidnapped and raped 18-year-old "Jane Doe."

1963 (March 13): Ernesto came home at about 8:30 A.M. from working the night shift and went to sleep. About an hour later, Officers Cooley and Young came to the house. Twila awakened him, and the officers asked Ernesto to come down to the station to talk about "a case they were investigating." He went with them.

The detective bureau set up a lineup, consisting of Ernesto and three Mexican jail inmates. Ernesto was the only one wearing a T-shirt. Jane Doe, looking through a two-way mirror, said she couldn't identify her kidnapper-rapist but that maybe Ernesto had a similar build and features. Afterward, Ernesto asked Detectives Cooley and Young, "How did I do?"

"You flunked," lied one of the officers.

Then the interrogation began. According to Officer Cooley, Ernesto soon admitted not only "that he was the person who had raped this girl" but also that he had raped another woman and tried to rob a third. Both Officers Cooley and Young testified that they made no threats or promises in exchange for Ernesto's confession. They had, without coercion of any kind, questioned him. Detective Cooley noted that Ernesto was "not unknowledgeable about his rights. He was an ex-convict...and had been through the routine before."

Ernesto told a different story. Here is his description of the interrogation:

> Once they get you in a little room and they start badgering you one way or the other, "you better tell us...or we're going to throw the book at you"...that is what they told me. They would throw the book at me. They would try to give me all the time they could. They thought there was even a possibility that there was something wrong with me. They would try to help me, get me medical care if I needed it....And I haven't had any sleep since the day before. I'm tired. I just got off work, and they have me and they are interrogating me. They mention first one crime, then another one, they are certain I am the person...knowing what a penitentiary is like, a person has to be frightened, scared. And not knowing if he'll be able to get back up and go home.

Unsure of her identification, Jane Doe asked to hear Ernesto's voice. The detectives brought her to the interrogation room. Ernesto looked up as she entered. "Is that the girl?" asked one of the officers.

"That's the girl," he answered, believing that she'd already identified him.

Then, Ernesto told them a story similar to Jane Doe's about the kidnapping and the rape. "Would you put the story in writing?" Detective Cooley asked. Ernesto agreed and wrote:

> Seen a girl walking up street stopped a little ahead of her got out of car walked towards her grabbed her by the arm and asked to get in the car. Got in car without force tied hands & ankles. Drove away for a few miles. Stopped asked to take clothes off. Did not, asked me to take her back home. I started to take clothes off her without any force, and with cooperation. Asked her to lay down and she did, could not get penis into vagina

got about ½ (half) inch in. Told her to get clothes back on. Drove her home. I couldn't say I was sorry for what I had done. But asked her to say a prayer for me.

It was 1:30 p.m. The whole interrogation took less than two hours. No brutality; no threats; no promises; no deprivations of water or toilet facilities; one lie; no advice about the right not to talk to the police—all pretty routine and civilized as far as interrogations go. Pressure, sure; but coercion—no. After all, interrogations aren't supposed to be social gatherings among friends.

1963 (June 20): Miranda was tried and convicted of kidnapping and raping Jane Doe. He was sent to the county jail to await his sentence.

1963 (June 27): Miranda was brought back to the courtroom, and Judge Yale McFate sentenced him to not less than twenty nor more than thirty years for each of the two crimes, kidnapping and rape. The sentences were to run concurrently.

1965 (April 22): The Arizona Supreme Court affirmed Miranda's conviction.

1966 (June 13): The U.S. Supreme Court reversed the Arizona Supreme Court's decision and remanded the case.

AFTER *MIRANDA V. ARIZONA*

1967 (February 15): Miranda's retrial for kidnapping and rape began without any chance that his confession would be admitted in evidence. The jury heard from two prosecution witnesses. First came the victim, Jane Doe, now 21 and married with two children. Doe told the jury how Ernesto Miranda had kidnapped and raped her four years earlier. However, on cross-examination, Miranda's lawyer, John Flynn, got her to admit that she couldn't positively identify Miranda as her attacker. Without the confession and Doe's uncertainty, things looked good for Miranda.

But the second witness—Twila Hoffman, Miranda's common-law wife and his daughter's mother—administered a crippling blow. Hoffman told the jury about a jail visit she made to Miranda on March 16, 1963, just three days after he confessed to kidnapping and raping Jane Doe. Hoffman testified that Miranda told her that he had taken Doe from the street and raped her. Miranda asked Hoffman to go to Doe and tell her that he'd marry her if she'd drop the charges against him. Hoffman angrily refused. Then, Miranda asked Hoffman to take their baby daughter Cleopatra, show the baby to Doe, and ask her to drop the charges so Cleopatra could be with her father. Again, Hoffman angrily refused. The jailhouse confession to Hoffman convinced the jury, and they found Miranda guilty. Judge McFate sentenced Miranda to the same twenty to thirty years that he did in the first trial.

1969–1972: A popular prisoner, Miranda earned a high-school diploma and some college credits. He became a prison barber.

1972 (December): Miranda was paroled on a split vote by the parole board. At 30, Miranda was free for the first time in nine years. He went back to Mesa and lived with his stepmother and two of his brothers. He worked in a car recycling plant and then in a produce warehouse. His bosses liked him in both jobs. He couldn't work as a barber because it's against the law in Arizona for convicted felons to get a barber's license.

1974 (July 23): Tempe police stopped Miranda for driving his car on the wrong side of the road. During a search, officers found a gun and illegal drugs, both of which violated the terms of his parole.

1975 (January 16): Miranda was sent back to prison for violating his parole.

1975 (April 28): Miranda was released on parole again. He got a job in a tire company. To get a little extra money he sold personally autographed *Miranda* warning cards for $1.50 apiece.

1976 (January 31): Saturday night: Miranda went to a bar and drank and played cards with two other men. "Three dollars," one of them yelled after they accused each other of cheating. The barmaid took the cards and the argument turned into a bloody fight. Miranda went to the men's room to wash off the blood. While he was in the men's room, one of the men handed a knife to the other. "Here, you finish it," he said and left the bar. When Miranda came out of the men's room, the two got into a scuffle. Miranda tried to get the knife. The man stabbed him in the stomach and chest. Someone called an ambulance, but Miranda was pronounced dead on arrival at Good Samaritan Hospital. When his attacker was arrested, the officer pulled out a warning card in the bar and said, "You have a right to remain silent...." Or so the records of the Phoenix police department say. (9–11, 13–14)

Just what impact do the *Miranda* warnings have on interrogation and confessions? To answer this, we'll examine the *Miranda* bright-line rules, the meaning of custody, the public safety exception to the rules, and what happens when the suspect waives the rights to counsel and to remain silent.

The *Miranda* "Bright-Line" Rules

The Supreme Court intended the *Miranda* warnings to provide a **bright-line rule**— sometimes called a *per se* rule—to prevent police coercion while still allowing police pressure. The rule is that whenever police officers conduct a custodial interrogation, they have to give suspects the now famous four warnings:

1. You have a right to remain silent.

2. Anything you say can and will be used against you in court.

3. You have a right to a lawyer.

4. If you can't afford a lawyer one will be appointed for you.

What's the reason for the bright-line rule? To avoid what the Court called the "inherently coercive nature of custodial interrogation."

The Court created five more bright-line rules for the interrogating officer, prosecutors, and judges. Police officers don't have to tell suspects about these rules:

1. Suspects can claim their right to remain silent at any time. If at any time they indicate in any way they don't want to talk, the interrogation has to stop immediately.

2. If, before interrogation begins, suspects indicate in any manner they want a lawyer, interrogation can't start; if it has already started, it has to stop immediately.

3. Any statement obtained without a lawyer present puts a "heavy burden" on the prosecution to prove defendants waived two constitutional rights: the right against self-incrimination and the right to a lawyer. Neither silence nor later confessions count as a waiver.

4. Statements obtained in violation of the rules can't be admitted into evidence.

5. Exercising the right against self-incrimination can't be penalized. So, prosecutors can't suggest or even hint at trial that the defendant's refusal to talk is a sign of guilt.

In *Commonweath v. Zook* (1989), these additional *Miranda* warnings were applied. Robert Zook confessed to two murders. He was charged with the murders, a jury found him guilty, and the trial court sentenced him to death. Zook appealed, claiming his confession was illegally obtained because the police denied his request for a lawyer during the interrogation. During the trial, the assistant district attorney elicited the following on direct examination of Lieutenant Landis (the interrogating officer):

Q: During the interview, did Mr. Zook ever request an attorney?
A: Approximately—I don't know, two-thirds of the way into the interview, something like that, right around the time we got through talking about whether he knew Conard or Wiker, he asked if he could use the phone to call his mother to see if she could get him an attorney. At that point, I said are you saying you want us to stop questioning you until you have an attorney present? And he said no, go ahead and finish with what you are doing. That was the only time that he came close to asking for an attorney, if that's what that was.

Did he waive his right to counsel? The Pennsylvania Supreme Court ruled:

We think that the trial court was in error in failing to suppress all statements made by Appellant after he made the request to use the phone to have his mother get an attorney. . . . It is inconsistent with *Miranda* and its progeny for the authorities, at their instance, to reinterrogate an accused in custody if he has clearly asserted his right to counsel. (920)

One final point about the bright-line *Miranda* rule: On TV "cop shows," whenever, wherever, and as soon as police officers arrest anyone, they "mirandize" them immediately, or say something like "Read him his rights." However, *Miranda v. Arizona* doesn't command officers to warn suspects whenever they arrest them. Officers have to give the famous warnings only if they intend to do both of the following: (1) take the suspects into custody *and* (2) interrogate them. These limits still leave the police a lot of leeway for questioning individuals who aren't in custody, including:

1. Questioning people at crime scenes

2. Questioning people before they become suspects

3. Questioning people during Fourth Amendment stops (Chapter 4)

The Meaning of *Custody*

In *Miranda,* the U.S. Supreme Court defined **custody** as being held by the police in a police station *or* depriving an individual of "freedom of action in any significant way." According to the Court, deciding whether suspects are in "custody" boils down to "whether there was a formal arrest or restraint on freedom of movement of the degree associated with a formal arrest." The Court used this language to prevent police officers from getting around the *Miranda* requirements by questioning suspects away from a police station. The Court was sending the message that *Miranda* targets coercive *atmospheres,* not just coercive *places.*

Whether suspects are in custody depends on a case-by-case evaluation of the totality of circumstances surrounding the interrogation. These circumstances include:

- Whether officers had probable cause to arrest
- Whether officers intended to detain suspects
- Whether suspects believed their freedom was significantly restricted
- Whether the investigation had focused on the suspect
- The language officers use to summon suspects
- The physical surroundings
- The amount of evidence of guilt officers present to suspects
- How long suspects are detained
- The amounts and kinds of pressure officers use to detain suspects

Three types of detentions don't qualify as being in custody:

- Drivers and passengers detained during routine traffic stops (*Berkemer v. McCarty* 1984)
- Probationers attending routine meetings with their probation officers (*Minnesota v. Murphy* 1984)
- Persons detained during the execution of search warrants (*Michigan v. Summers* 1981)

What about questioning suspects in their homes? It depends on the totality of the circumstances in each case. In *Orozco v. Texas,* four police officers entered Reyes Arias Orozco's bedroom at 4:00 A.M., woke him up, and immediately started questioning him about a shooting. The Court held that even though Orozco was at home in his own bed he was still in custody because he was "deprived of his liberty in a significant way." The Court relied heavily on the officers' testimony that from the moment Orozco gave them his name, he wasn't free to go anywhere.

In *Berkemer v. McCarty* (1984), the U.S. Supreme Court applied the totality-of-circumstances test to Richard McCarty, a suspect questioned about his sobriety while he was stopped for a traffic violation.

CASE | *Was He "in Custody"?*

Berkemer, Sheriff of Franklin County v. McCarty
468 U.S. 420 (1984)

Richard McCarty was convicted of operating a motor vehicle while under the influence of alcohol and/or drugs.

The U.S. District Court for the Southern District of Ohio denied his petition for habeas corpus. The U.S. Court of Appeals reversed. The U.S. Supreme Court granted certiorari and affirmed.

MARSHALL, J.

FACTS

On the evening of March 31, 1980, Trooper Williams of the Ohio State Highway Patrol observed Richard McCarty's car weaving in and out of a lane on Interstate Highway 270. After following the car for two miles, Williams forced McCarty to stop and asked him to get out of the vehicle. When McCarty complied, Williams noticed that he was having difficulty standing. At that point, "Williams concluded that McCarty would be charged with a traffic offense and, therefore, his freedom to leave the scene was terminated." However, McCarty was not told he would be taken into custody. Williams then asked McCarty to perform a field sobriety test, commonly known as a "balancing test." McCarty could not do so without falling.

While still at the scene of the traffic stop, Williams asked McCarty whether he had been using intoxicants. McCarty replied "he had consumed two beers and had smoked several joints of marijuana a short time before." McCarty's speech was slurred, and Williams had difficulty understanding him. Williams thereupon formally placed McCarty under arrest and transported him in the patrol car to the Franklin County Jail.

At the jail, McCarty was given an intoxilyzer test to determine the concentration of alcohol in his blood. The test did not detect any alcohol whatsoever in his system. Williams then resumed questioning McCarty in order to obtain information for inclusion in the State Highway Patrol Alcohol Influence Report. McCarty answered affirmatively a question whether he had been drinking. When then asked if he was under the influence of alcohol, he said, "I guess, barely." Williams next asked McCarty to indicate on the form whether the marihuana he had smoked had been treated with any chemicals. In the section of the report headed "Remarks," McCarty wrote, "No angel dust or PCP in the pot." At no point in this sequence of events did Williams or anyone else tell McCarty that he had a right to remain silent, to consult with an attorney, and to have an attorney appointed for him if he could not afford one.

McCarty was charged with operating a motor vehicle while under the influence of alcohol and/or drugs. Under Ohio law, that offense is a first-degree misdemeanor and is punishable by fine or imprisonment for up to six months. Incarceration for a minimum of three days is mandatory. McCarty moved to exclude the various incriminating statements he had made to Trooper Williams on the ground that introduction into evidence of those statements would violate the Fifth Amendment insofar as he had not been informed of his constitutional rights prior to his interrogation. When the trial court denied the motion, McCarty pleaded "no contest" and was found guilty. He was sentenced to 90 days in jail, 80 of which were suspended, and

was fined $300, $100 of which were suspended. [According to Ohio law] "The plea of no contest does not preclude a defendant from asserting upon appeal that the trial court prejudicially erred in ruling on a pretrial motion, including a pretrial motion to suppress evidence." * . . . We granted certiorari to resolve confusion in the federal and state courts regarding the applicability of our ruling in *Miranda* to . . . questioning of motorists detained pursuant to traffic stops. . . .

OPINION

In *Miranda v. Arizona* (1966), the Court addressed the problem of how the privilege against compelled self-incrimination guaranteed by the Fifth Amendment could be protected from the coercive pressures that can be brought to bear upon a suspect in the context of custodial interrogation. . . . In the years since the decision in *Miranda*, we have frequently reaffirmed the central principle established by that case: if the police take a suspect into custody and then ask him questions without informing him of the rights enumerated above, his responses cannot be introduced into evidence to establish his guilt. The one exception to this consistent line of decisions is *New York v. Quarles*, 467 U.S. 649 (1984). **

. . . There can be no question that McCarty was "in custody" at least as of the moment he was formally placed under arrest and instructed to get into the police car. Because he was not informed of his constitutional rights at that juncture, McCarty's subsequent admissions should not have been used against him.

To assess the admissibility of the self-incriminating statements made by McCarty prior to his formal arrest, we are obliged to decide . . . whether the roadside questioning of a motorist detained pursuant to a routine traffic stop should be considered "custodial interrogation.". . . A traffic stop significantly curtails the "freedom of action" of the driver and the passengers of the detained vehicle. . . . Certainly few motorists would feel free either to disobey a directive to pull over or to leave the scene of a traffic stop without being told they might do so. . . . Thus, we must decide whether a traffic stop exerts upon a detained person pressures that sufficiently impair his free exercise of his privilege against self-incrimination to require that he be warned of his constitutional rights.

Two features of an ordinary traffic stop mitigate the danger that a person questioned will be induced "to speak

---

*McCarty appealed through the Ohio courts and then petitioned the U.S. District court for a writ of habeas corpus. The case finally arrived at the U.S. Supreme Court on writ of certiorari.

**Excerpted on p. 294.

where he would not otherwise do so freely." First...the vast majority of roadside detentions last only a few minutes. A motorist's expectations, when he sees a policeman's light flashing behind him, are that he will be obliged to spend a short period of time answering questions and waiting while the officer checks his license and registration, that he may then be given a citation, but that in the end he most likely will be allowed to continue on his way. In this respect, questioning incident to an ordinary traffic stop is quite different from stationhouse interrogation, which frequently is prolonged, and in which the detainee often is aware that questioning will continue until he provides his interrogators the answers they seek.

Second, circumstances associated with the typical traffic stop are not such that the motorist feels completely at the mercy of the police. To be sure, the aura of authority surrounding an armed, uniformed officer and the knowledge that the officer has some discretion in deciding whether to issue a citation, in combination, exert some pressure on the detainee to respond to questions. But other aspects of the situation substantially offset these forces. Perhaps most importantly, the typical traffic stop is public....Passersby, on foot or in other cars, witness the interaction of officer and motorist. This exposure to public view both reduces the ability of an unscrupulous policeman to use illegitimate means to elicit self-incriminating statements and diminishes the motorist's fear that, if he does not cooperate, he will be subjected to abuse. The fact that the detained motorist typically is confronted by only one or at most two policemen further mutes his sense of vulnerability. In short, the atmosphere surrounding an ordinary traffic stop is substantially less "police dominated" than that surrounding the kinds of interrogation at issue in *Miranda*....

...The safeguards prescribed by *Miranda* become applicable as soon as a suspect's freedom of action is curtailed to a "degree associated with formal arrest." If a motorist who has been detained pursuant to a traffic stop thereafter is subjected to treatment that renders him "in custody" for practical purposes, he will be entitled to the full panoply of protections prescribed by *Miranda*....

Turning to the case before us, we find nothing in the record that indicates that McCarty should have been given *Miranda* warnings at any point prior to the time Trooper Williams placed him under arrest....We reject the contention that the initial stop of McCarty's car, by itself, rendered him "in custody." And McCarty has failed to demonstrate that, at any time between the initial stop and the arrest, he was subjected to restraints comparable to those associated with a formal arrest. Only a short period of time elapsed between the stop and the arrest. At no point during that interval was McCarty informed that his detention would not be temporary....Nor do other aspects of the interaction of Williams and McCarty support the contention that McCarty was exposed to "custodial interrogation" at the scene of the stop....A single police officer asked McCarty a modest number of questions and requested him to perform a simple balancing test at a location visible to passing motorists. Treatment of this sort cannot fairly be characterized as the functional equivalent of formal arrest.

We conclude...that McCarty was not taken into custody for the purposes of *Miranda* until Williams arrested him. Consequently, the statements McCarty made prior to that point were admissible against him.

AFFIRMED.

Questions

1. List all the facts relevant to deciding whether Richard McCarty's freedom was "limited in any significant way."

2. Summarize the arguments the Court gives for its rule that people stopped for traffic violations aren't typically in custody.

3. List the facts and circumstances in *Miranda* and McCarty that differ.

4. According to the Court, when can a noncustodial traffic stop turn into a custodial stop for purposes of *Miranda*?

5. Summarize how the Court applied its definition of "custody" to the stop of Richard McCarty.

The Public Safety Exception

What if "mirandizing" a suspect before questioning her would endanger an officer or someone nearby? Would officers have to give the warnings anyway? After all, *Miranda* said (and we've just learned in the last two sections) that officers have to give the warnings before custodial interrogation can start. No, said the U.S. Supreme Court in *New York v. Quarles* (1984), a case that created a **public safety exception** to *Miranda*.

In *Quarles,* a woman came up to two NYPD officers and told them she'd been raped by a man carrying a gun who had just gone into a supermarket across the street. Officer Kraft ran to the market and saw Benjamin Quarles, who fit the woman's description. Kraft briefly lost sight of Quarles, then saw him again, pulled his own gun, ordered Quarles to stop and put his hands over his head, frisked him, discovered an empty shoulder holster, and handcuffed him. Without mirandizing Quarles, Kraft asked him where the gun was. Nodding to some cartons, Quarles said, "The gun's over there." Among the cartons, Kraft found a loaded .38 caliber revolver.

By a 5–4 vote the Court decided Officer Kraft didn't have to warn Quarles. According to the Court, the cost of *Miranda* is that some guilty people will go free, a cost worth paying in most cases because of the premium we put on the right against coerced self-incrimination. But, the cost is too high if giving the warning endangers public safety:

> We conclude that the need for answers to questions in a situation posing a threat to the public safety outweighs the need for the...rule protecting the...privilege against self-incrimination. We decline to place officers such as Officer Kraft in the untenable position of having to consider, often in a matter of seconds, whether it best serves society for them to ask the necessary questions without the *Miranda* warnings and render whatever probative evidence they uncover inadmissible, or for them to give the warnings in order to preserve the admissibility of evidence they might uncover but possibly damage or destroy their ability to obtain that evidence and neutralize the volatile situation confronting them. (657–658)

So, the Court created the public safety exception to the *Miranda* rule:

> In recognizing a *narrow exception* [my emphasis] to the *Miranda* rule in this case, we acknowledge that to some degree we lessen the desirable clarity of that rule....The exception will not be difficult for police officers to apply because in each case it will be circumscribed by the exigency which justifies it. We think police officers can and will distinguish almost instinctively between questions necessary to secure their own safety or the safety of the public and questions designed solely to elicit testimonial evidence from a suspect. (658)

Justice O'Connor, who agreed the exception made sense, nonetheless dissented because of the confusion she believed making exceptions to *Miranda*'s bright-line rule would cause:

> Since the time *Miranda* was decided, the Court has repeatedly refused to bend the literal terms of that decision....Wherever an accused has been taken into "custody" and subjected to "interrogation" without warnings, the Court has consistently prohibited the use of his responses for prosecutorial purposes at trial. As a consequence, the "meaning of *Miranda* has become reasonably clear and law enforcement practices have adjusted to its strictures."...
>
> In my view, a "public safety" exception unnecessarily blurs the edges of the clear line heretofore established and makes *Miranda*'s requirements more difficult to understand... The end result will be a fine spun new doctrine on public safety exigencies incident to custodial interrogation, complete with the hair-splitting distinctions that currently plague our Fourth Amendment jurisprudence. (662–664)

The Supreme Court hasn't dealt with "blurring the edges of the clear line," but the U.S. District Court for the Southern District of New York tried to clarify just how "narrow" the public safety exception is in *U.S. v. Reyes* (2003).

United States v. Reyes

WL 346450 (S.D.N.Y.) (2003)

Ramon Reyes was indicted for possession of heroin with intent to distribute, carrying a firearm in connection with a narcotics crime, and possession of a firearm by a convicted felon. Reyes moved to suppress. The U.S. District Court granted the motion.

LYNCH, J.

FACTS

Reyes was arrested on October 17, 2001, based on probable cause to believe that he was in possession of heroin that he had brought to the place where he was arrested to sell to what turned out to be an undercover police officer. Detective Mark Moran, arriving on the scene in response to a prearranged signal that Reyes had come with the drugs and that an arrest was to be made, "pushed" Reyes "face down on the hood of the car" and prepared to search him incident to the arrest. According to Moran's testimony, corroborated by that of his partner who observed the interaction, before commencing the search Moran "asked [Reyes] if he had anything on him that can hurt me or anyone on my field team." Moran testified that this is standard police procedure before beginning a frisk or search of a person in a drug case, in order to protect the officer against the possibility of being harmed by sharp objects, such as hypodermic needles or razor blades, that a suspect might have in his pockets. Reyes responded that he had a gun in his pocket. Moran then repeated the question, asking if Reyes "had anything inside [his] pocket that could hurt me." Reyes, who does not speak English well, then "made the statement there was drugs inside the car, that was it."

It is undisputed that Moran did not advise Reyes of his rights before asking these questions. Reyes moves to suppress his answers, arguing that they were made in response to presumptively coercive custodial interrogation, without the required warnings, in violation of the rule of *Miranda v. Arizona*, (1966) The statements, and in particular the statement about the drugs, are potentially significant in the case, since they would help refute any claim that the drugs had been planted in the car without Reyes's knowledge by the confidential informant who had arranged the supposed heroin sale.

OPINION

Beyond any question, the statements made by Reyes were made in response to custodial interrogation. . . . Reyes was not free to leave; the officers had descended in response to a signal in order to arrest him, and he was being forcibly pinned to the car. The act of interrogation encompasses express questioning or its functional equivalent; words or actions of the police that are reasonably likely to elicit an incriminating response are regarded as tantamount to direct questioning. The statements at issue here were direct responses to express questioning by Detective Moran.

It would thus appear that *Miranda* requires suppression of the statements at issue. The government argues, however, that the statements are admissible because the questioning at issue falls within an exception to *Miranda* announced in *New York v. Quarles*, 467 U.S. 649 (1984). In *Quarles*, police officers in hot pursuit of a rapist armed with a firearm apprehended the apparent perpetrator, wearing an empty shoulder holster, in a supermarket. An officer handcuffed him and, without giving *Miranda* warnings, "asked [Quarles] where the gun was. Quarles nodded his head toward "some empty cartons" and said, "the gun is over there."

Reversing the state courts' suppression of Quarles's statement, a 5–4 majority of the Supreme Court held that *"on these facts,* there is a 'public safety' exception to the requirement that *Miranda* warnings be given before a suspect's answers may be admitted into evidence." (emphasis added). The Court based what it called "a narrow exception to the *Miranda* rule *in this case,*" (emphasis added), on the exigencies of the situation facing the arresting officers, including "the immediate necessity of ascertaining the whereabouts of a gun" that Quarles had removed from his holster and tossed aside in a public place where "an accomplice might make use of it" or "a customer or employee might later come upon it." In light of such a potential danger to public safety, the Court held, advising Quarles of his rights might have discouraged him from helping the police to locate the firearm before it could pose a danger to the public at large.

Although the *Quarles* Court made reference throughout the opinion to the narrowness of the "public safety" exception and its apparent limitation to the facts of the particular case, other language in the opinion suggests that the Court foresaw a potentially broader application of the new constitutional rule. For example, in clarifying that police officers could not employ the exception as a license to conduct an unfettered testimonial interrogation of a suspect who has not been read his *Miranda* rights, the Court noted that it would be acceptable for officers to ask "questions necessary to secure their own safety or the safety of the public." Moreover, the Court predicted that the exception would "free [officers] to follow their legitimate instincts when confronting situations presenting a danger to the public safety." The Court's opinion in *Quarles* thus leaves considerable uncertainty as to whether the Court intended its holding to be confined to the narrow factual circumstances of the case or, instead, to provide law enforcement officials with broader latitude to conduct limited custodial interrogations whenever public safety concerns might be implicated.

Pointing to this language, the government plausibly argues that Detective Moran, like the officers in *Quarles*, was simply asking "questions necessary to secure [his] own safety." Of course, Moran was authorized to (and almost immediately did) perform a search incident to the arrest of Reyes in order to determine whether Reyes had within reach any weapon that might be used against the arresting officers.* But the government contends that before performing such a search, an officer is entitled to ask the arrested person about dangerous objects in his pockets, because an officer searching a defendant might be injured by sharp objects such as knives, syringes, or razor blades kept there. Like the questioning at issue in *Quarles*, it argues, such queries are permissible not in order to elicit incriminating admissions, but simply in order to secure the safety of the officer.

The rule proposed by the government goes well beyond the facts of *Quarles*. There, the Court was concerned that a loaded firearm, carelessly discarded in a public place, posed an emergent threat to the general public, including children. Here, the situation was completely under police control, Reyes had been under observation since his arrival at the location, and any weapon he had with him would be immediately discovered and secured in a police search. Detective Moran testified that "numerous" people carry sharp objects in their pockets, and that he had stopped "a lot" of people who had uncapped hypodermic needles in their pockets but nothing in the record permits the Court to quantify this problem, and absolutely nothing of what was known about Reyes gave any particular reason to believe that his pockets in particular might have been booby-trapped. While the government's argument fits within the broader dicta in *Quarles*, it would be hard to consider the rule proposed a "narrow exception" that would apply only in situations marked by particular facts. Rather, what the

government appears to propose is that *whenever* officers arrest *anyone*, they are entitled to ask, before advising the defendant of his rights, what the person has about his person that might be "dangerous" or "harmful" to the officers and to use whatever he says in a subsequent prosecution.

This Court thus reads *Quarles* as the Supreme Court announced it: as a "narrow exception" to the *Miranda* doctrine, that carves out a circumscribed opportunity for law enforcement officials—in need of immediate information to protect themselves and members of the general public from harm—to conduct limited interrogations of suspects who, if apprised of their right against self-incrimination, might be unwilling to provide that information. Such an exception, however, does not accord officers an automatic right to interrogate suspects simply because it is possible that firearms are present at the arrest scene. In the context of searches for weapons, this doctrine requires, at a minimum, that the authorities have some real basis to believe that weapons are present, and some specific reason to believe that the weapon's undetected presence poses a danger to the police or to the public.

A similar standard must apply here. Unless every suspect in police custody can be interrogated, without *Miranda* warnings, about what the police might find in a search incident to arrest, the public safety exception can only be applied if the officers have some genuine, particularized reason to believe that conducting the search will be dangerous because of the possible presence of objects whose "undetected presence poses a danger to the police." There was no such reason here. Moreover, even to the extent that the generalized fear of sharp objects might justify a limited inquiry as to the presence of such objects, that would not render admissible statements made in response to a question as broad as whether "he had anything on him that can hurt me or anyone on my field team," a question that can reasonably be expected to lead to information about such matters as weapons in addition to or instead of the information about sharp objects that is the ostensible object of the inquiry. Accordingly, the *Quarles* exception is not applicable.

It should be noted that this conclusion implies no criticism of the officer's conduct. There is nothing terrible about the questions asked by Detective Moran. But there is nothing terrible about most questioning that takes place without *Miranda* warnings. The purpose of the warnings is to ensure that defendants are not led to waive their rights and respond to police interrogation in an atmosphere that is intrinsically coercive, even when the police have not behaved in a manner calculated to oppress. If ordinary stationhouse interrogation is inherently coercive, the questioning here, however legitimately intended to protect the officer, surely is far more likely to overbear the will of the most strong-

---

*Chapter 6.

willed defendant: not merely "in custody" but physically overpowered, forcibly bent over a car, and urgently (and repeatedly) asked what harmful objects he has on him, any reasonable person would feel compelled to answer. This particular defendant, with a limited command of English, quite naturally did not interpret the question as limited to sharp objects, and confessed to having a gun in his pocket; pressed yet again to provide more information about dangerous objects, he admitted to having drugs in the car. Such statements cannot, in the totality of the circumstances, be considered voluntary, nor can their admission into evidence be squared with the rule of *Miranda*.

Accordingly, the motion to suppress defendant's statements made at the scene of his arrest is granted.

Questions

1. List all the facts relevant to deciding whether Reyes was a danger to public safety.

2. List the specific differences in facts and circumstances between *Quarles* and this case.

3. Summarize the arguments the court gave for concluding that the public exception doesn't apply to this case.

4. Consider Justice O'Connor's warning in *New York v. Quarles* (p. 294) that we'd see "a fine spun new doctrine on public safety exigencies incident to custodial interrogation, complete with hair-splitting distinctions that currently plague our Fourth Amendment jurisprudence." Has Judge Lynch done here what Justice O'Connor predicted? Explain your answer.

5. If you favor a public safety exception, should it apply to the facts in this case?

 Go to Exercise 8-2 on the Criminal Procedure 6e CD to learn more about the public safety exception.

◆ ◆ ◆

THE WAIVER OF RIGHTS TO COUNSEL AND TO REMAIN SILENT

After *Miranda v. Arizona* was decided there was a lot of talk about handcuffing the police. The talk was created by a fear that suspects wouldn't talk if officers told them they had a right not to talk to police and to have lawyers with them if they did talk. As it turned out, these fears were greatly exaggerated. Most defendants talked to the police anyway. (They still do.) Because so many suspects waive their rights and talk to interrogators with no lawyer in sight, the questions, What is a valid waiver? and What is a voluntary confession? are important.

Valid Waivers

Miranda says courts can admit evidence obtained during custodial interrogation only if the government can prove that suspects "knowingly and intelligently" gave up their right to remain silent and to have a lawyer present if they decide to talk. (We'll just use the word *knowing* since in interrogation law they mean about the same thing.) According to the U.S. Supreme Court, a knowing waiver doesn't have to be an **expressed waiver,** which means you don't have to specifically say or write that you know your rights, know you're giving them up, and know the consequences of giving them up. Instead, the Court has adopted an **implied waiver** test, which says the totality of circumstances in each case has to prove that before suspects talked, they knew they had the rights and knew they were giving them up. Circumstances commonly considered

TABLE 8.3

Circumstances Relevant to Showing a Knowing Waiver

Intelligence

Education

Age

Familiarity with the criminal justice system

Physical condition

Mental condition

Ability to understand English

TABLE 8.4

Cases in Which Courts Found a Knowing Waiver

No evidence showed the suspect was threatened, tricked, or cajoled (*Connecticut v. Barrett* 1987).

The suspect invoked the right to counsel and then, after a five-hour ride in the back of a squad car, signed a waiver when police officers asked "if there was anything he would like to tell them" (*Henderson v. Florida* 1985).

The suspect asked for a lawyer, didn't get one, and then signed a waiver after repeated warnings and "nagging" by police officers (*Watkins v. Virginia* 1986).

After refusing to sign an expressed waiver, the defendant talked to the police (*U.S. v. Barahona* 1993).

The defendant said, "I don't got nothing to say" when he was presented with a waiver form but then answered questions during an interview that followed (*U.S. v. Banks* 1995).

in making this determination are listed in Table 8.3, and examples of cases in which courts ruled there was a knowing waiver appear in Table 8.4.

The U.S. Supreme Court applied the implied waiver test in *North Carolina v. Butler* (1979).

CASE | *Did He Waive His Right to Remain Silent?*

North Carolina v. Butler
441 U.S. 369 (1979)

Willie Butler was convicted in a North Carolina trial court of kidnapping, armed robbery and felonious assault. The North Carolina Supreme Court reversed. The U.S. Supreme Court vacated the judgment and remanded.

STEWART, J.

FACTS

Willie Thomas Butler and Elmer Lee robbed a gas station in Goldsboro, N.C., in December 1976, and had shot the sta-

tion attendant as he was attempting to escape. The attendant was paralyzed, but survived to testify against Butler.

The prosecution also produced evidence of incriminating statements made by Butler shortly after his arrest by Federal Bureau of Investigation agents in the Bronx, N.Y. Outside the presence of the jury, FBI Agent Martinez testified that at the time of the arrest he fully advised Butler of the rights delineated in the *Miranda* case. According to the uncontroverted testimony of Martinez, the agents then took Butler to the FBI office in nearby New Rochelle, N.Y. There, after the agents determined that Butler had an 11th grade education and was literate, he was given the Bureau's "Advice of Rights" form which he read. When asked if he understood his rights, he replied that he did. Butler refused to sign the waiver at the bottom of the form. He was told that he need neither speak nor sign the form, but that the agents would like him to talk to them. Butler replied: "I will talk to you but I am not signing any form." He then made inculpatory statements. Agent Martinez testified that Butler said nothing when advised of his right to the assistance of a lawyer. At no time did Butler request counsel or attempt to terminate the agents' questioning.

At the conclusion of this testimony the respondent moved to suppress the evidence of his incriminating statements on the ground that he had not waived his right to the assistance of counsel at the time the statements were made. The court denied the motion, finding that

> the statement made by the defendant, William Thomas Butler, to Agent David C. Martinez, was made freely and voluntarily to said agent after having been advised of his rights as required by the *Miranda* ruling, including his right to an attorney being present at the time of the inquiry and that the defendant, Butler, understood his rights; [and] that he effectively waived his rights, including the right to have an attorney present during the questioning by his indication that he was willing to answer questions, having read the rights form together with the Waiver of Rights.

Butler's statements were then admitted into evidence, and the jury ultimately found him guilty of each offense charged.

On appeal, the North Carolina Supreme Court reversed the convictions and ordered a new trial. It found that the statements had been admitted in violation of the requirements of the *Miranda* decision, noting that Butler had refused to waive in writing his right to have counsel present and that there had not been a *specific* oral waiver. As it had in at least two earlier cases, the court read the *Miranda* opinion as

> providing in plain language that waiver of the right to counsel during interrogation will not be recognized unless such waiver is 'specifically made' after the *Miranda* warnings have been given.

OPINION

We conclude that the North Carolina Supreme Court erred in its reading of the *Miranda* opinion. There, this Court said:

> If the interrogation continues without the presence of an attorney and a statement is taken, a heavy burden rests on the government to demonstrate that the defendant knowingly and intelligently waived his privilege

against self-incrimination and his right to retained or appointed counsel.

The Court's opinion went on to say:

> An express statement that the individual is willing to make a statement and does not want an attorney followed closely by a statement could constitute a waiver. But a valid waiver will not be presumed simply from the silence of the accused after warnings are given or simply from the fact that a confession was in fact eventually obtained.

Thus, the Court held that an express statement can constitute a waiver, and that silence alone after such warnings cannot do so. But the Court did not hold that such an express statement is indispensable to a finding of waiver.

An express written or oral statement of waiver of the right to remain silent or of the right to counsel is usually strong proof of the validity of that waiver, but is not inevitably either necessary or sufficient to establish waiver. The question is not one of form, but rather whether the defendant in fact knowingly and voluntarily waived the rights delineated in the *Miranda* case. As was unequivocally said in *Miranda*, mere silence is not enough. That does not mean that the defendant's silence, coupled with an understanding of his rights and a course of conduct indicating waiver, may never support a conclusion that a defendant has waived his rights. The courts must presume that a defendant did not waive his rights; the prosecution's burden is great; but in at least some cases waiver can be clearly inferred from the actions and words of the person interrogated.

The Court's opinion in *Miranda* explained the reasons for the prophylactic rules it created:

> We have concluded that without proper safeguards the process of in-custody interrogation of persons suspected or accused of crime contains inherently compelling pressures which work to undermine the individual's will to resist and to compel him to speak where he would not otherwise do so freely. In order to combat these pressures and to permit a full opportunity to exercise the privilege against self-incrimination, the accused must be adequately and effectively apprised of his rights and the exercise of those rights must be fully honored.

The per se rule that the North Carolina Supreme Court has found in *Miranda* does not speak to these concerns. There is no doubt that this respondent was adequately and effectively apprised of his rights. The only question is whether he waived the exercise of one of those rights, the right to the presence of a lawyer. Neither the state court nor Butler has offered any reason why there must be a negative answer to that question in the absence of an *express* waiver. This is not the first criminal case to question whether a defendant waived his constitutional rights. It is an issue with which courts must repeatedly deal. Even when a right so fundamental as that to counsel at trial is involved, the question of waiver must be determined on "the particular facts and circumstances surrounding that case, including the background, experience, and conduct of the accused."

> We see no reason to discard that standard and replace it with an inflexible *per se* rule in a case such as this. As stated at the outset of this opinion, it appears that every court that has considered this question has now reached the same conclusion. Ten of the eleven United States Courts of Appeals and the courts of at least 17 States have held that an explicit statement of waiver is not invariably necessary to support a finding that the defendant waived the right to remain silent or the right to counsel guaranteed by the *Miranda* case. By creating an inflexible rule that no implicit waiver can ever suffice, the North Carolina Supreme Court has gone beyond the requirements of federal organic law. It follows that its judgment cannot stand, since a state court can neither add to nor subtract from the mandates of the United States Constitution.

Accordingly, the judgment is vacated, and the case is REMANDED to the North Carolina Supreme Court for further proceedings not inconsistent with this opinion.

DISSENT

BRENNAN, J., joined by MARSHALL and STEVENS, JJ. *Miranda v. Arizona* held that "no effective waiver of the right to counsel during interrogation can be recognized unless *specifically* made after the warnings have been given." (Emphasis added.) There is no allegation of an affirmative waiver in this case. As the Court concedes, Butler refused to sign the waiver form, and "said nothing when advised of his right to the assistance of a lawyer." In the absence of an "affirmative waiver" in the form of an express written or oral statement, the Supreme Court of North Carolina correctly granted a new trial. I would, therefore, affirm its decision.

The rule announced by the Court today allows a finding of waiver based upon "inference from the actions and words of the person interrogated." The Court thus shrouds in half-light the question of waiver, allowing courts to construct inferences from ambiguous words and gestures. But the very premise of *Miranda* requires that ambiguity be interpreted against the interrogator. That premise is the recognition of the "compulsion inherent in custodial" interrogation, and of its purpose "to subjugate the individual to the will of his examiner." Under such conditions, only the most explicit waivers of rights can be considered knowingly and freely given....

Faced with "actions and words" of uncertain meaning, some judges may find waivers where none occurred. Others may fail to find them where they did.... A simple prophylactic rule requiring the police to obtain an express waiver of the right to counsel before proceeding with interrogation eliminates these difficulties. And since the Court agrees that *Miranda* requires the police to obtain some kind of waiver—whether express or implied—the requirement of an express waiver would impose no burden on the police not imposed by the Court's interpretation. It would merely make that burden explicit. Had Agent Martinez simply elicited a clear answer from Willie Butler to the question, "Do you waive your right to a lawyer?" this journey through three courts would not have been necessary.

Questions

1. State the elements of the implied waiver test adopted by the Court.

2. Summarize the arguments the Court gives for adopting the implied waiver test.

3. Summarize the arguments the dissent gives for adopting an explicit waiver test.

4. List all the facts relevant to deciding whether Willie Thomas Butler knowingly waived his rights.

5. How did the Court apply the implied waiver test to the facts?

6. What test would you adopt? Why? How would you apply it to the facts of this case?

Commonwealth v. Washington
393 Pa.Super. 132, 573 A.2d 1123 (1990)

How Does Washington State Define Waiver?

Joseph Washington was convicted of possession of a controlled substance with intent to deliver, and possession of drug paraphernalia. Washington was sentenced to two to twenty-three months in jail. At the time of this offense, Washington was thirty-four years old and had no criminal record. He appealed his conviction. The Washington Supreme Court reversed and remanded the case for a new trial.

CAVANAUGH, J.

FACTS

...A search of Joseph Washington's apartment yielded five and three-tenths grams of marijuana, a pipe, two scales, one of which was broken, plastic sandwich bags, cigarette rolling papers, and eighty-six dollars in cash. Washington turned himself into the Harrisburg Police Station on January 11, 1988. He was arrested by Detective Holland, who read him his constitutional rights. Another detective, Arnold, later re-read him his rights. Washington was asked if he understood his rights and he responded positively. However, he was never asked to waive his rights. He never signed a written waiver form.

Washington was then taken into a room for questioning. Police officers testified he said he didn't sell drugs as a business but would occasionally break up a $20.00 bag of marijuana into $5.00 bags and sell them to his friends.

OPINION

Washington asserts he never explicitly waived his rights. We are satisfied that Washington was given the proper *Miranda* warnings. However, there remains an issue as to whether he explicitly waived his rights. In *Commonwealth v. Bussey,* our Supreme Court rejected the implicit waiver rule of *North Carolina v. Butler,* * and held that, as a matter of state law, the Commonwealth must show

---

*Excerpted on p. 298.

that the accused explicitly waived his Miranda rights in order for self-incriminating statements made in the course of custodial interrogation to be admissible. The *Bussey* court rejected the *Butler* formulation which permitted a finding of waiver when the accused expresses an understanding of his *Miranda* rights and proceeds to give a statement.

The trial court and the Commonwealth both rely on *Commonwealth v. Speaks,* 505 A.2d 310 (1986) to show that Washington waived his rights. In *Commonwealth v. Speaks,* the accused was fully and adequately advised of his rights, explicitly manifested an understanding of those rights and answered a question posed to him immediately afterwards and within the course of the same dialogue. In that case, this court found that immediate, virtually contemporaneous response to questions following a manifestation that one understands one's rights suffices as an explicit waiver....

Because Washington did not explicitly waive his rights, we must look to the circumstances of the arrest, as found by the lower court, to see whether he was advised of his rights and manifested an understanding of his rights immediately before he began answering questions. According to the trial court, Washington appeared at the police station and was initially arrested by Detective Holland, who read him his rights. Detective Arnold, the investigating officer, was called to the booking desk and he arrived ten minutes later. Detective Arnold then re-read the arrest warrant and read appellant his rights. Afterwards, Washington was taken into a room and was asked questions to which police testified he gave incriminating responses. There was no signed statement taken.

Part of the *Speaks* rationale for not requiring the accused to state explicitly that he waives his rights is that the accused makes his incriminating statement within the course of the same dialogue in which he claims to have understood his rights. The *Speaks* court's use of the word "immediately" is very precise. It means within a second or two of having manifested an understanding of one's rights. From the trial court's synopsis of events in the instant case, it is unclear whether appellant expressed an understanding of his rights and began answering questions immediately and within the same dialogue....

REVERSED and REMANDED for a new trial.

Voluntary Self-Incrimination

Great fears and equally great hopes—depending on whether those who voiced them were more afraid of street criminals or of government abuse of power—were expressed that *Miranda v. Arizona* would kill police interrogation as a tool to collect evidence. But it didn't happen. As we've already learned (page 275), Richard Leo found that only 25 percent of suspects invoke their right to remain silent and/or to speak to a lawyer. One experienced interrogator, Sergeant James DeConcini (now retired), of the Minneapolis Police Department, suggests the reason is that knowledge is a two-way street. Not only do police officers want to find out what suspects know about crimes they're investigating, but suspects also want to know how much police officers know. Suspects believe that by cooperating with the police, they might find out if they "have something on them."

That most suspects waive their right to remain silent and agree to custodial interrogation brings us back to the due process requirement of voluntariness. Even if officers have warned suspects and have gotten a knowing waiver, they still may not have gotten voluntarily the incriminating statements that follow. To determine whether incriminating statements were made voluntarily, the U.S. Supreme Court adopted another of its totality-of-circumstances tests: Confessions are involuntary only if the totality of the circumstances proves two things:

1. Officers engaged in coercive conduct during the interrogation.

2. The coercive conduct caused the suspect to make incriminating statements.

According to Chief Justice Rehnquist, writing for a majority of the U.S. Supreme Court in *Colorado v. Connelly* (1986):

> ...The cases considered by this Court over the 50 years since *Brown v. Mississippi* have focused on the crucial element of police overreaching. While each confession case has turned on its own set of factors..., all have contained a substantial element of coercive police conduct. Absent police conduct causally related to the confession, there is simply no basis for concluding that any state actor has deprived a criminal defendant of due process of law.... As interrogators have turned to more subtle forms of psychological persuasion, courts have found the mental condition of the defendant a more significant factor in the "voluntariness" calculus. But this fact does not justify a conclusion that a defendant's mental condition, by itself apart from its relation to official coercion, should ever dispose of the inquiry into constitutional "voluntariness." (163)

The most common circumstances courts consider in determining whether coercive state action caused people to confess include the following:

- The location where the questioning took place
- Whether the suspect initiated the contact with law enforcement
- Whether the *Miranda* warnings were given
- The number of interrogators
- The length of the questioning
- Whether food, water, and toilet facilities were denied
- Whether the police used threats, promises, lies, or tricks

- Whether the suspect was denied access to a lawyer
- The suspect's characteristics, such as age, gender, race, physical and mental condition, education, drug problems, and experience with the criminal justice system

Courts have found that none of the following actions caused suspects to confess (Twenty-Sixth Annual Review of Criminal Procedure 1997, 967–968):

- Promises of leniency
- Promises of treatment
- Confronting the accused with other evidence of guilt
- The interrogator's appeal to the defendant's emotions
- False and misleading statements made by the interrogator

The U.S. Supreme Court applied the elements of coercion and cause to the totality of circumstances in *Colorado v. Connelly* (1986).

Colorado v. Connelly
479 U.S. 157, 107 S.Ct. 515 (1986)

The trial court suppressed statements made by Francis Barry Connelly. The state appealed. The Colorado Supreme Court affirmed. The U.S. Supreme Court granted certiorari, reversed, and remanded the case.

REHNQUIST, CJ., joined by WHITE, POWELL, O'CONNOR, and SCALIA, JJ. and, in all but Part III-A, BLACKMUN, J.

FACTS

On August 18, 1983, Officer Patrick Anderson of the Denver Police Department was in uniform, working in an off-duty capacity in downtown Denver. Francis Connelly approached Officer Anderson and, without any prompting, stated he had murdered someone and wanted to talk about it. Anderson immediately advised Connelly he had the right to remain silent, that anything he said could be used against him in court, and that he had the right to an attorney prior to any police questioning. Connelly stated that he understood these rights but he still wanted to talk about the murder. Understandably bewildered by this confession, Officer Anderson asked Connelly several questions. Connelly denied he had been drinking, denied he had been taking any drugs, and stated that, in the past, he had been a patient in several mental hospitals. Officer Anderson again told Connelly he was under no obligation to say anything. Connelly replied it was "all right," and that he would talk to Officer Anderson because his conscience had been bothering him. To Officer Anderson, Connelly appeared to understand fully the nature of his acts.

Shortly thereafter, Homicide Detective Stephen Antuna arrived. Connelly was again advised of his rights, and Detective Antuna asked him "what he had on his mind." Connelly answered that he had come all the way from Boston to confess to the murder of Mary Ann Junta, a young girl whom he had killed in Denver sometime during November 1982. Connelly was taken to police headquarters, and a search of police records revealed that the body of an unidentified female had been found in April 1983. Connelly openly detailed his story to Detective Antuna and Sergeant Thomas Haney, and readily agreed to take the officers to the scene of the killing. Under Connelly's sole direction, the two officers and Connelly proceeded in a police vehicle to the location of the crime. Connelly pointed out the exact location of the murder. Throughout this episode, Detective Antuna perceived no indication whatsoever that Connelly was suffering from any kind of mental illness.

Connelly was held overnight. During an interview with the public defender's office the following morning, he became visibly disoriented. He began giving confused answers to questions, and for the first time, stated "voices" had told him to come to Denver and he had followed the directions of these voices in confessing. Connelly was sent to a state hospital for evaluation. He was initially found incompetent to assist in his own defense. By March 1984, however, the doctors evaluating Connelly determined he was competent to proceed to trial.

At a preliminary hearing, Connelly moved to suppress all of his statements. Dr. Jeffrey Metzner, a psychiatrist employed by the state hospital, testified that Connelly was suffering from chronic schizophrenia and was in a psychotic state at least as of August 17, 1983, the day before he confessed. Metzner's interviews with Connelly revealed that he was following the "voice of God." This voice instructed him to withdraw money from the bank, to buy an airplane ticket, and to fly from Boston to Denver. When he arrived from Boston, God's voice became stronger and told him either to confess to the killing or to commit suicide. Reluctantly following the command of the voices, he approached Officer Anderson and confessed.

Dr. Metzner testified that, in his expert opinion, Connelly was experiencing "command hallucinations." This condition interfered with his "volitional abilities—that is, his ability to make free and rational choices." Dr. Metzner further testified that Connelly's illness did not significantly impair his cognitive abilities. Thus, he understood the rights he had when Officer Anderson and Detective Antuna advised him that he need not speak. Dr. Metzner admitted that the "voices" could in reality be Connelly's interpretation of his own guilt, but explained that in his opinion, Connelly's psychosis motivated his confession.

On the basis of this evidence the Colorado trial court decided that Connelly's statements must be suppressed because they were "involuntary." The court ruled that a confession is admissible only if it is a product of the defendant's rational intellect and "free will." Although the court found that the police had done nothing wrong or coercive in securing Connelly's confession, his illness destroyed his volition and compelled him to confess. The trial court also found that Connelly's mental state vitiated his attempted waiver of the right to counsel and the privilege against compulsory self-incrimination. Accordingly, Connelly's initial statements and his custodial confession were suppressed.

...The Colorado Supreme Court affirmed the trial court's decision to suppress all of Connelly's statements.

OPINION

...The cases considered by this Court over the 50 years since *Brown v. Mississippi* have focused upon the crucial element of police overreaching. While each confession case has turned on its own set of factors justifying the conclusion that police conduct was oppressive, all have contained a substantial element of coercive police conduct. Absent police conduct causally related to the confession, there is simply no basis for concluding that any state actor has deprived a criminal defendant of due process of law. Connelly correctly notes that as interrogators have turned to more subtle forms of psychological persuasion, courts have found the mental condition of the defendant a more significant factor in the "voluntariness" calculus. But this fact does not justify a conclusion that a defendant's mental condition, by itself and apart from its relation to official coercion, should ever dispose of the inquiry into constitutional "voluntariness."

...Our "involuntary confession" jurisprudence is entirely consistent with the settled law requiring some sort of "state action" to support a claim of violation of the Due Process Clause of the Fourteenth Amendment. The Colorado trial court found that the police committed no wrongful acts, and that finding has been neither challenged by Connelly nor disturbed by the Supreme Court of Colorado. The latter court, however, concluded that sufficient state action was present by virtue of the admission of the confession into evidence in a court of the State.

The difficulty with the approach of the Supreme Court of Colorado is that it fails to recognize the essential link between coercive activity of the State, on the one hand, and a resulting confession by a defendant, on the other. The flaw in Connelly's constitutional argument is that it would expand our previous line of "voluntariness" cases into a far-ranging requirement that courts must divine a defendant's motivation for speaking or acting as he did even though there be no claim that governmental conduct coerced his decision.

...We have previously cautioned against expanding "currently applicable exclusionary rules by erecting additional barriers to placing truthful and probative evidence before state juries.".... We abide by that counsel now. "The central purpose of a criminal trial is to decide the factual question of the defendant's guilt or innocence," and while we have previously held that exclusion of evidence may be necessary to protect constitutional guarantees, both the necessity for the collateral inquiry and the exclusion of evidence deflect a criminal trial from its basic purpose. Connelly would now have us require sweeping inquiries into the state of mind of a criminal defendant who has confessed, inquiries quite divorced from any coercion brought to bear on the defendant by the State. We think the Constitution rightly leaves this sort of inquiry to be resolved by state laws governing the admission of evidence and erects no standard of its own in this area. A statement rendered by one in the condition of Connelly might be proved to be quite unreliable, but this is a matter to be governed by the evidentiary laws of the forum, and not by the Due Process Clause of the Fourteenth Amendment....

We hold that coercive police activity is a necessary predicate to the finding that a confession is not "voluntary" within the meaning of the Due Process Clause of the Fourteenth Amendment. We also conclude that the taking of Connelly's statements, and their admission into evidence, constitute no violation of that Clause.

...We think that the Supreme Court of Colorado erred in importing into this area of constitutional law notions of "free will" that have no place there....The sole concern of the Fifth Amendment, on which *Miranda* was based, is governmental coercion. Indeed, the Fifth Amendment privilege is not concerned "with moral and psychological pressures to confess emanating from sources other than official coercion." The voluntariness of a waiver of this privilege has always depended on the absence of police overreaching, not on "free choice" in any broader sense of the word....

Connelly urges this Court to adopt his "free will" rationale, and to find an attempted waiver invalid whenever the defendant feels compelled to waive his rights by reason of any compulsion, even if the compulsion does not flow from the police. But such a treatment of the waiver issue would "cut this Court's holding in [*Miranda*] completely loose from its own explicitly stated rationale." *Miranda* protects defendants against government coercion leading them to surrender rights protected by the Fifth Amendment; it goes no further than that. Connelly's perception of coercion flowing from the "voice of God," however important or significant such a perception may be in other disciplines, is a matter to which the United States Constitution does not speak.

The judgment of the Supreme Court of Colorado is accordingly REVERSED, and the cause is REMANDED for further proceedings not inconsistent with this opinion....

DISSENT

BRENNAN, J. joined by MARSHALL, J.
Today the Court denies Mr. Connelly his fundamental right to make a vital choice with a sane mind, involving a determination that could allow the State to deprive him of liberty or even life. This holding is unprecedented: "Surely in the present stage of our civilization a most basic sense of justice is affronted by the spectacle of incarcerating a human being upon the basis of a statement he made while insane...." Because I believe that the use of a mentally ill person's involuntary confession is antithetical to the notion of fundamental fairness embodied in the Due Process Clause, I dissent.

Connelly's seriously impaired mental condition is clear on the record of this case. At the time of his confession, Mr. Connelly suffered from a "longstanding severe mental disorder," diagnosed as chronic paranoid schizophrenia. He had been hospitalized for psychiatric reasons five times prior to his confession; his longest hospitalization lasted for seven months. Mr. Connelly heard imaginary voices and saw nonexistent objects. He believed that his father was God, and that he was a reincarnation of Jesus.

...The state trial court found that the "overwhelming evidence presented by the Defense" indicated that the prosecution did not meet its burden of demonstrating by a preponderance of the evidence that the initial statement to Officer Anderson was voluntary. While the court found no police misconduct, it held:

> There's no question that the Defendant did not exercise free will in choosing to talk to the police. He exercised a choice both [*sic*] of which were mandated by auditory hallucination, had no basis in reality, and were the product of a psychotic break with reality. The Defendant at the time of the confession had absolutely in the Court's estimation no volition or choice to make.

...The absence of police wrongdoing should not, by itself, determine the voluntariness of a confession by a mentally ill person. The requirement that a confession be voluntary reflects a recognition of the importance of free will and of reliability in determining the admissibility of a confession, and thus demands an inquiry into the totality of the circumstances surrounding the confession.

Today's decision restricts the application of the term "involuntary" to those confessions obtained by police coercion. Confessions by mentally ill individuals or by persons coerced by parties other than police officers are now considered "voluntary." The Court's failure to recognize all forms of involuntariness or coercion as antithetical to due process reflects a refusal to acknowledge free will as a value of constitutional consequence. But due process derives much of its meaning from a conception of fundamental fairness that emphasizes the right to make vital choices voluntarily: "The Fourteenth Amendment secures against state invasion...the right of a person to remain silent unless he chooses to speak in the unfettered exercise of his own will...." This right requires vigilant protection if we are to safeguard the values of private conscience and human dignity....A true commitment to fundamental fairness requires that the inquiry be not whether the conduct of state officers in obtaining the confession is shocking, but whether the confession was "free and voluntary."

...Since the Court redefines voluntary confessions to include confessions by mentally ill individuals, the reliability of these confessions becomes a central concern. A concern for reliability is inherent in our criminal justice system, which relies upon accusatorial rather than inquisitorial practices. While an inquisitorial system prefers obtaining confessions from criminal defendants, an accusatorial system must place its faith in determinations of "guilt by evidence independently and freely secured." In *Escobedo v. Illinois,* 378 U.S. 478, 84 S.Ct. 1758, 12 L.Ed.2d 977 (1964), we justified our reliance upon accusatorial practices:

> We have learned the lesson of history, ancient and modern, that a system of criminal law enforcement which comes to depend on the "confession" will, in the long run, be less reliable and more subject to abuses than a system which depends on extrinsic evidence independently secured through skillful investigation.

I dissent.

Questions

1. List all the facts relevant to deciding whether Francis Connelly's confession was voluntary.

2. What are the two parts of the test that the U.S. Supreme Court announced for determining whether confessions are voluntary?

3. Do you agree with the majority that the confession was voluntary? If yes, what persuaded you? If no, do you agree with the dissent? Explain why.

 Go to Exercise 8-3 on the Criminal Procedure CD to learn more about voluntary confessions.

◆ **STATE CONSTITUTIONAL LAW** ◆

State v. Bowe
77 Hawai'i 51, 881 P.2d 538 (1994)

How Does Hawaii Define "Voluntary" Confession?

On September 17, 1991, Troy Bowe was charged with Assault in the Second Degree. The trial court granted Bowe's motion to suppress his confession. The Hawaii supreme court affirmed.

RAMIL, J., joined by KLEIN, Acting CJ., LEVINSON, NAKAYAMA, and RAMIL, JJ., and SOONG, Circuit Court J., in Place of MOON, CJ., recused.

FACTS

On January 21, 1990, a brawl involving a number of individuals occurred at one of the dormitory buildings on the University of Hawai'i-Manoa (UH) campus. During the fight, Steven Oshiro (Victim) was beaten and sustained physical injuries.

On February 9, 1990, Sergeant John Pinero (Sergeant Pinero) of the Honolulu Police Department (HPD) contacted Wallace, head coach of the UH Men's Basketball Team, and requested his assistance in making arrangements for the police to interview certain members of the basketball team suspected of being involved in the January 21, 1990 fight. Sergeant Pinero provided Wallace with a list of suspects that included Troy Bowe.

Wallace later told Bowe that he needed to go to the police station and that Wallace would go with Bowe if he required assistance. On February 12, 1990, Bowe went to the police station accompanied by Wallace. Bowe was given *Miranda* warnings and subsequently signed an HPD Form 81, waiving his constitutional rights to counsel and to remain silent. After waiving his constitutional rights, an interrogation commenced in which Bowe admitted assaulting the victim.

On September 17, 1991, an Oahu Grand Jury indicted Defendant and Vincent Smalls for Assault in the Second Degree. On November 21, 1991, Bowe filed a Motion to Suppress Evidence on the grounds that his February 12, 1990 statement to the police was involuntary because it was obtained through the use of official state coercion in violation of Bowe's constitutional right to due process. On May 8, 1992, the circuit court granted Bowe's motion to suppress.

In determining that Defendant's statement was coerced, the circuit court entered the following findings of fact:

1. On or about January or February of 1990, Sergeant John Pinero was an employee of the [HPD], who was at that time working on an investigation of an assault which allegedly involved TROY BOWE.

2. In his capacity as a police officer with the [HPD], Sergeant Pinero called Riley Wallace, at that time basketball coach of the University of Hawaii at Manoa Basketball Team (hereinafter "Basketball Team"), and gave Wallace a list of suspects who were on the Basketball Team that Sergeant Pinero wanted Wallace to bring down to the [HPD] (hereinafter "List").

3. Wallace, as head basketball coach, had the authority to suspend athletes or remove them from the

Basketball Team and, in the case of scholarship-athletes, to initiate procedures to withdraw their athletic-scholarships.

4. TROY BOWE was a scholarship-athlete on the Basketball Team.

5. TROY BOWE was on said List.

6. Sergeant Pinero specifically asked Wallace to locate the individuals on the List and have them meet with Sergeant Pinero.

7. Sergeant Pinero, however, did not request that Wallace use force or coercion while attempting to have individuals on the List meet with Sergeant Pinero.

8. Wallace then contacted Defendant TROY BOWE and informed him that he had to go down to the [HPD] to meet with Sergeant Pinero.

9. Wallace informed TROY BOWE that Wallace would accompany him to the [HPD] in place of an attorney and instructed TROY BOWE to make a statement to Sargeant Pinero.

10. Wallace did not inform TROY BOWE that he could or should have an attorney present with him when he went to be interviewed by Sargeant Pinero.

11. TROY BOWE believed that he could not refuse to follow Wallace's directions because if he did so Wallace could suspend him from the Basketball Team or institute procedures to revoke Defendant TROY BOWE's athletic-scholarship.

This timely appeal followed.

OPINION

The sole issue presented in this appeal is whether the coercive conduct of a private person is sufficient to render a confession inadmissible.

The Prosecution contends that the circuit court erred by granting Bowe's motion to suppress his February 12, 1990 confession to police because coercive police action is required for a confession to be found involuntary. Thus, the Prosecution maintains that the circuit court erred in concluding that Bowe's confession was involuntary as a result of Wallace's coercive influence.... The circuit court...concluded that coercive conduct of a private person, namely Wallace, was sufficient to render a confession inadmissible under HRS § 621-26. HRS § 621-26 (1985) which provides that

no confession shall be received in evidence unless it is first made to appear to the judge before whom the case is being tried that the confession was in fact voluntarily made.

We note, that the legislative history of HRS § 621-26 is silent as to whether coercive police conduct is a necessary predicate to finding a confession involuntary.

Whether the coercive conduct of a private person is sufficient to render a confession involuntary is a case of first impression in this jurisdiction. Thus, the Prosecution relies on *Colorado v. Connelly*, for support. In *Connelly*, the United States Supreme Court held that coercive police conduct is a necessary predicate to finding that a confession is not voluntary under the due process clause of the United States Constitution.

The Prosecution maintains that absent a finding that the police engaged in some coercive activity, Bowe's confession must be deemed voluntary. We begin our analysis with *Connelly*....[The court summarized the facts, majority, and dissenting opinions of *Colorado v. Connelly*.]...

When the United States Supreme Court's interpretation of a provision present in both the United States and Hawai'i Constitutions does not adequately preserve the rights and interests sought to be protected, we will not hesitate to recognize the appropriate protections as a matter of state constitutional law. Because the Supreme Court's decision in *Connelly* limits the interests protected by federal constitutional confession law, we find compelling reasons for rejecting *Connelly* as a model for interpreting our own state constitution. Thus, independent constitutional considerations arising under article I, sections 5 and 10 of the Hawai'i Constitution compel us to hold that the coercive conduct of a private person may be sufficient to render a Defendant's confession involuntary.

...The considerations underlying the right against self-incrimination under the Hawai'i Constitution are not limited to deterring government coercion, but are broader. While the Supreme Court in *Connelly* stated that, "the sole concern of the Fifth Amendment...is governmental coercion," we have recognized that one of the basic considerations underlying the exclusion of confessions obtained through coercion is the "inherent untrustworthiness of involuntary confessions." An involuntary confession is inherently untrustworthy because the free will of an individual is overborne by the external influence exerted in obtaining it. We have...learned the lesson of history...that a system of criminal law enforcement which comes to depend on the "confession" will, in the long run, be less reliable and more subject to abuses than a system which depends on extrinsic evidence independently secured through skillful investigation....

Our focus is not confined to deterring police misconduct, but rather, we have stressed other important considerations underlying the right against self-incrimination. Accordingly, we reject the Supreme Court's narrow focus on police coercion in *Connelly* and hold that the protections accorded under article I, section 10 of the Hawai'i Constitution are broader.... We recognize that an individual's capacity to make a rational and free choice between confessing and remaining silent may be overborne as much by the coercive conduct of a private individual as by the coercive conduct of the police. [Therefore,] we hold that the coercive conduct of a private person may be sufficient to render a confession inadmissible based on article 1, sections 5 and 10 of the Hawaii Constitution. We part company with the United States Supreme Court's decision in *Colorado v. Connelly*, that held that coercive police conduct is a necessary predicate to finding that a confession is not voluntary under principles of due process.

Nevertheless, we acknowledge that some sort of state action is required to support a defendant's claim that his due process rights were violated.... Although no state action is involved where an accused is coerced into making a confession by a private individual, we find that the state participates in that violation by allowing the coerced statements to be used as evidence.... Accordingly, we decline to follow the Supreme Court's rationale in *Connelly* and hold that official police coercion is not a necessary predicate to finding that a confession is involuntary under article I, sections 5 and 10 of the Hawai'i Constitution.

By rejecting *Connelly* as a matter of state constitutional law, we acknowledge that the absence of police coercion does not foreclose a finding of involuntariness. Rather, we recognize, as has been our prerogative, that the issue of voluntariness must be resolved by evaluating the "totality of circumstances" surrounding the making of the statement regardless of whether the source of the coercion was a private individual or the state. Against this background, we hold that the circuit court did not err in concluding as a matter of law that Defendant's confession was involuntary after finding coercive conduct by Wallace....

Accordingly, after reviewing the totality of circumstances surrounding Defendant's confession, we hold that the circuit court did not err in concluding that Defendant's confession was inadmissible.

 Go to Exercise 8-4 on the Criminal Procedure 6e CD to learn more about the application of the "totality of circumstances" test in deciding whether confessions are voluntary.

Voluntary doesn't mean "totally free of influence." The *Miranda* warnings were intended to remove *coercion* from police custodial interrogation. They weren't meant to eliminate all *pressure* on criminal suspects. The basic idea is, "Coercion no way; pressure OK." According to law professor Donald Dripps (1988):

> At trial, after establishing probable cause of guilt and when the defendant enjoys the protection of a neutral bench, a personal advocate, and public scrutiny, the government may not so much as put a polite question to the defendant. But, between arrest and commitment, the police may badger, trick, and manipulate the suspect in an environment solely within their control and to which no other witness is admitted. With respect to confessions, society insists on enjoying "at one and the same time the pleasures of indulgence and the dignity of disapproval." (701)

SUMMARY

    I. The interrogation and confession setting
        A. The right to remain silent (against self-incrimination) is ancient and controversial
            1. Jesus invoked it, and Talmudic law commanded it
            2. Controversy over the issue—three positions

a. All incommunicado interrogation is coercive—taken by people who fear abuse of police power more than crime

b. Only forced confessions are illegal—taken by those who fear crime more than abuse of police power

c. Pressure is ok; coercion isn't—taken by the U.S. Supreme Court

B. Popular portrayals of saintly cops and satanic criminals hide a complex reality

C. Interrogation isn't pleasant, and it's not supposed to be

D. Three justifications for interrogation

1. Can't solve crimes without them

2. Criminals don't confess unless they're caught or confess

3. Police have to use pressure or guilty people won't confess

E. Important empirical findings about interrogation based on Leo's direct observation

1. Interrogators rarely use coercion

2. Most interrogations last less than an hour

3. One in four suspects invokes his *Miranda* rights

4. Interrogators make up evidence and use tricks to undermine suspects' confidence

II. The Constitution and self-incrimination

A. Three constitutional approaches

1. Due process approach—applied in early cases of forced confessions by blacks in the South

a. Reliability rationale—admitting unreliable evidence to prove guilt denies defendants the right to their lives without due process of law

b. Accusatory system rationale—forced confessions violate due process even if they're true, because the government alone has the burden of proving guilt beyond a reasonable doubt

c. Fundamental fairness rationale—coerced confessions aren't just unreliable and contrary to the accusatory system of justice; they offend the fundamental fairness required by the due process clause

2. Right-to-counsel approach

a. Used for a brief period

b. Applied in *Escobedo v. Illinois*

c. Custodial interrogation is a critical stage in criminal prosecutions—the point when suspects' right to a lawyer kicks in

d. As soon as a police investigation focuses on a particular suspect (the accusatory stage), criminal prosecution begins and the right to counsel attaches

3. Self-incrimination approach

a. Custodial interrogation is inherently coercive without warnings

b. Applied in *Miranda v. Arizona*

B. "Witness against himself"—self-incrimination protection applies only to testimony, not to physical evidence

C. The meaning of *compelled*—according to the voluntariness test of self-incrimination, confessions violate due process if the totality of circumstances shows that suspects didn't confess voluntarily

III. *Miranda v. Arizona*

    A. Bright-line rules—custodial interrogation is inherently coercive without four warnings

        1. The right to remain silent

        2. Incriminating statements will be used

        3. The right to counsel

        4. A lawyer will be appointed for poor suspects

    B. Warnings not necessary except when two conditions are met:

        1. Suspects are in custody—custody usually means in police stations but includes any place where suspects are held against their will

        2. Suspects are interrogated—doesn't apply to interviews before interrogation begins or brief questioning during "stops" (Chapter 4)

    C. The meaning of *custody*

        1. Being held in a police interrogation room

        2. Wherever officers have deprived an individual of "freedom of action in any significant way" (*Miranda v. Arizona*)

        3. Circumstances that can form part of "totality of circumstances" showing custody

            a. Whether the officers had probable cause to arrest

            b. Whether the officers intended to detain the suspects

            c. Whether the suspects believed their freedom was significantly restricted

            d. Whether the investigation had focused on the suspect

            e. The language the officers used to summon the suspects

            f. The physical surroundings

            g. The amount of evidence of guilt the officers presented to the suspects

            h. How long suspects were detained

            i. The amounts and kinds of pressure the officers used to detain the suspects

        4. Circumstances *not* showing custody

            a. Drivers and passengers detained during routine traffic stops

            b. Probationers attending routine meetings with their probation officers

            c. Persons detained during the execution of search warrants

    D. The public safety exception

        1. Applied to *New York v. Quarles*

        2. No warnings are required if

            a. Officers are endangered

            b. Anyone else nearby is endangered

IV. The waiver of the right to counsel and to remain silent

    A. Government has to prove suspects waived two rights

        1. The right to counsel

        2. The right to remain silent

    B. A valid waiver has to be "knowing" and "voluntary"

        1. Knowing—knew the right and knew they were giving it up

        2. Voluntary—gave up the right without force, promise, or reward

        3. Can be an expressed or implied waiver

            a. Expressed—spoken or written

            b. Implied—the totality of circumstances shows it was voluntary and knowing

C. Voluntary self-incrimination
 1. Most suspects (about 75%) waive rights, so we're back to the due process requirement that suspects made incriminating statements voluntarily
 2. The two-prong test of confessions that violate the self-incrimination clause
    a. Police coercion was involved
    b. Police coercion *caused* the incriminating statements
 3. The totality of circumstances determines the two prongs

Go to the Criminal Procedure 6e CD to download this summary outline. The outline has been formatted so that you can add notes to it during class lectures, or later create a customized chapter outline to use while reviewing. Either way, the summary outline will help you understand the "big picture" and fill in the details as you study.

REVIEW QUESTIONS

1. What's the significance of *Dickerson v. U.S*?

2. Describe the popular picture of police officers and criminal suspects depicted on *NYPD Blue,* and then describe the complex reality behind the picture.

3. Identify three reasons Fred Inbau gave for the importance of confessions and police interrogation to get them.

4. List four findings of Richard Leo's research on police interrogation, and describe what his findings are based on.

5. What's the meaning and significance of the statement, "Pressure yes; coercion no"?

6. Identify the three provisions in the U.S. Constitution that govern police interrogation and confessions.

7. What's the basic idea behind the "due process approach" to confessions?

8. Describe and explain the significance of the U.S. Supreme Court case *Escobedo v. Illinois* to the right-to-counsel approach to confessions and police interrogation.

9. Define "witness against himself," and give examples of what's included and not included within the definition.

10. Identify three factors behind the decision in *Miranda v. Arizona.*

11. State and give the reason for the bright-line rule regarding warnings to suspects adopted in *Miranda v. Arizona.*

12. Identify two circumstances that have to be present before officers have to give the *Miranda* warnings.

13. List three types of questioning when officers *don't* have to give the *Miranda* warnings.

14. Identify nine circumstances that help determine whether suspects are "in custody."

15. Identify three detentions that don't qualify as "custodial."

16. State the facts and explain the significance of the U.S. Supreme Court case *New York v. Quarles.*

17. Summarize Justice O'Connor's dissent in the U.S. Supreme Court case *New York v. Quarles*.

18. Identify the two elements of a valid waiver of the rights to counsel and to remain silent.

19. Identify the two elements of involuntary confessions.

20. List the circumstances relevant to deciding whether confessions are voluntary.

KEY TERMS

accusatory stage p. 274
custodial interrogation p. 275
due process clause p. 277
right-to-counsel clause p. 277
self-incrimination clause p. 277
due process approach p. 277
reliability rationale p. 277
accusatory system rationale
    p. 277

fundamental fairness rationale
    p. 278
critical stage in criminal
    prosecution p. 279
testimony p. 280
voluntariness test of self-
    incrimination p. 282
bright-line rule (in *Miranda v. Arizona*) p. 289

custody p. 290
public safety exception (to
    Miranda v. Arizona) p. 293
expressed waiver p. 297
implied waiver p. 297

THE COMPANION WEB SITE
FOR *CRIMINAL PROCEDURE,* SIXTH EDITION

http://cj.wadsworth.com/samaha/crim_pro6e

Supplement your review of this chapter by going to the companion Web site to take one of the Tutorial Quizzes, use the flash cards to test yourself on the key terms from each chapter, and check out the many other study aids you'll find there. You'll find valuable data and resources at your fingertips to help you study for that big exam or write that important paper.

Identification Procedures

9

Chapter Main Points

- Proving a crime was committed is a lot easier than proving who committed it.
- Eyewitness identification of strangers is a very risky business; the risk of misidentification is high.
- Most mistaken identifications are due to the imperfections of human perception, memory, suggestion, and recall.
- Some risks of misidentification can be reduced by simple, inexpensive changes to procedures.
- The U.S. Constitution allows wide latitude in admitting eyewitness identification, leaving it to juries to sort out the reliability.
- Empirical evidence doesn't back up the assumptions the U.S. Supreme Court's test for the admissibility of eyewitness identification is based on.
- Lineups are least used and least unreliable; photo identifications are most unreliable and most widely used.
- Most courts admit DNA profile evidence, but they differ widely over the standards of admission.

Jimmy D. Glover was a trained African American undercover state police officer. Just after sunset, while there was still daylight, Glover and Henry Alton Brown, an informant, went to an apartment building at 201 Westland, in Hartford, to buy narcotics from "Dickie Boy" Cicero, a known narcotics dealer.

Glover knocked at the door of one of two apartments at the top of the stairs on the third floor. The door Glover knocked on might not have been to Cicero's apartment and the transaction that followed "was with some other person than" Cicero. Natural light from a window in the hallway illuminated the third floor hallway. Someone opened the door 12 to 18 inches in response to the knock. Glover observed a man standing at the door and, behind him, a woman. Glover asked for "two things" of narcotics. The man at the door held out his hand, and Glover gave him two $10 bills. The door closed. Soon the man returned and handed Glover two glassine bags.

Manson v. Brathwaite (1977), U.S. Supreme Court

IDENTIFYING STRANGERS

Proving a crime was committed is a lot easier than identifying who committed it. Of course, some suspects are caught red-handed; victims and witnesses personally know others; and some confess. Also, technological advances can identify some. Bite-mark evidence helped to convict the notorious serial rapist Ted Bundy, and fiber evidence led to the conviction of Wayne Williams for the murders of two young children in Atlanta. Many courts now admit DNA (deoxyribonucleic acid) evidence, touted as the "single greatest advance in the 'search for truth'... since... cross-examination," to prove the identity of the defendant as the perpetrator.

Despite technological advances, eyewitness identification remains the most widely used and sometimes the only way to identify and prove the guilt of **strangers** (perpetrators victims don't know). This chapter focuses on the three major procedures used to help victims identify strangers:

1. *Lineups.* Witnesses try to pick the suspect out of a group.

2. *Show-ups.* Witnesses try to match the suspect with one person.

3. *Photo identification.* Witnesses try to pick the suspect from one or many mug shots.

But, before we get into the procedures used for eyewitness identification of strangers, we'll look first at the reasons for mistaken identification and what the Constitution says about due process and identification procedures. Next, we'll examine the three major procedures used for the identification of strangers and how the court applies the due process test to assess their reliability. Last, we'll take at look at DNA, its reliability, and the standards for admitting it as evidence.

THE RISKS OF MISTAKEN EYEWITNESS IDENTIFICATION

Eyewitness identification of *strangers* is a very risky business in criminal cases. The risks of mistaken identification are high, even in ideal settings, and the most common identification procedures—lineups and photo ("mug shot") identifications—don't take place in ideal settings. According to one expert, mistaken identifications of strangers present the "greatest single threat to the achievement of our ideal that no innocent person shall be punished." Best guesses (there aren't any reliable exact figures) are that about half of all wrongful convictions were due to mistaken identifications by eyewitnesses. Take one famous example: Seven eyewitnesses swore that Bernard Pagano, a Roman Catholic priest, robbed them with a small, chrome-plated pistol. In a dramatic moment in the middle of Father Pagano's trial, Ronald Clouser confessed that he—not Father Pagano—committed the robberies (*National Law Journal* 1979, 1).

Mistakes in identifying criminals who are strangers to their victims are caused by four perfectly normal mental processes at three points in time:

1. *Perception.* Information the brain takes in at the time of the crime
2. *Memory.* Information the brain stores between the time of the crime and the lineup, show-up, or picture identification
3. *Suggestion.* The interpretation of events shaped by other people's suggestions
4. *Recall.* Information retrieved from memory at the time of the lineup, show-up, or picture identification

Perception

Let's start with perception. Contrary to common belief, the brain isn't a VCR that records what witnesses see. For well over a century, psychologists have proven repeatedly that the brain doesn't record exact images sent to it through our eyes. Why not? Because, unlike cameras, people have expectations, and our expectations and our highly developed thought processes heavily influence our perceptions. Like beauty, the physical characteristics of criminals are in the eye of the beholder.

Attention also shapes our observations. Observers—even trained ones—don't take in everything that happens during a crime. We all pay only selective attention to what's going on around us, and this selective attention leaves wide gaps in our memories. The degree of accuracy of witnesses' first perceptions of strangers during a crime depends on the interaction among five circumstances:

1. *Length of time* to observe the stranger
2. *Distractions* during the observation
3. *Focus* of the observation
4. *Stress* on the witness during the observation
5. *Race* of the witness and the stranger (Wells and Olson 2003, 279)

The longer the witness observes the stranger, the more reliable the perception. The problem is, most crimes are over in seconds. Even when they take longer, there are other obstacles to accurate observation. Descriptions of obvious (but crucial) details, like age, height, and weight, are highly inaccurate. Time estimates are also unreliable, particularly during stressful situations like getting robbed or raped. Witnesses also get distracted from physical description to other "details" like the gun a robber's waving or the knife of a rapist's in their victims' face. Understandable as this focus is, the weapon is obviously not as important as the description of the robber or rapist. Also, crimes aren't always committed under physical conditions ideal for accurately describing details; bad lighting is a good example. Equally important, stress distorts perceptions. It may sound convincing when a witness says, "I was so scared I could never forget that face," but, research convincingly demonstrates that accuracy goes way down during stressful events. According to C. Ronald Huff, an identification expert who conducted one study:

> Many of the cases we have identified involve errors by victims of robbery and rape, where the victim was close enough to the offender to get a look at him—but under conditions of extreme stress.... Such stress can significantly affect perception and memory and should give us cause to question the reliability of such eyewitness testimony.
>
> Yant 1991, 99

Discouraging as the natural limits of perception, distracted focus, poor lighting, and stress are to accurate identification, race complicates matters further. Researchers have demonstrated that identifying strangers of another race clearly raises the risk of mistaken identification. In one famous experiment, researchers showed observers a photo of a white man waving a razor blade in an altercation with a black man on a subway. When asked immediately afterward to describe what they saw, over half the subjects reported that the black man was carrying the weapon:

> Considerable evidence indicates that people are poorer at identifying members of another race than of their own. Some studies have found that, in the United States at least, whites have greater difficulty recognizing blacks than vice versa. Moreover, counterintuitively, the ability to perceive the physical characteristics of a person from another racial group apparently does not improve significantly upon increased contact with other members of that race. Because many crimes are cross-racial, these factors may play an important part in reducing the accuracy of eyewitness perception.
>
> Gross 1987, 398–399

Memory

Fading memory raises the already high risk of mistake caused by faulty perception. Memory fades most during the first few hours after an event (the very time when it's most important to keep it sharp); after that, it remains stable for several months. Curiously, at the same time witnesses' memory is fading, their confidence in their memory is rising. Unfortunately, courts and juries place enormous weight on witnesses' confidence, even in the face of clear proof that confidence is *not* related to accuracy.

Suggestion and Recall

As if faulty perception and fading memory aren't enough, suggestion is a powerful contributor to mistaken identification during the recall of information after crimes take place. According to the widely accepted findings of psychologists, most mistaken identifications happen because of a combination of the natural imperfections of perception and memory, and the normal susceptibility to innocent (and usually quite subtle) suggestion (Wells and Olson 2003, 277).

Suggestion is particularly powerful (and most threatening to accuracy) *after* a crime's committed. How does suggestion work? Witnesses store in one mental memory storage "bin" everything about the crime acquired by faulty perception at the time of the crime *and* what they learned later. According to psychologist and respected eyewitness expert Elizabeth Loftus, witnesses in her research add to their stories of crimes, and what they add depends on how *she* describes what happened. The power of Loftus's suggestions shapes what witnesses later take out of their memory "bin" and recall during the identification process. Steven Penrod, a psychologist at the University of Wisconsin, says witnesses (like all of us) embellish their stories: "A witness tells his story to the police, to the family, then to friends, then to the prosecutor." As the story gets retold, it becomes less reality and more legend. Witnesses "feel very confident about what they now think happened and that confidence is communicated to the jury" (Yant 1991, 100).

The very procedures used to identify strangers add to the problem created by the power of suggestion. Witnesses think of lineups and photo arrays as multiple-choice tests without a "none of the above" choice. And, they think of show-ups and single pictures as true/false tests. So, they feel like they have to choose the "best" likeness in the lineups and the right "true" or "false" likeness in the show-ups. They feel pressured by the possibility they might look foolish if they "don't know the answer." So, they're ripe for suggestion, particularly in uncomfortable or threatening situations. Suggestions (not *intended*, it should be stressed) by authority figures, like the police, aggravate these tendencies. For example, the very fact that police have arranged an identification procedure puts pressure on witnesses. They believe the police must have found the culprit or they wouldn't have gone to the trouble of arranging the identification event. So, they tell themselves, the culprit *has to be* in the lineup or the one person in the show-up or photo.

THE CONSTITUTION AND IDENTIFICATION PROCEDURES

Unreliable identification procedures can violate three constitutional rights—the Fifth and Fourteenth Amendment rights to due process and the Sixth Amendment right to counsel. The Court has decided defendants only have a right to have their lawyer present at lineups and show-ups *after* they're formally charged, and because almost all identification procedures take place *before* charges are filed, we won't discuss the Sixth Amendment right to counsel. The Court has relied almost exclusively on the Fifth and Fourteenth Amendment due process clauses to decide the constitutionality of eyewitness identification procedures. The due process clauses ban the federal and state governments from denying any person "life, liberty, or property without due process of law." The basic idea behind the application of the due process clause to identification procedures is that unreliable identification procedures can convict innocent people, and convicting innocent people deprives them of life (if they're executed), liberty (if they're imprisoned), and property (if they're fined) without due process of law.

The U.S. Supreme Court has rejected the claim that identification procedures "compel" defendants to be "witnesses against" themselves in violation of the Fifth Amendment due process clause [Chapter 8]. However, if suspects refuse to cooperate in identification procedures, they can face several consequences. Prosecutors can comment on such refusal at trial, urging jurors to read guilt into the refusal. Furthermore, courts sometimes put suspects who refuse to cooperate in contempt of court, a procedure that can result in both fines and incarceration. Finally, police may conduct the procedures over suspects' objections, as they did by subjecting the objecting defendant to a blood alcohol test in *Schmerber v. California* (Chapter 8). Officers can even use force, as long as they use only enough to conduct the identification procedure (LaFave and Israel 1984, 1:588–560).

Let's look at how the U.S. Supreme Court has applied the due process clauses to lineups, show-ups, and photographic identifications.

Lineups

The reliability of a lineup depends largely upon its makeup *and* the way the police conduct the identification process. We'll look at just how these factors can help reduce misidentifications. Then, we'll study how the courts apply due process to lineup reliability.

The Makeup of the Lineup

The lineup should comprise enough people and participants who resemble one another. The International Association of Chiefs of Police recommends the following characteristics:

1. Five to six participants

2. Same race, ethnicity, and skin color

3. Similar age, height, weight, hair color, and body build

4. Similar clothing

Unfortunately, real lineups often fall short of these recommendations. It's important for you to understand that this gap is hardly ever intentional; it's almost always because the only people available to put in lineups are police officers and jail inmates. But, no matter how wide the gap, most courts don't throw out lineup identifications. Why? Courts trust jurors' common sense and daily experience to detect wrong identifications.

Unfortunately, a significant, consistent, and convincing body of empirical research demonstrates that courts' trust in jurors' ability to discern lineup misidentifications is misplaced. Jennifer Davenport and Steven Penrod (1997) surveyed the state of our knowledge on the point and concluded:

> Jurors tend to rely on factors that are not diagnostic of eyewitness accuracy, such as an eyewitness's memory for peripheral details and eyewitness confidence, tend to overestimate eyewitness accuracy, and have difficulty applying their commonsense knowledge of lineup suggestiveness to their verdict decisions. (353)

And, according to one study in their survey, "[T]he numbers for inaccurate eyewitnesses are quite disturbing, because they suggest jurors may believe "three out of four mistaken identifications" (348).

Lineup Procedures and Reducing the Risk of Misidentification

The *way* police conduct lineups is also critical to reducing the risk of picking the wrong person. Most of the difficulties in administering the lineup come from the power of suggestion. Remember, most suggestion isn't intentional—it's not even conscious. Officers hardly ever conduct a lineup like the officer in charge of the notorious Lindburgh kidnapping murder case who told the witness, "We've got the right man. There isn't a man in this room who isn't convinced he's the man. Don't say anything until I ask you if he's the man" (Dressler 1997, 484). But, unconscious suggestion is no less powerful; maybe it's more powerful.

To weaken the power of suggestion, researchers recommend police departments follow these rules for conducting lineups (and for photo identifications—discussed later):

1. Tell the witness the offender may or may *not* be in the lineup.

2. Have someone who doesn't know who the suspect is conduct the lineup.

3. If a witness identifies the suspect, immediately ask the witness how sure she is of the identification *before* other information contaminates her decision. (Wells and Seelau 1995, 765)

Researchers have shown repeatedly that telling witnesses before they view lineups or mug shots that the "culprit might or might *not* be in the group" (the **might-or-might-not-be-present instruction**) improves the ratio of right-to-wrong identifications. Also, appointed **blind administrators**—administrators who don't know who the suspects are and therefore can't influence witnesses' identification by suggestion—should conduct lineups (Wells and Olson 2003, 286–287).

The need to reduce the risk of mistaken identification is crucial because once witnesses have positively identified a stranger, it's difficult to shake their conclusion— even if it's wrong. This fact is extremely important for at least three reasons. First, empirical research refutes the commonsense idea that confidence means accuracy. Second, courts rarely throw out eyewitness identifications, no matter how high the risk of misidentification is. Third, confident eyewitness testimony is particularly damning in front of juries. Jurors repeatedly dismiss even what should be convincing alibi evidence when they're faced with a confident eyewitness (*Stanford Law Review* 1977, 969). Jurors report over and over that they placed great confidence in witnesses who identified their victimizer. These in-court identifications are often given more weight by jurors than physical evidence—and more credibility than their reliability deserves.

 Go to Exercise 9-1 on the Criminal Procedure 6e CD to learn more about suggestions to law enforcement for improving the accuracy of stranger eyewitness identification.

The Due Process Test and Lineup Misidentification

Despite these research findings and recommendations (largely the work of psychologists), the U.S. Supreme Court has set a high standard for throwing out eyewitness identifications. To be thrown out, an identification has to deny a defendant "due process of law." The Court created a two-step test to implement the due process violation standard. The defendant has to prove by a **preponderance of the evidence** (more likely than not) that:

1. The lineup, show-up, or photographic array was unnecessarily and impermissibly suggestive (Twenty-Sixth Annual Review of Criminal Procedure 1997, 944–945)

2. The totality of circumstances proves the unnecessarily and impermissibly suggestive procedures created a very substantial likelihood of misidentification (Twenty-Sixth Annual Review of Criminal Procedure 1997, 944–945)

Five circumstances (factors) make up the "totality":

1. **Witnesses' opportunity to view** defendants at the time of the crime
2. **Witnesses' degree of attention** at the time of the crime
3. **Witnesses' accuracy of description** of defendants prior to the identification
4. **Witnesses' level of certainty** when identifying defendants at the time of the identification procedure
5. The **length of time between the crime and the identification** (Twenty-Sixth Annual Review of Criminal Procedure 1997, 945–946)

If the totality of circumstances shows the identification was reliable, it's admissible, even if it was unnecessarily or impermissibly suggestive (*Rodriguez v. Young* 1990). The U.S. Fifth Circuit Court of appeals applied the two-step, five-circumstances rule in *McFadden v. Cabana* (1988).

CASE | *Was the Lineup Identification Reliable?*

McFadden v. Cabana
851 F.2d 784 (Cal. Dist. 5, 1988)

Alan K. McFadden, a Mississippi state prisoner convicted of armed robbery and sentenced to life imprisonment, sought federal habeas corpus relief. The U.S. District Court for the Southern District of Mississippi denied the petition, and McFadden appealed. The Court of Appeals affirmed.

RUBIN, J.

FACTS

On September 11, 1980, Alan McFadden was in jail in Choctaw County, Mississippi, on charges unrelated to the conviction from which he now seeks relief. Officers from nearby Neshoba County came and took him to a police lineup. The lineup consisted of four men including McFadden, all of them black. McFadden claims, and the State does not dispute, that while he is only 5'6" and weighs 130 pounds, two of the other men in the lineup were 6'6" and 6'5" and weighed almost 200 pounds each; the fourth, McFadden's accomplice, was 5'10."

On September 16, McFadden and three other persons were indicted for the July 8 armed robbery of a jewelry store in Philadelphia, Mississippi, in Neshoba County. The

public denied a motion to suppress the identifications based on the lineup... The court denied the motion.

...At the one-day trial, four eyewitnesses to the robbery, including two store employees and two customers, 'positively and unequivocally' identified McFadden as one of the robbers. The robbery had taken place at about noon, the store had been well-lit, and the robbers had been in the store for about 15 minutes. McFadden's attorney cross-examined each eyewitness concerning her view of the robbers and her identification of them at the lineup. The attorney, however, called only three witnesses briefly to establish the disparity in the heights and weights of the lineup participants....

At the end of the day, the jury convicted McFadden and the other defendants of armed robbery and sentenced each to life imprisonment. The Mississippi Supreme Court affirmed McFadden's conviction and sentence by a 6–2 vote, and McFadden was later denied state habeas relief. In 1985, he filed a federal habeas petition. The district court referred the petition to a magistrate, who appointed counsel for McFadden in September 1986 and set an evidentiary hearing for February 1987....The magistrate recommended denying relief, finding...the lineup, while 'subject to criticism,' was permissible because the height and weight disparities did not undermine the reliability of the identifications.

After reviewing the record, the district court adopted the magistrate's report and denied the petition.

OPINION

McFadden claims he 'was denied due process of law by [among other things] being...placed in a lineup....

McFadden argues that the lineup at which the witnesses identified him, and which led to in-court identifications, was impermissibly suggestive and unreliable because he was so much smaller than all the others in the lineup. 'The identification of a defendant in a manner that suggests whom the witness should identify is a denial of the defendant's right to due process of law. Unnecessarily suggestive out-of-court identifications are not *per se* subject to exclusion, however; they are admissible if, under the totality of the circumstances, they are sufficiently reliable.' To evaluate reliability, the court should consider

(1) the opportunity of the witnesses to view the criminal at the crime;

(2) their degree of attention;

(3) the accuracy of their prior descriptions of the criminal;

(4) the level of certainty they demonstrated when confronted with the accused; and

(5) the length of time between crime and confrontation.

The State makes no claim that the disparities in height and weight would not have been suggestive to the identifying witnesses. It argues, instead...the identifications were sufficiently reliable to satisfy due process, as the magistrate found....McFadden does not question the historical facts found by the magistrate and by the Mississippi Supreme Court: that the witnesses were positive and emphatic, the store was well-lit, and the robbers were there for some time. Rather, he challenges the ultimate determination, based on these facts, that the identifications were sufficiently reliable to satisfy due process. Whatever standard of review the court should apply to the underlying facts concerning reliability—"clearly erroneous,"* "plain error"** or "not fairly supported by the record"†—the fact-findings of the state courts and the federal magistrate are amply supported by the record. The facts as found point strongly toward a determination of reliability: the witnesses had ample opportunity to view the criminals; the identifications were positive and emphatic; and the lineup occurred only a few weeks after the robbery. While the height and weight disparities were serious and unnecessary, they are the only tainted aspects of the lineup to which McFadden refers, and alone they are insufficient to overcome the indicia of reliability.

For these reasons, we AFFIRM the judgment of the district court.

Questions

1. List the characteristics of the members of the lineup.

2. Summarize the evidence of identification brought out during the trial.

3. Summarize the court's reasons for concluding the lineup didn't deny McFadden due process of law.

4. Assume you're the lawyer for the defense, and argue that the evidence supports the two-step test that the lineup denied McFadden due process of law.

---

*Reversible if the court "is left with the clear impression that an error has been committed."

**"So obvious and prejudicial the court should address it despite the party's failure to raise an objection to it."

†The facts don't point to substantial likelihood of misidentification.

EXPLORING LINEUP CHARACTERISTICS FURTHER

Go to the Criminal Procedure 6e CD to read the full text version of the case featured here.

Was the Makeup of the Lineup Fair?

FACTS

Hugh Houston and Patricia Roseboro were working at a grocery store when two men came in with dark scarves covering their faces from just under the eyes to below the mouth. One of the men also wore a toboggan that covered the top of his head and forehead to about an inch above the eyebrows, and he had a sawed-off shotgun. Though Houston did not know this defendant, he had seen him several times before either in the neighborhood or in the store, and he recognized the toboggan wearer as being the defendant. Houston was so sure he recognized the defendant that when told that it was a holdup he thought it was a joke, but he changed his mind when the robber knocked him down with the sawed-off shotgun. Houston then gave the robbers the money in the cash register, and they left.

Houston first described his assailant to the police as being 20 to 25 years old and 5'11", but his testimony at trial was that the defendant was only 5'4"; however, Houston readily chose the defendant's photograph from an array of six pictures shown to him by the police, and he picked the defendant out of a lineup as well. But Mrs. Roseboro, who told the officers shortly after the holdup that she would be able to identify the robbers if she saw them again, could not identify the defendant from either the photographs or the lineup, and though present during the trial she did not testify.

In this case the identification issue was not just a substantial feature of the state's case; it was the entire case. The only evidence linking the defendant to the crime was the testimony of one witness, Houston, who first described the culprit as being 7 inches taller than the defendant, even though he claimed to have seen the defendant on previous occasions. The only other person present when the crime was committed had as good an opportunity to observe the criminals, but she could not identify the defendant as being one of them. And, of course, the identification problem, never entirely free of difficulty, even when the subject's face is clearly visible, was greatly compounded here, since most of the criminal's head and face was covered.

As many judges and psychologists have noted, "convictions based solely on 'one eyewitness' identifications represent 'conceivably the greatest single threat to the achievement of our ideal that no innocent man shall be punished.'" This, of course, is because the human mind often plays tricks on us. One of the tricks that it sometimes plays is that a person seen briefly before in one place and situation is thought, even by the keenest of us, to be another person, seen in a different context altogether. This common experience of mankind, known to social scientists as "unconscious transference," has been much discussed in their literature, and the likelihood of the experience being repeated under various circumstances has been confirmed by experiments of different kinds.

That in this case Houston, in good conscience, could have picked the defendant out of the lineup not because he recognized him from the robbery but because he looked familiar from being in the area earlier is certainly quite possible. In an effort to guard against the baleful effects of this possibility, the defendant submitted a requested jury instruction, which included the following:

> I instruct you that the State has the burden of proving the identity of the defendant as the perpetrator of the crime charged beyond a reasonable doubt. This means that you, the jury, must be satisfied beyond a reasonable doubt that the defendant was the perpetrator of the crime charged before you may return a verdict of guilty.

> The main aspect of identification is the observation of the defendant by the witness at the time of the events.

> Examining the testimony of the witness, Hugh Houston, as to his observation of the perpetrator at the time of the crime, you should consider that the perpetrator was wearing a mask. However, your consideration must go further. The identification of the defendant by the witness, Hugh Houston, as the perpetrator of the offense must be purely the product of his recollection of the offender and derived only from the observation

made at the time of the offense. In making this determination, you should consider the manner in which the witness was confronted with the defendant after the offense, the conduct and comments of the persons in charge of the investigation and any circumstances or pressures which may have influenced the witness in making an identification, and which would cast out upon or reinforce the accuracy of the witness's identification of the defendant.

Should the trial judge have given this instruction?

DECISION AND REASONS

Yes, according to the North Carolina Court of Appeal:

Under the peculiar circumstances of the case, this was a proper instruction, and from defendant's viewpoint, a necessary one. It would have directed the jury's attention to the possibility that defendant had been identified because he looked familiar to the witness from being seen earlier in the area, rather than because the witness remembered him from the crime. Since this instruction was crucial to defendant's case, the circumstances supported it, and it had been timely and properly requested, defendant was entitled to have the substance of it presented to the jury....Thus, a new trial is required.

State v. Smith, 309 S.E.2d 695 (N.C.App. 1983)

A questionable assumption lies behind each of the five factors that make up the totality of circumstances that the U.S. Supreme Court established and the U.S. Fifth Circuit Court of Appeals applied in *McFadden v. Cabana*. When psychologist Gerald F. Uelman (1980) tested these assumptions in an experiment, he found some validity to the first assumption. Overall, however, none of the circumstances did much to improve the accuracy of identification. Between one-half and more than three-fourths of the identifications were wrong when witnesses had a good opportunity to observe, paid careful attention, gave an accurate description, had a high level of certainty, and were allowed a short interval between observation and identification (Table 9.1).

Show-Ups

Show-ups—identifications of a single person—are substantially less reliable than lineups because presenting only one person to identify is more suggestive than providing a group of people to choose from. Nevertheless, courts usually admit show-up identification evidence. Here are three common situations where courts are most likely to admit show-up identifications:

1. Witnesses accidentally run into suspects, such as in courthouse corridors

2. Emergencies, like when witnesses are hospitalized (see the Exploring Further case)

3. Suspects are loose, such as when police cruise crime scenes with witnesses (*McFadden v. Cabana* 1988)

The U.S. Supreme Court hasn't hesitated to affirm the use of show-up identifications, despite the strong empirical evidence of their unreliability. The Court applies the same totality-of-circumstances test to show-ups that it applies to lineups. The leading Supreme Court case on the point is *Neil v. Biggers* (1972), a rape case where the conviction depended heavily on a show-up to identify the defendant.

TABLE 9.1

Circumstances, Assumptions, and Validity of Five Factors

Factor	Assumption	Validity
1. The opportunity of the witnesses to view the criminal at the crime	The better the opportunity to view a person, the more accurate a later identification	Some validity
2. The witnesses' degree of attention	The greater the attention paid to a person, the more accurate a later identification	Between ½ and more than ¾ of the identifications were wrong
3. The accuracy of their prior descriptions of the criminal	The more accurate their description of a person, the more accurate a later identification	Between ½ and more than ¾ of the identifications were wrong
4. The level of certainty they demonstrated when confronted with the accused	The greater the level of certainty of identification, the more accurate the description	Between ½ and more than ¾ of the identifications were wrong
5. The length of time between the crime and the identification	The shorter the interval between an observation and a later identification, the more accurate the identification	Between ½ and more than ¾ of the identifications were wrong

Gerald F. Uelman. 1980. Testing the Assumptions of *Neil v. Biggers:* An Experiment in Eyewitness Identification. *Criminal Law Bulletin* 16:359–368.

CASE | *Was the Show-Up Reliable?*

Neil v. Biggers
409 U.S. 188 (1972)

Archie Biggers was convicted of rape and sentenced to twenty years in prison. The state's evidence consisted in part of testimony regarding the victim's identification of Biggers in the police station. The Tennessee Supreme Court affirmed. Biggers brought a federal habeas corpus action. The District Court issued the writ. The U.S. Court of Appeals affirmed. The U.S. Supreme Court reversed and remanded.

POWELL, J.

FACTS

The victim testified at trial that on the evening of January 22, 1965, a youth with a butcher knife grabbed her in the doorway to her kitchen:

A: He grabbed me from behind, and grappled—twisted me on the floor. Threw me down on the floor.

Q: And there was no light in the kitchen?

A: Not in the kitchen.

Q: So you couldn't have seen him then?

A: Yes, I could see him, when I looked up in his face.

Q: In the dark?

A: He was right in the doorway—it was enough light from the bedroom shining through. Yes, I could see who he was.

Q: You could see? No light? And you could see him and know him then?

A: Yes.

When the victim screamed, her 12-year-old daughter came out of her bedroom and also began to scream. The assailant directed the victim to "tell her (the daughter) to shut up, or I'll kill you both." She did so, and was then walked at knife point about two blocks along a railroad track, taken into a woods, and raped there. She testified that "the moon was shining brightly, full moon." After the rape, the assailant ran off, and she returned home, the whole incident having taken between 15 minutes and half an hour.

She then gave the police what the Federal District Court characterized as "only a very general description," describing him as "being fat and flabby with smooth skin, bushy hair and a youthful voice." Additionally, though not mentioned by the District Court, she testified at the habeas corpus hearing that she had described her assailant as being between 16 and 18 years old and between five feet ten inches and six feet tall, as weighing between 180 and 200 pounds, and as having a dark brown complexion. This testimony was substantially corroborated by that of a police officer who was testifying from his notes.

On several occasions over the course of the next seven months, she viewed suspects in her home or at the police station, some in lineups and others in showups, and was shown between 30 and 40 photographs. She told the police that a man pictured in one of the photographs had features similar to those of her assailant, but identified none of the suspects. On August 17, the police called her to the station to view respondent, who was being detained on another charge. In an effort to construct a suitable lineup, the police checked the city jail and the city juvenile home. Finding no one at either place fitting respondent's unusual physical description, they conducted a show up instead.

The showup itself consisted of two detectives walking respondent past the victim. At the victim's request, the police directed respondent to say "shut up or I'll kill you." The testimony at trial was not altogether clear as to whether the victim first identified him and then asked that he repeat the words or made her identification after he had spoken. In any event, the victim testified that she had "no doubt" about her identification. At the habeas corpus hearing, she elaborated in response to questioning.

The victim testified:

Q: What physical characteristics, if any, caused you to be able to identify him?

A: First of all,—uh—his size,—next I could remember his voice.

Q: What about his voice? Describe his voice to the Jury.

A: Well, he has the voice of an immature youth—I call it an immature youth. I have teen-age boys. And that was the first thing that made me think it was the boy.

The colloquy continued, with the victim describing the voice and other physical characteristics. At the habeas corpus hearing, the victim and all of the police witnesses testified that a visual identification preceded the voice identification.

A: That I have no doubt, I mean that I am sure that when I—see, when I first laid eyes on him, I knew it was the individual, because his face—well, there was just something that I don't think I could ever forget. I believe—

Q: You say when you first laid eyes on him, which time are you referring to?

A: When I identified him—when I seen him in the courthouse when I was took up to view the suspect.

OPINION

We must decide whether, as the courts below held, this identification and the circumstances surrounding it failed to comport with due process requirements. We have considered on four occasions the scope of due process protection against the admission of evidence deriving from suggestive identification procedures. In *Stovall v. Denno* (1967), the Court held that the defendant could claim that "the confrontation conducted . . . was so unnecessarily suggestive and conducive to irreparable mistaken identification that he was denied due process of law." This, we held, must be determined "on the totality of the circumstances." We went on to find that on the facts of the case then before us, due process was not violated, emphasizing that the critical condition of the injured witness justified a showup in her hospital room. At trial, the witness, whose view of the suspect at the time of the crime was brief, testified to the out-of-court identification, as did several police officers present in her hospital room, and also made an in-court identification. . . . *

The only case to date in which this Court has found identification procedures to be violative of due process is *Foster v. California* (1969). There, the witness failed to identify Foster the first time he confronted him, despite a suggestive lineup. The police then arranged a showup, at which the witness could make only a tentative identification. Ultimately, at yet another confrontation, this time a lineup, the witness was able to muster a definite identification. We held all of the identifications inadmissible, observing that the identifications were "all but inevitable" under the circumstances. . . .

Some general guidelines emerge from these cases as to the relationship between suggestiveness and misidentification. It is, first of all, apparent that the primary evil to be avoided is "a very substantial likelihood of irreparable misidentification.". . . It is the likelihood of misidentification which violates a defendant's right to due process. . . . Suggestive confrontations are disapproved because they increase the likelihood of misidentification, and unnecessarily suggestive ones are condemned for the further reason that the increased chance of misidentification is gratuitous. But . . . the admission of evidence of a showup without more does not violate due process. . . . [The Court then turned to whether] unnecessary suggestiveness alone requires the exclusion of evidence. ** . . .

While we are inclined to agree with the courts below that the police did not exhaust all possibilities in seeking

---

*The Court discussed other cases that upheld identification procedures under the totality-of-circumstances test.

**The District Court stated: "In this case it appears to the Court that a line-up, which both sides admit is generally more reliable than a show-up, could have been arranged. The fact that this was not done tended needlessly to decrease the fairness of the identification process to which petitioner was subjected."

persons physically comparable to respondent, we do not think that the evidence must therefore be excluded. The purpose of a strict rule barring evidence of unnecessarily suggestive confrontations would be to deter the police from using a less reliable procedure when a more reliable one may be available, and would not be based on the assumption that in every instance the admission of evidence of such a confrontation offends due process....

We turn, then, to the central question, whether under the "totality of the circumstances" the identification was reliable even though the confrontation procedure was suggestive. As indicated by our cases, the factors to be considered in evaluating the likelihood of misidentification include

1. the opportunity of the witness to view the criminal at the time of the crime,

2. the witness's degree of attention,

3. the accuracy of the witness's prior description of the criminal,

4. the level of certainty demonstrated by the witness at the confrontation, and

5. the length of time between the crime and the confrontation.

Applying these factors, we disagree with the District Court's conclusion. In part, as discussed above, we think the District Court focused unduly on the relative reliability of a lineup as opposed to a showup, the issue on which expert testimony was taken at the evidentiary hearing....

We find that the District Court's conclusions on the critical facts are unsupported by the record and clearly erroneous. The victim spent a considerable period of time with her assailant, up to half an hour. She was with him under adequate artificial light in her house and under a full moon outdoors, and at least twice, once in the house and later in the woods, faced him directly and intimately. She was no casual observer, but rather the victim of one of the most personally humiliating of all crimes. Her description to the police, which included the assailant's approximate age, height, weight, complexion, skin texture, build, and voice, might not have satisfied Proust* but was more than ordinarily thorough. She had "no doubt" that respondent was the person who raped her. In the nature of the crime, there are rarely witnesses to a rape other than the victim, who often has a limited opportunity for observation. The victim here, a practical nurse by profession, had an unusual opportunity to observe and identify her assailant. She testified at the habeas corpus hearing that there was something about his face "I don't think I could ever forget."

_____
*A novelist known for his highly detailed descriptions.

There was, to be sure, a lapse of seven months between the rape and the confrontation. This would be a seriously negative factor in most cases. Here, however, the testimony is undisputed that the victim made no previous identification at any of the showups, lineups, or photographic showings. Her record for reliability was thus a good one, as she had previously resisted whatever suggestiveness inheres in a showup. Weighing all the factors, we find no substantial likelihood of misidentification. The evidence was properly allowed to go to the jury.

REVERSED and REMANDED.

DISSENT

BRENNAN, J., joined by DOUGLAS and STEWART, JJ.
...As the Court recognizes..., an identification obtained as a result of an unnecessarily suggestive showup may still be introduced in evidence if, under the "totality of the circumstances," the identification retains strong indicia of reliability. After an extensive hearing and careful review of the state court record, however, the District Court found that, under the circumstances of this case, there existed an intolerable risk of misidentification. Moreover, in making this determination, the court specifically found that "the complaining witness did not get an opportunity to obtain a good view of the suspect during the commission of the crime," "the showup confrontation was not conducted near the time of the alleged crime, but rather, some seven months after its commission," and the complaining witness was unable to give "a good physical description of her assailant" to the police....

Questions

1. Summarize the details relevant to each of the five factors in deciding whether the identification satisfied the two prongs of the due process test regarding eyewitness identification.

2. Summarize the show-up of Biggers.

3. How could the police have improved this identification procedure?

4. What specific circumstances did the Court consider in determining the reliability of the show-up?

5. Why did the Court decide that the identification was reliable, despite its suggestiveness?

6. Do you agree? Explain.

7. Is the Court promoting the interest in correct result or perhaps satisfying the demand for crime control, particularly in a terrible crime like rape? If the latter, is this a proper interest for the Supreme Court to promote? Defend your answer.

8. Does the dissent have a point in arguing that the Supreme Court should not interfere with the findings of the courts closest to the proceedings? Also, do the lower court findings regarding the likelihood of misidentification make sense? Explain your answer.

EXPLORING SHOW-UPS FURTHER

 Go to the Criminal Procedure 6e CD to read the full text versions of the cases featured here.

1. *Was the Show-Up Fair?*

FACTS

Dr. Paul Behrendt was stabbed to death in the kitchen of his home in Garden City, Long Island, at about midnight, August 23. Mrs. Behrendt, his wife, followed her husband to the kitchen and jumped the assailant. The assailant knocked her to the floor and stabbed her eleven times. The police found a shirt on the kitchen floor with keys in the pocket, which they traced to Theodore Stovall. The police arrested Stovall on the afternoon of August 24. Mrs. Behrendt was hospitalized to save her life. The police arranged with Mrs. Behrendt's surgeon to allow them to bring Stovall to the hospital at noon on August 25. The police handcuffed Stovall to one of five officers who, with two members of the staff of the district attorney, brought him to the hospital room. Stovall was the only black person in the room. Mrs. Behrendt identified Stovall as her attacker after one of the officers asked her if Stovall "was the man" and after Stovall spoke a "few words for voice identification."

At Stovall's trial, Mrs. Behrendt testified about her hospital room identification, and she also identified him in court. He was convicted and sentenced to death. After several appeals upholding his conviction, Stovall eventually arrived in the U.S. Supreme Court in a habeas corpus proceeding. Did the way the show-up was done deny him due process?

DECISION AND REASONS

The Supreme Court held that the identification procedure did not deny Stovall due process. The Court conceded that show-ups—that is, procedures showing suspects singly to witnesses—are highly suggestive and widely condemned:

> We turn...to the question of whether petitioner...is entitled to relief on his claim that...the confrontation conducted in this case was so unnecessarily suggestive and conducive to irreparable mistaken identification that he was denied due process of law. This is a recognized ground of attack upon a conviction independent of any right to counsel claim. The practice of showing suspects singly to persons for the purpose of identification, and not as part of a lineup, has been widely condemned.

But, unreliable procedures alone don't deny due process. Even if the show-up was unreliable, it was not unnecessarily so. According to the Court:

> [A] claimed violation of due process of law in the conduct of a confrontation depends on the totality of the circumstances surrounding it, and the record in the present case reveals that the showing of Stovall to Mrs. Behrendt in an immediate hospital confrontation was imperative.

Here was the only person in the world who could possibly exonerate Stovall. Her words, and only her words, "He is not the man" could have resulted in freedom for Stovall. The hospital was not far distant from the courthouse and jail. No one knew how long Mrs. Behrendt might live. Faced with the responsibility of identifying her attacker, with the need for immediate action and with the knowledge that Mrs. Behrendt could not visit the jail, the police followed the only feasible procedure and took Stovall to the hospital room. Under these circumstances, the usual police station line-up, which Stovall now argues he should have had, was out of the question.

Stovall v. Denno, 388 U.S. 293 (1967)

2. Did the Show-Up Identification Deny Him Due Process of Law?

FACTS

Foster was convicted of robbing a Western Union office. The police put Foster, the only one wearing a leather jacket similar to the robber's, in a lineup with two other men who were considerably shorter than he. When the manager couldn't identify the robber, the police permitted a show-up. The witness–manager still made only a tentative identification. Ten days later, in a second lineup, the manager identified Foster, who was the only person from the first lineup to appear in the second. Did the identification procedure deny Foster due process?

DECISION AND REASONS

Yes, according to a majority (5–4) of the U.S. Supreme Court, in the only case where the Court has ever held that an identification procedure violated due process (and of course, four of the nine justices dissented). The Court decided that "the suggestive elements in this identification procedure made it all but inevitable" that the manager would identify Foster, "whether or not he was in fact the man. In effect, the police repeatedly said to the witness, 'This is the man.'" *Foster* is one of a very few cases in which any court, federal or state, has found that an identification procedure denied a defendant due process.

Foster v. California, 394 U.S. 440 (1969)

3. Was Being Handcuffed in the Show-Up a Denial of Due Process?

FACTS

The victims in this case had arranged to purchase marijuana from Ford's brother. Upon arriving at the apartment building where the transaction was to take place, Ford, his brother, and another man led the victims to a well-lighted basement storage room. There, the three men robbed the victims at gunpoint. The robbery took about four minutes. The victims identified Ford in a show-up conducted less than one-and-one-half hours after the crime. During the show-up, the appellant was wearing handcuffs, but the handcuffs were not visible to the victims. Ford's motion to suppress the identification evidence was denied, and he was convicted of aiding and abetting aggravated robbery in the first degree. Was he denied due process because he was handcuffed during the show-up?

DECISION AND REASONS

No, said the Minnesota Court of Appeals. Applying the five factors discussed in *Neil v. Biggers* [excerpted earlier], the court held:

> Application of the five factors in this case satisfies us that there was no substantial likelihood of misidentification. Both victims had several minutes to view the robbers in good lighting, both before and during the robbery. One victim testified that he saw appellant's face several times and made a special effort to remember it. Appellant matched the general description both victims had initially given to police. Both victims were certain of their identifications; indeed, one victim clearly distinguished between the robbers, expressing more certainty about the identification of appellant than of another individual who was displayed to the victims, but then not charged. Finally, the show-up was conducted less than one and one-half hours after the crime, leaving little opportunity for the victims to have forgotten their assailants.
>
> Appellant argues that the fact he was handcuffed during the identification procedure makes it impermissibly suggestive. We disagree. The handcuffs were not visible to the victims during the identification and no other circumstances suggest that the identification was tainted by use of the handcuffs.
>
> Appellant implies that the victims' identifications were not accurate because, although they both identified a third individual as a perpetrator, police concluded that there was not enough evidence to refer that individual for prosecution. The failure to prosecute, though, does not mean that the victims were wrong in their identification of that person.
>
> Finally, appellant cites social science authority for the proposition that the stress of being robbed makes it difficult to retain an accurate identification memory. We believe that, despite this assertion and whatever the merit that authority might have as applied in another circumstance, analysis of the *Biggers* factors indicates the identification procedure in this case did not create a substantial likelihood of irreparable misidentification. AFFIRMED.

State v. Ford, WL 278227 (Minn.App. 1996)

Photo Identification

The least reliable form of eyewitness identification is a picture display (sometimes called a **photo lineup** if there's more than one picture or a **photo show-up** if there's only one). The two-dimensional nature of photos distorts their accuracy, so they're naturally unreliable. Also, the fewer the photos, the less reliable the identifications because their suggestiveness grows as their numbers shrink. If the suspect stands out because of unique features, photos are even more suggestive and less reliable. Despite their widely recognized unreliability—and despite the urging of commentators that courts exclude them if lineups and show-ups can be substituted—photographs are the most widely used means of identification. The U.S. Supreme Court has given photo arrays a clear stamp of approval, because "this procedure has been used widely and effectively in criminal law enforcement" (LaFave and Israel 1984, 1:588–560).

The Court applies the same totality-of-circumstances test to photographic identification that it applies to lineups and show-ups. Not surprisingly, most photo identifications pass the test. The leading Supreme Court case on a single photo identification is *Manson v. Brathwaite* (1977).

Manson v. Brathwaite
432 U.S. 98 (1977)

Nowell Brathwaite was charged with possession and sale of heroin. The jury found him guilty, and the judge sentenced him to not less than six nor more than nine years. The Supreme Court of Connecticut affirmed. Fourteen months later, Brathwaite filed a petition for habeas corpus in the U.S. District Court for the District of Connecticut. The District Court dismissed his petition. On appeal, the U.S. Court of Appeals for the Second Circuit reversed. The U.S. District Court for the District of Connecticut denied relief, and Brathwaite appealed. The Court of Appeals, Second Circuit, reversed. The U.S. Supreme Court granted certiorari and reversed.

BLACKMUN, J.

FACTS

Jimmy D. Glover, a trained Negro undercover state police officer was assigned to the Narcotics Division in 1970. On May 5 of that year, at about 7:45 PM, EDT, and while there was still daylight, Glover and Henry Alton Brown, an informant, went to an apartment building at 201 Westland, in Hartford, to buy narcotics from "Dickie Boy" Cicero, a known narcotics dealer.

Cicero, it was thought, lived on the third floor of that apartment building. Glover and Brown entered the building, observed by back-up Officers D'Onofrio and Gaffey, and proceeded by stairs to the third floor. Glover knocked at the door of one of the two apartments served by the stairway. It appears that the door on which Glover knocked may not have been that of the Cicero apartment. Petitioner [John Manson, Commissioner of Corrections] concedes that the transaction "was with some other person than had been intended." The area was illuminated by natural light from a window in the third floor hallway.

The door opened 12 to 18 inches. Glover observed a man standing at the door and, behind him, a woman. Brown identified himself. Glover then asked for "two things" of narcotics. The man at the door held out his hand, and Glover gave him two $10 bills. The door closed. Soon the man returned and handed Glover two glassine bags.*...

---

*This was Glover's testimony. Brown later was called as a witness for the prosecution. He testified on direct examination that, due to his then use of heroin, he had no clear recollection of the details of the incident. On cross-examination, as in an interview

While the door was open, Glover stood within two feet of the person from whom he made the purchase and observed his face. Five to seven minutes elapsed from the time the door first opened until it closed the second time.

Glover and Brown then left the building. This was about eight minutes after their arrival. Glover drove to headquarters where he described the seller to D'Onofrio and Gaffey. Glover at that time did not know the identity of the seller. He described him as being "a colored man, approximately five feet eleven inches tall, dark complexion, black hair, short Afro style, and having high cheekbones, and of heavy build. He was wearing at the time blue pants and a plaid shirt."

D'Onofrio, suspecting from this description that respondent might be the seller, obtained a photograph of Brathwaite from the Records Division of the Hartford Police Department. He left it at Glover's office. D'Onofrio was not acquainted with Brathwaite personally but did know him by sight and had seen him "several times" prior to May 5. Glover, when alone, viewed the photograph for the first time upon his return to headquarters on May 7; he identified the person shown as the one from whom he had purchased the narcotics.

Brathwaite was arrested on July 27 while visiting at the apartment of a Mrs. Ramsey on the third floor of 201 Westland. This was the apartment where the narcotics sale took place on May 5. Brathwaite testified: "Lots of times I have been there before in that building." He also testified that Mrs. Ramsey was a friend of his wife, that her apartment was the only one in the building he ever visited, and that he and his family, consisting of his wife and five children, did not live there but at 453 Albany Avenue, Hartford.

Brathwaite was charged, in a two-count information, with possession and sale of heroin. At his trial in January 1971, the photograph from which Glover had identified Brathwaite was received in evidence without objection on the part of the defense. Glover also testified that, although he had not seen Brathwaite in the eight months that had elapsed since the sale, "there was no doubt whatsoever" in his mind that the person shown on the photograph was respondent. Glover also made a positive in-court identification without objection. No explanation was offered by the

---

with defense counsel the preceding day, he said that it was a woman who opened the door, received the money, and thereafter produced the narcotics. On redirect, he acknowledged that he was using heroin daily at the time, that he had had some that day, and that there was "an inability to recall and remember events."

prosecution for the failure to utilize a photographic array or to conduct a lineup.

Brathwaite, who took the stand in his own defense, testified that on May 5, the day in question, he had been ill at his Albany Avenue apartment ("a lot of back pains, muscle spasms . . . a bad heart . . . high blood pressure . . . neuralgia in my face, and sinus") and that at no time on that particular day had he been at 201 Westland.

His wife testified that she recalled, after her husband had refreshed her memory, that he was home all day on May 5.

Doctor Wesley M. Vietzke, an internist and assistant professor of medicine at the University of Connecticut, testified that Brathwaite had consulted him on April 15, 1970, and that he took a medical history from him, heard his complaints about his back and facial pain, and discovered that he had high blood pressure. The physician found Brathwaite, subjectively, "in great discomfort." Respondent in fact underwent surgery for a herniated disc at L5 and S1 on August 17.

The jury found Brathwaite guilty on both counts of the information. He received a sentence of not less than six nor more than nine years. His conviction was affirmed per curiam* by the Supreme Court of Connecticut. That court noted the absence of an objection to Glover's in-court identification and concluded that Brathwaite "has not shown that substantial injustice resulted from the admission of this evidence." Under Connecticut law, substantial injustice must be shown before a claim of error not made or passed on by the trial court will be considered on appeal.

Fourteen months later, Brathwaite filed a petition for habeas corpus in the U. S. District Court for the District of Connecticut. He alleged that the admission of the identification testimony at his state trial deprived him of due process of law to which he was entitled under the Fourteenth Amendment. The District Court dismissed Brathwaite's petition. On appeal, the United States Court of Appeals for the Second Circuit reversed. In brief summary, the court felt that evidence as to the photograph should have been excluded, regardless of reliability, because the examination of the single photograph was unnecessary and suggestive. And, in the court's view, the evidence was unreliable in any event. We granted certiorari.

OPINION

. . . The petitioner, Connecticut Commissioner of Corrections, acknowledges that "the procedure in the instant case was suggestive (because only one photograph was used) and unnecessary" (because there was no emergency or exigent circumstance). Brathwaite, in agreement with the Court of Appeals, proposes a per se rule of exclusion that he claims is dictated by the demands of the Fourteenth Amendment's guarantee of due process. He rightly observes this is the first case in which this Court has had occasion to rule upon . . . out-of-court identification evidence of the challenged kind.

Since the decision in *Biggers*,** the Courts of Appeals appear to have developed at least two approaches to such evidence. The first, or per se approach, employed by the Second Circuit in the present case, focuses on the procedures employed and requires exclusion of the out-of-court identification evidence, without regard to reliability, whenever it has been obtained through unnecessarily suggestive confrontation procedures. The justifications advanced are the elimination of evidence of uncertain reliability, deterrence of the police and prosecutors, and the stated "fair assurance against the awful risks of misidentification."

The second, or more lenient, approach is one that continues to rely on the totality of the circumstances. It permits the admission of the confrontation evidence if, despite the suggestive aspect, the out-of-court identification possesses certain features of reliability. Its adherents feel that the per se approach is not mandated by the Due Process Clause of the Fourteenth Amendment. This second approach, in contrast to the other, is ad hoc and serves to limit the societal costs imposed by a sanction that excludes relevant evidence from consideration and evaluation by the trier of fact.

Mr. Justice STEVENS, in writing for the Seventh Circuit in *Kirby v. Illinois*, observed: "There is surprising unanimity among scholars in regarding such a rule (the per se approach) as essential to avoid serious risk of miscarriage of justice." He pointed out that well-known federal judges have taken the position that "evidence of, or derived from, a showup identification should be inadmissible unless the prosecutor can justify his failure to use a more reliable identification procedure." Indeed, the ALI *Model Code of Pre-Arraignment Procedure* §§ 160.1 and 160.2 (1975) (hereafter *Model Code*), frowns upon the use of a showup or the display of only a single photograph."

The respondent here stresses the same theme and the need for deterrence of improper identification practice, a factor he regards as pre-eminent. Photographic identification, it is said, continues to be needlessly employed. He notes that the legislative regulation "the Court had hoped would engender," has not been forthcoming. He argues that a totality rule cannot be expected to have a significant deterrent impact; only a strict rule of exclusion will have direct and immediate impact on law enforcement agents. Identification evidence is so convincing to the jury that sweeping exclusionary rules are required. Fairness of the

---

*A brief opinion.

**Excerpted earlier in this chapter, on p. 324.

trial is threatened by suggestive confrontation evidence, and thus, it is said, an exclusionary rule has an established constitutional predicate.

There are, of course, several interests to be considered and taken into account. The driving force behind *United States v. Wade* (1967), *Gilbert v. California* (1967) (right to counsel at a post-indictment line-up), and *Stovall,* all decided on the same day, was the Court's concern with the problems of eyewitness identification. Usually the witness must testify about an encounter with a total stranger under circumstances of emergency or emotional stress. The witness' recollection of the stranger can be distorted easily by the circumstances or by later actions of the police. Thus, Wade and its companion cases reflect the concern that the jury not hear eyewitness testimony unless that evidence has aspects of reliability. It must be observed that both approaches before us are responsive to this concern. The per se rule, however, goes too far since its application automatically and peremptorily, and without consideration of alleviating factors, keeps evidence from the jury that is reliable and relevant.

The second factor is deterrence. Although the *per se* approach has the more significant deterrent effect, the totality approach also has an influence on police behavior. The police will guard against unnecessarily suggestive procedures under the totality rule, as well as the per se one, for fear that their actions will lead to the exclusion of identifications as unreliable.

The third factor is the effect on the administration of justice. Here the per se approach suffers serious drawbacks. Since it denies the trier reliable evidence, it may result, on occasion, in the guilty going free. Also, because of its rigidity, the per se approach may make error by the trial judge more likely than the totality approach. And in those cases in which the admission of identification evidence is error under the per se approach but not under the totality approach cases in which the identification is reliable despite an unnecessarily suggestive identification procedure reversal is a Draconian sanction. Unlike a warrantless search, a suggestive preindictment identification procedure does not in itself intrude upon a constitutionally protected interest. Thus, considerations urging the exclusion of evidence deriving from a constitutional violation do not bear on the instant problem. Certainly, inflexible rules of exclusion that may frustrate rather than promote justice have not been viewed recently by this Court with unlimited enthusiasm.... The standard, after all, is that of fairness as required by the Due Process Clause of the Fourteenth Amendment....

We turn, then, to the facts of this case and apply the analysis:

1. *The opportunity to view.* Glover testified that for two to three minutes he stood at the apartment door, within two feet of the respondent. The door opened twice, and each time the man stood at the door. The moments passed, the conversation took place, and payment was made. Glover looked directly at his vendor. It was near sunset, to be sure, but the sun had not yet set, so it was not dark or even dusk or twilight. Natural light from outside entered the hallway through a window. There was natural light, as well, from inside the apartment.

2. *The degree of attention.* Glover was not a casual or passing observer, as is so often the case with eyewitness identification. Trooper Glover was a trained police officer on duty and specialized and dangerous duty when he called at the third floor of 201 Westland in Hartford on May 5, 1970. Glover himself was a Negro and unlikely to perceive only general features of "hundreds of Hartford black males," as the Court of Appeals stated. 527 F.2d, at 371. It is true that Glover's duty was that of ferreting out narcotics offenders and that he would be expected in his work to produce results. But it is also true that, as a specially trained, assigned, and experienced officer, he could be expected to pay scrupulous attention to detail, for he knew that subsequently he would have to find and arrest his vendor. In addition, he knew that his claimed observations would be subject later to close scrutiny and examination at any trial.

3. *The accuracy of the description.* Glover's description was given to D'Onofrio within minutes after the transaction. It included the vendor's race, his height, his build, the color and style of his hair, and the high cheekbone facial feature. It also included clothing the vendor wore. No claim has been made that respondent did not possess the physical characteristics so described. D'Onofrio reacted positively at once. Two days later, when Glover was alone, he viewed the photograph D'Onofrio produced and identified its subject as the narcotics seller.

4. *The witness' level of certainty.* There is no dispute that the photograph in question was that of respondent. Glover, in response to a question whether the photograph was that of the person from whom he made the purchase, testified: "There is no question whatsoever." Tr. 38. This positive assurance was repeated.

5. *The time between the crime and the confrontation.* Glover's description of his vendor was given to D'Onofrio within minutes of the crime. The photographic identification took place only two days later. We do not have here the passage of weeks or months between the crime and the viewing of the photograph.

These indicators of Glover's ability to make an accurate identification are hardly outweighed by the corrupting effect of the challenged identification itself. Although identifications arising from single-photograph displays may be viewed in general with suspicion, we find in the instant case little pressure on the witness to acquiesce in the suggestion that such a display entails. D'Onofrio had left the photograph at Glover's office and was not present when Glover first viewed it two days after the event. There thus was little urgency and Glover could view the photograph at his leisure. And since Glover examined the photograph alone, there was no coercive pressure to make an identification arising from the presence of another. The identification was made in circumstances allowing care and reflection.

Although it plays no part in our analysis, all this assurance as to the reliability of the identification is hardly undermined by the facts that respondent was arrested in the very apartment where the sale had taken place, and that he acknowledged his frequent visits to that apartment. Mrs. Ramsey was not a witness at the trial.

Surely, we cannot say that under all the circumstances of this case there is "a very substantial likelihood of irreparable misidentification." Short of that point, such evidence is for the jury to weigh. We are content to rely upon the good sense and judgment of American juries, for evidence with some element of untrustworthiness is customary grist for the jury mill. Juries are not so susceptible that they cannot measure intelligently the weight of identification testimony that has some questionable feature.

Of course, it would have been better had D'Onofrio presented Glover with a photographic array including "so far as practicable . . . a reasonable number of persons similar to any person then suspected whose likeness is included in the array." Model Code, § 160.2(2). The use of that procedure would have enhanced the force of the identification at trial and would have avoided the risk that the evidence would be excluded as unreliable. But we are not disposed to view D'Onofrio's failure as one of constitutional dimension to be enforced by a rigorous and unbending exclusionary rule. The defect, if there be one, goes to weight and not to substance.

We conclude that the criteria laid down in Biggers are to be applied in determining the admissibility of evidence offered by the prosecution concerning a post-Stovall identification, and that those criteria are satisfactorily met and complied with here.

The judgment of the Court of Appeals is REVERSED.

CONCURRING OPINION

STEVENS, J.

. . . The arguments in favor of fashioning new rules to minimize the danger of convicting the innocent on the basis of unreliable eyewitness testimony carry substantial force. Nevertheless, . . . I am persuaded that this rulemaking function can be performed more effectively by the legislative process than by a somewhat clumsy judicial fiat and that the Federal Constitution does not foreclose experimentation by the States in the development of such rules. . . .

DISSENT

MARSHALL, J., joined by BRENNAN, J.

. . . It is distressing to see the Court virtually ignore the teaching of experience . . . and blindly uphold the conviction of a defendant who may well be innocent. . . . Relying on numerous studies made over many years by such scholars as Professor Wigmore and Mr. Justice Frankfurter, the Court in *U.S. v. Wade* concluded that "the vagaries of eyewitness identification are well-known; the annals of criminal law are rife with instances of mistaken identification."

It is, of course, impossible to control one source of such errors the faulty perceptions and unreliable memories of witnesses except through vigorously contested trials conducted by diligent counsel and judges. The Court acted, however, to minimize the more preventable threat posed to accurate identification by "the degree of suggestion inherent in the manner in which the prosecution presents the suspect to witnesses for pretrial identification." . . .

Despite my strong disagreement with the Court over the proper standards* to be applied in this case, . . . assuming applicability of the totality, the facts of the present case require [the exclusion of the identification in this case because it raises a very substantial likelihood of misidentification].

I consider first the opportunity that Officer Glover had to view the suspect. Careful review of the record shows he could see the heroin seller only for the time it took to speak three sentences of four or five short words, to hand over some money, and later after the door reopened, to receive the drugs in return. The entire face-to-face transaction could have taken as little as 15 or 20 seconds. But during this time, Glover's attention was not focused exclusively on the seller's face. He observed that the door was opened 12 to 18 inches, that there was a window in the room behind the door, and, most importantly, that there was a woman standing behind the man. Glover was, of course, also concentrating on the details of the transaction he must have looked away from the seller's face to hand him the money and receive the drugs. The observation during the conversation thus may have been as brief as 5 or 10 seconds.

As the Court notes, Glover was a police officer trained in and attentive to the need for making accurate identifications. Nevertheless, both common sense and scholarly study indicate that while a trained observer such as a police officer "is somewhat less likely to make an erroneous

_____

*The totality of the circumstances instead of the per se rule.

identification than the average untrained observer, the mere fact that he has been so trained is no guarantee that he is correct in a specific case. His identification testimony should be scrutinized just as carefully as that of the normal witness.". . .

Another factor on which the Court relies, the witness' degree of certainty in making the identification, is worthless as an indicator that he is correct. Even if Glover had been unsure initially about his identification of Brathwaite's picture, by the time he was called at trial to present a key piece of evidence for the State that paid his salary, it is impossible to imagine his responding negatively to such questions as "is there any doubt in your mind whatsoever" that the identification was correct. As the Court noted in *Wade:* "'It is a matter of common experience that, once a witness has picked out the accused at the (pretrial confrontation), he is not likely to go back on his word later on.'"

Next, the Court finds that because the identification procedure took place two days after the crime, its reliability is enhanced. While such nearness in time makes the identification more reliable than one occurring months later, the fact is that the greatest memory loss occurs within hours after an event. After that, the drop off continues much more slowly. Thus, the reliability of an identification is increased only if it was made within several hours of the crime. . . .

Finally, the Court makes much of the fact that Glover gave a description of the seller to D'Onofrio shortly after the incident. Despite the Court's assertion that because "Glover himself was a Negro and unlikely to perceive only general features of 'hundreds of Hartford black males,' as the Court of Appeals stated," the description given by Glover was actually no more than a general summary of the seller's appearance. We may discount entirely the seller's clothing, for that was of no significance later in the proceeding. Indeed, to the extent that Glover noticed clothes, his attention was diverted from the seller's face. Otherwise, Glover merely described vaguely the seller's height, skin color, hairstyle, and build. He did say that the seller had "high cheekbones," but there is no other mention of facial features, nor even an estimate of age. Conspicuously absent is any indication that the seller was a native of the West Indies, certainly something which a member of the black community could immediately recognize from both appearance and accent. Brathwaite had come to the United States from his native Barbados as an adult. . . .

In contrast, the procedure used to identify Brathwaite was both extraordinarily suggestive and strongly conducive to error. . . . By displaying a single photograph of Brathwaite to the witness Glover under the circumstances in this record almost everything that could have been done wrong was done wrong.

In the first place, there was no need to use a photograph at all. Because photos are static, two-dimensional, and often outdated, they are "clearly inferior in reliability" to live person lineups and showups. While the use of photographs is justifiable and often essential where the police have no knowledge of an offender's identity, the poor reliability of photos makes their use inexcusable where any other means of identification is available. Here, since Detective D'Onofrio believed he knew the seller's identity, further investigation without resort to a photographic showup was easily possible. With little inconvenience, a live person lineup including Brathwaite might have been arranged. Indeed, the police carefully staged Brathwaite's arrest in the same apartment that was used for the sale, indicating that they were fully capable of keeping track of his whereabouts and using this information in their investigation. . . .

Worse still than the failure to use an easily available live person identification was the display to Glover of only a single picture, rather than a photo array. With good reason, such single-suspect procedures have "been widely condemned." They give no assurance the witness can identify the criminal from among a number of persons of similar appearance, surely the strongest evidence that there was no misidentification. . . . The danger of error is at its greatest when "the police display to the witness only the picture of a single individual. . . ." The use of a single picture (or the display of a single live suspect, for that matter) is a grave error, of course, because it dramatically suggests to the witness that the person shown must be the culprit. Why else would the police choose the person? And it is deeply ingrained in human nature to agree with the expressed opinions of others particularly others who should be more knowledgeable when making a difficult decision.

In this case, moreover, the pressure was not limited to that inherent in the display of a single photograph. Glover, the identifying witness, was a state police officer on special assignment. He knew that D'Onofrio, an experienced Hartford narcotics detective, presumably familiar with local drug operations, believed respondent to be the seller. There was at work, then, both loyalty to another police officer and deference to a better-informed colleague. . . . While the Court is impressed by D'Onofrio's immediate response to Glover's description . . . the detective, who had not witnessed the transaction, acted on a wild guess that Brathwaite was the seller. D'Onofrio's hunch rested solely on Glover's vague description, yet D'Onofrio had seen respondent only "several times, mostly in his vehicle." There was no evidence that respondent was even a suspected narcotics dealer, and D'Onofrio thought that the drugs had been purchased at a different apartment from the one Glover actually went to. The identification of respondent provides a perfect example of the investigator and the witness bolstering each other's inadequate knowledge to produce a seemingly accurate but actually worthless identification.

The Court discounts this overwhelming evidence of suggestiveness, however. It reasons that because D'Onofrio was not present when Glover viewed the photograph, there was "little pressure on the witness to acquiesce in the suggestion." That conclusion blinks psychological reality. There is no doubt in my mind that even in D'Onofrio's absence, a clear and powerful message was telegraphed to Glover as he looked at respondent's photograph. He was emphatically told that "this is the man," and he responded by identifying respondent then and at trial "whether or not he was in fact 'the man.'"

I must conclude that this record presents compelling evidence that there was "a very substantial likelihood of misidentification" of respondent Brathwaite. The suggestive display of Brathwaite's photograph to the witness Glover likely erased any independent memory Glover had retained of the seller from his barely adequate opportunity to observe the criminal.

Accordingly, I dissent.

Questions

1. Describe the three approaches to dealing with misidentifications outlined by the majority opinion.

2. Which approach does the Court adopt, and why?

3. List the facts in each of the five factors and the majority opinion's assessment of them.

4. List the facts in the same way and the dissenting opinion's assessment of them.

5. Do you think the circumstances demonstrate "a very substantial likelihood of irreparable misidentification"?

6. Summarize the dissent's argument in favor of the per se test and against the totality test. Is the dissent correct in arguing that the Court wrongfully evaluated the impact of the exclusionary rule and the totality of circumstances? Evaluate those arguments.

7. Is the dissent's stress on Brathwaite's Barbados ancestry important? Explain.

8. Would you side with the dissent or the majority in this case? Defend your answer.

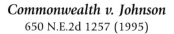

◆ STATE CONSTITUTIONAL LAW ◆

Commonwealth v. Johnson
650 N.E.2d 1257 (1995)

Did the Show-Up Violate Massachusetts Due Process?

Bruce Johnson was charged with larceny in the Boston Municipal Court. After the judge denied his motion to suppress the victim's pretrial identification of him in a "showup" procedure, and following a trial by jury, Johnson was convicted. He applied for direct appellate review. The Supreme Judicial Court granted the application and reversed.

LIACOS, CJ.

FACTS

On April 7, 1992, Leopoldino Goncalves was working at a parking lot on the corner of Traveler Street and Washington Street in Boston. After he finished work, at approximately 10:50 P.M., Goncalves walked across the street to use a public telephone that was located on Washington Street. Streetlights provided the only illumination. When Goncalves finished using the telephone, a white female with a limp approached him and asked him for a dollar. Goncalves told the woman that he did not have any money. A black male armed with a machete then approached. The man grabbed Goncalves's wallet and at the same time the woman snatched money from Goncalves's front pocket. The assailants discarded the wallet after removing the money. They left the area together in an automobile. Goncalves pursued them in his own automobile, but he lost sight of them in a public housing project. The entire incident described lasted only a few minutes.

Approximately forty-five minutes later, Goncalves went to the Area D-4 police station and reported the robbery. He described the male assailant as a twenty-seven to thirty year old black male, six feet tall with a medium build, weighing 170 pounds, and wearing a black cap, blue jeans, and a brown sweatshirt. Goncalves was shown about six books containing photographs of suspects, but was unable to identify his assailants. The record indicates that Goncalves looked at approximately 1,500 photographs while he was at the police station. Goncalves then accompanied a police officer to view a group of potential suspects. Once again, Goncalves did not make an identification.

The day following the incident, four police officers arrived at Goncalves's place of employment at approximately 5 P.M. They told Goncalves they wanted him to view two suspects. Goncalves accompanied the officers. When they arrived at the location where the suspects were being held, Goncalves saw a group of six to eight people. Only one adult black male, Bruce Johnson (the defendant), was present and a female with a limp was the only adult white female present. The two suspects were being "detained" by police officers but they were not handcuffed. The defendant and the woman were brought forward a few steps by the officers. Goncalves then identified the pair as his assailants. Goncalves based his identification in part on the fact that the clothing worn by the suspects was the same as that worn by his assailants.

Johnson possessed several characteristics that didn't match Goncalves's initial description of the male assailant. A booking photograph taken of Johnson at the time of his arrest, the day after the incident, shows Johnson with a moustache. Yet Goncalves had never mentioned the male assailant had a moustache. The booking sheet indicates Johnson is thirty-seven years old and weighs 220 pounds, whereas Goncalves described a man about twenty-seven years old, weighing 170 pounds, with a medium build. Finally, at the time of the hearing on the motion to suppress, Johnson was missing several front teeth. When describing his assailants to the police, Goncalves did not tell them the male assailant had missing teeth.

The judge ruled that Goncalves's identification of Johnson was tainted because it was made at an unnecessarily suggestive showup. The evidence presented at the motion hearing supports this conclusion. Although one-on-one confrontations are not per se excludable, they are disfavored because of their inherently suggestive nature. Showups have been permitted when conducted in the immediate aftermath of a crime and in exigent circumstances. The showup employed by the police in this case was conducted eighteen hours after the crime. It took place in the area of the housing project where Goncalves had seen his assailants drive the previous night; Johnson was brought forward from the group before Goncalves positively identified him; and Johnson was wearing clothes similar to those worn by

the male assailant. Based on these facts, the judge was warranted in concluding that the identification procedure was unnecessarily suggestive.

Although the judge found the identification procedure unnecessarily suggestive, he found that the identification was admissible because it was reliable. In concluding that the identification of Johnson was reliable, the judge cited Goncalves's good opportunity to view his assailants, his certainty in identifying the defendant, and his rejection of hundreds of other photographs as well as suspects presented to him prior to his identification of Johnson. In so doing, the judge relied on the "reliability test," set forth in *Manson v. Brathwaite*. This test is sometimes also referred to as the "totality" test or the "totality of the circumstances" test.

OPINION

This court has never accepted the reasoning in *Brathwaite* as an accurate interpretation of the due process requirements of art. 12 of the Declaration of Rights of the Massachusetts Constitution.... In cases involving an unnecessarily suggestive identification, we have adhered to the stricter rule of per se exclusion previously followed by the Supreme Court.... The Commonwealth now urges us to abandon the per se rule of exclusion and ... follow the reliability test of *Brathwaite*.... We have carefully considered the matter and, for the reasons set forth, we cannot accept *Brathwaite* as satisfying the requirements of art. 12. We conclude that art. 12 requires the application of the stricter per se approach.

Our past resistance to the so-called reliability test reflects this court's concern that the dangers present whenever eyewitness evidence is introduced against an accused require the utmost protection against mistaken identifications. There is no question that the danger of mistaken identification by a victim or a witness poses a real threat to the truth-finding process of criminal trials.... "[The] reliability test" is unacceptable because it provides little or no protection from unnecessarily suggestive identification procedures, from mistaken identifications and, ultimately, from wrongful convictions.

The *Brathwaite* Court examined three primary "interests" before holding that the per se rule should be abandoned in favor of the less protective "reliability" test. The first of these was the concern regarding the dangers presented by eyewitness evidence. The Court acknowledged that a witness's recollection "can be distorted easily by the circumstances or by later actions of the police." While the per se approach addresses this concern, the Court stated, it "goes too far since its application automatically and peremptorily, and without consideration of alleviating factors, keeps evidence from the jury that is reliable and relevant."

We believe that Justice Marshall, dissenting in *Brathwaite*, had a more realistic view of the trial process when he stated: "The dangers of mistaken identification are...simply too great to permit unnecessarily suggestive identifications.".... Indeed, studies conducted by psychologists and legal researchers since *Brathwaite* have confirmed that eyewitness testimony is often hopelessly unreliable....

The *Brathwaite* Court also discussed the public interest in deterring police from using identification procedures which are unnecessarily suggestive. The Court acknowledged that the per se rule is superior in promoting that interest because it provides greater deterrence against police misconduct. The Court nevertheless concluded: "The police will guard against unnecessarily suggestive procedures under the totality rule, as well as the per se one, for fear that their actions will lead to the exclusion of identifications as unreliable." To the contrary, it appears clear to us that the reliability test does little or nothing to discourage police from using suggestive identification procedures.... Indeed, an example of this result is seen in the instant case: the suggestion inherent in the showup procedure that was used to identify the defendant is plain. Furthermore, the showup was unnecessarily suggestive in that it was not conducted immediately after the crime or in exigent circumstances.... Rather than deterring unreliable identification procedures, the effect of the [totality of circumstances] reliability test has been, and would be in this Commonwealth, a message to police that, absent extremely aggravating circumstances, suggestive showups will not result in suppression. Whether or not to use a more fair and accurate identification procedure is, under that test, left to the officer's discretion.

Finally, the *Brathwaite* Court considered the impact of the two tests on the administration of justice. It was here that the Court found what it considered to be the most serious drawbacks of the per se approach. However, it is also here, in our view, that the Court erred most. The Court opined: "Since it denies the trier reliable evidence, [the per se approach] may result, on occasion, in the guilty going free." The opposite is probably more accurate: the admission of unnecessarily suggestive identification procedures under the reliability test would likely result in the innocent being jailed while the guilty remain free....

This case presents an example of why we should not abandon the per se rule of exclusion and replace it with the reliability test. There is absolutely no evidence that the in-court identification of the defendant was the result of anything independent of the unnecessarily suggestive showup. For example, Goncalves's description of his assailant, given to police just after the incident, did not match Johnson's appearance, in part because Johnson possessed the unique feature of several missing teeth. Regardless of this fact, following the showup Goncalves was able to "remember" that his assailant had missing teeth. Such flimsy evidence should not be permitted at trial. Only a rule of per se exclusion can ensure the continued protection against the danger of mistaken identification and wrongful convictions. Accordingly, we reject *Brathwaite* and affirm our confidence in the *Botelho* approach.

The verdict of guilty is vacated. The judgment of conviction is REVERSED. So ordered.

DISSENT

GREANEY, J., joined by LYNCH, J.
...What is important to me is that forty-seven States have adopted the reliability test to govern the admissibility of identification evidence.... The highest court of each of these States was aware of its right to fashion a different test under its State Constitution, but, significantly, each chose not to do so, opting instead for the reliability test. Underlying the choice made by the forty-seven States is tacit recognition of at least the following principles:

First, a criminal trial is meant to be a search for the truth in which the people (as represented by the prosecution) have the right to present reliable evidence tending to prove a defendant's guilt.

Second, since reliability is the linchpin governing the admission of all evidence, identification evidence which is found reliable by a judge, after a careful pretrial inquiry, should not be withheld from the jury.

Third, the jury is capable of sorting out issues of suggestiveness and reliability. It is not logical to deprive them of the antecedents of an in-court identification and to allow speculation on how a victim or identifying witness came to make his or her in-court identification.

DNA PROFILE IDENTIFICATION

DNA (deoxyribonucleic acid) testing can *potentially* identify suspects or *absolutely* exclude individuals as suspects in cases where perpetrators have left DNA at the scene of a crime or where victims have left DNA on items traceable to perpetrators. This capacity to use DNA to identify criminal suspects has come about because of rapid advances in molecular biology since DNA was discovered in 1953. DNA is a long, double-stranded molecule found in everyone's chromosomes. Chromosomes are carried in the nucleus of body cells that have nuclei. These include white blood cells, sperm cells, cells surrounding the hair roots, and saliva cells. DNA testing involves comparing the DNA samples in the nuclei of cells found at crime scenes with either similar DNA samples taken from the nuclei of cells of suspects or DNA samples left by victims on items traceable to perpetrators.

The most widely used test, in which long sections of DNA are broken into fragments, is called **DNA fingerprinting,** or **DNA profiling.** The test measures the fragments, which tend to vary from person to person. If samples from crime scenes have lengths that differ from those of the suspect, that excludes the suspect. If the sample at the scene and that of the suspect have the same lengths, the samples might have a common source. To reduce the element of chance, laboratories measure six or more distinct fragments. Two commercial laboratories (Cellmark Diagnostics Corporation and Lifecodes Corporation) and the FBI are the major sites for DNA testing in the United States (Kreiling 1993, 449; Thompson 1993, 26–27).

Let's look more closely at the reliability of DNA testing and the legal standards for admitting DNA profiles as evidence.

The Reliability of DNA Testing

DNA testing quickly entered the legal system, heralded by one court as "the greatest advance in crime fighting technology since fingerprinting." But then a serious scientific controversy broke out; some challenged the theory of DNA itself, and others challenged the testing methods. Most, however, accepted the soundness of the theory and the testing technology, attacking instead, the admission of the specific tests. According to Professor Edward Imwinkelried of the University of California Davis Law School:

> My reading of the proficiency studies of forensic DNA testing laboratories is that the most common cause of error is not the inherent limitations of the technique, but the way in which the specific test was conducted. What the courts don't understand is that no matter how impressive studies are of the validity of a scientific technique, they are worthless as a guarantee of reliability unless you replicate the variables of the experiment.
>
> Goldberg 1992, 85

In 1989, defense lawyers who were knowledgeable about DNA testing obtained the aid of disinterested scientists to successfully challenge DNA evidence in *People v. Castro* (1989). Lifecodes, the laboratory that did the testing, violated its own rules and was charged with scientific fraud. In the face of a unanimity of scientific opinion, including even experts hired by the prosecution, Lifecodes admitted that the testing didn't amount to a match. The wide coverage that the case received in both the popular and scientific press led to a full-scale debate. The controversy got so heated that John Hicks, head of the FBI Laboratory Division, contended "this is no longer a search for the truth; it is a war" (Thompson 1993, 23).

Legal Standards for Admitting DNA Profile Evidence

Most courts have admitted DNA tests as evidence, but the courts remain divided over the standards for admission. Some courts have adopted the *Frye* **standard.** Named after *Frye v. United States,* the *Frye* standard finds DNA evidence is admissible if the technique is "sufficiently established to have gained general acceptance in the particular field in which it belongs." Other courts have adopted a *Frye* **plus standard,** which finds that in addition to gaining general acceptance, admissibility requires showing that "the testing laboratory in the particular case performed the accepted scientific techniques in analyzing forensic samples." A third group of courts has adopted the *Federal Rules of Evidence standard,* which determines whether the relevancy of the evidence outweighs the tendency of the evidence to unfairly prejudice the defendant. A fourth group of courts has adopted a relevancy plus standard, a hybrid that adds the *Frye* standard and other requirements to the *Federal Rules of Evidence* standard (Goldberg 1992, 84).

The correct identification of criminal suspects by means of DNA testing, whatever the standard a particular court adopts, depends on the answers to the following three questions and the inferences that jurors or other fact finders make about them:

1. Is a reported match between the sample at the scene of the crime and the sample from the suspect a true match?

2. Is the suspect the source of the trace of DNA left at the scene of the crime?

3. Is the suspect the perpetrator of the crime?

A reported match strongly suggests a true match. However, mistakes in DNA processing do occur. Technical errors, such as enzyme failures, salt concentrations, and dirt spots, can produce misleading patterns. Human errors, including contaminations, mislabelings, misrecordings, misrepresentations, case mix-ups, and errors of interpretation, also occur. Assuming that the match is true, it strongly suggests that the suspect is the source of the trace of DNA left at the scene of the crime. Still, the match might be coincidental. The coincidence depends on the frequency of matching traits among the relevant population, usually the ethnic group of the suspect. However, the validity of this reference population isn't foolproof either; it depends on the correct identification of the suspect's ethnic group.

Further, prosecutors, experts, and jurors often exaggerate the weight to give to the match between the trace and the suspect by speaking in terms of odds. According to one trial transcript, after testifying that the blood of a victim matched a sample from a blanket, the following exchange took place:

Q [Prosecutor]: And in your profession and in the scientific field when you say match what do you mean?

A [Expert]: They are identical.

Q [Prosecutor]: So the blood on the blanket can you say it came from [the victim]?

A [Expert]: With great certainty I can say that those two DNA samples match and they are identical. And with population statistics we can derive a probability of it being anyone other than the victim.

Q [Prosecutor]: What is the probability in this case?

A [Expert]: In this case that probability is that it is one in 7 million chances that it could be anyone other than that victim. (Koehler 1995, 21)

But Professor Jonathan Koehler, at the University of Texas at Austin, says the expert's claim that population statistics can show the victim was probably *not* the source is false.

Finally, evidence the suspect is the source of the trace is also evidence the suspect committed the crime. But maybe not! The suspect could have left the trace innocently either before or after the commission of the crime. So the use of the match to prove guilt depends on an inference—perhaps a fair inference, but not an automatic or always correct inference.

Whatever the problems and criticisms of the use of DNA testing to identify suspects and link them to crimes, the impact of DNA (and other scientific evidence, too, for that matter) is substantial. According to one researcher, about 25 percent of jurors said they would have voted not guilty if scientific evidence had *not* been introduced. In another survey, 75 percent of judges and lawyers throughout the United States said that they believe judges believe scientific evidence more than other kinds of evidence, and 70 percent said they think jurors do, too (Giannelli 1991, 794).

The Minnesota Supreme Court considered these problems in *State v. Bloom* (1994).

CASE	*Is a DNA Profile Admissible?*

State v. Bloom
516 N.W.2d 159 (Minn. 1994)

Bloom was charged with rape. The district court, in a hearing on a motion to suppress, excluded evidence of DNA testing. The state appealed directly to the Minnesota Supreme Court, which reversed.

KEITH, CJ., joined by PAGE, TOMLJANOVICH, and GARDEBRING, JJ.

FACTS

Shortly after 1:00 A.M. on November 23, 1992, J. L. P., a 34-year-old woman, was entering her home in Brooklyn Park when she was grabbed from behind by a Caucasian man. The man, whom she did not see well enough to identify, forced her into her car, pulling a stocking cap over her face. He drove her to a different location, ordered her into the back seat, and told her if she did not comply with his demands he would penetrate her vagina with a screwdriver.

He forced her to submit to fellatio, digital penetration and ordinary sexual penetration. He also bit the victim on her breasts. After assaulting her, he drove her home and dropped her off, then abandoned her car nearby.

After preserving semen samples taken from the victim in the sexual assault examination and other semen samples found in the car, the BCA prepared a DNA profile of the samples. This consisted of six separate probes and resulting autorads for comparison with autorads made from probes of known DNA. James Liberty, who does forensic work at the BCA and has attended an FBI course on forensic aspects of DNA technology, testified that using information from two of the six probes to make a computer search of the BCA's sex-offender DNA database, he came up with five potential suspects, including defendant, whose DNA matched at those two loci. Comparing the probe data of the five potential suspects found in this manner, he determined that one of them, defendant, "stood out." Then, by comparing the database pattern of all five loci available in defendant's prior database profile he determined that there was a match with the pattern at all five loci on the autorads made from the assailant's semen.

Liberty then did another complete DNA test on both the assailant's semen and on a new sample of defendant's blood, taken after his arrest, as well as on blood from the victim's boyfriend and from another individual, and he produced new autorads. The victim's boyfriend and the other individual were excluded as possible sources. The defendant's DNA profile matched the crime scene sample at all nine loci tested. After using five loci and finding a match at each, Liberty made some calculations and concluded that there was a 1 in 93,700 chance that a randomly selected person would match at all five points.

Professor Daniel Hartl, a Professor of Biology at Harvard and an earlier critic of some of the statistical computations that forensic scientists were making based on FBI databases, testified (by telephone) for the state at the suppression hearing that, using the "interim ceiling method" recommended by the National Research Council, there was a 1 in 634,687 chance of a random match across the five loci. He testified that Liberty had obtained the less-impressive 1 in 93,700 figure by making some "adjustments" that were not needed because the interim ceiling approach, which Liberty too had used, had those adjustments built into it. Dr. Hartl, if permitted, would further testify at trial that in fact there was a nine-loci match and that in his opinion the nine-loci match constituted "overwhelming evidence that, to a reasonable degree of scientific certainty, the DNA from the victim's vaginal swab came from [defendant], to the exclusion of all others."

The trial court ... ruled (1) that the jury could be told (a) that defendant's DNA was consistent with crime scene samples on each of the nine bands tested, (b) the frequency of each individual band and (c) nonstatistical opinion testimony that defendant's DNA profile is consistent with that of the assailant, but (2) the jury could not be told (a) that the frequency of the profile in the population based on five tests is 1 in 634,687 (or, for that matter, 1 in 93,700) or (b) that the opinion of Dr. Hartl is as just quoted....

OPINION

This appeal gives this court an opportunity to revisit an issue that recently has been the focus of considerable controversy in the scientific community. The issue is not, as some have put it, the admissibility of DNA identification evidence in criminal prosecutions but the form the presentation of that evidence takes.

DNA ... occurs in all cells that have a nucleus, including white blood cells, sperm cells, cells surrounding hair roots, and cells in saliva. Most sections of DNA molecules vary little among individuals within a species. However, some

sections ... do vary. If two fragments do not match, they *could not* have a common source, but if they do match, they *might* have a common source. Researchers as yet have not developed DNA profiles that cannot be shared by two or more people. However, the theory underlying forensic use of DNA profiles is that "as the number and variability of the ... [variations increases], the odds of two people having the same profile become vanishingly small."

The "vanishingly small" probability figure that experts come up with in case after case is the probability of a random match. Carefully stated, it is the probability that a randomly selected person, if tested, would have the same DNA profile as that of the sample left at the scene. Thus, when the figure given is 1 in 1 billion, the expert is saying (if the expert chooses words carefully) that there is a 1 in 1 billion chance that a randomly selected person would have the same DNA profile as that of the sample left at the scene....

There are a number of potential sources of error in computing the probability figure. These include:

(a) The databases used may seriously underestimate the frequency in the population of a particular pattern of DNA at a particular locus.

(b) The databases may be unrepresentative, failing to take into account variations among population subgroups, or variations in particular geographical locales, in the frequency of certain DNA patterns at particular loci.

(c) The assumption of statistical independence may be invalid.... As stated by Lempert, "evidence of a DNA match is not nearly so probative as people have thought because suspect populations are not random agglomerations with respect to the likelihood of sharing the [traits] compared in DNA analysis."

(d) The laboratory's "false positive match rate" affects the reliability of the figure obtained using the product rule. False positive matches do occur, as the result of sloppy laboratory procedures, the poor quality of the materials used, the quality of the DNA sample obtained from the scene, the protocols calling for a match, and human error.

(e) If there was an error in concluding that there was a match at even one band in a particular case, then there is a very real chance that the jury will be told in that case that the chance of a random match is extremely small when in reality there is no match at all.

Because of these factors, the NRC [National Research Council Committee on DNA testing] in its 1992 report recommended the use of an extremely conservative "interim ceiling method" for estimating random match probabilities. (It is this method that the state's expert, Professor Hartl, used in this case to arrive at the 1 in 634,687 figure.)

One of the concerns expressed in our cases…has been that admission of the random match probability figure will confuse jurors. There is a chain of inferences that the jurors must make in order to get from the starting point, the testimony as to the probability of a random match, to the conclusion that the defendant is the perpetrator of the crime. Those inferential steps include: match report—true match—source—present at scene—perpetrator. Errors may occur at each step:

(a) *The inference that the reported match is a true match.* Most expert witnesses are technicians. Forensic scientists typically do not know much about the underlying statistical theory and, even if they do, "are often reluctant to acknowledge [for example,] that a reported match could be something other than a true match." This reluctance is not confined to forensic scientists: In courtroom testimony, forensic scientists and their academic supports often insist that the probability of a false positive is zero—that is, that false positives are impossible. Although the falsity of these claims has been demonstrated repeatedly, the claims still continue to be made. Currently, juries often hear nothing about false positives, other than broad assurance that they never occur. Jurors hear impressive numbers that appear to quantify with precision the frequency of the DNA profile, accompanied (when the issue is raised at all) by a vague, non-quantitative discussion of the chances of a false positive.

(b) *The inference that a true match means defendant is the source.* There is nothing inherently wrong in a jury using its inference that the match is a true match as the basis for another inference, specifically, that the defendant is the source. What is important is that the jury know that it has to go through the process of making the inference. The probability that a randomly selected person would have the same profile as the sample found at the scene is not the probability that someone other than the defendant is the source. But it is commonly assumed that it is the probability that someone other than defendant is the source. This is what is often referred to as "source probability error." In order to give an opinion as to the probability that someone other than defendant is the source, one would first have to estimate the size of the potential source population. "Source probability errors are frequently committed in the popular press." See e.g., "DNA Data: Letting Jurors Know the Whole Score," *Minneapolis Star-Tribune,* Feb. 1, 1994, at 10A (stating that, as the result of a trial judge's ruling, "jurors will hear testimony on the odds that the DNA evidence against [the defendant] actually belongs to someone else").

Unfortunately, source probability errors "are also committed by the courts and by experts who should know better."…One can understand attorneys and judges, who are not trained in statistics, making this mistake. And one can understand forensic scientists, most of whom are technicians, making this mistake. But even the best of the scientists make it occasionally.

(c) *The inference that defendant was the source means defendant was at the scene.* There is nothing inherently wrong in using the inference that defendant was the source to infer defendant was at the scene as long as jurors know that the one does not necessarily follow from the other.

(d) *The inferences that defendant was the source and that he was at the scene mean defendant committed the crime.* An even more egregious kind of error than "source probability error" is that which has been dubbed "prosecutor's fallacy," the fallacious equation of random match probability with the probability that the defendant is the perpetrator of the crime. As Koehler says, it really should not be called "prosecutor's fallacy" because experts, defense attorneys, judges and reporters also sometimes make the mistake; he therefore refers to it as "ultimate issue error." One has no way of knowing how often jurors make the error but it is quite possible that such error by jurors is common. Koehler explains, "[A] suspect who actually is the source of the trace may not be the perpetrator of the crime. The suspect may have left the trace innocently either before or after the crime was committed." Indeed, the use of a person's bodily fluids to frame that person is not beyond the realm of possibility.

Forensic use of DNA evidence is a very recent development. The first forensic use was in Great Britain less than 10 years ago. Those who are not by nature skeptical "rushed" to admit the evidence in criminal cases. In the "first wave of cases, expert testimony for the prosecution rarely was countered, and courts readily admitted RFLP findings."

Then law reviews began publishing critical articles dealing with a number of issues, including the standards used for determining individual matches, the adequacy of the studies estimating the frequency of individual traits in the population, the validity of the assumption of independence, the possibility of false matches, and the misleading presentation of things such as random match probability and the possibility of false matches. Unfortunately, the FBI and others advancing the "cause" of the easy admission of DNA evidence have not always behaved admirably.

Because of all the criticism, a Committee on DNA Technology in Forensic Sciences was formed by the National Research Council. The committee's report, which we referred to earlier, was released in 1992.... The NRC report has not put an end to the controversy. Indeed, it appears that the FBI is sufficiently concerned about the response of courts and critics to the NRC report that it has agreed to fund a new study by the NRC in the hope that that will help end what former-FBI Director Sessions called a "crisis."

While Minnesota was one of the first courts to admit DNA identification evidence in criminal trials, we took the cautious approach in doing so, insisting that the new forensic techniques receive adequate scrutiny and insisting that proper procedures be followed if the evidence is to be admitted.... As we said at the outset of this opinion, the issue in this case is not the admissibility of DNA evidence but the form that the presentation of the evidence takes....

... Notwithstanding the fact that the intense debate continues concerning the most reliable, accurate way of estimating random match probability and the proper role of statistical evidence in criminal trials, we now conclude, based on all the circumstances, including the very conservative nature of the probability figures obtained using the NRC's approach, that a DNA exception to the rule against admission of quantitative, statistical probability evidence in criminal prosecutions to prove identity is justified. Accordingly, any properly qualified prosecution or defense expert may, if evidentiary foundation is sufficient, give an opinion as to random match probability using the NRC's approach to computing that statistic.

We also conclude that, in an appropriate case, where there is an underlying statistical foundation for such an opinion, a properly qualified expert should be allowed to say more than that the DNA test results merely are consistent with the defendant's being the source of the physical evidence left behind by the assailant....

We have concluded that the DNA expert should be allowed to express the opinion that there is a "match" between the defendant's DNA profile and that left by the assailant at the scene or on the victim. The strength of the expert's opinion is something the jury should be told; it will depend in part on the degree of the expert's confidence in the opinion and in part on the underlying statistical foundation for the opinion. We also agree with Professor Kreiling that the expert should be allowed to phrase the opinion this way: that given a reliable multi-locus match, the probability that the match is random or coincidental is extremely low.

The expert should not, of course, be allowed to say that a particular profile is unique. Nor should the expert be allowed to say that defendant is the source to the exclusion of all others or to express an opinion as to the strength of the evidence. But should a properly qualified expert, assuming adequate foundation, be allowed to express an opinion that, to a reasonable scientific certainty, the defendant is (or is not) the source? We believe so....

We believe that allowing this sort of verbal, qualitative, non-statistical presentation of the underlying statistical evidence will lead to more agreement among reputable experts at trials and may decrease the likelihood of there being a battle of experts (over the reliability of the random match probability figure), with one expert canceling out or discrediting the other.

Needless to say, any rule of evidence "cuts both ways." The defendant in a criminal case has the same right as the state to present both quantitative and/or qualitative DNA evidence under the rules we today articulate. Moreover, the trial court of necessity retains its historic power under Minn.R.Evid. 403 and of course has the responsibility of crafting appropriate cautionary instructions. Prosecutors and trial courts are cautioned that we will not hesitate to award a new trial to a defendant if our review of the trial record reveals that quantitative or qualitative DNA identification evidence was presented in a misleading or improper way.

RESERVED IN PART and REMANDED for trial....

DISSENT

COYNE, J.

I dissent. I agree... that when a proper foundation has been laid—that is, when there has been a showing that the tests were performed in accordance with appropriate laboratory standards and controls—DNA test results are admissible into evidence.... [But there's a hedge,] the test data and methodology must be available for independent review by or on behalf of the opposing party, and the admissibility of statistical probability evidence should be limited to Rule 403 of the *Minnesota Rules of Evidence,* which permits the exclusion of relevant evidence if its probative value is substantially outweighed by the danger of unfair prejudice.

Today the majority has bulldozed that hedge into oblivion, ostensibly in the interest of "scientific proof," with only a backward glance at the reason for excluding statistical probability evidence. Statistical probabilities are certainly useful tools for... supporting certain conclusions with respect to the validity and use of the results of the research. Statistics have, however, been known to lie—either inadvertently or purposefully.... If... an erroneous statistical probability plays any significant role in the conviction of an innocent person, the error has not only destroyed the life of the innocent person but has in some sense dehumanized the community....

More to the point, perhaps, than the potential for error in these statistics is their potential for misuse. The state's imported expert witness is prepared . . . to testify that there is a 1 in 634,687 chance of a random match at the five loci in question. That figure is, in a sense, fictitious. . . . Statistical probabilities are, of course, only probabilities—estimates, not certainties. As the witness undoubtedly recognizes, however, the mere recitation of the number 634,687 conveys an aura of mathematical precision, lending the probability a credibility it may not deserve and a weight to which it has no logical claim. . . .

More inimical to our traditional system of legal proof in criminal trials than undeserved credibility is the danger that the fact finder will understand the statistic represents something which it does not—namely, that the probability refers to the odds that someone else than the defendant is the source of the specimen found at the scene of the crime. That mistake has so often found its way into the rhetoric of public figures and in erroneous reports in the public press that it may be impossible to erase it from the mind of the fact finder. Even the state's expert fell into that trap on cross-examination. . . .

That mine is the lone dissenting voice in this matter does not shake my conviction that the day will come when this court regrets today's decision.

Questions

1. According to the court, what inferences must jurors make when using DNA evidence, and what are the problems with each?

2. On the basis of this case, do you believe that DNA evidence should be admitted? If so, under what conditions?

3. Assume that you are a judge. Would you admit the evidence? What would you allow the experts to say?

4. Assume that you are the prosecutor, and argue for the admissibility of the evidence and for the expert to tell the jury the "odds" of a random person in the population having the same DNA.

5. Now assume that you are the defense attorney, and argue that the evidence isn't admissible or, if it is, that the experts shouldn't be allowed to talk about the odds.

SUMMARY

I. Identifying strangers
    A. It's easier to prove a crime was committed than who committed it
    B. Eyewitness identification is the most widely used identification procedure despite technological advances
    C. Three types
        1. Lineups (live and photo)—witnesses observe a row of individuals resembling one another; one is the suspect
        2. Show-ups—one suspect is observed by the witness
        3. Photo identification—the witness examines either an array of photos or an individual photo

II. The risk of mistaken eyewitness identification
    A. High risk of mistaken identification due to four normal mental processes:
        1. Perception (brains aren't cameras)
            a. Length—the longer the time to observe, the more accurate the observation
            b. Distractions—witnesses often are distracted
            c. Focus of observation—witnesses often focus on the weapons used against them and not on the criminal's physical characteristics
            d. Stress on witness during the observation, especially during criminal events
            e. Race of witness and stranger—interracial identifications are more inaccurate

2. Memory
    a. Falls off sharply during first few hours after the event
    b. Information is stored in the brain during and after the event
    c. After the event, memory remains stable for several months
3. Suggestion
    a. Other people's influence distorts interpretation of events
    b. Procedures are viewed by witnesses as multiple-choice (without "none of the above" choice) or as true/false questions
    c. Believe police wouldn't have set up the procedure unless they had the suspect present
4. Recall—information selectively retrieved from memory
B. Witnesses' confidence in their identification grows as time passes
C. Reducing risk of misidentification
    1. Better procedures can benefit recall and suggestion
    2. Avoid show-ups and single photo ID
    3. Include enough individuals and ones who resemble one another in lineups
    4. Warn witnesses the suspect might or might not be in the live or photo lineup
    5. Have blind administrators (ones who don't know if the suspect is there) manage the procedure

III. The Constitution and identification procedures
    A. Unreliable identification procedures can violate two constitutional provisions
        1. Fifth and Fourteenth Amendment due process clauses
        2. Sixth Amendment right to counsel *after* formal charges—right to have a lawyer present at lineups, show-ups, and photo IDs
        3. Court has ruled that ID procedures don't compel suspects to be witnesses against themselves in violation of the Fifth Amendment
        4. If suspects refuse to cooperate in identification procedures
            a. Prosecutors can comment at trial that jurors can infer guilt from the refusal
            b. Courts can hold those who refuse in contempt
            c. Police can conduct procedures over suspects' objections
        5. Courts apply a due process test of identification procedures
        6. Two-pronged totality of circumstances unreliability test—defendants have to prove by the totality of the circumstances that the
            a. Procedure was impermissibly and unnecessarily suggestive *and*
            b. Procedure caused a "very substantial likelihood" of misidentification
    B. Lineups
        1. Reliability depends on
            a. Composition of the lineup
                (1) Numbers—at least 5–6 for most accuracy
                (2) Similarity in physical characteristics and in dress
            b. Procedure—the way the lineup's conducted
                (1) High degree of inaccuracy due to power of suggestions
                (2) Recommendations for reducing unreliability
                    (a) Tell witnesses the suspect may or may not be in the lineup
                    (b) Have a blind administrator manage the lineup
                    (c) If the witness identifies the suspect, immediately ask how sure he is *before* other information affects the level of certainty

2. Due process and misidentification
   a. Two-pronged reliability test
   b. Totality of circumstances concerning five factors affecting eyewitness reliability
      (1) Opportunity to view
      (2) Degree of attention
      (3) Accuracy of description
      (4) Level of certainty
      (5) Length of time between crime and ID procedure
   c. Empirical research and due process test
      (1) Questionable assumption that reliability improves if witness' identification meets the reliability test
      (2) Some validity to the opportunity to view the suspect during the crime but none of the circumstances does much to improve reliability
C. Show-ups
   1. Substantially less reliable than lineups because suggestion is more powerful
   2. Three situations in which courts admit show-ups
      a. Chance encounters—witnesses accidentally see suspects
      b. Emergencies—witnesses are hospitalized
      c. Suspects aren't in custody
   3. Constitutionality depends on two-pronged due process reliability test
D. Photo identification
   1. The least reliable of all procedures (because the two-dimensional nature distorts accuracy)
   2. Most widely used
   3. Constitutionality
      a. U.S. Supreme Court has upheld their constitutionality
      b. Two-pronged due process reliability test determines admissibility

IV. DNA profile identification
   A. DNA can potentially identify individuals or absolutely exclude them as suspects
   B. Reliability issues arise not from technology but from DNA testing procedures
   C. Three legal standards for admitting DNA profiles as evidence
      1. *Frye* test—admissible if technique has gained general scientific acceptance
      2. *Frye* plus—general scientific acceptance + testing in a particular case that followed accepted scientific techniques
      3. *Federal Rules of Evidence*—relevance of the evidence outweighs any tendency to unfairly hurt the defendant's case
   D. Correct identification based on DNA depends on answers to three questions
      1. Is a reported match between the sample at the scene of the crime and the sample from the suspect a true match?
      2. Is the suspect the source of the trace of DNA left at the scene of the crime?
      3. Is the suspect the perpetrator of the crime?

E. Problems with use of DNA evidence in court
   1. Mistakes *do* happen
   2. Match might be coincidental
   3. Prosecutors, experts, and jurors exaggerate the weight of DNA evidence

 Go to the Criminal Procedure 6e CD to download this summary outline. The outline has been formatted so that you can add notes to it during class lectures, or later create a customized chapter outline to use while reviewing. Either way, the summary outline will help you understand the "big picture" and fill in the details as you study.

REVIEW QUESTIONS

1. Why is identification of strangers a risky business in criminal cases?
2. Identify and define four mental processes that account for mistakes in identifying strangers.
3. Identify five circumstances that affect the accuracy of perceptions in identifying strangers.
4. Describe how memory affects the accuracy of eyewitness identification.
5. Describe how suggestion works based on Elizabeth Loftus's research.
6. Describe how witnesses' descriptions of criminal events change over time.
7. When is the effect of suggestion most powerful and threatening, and why?
8. Explain why the procedures used to identify strangers add to the problem of misidentification.
9. Identify and describe three ways to reduce the inaccuracy of eyewitness identification by police procedures and legal rules.
10. Identify three constitutional provisions unreliable identification procedures can violate and when in the criminal process they kick in.
11. Identify four characteristics of lineups recommended by the International Association of Chiefs of Police.
12. Summarize what empirical research has shown about the reliability of lineups.
13. Describe and give an example of how the power of suggestion works in administering lineups.
14. List three rules for reducing misidentification in lineups recommended by Wells and Seelau.
15. Identify the two-steps in the totality-of-circumstances due process test of admissibility of eyewitness identification created by the U.S. Supreme Court.
16. Identify, describe, and give an example of the five circumstances in the totality-of-circumstances due process test you identified in (15).
17. Why are photo identifications the most unreliable eyewitness identification procedure?
18. Identify and compare the three legal tests for admitting DNA evidence in court.

19. Correct identification based on DNA depends on answers to three questions. Identify the three questions.

20. Summarize the importance jurors, lawyers, and judges attach to scientific evidence as proof of guilt.

KEY TERMS

strangers p. 314
lineup p. 314
show-up p. 314
photo identification p. 314
perception p. 315
memory p. 315
suggestion p. 315
recall p. 315
might-or-might-not-be-present instruction p. 319
blind administrator p. 319

preponderance of the evidence p. 319
witnesses' opportunity to view p. 320
witnesses' degree of attention p. 320
witnesses' accuracy of description p. 320
witnesses' level of certainty p. 320
length of time between the crime and the identification p. 320

photo lineup p. 329
photo show-up p. 329
DNA (deoxyribonucleic acid) testing p. 338
DNA fingerprinting p. 338
DNA profiling p. 338
Frye standard p. 339
Frye plus standard p. 339
Federal Rules of Evidence standard p. 339

THE COMPANION WEB SITE
FOR *CRIMINAL PROCEDURE,* SIXTH EDITION

http://cj.wadsworth.com/samaha/crim_pro6e

Supplement your review of this chapter by going to the companion Web site to take one of the Tutorial Quizzes, use the flash cards to test yourself on the key terms from each chapter, and check out the many other study aids you'll find there. You'll find valuable data and resources at your fingertips to help you study for that big exam or write that important paper.

Constitutional Violations: Exclusionary Rule and Entrapment

10

Chapter Main Points

- Individuals have numerous remedies against government misconduct (at least on paper).
- The two remedies discussed in this chapter—the exclusionary rule and the defense of entrapment—are *not* constitutional *rights*.
- The United States is the only criminal justice system in the world with the exclusionary rule, in which courts throw out good evidence for the purpose of preventing unconstitutional police behavior.
- The social cost of the exclusionary rule is that some guilty people go free, because keeping good evidence out of court undermines the prosecution's case.
- Because of the social cost of freeing guilty people, the scope of the exclusionary rule is restricted to cases where it's most likely to deter unconstitutional conduct by police (the government's case-in-chief against defendants).
- There's a lot of controversy over how high the social costs and how great the deterrent effects of the exclusionary rule are.
- Courts throw out cases where officers encouraged defendants to commit crimes they wouldn't have committed without the encouragement.
- Government encouragement of criminal behavior is an undercover police tactic directed mainly at consensual crimes like official corruption, drugs, pornography, and prostitution.

In January 1991, Phoenix police officer Bryan Sargent saw Isaac Evans driving the wrong way on a one-way street in front of the police station. The officer stopped Evans and asked to see his driver's license. After Evans told him that his license had been suspended, the officer entered Evans's name into a computer data terminal located in his patrol car. The computer inquiry confirmed that Evans's license had been suspended and also indicated that there was an outstanding misdemeanor warrant for his arrest. Based upon the outstanding warrant, Officer Sargent arrested Evans. While the police were handcuffing him, Evans dropped a hand-rolled cigarette that the officers determined smelled of marijuana. The officers proceeded to search his car and discovered a bag of marijuana under the passenger's seat.

The State charged Evans with possession of marijuana. When the police notified the Justice Court that they had arrested him, the Justice Court discovered that the arrest warrant previously had been quashed (vacated or voided) and notified the police. Evans argued that because his arrest was based on a warrant that had been quashed 17 days before his arrest, the marijuana seized incident to the arrest should be suppressed as the fruit of an unlawful arrest.

Arizona v. Evans (1995), U.S. Supreme Court

REMEDIES AGAINST OFFICER MISCONDUCT

As a very junior member of a Minneapolis mayor's committee to examine police misconduct, our committee held a neighborhood meeting to educate residents about our work. But *I* learned a lot more than the residents. One resident that night made a comment and then asked a great question. His comment: "We all know what happens when *we* break the law—*we* get arrested and prosecuted." And, then came the great question: "What I want to know is what happens when the *police* break the law against us? What recourse do we have?" The answer is, lots of remedies (on paper at least). We'll divide the discussion of the remedies into two types and between this chapter and the next. First, we'll look at remedies that can affect the outcome of the state's *criminal* case against defendants (the trial stage). Two of these remedies are the subject of this chapter:

1. *Exclusionary rule.* Throwing out illegally obtained evidence in the case against the defendant (by far the most frequently used remedy but of no use to innocent people)

2. *Defense of entrapment.* Dismissing cases against defendants who committed crimes they (or a hypothetical reasonable person) wouldn't have committed if law enforcement officers hadn't encouraged them to commit them

Second, remedies are granted in separate proceedings. Some of these proceedings are inside and some are outside the judicial system (Chapter 11). They include:

1. *Criminal prosecution* of police officers for their illegal actions

2. *Civil lawsuits* to sue officers, departments, and municipalities for official wrongdoing

3. *Administrative review of police misconduct* to discipline officers who break police rules

These remedies aren't mutually exclusive. For example, the government can prosecute police officers who damage property when they illegally break into a house to search it. The property owner can sue the same officers for both the damage to her property and the violation of her constitutional rights caused by the illegal search. The department can dismiss or suspend the officers from duty for conducting the illegal search. Courts can exclude the evidence the officers seized during the search, even if the defendant is guilty! Although this hardly ever happens, it *could* because the law doesn't force injured parties to choose one remedy.

One other point: There's no constitutional right to either the exclusionary rule or the defense of entrapment. The exclusionary rule is a device created by the U.S. Supreme Court to enforce constitutional rights, but it's not a right itself. The defense of entrapment is a right created by either federal and state statutes or court decisions.

THE EXCLUSIONARY RULE

The United States is the only country in the world that has an exclusionary rule (the rule that forces courts to throw out *good* evidence when the government gets it by using *bad* methods). Or, in Judge Cardozo's famous words, "The culprit goes free because the constable blundered" (*People v. Defore* 1926, 587). **Good evidence** refers to evidence that proves—or at least helps to prove—defendants committed the crimes they're charged with. **Bad methods** refers to police actions and procedures that violate procedures covered by five constitutional amendments:

- The Fourth Amendment ban on unreasonable searches and seizures (Chapters 3–7)

- The Fifth Amendment ban on coerced incriminating statements (Chapter 8)

- The Sixth Amendment right to counsel (Chapter 12)

- The Fifth and Fourteenth Amendment guarantees of due process of law in administering identification procedures (Chapter 9)

In this section, we'll trace the history of the exclusionary rule. Then, we'll examine the rationales for and the scope of the rule; what happens when people are brought to court by illegal arrests; the reasonable good-faith exception to the exclusionary rule; and the social costs of the rule.

History

The Bill of Rights to the U.S. Constitution doesn't mention the exclusionary rule (or for that matter any other remedies we'll be discussing in this chapter and Chapter 11). James Madison, in an address to Congress in 1789 (*Annals of Congress* 1789), explains this silence:

> If these rights are incorporated into the Constitution, independent tribunals of justice will consider themselves in a peculiar manner the guardians of those rights; they will be an impenetrable bulwark against every assumption of power in the Legislative or Executive; they will naturally be led to resist every encroachment upon rights expressly stipulated for in the Constitution by the declaration of rights. (457)

In other words, the Constitution didn't have to spell out the remedies because judges would create appropriate ones to fit the circumstances of each case.

Until the twentieth century, the only remedies for constitutional violations were private lawsuits against officials. All this dramatically changed in 1914, when the U.S. Supreme Court created the exclusionary rule in *Weeks v. U. S.* (1914). In that case, while Fremont Weeks was at work in Union Station, Kansas City, Kansas, police officers broke into his house without a warrant. They searched the house and seized "all of his books, letters, money, papers, notes, evidences of indebtedness, stock certificates, insurance policies, deeds, abstracts of title, bonds, candies, clothes, and other property." Then, the officers arrested Weeks while he was at work. Soon after, he was charged with illegal gambling. The trial court refused Weeks's motion to return the seized evidence, and he was convicted and sentenced to a fine and imprisonment. On appeal, the U.S. Supreme Court reversed the conviction because

> the letters . . . were taken from the house of the accused by an official of the United States, acting under color of his office, in direct violation of the constitutional rights of the defendant; that having made a seasonable application for their return, which was heard and passed upon by the court, there was involved in the order refusing the application a denial of the constitutional rights of the accused; and that the court should have restored these letters to the accused. In holding them and permitting their use upon the trial, we think prejudicial error was committed. (398)

Please notice two points here. First, the rule established in *Weeks* applied only to *federal* law enforcement; the states could choose any remedy they saw fit to enforce their own citizens' constitutional rights under their state constitutions. Second, the rule applied only to Weeks's *private papers* and other *belongings* he legally possessed. The Court said nothing about what it would've decided if Weeks had demanded the return of *contraband*. The importance of the case is that it started a trend toward the use of the exclusionary rule to enforce law enforcement violations of constitutional rights.

The Court broadened the *Weeks* rule in *Silverthorne Lumber Co. v. U.S.* (1920). After arresting Fred Silverthorne and his father, Justice Department officers and a U.S. marshal "without a shadow of authority" went to the Silverthornes' Lumber Company's office and "made a clean sweep of all the books, papers and documents found there." The officers immediately took all the stuff they seized to the office of the U.S. District Attorney's office. The Silverthornes demanded and got back their illegally seized books and papers, but, by that time, the government had already copied and photographed them. They used the copies and photographs to get a subpoena from the trial court ordering the Silverthornes to turn over the originals. When the Silverthornes refused to obey the subpoena, the trial court fined and jailed them for contempt. According to Justice Oliver Wendell Holmes, although the government's search and seizure "was an outrage," the government claims "it may study the papers before it returns them, copy them, and then . . . use the knowledge" to order the owners to turn over the papers. In other words, the Constitution protects the papers themselves from forbidden acts,

> but not any advantages the Government can gain from the forbidden act. . . . In our opinion such is not the law. It reduces the Fourth Amendment to a form of words. . . . The essence of a provision forbidding the acquisition of evidence in a certain way is that not merely evidence so acquired shall not be used before the Court but that it shall not be used at all. (392)

This expansion of the exclusionary rule to ban the use of evidence *indirectly* based on an illegal government action is called the **fruit-of-the-poisonous-tree doctrine.** The basic idea behind the doctrine is that the government should never be in a *better* position after violating the Constitution than it was before it broke the law. We'll discuss later the opposite idea: the government shouldn't be in a *worse* position after violating the Constitution than it was before. (See the "Attenuation," "Independent Source," and "Inevitable Discovery" sections later.)

Weeks and *Silverthorne* still restricted the exclusionary rule to *private* papers. In 1925, in *Agnello v. United States* (1925), the Court created "a full-blown rule of exclusion at federal trials." The government had illegally seized cocaine from Frank Agnello's house, and Agnello argued that the court should have suppressed the cocaine at his trial. The Supreme Court agreed, expanding the rule beyond papers to include the contraband cocaine. Years later, Justice Potter Stewart (1983, 1376–1377) contended that after the decision in *Agnello* in 1925, "the annexation of the exclusionary rule to the Fourth Amendment was complete."

As we've already noted *Weeks, Silverthorne,* and *Agnello* applied only to *federal* cases. States still were free to apply the exclusionary or not. (Remember, it wasn't until the 1930s that the Court began to apply the Bill of Rights to state criminal proceedings [Chapter 2]). So, the Court would have to decide in future cases whether the Fourteenth Amendment due process clause ("no state shall deny any person of life, liberty, or property without due process of law") applied to state criminal proceedings.

Do unreasonable searches and seizures violate the due process clause of the Fourteenth Amendment? It wasn't until 1949 that the Court took up the question in *Wolf v. Colorado* (1949). In fact, the Court was faced with two questions:

1. Does the Fourteenth Amendment due process clause apply the right against unreasonable searches and seizures to the states at all? and

2. If it does, is the exclusionary rule part of the right?

The Court answered "Yes" to the first question and "No" to the second. In other words, states have to enforce the ban on unreasonable searches and seizures, but the Fourth Amendment leaves it up to the states *how* to enforce it.

Eleven years later, in *Mapp v. Ohio* (1961), the Court changed its answer to the second question in *Wolf* to yes. The circumstances surrounding the decision to reverse itself were unusual, to put it mildly. The case started out and reached the Court as a free speech case. Dollree Mapp was convicted of possession of pornography in Ohio. The question the Supreme Court was asked to review—and which both the briefs and the oral argument were almost entirely devoted to—was whether Ohio's pornography statute violated Mapp's right to free speech. Until the first draft of the opinion circulated among the justices, the only mention of *Wolf* was in three sentences in an **amicus curiae brief** (an argument the Court allows to be submitted by someone—or more likely some interest group—who isn't a party but who has an interest in the case) of the American Civil Liberties Union. In fact, when asked about *Wolf v. Colorado* during oral arguments, Mapp's attorney admitted he'd never heard of the case. Justice Stewart (1983) later recalled:

> I was shocked when Justice [Tom C.] Clark's proposed Court opinion reached my desk. I immediately wrote him a note expressing my surprise and questioning the wisdom of overruling an important doctrine in a case in which the issue was not briefed, argued, or discussed by the state courts, by the parties' counsel, or at our conferences following the oral argument. After my shock subsided, I wrote a brief memorandum concurring in the judgment...and agreeing with Justice Harlan's dissent that the issue was not properly before the Court. The *Mapp* majority, however, stood its ground....The case...provides significant insight into the judicial process and the evolution of law—a first amendment controversy was transformed into perhaps the most important search-and-seizure case in history. (1367)

CASE	*Should the Court Exclude the Evidence?*

Mapp v. Ohio
367 U.S. 643 (1961)

Dollree Mapp was tried and convicted of illegal possession of pornography. Over her objection, the trial court admitted the pornography in evidence against her. On appeal, the Ohio Supreme Court affirmed. The U.S. Supreme Court reversed.

CLARK, J.

FACTS

On May 23, 1957, three Cleveland police officers arrived at Dollree Mapp's house pursuant to information that "a person was hiding out in the home, who was wanted for questioning in connection with a recent bombing, and that there was a large amount of policy paraphernalia being hidden in the home." Miss Mapp and her daughter by a former marriage lived on the top floor of the two-family dwelling. Upon their arrival at that house, the officers knocked on the door and demanded entrance but Mapp, after telephoning her attorney, refused to admit them without a search warrant. They advised their headquarters of the situation and undertook a surveillance of the house.

The officers again sought entrance some three hours later when four or more additional officers arrived on the scene. When Miss Mapp did not come to the door immediately, at least one of the several doors to the house was forcibly opened and the policemen gained admittance. Officer Carl DeLau testified that "we did pry the screen door to gain entrance"; the attorney on the scene testified that a policeman "tried...to kick the door" and then "broke the glass in the door and somebody reached in and opened the door and let them in"; Mapp testified that "The back door was broken."

Meanwhile Miss Mapp's attorney arrived, but the officers, having secured their own entry, and continuing in their defiance of the law, would permit him neither to see Miss Mapp nor to enter the house. It happens that Miss Mapp was halfway down the stairs from the upper floor to the front door when the officers, in this high-handed manner, broke into the hall. She demanded to see the search warrant. A paper, claimed to be a warrant, was held up by one of the officers. She grabbed the "warrant" and placed it in her bosom. A struggle ensued in which the officers recovered the piece of paper as a result of which they handcuffed Mapp because she had been "belligerent" in resisting their official rescue of the "warrant" from her person.

Running roughshod over Mapp, a policeman "grabbed" her, "twisted her hand," and she "yelled and pleaded with him" because "it was hurting." Mapp, in handcuffs, was then forcibly taken upstairs to her bedroom where the officers searched the dresser, a chest of drawers, a closet and some suitcases. They also looked in a photo album and through personal papers belonging to Mapp. The search spread to the rest of the second floor including the child's bedroom, the living room, the kitchen, and a dinette. The basement of the building and a trunk found therein were also searched. The obscene materials for possession of which she was ultimately convicted were discovered in the course of that widespread search.

At the trial no search warrant was produced by the prosecution, nor was the failure to produce one explained or accounted for. At best, "There is, in the record, considerable doubt as to whether there ever was any warrant for the search of defendant's home." The Ohio Supreme Court believed a "reasonable argument" could be made that the conviction should be reversed "because the 'methods' employed to obtain the evidence . . . were such as to 'offend a sense of justice,'" but the court found determinative the fact that the evidence had not been taken "from defendant's person by the use of brutal or offensive physical force against defendant."

OPINION

In 1949, 35 years after *Weeks v. United States* (1914) was announced, this Court, in *Wolf v. Colorado*, . . . for the first time, discussed the effect of the Fourth Amendment upon the States through the operation of the Due Process Clause of the Fourteenth Amendment. . . . The Court decided that the *Weeks* exclusionary rule would not then be imposed upon the States as "an essential ingredient of the right.". . .

The Court in *Wolf* . . . stated that "the contrariety of views of the States" on the adoption of the exclusionary rule . . . was "particularly impressive"; and . . . it could not "brush aside the experience of the States which deem the incidence of such conduct by the police too slight to call for a deterrent remedy . . . by overriding the States' relevant rules of evidence." While in 1949, prior to the *Wolf* case, almost two-thirds of the States were opposed to the use of the exclusionary rule, now . . . more than half . . . have wholly or partly adopted or adhered to the *Weeks* rule. Significantly, among those now following the rule is California which, according to its highest court, was "compelled to reach that conclusion because other remedies have completely failed to secure compliance with the constitutional provisions. . . ."

The second basis elaborated in *Wolf* in support of its failure to enforce the exclusionary doctrine against the States was that "other means of protection" have been afforded "the right of privacy." The experience of California that such other remedies have been worthless and futile is buttressed by the experience of other States. The obvious futility of relegating the Fourth Amendment to the protection of other remedies has, moreover, been recognized by this Court since *Wolf*. . . .

Since the Fourth Amendment's right of privacy has been declared enforceable against the States through the Due Process Clause of the Fourteenth, it is enforceable against them by the same sanction of exclusion as is used against the Federal Government. Were it otherwise, then . . . the assurance against unreasonable federal searches and seizures would be "a form of words," valueless and undeserving of mention in a perpetual charter of inestimable human liberties, so too, without that rule the freedom from state invasions of privacy would be so ephemeral and so neatly severed from its conceptual nexus with the freedom from all brutish means of coercing evidence as not to merit this Court's high regard as a freedom "implicit in the concept of ordered liberty.". . .

There are those who say, as did Justice (then Judge) Cardozo, that under our constitutional exclusionary doctrine "the criminal is to go free because the constable has blundered." In some cases this will undoubtedly be the result. But, "there is another consideration—the imperative of judicial integrity." "The criminal goes free, if he must, but it is the law that sets him free. Nothing can destroy a government more quickly than its failure to observe its own laws, or worse, its disregard of the charter of its own existence. . . ." [As Justice Brandeis, dissenting in *Olmstead v. United States*, 277 U.S. 438 (1928), 485, wrote:]

Our Government is the potent, the omnipresent teacher. For good or for ill, it teaches the whole people by its example. . . . If the Government becomes a lawbreaker, it breeds contempt for law; it invites every man to become a law unto himself; it invites anarchy.

Nor can it lightly be assumed that, as a practical matter, adoption of the exclusionary rule fetters law enforcement. Only last year this Court expressly considered that contention and found that "pragmatic evidence of a sort" to the contrary was not wanting. The Court noted that

the federal courts themselves have operated under the exclusionary rule . . . for almost half a century; yet it has not been suggested either that the Federal Bureau of Investigation has thereby been rendered ineffective, or that the administration of criminal justice in the federal courts has thereby been disrupted. Moreover, the experience of the states is impressive. . . . The movement towards the rule of exclusion has been halting but seemingly inexorable.

. . . Our decision, founded on reason and truth, gives to the individual no more than that which the Constitution guarantees him, to the police officer no less than that to which honest law enforcement is entitled, and, to the courts, that judicial integrity so necessary in the true administration of justice.

REVERSED and REMANDED.

DISSENT

HARLAN, J., joined by FRANKFURTER and WHITTAKER, JJ.

At the heart of the majority's opinion in this case is the following syllogism: (1) the rule excluding in federal criminal trial evidence which is the product of an illegal search and seizure is "part and parcel" of the Fourth Amendment; (2) *Wolf* held that the "privacy" assured against federal action by the Fourth Amendment is also protected against state action by the Fourteenth Amendment; and (3) it is therefore "logically and constitutionally necessary" that the *Weeks* exclusionary rule should also be enforced against the States.

This reasoning ultimately rests on the unsound premise that because *Wolf* carried into the States, as part of "the concept of ordered liberty" embodied in the Fourteenth Amendment, the principle of "privacy" underlying the Fourth Amendment, it must follow that whatever configurations of the Fourth Amendment have been developed in the...federal precedents are likewise to be deemed a part of "ordered liberty," and as such are enforceable against the States. For me, this does not follow at all.... Since there is not the slightest suggestion that Ohio's policy is "affirmatively to sanction...police incursion into privacy" what the Court is now doing is to impose upon the States not only federal substantive standards of "search and seizure" but also the basic federal remedy for violation of those standards. For I think it entirely clear that the Weeks exclusionary rule is but a remedy which, by penalizing past official misconduct, is aimed at deterring such conduct in the future.

I would not impose upon the States this federal exclusionary remedy.

Questions

1. List the reasons the Court gave for overruling *Wolf v. Colorado.* Do you agree?

2. Are Justice Stewart's recollections of any importance? Explain.

3. According to the Court majority, why should Dollree Mapp go free? Because the Cleveland police blundered?

4. What remedies are available to Dollree Mapp besides the exclusion of the evidence? Which would you recommend?

THE REST OF THE STORY

Mapp v. Ohio

April 1, 2000

Telephone conversation with Dollree Mapp:*

SAMAHA: I've heard various stories about how the police got into your house. What really happened?

MAPP: I was washing my hair when the police came to my house. They wanted to come in and I asked them what authority they had. They didn't have a warrant and I wouldn't let them in without one.

SAMAHA: I've heard various stories about the paper you grabbed from the officer. Can you tell me what it was?

MAPP: I'll tell you something about it. There was nothing on it. It was just a blank piece of paper.

SAMAHA: I've heard that after the police came in the house, they handcuffed and dragged you upstairs to your bedroom. Is that true?

MAPP: Of course they dragged me. That's the only way they could get me up those steps.

OFFICER CARL DELAU

May 30, 2000

Letter from Carl Delau:**

Dear Professor Samaha:
I became a member of the Cleveland Police Department on January 1, 1946 after serving nearly five years in the

---

*This conversation I had with Dollree Mapp in April 2000 wasn't recorded. It is based on my notes from the conversation.

**The letter from Captain Delau is essentially the way he wrote it except for some light editing for brevity, clarity, and readability.

Armed Forces (army) and overseas in Europe. I always had interesting assignments with the CPD but my most challenging one started in November 1949 when I was selected to be a member of the Bureau of Special Investigation. This small eight-man unit was headed by a very respected lieutenant, and his assignments came directly from the chief of police. Prior to the establishment of this unit, Cleveland was pretty much open as far as vice was concerned (horse wagering, numbers operations, and other illegal gambling activities). Our unit had citywide jurisdiction, and we reported only to the chief of police.

After putting a severe crimp in illegal horse wagering, we were assigned to work on the numbers racket due to complaints of police payoffs, car bombings, and other violence. When we started our inquiry and gained information on the numbers operation, I had just become a sergeant and I had two detectives working with me. Believe me, we soon became very knowledgeable about how the numbers racket operated, and we soon made many arrests of great importance. During these years and up to 1962 when I was promoted to lieutenant and transferred to another assignment, we got to know all of the operators in the clearinghouse racket and all of their key workers. Dollree Mapp was one of these key workers.

It was during our investigation of the clearinghouse (numbers) racket that we got to know Dollree Mapp. She was a top figure as a pickup person of numbers wagers from the various writers. Our three-man squad arrested her several times and had other conversations with her. You have to have had contact with her to understand her. She was a cunning, daring, audacious person. . . . She was referred to as a "foxy lady."

What led us to her home and arrest on May 23, 1957 was a bombing of the home of Donald King, a well-known clearinghouse figure. Yes, this is the same Donald King, the fight promoter who has made millions. Our three-man squad was responsible for the investigation into this bombing. King had contacted me and would talk only to me; he named the person who he stated was responsible for the bombing. This was a complicated and involved investigation as it involved extortion and payoffs to the city's number one hoodlum (white). A number of numbers figures were arrested and the persons were charged.

It was on a phone call for me to our office that the caller said that a person wanted in connection with the bombing was in this home of Mapp's on Milverton Avenue. We were familiar with this address and location and on arriving on the scene we observed the vehicle of another numbers figure in the drive, one Vergil Ogletree. As of that time, Ogletree did not figure in too strongly in our investigation. D. Mapp resided upstairs in this two-family home, which she did own. Knocking on the side door (the only entrance to the upstairs), Dollree answered from an open window in the landing to the upstairs. After telling her that we desired to speak to Ogletree, she stated that he was not there and that she would not permit us to enter the house. A side screen door was locked.

Knowing her nature and defiance, I did not want to force any entry unless I was armed with a search warrant. With this, I gained all needed information on the home and the reason for entry to the home and went to gain the use of a telephone to call my office and request the assistance in gaining a search warrant. My two partners remained on the scene (more information on the search warrant later in the letter).

A lieutenant (not my Lieutenant Cooney) arrived on the scene with a document. After informing D. Mapp that I had a search warrant and after she refused to open the door, I then forced the screen door by creating a small opening. We then met D. Mapp on this stair landing.

D. Mapp was still very hostile, which forced me to handcuff her to a uniform officer who had arrived on the scene. We then had her accompany us while we searched most of her upstairs home. It was at this time we found the pornographic literature. V. Ogletree was found in the first floor home where D. Mapp told him to hide and much policy evidence was found in the basement. The policy material was of a policy house operated by V. Ogletree. Both Mapp and Ogletree were placed under arrest, and the evidence was confiscated.

After further investigation, the next day, the prosecutor was consulted, at which time, Mapp was charged with a city ordinance of possession of policy slips. At a later date, her case for possession of the pornographic material was presented to the grand jury, and she was indicted for the possession of this material, a felony. V. Ogletree was released as we could not connect him to the policy paraphernalia, and he was not involved in the bombing of King's home.

Now, I will touch on several interesting highlights of the entire incident. Dollree Mapp after being indicted did plead guilty to the charge, and to our way of thinking and also to hers, she should have been placed on probation. The judge after reading the probation report did sentence her to the state's women's reformatory for 1 to 7 years. With this sentence, her attorney then fought to have her guilty plea withdrawn, which the judge granted.

During the trial, which was rather brief, our state's prosecutor was a woman who did a very commendable job. In fact, our county prosecutor, John T. Corrigan, was just about the best person anyone could find for this position, honest and fearless. The jury did not take much time to come up with a guilty verdict. . . . During the trial, when the jury viewed the presented evidence on pornography, the jury as a whole did not enjoy it—therefore the quick verdict.*

---

*Captain Delau is referring to how seriously pornography was regarded then compared with today.

Next, the search warrant. As you may have read, no search warrant was presented during the trial. The defense on several occasions brought up the subject of the search warrant, but on objection by the prosecutor, the objection was overruled. Now, this part may interest you as after the completion of the case, this information was made known. The search warrant was faulty probably due to the lack of knowledge of the lieutenant who obtained same and delivered it to me on the scene. I have admitted that when I received the document at the scene, I did not study it in its entirety. It was after we arrived at the police headquarters, I checked out the document and found the mistake. When the prosecutor was informed of this fact, he said no worry, we will proceed as if no warrant was issued.*

The question could be asked, why a faulty search warrant? Were not the police officers trained? Probably due to not having much need to obtain search warrants, everyone got a little rusty. In our small unit, we often obtained search warrants on complicated cases, and we were aware of what was needed to obtain a search warrant. In our state codebook of regulations it did spell out very clearly what was needed and how to obtain a search warrant.

Of interest, the Ohio Supreme Court did uphold the conviction and there was no question relative to the confiscation and the presentation of the evidence. They questioned the pornography statute.

What happened next you probably are well aware of. With the assistance of the ACLU, Mapp's attorney Kearns took the appeal to the U.S. Supreme Court. Gertrude Bauer Mahon argued the case for the state of Ohio, and it was reported that she had several heated exchanges with Justice F. Frankfurter. It was known that the appeal to this court was mostly on the merits of the state's obscenity statute. But, it was the feeling that the liberals of the U.S. court were waiting for a case similar to the Mapp case on the search issue.

Where is Dollree Mapp at present? Last I heard she was still in the vicinity of New York City. Why she left for New York no one knew, but in New York she did not become a law-abiding citizen. The way I recall it was that she was arrested once and while awaiting trail, she was arrested the second time. Later the first case was thrown out of court on an illegal search, but she was convicted on the second arrest.** Has the Mapp decision harmed police enforcement? A very definite Yes! Some law enforcement officers say it did not, and I have heard high-ranking officers say it has not, but I can only say that they have not performed police duties out in the street and prepared gambling cases for court.

Before Mapp and without search warrants, we at times forced doors but we always found violations that we knew were at that location. After Mapp, after much surveillance on a location, obtaining the needed information for a search warrant, then going back to the prosecutor's office for the affidavit, to the clerk's office for the warrant, then to a judge for his signature, we then went back out into the street, hoping that the clearing office was still at the location where it had been previously observed. There is so much room for leaks to the violators in the numbers racket. Prior to Mapp, we forced a few doors, but never did we fail to find a good-sized gambling operation. After Mapp and armed with a search warrant, often we failed to find the operation that had been at the address in question. Were there leaks, or was the time involved in gaining the search warrant working against the police?

We were a well-trained, innovative, aggressive squad, working to curtail the numbers racket to which we caused much harm....

> Respectfully,
> Carl Delau

---

*An Ohio case ruled that entries without warrants were legal.

**Captain Delau included a clipping from the *New York Daily News*, February 19, 1970, with the headline "Court Heroine from '61 Held in Big Dope Raid." The lead sentence reads, "A 42-year-old Queens woman who won a historic Court case in 1961 prohibiting the use of illegally seized evidence in state criminal cases yesterday was arrested for alleged possession of $800,000 worth of heroin."

Justifications

To put it mildly, the exclusionary rule is controversial. Critics say it sets criminals free on "technicalities." Supporters reply, these "technicalities" are rights our ancestors fought and died for. Why do we throw good evidence out of court? The U.S. Supreme Court has relied on three justifications:

1. *Constitutional right.* It's part of the constitutional rights *against* unreasonable seizure and coerced confessions and the rights to a lawyer and due process of law.

2. *Judicial integrity.* It preserves the honor and honesty of the courts.

3. *Deterrence.* It prevents officers from breaking the law.

The **constitutional right justification** stems from an ancient legal saying, "There's no right without a remedy" (Stewart 1983, 1380–1383). One commentator summed it up with this great image: "It's like one hand clapping" (Uviller 1988). In *Weeks v. United States* (1914), the case that created the exclusionary rule for the federal system, U.S. Supreme Court Justice William Rufus Day put it this way:

> If letters and private documents can...be seized and held and used in evidence against a citizen accused of an offense, the protection of the Fourth Amendment declaring his right to be secure against such searches and seizures is of no value, and...may as well be stricken from the Constitution. (393)

The **judicial integrity justification** maintains that the honor and honesty of courts forbid them to participate in unconstitutional conduct. Dissenting in *Olmstead v. U.S.* (1928), a famous case upholding the constitutionality of wiretapping decided in 1928 (Chapter 7), Justice Oliver Wendell Holmes spoke to the dilemma of throwing out good evidence because it was obtained by bad official behavior:

> We must consider two objects of desire, both of which we cannot have, and make up our minds which to choose. It is desirable that criminals should be detected, and to that end that all available evidence should be used. It also is desirable that the Government should not itself foster and pay for other crimes, when they are the means by which the evidence is to be obtained.... For my part, I think it is less evil that some criminals should escape than that the Government should play an ignoble part. (470)

The **deterrence justification** says throwing out good evidence because it was obtained illegally sends a strong message to law enforcement. Here's how the highly distinguished Justice Potter Stewart (who probably knew more about the Fourth Amendment than any other U.S. Supreme Court justice in our history) summed up the deterrence justification:

> The rule is calculated to prevent, not to repair. Its purpose is to deter—to compel respect for the constitutional guaranty in the only effective available way—by removing the incentive to disregard it.

Elkins v. U.S. 1960, 217

Since the 1980s, the Court has relied on deterrence as the only justification for excluding valid evidence. The Court has adopted another form of its old friend the balancing test in applying the deterrence justification. This form of the test weighs the **social cost of excluding "good" evidence**—namely, setting criminals free—against the deterrent effect that excluding good evidence might have on the illegal conduct of law enforcement officers. If the social costs outweigh the deterrent effect, then the evidence comes in. The constitutional significance of letting illegally seized evidence into court because the social cost of keeping it out is too high is that the exclusionary rule is not a constitutional right. (See "Social Costs and Deterrent Effects" later for more discussion.) According to the U.S. Supreme Court in *United States v. Leon* (1984; excerpted later in this section, on p. 367), excluding evidence is not a constitutional right, it's a **prophylactic rule**—a protective procedure against violations of constitutional rights (Schroeder 1981, 1378–1386).

The exclusionary rule brings into bold relief the tension between ends and means—namely, between result and process in the law of criminal procedure. By throwing out good evidence because of bad practices, the rule puts the search for truth second to fair procedures. No one has put the case for the exclusionary rule better than Associate Justice Louis D. Brandeis in his famous dissent in *Olmstead v. U.S.* (1928):

> Decency, security, and liberty alike demand that government officials shall be subjected to the same rules of conduct that are commands to the citizen. In a government of laws, existence of the government will be imperiled if it fails to observe the law scrupulously. Our government is the potent, the omnipresent teacher. For good or for ill, it teaches the whole people by its example. Crime is contagious. If the government becomes a lawbreaker, it breeds contempt for law; it invites every man to become a law unto himself; it invites anarchy. To declare that in the administration of the criminal law the end justifies the means—to declare that the government may commit crimes in order to secure the conviction of a private criminal—would bring terrible retribution. Against that pernicious doctrine this court should resolutely set its face. (468)

Scope

The social cost of freeing guilty people and of undermining the prosecution's case by keeping good evidence out of court has led the U.S. Supreme Court to limit the rule to cases the Court believes are most likely to deter police misconduct. The Court has decided that proceedings outside the trial of the defendant don't deter police misconduct, and it also has decided that even major parts of the trial itself have no deterrent effect on police misconduct. The Court has created numerous exceptions to the exclusionary rule to cover cases that it believes don't deter police misconduct. We'll discuss five of the major exceptions:

1. Collateral use
2. Cross-examination
3. Attenuation of the taint of unconstitutional official conduct
4. Independent source
5. Inevitable discovery

Collateral Use

The **collateral use exception** allows the use of illegally obtained evidence in nontrial proceedings (*U.S. v. Calandra* 1974). What proceedings does this include? The general answer is proceedings related to the case but not the trial of it. (The term **collateral proceedings** means proceedings "off to the side" of the main case.) Specifically, these include bail hearings (Chapter 12); preliminary hearings (Chapter 12); grand jury proceedings (Chapter 12); and some kinds of habeas corpus proceedings (Chapter 14). So, prosecutors can present illegally obtained evidence to deny defendants bail; get grand juries to indict defendants; and get judges in preliminary hearings to send cases on for trial.

Cross-Examination

The exclusionary rule applies only to one part (an extremely important part) of one very important criminal proceeding: the government's *case-in-chief* in the criminal trial. (**Case-in-chief** means the part of the trial where the government presents its evidence to prove the defendants' guilt.) The case-in-chief doesn't include cross-examination of defense witnesses. In *Walder v. United States* (1954), Walder was tried for purchasing and possessing heroin. During direct examination, Walder denied he'd ever bought or possessed heroin. The government then introduced heroin capsules seized during an illegal search to prove to the jury he was a liar. The trial court admitted the capsules but cautioned the jury not to use the heroin capsules to prove Walder's guilt, only to **impeach** (undermine the believability of) his testimony. The U.S. Supreme Court ruled that the exclusionary rule didn't apply:

> It is one thing to say that the Government cannot make an affirmative use of evidence unlawfully obtained. It is quite another to say that the defendant can turn the illegal method by which evidence in the Government's possession was obtained to his own advantage, and provide himself with a shield against contradiction of his untruths. Such an extension of the *Weeks* doctrine would be a perversion of the Fourth Amendment. (65)

Attenuation

The basic idea behind the fruit-of-the-poisonous-tree doctrine is that the government shouldn't be in a *better* position after (than before) it breaks the law. But, what if the government's position is *worse*? That's where the three complicated exceptions—attenuation, independent source, and inevitable discovery—come in. As you read and try to understand these exceptions, keep in mind they're exceptions to the poisonous-tree doctrine. So, their effect is to let more evidence into court. (Remember the effect of the doctrine is to keep evidence out of court). Maybe it'll help you to think of the exceptions as antidotes to (remedies to counteract) the poison of illegal government actions. As the U.S. Supreme Court said, not all evidence is "'fruit of the poisonous tree' simply because it would not have come to light but for the illegal actions of the police" (*Wong Sun v. U.S.* 1963, 488).

The noun "attenuation" (according to the dictionary) means "thinning, weakening, or emaciation." The **attenuation exception** says the illegally obtained evidence can come in if the poisonous connection between illegal police actions and the evidence they illegally got from their actions weakens (attenuates) enough. The U.S. Supreme Court hasn't written a bright-line attenuation rule. Instead, each case has to be decided on its own facts according to the totality of circumstances. One circumstance is the closeness in time between the poisonous tree (illegal government act) and getting its fruit (evidence). For example, in *Wong Sun v. U.S.* (1963, 491) federal narcotics officers in San Francisco illegally broke into James Wah Toy's home and chased him down the hall into his bedroom. Agent Wong pulled his gun, illegally arrested Toy, and handcuffed him. Toy then told the officers Johnny Yee sold him heroin. The officers immediately went to Yee's home. Yee admitted he had heroin and gave it to the officers. The Court ruled that the time between the illegal arrest and getting the heroin from Yee was too close to dissipate the poison of the arrest.

In the same case, the same narcotics officers illegally arrested another man by the name of Wong Sun. A few days later, after Wong Sun was charged and released on bail, he *voluntarily* went back to the Narcotics Bureau, where he told detectives he'd delivered heroin to Johnny Yee and smoked it with him. In his case, the U.S. Supreme Court decided "the connection between the arrest and the statement had become so attenuated as to dissipate the taint."

Another circumstance that might attenuate the poison enough to let the evidence in is an "intervening independent act of free will" after the illegal act. Let's go back to James Wah Toy in his bedroom after the illegal arrest. The government argued that when Toy told the officers that Yee sold him heroin, he did it of his own free will. But the Court rejected the argument, not because an independent act of free will *can't* attenuate the poison but because it didn't fit the facts of this case. According to the Court:

> Six or seven officers had broken the door and followed on Toy's heels into the bedroom where his wife and child were sleeping. He had been almost immediately handcuffed and arrested. Under such circumstances it is unreasonable to infer that Toy's response was sufficiently an act of free will to purge the primary taint of the unlawful invasion.
>
> *Wong Sun v. U.S.* 1963, 416–417

Independent Source

What if police officers violate the Constitution looking for evidence and, then, in a totally separate action, lawfully get the same evidence? It's admissible under the **independent source exception.** For example, in *U.S. v. Moscatiello* (1985), federal agents illegally entered a South Boston warehouse where they saw marijuana in plain view. They left the warehouse without touching the marijuana and kept the warehouse under surveillance while they went to get a search warrant. In applying for the warrant, the officers didn't build their probable cause on anything they'd learned during the unlawful entry of the warehouse. In ruling the marijuana was admissible as evidence, the U.S. Circuit Court of Appeals wrote:

> We can be absolutely certain that the warrantless entry in no way contributed in the slightest either to the issuance of a warrant or to the discovery of the evidence during the lawful search that occurred pursuant to the warrant. This is as clear a case as can be imagined where the discovery of the contraband in plain view was totally irrelevant to the later securing of a warrant and the successful search that ensued. As there was no causal link whatever between the illegal entry and the discovery of the challenged evidence, we find no error in the court's refusal to suppress.
>
> *U.S. v. Moscatiello* 1985, 603

In upholding the U.S. Court of Appeals, the U.S. Supreme Court wrote:

> While the government should not profit from its illegal activity, neither should it be placed in a worse position than it would otherwise have occupied. So long as a later, lawful seizure is genuinely independent of an earlier, tainted [one] . . . there is no reason why the independent source doctrine should not apply. . . .
>
> *Murray v. U.S.* 1988, 542–543

So, in a nutshell the independent source exception says, even if officers break the law, unless their law-breaking *causes* the seizure of evidence, the evidence is admissible in court.

Inevitable Discovery

But, what if official law-breaking *is* the cause of getting the evidence? Is the evidence banned from use? Not if officers, acting within the Constitution, would eventually find it anyway. And, this is the nub of the **inevitable discovery exception.** In *Nix v. Williams* (1984), Robert Williams was suspected of brutally murdering 10-year-old Pamela Powers. During an illegal police interrogation, Williams led police officers to the place where he hid the body. At the same time, a separate search party was combing the same area near where some of Pamela's clothing had been found. The search party took a break from the search only 2½ miles from where Williams led the officers to the body; the location was within the area they planned to search.

So, two searches were converging on the dead body. One search was being lawfully conducted by a search party. The other was the fruit of the poisonous illegal interrogation. The fruit-of-the-poisonous-tree search was the discovery of the body during the legal search party's break. Should the evidence be admitted? Yes, said the U.S. Supreme Court. Why? Because, the body would've been discovered anyway by the legal search party. Emphasizing the purpose of the fruit-of-the-poisonous-tree doctrine, and why the inevitable discovery exception was consistent with that purpose, the Court wrote:

> Exclusion of evidence that would inevitably have been discovered would . . . put the government in a worse position, because the police would have obtained that evidence if no misconduct had taken place. [This] rationale . . . justifies our adoption of the . . . inevitable discovery exception to the exclusionary rule. (444)

Illegally Seized (Arrested) Persons

The fruit of poisonous illegal government actions is usually either physical evidence or a confession. What if a *person* is the "fruit" of an illegal arrest? Does the fruit-of-the-poisonous-tree doctrine apply? How do we "suppress" or "exclude" a person? Specifically, these questions boil down to whether courts can (or should) dismiss a case against individuals who are in court because the police illegally arrested them. The answer given by the U.S. Supreme Court in *Ker v. Illinois* (1886) was, "No" (cited in *Frisbie v. Collins* 1952). (Based on my own survey of state cases, the answer in the 1800s was a loud "No!")

Why aren't illegally arrested persons fruit of a poisonous arrest? Because, as my research in the state cases made clear, courts historically have closed their eyes to how defendants got to court; they have opened them only when court proceedings began. The basic idea was (and still is) *how* defendants got into court was *police* business, not *court* business. The business of courts is to see to it that defendants get a fair trial. The exclusionary rule bans courts from admitting illegally seized evidence to prove defendants' guilt at trial, but there's no parallel rule that bans courts from claiming jurisdiction (power) over illegally seized persons; so, they can be tried. The practice of trying defendants who were brought to court by means of illegal seizures is controversial. The U.S. Supreme Court hasn't ruled on the point since *Frisbie v. Collins* in 1952, but the U.S. Second Circuit Court of Appeals dealt with the problem in *Matta-Ballesteros v. Henman* (1990).

Matta-Ballesteros v. Henman,
Warden U.S. Penitentiary, Marion, Indiana
896 F.2d 255 (Cal. Dist. 7 1990)

Juan Ramon Matta-Ballesteros ("Matta") petitions this Court by writ of habeas corpus claiming the United States illegally kidnapped him from his home in Honduras and tortured him before transporting him to the United States to face trial on pending criminal charges. Based on these allegations, Matta claims the United States violated the Honduran Constitution, international law, and the due process clause of the U.S. Constitution and as a result, the United States is without personal jurisdiction over him. The U.S. District Court denied his petition. Matta petitioned the Seventh Circuit U.S. Court of Appeals to remand the case to the district court for an evidentiary hearing. The Court of Appeals affirmed the U.S. District Court.

FLAUM, J.

FACTS

In 1971, Matta escaped from the United States Prison Camp at Eglin Air Force Base in Florida and fled to Honduras. He is a Honduran citizen and because Honduras does not extradite its own citizens, he believed he had found a safe haven from the reach of United States law enforcement officials. While he was in the Honduras, he allegedly became heavily involved in the narcotics trade and now faces criminal charges in the federal district courts of Arizona, Central California, and Southern California. At the time he filed the writ, he was also under indictment in the Northern District of Florida for escape pursuant to 18 U.S.C. § 751(a). He has since been convicted of that crime and sentenced to three years imprisonment.

At about 6:00 A.M. on the morning of April 5, 1988, Matta, accompanied by his bodyguards, arrived at his home in Tegucigalpa, Honduras. Upon his arrival, Matta was surrounded by armed members of the Honduran Special Troops or "Cobras," who were accompanied by at least four United States Marshals. He was arrested and handcuffed, allegedly at the direction of the United States Marshals. A black hood was placed over his head and he was pushed onto the floor of a car driven by the United States Marshals.

A United States Marshal immediately drove him to a United States Air Force base approximately an hour-and-a-half away. During the ride, Matta claims he was severely beaten and burned with a "stun gun" at the direction of the United States Marshals. (The stun gun or "Taser" is a non-lethal device commonly used to subdue individuals resisting arrest. It sends an electric pulse through the body of the victim causing immobilization, disorientation, loss of balance, and weakness. It leaves few, if any, marks on the body of the victim.) Once he arrived at the airport, Matta was flown to the United States. He claims that during this flight, he was once again beaten and shocked about the body, including on his testicles and feet, again by United States Marshals.

Upon his arrival in the United States, Matta was immediately transferred to Marion Penitentiary. Approximately 24 hours had passed from the time of his apprehension. Matta was subsequently examined by a physician who found abrasions on his head, face, scalp, neck, arms, feet, and penis, as well as blistering on his back. According to the examining physician, these injuries were consistent with those which could have been caused by a stun gun.

Based on these allegations, Matta filed a writ of habeas corpus in the Southern District of Illinois claiming the United States had acted in violation of the Honduran Constitution, international law, and the United States Constitution. He demanded his release back to Honduras on the basis the United States was without jurisdiction to prosecute him as a result of the alleged due process violations.

At the time he filed the writ, Matta faced indictment in the Northern District of Florida for escape from the United States Prison Camp at Eglin Air Force Base in 1971, along with indictments on various narcotics charges in the central and southern districts of California, and the district of Arizona. After filing the writ, he sought a preliminary injunction to prevent the government from transferring him from Marion to face prosecution in these districts. Matta did not face charges anywhere within the jurisdiction of the district court where he brought his petition. He was simply being held in Marion Penitentiary pending transfer to jurisdictions where he did face charges. The preliminary injunction was denied by the district court....

After denying the preliminary injunction, the district court ordered an expanded record from the parties, including affidavits from the petitioner and any occurrence witnesses. In addition to other documents, Matta filed affidavits from his bodyguards who were with him at the time of his arrest confirming his allegations. The government filed affidavits by various U.S. Marshals denying most of Matta's allegations, especially those concerning torture. The United States contended that the Honduran government, and not the United States, arrested Matta and was responsible for any mistreatment. Based on this expanded record, the district court found that Matta's claims failed as a matter of law, holding that even if the facts were as Matta alleged, he was not entitled to the relief he sought. The court, therefore, denied Matta's request for discovery and an evidentiary hearing, ruling on the pleadings and affidavits alone, much in the manner of a summary judgment. Since the district court's denial of the writ, Matta has been transferred to a prison in Florida, arraigned, tried, and convicted of escape from federal custody.

OPINION

...Matta...contends his abduction violated the fifth amendment due process clause. For the past 100 years, the Supreme Court has consistently held that the manner in which a defendant is brought to trial does not affect the ability of the government to try him. The *Ker-Frisbie* doctrine, as this rule has come to be known, states that "the power of a court to try a person for a crime is not impaired by the fact that he has been brought within the court's jurisdiction by reason of a 'forcible abduction.'" While notions of due process have been expanded since *Frisbie*, the Supreme Court has consistently reaffirmed the *Ker-Frisbie* doctrine. In *U.S. v. Crews*, the Court recognized that "[Crews] himself is not a suppressible 'fruit' and the illegality of his detention cannot deprive the Government of the opportunity to prove his guilt...." It is, therefore, inadequate for Matta to allege, without more, that the arrest was illegal.

To create a colorable argument in the face of this rule, Matta relies on an "exception" to the *Ker-Frisbie* doctrine carved out by the Second Circuit. Prior to trial for narcotics offences, Toscanino challenged the ability of the district court to try him, contending his presence had been illegally obtained through torture and kidnapping by the United States. Toscanino offered to prove in support of his motion that he and his pregnant wife had been lured from his home in Montevideo, Uruguay to a deserted area. There, Toscanino claimed, he was abducted by being knocked unconscious with a gun, placed into a car, bound and blindfolded and driven across the border to Brasilia where he was incessantly tortured and interrogated for seventeen days. After this ordeal Toscanino was drugged and placed on an American commercial flight. Once he arrived in the United States, he was taken into custody by waiting United States law enforcement officials.

Faced with these allegations, the Second Circuit held, "we view due process as now requiring a court to divest itself of jurisdiction over the person of a defendant where it has been acquired as the result of the government's delib-

erate, unnecessary and unreasonable invasion of the accused's constitutional rights." In so holding, that court relied on *Rochin v. California*** where the Supreme Court applied the due process clause, to "the whole course of the proceedings in order to ascertain whether they offend those canons of decency and fairness which express the notions of justice of English-speaking peoples even toward those charged with the most heinous offences."

...[Later, the Second Circuit narrowed *Toscanino* to apply only] where the defendant could prove "torture, brutality, and similar outrageous conduct."...The conduct must "shock the conscience" before a violation can occur. Matta asserts that he falls under [the torture and shock the conscience rule].

...The due process clause has been held to "protect a pre-trial detainee from the use of excessive force that amounts to punishment." Under this holding, if Matta could prove he was punished as a pre-trial detainee, then he might be entitled to some relief under the due process clause (although not necessarily the divestiture of jurisdiction by the United States). Matta, however, does not allege punishment during his pre-trial detention at Marion prison. Instead, he claims that he was tortured during the course of his arrest.... The remedy, however, for violations of the due process clause during pre-trial detention is not the divestiture of jurisdiction, but rather an injunction or money damages.

Claims such as Matta's involving constitutional violations during arrest, however, are properly analyzed under the fourth amendment rather than the fifth amendment.** Matta's requested relief, however, is not supported by the fourth amendment. His claim is essentially an exclusionary rule for the body of the defendant. Exclusionary rules are simply means of enforcing the provisions of the constitution. "The primary justification for the exclusionary rule then is the deterrence of police conduct that violates Fourth Amendment rights." In addition, the imperative of maintaining judicial integrity may play some role in the exclusionary rule calculus. We believe that neither rationale supports the application of the exclusionary rule to this case.

There are several reasons why the deterrence rationale fails to support the application of the exclusionary rule to the present case. First, the Supreme Court has explicitly rejected the use of the deterrence rationale in this situation. In *United States v. Crews*, the Court held:

The exclusionary principle...delimits what proof the Government may offer against the accused at trial,

---

*Chapter 2.

**See *Graham v. Connor*, Chapter 5, p. 181.

closing the courtroom door to evidence secured by official lawlessness. Respondent is not himself a suppressible "fruit," and the illegality of his detention cannot deprive the Government of the opportunity to prove guilt through the introduction of evidence wholly untainted by the police misconduct.

This decision is based on the Court's opinion that the deterrent effect of excluding the body of the defendant is not sufficient to warrant this extreme measure: "so drastic a step might advance marginally some of the ends served by exclusionary rules, but it would also increase to an intolerable degree interference with the public interest in having the guilty brought to book."

In addition, there are other means of deterring police misconduct in cases such as this that are less intrusive than a constitutionally based exclusionary rule. For example, Matta could file a *Bivens* action* alleging violation of his due process rights. Alternatively he could ask that the case be dismissed for prosecutorial misconduct.... Moreover, complaints from foreign nations of violations of international law as well as the loss of international standing provide an additional deterrent effect. We believe, that where the interference with the judicial process is so severe and where other means of deterrence are already in place, the additional deterrence created by the exclusionary rule is not enough to justify its use.

In *Stone*, the Court considered the judicial integrity rationale for the exclusionary rule. The Court stated that the imperative of judicial integrity plays a limited role, holding that judicial integrity itself is not enough to mandate a retreat "from the proposition that judicial proceedings need not abate when the defendant's person is unconstitutionally seized." In addition, reliance on the judicial integrity rationale has become suspect in recent years. In *Leon*, the Court held that "the question of whether the use of illegally obtained evidence in judicial proceedings represents judicial participation in a Fourth Amendment violation and offends the integrity of the courts is essentially the same as the inquiry into whether exclusion would serve a deterrence purpose...." Therefore, analysis of the judicial integrity rationale separate from the deterrence rationale may not be warranted. Moreover, judicial integrity can be protected through motions for prosecutorial misconduct....

While we do not condone government misconduct such as Matta alleges, we cannot create an exclusionary rule for the person of the defendant in light of our analysis and in the face of repeated re-affirmation by the Supreme Court that no such rule exists. The Court has rejected both the deterrence and the judicial integrity rationales for the exclusionary rule applied to this context. We therefore conclude that *Toscanino*, at least as far as it creates an exclusionary rule, no longer retains vitality and therefore decline to adopt it as the law of this circuit.

CONCURRING OPINION

WILL, J.

It is conceivable to me that, in the words of Justice Rehnquist, there may be cases "in which the conduct of law enforcement agents is so outrageous that due process principles would absolutely bar the government from invoking judicial process to obtain a conviction." This court has previously expressed skepticism about whether the government would ever, by outrageous conduct, surrender its authority to prosecute as a matter of due process. But we have never foreclosed that possibility—for entrapment cases, excessive force cases, or any other kind of case—and I see no reason to reject *Toscanino* and thereby foreclose it for future cases by our decision today.

I have no doubt that judges will disagree about the level of outrageousness, if any, that it should take to bar judicial process. But the simple fact of disagreement does not make the determination of what "outrageous" conduct would consist of somehow judicially more unmanageable or subjective than, for instance, the balancing that goes into distinguishing a reasonable from an unreasonable search or even guilt from innocence, and I would reserve the possibility that some day we may, given the facts, want the option of attempting that determination.

Questions

1. Summarize the illegal and other force used to bring Matta from Honduras to the United States.

2. Summarize the reasons the court gives for denying Matta's writ of habeas corpus.

3. Do you agree that how Matta got to court doesn't matter? Defend your answer with the reasoning in the case.

4. Should the amount of violence used to arrest and bring back Matta matter? Why? Why not? Back up your answer with reasoning from the majority and minority opinions.

---

*Chapter 11, p. 396.

The Reasonable Good-Faith Exception

The **reasonable good-faith exception** allows the government to use evidence obtained from searches based on unlawful search warrants if officers honestly and reasonably believed they were lawful. Although the good-faith exception is narrow, when the U.S. Supreme Court created it in *United States v. Leon* (1984) a firestorm of controversy broke out. Civil libertarians spun the exception to mean it would strangle the Fourth Amendment and blow a hole in the wall against government invasion of individual privacy. Law enforcement interest groups spun the exception just as much to mean the Court had finally taken the handcuffs off the police so that public safety would be the winner. But, when we slow down the spin so we can get a better look at reality, we see the reality hasn't changed much. The number of search warrants hasn't changed, and number of cases in which judges keep illegally seized evidence out of court hasn't changed either (Uchida and Bynum 1991, 1035). Keep this reality in mind as you read *United States v. Leon*, the case that created the good-faith exception (Ashdown 1983; Kamisar 1984; Schlag 1982).

| CASE | *Did They Act in Good Faith?* |

United States v. Leon
468 U.S. 897 (1984)

Police officers obtained a search warrant that led to the seizure of large quantities of methaqualone, heroin, and other evidence. Alberto Leon, "Patsy" Stewart, Ricardo del Castillo, and Armando Sanchez were indicted and moved to suppress the drugs and other evidence. The U.S. District Court granted the motion to suppress. The U.S. Court of Appeals affirmed. The U.S. Supreme Court granted certiorari and reversed.

WHITE, J, joined by BURGER, CJ., and BLACKMUN, POWELL, REHNQUIST, and O'CONNOR, JJ.

FACTS

In August 1981, a confidential informant of unproven reliability informed an officer of the Burbank Police Department that two persons known to him as "Armando" and "Patsy" were selling large quantities of cocaine and methaqualone from their residence at 620 Price Drive in Burbank, Cal. The informant also indicated that he'd witnessed a sale of methaqualone by "Patsy" at the residence approximately five months earlier and had observed at that time a shoebox containing a large amount of cash that belonged to "Patsy." He further declared that "Armando" and "Patsy" generally kept only small quantities of drugs at

their residence and stored the rest at another location in Burbank.

On the basis of this information, the Burbank police initiated an extensive investigation focusing first on the Price Drive residence and later on two other residences as well. Cars parked at the Price Drive residence were determined to belong to Armando Sanchez, who had previously been arrested for possession of marihuana, and Patsy Stewart, who had no criminal record. During the course of the investigation, officers observed an automobile belonging to Ricardo Del Castillo (who had previously been arrested for possession of 50 pounds of marihuana) arrive at the Price Drive residence. The driver of that car entered the house, exited shortly thereafter carrying a small paper sack, and drove away.

A check of Del Castillo's probation records led the officers to Alberto Leon, whose telephone number Del Castillo had listed as his employer's. Leon had been arrested in 1980 on drug charges, and a companion had informed the police at that time that Leon was heavily involved in the importation of drugs into this country. Before the current investigation began, the Burbank officers had learned that an informant had told a Glendale police officer Leon stored a large quantity of methaqualone at his residence in Glendale. During the course of this investigation, the Burbank officers learned that Leon was living at 716 South Sunset Canyon in Burbank.

Subsequently, the officers observed several persons, at least one of whom had prior drug involvement, arriving at the Price Drive residence and leaving with small packages; observed a variety of other material activity at the two residences as well as at a condominium at 7902 Via Magdalena; and witnessed a variety of relevant activity involving respondents' automobiles. The officers also observed Sanchez and Stewart board separate flights for Miami.

The pair later returned to Los Angeles together, consented to a search of their luggage that revealed only a small amount of marihuana, and left the airport. Based on these and other observations summarized in the affidavit, Officer Cyril Rombach of the Burbank Police Department, an experienced and well-trained narcotics investigator, prepared an application for a warrant to search 620 Price Drive, 716 South Sunset Canyon, 7902 Via Magdalena, and automobiles registered to each of the respondents for an extensive list of items believed to be related to respondents' drug-trafficking activities. Officer Rombach's extensive application was reviewed by several Deputy District Attorneys.

A facially valid search warrant* was issued in September 1981 by a State Superior Court Judge. The ensuing searches produced large quantities of drugs at the Via Magdalena and Sunset Canyon addresses and a small quantity at the Price Drive residence. Other evidence was discovered at each of the residences and in Stewart's and Del Castillo's automobiles.

Alberto Leon, "Patsy" Stewart, Ricardo del Castillo, and Armando Sanchez were indicted by a grand jury in the District Court for the Central District of California and charged with conspiracy to possess and distribute cocaine and a variety of substantive counts. They then filed motions to suppress the evidence seized pursuant to the warrant. The District Court held an evidentiary hearing and, while recognizing the case was close, granted the motions to suppress. It concluded that the affidavit was insufficient to establish probable cause.... The judge said:

I just cannot find this warrant sufficient for a showing of probable cause. There is no question of the reliability and credibility of the informant as not being established. Some details given tended to corroborate, maybe, the reliability of [the informant's] information about the previous transaction, but if it is not a stale transaction, it comes awfully close to it; and all the other material I think is as consistent with innocence as it is with guilt. So I just do not think this affidavit can withstand the test. I find, then, that there is no probable cause in this case for the issuance of the search warrant....

---

*Meaning the warrant looked as if it were legal.

In response to a request from the Government, the court made clear that Officer Rombach had acted in good faith, but it rejected the Government's suggestion that the Fourth Amendment exclusionary rule should not apply where evidence is seized in reasonable, good-faith reliance on a search warrant. [According to the judge:]

On the issue of good faith, obviously that is not the law of the Circuit, and I am not going to apply that law. I will say certainly in my view, there is not any question about good faith. [Officer Rombach] went to a Superior Court judge and got a warrant; obviously laid a meticulous trail. Had surveilled for a long period of time, and I believe his testimony—and I think he said he consulted with three Deputy District Attorneys before proceeding himself, and I certainly have no doubt about the fact that that is true.

The District Court denied the Government's motion for reconsideration, and a divided panel of the Court of Appeals for the Ninth Circuit affirmed....

OPINION

The Government's petition for certiorari... presented only the question "whether the Fourth Amendment exclusionary rule should be modified so as not to bar the admission of evidence seized in reasonable, good-faith reliance on a search warrant that is subsequently held to be defective." We granted certiorari to consider the propriety of such a modification....We have concluded that, in the Fourth Amendment context, the exclusionary rule can be modified somewhat without jeopardizing its ability to perform its intended functions....

...The Fourth Amendment contains no provision expressly precluding the use of evidence obtained in violation of its commands, and an examination of its origin and purposes makes clear that the use of fruits of a past unlawful search or seizure "works no new Fourth Amendment wrong." The wrong condemned by the Amendment is "fully accomplished" by the unlawful search or seizure itself, and the exclusionary rule is neither intended nor able to "cure the invasion of the defendant's rights which he has already suffered." The rule thus operates as "a judicially created remedy designed to safeguard Fourth Amendment rights generally through its deterrent effect, rather than a personal constitutional right of the party aggrieved."

Whether the exclusionary sanction is appropriately imposed in a particular case, our decisions make clear, is "an issue separate from the question whether the Fourth Amendment rights of the party seeking to invoke the rule were violated by police conduct." Only the former question is currently before us, and it must be resolved by weighing the costs and benefits of preventing the use in the prosecution's case in chief of inherently trustworthy tangible evidence obtained in reliance on a search warrant issued by a detached and neutral magistrate that ultimately is found to be defective.

The substantial social costs exacted by the exclusionary rule for the vindication of Fourth Amendment rights have long been a source of concern. "Our cases have consistently recognized that unbending application of the exclusionary sanction to enforce ideals of governmental rectitude would impede unacceptably the truth-finding functions of judge and jury." An objectionable collateral consequence of this interference with the criminal justice system's truth-finding function is that some guilty defendants may go free or receive reduced sentences as a result of favorable plea bargains.

Researchers have only recently begun to study extensively the effects of the exclusionary rule on the disposition of felony arrests. One study* suggests the rule results in the nonprosecution or nonconviction of between 0.6% and 2.35% of individuals arrested for felonies. The estimates are higher for particular crimes the prosecution of which depends heavily on physical evidence. Thus, the cumulative loss due to nonprosecution or nonconviction of individuals arrested on felony drug charges is probably in the range of 2.8% to 7.1%. Davies' analysis of California data suggests that screening by police and prosecutors results in the release because of illegal searches or seizures of as many as 1.4% of all felony arrestees, id., at 650, that 0.9% of felony arrestees are released, because of illegal searches or seizures, at the preliminary hearing or after trial, and that roughly 0.5% of all felony arrestees benefit from reversals on appeal because of illegal searches. The exclusionary rule also has been found to affect the plea-bargaining process.

Many of these researchers have concluded that the impact of the exclusionary rule is insubstantial, but the small percentages with which they deal mask a large absolute number of felons who are released because the cases against them were based in part on illegal searches or seizures. "'Any rule of evidence that denies the jury access to clearly probative and reliable evidence must bear a heavy burden of justification, and must be carefully limited to the circumstances in which it will pay its way by deterring official unlawlessness." Because we find that the rule can have no substantial deterrent effect in the sorts of

*By Thomas Davies. 1983. "A Hard Look at What We Know (and Still Need to Learn) about the 'Social Costs' of the Exclusionary Rule: The NIJ Study and Other Studies of 'Lost' Arrests." *American Bar Foundation Research Journal*, 640.

situations under consideration in this case, we conclude that it cannot pay its way in those situations.

Particularly when law enforcement officers have acted in objective good faith or their transgressions have been minor, the magnitude of the benefit conferred on such guilty defendants offends basic concepts of the criminal justice system. Indiscriminate application of the exclusionary rule, therefore, may well "generate disrespect for the law and administration of justice."...

As yet, we have not recognized any form of good-faith exception to the Fourth Amendment exclusionary rule. But the balancing approach that has evolved during the years of experience with the rule provides strong support for the modification currently urged upon us.... Because a search warrant "provides the detached scrutiny of a neutral magistrate"... we have expressed a strong preference for warrants... concluded that the preference for warrants is most appropriately effectuated by according "great deference" to a magistrate's determination.

Deference to the magistrate, however, is not boundless. It is clear... that the deference accorded to a magistrate's finding of probable cause does not preclude inquiry into the knowing or reckless falsity of the affidavit on which that determination was based.... To the extent proponents of exclusion rely on its behavioral effects on judges and magistrates... their reliance is misplaced. First, the exclusionary rule is designed to deter police misconduct rather than to punish the errors of judges and magistrates. Second, there exists no evidence suggesting that judges and magistrates are inclined to ignore or subvert the Fourth Amendment or that lawlessness among these actors requires application of the extreme sanction of exclusion. Third, and most important, we discern no basis, and are offered none, for believing that exclusion of evidence seized pursuant to a warrant will have a significant deterrent effect on the issuing judge or magistrate.... Judges and magistrates are not adjuncts to the law enforcement team; as neutral judicial officers, they have no stake in the outcome of particular criminal prosecutions. The threat of exclusion thus cannot be expected significantly to deter them....

We have frequently questioned whether the exclusionary rule can have any deterrent effect when the offending officers acted in the objectively reasonable belief their conduct did not violate the Fourth Amendment.... This is particularly true, we believe, when an officer acting with objective good faith has obtained a search warrant from a judge or magistrate and acted within its scope. In most such cases, there is no police illegality and thus nothing to deter.... "Once the warrant issues, there is literally nothing more the policeman can do in seeking to comply with the law." Penalizing the officer for the magistrate's error, rather than his own, cannot logically contribute to the deterrence of Fourth Amendment violations.

We conclude that the marginal or nonexistent benefits produced by suppressing evidence obtained in objectively reasonable reliance on a subsequently invalidated search warrant cannot justify the substantial costs of exclusion. We do not suggest, however, that exclusion is always inappropriate in cases where an officer has obtained a warrant and abided by its terms.... The officer's reliance on the magistrate's probable-cause determination and on the technical sufficiency of the warrant he issues must be objectively reasonable, and it is clear that in some circumstances the officer will have no reasonable grounds for believing that the warrant was properly issued.... The good-faith exception for searches conducted pursuant to warrants is not intended to signal our unwillingness strictly to enforce the requirements of the Fourth Amendment, and we do not believe it will have this effect....

We have now reexamined the purposes of the exclusionary rule and the propriety of its application in cases where officers have relied on a subsequently invalidated search warrant. Our conclusion is that the rule's purposes will only rarely be served by applying it in such circumstances.

...Officer Rombach's application for a warrant clearly was supported by much more than a "bare bones" affidavit. The affidavit related the results of an extensive investigation and...provided evidence sufficient to create disagreement among thoughtful and competent judges as to the existence of probable cause. Under these circumstances, the officers' reliance on the magistrate's determination of probable cause was objectively reasonable, and application of the extreme sanction of exclusion is inappropriate.

Accordingly, the judgment of the
Court of Appeals is REVERSED.

CONCURRING OPINION

BLACKMUN, J.

As the Court's opinion in this case makes clear, the Court has narrowed the scope of the exclusionary rule because of an empirical judgment that the rule has little appreciable effect in cases where officers act in objectively reasonable reliance on search warrants. Because I share the view that the exclusionary rule is not a constitutionally compelled corollary of the Fourth Amendment itself, I see no way to avoid making an empirical judgment of this sort, and I am satisfied the Court has made the correct one on the information before it. Like all courts, we face institutional limitations on our ability to gather information about "legislative facts," and the exclusionary rule itself has exacerbated the shortage of hard data concerning the behavior of police officers in the

absence of such a rule. Nonetheless, we cannot escape the responsibility to decide the question before us, however imperfect our information may be, and I am prepared to join the Court on the information now at hand.

What must be stressed, however, is that any empirical judgment about the effect of the exclusionary rule in a particular class of cases necessarily is a provisional one. By their very nature, the assumptions on which we proceed today cannot be cast in stone. To the contrary, they now will be tested in the real world of state and federal law enforcement, and this Court will attend to the results. If it should emerge from experience that, contrary to our expectations, the good-faith exception to the exclusionary rule results in a material change in police compliance with the Fourth Amendment, we shall have to reconsider what we have undertaken here. The logic of a decision that rests on untested predictions about police conduct demands no less.

DISSENT

BRENNAN, J. joined by MARSHALL, J.

Ten years ago, I expressed that the Court's decision "may signal that a majority of my colleagues have positioned themselves to reopen the door [to evidence secured by official lawlessness] still further and abandon altogether the exclusionary rule in search-and-seizure cases." Since then, in case after case, I have witnessed the Court's gradual but determined strangulation of the rule. It now appears that the Court's victory over the Fourth Amendment is complete.... Today the Court sanctions the use in the prosecution's case in chief of illegally obtained evidence against the individual whose rights have been violated—a result that had previously been thought to be foreclosed.

The Court seeks to justify this result on the ground that the "costs" of adhering to the exclusionary rule in cases like those before us exceed the "benefits." But the language of deterrence and of cost/benefit analysis, if used indiscriminately, can have a narcotic effect.... It suggests that not only constitutional principle but also empirical data support the majority's result. When the Court's analysis is examined carefully, however, it is clear that we have not been treated to an honest assessment of the merits of the exclusionary rule, but have instead been drawn into a curious world where the "costs" of excluding illegally obtained evidence loom to exaggerated heights and where the "benefits" of such exclusion are made to disappear with a mere wave of the hand....

...Since the Fourth Amendment became part of the Nation's fundamental law in 1791, what the Framers understood then remains true today—that the task of combating crime and convicting the guilty will in every era seem of such critical and pressing concern that we may be lured by the temptations of expediency into forsaking our commitment to protecting individual liberty and privacy. It was for that very reason that the Framers of the Bill of Rights insisted that law enforcement efforts be permanently and unambiguously restricted in order to preserve personal freedoms. In the constitutional scheme they ordained, the sometimes unpopular task of ensuring that the government's enforcement efforts remain within the strict boundaries fixed by the Fourth Amendment was entrusted to the courts. . . .

The Court's decisions over the past decade have made plain that the entire enterprise of attempting to assess the benefits and costs of the exclusionary rule in various contexts is a virtually impossible task for the judiciary to perform honestly or accurately. Although the Court's language in those cases suggests that some specific empirical basis may support its analyses, the reality is that the Court's opinions represent inherently unstable compounds of intuition, hunches, and occasional pieces of partial and often inconclusive data. . . . To the extent empirical data is available regarding the general costs and benefits of the exclusionary rule, it has shown, on the one hand . . . that the costs aren't as substantial as critics have asserted in the past, and, on the other hand, that while the exclusionary rule may well have certain deterrent effects, it is extremely difficult to determine with any degree of precision whether the incident of unlawful conduct by police is now lower than it was prior to *Mapp v. Ohio* (1961).

The Court has sought to turn this uncertainty to its advantage by casting the burden of proof upon proponents of the rule. . . . A doctrine that is explained as if it were an empirical proposition but for which there is only limited empirical support is both inherently unstable and an easy mark for critics. The extent of this Court's fidelity to Fourth Amendment requirements, however, should not turn on such statistical uncertainties. . . ."Personal liberties are not rooted in the law of averages." Rather than seeking to give effort to the liberties secured by the Fourth Amendment through guesswork about deterrence, the Court should restore to its proper place the principle framed 70 years ago in *Weeks* [*v. United States* (1914)] that an individual whose privacy has been invaded in violation of the Fourth Amendment has a right grounded in that Amendment to prevent the government from subsequently making use of any evidence so obtained.

Questions

1. According to the majority, is the exclusionary rule a constitutional right? Explain.

2. State exactly the Court's definition of the reasonable good-faith exception.

3. What two elements does the Court balance, and how does it weigh the balance to justify the creation of the good faith exception?

4. List all the facts the Court considers relevant to deciding whether the exception applies to Leon and the other defendants.

5. Summarize the empirical evidence the majority uses to back up its decision.

6. What is Justice Blackmun's main point in his concurring opinion?

7. List and state exactly Justice Brennan's objections to the exception.

8. Based on the majority, concurring, and the dissenting opinions, how much do *you* think we *really* know about the deterrent effect of the exclusionary rule?

◆ STATE CONSTITUTIONAL LAW ◆

State v. Novembrino
519 A.2d 820 (N.J. 1987)

Should New Jersey Reject the "Good Faith" Exception?

Ottavio Novembrino was charged with possession of controlled substances and possession with intent to distribute and moved to suppress evidence. The Superior Court, Law Division, Hudson County, granted the motion. The Superior Court, Appellate Division, affirmed. The New Jersey Supreme Court affirmed.

STEIN, J.

FACTS

. . . According to Detective Higgins, whose affidavit led to the issuance of the disputed search warrant, Novembrino was stopped by two officers from the Bayonne Police Department at about 6:15 P.M. on June 2, 1983.

The stop occurred shortly after Novembrino closed his service station and was proceeding home by automobile. One officer conducted a pat-down search, while the other officer conducted a limited inspection of the interior of Novembrino's automobile. Novembrino agreed to go with the officers to police headquarters. He drove to the station in his own car, accompanied by one of the officers. Detective Higgins testified that Novembrino was not placed under arrest and was free to leave, although neither officer advised him of his right to do so.

After being advised of his *Miranda* rights, Novembrino refused to consent to a search of his station. At about 6:30 P.M., Detective Higgins left a message requesting that the Bayonne municipal court judge telephone him. He then began to type an affidavit in support of a search warrant. Detective Higgins conceded that this was the first such affidavit he had ever prepared and estimated that its preparation took approximately ten or fifteen minutes. When the municipal court judge telephoned, Detective Higgins arranged to meet him at a shopping center. They met at approximately 6:50 P.M. The judge reviewed the affidavit and signed the warrant. Detective Higgins spoke with Detective Kelly by radio, and proceeded to the gas station where he met defendant and Detective Kelly. After Novembrino was shown the warrant, he unlocked the door to the service station and pointed out the location of the contraband....

At the suppression hearing, Novembrino argued that the affidavit did not establish probable cause....The trial court...suppressed the evidence on the ground that the affidavit submitted in support of the warrant failed to establish probable cause....In the Appellate Division, the State argued that the Higgins affidavit was sufficient to establish probable cause. The critical portion of the affidavit alleged:

> I received information from an informant who has proven reliable in several investigations (with the information he supplied), that "Otto" above description, is engaged in the illegal sales of cocaine and marijuana. My informant stated that Otto usually keeps the drugs in his gas station at above location. He (informant) also stated that he witnessed "Otto" dealing drugs from his gas station. I, along with Det. Ralph Scianni, conducted a surveillance of subject and his station on Thurs., 6/2/83, between the hours of 3:00 P.M. and 7:00 P.M., and observed Otto meeting with several persons, after leaving his station and making what we believed to be drug transactions. During the surveillance, we observed one person

making a transaction with Otto and checked on his vehicle and called the narcotics squad to inquire on his relationship with drugs. They told us that said person has been arrested for cocaine and other violations and they felt that Otto and the other person are involved in drug activity. From the information received from our informant and from our observations, we do feel that a search of Otto's gas station should be conducted for illegal contraband. We checked on ownership of the station and it belongs to Otto who we have presently in headquarters on this investigation. Otto was advised of his rights and refused a search of his station but appeared to be very nervous.

The Appellate Division concluded that the affidavit failed to establish probable cause:

> The affidavit here involved simply revealed that a police informant concluded for unknown reasons that defendant was a drug dealer, that a person previously arrested for possession of cocaine was seen at defendant's gas station engaged in some unspecified activities which caused a detective, whose education, training and experiences are unknown, to conclude that criminal activities in the form of violations of Title 24 were taking place at the gas station. The totality of the circumstances spelled out in the affidavit failed to contain a single objective fact tending to engender a "well grounded suspicion" that a crime was being committed.

OPINION

...It is an established principle of our federalist system that state constitutions may be a source of "individual liberties more expansive than those conferred by the Federal Constitution...." This Court has frequently resorted to our own State Constitution in order to afford our citizens broader protection of certain personal rights than that afforded by analogous or identical provisions of the federal Constitution.... Although the language of article I, paragraph 7 of the New Jersey Constitution is virtually identical with that of the fourth amendment, we have held in other contexts it affords our citizens greater protection against unreasonable searches and seizures than does the fourth amendment.

In this case, Novembrino urges that we construe our state-constitutional protection against unreasonable searches and seizures to preclude recognition of the good-faith exception to the exclusionary rule established in Leon. The Attorney General and the Hudson County Prosecutor argue that we should follow the Supreme

Court's* modification of the exclusionary rule and construe article I, paragraph 7 of our Constitution in a manner consistent with the good-faith exception. Our conclusion as to which of these courses to follow is strongly influenced by what we perceive to be the likely impact of our decision on the privacy rights of our citizens and the enforcement of our criminal laws, matters of "particular state interest" that afford an appropriate basis for resolving this issue on independent state grounds. . . .

Under the pre-*Leon* version of the exclusionary rule, police had finally come to learn that it was not enough that they had gotten a piece of paper called a warrant. Because that warrant was subject to challenge at the later motion to suppress, it was important to the police that the warrant be properly issued or that the warrant request be turned down at a time when it might be possible to acquire necessary additional information without compromising the investigation. Consequently, there had developed in many localities the very sound practice of going through the warrant-issuing process with the greatest of care, often by having the affidavit reviewed by individuals other than the magistrate.

But under *Leon* there is no reason to go through such cautious procedures and every reason not to. Why take the risk that some conscientious prosecutor or police supervisor will say the application is insufficient when, if some magistrate can be induced to issue a warrant on the basis of it, the affidavit is thereafter virtually immune from challenge? There is thus no escaping the fact that, as the *Leon* dissenters put it, the "long-run effect" of that case "unquestionably will be to undermine the integrity of the warrant process."

We find this criticism of the "good-faith" exception to be persuasive. One obvious consequence of the application of the exclusionary rule in New Jersey has been the encouragement of law-enforcement officials to comply with the constitutionally mandated probable-cause standard in order to avoid the suppression of evidence. The *Leon* rule avoids suppression of evidence even if the constitutional standard is violated, requiring only that the officer executing the defective warrant have an objectively reasonable basis for relying on it. Whatever else may be said for or against the *Leon* rule, the good-faith exception will inevitably and inexorably diminish the quality of evidence presented in search-warrant applications. By eliminating any cost for non-compliance with the constitutional requirement of probable cause, the good-faith exception assures us that the constitutional standard will be diluted. . . .

Our concern . . . is with the Constitution and with the basic and fundamental guarantees that document was intended to afford to all our citizens, particularly in times of public ferment. In our view, the citizen's right to be free from unreasonable searches and seizures conducted without probable cause is just such a fundamental principle, to be preserved and protected with vigilance. In our tripartite system of separate governmental powers, the primary responsibility for its preservation is that of the judiciary.

The exclusionary rule, by virtue of its consistent application over the past twenty-five years, has become an integral element of our state-constitutional guarantee that search warrants will not issue without probable cause. Its function is not merely to deter police misconduct. The rule also serves as the indispensable mechanism for vindicating the constitutional right to be free from unreasonable searches. Because we believe that the good-faith exception to the exclusionary rule adopted in *Leon* would tend to undermine the constitutionally guaranteed standard of probable cause, and in the process disrupt the highly effective procedures employed by our criminal justice system to accommodate that constitutional guarantee without impairing law enforcement, we decline to recognize a good-faith exception to the exclusionary rule. . . .

Justice Blackmun, concurring in *Leon*, cautioned us as to the "unavoidably provisional nature" of the decision, and warned that if "the good faith exception to the exclusionary rule results in a material change in police compliance with the Fourth Amendment, we shall have to reconsider what we have undertaken here." We suspect that Justice Blackmun's forebodings may be prophetic indeed. In our view, erosion of the probable-cause guarantee will be a corollary to the good-faith exception. We think it quite possible that the damage to the constitutional guarantee may reach such a level as to cause the Court to reconsider its experiment with the fourth amendment.

We see no need in New Jersey to experiment with the fundamental rights protected by the fourth-amendment counterpart of our State Constitution. We will not subject the procedures that vindicate the fundamental rights guaranteed by article I, paragraph 7 of our State Constitution—procedures that have not diluted the effectiveness of our criminal justice system—to the uncertain effects that we believe will inevitably accompany the good-faith exception to the federal exclusionary rule.

United States v. Leon, excerpted on p. 367.

The judgment of the Appellate Division is AFFIRMED.

"Bad Methods" by Non–Law Enforcement Government Officials

United States v. Leon made it clear that the good-faith exception was created to deter law enforcement officers—and no other government officials, like court employees and judges. Why?

1. There's "no evidence suggesting that judges and magistrates are inclined to ignore or subvert the Fourth Amendment or that lawlessness among these actors requires the application of the extreme sanction of exclusion."

2. There's "no basis for believing that exclusion of evidence seized pursuant to a warrant would have a significant deterrent effect on the issuing judge or magistrate."

Because, according to the Court, other officials aren't likely to get carried away with fighting crime, they're not susceptible to fooling around with evidence, and they're not deterred by threats of throwing out evidence if they make mistakes.

But the world of criminal justice began to change rapidly after the *Leon* decision in 1984. One change particularly caused concern that maybe limiting the reasonable good-faith exception to law enforcement officers should be reconsidered. In *Arizona v. Evans* (1995), Justice Ginsburg summarized the change:

> Widespread reliance on computers to store and convey information generates, along with manifold benefits, new possibilities of error, due to both computer malfunctions and operator mistakes. Most germane to this case, computerization greatly amplifies an error's effect, and correspondingly intensifies the need for prompt correction; for inaccurate data can infect not only one agency, but the many agencies that share access to the database. The computerized databases of the Federal Bureau of Investigation's National Crime Information Center (NCIC), to take a conspicuous example, contain over 23 million records, identifying, among other things, persons and vehicles sought by law enforcement agencies nationwide. NCIC information is available to approximately 71,000 federal, state, and local agencies. Thus, any mistake entered into the NCIC spreads nationwide in an instant.

Justice Ginsburg told of one horrible example of the effects of this explosion in computerized criminal justice data banks:

> The Los Angeles Police Department, in 1982, had entered into the NCIC computer an arrest warrant for a man suspected of robbery and murder. Because the suspect had been impersonating Terry Dean Rogan, the arrest warrant erroneously named Rogan. Compounding the error, the Los Angeles Police Department had failed to include a description of the suspect's physical characteristics. During the next two years, this incorrect and incomplete information caused Rogan to be arrested four times, three times at gunpoint, after stops for minor traffic infractions in Michigan and Oklahoma.

> *Rogan v. Los Angeles* 1987, 1384

Until 1990, all the Supreme Court exclusionary rule cases dealt with one kind of government behavior—unconstitutional acts by *police*. But, what if some other government official (like the magistrate who issued the warrant in *United States v. Leon*) was guilty of "bad methods? Does *Leon* mean the exclusionary rule can *only* apply to police? In 1995, the U.S. Supreme Court answered the question (sort of). In *Arizona v. Evans*, Isaac Evans was convicted of using marijuana seized during a search that was based on an invalid warrant that a justice of the peace court *clerk* should have removed from the court's database.

Was the Good-Faith Exception Intended Only to Deter Law Enforcement Officers?

Arizona v. Evans
514 U.S. 1 (1995)

Isaac Evans moved to suppress marijuana seized from his car. The motion was granted by the Superior Court, Maricopa County. The Arizona Court of Appeals reversed. The Arizona Supreme Court reversed. The U.S. Supreme Court granted certiorari and reversed and remanded.

REHNQUIST, CJ., joined by O'CONNOR, SCALIA, KENNEDY, SOUTER, THOMAS, and BREYER, JJ.

FACTS

In January 1991, Phoenix police officer Bryan Sargent observed Isaac Evans driving the wrong way on a one-way street in front of the police station. The officer stopped Evans and asked to see his driver's license. After Evans told him his license had been suspended, the officer entered Evans's name into a computer data terminal located in his patrol car. The computer inquiry confirmed Evans's license had been suspended and also indicated there was an outstanding misdemeanor warrant for his arrest. Based upon the outstanding warrant, Officer Sargent placed Evans under arrest. While being handcuffed, Evans dropped a hand-rolled cigarette the officers determined smelled of marijuana. Officers proceeded to search his car and discovered a bag of marijuana under the passenger's seat.

The State charged Evans with possession of marijuana. When the police notified the Justice Court they had arrested him, the Justice Court discovered the arrest warrant previously had been quashed* and so advised the police. Evans argued that because his arrest was based on a warrant that had been quashed 17 days prior to his arrest, the marijuana seized incident to the arrest should be suppressed as the fruit of an unlawful arrest. Evans also argued that "the 'good faith' exception to the exclusionary rule was inapplicable ... because it was police error, not judicial error, which caused the invalid arrest."

At the suppression hearing, the Chief Clerk of the Justice Court testified that a Justice of the Peace had issued the arrest warrant on December 13, 1990, because Evans had failed to appear to answer for several traffic violations. On December 19, 1990, Evans appeared before a substitute Justice of the Peace who entered a notation in Evans's file to "quash warrant."

The Chief Clerk also testified regarding the standard court procedure for quashing a warrant. Under that procedure:

1. A justice court clerk calls and informs the warrant section of the Sheriff's Office when a warrant has been quashed.

2. The Sheriff's Office then removes the warrant from its computer records.

3. After calling the Sheriff's Office, the clerk makes a note in the individual's file indicating the clerk who made the phone call and the person at the Sheriff's Office to whom the clerk spoke.

The Chief Clerk testified that there was no indication in Evans's file that a clerk had called and notified the Sheriff's Office his arrest warrant had been quashed. A records clerk from the Sheriff's Office also testified that the Sheriff's Office had no record of a telephone call informing it that respondent's arrest warrant had been quashed.

At the close of testimony, Evans argued that the evidence obtained as a result of the arrest should be suppressed because "the purposes of the exclusionary rule would be served here by making the clerks for the court, or the clerk for the Sheriff's office, whoever is responsible for this mistake, to be more careful about making sure that warrants are removed from the records."

The trial court granted the motion to suppress because it concluded the State had been at fault for failing to quash the warrant. Presumably because it could find no "distinction between State action, whether it happens to be the police department or not," the trial court made no factual finding as to whether the Justice Court or Sheriff's Office was responsible for the continued presence of the quashed warrant in the police records.

A divided panel of the Arizona Court of Appeals reversed because

> It believed the exclusionary rule was not intended to deter justice court employees or Sheriff's Office employees who are not directly associated with the arresting officers or the arresting officers' police department. [Therefore], "the purpose of the exclusionary rule would not be served by excluding the evidence obtained in this case."

---
*Voided or annulled.

The Arizona Supreme Court reversed. The court rejected the "distinction drawn by the court of appeals . . . between clerical errors committed by law enforcement personnel and similar mistakes by court employees." The court predicted that application of the exclusionary rule would "hopefully serve to improve the efficiency of those who keep records in our criminal justice system." Finally, the court concluded that "even assuming that deterrence is the principal reason for application of the exclusionary rule, we disagree with the court of appeals that such a purpose would not be served where carelessness by a court clerk results in an unlawful arrest."

We granted certiorari to determine whether the exclusionary rule requires suppression of evidence seized incident to an arrest resulting from an inaccurate computer record, regardless of whether police personnel or court personnel were responsible for the record's continued presence in the police computer. We now reverse.

OPINION

. . . In *Leon*,* we . . . determined there was no sound reason to apply the exclusionary rule as a means of deterring misconduct on the part of judicial officers who are responsible for issuing warrants.

First, we noted the exclusionary rule was historically designed "to deter police misconduct rather than to punish the errors of judges and magistrates."

Second, there was "no evidence suggesting that judges and magistrates are inclined to ignore or subvert the Fourth Amendment or that lawlessness among these actors requires the application of the extreme sanction of exclusion."

Third, and of greatest importance, there was no basis for believing that exclusion of evidence seized pursuant to a warrant would have a significant deterrent effect on the issuing judge or magistrate.

The *Leon* Court then examined whether application of the exclusionary rule could be expected to alter the behavior of the law enforcement officers. We concluded:

Where the officer's conduct is objectively reasonable, "excluding the evidence will not further the ends of the exclusionary rule in any appreciable way; for it is painfully apparent that . . . the officer is acting as a reasonable officer would and should act in similar circumstances. Excluding the evidence can in no way affect his future conduct unless it is to make him less willing to do his duty." Suppressing evidence because the judge

failed to make all the necessary clerical corrections despite his assurances that such changes would be made will not serve the deterrent function that the exclusionary rule was designed to achieve.

Thus, we held that the "marginal or nonexistent benefits produced by suppressing evidence obtained in objectively reasonable reliance on a subsequently invalidated search warrant cannot justify the substantial costs of exclusion. . . ."

Applying the reasoning of *Leon* to the facts of this case, we conclude that the decision of the Arizona Supreme Court must be reversed. . . . [The Arizona Supreme Court's] holding is contrary to the reasoning of *Leon*. If court employees were responsible for the erroneous computer record, the exclusion of evidence at trial would not sufficiently deter future errors so as to warrant such a severe sanction.

First, the exclusionary rule was historically designed as a means of deterring police misconduct, not mistakes by court employees.

Second, Evans offers no evidence that court employees are inclined to ignore or subvert the Fourth Amendment or that lawlessness among these actors requires application of the extreme sanction of exclusion. To the contrary, the Chief Clerk of the Justice Court testified at the suppression hearing that this type of error occurred once every three or four years.

Finally, and most important, there is no basis for believing that application of the exclusionary rule in these circumstances will have a significant effect on court employees responsible for informing the police that a warrant has been quashed. Because court clerks are not adjuncts to the law enforcement team engaged in the often competitive enterprise of ferreting out crime, they have no stake in the outcome of particular criminal prosecutions. The threat of exclusion of evidence could not be expected to deter such individuals from failing to inform police officials that a warrant had been quashed.

If it were indeed a court clerk who was responsible for the erroneous entry on the police computer, application of the exclusionary rule also could not be expected to alter the behavior of the arresting officer. As the trial court in this case stated: "I think the police officer was bound to arrest. I think he would have been derelict in his duty if he failed to arrest." "Excluding the evidence can in no way affect the officer's future conduct unless it is to make him less willing to do his duty."

The Chief Clerk of the Justice Court testified that this type of error occurred "once every three or four years." In fact, once the court clerks discovered the error, they imme-

---

*Excerpted earlier, on p. 367.

diately corrected it, and then proceeded to search their files to make sure that no similar mistakes had occurred. There is no indication the arresting officer was not acting objectively reasonably when he relied upon the police computer record. Application of the *Leon* framework supports a categorical exception to the exclusionary rule for clerical errors of court employees.

The judgment of the Supreme Court of Arizona is therefore REVERSED, and the case is REMANDED to that court for proceedings not inconsistent with this opinion.

CONCURRING OPINIONS

O'CONNOR, J., joined by SOUTER and BREYER, JJ.
... In recent years, we have witnessed the advent of powerful, computer-based record keeping systems that facilitate arrests in ways that have never before been possible. The police, of course, are entitled to enjoy the substantial advantages this technology confers. They may not, however, rely on it blindly. With the benefits of more efficient law enforcement mechanisms comes the burden of corresponding constitutional responsibilities.

SOUTER, J., joined by BREYER, J.
In joining the Court's opinion ... I add ... that we do not answer another question that may reach us in due course, that is, how far, in dealing with fruits of computerized error, our very concept of deterrence by exclusion of evidence should extend to the government as a whole, not merely the police, on the ground that there would otherwise be no reasonable expectation of keeping the number of resulting false arrests within an acceptable minimum limit.

DISSENTS

STEVENS, J.
... The Court seems to assume the Fourth Amendment—and particularly the exclusionary rule, which effectuates the Amendment's commands—has the limited purpose of deterring police misconduct. Both the constitutional text and the history of its adoption and interpretation identify a more majestic conception. ... The Amendment is a constraint on the power of the sovereign, not merely on some of its agents. The remedy for its violation imposes costs on that sovereign, motivating it to train all of its personnel to avoid future violations. ...

Even if one accepts deterrence as the sole rationale for the exclusionary rule, the Arizona Supreme Court's decision is correct on the merits. The majority's reliance on *United States v. Leon* is misplaced. The search in that case had been authorized by a presumptively valid warrant issued by a California Superior Court Judge. In contrast, this case involves a search pursuant to an arrest made when no warrant at all was outstanding against Evans. The holding in *Leon* rested on the majority's doubt "that exclusion of evidence seized pursuant to a warrant will have a significant deterrent effect on the issuing judge or magistrate." The reasoning in *Leon* assumed the existence of a warrant; it was, and remains, wholly inapplicable to warrantless searches and seizures. ...

The Phoenix Police Department was part of the chain of information that resulted in respondent's unlawful, warrantless arrest. We should reasonably presume that law enforcement officials, who stand in the best position to monitor such errors as occurred here, can influence mundane communication procedures in order to prevent those errors. That presumption comports with the notion that the exclusionary rule exists to deter future police misconduct *systemically* [italics added]. The deterrent purpose extends to law enforcement *as a whole* [italics added], not merely to "the arresting officer." Consequently, the Phoenix officers' good faith does not diminish the deterrent value of invalidating their arrest of respondent.

The Court seeks to minimize the impact of its holding on the security of the citizen by referring to the testimony of the Chief Clerk of the East Phoenix Number One Justice Court that in her "particular court" this type of error occurred "maybe once every three or four years."

Q: In your eight years as a chief clerk with the Justice of the Peace, have there been other occasions where a warrant was quashed but the police were not notified?

A: That does happen on rare occasions.

Q: And when you say rare occasions, about how many times in your eight years as chief clerk?

A: In my particular court, they would be like maybe one every three or four years.

Q: When something like this happens, is anything done by your office to correct that problem?

A: Well, when this one happened, we searched all the files to make sure that there were no other ones in there, which there were three other ones on that same day that it happened. Fortunately, they weren't all arrested.

Apart from the fact that the Clerk promptly contradicted herself, this is slim evidence on which to base a conclusion that computer error poses no appreciable threat to Fourth Amendment interests. For support, the Court cites a case from 1948. The Court overlooks the reality that computer technology has changed the nature of threats to citizens' privacy over the past half century. What has not changed is the reality that only that fraction of Fourth Amendment violations held to have resulted in unlawful arrests is ever noted and redressed. As Justice Jackson observed:

> There may be, and I am convinced that there are, many unlawful searches . . . of innocent people which turn up nothing incriminating, in which no arrest is made, about which courts do nothing, and about which we never hear.

Moreover, even if errors in computer records of warrants were rare, that would merely minimize the cost of enforcing the exclusionary rule in cases like this.

. . . One consequence of the Court's holding seems immediately obvious. Its most serious impact will be on the otherwise innocent citizen who is stopped for a minor traffic infraction and is wrongfully arrested based on erroneous information in a computer data base. I assume the police officer who reasonably relies on the computer information would be immune from liability in a § 1983 action.* Of course, the Court has held *respondeat superior*** is unavailable as a basis for imposing liability on his or her municipality. Thus, if courts are to have any power to discourage official error of this kind, it must be through application of the exclusionary rule.

. . . The offense to the dignity of the citizen who is arrested, handcuffed, and searched on a public street simply because some bureaucrat has failed to maintain an accurate computer data base strikes me as . . . outrageous. In this case, of course, such an error led to the fortuitous detection of respondent's unlawful possession of marijuana, and the suppression of the fruit of the error would prevent the prosecution of his crime. That cost, however, must be weighed against the interest in protecting other, wholly innocent citizens from unwarranted indignity. In my judgment, the cost is amply offset by an appropriately "jealous regard for maintaining the integrity of individual rights."

For this reason . . . I respectfully dissent.

GINSBURG, J., joined by STEVENS, J.

This case portrays the increasing use of computer technology in law enforcement. . . . Specifically, the Arizona Supreme Court saw the growing use of computerized records in law enforcement as a development presenting new dangers to individual liberty; excluding evidence seized as a result of incorrect computer data, the Arizona court anticipated, would reduce the incidence of uncorrected records. . . .

. . . Widespread reliance on computers to store and convey information generates, along with manifold benefits,

new possibilities of error, due to both computer malfunctions and operator mistakes. Most germane to this case, computerization greatly amplifies an error's effect, and correspondingly intensifies the need for prompt correction; for inaccurate data can infect not only one agency, but the many agencies that share access to the database. The computerized data bases of the Federal Bureau of Investigation's National Crime Information Center (NCIC), to take a conspicuous example, contain over 23 million records, identifying, among other things, persons and vehicles sought by law enforcement agencies nationwide. NCIC information is available to approximately 71,000 federal, state, and local agencies. Thus, any mistake entered into the NCIC spreads nationwide in an instant.

Isaac Evans' arrest exemplifies the risks associated with computerization of arrest warrants. Though his arrest was in fact warrantless—the warrant once issued having been quashed over two weeks before the episode in suit— the computer reported otherwise. Evans' case is not idiosyncratic. *Rogan v. Los Angeles*, 668 F.Supp. 1384 (CD Cal.1987), similarly indicates the problem. There, the Los Angeles Police Department, in 1982, had entered into the NCIC computer an arrest warrant for a man suspected of robbery and murder. Because the suspect had been impersonating Terry Dean Rogan, the arrest warrant erroneously named Rogan. Compounding the error, the Los Angeles Police Department had failed to include a description of the suspect's physical characteristics. During the next two years, this incorrect and incomplete information caused Rogan to be arrested four times, three times at gunpoint, after stops for minor traffic infractions in Michigan and Oklahoma.

. . . In this electronic age, particularly with respect to recordkeeping, court personnel and police officers are not neatly compartmentalized actors. Instead, they serve together to carry out the State's information-gathering objectives. Whether particular records are maintained by the police or the courts should not be dispositive where a single computer data base can answer all calls. Not only is it artificial to distinguish between court clerk and police clerk slips; in practice, it may be difficult to pinpoint whether one official, e.g., a court employee, or another, e.g., a police officer, caused the error to exist or to persist. Applying an exclusionary rule as the Arizona court did may well supply a powerful incentive to the State to promote the prompt updating of computer records. That was the Arizona Supreme Court's hardly unreasonable expectation. The incentive to update promptly would be diminished if court-initiated records were exempt from the rule's sway.

. . . The Arizona Supreme Court found it "repugnant to the principles of a free society," to take a person "into po-

---

*See Chapter 11 on suing the government.

**The rule that employers are legally responsible for their employees' wrongs.

lice custody because of a computer error precipitated by government carelessness." Few, I believe, would disagree. Whether, in order to guard against such errors, "the exclusionary rule is a 'cost' we cannot afford to be without," seems to me a question this Court should not rush to decide....

Questions

1. State the Court's reasons for limiting the deterrence justification to law enforcement officers.

2. Identify the dissenting justices reasons for arguing that the deterrence justification for the good-faith exception should be applied to all government officials.

3. Which of the opinions do you agree with? Support your answer.

4. How do you explain the differing interpretations of the clerk's testimony about the number of mistakes that the clerks made? Is this disagreement important? Should Chief Justice Rehnquist have included the whole testimony, as Justice Stevens did? Or, doesn't it make any difference?

Social Costs and Deterrent Effects

In 1960, in *Mapp v. Ohio*, the U.S. Supreme Court headed by Chief Justice Earl Warren applied the exclusionary rule to the states because the Court *assumed* (didn't know) the rule would deter illegal searches and seizures. Since the 1970s, in case after case, a majority of the Burger and then the Rehnquist Court has decided (on the basis of their *assumption*) the social cost of keeping good evidence from juries and letting criminals walk is too high a price to pay for deterring law enforcement officers from violating individuals' rights. Which Court's assumption is right?

Ever since the Court decided *Mapp*, a growing stack of empirical studies has tested the correctness of the two assumptions. What's the answer? According to Professor Christopher Slobogin (1999, 368–369), "No one is going to win the empirical debate over whether the exclusionary rule deters the police from committing a significant number of illegal searches and seizures." It's true, say most of the studies, police officers pay more attention to the Fourth Amendment than they did in 1960, but many officers don't take the rule into account when they're deciding whether to make a search or seizure. "In short, we do not know how much the rule deters" (369) either individual officers whose evidence courts throw out in cases the officer's responsible for (special deterrence) or other officers who might be thinking of illegally searching or seizing (general deterrence).

"We probably never will" (369). Why? Because it's hard to conduct empirical research. So, we have to rely on speculation (370). And, what's the speculation? Both supporters and opponents of the rule make plausible claims for their positions. It's reasonable for supporters to claim "officers who know illegally seized evidence will be excluded cannot help but try to avoid illegal searches because they will have nothing to gain from them." Equally reasonable,

> those who oppose the rule can point out that its most direct consequence is imposed on the prosecutor rather than the cop, that police know and count on the fact that the rule is rarely applied (for both legal and not-so-legal reasons), and that the rule cannot affect searches and seizures the police believe will not result in prosecution. (372)

Despite these limits to the empirical research, some of it provides us some things to think about. First, the social costs of letting guilty criminals go free by excluding credible evidence that would convict them may not be as high as is commonly thought. According to Thomas Y. Davies, who studied the exclusionary rule in California and whose research the Court cited in *United States v. Leon,* prosecutors almost never reject cases involving violent crimes because of the exclusionary rule. In that state, illegally seized evidence led to dismissals in a mere 0.8 percent of all criminal cases and only 4.8 percent of felonies. He found that prosecutors rejected for prosecution only 0.06 percent of homicide, 0.09 percent of forcible rape, and 0.13 percent of assault cases because of illegal searches and seizures. They rejected less than 0.50 percent of theft cases and only 0.19 percent of burglary cases. The largest number of cases rejected for prosecution due to illegal searches and seizures involved the possession of small amounts of drugs (Davies 1983). Other studies reached similar results—that is, the exclusionary rule affects only a small portion of cases, and most of those aren't crimes against persons (cited in Davies 1983). Less than one-tenth of 1 percent of all criminal cases will be dismissed because the police seized evidence illegally. The rule leaves violent crimes and serious property offenses virtually unaffected. Furthermore, not all cases that are rejected or lost involving illegally obtained evidence are lost because of the exclusionary rule. Peter F. Nardulli (1987) found, for example, that in some cases of drug possession, the police weren't interested in successful prosecution but rather in getting contraband off the street.

Most criminal justice professionals seem to agree that the exclusionary rule is worth the price. The American Bar Association (1988) gathered information from police officers, prosecutors, defense attorneys, and judges in representative urban and geographically distributed locations regarding the problems that they face in their work. They also conducted a telephone survey of eight hundred police administrators, prosecutors, judges, and defense attorneys based on a stratified random selection technique to obtain a representative group of small to large cities and counties. The results showed the following:

> Although the prosecutors and police . . . interviewed believe that a few Fourth Amendment restrictions are ambiguous or complex, and thus, present training and field application problems, they do not believe that Fourth Amendment rights or their protection via the exclusionary rule are a significant impediment to crime control. . . . A number of . . . police officials also report that the demands of the exclusionary rule and resulting police training on Fourth Amendment requirements have promoted professionalism in police departments across the country. Thus, the exclusionary rule appears to be providing a significant safeguard of Fourth Amendment protections for individuals at modest cost in terms of either crime control or effective prosecution. This "cost," for the most part, reflects the values expressed in the Fourth Amendment itself, for the Amendment manifests a preference for privacy and freedom over that level of law enforcement efficiency which could be achieved if police were permitted to arrest and search without probable cause or judicial authorization. (11)

In view of its limited application, restrictions on the exclusionary rule hardly seem adequate cause for either critics of the rule to rejoice that these restrictions will make society safer or for supporters to lament that they'll throttle individual liberties. Probably the strongest argument for the exclusionary rule is that it helps to ensure judicial integrity. Courts, by excluding illegally obtained evidence, announce publicly and in writing their refusal to participate in or condone illegal police practices. At the end of the day, what the exclusionary rule does is exact the price of setting a few criminals free to maintain the rule of law for everybody; it sacrifices the correct result in an individual case for the general interest in the essential fairness of constitutional government for all people.

Go to Exercise 10-1 on the Criminal Procedure 6e CD to learn more about the application of the reasonable good-faith exception.

THE DEFENSE OF ENTRAPMENT

What if law enforcement agents (usually undercover cops) get people to commit crimes they wouldn't have committed if the government hadn't encouraged them? Sometimes, defendants in such cases are entitled to the defense of **entrapment,** meaning courts will dismiss the criminal charges. For most of our history, U.S. courts didn't recognize entrapment as a defense. In 1864, a New York court explained why:

> Even if inducements to commit crime could be assumed to exist in this case, the allegation of the defendant would be but the repetition of the pleas as ancient as the world, and first interposed in Paradise: "The serpent beguiled me and I did eat." That defense was overruled by the great Lawgiver, and whatever estimate we may form, or whatever judgment pass upon the character or conduct of the tempter, this plea has never since availed to shield crime or give indemnity to the culprit, and it is safe to say that under any code of civilized, not say Christian ethics, it never will.
>
> *Board of Commissioners v. Backus* 1864, 42

Another court, in 1904, summed up this attitude toward entrapment:

> We are asked to protect the defendant, not because he is innocent, but because a zealous public officer exceeded his powers and held out a bait. The courts do not look to see who held out the bait, but to see who took it.
>
> *People v. Mills* 1904, 791

These attitudes stemmed from indifference to government enticements to commit crimes. After all, "once the crime is committed, why should it matter what particular incentives were involved and who offered them?" However, attitudes have shifted from indifference to "limited sympathy" toward entrapped defendants and a growing intolerance of government inducements to entrap individuals who are basically law-abiding people (Marcus 1986).

The present law of entrapment attempts to balance criminal predisposition and law enforcement practices; that is, it casts a net for habitual criminals, while trying not to capture law-abiding people in the net. The practice of entrapment wasn't a response to violent crime or other crimes with complaining victims. Rather, the practice arose because of the difficulty in detecting consensual crimes—namely, illegal drug offenses, gambling, pornography, and prostitution—because "victims" don't want to report the crimes to the police.

The use of government encouragement as a law enforcement tool is neither new nor limited to the United States. The practice has been associated with some highly unsavory characters throughout world history. Ancient tyrants and modern dictators alike have relied on government agents to get innocent people to commit crimes (the infamous agents provocateurs), so that these autocrats could silence and destroy their political opponents. From the days of Henry VIII to the era of Hitler, Mussolini, Franco, and Stalin to Manuel Noriega, Slobodan Milosevic, and Saddam Hussein (and too many others to list) in our own time, police states have used government inform-ers to get dissidents to admit their disloyalty.

Unfortunately, inducement isn't a tool used only by dictators to oppress their op-ponents. In all societies and political systems, it's used in ordinary law enforcement, too, creating the risk that law-abiding people will commit crimes they wouldn't have committed if they hadn't been encouraged. Enticement to commit crimes flies in the face of good government. The great Victorian British Prime Minister William Glad-stone admonished government to make it *easy* to do *right* and *hard* to do *wrong*. And, consider the plea in the Christian Lord's Prayer's to "lead us not into temptation, but deliver us from evil" (Carlson 1987).

Encouragement is likely to occur whenever law enforcement officers do any of the following:

1. Pretend they're victims

2. Intend to entice suspects to commit crimes

3. Communicate the enticement to suspects

4. Influence the decision to commit crimes

Here's how encouragement works in typical cases: One officer provides an oppor-tunity for targets to commit a crime while other officers witness the event; that way, they have proof of the target's guilt. But, it's usually not enough for officers just to present targets an opportunity, or even to "ask" them to commit a crime. In most cases, officers have to actively encourage their targets because like most of us, targets are wary of strangers. Active encouragement usually requires using tactics like

- Asking targets over and over to commit a crime

- Developing personal relationships with targets

- Appealing personally to targets

- Supplying or helping targets get contraband (LaFave and Israel 1984, 1:412–413)

The defense of entrapment is *not* a constitutional right; it's a defense to criminal liability created and defined by statutes and courts. It's what we call an **affirmative de-fense.** That means defendants have the burden of introducing *some* evidence they were entrapped. If they meet this burden, then the burden shifts to the government to prove defendants were *not* entrapped. The jury—or the judge in trials without juries—decides whether officers, in fact, entrapped defendants. The courts have adopted two types of tests for entrapment: one is subjective, and the other is objective.

Subjective Tests

Encouragement is entrapment only if it crosses the line from acceptable to unaccept-able encouragement. How do we know when officers have crossed that line? Most states and the federal government have adopted a **subjective test of entrapment,** which focuses on the predisposition of defendants to commit crimes. According to the subjective test, defendants are entitled to the defense of entrapment if they can show *some* evidence of two elements:

1. They had no desire to commit the crime before the government's encouragement.

2. The government's encouragement *caused* them to commit the crime.

The crucial question in the subjective test is, "Where did criminal intent originate?" If it originated with the defendant, then the government didn't entrap the defendant. If it originated with the government, then the government did entrap the defendant. Put another way, if the defendant was predisposed to commit the crime and the government only provided her with the opportunity to commit it, then she wasn't entrapped.

According to the Minnesota Court of Appeals, government encouragement has to "go beyond mere solicitation...; it requires something in the nature of persuasion, badgering or pressure by the state" (*State v. Fitiwi* 2003). The legal encyclopedia *Corpus Juris Secundum* (2003, § 61) says the government has to use "trickery, persuasion, or fraud." In a leading U.S. Supreme Court case, *Sherman v. U.S.* (1958), government informant and undercover agent Kalchinian and drug addict Joe Sherman met in a treatment center. Kalchinian struck up a friendship with Sherman and eventually asked Sherman to get him some heroin. At first Sherman refused. However, after Kalchinian begged and pleaded for several weeks, Sherman finally gave in and got Kalchinian the heroin. The police promptly arrested Sherman. The Court understandably found that the intent originated with the government. According to the Court, given that Sherman was in treatment for his addiction he was hardly predisposed to commit a drug offense.

Once defendants have produced some evidence the government agent persuaded the defendant to commit the crime, the government then has to prove the defendant was predisposed to commit it. The circumstances the government can use vary somewhat from state to state, but they usually boil down to either the defendants' *character* or their *behavior*. Minnesota's list is typical:

1. Active solicitation of the crime

2. Prior criminal convictions

3. Prior criminal activity not resulting in conviction

4. Defendant's criminal reputation

5. By any other adequate means (*State v. Wright* 2001)

The U.S. Supreme Court applied the predisposition test of entrapment in a child pornography case, *Jacobson v. United States* (1992).

CASE | *Did the Government Entrap Jacobson?*

Jacobson v. United States
503 U.S. 540 (1992)

Keith Jacobson was convicted in the U.S. District Court for the District of Nebraska of receiving child pornography through the mail. A panel (3 members) of the Court of Appeals for the Eighth Circuit reversed. On rehearing en banc (the full court) affirmed. The U.S. Supreme Court reversed.

WHITE, J., joined by BLACKMUN, STEVENS, SOUTER, and THOMAS, JJ.

FACTS

In February 1984, Keith Jacobson, a 56-year-old Korean War veteran-turned-farmer who supported his elderly father in Nebraska, ordered two magazines and a brochure from a California adult bookstore. The magazines, entitled Bare Boys I and Bare Boys II, contained photographs of nude preteen and teenage boys. The contents of the magazines startled petitioner, who testified that he had expected to receive photographs of "young men 18 years or older." On cross-examination, he explained his response to the magazines:

[PROSECUTOR]: You were shocked and surprised that there were pictures of very young boys without clothes on, is that correct?

[JACOBSON]: Yes, I was.

[PROSECUTOR]: Were you offended?

[JACOBSON]: I was not offended because I thought these were a nudist type publication. Many of the pictures were out in a rural or outdoor setting. There was— I didn't draw any sexual connotation or connection with that.

The young men depicted in the magazines were not engaged in sexual activity, and Jacobson's receipt of the magazines was legal under both federal and Nebraska law. Within three months, the law with respect to child pornography changed; Congress passed the Act illegalizing the receipt through the mails of sexually explicit depictions of children. In the very month the new provision became law, postal inspectors found Jacobson's name on the mailing list of the California bookstore that had mailed him Bare Boys I and II. There followed over the next 2½ years repeated efforts by two Government agencies, through five fictitious organizations and a bogus pen pal, to explore Jacobson's willingness to break the new law by ordering sexually explicit photographs of children through the mail.

The Government began its efforts in January 1985 when a postal inspector sent Jacobson a letter supposedly from the American Hedonist Society, which in fact was a fictitious organization. The letter included a membership application and stated the Society's doctrine: that members had the "right to read what we desire, the right to discuss similar interests with those who share our philosophy, and finally that we have the right to seek pleasure without restrictions being placed on us by outdated puritan morality." Jacobson enrolled in the organization and returned a sexual attitude questionnaire that asked him to rank on a scale of one to four his enjoyment of various sexual materials, with one being "really enjoy," two being "enjoy," three being "somewhat enjoy," and four being "do not enjoy." Jacobson ranked the entry "pre-teen sex" as a two, but indicated that he was opposed to pedophilia.

For a time, the Government left Jacobson alone. But then a new "prohibited mailing specialist" in the Postal Service found Jacobson's name in a file, and in May 1986, Jacobson received a solicitation from a second fictitious consumer research company, "Midlands Data Research," seeking a response from those who "believe in the joys of sex and the complete awareness of those lusty and youthful lads and lasses of the neophite [*sic*] age." Record, Government Exhibit 8. The letter never explained whether

"neophite" referred to minors or young adults. Jacobson responded: "Please feel free to send me more information, I am interested in teenage sexuality. Please keep my name confidential."

Jacobson then heard from yet another Government creation, "Heartland Institute for a New Tomorrow" (HINT), which proclaimed it was "an organization founded to protect and promote sexual freedom and freedom of choice. We believe that arbitrarily imposed legislative sanctions restricting your sexual freedom should be rescinded through the legislative process." The letter also enclosed a second survey. Jacobson indicated that his interest in "preteen sex–homosexual" material was above average, but not high. In response to another question, Jacobson wrote: "Not only sexual expression but freedom of the press is under attack. We must be ever vigilant to counter attack right wing fundamentalists who are determined to curtail our freedoms."

HINT replied, portraying itself as a lobbying organization seeking to repeal "all statutes which regulate sexual activities, except those laws which deal with violent behavior, such as rape. HINT is also lobbying to eliminate any legal definition of 'the age of consent.'" These lobbying efforts were to be funded by sales from a catalog to be published in the future "offering the sale of various items which we believe you will find to be both interesting and stimulating." HINT also provided computer matching of group members with similar survey responses; and, although petitioner was supplied with a list of potential "pen pals," he did not initiate any correspondence.

Nevertheless, the Government's "prohibited mailing specialist" began writing to Jacobson, using the pseudonym "Carl Long." The letters employed a tactic known as "mirroring," which the inspector described as "reflecting whatever the interests are of the person we are writing to." Jacobson responded at first, indicating that his interest was primarily in "male-male items." Inspector "Long" wrote back:

My interests too are primarily male-male items. Are you satisfied with the type of VCR tapes available? Personally, I like the amateur stuff better if it's well produced as it can get more kinky and also seems more real. I think the actors enjoy it more.

Jacobson responded:

As far as my likes are concerned, I like good looking young guys (in their late teens and early 20's) doing their thing together.

Jacobson's letters to "Long" made no reference to child pornography. After writing two letters, petitioner discontinued the correspondence.

By March 1987, 34 months had passed since the Government obtained Jacobson's name from the mailing list of the California bookstore, and 26 months had passed since the Postal Service had commenced its mailings to petitioner. Although Jacobson had responded to surveys and letters, the Government had no evidence that petitioner had ever intentionally possessed or been exposed to child pornography. The Postal Service had not checked Jacobson's mail to determine whether he was receiving questionable mailings from persons—other than the Government—involved in the child pornography industry.

At this point, a second Government agency, the Customs Service, included Jacobson in its own child pornography sting, "Operation Borderline," after receiving his name on lists submitted by the Postal Service. Using the name of a fictitious Canadian company called "Produit Outaouais," the Customs Service mailed petitioner a brochure advertising photographs of young boys engaging in sex. Jacobson placed an order that was never filled.

The Postal Service also continued its efforts in the Jacobson case, writing to petitioner as the "Far Eastern Trading Company Ltd." The letter began:

As many of you know, much hysterical nonsense has appeared in the American media concerning "pornography" and what must be done to stop it from coming across your borders. This brief letter does not allow us to give much comments; however, why is your government spending millions of dollars to exercise international censorship while tons of drugs, which makes yours the world's most crime ridden country are passed through easily.

The letter went on to say:

We have devised a method of getting these to you without prying eyes of U.S. Customs seizing your mail.... After consultations with American solicitors, we have been advised that once we have posted our material through your system, it cannot be opened for any inspection without authorization of a judge.

The letter invited Jacobson to send for more information. It also asked Jacobson to sign an affirmation that he was "not a law enforcement officer or agent of the U.S. Government acting in an undercover capacity for the purpose of entrapping Far Eastern Trading Company, its agents or customers." Jacobson responded. A catalog was sent, and Jacobson ordered Boys Who Love Boys, a pornographic magazine depicting young boys engaged in various sexual activities. Jacobson was arrested after a controlled delivery of a photocopy of the magazine.

When Jacobson was asked at trial why he placed such an order, he explained the Government had succeeded in piquing his curiosity:

Well, the statement was made of all the trouble and the hysteria over pornography and I wanted to see what the material was. It didn't describe the—I didn't know for sure what kind of sexual action they were referring to in the Canadian letter.

In Jacobson's home, the Government found the Bare Boys magazines and materials that the Government had sent to him in the course of its protracted investigation, but no other materials that would indicate Jacobson collected, or was actively interested in, child pornography.

Jacobson was indicted for violating 18 U.S.C. § 2252 (a)(2)(A). The trial court instructed the jury on the Jacobson's entrapment defense. The jury was instructed:

As mentioned, one of the issues in this case is whether the defendant was entrapped. If the defendant was entrapped he must be found not guilty. The government has the burden of proving beyond a reasonable doubt that the defendant was not entrapped.

If the defendant before contact with law-enforcement officers or their agents did not have any intent or disposition to commit the crime charged and was induced or persuaded by law-enforcement officers or their agents to commit that crime, then he was entrapped. On the other hand, if the defendant before contact with law-enforcement officers or their agents did have an intent or disposition to commit the crime charged, then he was not entrapped even though law-enforcement officers or their agents provided a favorable opportunity to commit the crime or made committing the crime easier or even participated in acts essential to the crime.

Jacobson was convicted, and a divided Court of Appeals for the Eighth Circuit, sitting en banc, affirmed, concluding "Jacobson was not entrapped as a matter of law." We granted certiorari.

OPINION

There can be no dispute about the evils of child pornography or the difficulties that laws and law enforcement have encountered in eliminating it. Likewise, there can be no dispute that the Government may use undercover agents to enforce the law.... Artifice and stratagem may be employed to catch those engaged in criminal enterprises." In their zeal to enforce the law, however, Government agents may not originate a criminal design, implant in an innocent person's mind the disposition to commit a criminal act, and then induce commission of the crime so that the Government may prosecute. Where the Government has induced an individual to break the law and the defense of entrapment is at issue, as it was in this case, the prosecution must prove beyond reasonable doubt that the defendant was disposed to commit the criminal act prior to first being approached by Government agents.

Inducement is not at issue in this case. The Government does not dispute that it induced Jacobson to commit the crime. The sole issue is whether the Government carried its burden of proving that Jacobson was predisposed to violate the law before the Government intervened. . . . The Government's internal guidelines for undercover operations provide that an inducement to commit a crime should not be offered unless:

> (a) There is a reasonable indication, based on information developed through informants or other means, that the subject is engaging, has engaged, or is likely to engage in illegal activity of a similar type; or
> (b) The opportunity for illegal activity has been structured so that there is reason for believing that persons drawn to the opportunity, or brought to it, are predisposed to engage in the contemplated illegal activity.

Thus, an agent deployed to stop the traffic in illegal drugs may offer the opportunity to buy or sell drugs and, if the offer is accepted, make an arrest on the spot or later. In such a typical case, or in a more elaborate "sting" operation involving government-sponsored fencing where the defendant is simply provided with the opportunity to commit a crime, the entrapment defense is of little use because the ready commission of the criminal act amply demonstrates the defendant's predisposition. Had the agents . . . simply offered Jacobson the opportunity to order child pornography through the mails, and Jacobson . . . had promptly availed himself of this criminal opportunity, it is unlikely his entrapment defense would have warranted a jury instruction.

But that is not what happened here. By the time Jacobson finally placed his order, he had already been the target of 26 months of repeated mailings and communications from Government agents and fictitious organizations. Therefore, although he had become predisposed to break the law by May 1987, it is our view that the Government did not prove this predisposition was independent and not the product of the attention the Government had directed at Jacobson since January 1985.

The prosecution's evidence of predisposition falls into two categories: evidence developed prior to the Postal Service's mail campaign, and that developed during the course of the investigation. The sole piece of preinvestiga-tion evidence is Jacobson's 1984 order and receipt of the Bare Boys magazines. But this is scant if any proof of Jacobson's predisposition to commit an illegal act. . . . It may indicate a predisposition to view sexually oriented photographs that are responsive to his sexual tastes; but evidence that merely indicates a generic inclination to act within a broad range, not all of which is criminal, is of little probative value in establishing predisposition.

Furthermore, Jacobson was acting within the law at the time he received these magazines. Receipt through the mails of sexually explicit depictions of children for non-commercial use did not become illegal under federal law until May 1984, and Nebraska had no law that forbade his possession of such material until 1988. Evidence of predisposition to do what once was lawful is not, by itself, sufficient to show predisposition to do what is now illegal, for there is a common understanding that most people obey the law even when they disapprove of it. . . . Hence, the fact that Jacobson legally ordered and received the Bare Boys magazines does little to further the Government's burden of proving he was predisposed to commit a criminal act. This is particularly true given Jacobson's unchallenged testimony that he did not know until they arrived that the magazines would depict minors.

The prosecution's evidence gathered during the investigation also fails to carry the Government's burden. Jacobson's responses to the many communications prior to the ultimate criminal act were at most indicative of certain personal inclinations, including a predisposition to view photographs of preteen sex and a willingness to promote a given agenda by supporting lobbying organizations. Even so, his responses hardly support an inference that he would commit the crime of receiving child pornography through the mails. Furthermore, a person's inclinations and "fantasies . . . are his own and beyond the reach of government. . . ."

On the other hand, the strong arguable inference is that, by waving the banner of individual rights and disparaging the legitimacy and constitutionality of efforts to restrict the availability of sexually explicit materials, the Government not only excited Jacobson's interest in sexually explicit materials banned by law but also exerted substantial pressure on Jacobson to obtain and read such material as part of a fight against censorship and the infringement of individual rights. For instance, HINT described itself as "an organization founded to protect and promote sexual freedom and freedom of choice" and stated that "the most appropriate means to accomplish its objectives is to promote honest dialogue among concerned individuals and to continue its lobbying efforts with State Legislators." These lobbying efforts were to be financed through catalog sales. Ibid. Mailings from the equally fictitious American Hedonist Society, and the correspondence from the nonexistent Carl Long, endorsed these themes.

Similarly, the two solicitations in the spring of 1987 raised the specter of censorship while suggesting Jacobson ought to be allowed to do what he had been solicited to do. The mailing from the Customs Service referred to "the worldwide ban and intense enforcement on this type of material," observed that "what was legal and commonplace is now an 'underground' and secretive service," and emphasized that "this environment forces us to take extreme measures" to ensure delivery. The Postal Service solicitation described the concern about child pornography as "hysterical nonsense," decried "international censorship," and assured petitioner, based on consultation with "American solicitors," that an order that had been posted could not be opened for inspection without authorization of a judge. It further asked petitioner to affirm he was not a Government agent attempting to entrap the mail order company or its customers. In these particulars, both Government solicitations suggested receiving this material was something Jacobson ought to be allowed to do.

Jacobson's ready response to these solicitations cannot be enough to establish beyond reasonable doubt he was predisposed, prior to the Government acts intended to create predisposition, to commit the crime of receiving child pornography through the mails. The evidence that he was ready and willing to commit the offense came only after the Government had devoted $2\frac{1}{2}$ years to convincing him he had or should have the right to engage in the very behavior proscribed by law. Rational jurors could not say beyond a reasonable doubt that Jacobson possessed the requisite predisposition prior to the Government's investigation and that it existed independent of the Government's many and varied approaches to him. As was explained in *Sherman*, where entrapment was found as a matter of law, "the Government may not play on the weaknesses of an innocent party and beguile him into committing crimes which he otherwise would not have attempted."

Law enforcement officials go too far when they "implant in the mind of an innocent person the disposition to commit the alleged offense and induce its commission in order that they may prosecute."... When the Government's quest for convictions leads to the apprehension of an otherwise law-abiding citizen who, if left to his own devices, likely would have never run afoul of the law, the courts should intervene. Because we conclude this is such a case and the prosecution failed... to adduce evidence to support the jury verdict Jacobson was predisposed, indepen-

dent of the Government's acts and beyond a reasonable doubt, to violate the law by receiving child pornography through the mails, we REVERSE the Court of Appeals' judgment affirming the conviction of Keith Jacobson.

DISSENT

O'CONNOR, J., joins with REHNQUIST, CJ.,
and KENNEDY AND SCALIA, JJ.

Keith Jacobson was offered only two opportunities to buy child pornography through the mail. Both times, he ordered. Both times, he asked for opportunities to buy more. He needed no Government agent to coax, threaten, or persuade him; no one played on his sympathies, friendship, or suggested that his committing the crime would further a greater good. In fact, no Government agent even contacted him face to face. The Government contends that from the enthusiasm with which Mr. Jacobson responded to the chance to commit a crime, a reasonable jury could permissibly infer beyond a reasonable doubt that he was predisposed to commit the crime. I agree.

The first time the Government sent Mr. Jacobson a catalog of illegal materials, he ordered a set of photographs advertised as picturing "young boys in sex action fun." He enclosed the following note with his order: "I received your brochure and decided to place an order. If I like your product, I will order more later."... Mr. Jacobson's order was never delivered.

The second time the Government sent a catalog of illegal materials, Mr. Jacobson ordered a magazine called "Boys Who Love Boys," described as: "11 year old and 14 year old boys get it on in every way possible. Oral, anal sex and heavy masturbation. If you love boys, you will be delighted with this." Along with his order, Mr. Jacobson sent the following note: "Will order other items later. I want to be discreet in order to protect you and me."

Government agents admittedly did not offer Mr. Jacobson the chance to buy child pornography right away. Instead, they first sent questionnaires in order to make sure he was generally interested in the subject matter. Indeed, a "cold call" in such a business would not only risk rebuff and suspicion, but might also shock and offend the uninitiated, or expose minors to suggestive materials. Mr. Jacobson's responses to the questionnaires gave the investigators reason to think he would be interested in photographs depicting preteen sex.

The Court, however, concludes that a reasonable jury could not have found Mr. Jacobson to be predisposed beyond a reasonable doubt on the basis of his responses to the Government's catalogs, even though it admits that, by that time, he was predisposed to commit the crime. The

Government, the Court holds, failed to provide evidence that Mr. Jacobson's obvious predisposition at the time of the crime "was independent and not the product of the attention that the Government had directed at petitioner." In so holding, I believe the Court fails to acknowledge the reasonableness of the jury's inference from the evidence, redefines "predisposition," and introduces a new requirement that Government sting operations have a reasonable suspicion of illegal activity before contacting a suspect....

Today, the Court holds that Government conduct may be considered to create a predisposition to commit a crime, even before any Government action to induce the commission of the crime. In my view, this holding changes entrapment doctrine. Generally, the inquiry is whether a suspect is predisposed before the Government induces the commission of the crime, not before the Government makes initial contact with him. There is no dispute here that the Government's questionnaires and letters were not sufficient to establish inducement; they did not even suggest that Mr. Jacobson should engage in any illegal activity. If all the Government had done was to send these materials, Mr. Jacobson's entrapment defense would fail. Yet the Court holds that the Government must prove not only that a suspect was predisposed to commit the crime before the opportunity to commit it arose, but also before the Government came on the scene.

The rule that preliminary Government contact can create a predisposition has the potential to be misread by lower courts as well as criminal investigators as requiring that the Government must have sufficient evidence of a defendant's predisposition before it ever seeks to contact him. Surely the Court cannot intend to impose such a requirement, for it would mean that the Government must have a reasonable suspicion of criminal activity before it begins an investigation, a condition that we have never before imposed....

The Court's rule is all the more troubling because it does not distinguish between Government conduct that merely highlights the temptation of the crime itself, and Government conduct that threatens, coerces, or leads a suspect to commit a crime... For example, in... *Sherman,* the Government agent played on the defendant's sympathies, pretending to be going through drug withdrawal and begging the defendant to relieve his distress by helping him buy drugs. The Government conduct in this case is not comparable.

While the Court states that the Government "exerted substantial pressure on petitioner to obtain and read such material as part of a fight against censorship and the in-

fringement of individual rights," one looks at the record in vain for evidence of such "substantial pressure." The most one finds is letters advocating legislative action to liberalize obscenity laws, letters which could easily be ignored or thrown away. Much later, the Government sent separate mailings of catalogs of illegal materials. Nowhere did the Government suggest that the proceeds of the sale of the illegal materials would be used to support legislative reforms. While one of the HINT letters suggested that lobbying efforts would be funded by sales from a catalog, the catalogs actually sent, nearly a year later, were from different fictitious entities (Produit Outaouais and Far Eastern Trading Company), and gave no suggestion that money would be used for any political purposes.

Nor did the Government claim to be organizing a civil disobedience movement, which would protest the pornography laws by breaking them:..."For those of you who have enjoyed youthful material...we have devised a method of getting these to you without prying eyes of U.S. Customs seizing your mail."...

In sum, the Court fails to construe the evidence in the light most favorable to the Government,* and fails to draw all reasonable inferences in the Government's favor.** It was surely reasonable for the jury to infer that Mr. Jacobson was predisposed beyond a reasonable doubt, even if other inferences from the evidence were also possible....

Because I believe there was sufficient evidence to uphold the jury's verdict, I respectfully dissent.

Questions

1. What specific facts demonstrate that the government induced Keith Jacobson to order the child pornography?

2. What evidence demonstrates that Keith Jacobson was predisposed to commit the crime?

3. Why did the Court reverse the conviction even though the jury convicted him?

4. What does the dissent mean when it says that the majority has changed the law of entrapment?

5. Commentary following the Court's decision claimed the decision "ties the hands of law enforcement officers." Do you agree? Defend your answer.

---

*Because the Government prevailed at the trial.

**For the same reason.

Objective Test

A minority (but growing number) of courts has adopted an **objective test of entrapment**, also called the **hypothetical person test** (*State v. Wilkins* 1983). The objective test of entrapment doesn't focus on the predisposition of the specific defendant in the case. Instead, it focuses on whether the actions of government officers would get a hypothetical "reasonable person" to commit a crime. According to the objective test, if the actions of the officer would induce an "ordinarily law-abiding" person to commit the crime, the court should dismiss the case. This test is a *prophylactic rule* aimed to deter "unsavory police methods." Courts (not juries) decide whether police methods would cause a hypothetical reasonable person to commit a crime they otherwise wouldn't commit. U.S. Supreme Court Justice Felix Frankfurter, concurring in *Sherman v. U.S.* (1958, discussed earlier) about the core idea behind the objective test, wrote:

> No matter what the defendant's past record and present inclinations to criminality, or the depths to which he has sunk in the estimation of society, certain police conduct to ensnare him into further crime is not to be tolerated by an advanced society. (382–383)

SUMMARY

I. Remedies against officer misconduct
  A. Two types of remedies
    1. Remedies affecting the outcome of the state's criminal case against defendants—exclusionary rule and defense of entrapment
    2. Remedies sought in separate proceedings
      a. Criminal prosecution of officers
      b. Civil lawsuits to sue officers, departments, and/or municipalities
      c. Administrative review of police misconduct
  B. Remedies aren't mutually exclusive (don't have to choose among them)
  C. No constitutional right to exclusionary rule or defense of entrapment

II. The exclusionary rule
  A. U.S. has the only criminal justice system in the world where courts throw out "good evidence" because government used "bad methods" to get it
    1. "Good evidence" means evidence that can help prove defendant's guilt
    2. "Bad methods" means conduct that violates
      a. Fourth Amendment ban on unreasonable searches and seizures
      b. Fifth Amendment right against self-incrimination
      c. Sixth Amendment right to counsel
      d. Fifth and Fourteenth Amendment rights to due process of law
  B. History
    1. No mention of the exclusionary rule in the Constitution; James Madison believed it was implied in the judicial power
    2. 1914, *Weeks v. U.S.*—U.S. Supreme Court created the rule
      a. Applied only to federal courts
      b. Covered only private papers and belongings

3. 1920, *Silverthorne Lumber Co. v. U.S.*—Court expanded rule to cover evidence indirectly based on illegal government action ("fruit of the poisonous tree")

4. 1925, *Agnello v. U.S.*—Court expanded the rule to cover contraband

5. 1949, *Wolf v. Colorado*—Court applied the Fourth Amendment but not the exclusionary rule to state proceedings; states could decide remedy for themselves

6. 1961, *Mapp v. Ohio*—Court applied the exclusionary rule to state criminal proceedings

7. 1984, *U.S. v. Leon*—exclusionary rule is *not* a constitutional righ; it's a device to protect constitutional rights

C. Justifications

1. Constitutional right—the 4th, 5th, 6th, and 14th Amendment rights wouldn't mean anything without the exclusion

2. Judicial integrity—courts shouldn't participate in unconstitutional behavior by approving it

3. Deterrence—prevent unconstitutional conduct by government officers

D. Scope

1. Scope of the rule is restricted because of the belief that the social costs of freeing guilty people and of undermining the prosecution's case are too high to keep good evidence out of court

2. Rule restricted to the government's case-in-chief at trial

3. Exceptions

   a. Collateral use—illegally obtained evidence is admissible in all nontrial settings (bail hearings, preliminary hearings, grand jury proceedings, habeas corpus proceedings)

   b. Cross-examination—prosecution can use illegally obtained evidence to undermine defense witness' (including defendant) credibility

   c. Exceptions to "fruit of the poisonous tree" rule; basic idea is government shouldn't be in a *worse* position after illegal conduct

      (1) Attenuation—originally tainted evidence is admissible if the totality of circumstances in the case proves that the poisonous connection between police illegality and the evidence has weakened enough

      (2) Independent source—originally tainted evidence is admissible if after violating the Constitution, officers get the same evidence in a totally separate lawful action

      (3) Inevitable discovery—originally tainted evidence is admissible if police law-breaking produced the evidence but the evidence would have eventually been discovered anyway

E. Illegally seized (arrested) persons

1. Illegally arrested persons aren't fruit of the poisonous tree, so they can be produced, tried, and convicted in court

2. Courts don't ask how individuals got to court (that's a police matter)

F. Reasonable good-faith exception

1. Applies only to evidence obtained by search warrants that later turn out to be illegal

2. Evidence obtained during execution of an illegal search warrant is admissible only if government can prove

        a. Officer honestly relied on the legality of the warrants

        b. It was reasonable for officers to believe the warrants were legal

     3. Rationale—there's no deterrent effect if officers honestly and reasonably believed the warrants were lawful

  G. Non–law enforcement government officials

     1. Prevention of government unconstitutional behavior is the only justification for the exclusionary rule

     2. Rule applies to police because they're deterred by exclusion

     3. Rule doesn't apply to judges and other court personnel (like clerks), because there's no evidence exclusion would deter their misconduct

III. The defense of entrapment

  A. Criminal cases are dismissed if the government pressured defendants to commit crimes they wouldn't have committed without pressure

  B. Encouragement isn't entrapment

  C. Line between entrapment and encouragement determined by two tests

     1. Subjective test focuses on defendants' predisposition to commit crime

        a. Defendants have the burden of presenting *some* evidence of two elements

           (1) They had *no* predisposition to commit the crime

           (2) Government pressure *caused* them to commit the crimes

        b. If defendants meet their burden, the government has to prove the defendants *were* predisposed

        c. The government can prove disposition by any of a variety of circumstances related to

           (1) Conduct of the defendants—prior criminal activity

           (2) Character of the defendants—reputation

     2. Objective test focuses on behavior of law enforcement

        a. If the government's actions would induce an ordinarily law-abiding person to commit the crime

        b. The case should be dismissed

Go to the Criminal Procedure 6e CD to download this summary outline. The outline has been formatted so that you can add notes to it during class lectures, or later create a customized chapter outline to use while reviewing. Either way, the summary outline will help you understand the "big picture" and fill in the details as you study.

REVIEW QUESTIONS

1. Identify two types of remedies against government wrongdoing and the differences between them, and give examples of each.

2. Is there a constitutional right to the exclusionary rule and the defense of entrapment? Explain your answer.

3. Briefly trace the history of the exclusionary rule through the leading U.S. Supreme Court cases that created and expanded it.

4. Identify and explain the rationales behind the three justifications for the exclusionary rule. Which justification does the U.S. Supreme Court use today?

5. Explain the balancing test the U.S. Supreme Court adopted to apply the deterrence justification.

6. Summarize U.S. Supreme Court Justice Louis Brandeis's arguments in favor of the exclusionary rule.

7. List and explain five exceptions to the exclusionary rule.

8. Identify the rationale for the attenuation, independent source, and inevitable discovery exceptions to the exclusionary rule.

9. Why aren't illegally arrested persons "fruit of a poisonous tree"?

10. State the narrow scope of the reasonable good-faith exception to the exclusionary rule.

11. Identify the assumptions of the Warren and Rehnquist courts regarding the exclusionary rule.

12. According to Professor Christopher Slobogin, why is no one likely to win the empirical debate over the accuracy of the assumptions you identified in (11)?

13. Describe and explain the U.S. Supreme Court's attitude toward the defense of entrapment throughout most of our history.

14. Identify four examples of active law enforcement encouragement.

15. Identify the difference between the subjective and objective tests of entrapment.

16. Identify two elements in the subjective test of entrapment.

17. What's the crucial question in the subjective test of entrapment?

18. Describe how the U.S. Supreme Court applied the subjective case to the facts of *Sherman v. U.S.*

19. Identify the two kinds of circumstances the government can use to prove defendants' predisposition to commit crimes. Give an example of each.

20. According to U.S. Supreme Court Justice Felix Frankfurter, what's the core idea behind the objective test of entrapment?

KEY TERMS

THE COMPANION WEB SITE
FOR *CRIMINAL PROCEDURE,* SIXTH EDITION

http://cj.wadsworth.com/samaha/crim_pro6e

 Supplement your review of this chapter by going to the companion Web site to take one of the Tutorial Quizzes, use the flash cards to test yourself on the key terms from each chapter, and check out the many other study aids you'll find there. You'll find valuable data and resources at your fingertips to help you study for that big exam or write that important paper.

11 Constitutional Violations: Other Remedies Against Government Misconduct

Chapter Main Points

- A wide range of remedies exists to hold officers, departments, and governments accountable for illegal acts.
- Most illegal police conduct is also a crime, but it's difficult (and should be) to prove criminal intent beyond a reasonable doubt.
- Most people who seek *compensation* for official wrongdoing don't succeed.
- Law enforcement officers and the governments responsible for them aren't liable for injuries if officers acted reasonably, in good faith, and without malice.
- Individual law enforcement officers and the governments responsible for them have no affirmative duty to protect individuals from other individuals who violate their constitutional rights.
- Judges are *absolutely* immune and prosecutors are *nearly* absolutely immune from damage suits.
- Internal department disciplinary procedures are based on the idea that the police can best enforce measures to deal with police misconduct.
- External civilian review of police misconduct is based on the idea that the police shouldn't police themselves.

A State's failure to protect an individual against private violence simply doesn't constitute a violation of the Due Process Clause.

Pinder v. Johnson (1995)

REMEDIES FOR OFFICIAL MISCONDUCT

We've talked about remedies that affect the determination of guilt (trial stage) in criminal cases against defendants (exclusionary rule and defense of entrapment [Chapter 10]). In this chapter, we discuss remedies against officers that aren't available in the criminal trial case against defendants. They result from three separate actions:

1. *Criminal law.* Prosecuting the officer.
2. *Civil law.* Suing the officer, the police department, or the government.
3. *Administrative.* Disciplining the officer outside the judicial system.

Let's look at these three actions and the remedies that flow from them.

CRIMINAL ACTIONS

Most police misconduct can be a crime. So, a police officer who *illegally* shoots and kills a person might have committed criminal homicide. Illegal arrests can be false imprisonment. Illegal searches can be trespasses—and maybe breaking and entering, too. How likely is it that police officers will be charged with crimes, convicted, and punished when they break the law? Not very. Why? Judges and juries don't see police misconduct as criminal. And with good reason. In our criminal justice system, the government has to prove criminal *intent* beyond a reasonable doubt. If police officers honestly believe they were enforcing the law and not committing a crime (which in most cases is either true or difficult to prove beyond a reasonable doubt), they're not guilty. And, this is the way it should be. The standard of proof has to be the same for officers as for everybody else. There's a second reason. Even if officers are guilty of criminal misconduct, prosecutors hesitate to prosecute, and juries are unwilling to convict police officers who are "only trying to do their job," especially when the "victims" might be criminals (or at least people who associate with criminals).

CIVIL ACTIONS

Most individuals seeking a remedy for official law-breaking (**plaintiffs**) want compensation (technically called **damages**) for the injuries caused by police misconduct. *How* do they get damages? The only way is by becoming plaintiffs in court in a **civil action** (meaning it's not a criminal case). *Who* can plaintiffs sue for money damages? Any or all of the following: individual law enforcement officers; the officers' superiors (like police chiefs and sheriffs); departments; and government units in charge of officers and departments. *Where* do they sue? In state and federal courts. We'll look separately at civil actions for damages against federal officers, state officers, departments and government units, and other government employees, because they're controlled by different statutes, court decisions, and governments. We'll also examine some of the hurdles to suing the government.

Suing U.S. Officers and the U.S. Government

Lawsuits against individual federal law enforcement officers are called **constitutional tort (*Bivens*) actions.** Lawsuits against the federal government for their officers' constitutional torts are called **Federal Tort Claims Act (FTCA) actions.** Let's look at each.

Suing U.S. Officers

Until 1971, individuals were banned from suing federal officers for violations of their constitutional rights. All that changed after the U.S. Supreme Court decided *Bivens v. Six Unnamed FBI Agents* (1971). In that case, on November 16, 1967, six FBI agents entered Webster Bivens's apartment without a search or arrest warrant. After they searched his apartment "from stem to stern," the agents arrested Bivens for violating federal drug laws and handcuffed him in the presence of his wife and children. The agents took Bivens first to the Federal Court Building in Brooklyn and then to the Federal Narcotic Bureau, "where he was interrogated, fingerprinted, photographed, subjected to search of his person, and booked." Bivens claimed these events caused him "great humiliation, embarrassment, and mental suffering," and would "continue to do so," and sought damages of $15,000 from each of the six officers (390). In *Bivens,* the Court created a constitutional tort, a private right to sue federal officers for violations of plaintiffs' constitutional rights. Called Bivens *actions,* plaintiffs have to prove two elements:

1. Officers were acting **under color of authority,** or appearance of power (Garner 1987, 123–124).

2. Officers' actions deprived the plaintiff of a constitutional right.

Even if plaintiffs prove these two elements, they don't automatically "win" their case. Law enforcement officers have a defense called **qualified immunity** (also called the **"good faith" defense**). According to this complex defense, individual officers can't be held personally liable for official action if

1. Their action meets the test of "objective legal reasonableness."

2. Reasonableness is measured by legal rules "clearly established" at the time the officers acted.

The reason for creating this easy test was to protect officers' broad discretion to do their job and keep them (and the courts) from being bombarded with frivolous lawsuits. The U.S. Supreme Court created and explained why it created the qualified immunity defense against constitutional torts in *Anderson v. Creighton* (1987).

Anderson v. Creighton

483 U.S. 635 (1987)

Robert E. Creighton Jr., his wife, and others sued FBI Agent Russell Anderson in the U.S. District Court for the District of Minnesota. The U.S. District Court granted summary judgment in favor of the agent. The Court of Appeals for the Eighth Circuit reversed and remanded. The U.S. Supreme Court granted certiorari, vacated the Circuit Court's judgment and remanded the case.

SCALIA, J., joined by REHNQUIST, CJ., and WHITE, BLACKMUN, POWELL, and O'CONNOR JJ.

FACTS

Russell Anderson is an agent of the Federal Bureau of Investigation. On November 11, 1983, Anderson and other state and federal law enforcement officers conducted a warrantless search of the Creighton family's home. The search was conducted because Anderson believed that Vadaain Dixon, a man suspected of a bank robbery committed earlier that day, might be found there. He was not.

...On the night of November 11, 1983, Sarisse and Robert Creighton and their three young daughters were spending a quiet evening at their home when a spotlight suddenly flashed through their front window. Mr. Creighton opened the door and was confronted by several uniformed and plain clothes officers, many of them brandishing shotguns. All of the officers were white; the Creightons are black. Mr. Creighton claims that none of the officers responded when he asked what they wanted. Instead, by his account (as verified by a St. Paul police report), one of the officers told him to 'keep his hands in sight' while the other officers rushed through the door. When Mr. Creighton asked if they had a search warrant, one of the officers told him, 'We don't have a search warrant [and] don't need [one]; you watch too much TV.'

Mr. Creighton asked the officers to put their guns away because his children were frightened, but the officers refused. Mrs. Creighton awoke to the shrieking of her children, and was confronted by an officer who pointed a shotgun at her. She allegedly observed the officers yelling at her three daughters to 'sit their damn asses down and stop screaming.' She asked the officer, 'What the hell is going on?' The officer allegedly did not explain the situation and simply said to her, 'Why don't you make your damn kids sit on the couch and make them shut up?' One

of the officers asked Mr. Creighton if he had a red and silver car. As Mr. Creighton led the officers downstairs to his garage, where his maroon Oldsmobile was parked, one of the officers punched him in the face, knocking him to the ground, and causing him to bleed from the mouth and the forehead. Mr. Creighton alleges that he was attempting to move past the officer to open the garage door when the officer panicked and hit him. The officer claims that Mr. Creighton attempted to grab his shotgun, even though Mr. Creighton was not a suspect in any crime and had no contraband in his home or on his person. Shaunda, the Creighton's ten-year-old daughter, witnessed the assault and screamed for her mother to come help. She claims that one of the officers then hit her.

Mrs. Creighton phoned her mother, but an officer allegedly kicked and grabbed the phone and told her to 'hang up that damn phone.' She told her children to run to their neighbor's house for safety. The children ran out and a plainclothes officer chased them. The Creightons' neighbor allegedly told Mrs. Creighton that the officer ran into her house and grabbed Shaunda by the shoulders and shook her. The neighbor allegedly told the officer, 'Can't you see she's in shock; leave her alone and get out of my house.' Mrs. Creighton's mother later brought Shaunda to the emergency room at Children's Hospital for an arm injury caused by the officer's rough handling.

During the melee, family members and friends began arriving at the Creighton's home. Mrs. Creighton claims that she was embarrassed in front of her family and friends by the invasion of their home and their rough treatment as if they were suspects in a major crime. At this time, she again asked Anderson for a search warrant. He allegedly replied, 'I don't need a damn search warrant when I'm looking for a fugitive.' The officers did not discover the allegedly unspecified 'fugitive' at the Creightons' home or any evidence whatsoever that he had been there or that the Creightons were involved in any type of criminal activity. Nonetheless, the officers then arrested and handcuffed Mr. Creighton for obstruction of justice and brought him to the police station where he was jailed overnight, then released without being charged.

The Creightons later filed suit against Anderson in a Minnesota state court, asserting among other things a claim for money damages under the Fourth Amendment. *Bivens v. Six Unknown Fed. Narcotics Agents*, 403 U.S. 388 (1971) After removing the suit to Federal District Court, Anderson filed a motion to dismiss or for summary judgment, arguing that the *Bivens* claim was barred by Anderson's qualified immunity from civil damages liability. Before any discovery took place, the District Court granted summary judgment on the ground that the search was lawful, holding that the undisputed facts revealed that Anderson had had probable cause to search the Creighton's home and that his failure to obtain a warrant was justified by the presence of exigent circumstances.

The Creightons appealed to the Court of Appeals for the Eighth Circuit, which reversed. The Court of Appeals held ... Anderson was not entitled to summary judgment on qualified immunity grounds, since the right Anderson was alleged to have violated—the right of persons to be protected from warrantless searches of their home unless the searching officers have probable cause and there are exigent circumstances—was clearly established.

Anderson filed a petition for certiorari, arguing that the Court of Appeals erred by refusing to consider his argument that he was entitled to summary judgment on qualified immunity grounds if he could establish as a matter of law that a reasonable officer could have believed the search to be lawful. We granted the petition, to consider that important question.

OPINION

When government officials abuse their offices, actions for damages may offer the only realistic avenue for vindication of constitutional guarantees. On the other hand, permitting damages suits against government officials can entail substantial social costs, including the risk that fear of personal monetary liability and harassing litigation will unduly inhibit officials in the discharge of their duties.

Our cases have accommodated these conflicting concerns by generally providing government officials performing discretionary functions with a qualified immunity, shielding them from civil damages liability as long as their actions could reasonably have been thought consistent with the rights they are alleged to have violated. Somewhat more concretely, whether an official protected by qualified immunity may be held personally liable for an allegedly unlawful official action generally turns on the 'objective legal reasonableness' of the action, assessed in light of the legal rules that were 'clearly established' at the time it was taken.... The contours of the right must be sufficiently clear that a reasonable official would understand that what he is doing violates that right. This is not to say that an official action is protected by qualified immunity unless the very action in question has previously been held unlawful, but it is to say that in the light of pre-existing law the unlawfulness must be apparent....

The Creightons [argue] ... that even if Anderson is entitled to qualified immunity under the usual principles of qualified immunity ... an exception should be made to those principles in the circumstances of this case.... We reject the Creightons ... proposal that no immunity should be provided to police officers who conduct unlawful warrantless searches of innocent third parties' homes in search of fugitives. They rest this proposal on the assertion that officers conducting such searches were strictly liable at English common law if the fugitive was not present. Although it is true that we have observed that our determinations as to the scope of official immunity are made in the light of the "common-law tradition," we have never suggested that the precise contours of official immunity can and should be slavishly derived from the often arcane rules of the common law....

The general rule of qualified immunity is intended to provide government officials with the ability reasonably to anticipate when their conduct may give rise to liability for damages. Where that rule is applicable, officials can know that they will not be held personally liable as long as their actions are reasonable in light of current American law. That security would be utterly defeated if officials were unable to determine whether they were protected by the rule without entangling themselves in the vagaries of the English and American common law. We are unwilling to Balkanize the rule of qualified immunity by carving exceptions at the level of detail the Creightons propose. We therefore decline to make an exception to the general rule of qualified immunity for cases involving allegedly unlawful warrantless searches of innocent third parties' homes in search of fugitives.

For the reasons stated, we vacate the judgment of the Court of Appeals and REMAND the case for further proceedings consistent with this opinion.

DISSENT

STEVENS, J., joined by BRENNAN and MARSHALL, JJ. ... The Court ... announces a new rule of law that protects federal agents who make forcible nighttime entries into the homes of innocent citizens without probable cause, without a warrant, and without any valid emergency justification for their warrantless search.... The Court of Appeals understood the principle of qualified immunity ... to shield government officials performing discretionary functions from exposure to damages liability unless their conduct violated clearly established statutory or constitutional rights of which a reasonable person would have known. Applying this principle, the Court of Appeals held that the Creightons' Fourth Amendment rights and the exigent circumstances doctrine were clearly established at the time of the search. Moreover, apparently referring to the 'extraordinary circumstances' defense...for a defendant who 'can prove that he neither knew nor should have known of the relevant legal standard,' the Court determined that Anderson could not reasonably have been unaware of these clearly established principles of law.

...The Court of Appeals' judgment rejecting Anderson's claim to immunity...raises the question whether this Court should approve a double standard of reasonableness—the constitutional standard already embodied in the Fourth Amendment and an even more generous standard that protects any officer who reasonably could have believed that his conduct was constitutionally reasonable.... Accepting for the moment the Court's double standard of reasonableness, I would affirm the judgment of the Court of Appeals because it correctly concluded that Anderson has not satisfied the...standard for immunity....

In this Court, Anderson has not argued that any relevant rule of law—whether the probable-cause requirement or the exigent-circumstances exception to the warrant requirement—was not 'clearly established' in November 1983. Rather, he argues that a competent officer might have concluded that the particular set of facts he faced did constitute 'probable cause' and 'exigent circumstances,' and that his own reasonable belief that the conduct engaged in was within the law suffices to establish immunity....

The Court's decision today represents a departure from the view we expressed two years ago in *Mitchell v. Forsyth*, 472 U.S. 511 (1985). We held that petitioner was entitled to qualified immunity for authorizing an unconstitutional wiretap because it was not clearly established that warrantless domestic security wiretapping violated the Fourth Amendment. We added in a footnote:

> 'We do not intend to suggest that an official is always immune from liability or suit for a warrantless search merely because the warrant requirement has never explicitly been held to apply to a search conducted in identical circumstances. But in cases where there is a legitimate question whether an exception to the warrant requirement exists, it cannot be said that a warrantless search violates clearly established law.'

Of course, the probable-cause requirement for an officer who faces the situation Anderson did was clearly established. In addition, an officer's belief that his particular warrantless search was justified (by exigent circumstances, in this case) is analytically no different from a situation in which the warrant requirement has not been explicitly held to apply to the particular search undertaken by the officer....

Although the question does not appear to have been argued in, or decided by, the Court of Appeals, this Court has decided to apply a double standard of reasonableness in damages actions against federal agents who are alleged to have violated an innocent citizen's Fourth Amendment rights. By double standard I mean a standard that affords a law enforcement official two layers of insulation from liability or other adverse consequence, such as suppression of evidence. Having already adopted such a double standard in applying the exclusionary rule to searches authorized by an invalid warrant, *United States v. Leon*, 468 U.S. 897 (1984), the Court seems prepared and even anxious in this case to remove any requirement that the officer must obey the Fourth Amendment when entering a private home. I remain convinced that in a suit for damages as well as in a hearing on a motion to suppress evidence, 'an official search and seizure cannot be both 'unreasonable' and 'reasonable' at the same time.'

A federal official may not with impunity ignore the limitations which the controlling law has placed on his powers. The effect of the Court's (literally unwarranted) extension of qualified immunity, I fear, is that it allows federal agents to ignore the limitations of the probable-cause and warrant requirements with impunity. The Court does so in the name of avoiding interference with legitimate law enforcement activities even though the probable-cause requirement, which limits the police's exercise of coercive authority, is itself a form of immunity that frees them to exercise that power without fear of strict liability....

The argument that police officers need special immunity to encourage them to take vigorous enforcement action when they are uncertain about their right to make a forcible entry into a private home has already been accepted in our jurisprudence. We have held that the police act reasonably in entering a house when they have probable cause to believe a fugitive is in the house and exigent circumstances make it impracticable to obtain a warrant. This interpretation of the Fourth Amendment allows room for police intrusion, without a warrant, on the privacy of even innocent citizens. In *Pierson v. Ray*, 386 U.S., at 555, we held that police officers would not be liable in an action brought under 42 U.S.C. § 1983 'if they acted in good faith and with probable cause....' We explained: 'Under the prevailing view in this country a peace officer who arrests someone with probable cause is not liable for false arrest simply because the innocence of the suspect is later proved. A policeman's lot is not so unhappy that he must choose between being charged with dereliction of duty if he does not arrest when he has probable cause, and being mulcted in damages if he does.'

Thus, until now the Court has not found intolerable the use of a probable-cause standard to protect the police officer from exposure to liability simply because his reasonable conduct is subsequently shown to have been mistaken.

Today, however, the Court counts the law enforcement interest twice and the individual's privacy interest only once.

The Court's double-counting approach reflects understandable sympathy for the plight of the officer and an overriding interest in unfettered law enforcement. It ascribes a far lesser importance to the privacy interest of innocent citizens than did the Framers of the Fourth Amendment. The importance of that interest and the possible magnitude of its invasion are both illustrated by the facts of this case. The home of an innocent family was invaded by several officers without a warrant, without the owner's consent, with a substantial show of force, and with blunt expressions of disrespect for the law and for the rights of the family members.

As the case comes to us, we must assume that the intrusion violated the Fourth Amendment. Proceeding on that assumption, I see no reason why the family's interest in the security of its own home should be accorded a lesser weight than the Government's interest in carrying out an invasion that was unlawful. Arguably, if the Government considers it important not to discourage such conduct, it should provide indemnity to its officers. Preferably, however, it should furnish the kind of training for its law enforcement agents that would entirely eliminate the necessity for the Court to distinguish between the conduct that a competent officer considers reasonable and the conduct that the Constitution deems reasonable. . . . On the other hand, surely an innocent family should not bear the entire risk that a trial court, with the benefit of hindsight, will find that a federal agent reasonably believed that he could break into their home equipped with force and arms but without probable cause or a warrant. . . .

The Fourth Amendment protects the individual's privacy in a variety of settings. In none is the zone of privacy more clearly defined than when bounded by the unambiguous physical dimensions of an individual's home—a zone that finds its roots in clear and specific constitutional terms: 'The right of the people to be secure in their houses . . . shall not be violated.' That language unequivocally establishes the proposition that at the very core of the Fourth Amendment stands the right of a man to retreat into his own home and there be free from unreasonable governmental intrusion. In terms that apply equally to seizures of property and to seizures of persons, the Fourth Amendment has drawn a firm line at the entrance to the house. Absent exigent circumstances, that threshold may not reasonably be crossed without a warrant.'

The warrant requirement safeguards this bedrock principle of the Fourth Amendment, while the immunity bestowed on a police officer who acts with probable cause permits him to do his job free of constant fear of monetary liability. The Court rests its doctrinally flawed opinion upon a double standard of reasonableness which unjustifiably and unnecessarily upsets the delicate balance between respect for individual privacy and protection of the public servants who enforce our laws.

I respectfully dissent.

Questions

1. State the test for qualified immunity adopted by the majority.

2. List the reasons the Court gives for defining qualified immunity the way it does.

3. Summarize the dissent's objections to the majority's definition of qualified immunity.

4. Which of the opinions do you agree with?

5. Do you believe the Robert and Sarisse Creighton and their children should receive damages for what happened? Defend your answer, relying on the facts and the arguments of the majority and the dissent.

Suing the U.S. Government

Bivens didn't decide whether Webster Bivens could also sue the U.S. government for the six FBI officers' constitutional torts. According to the doctrine of **sovereign immunity** (a holdover from the days when kings didn't have to appear in court), governments can't be sued without their consent. Most state and the U.S. governments have laws waiving their sovereign immunity (at least to some degree). That's what Congress did in the Federal Tort Claims Act (FTCA). After *Bivens*, Congress permitted FTCA suits against the U.S. government for the constitutional torts of federal law enforcement agents "empowered by law to execute searches, to seize evidence, or to make arrests for violations of Federal law."

The U.S. government's "deep pockets" make FTCA actions attractive to plaintiffs—probably more attractive than *Bivens* actions against individual officers. But, both remedies are available to plaintiffs. According to Professors Whitebread and Slobogin (2000):

> [T]he plaintiff whose constitutional rights have been violated by a federal police officer in bad faith can be assured of monetary compensation [in an FTCA action] at the same time he can expect direct "revenge" [in a *Bivens* action] against the official to the extent the official can afford it. (51–52)

Suing State Officers

Plaintiffs can sue individual state officers in two actions: *state* tort lawsuits and *federal* U.S. Civil Rights Act lawsuits. Let's look at each.

State Tort Actions

Most illegal acts by state police, county sheriffs' and their deputies, and local police officers and their chiefs are also **torts,** meaning plaintiffs can sue individual officers for damages for acts such as assault, false arrest/false imprisonment, and trespass/breaking and entering. But, the right to recover damages for injuries caused by officials' torts has to be balanced against law enforcement's job of protecting the public. So, although individual officers are liable for their own torts, there's a huge difference between suing an ordinary person and a cop. The **defense of official immunity** limits officers' liability for their torts. This doctrine says that "a public official charged by law with duties which call for the exercise of his judgment or discretion is not personally liable to an individual unless he is guilty of a willful or malicious wrong." Why? Because, "to encourage responsible law enforcement... police are afforded a wide degree of discretion precisely because a more stringent standard could inhibit action."

The Minnesota Supreme Court balanced the rights of injured individuals and the needs of law enforcement when the court decided a police officer wasn't liable for the death of a small boy he killed during a high-speed chase to catch a fleeing shoplifter. If the officer were held liable, the court said, officers in the future might shy away from vigorously enforcing the law (*Pletan v. Gaines et al.* 1992).

U.S. Civil Rights Act Actions

Civil Rights Act actions (called **1983 actions** because they're brought under Title 42, Section 1983 of the Civil Rights Act of 1871, which was passed just after the Civil War) allow plaintiffs to go into *federal* courts to sue *state* police officers and their agency heads; *county* sheriffs and their deputies; and *municipal* police officers and their chiefs for violating plaintiffs' *federal* constitutional rights. Here's what Section 1983 provides:

> Every person who, under color of any statute, ordinance, regulation, custom, or usage, of any State or Territory, subjects, or causes to be subjected, any citizen of the United States or other person within the jurisdiction thereof to the deprivation of any rights, privileges, or immunities secured by the Constitution and laws, shall be liable to the party injured....
>
> U.S. Code 2002, Title 42, § 1983

As interpreted by the U.S. Supreme Court, plaintiffs have to prove two elements similar to those in *Bivens* constitutional tort actions:

1. Officers acted "under color of state law," which includes all acts done within the scope of their employment.

2. Officers' actions *caused* a deprivation of plaintiffs' rights guaranteed by the U.S. Constitution.

Section 1983 doesn't mean officers are liable every time they violate individuals' constitutional rights. Far from it. The U.S. Supreme Court has read several limits into the statutory protection. First, plaintiffs can't recover for accidental or even negligent violations; violations have to be *deliberate*. Second, state and local officers are protected by the same qualified immunity under § 1983 that *federal* officers have under *Bivens* and the Federal Tort Claims Act (p. 400).

Suing State and Local Governments

Plaintiffs have two options in deciding to sue state and local governments instead of (or in addition to) suing individual officers. They can sue governments in state courts for the torts of their officers, or they can sue them under the U.S. Civil Rights Act (see the "Suing State Officers" section). Let's look at each of these complicated routes to recovering damages from governments instead of individuals.

State Tort Actions

What if the boy's parents in the Minnesota high-speed chase case (discussed earlier, p. 401) had sued the police department or the city instead of the individual officer? Under the **doctrine of *respondeat superior***, state and local governments and their agencies are liable for the torts of their employees *but* only if the employees committed the torts during the course of their employment. There's another catch; not all states have adopted the doctrine. In these states, government units enjoy the **defense of vicarious official immunity**, which means police departments and local governments can claim the official immunity of its employees. To determine whether government units are entitled to the defense of vicarious official immunity, courts apply a balancing test of local government liability. This test balances two elements: (1) the need for effective law enforcement and (2) the need to avoid putting the public at risk.

In the Minnesota Supreme Court's (*Pletan v. Gaines et al.* 1992, 42–43) application of the balancing test in the high-speed chase case, the court found the need to enforce the criminal law outweighed the risk to the public created by the high-speed chase. So, the court held, the municipality wasn't liable for the boy's death.

U.S. Civil Rights Actions

As you learned from *Anderson v. Creighton* (excerpted earlier, p. 397), suing individual officers for violating constitutional rights is a complicated business. Suing a department or a city under § 1983 is even more complicated. In fact, until the Court decided to undertake "a fresh analysis of debate on the Civil Rights Act of 1871" in *Monell v. New York City Department of Social Services* (1978), the Court interpreted § 1983 to mean Congress didn't intend to allow individuals to sue municipalities and counties at all. But in *Monell*, the Court changed its mind, deciding the legislative history of the act "compels the conclusion that Congress *did* intend municipalities and other local government units to be included among those persons to whom § 1983 applies."

According to the Court, individuals could sue local government units if they could prove two elements:

1. Officers *either* acted according to written policies, statements, ordinances, regulations, or decisions approved by authorized official bodies; *or* acted according to unwritten custom even though the custom wasn't formally approved through official decision making channels
2. *And* the action caused the violation of the plaintiff's constitutional right(s)

So, according to the Supreme Court in the *Monell* case:

> [A] local government cannot be sued for an injury inflicted solely by its employees or agents. Instead, it is when execution of a government's policy or custom, whether made by its lawmakers or by those whose edicts or acts may fairly be said to represent official policy, inflicts the injury that the government as an entity is responsible for it under § 1983. (695)

 Go to Exercise 11-1 on the Criminal Procedure 6e CD to learn more about suing local governments.

Law Enforcement Failure to Protect

Until now, we've talked only about remedies that protect individuals from *government* violations of their rights, but what about failure by the government to protect people from each other? Most police departments conceive their mission broadly: "To protect and serve." But, is their mission "to protect" a constitutional command? In other words, do governments and their officers have a constitutional duty to protect individuals from other private individuals who violate their rights? No. (At least not most of the time.) According to the U.S. Supreme Court, neither the language of the due process clauses nor the history of the Fifth and Fourteenth Amendments (the location of the due process clauses) imposes an affirmative duty on law enforcement to protect individuals from other private individuals who would deprive them of their right to life, liberty, or property (*DeShaney v. Winnegabo County* 1989). Nor does it bestow an affirmative right on individuals to be protected from those individuals. So, according to what we'll call the Supreme Court's **no-affirmative-duty-to-protect rule,** plaintiffs can't sue individual officers or government units for failing to stop private people from violating their rights by inflicting injuries on them.

But, there's at least one exception to the no-duty-to-protect rule—the **special relationship exception.** The special relationship is custody. When the government takes it upon itself to put people in jail, prison, or mental institutions against their will and keeps them there, it's cruel and unusual punishment (in violation of the Eighth Amendment to the U.S. Constitution) to fail to protect them when they can't protect themselves (*DeShaney v. Winnebago County* 1989, 199).

Some of the U.S. Courts of Appeals have created a **state-created-danger exception** (*Robinson v. Township of Redford* 2002, 929). This is a narrow exception, and, to qualify for it and collect damages under § 1983, plaintiffs have to prove three elements:

1. An officer's actions created a special danger of violent harm to the plaintiff in the lawsuit (not to the general public).

2. The officer knows or should have known her actions would encourage this plaintiff to rely on her actions.

3. The danger created by the officer's actions either
   a. Caused harm from the violence itself
   b. Or increased vulnerability to harm from violence

Other U.S. Courts of Appeals have soundly rejected the state-created-danger exception. The Fourth Circuit Court of Appeals stuck to the special relationship exception created by custody as the only exception to the no-affirmative-duty-to-protect rule and explained why in *Pinder v. Johnson* (1995).

| CASE | *Did the Police Have a Constitutional Duty to Protect Her and Her Children?* |

Pinder v. Johnson
54 F.3d 1169 (Cal. Dist. 4 1995)

Carol Pinder filed suit individually and as the survivor of her minor children against the municipality of Cambridge, Maryland, and Donald Johnson PFC, a police officer in the municipality of Cambridge. The U.S. District Court for the District of Maryland denied Johnson's motion for summary judgment.* A three-judge panel of the Fourth Circuit Court of Appeals affirmed. An en banc review** reversed.

WILKINSON, J. joined by HALL, WILKINS, NIEMEYER, and WILLIAMS, JJ. WIDENER, MOTZ, HAMILTON, and LUTTIG, JJ. concurred in part, and concurred in the judgment.

FACTS

The facts of this case are genuinely tragic. On the evening of March 10, 1989, Officer Donald Johnson responded to a call reporting a domestic disturbance at the home of Carol Pinder. When he arrived at the scene, Johnson discovered that Pinder's former boyfriend, Don Pittman, had broken into her home. Pinder told Officer Johnson that when Pittman broke in, he was abusive and violent. He pushed her, punched her, and threw various objects at her. Pittman was also screaming and threatening both Pinder

and her children, saying he would murder them all. A neighbor, Darnell Taylor, managed to subdue Pittman and restrain him until the police arrived.

Officer Johnson questioned Pittman, who was hostile and unresponsive. Johnson then placed Pittman under arrest. After confining Pittman in the squad car, Johnson returned to the house to speak with Pinder again. Pinder explained to Officer Johnson that Pittman had threatened her in the past, and that he had just been released from prison after being convicted of attempted arson at Pinder's residence some ten months earlier. She was naturally afraid for herself and her children, and wanted to know whether it would be safe for her to return to work that evening. Officer Johnson assured her that Pittman would be locked up overnight. He further indicated that Pinder had to wait until the next day to swear out a warrant against Pittman because a county commissioner would not be available to hear the charges before morning. Based on these assurances, Pinder returned to work.

That same evening, Johnson brought Pittman before Dorchester County Commissioner George Ames, Jr. for an initial appearance. Johnson only charged Pittman with trespassing and malicious destruction of property having a value of less than three hundred dollars, both of which are misdemeanor offenses. Consequently, Ames simply released Pittman on his own recognizance and warned him to stay away from Pinder's home.

Pittman did not heed this warning. Upon his release, he returned to Pinder's house and set fire to it. Pinder was still at work, but her three children were home asleep and died of smoke inhalation. Pittman was later arrested and charged

---

*A motion that the court enter a judgment without a trial because there's not enough evidence to support the plaintiff's claim.

**Full court.

with first degree murder. He was convicted and is currently serving three life sentences without possibility of parole.

Pinder brought this action for herself and for the estates of her three children, seeking damages under 42 U.S.C. § 1983, as well as state law theories, against the Commissioners of Cambridge and Officer Johnson. She alleged that defendants had violated their affirmative duty to protect her and her children, thereby depriving them of their constitutional right to due process under the Fourteenth Amendment. Johnson moved for summary judgment, arguing that he had no constitutionally imposed affirmative duty to protect the Pinders and that he was shielded from liability by the doctrine of qualified immunity. The district court, however, refused to dismiss plaintiff's due process claim, finding that Officer Johnson was not entitled to qualified immunity. Johnson brought an interlocutory appeal.*...A divided panel of this court affirmed, finding that Pinder had stated a cognizable substantive due process claim and that Johnson did not have a valid immunity defense. We granted rehearing en banc, and now reverse the judgment of the district court.

OPINION

...Qualified immunity under § 1983 shields officials from civil liability unless their actions violated "clearly established statutory or constitutional rights of which a reasonable person would have known." The linchpin of qualified immunity is objective reasonableness.... Important to this reasonableness inquiry is whether the rights alleged to have been violated were clearly established at the time of the challenged actions. If the law supporting the allegedly violated rights was not clearly established, then immunity must lie. Where the law is clearly established, and where no reasonable officer could believe he was acting in accordance with it, qualified immunity will not attach.

The purpose of this doctrine is to ensure that police officers and other government actors have notice of the extent of constitutional restrictions on their behavior. Thus, qualified immunity prevents officials from being blindsided by liability derived from newly invented rights or new, unforeseen applications of pre-existing rights. In short, officials cannot be held to have violated rights of which they could not have known.

Here, the question is simply whether the due process right Pinder claims was clearly established at the time of her dealings with Johnson. This inquiry depends upon an assessment of the settled law at the time, not the law as it currently exists. Also, the rights Pinder asserts must have been

clearly established in a particularized and relevant sense, not merely as an overarching entitlement to due process....

Pinder can point to no clearly established law supporting her claim at the time of the alleged violation. Pinder's claim is that Officer Johnson deprived her and her children of their due process rights by failing to protect them from the violent actions of Pittman. Eighteen days before the events giving rise to this action, the Supreme Court handed down its decision in *DeShaney v. Winnebago County Department of Social Services*, 489 U.S. 189, (1989) which squarely rejected liability under 42 U.S.C. § 1983 based on an affirmative duty theory.

The facts in *DeShaney* were as poignant as those in this case. There, the Winnebago County Department of Social Services (DSS) received a number of reports that a young boy, Joshua DeShaney, was being abused by his father. As this abuse went on, several DSS workers personally observed the injuries that had been inflicted on Joshua. They knew firsthand of the threat to the boy's safety, yet they failed to remove him from his father's custody or otherwise protect him from abuse. Ultimately, Joshua's father beat him so violently that the boy suffered serious brain damage. Joshua's mother brought a § 1983 action on his behalf, arguing that the County and its employees had deprived Joshua of his liberty interests without due process by failing to provide adequate protection against his father's violent acts.

Despite natural sympathy for the plaintiff, the Court held that there was no § 1983 liability under these circumstances. It noted that the Due Process Clause of the Fourteenth Amendment does not require governmental actors to affirmatively protect life, liberty, or property against intrusion by private third parties. Instead, the Due Process Clause works only as a negative prohibition on state action. "Its purpose was to protect the people from the State, not to ensure that the State protected them from each other." This view is consistent with our general conception of the Constitution as a document of negative restraints, not positive entitlements. The *DeShaney* Court concluded that:

> if the Due Process Clause does not require the State to provide its citizens with particular protective services, it follows that the State cannot be held liable under the Clause for injuries that could have been averted had it chosen to provide them. As a general matter, then, we conclude that a State's failure to protect an individual against private violence simply does not constitute a violation of the Due Process Clause.

The affirmative duty of protection that the Supreme Court rejected in *DeShaney* is precisely the duty Pinder relies on in this case. Joshua's mother wanted the state to be held liable for its lack of action, for merely standing by when it could have acted to prevent a tragedy. Likewise, Pinder

---

*An appeal that takes place before the trial court rules on the entire case.

argues Johnson could have, and thus should have, acted to prevent Pittman's crimes. *DeShaney* makes clear, however, that no affirmative duty was clearly established in these circumstances.

The *DeShaney* Court did indicate that an affirmative duty to protect may arise when the state restrains persons from acting on their own behalf. The Court explained that "when the State by the affirmative exercise of its power so restrains an individual's liberty that it renders him unable to care for himself, and at the same time fails to provide for his basic human needs . . . it transgresses the substantive limits on state action set by the Eighth Amendment and the Due Process Clause."

The specific source of an affirmative duty to protect, the Court emphasized, is the custodial nature of a "special relationship." *DeShaney* reasoned that "the affirmative duty to protect arises not from the State's knowledge of the individual's predicament or from its expressions of intent to help him, but from the limitation which it has imposed on his freedom to act on his own behalf." Some sort of confinement of the injured party—incarceration, institutionalization, or the like—is needed to trigger the affirmative duty. This Court has consistently read *DeShaney* to require a custodial context before any affirmative duty can arise under the Due Process Clause.

There was no custodial relationship with Carol Pinder and her children in this case. Neither Johnson nor any other state official had restrained Pinder's freedom to act on her own behalf. Pinder was never incarcerated, arrested, or otherwise restricted in any way. Without any such limitation imposed on her liberty, *DeShaney* indicates Pinder was due no affirmative constitutional duty of protection from the state, and Johnson would not be charged with liability for the criminal acts of a third party.

Pinder argues, however, that Johnson's explicit promises that Pittman would be incarcerated overnight created the requisite "special relationship." We do not agree. By requiring a custodial context as the condition for an affirmative duty, *DeShaney* rejected the idea that such a duty can arise solely from an official's awareness of a specific risk or from promises of aid. There, as here, plaintiff alleged that the state knew of the special risk of harm at the hands of a third party. There, as here, plaintiff alleged that the state had "specifically proclaimed, by word and by deed, its intention to protect" the victim. Neither allegation was sufficient to support the existence of an affirmative duty in *DeShaney*, and the same holds true in this case.

Promises do not create a special relationship—custody does. Unlike custody, a promise of aid does not actually place a person in a dangerous position and then cut off all outside sources of assistance. Promises from state officials can be ignored if the situation seems dire enough, whereas

custody cannot be ignored or changed by the persons it affects. It is for this reason that the Supreme Court made custody the crux of the special relationship rule. Lacking the slightest hint of a true "special relationship," Pinder's claim in this case boils down to an insufficient allegation of a failure to act.

We also cannot accept Pinder's attempt to escape the import of *DeShaney* by characterizing her claim as one of *affirmative* misconduct by the state in "creating or enhancing" the danger, instead of an omission. She emphasizes the "actions" that Johnson took in making assurances, and in deciding not to charge Pittman with any serious offense. By this measure, every representation by the police and every failure to incarcerate would constitute "affirmative actions," giving rise to civil liability. . . . No amount of semantics can disguise the fact that the real "affirmative act" here was committed by Pittman, not by Officer Johnson. . . . The most that can be said of the state functionaries . . . is that they stood by and did nothing when suspicious circumstances dictated a more active role for them.

Given the principles laid down by *DeShaney*, it can hardly be said that Johnson was faced with a clearly established duty to protect Pinder or her children in March of 1989. Indeed, it can be argued that *DeShaney* established exactly the opposite, *i.e.*, that no such affirmative duty existed because neither Pinder nor her children were confined by the state. . . .

It is true, as the district court noted, that some cases [have] found an "affirmative duty" arising outside the traditional custodial context. None of these cases, however, clearly establish the existence of the right Pinder alleges was violated. First, none of these cases found a particularized due process right to affirmative protection based solely on an official's assurances that the danger posed by a third party will be eliminated. All involved some circumstance wherein the state took a much larger and more direct role in "creating" the danger itself. These cases involve a wholly different paradigm than that presented here. When the state itself creates the dangerous situation that resulted in a victim's injury . . . the state is not merely accused of a failure to act; it becomes much more akin to an actor itself directly causing harm to the injured party. *See, e.g., Cornelius v. Town of Highland Lake*, 880 F.2d 348, 356 (11th Cir.1989) (duty when state brought inmates into victim's workplace); *Wells v. Walker*, 852 F.2d 368, 371 (8th Cir.1988) (duty when state brought dangerous prisoners to victim's store); *Nishiyama v. Dickson County*, 814 F.2d 277, 281 (6th Cir.1987) (duty when state provided unsupervised parolee with squad car). At most, these cases stand for the proposition that state actors may not disclaim liability when they themselves throw others to the lions. They do not, by contrast, entitle persons who rely on promises of aid to some greater degree of protection from lions at large. . . .

The extensive debate provoked by this case should be proof enough that the law in this area was anything but clearly established at the time Officer Johnson gave assurances to Pinder. To impose liability in the absence of a clearly established constitutional duty is to invite litigation over a limitless array of official acts.

. . . There are good reasons why the constitutional right to protection sought by Pinder was not clearly established by the courts. As the First Circuit noted in a similar case, "enormous economic consequences could follow from the reading of the Fourteenth Amendment that plaintiff here urges." The consequences, however, are not just economic, and their gravity indicates why the right Pinder asserts was never clearly established.

The recognition of a broad constitutional right to affirmative protection from the state would be the first step down the slippery slope of liability. Such a right potentially would be implicated in nearly every instance where a private actor inflicts injuries that the state could have prevented. Every time a police officer incorrectly decided it was not necessary to intervene in a domestic dispute, the victims of the ensuing violence could bring a § 1983 action. Every time a parolee committed a criminal act, the victims could argue the state had an affirmative duty to keep the prisoner incarcerated. Indeed, victims of virtually every crime could plausibly argue that if the authorities had done their job, they would not have suffered their loss. Broad affirmative duties thus provide a fertile bed for § 1983 litigation, and the resultant governmental liability would wholly defeat the purposes of qualified immunity.

If the right Pinder asserts were ever clearly established, it would entail other significant consequences. A general obligation of the state to protect private citizens . . . makes law enforcement officials constitutional guarantors of the conduct of others. . . . It is no solution to say that such a right to affirmative protection has its inherent limitations. It is no answer to contend that the duty here was created only by Johnson's promise and Pinder's reliance on that promise, and is limited by Johnson's awareness of the risk. Such "limitations" are no barrier to increased lawsuits. There are endless opportunities for disagreements over the exact nature of an official's promise, the intent behind it, the degree of the reliance, the causal link between the promise and the injury, and so on. Similarly, the extent of the state's affirmative duty to protect and the degree of the state's awareness of the risk are also subjects that would tie up state and local officials in endless federal litigation. . . .

In cases like this, it is always easy to second-guess. Tragic circumstances only sharpen our hindsight, and it is tempting to express our sense of outrage at the failure of Officer

Johnson to protect Pinder's children from Pittman's villainy. The Supreme Court in *DeShaney* specifically rejected the "shocks the conscience" test of *Rochin v. California*, 342 U.S. 165, 172 (1952) as a basis for imposing § 1983 liability in the affirmative duty context, however. We cannot simply ignore the lack of any clearly established constitutional duty to protect and the concomitant immunity from civil liability. Hard cases can make bad law, and it is to protect against that possibility that police officers possess the defense of qualified immunity.

For the foregoing reasons, the judgment of the district court denying qualified immunity to Officer Johnson is REVERSED.

CONCURRING OPINION

MOTZ, J.

I concur in the result reached in the majority opinion and admire its felicity of expression. I write separately to make it clear that its *sole* holding is that Officer Johnson was entitled to summary judgment on his qualified immunity defense. This is so because when this tragedy occurred in 1989, in view of *DeShaney v. Winnebago Dept. of Social Servs.*, 489 U.S. 189, 109 S.Ct. 998, 103 L.Ed.2d 249 (1989), a reasonable police officer could not have known that Officer Johnson's promise to Ms. Pinder created a special relationship making him liable to her. Thus, any suggestion . . . of the majority opinion that, even today, there is not and, as a matter of policy, should not be any "broad constitutional right to affirmative protection from the state" is dicta* and, in my view, erroneous dicta.

DISSENT

RUSSELL, J., joined by ERVIN, CJ., and MURNAGHAN and MICHAEL, JJ.

. . . Because I believe the Court casually disregards the very real ways in which Officer Johnson's conduct placed Pinder and her children in a position of danger, I respectfully dissent.

In March 1989, the time of the fire, the law "clearly established" that the state has a duty to protect an individual where the state, by its affirmative action, creates a dangerous situation or renders an individual more vulnerable to danger. As the Seventh Circuit stated in *Bowers v. DeVito*, 686 F.2d 616 (7th Cir.1982):

> If the state puts a man in a position of danger from private persons and then fails to protect him, it will not be heard to say that its role was merely passive; it is as

---

*A nonbinding opinion that's not binding as precedent.

much an active tort feasor [wrong doer] as if it had thrown him into a snake pit.

The Seventh Circuit and other circuits, including our own, have reaffirmed this duty.

The Supreme Court's decision in *DeShaney v. Winnebago County Department of Social Services* did not reject the state's clearly established duty to protect an individual where the state, through its affirmative action, has created a dangerous situation or rendered the individual more vulnerable to danger. In *DeShaney*, the Supreme Court held only that the state has no duty to protect an individual from the actions of third parties where the state was aware of the dangers but played no part in their creation. The fact that the state did not create the danger was central to the Court's holding.

In this case, Officer Johnson was not merely aware of the danger; he placed Pinder and her children in a position of danger. Officer Johnson knew Pittman had broken into Pinder's home and had been abusive and violent. Pittman had punched Pinder and thrown objects at her. When the officers arrived at the scene, Pittman was screaming and threatening that he "wasn't going to jail for nothing this time; this time it would be for murder." After the officers restrained Pittman, Pinder explained to Officer Johnson that Pittman had threatened Pinder before, that he had attempted to set fire to her house ten months earlier, and that he had just finished serving his sentence for the attempted arson.

Given Pittman's threats and violent behavior, Pinder was understandably concerned about the safety of herself and her children. She explained to Officer Johnson that she needed to return to work and specifically asked him whether it was safe to do so. Officer Johnson assured Pinder several times that Pittman would remain in police custody until morning. Officer Johnson indicated to Pinder that Pittman could not be released that night because a county commissioner would not be available until the morning.

Instead of remaining home with her children or making other arrangements for their safety, Pinder, relying on Officer Johnson's assurances, returned to work, leaving her children alone at home. At the police station, Officer Johnson charged Pittman only with two minor offenses, trespassing and malicious destruction of property having a value of less than three hundred dollars. Despite his previous representation to Pinder that no county commissioner would be available before the morning, Officer Johnson brought Pittman before a county commissioner that evening. Because Officer Johnson charged Pittman only with two misdemeanors, the county commissioner released Pittman on his own recognizance. Upon his release, Pittman went directly to Pinder's house and burned it down, killing the three children in the conflagration.

I cannot understand how the majority can recount these same events in its own opinion and not conclude that Officer Johnson placed Pinder and her children in a position of danger. Officer Johnson made assurances to Pinder that Pittman would remain in police custody overnight and falsely represented that no county commissioner would be available until morning. He induced Pinder to return to work and leave her children vulnerable to Pittman's violence. After witnessing Pittman's violent behavior and murderous threats, he charged Pittman with only minor offenses, assuring his release. Officer Johnson had a duty to protect Pinder and her children from Pittman, at least to an extent necessary to dispel the false sense of security that his actions created.

Unlike the majority, I believe that the law at the time of the incident clearly established that Officer Johnson had a duty to protect Pinder and her children upon Pittman's release. The Court finds it significant that no case before March 1989 contained the precise holding that due process creates a duty of affirmative protection based on an official's assurances that the danger posed by a third party will be eliminated. Such a particular holding, however, is not required in order to conclude that a right was clearly established. In *Anderson v. Creighton*, 483 U.S. 635 (1987), the Supreme Court...explained that "the contours of the right must be sufficiently clear that a reasonable official would understand that what he is doing violated that right." On the other hand, the Court also rejected the view that "an official action is protected by qualified immunity unless the very action in question has previously been held unlawful...." Requiring such a level of specificity would transform the defense of qualified immunity into a defense of absolute immunity. Instead, the Court held that the preexisting law had to be only specific enough that the unlawfulness of the official's conduct would be apparent to a reasonable person.

I believe that a reasonable officer in Officer Johnson's position would have recognized that, given his assurances to Pinder that Pittman would remain in police custody until morning and his failure to charge Pittman with an offense serious enough to ensure that he remained in custody overnight, he placed Pinder and her children in a dangerous position. He induced Pinder to let her guard down, dissuading her from taking actions to protect herself and her children from Pittman. Certainly, a reasonable officer would have recognized that he had a duty at least to phone Pinder and warn her that Pittman had been released from police custody.

Pinder's children were left alone at home, vulnerable to the rampage of a violent, intemperate man, and deprived of their mother's protection because of the hollow word of an irresponsible, thoughtless police officer. Today the

Court holds that this police officer, who took no action to correct a dangerous situation of his own creation, did not violate Pinder's due process rights and is otherwise immune from prosecution because he did not violate a clearly established right. I disagree.

Questions

1. List the facts relevant to deciding whether Donald Johnson is liable for damages to Carol Pinder.

2. Apply the facts you listed in (1) to the no-affirmative-duty-to-protect rule, the special relationship exception, and the state-created-danger exception.

3. Summarize the court's majority, concurring, and dissenting opinions' arguments in favor of or against the rule and exceptions in (3).

4. Which rule do you favor, and why?

Suing Judges and Prosecutors

Most plaintiffs in civil actions sue law enforcement officers, who enjoy qualified immunity from being sued for damages. What about prosecutors and judges? Can individuals sue them? The answer is "no" to suing a judge, and it's "hardly ever" to suing prosecutors. Why? Because judges enjoy **absolute immunity** from civil suits, meaning they can't be sued. The only remedy against misbehaving judges is either impeachment or, if they're elected, voting them out of office.

Prosecutors enjoy absolute immunity, too, as long as they're acting as advocates for the state in criminal prosecutions. For example, you can't sue a prosecutor for deciding to charge you with a specific crime instead of another, for refusing to plea-bargain, or for the way she handles the case against you in court. According to the decision in the leading case of prosecutorial immunity, *Imbler v. Pachtman* (1976), the absolute immunity granted to prosecutors extends to all conduct "intimately associated with the judicial phase of the criminal process." But, that case left open the question of whether absolute immunity extends to "those aspects of the prosecutor's responsibility that cast him in the role of an administrator or investigative officer rather than that of an advocate." In 1991, the Supreme Court reviewed the liability of prosecutors to civil lawsuits in *Burns v. Reed* (1991).

CASE	*Did the Prosecutor Enjoy Absolute Immunity?*

Burns v. Reed
500 U.S. 478 (1991)

Cathy Burns sued Richard Reed, an Indiana prosecutor. The U.S. District Court for the Southern District of Indiana granted the prosecutor's motion for a directed verdict. Burns appealed. The Court of Appeals for the Seventh Circuit affirmed. The U.S. Supreme Court granted certiorari. The Supreme Court affirmed in part and reversed in part.

WHITE, J., joined by REHNQUIST, CJ., and STEVENS, O'CONNOR, KENNEDY, and SOUTER, JJ.

FACTS

On the evening of September 2, 1982, Cathy Burns called the Muncie, Indiana, police and reported that an unknown assailant had entered her house, knocked her unconscious, and shot and wounded her two sons while they slept. Two police officers, Paul Cox and Donald Scroggins, were assigned to investigate the incident. The officers came to view Burns as their primary suspect, even though she passed a polygraph examination and a voice stress test, submitted exculpatory handwritten samples, and repeatedly denied shooting her sons. Speculating that Burns had multiple personalities, one of which was responsible for the shootings, the officers decided to interview Burns under hypnosis. They became concerned, however, that hypnosis might be an unacceptable investigation technique, and therefore sought the advice of the Chief Deputy Prosecutor, Richard Reed. Reed told the officers that they could proceed with the hypnosis.

While under hypnosis, Burns referred to the assailant as "Katie" and also referred to herself by that name. The officers interpreted that reference as supporting their multiple-personality theory. As a result, they detained Burns at the police station and sought Reed's advice about whether there was probable cause to arrest Burns. After hearing about the statements Burns had made while under hypnosis, Reed told the officers that they "probably had probable cause" to arrest Burns. Based on that assurance, the officers placed Burns under arrest. Following her arrest, Burns was placed in the psychiatric ward of a state hospital for four months. During that time, she was discharged from her employment, and the State obtained temporary custody of her sons. The medical experts at the hospital eventually concluded Burns did not have multiple personalities, and she was released.

The next day, Reed and Officer Scroggins appeared before a county court judge in a probable cause hearing, seeking to obtain a warrant to search Burns's house and car. During that hearing, Scroggins testified, in response to Reed's questioning, that Burns had confessed to shooting her children. Neither the officer nor Reed informed the judge that the "confession" was obtained under hypnosis or that Burns had otherwise consistently denied shooting her sons. On the basis of the misleading presentation, the judge issued a search warrant.

Burns was charged under Indiana law with attempted murder of her sons. Before trial, however, the trial judge granted Burns's motion to suppress the statements given under hypnosis. As a result, the prosecutor dropped all charges against Burns. On January 31, 1985, Burns filed an action in the U.S. District Court for the Southern District of Indiana against Reed, Officers Cox and Scroggins, and others. She alleged that the defendants were liable under 42 U.S.C. §1983 for violating her rights under the Fourth, Fifth, and Fourteenth Amendments to the United States Constitution, and she sought compensatory and punitive damages. Burns reached a settlement with several of the defendants, and the case proceeded to trial against Reed. After Burns presented her case, the District Court granted Reed a directed verdict, finding that Reed was absolutely immune from liability for his conduct.

Burns appealed to the U.S. Court of Appeals for the Seventh Circuit. That court affirmed. It held that "a prosecutor should be afforded absolute immunity for giving legal advice to police officers about the legality of their prospective investigative conduct." In a brief footnote, the court also held that Reed was absolutely immune from liability for his role in the probable cause hearing. Because the Courts of Appeals are divided regarding the scope of absolute prosecutorial immunity, we granted certiorari.

OPINION

Title 42 U.S.C. §1983 is written in broad terms. It purports to subject "every person" acting under color of state law to liability for depriving any other person in the United States of "rights, privileges, or immunities secured by the Constitution and laws." The Court has consistently recognized, however, that §1983 was not meant to abolish wholesale all common-law immunities. The section is to be read in harmony with general principles of tort immunities and defenses rather than in derogation of them. In addition, we have acknowledged that for "some special functions," it is "better to leave unredressed the wrongs done by dishonest officers than to subject those who try to do their duty to the constant dread of retaliation."

Imbler was the first case in which the Court addressed the immunity of state prosecutors from suits under §1983.... The Court observed that at common law prosecutors were immune from suits for malicious prosecution and for defamation, and that this immunity extended to the knowing use of false testimony before the grand jury and at trial.

The interests supporting the common-law immunity were held to be equally applicable to suits under §1983.... There was "concern that harassment by unfounded litigation would cause a deflection of the prosecutor's energies from his public duties, and the possibility that he would shade his decisions instead of exercising the independence of judgment required by his public trust."

The Court in *Imbler* declined to accord prosecutors only qualified immunity because, among other things, suits against prosecutors for initiating and conducting prosecutions "could be expected with some frequency, for a defendant often will transform his resentment at being prosecuted into the ascription of improper and malicious actions to the State's advocate," lawsuits would divert prosecutors' attention and energy away from their important duty of enforcing the criminal law, prosecutors would have more difficulty than other officials in meeting the standards for qualified immunity, and potential liability "would prevent the vigorous and fearless performance of the prosecutor's duty that is essential to the proper functioning of the criminal justice system." The Court also noted that there are other checks on prosecutorial misconduct, including the criminal law and professional discipline.

The Court therefore held that prosecutors are absolutely immune from liability under §1983 for their conduct in "initiating a prosecution and in presenting the State's case," insofar as that conduct is "intimately associated with the judicial phase of the criminal process." Each of the charges against the prosecutor in *Imbler* involved conduct having that association, including the alleged knowing use of false testimony at trial and the alleged deliberate suppression of exculpatory evidence. *The Court expressly declined to decide whether absolute immunity extends to "those aspects of the prosecutor's responsibility that cast him in the role of an administrator or investigative officer rather than that of an advocate." It was recognized, though, that "the duties of the prosecutor in his role as advocate for the State involve actions preliminary to the initiation of a prosecution and actions apart from the courtroom".* . . [emphasis added]. We have been "quite sparing" in our recognition of absolute immunity, and have refused to extend it any "further than its justification would warrant."

We now consider whether the absolute prosecutorial immunity recognized in *Imbler* is applicable to

1. Reed's participation in a probable cause hearing, which led to the issuance of a search warrant, and

2. Reed's legal advice to the police regarding the use of hypnosis and the existence of probable cause to arrest petitioner.

We address first Reed's appearance as a lawyer for the State in the probable cause hearing, where he examined a witness and successfully supported the application for a search warrant. The decision in *Imbler* leads to the conclusion that Reed is absolutely immune from liability in a §1983 suit for that conduct. . . . Like witnesses, prosecutors and other lawyers were absolutely immune from damages liability at common law for making false or defamatory statements in judicial proceedings (at least so long as the statements were related to the proceeding), and also for eliciting false and defamatory testimony from witnesses. . . .

The prosecutor's actions at issue here—appearing before a judge and presenting evidence in support of a motion for a search warrant—clearly involve the prosecutor's "role as advocate for the State," rather than his role as "administrator or investigative officer," the protection for which we reserved judgment in *Imbler*. Moreover, since the issuance of a search warrant is unquestionably a judicial act, appearing at a probable cause hearing is "intimately associated with the judicial phase of the criminal process." It is also connected with the initiation and conduct of a

prosecution, particularly where the hearing occurs after arrest, as was the case here. . . . Pretrial court appearances by the prosecutor in support of taking criminal action against a suspect present a substantial likelihood of vexatious litigation that might have an untoward effect on the independence of the prosecutor. Therefore, absolute immunity for this function serves the policy of protecting the judicial process, which underlies much of the Court's decision in *Imbler*. . . . Accordingly, we hold that Reed's appearance in court in support of an application for a search warrant and the presentation of evidence at that hearing are protected by absolute immunity.

Turning to Reed's acts of providing legal advice to the police, we note first that neither Reed nor the court below has identified any historical or common-law support for extending absolute immunity to such actions by prosecutors. . . . The next factor to be considered—risk of vexatious litigation—also does not support absolute immunity for giving legal advice. . . . In the first place, a suspect or defendant is not likely to be as aware of a prosecutor's role in giving advice as a prosecutor's role in initiating and conducting a prosecution. But even if a prosecutor's role in giving advice to the police does carry with it some risk of burdensome litigation, the concern with litigation in our immunity cases is not merely a generalized concern with interference with an official's duties, but rather is a concern with interference with the conduct closely related to the judicial process. Absolute immunity is designed to free the judicial process from the harassment and intimidation associated with litigation. That concern therefore justifies absolute prosecutorial immunity only for actions that are connected with the prosecutor's role in judicial proceedings, not for every litigation-inducing conduct.

The Court of Appeals speculated that anything short of absolute immunity would discourage prosecutors from performing their "vital obligation" of giving legal advice to the police. . . . Although the absence of absolute immunity for the act of giving legal advice may cause prosecutors to consider their advice more carefully, "where an official could be expected to know that his conduct would violate statutory or constitutional rights, he should be made to hesitate." Indeed, it is incongruous to allow prosecutors to be absolutely immune from liability for giving advice to the police, but to allow police officers only qualified immunity for following the advice. Ironically, it would mean that the police, who do not ordinarily hold law degrees, would be required to know the clearly established law, but prosecutors would not. . . .

We AFFIRM in part and REVERSE in part the judgment of the Court of Appeals. It is so ordered.

1. What reasons does the Court give for the absolute immunity of prosecutors?

2. Why do police enjoy only qualified immunity whereas prosecutors enjoy absolute immunity?

3. Why did the Court treat the prosecutor's appearance at the search warrant hearing differently from the prosecutor's provision of legal advice to the police?

4. Should the immunity cover both, neither, or one but not the other? Why?

Hurdles to Suing Officers and the Government

People who sue the government or its officers (even in the most brutal cases) rarely win. Why? According to Allison Patton (1993):

> There are three major weaknesses to section 1983 suits. First, these actions are difficult and expensive to pursue. Since most victims of misconduct are minorities without financial resources, only a small percentage of police brutality incidents become lawsuits. Those victims who are able to get legal representation face a long and arduous litigation process, because police departments rarely settle section 1983 suits. Second, the Supreme Court has severely limited the ability of plaintiffs to enjoin a particular police technique, even one that frequently results in the use of excessive force. Third, juries are more likely to believe the police officer's version of the incident than the plaintiff's. Often there are no witnesses, or each side has an equal number of supporting witnesses. For a variety of sociological and psychological reasons, juries do not want to believe that their police officers are bad people or liars. Thus, plaintiffs rarely win absent help from independent corroborative witnesses or physical evidence. (753–754)

There are other reasons. First, qualified immunity and absolute immunity present legal hurdles. Anthony Amsterdam (1974), defense attorney and constitutional law professor, adds several more:

> Where are the lawyers going to come from to handle these cases for the plaintiffs? ... What on earth would possess a lawyer to file a claim for damages ... in an ordinary search-and-seizure case? The prospect of a share in the substantial damages to be expected? The chance to earn a reputation as a police-hating lawyer, so that he can no longer count on straight testimony concerning the length of skid marks in his personal injury cases? The gratitude of his client when his filing of the claim causes the prosecutor to refuse a lesser-included-offense plea or to charge priors or pile on "cover" charges? The opportunity to represent his client without fee in these resulting criminal matters?
>
> Police cases are an unadulterated investigative and litigate nightmare. Taking on the police in any tribunal involves a commitment to the most frustrating and thankless legal work I know. And the idea that an unrepresented, inarticulate, prosecution-vulnerable citizen can make a case against a team of professional investigators and testifiers in any tribunal begs belief. Even in a tribunal having recognized responsibilities and some resources to conduct independent investigations, a plaintiff without assiduous counsel devoted to developing his side of the case would be utterly outmastered by the police. No, I think we shall have airings of police searches and seizures on suppression motions or not at all. (430)

Further, the no-affirmative-duty-to-protect rule protects most officials from being sued successfully. Finally, some plaintiffs *shouldn't* get damages, because their cases are frivolous (Slobogin 1998, 561).

ADMINISTRATIVE REMEDIES

Until now, we've dealt with court cases aimed at making police and other public officials accountable for their violations of individuals' constitutional rights, but accountability for official misconduct isn't limited to lawsuits. In fact, the most common accountability procedure for all kinds of police misconduct (not just violations of constitutional rights) is administrative review and discipline outside the courts. There are two types of administrative review:

1. *Internal affairs units (IAU)*. Review of police misconduct by special officers inside police departments

2. *External civilian review*. Review of complaints against police officers with participation by individuals who aren't sworn police officers

Internal Review

Most large and mid-sized police departments have special internal affairs units (IAU) that review police misconduct. According to Professor Douglas W. Perez (1994, 88–89), a former deputy sheriff, "most cops do not like internal affairs." They don't trust IAU, and some even think IAU investigators are traitors. Still, most officers believe IAU operations are a necessary evil. For one thing, they're a good defense against external review. As the famed Chicago chief of police O. W. Wilson said, "It is clearly apparent that if the police do not take a vigorous stand on the matter of internal investigation, outside groups—such as review boards consisting of laymen and other persons outside the police service—will step into the void" (Griswold 1994, 215–221).

Internal review consists of four successive stages:

1. Intake

2. Investigation

3. Deliberation

4. Disposition

The Internal Affairs Section of the Oakland, California, Police Department is considered an excellent unit, so we'll use it as an example of how internal review proceeds through these four stages. The unit is housed in the department building. The department intake policy is "anyone anywhere should accept a complaint if a citizen wishes it taken." All complaints alleging excessive force, police corruption, and racial discrimination are followed up (Perez 1994, 92–93). Then, someone besides the intake officer investigates complaints. The investigator gathers evidence, usually interviewing the officer involved last. If officers refuse to cooperate, they're subject to discipline, such as dismissal for refusing to obey an order of the chief.

Completed investigations go to the IAU supervisor. If the supervisor approves, complaints go to the decision-making, or deliberation, stage. Four possible decisions can be made in the deliberation stage (Figure 11.1):

1. *Unfounded.* The investigation proved that the act didn't take place.

2. *Exonerated.* The acts took place, but the investigation proved that they were justified, lawful, and proper.

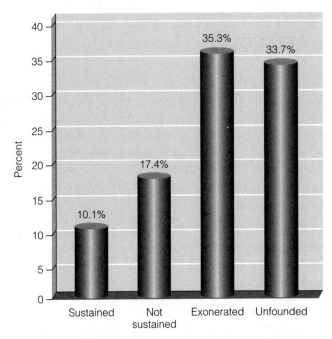

FIGURE 11.1 Decisions in Initial Disposition of Excessive Force Complaints
Source: Pate and Fridell 1993, 116.

3. *Not sustained.* The investigation failed to gather enough evidence to clearly prove the allegations in the complaint.

4. *Sustained.* The investigation disclosed enough evidence to clearly prove the allegations in the complaint. (Perez 1994, 96)

If the decision is "unfounded," "exonerated," or "not sustained," the case is disposed of by closing it. If the decision is "sustained," the supervisor recommends disciplinary action. Recommended disciplinary actions ranked from least to most severe include:

1. Reprimand

2. Written reprimand

3. Transfer

4. Retraining

5. Counseling

6. Suspension

7. Demotion

8. Fine

9. Dismissal

After the initial disposition, the case goes up the chain of command inside the department until it finally reaches the chief. In about half the cases, there's a discrepancy between the chief's recommendations and those of the immediate supervisor. These discrepancies are important because the immediate supervisor, usually a sergeant of patrol, works on the street with other patrol officers. The supervisors of sergeants usu-

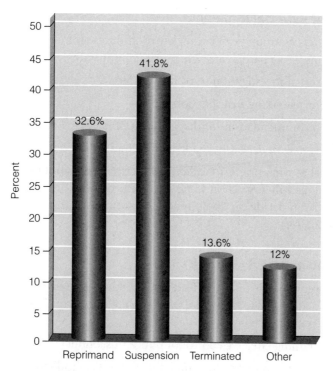

FIGURE 11.2 Distribution of Disciplinary Actions
Source: Pate and Fridell 1993, 116.

ally go along with the recommendations of sergeants. Chiefs of police, on the other hand, are removed from the day-to-day street operations of patrol officers and their immediate supervisors. They have departmentwide perspectives and are responsible to "local political elites" for their department's performance. So chiefs may find the disciplinary penalty too light and make it heavier. Figure 11.2 shows the distribution of disciplinary measures taken in a national sample of city police departments (Perez 1994, 96–97).

External Review

The basic objection to internal review is police shouldn't police themselves. To the question, "Who will watch the watchmen?" the answer is, "Not the watchmen!" So, external review has grown. In external review, individuals who aren't sworn police officers participate in the review of complaints against the police. Usually called *civilian review*, it has sparked controversy for nearly half a century. Police oppose external review because it interferes with their independence; they have no confidence outsiders know enough about police work to review it; and they know outside scrutiny could pierce the **blue curtain** that hides their "real" work from public view.

Strong police unions, chiefs who opposed external review, and the creation of internal review procedures (discussed in the last section) successfully prevented external review during the 1960s, when it became a popular proposal of some liberal reformers and citizen groups. However, by 1994, 72 percent of the fifty largest cities had created civilian review procedures of some sort (Walker and Bumpus 1992, 1, 3–4). Let's look at the types of external review and how well review by civilians has worked.

Types of External Review

The differences among civilian review procedures all turn on the point in the process when nonofficers participate. The possible points are:

1. The initial investigation to collect the facts

2. The review of the investigation reports

3. The recommendation for disposition to the chief

4. The review of decisions made by the chief

No matter at what point nonofficers participate, civilian review boards can only recommend disciplinary action to police chiefs, because under civil service laws only police chiefs can decide on disciplinary action against police officers (Walker and Bumpus 1992, 3–4).

Does Civilian Review Work?

The answer depends on the definition and the measures of effectiveness. Effectiveness can mean at least four things, all of which are important in determining the value of civilian review procedures:

1. Maintaining effective control of police misconduct

2. Providing resolutions to complaints that satisfy individual complainants

3. Preserving public confidence in the police

4. Influencing police management by providing "feedback from consumers" (Walker and Bumpus 1992, 8)

It's difficult to measure the effectiveness of civilian review because official data are ambiguous. Take the number of complaints, for example. A large number of complaints might mean a large volume of police misconduct, but it can also indicate confidence in the review procedures. Following the Rodney King incident in Los Angeles, observers noted that San Francisco, a city known for its strong review procedures, received more complaints than the much larger city of Los Angeles. In Los Angeles, the Independent Commission heard a number of citizen complaints that the LAPD created "significant hurdles" to filing complaints, that they were afraid of the process, and that the complaint process was "unnecessarily difficult or impossible." Further, the ACLU collected evidence suggesting that the LAPD "actively discouraged the filing of complaints." The beating of Rodney King, in fact, would never have come to public attention without the video, according to the Independent Commission. This is because, according to the commission, the efforts of Rodney King's brother Paul to file a complaint following the beating were "frustrated" by the LAPD (Pate and Fridell 1993, 39).

The numbers and rates of complaints are also difficult to assess because we don't know the numbers of incidents where people don't file complaints. In one national survey, of all the people who said the police mistreated them, only 30 percent said they filed complaints. One thing, however, is clear. Misconduct isn't distributed evenly among individuals and neighborhoods. In one survey, only 40 percent of the addresses in one city had any contact with the police in a year. Most contacts between private individuals and the police occur in poor neighborhoods. In New York City, the rate of complaints ranges from 1 to 5 for every 10,000 people, depending on the neighborhood.

Official data have consistently indicated racial minority males are disproportionately represented among complainants. So, the perception of a pattern of police harassment is a major factor in conflict between the police and racial minority communities (Walker and Bumpus 1992, 10).

Whatever the ambiguity of numbers and rates in the official statistics, observers have noted civilian review procedures rarely sustain complaints. Furthermore, the rates of complaints sustained in civilian review are about the same as the rates in internal affairs units (Walker and Bumpus 1992, 16–17).

SUMMARY

I. Remedies against official misconduct
   A. Remedies for official law-breaking are separate from trials of criminal defendants (discussed in Chapter 10)
   B. Three kinds of actions hold officers and government accountable for misconduct
      1. Criminal actions—prosecution of officers for criminal acts
      2. Civil actions—suing officers, departments, and governments for damages and/or injunctions
      3. Administrative remedies—internal department discipline of officers and external civilian review of police actions
   C. Remedies aren't mutually exclusive; all can be pursued at the same time

II. Criminal actions
   A. Most police misconduct *can* be a crime
   B. Most police officers aren't charged with, convicted of, or punished for criminal actions because
      1. Criminal intent doesn't exist, or it's difficult to prove beyond a reasonable doubt
      2. Officers who "honestly believe" their acts are lawful don't have criminal intent
      3. Unwillingness by prosecutors and juries to convict officers for "doing their job"
      4. Lack of sympathy for possible criminals and/or those they associate with

III. Civil actions
   A. General
      1. Most plaintiffs who sue officers and governments want compensation for injuries caused by police misconduct
      2. Plaintiffs can sue any or all of the following:
         a. Individual officers and their superiors (chiefs and sheriffs)
         b. Departments (police and sheriff's)
         c. Governments responsible for officers and departments (municipalities, counties, states, and U.S. government)
      3. Where can they sue?
         a. U.S. courts
         b. State courts

4. Laws governing damages vary depending on whether defendants are
   a. Individuals or departments and governments
   b. Federal or state, county, and municipal officers, departments, and governments
B. Suing federal officers and the U.S. government
   1. Suing individual officers (constitutional tort or *Bivens* actions)
      a. Individual federal officers are liable for their acts causing violations of plaintiffs' constitutional rights if plaintiffs can prove
         (1) Officers acted with apparent legal authority
         (2) Actions deprived plaintiffs of constitutional right
      b. Difficult to win *Bivens* cases because of defense of qualified immunity
         (1) Officers acted with objective reasonableness
         (2) Reasonableness measured by legal rules clearly established at time officers acted
      c. Reasons for difficulty
         (1) Preserve officers discretion to do their job
         (2) Prevent frivolous lawsuits
   2. Suing the U.S. government
      a. Sovereign immunity waived in Federal Tort Claims Act (FTCA)
      b. U.S. government's "deep pockets" make FTCA actions attractive
      c. Plaintiffs can pursue *Bivens* and FTCA actions
C. Suing state officers
   1. State tort actions
      a. Most illegal police acts are also state torts
      b. Tort law gives injured plaintiffs the right to recover damages
      c. Balance need for officer discretion and protecting officers
      d. Officers are liable only for "willful or deliberate wrong" (defense of official immunity)
   2. U.S. Civil Rights actions (§ 1983 actions)
      a. Plaintiffs can go into *federal* courts to sue *state, county,* and *municipal* officers for violations of plaintiffs' constitutional rights
      b. Elements of § 1983
         (1) Officers acted within the scope of their employment ("color of law")
         (2) Officers' actions *caused* deprivation of a constitutional right
      c. Limits on liability
         (1) Deliberate (not negligent or accidental) acts of officers
         (2) Qualified immunity defense (same as *Bivens* and FTCA)
D. Suing state and local governments
   1. State tort actions against state and local governments
      a. State and local governments are liable for their employees' torts (*respondeat superior*)
      b. Limits
         (1) Liability extends only to acts within the scope of employment
         (2) Not all states have adopted *respondeat superior,* in which case governments have same defense as individual officers (vicarious official immunity)

2. U.S. Civil Rights actions against state and local government
   a. Elements of state and local government liability
     (1) Officers acted according to either officially approved written policies *or* unwritten customs *and*
     (2) Officers actions *caused* the violation of a constitutional right of the plaintiff
   b. More complicated to prove liability of government than of individual (even though proving individual liability is also complicated)
E. Law enforcement duty to protect individuals
   1. No affirmative constitutional duty to protect individuals from each other
   2. Only individuals in custody have a constitutional right to protection (special relationship exception)
   3. Some U.S. Courts of Appeals have adopted a state-created-danger exception to the no-affirmative-duty-to-protect rule
   4. Elements of narrow exception
     a. Officer created danger of violent harm to plaintiff (not to the general public)
     b. Officer knew or should have known her actions encouraged this plaintiff to rely her actions
     c. Danger created by officer caused
       (1) Actual harm from violence *or*
       (2) Increased vulnerability to harm from violence
F. Suing judges and prosecutors
   1. Judges have absolute immunity from lawsuits—remedy is either impeachment or voting out of office
   2. Prosecutor liability
     a. Absolute liability when acting as advocates for the state in criminal prosecutions
     b. Limited liability when acting as administrators or investigators
G. Hurdles to suing officers and the government
   1. People who sue the government or its officers rarely win
   2. Reasons for failure
     a. Expensive
     b. Lengthy
     c. Juries more likely to believe police officers than plaintiffs
     d. Absolute, qualified, and official immunity
     e. No affirmative duty to protect
     f. Frivolous cases

IV. Administrative remedies
  A. Internal review
   1. Internal affairs unit (IAU) made up of department officers
   2. Four stages
     a. Intake—intake officers accept complaints
     b. Investigation—other officers gather evidence, interview witnesses
     c. Deliberation—other officers weigh evidence
     d. Disposition
       (1) First stage—deliberating officers decide among four dispositions

       (a) Unfounded—the act didn't take place

       (b) Exonerated—the act took place but was justified, lawful, and proper

       (c) Not sustained—not enough evidence to prove allegations in the complaint

       (d) Sustained—the evidence proved the allegations

    (2) Next stage—recommend disciplinary action for sustained complaints

       (a) Oral reprimand

       (b) Written reprimand

       (c) Transfer

       (d) Retraining

       (e) Counseling

       (f) Suspension

       (g) Demotion

       (h) Fine

       (i) Dismissal

    (3) Final stage—recommendations are forwarded and move up chain of command to chief for final disposition

3. Criticisms

  a. Police can't police themselves

  b. Some parts of public don't accept legitimacy of self-supervision

B. External review

  1. Overcome criticism of internal review: "Who will watch the watchman?"

  2. Civilians outside department review (or participate in reviewing) complaints

  3. Police criticisms of external civilian review

    a. Interferes with police independence

    b. Outsiders don't understand police work

    c. Pierces "blue curtain" that hides "real" police work from view

  4. The point in reviews when civilians (nonofficers) participate varies

    a. Collection of facts

    b. Review investigation report

    c. Recommend disciplinary action to chief

    d. Review of chief's disposition

  5. Only chiefs have the legal authority to order disciplinary action—required by most civil service laws

  6. Effectiveness of civilian review

    a. Definition of effectiveness varies

      (1) Controlling police misconduct

      (2) Resolving complaints to satisfy complainants

      (3) Preserving public confidence in police

      (4) Influencing police management by providing "feedback" from citizens

    b. Outcome

      (1) Civilian review rarely sustains complaints

      (2) Sustained rates are similar to those in internal review

c. Difficult to measure
   (1) Increased volume of complaints can mean either the level of misconduct or the level of confidence in the review process has risen (San Francisco example)
   (2) The number of incidents not reported isn't known

Go to the Criminal Procedure 6e CD to download this summary outline. The outline has been formatted so that you can add notes to it during class lectures, or later create a customized chapter outline to use while reviewing. Either way, the summary outline will help you understand the "big picture" and fill in the details as you study.

REVIEW QUESTIONS

1. How likely and why is it that police officers will be charged and convicted of criminal conduct?

2. Summarize the *Bivens v. Six Unnamed FBI Agents* case, and explain its significance.

3. Identify the two elements of the qualified immunity defense, and explain why the test is so easy for officers to pass.

4. What specific remedy does the Federal Tort Claims Act (FTCA) provide plaintiffs, and why is it attractive to plaintiffs?

5. Identify and describe the differences between two kinds of state civil lawsuits against individual state officers.

6. Describe the balance that has to be struck in state cases against state officers.

7. Identify two elements plaintiffs in § 1983 actions against state and local law enforcement officers have to prove.

8. Identify and describe two limits placed by the U.S. Supreme Court on § 1983 actions against state and local officers.

9. Describe the extent and limits of state tort actions against state and local governments.

10. Identify the elements in the balancing test used to decide whether to grant the defense of vicarious official immunity.

11. According to the U.S. Supreme Court in *Monell v. New York City Department of Social Services,* what two elements do plaintiffs have to prove to succeed in suing local government units?

12. According to the U.S. Supreme Court, what (if any) constitutional duty do law enforcement officers have to protect private individuals from each other?

13. Identify and explain the three elements in the state-created-danger exception to the no-affirmative-duty-to-protect rule.

14. Can you sue a judge for damages? A prosecutor? Explain.

15. Identify and explain the reasons for the hurdles plaintiffs have to overcome when they sue officers and the governments in charge of them.

16. Identify and briefly describe the two types of administrative remedies against police misconduct.

17. Identify and describe the stages, possible dispositions, and disciplinary actions in internal review procedures.

18. Identify the basic objection to internal review. How is external review supposed to overcome the objection?

19. Identify three reasons why police oppose civilian review.

20. Does civilian review work? Explain.

KEY TERMS

plaintiffs p. 395

damages p. 395

civil action p. 395

constitutional tort (*Bivens*) actions p. 396

Federal Tort Claims Act (FTCA) actions p. 396

under color of authority p. 396

qualified immunity p. 396

"good faith" defense p. 396

sovereign immunity p. 400

torts p. 401

defense of official immunity p. 401

Civil Rights Act actions p. 401

1983 actions p. 401

doctrine of *respondeat superior* p. 402

defense of vicarious official immunity p. 402

no-affirmative-duty-to-protect rule p. 403

special relationship exception p. 403

state-created-danger exception p. 403

absolute immunity p. 409

internal affairs units (IAU) p. 413

external civilian review p. 413

blue curtain p. 415

THE COMPANION WEB SITE FOR *CRIMINAL PROCEDURE*, SIXTH EDITION

http://cj.wadsworth.com/samaha/crim_pro6e

 Supplement your review of this chapter by going to the companion Web site to take one of the Tutorial Quizzes, use the flash cards to test yourself on the key terms from each chapter, and check out the many other study aids you'll find there. You'll find valuable data and resources at your fingertips to help you study for that big exam or write that important paper.

Starting Court Proceedings

Chapter Main Points

- After arrest, interrogation, and identification procedures at police stations, responsibility for criminal procedure changes hands from police to lawyers in courts.

- The power of prosecutors to transform suspects into defendants by charging them with crimes is the starting point of court proceedings.

- The "unreasonable seizure" ban in the Fourth Amendment commands that suspects detained after arrest be taken quickly before a magistrate to decide whether there's probable cause to back up their detention.

- The decision to bail or release defendants balances the needs to guarantee the appearance of defendants in court and protect public safety against the rights of defendants who haven't been convicted of crimes.

- The U.S. Supreme Court has interpreted the right to counsel to include the right to *effective* counsel for *all* defendants charged with *all* crimes with penalties of actual incarceration.

The prosecutor's power to charge gives her more control over life, liberty, and reputation than any other person in America.

U.S. Supreme Court Justice Robert Jackson, 1940

In all criminal prosecutions, the accused shall enjoy the right ... to have the assistance of counsel for his defense.

U.S. Constitution, Amendment VI

STARTING COURT PROCEEDINGS

After arrest, interrogation, and identification procedures, the action moves first from the police station to prosecutors' and defense attorneys' offices and then to the courts. In the interval between arrest and the first time defendants appear in court, both the police and the prosecutor make critical decisions. First, the police decide if the case should go forward or be dropped. Police drop cases for several reasons. The most obvious reason is they don't believe suspects are guilty. Even if they believe a suspect is guilty, they still might drop the case if they don't think they've got enough evidence to prove it. Or, they might release the suspect but *not* drop the case, with a warning that they'll be "watching her" and might "call her later." In misdemeanor cases, even if the police believe they can prove their case, they still might release suspects on the informal condition that they get "help," such as drug and alcohol treatment or family counseling, or "stay out of trouble."

Police take the strong cases they want prosecuted to the prosecutor's office. Prosecutors then make their own judgment about how to dispose of these cases. If they decide to prosecute, they start formal court proceedings by filing a complaint, information, or indictment (Chapter 13). All three proceedings have a single goal: to test the objective basis for the decision to charge. In these proceedings, either judges or grand juries consider the evidence the government has collected to prove its case. If the government has enough evidence, defendants have to appear and answer the criminal charges against them (called **arraignment**). The decision to start criminal court proceedings is not just a technicality. According to the U.S. Supreme Court in *Kirby v. Illinois* (1972):

> The initiation of judicial criminal proceedings is far from a mere formalism. It is the starting point of our whole system of adversary criminal justice. For it is only then that the Government has committed itself to prosecute, and only then that the adverse positions of Government and defendant have solidified. It is then that a defendant finds himself faced with the prosecutorial forces of organized society, and immersed in the intricacies of substantive and procedural criminal law. It is this point, therefore, that marks the commencement of the "criminal prosecutions." (689)

In this chapter, we'll look at the decision to charge, the rules regulating probable cause to detain, and what happens during defendants' first appearance in court after being charged.

THE DECISION TO CHARGE

Once the police bring a case to the prosecutor, lawyers take over the management of the criminal process. Although the police fade into the background, they don't disappear. Lawyers need them to clarify, investigate further, and perhaps testify in court. Prosecutors are likely to take at face value the recommendations from officers with a reputation for establishing "good" cases. They're just as likely to discount cases from officers with poor track records.

Prosecutors drop some cases without further action. If they don't think they can prove the case, they drop it and release the suspect outright. Even if they think they can prove their case, prosecutors don't automatically charge suspects. Why? Prosecutors have dual roles in our justice system. They represent the public in prosecuting criminal cases, but they're also officers of the court. In that capacity, their mission is to "do justice"—and doing justice doesn't always mean charging and prosecuting suspects. In *People v. Camargo* (1986), the defendant was charged with the criminal sale and possession of cocaine. By the time he was indicted, the defendant was in an advanced stage of AIDS and related complicating illnesses. He had *Pneumocystis carinii* pneumonia. The virus had invaded his brain and his stomach, and peripheral nerve damage caused him pain and suffering to the extent that doctors ordered him to limit his physical exercise to sitting in a chair for one hour a day. His doctors' prognosis was death within three to four months. The government dropped the case because "it did not appear that the interest of justice would be substantially served by the defendant's continued prosecution under this indictment." According to the court:

> [T]he uncompromising rampage of the multiple disease processes have condemned this defendant to a painful, imminent death. When the rationale for incarceration becomes unjustifiable because of . . . a deadly disease, it becomes imperative to allow the sufferer to live his last days in the best circumstances possible and with dignity and compassion.

In the interests of justice, prosecutors also can divert suspects into a program for community service, restitution, substance abuse, or family violence treatment. In these **diversion cases,** prosecutors agree to drop the case before formal judicial proceedings begin if suspects participate in and complete these programs. The number of cases prosecutors decide not to pursue ranges from a few in some jurisdictions to nearly half of all cases in others (Boland and others 1988).

Several reasons stand behind the **decision to charge** (to start formal court proceedings by filing a complaint, information, or indictment [Chapter 13]). Most important is the **strength of the case** against defendants. For example, if prosecutors don't have enough evidence to prosecute—no witnesses or weak witnesses, poor physical evidence, and no confessions or other admissions by suspects—they won't charge. Witnesses may be neither reliable nor convincing. Witness problems increase if victims know their assailants in violent crimes. In over half of these cases, witnesses and victims refuse to cooperate because they're either afraid or have a change of heart over prosecuting people they know (and often care about). Sometimes, prosecutors can't use evidence because the police seized it illegally (see Chapter 10). But, contrary to the popular belief that many guilty criminals go unpunished because of the exclusionary rule, fewer than 2 percent of all cases (and practically no violent crime cases) are dropped because of it (Davies 1983, n. 89; Nardulli 1983).

Selective prosecution is another reason behind the decision to charge. Lack of resources makes it impossible to prosecute every case, even when prosecutors have enough evidence and it's in the interests of justice to prosecute. Time and money make prosecutors set priorities: suspects guilty of petty thefts go to restitution to allow prosecutions for armed robbery, prosecuting violent sex offenses takes precedence over prostitution, and charging a few well-known tax evaders serves as examples to deter tax evasion. According to some critics, selective prosecution cuts into the legislature's power to make the laws. Others argue that selectively prosecuting only some individuals in a category—like "fat cats" or notorious tax evaders—undermines impartial law enforcement.

Which (if any) of the following suspects should a prosecutor selectively charge?

1. A student stole a cassette recorder to record his criminal procedure class because the professor talks too fast. He works part time to pay for school, and, although he could've paid for the recorder, it would've been difficult. He has never been in trouble with the law before and says he'll pay for the recorder.

2. A woman who works only occasionally stole a cordless phone for a friend who agreed to pay $35, half the phone's value. The woman has taken compact disks, tape cassettes, and an answering machine from the same store within the past six months.

3. A 50-year-old woman slipped a pair of stereo earphones into her purse. The woman is wealthy and indignantly denied that she intended to steal the earphones. She told the detective she put the device in her bag because she wanted to pick up some film, batteries, and other small items and simply forgot she had put it there.

You might want to review your decisions after completing this chapter.

Despite criticisms of the extent of prosecutorial power, U.S. Supreme Court Justice Robert Jackson's words in 1940 are still true: The prosecutor's power to charge gives her "more control over life, liberty, and reputation than any other person in America." So, except for violating due process by vindictively prosecuting individuals or violating equal protection by selectively prosecuting members of groups (Chapter 2)—violations rarely charged and hardly ever successfully when they are—the prosecutor's discretionary power to charge is practically unlimited.

PROBABLE CAUSE
TO DETAIN SUSPECTS

An urgent situation arises when the following circumstances combine: Defendants are arrested without warrants; they have no lawyers because they're too poor to hire one; they haven't been charged with any crime; and they're locked up in jail. The U.S. Constitution and state laws command that independent magistrates (not police officers whose zeal to root out crime might color their objectivity) have to decide soon whether there's probable cause to back up this severe deprivation of liberty. Of course, protecting public safety requires that police have the power to arrest suspects before a judge has decided there was probable cause for the arrest. Otherwise, suspects who turn out to be criminals might escape, commit further crimes, or destroy evidence. But, once suspects are in jail, these dangers evaporate. Now, the guarantees of due process and protection of innocent people take over. In *County of Riverside v. McLaughlin* (1991), the U.S. Supreme Court spoke about "reconciling these competing interests":

> On the one hand, States have a strong interest in protecting public safety by taking into custody those persons who are reasonably suspected of having engaged in criminal activity, even where there has been no opportunity for a prior judicial determination of probable cause. On the other hand, prolonged detention based on incorrect or unfounded suspicion may unjustly "imperil a suspect's job, interrupt his source of income, and impair his family relationships." We sought to balance these competing concerns by holding that States "must provide a fair and reliable determination of probable cause as a condition for any significant pretrial restraint of liberty, and this determination must be made by a judicial officer either before or promptly after arrest." (52)

Before we go on, let's clear up something that might confuse you—there are two kinds of probable cause. **Probable cause to detain a suspect** is decided at a court proceeding called the **first appearance** (sometimes the *probable cause hearing*). **Probable cause to go to trial** is decided in preliminary hearings or grand jury proceedings. Probable cause to detain (discussed in Chapter 5) requires fewer facts than probable cause to go to trial (Chapter 13).

In *Gerstein v. Pugh* (1975), the U.S. Supreme Court decided the Fourth Amendment "unreasonable seizure" ban demands that suspects locked up in jail be taken "promptly" to a magistrate to decide whether there are enough facts to back up the detention. The question is, How prompt is fast enough to satisfy the Fourth Amendment? Lower federal courts and state courts for a long time said the Fourth Amendment gives the police enough time to complete the "administrative steps incident to arrest." This usually means the police can do all of the following before they take suspects to court (*Sanders v. City of Houston* 1982, 700):

1. Complete paperwork
2. Search the suspect
3. Conduct an inventory search
4. Inventory property found
5. Fingerprint the suspect
6. Photograph the suspect
7. Check for a possible prior criminal record
8. Test laboratory samples
9. Interrogate the suspect
10. Check an alibi
11. Conduct a lineup
12. Compare the crime with similar crimes

Some jurisdictions are more specific; they spell out exactly how much time the police get to finish the administrative steps. Depending on the jurisdiction, times range from 24 to 36 hours (Brandes 1989). The U.S. Supreme Court defined "promptly" in *County of Riverside v. McLaughlin* (1991).

County of Riverside v. McLaughlin
500 U.S. 44 (1991)

Donald Lee McLaughlin and others brought a class action*
under 42 U.S.C. § 1983, challenging how the County of
Riverside, California, handles probable cause determina-
tions for individuals arrested without a warrant. The U.S.
District court granted a preliminary injunction. The Ninth
Circuit U.S. Court of Appeals affirmed. The U.S. Supreme
Court granted certiorari, vacated the judgment of the Court
of Appeals, and remanded the case.

O'CONNOR, J., joined by REHNQUIST, CJ.,
and WHITE, KENNEDY, and SOUTER, JJ.

FACTS

In August 1987, Donald Lee McLaughlin filed a complaint
in the U.S. District Court for the Central District of California. The complaint alleged that McLaughlin was then
currently incarcerated in the Riverside County Jail and had
not received a probable cause determination. He requested
"an order and judgment requiring that the defendants and
the County of Riverside provide in-custody arrestees, arrested without warrants, prompt probable cause, bail and
arraignment hearings." A second complaint named three
additional plaintiffs—Johnny E. James, Diana Ray Simon,
and Michael Scott Hyde....The complaint alleged that
each of the named plaintiffs had been arrested without a
warrant, had received neither prompt probable cause nor
bail hearings, and was still in custody....

In March 1989, plaintiffs asked the District Court to
issue a preliminary injunction requiring the County to
provide all persons arrested without a warrant a judicial
determination of probable cause within 36 hours of arrest.
The District Court issued the injunction, holding that the
County's existing practice violated this Court's decision in
Gerstein. Without discussion, the District Court adopted a
rule that the County provide probable cause determinations within 36 hours of arrest, except in exigent circumstances. The court "retained jurisdiction indefinitely" to
ensure that the County established new procedures that
complied with the injunction.

---

*An action in which one person or a small group of people rep-
resent the interests of a larger group.

The U.S. Court of Appeals for the Ninth Circuit consolidated this case with another challenging an identical
preliminary injunction issued against the County of San
Bernardino. On November 8, 1989, the Court of Appeals
affirmed the order granting the preliminary injunction
against Riverside County....The Court of Appeals...de-
termined that the County's policy of providing probable
cause determinations at arraignment within 48 hours was
"not in accord with *Gerstein*'s requirement of a determination 'promptly after arrest'" because no more than 36
hours were needed "to complete the administrative steps
incident to arrest." The Ninth Circuit thus joined the
Fourth and Seventh Circuits in interpreting *Gerstein* as
requiring a probable cause determination immediately
following completion of the administrative procedures
incident to arrest. By contrast, the Second Circuit understands *Gerstein* to "stress the need for flexibility" and to
permit States to combine probable cause determinations
with other pretrial proceedings. We granted certiorari to
resolve this conflict among the Circuits as to what constitutes a "prompt" probable cause determination under
Gerstein.

OPINION

...In *Gerstein v. Pugh* (1975), this Court held unconstitutional Florida procedures under which persons arrested
without a warrant could remain in police custody for 30
days or more without a judicial determination of probable cause. In reaching this conclusion we attempted to
reconcile important competing interests. On the one
hand, States have a strong interest in protecting public
safety by taking into custody those persons who are reasonably suspected of having engaged in criminal activity,
even where there has been no opportunity for a prior judicial determination of probable cause. On the other
hand, prolonged detention based on incorrect or unfounded suspicion may unjustly "imperil a suspect's job,
interrupt his source of income, and impair his family relationships." We sought to balance these competing concerns by holding that States "must provide a fair and reliable determination of probable cause as a condition for
any significant pretrial restraint of liberty, and this determination must be made by a judicial officer either before
or promptly after arrest."

The Court thus established a "practical compromise"
between the rights of individuals and the realities of law

enforcement.... We left it to the individual States to integrate prompt probable cause determinations into their differing systems of pretrial procedures....

Inherent in *Gerstein's* invitation to the States to experiment and adapt was the recognition that the Fourth Amendment does not compel an immediate determination of probable cause upon completing the administrative steps incident to arrest. Plainly, if a probable cause hearing is constitutionally compelled the moment a suspect is finished being "booked," there is no room whatsoever for "flexibility and experimentation by the States." Incorporating probable cause determinations "into the procedure for setting bail or fixing other conditions of pretrial release"—which *Gerstein* explicitly contemplated—would be impossible. Waiting even a few hours so that a bail hearing or arraignment could take place at the same time as the probable cause determination would amount to a constitutional violation. Clearly, *Gerstein* is not that inflexible....

But flexibility has its limits; *Gerstein* is not a blank check. A State has no legitimate interest in detaining for extended periods individuals who have been arrested without probable cause. The Court recognized in *Gerstein* that a person arrested without a warrant is entitled to a fair and reliable determination of probable cause and that this determination must be made promptly. Unfortunately, as lower court decisions applying *Gerstein* have demonstrated, it is not enough to say that probable cause determinations must be "prompt." This vague standard simply has not provided sufficient guidance. Instead, it has led to a flurry of systemic challenges to city and county practices, putting federal judges in the role of making legislative judgments and overseeing local jail house operations.

Our task in this case is to articulate more clearly the boundaries of what is permissible under the Fourth Amendment. Although we hesitate to announce that the Constitution compels a specific time limit, it is important to provide some degree of certainty so that States and counties may establish procedures with confidence that they fall within constitutional bounds. Taking into account the competing interests articulated in *Gerstein*, we believe that a jurisdiction that provides judicial determinations of probable cause within 48 hours of arrest will, as a general matter, comply with the promptness requirement of *Gerstein*. For this reason, such jurisdictions will be immune from systemic challenges.

This is not to say that the probable cause determination in a particular case passes constitutional muster simply because it is provided within 48 hours. Such a hearing may nonetheless violate *Gerstein* if the arrested individual can prove that his or her probable cause determination was delayed unreasonably. Examples of unreasonable delay are delays for the purpose of gathering additional evidence to justify the arrest, a delay motivated by ill will against the arrested individual, or delay for delay's sake. In evaluating whether the delay in a particular case is unreasonable, however, courts must allow a substantial degree of flexibility. Courts cannot ignore the often unavoidable delays in transporting arrested persons from one facility to another, handling late-night bookings where no magistrate is readily available, obtaining the presence of an arresting officer who may be busy processing other suspects or securing the premises of an arrest, and other practical realities.

Where an arrested individual does not receive a probable cause determination within 48 hours, the calculus changes. In such a case, the arrested individual does not bear the burden of proving an unreasonable delay. Rather, the burden shifts to the government to demonstrate the existence of a bona fide emergency or other extraordinary circumstance. The fact that in a particular case it may take longer than 48 hours to consolidate pretrial proceedings does not qualify as an extraordinary circumstance. Nor, for that matter, do intervening weekends. A jurisdiction that chooses to offer combined proceedings must do so as soon as is reasonably feasible, but in no event later than 48 hours after arrest....

For the reasons we have articulated, we conclude that Riverside County is entitled to combine probable cause determinations with arraignments. The record indicates, however, that the County's current policy and practice do not comport fully with the principles we have outlined. The County's current policy is to offer combined proceedings within two days, exclusive of Saturdays, Sundays, or holidays. As a result, persons arrested on Thursdays may have to wait until the following Monday before they receive a probable cause determination. The delay is even longer if there is an intervening holiday. Thus, the County's regular practice exceeds the 48-hour period we deem constitutionally permissible, meaning that the County is not immune from systemic challenges, such as this class action.

As to arrests that occur early in the week, the County's practice is that "arraignments usually take place on the last day" possible. There may well be legitimate reasons for this practice; alternatively, this may constitute delay for delay's sake. We leave it to the Court of Appeals and the District Court, on remand, to make this determination. The judgment of the Court of Appeals is vacated and the case is REMANDED for further proceedings consistent with this opinion.

DISSENT

SCALIA, J.

... "The Fourth Amendment requires a judicial determination of probable cause as a prerequisite to extended restraint of liberty," "either before or promptly after arrest." Though how "promptly" we did not say, it was plain enough that the requirement left no room for intentional delay unrelated to the completion of "the administrative steps incident to arrest." Plain enough, at least, that all but one federal court considering the question understood *Gerstein* that way. Today, however, the Court discerns something quite different in *Gerstein*. It finds that the plain statements set forth above (not to mention the common-law tradition of liberty upon which they were based) were trumped by the implication of a later dictum in the case which, according to the Court, manifests a "recognition that the Fourth Amendment does not compel an immediate determination of probable cause upon completing the administrative steps incident to arrest."

... Determining the outer boundary of reasonableness is an ... objective and ... manageable task. We were asked to undertake it in *Gerstein*, but declined—wisely, I think, since we had before us little data to support any figure we might choose.... The data available are enough to convince me, however, that certainly no more than 24-hours is needed. With one exception, no federal court considering the question has regarded 24 hours as an inadequate amount of time to complete arrest procedures, and with the same exception every court actually setting a limit for probable-cause determination based on those procedures has selected 24 hours. (The exception would not count Sunday within the 24-hour limit....) And state courts have similarly applied a 24-hour limit under state statutes requiring presentment without "unreasonable delay."...

... A few weeks before issuance of today's opinion there appeared in the *Washington Post* the story of protracted litigation arising from the arrest of a student who entered a restaurant in Charlottesville, Virginia, one evening to look for some friends. Failing to find them, he tried to leave—but refused to pay a $5 fee (required by the restaurant's posted rules) for failing to return a red tab he had been issued to keep track of his orders. According to the story, he "was taken by police to the Charlottesville jail" at the restaurant's request. "There, a magistrate refused to issue an arrest warrant," and he was released. That is how it used to be; but not, according to today's decision, how it must be in the future. If the Fourth Amendment meant then what the Court says it does now, the student could lawfully have been held for as long as it would have taken to arrange for his arraignment, up to a maximum of 48 hours.

Justice STORY wrote that the Fourth Amendment "is little more than the affirmance of a great constitutional doctrine of the common law." It should not become less than that. One hears the complaint, nowadays, that the Fourth Amendment has become constitutional law for the guilty; that it benefits the career criminal (through the exclusionary rule) often and directly, but the ordinary citizen remotely if at all. By failing to protect the innocent arrestee, today's opinion reinforces that view. The common-law rule of prompt hearing had as its primary beneficiaries the innocent—not those whose fully justified convictions must be overturned to scold the police; nor those who avoid conviction because the evidence, while convincing, does not establish guilt beyond a reasonable doubt; but those so blameless that there was not even good reason to arrest them. While in recent years we have invented novel applications of the Fourth Amendment to release the unquestionably guilty, we today repudiate one of its core applications so that the presumptively innocent may be left in jail. Hereafter, a law-abiding citizen wrongfully arrested may be compelled to await the grace of a Dickensian bureaucratic machine, as it churns its cycle for up to two days—never once given the opportunity to show a judge that there is absolutely no reason to hold him, that a mistake has been made. In my view, this is the image of a system of justice that has lost its ancient sense of priority, a system that few Americans would recognize as our own.

Questions

1. What reasons does the Court give for deciding that under ordinary circumstances, 48 hours is a reasonable time to satisfy the Fourth Amendment interest in providing a prompt determination of probable cause?

2. What interests did the Court balance in making its decision?

3. What administrative steps and specific circumstances did the Court consider in balancing these interests?

4. What does the history of the common law have to do with a decision made in 1991?

5. What rule would you adopt? Why?

FIRST APPEARANCE

The **criminal complaint** (the document that formally charges defendants with specific crimes) authorizes magistrates to conduct the *first appearance.* Magistrates complete four tasks at the first appearance:

1. Inform defendants of the charges against them
2. Inform defendants of their constitutional rights
3. Set bail or detain suspects
4. Appoint attorneys for indigent defendants

Felony defendants rarely enter a plea at their first appearance; they wait until their *arraignment* (a proceeding that orders defendants to come to court and plead to the charges against them [Chapter 13]). Misdemeanor defendants usually plead (almost always guilty) at their first appearance, especially if the penalty is a small fine. Let's look at the four things magistrates do at the first appearance.

Inform Suspects of the Charges Against Them

When suspects—now called defendants—first appear in court, magistrates tell them the charges against them. If defendants don't have a lawyer present, the court gives them copies of the complaint, the police report, and other papers supporting the complaint.

Inform Suspects of Their Constitutional Rights

Informing defendants of their constitutional rights follows this typical court rule in Minnesota's *Rules of Criminal Procedure* (Minnesota Rules of Court 1987, Rule 5.01, 112):

> The judge, judicial officer, or other duly appointed personnel shall advise the defendant substantially as follows:
>
> (a) That he is not required to say anything or submit to interrogation and that anything he says may be used against him in this or in any subsequent proceedings;
>
> (b) That he has a right to counsel in all subsequent proceedings, including police line-ups and interrogations, and if he appears without counsel and is financially unable to afford counsel, that counsel will forthwith be appointed without cost to him if he is charged with an offense punishable upon conviction by incarceration;
>
> (c) That he has a right to communicate with his counsel and that a continuance will be granted if necessary to enable defendant to obtain or speak to counsel;
>
> (d) That he has a right to a jury trial or a trial to the court;
>
> (e) That if the offense is a misdemeanor, he may either plead guilty or not guilty, or demand a complaint prior to entering a plea. The judge, judicial officer, or other duly authorized personnel may advise a number of defendants at once of these rights, but each defendant shall be asked individually before he is arraigned whether he heard and understood these rights as explained earlier.

Set Bail or Detain Suspects

Most defendants (in some places more than 90 percent) are released on bail while they wait for trial or the results of a plea bargain (see Chapter 13). Still, locking up even 10 percent of defendants adds to the never-ending problem of crowded jails. Pretrial detention can last for quite a while (more than 30 days for 33 percent of detainees; more than 90 days for 20 percent), and detention costs money ($30+ a day for every defendant). About 20 percent of defendants (charged with petty offenses) are released without even appearing before judges. These defendants receive a **citation release** (like a traffic ticket), or, they're released after posting bond according to **bail schedules** that list amounts for specific offenses (Toborg 1981).

Judges can attach a variety of conditions to release. Sometimes, defendants are **released on recognizance (ROR)**—their promise to appear in court on their court date. Some judges release defendants on the condition that they either report at scheduled times to a pretrial release program or promise not to leave town before their trial. Sometimes judges impose supervised release, like requiring defendants to report to relatives or their local police department; to participate in a treatment program for illegal drug, alcohol, or mental illness; or to attend employment programs (Toborg 1981).

Money bonds, in which defendants are released as soon as money is put up, come in several forms. With the **unsecured bond,** defendants have to pay only if they don't appear for their court date. With the **court-administered deposit bond,** defendants have to post 10 percent of the amount of the bond; if they appear, the court returns their deposit. Under **privately administered bail bonds,** bail bondsmen (most are men) or bondswomen charge 10 percent of the amount of the bond they turn over to the courts. Defendants forfeit the 10 percent fee even if they appear (Feeley 1979, chap. 4).

A typical state provision to guide judges in making the bail decision reads like this:

> The court, judge, or judicial officer shall impose the first of the following conditions of release which will reasonably assure the appearance of the person for trial or hearing, or when otherwise required, or, if no single condition gives that assurance, any combination of the following conditions:
> (a) Place the person in the care and supervision of a designated person or organization agreeing to supervise him;
> (b) Place restrictions on travel, association, or place of abode during his period of release;
> (c) Require the execution of an appearance bond in an amount set by the court with sufficient solvent sureties, or the deposit of cash or other sufficient security in lieu thereof; or
> (d) Impose any other condition deemed reasonably necessary to assure appearance as required, including a condition requiring that the person return to custody after specified hours. In any event, the court shall also fix the amount of money bail without other conditions upon which the defendant may obtain his release.
>
> Minnesota Rules of Court 1987, Rule 6.02, 188–189

Obviously, being locked up before trial is a major loss of freedom, but it's more than that. Temporary loss of wages and even permanent loss of a job, separation from family and friends, restrictions on aiding in their own defense, and loss of reputation are also possible for detained defendants. And—all of these take place *before* defendants are convicted. But, pretrial release is a risk for society. Defendants on bail can escape the jurisdiction of the court by fleeing; commit new crimes; and expose the community to anxiety, fear, and outrage over the threats to public safety. Clearly, the decision of whether to release or detain defendants before they're found guilty demands that courts strike the right balance between the right of defendants to be free until they're proved guilty and the need of the community to feel safe from crime and bring criminals to justice. Striking that balance boils down to two questions:

1. What are the constitutional rights of bailed and detained defendants?
2. What are the legitimate community interests in bailed and detained defendants?

To answer these questions, we'll look at how bail was viewed in the Constitution, whether preventive detention denies suspects their constitutional rights, and what rights defendants retain during pretrial detention.

Bail and the Constitution

There's no *absolute* constitutional right to bail, only a right against *excessive* bail. The Eighth Amendment to the U.S. Constitution provides that "Excessive bail shall not be required," but, the word "excessive" is subject to interpretation. So, legislatures and courts are left to spell out the precise constitutional limit. In a controversial case from the Cold War era, *Stack v. Boyle* (1951), U.S. Chief Justice Fred M. Vinson wrote for the majority:

> From the passage of the Judiciary Act of 1789, to the present...federal law has unequivocally provided that a person arrested for a non-capital offense shall be admitted to bail. This traditional right to freedom permits the unhampered preparation of a defense, and serves to prevent the infliction of punishment prior to conviction....Unless this right to bail before trial is preserved, the presumption of innocence, secured only after centuries of struggle, would lose its meaning. (4)

In *Stack*, twelve people were charged with conspiring to violate the Smith Act, which made it a crime to advocate the violent overthrow of the government. The case arose at the height of the Cold War, when anticommunism and fear of radicalism gripped the nation. The trial court fixed bail at $50,000 apiece. The U.S. Supreme Court ruled that amounts that are more than necessary to ensure that petitioners come to court for their trials are "excessive." The Court held that magistrates have to calculate how much money it will take to guarantee that defendants will appear.

Naturally, the amount will vary according to the circumstances of each case, but the main concerns include

1. The seriousness of the offense
2. The amount of the evidence against the defendant
3. The defendant's family ties, employment, financial resources, character, and mental condition
4. The length of the defendant's residence in the community
5. The defendant's criminal history
6. The defendant's prior record for appearing and/or "jumping" bail

Sometimes, no amount of money is enough to guarantee that rich defendants will come to court. In *U.S. v. Abrahams* (1978), Herbert Abrahams had three previous convictions; was an escaped prisoner from another state; had given false information at a prior bail hearing; had failed to appear on a former bail of $100,000; had failed to appear on a previous charge in California from which he was a fugitive; had several aliases; and had recently transferred $1.5 million to Bermuda! The U.S. First Circuit Court of Appeals upheld the U.S. District Court's conclusion that no condition "or any combination . . . will reasonably assure the appearance of defendant for trial if admitted to bail." In the 1980s, former U.S. Attorney General William French Smith maintained that the problem of rich defendants jumping bail is especially serious among major drug dealers, who can easily post bail in amounts of $1 million: "Some of these people net $250,000 to $500,000 a month from their drug sales. Paying bail of $100,000 is like getting rid of pocket money to these people."

At the other extreme (and a lot more common) any amount is too much for poor defendants to pay. Noted bail scholar Professor Caleb Foote (1965) believes our bail system violates the Constitution in three ways when it comes to poor defendants. It denies them:

1. *Due process of law* because defendants can't help with their own defense if they're locked up

2. *Equal protection of the law* because they're jailed because they're poor

3. *Right against excessive bail* because they can't raise any amount required

The U.S. Fifth Circuit Court of Appeals dealt with the problem of indigent defendants' bail in *Pugh v. Rainwater* (1977). Florida's bail system set up a range of release conditions. However, the system didn't create either a presumption in favor of release on recognizance or a priority for nonfinancial conditions. According to the Court:

> Because it gives the judge essentially unreviewable discretion to impose money bail, the rule is . . . discriminatory . . . : When a judge decides to set money bail, the indigent will be forced to remain in jail. We hold that equal protection standards are not satisfied unless the judge is required to consider less financially onerous forms of release before he imposes money bail. Requiring a presumption in favor of non-money bail accommodates the State's interest in assuring the defendant's appearance at trial as well as the defendant's right to be free pending trial, regardless of his financial status.

So, as the court put it later on rehearing the case, for

> an indigent, whose appearance at trial could reasonably be assured by one of the alternative forms of release, pretrial confinement for inability to post money bail would constitute imposition of an excessive restraint.

Pretrial detention is an obstacle to defendants trying to prepare their defense. They can't help investigators find witnesses and physical evidence. Cramped jail quarters and short visiting hours inhibit conferences with their lawyers. Jailing also affects defendants' appearance and demeanor; they can't conceal rumpled clothes and a pale complexion. Free defendants, on the other hand, can help their defense and show the court that they're working and otherwise responsible for themselves and their families.

Preventive Detention

Commentators, lawyers, judges, and criminal justice personnel have hotly debated whether the only acceptable purpose for bail and pretrial detention is to make sure defendants come to court. But, can courts also lock up "dangerous" defendants? Yes. **Preventive detention** allows judges to deny bail to defendants who might intimidate, hurt, and terrorize victims and witnesses or who might commit new crimes. To reduce these dangers, the U.S. Congress enacted the Bail Reform Act of 1984, which authorizes federal courts to jail arrested defendants when a judge determines, after a hearing, that no condition of release would "reasonably" guarantee the (1) appearance of the defendant *and* (2) the safety of the community. The Bail Reform Act guarantees at preventive detention hearings defendants' rights:

1. To have an appointed lawyer

2. To testify at the hearing

3. To present evidence

4. To cross-examine witnesses

If the judge decides there's **clear and convincing evidence** (more than probable cause but less than proof beyond a reasonable doubt), the defendant either won't appear or is a threat to public safety, the defendant can be "preventively detained" (jailed).

Preventive detention gives rise to both empirical and constitutional questions. The major empirical question is, Does probable cause to believe a person has committed a crime *predict* future dangerous behavior? The question is hard to answer because the word *dangerous* is vague, and because behavior, especially *violent* behavior, is hard to predict (Moore and others 1984, 1). The constitutional questions are, Does preventive detention violate the Eighth Amendment ban on "cruel and unusual punishment"? And, Does preventive detention violate the Fifth and Fourteenth Amendments and deny defendants liberty without due process of law? The U.S. Supreme Court answered "no" to both questions in *U.S. v. Salerno* (1987).

| CASE | *Were Their Pretrial Detentions "Punishment"?* |

United States v. Salerno
481 U.S. 739 (1987)

Anthony Salerno and Vincent Cafaro were committed for pretrial detention pursuant to the Bail Reform Act by a U.S. District Court. The U.S. Court of Appeals vacated the commitment and remanded the case. On writ of certiorari, the U.S. Supreme Court reversed.

REHNQUIST, CJ., joined by WHITE, BLACKMUN, POWELL, O'CONNOR, and SCALIA, JJ.

FACTS

Anthony Salerno and Vincent Cafaro were arrested on March 21, 1986, after being charged in a 29-count indictment alleging various Racketeer Influenced and Corrupt Organizations Act (RICO) violations, mail and wire fraud offenses, extortion, and various criminal gambling violations. The RICO counts alleged 35 acts of racketeering activity, including fraud, extortion, gambling, and conspiracy to commit murder. At their arraignment, the Government moved to have Salerno and Cafaro detained pursuant to § 3142(e) of the Bail Reform Act of 1984 on the ground that no condition of release would assure the safety of the community or any person. The District Court held a hearing at which the Government made a detailed proffer (offer) of evidence.

The Government's case showed that Salerno was the "boss" of the Genovese Crime Family of La Cosa Nostra and that Cafaro was a "captain" in the Genovese Family. According to the Government's proffer, based in large part on conversations intercepted by a court-ordered wiretap, the two respondents had participated in wide-ranging conspiracies to aid their illegitimate enterprises through violent means. The Government also offered the testimony of two of its trial witnesses, who would assert that Salerno personally participated in two murder conspiracies. Salerno opposed the motion for detention, challenging the credibility of the Government's witnesses. He offered the testimony of several character witnesses as well as a letter from his doctor stating that he was suffering from a serious medical condition. Cafaro presented no evidence at the hearing, but instead characterized the wiretap conversations as merely "tough talk."

OPINION

The Bail Reform Act of 1984 allows a federal court to detain an arrestee pending trial if the government demonstrates by clear and convincing evidence after an adversary hearing that no release conditions "will reasonably assure . . . the safety of any other person and the community." The United States Court of Appeals for the Second Circuit struck down this provision of the Act as facially unconstitutional, because, in that court's words, this type of pretrial detention violates "substantive due process." We granted certiorari because of a conflict among the Courts of Appeals regarding the validity of the Act. We hold that . . . the Act fully comports with constitutional requirements. We therefore reverse.

Responding to "the alarming problems of crimes committed by persons on release," Congress formulated the Bail Reform Act of 1984. . . . To this end, § 3141(a) of the Act requires a judicial officer to determine whether an arrestee shall be detained. § 3142(e) provides:

> If, after a hearing pursuant to the provisions of subsection (f), the judicial officer finds that no condition or combination of conditions will reasonably assure the appearance of the person as required and the safety of any other person and the community, he shall order the detention of the person prior to trial. . . .

The judicial officer is not given unbridled discretion in making the detention determination. Congress has specified the consideration relevant to that decision. These factors include the nature and seriousness of the charges, the substantiality of the government's evidence against the arrestee, the arrestee's background and characteristics, and the nature and seriousness of the danger posed by the suspect's release. Should a judicial officer order detention, the detainee is entitled to expedited appellate review of the detention order. . . .

Respondents present two grounds for invalidating the Bail Reform Act's provisions permitting pretrial detention on the basis of future dangerousness.

1. They rely upon the Court of Appeals' conclusion that the Act exceeds the limitations placed upon the Federal Government by the Due Process Clause of the Fifth Amendment.

2. They contend that the Act contravenes the Eighth Amendment's proscription against excessive bail.

We treat those contentions in turn. . . . Respondents first argue that the Act violates substantive due process because the pretrial detention it authorizes constitutes impermissible punishment before trial. The Government, however, has never argued that pretrial detention could be upheld if it were "punishment.". . . Pretrial detention under the Bail Reform Act is regulatory, not penal. . . .

The government's interest in preventing crime by arrestees is both legitimate and compelling. . . . On the other side of the scale, of course, is the individual's strong interest in liberty. We do not minimize the importance and fundamental nature of this right. But, as our cases hold, this right may, in circumstances where the government's interest is sufficiently weighty, be subordinated to the greater needs of society. . . .

Respondents also contend that the Bail Reform Act violates the Excessive Bail Clause of the Eighth Amendment. . . . We think that the Act survives a challenge founded upon the Eighth Amendment. . . . While we agree that a primary function of bail is to safeguard the courts' role in adjudicating the guilt or innocence of defendants, we reject the proposition that the Eighth Amendment categorically prohibits the government from pursuing other admittedly compelling interests through regulation of pretrial release. . . . Nothing in the text of the Bail Clause limits permissible government considerations solely to questions of flight. . . .

We believe that when Congress has mandated detention on the basis of a compelling interest other than prevention of flight, as it has here, the Eighth Amendment does not require release on bail.

In our society liberty is the norm, and detention prior to trial or without trial is the carefully limited exception. We hold that the provisions for pretrial detention in the Bail Reform Act of 1984 fall within that carefully limited exception. The Act authorizes the detention prior to trial of arrestees charged with serious felonies who are found after an adversary hearing to pose a threat to the safety of individuals or to the community which no condition of release can dispel. . . . We are unwilling to say that this congressional determination, based as it is upon that primary concern of every government—a concern for the safety and indeed the lives of its citizens—on its face violates either the Due Process Clause of the Fifth Amendment or the Excessive Bail Clause of the Eighth Amendment.

> The judgment of the Court of Appeals is
> therefore REVERSED.

DISSENT

MARSHALL, J., joined by BRENNAN, J.

The majority finds that "Congress did not formulate the pretrial detention provisions as punishment for dangerous individuals," but instead was pursuing the "legitimate regulatory goal" of "preventing danger to the community." Concluding that pretrial detention is not an excessive solution to the problem of preventing danger to the community, the majority thus finds that no substantive element of the guarantee of due process invalidates the statute.... The majority proceeds as though the only substantive right protected by the Due Process Clause is a right to be free from punishment before conviction. The majority's technique for infringing this right is simple: merely redefine any measure which is claimed to be punishment as "regulation," and, magically, the Constitution no longer prohibits its imposition....

The statute now before us declares that persons who have been indicted may be detained if a judicial officer finds clear and convincing evidence that they pose a danger to individuals or to the community.... The conclusion is inescapable that the indictment has been turned into evidence, if not that the defendant is guilty of the crime charged, then that left to his own devices he will soon be guilty of something else. "If it suffices to accuse, what will become of the innocent?"...

"It is a fair summary of history to say that the safeguards of liberty have frequently been forged in controversies involving not very nice people." Honoring the presumption of innocence is often difficult; sometimes we must pay substantial social costs as a result of our commitment to the values we espouse. But at the end of the day the presumption of innocence protects the innocent; the shortcuts we take with those whom we believe to be guilty injure only those wrongfully accused and, ultimately, ourselves.

Throughout the world today there are men, women, and children interned indefinitely, awaiting trials which may never come or which may be a mockery of the word, because their governments believe them to be "dangerous." Our Constitution, whose construction began two centuries ago, can shelter us forever from the evils of such unchecked power. Over two hundred years it has slowly, through our efforts, grown more durable, more expansive, and more just. But it cannot protect us if we lack the courage, and the self-restraint, to protect ourselves. Today, a majority of the Court applies itself to an ominous exercise in demolition. Theirs is truly a decision which will go forth without authority, and come back without respect.

Questions

1. In your opinion, is pretrial detention punishment or a "regulatory device"? What criteria do you use to answer this question?

2. What did Chief Justice John Marshall mean when he said, "If it suffices to accuse, what will become of the innocent?"

3. Does pretrial detention undermine the presumption of innocence?

4. What, in your opinion, is the proper purpose(s) of bail? Defend your answer.

Conditions of Pretrial Confinement

Detention prior to trial, whether to secure defendants' appearance or to protect public safety, is still confinement. Jailed defendants aren't free to leave; they're locked up in cells and subject to jail discipline; and they have to follow rules designed to maintain safety and order. But jailed defendants are *legally innocent*; they don't forfeit their constitutional rights just because they're in jail. A jail administrator was asked if surveillance in cells through two-way mirrors (prisoners didn't know they were two-way mirrors) violated the prisoners' right to privacy. The administrator replied, "They have no rights." The administrator was wrong. Jailed defendants do have rights, but they're watered down in jail. The U.S. Supreme Court addressed the questions, What rights? and How watered down? in *Bell v. Wolfish* (1979).

Bell v. Wolfish
441 U.S. 520 (1979)

Jailed defendants sued in federal district court challenging the constitutionality of numerous conditions of confinement and practices in the Metropolitan Correctional Center, a federally operated, short-term custodial facility for pretrial detainees in New York City. The U.S. District Court enjoined* various practices in the facility. The U.S. Court of Appeals affirmed. On writ of certiorari, the U.S. Supreme Court reversed.

REHNQUIST, J., joined by BURGER, CJ., and STEWART, WHITE, and BLACKMUN, JJ.

FACTS

The MCC (Metropolitan Correctional Center) differs markedly from the familiar image of a jail; there are no barred cells, dank, colorless corridors, or clanging steel gates. It was intended to include the most advanced and innovative features of modern design of detention facilities. "It represented the architectural embodiment of the best and most progressive penological planning." The key design element of the 12-story structure is the "modular" or "unit" concept, whereby each floor designed to house inmates has one or two largely self-contained residential units that replace the traditional cellblock jail construction. Each unit in turn has several clusters or corridors of private rooms or dormitories radiating from a central 2-story "multipurpose" or common room, to which each inmate has free access approximately 16 hours a day. Because our analysis does not turn on the particulars of the MCC concept design, we need not discuss them further.

When the MCC opened in August 1975, the planned capacity was 449 inmates, an increase of 50% over the former West Street facility. Despite some dormitory accommodations, the MCC was designed primarily to house these inmates in 389 rooms, which originally were intended for single occupancy. While the MCC was under construction, however, the number of persons committed to pretrial detention began to rise at an "unprecedented" rate. The Bureau of Prisons took several steps to accommodate this unexpected flow of persons assigned to the facility, but despite these efforts, the inmate population at the MCC rose above its planned capacity within a short time after its opening.

To provide sleeping space for this increased population, the MCC replaced the single bunks in many of the individual rooms and dormitories with double bunks. Also, each week some newly arrived inmates had to sleep on cots in the common areas until they could be transferred to residential rooms as space became available.

On November 28, 1975, less than four months after the MCC had opened, the named respondents initiated this action by filing in the District Court a petition for writ of habeas corpus.... The petition served up a variable potpourri of complaints that implicated virtually every facet of the institution's conditions and practices. Respondents charged they had been deprived of their statutory and constitutional rights because of overcrowded conditions, undue length of confinement, improper searches, inadequate recreational, educational, and employment opportunities, insufficient staff, and objectionable restrictions on the purchase and receipt of personal items and books.

The District Court, in the words of the Court of Appeals for the Second Circuit, "intervened broadly into almost every facet of the institution" and enjoined no fewer than 20 MCC practices on constitutional and statutory grounds. The Court of Appeals largely affirmed the District Court's constitutional rulings and in the process held that under the Due Process Clause of the Fifth Amendment, pretrial detainees may "be subjected to only those 'restrictions and privations' which 'inhere in their confinement itself or which are justified by compelling necessities of jail administration.' " We granted certiorari to consider the important constitutional questions raised by these decisions and to resolve an apparent conflict among the Circuits. We now reverse.

OPINION

...Not every disability imposed during pretrial detention amounts to "punishment" in the constitutional sense.... Once the Government has exercised its conceded authority to detain a person pending trial, it obviously is entitled to employ devices that are calculated to effectuate this detention. Traditionally, this has meant confinement in a facility which, no matter how modern or antiquated, results in restricting the movement of a detainee in a manner in which he would not be restricted if he simply were free to walk the streets pending trial. Whether it be called a jail, a prison, or a custodial center, the purpose of the facility is to detain. Loss of freedom of choice and privacy are inherent incidents of confinement in such a facility. And the fact that such detention interferes with the detainee's understandable desire

---

*Ordered to stop.

to live as comfortably as possible and with as little restraint as possible during confinement does not convert the conditions or restrictions of detention into "punishment.". . .

Judged by this analysis, respondents' claim that "double-bunking" violated their due process rights fails. . . . On this record, we are convinced as a matter of law that "double-bunking" as practiced at the MCC did not amount to punishment and did not, therefore, violate respondents' rights under the Due Process Clause of the Fifth Amendment.

Each of the rooms at the MCC that house pretrial detainees has a total floor space of approximately 75 square feet. Each of them designated for "double-bunking" contains a double bunkbed, certain other items of furniture, a wash basin, and an uncovered toilet. Inmates are generally locked into their rooms from 11 P.M. to 6:30 A.M. and for brief periods during the afternoon and evening head counts. During the rest of the day, they may move about freely between their rooms and the common areas. . . .

We disagree with both the District Court and the Court of Appeals that there is some sort of "one man, one cell" principle lurking in the Due Process Clause of the Fifth Amendment. While confining a given number of people in a given amount of space in such a manner as to cause them to endure genuine privations and hardships over an extended period of time might raise serious questions under the Due Process Clause as to whether those conditions amounted to punishment, nothing even approaching such hardship is shown by this record.

Detainees are required to spend only seven or eight hours each day in their rooms, during most or all of which they presumably are sleeping. During the remainder of the time, the detainees are free to move between their rooms and the common area. While "double-bunking" may have taxed some of the equipment or particular facilities in certain of the common areas, this does not mean that the conditions at the MCC failed to meet the standards required by the Constitution. Our conclusion in this regard is further buttressed by the detainees' length of stay at the MCC. Nearly all of the detainees are released within 60 days. We simply do not believe that requiring a detainee to share toilet facilities and this admittedly small sleeping space with another person for generally a maximum period of 60 days violates the Constitution. . . .

. . . Maintaining institutional security and preserving internal order and discipline are essential goals that may require limitation or retraction of the retained constitutional rights of both convicted prisoners and pretrial detainees. "Central to all other corrections goals is the institutional consideration of internal security within the corrections facilities themselves.". . .

Finally . . . the problems that arise in the day-to-day operations of the corrections facility are not susceptible to easy solutions. Prison administrators therefore should be accorded wide-ranging deference in the adoption and execution of policies and practices that in their judgment are needed to preserve internal order and discipline and to maintain institutional security. . . .

Inmates at all Bureau of Prison facilities, including the MCC, are required to expose their body cavities for visual inspection as part of a strip search conducted after every contact visit with a person from outside the institution. Corrections officials testified that visual cavity searches were necessary not only to discover but also to deter the smuggling of weapons, drugs, and other contraband into the institution. The District Court upheld the strip-search procedure but prohibited the body-cavity searches, absent probable cause to believe that the inmate is concealing contraband. Because petitioners proved only one instance in the MCC's short history where contraband was found during a body-cavity search, the Court of Appeals affirmed. In its view, the "gross violation of personal privacy inherent in such a search cannot be outweighed by the government's security interest in maintaining a practice of so little actual utility."

Admittedly, this practice instinctively gives us the most pause. However, assuming for present purposes that inmates, both convicted prisoners and pretrial detainees, retain some Fourth Amendment rights upon commitment to a corrections facility, we nonetheless conclude that these searches do not violate that Amendment. The Fourth Amendment prohibits only unreasonable searches, and under the circumstances, we do not believe that these searches are unreasonable. . . .

A detention facility is a unique place fraught with serious security dangers. Smuggling of money, drugs, weapons, and other contraband is all too common an occurrence. And inmate attempts to secrete these items into the facility by concealing them in body cavities is documented in this record. That there has been only one instance where an MCC inmate was discovered attempting to smuggle contraband into the institution on his person may be more a testament to the effectiveness of this search technique as a deterrent than to any lack of interest on the part of the inmates to secrete and import such items when the opportunity arises. . . .

There was a time not too long ago when the federal judiciary took a completely "hands-off" approach to the problem of prison administration. In recent years, however, these courts largely have discarded this "hands-off" attitude and have waded into this complex arena. . . . But many of these same courts have, in the name of the Constitution, become increasingly enmeshed in the minutiae of prison operations. Judges, after all, are human. They, no less than others in our society, have a natural tendency to believe that their individual solutions to often intractable problems are better and more workable than those of the persons who are actually charged with and trained in the running of the particular institution under examination. But under the Constitution, the first question to be answered is not whose plan is best, but in what branch of the Government is lodged the authority to initially devise the plan.... The wide range of "judgment calls" that meet constitutional and statutory requirements are confided to officials outside of the Judicial Branch of Government.

DISSENT

STEVENS, J., joined by BRENNAN, J.

This is not an equal protection case. An empirical judgment that most persons formally accused of criminal conduct are probably guilty would provide a rational basis for a set of rules that treat them like convicts until they establish their innocence. No matter how rational such an approach might be—no matter how acceptable in a community where equality of status is the dominant goal—it is obnoxious to the concept of individual freedom protected by the Due Process Clause. If ever accepted in this country, it would work a fundamental change in the character of our free society.

Nor is this an Eighth Amendment case. That provision of the Constitution protects individuals convicted of crimes from punishment that is cruel and unusual. The pretrial detainees whose rights are at stake in this case, however, are innocent men and women who have been convicted of no crimes. Their claim is not that they have been subjected to cruel and unusual punishment in violation of the Eighth Amendment, but that to subject them to any form of punishment at all is an unconstitutional deprivation of their liberty.

This is a due process case. The most significant—and I venture to suggest the most enduring—part of the Court's opinion today is its recognition of this initial constitutional premise. The Court squarely holds that "under the Due Process Clause, a detainee may not be punished prior to an adjudication of guilt in accordance with due process of law.".....

Prior to conviction every individual is entitled to the benefit of a presumption both that he is innocent of prior criminal conduct and that he has no present intention to commit any offense in the immediate future....

It is not always easy to determine whether a particular restraint serves the legitimate, regulatory goal of ensuring a detainee's presence at trial and his safety and security in the meantime, or the unlawful end of punishment....*

---

*Discussion of double-bunking, searches of mail, and cells is omitted.

The body-cavity search—clearly the greatest personal indignity—may be the least justifiable measure of all. After every contact visit a body-cavity search is mandated by the rule. The District Court's finding that searches have failed in practice to produce any demonstrable improvement in security is hardly surprising. Detainees and their visitors are in full view during all visits, and are fully clad. To insert contraband into one's private body cavities during such a visit would indeed be "an imposing challenge to nerves and agility." There is no reason to expect, and the petitioners have established none, that many pretrial detainees would attempt, let alone succeed, in surmounting this challenge absent the challenged rule. Moreover, as the District Court explicitly found, less severe alternatives are available to ensure that contraband is not transferred during visits. Weapons and other dangerous instruments, the items of greatest legitimate concern, may be discovered by the use of metal detecting devices or other equipment commonly used for airline security. In addition, inmates are required, even apart from the body-cavity searches, to disrobe, to have their clothing inspected, and to present open hands and arms to reveal the absence of any concealed objects. These alternative procedures "amply satisfy" the demands of security. In my judgment, there is no basis in this regard to disagree.

It may well be, as the Court finds, that the rules at issue here were not adopted by administrators eager to punish those detained at MCC. The rules can be explained as the easiest way for administrators to ensure security in the jail. But the easiest course for jail officials is not always one that our Constitution allows them to take. If fundamental rights are withdrawn and severe harms are indiscriminately inflicted on detainees merely to secure minimal savings in time and effort for administrators, the guarantee of due process is violated.

Questions

1. Summarize the arguments of the majority and the dissent. Which is better? Defend your answer, relying on the facts and arguments made in the case.

2. Distinguish between detention and punishment.

3. One critic said that it was all well and good for Supreme Court justices to say this case involved detention, not punishment, but it probably would be little comfort for the detainees to know that. Do you agree? Explain your answer.

4. Does it matter that most pretrial detainees are subject to confinement because they can't afford bail?

5. What interests are at stake in this case? How would you balance them?

Appoint Attorneys for Indigent Defendants

Lawyers are everywhere in the criminal justice system today, but that wasn't always true. During colonial times and for some time afterward, victims had to find and hire their own private prosecutors. Defendants in felony cases didn't even have the right to a lawyer to defend them during their trials. Until the 1960s due process revolution (Chapter 2), a lawyer's job was to represent people once they got to court, not before they were charged or after they were convicted. Since the due process revolution, even police departments and corrections agencies have to hire lawyers, because the Constitution protects people on the street, in police stations, and when they're locked up before trial. The remaining chapters will show that the right to a lawyer reaches even into prison cells and until the death penalty is carried out. This extension of constitutional protection (and the complex, technical legal rules accompanying it) has created the need for lawyers, not just for suspects, defendants, and convicts but also for police and corrections officers and departments. Here, we'll concentrate on counsel for suspects, defendants, and appellants.

The Sixth Amendment to the U.S. Constitution provides:

> In all criminal prosecutions, the accused shall enjoy the right...to have the assistance of counsel for his defense.

Courts have always recognized criminal defendants' Sixth Amendment right to **retained counsel** (a lawyer paid for by the client). But, they didn't recognize the right to **appointed counsel** (lawyers for people who can't afford to hire lawyers) until well into the 1900s. **Indigent defendants** (defendants too poor to hire their own lawyers) had to rely on **counsel pro bono** (lawyers willing to represent clients at no charge). Even today, many jurisdictions rely on lawyers who donate their services to represent poor defendants. But, most counties with large populations, and the U.S. government, have permanent defenders (called **public defenders**) paid by the public to defend poor clients.

As we saw in *Powell v. Alabama* (1932, Chapter 3) the U.S. Supreme Court ruled that "fundamental fairness" requires courts to appoint lawyers for indigent defendants. In *Johnson v. Zerbst* (1938), the Supreme Court elaborated the reasons for the right to counsel:

> [The right to counsel is] necessary to insure fundamental human rights of life and liberty. Omitted from the Constitution as originally adopted, provisions of this and other Amendments were submitted by the first Congress...as essential barriers against arbitrary or unjust deprivation of human rights. The Sixth Amendment stands as a constant admonition that if the constitutional safeguards it provides be lost, justice will not "still be done." It embodies a realistic recognition of the obvious truth that the average defendant doesn't have the necessary professional legal skills to protect himself when brought before a tribunal with power to take his life or liberty, wherein the prosecution is represented by experienced and learned counsel. That which is simple, orderly, and necessary to the lawyer—to the untrained layman—may appear intricate, complex, and mysterious. (462)

Zerbst, however, recognized only a narrow right to counsel: The Sixth Amendment guarantees poor defendants a right to a lawyer at their *trial* in *federal* courts. It says nothing about a right to counsel either *before* trial in federal courts or to any proceedings at all in *state* courts.

The U.S. Supreme Court confronted the right to counsel in *state* courts in *Betts v. Brady* (1942). Betts was convicted of robbery and sentenced to prison. At his trial, he asked for a lawyer, claiming that he was too poor to afford one. The judge denied his request because Carroll County, Maryland, the site of the trial, provided counsel only in murder and rape cases. Hearings on Betts's petition for habeas corpus eventually reached the Supreme Court. The Court, adopting the fundamental fairness approach, decided the due process clause didn't incorporate the Sixth Amendment right to counsel. The Court went further to hold that, except in "special circumstances," denial of counsel doesn't deprive a defendant of a fair trial. In other words, the right to counsel was not "inherent in the concept of ordered liberty" (Chapter 2).

The Court reviewed the history of representation by counsel, noting that English courts didn't allow defendants—even if they could afford to hire one—to have a lawyer in felony cases until 1843. The Court concluded that the Sixth Amendment right to counsel allowed defendants to have a lawyer but it didn't compel the state to provide one. The Court interpreted parallel state provisions of the right to counsel similarly:

> This material demonstrates that, in the great majority of the states, it has been the considered judgment of the people, their representatives and their courts that appointment of counsel is not a fundamental right, essential to a fair trial.... In the light of this evidence we are unable to say that the concept of due process incorporated in the Fourteenth Amendment obligates the states, whatever may be their own views, to furnish counsel in every such case. (471)

In *Gideon v. Wainwright* (1963), the Supreme Court accepted Clarence Gideon's petition for certiorari. The Court agreed to review the Florida Supreme Court's dismissal of Gideon's petition for habeas corpus based on a claim similar to that of Betts. The Court ordered the parties to argue the question of whether it should overrule *Betts v. Brady*.

CASE | *Did He Have a Right to a Lawyer?*

Gideon v. Wainwright
372 U.S. 335 (1963)

Clarence Gideon brought habeas corpus proceedings against the director of the Division of Corrections. The Florida Supreme Court denied all relief. The U.S. Supreme Court granted certiorari. The Court reversed and remanded the case to the Florida Supreme Court for further action.

BLACK, J., for a UNANIMOUS Court.

FACTS

Clarence Gideon was charged in a Florida state court with having broken and entered a poolroom with intent to commit a misdemeanor. This offense is a felony under Florida law. Appearing in court without funds and without a lawyer, Gideon asked the court to appoint counsel for him, whereupon the following colloquy took place:

THE COURT: Mr. Gideon, I am sorry, but I cannot appoint Counsel to represent you in this case. Under the laws of the State of Florida, the only time the Court can appoint Counsel to represent a Defendant is when that person is charged with a capital offense. I am sorry, but I will have to deny your request to appoint Counsel to defend you in this case.

THE DEFENDANT: The United States Supreme Court says I am entitled to be represented by Counsel.

Put to trial before a jury, Gideon conducted his defense about as well as could be expected from a layman. He made an opening statement to the jury, cross-examined the State's witnesses, presented witnesses in his own defense, declined to testify himself, and made a short argument "emphasizing his innocence to the charge contained in the Information filed in this case." The jury returned a verdict of guilty, and petitioner was sentenced to serve five years in the state prison. Later, petitioner filed in the Florida Supreme Court this habeas corpus petition attacking his conviction and sentence on the ground that the trial court's refusal to appoint counsel for him denied him rights "guaranteed by the Constitution and the Bill of Rights by the United States Government."

Later in the petition for habeas corpus, signed and apparently prepared by Gideon himself, he stated, "I, Clarence Earl Gideon, claim that I was denied the rights of the 4th, 5th and 14th Amendments of the Bill of Rights."

Treating the petition for habeas corpus as properly before it, the State Supreme Court, "upon consideration thereof" but without an opinion, denied all relief. Since 1942, when *Betts v. Brady* was decided by a divided Court, the problem of a defendant's federal constitutional right to counsel in a state court has been a continuing source of controversy and litigation in both state and federal courts. To give this problem another review here, we granted certiorari. Since Gideon was proceeding in forma pauperis,* we appointed counsel to represent him and requested both sides to discuss in their briefs and oral arguments the following: "Should this Court's holding in *Betts v. Brady* be overruled?"

OPINION

Treating due process as "a concept less rigid and more fluid than those envisaged in other specific and particular provisions of the Bill of Rights," the Court** held that refusal to appoint counsel under the particular facts and circumstances in the *Betts* case was not so "offensive to the common and fundamental ideas of fairness" as to amount to a denial of due process. Since the facts and circumstances of the two cases are so nearly indistinguishable, we think the *Betts v. Brady* holding if left standing would require us to reject Gideon's claim that the Constitution guarantees him the assistance of counsel.

Upon full consideration we conclude that *Betts v. Brady* should be overruled. The Sixth Amendment provides, "In all criminal prosecutions, the accused shall enjoy the right...to have the Assistance of Counsel for his defence."...

...In our adversary system of criminal justice, any person haled into court, who is too poor to hire a lawyer, cannot be assured a fair trial unless counsel is provided for him. This seems to us to be an obvious truth. Governments, both state and federal, quite properly spend vast sums of money to establish machinery to try defendants accused of crime. Lawyers to prosecute are everywhere deemed essential to protect the public's interest in an orderly society. Similarly, there are few defendants charged with crime, few indeed, who fail to hire the best lawyers they can get to prepare and present their defenses. That

government hires lawyers to prosecute and defendants who have the money hire lawyers to defend are the strongest indications of the wide-spread belief that lawyers in criminal courts are necessities, not luxuries.

The right of one charged with crime to counsel may not be deemed fundamental and essential to fair trials in some countries, but it is in ours. From the very beginning, our state and national constitutions and laws have laid great emphasis on procedural and substantive safeguards designed to assure fair trials before impartial tribunals in which every defendant stands equal before the law. This noble ideal cannot be realized if the poor man charged with crime has to face his accusers without a lawyer to assist him. A defendant's need for a lawyer is nowhere better stated than in the moving words of Mr. Justice Sutherland in *Powell v. Alabama:*

> The right to be heard would be, in many cases, of little avail if it did not comprehend the right to be heard by counsel. Even the intelligent and educated layman... requires the guiding hand of counsel at every step in the proceedings against him. Without it, though he be not guilty, he faces the danger of conviction because he does not know how to establish his innocence.

The Court in *Betts v. Brady* departed from the sound wisdom upon which the Court's holding in *Powell v. Alabama* rested. Florida, supported by two other States, has asked that *Betts v. Brady* be left intact. Twenty-two States, as friends of the Court, argue that *Betts* was "an anachronism when handed down" and that it should now be overruled. We agree. The judgment is reversed and the cause is remanded to the Supreme Court of Florida for further action not inconsistent with this opinion.

REVERSED.

Questions

1. What exactly did the Court decide that the right to counsel means?

2. On what theory did it apply the right to counsel to state proceedings?

3. Why did the Court take the unusual step of overruling its decision in *Betts v. Brady*?

4. Do you agree that the right to counsel should apply to state proceedings, or should states decide for themselves whether poor criminal defendants in their jurisdictions have a right to a lawyer assigned by the court?

5. Does the Court apply the right to counsel to state proceedings to further the interest in correct result? to further the interest in process? as a matter of efficiency? Explain your answer.

---

*As a poor person who can't afford a lawyer.

**In *Betts v. Brady*.

Gideon v. Wainwright

A. Balz

LIFE BEFORE THE CRIME

Clarence Gideon was born on August 30, 1910, in Hannibal, Missouri. At 14, Gideon ran away from home because he never felt at home in the strict Baptist working-class home where he was raised. His problems began early in life.

1924

Gideon was convicted of burglarizing a Missouri country store to get new clothes. He spent one year in a Missouri reformatory.

1928

He was convicted of burglary in Missouri; sentenced to ten years in prison; and paroled after serving three years.

1934

He was convicted of possession of U.S. government property and sentenced to three years in federal prison.

1940

Gideon was convicted of burglary in Missouri and sentenced to ten years. He escaped in 1943; was captured in 1944; and was released after serving his full term in 1950.

1952

Convicted of burglary in Texas, he was sentenced to two years. He was released on September 25.

1952–1961

After his release in 1952, Gideon stayed out of trouble with the law for nine years. He got married in 1955 and settled down in Louisiana. By 1961, they had six children, five of them from his wife's previous marriage. Gideon tried to support his family by working as a mechanic, but he was plagued by serious lung problems caused by tuberculosis. He spent most of 1959 in the hospital. During that time, his family

had to survive on their $81 a month welfare check. At the beginning of 1961, Gideon left Louisiana and ended up in Panama City, Florida, where the famous case of *Gideon v. Wainwright* began.

June 3, 1961

Shortly before dawn, a Panama City police officer while making his rounds, noticed the front door of the Bay Harbor Poolroom door was slightly open. He went inside and found someone had taken the money from the cigarette machine and jukebox. Henry Cook, who was standing outside the poolroom, told the officer that a little while before he looked through the poolroom window and saw Clarence Gideon, an acquaintance. Gideon was arrested and indicted for breaking and entering with intent to commit a misdemeanor.

August 4, 1961

Gideon was tried for breaking and entering. He represented himself after the judge refused to grant his request for a lawyer.

1961–1962

Gideon wrote his own appeal to the Florida Supreme Court and lost. Then he wrote out by hand his own petition for habeas corpus to the U.S. Supreme Court. The Court agreed to hear the case and appointed the well-known and respected lawyer Abe Fortas (who later became a U.S. Supreme Court justice) to represent Gideon. In a long letter to Fortas, Gideon wrote:

> I am not proud of my biography. I have no illusions about the law or courts or the people who are involved in them. I have read the complete history of law ever since the Romans first started writing them down and before the law of religions. I believe that each era finds a [*sic*] improvement in law [*sic*] each year brings some-

thing new for the benefit of mankind. Maybe this will be one of those small steps forward.*

April 5, 1963

Gideon was retried in the same courtroom for breaking and entering the Bay Harbor poolroom with intent to commit a misdemeanor. The same judge who presided over the first trial, Robert L. Mcrary, Jr., presided over the second trial. The prosecution presented the same witness, Henry Cook, to testify that he saw Gideon in the poolroom. But, this time Gideon had Fred Turner, a lawyer, to represent him. During an effective cross-examination, Turner asked Cook why he was hanging around the poolroom at 5:30 A.M. Turner also brought out that Cook had a criminal record and was picked up by the police for questioning about the poolroom break-in. None of this came out at Gideon's first trial. In his closing arguments, Turner accused Cook and some of his friends of committing the crime. The jury deliberated for an hour before bringing in its verdict—not guilty.**

1965

Employed pumping gas for a Fort Lauderdale gas station, Gideon told *Time*:

> I've seen ignorant white people accused of petty larceny, and if they had a lawyer they'd get six months, but without one they'd get 15 years. I tell you the prisons are full of lifers who wouldn't have got near that much if a lawyer had handled them. I didn't start out to do anything for anybody but myself, but this decision has done a helluva lot of good for those people.†

---

*Quoted in Anthony Lewis, "The Case of the Florida Drifter," in John A. Garraty, ed., *Quarrels That Shaped the Constitution* (New York: Harper and Row, 1988), 348.

**Ibid., 349.

†*Time*, December 17, 1965, 39.

Sometime in the 1960s

After a losing day at the Kentucky Derby, Gideon was charged with vagrancy. He showed the judge a book written about his famous case, and the judge said he was impressed to meet such a famous person. He told Gideon that he was going to let him go, but if Gideon would like, he'd sentence him to six months so Gideon could appeal the case to the Supreme Court to get the right to counsel extended to petty offenses like vagrancy. Gideon said, "No thanks, I'd just as soon go."‡

January 18, 1972

Gideon died in Fort Lauderdale, Florida. His mother brought his body back to Hannibal. His family wasn't proud of him, so they buried him in a grave without a marker. His mother said, "He could have been most anything if he'd gone to school as he ought to, and behaved himself."

1984

The American Civil Liberties Union arranged to put up a gravestone to commemorate a "man who proved that in this vast country one person can still make a difference." To the surprise of the ACLU, local and state dignitaries came to the commemoration. Hannibal mayor John Lyng said that the town had had many "cranky citizens," including Mark Twain. Gideon, Lyng said was "the kind of character we value in Hannibal. At one point in his life he decided to take a stand. We should all continue to have that kind of courage." On the gravestone are the words quoted earlier from Gideon's letter to Abe Fortas: "I believe that each era finds improvement in law. Maybe this will be one of those small steps forward."

---

‡Quoted in Anthony Lewis, "The Case of the Florida Drifter," in John A. Garraty, ed., *Quarrels That Shaped the Constitution* (New York: Harper and Row, 1988), 349.

Gideon left several Sixth Amendment questions unanswered, including:

1. When does the right to counsel attach; that is, at what proceedings does a citizen have a right to have a lawyer present? Or, more specifically, what does prosecution mean in the Sixth Amendment?

2. What is a criminal prosecution, according to the Sixth Amendment? Does "all criminal prosecutions" include even petty misdemeanors, such as disorderly conduct?

3. How poor is "indigent"?

4. Does "counsel" mean "effective" counsel?

TABLE 12.1

Critical Stages and the Right to Counsel

Stage of Criminal Process	Right to Counsel?
Investigative stop	No
Frisk for weapons	No
Arrest	No
Search following arrest	No
Custodial interrogation	Yes
Lineup before formal charges	No
First appearance	No
Lineup after formal charges	Yes
Grand jury review/Preliminary hearing	Yes
Arraignment	Yes
Pretrial hearings	Yes
Trial	Yes
Appeal/Collateral attack	Yes

When the Right to Counsel Attaches

The Sixth Amendment guarantees the right to counsel in all criminal "prosecutions," but what proceedings does prosecution include? Clearly, it includes the trial and appeal, when defendants most need special legal expertise. But what about before trial? The U.S. Supreme Court has ruled that the right to counsel attaches to all **critical stages of criminal proceedings.** Table 12.1 shows the stages in the criminal process and indicates the ones the U.S. Supreme Court has declared critical stages. It's clear from the table that defendants have the right to counsel to represent them at all procedures *after* the first appearance.

But what about what happens in the police station *before* the first appearance? Specifically, do you have a right to a lawyer during police interrogation and identification procedures (lineups, show-ups, and photo identification [Chapters 8 and 9])? The U.S. Supreme Court first applied the right to a lawyer in police stations in 1964, in *Escobedo v. Illinois* (1964). The Court held that the right to counsel attached at the accusatory stage of a criminal case—namely, when a general investigation focused on a specific suspect. According to the Court, that point was reached in *Escobedo* when the police made up their minds that Danny Escobedo had committed the murder they were investigating. After they made up their minds he was the murderer, Chicago police officers tried to get him to confess by interrogating him. During the interrogation, Escobedo asked to see his lawyer, who was in the police station. The officers refused. Eventually, he confessed and was tried and convicted with the help of the confession. The U.S. Supreme Court said the confession was not admissible because it was obtained during the accusatory stage without the help of Escobedo's lawyer. Just two years later, in *Miranda v. Arizona*, the Court had decided that police officers have to tell suspects that they have a right to a lawyer during cus-

TABLE 12.2

The Leading Right-to-Counsel Cases

Case	Year	Definition
Powell v. Alabama	1932	Appointed counsel for poor, illiterate, ignorant, isolated defendants in state capital cases
Johnson v. Zerbst	1938	Appointed counsel in federal cases at trial (not before or after)
Betts v. Brady	1942	Appointed counsel in state cases under "special circumstances"
Chandler v. Fretag	1954	Retained (paid for) counsel in all criminal cases
Gideon v. Wainwright	1963	Appointed counsel in state felony cases (overruled *Betts v. Brady*)
Argersinger v. Hamlin	1972	Appointed counsel in any offense punishable by incarceration
Scott v. Illinois	1979	No right to counsel for sentences that don't result in actual jail time

todial interrogation (Chapter 8). As for identification procedures, those conducted after indictment are a critical stage; those conducted before indictment are not (Chapter 9).

The Meaning of "All Criminal Prosecutions"

In 1932, *Powell v. Alabama* (Chapter 2) established the rule that due process commands that appointed counsel represent poor defendants in *capital* cases. In *Gideon v. Wainwright* (1963), the Court extended the right to counsel to poor defendants prosecuted for *felonies* against *property*. In 1972, the Court went further; all poor defendants prosecuted for *misdemeanors* punishable by jail terms have a right to an appointed lawyer. In *Argersinger v. Hamlin* (1972), Jon Richard Argersinger, a Florida indigent, was convicted of carrying a concealed weapon, a misdemeanor punishable by up to six months' imprisonment, a $1,000 fine, or both. A Florida rule limited assigned counsel to "non-petty offenses punishable by more than six months imprisonment." The Court struck down the rule, holding that states have to provide a lawyer for defendants charged with any offense punishable by incarceration no matter what the state's criminal code calls it (misdemeanor, petty misdemeanor, or felony). Table 12.2 summarizes the leading cases on the right to counsel.

Notice what the Court did *not* say in *Argersinger*: Poor people have a right to a lawyer paid for by the government in *all* criminal cases. Why? Because the Court was well aware of a practical problem: there isn't enough money to pay for everyone to have a lawyer. Of course, strictly speaking, constitutional rights can't depend on money, but as a practical matter, money definitely affects how many people get their rights in real life. We know many poor people who have a right to a lawyer don't get one because counties and other local governments simply don't have the money to pay for them. Why? Because taxpayers don't want their tax dollars spent on lawyers for "criminals." This mix of practical reality and constitutional rights surfaced in *Scott v. Illinois* (1979). The Court specifically addressed the question of whether the right to assigned counsel extends to offenses that don't actually result in prison sentences.

Do Indigents Have a Right to Assigned Counsel for Shoplifting?

Scott v. Illinois

440 U.S. 367 (1979)

Aubrey Scott, without a lawyer to defend him, was convicted of theft and fined $50 after a bench trial* in the Circuit Court of Cook County, Illinois. Scott appealed, contending that he had a constitutional right to a lawyer paid for by the state. The Illinois intermediate court of appeals affirmed the conviction. The Supreme Court affirmed. The U.S. Supreme Court granted certiorari and affirmed.

REHNQUIST, J., joined by BURGER, CJ., and STEWART, WHITE, and POWELL, JJ.

FACTS

Aubrey Scott was convicted of shoplifting merchandise valued at less than $150. An Illinois statute set the maximum penalty at a $500 fine or one year in jail, or both. Scott argues that a line of this Court's cases culminating in *Argersinger v. Hamlin* requires state provision of counsel whenever imprisonment is an authorized penalty.

The Supreme Court of Illinois rejected this contention, quoting the following language from *Argersinger:*

> We hold, therefore, that absent a knowing and intelligent waiver, no person may be imprisoned for any offense, whether classified as petty, misdemeanor, or felony, unless he was represented by counsel at his trial.

Under the rule we announce today, every judge will know when the trial of a misdemeanor starts that no imprisonment may be imposed, even though local law permits it, unless the accused is represented by counsel. He will have a measure of the seriousness and gravity of the offense and therefore know when to name a lawyer to represent the accused before the trial starts. The Supreme Court of Illinois went on to state that it was "not inclined to extend *Argersinger*" to the case where a defendant is charged with a statutory offense for which imprisonment upon conviction is authorized but not actually imposed upon the defendant. We agree with the Supreme Court of Illinois that the Federal Constitution does not require a state trial court to appoint counsel for a criminal defendant such as Scott, and we therefore affirm its judgment. . . .

There is considerable doubt that the Sixth Amendment itself, as originally drafted by the Framers of the Bill of Rights, contemplated any guarantee other than the right of an accused in a criminal prosecution in a federal court to employ a lawyer to assist in his defense. . . . In *Argersinger,* the State of Florida urged that . . . any offense punishable by less than six months in jail should not require appointment of counsel for an indigent defendant. . . .

In *Argersinger,* the Court rejected arguments that social cost or lack of available lawyers militated against its holding, in some part because it thought these arguments were factually incorrect. But they were rejected in much larger part because of the Court's conclusion that incarceration was so severe a sanction that it should not be imposed as a result of a criminal trial unless an indigent defendant had been offered appointed counsel to assist in his defense, regardless of the cost to the States implicit in such a rule. The Court in its opinion repeatedly referred to trials "where an accused is deprived of his liberty," and to "a case that actually leads to imprisonment even for a brief period." The Chief Justice in his opinion concurring in the result also observed that "any deprivation of liberty is a serious matter."

Although the intentions of the *Argersinger* Court are not unmistakably clear from its opinion, we conclude today that *Argersinger* did indeed delimit the constitutional right to appointed counsel in state criminal proceedings. Even were the matter [new], we believe the central premise of *Argersinger*—that actual imprisonment is a penalty different in kind from fines or the mere threat of imprisonment—is eminently sound and warrants adoption of actual imprisonment as the line defining the constitutional right to appointment of counsel. *Argersinger* has proved reasonably workable, whereas any extension would create confusion and impose unpredictable, but necessarily substantial, costs on 50 quite diverse States.

We therefore hold that the Sixth and Fourteenth Amendments to the United States Constitution require only that no indigent criminal defendant be sentenced to a term of imprisonment unless the State has afforded him the right to assistance of appointed counsel in his defense.

The judgment of the Supreme Court of Illinois is accordingly AFFIRMED. . . .

---

*Trial without a jury.

DISSENT

BRENNAN, J., joined by MARSHALL and STEVENS, JJ. ... In my view, the plain wording of the Sixth Amendment and the Court's precedents compel the conclusion that Scott's uncounseled conviction violated the Sixth and Fourteenth Amendments and should be reversed. ...

First, the "authorized imprisonment" standard more faithfully implements the principles of the Sixth Amendment identified in *Gideon*. The procedural rules established by state statutes are geared to the nature of the potential penalty for an offense, not to the actual penalty imposed in particular cases. The authorized penalty is also a better predictor of the stigma and other collateral consequences that attach to conviction of an offense. ... By contrast, the "actual imprisonment" standard ... denies the right to counsel in criminal prosecutions to accuseds who suffer the severe consequences of prosecution other than imprisonment.

Second, the "authorized imprisonment" test presents no problems of administration. It avoids the necessity for time-consuming consideration of the likely sentence in each individual case before trial and the attendant problems of inaccurate predictions, unequal treatment, and apparent and actual bias. ...

Finally, the "authorized imprisonment" test ensures that courts will not abrogate legislative judgments concerning the appropriate range of penalties to be considered for each offense. Under the "actual imprisonment" standard:

> The judge will ... be forced to decide in advance of trial—and without hearing the evidence—whether he will forego entirely his judicial discretion to impose some sentence of imprisonment and abandon his responsibility to consider the full range of punishments established by the legislature. His alternatives, assuming the availability of counsel, will be to appoint counsel and retain the discretion vested in him by law, or to abandon this discretion in advance and proceed without counsel.

... The apparent reason for the Court's adoption of the "actual imprisonment" standard for all misdemeanors is concern for the economic burden that an "authorized imprisonment" standard might place on the States. But, with all respect, that concern is both irrelevant and speculative. This Court's role in enforcing constitutional guarantees for criminal defendants cannot be made dependent on the budgetary decisions of state governments. A unanimous Court made that clear in *Mayer v. Chicago* (1971), in rejecting a proposed fiscal justification for providing free transcripts for appeals only when the appellant was subject to imprisonment:

> This argument misconceives the principle of *Griffin* [*v. Illinois* (1956)]. ... *Griffin* does not represent a balance between the needs of the accused and the interests of society; its principle is a flat prohibition against pricing indigent defendants out of as effective an appeal as would be available to others able to pay their own way. The invidiousness of the discrimination that exists when criminal procedures are made available only to those who can pay is not erased by any differences in the sentences that may be imposed. The State's fiscal interest is, therefore, irrelevant.

In any event, the extent of the alleged burden on the States is, as the Court admits, speculative. Although more persons are charged with misdemeanors punishable by incarceration than are charged with felonies, a smaller percentage of persons charged with misdemeanors qualify as indigent, and misdemeanor cases as a rule require far less attorney time.

Furthermore, public defender systems have proved economically feasible, and the establishment of such systems to replace appointment of private attorneys can keep costs at acceptable levels even when the number of cases requiring appointment of counsel increases dramatically. The public defender system alternative also answers the argument that an authorized imprisonment standard would clog the courts with inexperienced appointed counsel. A study conducted in the State of Wisconsin, which introduced a State Public Defender System after the Wisconsin Supreme Court in *State ex rel. Winnie v. Harris* (1977) extended the right to counsel in the way urged by Smith in this case, indicated that the average cost of providing counsel in a misdemeanor case was reduced from $150–$200 to $90 by using a public defender rather than appointing private counsel.

Perhaps the strongest refutation of Illinois' alarmist prophecies that an authorized imprisonment standard would wreak havoc on the States is that the standard has not produced that result in the substantial number of States that already provide counsel in all cases where imprisonment is authorized—States that include a large majority of the country's population and a great diversity of urban and rural environments. Moreover, of those States that do not yet provide counsel in all cases where any imprisonment is authorized, many provide counsel when periods of imprisonment longer than 30 days, 3 months, or 6 months are authorized. In fact, Scott would be entitled to appointed counsel under the current laws of at least 33 States. ...

BLACKMUN, J.

...I would hold that the right to counsel secured by the Sixth and Fourteenth Amendments extends at least as far as the right to jury trial secured by those Amendments. Accordingly, I would hold that an indigent defendant in a state criminal case must be afforded appointed counsel whenever the defendant is prosecuted for a criminal offense punishable by more than six months' imprisonment, or whenever the defendant is convicted of an offense and is actually subjected to a term of imprisonment. This resolution, I feel, would provide the "bright line" that defendants, prosecutors, and trial and appellate courts all deserve.... On this approach, of course, the judgment of the Supreme Court of Illinois upholding petitioner Scott's conviction should be reversed, since he was convicted of an offense for which he was constitutionally entitled to a jury trial. I therefore, dissent.

Questions

1. Should every defendant who cannot afford a lawyer have one in all criminal cases at state expense?

2. Would such an interpretation of the right to counsel promote the public interest in result over process? Or would it promote both result and process? Would it serve the societal interest in aiding the poor and weak in our society? Should it do so?

3. Should economic considerations be taken into account in deciding who should have constitutional rights? What interests does taking them into account promote? What interests does it sacrifice?

4. Is Justice Harry A. Blackmun's recommendation for a bright-line rule a good one?

The Standard of Indigence

The U.S. Supreme Court has never defined *indigence*. However, U.S. Courts of Appeals have established some general guidelines on how to determine whether defendants are poor enough to qualify for a lawyer paid for by the government:

1. Poor defendants don't have to be completely destitute.

2. Earnings and assets count; help from friends and relatives doesn't.

3. Actual, not potential, earnings are the measure.

4. The state can tap defendants' future earnings to get reimbursement for the costs of counsel, transcripts, and fees for expert witnesses and investigators.

Some states have set up detailed standards for determining indigence. Minnesota's rules (1987, Rule 5, 112–115) to help judges determine indigency at the first appearance are typical. They provide:

STANDARD OF INDIGENCE.

A defendant is financially unable to obtain counsel if he is financially unable to obtain adequate representation without substantial hardship for himself or his family.

1. *A defendant will be presumed to be financially unable to afford counsel* if:

a. his cash assets are less than $300.00 when entitled to only a court trial; or

b. his current weekly net income does not exceed $500.00 when entitled to a jury trial; and

c. his current weekly net income does not exceed forty times the federal minimum hourly wage ... if he is unmarried and without dependents; or,

d. his current weekly net income and that of his spouse do not exceed sixty times the federal minimum hourly wage ... if he is married and without dependents. In determining the amounts under either section (c) or section (d), for each dependent the amount shall be increased by $25.00 per week.

2. *A defendant who has cash assets or income exceeding the amounts* in paragraph (1) shall not be presumed to be financially able to obtain counsel. The determination shall be made by the court as a practical matter, taking into account such other factors as the defendant's length of employment or unemployment, prior income, the value and nature of his assets, number of children and other family responsibilities, number and nature of debts arising from any source, the amount customarily charged by members of the practicing bar for representation of the type in question, and any other relevant factor.

3. *In determining whether a defendant is financially able* to obtain adequate representation without substantial hardship to himself or his family:

    a. cash assets include those assets which may be readily converted to cash...without jeopardizing the defendant's ability to maintain his home or employment. A single family automobile shall not be considered an asset.

    b. the fact that defendant has posted or can post bail is irrelevant....

    c. the fact that the defendant is employable but unemployed shall not be in itself proof that he is financially able to obtain counsel without substantial hardship to himself or his family.

    d. the fact that parents or other relatives of the defendant have the financial ability to obtain counsel for the defendant is irrelevant, except under the following circumstances:

        i. where the defendant is unemancipated, under the age of 21 years, living with his parent or other relatives, and such parents or other relatives have the clear ability to obtain counsel; or

        ii. where the parents or other relatives of the defendant have the financial ability to obtain counsel for the defendant but are unwilling to do so only because of the relatively minor nature of the charge.

4. *Financial Inquiry.* An inquiry to determine financial eligibility of a defendant for the appointment of counsel shall be made whenever possible prior to the court appearance and by such persons as the court may direct.

The Right to "Effective" Counsel

In 1932, the U.S. Supreme Court said due process requires not just counsel but *effective* counsel, but the Court didn't say much to clarify what "effective" means. So, lower federal courts and state courts stepped in and adopted the **mockery of justice standard.** Under this standard, only lawyers whose behavior is so "shocking" that it turns the trial into a "joke" are constitutionally ineffective. One lawyer called it the "mirror test." (Put a mirror under the lawyer's nose; if it steams up he passes.) What prompted this professional "dissing"? In actual cases, appellate courts ruled that lawyers who slept through trials; came to court drunk; couldn't name a single precedent related to the case they were arguing; or were released from jail to represent their clients hadn't turned the proceedings into a joke and met the mockery of justice standard. When one defendant claimed he got ineffective representation because his lawyer slept through the trial, the judge said, "You have a right to a lawyer; that doesn't mean you have a right to one who's awake." That decision was affirmed by the reviewing court.

Courts and commentators have criticized the mockery of justice standard for being too subjective, vague, and narrow. The standard's focus on the trial excludes many serious errors that lawyers make in preparing for trial. Furthermore, in the overwhelming majority of cases disposed of by guilty pleas, the standard is totally irrelevant. Judge Bazelon, an experienced and respected federal judge, said the test requires "such a minimal level of performance from counsel that it is itself a mockery of the

Sixth Amendment." He continued, "I have often been told that if my court were to reverse in every case in which there was inadequate counsel, we would have to send back half the convictions in my jurisdiction."

Courts don't like to get involved in the touchy question of judging the performance of defense attorneys. Why? For one thing, too much interference can damage not only professional relationships but also the professional independence of defense lawyers and even the adversary system itself. Furthermore, judges who criticize defense lawyers are criticizing fellow professionals, lawyers who appear in their courts regularly.

Most jurisdictions have abandoned the mockery of justice standard, replacing it with the **reasonably competent attorney standard.** According to this standard, judges measure lawyers' performance against the "customary skills and diligence that a reasonably competent attorney would perform under similar circumstances." Attorneys have to be more diligent under the reasonably competent attorney standard than under the mockery of justice standard. Nevertheless, both the mockery of justice and the reasonably competent attorney standards are "vague to some appreciable degree and . . . susceptible to greatly varying subjective impressions" (LaFave and Israel 1984, 2:99–102).

The U.S. Supreme Court has tried to increase the clarity of the reasonably competent attorney test by announcing a new **two-pronged effective counsel test** to evaluate effectiveness of counsel. The test was announced in *Strickland v. Washington* (1984). In 1976, David Leroy Washington went on a 10-day crime spree that ended in three murders. After his lawyer, William Tunkey, was appointed, Washington confessed; he also pleaded guilty at his trial. Washington waived his right to an advisory jury to decide whether he should get the death penalty. During the sentencing phase of the proceedings, Tunkey didn't present any character evidence, didn't present any medical or psychiatric evidence, and only cross-examined some of the state's witnesses. The judge sentenced Washington to death. Washington went through the state and then the federal courts claiming ineffectiveness of counsel. The U.S. Court of Appeals for the Eleventh Circuit ruled in his favor and the state appealed.

The U.S. Supreme Court reversed, applying its new two-pronged test of ineffective counsel. Under the first prong, called the **reasonableness prong,** defendants have to prove that their lawyer's performance wasn't reasonably competent, meaning that the lawyer was so deficient that she "was not functioning as the 'counsel' guaranteed the defendant by the Sixth Amendment." Under the reasonableness prong, reviewing courts have to look at the totality of the facts and circumstances to decide whether the defense lawyer's performance was reasonably competent. Reviewing courts have to start with a presumption in favor of the defense lawyer's competence, meaning they have lots of leeway to make tactical and strategic decisions that fall within the wide range of available professional judgment. So, as long as defense counsel's choices fall within that wide range, representation is presumed reasonable.

If the defendant proves his lawyer's performance was unreasonable, he still has to prove the second-prong of the test, called the **prejudice prong** of the reasonable competence test. Under the prejudice prong, defendants have to prove that their lawyer's incompetence was *probably* responsible for their conviction. Some state courts have rejected the tough test of ineffectiveness announced in *Strickland v. Washington.* The Hawaii Supreme Court did so in *State v. Smith* (1986).

Did His Lawyer "Effectively" Represent Him?

State v. Smith
712 P.2d 496 (1986)

Michael Smith, aka Michael Calderon, was convicted in Third Circuit Court, Hawaii County, of attempted sodomy in the second degree, and he appealed. The Supreme Court vacated the judgment and remanded the case for a new trial.

Claiming a denial of his constitutional right to the effective assistance of counsel at trial, Michael Smith appeals from a judgment of conviction of Attempted Sodomy in the Second Degree entered by the Circuit Court of the Third Circuit.* Because we are convinced from a review of the record that the performance of defense counsel was not within the range of competence expected of lawyers in criminal cases, we vacate the judgment and remand the case for retrial.

NAKAMURA, J., joined by LUM, CJ., and PADGETT, HAYASHI, and WAKATSUKI, JJ.

FACTS

Michael Smith was charged with attempting to engage in deviate sexual conduct with a person below the age of fourteen in violation of §§ 705–500(1)(b) and 707–734(1)(b) Hawaii Revised Statutes (HRS), as amended. According to the criminal complaint:

> On or about the 8th day of October, 1983, in South Hilo, County and State of Hawaii, MICHAEL SMITH, aka MICHAEL CALDERON, did intentionally attempt to engage in deviate sexual intercourse with another person who is less than fourteen years old, by attempting to have [the victim], a person less than fourteen years old, suck his penis, and said act under the circumstances as he believed them to be constituted a substantial step in a course of conduct intended to culminate in the commission of the offense of Sodomy in the Second Degree, thereby committing the offense of Attempted Sodomy in the Second Degree, in violation of. He sought counsel to

*Smith's counsel on appeal wasn't his counsel at trial.

assist in his defense, and an attorney from the Public Defender's office was appointed to represent him.

Since Smith had been convicted previously of more than several offenses and arrested for others, including several sexually related offenses, the array of pre-trial motions filed by counsel included a motion . . . seeking to exclude testimony about other offenses allegedly committed by Smith.

The motion was granted in part. Essentially, counsel succeeded in preventing the introduction of evidence of prior offenses that did not result in convictions, as well as that of prior convictions for crimes in which "fraud, deceit or other forms of dishonesty" were not implicated. The order entered by the circuit court also precluded references by the State to any prior incarceration of Smith or any pending charge against him for lewdness or other sexually motivated conduct. Before the case proceeded to trial, however, the court found it necessary to appoint other counsel to represent Smith. The Public Defender also represented a witness the State intended to call. The possible conflict of interest was obviated by the replacement of the Public Defender.

At trial the State adduced evidence from which a reasonable inference could be drawn that Smith lured a five-year-old girl who had been playing at a playground in South Hilo to the "laundromat room" of a nearby hotel with intent to have the child perform an act of fellatio, but this design was foiled by the sudden appearance of the owner of the liquor establishment located above the basement room. The bar owner testified that when he opened the door to the room he saw the girl kneeling in a corner with her back to the wall. Smith, the witness said, was in a crouched position over the kneeling child; her face, according to the witness, was several inches away from the defendant's groin area. When the bar owner approached the pair he saw the defendant's exposed and erect penis and the victim's frightened countenance. Smith hurriedly attempted to cover the exposed organ and fled despite the witness' attempt to question him. However, he was apprehended shortly thereafter by the police and identified by the witness as the culprit.

Michael Smith testified he had no intention of engaging in deviate sexual activity with the victim, he did not ask her to perform an act of fellatio, and he was only exposing himself when the witness entered the "laundromat room." The testimony followed an opening statement delivered by counsel in which the defendant was characterized, inter alia, as a fantasizer, a former convict, a pervert, and an exhibitionist.

Counsel thus opened the defense of the charge of attempted sodomy by setting to naught his predecessor's effort to keep the jury from hearing evidence of certain aspects of Smith's criminal history, evidence which the former attorney and the trial court thought might be more prejudicial than probative. And he followed up by eliciting testimony from the defendant corroborating what he had imparted to the jury in his opening remarks. Though Michael Smith thereafter denied he had sodomy in mind and insisted he was only exposing his sexual organ to the little girl, the jury evidently found his testimony unworthy of belief and returned a guilty verdict.

Counsel's opening statement contained the following remarks:

> My client is a loner. He is in a sense a hermit, a fantasizer. My client will be telling you folks that he has had a very tragic and distorted background. He's never really had a family. His mother is an alcoholic. And he's always had a hang-up about sex. He's always fantasized being with either little boys or little girls. Sixty percent boys, forty percent girls. That's the kind of fantasies he's had.
>
> He served time in prison before. But not for anything close to what we're charged with today, Attempted Sodomy in the Second Degree. He served time in prison at Oahu Prison. Served five years there. Just got out last year. Served time for burglaries. Also committed thefts in the past. He's done a whole bunch of stuff that you folks are going to be terribly offended by. But we picked you today because we feel that you folks will stick to what the evidence shows and not what my client's past background is. I just want to let you folks know now through my opening statement of this so that you folks don't get shocked by the testimony that will come out from my client. Please understand that we say this to you only on the premise that we're giving you everything we got. We're putting everything out on the table. My client is not a nice guy. He's a pervert if you want to put it that way. But he's never, he's never committed anything like attempted sodomy before. He's flashed himself up on the U.H. Hilo campus before, he's been an exhibitionist, if you want to call it, but he's never done anything like go and attempt to sexually molest or commit a deviate

act such as having a little girl, you know, with her mouth over his penis. Nothing like that.

Although Smith urges a reversal of the judgment on grounds that the prosecution failed to demonstrate his intent to commit sodomy (this contention is devoid of any merit), his primary contentions on appeal are that he was deprived of his constitutional right to counsel and he should be afforded a new trial.

OPINION

The right of one accused of crime to be represented by an attorney "is a fundamental component of our criminal justice system." But this right "cannot be satisfied by mere formal appointment," for "the assistance of counsel...guaranteed by the United States and Hawaii Constitutions is satisfied only when such assistance is "effective."...Until 1984...the [U.S. Supreme] Court [did not] directly and fully address a claim of 'actual ineffectiveness' of counsel's assistance in a case going to trial." In addressing the claim of ineffectiveness in *Strickland v. Washington*, the Court held...a defendant's claim of ineffective assistance is upheld only if he shows "that counsel's representation fell below an objective standard of reasonableness" and "there is a reasonable probability that, but for counsel's unprofessional errors, the result of the proceeding would have been different." The *Strickland* test has been criticized as being unduly difficult for a defendant to meet....

The test for measuring ineffectiveness adopted by this court...[is] not that declared by the Supreme Court in *Strickland v. Washington*. For purposes of judging claims of inadequate representation brought under Article I, Section 14 of the Hawaii Constitution, we shall continue to apply [our own standard. According to the Hawaii standard], when a denial of this right is raised, the question is "whether, viewed as a whole, the assistance provided [the defendant was] 'within the range of competence demanded of attorneys in criminal cases.'" Of course, the "assistance need not be errorless nor will it be judged ineffective solely by hindsight."

The burden of establishing ineffectiveness rests with the defendant. And his claim of inadequate assistance will be upheld only if there were specific errors or omissions reflecting counsel's lack of skill, judgment or diligence, and these errors or omissions resulted in either the withdrawal or substantial impairment of a potentially meritorious defense.

We are convinced from a review of the record that the assistance rendered by trial counsel was not within the range of competence demanded of attorneys in criminal cases and there were errors or omissions reflecting a lack of skill or judgment that substantially impaired a potentially meritorious defense.

Michael Smith's defense to the charge of attempted sodomy was that he had no intention of committing such act and he was merely exposing himself to the five-year-old girl when the witness came upon them. Conceivably, the jury could have found the defendant guilty of a lesser crime if it believed this was all he had in mind when he inveigled the unsuspecting child into leaving the playground and accompanying him to the hotel. Counsel's opening statement and the elicitation of testimony regarding the defendant's criminal history, the State argues, were consistent with the defense Michael Smith was striving to establish. If the remarks concerning his past and...[eliciting] evidence of his prior convictions constituted error on the part of counsel, the State maintains, the jury was admonished by the trial court to disregard the offending remarks, the inadmissible evidence adduced by counsel was stricken, and proper cautionary instructions were given. We are also reminded that counsel's judgment ought not be subjected to judicial hindsight.

True, matters presumably within the judgment of counsel, like trial strategy, "will rarely be second-guessed by judicial hindsight. Attorneys "require and are permitted broad latitude to make on-the-spot strategic choices in the course of trying a case," and "[d]efense counsel's tactical decisions at trial normally will not be questioned by a reviewing court." Moreover, some of counsel's questionable decisions arguably could be deemed consistent with what defendant hoped would extenuate his crime. Yet, to say the circumstances here were uncommon would be an understatement.

With his opening remarks counsel nullified all of the spadework done by previous counsel to keep certain evidence of dubious value out of the jury's earshot. Even the trial judge's admonition to the jury that prior convictions, incarceration, or lewd conduct should not be considered in determining guilt in this case failed to deter him from following the announced plan of "putting everything out on the table." Though forewarned that this course of action was fraught with peril, he nonetheless urged the defendant to "tell us about the past five years of your life...." The following were among the questions asked and statements made by counsel in the course of his direct examination of the defendant: Michael, you've been in trouble with the law before, correct? Well let's not "BS" with the jury, okay. What have you been in trouble for? Tell us about the past five years of your life and then (inaudible).... Just tell it from your heart cause we don't hide nothing from the jury. [Defense counsel also]...adduced evidence of six prior burglary convictions and incarceration in the penitentiary as a consequence, as well as testimony about a "quirk" defendant had of exposing himself.

Where, as in this case, the success of the asserted defense hinged on defendant's credibility, we would be hard put to say instructions from the court probably had the desired curative effect, particularly when the damaging information of prior convictions and incarceration was conveyed to the jury by defense counsel and again by the defendant at the urging of counsel. We would have to say there were errors reflecting counsel's lack of skill or judgment and the errors substantially impaired a potentially meritorious defense. And there is more in the record to support the claim that counsel's performance at trial was not within the range of competence expected of Hawaii lawyers in criminal cases. For example, during the cross-examination of the young victim the following colloquy occurred:

Q. [DEFENSE COUNSEL]: How do you remember that the man said that? How do you remember that? You still remember?

A. [THE VICTIM]: I don't know.

Q. [DEFENSE COUNSEL]: I give you—I gonna give you one candy, one Valentines lollipop if you can tell us if you do remember or not, no?...

Thereafter, counsel sought permission to sit in the witness chair and continue his cross-examination while the victim sat in his lap. The transcript of the colloquy between court and counsel reads:

THE COURT: What do you propose to do?

[DEFENSE COUNSEL]: I'm going to be sitting on the chair and she can sit on my lap so she can see the jurors, so the jurors can see her.

THE COURT: What is this reference to candy or something?

[DEFENSE COUNSEL]: I have candy, you know, just to open things up a little bit more. It's up there....

Though the foregoing exchange occurred out of the jury's presence and counsel's request obviously was not granted, the incident hardly speaks well of his skill and judgment.

Concluding that the assistance rendered the defendant by trial counsel was ineffective, we vacate the judgment of conviction and REMAND the case for a new trial.

Questions

1. Describe everything Smith's lawyer did during the trial that's relevant to deciding whether he provided Smith "effective assistance of counsel."

2. State the rule the Hawaii Supreme Court follows in deciding whether defendants have received effective counsel under the Hawaii constitution.

3. How does the Hawaii rule differ from the two-pronged rule in *Strickland v. Washington*?

4. What reasons does the Hawaii Supreme Court give for not following the *Strickland v. Washington* test? Which test do you think is the better test? Why?

SUMMARY

I. Starting court proceedings
   A. Police decisions following arrest, interrogation, and identification procedures
      1. Police decide whether to the drop case or take it to prosecutor
      2. Elements in police decisions
         a. Belief suspects aren't guilty
         b. Belief they can't *prove* suspects are guilty
   B. Prosecutors' decisions after receiving the case from police
      1. Dispose
      2. Divert
      3. Charge

II. The decision to charge
   A. Dual roles of prosecutor
      1. Represent public in prosecuting defendants
      2. Represent court in doing justice to individual defendants—which can mean diverting suspects into restitution, treatment, or community service
   B. The decision to charge starts the adversary criminal justice process
   C. Elements of decision to charge
      1. Strength of case against suspect
      2. Wise use of limited resources (selective prosecution)

III. Probable cause to detain suspects
   A. Fourth Amendment commands against "unreasonable seizure"
      1. Prompt appearance of detained suspects before a neutral magistrate
      2. Magistrate decides whether there's probable cause to detain suspects
   B. Fourth Amendment allows detention long enough (usually no longer than 48 hours) for police to complete "administrative steps" before taking suspects to magistrates

IV. First appearance functions
   A. Inform suspects of charges against them
   B. Inform suspects of their constitutional rights
      1. Right to remain silent
      2. Right to counsel
      3. Right to a jury trial

C. Set bail or detain suspects
   1. Balance public safety and need to bring defendants to justice against the rights of defendants not yet convicted of crimes
   2. Conditions attached to release on bail
      a. Release on recognizance (ROR)—promise to appear in court
      b. Money bond—usually 10% of bond amount
      c. Supervised release—example: report to local police department
   3. Consequences of detention
      a. Lost wages and/or job affects defendants and families
      b. Restricts defendants' ability to aid lawyers with their own defense
   4. U.S. Constitution Eighth Amendment
      a. Bans "excessive," not *all*, bail
      b. Amount of bail depends on
         (1) The seriousness of the offense
         (2) The amount of the evidence against the defendant
         (3) The defendant's family ties, employment, financial resources, character, and mental condition
         (4) The length of the defendant's residence in the community
         (5) The defendant's criminal history
         (6) The defendant's prior record for appearing and/or "jumping" bail
      c. Preventive detention
         (1) Constitution permits detaining suspects who threaten public safety
         (2) Preventive detention doesn't violate the due process rights of defendants even though they're presumed innocent
         (3) Preventive detention isn't punishment, so the Eighth Amendment cruel and unusual punishment ban doesn't apply to it
D. Appoint attorneys for indigent defendants
   1. Right attaches to all "critical stages" in criminal proceedings
      a. All proceedings *after* the first appearance
      b. Police interrogation *before* the first appearance (Chapter 8)
   2. Right applies to "all criminal prosecutions"
      a. All felonies
      b. All misdemeanors punishable by incarceration
   3. Right to appointed counsel for indigent (poor) defendants
      a. Poor defendants don't have to be completely destitute
      b. Earnings and assets count; help from friends and relatives doesn't
      c. Actual, not potential, earnings are the measure
      d. The state can tap defendants' future earnings to get reimbursement for the costs of counsel, transcripts, and fees for expert witnesses and investigators
   4. Right to "effective" counsel (two-pronged test, *Strickland v. Washington*)
      a. Reasonableness prong—defendants have to prove lawyer's performance wasn't reasonably competent—presumption that lawyers are competent and have lots of leeway in tactics and strategy that courts will hardly ever question
      b. Prejudice prong—lawyer's incompetence was *probably* responsible for their conviction

Go to the Criminal Procedure 6e CD to download this summary outline. The outline has been formatted so that you can add notes to it during class lectures, or later create a customized chapter outline to use while reviewing. Either way, the summary outline will help you understand the "big picture" and fill in the details as you study.

REVIEW QUESTIONS

1. Describe what occurs following arrest, interrogation, and identification procedures.

2. List the reasons that affect whether police drop cases or take them to prosecutors.

3. Identify the two roles of prosecutors and how the roles affect their decisions.

4. According to the U.S. Supreme Court, why is the initiation of judicial proceedings not just a "mere formalism"?

5. List and explain the importance of the reasons behind the decision of prosecutors to charge, divert, or drop criminal cases.

6. Why and when do police officers have to take arrested suspects to a magistrate?

7. Explain the difference between probable cause to detain a suspect and probable cause to go to trial.

8. What's the significance of the U.S. Supreme Court case *Gerstein v. Pugh*?

9. List the "administrative steps" police officers can complete before they take detained suspects to magistrates.

10. Identify and describe the consequences of detention before trial.

11. Describe the balance struck in the decision to bail or detain defendants.

12. Exactly what does the constitutional right to bail consist of?

13. Identify three constitutional rights our bail system denies to poor defendants, and explain how each is denied.

14. Describe the obstacles pretrial detention creates for defendants trying to prepare their defense.

15. According to the 1984 Bail Reform Act, when can judges preventively detain defendants?

16. What constitutional rights do pretrial detainees have regarding the conditions of their confinement?

17. List the "critical changes" of criminal prosecutions.

18. Summarize the facts of the U.S. Supreme Court decision in *Argersinger v. Hamlin*.

19. List four guidelines for defining indigence developed by the U.S. Courts of Appeals, and summarize the detailed definition of *indigence* adopted in Minnesota.

20. Identify, define, and explain the two-prongs of the U.S. Supreme Court's test of "effective" counsel adopted in *Strickland v. Washington*.

KEY TERMS

THE COMPANION WEB SITE
FOR *CRIMINAL PROCEDURE,* SIXTH EDITION

http://cj.wadsworth.com/samaha/crim_pro6e

Supplement your review of this chapter by going to the companion Web site to take one of the Tutorial Quizzes, use the flash cards to test yourself on the key terms from each chapter, and check out the many other study aids you'll find there. You'll find valuable data and resources at your fingertips to help you study for that big exam or write that important paper.

13 Pretrial, Trial, and Conviction

Chapter Main Points

- Court proceedings are sharply divided into adversarial proceedings inside the courtroom and informal negotiation outside the courtroom.

- Most cases are decided by guilty pleas, not by trial.

- Before cases go to trial, the strength of the government's case is tested to make sure the public's resources and the hardships on defendants and their families are based on enough evidence.

- If the government passes the test of having enough evidence to go to trial, defendants have to come to court to hear and answer the charges against them.

- Before the trial begins, decisions not requiring a trial are disposed of in pretrial motions.

- Defendants have a constitutional right to a jury in all but trials of "petty" offenses.

- There's no constitutional right to a twelve-member jury or to a unanimous verdict.

- The government has the whole burden of proving defendants are guilty beyond a reasonable doubt; defendants have no burden at all to prove they're not guilty.

- There's a lot of debate over the benefits and costs of plea bargaining, but there's no empirical data to resolve the debate.

- Courts' acceptance of guilty pleas and plea bargaining is constitutional, even when defendants maintain they're innocent.

Claude Ballew was charged with "distributing obscene materials" in violation of the Georgia Code by knowingly showing the film "Behind the Green Door" that "contained obscene and indecent scenes." After a jury of 5 persons had been selected and sworn, Ballew moved to have the court impanel a jury of 12 persons. That court, however, tried its misdemeanor cases before juries of five persons pursuant to Ga. Const., Art. 6, paragraph 16, § 1. Ballew contended that for an obscenity trial, a jury of only five was constitutionally inadequate to assess the contemporary standards of the community. He also argued that the Sixth and Fourteenth Amendments required a jury of at least six members in criminal cases.

Ballew v. Georgia (1978), U.S. Supreme Court

AFTER THE DECISION TO CHARGE

Court proceedings are sharply divided into adversarial proceedings inside the courtroom and informal negotiation outside the courtroom. In this chapter, which examines what happens during the pretrial, the trial, and conviction phases of court proceedings, we'll look at several of the formal rules that govern criminal cases, including those that affect testing the government's case, arraignment, pretrial motions, jury trial convictions, the stages of a jury trial, and convictions by guilty pleas.

TESTING THE GOVERNMENT'S CASE

After the decision to charge, the action moves from the prosecutor's office into court. At this point, decisions *inside* the courtroom are based more on formal rules than informal discretion. These rules govern the pretrial proceedings to test the government's case and hear motions. **Testing the government's case** means deciding whether there's enough evidence to go to trial. Still more complex rules control the centerpiece of formal criminal justice, the criminal trial. But don't be deceived by these public formal proceedings. Discretionary decision making hasn't disappeared; it has just moved out of the courtroom and into the corridors in and around the courthouse. Here's where plea bargaining takes place—or, where defendants decide they just want to plead guilty without bargaining, hoping to get a lighter sentence by admitting their guilt and saving the court and lawyers time. In these cases (the vast majority by all counts), courtroom proceedings only ratify what was worked out by informal negotiations.

We saw in Chapter 12 that the decision to charge shows the government's commitment to criminal prosecution, and that the first appearance prepares defendants for the consequences of this decision. But, the government's commitment and the first appearance aren't enough by themselves to start a criminal trial. First, one of two procedures has to test the strength of the government's case against the defendant. There are good reasons for this test. According to the Seventh Circuit U.S. Court of Appeals in *U.S. v. Udziela* (1982):

> While in theory a trial provides a defendant with a full opportunity to contest and disprove charges against him, in practice, the handing up of an indictment will often have a devastating personal and professional impact that a later dismissal or acquittal can never undo. (1001)

Two procedures test the government's case against defendants: (1) preliminary hearings and (2) grand jury review. When prosecutors draw up a **criminal information** (a written formal charge made by prosecutors without a grand jury indictment), they test their case at a **preliminary hearing** before a judge. When they seek an **indictment,** they test the government's case by presenting it to a grand jury for **grand jury review.** If the government passes the test of the grand jury review, the grand jury returns the indictment as a **true bill,** which records the number of grand jurors voting for indictment. If the government passes the test in the preliminary hearing, the judge **binds over** the defendant, or sends the case on for trial.

Both preliminary hearings and grand jury review test the government's case, but they differ in several important respects (see Table 13.1).

Preliminary hearings are public; grand jury proceedings are secret. Preliminary hearings are adversarial proceedings, in which the defense can challenge the prosecution's case; grand juries hear only the prosecution's case without the defense's participation. Judges preside over preliminary hearings; prosecutors manage grand jury proceedings without judicial participation. In preliminary hearings, magistrates determine whether there's enough evidence to go to trial; grand jury review relies on **grand jurors** (citizens selected to serve a term) selected to decide whether there's enough evidence. Finally, defendants and their lawyers attend preliminary hearings; defendants and their lawyers are banned from grand jury review (**ex parte proceedings**).

The differences between preliminary hearings and grand jury proceedings reflect different values in the criminal process. The preliminary hearing stresses adversarial, open, accusatory values and control by experts (Chapter 1). Grand jury review, on the other hand, underscores the value of the democratic dimension of the criminal process: lay participation in criminal proceedings. But their goal is the same: deciding whether there's enough evidence to bring defendants to trial.

TABLE 13.1

Contrasts Between the Preliminary Hearing and Grand Jury Review

Preliminary Hearing	Grand Jury Review
Held in public	Secret proceeding
Adversarial hearing	Only the government's case is presented
Judge presides	Prosecutor presides
Judge determines the facts	Grand jurors decide the facts

The Preliminary Hearing

Preliminary hearings are held after the first appearance (Chapter 12). In most states, all judges are authorized to conduct preliminary hearings, but in practice it's done by magistrates, justices of the peace, municipal court judges, or other members of the lower court judiciary.

There's no constitutional right to a preliminary hearing. But, if states *do* provide for preliminary hearings, the Sixth Amendment guarantees defendants the right to have a lawyer represent them at the hearing (*Gerstein v. Pugh* 1975).

Preliminary hearings are adversarial proceedings. The prosecution presents evidence, and then the defense can challenge it and even present its own evidence. Preliminary hearings are also public. This may sound like a trial, but it's not. First, the rigid rules of evidence followed during trial are relaxed during preliminary hearings. In some states, preliminary hearing judges even admit illegally seized evidence and hearsay (LaFave and Israel 1984, 2:263–264). Prosecutors reveal only enough of the state's evidence (for example, a witness or two and minimal physical evidence) to satisfy the **bind-over standard** (there's enough evidence for the judge to decide to go to trial). Why? Because it takes time and, probably more important, prosecutors don't want to give away any more of their case than they have to. The defense typically introduces no evidence, because they don't want to give away their case either; instead defense attorneys limit their participation to cross-examining the state's witnesses.

The objective basis for going to trial is probable cause, but don't confuse this with probable cause to arrest (Chapter 6). Most courts hold that it takes more **probable cause to bind over** someone for trial than it does to arrest the person. Why? Because the consequences of going to trial are graver. Defendants are detained longer, and the ordeals of criminal prosecution, conviction, and punishment are greater. Even if they aren't convicted, defendants have to pay their lawyers; suffer the stigma of prosecution; and subject their families to hardships. As one prominent exonerated defendant asked, "How do I get my reputation back?" The consequences fall not only on defendants but also on the government. The state has to spend scarce resources to prove guilt, and that takes away resources for other services, like education and road repairs. The bind-over standard reflects the idea that the greater the invasions and deprivations against individuals, the more facts that are needed to back them up.

Just how many facts does it take to move a case to trial? Some courts have adopted a **prima facie case rule.** According to this standard, the judge can bind over a defendant if the prosecution presents evidence that could convict if the defense doesn't rebut it at trial. Others have adopted a **directed verdict rule.** According to this rule, preliminary hearing judges should look at the case like it's a trial and they're deciding whether there's enough believable evidence to send the case to the jury. If there isn't enough, then the judge should dismiss the case. The minimum amount of evidence required to bind over under the directed verdict rule is more than enough to add up to probable cause to arrest but less than enough to "prove the defendant's guilt beyond a reasonable doubt" (*Myers v. Commonwealth* 1973, 824).

Grand Jury Review

Grand jury review is ancient. Originating in medieval England as a council of local residents that helped the king look into matters of royal concern (crime, revenues, and official misconduct), the grand jury was an investigating body. However, by the time of the American Revolution, the grand jury had another duty: it screened criminal cases to protect individuals from malicious and unfounded prosecution. So, the grand jury had two functions: to act as a sword to root out crime and corruption and as a shield to protect innocent people from unwarranted state intrusion.

Colonists warmly approved of the **grand jury shield function,** because it "shielded" them from prosecution for their antiroyalist sentiments. For that reason, the Fifth Amendment to the U.S. Constitution provides that "no person shall be held to answer for a capital, or otherwise infamous crime, unless on a presentment or indictment by a Grand Jury...." But, grand jury indictment is one of the very few provisions in the Bill of Rights that *doesn't* apply to state court proceedings under the incorporation doctrine (Chapter 2). Grand juries vary from state to state both in their membership and in the procedures they follow. Let's look at grand jury membership, grand jury proceedings, and the debate over grand juries.

Members of the Grand Jury

We'll use as an example of choosing grand jury members the operation of the federal grand jury in the Southern District of New York, a jurisdiction that includes Manhattan, the Bronx, and several New York counties as far north as Albany (Frankel and Naftalis 1977, chap. 4).

Federal grand juries consist of not fewer than sixteen or more than twenty-three jurors. To qualify, prospective grand jurors have to

1. Be U.S. citizens
2. Be 18 or over
3. Reside in the jurisdiction
4. Have no felony convictions
5. Speak, write, and read English
6. Suffer from no physical impairments that might hamper their participation, such as impaired hearing or vision

The jurisdiction sometimes summons nearly two hundred citizens for jury service—many more than are needed. The process of narrowing down the number of potential jurors and selecting the final sixteen to twenty-three is called **purging the grand jury.** The process does eliminate prospective grand jurors with compelling reasons not to serve—business, family, and health obligations—but it often hinders the selection of a representative grand jury. The resulting composition of federal grand juries overrepresents retired persons and those not burdened with other responsibilities.

Grand Jury Proceedings

After swearing in the grand jurors, judges **charge the grand jury.** Some charges are calls to action against specific dangers. Others resemble stump speeches for law and order or constitutional rights. Almost all include a history and outline of grand jury duties and responsibilities, warnings about the secrecy of grand jury proceedings, and admonitions to protect the innocent and condemn the guilty. Following the charge, judges turn grand jurors over to prosecutors to conduct grand jury proceedings. Unlike preliminary hearings, grand jury proceedings don't require a judge's participation.

Grand jury secrecy severely restricts who's allowed to attend proceedings. In addition to the grand jurors themselves, only the prosecutor, witnesses called to testify, and stenographers appear in the grand jury room. Defendants are banned. So are witnesses' attorneys, even though these witnesses are often themselves **grand jury targets** (individuals who themselves are under suspicion and investigation). But witnesses may (and often do) bring their lawyers to the courthouse for consultation outside the grand jury room.

After all witnesses have testified and prosecutors have introduced any other evidence, prosecutors draw up an indictment and present it to the grand jury for consideration. Prosecutors then sum up the reasons the evidence amounts to a crime and leave during grand jury deliberations, which ordinarily take only a few minutes. Grand juries rarely disagree with prosecutors' recommendations. Forepersons sign both the indictment and the true bill, which records the number of jurors who voted to indict. Federal grand jury proceedings require twelve jurors' concurrence to indict.

The entire grand jury, accompanied by the prosecutor, then proceeds to a designated courtroom to **hand up the indictment,** an action that amounts to the formal filing of charges, requiring defendants to answer in court. After judges check to ensure all documents are in order, they accept the indictment, which becomes a matter of public record. They also accept the true bill, but it does not become a public record. The judges' acceptance initiates the criminal prosecution by indictment.

The Debate over the Grand Jury

Since the sixteenth century, observers have found a lot to criticize about the grand jury. The Elizabethan justice of the peace William Lambarde's charges to the Kent grand juries (Read 1962) have preserved these early criticisms. Justice Lambarde praised the grand juries' capacity to aid in law enforcement but scorned their conduct in carrying out their responsibilities. Mainly, Lambarde attacked their sword function, berating them for being too timid in rooting out crimes. But, he also criticized their shield function, too, attacking their weakness in screening cases.

In modern times, the debate has focused almost entirely on the grand jury's screening function. From the early 1900s, confidence in science and experts led many reformers to call for banning nonexperts from participating in criminal justice decision making. Those at the extreme wanted to abolish grand and trial juries and replace them with panels of "trained experts" to weigh evidence. More in the mainstream were two prestigious presidential commissions, the Wickersham Commission, appointed by President Herbert Hoover, and the National Advisory Commission, appointed by President Richard Nixon. Both urged the abolition only of mandatory grand jury review.

Since the early 1980s, most legal commentary has condemned the grand jury. Critics make several arguments against grand jury screening. One line of attack is that grand juries are prosecutors' rubber stamps. According to one former prosecutor, "A [prosecutor] can indict anybody, at any time, for almost anything before a grand jury." Statistics bear out this claim. Grand juries issue **no-bills** (refusals to indict) in only a tiny percentage of cases. Even the no-bills don't necessarily show grand jury independence. In sensitive or controversial cases, prosecutors choose grand jury review over preliminary hearings to put the burden for deciding whether or not to charge on the grand jury (LaFave and Israel 1984, 2:282–283).

Critics also condemn the nonadversarial nature of grand jury review, charging it prevents either effectively screening cases or adequately protecting citizens against unwarranted prosecutions. Also, the secrecy of grand jury proceedings creates doubts and suspicion. That defendants and their lawyers can't attend grand jury sessions provides further ammunition for critics' charges that this exclusion is both unfair and results in inadequate screening. Critics also argue grand jury review is inefficient, expensive, and time-consuming. Impaneling and servicing a grand jury is costly in terms of space, human resources, and money. The members have to be selected, notified, sworn, housed, fed, and provided other services.

Finally, grand jury screening takes more time than preliminary hearings. The law surrounding grand jury proceedings is complex and technical, creating delays in the proceedings themselves and, later, in successful challenges to grand jury proceedings. In several jurisdictions, the intricacies and complexities of impaneling a grand jury guarantee attack by a skilled defense attorney and frequently result in dismissal of charges for minor discrepancies in the impaneling procedure.

On the other side, supporters of grand jury review have their arguments, too. First, they maintain grand juries cost no more than preliminary hearings. Preliminary hearings, they charge, have turned into needless "minitrials," elaborate affairs to which lawyers, judges, other court personnel, and witnesses devote a great deal of court time. Furthermore, the number of requests that defense attorneys make for continuances leads to a greater delay in, and a better chance of successful challenges to, preliminary hearings than grand jury proceedings.

Grand jury supporters also reject the contention that the grand jury doesn't effectively screen cases. They cite prosecutors who believe that grand juries are valuable sounding boards and that grand jurors definitely have minds of their own. The high percentage of indictments grand juries return is not the important figure, according to supporters. Rather, the percentage of convictions—as high as 98 percent—based on indictments demonstrates that grand juries effectively screen out cases that shouldn't go to trial (Younger 1963).

Finally, grand jury review shows democracy at work. Supporters maintain that what grand jury review loses in secret and nonadversarial proceedings it more than recaptures in community participation in screening criminal cases. Citizen participation enhances public confidence in the criminal justice system. In a system where most cases don't go to trial, grand jury proceedings provide private citizens with their only opportunity to participate actively on the "front lines" of the criminal process. But, in fact, grand jurors aren't as representative of the community as trial jurors—who aren't all that representative either. Grand jury duty spans a long period of time, usually a year, and requires service at least two or three days a week. Only citizens with a lot of free time can devote such extended service in the criminal process (Graham and Letwin 1971, 681).

 Go to Exercise 13-1 on the Criminal Procedure 6e CD to learn more about testing the government's case.

ARRAIGNMENT

If defendants are indicted or bound over, the next step in the criminal process is arraignment. **Arraignment** means to bring defendants to court to hear *and* to answer (plead to) the charges against them. Don't confuse arraignment with the first appearance (Chapter 12). The first appearance takes place within days of arrest, and defendants don't have to answer the charges; arraignment happens sometimes months after arrest, and defendants have to answer something.

There are four possible pleas (answers) to the charges:

1. Not guilty
2. Not guilty by reason of insanity
3. Nolo contendere
4. Guilty (later in chapter)

Nolo contendere means defendants don't contest the issue of guilt or innocence. There's no *right* to plead nolo contendere; the court has to consent to it. Why do defendants plead nolo contendere? Because it might help them in civil lawsuits, a complicated matter we don't need to explore in a criminal procedure course. Also, if a defendant pleads guilty, the court has to decide whether the plea is knowing and voluntary (later in this chapter).

 Go to Exercise 13-2 on the Criminal Procedure 6e CD to learn more about your state's arraignment procedure.

PRETRIAL MOTIONS

Pretrial motions are written or oral requests asking the court to decide questions that don't require a trial to be ruled on. They're an important part of both prosecutors' and defense counsel's work. They definitely spend a lot more time on "motion practice" than they spend trying cases—and probably more time than they do on plea bargaining. Let's look briefly at the main pretrial motions:

1. Double jeopardy
2. Speedy trial
3. Change of venue
4. Suppression of evidence

Double Jeopardy

The Fifth Amendment to the U.S. Constitution provides guarantees that: "No person...shall...be subject for the same offence to be twice put in jeopardy of life or limb...." Although the words "life or limb" suggest only death and corporal punishment, this guarantee against **double jeopardy** applies to all crimes, including decisions in juvenile proceedings.

The ban on double jeopardy protects several interests both of the state and defendants (Table 13.2). It's supposed to allow the government "one fair shot" at convicting criminals. At the same time, it bans the government's use of its greater share of power and resources to subject less-powerful citizens accused of crimes to repeated attempts to convict them. Furthermore, it protects individuals from the embarrassment, expense, and ordeal—and the anxiety and insecurity—that repeated prosecutions generate. Defendants also have an interest in completing their trials under one tribunal and jury. In addition, both the state and defendants have an interest in the finality and

TABLE 13.2

Interests Protected by Double Jeopardy

Interest	State	Defendant
Allows one fair shot at convicting defendants	Yes	
Limits the advantage of greater resources		Yes
Reduces prolonged stress that multiple trials would lead to		Yes
Promotes finality (closure) in criminal cases	Yes	Yes
Reduces the costs that multiple trials would lead to	Yes	Yes

integrity of judgments that aren't susceptible to repeated reconsideration. Finally, the prohibition against double jeopardy reduces costs both to defendants and to the state. Retrials consume time and impede the efficient and economical disposition of other cases on crowded criminal court calendars.

The Fifth Amendment prohibition against double jeopardy kicks in as soon as the state "puts defendants to trial." In jury trials, this happens when the jury is impaneled *and* sworn in. The U.S. Supreme Court referred to the history of this definition of jury trials in *Crist v. Bretz* (1978), when it struck down Montana's rule that despite swearing in the jury, jeopardy didn't attach until the first witness commenced testifying:

> The reason for holding that jeopardy attaches when the jury is empaneled and sworn lies in the need to protect the interest of an accused in retaining a chosen jury. . . . It is an interest with roots deep in the historic development of trial by jury in the Anglo-American system of criminal justice. Throughout that history there ran a strong tradition that once banded together a jury should not be discharged until it had completed its solemn task of announcing a verdict. (36)

In trials without juries where judges find the facts (**bench trials**), jeopardy kicks in when the court begins to hear evidence. Why? Because until the court begins to hear evidence, the trial hasn't started. The point when *jeopardy* kicks in, or attaches, has been called the linchpin of the double jeopardy inquiry, but, the Fifth Amendment prohibits only *double* jeopardy. So, the attachment of jeopardy is necessary but not enough to kick in double jeopardy; it's only enough when defendants are exposed to *double* jeopardy.

What actions are protected by the ban on double jeopardy? Three, according to the U.S. Supreme Court:

1. A second *prosecution* for the same offense after *conviction*

2. A second *prosecution* for the same offense after *acquittal*

3. *Multiple punishments* for the same offense

Where jeopardy has kicked in but proceedings end before conviction or acquittal, the double jeopardy clause doesn't prevent a second prosecution for the same offense. This can happen in two types of cases. First, if the *defendant* moves to dismiss the case (or asks for or accepts a mistrial), and the judge rules in the defendant's favor, the prosecution can reprosecute. Second, even where defendants object to dismissal or a mistrial, the government can reprosecute for the same offense if the judge dismissed the case or ordered a mistrial because dismissal "serves the ends of justice" (**manifest necessity doctrine**). The classic example of manifest necessity is the **hung jury**—a jury unable to reach a verdict. Why? According to the U.S. Supreme Court (*U.S. v. Perez* 1824):

> We think that in cases of this nature, the law has invested Courts of justice with the authority to discharge a jury from giving any verdict, whenever, in their opinion, taking all the circumstances into consideration, there is a manifest necessity for the act, or the ends of public justice would otherwise be defeated. They are to exercise a sound discretion on the subject; and it is impossible to define all the circumstances, which would render it proper to interfere. To be sure, the power ought to be used with the greatest of caution, under urgent circumstances. (580)

The manifest necessity doctrine isn't limited to hung juries. It also applies to a range of situations where the prosecution is in a no-win situation. For example, when a court declared a mistrial because a defective indictment was enough to overturn a conviction, the U.S. Supreme Court (*Illinois v. Somerville* 1973) ruled that prosecuting the case again didn't violate the double jeopardy clause. The Court balanced two interests in reaching its decision, saying "a defendant's valued right to have his trial completed by a particular tribunal must in some instances be subordinated to the public's interests in fair trials designed to end in just judgments." According to the Court:

> A trial judge properly exercises his discretion to declare a mistrial . . . if a verdict of conviction could be reached but would have to be reversed on appeal due to an obvious procedural error in the trial. If an error would make reversal on appeal a certainty, it would not serve "the ends of public justice" to require that the Government proceed with its proof, when, if it succeeded before the jury, it would automatically be stripped of that success by an appellate court. (464)

The double jeopardy clause bans both multiple *punishments* and multiple *prosecutions*. The main purpose of the double jeopardy clause is to restrain prosecutors and judges. Although legislatures are free to define crimes and prescribe punishments, once they act "courts may not impose more than one punishment for the same offense and prosecutors ordinarily may not attempt to secure that punishment in more than one trial."

Still, it's not double jeopardy to prosecute and punish a defendant for the same acts in separate jurisdictions. According to the **dual sovereignty doctrine,** a crime arising out of the same facts in one state is not the same crime in another state. (In other words, "*same* offense" doesn't mean "*identical* offense.") The dual sovereignty doctrine arises most often when the same conduct is a crime under both state and federal law. In *Heath v. Alabama* (1985), Larry Heath (for $2,000) hired Charles Owens and Gregory Lumpkin to kill his wife, who was then nine months' pregnant. The killers fulfilled their part of the deal. Heath was sentenced to life imprisonment in a Georgia court after he pleaded guilty. However, part of the crime was committed in Alabama, so Alabama prosecuted Heath, too. He was convicted in Alabama of murder committed during a kidnapping and sentenced to death. He appealed the conviction on the grounds of double jeopardy. The U.S. Supreme Court affirmed the conviction, holding that successive prosecutions for the same crime in two different states didn't put him in jeopardy twice. According to Justice O'Connor, writing for the majority of the Court:

> To deny a State its power to enforce its criminal laws because another State has won the race to the courthouse "would be a shocking and untoward deprivation of the historic right and obligation of the States to maintain peace and order within their confines." Such a

deprivation of a State's sovereign powers cannot be justified by the assertion that under "interest analysis" the State's legitimate penal interests will be satisfied through a prosecution conducted by another State. A State's interest in vindicating its sovereign authority through enforcement of its laws by definition can never be satisfied by another State's enforcement of its own laws. The Court has always understood the words of the Double Jeopardy Clause to reflect this fundamental principle, and we see no reason why we should reconsider that understanding today. (93)

Also, it doesn't put defendants in double jeopardy to prosecute them in multiple trials for separate offenses arising out of the same incident. The U.S. Supreme Court decided this in the horrible multiple-murder case, *Ciucci v. Illinois* (1958). Vincent Ciucci was married and had three children. When he fell in love with a 21-year-old woman he wanted to marry, his wife wouldn't give him a divorce. So, he shot her and all three of his children in the head one-by-one while they slept. Illinois used the same evidence to convict Ciucci in three separate murder trials. The Court decided that the multiple trials, even if they stemmed from the same incident, didn't put Ciucci in jeopardy more than once.

A Speedy Trial

According to the Sixth Amendment, "In all criminal trials, the accused shall enjoy the right to a speedy... trial." The idea of speedy justice is more than nine hundred years older than the Bill of Rights. In 1187, King Henry II provided for "speedy justice" in the Assizes of Clarendon. King John promised in the Magna Carta in 1215 that "every subject of this realme...may...have justice...speedily without delay." In his *Institutes*—called by Thomas Jefferson, "the universal elementary book of law students" (*Klopfer v. North Carolina* 1967, 225)—Sir Edward Coke wrote that the English itinerant justices in 1600 "have not suffered the prisoner to be long detained, but at their next coming have given the prisoner full and speedy justice...without detaining him long in prison" ([Coke 1797 in] *Klopfer v. North Carolina* 1967). The Virginia Declaration of Rights in 1776 (the state's "bills of rights") and the speedy trial clause of the Sixth Amendment reflect this history. And even though the state constitutions guarantee a speedy trial, the U.S. Supreme Court has extended the federal speedy trial protection of the Sixth Amendment to the states (225).

The speedy trial clause promotes and balances several interests. For the accused, it prevents prolonged detention before trial; reduces the anxiety and uncertainty surrounding criminal prosecution; and guards against weakening the defense's case through loss of alibi witnesses and other evidence. The speedy trial provision also promotes the interest in obtaining the correct result. Delay means lost evidence and lost witnesses—or at least the loss of their memory—not only for the defense but also for the prosecution. The clause also promotes process goals, particularly that decisions should be made in a timely fashion. Organizational interests are at stake as well. Failure to provide prompt trials contributes to large case backlogs, particularly in urban areas. Furthermore, long pretrial detention is costly to taxpayers. In addition to feeding and housing detained defendants, lost wages and greater welfare burdens result from incarceration. Finally, because most detained defendants are poor, both the process interest in ensuring equal protection of the laws and the societal interest in protecting the poor and less powerful are at stake in speedy trial decisions (*Report to the Nation on Crime and Justice* 1988, 123).

According to the U.S. Supreme Court, the Sixth Amendment "speedy trial clock" doesn't start ticking until suspects are formally charged with crimes. Before they're charged, defendants have to depend on either statutes spelling out the length of time allowed between the commission of crimes and the filing of charges (**statutes of limitations**) or the due process clauses. So, in rejecting a speedy trial violation in a delay of three years between the commission of the crime and an indictment, the Court said:

> The due process clause of the Fifth Amendment would require dismissal of the indictment if it were shown at trial that the pre-indictment delay...caused substantial prejudice to appellants' rights to a fair trial and that the delay was an intentional device to gain tactical advantage over the accused.
>
> *U.S. v. Marion* 1971, 324

The speedy trial clause bans only *undue* delays. According to the U.S. Supreme Court, flexibility governs whether delays are undue enough to violate the speedy trial clause. The Court has adopted another one of its balancing tests to decide whether delays hurt (**prejudice,** if you want the technical term) defendants' cases. Four elements go into the balance:

1. The length of the delay
2. The reason for the delay
3. The defendant's assertion of his or her right to a speedy trial
4. The prejudice (harm) the delay causes to the defendant's case

What are the consequences of violating the speedy trial guarantee? According to the Court, there are only two remedies for the violation of the speedy trial clause:

1. *Dismissal without prejudice.* Allows a new prosecution for the same offense
2. *Dismissal with prejudice.* A more drastic remedy, it bars future prosecution for the same offense

According to a unanimous U.S. Supreme Court, even though there's enough evidence for conviction, undue delay subjects defendants to "emotional stress" that requires dismissal as "the only possible remedy." The Court's ruling has raised the strong objection that the high price of dismissal will make courts "extremely hesitant" to find speedy trial violations because judges don't want to be responsible for freeing criminals (*Strunk v. U.S.* 1973).

Although the Sixth Amendment doesn't require it, several states have enacted statutes or court rules that set time limits for bringing cases to trial. These limits vary widely among the states. The **Federal Speedy Trial Act** provides definite time periods for bringing defendants to trial. The government has to start *prosecution* within 30 days after arrest (60 days if there's no grand jury in session); *arraign* defendants within 10 days after filing indictments or informations; and bring defendants to *trial* within 60 days following arraignment. According to the act, the following delays don't count in computing days:

1. Delays needed to determine the defendant's competency to stand trial
2. Delays due to other trials of the defendant
3. Delays due to hearings on pretrial motions
4. Delays because of *interlocutory appeals*—provisional appeals that interrupt the proceedings, such as an appeal from a ruling on a pretrial motion

Change of Venue

The Sixth Amendment provides that "in all criminal prosecutions, the accused shall enjoy the right to a ... public trial, by an impartial jury of the State and district wherein the crime shall have been committed." A defendant's pretrial motion to change the **venue** (the place where the trial is held) waives the Sixth Amendment right to have a trial in the state and district where the crime was committed. Only defendants, not the prosecution, may move to change the venue, and changes of venue are not automatic. According to Rule 21(a) of the *Federal Rules of Criminal Procedure*:

> The court upon motion of the defendant shall transfer the proceeding as to that defendant to another district ... if the court is satisfied that there exists in the district where the prosecution is pending so great a prejudice against the defendant that the defendant cannot obtain a fair and impartial trial at any place fixed for holding court in that district.

Why do defendants give up their right to a trial in the place where the crime was committed? Because they believe they can't get an impartial public trial in that location. When courts rule on the motion, they balance the right to a public trial in the place where the crime was committed against the right to an impartial trial. In that respect, changing venue reflects the interest in obtaining a proper result in the individual case—prejudiced jurors can't find the truth. Process values are also at stake: the integrity of the judicial process requires a calm, dignified, reflective atmosphere; due process demands unbiased fact-finding; the equal protection clause prohibits trying defendants who are the object of public outrage differently from other defendants.

In *Sheppard v. Maxwell* (1966), the U.S. Supreme Court held that "where there is a reasonable likelihood that the prejudicial news prior to trial will prevent a fair trial, the judge should continue the case until the threat abates, or transfer it to another county not so permeated with publicity" (363). In this case, Ohio tried Dr. Sam Sheppard for the bludgeoning murder of his pregnant wife, Marilyn, a Cleveland socialite. The case dominated the news and gripped the public's attention before, during, and after the trial. Lurid headlines and long stories appeared regularly, detailing the brutality of the murder and Sheppard's failure to cooperate with authorities. The editorials accused Sheppard of the murder. One charged on the front page that "somebody is getting away with murder," alleging that Sheppard's wealth and prominent social position protected him from a full-fledged investigation by police. Finally, the papers printed detailed analyses of evidence that came to light during the investigation, editorializing about its credibility, relevance, and materiality to the case.

As for the trial itself, the press, the public, and other observers packed the courtroom every day. One local radio station set up broadcasting facilities on the third floor of the courthouse. Television and newsreel cameras waiting outside on the courthouse steps filmed jurors, lawyers, witnesses, and other participants in the trial. All the jurors were exposed to the heavy publicity prior to the trial. Referring to the "carnival atmosphere" at the trial, the Supreme Court concluded that Sheppard was entitled to a new trial without showing actual prejudice—a reasonable likelihood of prejudice was sufficient.

Fascination with the case didn't stop even after Sheppard's appeal to the U.S. Supreme Court. The popular 1960s television drama *The Fugitive* was based on the case. So was the 1990s movie with the same title. (The fascination continued for television viewers who watched a short-lived 2001 version of *The Fugitive*.)

TABLE 13.3
Factors Considered in Change-of-Venue Motions

Trials at distant locations burden witnesses.

Communities have a substantial interest in the trial taking place where the crime was committed.

Changing prosecutors disrupts the state's case.

Courts can't decide the partiality question until the jury has been impaneled.

Courts don't want to transfer a case after all the time spent in picking a jury.

In granting Sheppard a new trial, the U.S. Supreme Court ruled that the proceedings should have been postponed or the trial venue moved because of a reasonable likelihood of prejudice. The **reasonable-likelihood-of-prejudice test** requires courts to balance four elements in each change of venue case:

1. The kind and amount of community bias that endangers a fair trial

2. The size of the community where jury panels are selected

3. The details and seriousness of the offense

4. The status of the victim and the accused

These elements may vary in intensity, and they don't all have to be present in each case; they're guidelines for judges when they measure the likelihood the defendant will receive a fair trial.

Most courts don't grant changes of venue even if defendants show there's a reasonable-likelihood-of-prejudice. Instead, they adopt an **actual prejudice test** to determine whether to either change the venue or take less drastic measures. Under the actual prejudice test courts have to decide whether jurors were *in fact* prejudiced by harmful publicity. In *Swindler v. State* (1979), for example, John Edward Swindler proved that three jurors had read *and* heard about the case, and that over 80 percent of prospective jurors were excused for cause. This didn't stop the Arkansas Supreme Court from rejecting Swindler's claim that the trial court's refusal to grant his motion for change of venue denied him a fair trial and upholding Swindler's death sentence. Swindler's experience is an example of how rare change of venue is.

In deciding whether the venue should be changed, courts consider a number of issues (Table 13.3). Moving proceedings to jurisdictions farther away, providing for witnesses to appear, and working in unfamiliar court surroundings hinder smooth, efficient, economical resolution of criminal cases. Furthermore, society has a strong interest in maintaining public confidence in the criminal justice system and providing an outlet for community reaction to crime. Citizens resent moving trials both because they want to follow the proceedings, and they feel insulted by a ruling that their own jurisdiction can't guarantee a fair trial.

Suppression of Evidence

As you've already learned, almost every case excerpt dealing with police work is about a struggle between defendants who want to keep evidence out of court and prosecutors who want to get it in. And, you've also learned the reason for this struggle is the exclusionary rule (Chapter 11). Whether the exclusionary rule applies is decided in a pretrial hearing triggered by a defense **motion to suppress evidence** that law enforcement officers obtained by searches, seizures, confessions, or identification procedures (Chapters 4–9). The decision whether to let in evidence or keep it out is a **legal question,** meaning *judges,* not *juries* decide whether to exclude evidence.

CONVICTION BY JURY TRIAL

Three constitutional commands lie behind the conviction of defendants in criminal cases:

ARTICLE III, § 2

The Trial of all Crimes, except in Cases of Impeachment, shall be by Jury; and such Trial shall be held in the State where the Crimes shall have been committed.

THE FIFTH AMENDMENT

No person shall be . . . compelled in any criminal case to be a witness against himself. . . .

THE SIXTH AMENDMENT

In all criminal prosecutions, the accused shall enjoy the right to a speedy and public trial, by an impartial jury of the State and District wherein the crime shall have been committed . . . to be confronted with the witnesses against him, . . . and to have the assistance of Counsel for his defense.

These constitutional commands set high standards because conviction of a crime can result in the greatest deprivations (loss of property, liberty, privacy, and perhaps even life itself) in the criminal process. These commands are directed almost exclusively at criminal *trials,* but, in practice, only about 10 percent of criminal cases are decided in trials. The vast majority are disposed of by guilty pleas. Some of these guilty pleas result from negotiations, but many are **straight pleas** (pleas of guilty without negotiation). Trials and guilty pleas promote different interests. The trial promotes fact-finding by the adversarial process, procedural regularity, and public participation in criminal proceedings. The guilty plea promotes efficiency, economy, harmony, and speed. Plea negotiations also promote fact-finding by informal discussion and the give-and-take that occur in reaching an agreement over the plea.

Trial by jury is ancient, with roots in the societies of the Teutonic tribes in Germany and the Normans before their conquest of England. The Assizes of Clarendon in 1187 and the Magna Carta in 1215 also contain traces of its origins. The jury trial was provided for specifically in the English Bill of Rights in 1689, and, from that time, it became common practice in the British American colonies. From the start, the colonists resented royal interference with the right to a jury trial. Complaints regarding that interference appear in the Stamp Act, Congress's resolutions, the First Continental Congress's resolves, and the Declaration of Independence. Article III, § 2, in the body of the U.S. Constitution and the Sixth Amendment, reflects the new nation's commitment to jury trial. Every state constitution guarantees it, and the U.S. Supreme Court has interpreted the due process clause of the Fourteenth Amendment to require states to provide it (*Duncan v. Louisiana* 1968).

Trial by jury promotes several interests. It checks and balances government power by putting an independent community-dominated body between the state with all its resources and a single individual. Jury trial also balances official power with citizen participation in criminal law enforcement. In addition, it guarantees that accused citizens who prefer that other citizens decide their innocence or guilt will have that preference honored. In extending the Sixth Amendment's jury trial right to the states, Justice Byron R. White wrote the following:

> The guarantees of jury trial...reflect a profound judgment about the way in which law should be enforced and justice administered....Providing an accused with the right to be tried by a jury of his peers gave him an inestimable safeguard against the corrupt or overzealous prosecutor and against the compliant, biased, or eccentric judge....Beyond this, the jury trial...reflects a...reluctance to entrust plenary powers over the life and liberty of the citizen to one judge or to a group of judges. Fear of unchecked power, so typical of our State and Federal Governments in other respects, found expression in the criminal law in this insistence upon community participation in the determination of guilt or innocence.
>
> *Duncan v. Louisiana* 1968, 156

Let's explore more fully the meaning of the right to a trial by jury by examining how this right is affected by the moral seriousness standard, the issue of how many citizens are required to sit on a jury, the jury selection process, and the right to a public trial.

The Moral Seriousness Standard

According to the U.S. Supreme Court, there's one major exception to the right to a jury trial for "*all* crimes" in Article III, § 2, and "*all* criminal prosecutions" in the Sixth Amendment. That exception is for "petty offenses" (*Duncan v. Louisiana* 1968, 160). In jurisdictions where there's no specific law drawing a line between petty and other offenses, the Court has used six months' imprisonment as the dividing line (*Baldwin v. New York* 1970). But, by taking the "moral quality" of offenses into account, courts have declared some offenses serious even if the penalty is less than six months' imprisonment. So, under this **moral seriousness standard,** courts have decided defendants had a right to a jury trial when charged with conspiring to deceive immigration officials (*U.S. v. Sanchez-Meza* 1976), driving while intoxicated (*U.S. v. Craner* 1981), and shoplifting (*State v. Superior Court* 1978), even though the penalty for these offenses was less than six months in jail.

The Twelve-Member Jury Requirement

The twelve-member jury at one time was regarded by the U.S. Supreme Court as essential to the right to a jury trial (*Thompson v. Utah* 1898). The Court has since retreated from that position. Justice Byron R. White spelled out the reasons in *Williams v. Florida* (1970):

1. We can't "pretend" to know the Framers' intent.

2. The number 12 is based on superstition about the number (twelve apostles, twelve tribes of Israel, twelve stones).

3. History doesn't give good enough reasons to stick to twelve members in today's world.

So, according to the Court in *Williams v. Florida* (1970), the Sixth Amendment only demands enough jurors to achieve the goals of a jury trial: to find the truth and allow for community participation in criminal justice decision making. And that number isn't necessarily 12:

> That the jury at common law was composed of precisely 12 is a historical accident, unnecessary to effect the purposes of the jury system and wholly without significance "except to mystics." To read the Sixth Amendment as forever codifying a feature so incidental to the real purpose of the Amendment is to ascribe a blind formalism to the Framers which would require considerably more evidence than we have been able to discover in the history and language of the Constitution or in the reasoning of our past decisions. (102)

The twelve-member jury has strong supporters, despite the Court's dismissal of it as superstitious. Justice John Marshall Harlan called the accident of superstition argument "much too thin." If the number 12 was merely an accident, it was one that "has recurred without interruption since the 14th century." Also, according to Justice Harlan:

> If 12 jurors are not essential, why are six? Can it be doubted that a unanimous jury of 12 provides a greater safeguard than a majority vote of six? The uncertainty that will henceforth plague the meaning of trial by jury is itself a further reason for not hoisting the anchor of history.... The [Court's] circumvention of history is compounded by the cavalier disregard of numerous pronouncements of this Court that reflect the understanding of the jury as one of twelve members and have fixed expectations accordingly.
>
> *Baldwin v. New York* 1970, 126

Judges aren't the only ones who support the twelve-member jury. Social scientists have found that juries with twelve members are right more often, *and* they represent the community better than juries with fewer than twelve members. Hans Zeisel, a major authority on the jury, had this to say about the twelve-member jury:

> Suppose that in a given community, 90 percent of the people share one viewpoint and the remaining 10 percent have a different viewpoint. Suppose further that we draw 100 twelve-member and 100 six-member juries. Using standard statistical methods, it can be predicted that approximately 72 of the twelve-member juries will contain a representative of the 10 percent minority, as compared to only 47 juries composed of six persons. This difference is by no means negligible.
>
> LaFave and Israel 1984, 2:696, n. 57

Six-member juries are enough to satisfy the Sixth Amendment, but what about five? The Supreme Court answered this question in *Ballew v. Georgia* (1978).

| CASE | ***Does a Five-Member Jury Guarantee a Jury Trial?*** |

Ballew v. Georgia
435 U.S. 223 (1978)

Claude Ballew was charged with "distributing obscene matter" (a misdemeanor), tried by a five-member jury, convicted, and sentenced to a one-year incarceration and a fine of $1,000, the term of incarceration to be suspended upon payment of the fine. The Georgia Supreme Court denied certioraris. The U.S. Supreme Court granted certiorari, reversed the judgment, and remanded the case for proceedings consistent with the decision excerpted here.

BLACKMUN, J., joined by STEVENS, J.

FACTS

In November 1973, Claude Davis Ballew was the manager of the Paris Adult Theatre at 320 Peachtree Street, Atlanta, Ga. On November 9, two investigators from the Fulton County Solicitor General's office viewed at the theater a motion picture film entitled "Behind the Green Door."

On September 14, 1974, Ballew was charged with "distributing obscene materials" in violation of the Georgia Code by knowingly showing the film "Behind the Green Door" that "contained obscene and indecent scenes." Ballew was brought to trial in the Criminal Court of Fulton County. After a jury of 5 persons had been selected and sworn, Ballew moved to have the court impanel a jury of 12 persons. That court, however, tried its misdemeanor cases before juries of five persons pursuant to Ga. Const., Art. 6. paragraph 16, § 1. Ballew contended that for an obscenity trial, a jury of only five was constitutionally inadequate to assess the contemporary standards of the community. He also argued that the Sixth and Fourteenth Amendments required a jury of at least six members in criminal cases.

The motion for a 12-person jury was overruled, and the trial went on to its conclusion before the 5-person jury that had been impaneled. At the conclusion of the trial, the jury deliberated for 38 minutes and returned a verdict of guilty on both counts of the accusation. The court imposed a sentence of one year and a $1,000 fine on each count, the periods of incarceration to run concurrently and to be suspended upon payment of the fines.

The Supreme Court of Georgia denied certiorari and the U.S. Supreme Court granted certiorari.

OPINION

The Fourteenth Amendment guarantees the right of trial by jury in all state nonpetty criminal cases. The purpose of the jury trial is to prevent oppression by the Government. This purpose is attained by the participation of the community in determinations of guilt and by the application of the common sense of laymen who, as jurors, consider the case. Rather than requiring 12 members . . . the Sixth Amendment mandates a jury only of sufficient size to promote group deliberation, to insulate members from outside intimidation, and to provide a representative cross-section of the community.

When the Court in *Williams v. Florida* (1970) . . . held that a jury of six was not unconstitutional—it expressly reserved ruling on the issue whether a number smaller than six passed constitutional scrutiny. The Court refused to speculate when this so-called "slippery slope" would be-

come too steep. We face now, however, the two-fold question whether a further reduction in the size of the state criminal trial jury does make the grade too dangerous, that is, whether it inhibits the functioning of the jury as an institution to a significant degree, and, if so, whether any state interest counterbalances and justifies the disruption so as to preserve its constitutionality.

First, recent empirical data suggest that progressively smaller juries are less likely to foster effective group deliberation. At some point, this decline leads to inaccurate fact-finding and incorrect application of the common sense of the community to the facts. The smaller the group, the less likely are members to make critical contributions necessary for the solution of a given problem. As juries decrease in size, then, they are less likely to have members who remember each of the important pieces of evidence or argument. Furthermore, the smaller the group, the less likely it is to overcome the biases of its members to obtain an accurate result. When individual and group decision making were compared, it was seen that groups performed better because prejudices of individuals were frequently counterbalanced, and objectivity resulted.

Second, the data now raise doubts about the accuracy of the results achieved by smaller and smaller panels. Statistical studies suggest that the risk of convicting an innocent person rises as the size of the jury diminishes. Third, the data suggest that the verdicts of jury deliberation in criminal cases will vary as juries become smaller, and that the variance amounts to an imbalance to the detriment of one side, the defense. Fourth, a jury's decrease in size foretells problems not only for jury decision making, but also for the representation of minority groups in the community. The Court repeatedly has held that meaningful community participation cannot be attained with the exclusion of minorities or other identifiable groups from jury service.

While we adhere to, and reaffirm our holding in *Williams v. Florida*, these studies, most of which have been made since *Williams* was decided in 1970, lead us to conclude that the purpose and functioning of the jury in a criminal trial is seriously impaired, and to a constitutional degree, by a reduction in size to below six members. With the reduction in the number of jurors below six creating a substantial threat to Sixth and Fourteenth Amendment guarantees, we must consider whether any interest of the State justifies the reduction. We find no significant state advantage in reducing the number of jurors from six to five.

The States utilize juries of less than 12 primarily for administrative reasons. Savings in court time and in financial costs are claimed to justify the reductions. A reduction in size from six to five or four or even three would save the States little. They could reduce slightly the daily allowances, but with a reduction from six to five the saving would be minimal.

The judgment of the Court of Appeals is REVERSED, and the case is REMANDED for further proceedings not inconsistent with this opinion. It is so ordered.

Questions

1. Why does a six-member jury satisfy the Constitution but not a five-member jury, according to the Court?

2. How does the Court arrive at its conclusion?

3. Does social science research provide a better guide to how many jurors should constitute a jury than does history? Explain your answer.

Jury Selection

According to the U.S. Supreme Court, the Sixth Amendment right to an "impartial jury" requires that juries represent a "fair cross section" of the community. Furthermore, the equal protection clause of the Fourteenth Amendment prohibits the systematic exclusion of members of defendants' racial, gender, ethnic, or religious group. The **Federal Jury Selection and Service Act** meets these constitutional requirements by requiring that juries be

1. "Selected at random from a fair cross section of the community in the district or division wherein the court convenes," and

2. "No citizen shall be excluded from service as a grand or petit juror in the district courts of the United States on account of race, color, religion, sex, national origin, or economic status"

Most states have similar provisions. To implement them, jurisdictions select jurors at random from the following sources: local census reports, tax rolls, city directories, telephone books, and driver's license lists. Some states, mainly in New England and the South, use the **key-man system,** in which civic and political leaders recommend people from these lists whom they know personally or by reputation. Understandably, the key-man system faces repeated challenges that it doesn't represent a fair cross section of the community, and that it discriminates against various segments in the community (LaFave and Israel 1984, 2:708).

Jury service isn't popular; most prospective jurors ask to be excused (Table 13.4). Courts rarely refuse their requests because it's "easier, administratively and financially, to excuse unwilling people" (LaFave and Israel 1984, 2:708).

Some groups are ordinarily exempt from jury service: persons below voting age, convicted felons, and persons who can't write and read English. Some occupations are

TABLE 13.4
Common Excuses for Exemption from Jury Service
Economic hardship
Advanced age
Illness
Need to care for small children
Distance between home and the courthouse is too far

also exempt: doctors, pharmacists, teachers, clergy, lawyers, judges, criminal justice professionals, and some other public employees (LaFave and Israel 1984, 2:708–709).

From the **jury panel** (the potential jurors drawn from the list of eligible citizens not excused), the attorneys for the government and the defendant pick the jurors who will actually serve. The process of picking the actual jurors from the pool of potential jurors by questioning them is called the **voir dire**—literally, "to speak the truth." Both prosecutors and defense attorneys can remove jurors during the voir dire. There are two ways of removing (usually called "striking") potential jurors, **peremptory challenges** (striking without having to give a reason) and **challenges for cause** (striking by showing the juror is biased). Lawyers almost always use their peremptory challenges to strike potential jurors who look like they're going to sympathize with the other side. Attorneys use challenges for cause only when they can convince judges of juror bias.

The number of peremptory challenges depends on the jurisdiction; the number of challenges for cause is unlimited. In the federal courts, both the prosecution and the defense have twenty peremptories in capital offenses and three in misdemeanors. In felony cases, defendants have ten, and the government has six. Both sides rarely exercise their right to challenges for cause—usually one to three times to assemble a jury of twelve (Van Dyke 1977, 14).

Inquiring into race prejudice during voir dire is sensitive. In *Dukes v. Waitkevitch* (1976), for example, the First Circuit U.S. Court of Appeals ruled that the trial court didn't commit a constitutional error when it refused to inquire into race prejudice in a case where the black defendant was charged with participating in a gang rape of white women. In capital cases, however, the U.S. Supreme Court has ruled otherwise:

> The risk of racial prejudice infecting capital sentencing proceedings is especially serious in light of the complete finality of the death sentence.... We hold that a capital defendant accused of an interracial crime is entitled to have prospective jurors informed of the race of the victim and questioned on the issue of racial bias.
>
> *Turner v. Murray* 1986, 35

The problem of the bias—if not outright prejudice—of **death-qualified jurors** has troubled courts. Supporters of the death penalty believe that jurors who are opposed to the death penalty can't be impartial in death penalty cases. Opponents of the death penalty believe that jurors who support the death penalty are always biased toward conviction. The U.S. Supreme Court dealt with the issue of a death-qualified jury in *Lockhart v. McCree* (1986).

| CASE | *Are Death-Qualified Juries Impartial?* |

Lockhart v. McCree
476 U.S. 162 (1986)

Ardia McCree was convicted of capital murder. The Arkansas supreme court affirmed. McCree filed a habeas corpus petition. The U.S. District Court for the Eastern District of Arkansas granted the petition. The U.S. Circuit Court for the Eighth Circuit affirmed. On writ of certiorari, the U.S. Supreme Court reversed.

REHNQUIST, J., joined by BURGER, CJ., and WHITE, POWELL, and O'CONNOR, JJ.

FACTS

McCree was charged with capital felony murder. In accordance with Arkansas law, the trial judge at voir dire removed for cause, over McCree's objections, those prospective jurors who stated that they could not under any circumstances vote the imposition of the death penalty. Eight prospective jurors were excluded for this reason. The jury convicted McCree of capital felony murder, but rejected the State's request for the death penalty, instead setting McCree's punishment at life imprisonment without parole.

The District Court held a hearing on the "death qualification" issue in July 1981, receiving in evidence numerous social science studies concerning the attitudes and beliefs of **"Witherspoon-excludables,"** * along with the potential effects of excluding them from the jury prior to the guilt phase of a bifurcated capital trial. In August 1983, the court concluded, based on the social science evidence, that "death qualification" produced juries that "were more prone to convict" capital defendants than "non-death-qualified" juries.

The Eighth Circuit found "substantial evidentiary support" for the District Court's conclusion and affirmed the grant of habeas relief on the ground that such removal for cause violated McCree's constitutional right to a jury selected from a fair cross-section of the community.

OPINION

In the case we address the question, Does the Constitution prohibit the removal for cause, prior to the guilt phase of a bifurcated capital trial, of prospective jurors whose opposition to the death penalty is so strong that it would prevent or substantially impair the performance of their duties as jurors at the sentencing phase of the trial? We hold that it does not.

Of the six studies introduced by McCree that at least purported to deal with the central issue in this case, namely, the potential effects on the determination of guilt or innocence of excluding "Witherspoon-excludables" from the jury, three were also before this Court when it decided *Witherspoon*. There, this Court reviewed the studies and concluded:

> The data adduced by the petitioner ... are too tentative and fragmentary to establish that jurors not opposed to the death penalty tend to favor the prosecution in the determination of guilt. We simply cannot conclude, either on the basis of the record now before us or as a matter of judicial notice, that the exclusion of jurors op-

posed to capital punishment results in an unrepresentative jury on the issue of guilt or substantially increases the risk of conviction. In the light of the presently available information, we are not prepared to announce a per se constitutional rule requiring the reversal of every conviction returned by a jury selected as this one was.

It goes almost without saying that if these studies were "too tentative and fragmentary" to make out a claim of constitutional error in 1968, the same studies, unchanged but for having aged some eighteen years, are still not sufficient to make out such a claim in this case.

Nor do the three post-*Witherspoon* studies introduced by McCree on the "death qualification" issue provide substantial support for the "per se constitutional rule" McCree asks this Court to adopt. All three of the "new" studies were based on the responses of individuals randomly selected from some segment of the population, but who were not actual jurors sworn under oath to apply the law to the facts of an actual case involving the fate of an actual capital defendant. We have serious doubts about the value of these studies in predicting the behavior of actual jurors. In addition, two of the three "new" studies did not even attempt to simulate the process of jury deliberation, and none of the "new" studies was able to predict to what extent, if any, the presence of one or more "Witherspoon-excludables" on a guilt-phase jury would have altered the outcome of the guilt determination.

Finally, and most importantly, only one of the six "death qualification" studies introduced by McCree even attempted to identify and account for the presence of so-called "nullifiers," or individuals who, because of their deep-seated opposition to the death penalty, would be unable to decide a capital defendant's guilt or innocence fairly and impartially.

Having identified some of the more serious problems with McCree's studies, however, we will assume for purposes of this opinion that the studies are both methodologically valid and adequate to establish that "death qualification" in fact produces juries somewhat more "conviction-prone" than "non-death-qualified" juries. We hold, nonetheless, that the Constitution does not prohibit the States from "death qualifying" juries in capital cases.

We have never invoked the fair cross-section principle to invalidate the use of either for-cause or peremptory challenges to prospective jurors, or to require petit juries, as opposed to jury panels or venires, to reflect the composition of the community at large. We remain convinced that an extension of the fair cross-section requirement to petit juries would be unworkable and unsound, and we decline McCree's invitation to adopt such an extension.

---

*Jurors opposed to the death penalty.

The essence of a "fair cross-section" claim is the systematic exclusion of "a 'distinctive' group in the community." In our view, groups defined solely in terms of shared attitudes that would prevent or substantially impair members of the group from performing one of their duties as jurors, such as the "Witherspoon-excludables" at issue here, are not "distinctive groups" for fair cross-section purposes.

Our prior jury-representativeness cases have involved such groups as blacks, women, and Mexican-Americans. The wholesale exclusion of these large groups from jury service clearly contravened the fair cross-section requirement. The exclusion from jury service of large groups of individuals not on the basis of their inability to serve as jurors, but on the basis of some immutable characteristic such as race, gender, or ethnic background, undeniably gave rise to an "appearance of unfairness."

The group of "Witherspoon-excludables" involved in the case at bar differs significantly from the groups we have previously recognized as "distinctive." "Death qualification," unlike the wholesale exclusion of blacks, women, or Mexican-Americans from jury service, is carefully designed to serve the State's concededly legitimate interest in obtaining a single jury that can properly and impartially apply the law to the facts of the case at both the guilt and sentencing phases of a capital trial.

Furthermore, unlike blacks, women, and Mexican-Americans, "Witherspoon-excludables" are singled out for exclusion in capital cases on the basis of an attribute that is within the individual's control. It is important to remember that not all who oppose the death penalty are subject to removal for cause in capital cases; those who firmly believe that the death penalty is unjust may nevertheless serve as jurors in capital cases so long as they state clearly that they are willing to temporarily set aside their own beliefs in deference to the rule of law.

McCree argues that, even if we reject the Eighth Circuit's fair cross-section holding, we should affirm the judgment below on the alternative ground, adopted by the District Court, that "death qualification" violated his constitutional right to an impartial jury. We do not agree. According to McCree, when the State "tips the scales" by excluding prospective jurors with a particular viewpoint, an impermissibly partial jury results. We have consistently rejected this view of jury impartiality, including as recently as last Term when we squarely held that an impartial jury consists of nothing more than "jurors who will conscientiously apply the law and find the facts."

DISSENT

MARSHALL, J., joined by BRENNAN and STEVENS, JJ. The data strongly suggest that death qualification excludes a significantly large subset—at least 11% to 17%—of potential jurors who could be impartial during the guilt phase of trial. Among the members of this excludable class are a disproportionate number of blacks and women.

The perspectives on the criminal justice system of jurors who survive death qualification are systematically different from those of the excluded jurors. Death-qualified jurors are, for example, more likely to believe that a defendant's failure to testify is indicative of his guilt, more hostile to the insanity defense, more distrustful of defense attorneys, and less concerned about the danger of erroneous convictions. This pro-prosecution bias is reflected in the greater readiness of death-qualified jurors to convict or to convict on more serious charges. And, finally, the very process of death qualification—which focuses attention on the death penalty before the trial has even begun—has been found to predispose the jurors that survive it to believe that the defendant is guilty.

The evidence thus confirms, and is itself corroborated by, the more intuitive judgments of scholars and of so many of the participants in capital trials—judges, defense attorneys, and prosecutors. The chief strength of respondent's evidence lies in the essential unanimity of the results obtained by researchers using diverse subjects and varied methodologies. Even the Court's haphazard jabs cannot obscure the power of the array. Faced with the near unanimity of authority supporting respondent's claim that death qualification gives the prosecution a particular advantage in the guilt phase of capital trials, the majority here makes but a weak effort to contest that proposition.

Questions

1. Do death-qualified juries deny defendants fair trials?

2. Is the majority or the dissent "right" in interpreting the statistics?

3. Should juries represent a fair cross section of attitudes in the community? Why? Why not?

4. Why are attitudes different from race, ethnicity, and gender, according to the Court? Should they be? Explain.

5. How would you have decided this case? Defend your decision.

The Right to a Public Trial

Three constitutional Amendments guarantee defendants the right to a public trial:

1. The Sixth Amendment right to confront witnesses
2. The Fifth Amendment due process right
3. The Fourteenth Amendment due process right

Public trials protect two distinct rights:

1. *Public access.* The right of the public to attend the proceedings
2. *Defendants' rights.* The right of defendants to attend their own trials

The right to a public trial extends to "every stage of the trial," including jury selection, communications between judge and jury, jury instructions (judges' explanations of the law to the jury), and in-chamber conversations between judge and jurors. It doesn't include brief conferences at the bench outside the defendant's hearing or other brief conferences involving only questions of law.

Public trials support defendants' interests in avoiding persecution through secret proceedings, enhance community participation in law enforcement, and aid in the search for truth by encouraging witnesses to come forth who otherwise might not. These interests aren't absolute. Courtroom size limits public access. Furthermore, the need to protect threatened witnesses even justifies closing the courtroom. Protecting undercover agents also authorizes exclusion of the public during their testimony. Moreover, public trials may discourage shy and introverted witnesses from coming forward. Finally, judges can limit public access during sensitive proceedings. For example, it's justifiable to exclude spectators while alleged rape victims are testifying about the "lurid details" of the crime (*U.S. ex rel Latimore v. Sielaff* 1977).

Defendants don't have an *absolute* right to attend their own trials; they can forfeit that right by their disruptive behavior. For example, in *Illinois v. Allen* (1970), William Allen, while being tried for armed robbery, repeatedly interrupted the judge in a "most abusive and disrespectful manner." He also threatened him, "When I go out for lunchtime, you're going to be a corpse here." When the judge warned Allen that he could attend only as long as he behaved himself, Allen answered, "There is going to be no proceeding. I'm going to start talking all through the trial. There's not going to be no trial like this." According to the U.S. Supreme Court, the judge properly removed Allen from the courtroom:

> It is essential to the proper administration of criminal justice that dignity, order, and decorum be the hallmarks of all court proceedings in our country. The flagrant disregard in the courtroom of elementary standards of proper conduct should not and cannot be tolerated. We believe that trial judges confronted with disruptive, contumacious, stubbornly defiant defendants must be given sufficient discretion to meet the circumstances of each case. We think there are at least three constitutionally permissible ways for a trial judge to handle an obstreperous defendant like Allen: (1) bind and gag him, thereby keeping him present; (2) cite him for contempt; (3) take him out of the courtroom until he promises to conduct himself properly. (343)

Judges can also exclude defendants from questioning child witnesses in sexual abuse cases. For example, in *Kentucky v. Stincer* (1987), Sergio Stincer was on trial for sodomizing two children, ages 7 and 8. The trial court conducted an in-chambers hearing to determine whether the children could remember certain details and whether they understood the significance of telling the truth in court. The judge permitted his lawyer to attend but refused Stincer's request to do so. The U.S. Supreme Court upheld the judge's ruling because Stincer had an adequate opportunity to "confront" the children during the trial.

Courts can also require dangerous defendants to appear under guard to protect the public, witnesses, and court officials from harm and to prevent defendants from escaping. However, defendants ordinarily have the right not just to *be* at their trial but also to be *presented* in a way that doesn't prejudice their case. For example, the government can't bring defendants to court in jail dress (*Estelle v. Williams* 1976) or make defense witnesses testify in shackles because their dress prejudices the jury, furthers no state policy, and mainly hurts poor defendants (*Holbrook v. Flynn* 1986).

THE STAGES AND RULES OF JURY TRIALS

The adversarial process reaches its high point in the jury trial. Strict, technical rules control trials. The main stages in the criminal trial include:

1. Opening statements, with the prosecution first, followed by the defense
2. Presenting the evidence—the state's and the defendants' cases, including cross-examination
3. Closing arguments
4. Instructions to the jury
5. Jury deliberations
6. Jury verdict
7. Judgment of the court

We'll look at each of these stages and the issues of whether the law requires unanimous verdicts and jury nullification.

Opening Statements

Prosecutors and defense counsel can make **opening statements**—address the jury before they present their evidence. Prosecutors make their opening statements first; defense counsel address the jury either immediately after the prosecutor's opening statement or, in a few jurisdictions, following the presentation of the state's case. The opening statements have a narrow scope: to outline the case that the two sides hope to prove, not to prove the case. Proving the case takes place during the presentation-of-evidence phase of the criminal trial. In fact, it's unprofessional for either side to refer to any evidence they don't honestly believe will be admissible in court. Although it's rare for them to do so, appeals courts sometimes reverse cases in which prosecutors have referred to points they intend to prove with evidence they know is inadmissible, incompetent, or both (LaFave and Israel 1984, 3:12).

Presenting Evidence

The prosecution presents its case first because of its burden to prove defendants' guilt. In presenting its case, the rules of evidence restrict what evidence the state may use, mainly excluding illegally obtained testimony and physical evidence and most hearsay. The prosecution has to prove every element in the case, but the defense frequently *stipulates* (agrees not to contest) some facts, particularly those that might prejudice the defendant's case—detailed photographs and descriptions of a brutally murdered victim, for example. The prosecution can decline a stipulation. Most courts don't compel the prosecution to accept stipulations, because it might weaken the state's case (*People v. McClellan* 1969).

The state ordinarily presents all the available eyewitnesses to the crime. In some instances, if the prosecution doesn't call a material witness, particularly a victim, the defense can ask for a *missing witness instruction*—an instruction that jurors can infer that the witness's testimony would have been unfavorable to the prosecution. The prosecution can ask the court to inform the jury that a key witness is unavailable and not to draw negative inferences from his failure to testify. Prosecutors also may decide not to call witnesses—such as spouses, priests, and doctors—that they know will claim a valid privilege; doing so may result in reversible error (*Bowles v. U.S.* 1970).

Issues that affect the presenting of evidence include cross-examination, the admission of hearsay evidence, compelling witnesses to testify, the prosecutor's burden to prove all elements of a crime, and proof beyond a reasonable doubt.

Cross-Examination

The Sixth Amendment confrontation clause includes the right to cross-examine the prosecution's witnesses. In *Smith v. Illinois* (1968), when the prosecution's key witness, an informant, testified that he bought heroin from Smith, the trial court allowed him to use an alias, concealing his real name and address. The U.S. Supreme Court ruled that this violated Smith's right to confrontation:

> When the credibility of a witness is at issue, the very starting point in "exposing falsehood and bringing out the truth" through cross-examination must necessarily be to ask the witness who he is and where he lives. The witness's name and address open countless avenues of in-court examination and out-of-doors investigation.... It is of the essence of a fair trial that reasonable latitude be given to the cross-examiner, even though he is unable to state to the court what facts a reasonable cross-examination might develop.... To say that prejudice can be established only by showing that the cross-examination, if pursued, would necessarily have brought out facts tending to discredit testimony in chief, is to deny a substantial right and withdraw one of the safeguards essential to a fair trial. (132)

Hearsay Evidence

The confrontation clause also restricts the prosecution's use of **hearsay testimony**—out-of-court statements offered to prove the truth of the statements. Hearsay violates the confrontation clause because defendants can't ferret the truth through the adversarial process unless the defense can cross-examine the witnesses against them. Therefore, the jury can't have an adequate basis for fact-finding.

However, the confrontation clause doesn't bar hearsay testimony absolutely. The prosecution can introduce hearsay if it meets two tests:

1. It demonstrates the witness's unavailability and, hence, the necessity to use out-of-court statements.

2. It shows that the state obtained the evidence under circumstances that clearly establish its reliability.

In *Ohio v. Roberts* (1980), the majority of the Supreme Court found that the state satisfied the tests under these circumstances:

- The witness's mother said the witness, her daughter, had left home, saying she was going to Tucson, two years earlier.

- Shortly thereafter, a San Francisco social worker contacted the mother concerning a welfare claim her daughter had filed there.

- The mother was able to reach her daughter only once, by phone.

- When the daughter called a few months prior to the trial, she told her mother she was traveling but did not reveal her whereabouts.

The dissent argued that relying solely on the parents was not sufficient; the prosecution had the burden to go out and find the witness. The Court disagreed.

Compulsory Process

The Sixth Amendment guarantees the defendant's right "to have **compulsory process** for obtaining witnesses in [his or her] . . . favor. . . ." This means defendants can compel witnesses to come to court to testify for them. Most states pay for poor defendants' process, but they don't pay for process to get evidence that only corroborates (adds to) evidence already available. And, most states make defendants spell out exactly why they need the evidence.

The Burden of Proof

The Fifth Amendment provides that "no person . . . shall be compelled in any criminal case to be a witness against himself. . . ." This means the state can't call defendants to the witness stand in criminal trials. It also prohibits the prosecution from commenting on defendants' refusal to testify; it even entitles defendants to ask judges to instruct juries not to infer guilt from their silence. However, if defendants decide to take the stand to tell their side of the story, the prosecution can cross-examine them as they would any other witness.

The defense doesn't have to present a case; cross-examining the prosecution's witnesses by itself can raise a reasonable doubt about the proof against the defendant. Or, defendants may call their own witnesses for the sole purpose of rebutting the prosecution's witnesses. Of course, they may also call witnesses to create a reasonable doubt about their guilt—to establish alibis, for example. Defendants may also have affirmative defenses that justify or excuse what would otherwise be criminal conduct (self-defense, insanity, duress, and entrapment). Or, maybe they have evidence that reduces the grade of the offense, such as provocation to reduce murder to manslaughter or diminished capacity to reduce first-degree murder to second-degree murder. The prosecution, of course, has the right to cross-examine defense witnesses.

Proof Beyond a Reasonable Doubt

Defendants don't have to prove their innocence or help the government prove their guilt. The right against self-incrimination gives defendants an absolute right to say

TABLE 13.5

Sample of Trial Court Definitions of Proof Beyond a Reasonable Doubt

A doubt that would cause prudent people to hesitate before acting in a matter of importance to themselves

A doubt based on reason and common sense

A doubt that is neither frivolous nor fanciful and that can't be easily explained away

Substantial doubt

Persuasion to a reasonable or moral certainty

Doubt beyond that which is reasonable is about "7½ on a scale of 10" (rejected by the appellate court)

The reasonable doubt standard is met when the "scales of justice are substantially out of equipoise" (rejected by the appellate court)

---

nothing at all and not have it count against them. So, trials can proceed, and some do, where neither defendants nor their lawyers present a case. Sometimes, no defense is the best defense. The government, on the other hand, carries the whole burden to prove defendants are guilty beyond a reasonable doubt.

The U.S. Supreme Court ruled, in *In re Winship* (1970), that due process requires both federal and state prosecutors to prove every element of a crime beyond a reasonable doubt:

> The reasonable doubt standard is bottomed on a fundamental value determination of our society that it is far worse to convict an innocent man than to let a guilty man go free. [Two propositions cannot be disputed:] First, in a judicial proceeding in which there is a dispute about the facts of some earlier event, the factfinder cannot acquire unassailably accurate knowledge of what happened. Instead, all the factfinder can acquire is a belief of what probably happened. The intensity of this belief—the degree to which a factfinder is convinced that a given act actually occurred—can, of course, vary. In this regard, a standard of proof represents an attempt to instruct the factfinder concerning the degree of confidence our society thinks he should have in the correctness of factual conclusions for a particular type of adjudication. Although the phrases "preponderance of the evidence" and "proof beyond a reasonable doubt" are quantitatively imprecise, they do communicate to the finder of fact different notions concerning the degree of confidence he is expected to have in the correctness of his factual conclusions. (373)

Despite the constitutional requirement of proof beyond a reasonable doubt, the U.S. Supreme Court hasn't decided that due process requires judges to define proof beyond a reasonable doubt. Nevertheless, courts struggle to tell jurors what reasonable doubt means; Table 13.5 provides some examples of court definitions.

Closing Arguments

When they've presented their evidence, both the state and the defense make their closing arguments. Prosecutors close first, the defense follows, and then the prosecution rebuts. Prosecutors can't waive their right to make a closing argument and save their remarks for rebuttal. If they waive their right to make a closing argument, they're automatically barred from making a rebuttal. Prosecutors can't raise "new" matters in rebuttal either: they can only rebut what either they or the defense counsel brought up during closing arguments. Why? It's only fair that the defense should hear all the arguments in favor of conviction before responding to them.

Formally, prosecutors have the duty not only to convict criminals but also to seek justice. The American Bar Association's Standard for Criminal Justice (1980, § 3.5) includes the following guidelines for prosecutors. It is improper to

- Misstate intentionally the evidence or mislead the jury
- Refer to evidence excluded or not introduced at trial
- Express personal beliefs or opinions about the truth or falsity of the evidence or the defendant's guilt
- Engage in arguments that divert jurors' attention by injecting issues beyond the case or predicting consequences of the jury's verdict
- Make arguments calculated to inflame jurors' passions and prejudices

However, violating these standards rarely results in reversal: "If every remark made by counsel outside of the testimony were grounds for a reversal, comparatively few verdicts would stand, since in the ardor of advocacy, and in the excitement of the trial, even the most experienced counsel are occasionally carried away by this temptation" (*Dunlop v. U.S.* 1897).

When determining whether to reverse convictions based on improper closing arguments, appellate courts consider whether:

1. Defense counsel invited or provoked the remarks.
2. Defense counsel made timely objection to the remarks.
3. The trial judge took corrective action, such as instructing the jury to disregard the remarks.
4. The comments were brief and isolated in an otherwise proper argument.
5. Other errors occurred during the trial.
6. The evidence of guilt was overwhelming. (LaFave and Israel 1984, 3:15)

Although appellate courts rarely reverse convictions for these abuses, they frequently express their displeasure with prosecutors' improper remarks made during closing arguments. In *Bowen v. Kemp* (1985), Charlie Bowen was convicted of raping and murdering a 12-year-old girl. The prosecutor, in the course of the closing statement, made several comments focusing on the accused:

> And now we come up here with this idea that a man ... is subject to be rehabilitated and released back into society. Yeah, I guess he can be rehabilitated. Hitler could have been. I believe in about six or eight months if I'd had him chained to a wall and talked to him and beat him on one side of the head for a while with a stick telling him you believe this don't you then beat him on the other side with a stick telling him you believe that don't you I believe I could have rehabilitated Hitler. (678)

The prosecutor went on to call Bowen "a product of the devil," a "liar," who was "no better than a beast." And,

> You know for a criminal to go without proper punishment is a disgrace to the society we live in and it's shown to us every day by the fruits that we reap from day to day in our society when we have the bloody deeds such as this occur. (680)

Bowen appealed his conviction on the basis that the prosecutor's remarks affected the jury's verdict. While conceding that the remarks were improper, the circuit court of appeals affirmed the conviction. It found "no reasonable probability that, absent the improper statements of opinion, Bowen would not have been sentenced to death" (682).

Jury Instructions

Before jurors begin their deliberations, judges "instruct" them on what the law is and how they should apply it. Jury instructions usually inform the jury about the following subjects:

1. The respective roles of the judge to decide the law and the jury to decide the facts
2. The principle that defendants are presumed innocent until proven guilty
3. The principle that the state bears the burden of proving guilt beyond a reasonable doubt
4. The definition of all the elements of the crime with which the defendant is charged
5. Jury room procedures

Both the prosecution and the defense can ask the judge to provide the jury with specific instructions. And, they can object if the judge refuses to give the requested instruction and frequently do base appeals on such refusals. A number of jurisdictions use **pattern instructions**—published boilerplate instructions that fit most cases. Supporters praise the clarity, accuracy, impartiality, and efficiency of pattern instructions; critics say they're too general to help jurors. However, most empirical evaluations show that jurors understand only about half of judges' instructions, whether patterned or individually crafted (LaFave and Israel 3:39–40).

Jury Deliberations

After the judge instructs the jury, she orders them to retire to a separate room under supervision and without interruption to deliberate together until they reach a verdict. The jurors take the instructions, any exhibits received in evidence, and a list of the charges against the defendant with them into the jury room. During the course of their deliberations, they may ask the court for further instruction or information concerning the evidence or any other matter. The court can discharge *hung juries*—juries unable to reach a verdict after protracted deliberations.

Juries can return one of three verdicts:

1. Guilty
2. Not guilty
3. Special, mainly related to insanity or capital punishment

If the jury *acquits*, or issues the not guilty verdict, the defendants' ordeal with the criminal process stops immediately; they're free to go. If the jury convicts, the case continues to **judgment**—the court's final decision on the legal outcome of the case. Juries

TABLE 13.6
Arguments for Unanimous Verdicts

They instill confidence in the criminal justice process.

They guarantee that the jury carefully reviews the evidence.

They ensure the hearing and consideration of minority viewpoints.

They prevent government oppression.

They support the principle that convicting innocent defendants is worse than freeing guilty ones.

They fulfill the proof-beyond-a-reasonable-doubt requirement. (LaFave and Israel 1984, 698)

can't pass legal judgment; their word is final only as to the facts. Following the court's judgment of guilt or acquittal, the criminal trial ends.

The "Unanimous Verdict" Requirement

Like twelve-member juries (discussed earlier), unanimous verdicts are an ancient requirement and still enjoy strong support (Table 13.6). In 1900, the U.S. Supreme Court held that the Sixth Amendment demanded conviction by unanimous jury verdicts. The Court changed its mind in 1972 when it ruled in *Apodaca v. Oregon* that verdicts of 11–1 and 10–2 didn't violate two convicted felons' right to a jury trial:

> A requirement of unanimity...does not materially contribute to...[the jury's] common-sense judgment....A jury will come to such a verdict as long as it consists of a group of laymen representative of a cross section of the community who have the duty and the opportunity to deliberate, free from outside attempts at intimidation, on the question of a defendant's guilt. In terms of this function we perceive no difference between juries required to act unanimously and those permitted to convict or acquit by votes of 10 to two or 11 to one. Requiring unanimity would obviously produce hung juries in some situations where nonunanimous juries will convict or acquit. But in either case, the interest of the defendant in having the judgment of his peers interposed between himself and the officers of the state who prosecute and judge him is equally well served. (411)

In *Johnson v. Louisiana* (1972), in upholding a robbery conviction based on a 9–3 verdict, Justice Byron R. White wrote:

> Nine jurors—a substantial majority of the jury—were convinced by the evidence. Disagreement of the three jurors does not alone establish reasonable doubt, particularly when such a heavy majority of the jury, after having considered the dissenters' views, remains convinced of guilt. (362)

Still, the Supreme Court hasn't answered the question of how many votes short of unanimity are required to satisfy the Sixth Amendment.

What about less than unanimous verdicts by fewer than twelve-member juries? A unanimous U.S. Supreme Court in *Burch v. Louisiana* (1979) struck down a Louisiana statute providing that misdemeanors punishable by more than six months "shall be tried before a jury of six persons, five of whom must concur to render a verdict." According to the Court, to preserve the right to jury trial, it had to draw a line at non-unanimous verdicts of six-member juries—a line supported by the "near-uniform judgment of the nation" (only two other states had permitted these verdicts).

Jury Nullification

The jury's function is to decide the facts in a case and apply them to the law as the judge has defined the law. Nevertheless, juries have the power to acquit even when the facts clearly fit the law. Jury acquittals are final, meaning the prosecution can't appeal them. The practice of acquitting in the face of proof beyond a reasonable doubt is called **jury nullification.** Why do juries nullify? Usually, it's either because they sympathize with particular defendants (mercy killing) or because the state has prosecuted defendants for breaking unpopular laws (possession of small amounts of marijuana for personal use).

Jury nullification has an ancient lineage. The "pages of history shine on instances of the jury's exercise of its prerogative to disregard uncontradicted evidence and instructions of the judge." In the famous John Peter Zenger case (*New York v. Zenger* 1735), the jury ignored the facts and the judge's instructions and acquitted Zenger of the charge of sedition (LaFave and Israel 1984, 3:700). The U.S. Supreme Court has indirectly approved jury nullification. Although the Court obviously didn't like the jury's power, it conceded in *Sparf & Hansen v. U.S.* (1895):

> If a jury may rightfully disregard the direction of the court in matters of law and determine for themselves what the law is in the particular case before them, it is difficult to perceive any legal ground upon which a verdict of conviction can be set aside by the court as being against law. (101)

Nullification promotes (probably more than any other doctrine in criminal procedure we've studied) the interest in community participation in criminal law enforcement. As community representatives, juries act as safety valves in exceptional cases by allowing "informal communication from the total culture" to override the strict legal bonds of their instructions from the judge (*U.S. v. Dougherty* 1972).

 Go to Exercise 13-3 on the Criminal Procedure 6e CD to learn more about your state's trial procedures.

CONVICTION BY GUILTY PLEA

There are two types of guilty plea: (1) straight pleas and (2) negotiated pleas. **Straight guilty pleas** (pleading guilty without negotiation) are ordinarily made in what are called **"dead bang" cases,** meaning proof of guilt is overwhelming. **Negotiated pleas** (pleading guilty in exchange for concessions by the state) appear mainly in large urban courts. They arise when the state's case is weak, defendants have a strong defense, and/or they can gain the jury's sympathy. Although widely used for more than a century, negotiated pleas weren't formally recognized by courts until 1970. In that year, in *Brady v. United States,* the U.S. Supreme Court ruled that bargained pleas are constitutional. According to the U.S. Supreme Court, "the chief virtues of the plea system are speed, economy, and finality."

Whatever might be the situation in an ideal world, plea bargaining and guilty pleas are important (and can be beneficial) parts of our criminal justice system:

The defendant avoids lengthy incarceration and the anxieties and uncertainties of a trial; he gains a speedy disposition of his case, the chance to acknowledge his guilt, and a prompt start in realizing whatever potential there may be for rehabilitation. Judges and prosecutors conserve vital and scarce resources. The public is protected from the risks posed by those charged with criminal offense who are at large on bail while awaiting completion of criminal proceedings.

Blackledge v. Allison 1977, 71

Let's look further at the debate over plea bargaining and how guilty pleas impact defendants' Constitutional rights.

The Debate over Conviction by Guilty Plea

The arguments for and against conviction by guilty plea are heated, complex, and by no means empirically resolved. Some say negotiation better serves the search for truth; others argue the adversarial process best serves the ends of justice. Some maintain guilty pleas save time; others contend plea negotiations more than make up for the time it takes to go to trial. Some insist the criminal justice system would collapse under its own weight if only a few of the now vast majority of defendants who plead guilty asserted their right to trial; others contend banning plea bargaining would make little difference in how many defendants plead guilty. Some maintain the guilty plea intimidates the innocent and emboldens the guilty; others say outcomes between jury trials and guilty pleas don't differ all that much. The public and police officers oppose plea bargaining, because they believe it "lets criminals off"; however, the available empirical data don't resolve these questions.

The Constitution and Guilty Pleas

The social scientists and policy makers may not have resolved the empirical and policy questions surrounding conviction by plea, but the U.S. Supreme Court has settled the question of its constitutionality. When they plead guilty, defendants **waive** (give up) three constitutional rights:

1. The Fifth Amendment right to remain silent
2. The Sixth Amendment right to a trial by jury
3. The Sixth Amendment right to confront the witnesses against them

To give up these constitutional rights, defendants have to do so knowingly (also called intelligently) *and* voluntarily. According to the Court:

The criminal justice system enforces a minimum requirement that [a defendant's] plea be the voluntary expression of his own choice. But the plea is more than an admission of past conduct; it is the defendant's consent that judgment of conviction may be entered without a trial—a waiver of his right to trial before a jury or a judge. Waivers of constitutional rights not only must be voluntary but must be knowing, intelligent acts done with sufficient awareness of the relevant circumstances and likely consequences.

Brady v. U.S. 1970, 748

It's up to trial judges to make sure defendants pleas are voluntary *and* knowing. The Supreme Court has established the following standard for trial judges' inquiries:

A plea of guilty entered by one fully aware of the direct consequences, including the actual value of any commitments made to him by the court, prosecutor, or his own counsel, must stand unless induced by threats (or promises to discontinue improper harassment), misrepresentation (including unfulfilled or unfulfillable promises), or perhaps by promises that are by their nature improper as having no prior relationship to the prosecutor's business (e.g., bribes). (756)

The Supreme Court has held that a trial judge's failure to ask defendants questions concerning their plea is **reversible error**—grounds to reverse the trial court's judgment of guilt. Why? Because the trial court accepted the plea "without an affirmative showing that it was intelligent and voluntary" (*Boykin v. Alabama* 1969). A court can't presume that defendants give up fundamental rights by pleading guilty "from a silent record." Judges have to make clear to defendants when they plead guilty that they're giving up their rights to trial (Sixth Amendment), to confrontation (Sixth Amendment), and not to incriminate themselves (Fifth Amendment).

According to the Court, defendants have to know "the true nature of the charges" against them. For example, in one case, the defendant pleaded guilty to second-degree murder without knowing the elements of the crime. Neither his lawyer nor the trial judge had explained to him that second-degree murder required an intent to kill and that his version of what he did negated intent. The U.S. Supreme Court ruled that the record didn't establish a knowing plea. Most jurisdictions now require that judges determine that there's a **factual basis** for guilty pleas. To determine the factual basis, for example, judges might ask defendants to describe the conduct that led to the charges, ask prosecutor and defense attorneys similar questions, and consult presentence reports (*North Carolina v. Alford* 1970).

Brady v. U.S. (1970) established that guilty pleas aren't automatically involuntary but left it to lower courts to decide on a case-by-case basis whether the totality of circumstances shows that defendants voluntarily and knowingly pleaded guilty. What about defendants who are **factually innocent** (they didn't commit the crime) but **legally guilty** (the government has enough evidence to convict them) who plead guilty because they don't want to take the chance that by going to trial they'll get a harsher sentence than they can get by pleading guilty? Is their plea voluntary and knowing? The U.S. Supreme Court answered this question in *North Carolina v. Alford* (1970).

Was His Plea Voluntary?

North Carolina v. Alford
400 U.S. 25 (1970)

Henry Alford was indicted for the capital offense of first-degree murder. North Carolina law provided for three possible punishments for murder: (1) life imprisonment when a plea of guilty was accepted for first-degree murder; (2) death following a jury verdict of guilty of first-degree murder unless the jury recommended life imprisonment (3) two to thirty years' imprisonment for second-degree murder. Alford's attorney recommended that Alford plead guilty to second-degree murder, which the prosecutor accepted. Alford pleaded guilty and was sentenced to 30 years in prison. On writ of habeas corpus, the U.S. Court of Appeals found Alford's plea involuntary. On writ of certiorari, the U.S. Supreme Court reversed.

WHITE, J., joined by BURGER, CJ., and HARLAN, STEWART, and BLACKMUN, JJ.

FACTS

On December 2, 1963, Alford was indicted for first-degree murder, a capital offense under North Carolina law. The court appointed an attorney to represent him, and this attorney questioned all but one of the various witnesses who appellee said would substantiate his claim of innocence. The witnesses, however, did not support Alford's story but gave statements that strongly indicated his guilt. Faced with strong evidence of guilt and no substantial evidentiary support for the claim of innocence, Alford's attorney recommended that he plead guilty, but left the ultimate decision to Alford himself. The prosecutor agreed to accept a plea of guilty to a charge of second-degree murder, and on December 10, 1963, Alford pleaded guilty to the reduced charge.

Before the plea was finally accepted by the trial court, the court heard the sworn testimony of a police officer who summarized the State's case. Two other witnesses besides Alford were also heard. Although there was no eyewitness to the crime, the testimony indicated that shortly before the killing Alford took his gun from his house, stated his intention to kill the victim and returned home with the declaration that he had carried out the killing.

After the summary presentation of the State's case, Alford took the stand and testified that he had not committed the murder but that he was pleading guilty because he faced the threat of the death penalty if he did not do so. In response to the questions of his counsel, he acknowledged that his counsel had informed him of the difference between second- and first-degree murder and of his rights in case he chose to go to trial.

The trial court then asked Alford if, in light of his denial of guilt, he still desired to plead guilty to second-degree murder and appellee answered, "Yes, sir. I plead guilty on—from the circumstances that he [Alford's attorney] told me." After eliciting information about Alford's prior criminal record, which was a long one, the trial court sentenced him to 30 years' imprisonment, the maximum penalty for second-degree murder.

After giving his version of the events of the night of the murder, Alford stated: "I pleaded guilty on second degree murder because they said there is too much evidence, but I ain't shot no man, but I take the fault for the other man. We never had an argument in our life and I just pleaded

guilty because they said if I didn't they would gas me for it, and that is all."

In response to questions from his attorney, Alford affirmed that he had consulted several times with his attorney and with members of his family and had been informed of his rights if he chose to plead not guilty. Alford then reaffirmed his decision to plead guilty to second-degree murder:

Q: [by Alford's attorney] And you authorized me to tender a plea of guilty to second degree murder before the court?

A: Yes, sir.

Q: And in doing that, you have again affirmed your decision on that point?

A: Well, I'm still pleading that you all got me to plead guilty. I plead the other way, circumstantial evidence; that the jury will prosecute me on—on the second. You told me to plead guilty, right. I don't—I'm not guilty but I plead guilty.

On appeal, a divided panel of the Court of Appeals for the Fourth Circuit reversed on the ground that Alford's guilty plea was made involuntarily.

OPINION

The standard [for determining the validity of a quality plea is] whether the plea represents a voluntary and intelligent choice among the alternative courses of action open to the defendant. Ordinarily, a judgment of conviction resting on a plea of guilty is justified by the defendant's admission that he committed the crime charged against him and his consent that judgment be entered without a trial of any kind. The plea usually subsumes both elements, and justifiably so, even though there is no separate, express admission by the defendant that he committed the particular acts claimed to constitute the crime charged in the indictment. Here Alford entered his plea but accompanied it with the statement that he had not shot the victim. . . .

While most pleas of guilty consist of both a waiver of trial and an express admission of guilt, the latter element is not a constitutional requisite to the imposition of criminal penalty. An individual accused of crime may voluntarily, knowingly, and understandably consent to the imposition of a prison sentence even if he is unwilling or unable to admit his participation in the acts constituting the crime.

Nor can we perceive any material difference between a plea that refuses to admit commission of the criminal act and a plea containing a protestation of innocence when, as in the instant case, a defendant intelligently concludes that his interests require entry of a guilty plea and the record before the judge contains strong evidence of actual guilt. Here the State had a strong case of first-degree murder against Alford. Whether he realized or disbelieved his guilt, he insisted on his plea because in his view he had absolutely nothing to gain by a trial and much to gain by pleading. Because of the overwhelming evidence against him, a trial was precisely what neither Alford nor his attorney desired.

Confronted with the choice between a trial for first-degree murder, on the one hand, and a plea of guilty to second-degree murder, on the other, Alford quite reasonably chose the latter and thereby limited the maximum penalty to a 30-year term. When his plea is viewed in light of the evidence against him, which substantially negated his claim of innocence and which further provided a means by which the judge could test whether the plea was being intelligently entered, its validity cannot be seriously questioned. In view of the strong factual basis for the plea demonstrated by the State and Alford's clearly expressed desire to enter it despite his professed belief in his innocence, we hold that the trial judge did not commit constitutional error in accepting it.

Alford now argues in effect that the State should not have allowed him this choice but should have insisted on proving him guilty of murder in the first degree. The States in their wisdom may take this course by statute or otherwise and may prohibit the practice of accepting pleas to lesser included offenses under any circumstances. But this is not the mandate of the Fourteenth Amendment and the Bill of Rights. The prohibitions against involuntary or unintelligent pleas should not be relaxed, but neither should an exercise in arid logic render those constitutional guarantees counterproductive and put in jeopardy the very human values they were meant to preserve.

The Court of Appeals judgment directing the issuance of the writ of habeas corpus is vacated and the case is REMANDED to the Court of Appeals for further proceedings consistent with this opinion. It is so ordered.

DISSENT

BRENNAN, J., joined by DOUGLAS and MARSHALL, JJ. Last Term, this Court held, over my dissent, that a plea of guilty may validly be induced by an unconstitutional threat to subject the defendant to the risk to death, so long as the plea is entered in open court and the defendant is represented by competent counsel who is aware of the threat, albeit not of its unconstitutionality. *Brady v. United States,* 397 U.S. 742, 745–758 (1970). Today the Court makes clear that its previous holding was intended to apply even when the record demonstrates that the actual effect of the unconstitutional threat was to induce a guilty plea from a defendant who was unwilling to admit his guilt.

I adhere to the view that, in any given case, the influence of such an unconstitutional threat must necessarily be given weight in determining the voluntariness of a plea....I believe that at the very least such a denial of guilt is...a relevant factor in determining whether the plea was voluntarily and intelligently made. With these factors in mind, it is sufficient in my view to state that the facts set out in the majority opinion demonstrate that Alford was "so gripped by fear of the death penalty" that his decision to plead guilty was not voluntary but was "the product of duress as much so as choice reflecting physical constraint."

Questions

1. Did Henry Alford knowingly and voluntarily plead guilty?

2. Consider the dissent's comment that Henry Alford was "so gripped by fear of the death penalty" that his decision was "the product of duress." Should defendants ever be allowed to plead guilty if they believe they're innocent? Why? Why not? Back up your answer with arguments from the majority and dissenting opinions.

SUMMARY

    I. After the decision to charge

        A. Court proceedings divided into

            1. Adversarial proceedings inside the courtroom

            2. Informal negotiation outside the courtroom

        B. Chapter examines what happens during the pretrial, the trial, and conviction phases of court proceedings

1. Testing the government's case
2. Arraignment
3. Pretrial motions
4. Jury trial convictions
5. The stages of a jury trial
6. Convictions by guilty pleas

II. Testing the government's case
A. After decision to charge, the case moves from the prosecutor's office to the court
B. Two procedures to test the government's case (determine whether there's enough evidence to go to trial)
1. Preliminary hearing
a. Is public
b. Tests both government and defense cases (not a minitrial)
c. The judge presides
d. The judge decides whether the government's case passes the test (bind-over)
2. Grand jury review
a. Is secret
b. Hears only government's case
c. The prosecutor presides
d. Grand jurors decide whether the government's case passes the test (indictment)
e. Membership requirements
(1) U.S. citizens over 18
(2) Jurisdiction resident
(3) No felony convictions
(4) Speak, read, and write English
(5) No physical impairments to hinder participation (hearing, vision)

III. Arraignment
A. Brings defendants to court to hear *and* answer (plead to) charges
B. Four possible pleas (answers)
1. Not guilty
2. Not guilty by reason of insanity
3. Nolo contendere (no contest)
4. Guilty

IV. Pretrial motions
A. Decide questions before trial that don't require a trial to answer
B. Double jeopardy (Fifth Amendment bans it)
1. Interests protected
a. Government
(1) Allows one fair shot to convict
(2) Finality—promotes closure
(3) Reduces costs that multiple trials would lead to
b. Defendants
(1) Limits the government's advantage of greater resources
(2) Reduces prolonged stress that multiple trials would lead to

(3) Finality—acquittals can't be overturned

(4) Reduces costs that multiple trials would lead to

2. Jeopardy begins

a. Jury trial—when the jury is sworn in

b. Bench trial (by judge without jury)—when the judge begins to hear evidence

3. Double jeopardy doesn't prevent a second prosecution if

a. The judge grants the *defendant's* motion to dismiss

b. The judge dismisses or orders a mistrial to "serve the ends of justice"—(hung jury)

C. A speedy trial (Sixth Amendment requirement)

1. Begins when the government formally charges suspects

2. Bans only *undue* delays

3. The balancing test

a. Length of the delay

b. Reason for the delay

c. Defendant's assertion of right to a speedy trial

d. Prejudice (harm) the delay causes to the defendant's case

4. Consequences of undue delay

a. Dismissal without prejudice—allows new prosecution

b. Dismissal with prejudice—bars new prosecution

5. The Federal Speedy Trial Act

a. Prosecution has to begin 30 days after arrest (60 if no grand jury in session)

b. Arraignment has to take place 10 days after indictment or information

c. The trial has to begin within 60 days of arraignment

D. Change of venue

1. Motion waives the defendant's Sixth Amendment right to trial in the district where the crime was committed

2. Only defendants can file a motion to change venue

3. Interests protected

a. The defendant's right to a fair and impartial trial

b. The community's interest in administering justice where the crime was committed

4. Tests for granting motions to change venue because of harmful publicity

a. Reasonable-likelihood-of-prejudice test balances (minority of courts)

(1) The kind and amount of bias

(2) The size of the community where juries are selected

(3) The details and seriousness of the offense

(4) The status of the victim and the accused

b. Actual prejudice test requires proof jurors were *in fact* (not just reasonably likely to have been) prejudiced by harmful publicity (majority of courts)

E. Motion to suppress

1. An inquiry regarding the exclusionary rule (Chapter 10) triggers the motion

2. Exclusion is a legal question decided by judges

V. Conviction by jury trial
  A. The Constitution creates a right to trial by jury
    1. Protects the right in *all* crimes
    2. Except "petty offenses"—moral seriousness standard
  B. Twelve-member requirement
    1. No constitutional right to a twelve-member jury
      a. Two elements of constitutional test
        (1) Are there enough jurors to find the truth?
        (2) Are there enough to allow community participation in decision making?
      b. U.S. Supreme Court: five jurors aren't enough (*Ballew v. Georgia* 1978)
    2. Jury selection: Federal Jury Selection Act is followed in most states
      a. Random selection from a "fair cross section of community"
      b. No exclusions based on "race, color, religion, sex, national origin, or economic status"
      c. Jury list sources: local census reports, tax rolls, city directories, telephone books, and driver's license lists
    3. Selecting jurors from the jury panel (voir dire)
      a. Peremptory challenges (striking without having to give a reason)—limited by statute
      b. Challenges for cause (striking biased jurors)—unlimited number
      c. Prospective jurors in death penalty cases can be struck for cause if they're opposed to the death penalty
  C. The right to a public trial
    1. Rights involved
      a. The right of public access
      b. The right of defendants to attend their own trials
    2. Defendants' rights aren't absolute
      a. Their appearance has to comport with the dignity of the proceedings
      b. They can't be disruptive
    3. The right applies to all stages of a trial (see D. 1–7)
  D. The stages and rules of jury trials
    1. Opening statements
    2. Presenting evidence (first state, then defendant)
      a. State
        (1) Presents first
        (2) Presents admissible evidence to prove guilt beyond a reasonable doubt
      b. Defendant
        (1) Presents after the state
        (2) Raises a reasonable doubt of guilt
    3. Closing arguments
      a. Prosecutors first, defense next, finally prosecution rebuts
      b. Appellate courts frequently express disapproval of prosecutors' "improper" remarks
      c. Appellate courts rarely reverse for improper remarks by prosecutors

4. Instructing the jury
    a. Juries decide facts; the judge decides the law
    b. Principles
        (1) Defendants are innocent until proven guilty
        (2) The state has burden to prove guilt beyond a reasonable doubt
    c. Defines all the elements of the crime the prosecution has to prove
    d. Jury room procedures
5. Jury deliberations
6. Jury verdict
    a. Types—guilty, not guilty, special (insanity, capital punishment)
    b. No constitutional requirement for a unanimous verdict (11–1, 10–2, 9–3 OK)
7. Judgment of the court
E. Jury nullification
    1. Juries nullify the law when they acquit defendants even though they believe they're guilty beyond a reasonable doubt
    2. Reflects a community role as a safety valve to relax the law's rigidity and provide justice in individual cases

VI. Conviction by guilty plea
    A. Two types
        1. Straight—pleading guilty without concessions
        2. Negotiated—pleading guilty after getting concessions through negotiation
    B. The debate
        1. Empirical studies don't answer questions of accuracy, need, and fairness of pleas
        2. U.S. Supreme Court decided guilty pleas and plea bargaining are constitutional
    C. Constitutional requirements
        1. Pleas must be voluntary *and* knowing
        2. Judges must determine there's a factual basis for the plea
        3. Courts can accept guilty pleas from defendants even if they maintain their innocence

 Go to the Criminal Procedure 6e CD to download this summary outline. The outline has been formatted so that you can add notes to it during class lectures, or later create a customized chapter outline to use while reviewing. Either way, the summary outline will help you understand the "big picture" and fill in the details as you study.

REVIEW QUESTIONS

1. List and describe the differences between testing the government's case by grand jury review and by preliminary hearing.

2. Identify the four possible pleas defendants can enter at their arraignment.

3. Describe and explain the significance of the U.S. Supreme Court decisions in *Heath v. Alabama* and *Ciucci v. Illinois*.

4. According to the Federal Speedy Trial Act, when does the government have to begin prosecution? arraign defendants? bring defendants to trial?

5. Summarize the arguments against changes of venue.

6. Describe and summarize the significance of the U.S. Supreme Court decision in *Sheppard v. Maxwell.*

7. What kind of question is answered by the motion to suppress evidence?

8. Contrast conviction by trial with conviction by guilty plea.

9. Identify five sources most jurisdictions use to draw up jury lists, and list six reasons jurors give to be excused from jury service. Why do most courts accept their excuses?

10. Explain the difference between peremptory challenges and challenges for cause.

11. Summarize the controversy over death-qualified jurors.

12. List and briefly summarize the stages in the criminal trial.

13. Describe and explain the significance of the U.S. Supreme Court case of *In re Winship.*

14. What's the difference between the jury's verdict and the judgment of the court?

15. Describe and explain the significance of the U.S. Supreme Court decisions in *Apodaca v. Oregon* and *Johnson v. Louisiana.*

16. Explain the difference between straight and negotiated guilty pleas.

17. Summarize the arguments for and against plea bargaining.

18. List three constitutional rights defendants waive when they plead guilty.

19. Explain how a defendant can be factually innocent but legally guilty.

20. Describe and explain the significance of the U.S. Supreme Court decision in *Brady v. U.S.*

KEY TERMS

testing the government's case p. 461
criminal information p. 462
preliminary hearing p. 462
indictment p. 462
grand jury review p. 462
true bill p. 462
bind over p. 462
grand jurors p. 462
ex parte proceedings p. 462
bind-over standard p. 463
probable cause to bind over p. 463
prima facie case rule p. 463

directed verdict rule p. 463
grand jury shield function p. 464
purging the grand jury p. 464
charge the grand jury p. 464
grand jury targets p. 465
hand up the indictment p. 465
no-bills p. 465
arraignment p. 466
nolo contendere p. 467
pretrial motions p. 467
double jeopardy p. 467
bench trials p. 468
manifest necessity doctrine p. 468

hung jury p. 468
dual sovereignty doctrine p. 469
statutes of limitations p. 471
prejudice p. 471
dismissal without prejudice p. 471
dismissal with prejudice p. 471
Federal Speedy Trial Act p. 471
venue p. 472
reasonable-likelihood-of-prejudice test p. 473
actual prejudice test p. 473
motion to suppress evidence p. 474

THE COMPANION WEB SITE
FOR *CRIMINAL PROCEDURE,* SIXTH EDITION

http://cj.wadsworth.com/samaha/crim_pro6e

Supplement your review of this chapter by going to the companion Web site to take one of the Tutorial Quizzes, use the flash cards to test yourself on the key terms from each chapter, and check out the many other study aids you'll find there. You'll find valuable data and resources at your fingertips to help you study for that big exam or write that important paper.

After Conviction

14

Chapter Main Points

- After conviction, the presumption of innocence enjoyed by defendants shifts to a strong presumption of guilt against offenders.
- Retribution aims at punishing past crimes; deterrence looks ahead to preventing future crimes.
- The history of sentencing is a pendulum swing between fitting sentences to punish crimes and tailoring sentences to suit offenders.
- Empirical evaluations suggest that mandatory minimum sentences, in practice, aren't as effective as their supporters hoped they'd be.
- The U.S. Supreme Court has ruled that death sentences aren't "cruel and unusual punishment."
- There's no *constitutional* right to appeal a conviction.
- There's an extremely limited right to attack a conviction indirectly by habeas corpus.

Ms. Rivera carried one pound of cocaine owned by a New York dealer and delivered it to a buyer in Providence, Rhode Island. She was caught and convicted of "transporting with intent to distribute" the cocaine. The U.S. Sentencing Guidelines provide a sentence of 33 to 41 months' imprisonment for first-time offenders. Ms. Rivera argued to the U.S. District Court that it should depart downward from this Guidelines sentence because: First, she has three small children, ages three, five, and six, who need a mother's care. Second, she has to live solely on welfare without any financial aid from her former husband. Third, she has virtually no contact with any other family member (except for a sister, with five children, also on welfare). Fourth, she's never before engaged in any criminal activity. Finally, she committed this single offense because of an "unwise wish" to get money for Christmas presents for her children.

U.S. v. Rivera (1993), First Circuit U.S. Court of Appeals

PROCEDURES AFTER CONVICTION

After conviction defendants become "offenders." You might think this is just a change of words. But you'd be wrong. It's a dramatic shift in status with grave consequences. In court *before* conviction, the shield of constitutional rights protects defendants by the presumption of innocence and all that goes with it (Chapters 12 and 13). *After* conviction, a very tough to overcome presumption of guilt rules the day. Convicted offenders have some rights after conviction, but they're greatly shrunken. Due process limits the power to sentence only to a very small degree. There's no constitutional right to appeal. And, the right of **habeas corpus**—a civil action to determine if the offender is being lawfully detained—is extremely limited.

There's a powerful assumption (not necessarily backed up by reality) that the state and defendants have had one shot at justice, and that's enough. Why? Because there's a further assumption that both sides have had a *fair* shot. Lots of time, energy, and money are devoted to deciding guilt. For their part, prosecutors have enormous resources at their command—the whole law enforcement machinery—to help them make their case. To offset the state's advantage, defendants are shielded by an array of constitutional rights (we've examined them in every chapter). After that fair shot, the assumption is we're wasting time, money, and energy to climb up, first, the ladder of appeals and then up a second ladder of **collateral attack** (habeas corpus review of convictions by offenders in a separate civil action) to decide if offenders are being lawfully detained. As in all things (even the pursuit of justice), there comes a time to call it quits and move on—for the state, to fighting other crimes, and for offenders, to paying for their crimes, putting their lives together, and getting back into society as productive members of their community.

Let's look now at the three main procedures that take place after conviction:

1. Sentencing
2. Appeal
3. Collateral attack (habeas corpus)

SENTENCING

For more than a thousand years, policy makers have debated whether to fit sentences to the crime or to tailor sentences to suit the criminal. As early as 700 A.D., the Roman Catholic Church's penitential books revealed a tension between prescribing penance strictly according to the sin and tailoring it to suit individual sinners. **Determinate, or fixed, sentencing** (fitting punishment to the crime) puts sentencing authority in the hands of legislators. **Indeterminate sentencing** (tailoring punishment to suit the criminal) puts the power to sentence in the hands of judges and parole boards.

Like the ancient tension between fixed and indeterminate sentencing, there's an ancient debate about judicial discretion in sentencing. Arguments over who should impose sentences indelibly mark the history of sentencing. Finally, there's an ancient debate over what sentences to impose—about capital and corporal punishment, the length of imprisonment, what kinds of prisons to put prisoners in, and how to treat them while they're there. The early arguments regarding sinners and penance, judges and punishment, and the aims and kinds of punishment all sound a lot like current debates over the proper authority, aims, kinds, and amounts of punishment sentences ought to reflect.

In this section, we'll concentrate on fixed and indeterminate sentencing (Samaha 1978). We'll begin by looking at the history of sentencing, then examine more closely the division of sentencing authority, sentencing guidelines, offenders' rights at sentencing, and, finally, the ultimate punishment—the death sentence.

The History of Sentencing

Fixed sentencing, tailored to fit the crime, prevailed from the 1600s to the latter 1800s. Then a shift toward *indeterminate sentencing*, tailored to fit individual criminals, began. However, neither fixed nor indeterminate sentences have ever totally dominated criminal sentencing. The tension between the need for certainty and flexibility in sentencing decisions has always required both a measure of predictability (fixed sentences) and a degree of flexibility (indeterminate sentences). Shifting ideological commitments and other informed influences on sentencing ensure that neither fixed nor indeterminate sentences will ever exclusively prevail in sentencing policies and practices.

Following the American Revolution, fixed but relatively moderate penalties became the rule. States abolished the death penalty for many offenses. The rare use of corporal punishment (whipping), mutilation (cutting off ears and slitting tongues), and shaming (the ducking stool) led to their extinction. Imprisonment, which up to that time had been used mainly to detain accused people while they waited for their trial, by 1850 had become the dominant form of criminal punishment after conviction.

Statutes fixed prison terms for most felonies. In practice, liberal use of pardons, early release for "good time," and other devices permitted judges to use informal discretionary judgment in altering formally fixed sentences (Rothman 1971).

The modern history of sentencing began around 1870. Ironically, demands for reform at that time were the opposite of those today; they grew out of deep dissatisfaction with legislatively fixed harsh prison sentences. Reformers complained that prisons were nothing more than warehouses for the poor and the undesirable, and that harsh prison punishment didn't work. Proof of that, the reformers maintained, were the crime rates that continued to grow at unacceptable rates despite harsh, fixed prison sentences. Furthermore, the reformers documented that the prisons were full of recent immigrants and others on the lower rungs of society. Many public officials and concerned citizens agreed. Particularly instrumental in demanding reform were prison administrators and other criminal justice officials. By 1922, all but four states had adopted some form of indeterminate sentencing law.

When the indeterminate sentence became the prevailing practice, administrative sentencing by parole boards and prison officials took precedence over legislative and judicial sentence fixing. At its extreme, judges set no time on sentencing, leaving it wholly to parole boards and correctional officers to determine informally the length of a prisoner's incarceration. More commonly, judges were free to grant probation, suspend sentences in favor of alternatives to incarceration such as community service, or pick confinement times within minimums and maximums prescribed by statutes. Parole boards and corrections officers then determined the exact release time.

Indeterminate sentencing remained dominant until the 1970s, when several forces coalesced to oppose it. Prison uprisings, especially at Attica and the Tombs in New York in the late 1960s, dramatically portrayed rehabilitation as little more than rhetoric and prisoners as deeply and dangerously discontented. Advocates for individuals' rights challenged the widespread and unreviewable informal discretionary powers exercised by criminal justice officials in general and judges in particular. Demands for increased formal accountability spread throughout the criminal justice system. Courts required public officials to justify their decisions in writing and empowered defendants to dispute allegations against them at sentencing. The courts required even prisons to publish their rules and grant prisoners the right to challenge rules that they were accused of breaking.

Several statistical and experimental studies showed a pernicious discrimination in sentencing. In particular, some research strongly suggested that the poor and blacks were sentenced more harshly than whites and middle- and upper-class Americans. Finally, official reports showed steeply rising street-crime rates. The National Research Council created a distinguished panel to review sentencing. It concluded that by the early 1970s, a "remarkable consensus emerged along left and right, law enforcement officials and prisoners groups, reformers and bureaucrats that the indeterminate sentencing era was at its end" (Blumstein 1983, 48–52).

By the late 1970s, the emphasis in crime policy had shifted from fairness to crime prevention. Crime prevention was based on incarceration, general deterrence, and retribution; prevention by rehabilitation was definitely losing ground. Civil libertarians and "law and order" supporters alike called for sentencing practices that would advance swift and certain punishment. They differed only on the *length* of sentences. To civil libertarians, determinate sentencing meant short, fixed sentences; to conservatives, it meant long, fixed sentences.

Three ideas came to dominate thinking about sentencing:

1. Many offenders deserve severe punishment, because they have committed serious crimes.

2. Repeat career offenders require severe punishment to incapacitate them.

3. All crimes deserve some punishment to retain the deterrent potency of the criminal law.

According to the National Council on Crime and Delinquency (1992):

> [B]y 1990, the shift in goals of sentencing reform was complete. Virtually all new sentencing law was designed to increase the certainty and length of prison sentences to incapacitate the active criminal and deter the rest. (6)

Harsher penalties accompanied the shift in the philosophy of punishment. Public support for the death penalty grew, the U.S. Supreme Court ruled that the death penalty was not cruel and unusual punishment, courts sentenced more people to death, and the states began to execute criminals. Judges sentenced more people to prison and to longer prison terms; by 1990, the United States sentenced more people to prison for longer terms than any other country in the world.

The Division of Sentencing Authority

Throughout American history, three institutions—legislatures, courts, and administrative agencies—have exercised sentencing power. In the **legislative sentencing model,** legislatures prescribe specific penalties for crimes without regard to the persons who committed them. The punishment fits the crime, not the criminal, and judges and parole boards can't alter these penalties. Removing discretion from judges and parole boards doesn't eliminate evils arising from prejudicial laws that criminalize conduct peculiar to certain groups in society, but it does limit the making of criminal law to legislatures.

In the **judicial sentencing model,** judges prescribe sentences within broad formal contours set by legislative acts. Typically, a statute prescribes a range, such as 1 to 10 years, 0 to 5 years, or 20 years to life. Judges then fix the exact time that convicted criminals serve.

In the **administrative sentencing model,** both the legislature and the judge prescribe a wide range of allowable prison times for particular crimes. Administrative agencies, typically parole boards and prison administrators, determine the exact release date. Under this model, administrative agencies have broad discretion to determine how long prisoners serve and under what conditions they can be released.

As models, these sentencing schemes never operate in pure form. At all times in U.S. history, all three sentencing institutions have overlapped considerably; all have included the exercise of wide discretion. For example, plea bargaining (Chapter 13) has prevented fixing sentencing authority in any of these three. Charge bargaining gets around legislatively fixed sentences, sentence bargaining avoids judicially fixed sentencing, and both alter administratively fixed sentences. But until sentencing reforms in the 1970s began to change policy and practice, legislatures set the general range of penalties, judges picked a specific penalty within that range, and parole boards released offenders after some time spent in prison. Under this practice, judges, parole boards, and prison authorities had considerable discretion in sentencing criminal defendants.

Sentencing Guidelines and Mandatory Minimum Sentences

The indeterminate sentence, parole boards, and good time remain a part of the sentencing structure of many states. But, fixed sentences are catching up. Fixed sentencing has taken two primary forms—**sentencing guidelines** and **mandatory minimum prison sentences.** The federal government and most states have adopted both forms. Both are based, at least in theory, on limiting or even eliminating discretion in sentencing. Both respond to three demands from experts and the public:

1. *Uniformity.* Similar offenses should receive similar punishment.

2. *Certainty and truth in sentencing.* Convicted offenders, victims, and the public should know that the sentence imposed is similar to the sentence actually served. ("Do the crime; do the time.")

3. *Retribution, deterrence, and incapacitation.* The rehabilitation of individual offenders isn't the primary aim of punishment.

Let's look more closely at sentencing guidelines and mandatory minimum prison sentences.

Sentencing Guidelines

In sentencing guidelines, a commission establishes a relatively narrow range of penalties, and judges are supposed to choose a specific sentence within that range. The guideline sentence depends on a combination of the seriousness of the crime and the offender's criminal history. Sentences are either presumptively incarceration or presumptively probation. Judges can depart from the range set in the guidelines, but usually they have to give written reasons for their departure. Letting judges choose within a range without departing from the guidelines builds a flexibility into the system that allows for differences in individual cases. Characteristics such as the amount of money stolen, the extent of personal injury inflicted, and the criminal history of the offender can affect the sentence that judges impose without undermining the basic goals of uniformity and equity.

The First Circuit U.S. Court of Appeals applied the U.S. Sentencing Guidelines to departures from the permissible range of sentences in two cases. Chief Judge Breyer (now Associate U.S. Supreme Court Justice Breyer) discussed the philosophy of the guidelines and how that philosophy affects departures from the guidelines in two cases reported together, *U.S. v. Rivera* (1993) and *U.S. v. Adamo* (1993).

CASE | *Were Departures Justified?*

U.S. v. Rivera
U.S. v. Adamo
994 F.2d 942 (Cal. Dist.1 1993)

Mirna Rivera, a single mother of three children, was convicted of carrying a pound of cocaine from New York to Providence, Rhode Island, and sentenced to thirty-three months in prison by the U.S. District Court for the District of Rhode Island. Robert Adamo, a union official, was convicted of embezzlement from the union's health and welfare fund and was sentenced by the district court to a term of probation without confinement so that he could continue to work and make restitution to the fund. In a consolidated appeal, the Court of Appeals vacated both sentences and remanded the cases.

BREYER, CJ., joined by CAMPBELL and BOWNES, JJ.

FACTS

Mirna Rivera, a single mother of three small children, was convicted of carrying about a pound of cocaine from New York to Providence. She appeals her 33 month sentence of imprisonment. She argues the district court would have departed downward from the minimum 33 month Guidelines prison term if it weren't for the court's view that it lacked the legal "authority" to depart. She says this view is legally "incorrect" and she asks us to set aside her sentence.

The second case involves a union official, Robert Adamo, who embezzled about $100,000 from his union's Health and Welfare Fund. The district court departed downward from the fifteen to twenty-one month prison term that the Guidelines themselves would have required. Instead, the court imposed a term of probation without confinement. The court said that it was departing downward so that Mr. Adamo could continue to work and to make restitution to the Fund. The Government appeals. It argues that Adamo's circumstances are insufficiently unusual to warrant the departure.

We agree with the appellants in both cases. In our view, the district court sentencing Ms. Rivera held an unduly narrow view of its departure powers. The district court sentencing Mr. Adamo failed to analyze the need for departure in the way that the law requires. We consider both cases in this single opinion because doing so may help to illustrate an appropriate legal analysis for "departures." We shall first set forth our view of the portion of the law here applicable; and we shall then apply that law to the two appeals.

OPINION

I. Departures

The basic theory of the Sentencing Guidelines is a simple one. In order to lessen the degree to which different judges imposed different sentences in comparable cases, an expert Sentencing Commission would write Guidelines, applicable to most ordinary sentencing situations. In an ordinary situation, the statutes, and the Guidelines themselves, would require the judge to apply the appropriate guideline—a guideline that would normally cabin, within fairly narrow limits, the judge's power to choose the length of a prison term. Should the judge face a situation that was not ordinary, the judge could depart from the Guidelines sentence, provided that the judge then sets forth the reasons for departure. A court of appeals would review the departure for "reason-

ableness." And, the Commission itself would collect and study both the district courts' departure determinations and the courts of appeals' decisions, thereby learning about the Guidelines' actual workings and using that knowledge to help revise or clarify the Guidelines for the future....

A. The Statute

The Sentencing Statute itself sets forth the basic law governing departures. It tells the sentencing court that it shall impose a sentence of the kind, and within the range... established for the applicable category of offense committed by the applicable category of defendant as set forth in the Guidelines....The statute goes on immediately to create an exception for departures by adding that the sentencing court shall "impose" this Guidelines sentence unless the court finds that there exists an aggravating or mitigating circumstance of a kind, or to a degree, not adequately taken into consideration by the Sentencing Commission in formulating the Guidelines that should result in a sentence different from that described....If the sentencing court makes this finding and sentences "outside the [Guidelines'] range," it must state in open court... the specific reason for the imposition of a sentence different from that described [in the Guidelines]. The defendant may then appeal an upward departure, and the Government may appeal a downward departure. On appeal, if the court of appeals determines that the sentence...is unreasonable,...it shall state specific reasons for its conclusions and...set aside the sentence and remand the case for further sentencing proceedings with such instructions as the court considers appropriate....

B. The Guidelines

The Guidelines deal with departures in four basic ways.

1. *Cases Outside the "Heartland."* The Introduction to the Guidelines (which the Commission calls a "Policy Statement") makes an important distinction between a "heartland case" and an "unusual case." The Introduction says the Commission intends the sentencing courts to treat each guideline as carving out a "heartland," a set of typical cases embodying the conduct that each guideline describes. The Introduction goes on to say that when a court finds an atypical case, one to which a particular guideline linguistically applies, but where conduct significantly differs from the norm, the court may consider whether a departure is warranted. The Introduction further adds that, with a few stated exceptions, the Commission does not intend to limit the kinds of factors, whether or not mentioned anywhere else in the guidelines, that could constitute grounds for departure in an unusual case.

The Introduction thus makes clear that (with a few exceptions) a case that falls outside the linguistically applicable guideline's "heartland" is a candidate for departure. It is, by definition, an "unusual case." And, the sentencing court may then go on to consider, in light of the sentencing system's purposes, whether or not the "unusual" features of the case justify departure.... Thus, (with a few exceptions) the law tells the judge, considering departure, to ask basically, "Does this case fall within the 'heartland,' or is it an 'unusual case'?"

2. *Encouraged Departures.* In certain circumstances, the Guidelines offer the district court, which is considering whether to depart, special assistance, by specifically encouraging departures. Part 5K lists a host of considerations that may take a particular case outside the "heartland" of any individual guideline and, in doing so, may warrant a departure. The individual guidelines do not take account, for example, of an offender's "diminished capacity," which circumstance, in the Commission's view would normally warrant a downward departure. Nor do certain guidelines (say, immigration offense guidelines) take account of, say, use of a gun, which circumstance would remove the situation (the immigration offense) from that guideline's "heartland" and would normally warrant an upward departure....

3. *Discouraged Departures.* The Guidelines sometimes discourage departures. Part 5H, for example, lists various "specific offender" characteristics, such as age, education, employment record, family ties and responsibilities, mental and physical conditions, and various good works. The Guidelines say that these features are "not ordinarily relevant" in determining departures....

At the same time, the Commission recognizes that such circumstances could remove a case from the heartland, but only if they are present in a manner that is unusual or special, rather than "ordinary." It may not be unusual, for example, to find that a convicted drug offender is a single mother with family responsibilities, but, at some point, the nature and magnitude of family responsibilities (many children? with handicaps? no money? no place for children to go?) may transform the "ordinary" case of such circumstances into a case that is not at all ordinary. Thus, a sentencing court, considering whether or not the presence of these "discouraged" factors warrants departure, must ask whether the factors themselves are present in unusual kind or degree. The Commission, in stating that those factors do not "ordinarily" take a case outside the heartland, discourages, but does not absolutely forbid, their use.

4. *Forbidden Departures.* The Commission has made several explicit exceptions to the basic principle that a sentenc-ing court can consider any "unusual case" (any case outside the heartland) as a candidate for departure. The Guidelines state that a sentencing court "cannot take into account as grounds for departure" race, sex, national origin, creed, religion, and socio-economic status. The Guidelines also state that "lack of guidance as a youth" cannot justify departure, that drug or alcohol abuse is not a reason for imposing a sentence below the Guidelines range, and that personal financial difficulties and economic pressure upon a trade or business do not warrant a decrease in sentence. Thus, even if these factors make a case "unusual," taking it outside an individual guideline's heartland, the sentencing court is not free to consider departing. But, with these... exceptions, the sentencing court is free to consider, in an "unusual case," whether or not the factors that make it unusual (which remove it from the heartland) are present in sufficient kind or degree to warrant a departure. The court retains this freedom to depart whether such departure is encouraged, discouraged, or unconsidered by the Guidelines.

C. The Sentencing Court's Departure Decision

Given the statutory provisions, and the relevant Guidelines statements, we suggest (but we do not require) that, as an initial matter, a sentencing court considering departure analyze the case along the following lines:

1. What features of this case, potentially, take it outside the Guidelines' "heartland" and make of it a special, or unusual, case?

2. Has the Commission forbidden departures based on those features?

3. If not, has the Commission encouraged departures based on those features?

If not, has the Commission discouraged departures based on those features? If no special features are present, or if special features are also "forbidden" features, then the sentencing court, in all likelihood, simply would apply the relevant guidelines. If the special features are "encouraged" features, the court would likely depart, sentencing in accordance with the Guidelines' suggestions. If the special features are "discouraged" features, the court would go on to decide whether the case is nonetheless not "ordinary," i.e., whether the case differs from the ordinary case in which those features are present. If the case is ordinary, the court would not depart. If it is not ordinary, the court would go on to consider departure....

D. Review on Appeal

If the district court decides to depart, the defendant may appeal (an upward departure) or the Government may appeal (a downward departure). The statute then provides the appellate court with two important instructions. First, the court of appeals must decide if the resulting sentence is "unreasonable, having regard for" the sentencing court's reasons and the statute's general sentencing factors. Second, the court of appeals must (as it ordinarily does) give "specific reasons" for its decision. . . .

II. Applying the Analysis

We now apply our "departure" analysis to the circumstances of the two cases before us, the appeal of Ms. Mirna Rivera, and that of Mr. Robert Adamo.

A. Mirna Rivera

For purposes of this appeal, we take Ms. Rivera to have transported about one pound of cocaine, from New York to Providence, with intent to distribute it, in violation of 21 U.S.C. § 841(a)(1), (b)(1)(B). The Guidelines provide a sentence of 33 to 41 months' imprisonment for a first time offender who has engaged in this conduct. See U.S.S.G. § 2D1.1(a)(3), (c)(10) (base offense level of 24); U.S.S.G. § 3B1.2(a) (reduction of 4 points for minimal participation); U.S.S.G. Ch. 5, Pt. A (sentencing table). Ms. Rivera argued to the district court that it should depart downward from this Guidelines sentence for the following reasons:

1. She has three small children, ages three, five, and six, who need a mother's care.

2. She lives solely on welfare, receiving no financial aid from her former husband.

3. She has virtually no contact with any other family member (except for a sister, with five children, also on welfare).

4. She has never before engaged in any criminal activity.

5. She committed this single offense because of an unwise wish to obtain money for Christmas presents for her children.

The district court decided not to depart. Rivera claims that this decision reflects the court's incorrect belief that it lacked the legal authority to depart. And, she asks us to order a new proceeding.

After reviewing the record of the sentencing proceeding, we conclude that Rivera is correct. The district court's analysis of the nature of its power to depart is not consistent with the view of departures that we set forth in this opinion. We recognize a difference between "forbidden departures," and "discouraged departures." And, we believe that the district court did not realize that it had the legal power to consider departure, where departure is discouraged (but not forbidden), if it finds features of the case that show it is not ordinary.

At the sentencing hearing, the district court said:

With respect to Defendant's argument that the Defendant's family situation, economic situation, warrants a departure, I must say that the guidelines are drawn to apply to everyone in exactly the same way, that it is clear from the guidelines that the economic situation and the family situation of the Defendant is not a consideration. There are those who certainly would disagree with that, but that is the principle that is embodied in the guidelines. They are age blind, they are sex blind, they are blind to family circumstances, and can result in their application in a certain amount of cruelty. But, that isn't a basis for making a departure. It's a situation where somebody tries to draw a straight line that applies to every situation that can possibly arise and this Court is without discretion to take what might well be thought by most people, at least, legitimate concerns into consideration. Simply put, I can't do that because the guidelines do not permit me to do that. So that Defendant's objection or request to make a downward departure is denied. . . . Your Counsel says that a court somewhere observed that these guidelines are not a straightjacket for a District Court. Well, I don't agree with that. Here is a circumstance where I'm satisfied that the reason you did this was to buy toys for your children at Christmas. It was a serious mistake. The pre-sentence report says this: There is no information suggesting that Ms. Rivera had any previous participation in a similar type criminal activity. The Defendant's lifestyle is not indicative of that of a drug dealer who has profited from ongoing criminal activity. Rather she appears destitute, relying on public assistance to support herself and her children. . . . If I had the authority to do it, I would not impose the sentence that I am about to impose. I would impose a lesser sentence because I think that these guidelines simply are unrealistic when applied to real life situations like this. They may work in many circumstances, but they certainly don't work here.

In these statements, the court repeatedly said it lacked the legal power to depart; it characterized the case before it as different from the "many circumstances" where the Guidelines might work; it added that it would depart if it could; it set forth several circumstances that might make the case a special one; and it described as identical ("sex blind" and "blind to family circumstances") guidelines that, in fact, differ significantly, the former involving a "forbidden" departure, and the latter a "discouraged" departure. Taken together, these features of the case warrant a new sentencing proceeding, conducted with the district court fully aware of its power to depart in "unusual cases" and where family circumstances are out of the "ordinary." . . .

... The upshot is a difficult departure decision. On the one hand lie a host of quite special circumstances (though many are of the "discouraged" sort), and on the other hand lies the simple fact that Ms. Mirna Rivera did transport a pound of cocaine from New York to Providence. This is the kind of case in which, if the district court departs, its informed views as to why the case is special would seem especially useful and would warrant appellate court "respect."

We REMAND the case for further proceedings.

B. Robert Adamo

Mr. Adamo was convicted of embezzling about $100,000 belonging to the union Health and Welfare Fund of which he was a fiduciary, in violation of 18 U.S.C. § 664. He accepted responsibility for the crime, U.S.S.G. § 3E1.1. It was his first offense. The Guidelines provided a minimum prison term of fifteen months. See U.S.S.G. §§ 2E5.2, 2B1.1, 3B1.3 (base offense level of 4; increase of 8 points for amount of loss; 2 level enhancement for more than minimal planning; 2 level enhancement for fiduciary); U.S.S.G. Ch. 5, Pt. A (sentencing table). The district court, departing downward from the Guidelines, sentenced Mr. Adamo to probation alone, without any imprisonment.

The court gave the following reasons for its downward departure:

When I look at these cases of sentencing, the first thing I ask myself is, "What sentence would I impose if there were no guidelines?" That's what I did for more than 20 years. And then I ask myself, "What's a just sentence in these circumstances? Am I going to be limited by these artificial guidelines made by people who have no idea of what kind of a case I'm going to have to decide?" No two cases are the same.... So that's where justice is in this case, having restitution made to this Health & Welfare Fund. If I send this defendant to prison I think it's foreordained that restitution will not be made. It may be made in some respect, but I'm sure the defendant would lose both his jobs and would find it very difficult to have employment which would allow him to make restitution. And a time in prison would serve no useful purpose in this case. The only factor in sentencing which would be accomplished is punishment, but the defendant has been punished just by being here—just being here and what's he's gone through in the last 6 months, and the notoriety of this. So, imprisonment serves no useful purpose in this case. It certainly isn't a matter of deterrence. I'm sure the defendant will never do anything like this again. Here is a man who has lived an exemplary life, he's worked two jobs to take care of his family. His wife has worked, and although they were making in the range of $70,000 a year, the problem of educating two children came up. It's a problem that everyone faces. This is where the error of judgment comes in. He took this money, not out of greed, not out of desire to own a fancy car or a palatial home and a boat, but to educate his children. He didn't think about the other alternatives. His daughter wanted to go to an expensive private school, instead of going to a local state school of some sort, and he thought that's what she should have. He didn't consider loans and other types of programs. This money was available, he took it—a terrible mistake. But that's the only mistake that he seems to have made, and I just don't think he should spend time in prison because of this one mistake. I want restitution made, so I'm going to exercise my best judgment in these circumstances. My best judgment is to have as long a term of probation as possible so that restitution can be made with the guidance of the probation office. So, I'm going to depart downward and impose a term of probation of 5 years. That's the maximum that I can impose. And one of the conditions of probation will be, and is, that the defendant shall pay restitution in the amount of $91,125.62 to the Health & Welfare Fund of the Building Service Employees International Union, AFL-CIO Local 334.

The court's explication of its reasons is useful, for it produces understanding and permits evaluation, both by appellate courts and by the Commission. We nonetheless believe the analysis does not permit the departure before us.

First, we believe... the embezzlement guidelines encompass, within their "heartland," embezzlement accompanied by normal restitution needs and practicalities (i.e., the simple facts that restitution is desirable and that a prison term will make restitution harder to achieve). It would seem obvious, and no one denies, that the embezzlement guidelines are written for ordinary cases of embezzlement, that restitution is called for in many such cases, and that prison terms often make restitution somewhat more difficult to achieve. Moreover, the embezzlement guideline reflects the Commission's intent to equalize punishments for "white collar" and "blue collar" crime.... Further, the district court itself, stating that it did not wish "to be limited by these artificial guidelines," and that "no two cases are alike," seemed to disregard, rather than to deny, the scope of the embezzlement guideline.... [We hold] that ordinary restitution circumstances of this sort do not fall outside the embezzlement guideline's "heartland," and therefore do not warrant a downward departure.

Second, we recognize a special need of a victim for restitution, and the surrounding practicalities, might, in an unusual case, justify a departure. But, we cannot review a district court determination to that effect here, for the district court made no such determination.... We mention this fact because the defendant has pointed to one unusual feature of the case. The record before us contains a suggestion that Mr. Adamo could keep his job (and therefore remain able to make restitution) were his prison term only one year, but he could not keep his job (and thus would lose his ability to make restitution) were he sentenced to the Guidelines prison term of one year and three months. We can imagine an argument for departure resting upon a strong need for restitution, an important practical advantage to the lesser sentence, and a departure limited to three months.

We are not arguing such a departure or saying that we would eventually find it lawful. We mention the special circumstance to underscore the need for reasoned departure analysis, sensitive to the way in which the Guidelines seek to structure departure decisions and to the role that such departures, and their accompanying reasons, can play in the continued development of the Sentencing Guidelines.... The district court, in Mr. Adamo's case, may wish to conduct such an analysis in light of the special features of the case to which the defendant has pointed. We therefore remand this case for new sentencing proceedings.

The sentences in both cases are vacated and the cases are REMANDED to the district court for resentencing.

Questions

1. What is the basic philosophy of the federal sentencing guidelines, according to Chief Judge Breyer?

2. Explain the difference between "heartland" cases and "unusual" cases and this difference's effect on sentencing under the guidelines.

3. What specific facts justify the departure in the case of Mirna Rivera? Would you allow the departure? Argue the case for and against the departure, and then give your reasons for departing or not departing.

4. What facts don't justify the departure in the case of Robert Adamo? Would you disallow the departure? Give reasons why or why not.

Mandatory Minimum Sentences

The other type of fixed sentence, mandatory minimum sentences, requires judges to impose a nondiscretionary minimum amount of prison time that all offenders convicted of the offense have to serve. Judges can sentence offenders to more than the minimum but not less. Mandatory minimum sentence laws promise that "If you do the crime, you *will* do the time." Mandatory penalties are very old. The "eye for an eye" and "tooth for a tooth" in the Old Testament were mandatory penalties. The Anglo-Saxon king Alfred prescribed a detailed mandatory penal code, including such provisions as "If one knocks out another's eye, he shall pay 66 shillings, $6\frac{1}{3}$ pence. If the eye is still in the head, but the injured man can see nothing with it, one-third of the payment shall be withheld" (Lee n.d.). And, as early as 1790 in the United States, most states had established mandatory penalties for capital crimes. Throughout the nineteenth century, Congress enacted mandatory penalties—usually short prison sentences—for a long list of crimes, including refusal to testify before Congress, failure to report seaboard saloon purchases, or causing a ship to run aground by use of a false light (Wallace 1993, 9).

From 1900 to the 1950s, the use of mandatory minimum penalties fell into disuse. In the 1950s, fear that crime and drug problems were caused by a Communist plot to get Americans "hooked" on especially potent "pure Communist heroin" from China led Congress to enact the Narcotic Control Act of 1956 (U.S. Congress 1954, 7). The Boggs Act, named after its sponsor Alabama Representative Hale Boggs, signaled a shift to mandatory minimum sentences. The Senate Judiciary explained why Congress needed a mandatory minimum sentence drug law:

There is a need for the continuation of the policy of punishment of a severe character as a deterrent to narcotic law violations. [The Committee] therefore recommends an increase in maximum sentences for first as well as subsequent offenses. With respect to the mandatory minimum features of such penalties, and prohibition of suspended sentences or probation, the Committee recognizes objections in principle. It feels, however, that, in order to define the gravity of this class of crime and the assured penalty to follow, these features of the law must be regarded as essential elements of the desired deterrents, although some differences of opinion still exist regarding their application to first offenses of certain types.

U.S. Sentencing Commission 1991, 5–7

The statute imposed stiff mandatory minimum sentences for narcotics offenses, requiring judges to pick within a range of penalties. Judges couldn't suspend sentences or put convicted offenders on probation. In addition, offenders weren't eligible for parole if they were convicted under the act. For example, the act punished the first conviction for selling heroin by a term of from 5 to 10 years of imprisonment. Judges had to sentence offenders to at least 5 years in prison, judges couldn't suspend the sentence or put offenders on probation, and offenders weren't eligible for parole for at least the minimum period of the sentence. For second offenders, the mandatory minimum was raised to 10 years. The penalty for the sale of narcotics to persons under 18 ranged from a mandatory minimum of 10 years to a maximum of life imprisonment or death (U.S. Sentencing Commission 1991, 6).

In 1970, Congress retreated from the mandatory minimum sentence approach. In the Comprehensive Drug Abuse Prevention and Control Act of 1970, Congress repealed virtually all of the mandatory minimum provisions adopted in the 1956 act because the increased sentence lengths "had not shown the expected overall reduction in drug law violations." Among the reasons for the repeal of mandatory minimum penalties for drug law offenses were that they

- Alienated youths from the general society

- Hampered the rehabilitation of drug offenders

- Infringed on judicial authority by drastically reducing discretion in sentencing

- Reduced the deterrent effect of drug laws because even prosecutors thought the laws were too severe

According to the House committee that considered the repeal of the bill:

The severity of existing penalties, involving in many instances minimum sentences, have [sic] led in many instances to reluctance on the part of prosecutors to prosecute some violations, where the penalties seem to be out of line with the seriousness of the offenses. In addition, severe penalties, which do not take into account individual circumstances, and which treat casual violators as severely as they treat hardened criminals, tend to make conviction more difficult to obtain.

U.S. Congress 1970, 11

The retreat from mandatory minimum sentences was short-lived, because public concern about violence and drugs again rose to the top of the national agenda. The public and legislatures blamed rising crime rates on the uncertainty and "leniency" of indeterminate sentences. Beginning in the early 1970s, the states and the federal government enacted more and longer mandatory minimum prison sentences. By 1991, forty-six states and the federal government had enacted mandatory minimum sentencing laws. Although the list of mandatory minimum laws is long (the U.S. Criminal Code contains at least one hundred), the main targets of mandatory minimum sentences are drug offenses, violent crimes, and crimes committed with a weapon (Wallace 1993, 11).

Mandatory minimum sentences are supposed to satisfy three basic aims of criminal punishment: retribution, incapacitation, and deterrence. According to supporters, mandatory minimum sentence laws mean those committing serious crimes will receive severe punishment. Furthermore, violent criminals, criminals who use weapons, and drug offenders can't harm the public if they're in prison. And the knowledge that committing mandatory minimum crimes will bring certain, swift, and severe punishment should deter these types of crimes.

Several evaluations, however, suggest that, in practice, mandatory minimum penalties don't always achieve the goals their supporters hoped they would. In 1990, Congress ordered the U.S. Sentencing Commission to evaluate the rapidly increasing number of mandatory minimum sentencing provisions in the federal system. The results of the commission's study provided little empirical support for the success of mandatory sentencing laws, as these findings demonstrate:

1. *Only a few of the mandatory minimum sentencing provisions are ever used.* Nearly all those used relate to drug and weapons offenses.

2. Only *41 percent* of defendants whose characteristics and behavior qualify them for mandatory minimum sentences actually receive them.

3. *Mandatory minimum sentences actually introduce disparity in sentencing.* For example, the commission found that race influences disparity in a number of ways. Whites are less likely than blacks and Hispanics to be indicted or convicted at the mandatory minimum. Whites are also more likely than blacks and Hispanics to receive reductions for "substantial assistance" in aiding in the prosecution of other offenders. The mandatory minimum sentence laws allow an exception for offenders who provide "substantial assistance" in investigating other offenders. But, judges can reduce the minimum for substantial assistance only on the motion of the prosecutors.

4. *Substantial assistance also leads to disparities quite apart from race.* It tends to favor the very people the law was intended to reach—those higher up in the chain of drug dealing, because underlings have less to offer the government. In one case, for example, Stanley Marshall, who sold less than one gram of LSD, got a 20-year mandatory prison sentence. Jose Cabrera, on the other hand, who the government estimated made more than $40 million from importing cocaine and who would have qualified for life plus 200 years, received a prison term of 8 years for providing "substantial assistance" in the case of Manuel Noriega. According to Judge Terry J. Hatter, Jr., "The people at the very bottom who can't provide substantial assistance end up getting [punished] more severely than those at the top" (*Criminal Justice Newsletter* 1993, 5; Wallace 1993, 11).

5. *Mandatory minimum sentences don't eliminate discretion;* they just shift it from judges to prosecutors. Prosecutors can use their discretion in a number of ways, including manipulating the "substantial assistance" exception and deciding not to charge defendants with crimes carrying mandatory minimum sentences, or to charge them with mandatory minimum crimes of lesser degree.

The U.S. Sentencing Commission recommended further study before making any final conclusions about the effectiveness of mandatory penalties. But their findings, along with other research on federal and state mandatory minimum sentences, suggest that mandatory minimum penalties aren't the easy answer to the crime problem that politicians promise and the public hopes for (Campaign for an Effective Crime Policy 1993; Schulhofer 1993, 199).

Objections to mandatory minimum sentences also arise from the experiences of judges who administer them. In *U.S. v. Brigham,* Judge Easterbrook of the Seventh Circuit U.S. Court of Appeals revealed why some judges object to the mandatory minimum sentences.

CASE	*Was the Mandatory Minimum Sentence Appropriate?*

U.S. v. Brigham
977 F.2d 317 (7th Cir. 1992)

Anthony Brigham was convicted in the U.S. District Court for the Northern District of Illinois of conspiracy to sell cocaine. He appealed. The Seventh Circuit U.S. Court of Appeals affirmed.

EASTERBROOK, J., joined by POSNER, J.

FACTS

Steep penalties await those who deal in drugs. Buying or selling 10 kilograms of cocaine—even agreeing to do so, without carrying through—means a minimum penalty of 10 years' imprisonment, without possibility of parole. 21 U.S.C. §§ 841(b)(1)(A), 846. The "mandatory" minimum is mandatory only from the perspective of judges. To the parties, the sentence is negotiable. Did a marginal participant in a conspiracy really understand that a 10-kilo deal lay in store? A prosecutor may charge a lesser crime, if he offers something in return. Let's make a deal. Does the participant have valuable information; can he offer other assistance? Congress authorized prosecutors to pay for aid with sentences below the "floor." Let's make a deal.

Bold dealers may turn on their former comrades, setting up phony sales and testifying at the ensuing trials. Timorous dealers may provide information about their sources and customers. Drones of the organization—the runners, mules, drivers, and lookouts—have nothing comparable to offer. They lack the contacts and trust necessary to set up big deals, and they know little information of value. Whatever tales they have to tell, their bosses will have related. Defendants unlucky enough to be innocent have no information at all and are more likely to want vin-

dication at trial, losing not only the opportunity to make a deal but also the 2-level reduction the sentencing guidelines provide for accepting responsibility.

Mandatory minimum penalties, combined with a power to grant exceptions, create a prospect of inverted sentencing. The more serious the defendant's crimes, the lower the sentence—because the greater his wrongs, the more information and assistance he has to offer to a prosecutor. Discounts for the top dogs have the virtue of necessity, because rewards for assistance are essential to the business of detecting and punishing crime. But what makes the post-discount sentencing structure topsy-turvy is the mandatory minimum, binding only for the hangers on. What is to be said for such terms, which can visit draconian penalties on the small fry without increasing prosecutors' ability to wring information from their bosses?

Our case illustrates a sentencing inversion. Such an outcome is neither illegal nor unconstitutional, because offenders have no right to be sentenced in proportion to their wrongs. Still, meting out the harshest penalties to those least culpable is troubling, because it accords with no one's theory of appropriate punishments.

Agents of the Drug Enforcement Agency learned from an informant that Craig Thompson was in the market to buy 10 kilograms of cocaine. The DEA's undercover agents feigned willingness to supply him. During negotiations, Thompson said that he had just sold 17 kilograms and needed 10 more that very day to tide his organization over until the arrival of a shipment that he was expecting. Thompson and the agents did not trust one another. Jeffrey Carter, one of Thompson's goons, searched an agent; the agent's gun, normal in the business, did not trouble Carter, but a transmitter or recorder would mean big trouble. Carter was not very good at his job; he didn't find the concealed recorder. Thompson ultimately agreed to pay $30,000 per kilogram, a premium price for quick service. After the agents let on that they didn't trust Thompson any more than Thompson trusted them, Thompson agreed to let the agents hold his Rolls Royce as collateral until payment. In the agents' presence, Thompson called Tyrone Amos and told him to pick up "ten of those things today" at a suburban motel. Thompson and Carter would hand over the Rolls in a different suburb.

At the appointed time, less than five hours after the agents first met Thompson, one team descended on a restaurant to receive the Rolls Royce and another decamped to the motel to "deliver" the cocaine. Amos arrived at the motel in a car driven by Anthony Brigham. Amos and the agents at the motel had a conversation; Brigham stayed in the car. Carter had not appeared at the restaurant with the Rolls Royce, so everyone settled down to wait. Brigham looked around the parking lot but scrunched down in his seat when the agents' Corvette drove slowly by. At the restaurant Thompson and the agents discussed future deals of 50–100 kilograms per month. At the motel Brigham paced nervously in the lobby. After touring the parking lot again, lingering over the Corvette, Brigham joined Amos at a nearby gas station, where Amos placed a phone call. The two had a conversation and returned to the motel, where Amos told the agents that Carter and the Rolls were still missing. While Amos and one agent were dining together some distance from the motel, Thompson paged Amos with news that the Rolls had arrived.

Back at the motel, the agents went through the motions of delivering cocaine. As Amos headed for the agents' car to retrieve the drug from the trunk, Brigham moved his car to a location from which he could keep the delivery in sight. But there was no cocaine. Before Amos could open the trunk other agents moved in, arresting Amos and Brigham, just as they pinched Thompson and Carter at the restaurant.

All but Brigham pleaded guilty and provided valuable assistance to prosecutors. All but Brigham were sentenced to less than the "mandatory" minimums. Thompson received 84 months' imprisonment and Amos 75 months, after the prosecutor made motions under § 3553(e). Carter, who was allowed to plead to a charge that did not carry a minimum term, received 4 years' probation, 4 months of which were to be in a work-release program run by the Salvation Army. That left Brigham, who went to trial, was convicted, and received the "mandatory" term of 120 months' imprisonment.

OPINION

Was the evidence sufficient? Appellate judges do not serve as additional jurors. After a jury convicts, the question be-

comes whether any sensible person could find, beyond a reasonable doubt, that the defendant committed the crime. That is a steep burden, for 12 persons, presumably sensible and having a more direct appreciation of the evidence than the written record affords to appellate judges, have unanimously found exactly that.

Brigham emphasizes that "mere" presence at a crime does not implicate the bystander in that offense. Conspiracy is agreement, and what proof of agreement did the prosecutor present? Brigham arrived with Amos, conferred with Amos, and was in position to watch an exchange occur. No one testified that Brigham had any role in the exchange or Thompson's organization. Although the prosecutor portrayed Brigham as a lookout, he asks: What kind of lookout would be unarmed, without radio, pager, cellular phone, or any other way to give or receive alerts? What counter surveillance operative would hunker down in the car rather than keep a hawk-eyed watch? Thompson, Carter, and Amos, who reaped rewards for their assistance, were conspicuously absent at Brigham's trial. Had they no evidence to offer against him?

No one questions the rule that "mere presence" at the scene of a crime does not prove conspiracy. "Mere" presence differs from, say, "revealing" presence. Like many a weasel word, "mere" summarizes a conclusion rather than assisting in analysis. When the evidence does not permit an inference that the defendant was part of the criminal organization, the court applies the label "mere presence." So we must examine the evidence, taking inferences in the light most favorable to the jury's verdict, rather than resting content with slogans.

Brigham shows up on short notice with Amos, who the jury could conclude was there to receive 10 kilograms of cocaine from strangers whom Thompson and Amos do not trust. Is Amos likely to come alone? Is a companion apt to be ignorant of the nature and risks of the transaction? For almost three hours Brigham remains at the motel, generally observant and generally nervous; he follows Amos to a pay phone where a telephone call and conversation ensue. Amos reveals the contents of this conversation to the agents; the jury could conclude that he revealed it to Brigham too. While Amos and an agent go to dinner, Brigham keeps watch. After Amos returns, eye contact and a nod from Amos lead Brigham to take up position where he can watch the trunk of the agents' car. Just what was Brigham doing for three hours in the lobby and parking lot of the motel, if not assisting Amos? He was not exactly passing through while a drug deal went down around him. Brigham did not testify, and his lawyer offered no hypothesis at trial. At oral argument of this appeal the best his counsel could do was to suggest that Brigham might have believed that Amos was picking up counterfeit money rather than drugs. Tell us another! The jury was entitled to conclude that Brigham knew about, and joined, a conspiracy to distribute cocaine.

Thin the evidence was, but it was also sufficient. Evidence at sentencing shows that the jury drew the right inference. Amos related that he brought Brigham as a lookout. Brigham told the prosecutor that he was part of the organization and had been involved in some big-stakes transactions. But he was unable to provide enough information to induce the prosecutor to make the motion under § 3553(e) that unlocks the trap door in the sentencing "floor." Pleading guilty would have produced the 10-year minimum term, so Brigham went to trial; he had nothing to lose and some chance of being acquitted. The evidence at sentencing showed that Brigham knew that Thompson's organization dealt in multi-kilogram quantities, which supports the judge's conclusion that Brigham qualifies for the 10-year minimum.

All that remains is Brigham's argument that the judge should have invoked U.S.S.G. § 5K2.0 to give him a break. Section 5K2.0 describes appropriate departures from the guidelines, but Brigham needed a departure from a minimum sentence prescribed by statute. That was available only on motion of the prosecutor under § 3553(e). Brigham does not contend that in declining to make the motion the prosecutor violated the Constitution....

Wise exercise of prosecutorial discretion can prevent egregious sentencing inversions. How that discretion is to be exercised is a subject for the political branches. Brigham joined the conspiracy and received a sentence authorized by Congress. His judicial remedies are at a close.

AFFIRMED.

DISSENT

BAUER, CJ.

Taking all the evidence as described in the majority opinion as absolutely true, and viewing it in the light most favorable to the government, I still do not find that any sensible juror could find Brigham guilty of the crime of conspiracy beyond a reasonable doubt. At oral argument, counsel for Brigham could only suggest, in answer to a question from the bench as to what explanation he could give for Brigham's actions on the day in question, "that Brigham might have believed that Amos was picking up counterfeit money rather than drugs." An unbelievable scenario. The fact is, no one testified as to what exactly Brigham was doing or why he was doing it; no one, in spite of the marvelous totally cooperating witnesses who, if the government's theory is correct, could have nailed Brigham's hide to the jailhouse wall. But they didn't. And it is not Brigham's missing explanation that is fatal; it is the government's inability to explain that creates the problem.

Tell us another, indeed, but only if it is the government tale; the accused has absolutely no burden to explain anything. The government accuses, the defendant says "prove it," and the government says the suspicious activity is enough to convince and convict. And so it proved.

I would have directed a verdict of "not guilty" had I been the trial judge and I construe my role in review to be the same. I do not believe the evidence sufficient to convince a sensible juror of proof beyond a reasonable doubt. The existence of cooperating witnesses who knew all and told nothing virtually implies the missing witness analysis: you had the control, you didn't produce, I infer the testimony would have been adverse to you.

Questions

1. What are Judge Easterbrook's exact objections to the mandatory minimum sentence that he was obliged to impose in this case? Do you agree? Defend your answer.

2. Summarize Judge Bauer's dissenting opinion. Would you have joined this dissent? Defend your answer.

Offenders' Rights at Sentencing

As you read at the beginning of the chapter, when defendants become convicted offenders, they lose many safeguards they had during trial. Why? In addition to the reasons described at the beginning of the chapter, there are a few others related specifically to sentencing. One reason is that most of the procedural safeguards written into the Constitution were originally intended to protect abuses of defendants' rights during the trial itself. Also, too much attention to defendants' rights would restrict the flexibility judges need to impose the right sentence, one that will satisfy the objectives of retribution and prevention.

This increased flexibility allows trial judges to use information outside the official record of the trial, such as the reports of probation officers or of others who know about an offender's personal life and the circumstances of the crime but who don't appear in court. Offenders have no right either to confront or to cross-examine persons who have supplied unfavorable information about them. Trial judges can also consider the conduct of defendants during the trial. For example, one trial judge considered the defendant's refusal to help officers investigate a conspiracy the defendant admitted he was part of.

One right offenders don't give up is to have counsel at sentencing (*Mempa v. Rhay* 1967). That right remains in full force. So does their right to equal protection of the laws. For example, it violates equal protection to fine only those convicted offenders who can afford to pay but to convert fines to imprisonment for those who can't pay (*Tate v. Short* 1971). Also, a court can't revoke offenders' probation and imprison them because they fail to pay a fine they can't afford to pay (*Bearden v. Georgia* 1983; *Gagnon v. Scarpelli* 1973).

Death Sentences

"Death is different" from all other punishments says the Supreme Court, which means death sentences are different, too. So, the cruel-and-unusual-punishment clause applies to the death *penalty* and to death *sentences.* The U.S. Supreme Court has made it clear that the penalty of death isn't cruel and unusual punishment, at least when it's administered to murderers (*Gregg v. Georgia* 1976). The Court has held that capital punishment for murder isn't cruel and unusual punishment, *if* the sentencing process allows the judge or jury to consider—and offers adequate guidance in weighing—mitigating and aggravating circumstances (see Table 14.1) and provides for a review procedure to ensure against discriminatory application of the death penalty (*Lockett v. Ohio* 1978). According to the Supreme Court, the rationale for this is that "it is of vital importance to the defendant and to the community that any decision to impose the death sentence be, and appear to be, based on reason rather than caprice or emotion" (*Gardner v. Florida* 1977).

TABLE 14.1	
Aggravating and Mitigating Circumstances in Death Penalty Cases	
Aggravating Circumstances	**Mitigating Circumstances**
Prior record of violent felony	No significant prior criminal record
Felony murder	Extreme mental or emotional disturbance
Murder of more than one person	Minor participant in the murder
Murder of police officer or other public official	Youth at the time of the murder
Torture or other heinous killing	
Killing to avoid arrest	
Killing during escape from lawful custody	

Statistics indicate there's a pronounced racial disparity in death sentences. Blacks who kill whites are more likely to receive the death sentence than either blacks who kill blacks or whites who kill blacks. The U.S. Supreme Court has held that these numbers may well prove that race infects death sentencing decisions in *general*, but that it's not enough to prove cruel and unusual punishment in individual cases. To overturn a death sentence, individual defendants have to prove the death sentencing decision in *their* case was infected by racial views. Specifically, they have to prove the prosecutor, the jury, or their lawyer's decisions were motivated by race (*McCleskey v. Kemp* 1987).

APPEALS

It may surprise you to learn (as it surprises most of my students) that convicted offenders don't have a constitutional right to appeal their convictions. According to the U.S. Supreme Court in *Ross v. Moffitt* (1974), "It is clear that the State need not provide any appeal at all." According to that principle, the Court upheld a state court decision that denied a poor defendant a right to a lawyer for his appeal to the state supreme court. According to the Court:

> There are significant differences between the trial and appellate stages of a criminal proceeding. The purpose of the trial stage from the State's point of view is to convert a criminal defendant from a person presumed innocent to one found guilty beyond a reasonable doubt. To accomplish this purpose, the State employs a prosecuting attorney who presents evidence to the court, challenges any witnesses offered by the defendant, argues rulings of the court, and makes direct arguments to the court and jury seeking to persuade them of the defendant's guilt. Under these circumstances "reason and reflection require us to recognize that in our adversary system of criminal justice, any person haled into court, who is too poor to hire a lawyer, cannot be assured a fair trial unless counsel is provided for him."
>
> By contrast, it is ordinarily the defendant, rather than the state, who initiates the appellate process, seeking not to fend off the efforts of the state's prosecutor but rather to overturn a finding of guilty made by a judge or a jury below. The defendant needs an attorney on appeal not as a shield to protect him against being "haled into court" by the state and stripped of his presumption of innocence, but rather as a sword to upset the prior determination of guilt. This difference is significant for, while no one would agree that the state may simply dispense with the trial stage of proceedings without a criminal defendant's consent, it is clear that the state need not provide any appeal at all. (609)

Even though there's no *constitutional* right to appeal, every jurisdiction has created a **statutory right to appeal.** To understand this statutory right, refer to Figure 1.2 in Chapter 1, which depicts our three-tiered judicial system: trial courts, intermediate appeals courts, and supreme courts of appeal. The statutory right to appeal applies only to the intermediate appellate courts (and in capital cases to the supreme courts). On the other hand, appeals to the supreme courts are discretionary. Most of the cases in this book, like those to the U.S. Supreme Court, are discretionary appeal cases. The **writ of certiorari** is a discretionary writ, allowing appeals only in cases the U.S. Supreme Court or the state supreme courts decide are of significance beyond the interests of the particular defendants appealing them (Chapter 1, "Appellate Cases," p. 18).

Since the late 1980s, the U.S. Supreme Court has sharply reduced the number of cases it accepts by means of certiorari. By this reduction, the Court has reaffirmed the principle that final appeal isn't a right; it's a matter of discretionary judgment.

Three principal doctrines define the scope of appellate review of criminal cases in state courts:

1. Mootness

2. Raise or waive

3. Plain error

Traditionally, the **mootness doctrine** banned appeals by offenders who had finished their prison sentences or who had paid their fines. Some jurisdictions have retained this **traditional definition of mootness.** Several others have gone to the other extreme, holding that criminal cases are never moot, because defendants always have an interest in removing the "stigma of guilt." Most jurisdictions have taken a middle ground, retaining the mootness doctrine but carving out exceptions to it.

The **collateral consequences exception** says that if defendants might suffer legal consequences from a criminal conviction, then even if they've fully served their sentence the case isn't moot. These consequences include the possibility of the loss of a professional license, rejection for admission to a professional school, or loss of employment.

The **raise-or-waive doctrine** says defendants have to raise their objections at trial; if they don't, they give up their right to appeal. Why? The **doctrine of judicial economy** says we shouldn't spend time and money on appeals defendants could've avoided by objecting during the trial. However, defendants don't always waive their right to appeal when they fail to object at trial. When procedural requirements don't provide adequate time for a defendant to object to a trial court error, the defendant doesn't waive the right to appeal the error. Also, circumstances can make it impossible for a defendant to comply with the raise-or-waive rule. And obviously, incompetent lawyers don't object to their own ineffectiveness (LaFave and Israel 1984, 3:252–254).

A major exception to the raise-or-waive rule is the **plain-error doctrine,** which applies even if defendants don't object to the errors at trial. The plain-error doctrine applies when "plain errors affecting substantial rights" cause "manifest injustice or miscarriage of justice." Most courts apply the doctrine "sparingly." Plain error doesn't require or justify a review "of every alleged trial error that has not been properly preserved for appellate review." Furthermore, in most jurisdictions, the "defendant bears the burden of proving that an alleged error is of such magnitude that it constitutes plain error." According to one commentator, "'Plain error' is a concept appellate courts find impossible to define, save that they know it when they see it."

COLLATERAL ATTACK (HABEAS CORPUS)

Appeals are called **direct attacks,** because they attack the decisions made by the trial court and/or the jury's guilty verdict as part of the same case, the defendants' criminal trial. **Habeas corpus proceedings** are called collateral attacks, because they indirectly attack the judgment in a new noncriminal (civil) lawsuit. In that new case, the defendant in the criminal case (now the petitioner or plaintiff in the habeas case) asks (petitions the court) for the writ on the ground that the plaintiff is being unlawfully detained. If the court issues the writ, the writ orders the person (usually a prison warden) to bring the plaintiff before the judge and "show cause" for the detention. The object is to find out if the court in the criminal case had the authority (**jurisdiction**) to enter the judgment that put the plaintiff in prison and, if so, whether the judgment was properly reached. Depending on the evidence produced, the plaintiff is either set free, bailed, tried, or sent back to prison (Fisher 1888, 454).

Habeas corpus ("the great writ of liberty") has a long and distinguished history. It's called the "great writ of liberty" because it originated as a bulwark against tyrannical English kings. According to the nineteenth-century historian of habeas corpus, Sydney George Fisher (1888):

> These rulers of men often want to rid themselves quickly of their personal enemies or of those whom they choose to consider enemies of their country, and of the easiest methods is to arrest on any sort of charge or suspicion, and keep the victim in confinement simply by not allowing him to be brought to trial. And it has often been said,—and the Bastille and the Tower of London will warrant the assertion—that the power to secretly hurry a man to jail, where his sufferings will be unknown or soon forgotten, is more dangerous than all the engines of tyranny. (454)

Fisher contrasted this abuse of the English kings' power with President Lincoln's suspension of the writ of habeas corpus during the Civil War. Fisher vigorously defended Lincoln and scoffed at Lincoln's critics who called him a dictator because, Fisher argued, it was right to take extreme measures to save the Union.

Of course, we're a long way from tyrannical kings and even from Lincoln's use of the writ. Today, most habeas corpus proceedings begin only after criminal cases run through their full course of direct attack in state trial and appellate courts. After all this long and involved process, habeas proceedings start in U.S. District Court, proceed through the U.S. Court of Appeals, and can eventually reach the U.S. Supreme Court for final review.

According to the U.S. Constitution Article I, "The privilege of the Writ of Habeas Corpus shall not be suspended, unless when in Cases of Rebellion or Invasion the public Safety may require it." Two U.S. statutes elaborated on Article I by granting power to U.S. courts to hear petitions of habeas corpus and issue writs of habeas corpus. The U.S. Judiciary Act of 1789 authorized U.S. courts to deal with the petitions of *federal* prisoners. The Habeas Corpus Act of 1867 (LaFave and Israel 1984, 292) extended the power of U.S. Courts to deal with habeas corpus petitions of *state* prisoners.

According to the 1867 act:

> [T]he several courts of the United States . . . within their respective jurisdictions, in addition to the authority already conferred by law, shall have power to grant writs of habeas corpus in all cases where any person may be restrained of his or her liberty in violation of the Constitution, or of any treaty or law of the United States. (292)

The language of the 1867 act lends itself to both a narrow interpretation and a broad interpretation of the power of the federal courts to review the imprisonment of state prisoners. According to the narrow view, the act authorizes the courts only to review the jurisdiction of the court—that is, its authority over the person and the subject matter of the case. The review asks only whether the court has the power to hear criminal cases and whether it can decide criminal cases involving the prisoner. According to the broader view, the act empowers the federal courts to review the whole state proceeding to determine possible violations of federal law and constitutional provisions (LaFave and Israel 1984, 3:292–294).

During the years of the Warren Court (Chief Justice Earl Warren, 1953–1969), when federal rights were expanding through the incorporation doctrine (Chapter 3), the Court opted for a **broad view of habeas corpus.** The leader of the broad view, Associate Justice William Brennan, argued that the broader view fulfilled the historical purpose of habeas corpus, "providing relief against the detention of persons in violation of their fundamental liberties." As to objections that such expansive review of lower court proceedings threatened the interest in finality, he argued that "conventional notions of finality of litigation" should "have no place where life or liberty is at stake and infringement of constitutional rights is alleged." In addition to preserving fundamental liberties, the broader view, according to its supporters, furthers the interest in correct results. The more chances to review, the greater the accuracy of the final decision.

According to one judge:

> We would not send two astronauts to the moon without providing them with at least three or four back-up systems. Should we send literally thousands of men to prison with even less reserves? . . . With knowledge of our fallibility and a realization of past errors, we can hardly insure our confidence by creating an irrevocable end to the guilt determining process.
>
> LaFave and Israel 1984, 3:298–299

Justice Brennan's and the Warren Court majority's view have received strong criticism from judges and commentators. Most of the criticism focuses on the threat to finality and the costs of "endless" reviews of legal issues, which sometimes go on for years. No one has put the argument for finality better than the great advocate John W. Davis in his last argument before the U.S. Supreme Court:

> Somewhere, sometime to every principle comes a moment of repose when it has been so often announced, so confidently relied upon, so long continued, that it passes the limits of judicial discretion and disturbance.
>
> *Brown v. Board of Education* 1954

Others doubt that the broad view really protects prisoners' fundamental rights. Associate Supreme Court Justice Robert H. Jackson in *Brown v. Allen* (1953) argued that we have no reason to expect more accuracy in a second review than in the initial decision:

> Reversal by a higher court is not proof that justice is thereby better done. There is no doubt that if there were a super-Supreme Court, a substantial proportion of our reversals of state courts would also be reversed. We are not final because we are infallible, but we are infallible only because we are final.

Justice Jackson attributed the controversy over habeas corpus to three causes:

1. The Supreme Court's use of the due process clause of the Fourteenth Amendment to "subject state courts to increasing federal control"

2. The determination of what due process means by "personal notions of justice instead of by known rules of law"

3. The "breakdown of procedural safeguards against abuse of the writ"

The Burger (Chief Justice Warren Burger, 1969–1986) and Rehnquist (Chief Justice William Rehnquist, 1986–) Courts adopted the **narrow view of habeas corpus**—the power to review only the jurisdiction of the court over the person and the subject matter of the case.

The Rehnquist Court emphasizes the balance of interests that habeas corpus proceedings require. On one side of the balance are the constitutional rights of individuals and the need to control government misconduct. On the other side are the following interests:

- The finality of decisions

- Reliability, or obtaining the correct result

- Certainty in decisions, or promoting reliance on decisions

- The stability of decisions, or promoting the permanence of decisions

- Federalism, or respect for state criminal court decisions

- The burden on federal judicial resources in hearing repeated challenges

- Contempt for the system from repeated and long-drawn-out proceedings

- The impediment that many frivolous claims are to the success of meritorious claims

To the Rehnquist Court, the main problem in habeas corpus is an "endless succession of writs." Historically, an English subject could take a petition to every judge in England. The rule of *res judicata*—that once a matter is decided it cannot be reopened—didn't apply to habeas corpus. The remnants of that rule linger in the rule that denial of a first petition for habeas corpus doesn't prohibit filing a second petition. But, according to the Court in *McCleskey v. Zant* (1991), just because the rule of res judicata doesn't apply doesn't mean that prisoners can file an unlimited number of petitions. Courts have the discretion to deny successive petitions, especially if petitioners try to raise issues they failed to raise in their first petition.

The **abuse-of-the-writ rule** requires petitioners to prove they didn't fail deliberately or negligently to raise an issue in their first petition. Tactical decisions by attorneys and the accidental failure of competent counsel to raise claims aren't enough to avoid the abuse-of-the-writ rule. However, the rule doesn't apply to a failure to raise a claim of ineffective counsel. According to the **cause-and-prejudice rule,** in addition to proving they didn't fail deliberately or negligently to raise an issue in the first petition (cause), petitioners have to prove the failure to raise the issue *probably* affected the outcome of the case. Placing this burden of proof on habeas petitioners discourages baseless petitions while at the same time, according to the Court, it keeps the system open for genuine claims for relief.

The cause-and-prejudice rule isn't hard and fast. It permits, but doesn't require, courts to deny petitions if defendants fail to satisfy its requirements. For example, **cases of manifest injustice,** those in which the petitioner is probably innocent, are an exception to the rule. The word "innocent" refers to factual innocence—that is, a case in which the petitioner didn't commit the crime. It doesn't refer to cases where the petitioner may be entitled to an acquittal because of either procedural irregularities or to the government's inability to prove legal guilt beyond a reasonable doubt.

Other obstacles stand in the way of state prisoners' hopes to get federal habeas relief. According to the **exhaustion-of-remedies rule,** when a state prisoner files a petition in a federal court containing any claim for which a state remedy remains available, the court has to dismiss the petition. In such a case, the state prisoner may either strike the unexhausted state claim and file again in federal court or exhaust the claim by filing in state court. Furthermore, the claim has to violate a federal right. Errors in state proceedings that don't violate a federal right have to be pursued in state courts. Also, federal courts have to respect state court findings of fact. For example, federal courts, in reviewing petitions of state court convictions, can't review the credibility of witnesses (*Marshall v. Lonberger* 1983; *Rose v. Lundy* 1982).

The Supreme Court placed perhaps the most significant limit on federal review of state habeas corpus petitions in *Stone v. Powell* (1976). In *Stone*, the Court held that a state prisoner can't raise a Fourth Amendment illegal-search-and-seizure claim in a federal habeas corpus proceeding if the state has already provided an opportunity for the petitioner to raise the issue in state court. The Court held that the interests in finality and economy outweighed the costs of the exclusionary rule.

SUMMARY

I. Procedures after conviction
  A. Change of status from defendant to offender
    1. Presumption of innocence enjoyed by defendants
    2. Presumption of guilt against offenders
    3. Government and defendants get one *fair* shot at justice
  B. Three main procedures follow conviction
    1. Sentencing
    2. Appeals
    3. Habeas corpus, or collateral attack

II. Sentencing
  A. Aims
    1. Fit the sentence to the crime—look back to crime
    2. Tailor the sentence to suit the offender—look forward to prevention
  B. History—pendulum swing from fixed to indeterminate sentencing
  C. Division of sentencing authority among legislature, judges, and administrative agencies
  D. Fixed sentences
    1. Goals—uniformity; certainty; retribution, deterrence, and incapacitation
    2. Guidelines
      a. Weigh seriousness of crime *and* criminal history of offender
      b. Judges choose within a specified range
      c. Departures from the range are permitted if backed up with written reasons
      d. Prosecutors can appeal downward departures, and defendants can appeal upward departures
    3. Mandatory minimums
      a. Prescribe a nondiscretionary minimum amount of prison time
      b. Empirical support for the effectiveness is weak

E. Offenders' rights at sentencing
  1. Constitutional rights are aimed at defendants, not offenders
  2. The right to counsel is retained
F. Death sentences
  1. The death sentence isn't "cruel and unusual punishment" (Eighth Amendment)
  2. The sentencing process has to allow judges and/or juries to consider mitigating and aggravating circumstances
  3. Race disparity in death sentences generally doesn't prove discrimination against specific defendants

III. Appeals
  A. Convictions are reviewed for errors in the criminal case
  B. No *constitutional* right to appeal conviction
  C. All states and the U.S. government have a *statutory* right to appeal
    1. The right applies only to *intermediate* appellate courts
    2. Appeals to supreme courts are wholly discretionary
    3. The U.S. Supreme Court sharply limits discretionary appeals through writs of certiorari
    4. State supreme court discretionary appeals are limited by
      a. Mootness—the sentence has been served or the fine paid
      b. Failure to raise objections during the trial—"raise or waive"

IV. Collateral attack (habeas corpus)
  A. Suing official (warden or jailer) to challenge the lawfulness of detention
  B. Broad view (Warren Court in 1960s)—review the *whole* state court proceeding to decide whether federal law and the Constitution were violated
  C. Narrow view (present view)—review only whether the state court had jurisdiction (authority over person and subject matter) to hear the case
  D. Finality and efficiency objectives resulted in severe limitations placed on collateral attack
  E. Two review processes—first appeal and then habeas corpus

 Go to the Criminal Procedure 6e CD to download this summary outline. The outline has been formatted so that you can add notes to it during class lectures, or later create a customized chapter outline to use while reviewing. Either way, the summary outline will help you understand the "big picture" and fill in the details as you study.

REVIEW QUESTIONS

1. Why is the change of status from defendant to offender more than "just a change of words"?

2. Describe the reasons for the assumption that one shot of justice is enough.

3. In the debate over sentencing, identify the two sides that have characterized its history for more than a thousand years.

4. Trace the history of sentencing from 700 to the present.

5. List three ideas that came to dominate thinking about sentencing in the 1970s.

6. Identify and describe the three divisions of sentencing authority.

7. Identify three aims of both sentencing guidelines and mandatory minimum sentences.

8. Compare and contrast sentencing guidelines and mandatory minimum sentences.

9. What two elements are balanced in sentencing guidelines?

10. List the reasons for the revival of mandatory minimum sentences in the 1950s.

11. List the reasons for the abandonment of mandatory minimum sentences in the 1970s.

12. Identify the two main targets of current mandatory minimum sentences.

13. Identify the three aims of criminal punishment that mandatory minimum sentences are supposed to satisfy.

14. List and summarize the five main findings of empirical research on the effectiveness of mandatory minimum sentences.

15. Summarize the limits on the rights of offenders at sentencing, and explain the reasons for the limits.

16. When is the sentence of death *not* cruel and unusual punishment?

17. Identify the nature and circumstances of the right to appeal a conviction.

18. What's the difference between an appeal and a collateral attack?

19. Describe the progress through direct appeal and collateral attack.

20. Summarize the difference between the broad and narrow views of habeas corpus review.

21. List the three causes of the controversy over habeas corpus identified by U.S. Supreme Court Justice Robert Jackson.

22. Identify eight interests furthered by limits to habeas corpus review.

23. According to the Rehnquist Court, what's the main problem in habeas corpus review?

24. What's the significance of the U.S. Supreme Court decision in *Stone v. Powell?*

KEY TERMS

habeas corpus p. 502
collateral attack p. 502
fixed (determinate) sentencing
   p. 503
indeterminate sentencing p. 503
legislative sentencing model
   p. 505
judicial sentencing model p. 505
administrative sentencing model
   p. 505

sentencing guidelines p. 506
mandatory minimum prison
   sentences p. 506
statutory right to appeal p. 518
writ of certiorari p. 518
mootness doctrine p. 519
traditional definition of mootness
   p. 519
collateral consequences exception
   p. 519

raise-or-waive doctrine p. 519
doctrine of judicial economy
   p. 519
plain-error doctrine p. 519
direct attacks p. 519
habeas corpus proceedings
   p. 519
jurisdiction p. 520
broad view of habeas corpus
   p. 521

narrow view of habeas corpus
p. 522

abuse-of-the-writ rule p. 522
cause-and-prejudice rule p. 522

cases of manifest injustice p. 522
exhaustion-of-remedies rule p. 522

THE COMPANION WEB SITE
FOR *CRIMINAL PROCEDURE,* SIXTH EDITION

http://cj.wadsworth.com/samaha/crim_pro6e

 Supplement your review of this chapter by going to the companion Web site to take one of the Tutorial Quizzes, use the flash cards to test yourself on the key terms from each chapter, and check out the many other study aids you'll find there. You'll find valuable data and resources at your fingertips to help you study for that big exam or write that important paper.

Criminal Procedure in Crisis Times

15

Chapter Main Points

- The balance between government power and individual liberty and privacy always tips toward more government power during national emergencies.
- Since 9/11, the government has shifted its primary goal from gathering evidence to prosecute terrorists for their crimes to gathering intelligence to prevent their future attacks.
- The USA Patriot Act *modifies* in the government's favor (but doesn't eliminate) the constitutional balance between government power and individual privacy and liberty.
- The Patriot Act adds terrorist crimes to the list of "serious crimes" Congress has made eligible for electronic surveillance and "sneak and peek" searches.
- The president's power to detain suspected terrorists is clear. Decisions about how long and under what conditions they can be detained and whether there are different rules for citizens and noncitizens are making their way through the courts right now.
- Decisions about the extent of suspects' right to a lawyer, under what conditions and for what purposes the right exists, and whether the rules are different for citizens and noncitizens are making their way through the courts right now, too.
- Suspected terrorists can be tried either for crimes in ordinary courts or for *war* crimes in special *military* courts.
- Presidents are authorized to establish military courts to try *anyone* suspected of war crimes; President Bush's order creating military courts after 9/11 limits their jurisdiction to trials of *noncitizens*.
- Trials in military courts aren't bound by the constitutional requirements that apply to criminal trials in ordinary courts, but the Department of Defense has guaranteed defendants in 9/11 military court proceedings most of the rights defendants enjoy in ordinary criminal trials.

As terrible as 9/11 was, it didn't repeal the Constitution.

Judge Rosemary Pooler, November 17, 2003 (Hamblett 2003, 12)

A strict observance of the written laws is doubtless one of the high duties of a good citizen, but it is not the highest. The laws of necessity, of self-preservation, of saving our country when in danger, are of higher obligation. To lose our country by a scrupulous adherence to written law, would be to lose the law itself, with life, liberty, property and all those who are enjoying them with us; thus absurdly sacrificing the ends to the means.

Thomas Jefferson, September 20, 1810 (1904, I:146)

The law is not dead, but sleepeth; the Constitution is eclipsed, but the dark ... which intercepted its light ... will soon pass away, and we shall again behold the glorious luminary shining forth in all its original splendor.

Edward Livingston, 1815 (Gayarré 1903, 601)

The Constitution of the United States is a law for rulers and people, equally in war and in peace, and covers with the shield of its protection all classes of men, at all times, and under all circumstances.

Ex Parte Milligan (1866)

BALANCING RIGHTS AND SECURITY DURING EMERGENCIES

We end our journey through the criminal process the way we began—by looking at the balance between government power and individual liberty and privacy. But this time, we're going to look at the balance when it's most stressed—during emergencies. We're all familiar with governors who declare state emergencies during floods and fires and call out the state National Guard to enforce government orders to stay out of the danger areas or to leave them (even their homes). Even local governments can declare emergencies and take extraordinary measures. For example, for those of us who live in Minnesota, the city or town government infringes on our freedom by ordering us not to park on the streets during "snow emergencies." The simple lesson of these examples is that emergency times call for recalibrating the balance between government power and individual liberty and privacy. The balance tips to expanding government power and limiting individual liberty and privacy.

But, emergency powers are limited by two conditions:

1. *Necessity.* Government can exercise extraordinary power only *when* and *to the extent* it's absolutely needed to protect the people from the dangers created by the emergency.

2. *Temporary nature.* Government has to give up its extraordinary power as soon as the emergency's over.

In this chapter, we'll examine how emergencies affect criminal procedure by looking at the history of criminal procedure during wartime, how terrorism has impacted surveillance laws, "sneak and peek" searches in terrorist cases, the detention of terrorist suspects, and trials for those suspected of terrorism.

THE HISTORY OF CRIMINAL PROCEDURE DURING WARTIME

In floods, fires, snow emergencies, and the like, it's easy to apply the conditions that limit emergency powers because the emergencies are easy to define (our senses clearly tell us the fires, floods, and snow are here); the responses to them are widely known and followed (build firewalls and levies; plow the snow); and it's easy to tell when they're over (we can see the fires and floods have stopped and the snow's gone, or at least it's under control).

What's just been said about flood, fire, and snow emergencies used to be true of the subject of this chapter—wartime emergencies. Wars began when governments of one country declared war on another country. They were fought according to long-standing **laws of war**—rules written, understood, and agreed to by almost all the countries fighting the wars (Avalon Project 2003). And, they ended when the countries signed peace treaties. Of course, not all nations always followed the laws of war, and even if they did, there was plenty of play in the joints for interpreting many of the rules. Also, arguments have been made that the "new" wars, those since World War I, differed from when the rules were made. In the world wars, I and II, the difference was that these were **"total wars,"** meaning the whole people, the governments, and the countries' resources were mobilized for fighting and winning the war. The rules had to change to meet the changes brought about by total war.

But even in total wars, most of the basics were the same as they'd always been. The enemies were identifiable foreign nations. Wars began with declarations of war (even if the declaration was by a "sneak attack" like the Japanese attack on Pearl Harbor). Wars ended when treaties were signed between the warring nations.

Then came the Cold War. International communism crossed national boundaries. Communist spies came to the United States. They looked and acted like non-Communists. They got jobs in strategic industries and government for the purpose of "boring from within" to learn secrets and pass them on to Communist governments. They became the feared "invisible enemy within." Waging the Cold War required great emphasis on an old feature of war—**intelligence** (gathering information about the enemy).

The government took strong measures to respond to the Communist "hidden enemy within." These measures were of two types. First, the government sought to get evidence either to prosecute and convict them of crimes or to find and deport them. Second, but far more important, law enforcement focused on gathering intelligence to *prevent* further Communist infiltration and activity in the United States. The emphasis on intelligence gathering for the purpose of prevention was very different from what we've studied throughout this book—balancing the need for getting evidence for criminal prosecution against the rights of individuals to fair proceedings.

This shift in emphasis from prosecuting terrorists for crimes to preventing them from committing more terrorist attacks continues to be reflected in most of the measures being used (with some modifications) to respond to domestic and international terrorism today. We'll examine both the terrorism prevention and criminal prosecution elements of anti-terrorism laws, court decisions, and procedures before September 11, 2001; look at modifications made after September 11 by the 2001 **USA Patriot Act** (short for **U**niting and **S**trengthening **A**merica by **P**roviding **A**ppropriate **T**ools **R**equired to **I**ntercept and **O**bstruct **T**errorism); and then see how the efforts have fared in a few court cases.

U.S. Attorney General John Ashcroft (Attorney General's Guidelines 2002) stated clearly the shift in the FBI's role brought about by the September 11 attacks:

> The FBI...plays a central role in the enforcement of federal laws and in the proper administration of justice in the United States. In discharging this function, the highest priority is to protect the security of the nation and the safety of the American people against...terrorists and foreign aggressors. Investigations by the FBI are premised on the fundamental duty of government to protect the public against...those who would threaten the fabric of society through terrorism or mass destruction. (2)

As I'm writing this, we're limited to studying what these laws *say*, not to how they're *operating*. Why? First, there's the need for secrecy. The government can't tell us things that might tip off terrorists—things that might help us learn more about the laws but also help terrorists plan future attacks. Second, September 11, 2001, is too recent to have produced more than a few officially reported court cases to analyze. In other words, we have to face a problem (aggravated by current necessity) social scientists have recognized for nearly two centuries: the gap between the **"law in books"** (the way laws are *supposed* to work) and the **"law in action"** (the way the law *really* works).

Let's look at what the anti-terrorism laws say and (as much as possible) how they're operating regarding four issues you've already studied:

1. Surveillance (Chapter 3)

2. Search and seizure (Chapters 4–7)

3. Right to counsel (Chapter 12)

4. Trial (Chapter 13)

As you read about these four issues, remember that just as in ordinary criminal procedure, federal anti-terrorism procedure laws are based on the requirement in a constitutional democracy to balance the need for enough government power to prevent and prosecute terrorist acts and the rights of individuals guaranteed by the U.S. Constitution. Comments from Charles Doyle (2002), senior specialist at the Congressional Research Center, on the intelligence gathering provisions of the Patriot Act underscore this emphasis:

[The Patriot Act was] erected for the dual purpose of protecting the confidentiality of private telephone, face-to-face, and computer communications while enabling authorities to identify and intercept criminal communications. (2)

One last point before we begin our journey through the national security law and its application to anti-terrorism. There's a lot of chatter about the dramatic changes in the balance between power and liberty brought about by the USA Patriot Act. On one side, we're warned that *with* the expanded government powers authorized by the act, we'll lose our liberty and privacy to our own government. On the other side, we're warned that *without* the expanded powers established in the act we'll lose our liberty and privacy to foreign terrorist organizations. You can decide for yourselves whether these extreme positions on the anti-terrorism laws are correct or whether the changes in the law are modest adjustments to existing laws.

SURVEILLANCE AND TERRORISM

You're already familiar with law enforcement's use of surveillance to gather evidence in criminal cases, especially in illegal drug cases. You learned in Chapter 3 that, according to the U.S. Supreme Court, the Fourth Amendment ban on unreasonable searches and seizures doesn't protect any of the following highly personal information from law enforcement officers who intercept communications and capture it without warrants or probable cause:

1. Conversations of private individuals secretly listened to after wiring informants for sound (*U.S. v. White*, case excerpt Chapter 3)

2. Telephone company lists of the phone numbers of outgoing calls (**pen registers**) (*Smith v. Maryland*, "Exploring the Expectation of Privacy Further," Chapter 3) and incoming calls (**trap and trace**) of a specific telephone

3. Bank records of individuals' financial dealings (*U.S. v. Miller*, "Exploring the Expectation of Privacy Further," Chapter 3)

The rationale for the Court's decisions in these cases goes like this: The Fourth Amendment bans "unreasonable searches and seizures" by the government. But not all government actions are searches and seizures. If a government action isn't a search or seizure, the ban doesn't apply at all. In other words, it's left to government discretionary judgment whether to act. Here's another "but": Legislatures can control this discretion. And, Congress has decided to control government's discretion not just in ordinary criminal cases but in anti-terrorism cases, too. Let's look at the legislation balancing government power to use electronic surveillance and individual privacy and how the USA Patriot Act has modified the general legislation.

Federal law has established a three-tiered system to balance government power and individual privacy in government surveillance (see Table 15.1). Tier 1 restricts government power and protects privacy most. Tier 2 authorizes more government power and provides less protection for individual privacy. Tier 3 authorizes the most government power and provides the least protection for individual privacy. The tiers are nothing new; they've been around since the 1960s.

We'll look at how terrorism has affected surveillance procedures for each of the three tiers.

TABLE 15.1

Three Tiers of Federal Law Balancing Government Power and Individual Privacy

Tier 1 Least Government Power/ Most Privacy Protection	Tier 2 More Government Power/ Less Privacy Protection	Tier 3 Most Government Power/ Least Privacy Protection
1. General ban on electronic surveillance, interception, and capture	1. Stored communications and transactions are subject to surveillance, interception, and capture of information	1. Pen registers and trap and trace devices are allowed for surveillance, interception, and capture of information
2. Exception: serious crime	2. Applies to all crimes, not just "serious" crimes	2. Applies to all crimes, not just "serious" crimes
3. Safeguards: detailed and approved by courts	3. Safeguards: court order, warrant, or subpoena	3. Safeguard: certification by law enforcement agency supervisory officer without the need for approval by court order

Tier 1: "Real Time" Electronic Surveillance

The first tier was established in 1968 by the **Crime Control and Safe Streets Act** (U.S. Code 2003, Title 18, Chapter 119, §§ 2510/2522). This act provides the most protection for individual privacy by placing a general ban on the interception of "wire, oral, or electronic communications" while they're taking place (§ 2511). However, there's a **serious crime exception** to the ban. *Serious crimes* are defined as crimes punishable by death or more than one year in prison (§ 2516). The exception comes attached with specific conditions aimed at protecting individual privacy. Here are a few of the more important conditions:

1. The U.S. Attorney General or other senior Department of Justice officials have to approve a law enforcement officer's application for a court order from a federal judge to allow the officer to secretly intercept and capture conversations.

2. The judge may issue the order if the interception "may provide or has provided evidence of any offense punishable by death or imprisonment for more than one year."

3. The application includes
   a. A "full and complete statement of the facts and circumstances relied upon by the applicant, to justify the belief that an order should be issued"
   b. "A full and complete statement as to whether other investigative procedures have been tried and failed or why they reasonably appear to be unlikely to succeed if tried or to be too dangerous"
   c. A statement of how long the interception is going to last

The Patriot Act adds several terrorist crimes to the list of serious crimes excepted from the ban on electronic surveillance (Table 15.2).

Tier 2: Surveilling Stored Electronic Communications

Tier 2 legislation (the USA Patriot Act) tips the balance somewhat in favor of government power and guarantees somewhat less protection for individual privacy. The Patriot Act has significantly expanded government surveillance power beyond the Crime

TABLE 15.2		
Terrorist Crimes not Subject to a Ban on Electronic Surveillance		
Chemical weapons offenses (18 U.S. Code 229)		
Terrorist acts of violence against Americans overseas (§ 2332)		
Use of weapons of mass destruction (§ 2332(a))		
Financial transactions with countries that support terrorists (§ 2332(d))		
Providing material support for terrorists (§ 2339A)		
Providing material support for terrorist organizations (§ 2339B)		

Control and Safe Streets Act of 1968. First, it allows the government to access *stored* "wire and electronic communications" like voice mail and e-mail. Second, the power applies to *"any* criminal investigation," not just to the *serious* crimes in Tier 1.

The Patriot Act does include definite limits to the government's Tier 2 power. The decision to intercept and capture stored information isn't left to law enforcement's discretionary judgment. If the e-mail and voice mail messages are stored under six months, officers have to get a warrant based on probable cause (U.S. Code 2003, Title 18 §2703; see Chapter 6, "Search," on search warrants). For communications stored over six months, the government still needs a warrant to access the information. But, they don't have to tell subscribers about the warrant for 90 days, "if the court determines" there's "reason to believe" this "may have an adverse result" on the investigation (§2705(a)(1)(A)). "Adverse results" include endangering life; flight from prosecution; destruction of evidence; intimidating potential witnesses; or "otherwise seriously jeopardizing an investigation or unduly delaying a trial" (§2705(a)(2)).

Tier 3: Secret "Caller ID"

Government power in Tier 3 legislation is *broader* than in Tiers 1 and 2 but doesn't invade individual privacy as deeply as they do. Tier 3 grants the power to capture a record of all telephone *numbers* (not *conversations*) *from* a subscriber's phone, using pen registers and trap and trace devices (U.S. Code Title 18, §§ 3121–3127). This **secret "caller ID"** is available to investigate "any crime"; without court approval; and without officers' ever notifying subscribers they have it or what they learned from it. Officers are limited in getting and using the secret caller IDs only by having to get the approval of a department senior official.

The Patriot Act expands pen register and trap and trace in two ways (§§ 3121, 3123). First, it allows the use of pen registers and trap and trace devices to capture e-mail *headers* (not messages). Before the act, pen registers and trap and trace were authorized only to capture *telephone* numbers. Second, it expands the geographical area the pen register and trap and trace order covers. Before the act, the court's power was limited to issuing orders only within its own district; the act empowers the court to issue orders to "anywhere in the United States" (§ 3123(b)(1)(C)).

To address objections that e-mail headers reveal more information than telephone numbers, the act (§ 3123(a)(3)) requires any agency getting the court order to submit a detailed report to the court showing:

1. The name of the officer who installed and/or accessed the device

2. The date and time the device was installed, accessed, and uninstalled

3. The configuration of the device when it was installed and any modifications made after installation

4. Information captured by the device

"SNEAK AND PEEK" SEARCHES

You've already learned that searches of private places are "unreasonable searches," banned by the Fourth Amendment unless officers are backed up by warrants based on probable cause *and* they "knock and announce" their presence before they enter and search (Chapter 6). But, you also learned that there's a "no knock" emergency exception to the knock-and-announce rule. **"Sneak and peek" searches** are a variation of no-knock entries. Sneak-and-peek search warrants allow officers to enter private places without the owner or (occupant) consenting or knowing about it. They're not new. During the 1980s, the FBI and DEA (Drug Enforcement Agency) asked for and judges issued at least thirty-five sneak-and-peek warrants (*Georgia Defender* 2002, 1). Here's a description of these warrants from the 1980s:

> Under those warrants the search occurred only when the occupants were absent from the premises. The entry and the search were conducted in such a way as to keep them secret. The warrants prohibited seizures of anything except intangible evidence, i.e., information concerning what had been going on, or now was located, inside the premises. No tangible evidence was seized. The searching officers usually took photographs inside the premises searched. No copy of the warrant or receipt was left on the premises. The time for giving notice of the covert entry might be postponed by the court one or more times. The same premises might be subjected to repeated covert entries under successive warrants. At the end of the criminal investigation the premises previously searched under a sneak and peek warrant were usually searched under a conventional search warrant and tangible evidence was then seized. Generally, it was not until after the police made an arrest or returned with a conventional search warrant that the existence of any covert entries was disclosed. Sometimes this was weeks or even months after the surreptitious search or searches. (1)

Both the Second and Ninth Circuit U.S. Courts of Appeals have upheld the admission of evidence obtained during sneak-and-peek searches. The Second Circuit said they were reasonable searches (*U.S. v. Villegas* 1990; Chapter 6); the Ninth Circuit said the evidence was admissible under the "good faith" exception to the exclusionary rule (*U.S. v. Freitas* 1988; Chapter 11).

The Patriot Act was the first time sneak-and-peek warrants became part of a statute (§ 213). Section 213 authorizes judges to issue sneak-and-peek warrants if:

1. The court finds reasonable cause to believe that providing immediate notification of the execution of the warrant may have an adverse effect; ["adverse effect" includes: "endangering life; flight from prosecution; destruction of evidence; intimidating potential witnesses; or otherwise seriously jeopardizing an investigation or unduly delaying a trial"]

2. The warrant prohibits the seizure of any tangible [personal] property... except where the court finds reasonable necessity for the seizure

3. The warrant provides for the giving of such notice within a reasonable time of its execution, which period may be extended by the court for good cause shown

Section 213 set off a storm of protest from politicians from both the Democratic and Republican parties, defense lawyers, and civil libertarians. Here's what the *Georgia Defender* (2002; the publication of the Georgia defense bar) wrote:

> It is obvious that these restrictions [reasonable cause, property seizure, and notice] on issuing sneak and peek search warrants border on the meaningless, especially in light of the somber reality that search warrants are issued secretly and **ex parte** [in the defendant's absence from the proceeding], that they are typically issued on the basis of recurring, generalized, boilerplate allegations, and that the judicial officials who issue them tend to be rubber stamps for law enforcement.
>
> Take, for example, the "adverse result" requirement. The statutory definition of adverse result is so all-encompassing that it is difficult to imagine many criminal investigations where at least one form of such a result is not going to be arguably applicable; furthermore, to satisfy the requirement the court need not have reasonable cause to believe that there will be an adverse result, only that there "may" be an adverse result.
>
> The second requirement, that the warrant prohibit the seizure of tangible property, is drained of significance by the gigantic exception allowing seizure of such property "where the court finds reasonable necessity for the seizure." It will be a rare case indeed where such necessity, if alleged, will not be determined to exist by the issuing court; and it may be confidently predicted that, with the passage of time, requests for seizure of tangible evidence will become the rule rather than the exception in connection with sneak and peek warrants.
>
> The final requirement, that the warrant provide for the giving of notice within a reasonable period, involves merely a question of the wording of a sneak and peek warrant, and the provision permitting the court (acting ex parte) to extend the period (one or more times) "for good cause shown," a standard easily met, makes it likely that such extensions will become routine and pro forma.

On the other side, Massachusetts U.S. Attorney Michael Sullivan told the Boston Anti-Terrorism Task Force that sneak and peek is part of the Patriot Act's "series of necessary, measured, and limited tools without which we would be greatly hampered in the struggle against terrorism" (Murphy 2003). We can't settle this debate here, but keep in mind that all Section 213 did was write into a statute combating terrorism what law enforcement had been doing in enforcing drug laws for twenty years (and off the record probably a lot longer). Further, courts also previously admitted evidence obtained from these searches either because they were "reasonable" Fourth Amendment "searches" or qualified as a "good faith" exception to the exclusionary rule.

THE DETENTION OF TERRORIST SUSPECTS

You already know that in ordinary times, under ordinary circumstances, detaining someone on the street for just a few minutes is an "unreasonable" Fourth Amendment seizure (a stop) unless it's backed up by enough facts to amount to reasonable suspicion

(Chapter 4). You know that arresting and detaining someone for hours (and maybe a few days) at a police station is an "unreasonable seizure" if it's not backed up by more facts (probable cause) (Chapter 5). You also know that both the Fourth Amendment and the Sixth Amendment "speedy trial" clause require officers to take detained suspects before a judge promptly (usually within 48 hours) so the judge can decide whether there's probable cause to detain them; to inform them of their rights; to set or deny them bail; and to provide them with a lawyer if they can't afford one (Chapter 12).

But, we aren't living in *ordinary* times under *ordinary* circumstances anymore. September 11 changed all that. Three official acts document the changes in the balance between preserving national security and the right of individuals to come and go as they please.

1. Presidential Proclamation 7463

2. Congressional "Authorization for Use of Military Force" (Joint Resolution)

3. The president's Military Order of November 13, 2001, "Detention, Treatment, and Trial of Certain Non-Citizens in the War Against Terrorism"

On September 14, President George W. Bush declared a "national emergency by reason of certain terrorist attacks" in **Presidential Proclamation 7463** (*Federal Register* 2001, 48199). On that same day, Congress threw its weight behind the president's war power in a Joint Resolution, **Authorization for Use of Military Force.** Section 2 power provides:

> That the President is authorized to use all necessary and appropriate force against those nations, organizations, or persons he determines planned, authorized, committed, or aided the terrorist attacks that occurred on September 11, 2001, or harbored such organizations or persons, in order to prevent any future acts of international terrorism against the United States by such nations, organizations or persons.

Third, President George W. Bush issued the **Military Order of November 13, 2001,** "Detention, Treatment, and Trial of Certain Non-Citizens in the War Against Terrorism" (*Federal Register* 2001, 57831–57836). According to the order, "certain noncitizens" included "any individual who is not a U.S. citizen ... that there is reason to believe:

1. Is or was a member of ... al Qaida

2. Has engaged in, aided or abetted, or conspired to commit, acts of international terrorism, or acts in preparation therefore, that have caused, threaten to cause, or have as their aim to cause, injury to or adverse effects on the U.S., its citizens, national security, foreign policy, or economy, or

3. Has knowingly harbored one or more individuals described in 1 or 2 ... shall be detained by the secretary of defense.

After defining whom it includes, the order spells out the conditions of detention and the treatment of detainees. Persons detained shall be:

    a. Treated humanely, without any adverse distinction based on race, color, religion, gender, birth, wealth, or any similar criteria;

    b. Afforded adequate food, drinking water, shelter, clothing, and medical treatment;

c. Allowed the free exercise of religion consistent with the requirements of such detention; and

d. Detained in accordance with *such other conditions as the secretary of defense shall prescribe.*

The Military Order of November 13, 2001 applies only to *noncitizens.* But, can citizens be detained under the same circumstances as those outlined in the order? In *Padilla v. Rumsfeld* (2003), the U.S. Second Circuit Court of Appeals dealt with "whether the Constitution gives the President the power to detain an American citizen seized in this country until the war with al Qaeda ends."

| CASE | Can U.S. Citizens Suspected of Aiding Terrorists Be Detained Indefinitely? |

Padilla v. Rumsfeld

2003 WL 22965085 (2nd Cir., N.Y.)

Donald Rumsfeld, the Secretary of Defense, and Jose Padilla, by his next friend Donna R. Newman, Esq., cross-appeal on questions certified by the District Court for the Southern District of New York (Mukasey, CJ.) arising from a petition for a writ of habeas corpus filed on behalf of Padilla challenging his detention as an enemy combatant. Affirmed in part, reversed in part, and remanded. Judge Wesley dissents in part in a separate opinion.

POOLER and PARKER, JJ.

FACTS

I. The Initial Detention

On May 8, 2002, Jose Padilla, an American citizen, flew on his American passport from Pakistan, via Switzerland, to Chicago's O'Hare International Airport. There he was arrested by FBI agents pursuant to a material witness warrant issued by the Chief Judge of the Southern District of New York in connection with a grand jury investigation of the terrorist attacks of September 11. Padilla carried no weapons or explosives.*

---

*These details should not be read to suggest that Padilla is in fact innocent or that the government lacked substantial reasons to be suspicious of him. We include them because they are relevant to our analysis of the President's power to detain Padilla as an enemy combatant. As is evident from the government investigation, described below, the government had ample cause to suspect Padilla of involvement in a terrorist plot. We, of course, reach no conclusion as to Padilla's guilt or innocence.

The agents brought Padilla to New York where he was held as a civilian material witness in the maximum security wing of the Metropolitan Correctional Center (MCC). At that point, Padilla was under the control of the Bureau of Prisons and the United States Marshal Service. Any immediate threat he posed to national security had effectively been neutralized. On May 15, 2002, he appeared before Chief Judge Mukasey, who appointed Donna R. Newman, Esq., to represent Padilla. Newman "conferred with [Padilla] over a period of weeks in...an effort to end [his] confinement." She also conferred with Padilla's relatives and with government representatives on Padilla's behalf.

On May 22, Newman moved to vacate the material witness warrant. By June 7, the motion had been submitted for decision. A conference on the motion was scheduled for June 11. However, on June 9, the government notified the court ex parte that (1) it wished to withdraw its subpoena and (2) the President had issued an Order (the "June 9 Order") designating Padilla as an enemy combatant and directing Secretary Rumsfeld to detain him. Chief Judge Mukasey vacated the warrant, and Padilla was taken into custody by Department of Defense (DOD) personnel and transported from New York to the high-security Consolidated Naval Brig in Charleston, South Carolina. At the scheduled June 11 conference, Newman, unable to secure Padilla's signature on a habeas corpus petition, nonetheless filed one on his behalf as "next friend."**

For the past eighteen months, Padilla has been held in the Brig in Charleston. He has not been permitted any

---

**A person who appears in a lawsuit to act for the benefit of someone else but is not a party to the lawsuit.

contact with his counsel, his family or any other non-military personnel. During this period he has been the subject of ongoing questioning regarding the al Qaeda network and its terrorist activities in an effort to obtain intelligence.

II. The Order Authorizing the Detention

In his June 9 Order, the President directed Secretary Rumsfeld to detain Padilla based on findings that Padilla was an enemy combatant who

(1) was "closely associated with al Qaeda, an international terrorist organization with which the United States is at war";

(2) had engaged in "war-like acts, including conduct in preparation for acts of international terrorism" against the United States;

(3) had intelligence that could assist the United States to ward off future terrorist attacks; and

(4) was a continuing threat to United States security. As authority for the detention, the President relied on "the Constitution and . . . the laws of the United States, including the [Joint Resolution]."

In an unsealed declaration submitted to the District Court, Michael H. Mobbs, a special advisor to the Under Secretary of Defense for Policy (who claims no direct knowledge of Padilla's actions or of the interrogations that produced the information discussed in his declaration), set forth the information the President received before he designated Padilla as an enemy combatant. According to the declaration, Padilla was born in New York, was convicted of murder in 1983, and remained incarcerated until his eighteenth birthday. In 1991, he was convicted on a handgun charge and again sent to prison. He moved to Egypt in 1998 and traveled to several countries in the Middle East and Southwest Asia between 1999 and 2000. During this period, he was closely associated with known members and leaders of al Qaeda. While in Afghanistan in 2001, Padilla became involved with a plan to build and detonate a "dirty bomb" within the United States, and went to Pakistan to receive training on explosives from al Qaeda operatives. There he was instructed by senior al Qaeda officials to return to the United States to conduct reconnaissance and/or other attacks on behalf of al Qaeda. He then traveled to Chicago, where he was arrested upon arrival into the United States on May 8, 2002. Notwithstanding Padilla's extensive contacts with al Qaeda members and his actions under their direction, the government does not allege that Padilla was a member of al Qaeda.

The government also offered for the District Court's review Mobbs' sealed declaration, which the District Court characterized as "identifying one or more of the sources referred to only in cryptic terms in the [unsealed] Mobbs Declaration" and "setting forth objective circumstantial evidence that corroborates the factual allegations in the unsealed Mobbs Declaration."* . . .

OPINION

[This excerpt includes only the parts of the opinion having to do with Padilla's detention and access to his lawyer.]

II. Power to Detain

A. Introduction

The District Court concluded, and the government maintains here, that the indefinite detention of Padilla was a proper exercise of the President's power as Commander-in-Chief. The power to detain Padilla is said to derive from the President's authority, settled by *Ex parte Quirin*, 317 U.S. 1 (1942), to detain enemy combatants in wartime—authority that is argued to encompass the detention of United States citizens seized on United States soil. This power, the court below reasoned, may be exercised without a formal declaration of war by Congress and "even if Congressional authorization were deemed necessary, the Joint Resolution, passed by both houses of Congress, . . . engages the President's full powers as Commander in Chief. *Padilla I*, 233 F.Supp.2d at 590. Specifically, the District Court found that the Joint Resolution acted as express congressional authorization under 18 U.S.C. § 4001(a), which prohibits the detention of American citizens absent such authorization. In addition, the government claims that 10 U.S.C. § 956(5), a statute that allows the military to use authorized funds for certain detentions, grants authority to detain American citizens.

These alternative arguments require us to examine the scope of the President's inherent power and, if this is found insufficient to support Padilla's detention, whether Congress has authorized such detentions of American citizens. We reemphasize, however, that our review is limited to the case of an American citizen arrested in the United States, not on a foreign battlefield or while actively engaged in armed conflict against the United States. As the Fourth Circuit recently—and accurately—noted in *Hamdi v. Rumsfeld*, "to compare this battlefield capture of Hamdi to the domestic arrest in *Padilla v. Rumsfeld* is to compare apples and oranges." . . .

---

*Prior to oral argument, we reviewed the sealed Mobbs declaration as well as a sealed declaration of Vice Admiral Lowell E. Jacoby, the Director of the Defense Intelligence Agency, which was submitted to the District Court in connection with Secretary Rumsfeld's motion for reconsideration. Nothing in the ensuing discussion or holdings relies on either of these sealed documents.

I. INHERENT POWER

...Great deference is afforded the President's exercise of his authority as Commander-in-Chief....Whether a state of armed conflict exists against an enemy to which the laws of war apply is a political question for the President, not the courts....We have no quarrel with the former chief of the Justice Department's Criminal Division, who said:

> For [al Qaeda] chose not to violate the law but to attack the law and its institutions directly. Their proclaimed goal, however unrealistic, was to destroy the United States. They used powerful weapons of destructive force and openly declared their willingness to employ even more powerful weapons of mass destruction if they could lay hold of them. They were as serious a threat to the national security of the United States as one could envision. Michael Chertoff, "Law, Loyalty, and Terror: Our Legal Response to the Post-9-11 World," *Wkly. Standard*, Dec. 1, 2003, at 15.

However, it is a different proposition entirely to argue that the President even in times of grave national security threats or war, whether declared or undeclared, can lay claim to any of the powers, express or implied, allocated to Congress. The deference due to the Executive in its exercise of its war powers therefore only starts the inquiry; it does not end it. Where the exercise of Commander-in-Chief powers, no matter how well intentioned, is challenged on the ground that it collides with the powers assigned by the Constitution to Congress, a fundamental role exists for the courts. To be sure, when Congress and the President act together in the conduct of war, "it is not for any court to sit in review of the wisdom of their action or substitute its judgment for theirs." But when the Executive acts, even in the conduct of war, in the face of apparent congressional disapproval, challenges to his authority must be examined and resolved by the Article III courts.

These separation of powers concerns are heightened when the Commander-in-Chief's powers are exercised in the domestic sphere. The Supreme Court has long counseled that while the Executive should be "indulge[d] the widest latitude of interpretation to sustain his exclusive function to command the instruments of national force, at least when turned against the outside world for the security of our society," he enjoys "no such indulgence" when "it is turned inward." This is because "the federal power over external affairs [is] in origin and essential character different from that over internal affairs," and "congressional legislation which is to be made effective through negotiation and inquiry within the international field must often accord to the President a degree of discretion and freedom from statutory restriction which would not be admissible were domestic affairs alone involved." Thus, we

do not concern ourselves with the Executive's inherent wartime power, generally, to detain enemy combatants on the battlefield. Rather, we are called on to decide whether the Constitution gives the President the power to detain an American citizen seized in this country until the war with al Qaeda ends.

The government contends that the Constitution authorizes the President to detain Padilla as an enemy combatant as an exercise of inherent executive authority. Padilla contends that, in the absence of express congressional authorization, the President, by his June 9 Order denominating Padilla an enemy combatant, has engaged in the "lawmaking" function entrusted by the Constitution to Congress in violation of the separation of powers....

The Constitution entrusts the ability to define and punish offenses against the law of nations to the Congress, not the Executive. U.S. Const. art. II, § 8, cl. 10....The Constitution envisions grave national emergencies and contemplates significant domestic abridgements of individual liberties during such times. Here, the Executive lays claim to the inherent emergency powers necessary to effect such abridgements, but...the Constitution lodges these powers with Congress, not the President.

First, the Constitution explicitly provides for the suspension of the writ of habeas corpus "when in Cases of Rebellion or Invasion the public Safety may require it." U.S. Const. art. I, § 9, cl. 2. This power, however, lies only with Congress. Further, determinations about the scope of the writ are for Congress. Moreover, the Third Amendment's prohibition on the quartering of troops during times of peace* reflected the Framers' deep-seated beliefs about the sanctity of the home and the need to prevent military intrusion into civilian life. At the same time they understood that in times of war—of serious national crisis—military concerns prevailed and such intrusions could occur. But significantly, decisions as to the nature and scope of these intrusions were to be made "in a manner to be prescribed by law." U.S. Const. amend. III. The only valid process for making "law" under the Constitution is, of course, via bicameral passage and presentment to the President, whose possible veto is subject to congressional override, provided in Article I, Section 7.

The Constitution's explicit grant of the powers authorized in the Offenses Clause, the Suspension Clause, and the Third Amendment, to Congress is a powerful indication that, absent express congressional authorization, the President's Commander-in-Chief powers do not support Padilla's confinement. The level of specificity with which

---

*"No Soldier shall, in time of peace be quartered in any house, without the consent of the Owner, nor in time of war, but in a manner to be prescribed by law." U.S. Const. amend. III.

the Framers allocated these domestic powers to Congress and the lack of any even near-equivalent grant of authority in Article II's catalogue of executive powers compels us to decline to read any such power into the Commander-in-Chief Clause. In sum, while Congress—otherwise acting consistently with the Constitution—may have the power to authorize the detention of United States citizens under the circumstances of Padilla's case, the President, acting alone, does not.

The government argues that *Quirin* established the President's inherent authority to detain Padilla. In *Quirin*, the Supreme Court reviewed the habeas petitions of German soldiers captured on United States soil during World War II. All of the petitioners had lived in the United States at some point in their lives and had been trained in the German Army in the use of explosives. These soldiers, one of whom would later claim American citizenship, landed in the United States and shed their uniforms intending to engage in acts of military sabotage. They were arrested in New York and Chicago, tried by a military commission as "unlawful combatants," and sentenced to death. The Court denied the soldiers' petitions for habeas corpus, holding that the alleged American citizenship of one of the saboteurs was immaterial to its judgment: "Citizenship in the United States of an enemy belligerent does not relieve him from the consequences of a belligerency which is unlawful because in violation of the law of war." The government contends that *Quirin* conclusively establishes the President's authority to exercise military jurisdiction over American citizens.

We do not agree that *Quirin* controls. First, and most importantly, the *Quirin* Court's decision to uphold military jurisdiction rested on express congressional authorization of the use of military tribunals to try combatants who violated the laws of war. Specifically, the Court found it "unnecessary for present purposes to determine to what extent the President as Commander in Chief has constitutional power to create military commissions without the support of Congressional legislation." Accordingly, *Quirin* does not speak to whether, or to what degree, the President may impose military authority upon United States citizens domestically without clear congressional authorization. We are reluctant to read into *Quirin* a principle that the *Quirin* Court itself specifically declined to promulgate.

Moreover, there are other important distinctions between *Quirin* and this case. . . . The petitioners in *Quirin* admitted that they were soldiers in the armed forces of a nation against whom the United States had formally declared war. The *Quirin* Court deemed it unnecessary to consider the dispositive issue here—the boundaries of the Executive's military jurisdiction—because the *Quirin* petitioners "upon the conceded facts, were plainly within those boundaries." Padilla makes no such concession. To the contrary, he, from all indications, intends to dispute his designation as an enemy combatant, and points to the fact that the civilian accomplices of the *Quirin* saboteurs—citizens who advanced the sabotage plots but who were not members of the German armed forces—were charged and tried as civilians in civilian courts, not as enemy combatants subject to military authority. . . .

The government's argument for the legality of Padilla's detention . . . relies heavily on the Fourth Circuit's decisions in *Hamdi II* and *Hamdi III*. These decisions are inapposite. The Fourth Circuit directly predicated its holdings on the undisputed fact that Hamdi was captured in a zone of active combat in Afghanistan: The court said:

> We have no occasion . . . to address the designation as an enemy combatant of an American citizen captured on American soil or the role that counsel might play in such a proceeding. We shall, in fact, go no further in this case than the specific context before us—that of the undisputed detention of a citizen during a combat operation undertaken in a foreign country.

. . . Based on the text of the Constitution and the cases interpreting it, we reject the government's contention that the President has inherent constitutional power to detain Padilla under the circumstances presented here. Therefore, . . . we must now consider whether Congress has authorized such detentions.

II. CONGRESSIONAL ACTS

a. The Non-Detention Act

. . . The Non-Detention Act provides: "No citizen shall be imprisoned or otherwise detained by the United States except pursuant to an Act of Congress." 18 U.S.C. § 4001(a). . . . We read the plain language of section 4001(a) to prohibit all detentions of citizens. . . . [Congress passed the Act only] after ample warning that both the sponsor of the amendment and its primary opponent believed it would limit detentions in times of war and peace alike. [This] is strong evidence that the amendment means what it says, that is that no American citizen can be detained without a congressional act authorizing the detention. . . .

b. Specific Statutory Authorization

Since we conclude that the Non-Detention Act applies to military detentions such as Padilla's, we would need to find specific statutory authorization in order to uphold the detention. The government claims that . . . the Joint Resolution, which authorized the use of force against the perpetrators of the September 11 terrorist attacks . . . authorize[s] the detention of enemy combatants. . . . [W]ith respect to the Joint Resolution . . . we disagree with the District Court, which held that it must be read to confer authority for

Padilla's detention. It found that the "language [of the Joint Resolution] authorizes action against not only those connected to the subject organizations who are directly responsible for the September 11 attacks, but also against those who would engage in 'future acts of international Terrorism' as part of 'such . . . organizations.'"

We disagree with the assumption that the authority to use military force against these organizations includes the authority to detain American citizens seized on American soil and not actively engaged in combat. First, we note that the Joint Resolution contains no language authorizing detention. It provides:

> That the President is authorized to use all necessary and appropriate force against those nations, organizations, or persons he determines planned, authorized, committed, or aided the terrorist attacks that occurred on September 11, 2001, or harbored such organizations or persons, in order to prevent any future acts of international terrorism against the United States by such nations, organizations or persons. Joint Resolution § 2(a).

. . . The plain language of the Joint Resolution contains nothing authorizing the detention of American citizens captured on United States soil, much less the express authorization required by section 4001(a) and the "clear," "unmistakable" language required by *Endo*. While it may be possible to infer a power of detention from the Joint Resolution in the battlefield context where detentions are necessary to carry out the war, there is no reason to suspect from the language of the Joint Resolution that Congress believed it would be authorizing the detention of an American citizen already held in a federal correctional institution and not "arrayed against our troops" in the field of battle.* . . .

_____

*FN31. The debates on the Joint Resolution are at best equivocal as to the President's powers and never mention the issue of detention. Therefore, even assuming they could overcome the lack of a specific grant to the President, they do not suggest that Congress authorized the detention of United States citizens captured on United States soil. Some legislators believed the President's authority was strictly limited. *See, e.g.,* 147 Cong. Rec. H5639 (Rep. Lantos: "to bring to bear the full force of American power abroad"). Supporters of the President's power argued that it was too limited. *See, e.g., id.* at H5653 (Rep. Barr arguing that in addition to the joint resolution, Congress should declare war to "[g]ive the President the tools, the absolute flexibility he needs under international law and The Hague Convention to ferret these people out wherever they are, however he finds them, and get it done as quickly as possible"); *id.* at H5654 (Rep. Smith: "This resolution should have authorized the President to attack, apprehend, and punish terrorists whenever it is in the best interests of America to do so. Instead, the resolution limits the President to using force only against those responsible for the terrorist attacks last Tuesday. This is a significant restraint on the President's ability to root out terrorism wherever it may be found.")

Conclusion

In sum, we hold that . . .

(3) in the domestic context, the President's inherent constitutional powers do not extend to the detention as an enemy combatant of an American citizen seized within the country away from a zone of combat;

(4) the Non-Detention Act prohibits the detention of American citizens without express congressional authorization; and

(5) neither the Joint Resolution nor 10 U.S.C. § 956(5) constitutes such authorization under section 4001(a).

These conclusions are compelled by the constitutional and statutory provisions we have discussed above. The offenses Padilla is alleged to have committed are heinous crimes severely punishable under the criminal laws [which the government is free to prosecute him under]. Further, under those laws the Executive has the power to protect national security and the classified information upon which it depends. And if the President believes this authority to be insufficient, he can ask Congress—which has shown its responsiveness—to authorize additional powers. To reiterate, we remand to the District Court with instructions to issue a writ of habeas corpus directing the Secretary of Defense to release Padilla from military custody within 30 days. The government can transfer Padilla to appropriate civilian authorities who can bring criminal charges against him. Also, if appropriate, Padilla can be held as a material witness in connection with grand jury proceedings. In any case, Padilla will be entitled to the constitutional protections extended to other citizens.

DISSENT

WESLEY, J.

I respectfully dissent from that aspect of the majority's opinion that concludes the President is without authority from Congress or the Constitution to order the detention and interrogation of Mr. Padilla. In my view, the President as Commander in Chief has the inherent authority to thwart acts of belligerency at home or abroad that would do harm to United States citizens. But even if Mr. Padilla's status as a United States citizen on United States soil somehow changes the constitutional calculus, I cannot see how the Non-Detention Act precludes an affirmance.

. . . My disagreement with the majority is two-fold. In my view, the President, as Commander in Chief, has inherent authority to thwart acts of belligerency on U.S. soil that would cause harm to U.S. citizens, and, in this case, Congress through the Joint Resolution specifically and directly authorized the President to take the actions herein contested. . . .

But the scope of the President's inherent war powers under Article II does not end the matter, for in my view Congress clearly and specifically authorized the President's actions here. As Chief Judge Mukasey noted, the Joint Resolution, passed by both houses of Congress, "authorizes the President to use necessary and appropriate force in order, among other things, 'to prevent any future acts of international terrorism against the United States,' and thereby engages the President's full powers as Commander in Chief." The Joint Resolution authorized the President to take the action herein challenged; his powers were at their apogee.

. . . It is quite clear from the President's Order of June 9, 2002 that Mr. Padilla falls within the Joint Resolution's intended sweep. As relevant here, the Joint Resolution authorizes the President

(1) to use appropriate and necessary force—detention would seem to be an appropriate level of force in Mr. Padilla's situation,

(2) against those organizations that planned, authorized, or committed the terrorist attacks of 9-11—none of us disputes al Qaeda is responsible for the carnage of that day,

(3) in order to prevent future attacks of terrorism against the United States—Padilla is alleged to be closely associated with an al Qaeda plan to carry out an attack in the United States *and* to possess information that if obtained by the U.S. would prevent future terrorist attacks.

The majority contends that 18 U.S.C. § 4001(a) prohibits detention of U.S. citizens on U.S. soil as enemy combatants absent a precise and specific statutory authorization from Congress. . . . I share their view that the plain language of the statute appears to apply to military and civil detentions and that its placement in the U.S. Code does not rebut that conclusion. However, I find it somewhat puzzling that despite the statute's obvious and conceded clarity, the majority, based solely on the statement of one Member of Congress sees fit to add a condition not found in the words of the section.

The statute is quite clear: "No citizen shall be imprisoned or otherwise detained by the United States except pursuant to an Act of Congress." 18 U.S.C. § 4001(a). The section neither defines an "Act of Congress" nor contains a requirement that the authorizing enactment use the word "detention." The majority does not contest that the Joint Resolution is an Act of Congress. However, they chafe at its lack of specificity. As noted above, I think it would be quite difficult to conclude that Congress did not envision that

detaining a terrorist was a possibility. It is apparent from the legislative record of § 4001(a) and the Joint Resolution that the efforts of Congress in each instance meant and implied many different things to individual Members. That is not unusual. It would be quite a surprise to see that Congress was of one mind on any issue; that is the nature of a representative democracy. But one thing is clear, both enactments have the force of law. It is the words used, not the individual motives of legislators, that should serve as the guide. Thus, I think it best to trace a course of legislative intent using the plain and powerful language employed.

The problem with the majority's view of the Joint Resolution of September 18, 2001 is that it reduces the legislative efforts contained therein to a general policy statement. . . . Congress passed the Joint Resolution and agreed that the President should utilize his war powers with regard to an identified threat. Of course, identifying the threat made sense. Only days earlier the nation had been attacked—American lives had been lost on American soil. Congress responded and invested the President with authority to pursue those responsible for the attacks in order to prevent future attacks. Contrary to the implication of the majority, the Joint Resolution was *not* limited in geographic scope. It did not limit the President's authority to foreign theaters. Congress clearly recognized that the events of 9-11 signaled a war with al Qaeda that could be waged on U.S. soil.

The President's authority to detain an enemy combatant in wartime is undiminished by the individual's U.S. citizenship. Consequently, Padilla's citizenship here is irrelevant. Moreover, the fact that he was captured on U.S. soil is a distinction without a difference. While Mr. Padilla's conduct may have been criminal, it was well within the threat identified in the Joint Resolution. The resolution recognizes the painful reality of 9-11; it seeks to protect U.S. citizens from terrorist attacks at home and abroad. "[E]ntry upon our territory in time of war by enemy belligerents, including those acting under the direction of armed forces of the enemy . . . is a warlike act." *

Congress presumably was aware of § 4001(a) when it passed the Joint Resolution. The resolution was congressional confirmation that the nation was in crisis. Congress called upon the President to utilize his Article II war powers to deal with the emergency. By authorizing the President to use necessary and appropriate force against al

---

*Under the Geneva Convention Relative to the Treatment of Prisoners of War, Aug. 12, 1949, art. 4(A)(4), 6 U.S.T. 3317, 75 U.N.T.S. 135, prisoners of war subject to capture include all "persons who accompany the armed forces without actually being members thereof."

Qaeda and its operatives, Congress had to know the President might detain someone who fell within the categories of identified belligerents in carrying out his charge. A different view requires a strained reading of the plain language of the resolution and cabins the theater of the President's powers as Commander in Chief to foreign soil. If that was the intent of Congress it was masked by the strong and direct language of the Joint Resolution. And if, as the majority asserts, § 4001(a) is an impenetrable barrier to the President detaining a U.S. citizen who is alleged to have ties to the belligerent and who is part of a plan for belligerency on U.S. soil, then § 4001(a), in my view, is unconstitutional....

Questions

1. Summarize the facts of Jose Padilla's detention.

2. List his suspected ties to terrorists, and the basis for believing he has the ties.

3. Summarize the government's arguments in favor of Padilla's detention.

4. Summarize the defendant's arguments against his detention.

5. Summarize the court's reasons for its decision that Padilla's detention was unlawful.

TERRORIST SUSPECTS' RIGHT TO COUNSEL

The Sixth Amendment to the U.S. Constitution guarantees the accused the right to "the assistance of counsel for his defense." According to the U.S. Supreme Court, this right is "necessary to insure fundamental human rights of life and liberty" (*Powell v. Alabama* 1932, 432):

> The Sixth Amendment stands as a constant admonition that if the constitutional safeguards it provides be lost, justice will not be done. It embodies a realistic recognition of the obvious truth that the average defendant doesn't have the necessary professional legal skills to protect himself when brought before a tribunal with power to take his life or liberty, wherein the prosecution is represented by experienced and learned counsel. That which is simple, orderly, and necessary to the lawyer—to the untrained layman—may appear intricate, complex, and mysterious. (462)

The right to counsel applies to "all *criminal* prosecutions." According to the U.S. District Court in *Padilla v. Bush* (2002), this excludes the right to counsel in terrorist cases (like *Padilla v. Bush*) because they're not *criminal* cases. The government plan in terrorist cases isn't to prosecute individual terrorists for terrorist crimes; it's to prevent future terrorist attacks by detaining suspected terrorists and getting intelligence from them about other terrorists, terrorist organizations, their operations, and plans. This very important question of what, if any, right to counsel terrorists have remains to be decided finally by the U.S. Supreme Court.

But whatever the Court may decide, the Sixth Amendment isn't the only source of the right to counsel; there's also a statutory right. The federal habeas corpus statutes (U.S. Code 2003, Title 28 §§ 2241, 2243) allow petitioners seeking writs of habeas corpus to present facts to courts conducting the proceedings. Although the habeas corpus statutes don't provide for appointing counsel, another federal statute, the All Writs

Act (U.S. Code 2003, Title 18 §3006A(2)(B)) permits courts conducting habeas corpus proceedings to appoint counsel if "the interests of justice so require." The U.S. District Court for the Southern District Court of New York considered this statutory right in *Padilla v. Rumsfeld* (2002), in another decision growing out of the same case excerpted in the last section.

CASE	*Does He Have a Right to a Lawyer?*

Padilla v. Rumsfeld
233 F.Supp.2d 564 (USDC SDNY, 2002)

FACTS

[See *Padilla v. Rumsfeld* excerpt, pp. 537–538 for the Facts of this case.]

OPINION

The government has not disputed Padilla's right to challenge his detention by means of a habeas corpus petition. Although Padilla has the ability, through his lawyer, to challenge the government's naked legal right to hold him as an unlawful combatant on any set of facts whatsoever, he has no ability to make fact-based arguments because, as is not disputed, he has been held incommunicado during his confinement at the Consolidated Naval Brig in Charleston, and has not been permitted to consult with counsel. Therefore, unless I find that the only fact issue Padilla has a right to be heard on is whether the government's proffered facts, taken alone and without right of response, are sufficient to warrant his detention...—an argument that can be presented by counsel without access to Padilla—I must address the question of whether he may present facts, and how he may do so. As explained below:

(i)   Padilla does have the right to present facts;

(ii) the most convenient way for him to go about that, and the way most useful to the court, is to present them through counsel; and

(iii) the government's arguments are insufficient to warrant denying him access to counsel.

Therefore, to the extent set forth below, Padilla will be permitted to consult with counsel in aid of prosecuting this petition.

Padilla's right to present facts is rooted firmly in the statutes that provide the basis for his petition. Padilla has petitioned pursuant to [the federal habeas corpus statute]

28 U.S.C. § 2241, which...grants to district courts the power to issue writs of habeas corpus; a related section, 28 U.S.C. § 2243, provides the skeletal outline of procedures to be followed in a § 2241 case:

A court, justice or judge entertaining an application for a writ of habeas corpus shall forthwith award the writ or issue an order directing the respondent to show cause why the writ should not be granted.... The writ, or order to show cause shall be directed to the person having custody of the person detained. It shall be returned within three days unless for good cause additional time, not exceeding twenty days, is allowed.

The person to whom the writ or order is directed shall make a return certifying the true cause of the detention.

When the writ or order is returned a day shall be set for a hearing, not more than five days after the return unless for good cause additional time is allowed.

Unless the application for the writ and the return present only issues of law the person to whom the writ is directed shall be required to produce at the hearing the body of the person detained.

The applicant or the person detained may, under oath, deny any of the facts set forth in the return or allege any other material facts.

The return and all suggestions made against it may be amended, by leave of court, before or after being filed.

The court shall summarily hear and determine the facts, and dispose of the matter as law and justice require.

A related section, 28 U.S.C. § 2246, allows the taking of evidence in habeas corpus cases by deposition, affidavit, or interrogatories.... Quite plainly, Congress intended that a § 2241 [habeas corpus] petitioner would be able to place facts, and issues of fact, before the reviewing court, and it would frustrate the purpose of the remedy to prevent him from doing so.

The habeas corpus statutes do not explicitly provide a right to counsel for a petitioner in Padilla's circumstances, but 18 U.S.C. § 3006A(2)(B) (2000) permits a court to which a § 2241 [habeas corpus] petition is addressed to appoint counsel for the petitioner if the court determines that "the interests of justice so require." I have already so determined, and have continued the appointment of Newman and appointed also Andrew Patel, Esq., as co-counsel.

Of course, Padilla has no Sixth Amendment* right to counsel in this proceeding. The Sixth Amendment grants that right to the "accused" in a "criminal proceeding"; Padilla is in the custody of the Department of Defense; there is no "criminal proceeding" in which Padilla is detained; therefore, the Sixth Amendment does not speak to Padilla's situation. Beyond the plain language of the Amendment, "even in the civilian community a proceeding which may result in deprivation of liberty is nonetheless not a 'criminal proceeding' within the meaning of the Sixth Amendment if there are elements about it which sufficiently distinguish it from a traditional civilian criminal trial." Such "elements" are present here—notably, that Padilla's detention "does not implicate either of the two primary objectives of criminal punishment: retribution or deterrence." There being no criminal proceeding here, Padilla could not enforce this right now even if he had it.

Nor does the self-incrimination clause of the Fifth Amendment** provide any more help to Padilla than the Sixth Amendment in his effort to confer with counsel. Although the Supreme Court in *Miranda v. Arizona*, 384 U.S. 436 (1966),[†] found in that clause a right to counsel, calling the presence of counsel "the adequate protective device necessary to make the process of police interrogation conform to the dictates of the privilege," and "although conduct by law enforcement officials prior to trial may significantly impair that right [to avoid self-incrimination], a constitutional violation occurs only at trial." That is of no help to Padilla, who does not face the prospect of a trial....

However..., the provisions and characteristics of the habeas corpus statute..., and the court's power under the All Writs Act, 28 U.S.C. § 1651(a) (2000), to issue writs in aid of its jurisdiction, provide a statutory basis for decision. Considerations of prudence require that a court avoid a constitutional basis for decision when there exists a non-constitutional alternative.

Part of that non-constitutional alternative lies in the provisions of the habeas corpus statute..., which make it clear that Congress intended habeas corpus petitioners to have an opportunity to present and contest facts, and courts to have the flexibility to permit them to do so under proper safeguards. Padilla's need to consult with a lawyer to help him do what the statute permits him to do is obvious. He is held incommunicado at a military facility. His lawyer has been told that there is no guarantee even that her correspondence to him would get through.

Although it is not uncommon for habeas corpus cases to be pursued by petitioners **pro se**,[‡] such cases, usually involving challenges to either state convictions under 28 U.S.C. § 2254 or federal convictions under 28 U.S.C. § 2255, almost always are filed after the petitioners already have had the benefit of completed criminal proceedings, and appeals, in which they were represented by counsel. Padilla has had no such benefit here. It would frustrate the purpose of the procedure Congress established in habeas corpus cases, and of the remedy itself, to leave Padilla with no practical means whatever for following that procedure.

The All Writs Act provides that "all courts established by Act of Congress may issue all writs necessary or appropriate in aid of their respective jurisdictions and agreeable to the usages and principles of law." 28 U.S.C. § 1651(a) (2000)....In *Harris v. Nelson*, 394 U.S. 286 (1969), the Supreme Court...appears to have read broadly the power of a court hearing a habeas corpus petition to fashion remedies under the All Writs Act:

> [T]he habeas corpus jurisdiction and the duty to exercise it being present, the courts may fashion appropriate modes of procedure, by analogy to existing rules or otherwise in conformity with judicial usage. Where their duties require it, this is the inescapable obligation of the courts. Their authority is expressly confirmed in the All Writs Act, 28 U.S.C. § 1651.

...The decision whether to grant or withhold an order under the All Writs Act lies "in the sound discretion of the court."...Although the Sixth Amendment does not control Padilla's case..., [the Supreme Court's cases suggest] that discretion under the All Writs Act should be exercised in favor of permitting him to consult with counsel in aid of his petition and, in particular, in aid of responding to the Mobbs Declaration should he choose to do so.

The government has argued that affording access to counsel would "jeopardize the two core purposes of detaining enemy combatants—gathering intelligence about the enemy, and preventing the detainee from aiding in any further attacks against America." This would happen, the

---

*The Sixth Amendment to the Constitution states that "[i]n all criminal prosecutions, the accused shall enjoy the right...to have the Assistance of Counsel for his defence." U.S. Const., amend. VI.

**That clause states that "[n]o person...shall be compelled in any criminal case to be a witness against himself." U.S. Const., amend. V.

[†]Chapter 8.

[‡]Without a lawyer.

government argues, because access to counsel would interfere with questioning, and because al Qaeda operatives are trained to use third parties as intermediaries to pass messages to fellow terrorists, even if "the intermediaries may be unaware that they are being so used."

However, access to counsel need be granted only for purposes of presenting facts to the court in connection with this petition if Padilla wishes to do so; no general right to counsel in connection with questioning has been hypothesized here, and thus the interference with interrogation would be minimal or nonexistent.

As to the possibility that Padilla might use his lawyers to pass messages to others, there are several responses to that conjecture.

First, accepting that conjecture at face value and across the board proves far too much: by the government's logic, no indicted member of al Qaeda facing trial in an Article III court should be allowed to consult with counsel—a result barred by the Sixth Amendment.

Second, I have read both the Mobbs Declaration and the Sealed Mobbs Declaration, the latter only for the purpose of assessing the government's access-to-counsel argument; the government's conjecture is, on the facts presented to me in those documents, gossamer* speculation. Although the government presents facts showing that Padilla had contact with and was acting on behalf of al Qaeda, there is nothing to indicate that Padilla in particular was trained to transmit information in the way the government suggests, or that he had information to transmit.

Third, Padilla has already had meetings with counsel in New York, and thus whatever speculative damage the government seeks to prevent may already have been done.

Fourth, there is no reason that military personnel cannot monitor Padilla's contacts with counsel, so long as those who participate in the monitoring are insulated from any activity in connection with this petition, or in connection with a future criminal prosecution of Padilla, if there should ever be one. The U.S. Bureau of Prisons has adopted such procedures with respect to incarcerated defendants who present a similar danger. See Prevention of Acts of Violence and Terrorism, 28 C.F.R. § 501.3(a) (2002) (special procedures to be used if "there is a substantial risk that a prisoner's communications or contacts with persons could result in death or serious bodily harm to persons, or substantial damage to property that would entail the risk of death or serious bodily injury to

persons"). One would think that such procedures would go a long way toward preventing Padilla from transmitting information through his lawyers to others.

Finally, Padilla's lawyers themselves are members of this court's Criminal Justice Act panel who have appeared before this court in numerous cases. In addition to being able advocates, they have conducted themselves at all times in a fashion consistent with their status as—to use the antique phrase—officers of the court. There is nothing in their past conduct to suggest that they would be inclined to act as conduits for their client, even if he wanted them to do so.

Even giving substantial weight, as I do, to the President's statement in the June 9 Order that Padilla is "a continuing, present and grave danger to the national security of the United States" and that his detention "is necessary to prevent him from siding with al Qaeda in its efforts to attack the United States," there has been no fact presented to me that shows that the source of that danger is the possibility that Padilla will transmit information to others through his lawyers.

By contrast, Padilla's statutorily granted right to present facts to the court in connection with this petition will be destroyed utterly if he is not allowed to consult with counsel. On the facts presented in this case, the balance weighs heavily in Padilla's favor.

I do not believe that the decision in *Hamdi v. Rumsfeld*, 296 F.3d 278 (4th Cir.2002), alters the balance in the government's favor. In that case, the Court of Appeals for the Fourth Circuit reversed the order of a district court directing the government to permit unmonitored access by counsel to a detainee captured in Afghanistan and held at a Navy brig in Norfolk, Virginia. The order was rendered without benefit of briefing or argument, and with "little indication in the order (or elsewhere in the record for that matter) that the court gave proper weight to national security concerns." According to the Fourth Circuit, "the peremptory nature of the [District Court's] proceedings stood in contrast to the significance of the issues before the court."

No such access is to be granted here, and the court has had the full benefit of the government's submissions, both sealed and unsealed. Further, Padilla's situation appears to differ from Hamdi's in that he had access to counsel after his capture but before his designation as an enemy combatant, and thus no potential prophylactic effect of an order barring access by counsel could have been lost.

Because this court has jurisdiction over Padilla's petition, and because the procedure outlined by the applicable statutes cannot be followed unless Padilla is permitted to consult with counsel, respondent Secretary Rumsfeld will be directed to permit Padilla to consult with counsel solely

---

*Sounds good but doesn't mean much.

for the purpose of submitting to the court facts bearing upon his petition, under such conditions as the parties may agree to, or, absent agreement, such conditions as the court may direct so as to foreclose, so far as possible, the danger that Padilla will use his attorneys for the purpose of conveying information to others.

Questions

1. According to the court, why doesn't Padilla have a Fifth Amendment right to a lawyer in this case?

2. According to the court, why doesn't he have a right to a lawyer under either the Fifth Amendment self-incrimination or due process clause?

3. According to the court, what statutes provide Padilla with a right to a lawyer in this case?

4. According to the government's lawyer, what's the source of the president's power over Padilla's right to a lawyer?

5. According to the government, how broad is the president's power over Padilla's rights in this case?

6. According to the government, what are the dangers of providing Padilla with a lawyer in this case?

7. According to the court, what measures to prevent the dangers are already in place and/or can be easily put in place?

TERRORIST TRIALS BY MILITARY COURTS AFTER 9/11

Suspected terrorists can be tried either for crimes (like treason and murder) in the ordinary courts (called **Article III courts** because their authority comes from Article III of the U.S. Constitution, which created the judiciary) or for *war crimes* (such as fighting for a terrorist organization) in special military courts (usually called military commissions or sometimes military tribunals). If they're tried for ordinary crimes in ordinary courts, all that you've learned in Chapters 10 through 14 applies so we don't need to go over it again.

Here, we'll examine the relaxed rules of procedure and proof and diminished rights for defendants that apply to *military commissions*. A **military commission** consists of a panel of military officers acting under military authority to try enemy combatants for **war crimes**—acts committed during wartime that inflict "needless and disproportionate suffering and damages" in pursuit of a "military objective." Don't confuse military commissions with military **court martials**, which are also made up military officers but to try members of U.S. armed forces for violating the Uniform Code of Military Justice (Elsea 2001, 16, 7).

The Military Order of November 13, 2001 (*Federal Register* 2001, 57831–57836) spells out the rules governing military commissions to try suspected terrorists. Let's look at the main points in the Military Order that are relevant to military commissions: the source and jurisdiction of their authority and the trial proceedings before them.

Sources of Military Commission Authority

The president bases his authority to establish military commissions on three sources. First, the U.S. Constitution, Article II, Section 2 makes the president the "commander in chief" of the armed forces. As commander in chief, he's responsible for trying terrorists. Second, Article II, Section 2 also imposes responsibility on the president to "take care that the laws shall be faithfully executed." In this case, according to the Military Order, the laws include trying war crimes under the Articles of War and the Authorization for Use of Military Force, passed by a joint resolution of Congress on September 14, 2001 (page 536). Third, the joint resolution authorized the president to use "all necessary and appropriate force against those nations, organizations, or persons he determines planned, authorized committed, or aided" or "harbored" them.

Jurisdiction of Military Commissions

The provisions of the order apply only to "certain Non-Citizens in the War Against Terrorism" (*Federal Register* 2001, 57833). This means the military commission's authority only applies to noncitizens. Here's how Section 2 of the order defines noncitizens and outlines restrictions on their rights, including taking away the power (jurisdiction) of ordinary courts to review military commission decisions regarding noncitizens.

> (a)...any individual who is not a United States citizen with respect to whom I determine from time to time in writing that:
>> (1) there is reason to believe that such individual, at the relevant times,
>>> (i) is or was a member of the organization known as al Qaida;
>>> (ii) has engaged in, aided or abetted, or conspired to commit, acts of international terrorism, or acts in preparation therefor, that have caused, threaten to cause, or have as their aim to cause, injury to or adverse effects on the United States, its citizens, national security, foreign policy, or economy; or
>>> (iii) has knowingly harbored one or more individuals described in subparagraphs (i) or (ii) of subsection 2(a)(1) of this order; and
>> (2) it is in the interest of the United States that such individual be subject to this order. (57834)

As noncitizens, the individuals the order applies to don't "necessarily enjoy the same constitutional rights as citizens" even if they're legally in the country. During wartime, aliens of enemy nations can be

> detained and deported, and their property can be confiscated.... They may also be denied access to the courts of the United States if they would use the courts to the advantage of the enemy or to impede the U.S. prosecution of a war.
>
> Elsea 2001, 28–29

The order takes away the jurisdiction of all courts in and outside the United States to try any cases covered by the order. According to Order Section 7(b)(1), "military tribunals shall have exclusive jurisdiction with respect to offenses by the individual..." (57835). The order also strips individuals of the right to have their cases reviewed by any other courts. According to Sections 7(b)(2) and (c):

> [T]he individual shall not be privileged to seek any remedy or maintain any proceeding, directly or indirectly, or to have any such remedy or proceeding sought on the individual's behalf, in
>> (i) any court of the United States, or any State thereof,
>> (ii) any court of any foreign nation, or

(iii) any international tribunal.

(c) This order is not intended to and does not create any right, benefit, or privilege, substantive or procedural, enforceable . . . by any party against the United States, its departments, agencies, or other entities, its officers or employees, or any other person. (57836)

If the order's provision takes away ordinary courts' habeas corpus jurisdiction (power) to review the legality of detention (Chapter 14), it might not survive a constitutional challenge because of *Ex Parte Quirin* (1942), the leading U.S. Supreme Court case on the subject. In *Quirin,* the Court specifically ruled that the legality of detention by military commissions was subject to habeas corpus review. *Quirin* took place in the darkest days of World War II when the Allies were losing most of the battles against both Germany and Japan. Hitler brazenly sent two groups of four saboteurs by submarine to the United States, with one group sneaking ashore in New York and the other in Florida. They carried explosives and other materials of sabotage, which they intended to use to blow up strategic targets and to terrorize and demoralize the populace.

They quickly turned themselves in to the FBI for reasons not yet clear and were set for trial by secret military commission. Before the trials began, their lawyers filed habeas corpus petitions, challenging their detention and the jurisdiction of the secret commission. The U.S. Supreme Court denied their petitions *but* made it clear it had the authority (jurisdiction) to hear their petition. In other words, even Nazis were entitled to *some* review by ordinary courts. We'll have to wait for cases like *Padilla* and others now making their way through the U.S. courts to find out to what extent, if any, the Constitution limits the power of the president alone (or backed up by congressional action) to define the status of noncitizens and their rights to review of their detention before and during proceedings in military commissions.

Trial Proceedings of Military Commissions

Military commissions aren't bound by the constitutional requirements that apply to ordinary (Article III) courts. So, defendants have no *constitutional* right to a speedy trial, to trial by jury, to counsel, to remain silent, or to proof beyond a reasonable doubt. Nevertheless, the Department of Defense, authorized by the Military Order to establish rules for military commissions, guarantees "each accused tried by Military Commission":

1. The presumption of innocence

2. Proof of guilt beyond a reasonable doubt

3. The right to call and cross-examine witnesses (subject to the rules regarding production of witnesses and protection of information)

4. That nothing said by an accused to his attorney, or anything derived therefrom, may be used against him at trial

5. No adverse inference for remaining silent

6. That any military commission proceeding will be full and fair

7. Military Defense Counsel to assist him in preparing a defense will be provided at no cost to him

The accused may also hire a civilian defense counsel at no cost to the government as long as that counsel:

1. Is a United States citizen

2. Is admitted to practice in a United States jurisdiction

3. Has not been the subject of sanction or disciplinary action

4. Is eligible for and obtains at least a SECRET level clearance

5. Agrees to follow the Military Commission rules (Military Commission Procedures 2002, 2)

As for *proving* guilt, here's the Defense Department's standard:

The Presiding Officer may admit any evidence that "would have probative value to a reasonable person." This standard of evidence takes into account the unique battlefield environment that is different than traditional peacetime law enforcement practices in the U.S. For example, soldiers are not required to obtain a search warrant when someone is shooting at them from a cave. This standard of evidence allows both the defense and the prosecution to admit evidence that was acquired during military operations. (2)

And, as to *finding* guilt:

A finding of guilt and the imposition of a sentence must be with the concurrence of two-thirds of the Military Commission panel members. (2)

If the commission finds the defendant guilty, the commission panel members may impose any appropriate sentence, including death. A sentence of death requires a unanimous vote from a seven-member Military Commission panel (2).

The Department of Defense has also established a review process that follows the verdict and sentence:

1. A three-member Review Panel of Military Officers, one of whom must have prior experience as a judge, will review all cases for material errors of law, and may consider matters submitted by the Prosecution and Defense. Review Panel members may be civilians who were specifically commissioned to serve on the panel. If a majority of the Review Panel members believe a material error of law has occurred, they may return the case to the Military Commission for further proceedings.

2. The Secretary of Defense will review the record of trial and, if appropriate, may return it to the Military Commission for further proceedings, or forward the case to the President with a recommendation as to disposition.

3. The President may either return the case to the Military Commission for further proceedings or make the final decision as to its disposition.

4. The President may delegate final decision authority to the Secretary of Defense, in which case the Secretary may approve or disapprove the findings or change a finding of Guilty to a finding of Guilty to a lesser-included offense, or mitigate, commute, defer, or suspend the sentence imposed, or any portion thereof. A finding of Not Guilty as to a charge shall not be changed to a finding of Guilty. (3)

After the final decision is made, "a sentence shall be carried out promptly" (3).

The steps in the process of investigating, charging, trying, convicting, sentencing, and appealing military commission decisions are outlined in Figure 15.1.

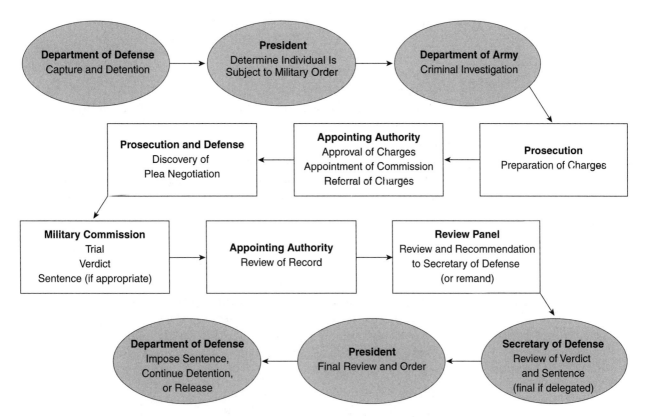

FIGURE 15.1 Steps in Military Commission Procedures
Source: Military Commission Procedures. 2002. Department of Defense Fact Sheet. Washington, D.C.: U.S. Government, 4.

SUMMARY

I. Balancing rights and security during emergencies
   A. Is most challenging during emergencies
   B. The balance tips toward government power over individual liberty and privacy during emergencies
   C. Limits on government power
      1. Necessity—emergency power only when and to the extent necessary
      2. Temporary—extraordinary power ends as soon as the emergency ends

II. The history of criminal procedure in wartime
   A. Clear principles applied to wars fought between two nations
      1. Declarations of war defined the beginning
      2. Laws of war controlled fighting
      3. Peace treaties defined the end
   B. Total war (World Wars I and II)
      1. Required commitment of whole people, government, and people
      2. Otherwise resembled earlier wars
   C. Cold War
      1. International communism crossed national borders

2. Spies came to U.S. and looked and acted like non-Communists
3. A hidden enemy "bored from within" to learn our secrets and pass them on to Communist governments
4. Fighting them required not military combat but intelligence gathering about Communists, their actions, and their plans
5. Goal sometimes was to prosecute but more often to deport them and prevent further infiltration into the U.S.

D. War on terror
1. Major shift from prosecution to prevention
2. Primary mission shift in law enforcement from gathering evidence to prosecute terrorists for past attacks to gathering intelligence to prevent future attacks
3. Prosecution is still a mission
4. New laws—USA Patriot Act, other laws, regulations, court opinions
   a. Knowledge limited to what laws *say* (not how they're operating)
      (1) Need for secrecy to guard against future attacks
      (2) Too recent to produce more than a few court cases
   b. Based on a constitutional requirement to balance need for government power to prevent and prosecute terrorist acts and rights of individuals guaranteed by the U.S. Constitution

III. Surveillance and terrorism
A. Fourth Amendment (Chapter 3) doesn't protect
1. Wiring informants for sound (*U.S. v. White*)
2. Retrieving lists of telephone numbers of outgoing (pen registers, *Smith v. Maryland*) and incoming (trap and trace) calls
3. Bank records of individuals' financial dealings (*U.S. v. Miller*)

B. Three-tiered system of balancing government power and individual privacy
1. Tier 1: "Real-time" electronic surveillance
   a. Protects individual privacy most
   b. Ban on the interception of "wire, oral, or electronic communications" while they're taking place
   c. Established in 1968 by the Crime Control and Safe Streets Act
   d. "Serious crime" exception to ban under conditions:
      (1) Approval of application by high official
      (2) Judge's approval of application
      (3) Application includes
         (a) Statement of facts and circumstances
         (b) Statement as to whether other investigative procedures tried and failed
         (c) Statement as to projected length of interception
   e. Patriot Act adds terrorist crimes to list of "serious crimes" ban
2. Tier 2: Surveillance of stored electronic communications
   a. Patriot Act significantly expands government electronic surveillance power
   b. Allows government access to *stored* communications—voice mail and e-mail messages, not just telephone numbers and e-mail addresses
   c. Applies to "*any* criminal investigation"

   d. Limits to government's Tier 2 surveillance power
    (1) Messages stored less than 6 months—warrant and probable cause required
    (2) Messages stored over 6 months—warrant required but 90-day delay in notification to subscriber is allowed if the court determines notification "may have an adverse result"
  C. Tier 3: Secret "caller ID"
   1. Government power broader than in Tier 2 but invades individual privacy less
   2. The power of secret "caller ID" allows government to access pen registers and trap and trace telephone numbers
    a. To investigate *any* crime
    b. Without court approval
    c. Without ever notifying subscribers
   3. Limitation—approval of department superior required
   4. Patriot Act expansions
    a. Creates power to seek court order to retrieve e-mail headers, not messages
    b. Orders apply to "anywhere in the U.S.," not just the district where the order is approved
   5. Patriot Act limits—government is required to submit report to the court showing
    a. The name of the officer who installed and/or accessed the device
    b. The date and time of the device installation, access, disconnection
    c. The device configuration and modification
    d. Information captured

IV. "Sneak and peek" searches
  A. Variation of "no knock" entries (Chapter 6)
  B. Allow officers to enter private places without the owner consenting or knowing about the entry
  C. Until 9/11, used mainly in drug cases with court approval but no statute
  D. Patriot Act included the use of sneak-and-peek warrants if
   1. Court finds reasonable cause to believe notification may have an "adverse effect"
   2. Warrant prohibits seizure of any property except where court finds reasonable necessity for seizure
   3. Warrant provides for giving notice within a reasonable time of execution
  E. Controversy over Patriot Act provision
   1. Against—gives government too much power
   2. For—reasonably balances government need and individual privacy in the fight against terrorism

V. Detention of terrorist suspects
  A. Ordinary times—even brief detentions are unreasonable Fourth Amendment seizures without an objective basis to back them up (Chapters 4, 5, 12)
  B. Balancing security and rights after 9/11
   1. Presidential Proclamation 7463 (September 14, 2001) declared "national emergency"

2. Congressional joint resolution Authorization for Use of Military Force (September 14, 2001) to catch 9/11 attackers and their supporters and to prevent future terrorist attacks
3. President's Military Order of November 13, 2001 provided for rules of detention, treatment, and trial of "certain noncitizens" in the "war against terrorism"
   a. Broad definition of noncitizens to include any person who there's reason to believe
      (1) Is a past or present al Qaeda member
      (2) Has acted in some connection with acts of international terrorism or
      (3) Has knowingly harbored one or more individuals described in 1 or 2 . . .
   b. Conditions of confinement and treatment of detainees
      (1) Provide humane and nondiscriminatory treatment
      (2) Afford adequate food, water, shelter, clothing, and medical treatment
      (3) Allow free exercise of religion
      (4) Secretary of Defense may prescribe other conditions
C. Detaining citizens after 9/11 (*Padilla v. Rumsfeld* 2003)
   1. U.S. Circuit Court affirms the right to detain citizens
   2. No right to detain citizens indefinitely
   3. Detained citizens have a right to challenge detention

VI. Terrorist suspects' right to counsel
A. Sixth Amendment guarantees the right to the assistance of counsel in "all criminal prosecution," so all persons detained for prosecution of terrorist-related *crimes* are protected by the right to counsel (Chapter 12)
B. Terrorist detention cases aren't all criminal cases, so detainees don't have a Sixth Amendment right to counsel
C. But terrorists have a right to counsel created by statutes
   1. Habeas corpus statute implies right to assistance of a lawyer to help challenge detention
   2. All Writs Act permits appointment of counsel in habeas proceedings "if the interests of justice so require"

VII. Terrorist trials by military courts after 9/11
A. Suspected terrorists can be tried either for crimes in ordinary (Article III) courts or for war crimes (acts during wartime that inflict "needless and disproportionate suffering and damages" in pursuit of a "military objective") by military commissions (courts)
B. Ordinary rules govern trials in Article III courts (Chapters 10–14)
C. Special rules with fewer rights and more relaxed procedures and standards of proof govern military commissions
D. Sources of military commission authority according to Military Order of November 13, 2001
   1. U.S. Constitution, Article II, Section 2—commander-in-chief
   2. U.S. Constitution, Article II, Section 2—president to "faithfully" execute the laws
   3. Laws include (according to the president) Articles of War and Authorization for Use of Military Force

E. Jurisdiction of military commission according to Military Order of November 13, 2001
   1. Applies only to noncitizens as defined in order
   2. Individuals subject to the order don't "necessarily enjoy the same constitutional rights as citizens"
   3. Strips Article III courts of jurisdiction either to hear or review military commission cases (may not survive constitutional challenges)
F. Trial proceedings according to Military Order of November 13, 2001
   1. Defendants have no constitutional rights to speedy trial, trial by jury, right to counsel, remain silent, or proof beyond a reasonable doubt
   2. Defendants trial rights under the order:
      a. The presumption of innocence
      b. Proof of guilt beyond a reasonable doubt
      c. The right to call and cross-examine witnesses
      d. Nothing said by an accused to his attorney may be used against defendants
      e. No adverse inference for remaining silent
      f. Overall requirement that any military commission proceeding be full and fair
      g. Military Defense Counsel provided at no cost to the defendant
      h. Accused may also hire a civilian defense counsel at no cost to the government under listed conditions
   3. Finding of guilt
      a. Two-thirds of Military Commission members required to find guilt
      b. Unanimous vote required for imposing death penalty
   4. Review of commission proceedings
      a. Panel of three military officers reviews cases
      b. Secretary of defense reviews trial record and either
         (1) Sends it back to the commission for further proceedings
         (2) Forwards it to the president with a recommended disposition
      c. President may return the case to the commission or make the final decision
      d. After the final decision, the sentence is to be "promptly carried out"

Go to the Criminal Procedure 6e CD to download this summary outline. The outline has been formatted so that you can add notes to it during class lectures, or later create a customized chapter outline to use while reviewing. Either way, the summary outline will help you understand the "big picture" and fill in the details as you study.

REVIEW QUESTIONS

1. Identify and describe two limits on government's emergency powers.
2. Summarize the history of criminal procedure in wartime.
3. Identify the difference between the responses to ordinary crime we've studied in previous chapters and the responses to domestic and international terrorism.

4. Describe how our study of anti-terrorism laws is limited, and give two reasons for this limitation.

5. What requirement of a constitutional democracy are all federal anti-terrorism procedure laws based on?

6. Describe both sides of the argument about the changes in the balance between power and liberty brought about by the September 11 attacks.

7. Identify three types of personal information not protected from electronic surveillance by the Fourth Amendment.

8. According to the U.S. Supreme Court, why aren't they protected?

9. Identify and describe the three tiers of the surveillance system designed to balance government power and individual privacy. Include in your description both government powers and the limits on that power in each tier.

10. How, if at all, has the Patriot Act modified this balance?

11. What were "sneak and peek" searches originally used for, and how has their legal status and definition changed since 9/11?

12. List and describe the three conditions under which the Patriot Act authorizes judges to issue sneak-and-peek warrants.

13. Summarize the two sides of the argument over sneak-and-peek warrants that followed passage of the Patriot Act.

14. Identify and describe the significance of the three sources that have affected the balance between security and rights in the detention of terrorist suspects since 9/11.

15. Explain the difference between how the Sixth Amendment right to counsel works in ordinary criminal cases and terrorist cases where the object is not to prosecute suspects.

16. Identify and describe two sources for the right to counsel *other than* the Sixth Amendment.

17. Identify and describe the two kinds of proceedings for the trial of suspected terrorists.

18. Identify the sources of authority for the Military Order of November 13, 2001, and describe the jurisdiction of military commissions created by the order.

19. How do the constitutional requirements that apply to Article III (ordinary) criminal courts differ from those of military commissions?

20. According to the Military Order of November 13, 2001, describe the following elements of a military trial: (a) the standard of proof; (b) the rule for votes in finding guilt; (c) the rights of the accused; and (d) the review process.

KEY TERMS

THE COMPANION WEB SITE
FOR *CRIMINAL PROCEDURE,* SIXTH EDITION

http://cj.wadsworth.com/samaha/crim_pro6e

 Supplement your review of this chapter by going to the companion Web site to take one of the
Tutorial Quizzes, use the flash cards to test yourself on the key terms from each chapter, and
check out the many other study aids you'll find there. You'll find valuable data and resources
at your fingertips to help you study for that big exam or write that important paper.

Selected Amendments of the Constitution of the United States

Amendment IV [1791]

The right of the people to be secure in their persons, houses, papers, and effects, against unreasonable searches and seizures, shall not be violated, and no Warrants shall issue, but upon probable cause, supported by Oath or affirmation, and particularly describing the place to be searched, and the persons or things to be seized.

Amendment V [1791]

No person shall be held to answer for a capital, or otherwise infamous crime, unless on a presentment or indictment of a Grand Jury, except in cases arising in the land or naval forces, or in the Militia, when in actual service in time of War or public danger; nor shall any person be subject for the same offence to be twice put in jeopardy of life or limb; nor shall be compelled in any criminal case to be a witness against himself, nor be deprived of life, liberty, or property, without due process of law; nor shall private property be taken for public use, without just compensation.

Amendment VI [1791]

In all criminal prosecutions, the accused shall enjoy the right to a speedy and public trial, by an impartial jury of the State and district wherein the crime shall have been committed, which district shall have been previously ascertained by law, and to be informed of the nature and cause of the accusation; to be confronted with the witnesses against him; to have compulsory process for obtaining witnesses in his favor, and to have the Assistance of Counsel for his defence.

Amendment VIII [1791]

Excessive bail shall not be required, nor excessive fines imposed, nor cruel and unusual punishments inflicted.

Amendment XIV [1868]

Section 1 All persons born or naturalized in the United States, and subject to the jurisdiction thereof, are citizens of the United States and of the State wherein they reside. No State shall make or enforce any law which shall abridge the privileges or immunities of citizens of the United States; nor shall any State deprive any person of life, liberty, or property, without due process of law; nor deny to any person within its jurisdiction the equal protection of the laws.

Section 2 Representatives shall be apportioned among the several States according to their respective numbers, counting the whole number of persons in each State, excluding Indians not taxed. But when the right to vote at any election for the choice of electors for President and Vice President of the United States, Representatives in Congress, the Executive and Judicial officers of a State, or the members of the Legislature thereof, is denied to any of the male inhabitants of such State, being twenty-one years of age, and citizens of the United States, or in any way abridged, except for participation in rebellion, or other crime, the basis of representation therein shall be reduced in the proportion which the number of such male citizens shall bear to the whole number of male citizens twenty-one years of age in such State.

Section 3 No person shall be a Senator or Representative in Congress, or elector of President and Vice-President, or hold any office, civil or military, under the United States, or under any State, who having previously taken an oath, as a member of Congress, or as an officer of the United States, or as a member of any State legislature, or as an executive or judicial officer of any State, to support the Constitution of the United States, shall have engaged in insurrection or rebellion against the same, or given aid or comfort to the enemies thereof. But Congress may by a vote of two thirds of each House, remove such disability.

Section 4 The validity of the public debt of the United States, authorized by law, including debts incurred for payment of pensions and bounties for services in suppressing insurrection or rebellion, shall not be questioned. But neither the United States nor any State shall assume or pay any debt or obligation incurred in aid of insurrection or rebellion against the United States, or any claim for the loss or emancipation of any slave; but all such debts, obligations and claims shall be held illegal and void.

Section 5 The Congress shall have power to enforce, by appropriate legislation, the provisions of this article.

 Go to the Criminal Procedure 6e CD for the full text of the Constitution of the United States.

Glossary

abandoned property property the owner has intentionally given up possession of.

absolute immunity the absence of liability for actions within the scope of duties.

abuse-of-writ rule the rule that habeas corpus petitioners must demonstrate that they neither deliberately nor negligently failed to raise an issue in a prior habeas petition.

accusatorial system rationale a system in which the government bears the burden of proof.

accusatory stage the point at which the criminal process focuses on a specific suspect.

actual authority (objective) third-party consent third-party consent searches aren't valid unless the person consenting had actual authority to consent for another person.

actual prejudice test proof that a defendant can't get a fair trial because pretrial publicity has led to jury impartiality.

actual-seizure stops the physical grabbing of a suspect.

administrative sentencing model a sentencing structure in which parole boards and prison administrators determine the exact release date within sentences prescribed by legislatures and judges.

affirmative defense a defense, such as self-defense or insanity, that requires defendants to present facts in addition to denying the charge.

affirmed an appellate court decision upholding the decision of a lower court.

airport searches searches of passengers and their baggage passing through detectors before entering airplanes are reasonable without warrants or prob-

able cause because the need for security outweighs the minimal invasion of individual privacy.

American Law Institute group of distinguished judges, lawyers, criminal justice professionals, law enforcement professionals, and scholars.

amicus curiae brief brief filed in court by someone interested but not a party in the case.

apparent authority (subjective) third-party consent individuals who it's reasonable to believe (but in fact don't) have authority to consent to a search.

Article III courts regular federal courts created by the Judiciary Act.

attenuation exception illegally seized evidence is admissible in court if the poisonous connection between illegal police actions and the evidence they illegally got from their actions weakens enough.

Authorization for Use of Military Force (Joint Resolution) joint resolution of Congress passed following the September 11 attacks supporting the president's war power to use "all necessary and appropriate force."

"bad" methods using unconstitutional means to obtain evidence.

balance between result and process the criminal procedure version of "the ends don't justify the means."

balancing element (of reasonableness test) the need to search and/or seize outweighs the invasion of individual liberty and/or privacy.

balloon swallowers drug couriers who conceal drugs in their digestive tracts.

bills of rights guarantee individuals' rights against government power.

bind over to decide to send a case to trial.

bind-over standard enough evidence exists for the judge in a preliminary hearing to decide to send the case to trial.

blind administrator a person conducting a lineup who doesn't know which person in the lineup is the suspect.

blue curtain wall of protection that hides "real" police work from public view.

border search exception searches at international borders are reasonable without probable cause or warrants because the government interest in what and who enters the country outweighs the invasion of privacy of persons entering.

"bright line" (clear) rule rule that spells out specifically officers' power; rule applying to all cases instead of by assessing the totality of circumstances on a case-by-case basis.

broad view of habeas corpus view that courts should review all claims that persons are being detained in violation of their fundamental liberties.

case-by-case basis deciding whether constitutional requirements were satisfied in each case.

case-in-chief the part of the trial where the government presents its evidence to prove the defendants' guilt; not the part where the government cross-examines defense witnesses or otherwise challenges the defense case.

cases of manifest injustice cases in which defendants are probably factually innocent.

cause-and-prejudice rule the rule that permits but does not require courts to deny habeas petitions if defendants fail to show cause and prejudice; petitioners must show they didn't deliberately or negligently fail to raise issues and that the prejudice probably changed the outcome of their trials.

certiorari a discretionary order of the Supreme Court to review a lower court decision.

challenges for cause removals of prospective jurors upon showing their partiality.

charge the grand jury the address of the judge to the grand jury.

charging by information formal criminal charge by a prosecutor.

Civil Rights Act actions lawsuits initiated by private individuals in federal court against state officers for violating the individuals' constitutional rights.

clear and convincing evidence more than probable cause but less than proof beyond a reasonable doubt.

collateral attack a proceeding to review the constitutionality of detention or imprisonment.

collateral consequences exception the principle that cases aren't moot if conviction can still cause legal consequences despite completion of the sentence.

collateral proceedings (in exclusionary rule) proceedings "off to the side" of the main case (for example, grand jury proceedings and bail hearings).

collateral use exception allows the use of illegally obtained evidence when it's not a part of the prosecution's case-in-chief at trial.

community security the safety side of the balance between security and individual autonomy in a constitutional democracy.

compulsory process Sixth Amendment guarantee of defendants' right to compel the appearance of witnesses in their favor.

concurring opinion statements in which justices agree with the decision but not the reasoning of a court's opinion.

consent search searches the government can prove by the totality of the circumstances suspects consented to don't require probable cause or warrants.

constitutional democracy the balance between the power of government and the rights of individuals.

constitutionalism refers to the idea that the U.S. Constitution is a document that differs from statutes.

constitutional right justification the idea that the exclusionary rule is an essential part of constitutional rights.

constitutional tort (*Bivens*) actions lawsuits against individual federal law enforcement officers.

constitutions permanent (or hard to change) general principles.

containers (in searches) include vehicles, purses, clothing, or anything else where people might put their "stuff."

conventional Fourth Amendment approach wherein the warrant and reasonableness clauses are firmly connected, according to the Court when ruling on stop-and-frisk law cases.

counsel pro bono lawyers willing to represent clients at no charge.

court-administered deposit bond defendants have to post 10 percent of the amount of the bond; if they appear, the court returns their deposit.

court martial a military court made up of military officers to try members of the U.S. armed forces for violating the Uniform Code of Military Justice.

court opinions written explanation for a court's decision.

Crime Control and Safe Streets Act provides for a general ban on the interception of "wire, oral, or electronic communications" when they're taking place.

criminal complaint the formal charging document.

criminal information written formal charge made by prosecutors without a grand jury indictment.

criminal procedures the methods that the government uses to detect, investigate, apprehend, prosecute, convict, and punish criminals.

critical stage in criminal prosecution includes all those stages that occur after the government files formal charges; the view that custodial interrogation is so important in criminal prosecutions that during it suspects have a right to a lawyer.

critical stages of criminal proceedings proceedings where individuals especially need the legal expertise of a lawyer.

curtilage the area immediately surrounding a house that's not part of the open fields doctrine.

custodial interrogation the questioning that occurs after the police have taken suspects into custody.

custody depriving people of their "freedom of action in any significant way."

custody-related searches searches taking place in jail, prison, and other detention facilities.

damages a remedy in private lawsuits in the form of money for injuries.

"dead bang" case cases in which defendants are clearly guilty.

death-qualified jurors jurors who aren't opposed to the death penalty.

decision of the court court's answer to the legal question or issue in a case before it.

decision to charge prosecutor's decision to begin formal proceedings against a suspect.

defense of entrapment defense to criminal liability based on proof that the government induced the defendant to commit a crime she wouldn't have otherwise committed.

defense of official immunity a public official charged by law with duties calling for discretionary decision making isn't personally liable to an individual except for willful or malicious wrongdoing.

defense of vicarious official immunity police departments and local governments can claim the official immunity of their employees.

deterrence justification the justification that excluding evidence obtained in violation of the Constitution prevents illegal law enforcement.

direct attacks appeals attacking directly decisions made by trial courts.

directed verdict rule enough evidence exists to decide a case without submitting it to the jury.

direct information information that officers know firsthand, acquired directly from their physical senses.

discretionary decision making informal decision making based on professional judgment and experience.

dismissal without prejudice the termination of a case with the provision that it can be prosecuted again.

dismissal with prejudice the termination of a case with the provision that it can't be prosecuted again.

dissenting opinion part of an appellate court case in which justices write opinions disagreeing with the decision and reasoning of a court.

diversion cases prosecutors agree to drop a case before formal judicial proceedings begin if suspects participate in specified programs (for example, community service, restitution, substance abuse, or family violence treatment).

DNA (deoxyribonucleic acid) fingerprinting measuring and comparing the lengths of selected strands of DNA in chromosomes.

DNA profiling a special type of DNA pattern that distinguishes one individual from all others.

DNA testing can potentially identify suspects or absolutely exclude individuals as suspects in cases where perpetrators have left DNA at the scene of a crime or where victims have left DNA on items traceable to perpetrators.

doctrine of judicial economy rule that says that time and money shouldn't be spent on appeals defendants could've avoided by objecting during the trial.

doctrine of *respondeat superior* employers are legally liable for their employees' illegal acts.

double jeopardy constitutional protection against being subject to liability for the same offense more than once.

drug courier profile general characteristics that alert officers to possible illegal drug activity.

dual sovereignty doctrine the principle that holds that a crime arising out of the same facts in one state isn't the same crime in another state.

due process broad and vague guarantee of fair procedures.

due process approach confessions must be voluntary; involuntary confessions violate due process, not because they are compelled but because they may not be true.

due process clause the Fifth and Fourteenth Amendment provisions prohibiting the federal government and the states, respectively, from depriving citizens of life, liberty, or property without due process of law.

due process revolution U.S. Supreme Court application of the Bill of Rights to state criminal proceedings.

emergency searches (also called exigent circumstance searches) searches without warrants or probable cause are reasonable because it's impractical (even dangerous) to require officers to obtain warrants before they search.

employee drug testing testing employees for drug use to increase workplace safety.

ends-means balance criminal procedure balances crime control (ends) against due process (means).

entrapment a defense to crime based on a law enforcement officer's illegal inducement to commit the crime.

equal protection of the law state officials can't investigate, apprehend, convict, and punish people for unacceptable reasons.

exclusionary rule the rule that illegally seized evidence can't be admitted in criminal trials.

exhaustion-of-remedies rule when a state prisoner files a petition containing any claim for which a state remedy remains available, the court has to dismiss the petition.

exigent circumstance searches circumstances requiring prompt action, which eliminates the warrant requirement for a search.

ex parte proceedings where the individual involved isn't present.

ex parte proceedings see ex parte.

expressed waiver suspect specifically says or writes that she knows her rights, knows she's giving them up, and knows the consequences of giving them up.

external civilian review review of complaints against police officers with participation by individuals who aren't sworn police officers.

factual basis requirement that judges not accept guilty pleas unless there are facts to back up the defendants' guilt.

factually innocent defendants who didn't commit the crime.

Federal Jury Selection and Service Act requires that juries represent a "fair cross section" of the community and bans the systematic exclusion of members of defendants' racial, gender, ethnic, or religious group.

***Federal Rules of Evidence* standard** the test of admissibility of DNA testing by considering whether the relevancy of the evidence outweighs the tendency of the evidence to unfairly prejudice jurors against the defendant.

Federal Speedy Trial Act sets definite time frames for bringing defendants to trial.

Federal Tort Claims Act (FTCA) lawsuits against the federal government for their officers' constitutional torts.

first appearance the appearance of a defendant in court for determination of probable cause, determination of bail, assignment of attorney, and notification of rights.

first party the party that succeeded in the lower court.

fixed (determinate) sentencing sentences that fit the punishment to the crime.

formal criminal procedure decision making according to the formal rules of criminal procedure.

Fourth Amendment frisks pat-downs of the outer clothing for weapons.

Fourth Amendment stops brief, on-the-spot detentions that freeze suspicious situations so that law enforcement officers can determine whether to arrest, investigate further, or terminate further action.

frisks pat-down searches for weapons.

fruit-of-the-poisonous-tree doctrine the principle that evidence derived from illegally obtained sources isn't admissible.

Frye **plus standard** the test of DNA admissibility that requires showing not only general acceptance of DNA theory but also that "the testing laboratory in the particular case performed the accepted scientific techniques in analyzing forensic samples."

Frye **standard** the rule that DNA evidence is admissible if the technique is "sufficiently established to have gained general acceptance in the particular field in which it belongs."

full custodial arrest taking arrested suspect to the police station.

fundamental fairness rationale the principle that state procedures can't violate basic standards of ordered liberty.

general warrant documents that gave the monarch and its officials the power to enter, search, seize, and enforce taxes; usually a writ of assistance.

"good" evidence proof of guilt.

"good faith" defense officers can't be held personally liable for their actions if they acted according to rules clearly established at the time of their actions.

grabbable area (in search incident to arrest) the arrestee's person and area within his reach.

graduated objective basis requirement the greater the government invasion, the more facts required to back it up.

grand jurors members of the grand jury.

grand jury review a secret proceeding to test a government case.

grand jury shield function grand jury protects against frivolous and/or malicious prosecution.

grand jury targets witnesses who are also targets of grand jury investigations.

habeas corpus an action that asks those who hold defendants to justify their detention.

habeas corpus proceedings civil action brought by defendants attacking the lawfulness of their detention.

hand up the indictment to deliver an indictment to the judge.

hearing before condemnation a law that deprives persons of life, liberty, privacy, and property only according to fair procedures.

hearsay testimony evidence not coming from the personal knowledge of witnesses but from the repetition of what they have heard others say.

hot pursuit the exigent circumstance constituting the need to apprehend a fleeing suspect.

hung jury a jury that's unable to reach a verdict after protracted deliberations.

hypothetical person test (also known as objective test of entrapment) looks at government actions that would induce a hypothetical reasonable person to commit crimes. According to the test, if the actions of the officer would induce an "ordinarily law-abiding" person to commit the crime, the court should dismiss the case.

impeach to show that a witness's credibility is suspect.

implied waiver (in self-incrimination) the totality of circumstances in each case adds up to proof that before suspects talked, they knew they had the right to remain silent and knew they were giving up the right.

incorporation doctrine the principle that the Fourteenth Amendment due process clause incorporates the provisions of the Bill of Rights and applies them to state criminal procedure.

independent source exception (exclusionary rule) evidence is admissible even if police officers violate the Constitution to obtain it if then in a totally separate action, they lawfully get the same evidence.

indeterminate sentencing tailoring punishment to suit the criminal; sentencing that relies heavily on the discretion of judges and parole boards in exercising sentencing authority.

indictment a formal criminal charge issued by a grand jury.

indigent defendants defendants too poor to hire their own lawyers.

individual autonomy the autonomy side of the balance between security and autonomy in a constitutional democracy.

individualized suspicion suspicion that points to specific individuals.

inevitable discovery exception (exclusionary rule) evidence illegally obtained is admissible if officers would've legally discovered the evidence eventually.

in loco parentis the principle by which the government stands in place of parents; school administrators are a substitute parent while students are in school and have the legal authority to search students and their stuff during school hours and activities.

intelligence gathering all kinds of information (not just criminal evidence) about enemies.

internal affairs units (IAU) review of police misconduct by special officers inside police departments.

inventory searches doing searches of suspects' personal items, officers are required to list the valuables and confiscate weapons, contraband, and evidence; searches conducted without probable cause or warrants to protect property and the safety of police and to prevent claims against police.

issue in criminal procedure cases legal question in a case.

"jot for jot" approach incorporated rights apply to the states exactly as they apply to federal proceedings.

judgment the final outcome of a case.

judicial integrity justification the idea that the honor and honesty of the courts justify the exclusionary rule.

judicial restraint the principle that judges are bound to defer to the will of the majority as expressed through their elected representatives.

judicial review the power of courts to review legislation.

judicial sentencing model a structure in which judges prescribe sentences within broad contours set by legislative acts.

jurisdiction the authority of a court to hear and decide cases.

jury nullification the jury's authority to reach a not guilty verdict despite proof of guilt.

jury panel potential jurors drawn from the list of eligible citizens not excused.

key-man system jury lists made up by civic and political leaders selected from individuals they know personally or by reputation.

knock-and-announce rule the practice of law enforcement officers knocking and announcing their presence before entering a home to search it.

law in action law as it operates in practice.

law in books formal enacted laws and court decisions.

laws detailed easily changed rules passed by legislatures.

laws of war rules written, understood, and agreed to by almost all the countries fighting the wars.

legal question issue in a criminal case; questions *judges*, not *juries*, decide.

legal question in the case see legal question.

legally guilty the cases in which the government has proved beyond a reasonable doubt the guilt of defendants.

legislative sentencing model a structure in which legislatures exercise sentencing authority.

length of time between the crime and the identification one of the factors used to determine the reliability of eyewitness identification of strangers.

liberty the right of citizens to come and go as they please (locomotion) without government interference.

lineup an identification procedure in which the suspect stands in a line with other individuals.

majority opinion the law of a case in an appellate court.

mandatory minimum prison sentences the legislatively prescribed, nondiscretionary amount of prison time that all offenders convicted of the offense must serve.

manifest necessity doctrine (in double jeopardy) the government can reprosecute a defendant for the same offense if the judge dismissed the case or ordered a mistrial because dismissal "served the ends of justice."

memory (in eyewitness identification) information the brain stores between the crime and the lineup, show-up, or picture identification.

***Mendenhall* test** a Fourth Amendment seizure takes place when a reasonable person wouldn't feel free to leave the presence of an officer.

might-or-might-not-be-present instruction (in eyewitness identification procedures) one of the ways to improve the reliability of eyewitness identification of strangers is to tell witnesses the suspect may or may not be among the photos or members of a lineup.

military commission non–Article III courts consisting of a panel of military officers acting under military authority to try enemy combatants for war crimes.

Military Order of November 13, 2001 president's order defining who could be detained following September 11, 2001, and prescribing the conditions of their detention.

mockery of justice standard the standard under which counsel is deemed ineffective only if circumstances reduced the trial to a farce.

mootness doctrine ban on appeals by offenders who have finished their prison sentences or paid their fines.

moral seriousness standard the principle that the Sixth Amendment right to a jury trial extends to morally serious misdemeanors.

motion to suppress evidence beginning of proceeding to determine whether evidence is admissible in court.

narrow view of habeas corpus power to review only the jurisdiction of the court over the person and the subject matter of the case.

negotiated plea a plea of guilty in exchange for a concession to the defendant by the government.

no-affirmative-duty-to-protect rule plaintiffs can't sue individual officers or government units for failing to stop private people from violating their rights.

no arrests in homes without a warrant rule exception to the rule that officers don't need warrants to arrest suspects.

no-bills a grand jury finding of insufficient evidence.

no-knock entry an exception to the requirement of the Fourth Amendment that officers have to knock-and-announce their presence before entering homes.

nolo contendere a plea by which a defendant accepts but doesn't admit charges.

objective basis the factual justification for government invasions of individual privacy, liberty, and property.

objective basis requirement facts, not hunches, have to back up government invasions of individual liberty and privacy.

objective privacy prong whether the subjective expectation of privacy is "one that society is prepared to recognize as 'reasonable.'"

objective standard of reasonable force (in arrest) Fourth Amendment reasonableness requirement allows officers to use only the amount of force reasonably required to get control of an arrested person under the totality of circumstances in the particular case.

objective test of entrapment focuses on the actions of government agents to induce defendants to commit crimes.

"on the spot" requirement during Fourth Amendment stops, officers can't move suspects from the place where they stopped them.

open fields any privately owned land not included within the area immediately surrounding a house.

open fields doctrine the rule that the Fourth Amendment doesn't prevent government officials from gathering and using information they see, hear, smell, or touch in open fields.

opening statements addresses to the jury by the prosecution and defense counsel before they present their evidence.

parallel rights state-granted rights similar to those in the U.S. Constitution and Bill of Rights.

particularity requirement the requirement that a warrant must identify the person or place to be searched and the items or persons to be seized.

pattern instructions published, standard jury instructions.

pen register telephone company lists of the phone numbers of outgoing calls from a particular telephone number.

perception (in reliability of eyewitness identification) information the brain takes in at the time of the crime.

peremptory challenges removals of jurors without showing cause.

perjury lying under oath about a material element in a crime.

petitioner a party whose case has come to court by judicial writ.

photo identification witnesses try to pick the suspect from one or many mug shots (the least reliable form of eyewitness identification of suspects).

photo lineup a photo identification with more than one photo in the array.

photo show-up showing a suspect only one photo.

plain-error doctrine rule that review of convictions should take place only when "plain errors affecting substantial rights" cause "manifest injustice or miscarriage of justice."

plaintiffs party who brings a civil action.

plainview doctrine doctrine that it's not a "search" to discover evidence inadvertently obtained through ordinary senses if the officers are where they have a right to be and are doing what they have a right to do.

plainview searches evidence obtained by officers' ordinary senses of seeing, touching, smelling, and hearing.

plurality opinion a statement in which the greatest number, but not a majority, of the justices favor a court's decision.

precedent a prior decision that's binding on a similar present case.

prejudice decisions that hurt the defendant's case; defendants have to show that bad lawyering deprived them of a fair trial with a reliable result.

preliminary hearing the adversary proceeding that tests the government's case.

preponderance of the evidence more evidence than not supports a conclusion.

Presidential Proclamation 1763 proclamation declaring a national emergency by reason of the terrorist attacks of September 11, 2001.

presumption of regularity presumes government actions are lawful in the absence of "clear evidence to the contrary."

pretext arrests arrests made only for the purpose of conducting a search there's no probable cause to search for.

pretrial motions between arraignment and trial, prosecutors and defense counsel can file motions that ask the court to act on a range of questions; written or oral requests to the court to decide a question before the trial begins.

preventive detention confinement of defendants to jail before conviction based on their threat to public safety.

prima facie case rule enough evidence exists to make a decision unless the evidence is contradicted.

privacy the value that's sometimes referred to as "the right to be let alone from government invasions."

privacy doctrine the doctrine that holds that the Fourth Amendment protects persons, not places, when persons have an expectation of privacy that society is prepared to recognize.

privately administered bail bonds private businesses that charge a percentage of the amount of the bond money they turn over to the courts.

probable cause objective basis for arrest.

probable cause to bind over amount of evidence of guilt needed to justify sending a case to trial.

probable cause to detain a suspect objective basis for detaining a suspect following arrest.

probable cause to go to trial higher objective basis than probable cause to detain and tested by a preliminary hearing or grand jury review.

procedural due process guarantee of fair procedures.

prophylatic rule mechanisms that aren't themselves constitutional rights but are used to guarantee those rights.

pro se defendants who represent themselves.

public defenders permanently employed defense lawyers paid for at public expense.

public places streets, parks, and other publicly owned areas; also include privately owned businesses that are open to the public.

public safety exception (to *Miranda v. Arizona*) the rule that *Miranda* warnings need not be administered if doing so endangers the public.

purging the grand jury eliminating prospective grand jurors who have compelling reasons not to serve.

qualified immunity immunity from tort action granted if a party was acting reasonably within the scope of duties.

quantum of proof amount of evidence backing up a government invasion.

raise-or-waive doctrine the rule that defendants must raise and preserve objections to errors at trial or waive their right to appeal the errors.

reasonable good-faith exception (exclusionary rule) searches conducted by officers with warrants they honestly and reasonably believe satisfy the Fourth Amendment requirements.

reasonable-likelihood-of-prejudice test the determination that circumstances may prevent a fair trial.

reasonable manner of arrest requirement to satisfy the Fourth Amendment arrests have to be executed in a reasonable manner.

reasonableness clause the clause in the Fourth Amendment that bans "unreasonable searches and seizures" as opposed to the "warrant clause," which outlines the requirements for obtaining arrest and search warrants.

reasonableness clause prong see reasonableness prong.

reasonableness Fourth Amendment approach the warrant and the reasonableness parts of the Fourth Amendment are separate elements that address separate problems.

reasonableness prong defendants have to prove that their lawyer's performance wasn't reasonably competent, meaning that the lawyer was so deficient that she "was not functioning as the 'counsel' guaranteed the defendant by the Sixth Amendment."

reasonableness test (Fourth Amendment) the reasonableness of searches and seizures depends on balancing government and individual interests and the objective basis of the searches and seizures.

reasonableness test of Fourth Amendment stops the totality of circumstances in each case must satisfy the balancing and objective basis elements required by the reasonableness clause of the Fourth Amendment.

reasonable suspicion facts, apparent facts, or circumstances that would lead a reasonable person to suspect that a crime may have been, may be about to be, or may be in the process of being committed.

reasonably competent attorney standard performance measured by customary skills and diligence.

recall information retrieved from memory at the time of the lineup, show-up, or picture identification.

release on recognizance (ROR) release from custody on a mere promise to appear.

relevant facts facts about the acts of government officials and the objective basis for those actions.

reliability rationale the justification for reviewing state confessions based on their untrustworthiness.

remanded sent back to a lower court for further proceedings.

retained counsel a lawyer paid for by the client.

reversed overturned by an appellate court.

reversible error an error that requires an appellate court to reverse the trial court's judgment in the case; errors that affect the outcome of a case.

right of locomotion individual freedom to come and go as you please without unreasonable government interference.

right-to-counsel clause the clause in the Sixth Amendment that guarantees the right to a lawyer in "all criminal prosecutions."

roadblocks barricades for stopping vehicles so officers can question their occupants.

Robinson **rule (searches incident to arrest)** bright-line rule that officers can always search anyone they're authorized to take into custody.

routine written procedure requirement inventory searches are reasonable if officers follow department guidelines in conducting them.

rule of four the requirement that four Supreme Court justices must vote to review a case for its appeal to be heard by the Supreme Court.

searches incident to arrest a search made of a lawfully arrested suspect without probable cause or warrant.

second party the party that succeeded in the lower court.

secret "caller ID" power of government to capture a record of all telephone *numbers* (not *conversations*) from a subscriber's phone in the investigation of "any crime."

§ 1983 actions lawsuits brought by private individuals against law enforcement officers under the § 1983 of the U.S. Civil Rights Act.

seditious libels printed criticisms of government.

seizure (Fourth Amendment) physical seizure or submission to government show of authority.

selective incorporation the concept that only some federal rights are incorporated by the due process clause.

selective prosecution decision to prosecute based on interests of justice and resources.

self-incrimination clause Fifth Amendment guarantee that defendants in criminal cases can't be compelled to be witnesses against themselves.

sentencing guidelines a narrow range of penalties established by a commission within which judges are supposed to choose a specific sentence.

serious crime exception (to Crime Control and Safe Streets Act) provides for an exception for serious crimes to the act's general ban on the interception of "wire, oral, or electronic communications" when they're taking place.

shakedown routine, unannounced searches of prisoners and their cells for weapons and contraband aren't searches according to the U.S. Supreme Court.

show-of-authority stops submissions to the display of official force.

show-up a procedure in which the witness identifies the suspect without other possible suspects present.

sneak-and-peek searches warrants that allow officers to enter private places without the owner or (occupant) consenting or knowing about it.

social cost of excluding "good" evidence the number of guilty persons who go free because of the exclusionary rule.

sovereign immunity governments can't be sued by individuals without the consent of the government.

special-needs searches government inspections and other regulatory measures not conducted to gather criminal evidence.

special relationship exception (to the no-affirmative-duty-to-protect rule) governments have a duty to protect individuals they hold in custody.

Spinelli-Aguilar **test (in probable cause)** two-pronged test (veracity and basis-of-knowledge) of the reliability of informants' information used as a basis for establishing probable cause.

stare decisis the doctrine in which a prior decision binds a present case with similar facts.

state-created-danger exception (to the no-affirmative-duty-to-protect rule) the officer's actions created a special danger of violent harm to the plaintiff in the lawsuit; the officer knows or should have known her actions would encourage this plaintiff to rely on her actions; and the danger created by the officer's actions caused either harm or vulnerability to harm.

statutes of limitations laws specifying the length of time permitted to lapse between the commission of a crime and the initiation of prosecution.

statutory right to appeal non-constitutional right to appeal a criminal conviction.

stops brief "seizures" that require reasonable suspicion to back them up.

straight guilty plea see straight pleas.

straight pleas plea of guilty not based on negotiation.

strangers (in identification procedures) refers to eyewitness identification of strangers.

strength of the case the amount of evidence of guilt that's admissible in court.

student searches searches of primary and secondary students, who have a reduced expectation of privacy because school officials are *in loco parentis* (substitute parents) during school hours.

subjective privacy prong whether a "person exhibited an actual [personal] expectation of privacy."

subjective test of entrapment the test of entrapment that focuses on the predisposition of defendants to commit crimes.

substantive due process guarantee against arbitrary laws.

suggestion (in eyewitness identification) interpretation of events shaped by other people's suggestions.

supervisory power the ability of the U.S. Supreme Court to oversee lower federal court and state court proceedings.

suppression hearing hearings held before trial on the defendant's motions to exclude evidence.

supremacy clause the principle that the U.S. Constitution and laws are supreme over state law.

testimony the content of what you say and write against yourself.

testing the government's case deciding whether there's enough evidence to go to trial.

thermal imagers devices that detect, measure, and record infrared radiation not visible to the naked eye.

third-party consent searches one person can consent for another person to a search.

torts private wrongs; civil lawsuits for damages.

total incorporation the principle that all federal rights are incorporated by the due process clause.

totality of circumstances all the facts surrounding a government invasion of privacy, liberty, or property.

totality of circumstances of informant reliability test (in probable cause) in evaluating informants' information, this test takes veracity and basis of knowledge into account as two of many pieces of information that might add up to probable cause.

totality-of-circumstances test the conditions used to determine both the voluntariness of a waiver of rights and of incriminating statements.

total wars wars where the whole people, the governments, and the countries' resources are mobilized for fighting and winning the war.

traditional definition of mootness ban on appeals by offenders who have finished their prison sentences or paid their fines.

trap and trace telephone company lists of the phone numbers of incoming calls to a particular phone number.

trespass doctrine the Fourth Amendment doctrine that requires physical intrusions into a "constitutionally protected area" to qualify as a search.

trial courts courts that conduct trials.

true bill the record of the number of grand jurors voting for indictment.

two-pronged effective counsel test U.S. Supreme Court test of "effectiveness of counsel," which requires the defense to prove a lawyer's performance wasn't reasonably competent and that the incompetence affected the outcome of the case in favor of conviction.

two-pronged test of reliability (Spinelli–Aguilar test) the test used to establish the veracity and basis of knowledge of an informant.

under color of authority officers acting under the appearance of their official power.

unsecured bonds money bonds that defendants have to pay only if they don't appear for their court date.

USA Patriot Act short for Uniting and Strengthening America by Providing Appropriate Tools Required to Intercept and Obstruct Terrorism; bill passed after 9/11 giving the government more powers.

U.S. Courts of Appeals intermediate appeals court in the federal judicial system.

U.S. District Court trial court in the federal judicial system.

venue the place where a trial is held.

voir dire the examination of prospective jurors.

voluntariness test of consent searches a test in which the totality of circumstances is used to determine whether a consent to search was obtained without coercion, deception, or promises.

voluntariness test of self-incrimination the standard that relies on the totality of circumstances to determine whether waivers and confessions were voluntary.

voluntary encounters "communication between police and individuals involving no coercion or detection."

waive knowing you have a right and voluntarily giving it up.

war crimes crimes committed during wartime that inflict "needless and disproportionate suffering and damages" in pursuit of a "military objective."

warrant clause part of the Fourth Amendment stating the requirements for search and arrest warrants.

wartime emergency exception to the Bill of Rights putting aside ordinary rules during emergencies.

whole picture test looking at all the facts and circumstances in each case to determine the constitutionality of government actions.

Witherspoon-**excludables** potential jurors opposed to the death penalty.

witnesses' accuracy of description one of five factors in the totality of circumstances used to assess the reliability of witness identification.

witnesses' degree of attention one of five factors in the totality of circumstances used to assess the reliability of witness identification.

witnesses' level of certainty one of five factors in the totality of circumstances used to assess the reliability of witness identification.

witnesses' opportunity to view one of five factors in the totality of circumstances used to assess the reliability of witness identification.

writ of assistance warrants giving royal agents the power to search anyone, anywhere, anytime.

writ of certiorari discretionary proceeding to review a lower court decision.

Bibliography

Abel v. U.S. 1960. 362 U.S. 217.

Adams v. Williams. 1972. 407 U.S. 143.

Adamson v. California. 1947. 332 U.S. 46.

Agnello v. U.S. 1925. 269 U.S. 20.

Allen, Francis A. 1978. "The Law as a Path to the World." *Michigan Law Review* 77.

Allison v. State. 1974. 214 N.W.2d 437.

American Academy of Political and Social Science. 1910. *Annals* 46.

American Bar Association. 1980. *Standards for Criminal Justice.* 2nd ed. Chicago: ABA.

American Bar Association. 1988. *Criminal Justice in Crisis.* Chicago: ABA.

American Law Institute. 1975. *Model Code of Pre-Arraignment Procedure.* Philadelphia: ALI.

Amsterdam, Anthony. 1970. "The Supreme Court and the Rights of Suspects in Criminal Cases." *New York University Law Review* 45:785.

Amsterdam, Anthony. 1974. "Perspectives on the Fourth Amendment." *Minnesota Law Review* 58:430.

Anderson v. Creighton. 1987. 483 U.S. 635.

Annals of Congress. 1789. House of Representatives, 1st Cont. 1st Sess. http://memory.loc.gov/cgi-bin/ampage.

Apodaca v. Oregon. 1972. 406 U.S. 404.

Argersinger v. Hamlin. 1972. 407 U.S. 25.

Arizona v. Evans. 1995. 514 U.S. 1.

Ashcroft v. Tennessee. 1944. 322 U.S. 143.

Ashdown, Sue. 1983. "Good Faith, the Exclusionary Remedy, and Rule-Oriented Adjudication in the Criminal Process." *William and Mary Law Review* 24: 335.

Atwater v. City of Lago Vista. 2001. 532 U.S. 318.

Avalon Project at the Yale Law School. 2003. *The Laws of War.* http://www.yale.edu/lawweb/avalon/lawofwar/lawwar.htm.

Baker, Liva. 1985. *Miranda: Crime, Law, and Politics.* New York: Atheneum.

Baldwin v. New York. 1970. 399 U.S. 66.

Ballew v. Georgia. 1978. 435 U.S. 223.

Barnes v. State. 1975. 520 S.W.2d 401 (Tex.Crim.App.).

Barron v. Baltimore. 1833. 32 U.S. (7 Pet.) 243.

Bearden v. Georgia. 1983. 461 U.S. 660.

Bell v. Wolfish. 1979. 441 U.S. 520.

Berkemer v. McCarty. 1984. 468 U.S. 420.

Betts v. Brady. 1942. 316 U.S. 455.

Bivens v. Six Unnamed FBI Agents. 1971. 403 U.S. 388.

Black v. Amico. 1974. 387 F.Supp. 88 (W.D.N.Y.).

Blackledge v. Allison. 1977. 431 U.S. 63.

Blumstein, Alfred et al. 1983. *Research on Sentencing: The Search for Reform.* Washington, D.C.: National Academy Press.

Board of Commissioners v. Backus. 1864. 29 How. Pr. 33.

Boland, Barbara et al. 1988 (May). *The Prosecution of Felony Arrests, 1982.* Washington, D.C.: National Institute of Justice.

Bostick v. State. 1989. 554 So.2d 1153 (Fla.).

Bowen v. Kemp. 1985. 769 F.2d 672 (11th Cir., Ga.).

Bowles v. U.S. 1970. 439 F.2d 536 (D.C. Cir.).

Boykin v. Alabama. 1969. 395 U.S. 238.

Bradley, Craig M. 1985. "Two Models of the Fourth Amendment." *Michigan Law Review* 83:1471.

Brady v. U.S. 1970. 397 U.S. 742.

Brandes, Wendy. 1989. "Post-Arrest Detention and the Fourth Amendment: Refining the Standard of *Gerstein v. Pugh.*" *Columbia Journal of Law and Contemporary Problems* 22:445–88.

Brinegar v. United States. 1949. 338 U.S. 160.

Brown v. Allen. 1953. 344 U.S. 443.

Brown v. Board of Education. 1954. Oral Argument.

Brown v. Mississippi. 1936. 297 U.S. 278.

Burch v. Louisiana. 1979. 441 U.S. 130.

Burns v. Reed. 1991. 500 U.S. 478.

California v. Acevedo. 1991. 500 U.S. 565.

California v. Ciraolo. 1986. 476 U.S. 207.

California v. Greenwood. 1988. 486 U.S. 35.

California v. Hodari D. 1991. 499 U.S. 621.

Campaign for an Effective Crime Policy. 1993 (October). "Evaluating Mandatory Minimum Sentences." Washington, D.C.: Campaign for an Effective Crime Policy (unpublished manuscript).

Caplan, Gerald M. 1985. "Questioning *Miranda.*" *Vanderbilt Law Review* 38:1417–1476.

Cardozo, Benjamin. 1921. *The Nature of the Judicial Process.* New Haven, Conn.: Yale University Press.

Carlson, Jonathan. 1987. "The Act Requirement and the Foundations of the Entrapment Defense." *Virginia Law Review* 73: 1011.

Carroll v. U.S. 1925. 267 U.S. 132.

Chandler v. Florida. 1981. 499 U.S. 560.

Chimel v. California. 1969. 395 U.S. 752.

Ciucci v. Illinois. 1958. 356 U.S. 571.

Cloud, Morgan. 1985. "Search and Seizure by the Numbers: The Drug Courier Profile and Judicial Review of Investigative Formulas." *Boston University Law Review* 65:843.

Cochrane v. Quattrocchi. 1991. 949 F.2d 11 (1st Cir.).

Coke, Edward. 1797. *The Second Part of the Institutes of the Laws of England.* 5th ed. London: Brooke.

Colorado v. Bertine. 1987. 479 U.S. 367.

Colorado v. Connelly. 1986. 479 U. S. 157.

Commonwealth v. Gonsalves. 1999. 429 Mass. 658, 711 N.E.2d 108.

Commonwealth v. Guillespie. 2000. 392MDA99 Pa.Super.

Commonwealth v. Neilson. 1996. 666 N.E.2d 984 (Mass.).

Commonwealth v. Washington. 1990. 393 Pa.Super. 132, 573 A.2d 1123.

Commonwealth v. Zook. 1989. 553 A.2d 920 (Pa.).

Connecticut v. Barrett. 1987. 479 U.S. 523.

Copacino, John M. 1994. "Suspicionless Criminal Seizures after Michigan Department of State *Police v. Sitz.*" *American Criminal Law Review* 31: 215.

Corpus Juris Secundum. 2003. St Paul, Minn.: West, § 61.

Cortner, Richard C. 1981. *The Supreme Court and the Second Bill of Rights.* Madison, Wisc.: University of Wisconsin Press.

County of Riverside v. McLaughlin. 1991. 500 U.S. 44.

Criminal Justice Newsletter. 1993 (November 15). Washington, D.C.: Pace Publications.

Criminal Law Reporter. 1989. May 3.

Crist v. Bretz. 1978. 437 U.S. 28.

Cronin, Thomas E. et al. 1981. *U.S. v. Crime in the Streets.* Bloomington, Ind.: Indiana University Press.

Crooker v. California. 1958. 357 U.S. 433.

Culombe v. Connecticut. 1961. 367 U.S. 568.

Cupp v. Murphy. 1973. 412 U.S. 291.

Davenport, Jennifer L., and Steven Penrod. 1997. "Eyewitness Identification Evidence: Evaluating Commonsense Evaluations." *Psychology, Public Policy, and Law* 3:338–361.

Davies, Thomas A. 1983. "A Hard Look at What We Know (and Still Need to Learn) about the 'Social Costs' of the Exclusionary Rule: The NIJ Study and Other Studies of 'Lost' Arrests." *American Bar Foundation Research Journal* 640.

DeShaney v. Winnebago County. 1989. 489 U.S. 189.

Dickerson v. U. S. 2000. 530 U.S. 428.

Dix, George E. 1985. "Nonarrest Investigatory Detentions in Search and Seizure Law." *Duke Law Journal* 849.

Dow Chemical Co. v. U.S. 1986. 476 U.S. 227.

Doyle, Charles. 2002. *The USA Patriot Act: A Legal Analysis.* Congressional Research Service.

Draper v. U.S. 1959. 358 U.S. 307.

Dressler, Joshua. 1997. *Understanding Criminal Procedure.* New York: Matthew Bender.

Dripps, Donald A. 1988. "Forward: Against Police Interrogation—and the Privilege Against Self-Incrimination." *Journal of Criminal Law and Criminology* 78.

Dukes v. Waitkevitch. 1976. 536 F.2d 469 (1st Cir.).

Duncan v. Louisiana. 1968. 391 U.S. 145.

Dunlop v. U.S. 1897. 165 U.S. 486.

Elkins v. U.S. 1960. 364 U.S. 206.

Elsea, Jennifer. 2001. *Terrorism and the Law of War: Trying Terrorists as War Criminals Before Military Commissions.* Washington, D.C.: Congressional Research Service.

Ervin, Sam J. 1983. "The Exclusionary Rule: An Essential Ingredient of the Fourth Amendment." *Supreme Court Review.*

Escobedo v. Illinois. 1964. 378 U.S. 478.

Estelle v. Williams. 1976. 425 U.S. 501.

Ex Parte Milligan. 1866. 71 U.S. 2.

Federal Criminal Code and Rules. 1987. St. Paul, Minn.: West.

Federal Register. 2001 (September 18). "Proclamation 7463 of September 14, 2001." Presidential Documents.

Federal Rules of Criminal Procedure. 2002. 41(d)(3). http://www.law.cornell.edu/rules/frcrmp/Rule4.htm.

Federalist Papers. 1961. Middletown, Conn.: Wesleyan University Press.

Feeley, Malcolm M. 1979. *The Process Is the Punishment: Handling Cases in a Lower Criminal Court.* New York: Russell Sage Foundation.

Fisher, Sydney George F. 1888. "The Suspension of Habeas Corpus During the War of Rebellion." *Political Science Quarterly* 3.

Florida v. Jimeno. 1991. 500 U.S. 248.

Florida v. J.L. 2000. 529 U.S. 266.

Florida v. Royer. 1983. 460 U.S.491.

Foote, Caleb. 1965. "The Coming Constitutional Crisis in Bail." *University of Pennsylvania Law Review* 113: 959–1185.

Foster v. California. 1969. 394 U.S. 440.

Fraenkel, Osmond K. 1942. "From Suspicion to Accusation." *Yale Law Journal* 51.

Fraizer v. Roberts. 1971. 441 F.2d 1224 (8th Cir.).

Frankel, Marvin E., and Gary F. Naftalis. 1977. *The Grand Jury: An Institution on Trial.* New York: Hill and Wang.

Friendly, Henry J. 1965. "The Bill of Rights as a Code of Criminal Procedure." *California Law Review* 53:929.

Frisbie v. Collins. 1952. 342 U.S. 519.

Gagnon v. Scarpelli. 1973. 411 U.S. 778.

Gardner v. Florida. 1977. 430 U.S. 349.

Gardner, James A. 1991. "The Failed Discourse of State Constitutionalism." *Michigan Law Review* 90: 761.

Garner, Bryan A. 1987. *Dictionary of Modern Legal Usage.* New York: Oxford University Press.

Gayarré, Charles. 1903. *History of Louisiana,* vol. IV. New Orleans: F.F. Hansell & Bro.

Georgia Defender. 2002 (September). "Sneak and Peek Warrants and the USA Patriot Act."

Gerstein v. Pugh. 1975. 420 U.S. 103.

Giannelli, Paul C. 1991. "Criminal Discovery, Scientific Evidence, and DNA." *Vanderbilt Law Review* 44.

Gideon v. Wainwright. 1963. 372 U.S. 335.

Goldberg, Stephanie. 1992 (April). "A New Day for DNA?" *American Bar Association Journal* 78.

Goldstein, Abraham S. 1987. "The Search Warrant, the Magistrate, and Judicial Review." *New York University Law Review* 62:1173.

Goldstein, Joseph. 1960. "The State and the Accused: Balance and Advantage in Criminal Procedure." *Yale Law Journal* 69.

Graham v. Connor. 1989. 490 U.S. 386.

Graham, Fred. 1970. *The Self-Inflicted Wound.* New York: Macmillan.

Graham, Kenneth, and Leon Letwin. "The Preliminary Hearing in Los Angeles: Some Field Findings and Legal-Policy Questions." *UCLA Law Review* 18: 636.

Gregg v. Georgia. 1976. 428 U.S. 153.

Griswold, David B. 1994. "Complaints Against the Police: Predicting Dispositions." *Journal of Criminal Justice* 22.

Gross, Samuel R. 1987. "Loss of Innocence: Eyewitness Identification and Proof of Guilt." *Journal of Legal Studies* 16.

Haddad, James B. 1977. "Well-Delineated Exceptions, Claims of Sham, and Fourfold Probable Cause." *Journal of Criminal Law and Criminology* 68:198–225.

Hall, Jerome. 1942. "Objectives of Federal Criminal Rules Revision." *Yale Law Journal* 725.

Hall, John Wesley, Jr. 1993. *Search and Seizure.* 2nd ed. New York: Clark, Boardman, Callaghan.

Hamblett, Mark. 2003. "Tough Questions for U.S. on Detention." *Legal Times,* 24 November.

Hamilton, Alexander. 1788. "The Federalist No. 78: The Judiciary Department." Hancock, Catherine. 1982. "State Court Activism and Searches Incident to Arrest." *Virginia Law Review* 68:1085.

Hand, Learned. 1922. *U.S. v. Garsson.* 291 Fed. 646 (S.D.N.Y.).

Harris v. U.S. 1947. 331 U.S. 145.

Hayes v. Florida. 1985. 470 U.S. 811.

Heath v. Alabama. 1985. 474 U.S. 82.

Henderson v. Florida. 1985. 473 U.S. 916.

Hester v. U.S. 1924. 265 U.S. 57.

Hickey, Thomas, and Michael Axline. 1992. "Drunk-Driving Roadblocks Under State Constitutions: A Reasonable Alternative to *Michigan v. Sitz.*" *Criminal Law Bulletin* 28.

Hockett, Jeffrey D. 1991. "Justice Robert H. Jackson, the Supreme Court, and the Nuremberg Trial." *Supreme Court Review.* Chicago: University of Chicago Press.

Holbrook v. Flynn. 1986. 475 U.S. 560.

Hudson v. Palmer. 1984. 468 U.S. 523.

Hurtado v. California. 1884. 110 U.S. 516.

Illinois v. Allen. 1970. 397 U.S. 337.

Illinois v. Rodriquez. 1990. 497 U.S. 177.

Illinois v. Somerville. 1973. 410 U.S. 458.

Illinois v. Wardlow. 2000. 528 U.S. 119.

Imbler v. Pachtman. 1976. 424 U.S. 409.

In the Matter of the Welfare of E.D.J. 1993. 502 N.W.2d. 779 (Minn.)

In re Winship. 1970. 397 U.S. 358.

Inbau, Fred E. 1961. "Police Interrogation and Limitations." *Journal of Criminal Law, Criminology, and Police Science* 52:19.

Inbau, Fred E. and others. 1980. *Criminal Law and Its Administration.* 4th ed. Mineola, N.Y.: Foundation Press.

INS v. Delgado. 1984. 466 U.S. 210.

Israel, Jerold H. 1982. "Selective Incorporation: Revisited." *Georgetown Law Journal* 71:274.

Jacobson v. U.S. 1992. 503 U.S. 540.

Jefferson, Thomas. 1904. *Works.* London: Putnam and Sons.

Johnson v. Louisiana. 1972. 406 U.S. 356.

Johnson v. Zerbst. 1938. 304 U.S. 458.

Jonas, Daniel S. 1989. "Comment, Pretextual Searches and the Fourth Amendment: Unconstitutional Abuses of Power." *University of Pennsylvania Law Review* 137:1791.

Jones v. U.S. 1959. 266 F.2d 924 (D.C. Cir.).

Kamisar, Yale. 1977. "The Importance of Being Guilty." *Journal of Criminal Law and Criminology* 68:190.

Kamisar, Yale. 1984. "*Gates,* 'Probable Cause,' 'Good Faith,' and Beyond." *Iowa Law Review* 69: 551.

Katz v. U.S. 1967. 389 U.S. 347, 88 S.Ct. 507, 19 L.Ed.2d 576.

Kennedy, Randall. 1997. *Race, Crime, and the Law.* New York: Random House.

Kentucky v. Stincer. 1987. 107 S.Ct. 2658.

Ker v. California. 1963. 374 U.S. 23.

Ker v. Illinois. 1886. 119 U.S. 436.

Kirby v. Illinois. 1972. 406 U.S. 682.

Klopfer v. North Carolina. 1967. 386 U.S. 213.

Knowles v. Iowa. 1998. 525 U.S. 113.

Koehler, Jonathan J. 1995. "Error and Exaggeration in the Presentation of DNA Evidence at Trial." *Jurimetrics Journal* 34.

Kreiling, Kenneth R. 1993. "DNA Technology in Forensic Science." *Jurimetrics Journal* 33.

Kurland, Philip B., and Gerhard Casper, eds. 1975. "Brief for the NAACP Legal Defense and Educational Fund, Inc., as Amicus Curiae." In the case of *Terry v. Ohio, Landmark Briefs and Arguments of the Supreme Court of the United States.* Washington, D.C.: University Publications of America.

Kyllo v. U.S. 2001. 533 U.S. 27.

LaFave, Wayne. 1993. "Police Rule Making and the Fourth Amendment. In *Discretion in Criminal Justice.* Edited by Lloyd Ohlin and Frank Remington. Albany, N.Y.: State University of New York Press.

LaFave, Wayne, and Jerold Israel. 1984. *Criminal Procedure.* St. Paul, Minn.: West.

LaFave, Wayne, and Jerold Israel. 1987. *Search and Seizure.* St. Paul, Minn.: West.

Lanza v. New York. 1962. 370 U.S.139.

Latzer, Barry. 1991. *State Constitutions and Criminal Justice.* Westport, Conn.: Greenwood.

Lee, F.N. n.d. *King Alfred the Great and Our Common Law.* http://www.dr-fnlee.org/docs6/alfred/alfred.pdf.

Leo, Richard. 1998. "From Coercion to Deception: The Changing Nature of Police Interrogation in America." *In The Miranda Debate: Law, Justice and Policing.* Edited by Richard Leo and George C. Thomas III. Boston: Northeastern University, 2002.

Levy, Leonard. 1968. *The Origins of the Fifth Amendment.* New York: Oxford University Press.

Lewis, Anthony. 1994. "The Blackmun Legacy." *New York Times,* 8 April.

Lisenba v. California. 1941. 314 U.S. 219.

Lockett v. Ohio. 1978. 438 U.S. 586.

Lockhart v. McCree. 1986. 476 U.S. 162.

Madison, James. 1787. "The Federalist No. 51." In *The Federalist.* Edited by Jacob E. Cooke. Middletown, Conn.: Wesleyan University Press, 1961, 349.

Manson v. Brathwaite. 1977. 432 U.S. 98.

Mapp v. Ohio. 1961. 367 U.S. 643.

Marbury v. Madison. 1803. 5 U.S. 137.

Marcus, Paul. 1986. "The Development of Entrapment Law." *Wayne Law Review* 336: 5.

Marshall v. Lonberger. 1983. 459 U.S. 422.

Mary Beth G. v. City of Chicago. 1983. 723 F.2d 1262 (7th Cir.).

Maryland v. Garrison. 1987. 480 U.S. 79.

Maryland v. Wilson. 1997. 519 U.S. 408.

Massiah v. U.S. 1964. 377 U.S. 201.

Matta-Ballesteros v. Henman. 1990. 896 F.2d 255 (Cal. Dist. 7).

McCauliff, C.M.A. 1982. "Burdens of Proof: Degrees of Certainty, Quanta of Evidence, or Constitutional Guarantees?" *Vanderbilt Law Review* 35:1293.

McCleskey v. Kemp. 1987. 481 U.S. 279.

McCleskey v. Zant. 1991. 499 U.S. 467.

McCray v. Illinois. 1967. 386 U.S. 300.

McCulloch v. Maryland. 1819. 17 U.S. 316.

McDonald, Forrest. 1985. *Novus Ordo Seclorum.* Lawrence, Kans.: University of Kansas Press.

McFadden v. Cabana. 1988. 851 F.2d 784 (5th Cir.).

Mempa v. Rhay. 1967. 389 U.S. 128.

Michigan v. Clifford. 1984. 464 U.S. 287.

Michigan v. Sitz. 1993. 506 N.W.2d 209.

Michigan v. Summers. 1981. 452 U.S. 692.

Military Commission Procedures. 2002. Department of Defense Fact Sheet. Washington, D.C.: U.S. Government.

Miller, Frank W., and Robert O. Dawson, George E. Dix, and Raymond I. Parnas. 2000. *Criminal Justice Administration.* New York: Foundation Press.

Minnesota v. Murphy. 1984. 465 U.S. 420.

Minnesota Rules of Court. 1987. *Rules of Criminal Procedure.* St. Paul, Minn.: West.

Miranda v. Arizona. 1966. 384 U.S. 436, 86 S.Ct. 1602.

Monell v. New York City Department of Social Services. 1978. 436 U.S. 658.

Moore, Mark H. et al. 1984. *Dangerous Offenders: The Elusive Target of Justice.* Cambridge, Mass.: Harvard University Press.

Mueller, Gerhard O. W. 1966. Foreword. In *Criminal Procedure Under the Federal Rules* by Lester B. Orfield. Rochester, N.Y.: Lawyers Co-operative Publishing Company 1.

Murray v. U.S. 1988. 487 U.S. 533.

Myers v. Commonwealth. 1973. 298 N.E.2d 819.

Nardulli, Peter F. 1983 (Summer). "The Societal Cost of the Exclusionary Rule: An Empirical Assessment." *American Bar Foundation Research Journal,* 585–609.

Nardulli, Peter F. 1987. "The Societal Cost of the Exclusionary Rule: Revisited." *University of Illinois Law Review,* 585–609.

National Council on Crime and Delinquency. 1992. *Criminal Justice Sentencing Policy Statement.* San Francisco: NCCD.

National Treasury Employees Union v. Von Raab. 1989. 489 U.S. 656, 109 S.Ct. 1384, 103 L.Ed.2d 685.

National Law Journal. 1979 (September 10). "Pagano Case Points Finger at Lineups."

Neil v. Biggers. 1972. 409 U.S. 188.

Nelson, William E. 1988. *The Fourteenth Amendment: From Political Principle to Judicial Doctrine.* Cambridge, Mass.: Harvard University Press.

New Jersey v. T.L.O. 1985. 469 U.S. 325.

New York v. Belton. 1981. 453 U.S. 454.

New York v. Quarles. 1984. 467 U.S. 649.

New York v. Zenger. 1735. 17 Howell's St. Tr. 675, 721–722.

Nix v. Williams. 1984. 467 U.S. 431.

North Carolina v. Alford. 1970. 400 U.S. 25.

North Carolina v. Butler. 1979. 441 U.S. 369.

Ohio v. Roberts. 1980. 448 U.S. 56.

Ohio v. Robinette. 1996. 117 S.Ct. 417.

Oliver v. U.S. 1984. 466 U.S. 170.

Olmstead v. U.S. 1928. 277 U.S. 438.

Orozco v. Texas. 1969. 394 U.S. 324.

Orr v. State. 1980. 382 So.2d 860 (Fla.App.).

Packer, Herbert. 1968. *The Limits of the Criminal Sanction.* Stanford, Cal: Stanford University Press.

Padilla v. Bush. 2002. 233 F.Supp. 564.

Padilla v. Rumsfeld. 2002. 233 F.Supp.2d 564 (U.S.D.C. S.D.N.Y.).

Padilla v. Rumsfeld. 2003. WL 22965085 (2nd Cir., N.Y.).

Palko v. Connecticut. 1937. 302 U.S. 319.

Pate, Anthony M., and Lorie A Fridell. 1993. Police Use of Force: Official Reports, Citizen Complaints, and Legal Consequences. Washington, D.C.: Police Foundation.

Patton, Allison. 1993. "The Endless Cycle of Abuse: Why 42 U.S.C. § 1983 Is Ineffective in Deterring Police Brutality." *Hastings Law Journal* 44:753.

Payton v. New York. 1980. 445 U.S. 573.

Pennsylvania v. Mimms. 1977. 434 U.S. 106.

People v. Brooks. 1989. 257 Cal.Rptr. 840 (Cal.App.).

People v. Brown. 1969. 248 N.E.2d 867 (N.Y.).

People v. Camargo. 1986. 516 N.Y.S.2d 1004.

People v. Castro. 1989. 545 N.Y.S.2d 985 (Bronx Cty.).

People v. Courtney. 1970. 90 Cal.Rptr. 370. (Cal.App.3d).

People v. Defore. 1926. 150 N.E.2d 585.

People v. Martinez. 1968. 65 Cal.Rptr. 920 (Cal.).

People v. McClellan. 1969. 457 P.2d 871 (Cal.).

People v. Mills. 1904. 70 N.E. 786.

People v. Rivera. 1964. 201 N.E.2d 32.

People v. Washington. 1987. 236 Cal.Rptr. 840 (Cal.App).

Perez, Douglas W. 1994. *Common Sense About Police Review.* Philadelphia: Temple University Press.

Petitioner's Brief. 1996. U.S. S.Ct., February 16.

Pilcher, Wayland D. 1967. "The Law and Practice of Field Interrogation." *Journal of Criminal Law, Criminology, and Police Science* 58.

Pinder v. Johnson. 1995. 54 F.3d 1169 (Cal. Dist. 4).

Pletan v. Gaines et al. 1992. 494 N.W.2d 38 (Minn.).

Pound, Roscoe. 1921. "The Future of the Criminal Law." *Columbia Law Review* 21.

Powell v. Alabama. 1932. 287 U.S. 45.

Pugh v. Rainwater. 1977. 557 F.2d 1189 (5th Cir.).

Read, Conyers, ed. 1962. *William Lambarde and Local Government.* Ithaca, N.Y.: Cornell University Press.

Rehnquist, William H. 1974. "Is An Expanded Right of Privacy Consistent with Fair and Effective Law Enforcement? Or: Privacy, You've Come a Long Way Baby." *Kansas Law Review* 23.

Remington, Frank. 1960. "The Law Relating to 'On the Street' Detention, Questioning, and Frisking of Suspected Persons and Police Arrest Privileges in General." *Journal of Criminal Law, Criminology, and Police Science* 50.

Remme, Tilman. 2000. Conversation with author. London: British Broadcasting Company.

Richards v. Wisconsin. 1997. 520 U.S. 385.

Report to the Nation on Crime and Justice. 1988. 2nd ed. Washington, D.C.: Bureau of Justice Statistics.

Robinson v. Township of Redford. 2002. 48 Fed. Appx. 925.

Rochin v. California. 1952. 342 U.S. 165.

Rodriguez v. Young. 1990. 906 F.2d 1153 (7th Cir.).

Rogan v. Los Angeles. 1987. 668 F.Supp. 1384 (C.D. Cal.).

Rogers v. Richmond. 1961. 365 U.S. 534.

Rose v. Lundy. 1982. 455 U.S. 509.

Ross v. Moffitt. 1974. 417 U.S. 600.

Rossiter, Clinton. 1948. *Constitutional Dictatorship.* Princeton, N.J.: Princeton University Press.

Rothman, David. 1971. *The Discovery of the Asylum.* Boston: Little, Brown.

Rudstein, David S. 1991. "White on White: Anonymous Tips, Reasonable Suspicion and the Constitution." *Kentucky Law Journal* 79:661.

Ruffin v. Commonwealth. 1871. 62 Va. 1025.

Rutland, Robert Allen. 1955. *The Birth of the Bill of Rights.* Boston: Northeastern University Press.

Samaha, Joel. 1978. "Discretion and Law in the Early Penitential Books." In *Social Psychology and Discretionary Law.* Edited by Richard Abt. New York: Norton.

Samaha, Joel. 2003. *Criminal Justice.* 6th ed. Belmont, Cal.: Wadsworth.

Sanders v. City of Houston. 1982. 543 F.Supp. 694 (S.D. Texas).

Sanders v. United States. 1963. 373 U.S. 1.

Schauer, Frederick. 1987. "Precedent." *Stanford Law Review* 39.

Schlag, Pierre. 1982. "Assaults on the Exclusionary Rule: Good Faith, Limitations, and Damage Remedies." *Journal of Criminal Law and Criminology* 73: 875.

Schmerber v. California. 1966. 384 U.S. 757.

Schneckloth v. Bustamonte. 1973. 412 U.S. 218.

Schroeder, William A. 1981. "Deterring Fourth Amendment Violations." *Georgetown Law Journal* 69:1361.

Schulhofer, Stephen J. 1993. "Rethinking Mandatory Minimums." *Wake Forest Law Review* 28.

Schulhofer, Steven J. 1981. "Confessions and the Court." *Michigan Law Review* 79:865–893.

Schulhofer, Steven J. 1985. "Reconsidering *Miranda.*" *University of Chicago Law Review* 54:435–461.

Scott v. Illinois. 1979. 440 U.S. 367.

Seidman, Louis Michael. 1980. "Factual Guilt and the Burger Court: An Examination of Continuity and Change in Criminal Procedure." *Columbia Law Review.*

Sheppard v Maxwell. 1966. 384 U.S. 333.

Sherman v. U.S. 1958. 356 U.S. 369.

Sibron v. New York. 1968. 392 U.S. 40.

Silverman v. U.S. 1961. 365 U.S. 505.

Silverthorne Lumber Company v. U.S. 1920. 251 U.S. 385.

Sitz v. Michigan. 1993. 506 N.W.2d 219.

Skolnick, Jerome. 1994. *Justice Without Trial: Law Enforcement in a Democratic Society.* 3rd ed. New York: Macmillan.

Slobogin, Christopher. 1998. *Criminal Procedure: Regulation of Police Investigation.* Charlottesville, Va.: LEXIS Law Publishing.

Slobogin, Christopher. 1999. "Why Liberals Should Chuck the Exclusionary Rule." *University of Illinois Law Review* 363.

Smith v. Illinois. 1968. 390 U.S. 129.

Smith v. Maryland. 1979. 442 U.S. 745.

Smith, Page. 1962. *John Adams.* New York: Doubleday.

Sorrells v. U.S. 1932. 287 U.S. 435.

South Dakota v. Opperman. 1976. 428 U.S. 364; 228 N.W.2d 152.

Spano v. New York. 1959. 360 U.S. 315.

Sparf and Hansen v. U.S. 1895. 156 U.S. 51.

Spitzer, Eliot. 1999. *The New York City Police Department's "Stop & Frisk" Practices: A Report to the People of the State of New York from the Attorney General.* New York: Civil Rights Bureau.

St. Johns Law Review. 1998. "*Terry v. Ohio* 30 Years Later: A Symposium on the Fourth Amendment, Law Enforcement and Police-Citizen Encounters." New York: St. Johns Law Review.

Stack v. Boyle. 1951. 342 U.S. 1.

Stanford Law Review. 1977. "Notes: Did Your Eyes Deceive You? Expert Psychological Testimony on the Unreliability of Eyewitness Identification." *Stanford Law Review* 29.

State v. Bloom. 1994. 516 N.W.2d 159 (Minn.).

State v. Bowe. 1994. 77 Hawaii 51, 53; 881 P.2d 538 541.

State v. Bumpus. 1990. 459 N.W.2d 619 (Iowa).

State v. Fitiwi. 2003. Minnesota Court of Appeals (not reported).

State v. Ford. 1996. WL 278227 (Minn.App.).

State v. Ladson. 1999. 979 P.2d 833.

State v. McLees. 2000. 994 P.2d 683.

State v. Morris. 1996. 165 Vt. 111, 680 A.2d 90.

State v. Novembrino. 1987. 519 A.2d 820 (N.J.).

State v. Putt. 1997. 955 S.W.2d 640 (Tenn.Crim.App.).

State v. Richards. 1996. 549 N.W.2d 218.

State v. Ricks. 1989. 771 P.2d 1364 (Alaska.App.).

State v. Ross. 2001. 639 N.W.2d 225 (Wisc.App.).

State v. Smith. 1986.712 P.2d 496.

State v. Superior Court. 1978. 589 P.2d 48 (Ariz.App.).

State v. Wilkins. 1983. 473 A.2d 295.

State v. Wright. 2001. 2001 WL 96203 (Minn.App.).

Steagold v. U.S. 1981. 451 U.S. 204.

Stein v. New York. 1953. 346 U.S. 156.

Stern, Loren G. 1967. "Stop and Frisk: An Historical Answer to a Modern Problem." *Journal of Criminal Law, Criminology, and Police Science* 58.

Stewart, Potter. 1983. "The Road to *Mapp v. Ohio* and Beyond: The Origins, Development, and Future of the Exclusionary Rule in Search-and-Seizure Cases." *Columbia Law Review* 83.

Stone v. Powell. 1976. 428 U.S. 465.

Storing, Herbert J. 1981. *The Complete Anti-Federalist.* Chicago: University of Chicago Press.

Stovall v. Denno. 1967. 388 U.S. 293.

Strachan-Davidson, James L. *Problems of the Roman Criminal Law.* 1912. London: Oxford University Press.

Strickland v. Washington. 1984. 104 S.Ct. 2052.

Strunk v. U.S. 1973. 412 U.S. 434.

Susla v. State. 1976. 247 N.W.2d 907.

Sutton, Paul. 1986. "The Fourth Amendment in Action: An Empirical View of the Search Warrant Process." *Criminal Law Bulletin* 22:405.

Swindler v. State. 1979. 592 S.W.2d 91 (Ark.).

Tate v. Short. 1971. 401 U.S. 395.

Taylor, Telford. 1969. *Two Studies in Constitutional Interpretation.* Columbus: Ohio State University Press.

Tennessee v. Garner. 1985. 471 U.S. 1.

Terry v. Ohio. 1968. 392 U.S. 1.

Thompson, William C. 1993. "Evaluating the Admissibility of New Genetic Identification Tests: Lessons from the 'DNA War.'" *Journal of Criminal Law and Criminology* 84.

Thurman v. City of Torrington. 1984. 595 F.Supp. 1521.

Tiffany, Lawrence P., Donald M. McIntyre, Jr., and Daniel L. Rotenberg. 1967. *Detection of Crime: Stopping and Questioning, Search and Seizure, Encouragement, and Entrapment.* Boston: Little, Brown.

Toborg, Mary A. 1981. *Pretrial Release: A National Evaluation of Practices and Outcomes.* Washington, D.C.: National Institute of Justice.

Turner v. Murray. 1986. 476 U.S. 28.

Twenty-Sixth Annual Review of Criminal Procedure. 1997. *Georgetown Law Journal* 85.

Uchida, Craig, and Timothy Bynum. 1991. "Criminology: Search Warrants, Motions to Suppress and 'Lost Cases': The Effects of the Exclusionary Rule in Seven Jurisdictions." *Journal of Criminal Law and Criminology* 81:103.

Uelman, Gerald F. 1980. "Testing the Assumptions of *Neil v. Biggers*: An Experiment in Eyewitness Identification." *Criminal Law Bulletin* 16:359–368.

U.S. v. Abrahams. 1978. 575 F.2d 3 (1st Cir.).

U.S. v. Adamo. 1993. 994 F.2d 942 (Cal. Dist. 1).

U.S. v. Armstrong. 1996. 517 U.S. 456.

U.S. v. Banks. 1995. 78 F.3d 1190 (7th Cir.).

U.S. v. Barahona. 1993. 990 F.2d 412 (8th Cir.).

U.S. v. Blake. 1988. 718 F.Supp. (S.D.Fla.).

U.S. v. Brigham. 1992. 977 F.2d 317 (7th Cir.).

U.S. v. Calandra. 1974. 414 U.S. 338.

U.S. v. Ceballos. 1987. 812 F.2d 42 (2nd Cir.).

U.S. v. Chavez. 1987. 812 F.2d 1295 (10th Cir. 1987).

U.S. v. Craner. 1981. 652 F.2d 23 (9th Cir.).

U.S. v. Doe. 1985. 819 F.2d 206 (9th Cir.).

U.S. v. Dougherty. 1972. 473 F.2d 1113 (D.C. Cir.).

U.S. v. Dunn. 1987. 480 U.S. 294.

U.S. v. Edwards. 1974. 415 U.S. 800.

U.S. v. Elmore. 1979. 595 F.2d 1036.

U.S. v. Freitas. 1988. 800 F.2d 1451.

U.S. v. Harris. 1971. 403 U.S. 573.

U.S. v. Henry. 1980. 447 U.S. 264.

U.S. v. Kim. 1976. 415 F.Supp. 1252 (D.Hawaii).

U.S. v. Leon. 1984. 468 U.S. 897.

U.S. v. Lindsey. 1989. 877 F.2d 777 (9th Cir.).

U.S. v. Marion. 1971. 404 U.S. 307.

U.S. v. Mendenhall. 1980. 446 U.S. 544, 100 S.Ct. 1870, 64 L.Ed.2d 497.

U.S. v. Miller. 1976. 425 U.S. 435.

U.S. v. Montoya de Hernandez. 1985. 473 U.S. 531.

U.S. v. Moscatiello. 1985. 771 F.2d 589 (Cal. Dist. 1, Mass.)

U.S. v. Perez. 1824. 22 U.S. (9 Wheat.) 579.

U.S. v. Ramsey. 1977. 431 U.S. 606.

U.S. v. Reyes. 2002. 283 F.3d 446.

U.S. v. Rivera. 1993. 994 F.2d 942 (Cal. Dist. 1).

U.S. v. Robinson. 1973. 414 U.S. 218.

U.S. v. Robinson. 1998. 149 F.3d 1185 (6th Cir., Ohio).

U.S. v. Rodney. 1992. 956 F.2d 295 (CADC).

U.S. v. Salerno. 1987. 481 U.S. 739.

U.S. v. Sanchez-Meza. 1976. 547 F.2d 461 (9th Cir.).

U.S. v. Santana. 1976. 427 U.S. 38.

U.S. v. Sharpe and Savage. 1985. 470 U.S. 675.

U.S. v. Sokolow. 1989. 490 U.S. 1.

U.S. v. Teslim. 1989. 869 F.2d 316 (7th Cir.).

U.S. v. Udziela. 1982. 671 F.2d 995 (7th Cir.).

U.S. v. Villegas. 1990. 899 F.2d 1324 (2nd Cir.).

U.S. v. Warner. 1988. 843 F.2d 401 (9th Cir.).

U.S. v. Watson. 1976. 423 U.S. 411.

U.S. v. Weaver. 1992. 966 F.2d 391.

U.S. v. Werbrouck. 1978. 589 F.2d 273 (7th Cir.).

U.S. v. White. 1971. 401 U.S. 745.

U.S. v. Winsor. 1988. 846 F.2d 1569 (9th Cir.).

USA Patriot Act. 2001. P.L. 107-156, 115 Stat. 272.

U.S. Code. 1867. 14 Stat. 385.

U.S. Code. 2002. Title 42. http://uscode.house.gov/uscode-cgi/fastweb.exe?search.

U.S. Code. 2003. Chapter 119, Wire and Electronic Communications Interceptions and Interceptions of Oral Communications. http://www4.law.cornell.edu/uscode/18/pIch119.html.

U.S. Congress. 1954. Senate, Committee on the Judiciary, Hearing Before the Subcommittee to Investigate Juvenile Delinquency, Miami, Florida, 83d Cong., 2d sess. Washington, D.C.: Government Printing Office.

U.S. Congress. 1970. H. Rep. No. 1444, 91st Cong., 2d Sess. Washington, D.C.: Government Printing Office.

U.S. Department of Justice. 2002. *The Attorney General's Guidelines on General Crimes, Racketeering Enterprise and Terrorism Enterprise Investigations.* Washington D.C.: U.S. Department of Justice.

U.S. ex rel. Latimore v. Sielaff. 1977. 561 F.2d 691 (7th Cir.).

U.S. Sentencing Commission. 1991. *Mandatory Minimum Penalties in the Federal Criminal Justice System.* Washington, D.C.: U.S. Sentencing Commission.

Uviller, H. Richard. 1986. "Seizure by Gunshot: The Riddle of the Fleeing Felon." *New York University Review of Law of Social Change* 14:705.

Uviller, H. Richard. 1988. *Tempered Zeal.* Chicago/New York: Contemporary Books.

Van Dyke, Jon. 1977. *Jury Selection Procedures.* Cambridge, Mass.: Ballinger.

Vernonia School District v. Acton. 1995. 515 U.S. 646.

Walder v. U.S. 1954. 347 U.S. 62.

Walker, Samuel. 1980. *Popular Justice.* New York: Oxford University Press.

Walker, Samuel, and Vic W. Bumpus. 1992. "The Effectiveness of Civilian Review." *American Journal of Police* 11.

Wallace, Henry Scott. 1993 (September). "Mandatory Minimums and the Betrayal of Sentencing Reform: A Legislative Dr. Jekyll and Mr. Hyde." *Federal Probation.*

Warden v. Hayden. 1967. 387 U.S. 294.

Watkins v. Virginia. 1986. 475 U.S. 1099.

Watts v. Indiana. 1949. 338 U.S. 49.

Weeks v. U.S. 1914. 232 U.S. 383.

Weiner, William P., and Larry S. Royster. 1991. "Sobriety Checkpoints in Michigan: The *Sitz* Case and Its Aftermath." *T. M. Cooley Law Review* 8:243.

Wells, Gary, and Eric Seelau. 1995. "Eyewitness Identification: Psychological Research and Legal Policy on Lineups." *Psychology, Public Policy, and Law* 1:765.

Wells, Gary L., and Elizabeth A. Olson. 2003. "Eyewitness Testimony." *Annual Review of Psychology* 54:277–295.

Welsh v. Wisconsin. 1984. 466 U.S. 740.

White, Welsh S. 1986. "Defending *Miranda*" Vanderbilt *Law Review* 39:1–22.

Whitebread, Charles H., and Christopher Slobogin. 2000. *Criminal Procedure.* New York: Foundation Press.

Whren v. U.S. 1996. 517 U.S. 806.

Williams v. Beto. 1965. 354 F.2d 698 (5th Cir.).

Williams v. Florida. 1970. 399 U.S. 78.

Wilson v. Arkansas. 1995. 514 U.S. 927.

Wilson v. Commonwealth of Virginia. 1999. 509 S.E.2d 540.

Wolf v. Colorado. 1949. 338 U.S. 25.

Wong Sun v. U.S. 1963. 371 U.S. 471.

Wyoming v. Houghton. 1999. 526 U.S. 295.

Yant, Martin. 1991. *Presumed Guilty: When Innocent People Are Wrongly Convicted.* Buffalo: Prometheus Books.

Ybarra v. Illinois. 1979. 44 U.S. 85.

Younger, Richard D. 1963. *The People's Panel.* Providence, R.I.: Brown University Press.

Case Index

Index